John Wilkens

An essay towards a real character and a philosophical language

John Wilkens

An essay towards a real character and a philosophical language

ISBN/EAN: 9783741171956

Manufactured in Europe, USA, Canada, Australia, Japa

Cover: Foto ©Andreas Hilbeck / pixelio.de

Manufactured and distributed by brebook publishing software (www.brebook.com)

John Wilkens

An essay towards a real character and a philosophical language

AN ESSAY
Towards a
REAL CHARACTER,
And a
PHILOSOPHICAL
LANGUAGE.

By JOHN WILKINS D.D. *Dean of* RIPON, *And Fellow of the* ROYAL SOCIETY.

LONDON,
Printed for SA: GELLIBRAND, and for
JOHN MARTYN Printer to the ROYAL
SOCIETY, 1668.

To the Right Honourable
WILLIAM
LORD VISCOUNT
BROUNCKER,
PRESIDENT;

Together with the reſt of the *COUNCIL* and *FELLOWS* of the *ROYAL SOCIETY.*

My Lord,

NOW *at length preſent to your Lordſhip thoſe Papers I had drawn up concerning a* Real Character, *and a* Philoſophicall Language; *which by ſeverall Orders of the Society have been required of Me. I have been the longer about it, partly becauſe it required ſome conſiderable time to reduce the Collections I had by me to this purpoſe, into a tolerable order; and partly becauſe when this work was done in Writing, and the Impreſſion of it well nigh finiſhed, it hapned (amongſt many other better things) to be burnt in the late dreadfull Fire; by which, all that was Printed (excepting only two Copies) and a great part of the unprinted Original was deſtroyed: The repairing of which, hath taken up the greateſt part of my time ever ſince. I mention this by way of Apology for that ſlackneſs and delay, I may ſeem to be guilty of in my obedience to your Orders.*

d   *I am*

The Epistle

 I am not so vain as to think that I have here completely finished this great undertaking, with all the advantages of which such a design is capable. Nor on the other hand, am I so diffident of this Essay, *as not to believe it sufficient for the business to which it pretends, namely the distinct expression of all things and notions that fall under discourse.*

 I am sensible of sundry defects in the severall parts of this Book: And therefore would make it my humble motion to your Lordship and this Society, that you would by your Order appoint some of our number, thoroughly to examin & consider the whole, and to offer their thoughts concerning what they judge fit to be amended in it. Particularly in those Tables that concern the species of Natural bodies; *which, if they were (so far as they are yet known and discovered) distinctly reduced and described, This would very much promote and facilitate the knowledg of Nature, which is one great end of your Institution. And besides, the ranging of these things into such an order as the Society shall approve, would afford a very good method for your* Repository, *both for the disposal of what you have already, and the supplying of what you want, towards the compleating of that Collection, so generously begun of late, by the bounty of* M^r· Daniel Collwal, *a worthy Member of this* Society. *And by this means, I should not doubt, but that in a very short space, you would have the most usefull* Repository *in the* World.

 It is no easie undertaking to Enumerate *all such matters as are to be provided for in such a design; But the business of* Defining, *being amongst all others the most nice and difficult, must needs render it a very hard task for any one to attempt the doing of this, for all kinde of*·
Things,

DEDICATORY.

Things, Notions, *and* Words, *which yet is necessary to the design here proposed.*

Upon which account I may be excused for being so sollicitous about the assistance of others in these matters, because of their great difficulty and importance. The compleating of such a design, being rather the work of a College *and an* Age, *then of any single Person: I mean, the combined Studies of many Students, amongst whom, the severall shares of such a* Work *should be distributed; And that for so long a course of time, wherein sufficient experiments might be made of it by practice.*

It has been sayd concerning that famous Italian *Academy styled* de la Crusca, *consisting of many choice Men of great Learning, that they bestowed forty years in finishing their* Vocabulary. *And 'tis well enough known, that those great* Wits *of the* French Academy, *did begin their* Dictionary *in the year* 1639. *And for the hastning of the* Work, *did distribute the parts of it amongst severall Committees; and yet that undertaking is (for ought I can understand) far enough from being finished.*

Now if those famous Assemblies consisting of the great Wits *of their* Age *and* Nations, *did judge this* Work *of* Dictionary-making, *for the polishing of their* Language, *worthy of their united labour and studies; Certainly then, the Design here proposed, ought not to be thought unworthy of such assistance; it being as much to be preferred before that, as* things are better then words, *as* real knowledge *is beyond* elegancy of speech, *as the* general good of mankind, *is beyond that of any particular* Countrey *or* Nation.

I am very sensible that the most usefull inventions do at their first appearance, make but a very slow progress in the World, unless helped forward by some particular advantage

vantage. Logarithms *were an Invention of excellent Art and usefulness; And yet it was a considerable time, before the Learned Men in other parts, did so farr take notice of them, as to bring them into use.* The Art of Shorthand, *is in its kind an Ingenious device, and of considerable usefulness, applicable to any Language, much wondered at by Travailers, that have seen the experience of it in* England: *And yet though it be above Threescore years, since it was first Invented,* 'tis *not to this day (for ought I can learn) brought into common practice in any other Nation. And there is reason enough to expect the like Fate for the design here proposed.*

The only expedient I can think of against it, is, That it be sent abroad into the World, with the reputation of having bin considered and approved of, by such a Society *as this; which may provoke, at least, the Learned part of the World, to take notice of it, and to give it such encouragement, as it shall appear to deserve.*

And if upon such an amendment and recommendation by this Society, *the design here proposed, should happen to come into common use, It would requite the Honour you bestow upon it, with abundant Interest. The being Instrumental in any such discovery as does tend to the Universal good of Mankind, being sufficient not only to make the* Authors *of it famous, but also the* Times *and* Places *wherein they live.*

He that knows how to estimate, that judgment inflicted on Mankind in the Curse of the Confusion, *with all the unhappy consequences of it, may thereby judge, what great advantage and benefit there will be, in a remedy against it. Men are content to bestow much time and pains in the Study of Languages, in order to their more easy conversing with those of other Nations.* 'Tis

said

Dedicatory.

said of Mithridates *King of* Pontus, *that he was skilled in Two and twenty several Tongues, which were spoken in the several Provinces under his Dominion:* Which, *tho it were a very extraordinary attainment, yet how short a remedy was it against the Curse of the Confusion, considering the vast multitude of Languages that are in the World.*

Besides that most obvious advantage which would ensue, of facilitating mutual Commerce, *amongst the several Nations of the World, and the improving of all* Natural knowledge ; *It would likewise very much conduce to the spreading of the knowledge of* Religion. *Next to the Gift of Miracles, and particularly that of Tongues, powred out upon the Apostles in the first planting of Christianity, There is nothing that can more effectually conduce to the further accomplishment of those Promises, which concern the diffusion of it, through all Nations, then the design which is here proposed.*

To which it will be proper for me to add, That this design will likewise contribute much to the clearing of some of our Modern differences in Religion, *by unmasking many wild errors, that shelter themselves under the disguise of affected phrases; which being Philosophically unfolded, and rendered according to the genuine and natural importance of Words, will appear to be inconsistencies and contradictions. And several of those pretended, mysterious, profound notions, expressed in great swelling words, whereby some men set up for reputation, being this way examined, will appear to be, either nonsence, or very flat and jejune.*

And tho it should be of no other use but this, yet were it in these days well worth a mans pains and study, considering the Common mischief that is done, and the many

b *impostures*

impoſtures and cheats that are put upon men, under the diſguiſe of affected inſignificant Phraſes.

But what ever may be the iſſue of this attempt, as to the eſtabliſhing of a real Character, and the bringing of it into Common uſe, amongſt ſeveral Nations of the World (of which I have but very ſlender expectations;) yet this I ſhall aſſert with greater confidence, That the reducing of all things and notions, to ſuch kind of Tables, as are here propoſed (were it as compleatly done as it might be) would prove the ſhorteſt and plaineſt way for the attainment of real Knowledge, that hath been yet offered to the World. And I ſhall add further, that theſe very Tables (as now they are) do ſeem to me a much better and readier courſe, for the entring and training up of men in the knowledge of things, then any other way of Inſtitution that I know of; which I ſhould not preſume to aſſert, before ſuch able Judges as thoſe of this Society, were it not a thing I had well conſidered and were convinced of.

I have nothing further to add, but only the declaring my ſelf to be moſt Zealouſly devoted to the Honour and Welfare of the Royal Society,

And particularly (My Lord,)

       Your Lordſhips moſt

          Humble Servant,

             Jo. Wilkins.

TO THE
READER.

IT may perhaps be expected by some, that I should give an account of my ingaging in a Work of this nature so unsuitable to my Calling and Business.

For the satisfaction of such, they may please to take notice, that this Work was first undertaken, during that vacancy and leasure which I formerly enjoyed in an Academicall station, to which the endeavours of promoting all kind of usefull knowledge, whereby Learning may be improved, is a very suitable imployment. In the time of that daily and intimate converse which I then injoyed, with that most Learned and excellent Person Dr. Seth Ward, the present Bishop of Salisbury. I had frequent occasion of conferring with him, concerning the various Desiderata, proposed by Learned men, or such things as were conceived yet wanting to the advancement of several parts of Learning; amongst which, this of the Universal Character, was one of the principal, most of which he had more deeply considered, than any other Person that I knew. And in reference to this particular, he would say, That as it was one of the most usefull, so he judged it to be one of the most feasible, amongst all the rest, if prosecuted in a regular way. But for all such attempts to this purpose, which he had either seen or heard of, the Authors of them did generally mistake in their first foundations; whilst they did propose to themselves the framing of such a Character, from a Dictionary of Words, according to some particular Language, without reference to the nature of things, and that common Notion of them, wherein Mankind does agree, which must chiefly be respected, before any attempt of this nature cou'd signifie any thing, as to the main end of it.

It was from this suggestion of his, that I first had any distinct apprehension of the proper course to be observed, in such an undertaking; having in a Treatise I had published some years before, proposed the Hebrew Tongue as consisting of fewest Radicals, to be the fittest ground work for such a design.

Besides

The Epistle

Besides the many Private conferences to this purpose, I must not forget to mention, that Publique account which he hath given to the World, of his thoughts upon this subject, in that Learned and Ingenious discourse styled Vindiciæ Academiarum; wherein he endeavours to Vindicate those Ancient and famous Schools of Learning, from such reproaches, whereby some Ignorant and ill-natured men (taking the advantage of those bad Times) would have exposed them to contempt and ruine. In which Treatise there is mention made of some considerable preparations, towards the Design here proposed, which if his other necessary imployments would have permitted him to have prosecuted, would without doubt, long ere this, have been advanced to as great a Perfection, as the first Essay in so difficult a matter could have attained.

It was some considerable time after this, before I had any thought of attempting any thing in this kind: The first occasion of it was, from a desire I had, to give some assistance to another person, who was willing to ingage in this design of framing a real Character, from the Natural notion of things; for the helping of whom in so worthy an undertaking, I did offer to draw up for him, the Tables of Substance, or the species of Natural Bodies, reduced under their several Heads; which I did accordingly perform, much after the same Method, as they are hereafter set down: Though in the doing of it, I found much more labour and difficulty, then I expected, when I undertook it. But he for whom I had done this, not liking this method, as being of too great a Compass, conceiving that he could sufficiently provide for all the chief Radicals, in a much briefer and more easy way, did not think fit to make use of these Tables. Upon which, being my self convinced, That this which I had begun, was the only course for the effecting of such a work, and being withal unwilling to loose so much pains as I had already taken towards it, I resolved (as my leasure would permit) to go on with the other Tables of Accidents. And when after many reviews and changes I had reduced (as well as I could) into these Tables, all simple things and notions, by a Consideration of them à Priori, I then judged it necessary to attempt the reduction of all other Words in the Dictionary to these Tables; either as they were Synonymous to them, or to be defined by them, which would be a means to try the fulness of these Tables, and consequently to supply their defects; And besides a great help to Learners, who without such a direction, might not perhaps at first be able to find out the true place and notion of many Words.

For the farther compleating of this Work, I found it necessary to take into consideration, the framing of such a Natural Grammar, as might be suited to the Philosophy of Speech, abstracting from those many unnecessary rules belonging to instituted Language; which proved a matter of no small difficulty, considering the little help to be had for it, from those few Authors who had before undertaken to do any thing in this kind.

In the doing of these things, I have not neglected any help that I could procure from others, and must acknowledge my self much ingaged to sundry Learned Men of my acquaintance, for their directions, and furtherance in such matters, as were most suitable to their several Studies and Professions.

Amongst the rest, I must not forget to make particular mention of the special assistance I have received, in drawing up the Tables of Animals

from

To the READER.

from that most Learned and Inquisitive Gentleman, a worthy Member of the Royal Society, Mr. Francis Willoughby, who hath made it his particular business, in his late Travails through the most considerable parts of Europe, to inquire after and understand the several species of Animals, *and by his own Observations is able to advance that part of Learning, and to add many things, to what hath been formerly done, by the most Learned Authors in this kind.*

And as for those most difficult Tables of Plants, *I have received the like assistance, from one of his Companions in Travail, Mr.* John Wray, *Late Fellow of* Trinity Colledge *in* Cambridge, *who besides his other general Knowledge, hath with great success applyed himself to the Cultivating of that part of Learning.*

And as for the principal difficulties, which I met with in any other part of this Work, I must acknowledge my self obliged to the continual assistance I have had, from my most Learned and worthy Friend, Dr. William Lloyd, *then whom (so far as I am able to judge,) this Nation could not have afforded a fitter Person, either for that great Industry, or Accurate judgment, both in* Philological, *and* Philosophical *matters, required to such a Work. And particularly I must wholy ascribe to him that tedious and difficult task, of suiting the Tables to the* Dictionary, *and the drawing up of the* Dictionary *it self, which upon tryal, I doubt not, will be found to be the most perfect, that was ever yet made for the* English Tongue.

And here I think it proper to give notice that there are several Words mentioned in the Dictionary, *and frequently used amongst some Authors, which are yet very questionable as to their fitness and propriety: Each of these were in the Original Coppy marked with an Asterisk, for the better distinction of them; but by some oversight, these marks have been omitted in the Impression.*

If any shall suggest, that some of the Enquiries here insisted upon (as particularly those about the Letters of the Alphabet) do seem too minute and trivial, for any prudent Man to bestow his serious thoughts and time about. Such Persons may know, that the discovery of the true nature and Cause of any the most minute thing, doth promote real Knowledge, and therefore cannot be unfit for any Mans endeavours, who is willing to contribute to the advancement of Learning. Upon which Account some of the most eminent Persons, in several Ages, who were Men of business, have not disdained to bestow their pains about the First Elements of Speech.

Julius Cæsar, *is said to have written a Book* de Analogia. *And the Emperour* Charles the Great, *to have made a Grammar of his vulgar Tongue. So did St.* Basil *for the* Greek; *and St.* Austin *for the* Latin, *both extant in their Works.*

Besides divers of great reputation both Ancient *and* Modern, *who have Written whole Books on purpose, concerning the just Number of the Letters in the Alphabet; Others have applyed their disquisitions to some particular Letters:* Messala Corvinus, *a Great Man, and a famous* Orator *amongst the* Romans, *Writ a Book concerning the Letter* S. Adamantius Martyr, *was the Author of another Book, concerning the Letters* V. *and* B. *Our Learned* Gataker *has Published a Book concerning* Dipthongs. *And* Jovianus Pontanus *esteemed a Learned Man, hath Two Books* de Adspiratione, *or the Letter* H.

Mr. Franklyn *hath published a particular Discourse concerning* Accents, *And* Erycius Puteanus *hath Written a Book purposely,* de Interpunctione, *of the true way of Pointing Clauses and Sentences. And these Generally well esteemed for their great usefulness in the Promoting of Learning: Which may be a sufficient Vindication against any Prejudices of this Nature.*

THE

THE CONTENTS.

The First Part Containing the Prolegomena.

CHAPTER, I.
I. THE Introduction. II. The Original of Languages. III. The First Mother Tongues. IV. Their several Offsprings. Page, 1

CHAP. II.
I. Concerning the various Changes and Corruptions, to which all vulgar Languages are obnoxious. II. Particularly concerning the Change of the *English* Tongue. III. Whether any Language formerly in use, be now wholly lost. IV. Concerning the first rise and occasion of New Languages. pag. 6

CHAP. III.
I. The Original of Letters and Writing. II. That all Letters were derived from the Hebrew. III. The use of Letters is less *Antient*, and the Kinds of them less numerous, than of Languages themselves. IV. Of Notes for secrecy or brevity. V. Of a Real Character. VI. Of Alphabets in General. pag. 10

CHAP. IV.
I. Of the defects in Common Alphabets, as to the true Order of the Letters, II. Their just Number, III. Determinate Powers, V. Fitting Names, V. Proper Figures. VI. Of the Imperfections belonging to the Words of Languages, as to their Equivocalness, Variety of Synonymous Words, Uncertain Phraseologies, Improper way of Writing. pag. 14

CHAP. V.
I. That neither Letters nor Languages, have been regularly established by the Rules of Art. II. The Natural ground or Principle of the several ways of Communication amongst Men. III. The first thing to be provided for, in the establishing of a Philosophical Character or Language, is a just enumeration of all such Things and Notions, to which Names are to be assigned. pag. 19

The Second Part Containing Universal Philosophy.

CHAPTER. I.
I. THE Scheme of Genus's. II. Concerning the more General Notions of Things, The difficulty of Establishing these aright. III. Of Transcendentals General. IV. Of Transcendentals Mixed. V. Of

The Contents of the CHAPTERS.

V. Of Transcendental Relations of Action. VI. Of the several Notions belonging to Grammar, or Logic. Page, 22

CHAP. II.
I. Concerning God. II. Of the several Things and Notions reducible under that Collective Genus of the World. pag 51

CHAP. III.
I. Of Elements and Meteors. II. Of Stones. III. Of Metals. pag. 56

CHAP. IV.
I. Of Plants, The difficulty of enumerating and describing these. II. The more general distribution of them. III. Of Herbs considered according to their Leaves. IV. Of Herbs considered according to their Flowers. V. Of Herbs considered according to their Seed Vessels. VI. Of Shrubs. VII. Of Trees. pag. 67

CHAP. V.
I. Concerning Animals, The General distribution of them. II. Of Exanguious Animals. III. Of *Fishes*. IV. Of *Birds*. V. Of *Beasts*. VI. A Digression concerning the capacity of *Noah's* Ark. pag. 121

CHAP. VI.
I. Of Parts of Animate Bodies, whether I. *Peculiar*, or II. *General*. p. 168

CHAP. VII.
I. Concerning the Predicament of *Quantitie*. I. Of *Magnitude*. II. Of *Space*. III. Of *Measure*. pag. 181

CHAP. VIII.
Concerning the Predicament of *Quality*, and the several Genus's belonging to it. I. Of *Natural Power*. II. Of *Habit*. III. Of *Manners*. IV. Of *Sensible Quality*. V. Of *Disease*; with the various differences and species under each of these. pag. 194

CHAP. IX.
Of the Predicament of *Action*; The several Genus's under it. viz. I. *Spiritual Action*. II. *Corporeal Action*. III. *Motion*. IV. *Operation*. p. 225

CHAP. X.
Concerning *Relation* more private, namely I. *Oeconomical*, or Family Relation; together with the several kinds of things belonging to those in that capacity, either as II. *Possessions*, or III. *Provisions*. pag. 249

CHAP. XI.
Concerning *Relation* more Publike, whether I. *Civil*. II. *Judiciary*. III. *Naval*. IV. *Military*. V. *Ecclesiastical*. pag. 263

CHAP. XII.
I. A General Explication of the design of the fore-going Tables. II. Particular Instances in the six principal Genus's of it. III. Something to be noted concerning *Opposites* and *Synonyma's*. IV. An Account of what kind of things ought not to be provided for in such Tables. p. 289

The

The Contents of the CHAPTERS.

The Third Part Containing Philosophical Grammar.

CHAPTER. I.
I. Concerning the several *Kinds* and *Parts* of Grammar. II. Of *Etymologie*, The more general Scheme of *Integrals* and *Particles*. III. Of *Nouns* in General. IV. Of *Substantives* common, denoting either *Things*, *Actions*, or *Persons*. V. Rules concerning *Nouns of Action*. VI. Of *Substantives Abstracts*. VII. Of *Adjectives* according to the true Philosophical notion of them. VIII. The true notion of a *Verb*. IX. Of derived *Adverbs*. X. A general Scheme of the forementioned Derivations. page, 297

CHAP. II.
I. Of *Particles* in General. II. Of the *Copula*. III. Of *Pronouns* more generally. IV. More particularly. V. Of *Interjections* more generally. VI. More particularly. p. 304

CHAP. III.
I. Of Prepositions in general. II. The particular kinds of them enumerated. III. An Explication of the four last Combinations of them, relating to Place or Time. p. 309

CHAP. IV.
I. Of Adverbs in general. II. The particular kinds of them. III. Of Conjunctions. p. 312

CHAP. V.
I. Of Articles. II. Of Modes. III. Of Tenses. IV. The most distinct way of expressing the differences of Time. p. 315

CHAP. VI.
I. Of Transcendental particles, The end and use of them. II. The usual ways for inlarging the sense of Words in instituted Languages. III. The general Heads of Transcendental Particles. p. 318

CHAP. VII.
Instances of the great usefulness of these Transcendental Particles, with directions how they are to be applyed. p. 323

CHAP. VIII.
Of the Accidental differences of Words. I. Inflexion. II. Derivation. III. Composition. p. 352

CHAP. IX.
Of the second part of Grammar called Syntax. p. 354

CHAP. X.
Of Orthography. I. Concerning Letters. The Authors who have treated of this Subject. II. A brief Table of all such kinds of Simple found, which can be framed by the mouths of Men. III. A further Explication of this Table, as to the Organs of Speech, and as to the Letters framed by these Organs. p. 357

d   CHAP.

The Contents of the CHAPTERS.

CHAP. XI.
Of Vowels. p. 363

CHAP. XII.
Of Confonants. p. 366

CHAP. XIII.
Of Compound Vowels, and Confonants. p. 370

CHAP. XIV.
I. Of the Accidents of Letters, I. Their Names. II. Their Order. III. Affinities and Oppofitions. IV. Their Figures, with a twofold Inftance of a more regular Character for the Letters, The later of which may be ftyled Natural. V. Of Pronunciation. VI. The feveral Letters dif-ufed by feveral Nations. p. 347.

The Fourth Part Containing a Real Character, *and a* Philofophical Language.

CHAPTER I.
The propofal of one kind of Real Character (amongft many other which might be offered) both for all *Integrals*, whether *Genus's*, *Differences* or *Species*; together with the derivations and Inflexions belonging to them, as likewife for all the feveral kinds of *Particles*. page, 385

CHAP. II.
An Inftance of this Real Character, in the Lord's Prayer and the Creed. p. 395

CHAP. III.
How this Real Character may be made effable in a diftinct Language, and what kind of Letters or Syllables may be conveniently affigned to each Character. p. 414

CAHP. IV.
Inftance of this Philofohical Language, both in the Lord's Prayer and the Creed: A comparifon of the Language here propofed, with fifty others, as to the facility and Euphonicalnefs of it. p. 421

CHAP. V.
Directions for the more eafy learning of this Character and Language, with a brief Table containing the Radicals, both *Integrals* and *Particles*; together with the Character and Language, by which each of them are to be expreffed. p. 439

CHAP. VI.
The *Appendix* containing a Comparifon betwixt this Natural *Philofophical Grammar* and that of other *Inftituted* Languages, particularly the *Latin*, in refpect of the multitude of *unneceffary Rules* and of *Anomalifms*, concerning the *China* Character: The feveral Attemps and Propofals made by others, towards a new kind of Character and Language. The advantage in refpect of facility, which this Philofophical Language hath above the *Latin*. p. 441

ERRATA.

PAGE 6. Line 17. Read *Instituted by Art.* p. 15. l. 9. r. 3 *By aſigning*, &c. p. 16. l. 11. (y) p. 27. l. 39. dele *relief.* p. 32. l. 43. dele *poor.* p. 40. l. 28. r. *defer.* p. 41. l. 21, 22. add *adminiſter, diſperſe, diſtribute Token, Fairing* to the preceding line. p. 70. l. 38. r. *dryer.* p. 73. l. 3. r. *Lacinia.* p. 91. l. 7, 8. r. *of this Tribe.* p. 94. l. 19. r. *expand.* p. 97. l. 21; 31. r. *Chickling.* p. 133. l. 31. r. *Oxyrhynchus.* p. 134. l. 48. r. *ſorg.* p. 139. l. 18. *Chamma.* p. 147. l. 20. r. *Cariocataƈtes.* p. 150. l. 20, 21. r. *Cuccothrauſtes.* p. 153. *Of Birds.* p. 156. l. 13. *Avoſetta.* p. 157. l. 48. *Strepſiceros.* p. 159. l. 5. r. *Shrewmouſe.* p. 177. l. 10, &c. r. *More properly Organical ; Whether ſuch parts as are* p. 181. l. 40. after ſuperficies add *imply-*
{ External ; *uſed for the Ɛenſes,* &c. *ing a reſpect to the ſides or limits of it.*
{ Internal ; *uſed for* Taſting, Speaking, *or* Eating. p. 201. l. 49. dele *the,* l. 50. r. the word *Change.* p. 292. l. 22. r. *Arts.* p. 299. l 35. r. *Lux.* p. 301. l. 14. r. *Quantity.* p. 309. l. 19. r. *this.* p. 324. l. 38. r. *jabber.* p. 346. l. 29. r. *Flat.* p. 368. l. 12. r. *Thin.* p. 390. l. 8, 9. r. *upward, downward, above, below.*

Pag. 391. lin. 13. ⸺ p. 395. number, 71. ⸺ n. 74. ⸺ p. 399. n. 33. ⸺ p. 400. n. 37, 45. ⸺ p. 404. l. 3. n. 23. ⸺ n. 27. ⸺ n. 37. ⸺ n. 109. ⸺ p. 413. l. 20. ⸺ p. 422. l. 3. *at.* p. 427. n. 37. c ४ *abys*, p. 428. l. 2. dele 86. l. 6. t ४ ulti. p 429 l. 19. for ४. r. ſ.

In the MARGIN.

Page 70. Read *Muſcus.* p. 72. *Oryza.* p. 76. *Petaſites.* p. 86. *Conyza.* p. 89. *Perfoliata. Erynginm. Spondylinm.* p. 90. *Cherophyllon.* p. 91. *Thyſſelinum. Chamadrys.* p. 92. *Chamapitis.* p. 93. *Stachis. Bugula.* p. 95. *Caryophyllata.* p. 99. *Scorpioides. Bupleurifolio.* p. 102. *Caryophyllus Aſcyrum.* p. 103. *Chamædrys.* p. 104. *Vola. Hyoſcyamus.* p. 106. *Ebulus.* p. 107. *Groſſularia.* p. 108. *Mahaleb.* p. 109. *Philyrhea. Pyracantha. Thymelæa.* p. 115. *Laurocerasus.* p. 116. *Piſtacia. Corylus.* p. 123. *Proſcarabæus.* p. 142. *Lentiſcus.* p. 148. *Ruſſa. Corylorum.* p. 150. *Alauda. Gruchramus.* p. 152. *Troglodytes.* p. 158. *Gazellnsı*

CHAP. I.

I. *The Introduction.* II. *The Original of Languages.* III. *The first Mother-tongues.* IV. *Their several Off-springs.*

IN the handling of that subject, I have here §. I. proposed to treat of, I shall digest the things which to me seem most proper and material to be said upon this occasion, into four parts; according to this following Method.

In the first Part I shall premise some things as *Præcognita*, concerning such Tongues and Letters as are already in being, particularly concerning those various *defects* and *imperfections* in them, which ought to be *supplyed* and *provided against*, in any such Language or Character, as is to be invented according to the rules of Art.

The second Part shall contein that which is the great foundation of the thing here designed, namely a regular *enumeration* and *description* of all those things and notions, to which marks or names ought to be assigned according to their respective natures, which may be styled the *Scientifical* Part, comprehending *Universal Philosophy*. It being the proper end and design of the several branches of Philosophy to reduce all things and notions unto such a frame, as may express their natural order, dependence, and relations.

The third Part shall treat concerning such helps and Instruments, as are requisite for the framing of these more simple notions into continued Speech or Discourse, which may therefore be stiled the Organical or *Instrumental* Part, and doth comprehend the Art of Natural or *Philosophical Grammar*.

In the fourth Part I shall shew how these more generall Rules may be applyed to particular kinds of Characters, and Languages, giving an instance of each. To which shall be adjoyned by way of *Appendix*, a Discourse shewing the advantage of such a kind of Philosophical Character and Language, above any of those which are now known, more particularly above that which is of most general use in these parts of the World; namely, the *Latine*.

Lastly, There shall be added a *Dictionary* of the English tongue, in which shall be shown how all the words of this Language, according to

the various equivocal senses of them, may be sufficiently expressed by the Philosophical Tables here proposed.
I begin with the first of these.

§. II. The design of this Treatise being an attempt towards a *new* kind of *Character* and *Language*, it cannot therefore be improper to premise somewhat concerning those already *in being*; the first *Original* of them, their several *kinds*, the various *changes* and *corruptions* to which they are lyable, together with the manifold *defects* belonging to them. This I shall endeavour to do in the former part of this Discourse.

There is scarce any subject that hath been more throughly scanned and debated amongst Learned men, than the *Original* of *Languages* and *Letters*. 'Tis evident enough that no one Language is *natural* to mankind, because the knowledge which is natural would generally remain amongst men, notwithstanding the superinduction of any other particular Tongue, wherein they might be by *Art*. Nor is it much to be wondred at, that the ancient Heathen, who knew nothing of Scripture-revelation, should be inclined to believe, that either *Men* and *Languages* were *eternal*; or, that if there were any particular time when men did spring out of the Earth, and after inhabit alone and dispersedly in Woods and Caves, they had at first no Articulate voice, but only such rude sounds as Beasts have; till afterwards particular Families increasing, or several Families joyning together for mutual safety and defence, under Government and Societies, they began by degrees and long practice to consent in certain Articulate sounds, whereby to communicate their thoughts, which in several Countries made several Languages, according to that in the Poet,

Horat. lib. 1. Sat. 3.

Cùm prorepserunt primis animalia terris,
Mutum & turpe pecus, glandem atque cubilia propter
Unguibus & pugnis, dein fustibus, atque ita porro
Pugnabant armis, quæ post fabricaverat usus,
Donec verba quibus voces sensúsque notarent
Nomináque invenêre; dehinc absistere bello,
Oppida cœperunt munire, & ponere leges,
Ne quis fur esset, neu latro, neu quis adulter, &c.

But to us, who have the revelation of Scripture, these kind of scruples and conjectures are sufficiently stated. And 'tis evident enough that the first Language was *con-created* with our first Parents, they immediately understanding the voice of God speaking to them in the Garden. And how Languages came to be *multiplyed*, is likewise manifested in the Story of the *Confusion of Babel*. How many Languages, and which they were that sprang up at that Confusion, is altogether uncertain; whether many of them that were then in being, be not now wholly lost; and many others, which had not the same original, have not since arisen in the world, is not (I think) to be doubted.

Gen. 11. 1, 6.

The most received Conjecture is, that the Languages of the Confusion were according to the several Families from *Noah*, which were 70 or 72. though there be very strong probabilities to prove that they were not so many, and that the first Dispersion did not divide mankind into so

many

Chap. I. *The first Mother-tongues.* 3

many Colonies. But now the several Languages that are used in the world do farre exceed this number. *Pliny* and *Strabo* do both make mention of a great Mart-Town in *Colchos* named *Dioscuria*, to which men of three hundred Nations, and of so many several Languages, were wont to resort for Trading. Which, considering the narrow compass of Traffick before the invention of the magnetic Needle, must needs be but a small proportion, in comparison to those many of the remoter and unknown parts of the world.

<small>Nat. Hist. lib. 6.cap. 5. Strabo,lib.11.</small>

Some of the *American* Histories relate, that in every fourscore miles of that vast Country, and almost in every particular valley of *Peru*, the Inhabitants have a distinct Language. And one who for several years travelled the Northern parts of *America* about *Florida*, and could speak six several Languages of those people, doth affirm, that he found, upon his enquiry and converse with them, more than a thousand different Languages amongst them.

<small>Mr. *Cambden's* Remains.

Purchas Pilg. lib. 8. sect. 4. chap. 1.</small>

As for those Languages which seem to have no derivation from, or dependance upon, or affinity with one another, they are styled *Lingua matrices*, or *Mother-tongues*. Of these *Joseph Scaliger* affirms there are eleven, and not more, used in *Europe*; whereof four are of more general and large extent, and the other seven of a narrower compass and use. Of the more general Tongues.

<small>§. III.

Diatribe de Europæorum linguis.</small>

1. The *Greek* was anciently of very great extent, not onely in *Europe*, but in *Asia* too, and *Afric*, where several Colonies of that Nation were planted; by which dispersion and mixture with other people it did degenerate into several *Dialects*. Besides those four that are commonly noted, the *Doric, Ionic, Æolic, Attic*, *Herodotus* doth mention four several Dialects of the *Ionic*. The inhabitants of *Rhodes, Cyprus, Crete*, had each of them some peculiarity in their Language. And the present *Coptic* or *Ægyptian* seems, both from the *words* and the *character*, to be a branch of this family, and was probably spred amongst that people in the days of *Alexander* the Great, upon his conquering of them: Though some conceive that there were at least 30000 families of *Greeks* planted in that Country long before his time.

<small>*Brerewood's* Enquiries, chap. 1.</small>

2. The *Latin*, though this be much of it a derivation from the *Greek*, (of which the now *French, Spanish*, and *Italian* are several off-springs and derivations) had anciently four several Dialects, as *Petrus Crinitus* shews out of *Varro*.

<small>De honesta disciplina, lib. 3. cap. 3.</small>

3. The *Teutonic* or *German* is now distinguished into *Upper* and *Lower*. The *Upper* hath two notable Dialects. 1. The *Danish, Scandian*, or perhaps the *Gothic*, to which belongs the Language used in *Denmark, Norway, Swedeland*, and *Island*. 2. The *Saxon*, to which appertain the several Languages of the *English*, the *Scots*, the *Frisians*, and those on the North of *Elve*.

<small>*Virstegans* chap. 7.</small>

4. The *Slavonic* is extended, though with some variation, through many large Territories, *Muscovia, Russia, Poland, Bohemia, Vandalia, Croatia, Lithuania, Dalmatia*; and is said to be the vulgar Language used amongst 60 several Nations.

<small>*Gesner.* Mithridates, cap. 21.</small>

The Languages of lesser extent are, 1. The *Albanese*, or old *Epirotic*, now used in the mountainous parts of *Epirus*.

2. The *European Tartar*, or *Scythian*, from which some conceive our

B 2 *Irish*

Irish to have had its original. As for the *Turkish* Tongue, that is originally no other but the *Asiatic Tartar*, mixed with *Armenian* and *Persian*, some *Greek*, and much *Arabic*.

3. The *Hungarian*, used in the greatest part of that Kingdom.
4. The *Finnic*, used in *Finland* and *Lapland*.
5. The *Cantabrian*, used amongst the *Biscainers*, who live near the Ocean on the *Pyrene* hills, bordering both upon *France* and *Spain*.
6. The *Irish*, in *Ireland*, and from thence brought over into some parts of *Scotland*. Though Mr. *Camden* would have this to be a derivation from the *Welsh*.
7. The old *Gaulish* or *British*, which is yet preserved in *Wales*, *Cornwall*, and *Britain* in *France*.

Enquiries, chap. 4.

To this number Mr. *Brerewood* doth add four others, *viz.*
1. The *Arabic*, now used in the steep mountains of *Granata*; which yet is a Dialect from the *Hebrew*, and not a *Mother-tongue*.
2. The *Cauchian*, in *East-Friseland*.
3. The *Illyrian*, in the Isle of *Veggia*.
4. The *Jazygian*, on the North side of *Hungary*.

§. IV.

Besides this difference of Languages in their first derivation, every particular Tongue hath its several Dialects. Though *Judea* were a region of a very narrow compass, yet was it not without its varieties of this kind: witness the story concerning *Shibboleth* and *Sibboleth*; and that

Judges 12.
Judges 18.3.
Matth. 26.73.

of the *Levite*, who was discovered by his manner of speech; and S. *Peter*'s being known for a *Galilean*. 'Tis so generally in other Countries, and particularly with us in *England*, where the Northern and Western inhabitants do observe a different dialect from other parts of the Nation, as may appear from that particular instance mentioned by *Verstegan*. Whereas the inhabitants about *London* would say, *I would eat more cheese if I had it*. A Northern man would speak it thus, *Ay sud eat mare cheese gyn ay had et*. And a Western man thus, *Chud eat more cheese an chad it*.

Every one of these reputed Mother-tongues, except the *Arabic*, (and perhaps the *Hungarian*) was used in *Europe* during the time of the *Roman* Empire. But whether they were all of them so ancient as the Confusion of *Babel*, doth not appear; there wants not good probability to the contrary for some of them.

Georg. Hornii Epist. in Bos-hornii Origines Gallic.

It hath been the opinion of some, particularly *Boxhornius*, that the *Scythian* Tongue was the common mother from which both the *Greek*, *Latin*, *German* and *Persian* were derived, as so many Dialects; and 'tis said that *Salmasius* did incline to the same judgment. And *Philip Cluverius* conjectures, that both *Germans*, *Gauls*, *Spaniards*, *Britans*, *Swedes* and *Norwegians*, did anciently use one and the same Language. One principal argument used for this is, the agreement of those remote Nations in some radical words. *Joseph Scaliger* observes that the words, *Father*, *Mother*, *Brother*, *Bond*, &c. are used in the *Persian* tongue, with some little variety, in the same sense and signification as they are used with us.

In Epist.

And *Busbequius* relates, that the inhabitants of *Taurica Chersonesus* have divers words in the same sense common with us, as *Wine*, *Silver*, *Corn*, *Salt*, *Fish*, *Apple*, &c. But this might be merely casual, or else occasioned by a mixture of Colonies, and will not argue a derivation of one from another.

Chap. I.   *And their Off-spring.*   5

another. So there are several words common to the *Turks*, *Germans*, *Greeks*, *French*, sometimes of the same, and sometimes of several significations; which is not sufficient to argue that all these were of the same Original.   <small>Boxhorn. Origin. Gallic. cap. 6. & 8.</small>

Besides these *European*, there is likewise great variety of Languages in other parts of the world. As for the *Hebrew* Tongue, which is by many learned men supposed to be the same that *Abraham* learnt when he came into *Canaan*, to which that expression *Isai.* 19. 18. *The language of Canaan*, is thought to allude; this is supposed to be the first *Mother tongue* amongst all those that are now known in the world, from which there are sundry *derivations*, as the *Chaldee*, *Syriac*, *Punic*, *Arabic*, *Persian*, *Æthiopic*.

When the *Jews* were in Captivity at *Babylon*, mixed with the *Chaldeans* for 70 years, in that tract of time they made up a Language distinct from both, which is sometimes called *Syriac*, and sometimes *Chaldee*, and sometimes *Hebrew*. Those passages in the Gospel, which are said to be in the *Hebrew* tongue, as *Talitha Kumi*; *Elohi*, *Elohi*, *Lamma sabachthani*, are properly *Syriac*; onely they are called *Hebrew*, because that was the Language which the *Hebrews* then used. A great part of this *Syriac* tongue is for the *substance* of the words *Chaldee*, and *Hebrew* for the *fashion*, Yet degenerating much from both. After the Captivity the pure *Hebrew* ceased to be *vulgar*, remaining onely amongst learned men, as appears by that place in *Nehem.* 8. 7, 8. where we find the Priests, upon reading of the Law to the people after their coming out of *Babylon*, were fain to expound it distinctly to them, and to make them understand the meaning of it; the common people, by long disuse, being grown strangers to the Language wherein 'twas written. So in our Saviour's time, the unlearned *Jews*, whose vulgar Tongue the *Syriac* was, could not understand those parts of *Moses* and the *Prophets* read to them in *Hebrew* every Sabbath-day. Which was the reason of those public speeches and declarations of any learned men, who occasionally came into the Synagogues, after the reading of the Law: though neither Priests, nor Levites, nor Scribes, yet was it ordinary for them to expound unto the people the meaning of those portions of Scripture that were appointed to be read out of the *Hebrew*, which the people did not understand; and to render their meaning in *Syriac*, which was their *vulgar* Tongue.   <small>Brerewood's Enquiries, chap. 9.
John 5. 2. & 19. 13, 17. Acts 21. 40.
Bochart. Geog. l. 1. cap. 15.

Luke 4. 15, 16. Acts 13. 19.</small>

As for so much of the pure *Hebrew* as is now in being, which is onely that in the old Testament, though it be sufficient to express what is there intended, yet it is so exceedingly defective in many other words requisite to humane discourse, that the Rabbins are fain to borrow words from many other Languages, *Greek*, *Latin*, *Spanish*, &c. as may appear at large in *Buxtorf's Lexicon Rabbinicum*, and a particular Discourse written to this very purpose by *David Cohen de Lara*. And, from the several defects and imperfections which seem to be in this Language, it may be guessed not to be the same which was con-created with our first Parents, and spoken by *Adam* in *Paradise*.

What other varieties of Tongues there have been, or are, in *Asia*, *Afric*, or *America*, I shall not now enquire.

CHAP.

CHAP. II.

I. *Concerning the various changes and corruptions to which all vulgar Languages are obnoxious.* II. *Particularly concerning the changes of the* English *tongue.* III. *Whether any Language, formerly in use, be now wholly lost.* IV. *Concerning the first rise and occasion of new Languages.*

§. I.

THere are three Queres which may deserve some farther disquisition. 1. Whether the purest of those *Mother-tongues*, which yet remain, be not now much changed from what they were at the first Confusion. 2. Whether and how any of the *Mother-tongues* have been quite lost since the Confusion. 3. Whether and how other new Languages have since arisen in the world.

1. To the first, Besides the common fate and corruption to which Languages as well as all other humane things are subject, there are many other particular causes which may occasion such a change: The mixture with other Nations in Commerce; Marriages in Regal Families, which doth usually bring some common words into a Court fashion; that affectation incident to some eminent men in all ages, of coining new words, and altering the common forms of speech, for greater elegance; the necessity of making other words, according as new things and inventions are discovered. Besides, the Laws of forein Conquests usually extend to Letters and Speech as well as Territories; the Victor commonly endeavouring to propagate his own Language as farre as his Dominions; which is the reason why the *Greek* and *Latin* are so universally known. And when a Nation is overspread with several Colonies of foreiners, though this do not alwaies prevail to *abolish* the former Language, yet if they make any long abode, this must needs make such a considerable *change* and *mixture* of speech as will very much alter it from its original Purity.

Those *learned* Languages which have now ceased to be *vulgar*, and remain onely in Books, by which the purity of them is regulated, may, whilst those Books are extant and studied, continue the same without change. But all Languages that are vulgar, as those learned ones formerly were, are upon the fore-mentioned occasions, subject to so many alterations, that in tract of time they will appear to be quite another thing then what they were at first.

Brerewood's Enquiries, chap. 2. & 6.

The Liturgies of S. *Basil* and S. *Chrysostom*, which are yet used in the *Greek* Churches in their publick worship, the one for *solemn*, the other for *common* days, have been a long time unintelligible to that people; so much is the *vulgar Greek* degenerated from its former purity.

Hist. lib. 3.

And *Polibius* testifies, that the Articles of truce betwixt the *Romans* and *Carthaginians* could scarce be understood by the most learned *Roman* Antiquaries 350 years after the time of their making.

§. II.
Alex. Gil Logonom. Anglican. Preface.

If any *English* man should now write or speak as our forefathers did about six or seven hundred years past, we should as little understand him as if he were a forciner; of which it were easie to give several proofs

by

Chap. II.   *The Alterations of Languages.*

by inſtance, if it were not inconſiſtent with my preſent deſign of brevity. What the *Saxons* Language was at their firſt arrival into *England* about the year 440, doth not appear; but 'tis moſt probable that the *changes* and *differences* of it, have been ſomewhat proportionable in ſeveral Ages.

About the year of Chriſt 700 the Lord's Prayer in *Engliſh* was thus rendred:

Uren fader thic arth in heofnas, ſic gehalgud thin noma: to cymeth thin ric: ſic thin willa ſue is in heofnas and in eortho. Uren hlaf ofer wirtlic ſel us to daeg; and forgef us ſcylda urna, ſue we forgefen ſcyldgum urum; and no inlead uſith in cuſtnung. Ah gefrig urich from iſle. Amen.   *Cambden's Remains, pag. 23.*

About 200 years after, it was changed thus:

Thu ure fader the eart on heofenum. Si thin nama gehalgod. Cum thin ric. Si thin willa on eorthen ſwa, ſwa on heofenum. Syle us to dæg urn dægthanlican hlaf. And forgif us ure gyltas ſwa, ſwa we forgifath tham the with us agyltath. And ne led the us on coſtnung. Ac alys us from yſle. Si it ſwa.   *Liſle's Saxon Monuments.*

About the ſame time it was rendred in the Saxon Goſpels, ſaid to be Tranſlated by King *Alfred*, after this manner.

Fæder ure thu the earth on heofenum, ſi thin nama Gehalgod to be cume thin Rice, Gewurthe thin willa on eorthan ſwa ſwa on heofnum, urne ge dæghwanlican hlaf ſyle us to dæg. And forgyf us ure gyltas, ſwa ſwa we forgivath urum gyltendum. And ne gelædde thu us on coſtnung. Ac Alyſe us of yſle.

About 260 years after, in the time of King *Henry* the 2d, it was rendred thus, and ſent over by Pope *Adrian*, an *Engliſh*-man, turned into meter, that the people might more eaſily learn and remember it.

   Ure fadyr in heaven rich,
   Thy name be hallyed ever lich,
   Thou bring us thy michell bliſſe:
   Als hit in heaven y-doe,
   Evar in pearth beene it alſo.
   That holy bread that laſteth ay,
   Thou ſend it ous this ilke day,
   Forgive ous all that we have don,
   As we forgivet uch other mon:
   Ne let ous fall into no founding,
   Ac ſhield ous fro the fowle thing. Amen.

And about a hundred years after, in the time of *Henry* the third, it was rendred thus:

   Fader that art in heavin bliſſe,
   Thin helge nam it wurth the bliſſe,
   Cumen and mot thy kingdom,
   Thin holy will it be all don,
   In heaven and in eroth alſo,
   So it ſhall bin full well Ic tro,
   Gif us all bread on this day,
   And forgif us ure ſinnes,
   As we do ure wider winnes:
   Let us not in fonding fall,
   Oac fro evil thu ſyld us all. Amen.

About two hundred years after this in the time of *Henry* the VI. (as appears by a large manuscript Velume Bible in the *Oxford*-Library, said to have been this Kings, and by him to have been given to the *Carthusians* in *London*;) It was rendred thus.

Oure fadir that art in hevenes, halewid be thi name, thi kingdom come to thee, be thi wil don in eerthe, as in hevene, give to us this day oure breed over othre substanc, and forgive to us oure dettis, as we forgiven oure dettouris, and lede us not into temptation, but delivere us from ivel. Amen.

In another M.S. of *Wickliffes* Translation, who lived in *Richard* the 2^d time, it is rendred with very small difference from this.

About a hundred years after this, In a Bible set forth with the Kings licens, translated by *Thomas Mathew*, and printed in the year 1537, it was rendered thus:

O oure father which arte in hevēn halowed be thy name. Let thy kingdome come. Thy will be fulfilled, as well in erth, as it is in heven. Geve us this daye oure dayly bred. And forgeve us our treaspases, even as we forgeve oure trespacers. And lead us not into temptacion, but delyver us from evyll. Amen.

After the same manner it is rendered in the Translation of *William Tyndall*, with some little differences in the spelling.

This one instance may sufficiently manifest by what degrees this Language did receive its several Changes, and how much altered it is *now* from what it *hath been*, and consequently what is to be expected in *future times*. Since Learning began to flourish in our Nation, there have been more then ordinary Changes introduced in our Language: partly by new artificial *Compositions*; partly by *enfranchising* strange forein words, for their elegance and significancy, which now make one third part of our Language; and partly by *refining* and *mollifying* old words, for the more easie and graceful sound: by which means this last Century may be conjectured to have made a greater change in our Tongue, then any of the former, as to the addition of new words.

And thus, in all probability, must it have been with all other *vulgar* Languages. So that 'tis not likely that any of these *Mother-tongues* now in being, are the same that they were at the first Confusion. So true is that of the Poet:

Horat. de arte poëtica.

Ut sylva foliis pronos mutantur in annos,
Prima cadunt; ita verborum vetus interit ætas,
Et, juvenum ritu, florent modò nata vigéntque.
Debemur morti nos nostrdque----

And a little after,

Multa renascentur quæ jam cecidere, cadéntque
Quæ nunc sunt in honore vocabula, si volet usus;
Quem penes arbitrium est, & vis, & norma loquendi.

§. III. 2. As to the second Quere, Whether any of the Ancient Languages be now *quite lost*; it may be answered, That if in some few hundreds of years a Language may be so *changed* as to be scarce intelligible; then, in a much longer tract of time it may be quite *abolished*, none of the most radical and substantial parts remaining: For every *change* is a *gradual corruption*.

Before

Chap. II. *Of new Languages.* 9

Before the flourishing of the *Roman Empire*, there were several native Languages used in *Italy*, *France*, *Spain*. In *Italy* we read of the *Messapian*, the *Hetruscan*, the *Sabine*, the *Oscan*, the *Hetrurian* or *Tuscan* Languages; which are now thought by Learned men to be utterly lost, and no-where to be found in the World. *Ludov. Vives* Annot. in *Au-gust.* Civ.Dei, lib. 19. cap. 17.

'Tis probable that there was not onely one Language in so vast a Territory as *France*, but that several Provinces spake several Languages: But what those Languages were, or whether yet extant, is uncertain. As for the *Celta*, who, inhabiting the inner part of the Country, were less subject to forein mixtures, 'tis most probable that their Language might be the *British* or *Welsh*, which is yet spoken in some parts of *France*. *Cæsar* reports that the *Gauls* were wont often to pass over into *Britain*, to be instructed by the *Druids*, amongst whom there was then no use of Books or Writing, and therefore they must communicate by Discourse. And *Tacitus* affirms that the Speech of the *British* and *Gauls*, differed but little. *Brerewood's* Enquiries, chap. 6.
De Bello Gallico, lib. 6.

It is conceived that one of the ancient Tongues of *Spain* was the *Cantabrian*, which doth now there remain in the more barren mountainous, inaccessible parts, where Conquerors are less willing to pursue, or desirous to plant; as our *British* doth in *Wales*. But 'tis probable that there might be several other Languages besides this in so great a Continent, as well as in *Italy*, which are now wholly lost and unknown.

3. As to the third Quere, concerning the *first Rise* and occasion of *new Languages*, that may be sufficiently answered by what was before suggested, concerning those many particular emergencies which may contribute to the introducing a *change* in Languages. § IV.

Some think that the *Italians*, *Spaniards* and *French*, after they were totally subdued by the *Romans*, and planted with their Colonies, did, after a certain space of time, receive the *Latin* Tongue as their most vulgar Speech, and retained it; till afterwards, being several times overrun by the Northern barbarous Nations, the *Goths* and *Vandals*, and other Tribes of the *Germans*, who mixed with them, and after several Conquests resided amongst them, sometimes 20, 60, 200 years together; this afforded time enough for such a thorough coalition betwixt them and the Natives, as could not but introduce a great *change* in the common Language, whilst the Nations were forced to attemper their Speech for the mutual understanding of one another.

Others conceive that those Countries did not at first perfectly receive the *Latin* from the *Romans*, but did onely make use of the most principal *radical words*; neglecting the Grammatical rules of *composition* and *inflection*, and withall varying the way of *pronunciation*, according to the unusualness and difficulty of several sounds to several Countries: And that this was the first and chief occasion of those various *Medleys* or several *Dialects* now in use; which were afterwards somewhat farther changed from their Originals, by those several Inundations of the *Barbarians*.

'Tis not much material to dispute, which of these causes had the principal influence in the extraction of these modern Tongues, so long as 'tis granted that both of them might contribute and suffice for this effect. As for our present *English*, this seems to be a mixture of the *British*, *Roman*,

Cambden's Remains. *man*, *Saxon*, *Danish*, *Norman*, according to the several vicissitudes of Plantations and Conquests, that this Nation hath undergone. And according as such Conquests have been more or less compleat and absolute, so have the *Languages* been more or less generally altered: which is the reason why the *Saxon* Tongue was by our progenitors more fully introduced in *England*, then either that of the *Franks* amongst the *Gauls*, or that of the *Goths* or *Lumbards* in *Italy*, or that of the *Goths*, *Vandals* or *Moors* in *Spain*.

Linschoten voiage, chap. 18. That which seems to be the *newest Language* in the World, is the *Malayan*, which is now as general and common amongst the Natives of the *East-Indies*, as *Latin* or *French* is in these parts of the World. 'Tis said to be but of late invention, occasioned by the concourse of Fishermen from *Pegu*, *Siam*, *Bengala*, and several other Nations, who meeting together at a place convenient for Fishing, and finding that it was by situation exceeding commodious for Traffick from several parts, did agree to settle there a Plantation; and accordingly built the Town of *Malacca*, which hath since, for many years, been governed by the *Portuguez*, and is now under the power of the *Hollander*. And, for the more facil *converse* with one another, they agreed upon a distinct *Language*, which probably was made up by selecting the most soft and easy words belonging to each several Nation. And this is the onely *Language* (for ought I know) that hath ever been at once *invented*; if it may properly be styled a distinct Language, and not rather a *Medley* of many. But this being invented by rude Fishermen, it cannot be expected that it should have all those advantages, with which it might have been furnished by the rules of Philosophy.

Additamentum de Regno. atoya. I know that the Learned *Golius* doth affirm the *China* Language to be invented by *Art*; but, upon the best discovery to be made of it at this distance, from those who have lived many years in that Country, and pretend to understand the Language, it appears to be so exceedingly *equivocal*, and in many respects so very *imperfect*, that there is little reason to believe it had any such Original.

CHAP. III.

I. *The Original of Letters and Writing.* II. *That all Letters were derived from the* Hebrew. III. *The use of Letters is less ancient, and the kinds of them less numerous, then of the Languages themselves.* IV. *Of Notes for Secrecy or Brevity.* V. *Of real Characters.* VI. *Of Alphabets in general.*

§. I.

Tuscul. Qu. lib. 1. HAving laid down this brief and general View of *Languages*, 'tis requisite that something should be also premised concerning *Letters*, the *Invention* of which was a thing of so great Art and exquisiteness, that *Tully* doth from hence inferr the divinity and spirituality of the humane *soul*, and that it must needs be of a farr more excellent and abstracted Essence then mere Matter or Body, in that it was able to reduce all articulate sounds to 24 *Letters*.

Though

Chap. III.   *All Letters from the Hebrew.*   11

Though the Scripture doth not mention any thing concerning the invention of these; yet 'tis most generally agreed, that *Adam*, (though not immediately after his Creation, yet) in process of time, upon his experience of their great necessity and usefulness, did first invent the ancient *Hebrew* Character: whether that which we now call the *Hebrew*, or else the *Samaritan*, is a question much debated by several Learned men, which I shall not now inquire into, or offer to determine.

As for those particular *Alphabets* which are by some ascribed to *Adam*, *Enoch* and *Noah*, mentioned by several Authors, and in a late Discourse by *Thomas Bangius*, they have so little foundation in any probable reason or story, that I shall not so much as make any farther mention of them.

Cœlum Orientis.

It hath been abundantly cleared up by many Learned men, that the ancient *Hebrew* Character hath the *priority* before any other now known; which is confirmed by the concurrent testimony of the best and most ancient Heathen Writers. And 'tis amongst rational arguments none of the least, for the Truth and Divine Authority of Scripture, to consider the general concurrence of all manner of evidence for the Antiquity of the *Hebrew*, and the derivation of all other Letters from it.

§. II.

Grotius de Veritate Relig. lib. 1.

Pliny affirms in one place, that the first *invention* of Letters ought to be ascribed unto the *Assyrians*; and in another place he saith, that under the name of *Syria* he understands the Regions which were styled *Palestine*, *Judaea* and *Phœnicia*; and in the same Chapter he ascribes the *invention* of Letters to the *Phœnicians*. So doth *Lucan* likewise;

Nat. Hist. L 7. cap. 56. Lib. 5. cap. 12.

Bell. Pharsal. lib. 3.

Phœnices primi (fame si credimus) ausi Mansuram rudibus vocem signare figuris.

With these agree [a] *Herodotus*, *Strabo*, [b] *Plutarch*, [c] *Curtius*, *Mela*, &c. who all consent, that the *Grecians* did first receive their Letters from the *Phœnicians* by *Cadmus*, who lived about the time of *Joshua*. And that the *Punic* or *Phœnician* Tongue was the *Canaanitish* or the *Hebrew*, though somewhat altered from its original pronunciation, (as is wont in tract of time to befall Colonies planted far from home, amongst strangers,) is sufficiently manifested from the remainders of it that are extant in *Plautus* and other prophane Authors, as they are cited by the learned *Bochart*. And that the *Phœnicians* were *Canaanites* hath proof also in Scripture, because the same woman who in *Mark* 7. 26. is styled a *Syrophœnician*, is said *Matth.* 15. 22. to be a *Canaanite*.

[a] *Terpsichore.*
[b] *Symposiac. lib. 9.*
[c] *Hist. lib. 4.*
Scaliger. Appendix de Emendat. Temp.
Brerewood's Enquiries, chap. 7.
Geograph. l. 2.

That the ancient *Greek* Character was of very near affinity to the *Samaritan*, and that the *Latin* Letters were of such an affinity to the *Greek*, and derived from them, being in a manner the same with the ancient *Ionic* Letters, is made very plain by *Scaliger*, and owned by *Pliny* and *Dionysius Halicarnassensis*. And *Tacitus* doth acknowledge that the ancient *Latin* Characters were in their shape and figure almost the same with the *Greek*. And as for the other Letters that are known, namely, the *Syriac*, *Arabic*, *Æthiopic*, *Armenian*, *Coptic*, *Illyric*, *Georgian*, *Gothic*, there is this cogent Argument to prove them to be of the same Original, because their *Alphabets* do generally observe the same order of Letters, which, being in it self exceedingly irrational, cannot probably have any other reason but *imitation*. Except onely that of the *Arabs*, saith *Hermannus Hugo*, who, that they might not seem to have borrowed Letters from

Animadvers. in Eusebium, Anno 1617.
Nat. Hist. lib. 7. cap. 56.
Hist. lib. 1.
Annal. 11.

De Origine Scribendi, cap. 5.

C 2

from others, did purposely disturb the order of the *Alphabet*; to which he might have added the *Æthiopic* and *Armenian*.

§. III. There are two general things to be observed concerning these derived Letters. 1. That they are not of so great *Antiquity*. 2. That they are not so *numerous* as Languages are.

1. They are not so *ancient*, many Nations remaining a long while before they grew so far civilized as to understand the use of Letters, which to this day are not known amongst many of the *American* Nations, nor the Inhabitants of *Lapland*: and after they have been known, and of some public use, it hath been yet a considerable space, before persons have written any Discourse in their own Language. 'Tis observed by *Tschudas* of the *German*, and by *Genebrard* of the *French* Tongue, (saith Mr. *Brerewood*) that 'tis not much above 400 years, since Books began to be written in those Languages.

Enquiries, chap. 5.

2. And because the use of *Letters* in particular Countries is not so ancient as *Language*, therefore are they not of so *numerous* kinds; several Nations taking up the use of *Letters* from their neighbours, and adapting them to their own Tongue. Thus the *Spanish*, *French*, *Italian*, *German*, *British*, *English*, *Irish*, &c. do all of them use the same *Latine* Character, it being probable that they had none of their own, before they learnt this of the *Romans*. The *Coptic* or *Egyptian* Character, ever since *Egypt* came under the Dominion of *Macedon*, hath been the *Greek*, excepting only seven *Letters* proper to their Tongue, which the *Greek* Alphabet did not sufficiently express; The *Muscovites* likewise and the *Russians*, the *Georgians* and *Jacobins*, do use the *Greek* Character; the *Persians* and *Turks* use the *Arabick*: though the *Letters* of any Tongue do not alwaies remain the same, but are subject to the like fate and mutability, to which Languages are exposed.

§. IV. Besides this common way of Writing by the ordinary *Letters*, the Ancients have sometimes used to communicate by other *Notes*, which were either for *Secrecy*, or *Brevity*.

1. For *Secrecy*: such were the *Egyptian Hieroglyphicks*, (as they are commonly esteemed) being the representation of certain living Creatures, and other Bodies, whereby they were wont to conceal from the vulgar the Mysteries of their Religion. But there is reason to doubt whether there be any thing in these worth the enquiry, the discoveries that have been hitherto made out of them being but very few and insignificant. They seem to be but a slight, imperfect invention, sutable to those first and ruder Ages; much of the same nature with that *Mexican* way of writing by Picture, which was a mere shift they were put to for want of the knowledge of *Letters*. And it seems to me questionable, whether the *Egyptians* did not at first use their *Hieroglyphicks* upon the same account, namely, for the want of *Letters*.

Vid. Purchas book 5. chap. 7. sect. 1.

Those waies of writing treated of by the Abbot *Trithemius*, were likewise for *occult* or *secret* communication: And though some Learned men have suspected and accused him to have thereby delivered the Art of *Magic*, or Conjuring; yet he is sufficiently cleared and vindicated from any such prejudice in that very learned and ingenious Discourse *de Cryptographia*, under the feigned name of *Gustavus Selenus*,

by

Chap. III.   *Of a Reall Character.*   13

by which the noble Author, the Duke of *Lunenburg*, did disguise his true name of *Augustus Lunæburgicus*.

2. For *Brevity*: There were single *Letters* or *marks*, whereby the *Romans* were wont to express whole words. *Ennius* is said to have invented 1100 of these; to which number *Tullius Tyro*, *Cicero's Libertus*, (Others say *Cicero* himself,) added divers others, to signifie the *particles* of speech; after whom *Philargyrus* the *Samian* and *Mecænas*, added yet more. After these *Annæus Seneca* is said to have laboured in the regulating and digesting of those former notes; to which adding many of his own, he augmented the whole number to 5000, published by *Janus Gruterus*; though amongst his there are divers of a later invention, relating to Christian institutions, which have been added since (as 'tis said) by S. *Cyprian* the Martyr. The way of writing by these did require a vast memory and labour; yet it was far short of expressing all things and Notions, and besides, had no provision for Grammatical variations.   *Tritbemius de Polygraphia.*

Of this nature is that *Short-hand-writing* by Characters so frequent with us in *England*, and much wondered at by Foreiners; which hath a great advantage for speed and swiftness in writing; those who are expert in it being able this way to take any ordinary discourse *verbatim*.

Besides these, there have been some other proposals and attempts about a *Real universal Character*, that should not signifie *words*, but *things* and *notions*, and consequently might be legible by any Nation in their own Tongue; which is the principal design of this Treatise. That such a Real Character is possible, and hath been reckoned by Learned men amongst the *Desiderata*, were easie to make out by abundance of Testimonies. To this purpose is that which *Piso* mentions to be somewhere the wish of *Galen*, That some way might be found out to represent things by such peculiar *signs* and *names* as should express their *natures*; *ut Sophistis eriperetur decertandi & calumniandi occasio*. There are several other passages to this purpose in the Learned *Verulam*, in *Vossius*, in *Hermannus Hugo*, &c. besides what is commonly reported of the men of *China*, who do now, and have for many Ages used such a general Character, by which the Inhabitants of that large Kingdom, many of them of different Tongues, do communicate with one another, every one understanding this common Character, and reading it in his own Language.   §. V.   *Histor. Nat. India, lib. 4. c. 3.*   *De Augment. lib. 6. cap. 1. Orig. scribendi, cap. 4.*

It cannot be denied, but that the *variety* of *Letters* is an appendix to the Curse of *Babel*, namely, the multitude and variety of *Languages*. And therefore, for any man to go about to add to their number, will be but like the inventing of a Disease, for which he can expect but little thanks from the world. But this Consideration ought to be no discouragement: For supposing such a thing as is here proposed, could be well established, it would be the surest remedy that could be against the Curse of the Confusion, by rendring all other *Languages* and *Characters* useless.

It doth not appear that any *Alphabet* now in being, was *invented at once* or by the *rules of Art*; but rather that all, except the *Hebrew*, were taken   §. VI.

taken up by Imitation, and paſt by degrees through ſeveral Changes; which is the reaſon that they are leſs complete, and liable to ſeveral exceptions. The *Hebrew* Character, as to the ſhape of it, though it appear ſolemn and grave, yet hath it not its *Letters* ſufficiently diſtinguiſhed from one another, and withall it appears ſomewhat harſh and rugged. The *Arabic* Character, though it ſhew beautiful, yet is it too elaborate, and takes up too much room, and cannot well be written ſmall. The *Greek* and the *Latin* are both of them graceful and indifferent eaſie, though not without their ſeveral imperfections.

As for the *Æthiopic*, it hath no leſs then 202 *Letters* in its Alphabet; namely, 7 Vowels, which they apply to every one of their 26 Conſonants, to which they add 20 other aſpirated Syllables. All their Characters are exceedingly complicated and perplexed, and much more difficult then thoſe propoſed in this following Diſcourſe for the expreſſing of things and notions.

Martinii Atlas Sinenſis.

This is ſaid likewiſe of the *Tartarian*, that every Character with them is a Syllable, having each of the Vowels joyned to its Conſonant, as *La, Le, Li,* &c. which muſt needs make a long and troubleſome *Alphabet*.

But it is not my purpoſe to animadvert upon theſe Tongues that are leſs known, ſo much as thoſe with which theſe parts of the world are better acquainted.

CHAP. IV.

I. *The Defects in the common Alphabets, as to their true Order.* II. *Juſt Number.* III. *Determinate Powers.* IV. *Fitting Names.* V. *Proper Figures of the Letters.* VI. *The Imperfections belonging to the Words of Language, as to their Equivocalneſs, variety of Synonymous words, uncertain Phraſeologies, improper way of Writing.*

§. I.

ONe ſpecial Circumſtance which adds to the Curſe of *Babel* is that *difficulty* which there is in all *Languages*, ariſing from the various *Imperfections* belonging to them, both in reſpect of 1. their firſt *Elements* or *Alphabets*, 2. their *Words*.

1. For *Alphabets*, they are all of them, in many reſpects, liable to juſt exception.

1. As to the *Order* of them, they are inartificial and *confuſed*, without any ſuch methodical diſtribution as were requiſite for their particular natures and differences; the *Vowels* and *Conſonants* being promiſcuouſly huddled together, without any diſtinction: Whereas in a regular *Alphabet*, the *Vowels* and *Conſonants* ſhould be reduced into *Claſſes*, according to their ſeveral kinds, with ſuch an order of precedence and ſubſequence as their natures will bear; this being the proper end and deſign of that which we call *Method*, to ſeparate the Heterogeneous, and put the Homogeneous together, according to ſome rule of precedency.

The *Hebrew* Alphabet, (the order of which is obſerved in ſeveral Scriptures, *Pſal.* 119. and in the Book of *Lamentations*) from whence the others are derived, is not free from this Imperfection.

2. For

Chap. IV.   *Defects in Alphabets.*   15

2. For their *Number*, they are in several respects both *Redundant*, and §. II.
Deficient.
  1. *Redundant* and superfluous; either 1. By allotting *several Letters* to the *same power* and sound. So in the *Hebrew* (ב & ו) and so perhaps (ב & ו) (ת & ט) (ס & ש) (כ & ק) So in the ordinary *Latin*, (*C* & *K*) (*F* & *Ph*.) Or 2. by reckoning *double Letters* amongst the most simple elements of Speech: as in the *Hebrew* ש; in the *Greek* ξ and ψ; in the *Latin* (*Q. Cu*) (*X. cs*.) and *J* Consonant or Jod which is made up of (*dzh*) by assigning several Letters to represent one simple power, as *th*, *sh*, &c. So that none of these can regularly be reckoned amongst the simple elements of Speech.
  2. *Deficient* in other respects, especially *in regard of Vowels*, of which there are 7 or 8 several kinds commonly used, (as I shall shew afterwards) though the *Latin* Alphabet take notice but of *five*, whereof two, namely (*i* and *u*.) according to our *English* pronunciation of them, are not properly Vowels, but *Diphthongs*. And besides, that gradual difference amongst Vowels of *long* and *short* is not sufficiently provided for. The Ancients were wont to express a *long* Vowel by *doubling* the Character of it ; as *Amaabam, Naata, Ree, Seedes, Sanctissimiis, Mariinas :* *Vossius*. though oftentimes the Vowel *I*, instead of being doubled, was onely *prolonged* in the figure of it; as ÆDILIS, PISO, VIVUS. For the ways used by us *English* for lengthning and abbreviating Vowels, *viz*. by adding *E* quiescent to the end of a word for *prolonging* a Syllable, and *doubling* the following Consonant for the *shortning* of a Vowel, as *Wane, Wann ; Ware, Warr*, &c. or else by *inserting* some other Vowel, for the *lengthning* of it, as *Meat, Met ; Read, Red*, &c. both these are upon this account *improper*, because the sign ought to be where the sound is. Nor would it be so fit to express this by a distinct *Character*, because it denotes onely an *accidental* or *gradual difference*, as by an *Accent* ; the chief use of *Accents*, for which they are necessary in ordinary speech, being to signifie *Quantities* and Elevations of voice.

3. For their *Powers*, they are very *uncertain*, not alwaies fixed and determined to the same signification : which as to our *English* pronunciation may be made to appear by abundance of Instances both in the Vowels and Consonants.
  1. As to the *Vowels* : It is generally acknowledged that each of them have several sounds. *Vocales omnes plurisona*, saith *Lipsius*. And the learn- De Pronunc. ed *Vossius* doth assure us, that the Ancients did use their Vowels in very cap. 5.
different wayes, *aliquando tenuius exiliúsque, nunc crassius, nunc inter-* lib. 1. cap. 12. *medio sono*. Jos.Scal.Diat.
  The power of the Vowel (*i*) treated of afterwards, is expressed in De varia pro-
writing no less then six several waies ; by nunciat.one.
    e. He, me, she, ye.
    ee. Thee, free, wee.
    ie. Field, yield, shield, chief.
    ea. Near, dear, bear.
    eo. People.
    i. Privilege.
  So is the *Power* of the Vowel (*a*) as in *All, aul, aw, fault, caught, brought*.

brought. These are all various waies of writing the same long Vowel; besides which there are other distinct waies of expressing the same Vowel when it is used short, as in the words *of, for,* &c.

And for the *Power* of the Vowel (*u*) that is likewise written five several waies.

    o. To, who, move.
    oe. Doe.
    oo. Shoo, moon, noon.
    ou. Could, would.
    wo. Two.

And as for the *Power* of the Vowel (*u*) this also is written five several waies; namely, by the Letters

    i. Sir, stir, firmament, &c.
    o. Hony, mony, come, some, love, &c.
    oo. Blood, flood.
    u. Turn, burn, burthen.
    ou. Country, couple.

2. As to the *Consonants*, these likewise are of very *uncertain Powers*: witness the different pronunciation of the letter (*C*) in the word *Circo*, and (*G*) in the word *Negligence*. I know 'tis said that the letter (*C*) before the Vowels *a, o, u,* must be pronounced like (*K,*) as in the words *cado, coram, cudo*; and before the Vowels *e, i,* as *S,* as in the words *cedo, cilium.* But there is no reason why it should be so. Upon which account our learned Countryman, Sir *Tho. Smith,* doth justly censure it as *monstrum litera, non litera; ignorantiæ specimen, non artis; modò serpens, modò cornix.*

De Linguæ Anglicanæ pronunciatione.

The letters *C, S, T,* are often used alike, to denote the same *Power*, and that both in *English* and *French*; and the letter (*S*) is most frequently used for (*Z*) which must needs be very improper. And, which is yet more irrational, some Letters of the same name and shape are used sometimes for *Vowels*, and sometimes for *Consonants*; as *J, V, W, Y*; which yet differ from one another *sicut corpus & anima,* and ought by no means to be confounded.

Cessio, Sessio, Gratia.

Priscian.

To which may be added, that from this equivocal *power* of Letters, it so falls out, that

1. Some words are *distinguished* in writing, and *not* in *pronunciation*: as *Sessio, Cessio*; *Sera, Cera*; *Servus, Cervus*; *Syrus, Cyrus*; *Boar, Bore*; *Come,* Lat. *Cum*; *Dome, Dum*; *Dear, Deer*; *Hear, Here*; *Heart, Hart*; *Meat, Mete*; *Son, Sun*; *Some,* Lat. *Sum*; *Toes, Toze*; *Toe, Towe*; *To, Too, Two.*

2. Some words are *distinguished* in *pronunciation*, but *not* in *writing*; as the words *Give,* i. *Dare, Give,* i. *Vinculum*; *Get.* i. *Acquirere, Get,* i. *Gagates*; *is* and *his* in *English,* and *is* and *his* in *Latin*. So the *Latin* word *Malè,* i. *evilly,* is a dissyllable; whereas the *English* word *Male,* which signifies the masculine Sex, is but a monosyllable. All which are very great incongruities, and such as ought to be avoided in any regular establishment of Letters.

§. IV.

4. Their *Names* in most Alphabets, are very *improperly expressed* by words of several syllables; as *Aleph, Beth, Gimel,* &c. *Alpha, Beta, Gamma,* &c. And thus it is in 15 several Alphabets mentioned by *Hermannus*

Chap. IV.   *Imperfection in Words.*   17

mannus Hugo. In which respect the *Roman Alphabet*, and our *English,*   De Origine
which follows it very near, are much more convenient then the rest,   Scribendi
where each Letter is named simply by its Power. Though herein like-   c. 7.
wise there be some defects : for the letter *C* should not be named *See*,
but *Kee* ; and *G*, not, as usually we do, *Jee*, but Гн: and so *R*, to conform it with the rest, should be called *er*, not *ar* ; and Z should be styled
ez, not *zad*.

5. Their *Figures* have not that *correspondency* to their Natures and   §. V.
Powers which were desirable in an artificially-invented Alphabet,
wherein the *Vowels* ought to have something answerable in their *Chara-
cter* unto the several kinds of *Apertion* which they have in their *sound*.
And so for the *Consonants*, they should have some such affinity in their
Figures as they have in their *Powers*. 'Tis so in some of them, whether
purposely or casually, I know not ; as B P. b p. CG. SZ. and perhaps
T D, t d : but not in others.

To this may be added, the *manner of writing* as to the *Oriental*
Tongues, from the right hand to the left, which is as *unnatural* and inconvenient, as to write with the light on the wrong side. The *Jews* them-   Scaliger de
selves write their particular strokes of Letters from the left to the right   Caufis L. L.
hand ; and therefore it would be much more rational, that their words   cap. 46.
should be written so too.

Besides these Defects in the usual *Alphabets* or *Letters*, there are seve-   §. VI.
ral others likewise in the *Words* of Language, and their Accidents and
Constructions.

1. In regard of *Equivocals*, which are of several significations, and
therefore must needs render speech doubtful and obscure ; and that argues a *deficiency*, or want of a sufficient number of *words*. These are either *absolutely* so, or in their *figurative* construction, or by reason of *Phraseologies*.

Of the first kind there are great variety in *Latin*. So the word

LIBER *apud* ⎧ Literatos ⎫ *significat* ⎧ Codicem. ⎫
⎨ Politicos ⎬   ⎨ Libertate fruentem. ⎬
⎩ Oratores ⎭   ⎩ Filium. ⎭
⎩ Rusticos ⎭   ⎩ Arboris corticem. ⎭

So the word *Malus* signifies both an *Apple-tree*, and *Evil*, and *the Mast
of a ship* ; and *Populus* signifies both a *Poplar-tree*, and the *People*, &c.
Besides such Equivocals as are made by the *inflexion* of words : as *Lex,
legis, legi* ; *Lego, legis, legi* : *Sus, suis* ; *Suo, suis* ; *Suus, suis* : *Amare* the
Adverb ; *Amo, amas, amavi, amare* ; and *Amor, amaris vel amare* : with
abundance of the like of each kind.

Nor is it better with the *English* Tongue in this respect, in which there
is great variety of Equivocals. So the word *Bill* signifies both a *Weapon*,
a Bird's *Beak*, and a written *Scroul* : The word *Grave* signifies both *Sober*, and *Sepulcher*, and to *Carve*, &c.

As for the ambiguity of words by reason of *Metaphor* and *Phraseology*,
this is in all instituted Languages so obvious and so various, that it is needless to give any instances of it ; every Language having some peculiar
phrases belonging to it, which, if they were to be translated *verbatim* into another Tongue, would seem wild and insignificant. In which our

D   English

English doth too much abound, witness those words of *Break, Bring, Cast, Cleare, Come, Cut, Draw, Fall, Hand, Keep, Lay, make, Pass, Put, Run, Set, Stand, Take*, none of which have less then thirty or forty, and some of them about a hundred several senses, according to their use in Phrases, as may be seen in the Dictionary. And though the varieties of Phrases in Language may seem to contribute to the elegance and ornament of Speech; yet, like other affected ornaments, they prejudice the native simplicity of it, and contribute to the disguising of it with false appearances. Besides that, like other things of fashion, they are very changeable, every generation producing new ones; witness the present Age, especially the late times, wherein this grand imposture of Phrases hath almost eaten out solid Knowledge in all professions; such men generally being of most esteem who are skilled in these Canting forms of speech, though in nothing else.

2. In respect of *Synonymous* words, which make Language tedious, and are generally *superfluities*, since the end and use of Speech is for humane utility and mutual converse; *magis igitur refert ut brevis, & rectus, & simplex fit, quàm longus & varius.* And yet there is no particular Language but what is very obnoxious in this kind. 'Tis said that the *Arabic* hath above a thousand several names for a *Sword*, and 500 for a *Lion*, and 200 for a *Serpent*, and fourscore for *Hony*. And though perhaps no other Language do exceed at this rate, as to any particular; yet do they all of them abound more then enough in the general. The examples of this kind, for our *English*, may be seen in the following Tables. To this may be added, that there are in most Languages several words that are mere *Expletives*, not adding any thing to the Sense.

Scaliger de Caussis L. L. cap. 188.
Bp. Walton Prolegomena de Lingua Arabica, sect. 6.

3. For the *Anomalisms* and Irregularities in Grammatical construction, which abound in every Language, and in some of them are so numerous, that Learned men have scrupled whether there be any such thing as *Analogy*.

4. For that *Difference* which there is in very many words betwixt the writing and pronouncing of them, mentioned before. *Scriptio est vocum pictura:* And it should seem very reasonable, that men should either speak as they write, or write as they speak. And yet Custom hath so rivetted this incongruity and imperfection in all Languages, that it were an hopeless attempt for any man to go about to repair and amend it. 'Tis needless to give instances of this, there being in divers Languages as many words whose sounds do disagree with their way of writing, as those are that agree. What is said of our *English* Tongue is proportionably true of most other Languages, That if ten Scribes (not acquainted with the particular Speech) should set themselves to write according to pronunciation, not any two of them would agree in the same way of spelling.

'Tis an observation of a Learned man concerning the *French* Tongue, that it is *ineptissimè confusa, aliàs ad fastidium otiosis suffarcta literis; aliàs ad mendicitatem inops & jejuna; nunquam sibi constans, & raro rationi consona.* 'Tis said that *Peter Ramus* did labour much in reducing it to a new *Orthography*, but met with much discouragement in this attempt from Learned men; besides the invincibleness of general Custom, against which (for the most part) men strive in vain. What better success those Learned ingenuous persons of the *French Academy* may have, who

Sir Tho. Smith de rectâ Scriptione.

Chap. V. *Neither established by Rules of Art.* 19

who have been for several years ingaged in this Work, I cannot conjecture. 'Tis well observed of *Chilperick* King of *France*, than he did, for the compendiousness of writing, add to the *French* Alphabet, these five Letters, अ, ψ, ω, Ʒ, ↄ, conjoyning his Edict with Solomon Edict, the reception and use of them through his Dominions; and that in all Schools Youths should be instructed in the use of them. And yet, notwithstanding his Authority in imposing of them, they were presently after his death laid aside and disused.

As to *our own Language*, several persons have taken much pains about the *Orthography* of it. That learned Knight Sir *Thomas Smith*, Secretary to Queen *Elizabeth*, and sometimes her Embassadour into *France*, hath published an elegant Discourse in *Latin*, *De recta & emendata Linguæ Anglicanæ Scriptione*. After him, this Subject was in another discourse prosecuted by one of the *Heralds*, who calls himself *Chester*; who was followed by one *Wade*, that writ to the same purpose. After these, *Bullaker* endeavoured to add to, and alter divers things in those others that preceded him; which was succeeded in the same attempt by *Alexander Gill*, in his *English Grammar*. And yet so invincible is Custom, that still we retain the same errors and incongruities in writing which our Forefathers taught us.

Gregorius Thuronensis

CHAP. V.

I. *That neither Letters nor Languages have been regularly established by the rules of Art.* II. *The natural Ground or Principle of the several ways of Communication amongst men.* III. *The first thing to be provided for in the establishing of a Philosophical Character or Language, is a just enumeration of all such things and notions to which names are to be assigned.*

FRom what hath been already said it may appear, that there are no Letters or Languages that have been at once invented and established according to the Rules of Art; but that all, except the first, (of which we know nothing so certain as, that it was not made by human Art upon Experience) have been either taken up from that first, and derived by way of *Imitation*; or else, in a long tract of time, have, upon several emergencies, admitted various and *casual alterations*; by which means they must needs be liable to manifold defects and imperfections, that in a Language at once invented and according to the *rules of Art* might be easily avoided. Nor could this otherwise be, because that very Art by which Language should be regulated, viz. *Grammar*, is of much *later* invention then Languages themselves, being adapted to what was already in being, rather then the Rule of making it so.

§. I.

Though the *Hebrew* Tongue be the most ancient, yet *Rabbi Judah Chiug* of *Fez* in *Afric*, who lived *A. D.* 1040. was the first that reduced it to the Art of *Grammar*. And though there were both *Greek* and *Latin* Grammarians much more ancient; yet were there none in either, till a long time after those Languages flourished: which is the true reason of all

Vossius de Arte Grammat. lib. 1. *cap.* 4.

D 2

all those *Anomalisms* in *Grammar*; because the *Art* was suted to *Language*, and not *Language* to the *Art*. *Plato* is said to be the first that considered *Grammar*: *Aristotle* the first that by *writing* did reduce it into an Art: and *Epicurus* the first that publickly taught it amongst the *Grecians*.

Vossius ibid. cap. 3. Polydor. Virgil. lib.1.cap.7.

And for the *Latin*, *Crates Malloten*, Embassador to the *Roman* Senate from King *Attalus*, betwixt the second and third *Punic* War, presently after the death of *Ennius*, U. C. 583. was the first that brought in the Art of Grammar amongst the *Romans*, saith *Suetonius*.

These being some of the Defects or Imperfections in those Letters or Languages, which are already known, may afford direction, what is to be avoided by those who propose to themselves the Invention of a new *Character* or *Language*, which being the principal end of this Discourse, I shall in the next place proceed to lay down the first Foundations of it.

§. II. As men do generally agree in the same Principle of Reason, so do they likewise agree in the same *Internal Notion* or *Apprehension of things*.

The *External Expression* of these Mental notions, whereby men communicate their thoughts to one another, is either to the *Ear*, or to the *Eye*.

To the *Ear* by *Sounds*, and more particularly by Articulate *Voice* and *Words*.

To the *Eye* by any thing that is *visible*, Motion, Light, Colour, Figure; and more particularly by *Writing*.

That *conceit* which men have in their minds concerning a Horse or Tree, is the Notion or *mental Image* of that Beast, or natural thing, of such a nature, shape and use. The *Names* given to these in several Languages, are such arbitrary *sounds* or *words*, as Nations of men have agreed upon, either casually or designedly, to express their Mental notions of them. The *Written word* is the figure or picture of that Sound.

So that if men should generally consent upon the same way or manner of *Expression*, as they do agree in the same *Notion*, we should then be freed from that Curse in the Confusion of Tongues, with all the unhappy consequences of it.

Now this can onely be done, either by *enjoyning* some one Language and Character to be universally learnt and practised, (which is not to be expected, till some person attain to the *Universal Monarchy*; and perhaps would not be done then:) or else by *proposing* some such way as, by its facility and usefulness, (without the imposition of Authority) might *invite* and ingage men to the learning of it; which is the thing here attempted.

§. III. In order to this, The first thing to be considered and enquired into is, Concerning a just *Enumeration* and description of such things or notions as are to have *Marks* or *Names* assigned to them.

The chief Difficulty and Labour will be so to contrive the Enumeration of things and notions, as that they may be full and *adequate*, without any *Redundancy* or *Deficiency* as to the Number of them, and *regular* as to their Place and Order.

If

If to every thing and notion there were assigned a distinct *Mark*, together with some *provision* to express Grammatical *Derivations* and *Inflexions*; this might suffice as to one great end of a *Real Character*, namely, the expression of our Conceptions by *Marks* which should signifie *things*, and not *words*. And so likewise if several distinct *words* were assigned for the *names* of such things, with certain invariable *Rules* for all such Grammatical *Derivations* and *Inflexions*, and such onely, as are natural and necessary; this would make a much more easie and convenient Language then is yet in being.

But now if these *Marks* or *Notes* could be so contrived, as to have such a *dependance* upon, and relation to, one another, as might be sutable to the nature of the things and notions which they represented; and so likewise, if the *Names* of things could be so ordered, as to contain such a kind of *affinity* or *opposition* in their letters and sounds, as might be some way answerable to the nature of the things which they signified; This would yet be a farther advantage superadded: by which, besides the best way of helping the *Memory* by natural Method, the *Understanding* likewise would be highly improved; and we should, by learning the *Character* and the *Names* of things, be instructed likewise in their *Natures*, the knowledg of both which ought to be conjoyned.

For the accurate effecting of this, it would be necessary, that the *Theory* it self, upon which such a design were to be founded, should be exactly *suted to the nature of things*. But, upon supposal that this Theory is *defective*, either as to the *Fulness* or the *Order* of it, this must needs add much *perplexity* to any such Attempt, and render it *imperfect*. And that this is the case with that common Theory already received, need not much be doubted; which may afford some excuse as to several of those things which may seem to be less conveniently disposed of, in the following Tables, or Schemes proposed in the next part.

The End of the First Part.

The

The Second Part,

Conteining a regular enumeration and description of all those things and notions to which names are to be assigned.

CHAP. I.

I. *The Scheme of Genus's.* II. *Concerning the more general notions of things, the difficulty of establishing these aright.* III. *Of Transcendentals general.* IV. *Of Transcendental relations mixed.* V. *Of Transcendental relations of Action.* VI. *Of the several notions belonging to Grammar or Logic.*

HAVING dispatched the *Prolegomena* in the former part, I proceed (according to the method proposed) to that more difficult attempt of enumerating and describing all such things and notions as fall under discourse.

In treating concerning this, I shall first lay down a Scheme or *Analysis* of all the *Genus*'s or more common heads of things belonging to this design; And then shew how each of these may be subdivided by its peculiar *Differences*; which for the better convenience of this institution, I take leave to determine (for the most part) to the number of six. Unless it be in those numerous tribes, of *Herbs, Trees, Exanguious Animals, Fishes* and *Birds*; which are of too great variety to be comprehended in so narrow a compass. After which I shall proceed to enumerate the several *Species* belonging to each of these *Differences*, according to such an order and dependance amongst them, as may contribute to the *defining* of them, and determining their primary significations These *Species* are commonly joyned together by *pairs*, for the better helping of the Memory, (and so likewise are some of the *Genus*'s and *Differences*.) Those things which naturally have *Opposites*, are joyned with them, according to such Opposition, whether *single* or *Double*. Those things that have no Opposites, are paired together with respect to some *Affinity* which they have one to another. Tho it must be acknowledged that these Affinities are sometimes less proper and more remote, there being several things shifted into these places, because I knew not how to provide for them better.

All

Chap. I. *The General Scheme.*

All kinds of things and notions, to which names are to be assigned, may be distributed into such as are either more

- *General*; namely those Universal notions, whether belonging more properly to
  - *Things*; called TRANSCENDENTAL
    - GENERAL. I
    - RELATION MIXED. II
    - RELATION OF ACTION. III
  - *Words*; DISCOURSE. IV
- *Special*; denoting either
  - CREATOR. V
  - *Creature*; namely such things as were either *created* or *concreated* by God, not excluding several of those notions, which are framed by the minds of men, considered either
    - *Collectively*; WORLD. VI
    - *Distributively*; according to the several kinds of Beings, whether such as do belong to
      - *Substance*;
        - *Inanimate*; ELEMENT. VII
        - *Animate*; considered according to their several
          - *Species*; whether
            - *Vegetative*
              - *Imperfect*; as *Minerals*,
                - STONE. VIII
                - METAL. IX
              - *Perfect*; as *Plant*,
                - HERB consid. accord. to the
                  - LEAF. X
                  - FLOWER. XI
                  - SEED-VESSEL. XII
                - SHRUB. XIII
                - TREE. XIV
            - *Sensitive*;
              - EXANGUIOUS. XV
              - *Sanguineous*;
                - FISH. XVI
                - BIRD. XVII
                - BEAST. XVIII
          - *Parts*;
            - PECULIAR. XIX
            - GENERAL. XX
      - *Accident*;
        - *Quantity*;
          - MAGNITUDE. XXI
          - SPACE. XXII
          - MEASURE. XXIII
        - *Quality*; whether
          - NATURAL POWER. XXIV
          - HABIT. XXV
          - MANNERS. XXVI
          - SENSIBLE QUALITY. XXVII
          - SICKNESS. XXVIII
        - *Action*;
          - SPIRITUAL. XXIX
          - CORPOREAL. XXX
          - MOTION. XXXI
          - OPERATION. XXXII
        - *Relation*; whether more
          - *Private*.
            - OECONOMICAL. XXXIII
            - POSSESSIONS. XXXIV
            - PROVISIONS. XXXV
          - *Publick*.
            - CIVIL. XXXVI.
            - JUDICIAL. XXXVII
            - MILITARY. XXXVIII
            - NAVAL. XXXIX
            - ECCLESIASTICAL. XL.

In this precedent Scheme, all the several things or notions, to which names are to be assigned, are reduced to forty *Genus's*. The first six of which do comprehend such matters, as by reason of their Generalness, or in some other respect, are above all those common heads of things called Predicaments; The rest belonging to the several *Predicaments*, of which I reckon only five. Amongst these, *Substance* doth take in fourteen *Genus's*, *Quantity* three, *Quality* five, *Action* four, and *Relation* eight.

This being supposed to be a sufficient general Scheme of things, that which is next to be enquired after, is how each of those *Genus's* may be subdivided into its proper differences and species. In order to which I shall offer that which follows.

In the enumeration of all such things and notions as fall under discourse, those are first to be considered which are more general or comprehensive, belonging either to *Metaphysic*, or to *Grammar* and *Logic*. Tho *particulars* are first in the order of *Being*, yet *Generals* are first in the order of *Knowing*, because by these, such things and notions as are less general, are to be distinguished and defined.

Now the proper end and design of *Metaphysic* should be to enumerate and explain those more general terms, which by reason of their Universality and Comprehensiveness, are either *above* all those Heads of things stiled Predicaments, or else *common to several of them*. And if this Science had been so ordered, as to have conteined a plain regular enumeration and description of these general terms, without the mixture of nice and subtle disputes about them; It might have been proper enough for learners to have begun with. But men having purposely strained their Wits to frame and discuss so many intricate questions, as are commonly treated of in it : 'Tis no wonder that it should hereby be rendred, not onely less fit for young beginners, but liable also to the prejudice and neglect of those of riper judgments. That which I aim at in treating concerning these things, is to offer some brief and plain description of them, as being conscious that such matters as are *primo nota*, and most obvious, are most hard to be defined. And the multiplying of words, about things that are plain enough of themselves, doth but contribute to the making of them more obscure.

The right ordering of these Transcendentals is a business of no small difficulty; because there is so little assistance or help to be had for it in the Common Systems, according to which this part of Philosophy (as it seems to me) is rendred the most rude and imperfect in the whole body of Sciences; as if the compilers of it had taken no other care for those General notions, which did not fall within the ordinary series of things, and were not explicable in other particular Sciences, but only to tumble them together in several confused heaps, which they stiled the Science of *Metaphysic*. And this is one reason why the usual enumeration of such Terms is very short and deficient in respect of what it ought to be, many of those things being left out, which do properly belong to this number; which defects are here intended to be in some measure supplied. Tho it must be granted, that by reason of the exceeding *comprehensiveness* of some notions, and the extreme *subtilty* of others, as likewise because of the streightness of that method which I am bound up to

by

Chap. I. *Concerning Metaphysic.*

by these Tables it will so fall out, that several things cannot be disposed of so accurately as they ought to be.

The several things belonging to Metaphysical or Transcendental notions may be comprehended under these three Heads, namely such as are either more

{ *Absolute*; conteining the *Kinds, Causes, Differences* and *Modes* of things, which I take the liberty to call TRANSCENDENTAL GENERAL.
{ *Relative*; whether
  { *Mixed*; and common both to Quantity, Quality, Whole and Part, stiled TRANSCENDENTAL MIXED.
  { *Simple*; and proper to Action, viz. TRANSCENDENTAL relation of ACTION.

The most Universal conceptions of Things are usually stiled TRANSCENDENTAL, *Metaphysic-all*.

To which may be annexed by way of affinity, that general name which denotes those highest and most common heads, under which the several kinds of things may be reduced in an orderly series: viz. PREDICAMENT, *Category*.

Transcendentals general may be distributed into such as do concern the nature of things according to their

{ KINDS. I.
{ CAUSES. II.
{ *Differences*; more
{ { ABSOLUTE and Common. III.
{ { *Relative to Action*; considering
{   { THE END. IV.
{   { THE MEANS. V.
{ MODES. VI.

E   I. That

I. KIND. 1. That common Essence *wherein things of different natures do agree*, is called GENUS, *general, common Kind.*

That common nature which is communicable to several *Individuals,* is called SPECIES, *Sort* or *special kind, specifie, specifical. Breed.*

These common kinds may be distinguished into such as are either more properly
- *Transcendental*; namely, those most universal and comprehensive Terms which fall under Discourse; relating to
  - *The first and most general Conception, of which the Understanding takes notice,* as most known.
    1. { BEING, *Entity, Essence, Existence, subsist, am, is, extant.*
       { NOTHING, *Nought, null, none, annul, disannul, annihilate, abrogate, abolish, void, undoe, cancel, evacuate, Ciphre.*
  - *Those Beings which* || *are truly such,* or *those which our Senses mistake for Beings.*
    2. { THING, *Affair, Matter, Business, Case, real-ly, indeed.*
       { APPARENCE, *Apparition, Phantasm, Shew, Vision, Elusion and vanish.*
  - *Similitudes of Beings; formed in our Minds* either || *by apprehension of things that are,* or *imagination of things that are not.*
    3. { NOTION, *Conception.*
       { FICTION, *Figment, make, feign, frame, devise, counterfet, forge coin, mint, Fable, Apologue, Romance, Tale, Legend, Mythology, Fairy, Nymph, Centaur, Griffin, Bugbear, Goblin, Chymera, Atlantis, Utopia.*
  - *The words assigned for the signifying of several Things and Notions:* to which that common name for the signifying *of particular rational Beings* may be annexed, though less properly.
    4. { NAME, *Style, Title, Titular, Compellation, Appellation, nominate, denominate, Sirname, Inscription, Nomenclator, anonymous, call, Noun, Term.*
       { PERSON, *Age, Party, No-body, Wight.*
- *Predicamental*; those chief Heads, under which other Terms may be reduced; denoting either
  - *Such things as* || *subsist by themselves,* or which (according to the old Logical definition) *require a subject of inhesion:* Though they are indeed nothing but the modes of Substance.
    5. { SUBSTANCE, *subsist.*
       { ACCIDENT-*all.*
  - *That habitude of things whereby they may be said* to have parts distinct and capable of division, or *the general disposition of things either to Action or Passion.*
    6. { QUANTITY, *Much, Deale, Mathematick.*
       { QUALITY, *Disposition, Endowment, indue, parts, qualification, manner, condition, estate.*
  - *The application of the Agent to the Patient,* or *the reception of the force of the Agent.*
    7. { ACTION, *doe, perform, commit, practise, proceeding, function, exercise, atchieve, dealing, Act, Fact, Deed, Feat, Exploit, Passage, Prank, Trick,* play the Part.
       { PASSION, *abide, ail, bear, endure, suffer, undergo, sustain, feel, capable.*
  - *Such things as* || *cannot be,* or *cannot be known, without a respect to something else;* or *which may be,* or *may be understood of themselves,* without any such reference.
    8. { RELATION, *refer, Regard, Respect, Habitude, correlative.*
       { ABSOLUTENESS, *irrespective, peremptory, flat, positive.*

II. That

Chap. I.   *Transcendentals General.*   27

II. That which any way contributes to the producing of an effect, is styled CAUSE, *Reason, Ground, Principle, proceed from, procure, produce, make, constitute, Influence, raise, put, set, bring to pass.*

That which proceeds from, or depends upon the Cause, is styled EFFECT, *Event, Issue, Fruit, accrue, Success, spring from, become, grow, come of it, impression, Product.*

11. CAUSE.

Causes are commonly distributed into

- *External*, such as are without the Effect.
  - *By which things are done;* whether
    - *More immediate* and absolute; either ‖ *more principal*, of which the first Action is, or *less principal*, and subservient to the chief Agent.
      1. { EFFICIENT, *Author, Maker, Efficacy, effectual, Energy, Virtue, Validity, Force, Vigour, Operation, Influence, frame, constitute, beget, effect, do, make, cause, work, render, create, bring to pass.*
           INSTRUMENT, *Tool, Organ-ical, Implement;*
    - *More remote* and relative; being either in
      - *The Agent;* serving either to
        - *Excite*, or *restrain* it.
          2. { IMPULSIVE, *Incentive, Motive, Reason, Ground, Concitation, Instigation, Inducement, impell, stimulate, stir up, prick forward, spur on, rouse, quicken, irritate, provoke, excite, egging, incite, Instinct, Consideration, put on, set at or on, move, urge, draw in.*
               COHIBITIVE, *restrain, check, curb, with-hold, keep short or back, inhibit, repress, hold in, bridling, stint, coerce, confine, limit, no ho, stay, staunch, moderate, master, controle.*
        - *Direct* and regulate its *Action*; either ‖ by that *Idea* which the Agent hath in his mind of some like case, or by some *Pattern* before his eyes.
          3. { EXEMPLAR, *Example, Instance, Idea, Precedent, Cause.*
               TYPE, *Pattern, Platform, Model, Last, Mold, Prototype, Antitype, Extract, Original, Copy, Counterpart, Draught, Sampler, Proof, Duplicate, exemplifie, prefigure.*
      - *The Patient;* relating to ‖ *some peculiar capacity in the thing,* or *some fitness in respect of time.* (*lification.*
        4. { CONDITION, *Proviso, Salvo, in case, Term, Case, State, liking, Habit, Qua-*
             OCCASION *-al, Exigence, Emergence, Advantage, Opportunity, draw, provoke, scandal.* (*abated,*
      - *Some third thing, by which the force of the Efficient is either* ‖ *increased* or
        5. { ADJUVANT, *Help, Aid, Assistance, Succour, Relief, Support, Advantage, auxiliary, subsidiary, avail, conduce, promote, farther, stand in stead, supply, accommodate, serve, Co-adjutor, abet, take ones part, stand by, a stay to one, forward, minister, relief, back one.*
             IMPEDIENT, *hinder, Obstacle, Remora, Clog, Bar, debar, obstruct, cumber, Rub, Check, Dam, Luggage, Lumber, Baggage, Prejudice, Disadvantage, foreslow, lett, stop, Disservice, stay, stand in the way, trigg, keep back, restrain, with-hold, interfere.*
  - *For whose sake a thing is:* to which may be annexed *the general name of such things as have any tendency to the promoting of it.* (*Reason, final, tend.*
    6. { END, *Aim, Mark, Goal, Drift, Intent, Effect, Purpose, Design, Scope, sake, Reach,*
         MEANS, *Way, Shift, Expedient, accommodate.*
- *Internal*, such as are within the Effect as its chief constituent parts; ‖ *out of which a thing is made,* and of which it consists; or *by which a thing is constituted in its being, and distinguished from all other things.*
  7. { MATTER-*ial, Stuff, Substance, Argument, Subject, Boot as fire-boot,* &c.
       FORM-*al, Essence.*

E 2   III. Those

III. DIVERSITY.

III. Those general Names which may be styled Differences, are too numerous to be placed under one common Head according to the method designed in these Tables, and therefore are they here reduced unto three Heads: whereof the first contains such as do not immediately imply any relation to Action, and are therefore styled more *absolute* and *common*; namely, those more universal Affections of Entity whereby several things are differenced, so as to make them DIVERS from one another, (*another, several, sundry, variety, dissonant, to and fro, up and down, multiplicity, choice, different, others, Heterogeneous*;) to which the notion of IDENTITY, *Very, sameness, all one, unvaried,* may be properly opposed, importing an Unity or *Agreement in the same Essence.*

These are distinguishable into *such Differences* of things *as imply a respect unto*
{ *Something without the things themselves.* (*prehensions of them.*
  The Understanding; in regard of the ‖ *congruity,* or *incongruity of things to our apprehension.*
  1. { TRUTH, *true, Verity, verifie, very, Right, Sooth, irrefragably, likely, probable.*
     FALSHOOD, *false-ifie, Error, erroneous, untrue.*
  The Will; as to the ‖ *agreement,* or *disagreement* of things with that Faculty, so as to be rendred *desirable* or *avoidable.*
  2. { GOODNESS, *Weal, Welfare, right, regular, well, rectifie, better, best.*
     EVILNESS, *ill, bad, naught, wrong, amiss, shrewd, scurvy, lewd, horrid horrible, corrupt, Pravity, deprave, Sin, Fault, Trespass, Transgress-ion, Peccadillo, worse.*
The nature of things in themselves; as to ‖
  Their naked being, or *not being.*
  3. { POSITIVENESS, *Thesis.*
     PRIVATIVENESS, *Privation, bereave, deprive, depose, put out,* or *forth, take away, strip, devest, disseise, dispossess, disfurnish.*
  Their being, or *not being what they are pretended to be.*
  4. { GENUINENESS, *right, arrant, rank, very, native, legitimate, true, currant.*
     SPURIOUSNESS, *mongrel, bastard, false, illegitimate, improper, adulterine, base, misbegot, sophisticated.*
  Their degrees of being; whether ‖ *present,* or *future* and *in possibility.*
  5. { ACTUALNESS, *Existence, extant.*
     POTENTIALNESS, *Reversion, may, can.*
  Their Extension; being ‖ *circumscribed by bounds,* or *not so circumscribed,* (ded.
  6. { FINITENESS, *definite, determined, limited, bounded, Term, Confine, Stint, conclu-*
     INFINITENESS, *endless, indefinite, unbounded, immense, indeterminate, unlimited, unmeasurable, inexhaustible.*
{ *Their Causes.* (*seriour Agent.*
  Efficient; whether ‖ *the order of common Providence,* or *the skill of some in-*
  7. { NATURALNESS, *right, native, wild, carnal, præternatural, supernatural.*
     FACTITIOUSNESS, *artificial, technical, made.*
  Material; being either ‖ *without all parts and composition,* or *being such, to the framing of which several parts and ingredients do concurr.*
  8. { SIMPLICITY, *mere, sheer, clear, fine, plain, right, pure, unmixed, Ingredient, single, uncompounded.*
     MIXEDNESS, *mingle, compound, blend, shuffle, Medly, Miscellany, promiscuous, temper, Commixtion, complex, complicate, confound, intermingle, Hodg-podge, Gallimaufry, Rhapsody, Centon, dash, brew.*
  Formal; ‖ *being in such a state to which nothing is wanting,* or *else wanting something of what they may and should have.*
  9. { PERFECTION, *absolute, intire, full, accurate, exact, exquisite, punctual, precise, complete, consummate, accomplish, strict, plenary, throughly, mature, up, at the top.*
     IMPERFECTION, *incomplete, lame.*   IV. That

IV. That kind of Difference betwixt things, which relates to Actions considering the End, may be stiled DISAGREEABLENESS, *unsuitable, discrepant.*

To which may be opposed the Notion of CONVENIENCY, *agreement, agreable, sutable, serving, commodious.*

These may be distinguished into such as are

More *Simple*; denoting *their*

  Fitness to ‖ promote, or hinder our well-being.

1. { PROFITABLENESS, *Advantage, Benefit, Emolument, Interest, Concern, Boot, Fruit, Utility, Commodious, Edifie, stand insted, good for, avail.*
   HURTFULNESS, *Harm, Prejudice, Disadvantage, Dammage, Disprofit, Nusance, Mischief discommodious, nocent, shrewd turn, pernitious, noxious, noisom, damnifie, endammage, impair, annoy, displeasure, naught for, vermin, weed.*

  Sutableness or unsutableness to our appetites.

2. { PLEASANTNESS, *Delight, Complacence, injoyment, satisfaction, sweet, taking, delicious, Paradise.*
   UNPLEASANTNESS, *Regret, displeasing, offensive, trouble, grievous, uneasie, painful.*

  Agreableness or Disagreableness of things to Right reason.

3. { DUENESS, *Duty, ought, should, Honest, owe, part, incumbent on:*
   UNDUENESS, *ought not, dishonest.*

More *mixed* implying a respect to the nature of the end, as to its

  Capacity or Incapacity of existing.

4. { POSSIBILITY, *Feasible, may, can.*
   IMPOSSIBILITY, *cannot be.*

Degrees of goodness; whether such as are like to answer the desires, by proving *very great* and considerable, or such as are like to disappoint the desires, by proving to be *very little* or none.

5. { IMPORTANCE, *of Moment, Consequence, Strength, Force, Weight, material, considerable, pithy, pregnant, essential, it mattereth.*
   VANITY, *Trifle, trivial, frivolous, Foppery, Gewgaw, Knack, Toy, sleeveless, slight, light, fruitless, fidling, void, Trumpery, Bauble, Quillet, Quirk, Gambol, to no boot, to no purpose,*

Esteem amongst good men; whether such as they are like to think *well of,* as deserving praise and reward, or to think *ill of,* as deserving shame and punishment.

6. { WORTHINESS, *Merit, Desert, Value, demerit, cheap, dear, price, precious, depreciate.*
   UNWORTHINESS, *Vile, Mean, Poor, undeserving, indign.*

V. DIFFE-RENCE relating to the MEANS.

V. DIFFERENCES of things relating to the MEANS, may be distributed into such as are

More *Simple*, denoting the being of things
- *Good*; as good is determined by
  - *Law*; whether *according to Law*, or *not against it*.
    1. { LAWFULNESS, *legitimate, right, legal, canonical, orderly.*
       { INDIFFERENCE, *adiaphorous.*
  - *Custom* or opinion; whether such as the generality of men do think *well of* and practise, or *dislike* and avoid.
    2. { DECENCY, *Decorum, meet, fit, seemly, handsome, becoming, comely, goodly.*
       { INDECENCY, *Indecorum, unmeet, unfit, unseemly, unhandsome, uncomely, misbeseeming, ugly.*
- *Free from evil*; whether of
  - *Hurt*;
    3. { SAFETY, *Security, sure, tutelary, innoxious, save, protect, insure, indemnifie, warrant, Sanctuary, Shelter, Refuge.*
       { DANGER, *Hazard, Peril, Jeopardy, unsafe, risk, venture, adventure, endanger, expose, incur.*
  - *Labor* and *Pain*; in the
    - *Agent*; the *Doing* of things with *little* or *much labor*.
      4. { EASINESS, *Facil -ity -itate, clear, gentle, light,*
         { DIFFICULTY, *Hard, uneasie, crabbed, intricate, laborious, streight, Perplexity, rub, knot, graveling, hard put to it.*
    - *Patient*; The *suffering* of things with *little or no labor*, or *with much*.
      5. { GENTLENESS, *Easiness, softness, still, tenderly, gingerly.*
         { VIOLENCE, *boisterous, rough, harsh, blustering, impetuous, force, ravish.*

Comparative; of the
- *Nature of the means* to one another; whether *mutually agreeing* as having the same kind of affections, or *disagreeing* as having such kind of affections as are apt to exclude one another out of the same subject.
  6. { CONGRUITY, *Suitableness, Agreeableness, Sympathy, consonant, compatible, right, apposite, fit, meet, apt, adapt, consistent, accord, conform, accommodate, comply.*
     { CONTRARIETY, *Repugnance, withstand, against, unsutable, Antiperistasis, counter, cross, incongruous, inconsistent, incompatible, interfere.*
- *Usefulness* or *Unusefulness* of means to an end, whether in
  - *Lower degrees*; when there is a fair probability that a means may either *promote* or *hinder* the end.
    7. { EXPEDIENCE, *Convenience, behoovful, meet, fit, perquisite, requisite.*
       { INCONVENIENCE, *Inexpedience, unmeet, unfit, incommodious.*
  - *Higher degree*; when there is a *certain dependance* betwixt the means and the end.
  - To which may be opposed that kind of *nexus* betwixt means and end, which is altogether *uncertain* and doubtful.
    8. { NECESSITY, *needful, requisite, essential, should, must, streight, exigent, force, perquisite, pressing.*
       { CONTINGENCE, *Venture, adventure, may, Accident, peradventure, adventitious, fortuitous, incident, happen, perhaps.*

6. Those

VI. Those more general respects and habitudes which several things **VI. MODE.** or notions have to one another, are stiled by the name of MODE, *manner, way, sort, fashion, guise, wise, garb, course, form-ality, kind.*
These may be distinguished into such as are

Internal; denoting that

1. { In which another thing *exists*, or *the thing so existing in another*
    SUBJECT, *liable, obnoxious, exposed, matter, Text, Theme, undergoe, capable.*
    ADJUNCT, *Epithete, inherent.*
   About which a thing is imployed.

2. OBJECT, *mark, scope, butt, treat, handle, meddle with, have to do with.*

External;

With which things are accompanied or done; according to the

Kinds of them, either in *General*, or *specially* of such things, as are remarkable for Extraordinariness and Greatness.

3. { CIRCUMSTANCE, *Rite, Ceremony.*
    SOLEMNITY, *Grandeur, state, Pomp, Port, celebrate, solemnize, Rite.*

Consequence of them; or that habitude resulting to any thing from the consideration of all its circumstances together.

4. STATE, *Estate, Condition, Case, Juncture, Liking, manner, pass, pickle, plight, point, in good repair.*

By which any thing is known.

5. SIGN, *Badge, Token, Mark, Note, Symptome, Symbol, Index, Indication, Cue, Print, Scarr, Track, Signature, signifie, Beacon, becken, Boad, foretoken, presage, Prodigie, portentous, ominous, auspicious.*

According to which any thing is, or is done; relating either to the

Order observed in the being or doing of things; whether by

One person or thing *after* another who hath *left his place*, or *for* another who is onely *absent* from his place.

6. { ROOM, as *Successor, Caliph, supply, place.*
    STEAD, as *substitute, subditious, serve for, succedaneous, Deputy, Surrogate, Vicar, Delegate, Vice-gerent, Attourney, Broaker, Factor, in lieu, Lieutenant, Proctor, Proxy.*

Two persons or things either one *after another*, or one *with another*.

7. { TURN, *Course, alternate, second, bout.*
    RECIPROCATION, *mutual, interchangeable, intercourse, correspond.*

Measures of Being; whether the more *General name* for such measures, differenced according to more and less, or that *special kind* which denotes the *sodain* and *short Being or Doing* of any thing according to a greater measure. *(and little.*

8. { DEGREE, *gradual, a spice, a strein, gradation, leasurely, by little*
    IMPETUS, *Fit, Paroxysm, brunt, crash, effort, pang.*

Affections of Being; with reference either to some common *agreement and mutual dependance*, or to some *inconsistency betwixt them*.

9. { COGNATION, *Affinity, Nearness.*
    OPPOSITION, *Disagreableness, contrary, counter, repugnant, withstand, against, cross, thwart, other side, adverse, Antagonist, Antithesis, confront, impugn, oppugn.*

Transcendentals Mixt. Part. II.

TRANSCENDENTAL Relations MIXED, may be distributed into such as do belong either
QUANTITY, as considered (to
{ More GENERALLY. I
More restrainedly, to
{ CONTINUED QUANTITY. II
{ DISCONTINUED QUANTITY. III
QUALITY, as considered more
{ LARGELY IV
{ STRICTLY. V
WHOLE and PART. VI

I. Transcend. Relations of QUANTITY MORE GENERAL.

I. TRANSCENDENTAL mixed *Relations* belonging to QUANTITY considered MORE GENERALLY, may be distributed into such as do concern the measure of things compared either *Other things* of the same kind or company (ther with
Indefinitely; as to
Being or *Substance*, namely when the things compared are considered
Singly and intire, Being either of an ordinary size, or *more* or *less* than *ordinary*.

1. { INDIFFERENCE, *Pretty big, passable, reasonable, so so.*
   { GREATNESS, *Magnitude, ample, large, vast, huge, immense, grand, monstrous, prodigious, sound, swinging, whisker, main, much, magnifie, aggravate, exaggerate, a filthy deal, a foul deal, Gyant.*
   { LITTLENESS, *Smalness, Petty, Minute, Medicum, Scantling, diminutive, least, poor, abate, allay, extenuate, Elf, Dwarf, Shrimp, Tit, Daudiprat, Pigmy.*

Conjunctly; as consisting of several individuals or parts, whereof there are together an *ordinary* number, or *more* or *less* then *ordinary*.

2. { MEDIOCRITY, *a pretty deal, an indifferent quantity, mean, reasonable.*
   { ABOUNDANCE, *a great deal, much, a world, affluence, plenty, store, copious, flush, satiate, flow, fluent, luxuriant, enough and to spare.*
   { SCARCITY, *Little, want, dearth, pinching, scant, bare, jejune, lack.*

Use, with respect to the quantity of it, whether such as may by its *just* proportion promote the end, or such as may hinder it, by being *too much*, or *too little.*

3. { SUFFICIENCY, *enough, big* or *much enough, competency, moderate, satisfie, serve, well, full.*
   { EXCESS, *Redundance, superfluity, needless, exuberance, too much, overmuch, overcharge, cloy, glutt, surfet, satiety, extreme, immoderate, luxuriant, rank, out of reason, wast, fly out, lash out.*
   { DEFECT, *Not enough, lack, need, penury, indigent, necessitous, destitute, want, fail, fall short of, slender, jejune, incompetent, insufficient.*

Quality of it, denoting the being of a thing of an *ordinary goodness*, or *more* or *less* then

4. { INDIFFERENCY, *Pretty well, tolerable, not amiss.* (*ordinary.*
   { EXCELLENCY, *extraordinary good, eminence, preheminence, egregious, eximious, incomparable, superlative, sovereign, transcendent, singular, heroic, high, noble, gallant, choice, passing, rare, remarkable, notable, Paragon, Mirrour.*
   { SORRINESS, *mean, poor, vile, trivial, contemptible, despicable, frippery, Trash, Trumpery, Raff, Scum, Drugg, silly, slight, paultry, scurvy, poor, course, flat, pedling, cheap, worthless, Fellow, Sirrah, Companion, Rascal, Varlet, Wretch, Scoundril, Skip-jack, Scrub, Urchin, Flirt, Gill, Jade.*

Definitely; as to
Being; either of the *same degree*, or *more* or *less*.

5. { EQUALITY, *Evenness, parity, peer, match, fellow, adaequate, aequipollent, adjust,*
   { INEQUALITY, *unequal, odds.* (*halves with, as many, all one.*
   { SUPERIORITY, *above, upper, advantage, odds, preheminence, surmount, overpass, surpass, exceed, go beyond, out-go, get the start, top, excell, prevail, predominant.*
   { INFERIORITY, *under-ling, disadvantage, allay, come short of, low.*

Use; as means to an end, when one thing hath the *same degrees* of fitness for an end as another, or *more* or *less*.

6. { EQUIVALENCE, *countervail.*
   { BETTERNESS.
   { WORSENESS.

Themselves; in respect of their
Being or *substance*, either *continued* the same, or *changed* to *more* or *less*.

7. { AT A STAND. (*prove, rise, grow, gain, come forward, crescent.*
   { INCREASE, *Augmentation, progress, increment, enlarge, magnifie, amplifie, aggravate, improve.*
   { DIMINUTION, *Abate, Bate, swage, asswage, decrease, extenuate, mince, mitigate, allay, retrench, rebate, shrink.*

QUALITY in general, either *continuing* in an ordinary degree, or being *changed* to *more* or *less*.

8. { JUST TEMPER.
   { INTENTION, *heighten, strein, raise, aggravate, exaggerate, exasperate, enhaunce, acute, cutting, keen, sore, piercing, vehement, urgent, eager, earnest, deep sleep, amain, greatly, much.* (*slender, weak, dead, dilute, dull, faint, gentle, light.*
   { REMISSION, *Abate, allay, slake, slacken, swage, asswage, diminish, mitigate, slight, cold,*

Use; when things either *continue* as they were, or else become *more* or *less good.*

9. { KEEPING AT A STAY. (*Improve, Edifie, botch, cobble, clout, patch, Progress, advance.*
   { MENDING, *emendation, bettering, Reparation, Reformation, Restauration, correct, redress,*
   { MARRING, *Spoiling, Deprave, Impair, spill, taint, allay, wear, corrupt, vitiate, wast,*

II. Tran-

II. *Transcendental* Mixed *Relations* belonging to CONTINUED QUANTITY, may be distinguished into those various measures of distance according to the difference of *more* or *less*, with respect either to

- *Line*; from END to End.
  1. { LENGTH, -*en*, *Longitude*, *prolong*, *protract*, *eeke out*, *extend*, *tedious*, *prolixness*.
     SHORTNESS, *Brevity*, *Conciseness*, *abbreviate*, *curtal*, *abridge*, *restrain*, *compendious*, *succinct*.
- *Superficies*; from side to side.
  2. { BREDTH, *Wideness*, *Latitude*, *Largeness*, *Ampleness*, *spacious*, *dilate*, *enlarge*, *extend*.
     NARROWNESS, *Streightness*, *Scantness*, *close*, *compressed*, *pink-eyed*, *restrain*.
- *Body*; reckoning from
  - *Top to Bottom.*
    3. { DEEPNESS, *profound*, *Abyss*, *farr into*, *high*.
       SHALLOWNESS, *Ford*, *Scoure*, *Depression*, *low*, *flat*.
  - *Bottom to Top.*
    4. { HIGHNESS, *Altitude*, *exalt*, *elevate*, *Soar*, *sublime*, *tall*, *lofty*, *proper*, *towring*, *advance*, *raise*, *aloft*.
       LOWNESS, *abase*, *bring down*, *depress*, *demiss*, *nether*
  - *Any Superficies to the opposite.*
    5. { THICKNESS, *Crassitude*, *gross*, *deep*, *incrassate*, *rouncival*.
       THINNESS, *slender*, *fine*, *slim*, *lank*, *flank*, *slight*, *tenuity*, *gaunt*, *rare*, *subtle*, *attenuate*.

Transcendentals Mixt.   Part. II

III. Transcen-dental Relations of DISCON-TINUED QUANTITY.

III. *Transcendental Relations* of DISCONTINUED QUANTITY or Number, may be distributed into such as are either

- *Comparative*; denoting either a *greater* or *lesser* number then ordinary.
  - 1. { MULTITUDE, *many, numerous, a world of, multiply, increase, propagate, store, swarm, thick, press, crowd, throng, rout.*
       FEWNESS, *Paucity, decrease, small number, thin, diminishing.*
- *Positive*; concerning the
  - *Number* of things, whether
    - *One,* or *more* then one.
      - 2. { SINGULARITY, *Individual, numerical, single.*
           PLURALITY, *more.*
    - *Some* or *All.*
      - 3. { PARTICULARITY, *special, peculiar.*
           UNIVERSALITY, *Generality, Catholick, Oecumenical, utmost.*
  - *Kinds* of things, whether *One* kind, or *All* kinds.
    - 4. { SPECIALNESS, *peculiar, particular.*
         GENERALNESS, *All.*
  - *Parts* of which number consists, whether *Equal* or *Unequal* Units.
    - 5. { EVENNESS, *Parity.*
         ODDNESS, *Imparity, uneven.*
  - *Position* of things numbred, denoting their
    - Being in a state of *separation* from others, or in a state of *conjunction* with several others.
      - 6. { SEGREGATENESS, *sever, set apart* or *aside, Analysis, Anatomy, piece-meal, by retail, dispence, distribute, one by one, Parcels, by pole.*
           AGGREGATENESS, *Train, Troop, Company, Party, Scull, Swarm, Team, Flock, Heard, Pack, Covy, Sheaf, Bale, Bundle, Fardle, Bunch, Cluster, Gross, by the great.*
    - *Order,* belonging either to *Things,* or to *Words.*
      - 7. { SERIES, *Rank, Row, Class, successive, Chain, Course, Race, collateral, Concatenation, Alphabet.*
           CATALOGUE, *Index, Table, List, Role, Bill, Scrole, Terrier, a particular, Cargo, Inventory, Muster, impannel, Genealogy, Pedigree, Vocabulary, Dictionary, Lexicon, Nomenclator, Almanack, Calendar.*
  - *Parts* of an aggregate being *all together.*
    - 8. SUIT, *Pack, Set, Mess, a Ring.*

IV. *Tran-*

IV. *Transcendental Relations* belonging to QUALITY, *as considered MORE LARGELY*, may be distributed into such kind of Relations as are either

- *Single*; containing a respect to the
  - *Cause* of a thing, whether *none* or *any*, The being of a thing, the first of its kind, or not.
    1. { PRIMITIVENESS, *Root, original, simple, underived.*
         DERIVATIVENESS, *conjugate, Notation, Etymology, transmission.*
  - *Distance* of a thing, whether *without* or *with* any other between.
    2. { IMMEDIATENESS, *Next.*
         MEDIATENESS.
  - *Manner of being*, whether *intirely of it self*, or *by* virtue of *something else*.
    3. { ABSOLUTENESS, *Independent, Freehold.*
         DEPENDENCY, *Under.*
  - *Degrees of Being* or Causality, whether *superior* and before all others, or *inferior*, and after some others.
    4. { PRINCIPALNESS, *Chief, Special, Ring-leader, soveraign, supreme, paramount, first, main, arch, prime, primary, capital, cardinal, fundamental, Top, Head, Master.*
         ACCESSORINESS, *Abet, adherent, second, Companion, Party, Copartner, Complice, Appendage, Label, Appurtenance, adventitious, collateral, conscious, privy, side with, back, partake, participate, by the way, by the by.*
- *Mutual*; whether more
  - *Positive*; signifying one thing either to have or not to have Relation to some other.
    5. { PERTINENCY, *belong, appertain, apposite, to the purpose, touching, concern, material, relate to, serve for, incumbent on.*
         IMPERTINENCY, *not to the purpose, extravagant, sleeveless, wide from the matter, wild, idle, improper.*
  - *Comparative*, denoting such relation to belong onely *to one or few*, or *to many*.
    6. { PROPERNESS, *incommunicable, owner, peculiar, concern.*
         COMMONNESS, *usual, vulgar, currant, general, prostitute.*

IV. Transcen. Relations of QUALITY at large.

V. *Tran-*

V.Tranſcend. Relations more ſtrictly.

V. *Tranſcendental Relations* of QUALITY *conſidered* MORE STRICTLY, may be diſtributed into ſuch as do concern either their
- *Being* ; *The ſame* or *divers.*
  - 1. ⎧ LIKENESS, *Similitude, ſimilar, aſſimilate, reſemble, repreſentation* ⎫
       ⎨ *Species, Idea, Image, Effigies, Portraiture.* ⎬
       ⎩ UNLIKENESS, *Diſſimilitude, diſſimilar, degenerous.* ⎭
- *Circumſtances* ; whether
  - *Special,* relating to their
    - *Place,* either the being of things *in* their due *poſitions,* or *out* of their due places.
      - 2. ⎧ ORDER, *Regular, Method, array, imbattle, marſhal, rally, in frame,* ⎫
           ⎨ *diſpoſe, digeſt, range.* ⎬
           ⎩ CONFUSION, *Diſorder, Rhapſody, Chaos, Gallimaufry, tumult, rout, coyl, diſhevelled, diſranked, out of frame* or *order, promiſcuous, Prepoſterous, Ruffle, Shuffle, ſcamble, clutter, blunder, jumble, hurry, hurly burly, pell mell.* ⎭
    - *Time,* either the being of things *as uſually they are,* or their being *otherwiſe then commonly they uſe to be.*
      - 3. ⎧ ORDINARINESS, *common, uſual, trivial, currant.* ⎫
           ⎩ EXTRAORDINARINESS, *ſtrange, uncouth, unuſual, unwonted, of note, notable, notorious, Odneſs, Paradox.* ⎭
  - *General,* The *being* of things *according to certain rules* or not ſo.
    - 4. ⎧ REGULARNESS, *right, rectifie, rule.* ⎫
         ⎩ EXORBITANCY, *Irregularneſs, Enormity, Diſorder, extravagant, licentious, wild, faulty, wrong, looſe, immoderate, unruly, unbridled, out of ſquare, laſh out, Heteroclyte, Anomalous.* ⎭
- *Being known* ; either to *many* or *few.*
  - 5. ⎧ PUBLICKNESS, *Notorious, famous, common, extant, open, being out, or abroad, Declaration, Manifeſto, Remonſtrance, Edition, Promulgation, ſet forth* or *out, ſhew, ſpread, blazon, publiſh, proclaim, divulge, denounce, produce, poſt up, come to light, high way.* ⎫
       ⎩ PRIVATENESS, *underhand, clancular, clandeſtine, retire, between themſelves.* ⎭
- *Mixture* with or addition of other things ; when they are
  - *Better for ſuch mixture,* or *Worſe for being without it*
    - 6. ⎧ ORNATENESS, *adorn, ſet out, Deck, beautifie, embelliſh, trimm, trick, tire, garniſh, flouriſh, dreſs. prank, Ornament, Grace, florid, neat, ſmug, ſpruce, elegant, quaint. fine, polite, gay, gaudy. gorgeous, flaring, gariſh, flaunting, Gallant, Spark, Bracelet, Plume, Garland, Ouch,* &c. ⎫
         ⎩ HOMELINESS, *ſimple, rough, rude, untrimmed, plain, bald.* ⎭
  - *Better for being without ſuch mixture,* or *worſe for it.*
    - 7. ⎧ PURITY, *Cleanneſs, undefiled, defecate, fine, refine, try, furbuſh, ſcoure, purge, purifie, clarifie, depuration, neat, abſterſive.* ⎫
         ⎩ DEFILEMENT, *Filthineſs, Impurity, unclean, fowl, ſqualid, bedawb, beſmear, bewray, contaminate, ſlabber, ſlubber, ſmear, ſoil, ſully, pollute, daggle, ſlurry, ſmutch, ſmutt, ſtain, alloy, embaſe, daſh.* ⎭

VI. That

Chap. I. *Transcendentals Mixt.*

VI. That thing which is made up of several lesser things united together is called by the name of WHOLE, *Total, Integral, Intire, Summ, All, Utterly, Quite and clean, full, plenary.* VI. Transcen. Relations of WHOLE and PART.

Those lesser things, by the union of which another greater thing is made up, are stiled by the common name of *PARTS. Particle, Parcel, partial, Divide, share, distribute, driblet, portion, piece, pittance.*

The transcendental relations of *whole* and *part* are such as denote a respect to *Quantity*

Continued; in regard of the

  Quality; of *Goodness* or *Badness* of such parts.
1. { BEST PART, *Quintessence, Cream, Flower, the heart, Top.*
    WORST PART, *Refuse, Scumm, Dreggs, Raff, draft, dross, rubbish, tare, bran, chaff, recrement, trash, garbage, offal.*

  Time; either that which is *first taken*, whereby the goodness of the whole is to be measured, or that which is *superadded* after the (whole.
2. { SAY, *taste, touch, scantling.*
    VANTAGE, *surplus, overplus, to boot, over and above, over-weight, corollary, supplement, vails.*

  Place; specially in *liquids*, either that part which in separation doth rise to the top, or that which *falls to the bottom.* (defecate.
3. { SCUM, *Sandever, Mother.*
    SEDIMENT, *setling, caput mort, grounds, lees, dregs, feculent, rack,*

  Figure; specially in solids; whether
    Roundish; in greater parts, or in *lesser* parts.
4. { LUMP, *Bole, Morsel, Bit, Cantle, Luncheon, Gobbet, Mammock, Stub, stump, grumous, clotted, clod, turfe, sod.*
    POWDER, *Mote, Dust, Corn, Grain, Crum, Grate, moulder.*

  Oblong; made || either by *Cutting*, or by *Breaking,*
5. { CHIP, *Lamin, Scale, Flake, Flaw, Flitter, shive, shiver, splinter.*
    FRAGMENT, *Piece, Scrap, Sheard, tatter, Flitter, rag, shread, snip, slive, slice, collop, cut.*

Discontinued; denoting the respect of

  A Part put to another, or the *whole* as being *made up of such parts.*
6. { ADDITUM, *item, put to, insert, eke out.*
    SUMM, *lay or couch together, cast up, count, draw to a head, come to, amount, result, total, in the whole.*

  A Part taken out from others, or the *whole* remaining *after such taking out.*
7. { ABLATUM, *abate, defalk, retrench, deduct, subduct, substract, take away.*
    RESIDUE, *overplus, surplussage, arrear, remainer, remnant, left behind, the other, the rest, relicks, orts, scraps, reversions, gleaning, offal, odd-ends, stubs, stumps, stubble.*

  A Part repeated a certain *number of times, so as to equal the whole*, or the *whole* considered *as it is so made up.*
8. { MULTIPLIER, *side.*
    PRODUCT, *rectangle.*

  A Part taken out such a certain *number of times as leaves nothing of the whole*, or *that number of times which is the correspondent* (part.
9 { DIVISOR.
    QUOTIENT.

TRANSCENDENTAL RELATIONS OF ACTION, may be distributed into such as are more ⎰SIMPLE. I
⎰General.————————————— ⎱COMPARATE. II
⎱Special; denoting either
   ⎧Kinds of Action.   (BUSINESS. III.
   ⎪⎰Solitary; wherein more then one person is not necessarily supposed.
   ⎨⎱Social; wherein more then one person is necessarily supposed.
   ⎪EVENTS. V   (COMMERCE. IV
   ⎩ITION. VI   (things, are such as do concern

I. TRANS. RELAT. of ACT ON SIMPLE.

I. *Transcendental* respects of ACTION SIMPLE or relating to *single*
The *General condition* of a thing, denoting the *making* of it ‖ *to be so*, or
⎧PUTTING, Set, Lay, Make.   (*to be otherwise*.
1.⎨ALTERING, *Change, Vary, Mutation, shift, Revolution, Vicissitude,*
  ⎩*Ones right in a thing;* whether   (*Catastrophe, Metamorphosis.*
   ⎧*Making it* ‖ *to be his*, or *not to be his.*
   ⎪⎰APPROPRIATING, *own. set apart, engross, monopolize.*
2.⎨⎱ALIENATING, *transferr. estrange, pass away ones right.*
   ⎩*Declaring it to be his,* or *not to be his.*
   ⎧CLAIMING, *Owning, Challenging, Demand, arrogate, assume, profess,*
3.⎨ *attribute. ascribe, take upon him, declare for.*
   ⎩ABDICATING, *disclaim, disown, renounce, relinquish, refuse, reject,*
    repudiate, desert, forsake, disavow, disherit, execrate, forswear, de-
    stitute. cast off, lay aside, put away.
Ones Possession; with respect to the
   ⎧*Causing of a thing to be in ones Possession* or *not.*
4.⎨⎰TAKING, *Seising, Apprehending, resume, surprize, assume, intercept.*
   ⎱LEAVING, *Relinquish, Residue, forsake, spare.*
   ⎩*Being of a thing in ones possession,* or *the not being of such a thing in ones*
    possession as he ought to have.
5.⎰HAVING, *in hand, hold, possess.*
  ⎱WANTING, *indigent, lack, miss, necessity, need, penury.*
Continuing a thing in ones Possession or *not.*
6.⎰HOLDING, *Detain, Retain, Keep.*
  ⎱LETTING GO, *Dismiss surrender, give up, Shed, Cast, mew, resign.*
The Knowledge of things, with respect to the
   ⎧*Endeavour of knowing,* or *the good success of such endeavour.*
7.⎨⎰SEEKING, *search, feel for, grope, ransack, rummage, Quest.*
   ⎱FINDING, *retrive, sift out, smell out, Foundling.*
   ⎩*Causing a thing to be known,* or *hindring it from being known.*
8.⎰SHEWING, *disclose, detect, betray, reveal, discover, declare, de-*
  ⎱ *monstrate, remonstrate, render.*
   ⎩CONCEALING, *Hide, Shelter, Suppress, Sculk, lurk. Secret, Private,*
    Latent, occult, underhand, close, clancular, clandestine. in a corner,
    in hugger mugger, recess. retire. slink, mich. sneak, slip, or *steal away,*
    cloke, veil, hoodwink, mask, muffle.
Causing others to be perfectly known, or *to be thought so.*
   ⎧MANIFESTING, *Apparent, Evident, plain, flat, open, conspicuous,*
9.⎨ *perspicuous, obvious, certain, clear, palpable, shew, declare, certifie*
   ⎪ *set forth, come to light.*
   ⎩SEEMING, *Semblance, Shew, Pretence, Pretext, Umbrage, Colour,*
    a shew, a blind, Formal, Appear, palliate, fain, bear in hand, make
    as if, make shew of, specious, disguise, Ey-service.   II. Tran-

Chap. I.   *Transcendental Relations of Action*   39

II. *Transcendental Relations of Action* COMPARATE, are such as do concern *II. Transcendental Relations of Actions COMPARATE.*
Divers things at the same time; whether such kind of Actions as from the nature of the Agents or Patients, may be called

Corporeal; denoting the
  Causing of things to be together or asunder.
  1. { JOINING, *annex, Connexion, couple, link, copulation, concatenation, conjunction, Coalition, coherent, copulative, conglutinate, combine, compact, set or put together.*
     SEPARATING, *Segregate, sunder, sever, dissever, divide, disjoin, disunite, dissect, dissolve, part, take in pieces, disjunctive.*
  Continuing them together or asunder.
  2. { ADHEARING, *Cleave, stick to, cling to, hang together, coherent, inseparable.*
     ABANDONING, *Forsake, Desert, Relinquish, Leave, Forgo, Flinch, Quit, Dereliction, forlorn, destitute, shake or cast off, start back, give over.*

Mental; *Putting of things together or asunder*
  3. { APPLYING, *lay or put to.*
     ABSTRACTING.

Both *Corporeal and Mental*; with respect to the
  Taking in of several things, or the leaving out of some.
  4. { COMPREHENDING, *Contain, Comprize, Imply, Involve, Inclose, Include, inclusive, hold, Complication.*
     EXEMPTING, *Except, restrain, seclude, exclude, save, salvo, set aside.*
  Putting of things together, the better to judge of their likeness or unlikeness, or examining of them for the distinguishing of that which is right and true.
  5. { COMPARING, *Conferr, Collation, resemble.*
     TRY, *Prove, Search, Temptation, Experiment, test, touch, examin, gage, poise, pose, probe.*

The same things at divers times, whether the same as to

Substance; signifying either the *doing of the same thing several times*, or the *making of a thing to be different* at one time *from what it was* before.
  6. { REPEATING, *Iterate, reiterate, recite, render, rehearse, redouble, reduplicate, inculcate, ingeminate, recapitulate, renew, afresh, again, Tautology, the burden.*
     CHANGING, *Mutation, Vary, Alter, Shift.*

Quantity; The *giving back* of *the very same* thing, or of *something* else equal to it.
  7. { RESTORING, *Give back, Restitution, refund, return, Restauration.*
     COMPENSATING, *Recompense, award, make amends, remunerate, quit, requite, retaliate, retribute, reparation, paying, fit, being even with, meet with, make good, cry quittance, like for like, one for another.*

Quality; endeavouring to *shew how another thing is*, or to *do the like*.
  8. { REPRESENTING, *declare, shew, exhibit, present.*
     IMITATING, *Mimick, personate, take forth, follow.*

Use; as means to an end, The *making* of *a thing more fit* or *less fit for its end*.
  9. { REPAIRING, *Mending, Bettering, Improving, correct, rectifie, renew, reedifie, Emendation, Instauration, Redress, set to right, make good, make up, patch up, piece up.*
     SPOILING, *Marring, corrupting, deprave, impaire, raze, scrape or cross out, sleight works.*

III. Those

III. Those kind of Actions about which men bestow their time and labour, are called by the general name of BUSINESS, *Affair, Task, Chare, Transaction. Matter, Factor, Agent, negotiate, occupie, stickle, meddle, intermeddle, dealing, imployment, active.*

To which may be opposed the Negation or being free from such Actions stiled LEASURE, *Vacation vacant, idle or spare time, unoccupied, respite.*

Transcendental relations of BUSINESS, may be distributed into such as are

Previous to it.
  Mental or *Verbal.*
1. DESIGNING, *allot, appoint, plot, preordein, project.*
  UNDERTAKING, *enterprize, take in hand, set upon, task.* (fite materials.
  Real; either more *general* or more *special*, with respect to the providing of requi-
2. PREPARING, *Parade, previous, ready, make way, fitting, Tuning, Harbinger.*
  FURNISHING, *Æquipage, fitting, ready.*

Parts of it; whether
  Initial; with respect to the
    First entrance upon a business; either *Real* or *Seeming.*
3. BEGIINNING, *Inchoate, initiate, commence, Inceptor, Spring, Rise, Original, first, set about, set forth, set a foot, go in hand with, enter upon.*
  OFFERING, *Propose, profer, tender, bid, propound, overture.* (be done.
  Application of the labor, either *to the doing* of any thing, or *to know whether it can*
4. ENDEAVOURING, *Devoir, bestir, adoo, coyl, stickle, strein, strive, struggle, effort, make a stir, do ones best, reach after, lay out for.*
  ESSAYING, *Trying, say, attempt, prove, tempt-ation, Test, Experience, enterprize, venture, sound, tast, touch, run the risk or adventure.* (longer time.

Medial; with respect to the time bestow'd in the doing of it, whether *shorter* or
5. DISPATCHING, *Hasten, quick, high, forward, hurry, precipitate, speed, Celerity, Expedition, sodain, apace, out of hand, cut short.*
  PROTRACTING, *Delay, desert, retard, slacken, respite, tarry, foreslow, linger, prolong, lengthen, prorogue, procrastinate, dally, lagg, stand about, whiling about, shift off, put off, post off, spin out time;*

Final; with respect to the
  End of the Action; ‖ either the *effecting* of what we undertake and profess, or our failing in it.
6. PERFORMING, *Accomplishing, Atchieve, fulfil, verifie, discharge, execute, keep, observe, exploit, make good, bring to pass.*
  VIOLATING, *infringe, break, trespass, transgress.*

Action it self; whether *Perfect* or *Imperfect.*
7. FINISHING, *Concluding, ending, accomplishing, fulfil, performing, cease, give over, Period, Term, ultimate, last, consummate, determine, dispatched, done, Catastrophe, clap up, shut up, wind up, close up, draw to an issue, go through*
  MISCARRYING, *Failing.* (with, run his course.

Hinderances of it; either not *rightly using the means,* or *not using some of them.*
  ERRING, *Swerve, slip, stray, astray, mistake, oversight, deviate, falter, fallible, heterodox, Fallacy, wrong, amiss, awry, being out, beside the mark.*
  OMITTING, *Pretermit, Wave, decline, default, escape, lapse, leave, miss, forbear, balk, supersede, overlook, overpass, preterition, overslip, overskip, let pass, pass by or over, lay aside, hold ones hand.*

Helps of it; denoting either *avoiding mistakes at the beginning,* or *rectifying mistakes afterwards.*
9. PREVENTING, *Anticipate, Previous, aforehand, forestal, Foregame.*
  REMEDYING, *Redress, Shift, Aftergame, Help.*

IV. Tran-

Chap. I. *Transcendental Relations of Action.* 41

IV. Transcendental relations of Action concerning such things as are alienated from one Person to another, are usually called by the General Name of COMMERCE, *Entercourse, Traffick, Prattick, have to do with.*

[sidenote: IV. Transcen. Relations of COMMERCE.]

These may be distributed into such as are

- **Free**; and not upon consideration
  - *Passive*; Not hindring one to take or to do.
    1. { YIELDING, *Suffering, permitting, give way, give place.*
       { SUBMITTING to.
  - *Active*;
    - *Imperfect*; denoting a *willingness to part with*, or a *desire to have a thing.*
      2. { OFFERING, *Proffer, tender, exhibit, present, recommend, Oblation.*
         { DEMANDING, *Require, Challenge.*
    - *Perfect*; with respect to the
      - *Possession* of a thing; the *Parting with it*, or *Taking of it.*
        3. { DELIVERING, *Surrender, transferr, resign.*
           { RECEIVING, *Take, entertain, capable, reception, receptacle.*
      - *Right* of a thing; the *Parting with it*, or *Taking of it.*
        4. { GIVING, *Bestow, confer, render, grant, contribute, endow, consign, Gift, Boon, Largess, Collation, Donation, Donative, Gratis.*
           { ACCEPTING, *Receiving, administer, dispense, distribute, Token, Fairing, take in good part.*
- **Conditional**; and upon consideration, whether such as concern the
  - *Causing of Relations* by Actions that are
    - *Real*; The *Parting with something of ones own* for the use and in the stead of *another*, or the *restoring what another hath so parted with.*
      5. { DISBURSING, *Bestow, defray, extend, lay out, Bursar, Principal.*
         { REFUNDING, *Repay, return, reimburse.*
    - *Verbal*; the *Comparing and measuring of particulars*, or *reducing them to an equality.*
      6. { RECKONING, *Compute-ation, count, account, cast account, Calculate, Audit, Score, Tally.*
         { BALLANCING, *Evening of Accounts, Quitting scores, Adjust.*
  - *Relations themselves* ensuing upon such Actions, whether as *having somewhat of ones own in anothers possession*, or *something of anothers in ones own possession.*
    7. { BEING CREDITOR, *Lending, Loan.*
       { BEING DEBTOR, *Owing, Debt, upon score, in ones books, behind hand, Arrear.*
  - *Ceasing* or *dissolution of such relations* by some Act of the
    - *Debitor*; either by *restoring what is due*, or by being *rendred unable for it.*
      8. { PAYING, *Defray, discharge, satisfie, reimburse, Annuity, Poundage, Shot, responsible.*
         { FAILING, *Break, Bankrout.*
    - *Creditor*; *Acknowledging restitution*, or *Giving away his right to it.*
      9. { ACQUITTING, *Discharge, Quittance, Receipt, clear accounts.*
         { FORGIVING, *Remitting, pardoning, put up,*

V. The

Transcendental Relations of Action. Part. II

V. EVENT. V. The General name for that which follows upon Actions, especially as it relates to the end for which Actions are done, is EVENT, *Upshot, issue, result, emergence, accrue, occurr, come to pass, fall out, befall, betide, ensue, prove, redound, happen, light, succede, Luck, Fortune, End, Sequel, Success, incident, coincident, intervene, supervene, take effect, how fares, goes, speeds it, come of it, come to good* or *to naught.*

Transcendental relations of Action belonging to *Event*, may be distributed into such as do concern the

Existing or *not existing of the End* designed.

1. {
   OBTEINING, *Acquire, get, procure, attain, reach, gain, compass, recover, take, win, catch, come by, pick up.*
   FRUSTRATING, *Fail, disappoint miss, defeat, deceive, elude, cross, come short of, shift off, put by, of no effect, to no purpose, vain, void, nullity.*
   }

Good or *Evil* accrewing to us by it, with respect to the

Increasing or *Diminishing of our Possessions.*

2. {
   GAINING, *Lucre, Advantage, Profit, Emolument, Stock; the proceed, acquire, get, win, recover, extort.*
   LOOSING, *Dammage, decrement, detriment, disadvantage, disprofit, wrack, spoil hurt, hinderance, out of ones way.*
   }

Diminishing or *Increasing of our Want.*

3. {
   SAVING, *Sparing, take up.* (*sumptuary, run out.*
   SPENDING, *Lay out, bestow, expend, dispend, expence, charges, cost,*
   }

Continuing, or *not Continuing of a thing in our Possession.*

Imperfect; denoting the *Endeavour* and care we use about it, whether *any* or *none.* (*pository.*

4. {
   LAYING UP, *Treasuring, Preserving, Stow, Hoord, Store, Re-*
   SQANDRING, *Lavish, profuse, careless, misspend, embezel, wast, unthrifty, ill husbandry, spendthrift, flying out.*
   }

Perfect; Consisting in the *Good* or *Ill success* of such Endeavour.

5. {
   KEEPING, *Preserve, retain, Custody, holding, promptuary, Cellar.*
   LOOSING, *Perdition, loss, wrack, shed, spil.*
   }

Applying of a thing; whether more

Simply; denoting the *applying* of a thing *to its proper end,* or *the not applying of it so.*

6. {
   USING, *Imploy, improve, exercise, occupy, manage, treat, handle, entertain, useful, serviceable, stand in good stead.* (*hand.*
   ABSTEINING, *Forbear, refrain, spare, withdraw, wean, hold ones*
   }

Relatively; as to that *satisfaction* or *dissatisfaction* of mind which we have in the *use of a thing.*

7. {
   INJOYING, *Fruition.*
   BEING SICK OF, *Nauseate, loath, tedious, surfet, weary of.*
   }

Result of such application, in the *diminishing* or *increasing* of our

Pain.

8. {
   REFRESHING, *Recreate, relieve, recruit, relaxation, refection, Bait.*
   WEARYING, *Lassitude, tyring, tedious, faint, fatigue.*
   }

Hinderances.

9. {
   QUIETING, *Tranquillity, rest, compose, sedate, serene, still, calm, set or be at rest.*
   TROUBLING, *Molest, disturb, annoy, disquiet, incumber, infest, interrupt, pester, cumber, turbulent, stirs, coil, broil, turmoil, garboil, perturbation.*
   }

VI. The

Chap. I. *Transcendental Relations of Action.* 43

VI. The General name denoting Transcendental Motion or rest, is **VI. ITION.**
ITION, *Going, Passing, Remove, betake, repair, transmission, Penetrate, Fiitt.*
STATING, *Abide, remain, tarry, continue, reside, rest, stop, stick, damm, detain, hold at a bay, Mansion, Stage, Remora.*

The Relations belonging to this motion, may be distinguished into such as are

Solitary, supposing but one Person or Thing, with respect to its

Moving *towards* or *from* the Speaker.

1. { COMING, *Arrive, Access, Resort, repair to, frequent, recourse, concourse, confluence, return.*
    GOING, *Depart, recede, return, regress, ingress, egress, be packing, be jogging, retire, retrograde, withdraw, dislodge, avant, void, slip away, slink or sneak away, fling away, fall off, get gone, set forth, rub along.*

Continuing of Motion; whether

Simply; Towards *the same* term, or *changing of the Term.*

2. { PROCEEDING, *Persist, prosecute, persevere, progress, pass, advance, hold or go on, set forward or on.*
    TURNING, *Winding, Veare, Double, tack, about, face about, wheel about.*

With Design; either to *some certain place,* or to *no certain place.*

3. { TRAVAILING, *Expedition, Voyage, Journey, Progress, Peregrination, Itinerant, Passenger, Wayfaring, March, set out, Palmer, Pilgrim, Pass, Passport.*
    WANDRING, *Stray, astray, range, rove, straggle, err-ant, Vagrant, Vagabond, random, ramble, rome, prole, gad, Gypsie, Rogue, Landloper, Labyrinth, Ambages.*

Social; supposing several persons or things.

Causing another

To *go* or to *come,*

4. { SENDING, *Mission, missive, Token, convey, dismiss, Remit, dispatch, Messenger, Embassador, Legat, Envoy, Lieger, Emissary, Currier, Arrant.*
    FETCHING, *Bring, reduce, forth-coming.*

To *come after,* or to *go before.*

5. { LEADING, *Guide, Conduct, bring, convey, draw, Manuduction.*
    DRIVING, *Chase, drift, expel, repel, repulse, goad, beat back, Ferret out.*

Coming after another thing in motion, or *coming up* equal *to* it.

6. { FOLLOWING, *Ensue, come after, pursue, dogging, trace.*
    OVERTAKING, *Reach, Top, Catch, fetch up.*

Coming of things together from several terms, or the *Preterition of something* in our way.

7. { MEETING, *Obviate, obvious, encounter, occurr, Randevouze.*
    AVOIDING, *Decline, Fly, shun, eschew, Wave, beware, escape, evade, shift off, out of the way.*

G 2 Of

Of DISCOURSE;

Or the several notions belonging to *Grammar* or *Logick*.

§. VI. THE most general name for those external expressions, whereby men do make known their thoughts to one another, is DISCOURSE, *Commune, Communication, Parly, Talk, Colloquie, Tract, Treatise, handle, Stile.*

To which may be annexed that particular way of discourse, most in use, namely by articulate voice and words, called LANGUAGE, *Tongue, Speech, Linguist, dialect.*

The several things and notions belonging to discourse, may be distributed into such as do concern either the

- *Parts of it*; or those primary ingredients of which it consists, whether
  - *More Simple*; stiled ELEMENTS. I
  - *Less Simple*; WORDS. II
- *Kinds of it*; or those secondary parts belonging to it, whether such as are
  - *Proper*, to
    - GRAMMAR. III.
    - LOGIC. IV.
  - COMMON TO BOTH. V
- MODES *of it*. VI

Chap. I. *Discourse.*

1. The first and more simple ingredients required to the framing of Discourse or Language, are stiled ELEMENTS. *Abcdarian.* **I. ELEMENTS.**

These may be distinguished into such as do concern either the
Sounds made by the Organs of speech, according to the
- General name; denoting either ‖ that which is *spoken,* or *the picture of it* in writing.
  - 1. { LETTER, *literal.*
       { CHARACTER, *Figure, Note, Letter, Cyphre, Orthography.*
- Particular kinds; relating to such as are
  - More primary and *simple*; whether ‖ such *apert sounds* as are framed *by a free emission of the breath* through the organs of speech, or such *closed sounds* in the pronouncing of which *the breath is intercepted* by some collision or closure amongst the instruments of speech.
    - 2. { VOWEL.
         { CONSONANT.
  - Less primary and *mixed*; either that which (for the most part) doth consist of *several letters pronounced in one* continued *motion,* or of more *Vowels* coalescing *in one sound.*
    - 3. { SYLLABLE.
         { DIPHTHONG.

Time or pause to be observed in the pronouncing of several words or sentences, according to the
- General name; denoting that mark which serves, either ‖ for *separating such words as belong to several clauses or sentences,* or for *uniting* those *words* which are *to be pronounced as one.*
  - 4. { INTERPUNCTION, *Period, Point.*
       { HYPHEN, *Maccaph.*
- Particular kinds;
  - *Lesser*; according to the degrees of *Less* or *More*
    - 5. { COMMA.
         { SEMICOLON.
  - *Greater*; according to the degrees of *Less* or *More.*
    - 6. { COLON.
         { PERIOD, *full point, stop, pause, rest.*

Manner of Pronouncing; with reference to
- Distinction of such words or clauses as are
  - *Less material*; denoting that such a passage, either ‖ is *not necessary to make the sense perfect,* or is *added by way of Explication* of something preceding.
    - 7. { PARENTHESIS.
         { PARATHESIS, *Exposition.*
  - *More material*; either that which serves to *distinguish such words, wherein the force of the sense doth* more peculiarly *consist,* or that which *denotes the words to be intended to a contrary sense,* to what they naturally signifie.
    - 8. { EMPHASIS.
         { IRONY --*call.*
- *Prolongation of Vowels,* or *Elevation of voice* in the pronouncing of any syllable.
  - 9. { ACCENT.
       { ACCENT, *elevate.*

II. *Those*

II. WORDS. II. Those particular *sounds* or *Characters*, which are agreed upon to *signifie any one thing or notion*, are called by the general name of WORD, *Verbal, verbatim, term, eudite.*

That which is intended by any such sound or Character, is called MEANING, *Sense, Signification, Purport, Acception, Import, tenor, denote, moral.* Words may be distinguished according to the

General name; given to the chief kinds of them, whether ‖ the *more Principal* such as signifie some intire thing or notion, or the *Less Principal*, such as consignifie and serve to circumstantiate other words with (which they are joyned.
1. { INTEGRAL.
   { PARTICLE.

Particular kinds; whether of

Integrals; considered according to their

Natures; being either more

Absolute; denoting either ‖ the *naked Essence* of a thing, or the *End*
2. { ABSTRACT, *separate*. (and thing it self.
   { CONCRETE, *complex*.

Relative; to the

Names of things; whether such as signifie more simply and of themselves, or such whose signification doth import their being ad-
3. { SUBSTANTIVE. (*joyned to something else.*
   { ADJECTIVE.

Actions or Passions of things; (which is here taken notice of in compliance with Instituted Grammar, tho it be not properly one simple part of speech, but rather a mixture of two, namely the Predicate and Copula.) To which may be annexed that which is commonly adjoyned unto this, to signifie the *Quality* or affe-
4. { VERBE. (ction *of the Action or Passion*.
   { ADVERBE DERIVED.

Place and Order in a proposition, whether that which according to natural construction doth *precede the Copula*, or that which doth (*follow it*.
5. { SUBJECT.
   { PREDICATE, *Attribute, ascribe, impute*.

Particles; whether the

Most necessary and essential *to every proposition*.
6. COPULA.

Less necessary;

Substantive; in the room either of some *Integral word*, or of some
7. { PRONOUN. (*sentence* or complex part of it.
   { INTERJECTION.

Connexive or declarative; whether such as are more

Proper to Substantives; being usually prefixed before them, either ‖ that whose office it is to *join integral with integral on the same side of the Copula*, or that which *serves for the more* full and
8. { PREPOSITION. (*distinct expression of Substantives*.
   { ARTICLE.

Common to other words; either that kind of particle which is usually adjoined to Verbs, to *signifie some kind of Mode* or Circumstance belonging to them, or that which *serves chiefly for the joyning of clauses* or *sentences*.
9. { ADVERBE UNDERIVED. III. COM-
   { CONJUNCTION.

Chap. I.   *Discourse.*   47

III. COMPLEX GRAMMATICAL NOTIONS. of Speech, may be distinguished into such as concern the

- Portions into which a discourse may be divided, whether more
  - *Imperfect*;
    - *Absolute*; either that which *denotes* onely *some part of the sense*, or that which signifies some *complete sense*.
      - 1. { CLAUSE, *Passage.*
        - SENTENCE, *Period, Text, Aphorism, Apophthegm, Axiom, Impress, Motto, Posie, Phrase, Stile.*
    - *Relative*; to the number and order of such parts, either the *less*, consisting of *one or more sentences*, or the *Greater* being an *Aggregate of these*.
      - 2. { VERSE, *Staffe, Stanza.*
        - SECTION, *Paragraff, Article, Scene.*
  - *Perfect*; conteining either a *Principal part*, or an *Intire discourse*.
    - 3. { CHAPTER, *Act.*
      - BOOK, *Tract, Treatise.*
- Kinds of such discourse; with respect to the
  - *Matter* or Words, according to the
    - *General name*; denoting either a more loose and *free way of putting the words together*, or that which is *bound up to measure*.
      - 4. { PROSE.
        - VERSE, *Lyrick, Pindarick, Ode.*
    - *Particular kinds of Verse*; either that which depends only upon *some stated measure of words*, or that which doth likewise suppose a *similitude in the sound of the ending Syllables*.
      - 5. { MEETRE-*ical.*
        - RIME.
  - *Form* or signification of words, whether
    - *Natural* and according to the first intention of them, or *Artificial* and borrowed, containing a reference to something else of near affinity and similitude.
      - 6. { PROPER.
        - TRALATITIOUS, *Metaphor, Trope, Parable, Simile, Homely,* or *Ornate.*
    - 7. { SIMPLE.
      - FIGURATE. *Allegory, Improper, Riddle, Ænigmatical.*
    - *Full*, or *Defective*; having something left out.
      - 8. { EXPRESS, *Plain, open, flat, explicite, Hint, Inkling, mention, set form.*
        - UNDERSTOOD, *Implied, implicite, tacit, intimated.*
    - *Easie*, or *Difficult* to be understood.
      - 9. { PLAIN, *Evident, Perspicuous, clear, express, obvious, easie, facil, explain, explicate, unfold, illustrate, open, make out.*
        - OBSCURE, *Dark, abstruse, riddle, ænigmatical, deep, profound, hard, difficult, mysterious, intrigue.*

IV. COMPLEX LOGICAL NOTIONS of discourse, may be distributed into such as are

- *Positive*; concerning
  - *Words*; with respect to their
    - *Ambiguity*; *Shewing the different senses which they are capable of, or using them in a fallacious sense.*
      1. { DISTINCTION, *discriminate.*
           ÆQUIVOCATION, *Ambiguous, Amphibole.*
    - *Universality*; *Restraining a word unto some more proper and peculiar sense, or enlarging of it as there may be occasion, to its full scope and comprehensiveness.*
      2. { LIMITATION, *Restriction, stint, bound, terminate, determine.*
           AMPLIATION, *Inlarge, dilate, expatiate.*
  - *Things*; declaring either their
    - *Natures*; more or less perfectly.
      3. { DEFINITION.
           DESCRIPTION, *Character, delineate, pourtray, plot, platform, model.*
    - *Kinds*; more or less perfectly.
      4. { DIVISION, *Parting, Dichotomy.*
           PARTITION, *Distribution, parting.*
    - *Affections*; namely such *common principles of knowledge* whereby men are to be directed in their judging. To which may be opposed the *excluding of such particulars as do not properly belong to those generals.*
      5. { RULE, *Maxim, Axiom, Principle, Theorem, Canon, Rubric, Aphorism, regulate.*
           EXCEPTION, *Exempt, reservation, restrain, exclude, seclude, salvo, save, set aside.*
- *Comparate* or disputative,
  - *General*; *when from somethings already known and granted, we endeavour to prove some other thing, or the taking of that other thing as being so proved.*
    6. { ARGUMENTATION, *Reason, argue, dispute, debate, discuss, dissertation, ratiocination, demonstration, sophistry, captious, cavil, polemic, mooting, Problem, chop Logic.*
         ILLATION, *Inference, consequence, consectary, deduction, sequel, Conclusion, Corollary, result, follow, imply.*
  - *Special*; as respecting the
    - *Forms* most *Artificial*, whether that which is most *full*, or that which is *defective.*
      7. { SYLLOGISM.
           ENTHYMEM.
    - *Matter*;
      - *Intrinsic* from the nature of the things themselves, signifying the *proving of a General*, whether ‖ *from many or all the particulars*, or *from some one or few particulars.*
        8. { INDUCTION, *Particularize.*
             EXAMPLE, *Instance, exemplify, specifie, leading case.*
      - *Extrinsic*; from the *Authority* of some other person, or a *resemblance* to some other thing.
        9. { CITATION, *Quotation, testimonies, alledge.*
             ALLUSION, *Glance.*

V. MIXED

Chap. I. *Discourse.* 49

V. MIXED NOTIONS OF DISCOURSE belonging both to **V. MIXED**
Grammar and *Logic* may be distributed into such as are **NOTIONS OF DISCOURSE.**

Less complex; denoting such *a compleat sentence, wherein something is either affirmed or denied,* To which may be adjoyned such kind of sentences, *as* by common use and long experience *have obtained to be of authority amongst men.*

1. {
PROPOSITION, *Thesis, Assertion, Point, Doctrine, Observation, Position, Problem.*
ADAGE, *Proverb, Old-say* or *saw, By-word.*
}

More complex; whether

Kinds of discourse;

Positive:

More general; denoting something to be *spoken in presence, or written to be sent to others.*

2. {
ORATION, *Speech, Harangue, Declamation, Oratory, Panegyric.*
EPISTLE, *Letter.*
}

More special; relating to matters of Fact, ‖ either the *more usual name, or that which denotes what is commonly said by many.*

3. {
NARRATION, *Relate, Story, History, Tale, tell, Tidings, Report, recite, recount, rehearse, impart, inform, Tradition, Annunciation, Commemoration, Diary, Diurnal, Gazet, Chronicle, Legend, bring word, give notice,* or *intelligence.*
RUMOR, *Brute, Hear-say, Report, common Fame, Noise, Vogue.*
}

Explicative; according to the

General name;

4. INTERPRETATION, *Exposition, construction, explain, explicate, unfold, Trouchman.*

Particular kinds; whereby the words are

Altered; by *putting* them *into another language*, or *into other words of the same language.*

5. {
TRANSLATION, *Construe, version, interpret, turn, render.*
PARAPHRASE, *Descant, Metaphrase, Circumlocution.*
}

Enlarged; by adding several other words for further explication, or *Contracted*; into fewer words.

6. {
COMMENTARY, *Gloss, Note, Annotation, Stricture, Scholiast, Expositor.*
EPITOME, *Compendium, Brief, abbreviate, breviate, abridge, Breviary, succinct, concise, Abstract, Synopsis, System, couch, contract, Summary, extract, recapitulate.*
}

Appendages of discourse, whether the

Extreme; either the *Beginning* or the *End.*

7. {
PROLOGUE, *Exordium, Preamble, Proem, Introduction, Preface, Prelude.*
EPILOGUE, *Conclusion.*
}

Intermediate; either that which is more necessary, *whereby one part is to be connected to another*, or such *additional part* as is less necessary to the main scope of the discourse.

8. {
TRANSITION, *Passage.*
DIGRESSION, *On the by, by the way, Diversion, Excursion, Extravagant, glance.*
}

H VI. MODES

VI. MODES OF DISCOURSE may be distributed into such as concern the business of proving or perswading, either

- *Antecedently*; denoting such forms of speech as imply
  - *Doubting, or a desire of being informed by others*, to which may be opposed the general name for *those returns which others make to such forms of speech*.
    - 1. { QUESTION, *Ask, Interrogate, demand, examin, expostulate, Inquisition.*
      ANSWER, *Responsal, Reply, Rejoinder, Return.*
  - *Knowing* or acknowledging, whether
    - *Positive*; saying a thing to be so, or not to be so.
      - 2. { AFFIRMATION, *Assert, averr, avouch, profess, Asseveration, Position.*
        NEGATION, *Deny, renounce, refuse, Recusant, disavow, gainsay, repulse, say nay.*
    - *Conditional*; allowing a thing to be so for the present, that we may thereby the better judge of the consequences from it, or owning the truth asserted by another.
      - 3. { SUPPOSITION, *Admit, premise, presuppose, Condition, Proviso, Hypothesis, put case.*
        CONCESSION, *Grant, yield, allow, acknowledge, admit, agree.*
- *Concomitantly*; as the Acts or parts of it.
  - *More general*;
    - *Saying something against what another affirms*, or *saying what is most contrary to it.*
      - 4. { OPPOSITION, *Gainsay, thwart.*
        CONTRADICTION.
    - *Arguing against another*, to which is opposed, *The shewing an insufficiency in such arguments.*
      - 5. { OBJECTION, *Impugn, Cavil.*
        SOLUTION, *Solve, Answer, Resolve, Subterfuge, Evasion, Casuist.*
  - *More special*; relating to
    - *Our own arguments* or *opinions, by shewing the truth of them*, or *seconding such proof, by further evidence.*
      - 6. { PROBATION, *Prove, demonstrate, evince, Evidence, verifie, Reason, Presumption.*
        CONFIRMATION, *Stablish, establish, ratifie.*
    - *Our adversaries arguments, by shewing the weakness of them*, or *turning the force of them against himself.*
      - 7. { CONFUTATION, *Refell, refute, disprove, reason against.*
        RETORTION, *Invert, recriminate.*
- *Subsequently*; whether
  - *Reall*; by *rendring an adversary unable to defend his own opinion*, or *making him to submit to ours.*
    - 8. { POSING, *Puzzle, nonplus, baffle, confound, gravel, run down.*
      CONVICTION, *Satisfie, evince.*
  - *Verbal*; *acknowledging the truth of our opinion*, or *renouncing the error of his own.*
    - 9. { CONFESSION, *Acknowledge, own, yield, grant, profess, cry mercy.*
      RECANTATION, *Renounce, retract, recal, revoke, unsay, bite in.*

CHAP. II.
I. Concerning GOD. II. Of the several things and notions reducible under that collective Genus of WORLD.

§. I.

THose more special kinds of beings to be treated of Antecedaneously to the Predicaments, because they are not (as Predicaments are) capable of any subordinate species, are GOD and WORLD.

That which the Heathen Philosophers stile the first Mover, the first and supreme cause of all things, and suppose to be *a Being of all possible perfections*, is GOD, *Lord, Jehovah, Deity, Divine -ity, Deifie*.

And because of that absolute Simplicity and Purity of the Divine nature, whereby 'tis distinguished from all other things, and therefore *incapable of* being divided by *Parts*, or by *Differences* and *Species* as the rest are; hereupon, under this Head there is onely provision to be made for that great Mystery of Christianity, the Sacred Persons of the Blessed

Trinity { FATHER.
         SON, *Christ, Jesus.*
         HOLY GHOST, *Holy Spirit.*

To the name of *God* that of *IDOL* may be opposed, by which is meant any *False God*; according to the Acception of the word in that Scripture, *All the Gods of the Heathen are Idols.*

To the *Second Person* the name *ANTICHRIST* may be adjoyned by way of *Opposition*; the true Notion and Importance of the word so requiring.

§. II.

By WORLD, *Universe*, is meant the *Compages* or *Frame of the whole Creation*, with more especial reference to those *Principal* and more *General parts* of which it consists; whether
{ SPIRITUAL and immaterial. I.
  Corporeal, considered according to the
  Parts into which it is divided, whether
    CELESTIAL. II.
    Terrestrial: either
      { Inanimate. ——— { LAND. III.
        ANIMATE. V.   WATER. IV.
    CIRCLES by which it is divided. VI.

I. SPIRIT.

I. By SPIRIT is meant *Immaterial Substance*: to which may be adjoyned, as its proper Opposite, the word *BODY, Corporeal, Matter -ial, Carcass, Corps, corpulent.*
A Created Spirit is either such as
{ Doth not relate to a Body; and that considered according to its
  General Name, as being *a ministring Spirit.*
  1. ANGEL -ical, *Dæmon.*
  Special kinds, as *Good* or *Evil.*
  2. { GOOD ANGEL, *Cherub, Seraphim, Good Genius.*
      DEVIL, *Satan, Fiend, Diabolical, Dæmon, Fury, Goblin, bad Genius.*
  Doth relate to a Body; and that considered according to its
  General Name, as being *designed for the enlivening and quickning of a Body.*
  3. SOUL, *Animate, Spirit, Mind.*
  Special kinds, as *rendring its Body capable of*
    Nutrition and Growth;
    4. VEGETATIVE, *grow.*
    Sense;
    5. SENSITIVE.
    Discourse and Religion, together with a sense of moral good and evil.
    6. RATIONAL, *reasonable.*

II. A-

II. HEAVEN. II. *Amongſt Corporeal Subſtances, that which is eſteemed moſt Simple and moſt Perfect*, whoſe general name is therefore frequently uſed to ſignifie a *place* or a *ſtate* of the greateſt Perfection and Happineſs, together with that which in both theſe reſpects is *oppoſite*, are commonly ſtyled
- HEAVEN, *Celeſtial, Firmament, Skie.*
- HELL, *Infernal, Stygian.*

Thoſe *parts of Heaven which fall under our Senſes* may be conſidered according to their.

- General Name; denoting ſuch parts as are *more Solid and Luminous.*
  - 1. STARR, *Stellate.*
  - Particular kinds; either
    - *Fixed,* that is to ſay, *which do alwayes keep the ſame diſtance from one another.* And theſe, for the better diſtinction and remembrance of them, are uſually diſtributed into divers parcels or little Aggregates, called *Conſtellations*: the received names of which are, according to their imaginary Reſemblances, either the proper names of *Perſons,* as *Perſeus, Andromeda, Orion,* &c. or the names of brute *Animals,* as *Bear, Lion, Ram,* &c. or the names of *Inanimate* things, as *Balance, Arrow,* &c. which may each of them be ſufficiently expreſſed, as the things themſelves are to which they are reſembled, without being particularly provided for in the Table. And becauſe that great *Luminary which rules the Day,* with us in this Syſtem is, by the moſt received Hypotheſis, thought to belong to this number; therefore may it be adjoyned, as the moſt conſiderable Particular belonging to this General.
      - 2. { FIXED STARR, *Conſtellation.*
          { SUN, *Solar.*
    - *Wandring,* viz. *which do not alwaies keep the ſame diſtance from one another;* to which may be adjoyned that other kind of *Luminous Body, which is now by ſufficient obſervation and experiment diſcovered to be above the Atmoſphere;* according to the
      - General names.
        - 3. { PLANET, *Wandring ſtarr.*
            { COMET, *Blazing ſtarr.*
      - Particular kinds of *Planets,* being either
        - *Primary;*
          - *Seen by us at a diſtance,* either *more*
            - *Frequently,*
              - *Higher* pair
                - 4. { SATURN-*ine.*
                    { JUPITER, *Jovial.*
              - *Lower* pair,
                - 5. { MARS.
                    { VENUS, *Morning ſtar, Evening ſtar, Day ſtarr.*
            - *Rarely,* as being *near the Sun,*
              - 6. MERCURY-*ial.*
          - *Inhabited by us,*
            - 7. The GLOBE of SEA AND LAND, *Earth, World, Oecumenical, Terreſtrial, Terrene, Univerſe, Geography.*
        - *Secondary;* whether *moving* || *about the Earth,* or *about any other Planet,*
          - 8. { MOON, *Lunar.*
              { SATELLES.

III. By

III. By EARTH, *Land, World,* is meant the *habitable parts of this* III. EARTH. *Globe*; to which may be adjoyned the more general name of the *Greater parts of the Earth,* denoted by the word COUNTRY, *Region, Land, Tract, Quarter, Coast.*

The most considerable Notions belonging to Discourse, which refer to this, may be distinguished *with respect to its*

Figure, || whether *equal* or *unequal,* Convex or *Concave.*

1. { PLAIN, *Champion, Level, Flat, Even.*
{ MOUNTAIN, *Hill, Ascent, Rising, Upland, Downs, Knoll.*
{ VALLEY, *Vale, Dale, Bottom.*

Boundaries, or *adjacent Waters*; which are either

On *all sides,* whether

Great, || *more* great, or *less* great.

2. { CONTINENT, *Firm-land, Main-land.*
{ ISLAND, *Isle, Insular.*

Less, || whether *roundish* and *high,* or *oblong.*

3. { ROCK, *Cragg.*
{ CLIFF.

On *three sides,* which, according to a higher or lower situation, as it is *conspicuous* || *more* or *less,* is called

4. { PROMONTORY, *Cape, Fore-land, Head-land, Point,*
{ PENE-ISLE.

On *two sides, conspicuous,* || *more* or *less.*

5. { ISTHMUS, *streight, Neck of land.*
{ BANK, *Shelf, Flat, Ridge, Shallow, Shole.*

On *one side,* either according to the more general name, or that particular kind which is *sometimes covered with Sea.*

6. { SHORE, *Strand, Sea-coast, Bank-side.*
{ WASHES, *Sands.*

Motion or *Rest.*

7. { QUICKSANDS, *Drift, Syrtis.*
{ OAZ.

IV. To

IV. WATER.

IV. To the word WATER, as it denotes the *watry part of this Terrestrial Globe*, may be adjoyned the word SEA, *Marine, Maritim*; which denotes the more general name of the *greater parts* of *Water*, as Country or Region does of Land. (as the other, *with respect to its*

The more considerable Notions under this Head may be distinguished

Figure, ‖ whether *equal* or *unequal*, *Convex* or *Concave*.
1. { ÆQUOR, *Calm Sea, Smooth Sea.*
   { WAVE, *Billow, Surge, Undulation, Rough.*
   { WHIRL-POOL, *Vorago, Gulf, Swallow*

Boundaries, or *adjacent Land*; which is either

On all sides, whether
  Great, ‖ *more* great, or *less* great.
2. { OCEAN, *Main-sea.*
   { LAKE, *Meer, Pond, Plash.*
  Less, ‖ whether *obround* and *deep*, or *oblong*.
3. { WELL, *Head.*
   { SPRING, *Fountain, Source, Rivulet.*

On three sides, ‖ *greater*, or *less*.
4. { BAY, *Gulf, Creek, Arm of the Sea, Harbour, Port, Key.*
   { PENE-LAKE, *Haven, Harbour, Port, Key.*

On two sides, ‖ *greater*, or *less*.
5. { FRETUM, *Streight, Narrow sea, Sound.*
   { CHANNEL.

On one side, either according to the more *general* name, or that *particular* kind which is *sometimes higher, and sometimes lower upon the*
6. { SHORE, *Margo aquæ.* (*Land.*
   { TIDE, *Ebb, Flow, High-water, Low-water, Neap-tide, Spring-tide.*

Motion or *Rest*; whether constantly moving, or generally at rest
7. { STREAM, *River, Brook, Current, flow, pour, gush, Bourn, Rill, Rivulet, Eddy, Gullet, Flood, Deluge, Inundation, Torrent, Cataract, Water-course, Running-water.* (*water.*
   { STAGNUM, *Pool, Puddle, Pond, stagnate, standing-water, Dead-*

V. ANIMATE PARTS OF THE WORLD.

V. The ANIMATE PARTS of the World do comprehend *such Bodies*
Vegetative, more (*as are endowed with Life or Spirit*; whether
Imperfect; such Bodies as grow in Veins of the Earth, which though they are not commonly owned and reckoned under this Rank, yet several Learned men have heretofore reduced them hither, as being a more imperfect kind of *Vegetable*; because when Mines have seemed to be totally exhausted of them, yet there hath remained behind some kind of Seminal or Spermatic parts, whereby they have in process of time been renewed again, and continued to propagate their
1. MINERAL. (*kinds.*

Perfect; whether according to the
General name;
2. PLANT, *Vegetable.*

Special kinds; denoting either, that tribe of Plants that are *most small, tender and numerous*; Or those kinds, amongst these, which are com-
   { HERB, *Wort, Weed, Botanic.* (monly fed upon by beasts, &c.
3. { GRASS, *Grase, Greensword.*

Sensitive,
4. ANIMAL, *Brute -ish.*

Rational,
5. MAN, *Woman, Human -ity, Folk.*

VI. Be-

Chap. II.   World.

VI. Besides those General parts *into which* the World may be divided, there is likewise consideration to be had of those Imaginary CIRCLES *by which men have agreed to divide both the Celestial and Terrestrial Globe, for the better explaining of the Distances and Motions of the Starrs, and the several Climates of the Earth*; to which may be adjoyned for Affinity the Notion of ORBE, *Sphere*.

VI. IMAGINARY CIRCLES.

These Circles are either

Greater, *dividing the Sphere into two equal parts*;
- *Indeterminately*; namely that which *separates the upper and visible part* of the Globe, *from that which* by reason of its being below us, we cannot see, terminating our vision.
  1. HORIZON -*tall*.
- *Determinately*; as to
  - *Northern* and *Southern* parts; whether
    - *Directly*; wherein the Sun makes every-where equal day and night:
      2. ÆQUATOR, *Æquinoctial, the Line*.
    - *Obliquely*, namely, that Line wherein the Sun is supposed constantly to move in its Annual course: to which may be adjoyned that *Circular superficies, on each side of this*, which terminates the motion of the Planets;
      3. { ECLIPTIC.
           ZODIAC.
  - *Eastern* and *Western* parts; wherein the Sun makes mid-day or midnight: to which those other *Circles* correspond *which pass through the Poles of the Horizon*, as the former do through the Poles of the World;
      4. { MERIDIAN, *Colure*.
           AZIMUTH.

Lesser, *dividing the Sphere into two unequal parts*; whether
- Polar *described by the supposed motion of the Poles of the Ecliptic*; ‖ either *Northern* or *Southern*.
  5. { ARTIC.
        ANTARTIC.
- Tropic, *terminating the motion of the Sun in its greatest Declination*; ‖ *Northern*, or *Southern*.
  6. { TROPIC of ♋ *Summer Solstice*.
        TROPIC of ♑ *Winter Solstice*.
- *Parallels*, relating ‖ either *to the Æquator*, or *to the Horizon*.
  7. { PARALLEL.
        ALMACANTAR.

CHAP.

CHAP. III.

I. *Of Elements and Meteors*. II. *Of Stones*. III. *Of Metals*.

§. I. VVHereas men do now begin to doubt, whether those that are called the Four ELEMENTS be really the *Primordia rerum*, First Principles, of which all mixed Bodies are compounded; therefore may they here be taken notice of and enumerated, without particular restriction to that Notion of them, as being onely the *great Masses of natural Bodies, which are of a more simple Fabric then the rest:* For which reason the word METEOR may be annexed to Element, for its affinity in this respect, signifying the several *kinds of Bodies which are of a more imperfect mixture*. These are, according to the common Theory, distinguishable into

⎧ More *simple*; whether
⎪ ⎧ *Real*, such as do actually exist.
⎪ ⎪ ⎧ *Lighter*;
⎪ ⎪ ⎨ ⎧ FIRE. I.
⎨ ⎨ ⎩ AIR. II.
⎪ ⎪ ⎩ *Heavier*;
⎪ ⎪ ⎧ WATER. III.
⎪ ⎪ ⎩ EARTH. IV.
⎪ ⎩ APPARENT. V.
⎩ More *mixed*; denoting various modes of Air.
 WEATHER. VI.

I. The

Chap. III.   Element.   57

I. The *hottest and lightest* kind of those that are counted *Elements*, is called FIRE: *Burn, Scald, Singe, Kindle, Tind, Light*.   I. FIRE.

The several Notions referring to the Parts or Kinds of It, are distinguishable by their Magnitude, Place, Duration, Shape, &c.

The *General* parts or *kinds of Fire*, are ‖ either greater, which seem to be *enkindled Air*; or *less*, being a *small separated portion of Fire*.

1. { FLAME, *Blaze, Coruscation, Flash, Leam, Light fire*.
    SPARK, *Strike fire*.

The *Special* sorts of Fiery Bodies, to which custom hath given particular names, are such as are either

More considerable; in respect of their

Lastingness, continuing for *some time in the same place*; and then ‖ *vanishing*, or *falling*.

2. { COMET, *Standing, Blazing starr*.
    FALLING STARR.

Suddenness; being ‖ either the *Shining and flash of inflamed Exhalations*, or the *Sound made by such Inflammations*,

3. { LIGHTNING, *Flash, Coruscation*.
    THUNDER, *Fulminate*.

Less considerable;

More *high in the Air*;

Of *Coherent* parts, in the shape of ‖ a standing *perpendicular Column*, or of a *Dart in motion*.

4. { BEAM, *Trabs*.
    DART, *Jaculum*.

Of *Disjoyned* parts, of a shape ‖ *bigger*, or *lesser*.

5. { CAPRA SALTANS.
    SCINTILLÆ VOLANTES.

More *low in the Air, loose, wandring*; ‖ as that which appears often to Mariners at Sea: and if *single*, it is called *St. Hermo, Helena*, and is thought to portend Storms; if *double*, 'tis styled *Castor and Pollux*, signifying good weather: Or *that which adheres to, and encompasses* several *Animals*, without hurting them, being probably *an Inflammation of their Effluvia*.

6. { IGNIS FATUUS, *Will with a Wisp, Jack with a Lanthorn*.
    IGNIS LAMBENS.

Within the Earth;

7. DAMP.

II. The

| | | Element. | Part. II. |

II. AIR. II. The General name for that kind of *Body*, which, *for its Levity and Warmth*, is counted *the next Element to that of Fire*, is AER, *œl, Wind, Breath.*
It is *distinguishable by its*
Purity; being ‖ either more *remote from the Earth and its Exhalations*; or *adjoyning to the Terrestrial Globe, and impregnated by the Steams and Effluvia that proceed from it.*

1. { Æ̈THER, or *ethereal Air, Firmament, Skie, Welkin.*
   { ATMOSPHERE.

Kinds of *mixture*, according to the more
General name, or that *particular* kind which signifies a *mixture of Watry* (parts.
2. { EXHALATION, *Steam, Reek, Effluvium, volatile.*
   { VAPOR, *Evaporate, Breathe.*
Particular kinds in respect of its mixture with ‖ *Earthy*, or *Fiery* parts.
3. { FUME.
   { SMOKE, *Suffumigation, bloting, fume.*

Motion,
Above ground; ‖ *Direct*, or *Circular.*
4. { WIND, *Blow, Gale, Breath, Blast, Puff, Gust, Flaw, Monsoon, Trade-wind, Bellows, Eolipile, Fan, Ventiduct.*
   { WHIRLWIND, *Herricano, Tornado.*
Under ground; ‖ *Violent*, or *Gentle.*
5. { EARTHQUAKE.
   { DAMP.

III. WATER. III. The third of those greater *Masses* of *Body*, *considerable for its Gravity and Moisture*, is styled WATER: *Aqueous, Dip, padle, Drein.*
The names belonging to this are such as concern either
The *smaller Particles of it*; ‖ whether *Solid*, or *Hollow.*
1. { DROP, *Drip, drible, drizle, trickle, sprinkle, run, shed, instil.*
   { BUBBLE, *Froth, Spume, Fome, Mantle, Ebullition.*
The *Mixture of it with Air*, ‖ *Upper*, or *Lower.*
2. { CLOUD, *Overcast, gloomy.*
   { MIST, *Fogg, nebulous.*
The *Condensation of it*, ‖ *from a Cloud*, or *from a Mist.*
3. { RAIN, *Drizle.*
   { DEW.
The *Congelation of it, according to its more*
General acception, or according to that *special kind* of it relating to the smaller *particles of a Cloud*, styled
4. { FROST, *Freeze, Ice, congele, Isicle.*
   { SNOW.
Particular restriction to the Drops ‖ of *Rain*, or of *Dew.*
5. { HAIL.
   { RIME, *Hoar-frost.*
The *Kinds of Dew*:
More *Concrete*; of a *sweet taft*: to which may be adjoyned that peculiar kind of *physical Dew* mixed with the *Exudations* of the Plant
6. { MANNA.   (*Ladanum.*
   { LADANUM.
More *Liquid*; gathered *from Plants by Bees*: to which may be adjoyned for its affinity, that other natural Body *gathered* likewise *by*
7. { HONY.   (*Bees*, and of a *clammy* consistence.
   { WAX.

IV. That

Chap. III.   *Element.*   59

IV. That which is commonly described to be the *Coldest, Thickest,* IV. EARTH.
Heaviest, of any of those Bodies counted *Elements,* is called EARTH,
Land, Mold.
This is distinguishable by its
{ Smaller *Particles*;
  { *Alone* and without mixture.
    1. DUST.
    Mixed with Water.
    2. DURT, *Mud, Mire, daggle, puddle:*
    Separated by Fire, ||*descending,* or *ascending.*
  3. { ASHES, *Embers, Cinders.*
      SOOT, *Fuliginous.*
  Bigger *Masses* of it, *serviceable for building,* and *of a*
  Cold, clammy consistence, to which that common *mixture which is made
  of this* may be adjoyned for its affinity.
  4. { CLAY.
      MORTAR, *Lome.*
  Hot and *dry consistence,* usually *made of burnt Stone*; to which, for the
  same reason, may be adjoyned that other common *mixture made of
  this.*
  5. { LIME.
      PLASTER, *Parget, Tarras, daube.*

The placing of that Pair, *Flame, spark* under the first Difference; NOTE.
and that other Pair, *Drop, Bubble,* under the third Difference; with
those other Species under the fourth Difference, must be granted to be
besides the common Theory; But there is this account to be given of it,
That there seems to be the like kind of resemblance and affinity in these
to their *Genus'es,* as there is in some of the other Species, which are commonly received.

V. APPEARING METEORS are such as onely seem to be, and have V. APPEAR-
not any real existence. ING METE-
These are either *of* a ORS.
{ *Determined Shape*;
  Part of a round.
  1. RAINBOW, *Iris.*
  Round wholly;
  { *Encompassing* any of the Planets or bigger *Starrs.*
    2. HALO.
    Representing || *the Sun,* or *the Moon.*
  3. { PARELIUS.
      PARASELENE.
  Straight.
  4. VIRGÆ, *Streaks, Rays of Light.*
  Undetermined shape, being a *seeming* Hollowness or *Opening in the
  Heavens*
  5. CHASM, *Gaping.*

VI. **By WEATHER** is meant the state and *condition of the Air*; the several kinds of which, not sufficiently expressible by any words in the precedent Table, are considered either *as to*

- The Air's || *Transparency*, or *Opacity*.
  - 1. ⎰ CLEARNESS, *Open, serene.*
       ⎱ HAZINESS.
- The various *Meteors wherewith* it may be *affected*; whether
  - *Rain*;
    - *simply* and by it self; either
      - *Drops*, || *little*, or *great*.
        - 2. ⎰ MIZLING, *Drizzle.*
             ⎱ SHOWR.
      - *Stream*.
        - 3. SPOUT.
    - *Mixed*, || *with* violent *Winds*, or *with Snow*.
      - 4. ⎰ STORM.
           ⎱ SLEET.
  - *Winde*, considered *according to* its
    - *Quality*; whether *excessively cold*, or *mixed with noxious vapours*.
      - 5. BLASTING.
    - *Quantity*; being either
      - *Little*, or *not sufficient to ruffle the waters*.
        - 6. ⎰ GENTLE GALE, *Breez.*
             ⎱ CALM, *Still, Halcyon.*
      - *Much*; whether *equal*, or *unequal*.
        - 7. ⎰ STIFF GALE, *High wind.*
             ⎱ TEMPEST, *Storm, Flaw, blustering, boisterous.*

OF STONES.

SUch kind of *Minerals* as are *hard and friable* are called STONES, §. II. *Petrifie, Quarry:* to which EARTHY CONCRETIONS may be annexed by way of affinity, being more *soft* and *brittle*, and of a middle nature *betwixt Stones and Metals*.

Stones may be distinguished into such as are
- VULGAR, and of no price. I.
- MIDDLE-prized. II.
- PRECIOUS; either
  - LESS TRANSPARENT. III.
  - MORE TRANSPARENT. IV.

Earthy Concretions are either
- DISSOLVIBLE. V.
- NOT DISSOLVIBLE. VI.

I. VULGAR STONES, or such as are of little or no price, are distinguishable from their different Magnitudes, Uses, Consistences, *into* the

Greater Magnitudes of Stone; *used* either *about*
- *Buildings*; whether of
  - *Walls*; chiefly, being of a
    - *Softer* consistence; || whether *natural*, or *factitious*.
      1. FREE-STONE.
         BRICK.
    - *Harder* consistence; not easily yielding to the Tool of the Workman, growing || either in
      - *Greater* masses;
        2. RAGG.
      - *Lesser* masses; whether such as are for their figure
        - More *knobbed* and unequal; used for the striking of fire, || either the more common which is *less heavy*, or the less common which is *more heavy*, as having something in it of a metalline (mixture.
          3. FLINT.
             MARCHASITE, *Fire-stone*.
        - More *round* and even;
          4. PIBBLE, *Thunderbolt*.
  - *Roof* or *Pavement*; being of a *laminated* figure, || either *natural*, or *factitious*.
    5. SLATE.
       TILE.
- *Metals*, either *for* the
  - *Sharpning* or *trying* of them.
    6. WHET-STONE.
       TOUCH-STONE.
  - *Polishing* or *cutting* of them; || being either of a more spungy and *soft*, or of a more *hard* consistence.
    7. PUMICE.
       EMRY.

Lesser Magnitudes; || either *more*, or *less* minute.
  8. SAND, *Grit*.
     GRAVEL.

II. MID-

II. MIDDLE-PRIZED STONES are either *of a Shining Politure*, or capable of it; whether of a
- *Simple white* colour, and more *soft* confiftence.
  1. ALABASTER.
- *Sometime white, fometime black*, or *green*, and *fometime variegated* with veins; growing in ||*greater*, or *leffer* Maffes.
  2. { MARBLE, *Porphyrie.*
     { AGAT.
- *Spotted*; || with *Red* upon a *Greenifh* colour, or with fpots of *Gold*-colour upon *Blew*.
  3. { JASPIS, *Heliotrope.*
     { LAZUL, *Azure-ftone.*
- *Tranfparency*: either
- *Brittle*; || whether *natural*, or *factitious*.
  4. { CRYSTAL-*ine.*
     { GLASS, *Vitrifie.*
- *Fiffil, into Flakes*, || either *greater*, or *leffer*.
  5. { SELENITE, *Mufcovia glaff, Ifingglaff, Sparr.*
     { TALC.
- *Relation to Metals*; || *attracting of Iron*, or *making of Braff.*
  6. { LOAD-STONE, *Magnet-ical, Compaff.*
     { CADMIA, *Calaminaris.*
- *Incombuftible nature.*
  7. AMIANTUS, *Asbeftus.*
- *Strange Original*; not being properly Minerals, though ufually reckoned amongft them; but either a *fub-marine Plant*; or fuppofed to proceed from a *liquid Bitumen.*
  8. { CORAL-*ine.*
     { AMBER.

There are feveral other kinds of Stony Confiftences mentioned in the Authors who write *de Lapidibus.* Some that are found in the Bodies of Animals, their Stomachs, Guts, Bladders, Kidneys, *&c.* feveral of which are *denominated* from the *Animals* in which they are found; as *Alectorius, Chelidonius, Bezoar, &c.* Others have peculiar names *from* their *fhapes*; as *Aftroides, Gloffopetra, &c.* Others made of *Animals* or parts of *Animals* petrified, which may be fufficiently expreffed, without being particularly provided for in the Tables.

Chap. III.   Stone.

III. PRECIOUS STONES, *Gemms*, *Jewels*, are such as, for their *rarity* and *beauty*, are every where more *esteemed*: amongst which some are LESS TRANSPARENT, which are distinguishable chiefly by their Colours: either

- Representing variety of *Colours with dimness*, ∥ *less*, or *more*.
    1. { OPAL.
         CATS-EYES.
- Of *particular Colours*.
  - *Whitish and shining*; though this be not properly a Mineral, but a part of *a testaceous Fish*.
    2. PEARL.
  - *Red*.
    3. SARDIUS, *Cornelian*, *Bloud-stone*.
  - *Pale Fleshy* colour, like that of a man's nail.
    4. ONYX.
  - *Blewish*.
    5. TURCOIS.
  - *Pale Purple*.
    6. CHALCEDONY.

As for that which is commonly styled a *Toadstone*; this is properly *a tooth* of the Fish called *Lupus marinus*, as hath been made evident to the Royal Society by that Learned and inquisitive person Dr *Merit*.

IV. MORE TRANSPARENT *Gemms*; may be distinguished into such as are either

- *Colourless*: ∥ either *most hard and bright*; or that which is very like to this in other respects, but onely *less hard and bright*.
    1. { DIAMOND, *Adamant*.
         SAPHIRE WHITE.
- *Coloured*; to be ranged according to the order of the colours in the Rainbow.
  - *Red*; of *a lustre* ∥ *greater*, or *less*.
    2. { RUBY, *Carbuncle*.
         GRANATE.
  - *Yellow*; whether *paler*, or *deeper*.
    3. { CHRYSOLITE.
         TOPAZ.
  - *Green*; ∥ either most *bright* and pleasant, or of a *darker* kind of *Sea-green*.
    4. { EMERALD, *Smaragd*.
         BERYL.
  - *Blewish*.
    5. SAPHIRE.
  - *Purple* or Violaceous; *more inclining* ∥ *to Blew*, or *to Yellow*.
    6. { AMETHYST.
         HYACINTH.

V. Such

V. EARTHY CONCRETIONS DISSOLVIBLE.

V. Such EARTHY CONCRETIONS as commonly grow *in Mines*, together with such *other factitious Substances* as have some analogy to these, and are DISSOLVIBLE by Fire or Water, may be distinguished by their being

Not inflammable:
- *More simple*; being several kinds of *Salt*, ‖ whether of the
  - *Sea-water*, the most necessary *Condiment for Meat*; or of the *Air*, used as a chief ingredient *in the making of Gunpowder*.
    1. { SALT, *Brine*.
       { NITRE, *Salt-peter*.
  - *Earth*; ‖ of a *styptic* quality and abstersive, proper for the drying of Wounds, commonly *boiled* up into a consistence *from a mineral water*; or that other kind of Earthy Salt *dug up in* great *lumps*.
    2. { ALUME.
       { SAL GEMMÆ.
  - *Metals* of all kinds, sometimes called Sugars and Crystals; but agreeing in the common nature with that which is styled
    3. VITRIOL, *Chalchanthus, Copperas*.
  - *Vegetables*; made ‖ either *by fermentation*, or *by burning*.
    4. { TARTAR.
       { Al CALI.
  - *Animal Substances*, made *by Distillation*, called
    5. URINOUS SALT.
  - *More mixed* of other Salts; ‖ more *volatile*, or *fixed*.
    6. { SAL AMMONIAC.
       { CHRYSOCOLLA, *Borax*.

Inflammable; of a more
- *Dry* consistence, and *Yellowish* colour.
  7. SULPHUR, *Brimstone*.
- *Clammy* and tenacious consistence
  - *Not sweet*-sented; ‖ more *solid*, or more *liquid*.
    8. { BITUMEN -*inous*.
       { NAPHTHA.
  - *Sweet*-sented.
    9. AMBERGRIS.

VI. EARTHY CONCRETIONS NOT DISSOLVIBLE.

VI. EARTHY CONCRETIONS NOT DISSOLVIBLE may be distinguished by their various Colours; being either

- *White* and soft according to degrees, ‖ *more*, or *less*.
  1. { CHALK.
     { MARLE.
- *Yellowish red*, whether more *yellow*, or more *red*.
  2. { OKER, *Yellow oker*.
     { RED OKER, *Ruddle*.
- *Black*; of a *finer* or *courser* grain.
  3. { JETT.
     { PIT-COAL, *Sea-coal*.
- *Gold*-colour, of a *poisonous* nature, ‖ either *as* it is *dug* out of the Earth,
  4. { ORPIMENT, *Auripigmentum*.   (or *as* it is *sublimed*.
     { ARSENIC, *Rats-bane*.
- *Reddish*; often found in the same Mines with Orpiment.
  5. SANDARACH.

OF METALS.

METAL is a *Mineral*, for the most part, of a *hard* consistence, close, *ductil*, and *fusil*: It is distinguishable into
{ *Perfect*,
  { NATURAL. I.
    FACTITIOUS. II.
  Imperfect, with reference to
  { METALLINE KINDS. III.
    RECREMENTITIOUS PARTS. IV.

§. III.

I. By NATURAL METALS are meant *such as* of themselves *grow in the Earth*, without any kind of mixture, or other help by the Art of men. These are either

I. NATURAL METALS.

More *rare* and *precious*; of a
{ *Yellowish* colour, most *heavy*, not growing in any particular Mines, where 'tis imbased with any drossy mixture: but found pure, either in small sands, or rocky branches.
  1. GOLD, *Gilt, Or.*
  Whitish, and next in value to Gold, not subject to rust, and *of a pleasant sound*.
  2. SILVER, *Argent.*
Of a *middle* value; of a
{ *Whitish* colour, and more *soft* consistence.
  3. TINN, *Stannery.*
  Reddish colour, the first material of Mony.
  4. COPPER.
Most *base* and *common*:
{ Of a *softer* consistence, and a *darkish* colour, not *sonorous*.
  5. LEAD, *Plummer.*
  Of a *harder* consistence, being the common matter for Weapons and Tools.
  6. IRON.

II. By FACTITIOUS METALS are meant such as are made by the Art of men. These may be distinguished into such as are *made of*

II. FACTITIOUS METALS.

{ *Copper* and *Lapis calaminaris*.
  1. BRASS, *Brasier.*
  Tinn, Lead, and *Tin-glass.*
  2. PEWTER·*er.*
  Iron depurated by frequent heating, and beating, and boiling *with Salts.*
  3. STEEL.

III. IMPER-

III. IMPERFECT kinds of METAL, are either
- Fluid;
  - 1. MERCURY, *Quick-silver.*
- Solid and consistent; used for
  - Purging, and chiefly for Vomiting.
    - 2. ANTIMONY *-al.*
  - Making of *Pewter*, being of *shining brittle* substance.
    - 3. BISMUTE, *Tin-glass.*
  - Making of *Soder*, being like Tinn, but more *hard* and *brittle.*
    - 4. SPELTER, *Zink, Spalt.*
  - Painting; ‖considered according to its *natural* state, being *the Oar of Quick-silver*, and of a *Dark red*: or else as it is *prepared by grinding*, which renders it of a *Bright red.*
    - 5. { CINNABAR, *Rudle.*
         VERMILION.
  - Writing; not known to the Ancients, and therefore without any Latin or Greek name.
    - 6. BLACK-LEAD.

IV. RECREMENTITIOUS PARTS OF METAL, are such as are cast off; either *in* the
- Preparation *of them,* by
  - Melting; being *of parts*
    - More *large and united*; a *kind of scum* arising from the separation of impurer mixtures in the fusion of Metals, chiefly in the purging of Silver from Lead.
      - 1. LITHARGE.
    - More *minute and separate*; being a concretion of the *lesser parts of Copper*, which fly out when that Metal is *in fusion*; ‖either the *heavier* parts, which by their gravity descend to the floor: or *the more light and volatile* parts, which adhere to the roof or walls.
      - 2. { SPODIUM.
           POMPHOLYX.
  - Beating or hammering.
    - 3. SCORIA, *Scales.*
- Corruption *of them*; according to the
  - General name.
    - 4. RUST, *Canker.*
  - Particular kinds; proceeding either *of Copper* and Brass, or *of Lead.*
    - 5. { VERDIGREECE, *Ærugo.*
         CERUSE, *White lead.*

CHAP.

CHAP. IV.

1. *Of Plants, The difficulty of enumerating and describing these.* II. *The more general distribution of them.* III. *Of Herbs considered according to their Leaves.* IV. *Of Herbs considered according to their Flowers.* V. *Of Herbs considered according to their Seed-vessels.* VI. *Of Shrubs.* VII. *Of Trees.*

§. I.

The more *perfect* kind of *Vegetables* are called by the name of *Plants*, the several kinds of which are so exceeding numerous, as must needs render it a very difficult task for any man who is most versed in the study of them, either to *enumerate* them so fully or to *order* them so acurately, as will not be liable to many exceptions; especially considering the streining and force that must sometimes be used, to make things comply with the institution of these tables into which they are to be reduced.

Gaspar Bauhinus doth in his *Pinax* reckon up about six thousand several plants, the particular names of which do amount to almost twice the number of words here intended for the whole body of language. And there is reason enough to believe, that there are many more besides those he mentions, since we find by daily experience, in sowing the seeds of Flowers and of Trees, and the different wayes of culture used about them, that new kinds of Flowers and of Fruits are continually produced, such as were not before described by any Author, and such as do afterwards propagate their kinds; insomuch that it may well be doubted whether there be any determinate number of these subordinate Species.

I design in these following tables to take notice only of the *chief families* of Plants, to which the others are to be reduced. In the descriptions of which, there will be no small difficulty, by reason of their great number, and the want of proper words to express the more minute differences betwixt them, in respect of shape, colour, tast, smell, *&c.* to which instituted languages have not assigned particular names. I mention this by way of Apology for the several defects, which I am sensible of in the following tables.

In the description of those Plants which are heads of *numerous families*, I take notice only of that *Communis ratio*, which belongs to all the subordinate varieties of them, unless it be when there is no such common agreement belonging to them all: or where several things are reduced under the same head, some for their agreement in one Accident, and others for their agreement in some other Accident; in which cases the descriptions here mentioned, are to be understood of the chief and most common Plants of that name.

As for the various *particulars contained under each family*, as suppose Tulips, Roses, Apples, Pears, Plums, *&c.* These need not be particularly provided for, both because the just number of them is not yet stated, every year producing new ones: And because they may as well be expressed Periphrastically here as in all other Languages; either by their

- *Seasons*; whether Early or Late, Vernal, Autumnal, Hyemal.
- *Lastingness*; being either Annual or Perennial.
- *Bigness or Littleness*, Talness or Lowness.
- *Manner of growth*; whether Erect, Trailing, Creeping, Climbing, Twisting.
- *Place of growth*; either *Terrestrial*, Hilly, Sandy, Stony, Clay, &c. *Aquatic*, belonging either to Sea or Rivers, Marish, Moorish, Fenny grounds.
- *Several parts*; whether in respect of the
  - *Root*; being either *Fibrous*, of bigger or lesser strings, more or less numerous, spreading sidewise or tending more directly downwards: Or *Bulbous*, of one single bulb or several, whether Obround, Compressed, Oblong, Coated or Scaly: Or *Tuberous*, having its thicker parts contiguous, or hanging more at a distance by small strings.
  - *Stemm* or stalk; whether Solid or Hollow, Smooth or Rugged, Round or Angular, Knotted or Jointed more or less frequently, being free from leaves, or having leaves.
  - *Leaves*; whether as to their
    - *Superficies*; being Smooth, Unctuous, Shining, Rough, Prickly, Hairy, Woolly, &c.
    - *Shape and figure*; Round Angular, Broad Narrow, Long Short, of smooth or of indented, jagged, waved, curled edges, being either sharp or round pointed.
    - *Substance or Bulk*; Thick Succulent, or Thin Dry, being interspersed with nerves either direct or transverse.
    - *Colour*; whether the same on both sides or different, clear or spotted, of a brighter or darker green.
    - *Number*; One, Two, Three, &c.
    - *Manner of growth*; whether singly, or in pairs opposite to each other: or having more then two encompassing the stalk, Winged, Fingered, &c.
  - *Flowers*; as to their
    - *Shapes*; consisting of one single undivided leaf, either divided at the edge or not: or having several leaves, three, four, five or more.
    - *Colour*; whether simple, as Red, Yellow, Purple, &c. or Mixed, Striped, Speckled, Edged.
    - *Number*; Bearing either One or Many, and these either single or double.
    - *Manner of growth*; whether of single flowers, being Erect, Hanging, Reversed, &c. or of several flowers, Verticillate, Spicate, Umbelliferous.
  - *Seed-vessels*; whether *Oblong*, Closed or Open, *Round*, Hollow, Solid, Smooth, Rugged, Prickly, Scaly, conteining few or many seeds.
  - *Seeds themselves*; Round, square, flat, oblong, downy, &c. smooth, Echinate, black, white, shining, &c.
  - *Fruits*; Apples, Berries, &c.
  - *Juice*; Waterish, Gummy, Milky, Yellow.

Chap. IV. Plants.

To all which may be added their different smells and taits, and the several uses they are commonly applyed unto; by some of which Accidents all other Plants may be sufficiently described.

I had formerly distributed the kinds of Herbs, according to those several ends and purposes for which they are commonly used, into these three heads; 1. Such as are for *pleasure*, being usually cherished in Gardens, for their flowers, or beauty, or sweet sent. 2. Such as are *Alimentary*, being used by men for food, either in respect of their Roots, their Leaves or Stalks, their Fruit or their Seed. 3. Such as are *Medicinal*, being either Hot and biting, or Cold and Stupefying, Purgative, Alterative, Vulnerary. But upon further consideration I am satisfied, that though these heads may seem more facil and vulgar; yet are they not so truly Philosophical, but depend too much upon the Opinions and customs of several times and Countries.

As for the usual distinction betwixt *Shrubbs* and *Trees*, it doth not seem (at least so farr as these things have been hitherto described) to have any such distinct limits in nature, as were to be desired, and as is to be found betwixt other things, there being several under each head, which seem to be of a doubtful condition. Some that are reckoned for *Shrubbs*, which have a fair pretence to be placed amongst *Trees*: and others accounted *Trees*, which without any injury might be reduced to the Genus of *Shrubbs*. I do in the following tables comply with that opinion, which seems most common and probable.

The reason why the two last differences of *Trees*, is not from their *fruit* (as the others are) but from their *Woods* and *Rines*, or from their *Rosins* and *Gumms*, is because these are the only things that we yet know of them, their natures in other respects being not yet (for ought I know) described by any Authors.

As for any *new species* of Plants that shall hereafter be discovered, 'tis probable they may by analogie be reduced either to some of the *families*, here mentioned, or at least to some of the *Tribes*.

I have added to the several species of *Plants* and *Animals*, their Latin names in the Margin, because many of them are as well, if not better, known by such compellations; and because they are most frequently treated of by the Authors who write in that Language.

§. II.

Plants may be distinguished into such as are more
{ *Minute* and *tender*, called *Herbs*, to be considered according to their
  { *Leaves*.
  { *Flowers*.
  { *Seed-vessels*.
{ *Large* and *hard* being wooddy plants, whether the
  { *Lesser*, which commonly grow up from the root in several stemms called *Shrubbs*.
  { *Larger*, which of themselves do grow up in one single stemm, called *Trees*.

Herbs

§. III, HERBS CONSIDERED ACCORDING TO THEIR LEAVES, may be diſtinguiſhed into ſuch as are
- *Imperfect*; which either do want, or ſeem to want ſome of the more eſſential parts of Plants, *viz.* either Root, Stalk or Seed. I.
- *Perfect*; having all the eſſential parts belonging to a Plant, to be diſtinguiſhed by the
  - *Faſhion of the leaf*; whether
    - *Long*; as all Gramineous herbs, having a long narrow leaf without any foot-ſtalk.
      - (*Not flowring*; (i.) not having any foliaceous flower.
        - FRUMENTACEOUS; Such whoſe ſeed is uſed by men for food, either Bread, Pudding, Broth, or Drink. II.
        - NOT FRUMENTACEOUS; III.
      - *Flowring*; Being of
        - BULBOUS ROOTS; Having no fibers from the ſide, but only from the Bottom or the Top; whoſe leaves are more thick, undivided, ſmooth-edged, and generally deciduous. IV.
        - AFFINITY TO BULBOUS ROOTS; V.
    - ROUND; VI.
  - *Texture of the Leaf*; being either
    - NERVOUS; having ſeveral prominent Fibers. VII.
    - SUCCULENT; having thick juicie leaves, covered with a cloſe membrane, through which the moiſture cannot eaſily tranſpire, which makes them continue in dry places. VIII.
  - SUPERFICIES of the Leaf, or MANNER of Growing. IX.

1. IMPERFECT HERBS.

1. IMPERFECT HERBS may be diſtinguiſhed into
- *Terreſtrial*; whether
  - *Moſt imperfect*; which ſeem to be of a ſpontaneous generation.
    - *Having no leaf*,
      - *With a Stemm* and *Head*; the *Greater* or the *Leſſ*. The later of which hath by Mr. *Hook* been firſt diſcovered to conſiſt of ſmall ſtemms with little balls at the top, which flitte* out when 1. *Fungus. Mucor.*
        - MUSHROOM, *Toadſtool, Fungus, Touchwood, Spunke.* (ripe.
        - MOULD, *Horineſſ, Vinnewd.*
      - *Without a Stem*, of a roundiſh figure ‖ growing either *in the ground*, being eſculent, & counted a great delicate: or *on the ground*, being 2. *Tuber. Fungus pulverulentus.*
        - TRUBS, *Truffle.* (when dry) full of an unſavory hurtful duſt.
        - FUZBALL, *Puchfiſt.*
    - *Having a leaf*; being generally *deeper* then other plants and *curled*, growing *in ſuch barren places* where no other plants will thrive, ‖ either that which grows, both on the *ground*, and *on walls and trees*, of which there are great varieties: or that which grows *Moſchus. Lichen.*
      - 3. MOSS. (only *in moiſt grounds and ſhady places.*
      - LIVERWORT.
  - *Leſſ Imperfect*; being counted Infœcund, whoſe ſeed and flower (if there be any) is ſcarce diſcernable, commonly called *Capillary*
    - *Have ſeveral leaves*; (*Plants*, whether ſuch as
      - *Divided*;
        - *Doubly*; or ſubdivided,
          - *Greater*; of a *brighter* or a *darker* green, the later being leſs and *Filix. Dryopteris.*
            - 4. FEARN, *Brake.* (more finely cut.
            - OAK-FEARN.
          - *Leſſer*; either that which *grows* commonly *on walls and dry places,*

Chap. IV.   *Herbs according to their Leaves.*   71

ces, somewhat resembling Rue both in the colour and figure of the leaf: or that which *grows in moist shady places,* having small slender black stalks.

5. { WHITE MAIDENHAIR, *Wall-rue, Tentwort*   *Adiantum album.*
   { BLACK MAIDENHAIR.   *Capillus Veneris.*

Singly; or not subdivided,

Greater; of a *broader leaf,* and *purgative root*: or of a *narrower and longer leaf.*

6. { POLYPODI.   *Polypodium.*
   { ROUGH SPLEENWORT.   *Lonchitis.*

Lesser; either that which hath a *black stalk and winged leaves* like those of a *Vetch*: or that which hath a *thicker shorter leaf,* not divided to the middle ribb.

7. { ENGLISH BLACK MAIDENHAIR.   *Trichomanes.*
   { SPLEENWORT, *Miltwast.*   *Asplenium.*

Undivided; either that whose *leaves* are somewhat *broader towards the bottom,* where they encompass the stalk like a half moon: Or (that whose *leaf is more equal.*

8. { MULE FEARN.   *Hemionitis.*
   { HARTSTONGUE.   *Phyllitis.*

Have but one leaf; either that whose leaf is like the others of this tribe, with a *tuft of very small flowers*: or that which hath an *undivided succulent leaf,* with a small *spike* standing off from it.

9. { MOON WORT.   *Lunaria.*
   { ADDERS TONGUE.   *Ophioglossum.*

Aquatic; belonging to

Fresh water; either that which consists of *small round leaves,* floting on the top or immersed in the water, having little strings shooting down from them : Or that which consists of *long small slimy filaments,* resembling green raw silk.

10. { DUCKWEED.   *Lens palustris.*
    { HAIRY RIVERWEED.   *Conferva.*

Salt water; being either of a

Softer consistence; having some resemblance to

Mushrooms; either the *Greater,* being more *round and thick,* with pores every way: or the *Less,* having *long slender stalks* with round *leaves* growing at the top of them.

11. { SPUNGE.   *Spongia.*
    { SEA NAVELWORT.   *Androsace.*

Moss, or ground Liverwort, having green *curled leaves* spreading

12. SEA-LETTICE.   (on the ground.   *Lactuca marina.*

Mushrooms and Moss; either that which is *flat and roundish, hard* and *tough,* with several *lines parallel* to the circumference: or that whose *leaves grow out of one another without any stemm.*

13. { SEA-EAR.   *Auris marina.*
    { ROUND LEAVED OYSTERWEED.   *Opuntia marina.*

Capillary Plants; having a *soft membranaceous tough leaf,* growing commonly upon Stones and Rocks in the Sea.

14. WRACK.   *Alga.*

Harder consistence; being tough, with many *fibres* or ribbs *elegantly distributed* somewhat like the Mashes of a Net, growing to a great bredth.   *Corallina marina Reticulata.*

15. SEA FANN.

H. GRA-

II. GRAMINEOUS FRUMENTACEOUS HERBS.

11. GRAMINEOUS FRUMENTACEOUS HERBS, may be distinguished into such, whose seeds are
- Greater; being covered either with a
  - Thin membrane; without any husk adhering, of a figure.
    - Oblong; either that of a more *turgid* grain and *brighter* colour, every seed in the ear being covered with three loose husks: Or that which bears a more *black*, *lank*, *oblong seed*, having always a beard adhering to the husk of each grain in the growth.

    1. { WHEAT. *Triticum.*
         RY. *Secale.*

    - Roundish and somewhat *compressed*; being the biggest of this tribe, the ears growing out of the sides of the stalk, the top of it having a chaffy panicle without any seed.

    2. MAIZE, *Indian-wheat.* *Frumentum Indicum.*
  - Husk; growing in a
    - Spike; either that whose grains in the growth of them are *bearded*, their husks adhering close to them, being the *lowest*: Or that whose grains are more *turgid and round*, growing at a greater distance in a kind of compounded ear, which seems to consist of several lesser spikes.

    3. { BARLY, *Malt.* *Hordeum.*
         RICE. *Oriza.*

    - Panicle; or dispersed tuft, *at a distance* from each other, *upon long weak stemms*, not above two together, hanging down.

    4. OAT. *Avena.*
- Lesser; growing either in a
  - Spike; or ear, having *short beards*, the grain being of a *yellowish* colour.

  5. PANIC. *Panicum.*

  - Panicle or tuft; having a *roundish shining seed*, || either that which is a more *tall large Plant*, whose panicle *stands upright*: or that which is a *less Plant*, whose panicle *hangs down*.

  6. { INDIAN MILLET. *Sorgum.*
       MILLET. *Milium.*

Chap. IV.   Herbs according to their Leaves.   73

III. GRAMINEOUS PLANTS NOT used by men FOR FOOD, may be distributed into III GRAMI-
such as are   NEOUS
  More properly called Grasses; (i.) such as have a hollow jointed, and not branched stalk, and PLANTS
  a stamineous flower, whether such as are   NOT USED
    Spicate; considerable for the   BY MEN
      Largeness of the seed; being nearest to those of the frumentaceous kind; either ‖ that of FOR FOOD.
      a *short spike, squamous* and shining seed: or that *resembling Panic*.
        1. {CANARY-GRASS.   *Phalaris.*
           {PANIC-GRASS.   *Gra. Paniceum.*
      Figure of the spike; whether
        Full, compact and round; either that whose spike is more *soft and downy*, resembling
        a fox-tail: or that which is like this but *more rough*.
        2. {FOX-TAIL.   *Alopecuros.*
           {CATS-TAIL.   *Gr. Typhinum.*
        Not full, but lank; resembling either
          Wheat;
          3. WHEAT-GRASS.   *Gr. Triticeum.*
          Rye; either ‖ the *greater* used for the making of trails: or the *lesser*.
          4. {MATWEED.   *Spartum.*
             {WILD BARLY.   *Gr. Hordeaceum.*
        Not compact, but loose, in which the parts are not close set together; ‖ either that
        whose spike is more *flat and long*, the seeds growing only on two sides alternately,
        having an inebriating quality: or that whose spike hath some *resemblance to wheat*,
        the plant being apt to spread it self by the root.
          5. {DARNELL, *Toret*.   *Lolium.*
             {DOGS-GRASS, *Quitch, Couch*.   *Gr. Caninum.*
        Not round; but having the husks *inclining one way*, being divided into many parts,
        each whereof resembles the comb of a Cock.
          6. CRESTED-GRASS.   *Gr. Cristatum.*
    Paniculate; considerable for the
      Largeness of the Leaves; having jointed stalks; either ‖ that whose stalks is commonly
      bigger and taller then other Grasses: or that which bears a *large perforate shining seed*
      of an ash colour.
        7. {REED.   *Arundo.*
           {JOB'S-TEARS.   *Lathrima Job.*
      Figure of the Panicle; comprehending such kind of plants as are
        Less common; whether such as have
          Some resemblance to the panicle of Oats, or to the *claws of a bird*.
          8. {OAT-GRASS.   *Gr. Avenaceum.*
             {FINGER-GRASS.
          Many squamous shining hollow heads hanging upon slender stalks: or having *hairy* *Dactyloides.*
          leaves, with long woolly strings on the sides of them, the seed being conteined in a
          close seed-vessel.
          9. {PEARL-GRASS, *Quaking-grass.*   *Gr. tremulum.*
             {HAIRY-GRASS.   *Gr. hirsutum.*
        Most common; both in Pastures and Meadows, yielding the best food for Cattel, both
        when growing, and when made into hay.
          10. MEADOW-GRASS.   *Gr. pratense*
  Less properly called Grasses; considerable either for the   *paniculatum.*
    Sent of the plant being sweet; either that which grows in *watery places*, having a *leaf like*
    a flag, bearing a *Julus* hard and close: or that whose *stalks* have *a spongy pith*, bearing
    flowers like those of Reeds.
      11. {SWEET SMELLING REED.   *Calamus Aro-*
          {CAMELS HAY.   *maticus,*
                                                                           Schœnanthum,
    Stalk; being
      Lesser; either that which is *triangular*: or that which is *round*, being full of a spongy
      pith
      12. {GALINGALE.   *Cyperus.*
          {RUSH.   *Juncus.*
      Greater; of a *woody* substance, *porous*, used *for walking staves*.
      13. CANE.   *Canna.*
    Head or spike; whether more
      Loose; having a soft downy substance, ‖ either *on each side of the spike*, making it to re-
      semble a feather: or *intermixed with the panicle*.
      14. {FEATHER GRASS.   *Gr. plumosum.*
          {COTTON GRASS.   *Gr. tomento-*
      Close; whether   *sum.*
        Greater; either that which hath a round *cylindrical head*, being a tall plant, whose
        spike is *blackish* and *soft like velvet*: or that which bears several *spherical burrs*.
        15. {REED MACE.   *Typha.*
            {BURR REED.   *Sparganium.*
        Lesser; having a naked stalk, bearing a *small spike resembling the tail of a Mouse*.
        16. MOUSE-TAIL.   *Myosurus.*

L   IV. GRA-

IV. GRAMI-NEOUS HERBS of BULBOUS ROOTS.	IV. GRAMINEOUS HERBS of BULBOUS ROOTS, may be distinguished into such as are considerable for their *Flowers*; which are generally made up of six leaves, or divided into six *lascinia*: either these whose fibres grow from the *Bottom of the bulb*; having the Roots

- *Scaly*; divided into many squamous *lamina*.
  - The *Greater*; whose root hath a strong sent like that of a Fox, the flowers hanging down round the top of the stalk, with a tuft of green leaves above them.

Corona Imperialis. — 1. CROWN IMPERIAL.

- The *Lesser*; having the stalk set with leaves, ‖ either that whose flower is more *large and hollow*: or that whose flowers are *smaller*, having the leaves *reversed backwards*.

Lilium Martagon. — 2. { LILLY. MARTAGON, *Turks-cap.*

- *Coated*; made up of several coats encompassing one another.
  - *Bearing the flower upon a stem*; to be further distinguished by the
    - *Shape of the flower*; whether
      - *Large and Hollow*; resembling a cup, | either that which doth generally bear but *one flower* upon a stalk, *standing upright*, having an *esculent root*: or that which doth sometimes bear *two flowers* upon a stalk, with *checkered streaks*, hanging down their heads, the root consisting of *two lobes*.

Tulipa. Fritillaria. — 3. { TULIP. FRITILLARY.

  - *Having a cup in the middle of the flower*, which comes out of a *skinny husk*: or that which hath *many small flowers* together upon the same stalk.

Narcissus. Hyacinthus. — 4. { DAFFODILL. HYACINTH.

  - *Colour of the flower*; being generally *white* and *marked with green*, ‖ either that with a *starr-like flower*, marked with a streak of *green on the back* of the leaf: or that which hath a hanging *pendulous flower*, whose leaves are *tipt with green*.

Ornithogalum. Viola bulbosa. — 5. { STARR OF BETHLEHEM. BULBOUS VIOLET, *Snow-drop.*

  - *Figure of the leaf*; resembling the blade of a sword, ‖ either that which bears a *Flow.r de luce*, having *nine leaves*, three of which stand up: or that whose flowers grow in a row under one another.

Iris bulbosa. Gladiolus segetum. — 6. { BULBOUS IRIS, *Flower de luce.* CORNFLAGG.

- *Having naked flowers, without any stem*; whether that of a *larger flower* and *broader leaf*: or that of a *lesser flower* and *narrower leaf*.

Colchicum. Crocus. — 7. { MEDOW SAFFRON, *Naked Lady.* CROCUS, *Saffron.*

- *Top of the Bulb*; whose root doth usually consist of *two bulbs*, the flowers growing in a kind of spike, of great variety of colours and shapes.

Orch's. — 8. ORCHIS, *Satyrion.*

- *Strong sent*; whether such whose leaves are more.
  - *Long*; their sent being
    - *Less strong*; the
      - *Greater*; whose roots grow single, ‖ either that with *hollow tubulous leaves*, the st. lk swelling out in the middle: or that of a *broader leaf*, rising higher in the stalk and continuing green all winter.

Cepa. Porrum. — 9. { ONYON. LEEK.

    - *Lesser*; whose roots grow commonly in clusters, ‖ either that which bears *no seed*: or that which doth *bear seed*, having very small tubulous leaves.

Ascalonitis. Porrum sect.le. — 10. { SHALOT, *Echalote.* CIVES.

  - *More strong*; either that whose *root is divided into Cloves*: or that of an *entire root*, and in some esteem for the flower.

Allium sativum. Moly. — 11. { GARLICK. MOLY.

  - *Broad*; having the root either
    - *Oblong and small*; either that which is *lower* with an *Umbell of large flowers*: or that which is *taller*, having *a round head*.

Allium Ursinum. Victorialis longa. — 12. { RAMSON. MOUNTAIN RAMSON.

    - *Round and great*; growing upon the Sea-coasts.

Scylla. — 13. SQUILL, *Sea-onyon.*

V. HERBS

V. HERBS OF AFFINITY TO BULBOUS PLANTS, upon account of their leaves or flowers, may be diftinguifhed into fuch as are either
- Efteemed for their flowers; growing in
  - Dryer places; whether fuch Plants as are more properly
    - Europæan; whofe flowers are
      - Leſſer; bearing
        - Many flowers; Starr-like, ‖ either that of a *Tuberous root*, whofe flowers grow in a fpike: or that of a *Fibrous root*.
          1. { KINGS SPEAR. *Aſphodelus*.
             { SPIDER WORT. *Phalangium*.
        - One ſingle flower; hanging the head, having a *tuberous root*, bearing *two long ſpotted leaves*.
          2. DOGSTOOTH. *Dens caninus*.
      - Larger; of a tuberous root, ‖ either that of a *fading flower* reſembling a Lilly: or that whofe *leaf is like the blade of a ſword*.
        3. { DAY-LILLY. *Lilia ſphodelus*.
           { TUBEROUS FLOWER DE LUCE. *Iris tuberoſa*.
    - American; of a tuberous root, ‖ whofe flowers are either
      - Leſſ ſweet; either that of *broad leaves*, bearing a *ſcarlet flower* like that of Corn-flagg, with a geniculate ſtalk: or that which hath *long thick dry leaves, ſharp pointed*, growing immediately from the root, bearing a ſtem of large flowers, hanging down their heads.
        4. { FLOWRING REED. *Canna Indica*.
           { JUCCA, *Indian bread*. *Jucca*.
      - More ſweet; growing *in a ſpike*, reſembling the flowers of a Hyacinth.
        5. INDIAN HYACINTH. *Hyacinthus Indicus tuberoſus*.
  - Watery places; the flowers coming forth in an Umbell, being of a purpliſh colour, having fix leaves; *the leaves* of the Plant being *long and triangular*.
    6. FLOWRING RUSH. *Juncus floridus*.
- Not esteemed for their flowers; being diſtinguiſhable by their
  - Having *no perfect leaves*; but ſome little ſcaly ſubſtances reſembling leaves, whether of
    - Fibrous roots; matted together, reſembling a birds neſt.
      7. BIRDS NEST. *Nidus avis*.
    - Scaly roots; with little *protuberances* ſomewhat *reſembling teeth*, ‖ either that whoſe root is more *Round* or more *Branched*.
      8. { BROOMRAPE. *Orobanche*.
         { TOOTHWORT. *Dentaria aphyllos*.
  - Having *a naked ſtile* or peſtle *inſtead of a flower*, whether the
    - Greater; of a Tuberous root, ‖ either that which hath a *ſpotted thick ſtalk* like a Snake, with a *jagged leaf*: or that of a *Triangular undivided leaf*.
      9. { DRAGON. *Dracontium*.
         { WAKE ROBIN, *Cuckoo-pintle*. *Arum*.
    - Leſſer; having either *Broad* or *Narrow leaves*.
      10. { BROAD LEAVED FRIARS COWLE. *Ariſarum latifol*.
          { NARROW LEAVED FRIARS-COWLE. *Ariſarum anguſtifol*.

VI. HERBS

VI. HERBS OF ROUND LEAVES, may be distinguished into such whose leaves are

- Larger;
  - Terrestrial;
    - Lying on the ground; the *flower* coming up *before the leaf* and *soon fading*, ‖ either that whose leaf is *white underneath*, of a *yellow flower*, growing *one upon a stalk*: or that which hath a *spike of purplish flowers*, being the *larger plant*.
      1. { COLTSFOOT. *Tussilago.*
         { BUTTERBURR. *Petasitis.*
    - Standing from the ground; bearing *Burrs*, the *Greater* or the *Lesser*.
      2. { GREAT BURDOCK. *Bardana major.*
         { LITTLE BURDOCK. *Bardana minor.*
    - Growing upon *mountainous places*; having a *purplish flower*, and a *pappous seed*.
      3. HORSEFOOT, *Mountain-Coltsfoot.* *Cacalia.*
    - Aquatic; of *smooth shining leaves*, ‖ either that whose leaves are of a *light green* and not *serrate*: or of a *dark green* and *serrate*, bearing yellow flowers.
      4. { WATER-LILLY. *Nymphæa.*
         { MARSH-MARIGOLD. *Caltha palustris.*
- Lesser; whose flowers do stand either
  - Singly; on *long foot-stalks*, growing in
    - Dryer places; distinguishable by the
      - Flower; having a *bending head* and a *short heel*, ‖ either that of a *bigger leaf* and the flower of a more *simple colour*: or that of a *lesser oblong leaf* and the flower of *several colours*.
        5. { VIOLET. *Viola.*
           { PANSY, *Hearts-ease.* *Herba Trinitatis.*
      - Leaf; being more thick, somewhat resembling Ivy, ‖ either that whose leaves are of a strong *purgative quality*, the *flowers small*, of a dirty purple: or that which is *esteemed for the flower*, having a great *tuberous root*, the *leaf* for the most part *spotted*.
        6. { ASARABACCA. *Asarum.*
           { SOWBREAD. *Cyclamen.*
    - Fenny and boggy places; either that of *pale yellowish leaves*, which feel *unctuously*, the *flower like a Violet*: or that which hath a *large white flower*, the leaves being like those of a Violet, but less.
      7. { BUTTERWORT, *York-shire Sanicle.* *Pinguicula.*
         { GRASS OF PARNASSUS. *Gramen Parnassii.*
  - Many together;
    - Terrestrial; distinguishable by
      - The flowers; growing in a *Spike*, being *white*, ‖ either that which is *bigger*, having *green leaves* like those of a *Pear-tree*: or that which is *less*, with *red hairs* upon the leaves retaining the Dew, growing in moist places.
        8. { WINTERGREEN. *Pyrola.*
           { SUN-DEW. *Ros solis.*

Chap. IV.   Herbs according to their Leaves.   77

The leaves;

Indented; and divided into several Angles, || either that which hath *smooth shining leaves* and *seeds like* small *burrs*: or that whose leaves are *somewhat hairy*, being of an elegant structure, bearing yellowish green flowers.

9. { SANICLE.   *Sanicula.*
   { LADIES MANTLE.   *Alchymilla.*

Scolloped about the edges; || either that which is *taller*, of a *white flower*, the root consisting of many small reddish kernels: or that which is *lower*, of a *yellow flower* and fibrous root, growing in moist places.

10. { WHITE SAXIFRAGE.   *Saxifraga alba.*
    { GOLDEN SAXIFRAGE.   *Saxifraga aurea.*

The manner of growing; whether

Creeping on the ground; either that with a *hairy leaf*, of an ill sent, bearing a *blew hooded flower*: or that of a *small leaf*, bearing a *yellow flower*.

11. { GROUND IVY, *Aleboof, Tunnhoof.*   *Hedera terrestris.*
    { MONYWORT, *Herb twopence.*   *Nummularia.*

Climbing; of a *hot biting tast*, and an *elegant flower* with a long heel.

12. INDIAN CRESS.   *Nasturtium Indicum.*

Marine; growing in salt places near the Sea, || either that of a *salt juicy leaf*, bearing a spike of small white flowers: or that which hath a *large bell flower*, the plant running upon the ground, being Purgative.

13. { SCURVY-GRASS.   *Cochlearia.*
    { SEA-BINDWEED.   *Soldanella.*

Herbs according to their Leaves. Part. II.

VII. HERBS OF NERVOUS LEAVES.

VII. HERBS OF NERVOUS LEAVES, may be diftributed into such as are

Terreftrial; growing in dryer places, which are diftinguifhable according to the

Fafhion of their leaves; whether

More broad; to be further confidered according to their

Manner of growth; having

Leavy ftalks; viz. the leaves embracing the ftalk, || either that which hath *pleited leaves,* whofe *root* is a vehement *purgative*: or that other, having a *fpike of flowers* like thofe of *Orchis.*

Helleborus albus.
Helleborine.

1. { WHITE HELLEBORE, *Neezwort.*
    { HELLEBORINE, *Baftard white Hellebore.*

Naked ftalks; and flowers in a fpike, || either that whofe *leaves* are *undivided*: or that whofe *leaves* are fo *divided into jaggs,* as to reprefent a Staggs horn.

Plantago.
Coronopus.

2. { PLANTAIN.
    { BUCKSHORN.

Colour of the leaves; whether that whofe leaves are of a *dark green above* and *afh-coloured underneath,* bearing a *fpike* of flowers: or that whofe leaves are of a *paler green,* bearing the flowers in a kind of *Umbel.*

Biftorta.
Saponaria.

3. { SNAKEWEED, *Biftort.*
    { SOPEWORT.

More narrow; either that whofe *fpike* is round and more *long*: or that whofe *fpike* is more *fhort,* conteining feeds refembling fleas.

Holofteum.
Pfyllium.

4. { SEA-PLANTAIN.
    { FLEAWORT.

Number of their leaves; either that which hath only *one leaf*: or that which hath only *two leaves.*

Monophyllon.
Bifolium.

5. { ONE-BLADE.
    { TWAY-BLADE.

Flower; of one leaf, whether

Greater; in the *fafhion of a Bell,* the plant having a *bitter taft,* || either the *Taller and larger*: or the *Lower and fmaller.*

Gentiana.
Gentianella.

6. { GENTIAN, *Fellwort.*
    { DWARF-GENTIAN.

Leffer; having fmall *one leaved flowers, hanging down* their heads and bearing berries; || either the *Higher* or the *Lower.*

Sigillum Salomonis.
Lilium convallium.

7. { SOLOMONS-SEAL.
    { LILLY OF THE VALLEY.

Aquatic; growing in the water, bearing fpikes of flowers from the joynts of the ftalk; || either that of *fmooth edged leaves*: or that whofe leaves are either *curled or waved about the edges.*

Potamogeiton.
Tribulus aquaticus.

8. { PONDWEED.
    { WATER-CALTROPE.

VIII. SUC-

Chap. IV.   Herbs according to their Leaves.   79

VIII. SUCCULENT HERBS may be diſtributed into ſuch as are **VIII. SUC-**
Biggeſt, either that whoſe *leaf* is more *broad* and *not indented*: or that **CULENT**
whoſe *leaf is long, ſharp and indented.* **HERBS.**

1. { HOUSELEEK, *Sengreen.*   *Sedum majus.*
   { ALOE.   *Aloe.*

Leſſer ;
Terreſtrial ; conſiderable for having

Broad and commonly *crenated leaves*, a *round ſtalk*, the flowers growing in the faſhion of an Umbell, || either that whoſe *leaves are more blunt pointed* : or that whoſe leaves are more *ſharp pointed,* the root having a ſent like that of Roſes.

2. { ORPINE,   *Telephium.*
   { ROSEWORT.   *Rhodia radix.*

Round pointed leaves not indented, || either that which is *greater*, having *reddiſh ſtalks,* bearing *yellowiſh flowers,* being eſculent: or that which is *leſs*, bearing *ſmall white flowers* of five leaves.

3. { PURSLAIN.   *Portulaca.*
   { GARDEN BROOKLIME.   *Cepaa.*

White flowers, ſpeckled with red, the *leaves ſerrate,* || either that which hath a more *round leaf,* and *larger flower* : or that whoſe *leaf* is more *oblong* and *flower leſs.*

4. { SPOTTED SANICLE.   *Sanicula guttata.*
   { INDENTED SENGREEN.   *Sedum ſerratum.*

Narrow leaves ; growing in dry places: the *Greater* or the *Leſſer.*

5. { STONE CROPP.   *Sedum minus.*
   { WALL PEPPER.   *Illecebra.*

Small round leaves ; the *ſtalk* proceeding *from the middle* or *Center* of it, bearing a *ſpike of ſmall flowers.*

6. NAVELWORT, *Wall-pennywort,*   *Umbilicus Veneris.*

Marine ; growing in *ſalt places,* whoſe *leaf* is *cylindrical,* the aſhes of it being uſed in making of Glaſs.

7. GLASSWORT.   *Cali.*

IX. HERBS

Herbs according to their Leaves. Part. II.

IX. HERBS considered according to their SUPERFICIES, or MANNER OF GROWING.

IX, HERBS considered according to the SUPERFICIES of their Leaves, or their MANNER OF GROWING, may be distinguished in-
Rough leaved; whether (to such as are
More rough; having

Borago.
Buglossum.
1. { *Blew flowers*; either ‖ that whose *leaves* are *broader*, having black streaked seed: or that whose *leaves* are *longer*, the Segments of the flower being not so sharp pointed as the other.
   { BURRAGE.
   { BUGLOSS.

Anchusa.
Echium.
2. { *Long narrow leaves*; either ‖ that which hath a *red root* commonly used in Dying: or that which bears *larger flowers*, which before (they are explicated, do turn like a Scorpions tail.
   { ALKANET.
   { VIPERS BUGLOSS.

Less rough; distinguishable by their having

Pulmonaria.
Cerinthe.
3. { *Spotted leaves*; bearing one entire flower of different colours, *viz.* White and Purple on the same root: or that whose *flower is a round tube, hanging* downwards, the leaves embracing the stalk.
   { SAGE OF JERUSALEM, *Ladies-glove.*
   { HONYWORT.

Symphytum.
Cynoglossum.
4. { *Broad leaves*, sharp pointed, being large plants; either ‖ that whose *flower is long, hollow, and of one leaf,* divided into five segments: or that which is of an *offensive sent,* the flower of *a dirty red,* the flower
   { COMFREY. (succeeded by 4 seeds in the shape of little burrs.
   { DOGS-TONGUE, *Hounds-tongue.*

Lithospermum.
Heliotropium.
5. { *Small leaves*; either ‖ that whose *seed* is of an *ash colour, hard and shining,* like a polished stone: or that the *spike* of whose flowers is
   { GRUMMELL. (*crooked* and supposed to turn *towards the Sun.*
   { HELIOTROPE.

Stellate; so stiled from the manner of the growth of their leaves, which encompass the stalk at intervals, like the rays of a Starr; distin-
Lesser flowers; (guishable by bearing.
Erect; having slender long leaves; of

Asparagus.
Galium.
6. { *Solid stalks*; either ‖ the *taller* bearing red berries, the shoots of which are used for food: or the *lower* of an ill sent, bearing yellow flow-
   { ASPARAGUS. (ers, used in some places to coagulate Milk.
   { LADIES-BEDSTRAW, *Cheeserunning.*

Equisetum.
Millefolium cornutum aquaticum.
7. { *Hollow stalks*; jointed without any leavy flowers, either ‖ that whose leaves are *like bristles*: or that whose leaves are *branched like*
   { HORSE-TAIL. (the horns of a Stagg.
   { HORNED WATER-MILFOIL.

Ramping; of

Rubia tinctorum.
Cruciata.
8. { *Broader leaves*; either ‖ that which hath *a red root used for Dying*: or that whose leaf is more *hairy,* having four leaves opposite to one
   { MADDER. (another at a joint, bearing yellow flowers.
   { CROSSWORT.

Mollugo.
Aparine.
9. { *Narrower leaves*; either ‖ that which is *like Madder*: or that common weed, whose *stalks* and little *burrs* are apt *to stick to a man's clothes.*
   { BASTARD MADDER.
   { GOOSE-GRASS, *Cleavers.*

Asperula.
Spergula.
10. { *Larger flowers*; growing on the top of the branches; either ‖ that of *broader leaves,* growing commonly in woods, having a tuft of white *four-leaved flowers* of a sweet sent: or that of *narrower leaves,* the
   { WOODROF. (flower consisting of *five leaves.*
   { SPURRY.

Of

Chap. IV. *Herbs according to their Flowers.*   81

Of Herbs considered according to their Flowers.

§. IV.

Herbs considered according to their flower, having no seed-vessel besides the Cup which covers the flower, may be distinguished into
- STAMINEOUS; whose flower doth consist of threddy Filaments or Stamina, having no leaves besides the *Perianthium*: or those herbaceous leaves encompassing these stamina, which do not wither or fall away before the seed is ripe. I.
- *Foliaceous*; which besides the Stamina have leaves, being either of
  - *Compound flowers*; consisting of many leaves: or a circle of Leaves, and a Thrumm of short stamina, close set together; whether
    - NOT PAPPOUS. II.
    - PAPPOUS, whose seeds do either ly in down: or have some downy parts. III.
  - *Simple flowers*; which besides a circle or border of leaves, have only some fewer longer stamina more sparsedly set together, like threds or strings, to be distinguished by the manner of the growing of the
    - *Flower*; into
      - *Umbelliferous*; such as grow in the fashion of an Umbel on several little stalks, proceeding from the top of a bigger stalk, which all together represent the figure of an inverted Cone, the flowers being the Basis, which have generally two seeds growing together, and a compound leaf, whether of
        - BROADER LEAVES; under which are comprehended all such whose leaves are about the same bredth, or broader then Parsly. IV.
        - FINER LEAVES; under which are comprehended all such, whose leaves are divided into narrower segments then those of Parsley. V.
      - *Verticillate*; by which those kinds of Plants are meant, whose flowers grow in rundles or whirles about the stalk, being of the shape of a Hood or Helmet; as likewise those whose flowers are of the like shape, namely Galeated, having the like open seed-vessel, but their leaves growing by pairs, whether
        - FRUTICOSE; having stalks of a hard woody consistence. VI.
        - NOT FRUTICOSE. VII.
      - SPICATE. VIII.
    - SEED; growing MANY TOGETHER IN A Cluster or BUTTON. IX.

I. HERBS

Herbs according to their Flowers. Part. II.

I. HERBS OF STAMINEOUS FLOWERS.

I. HERBS OF STAMINEOUS FLOWERS, and not of grassy leaves, may be distributed into such whose seeds are

Triangular; the plants to which they belong being either

Perennial;

  Bigger; having a *great leaf* not jagged about the edges; || either that whose *leaf* is *more large*, and the *root used for purging*: or that whose *leaf* is *more oblong*.

Rhabarbarum.
Lapathum.

1. { RUBARB.
   { DOCK.

  Lesser; having a *grateful acidity* in the taste of the leaf; || either that whose *leaf* is *oblong*: or *roundish*.

Acetosa.
Acetosa Romana.

2. { SORREL.
   { FRENCH SORREL.

Annual; having leaves.

  Triangular; and black seed; || either that which is *Erect*, whose seed is *Esculent*: or that which is *Climbing*.

Tragopyrum.
Convolvulus niger.

3. { BUCK-WHEAT, *Brank*.
   { BLACK BINDWEED.

  Not Angular; being short and slender, upon *weak procumbent stalks*, full of joynts.

Polygonum.

4. KNOT-GRASS.

Round;

Distinguishable by Sex; of *male and female*; because from the same seed some plants are produced, which bear flowers and no seeds, and others which bear seeds and no flowers.

  The *bigger*; having a divided leaf; || either that which hath a *large hollow stalk*, and a compound or *fingered leaf, of the rine* of which Linnen is made: or that which is a *climbing Plant* twisting about such things as are next to it, from the right hand towards the left, contrary to the manner of other twining Plants, of a *rough roundish leaf*, divided into many segments, with a *head of scaly tufts* growing in a cluster or bunch, commonly used to preserve drink from sowring.

Cannabis.
Lupulus.

5. { HEMP, *Tow, Canvas*.
   { HOPP.

The *Lesser*; whose leaves are

Shorter; either that which hath *smooth leaves* and is *annual*: or that which hath *hoary leaves* being *perennial*.

Mercurialis.
Phyllon.

6. { MERCURY.
   { CHILDING MERCURY.

Longer; of serrate edges, the root being perennial.

Cynocrambe.

7. DOGS MERCURY.

Not distinguishable by Sex; but either by their

Leaf; being

Triangular; considerable for

Being of an *unctuous* touch, and used for Sallets: || either that which hath a *bigger and echinate seed*: or that which hath a *less and smooth seed*.

Spinachia.
Bonus Henricus.

7. { SPINAGE.
   { ENGLISH MERCURY.

Chap. IV. Herbs according to their Flowers.

Having a *seed vessel* made up *of two leaves closing* together: or having the *leaf sinuate* about the edges.

9. {ORRAGE.   *Atriplex.*
   {GOOS-FOOT.   *Pes Anserinus.*

Broad; with smooth edges of a dull *insipid tast*, with a *large long root*, the *seed-vessel* being *round, rugged and hard*, conteining two or three seeds.

10. BEET.   *Beta.*

Narrow and long, having a spicate head; ‖ either that used by Dyers, having *undivided leaves*, and *longer spikes*: or that which hath *divided leaves*, and *shorter spikes*.

11. {DYERS-WEED.   *Luteola.*
    {BASE ROCKET.   *Reseda.*

Winged leaves; with a *stiffe stalk*, growing to a good stature, and bearing *Triangular Cods*.

12. MEADOW-RUE.   *Thalictrum.*

Sent or smell.

Pleasant; either that whose *leaves resemble* those of an *Oak*, with red veins: or that whose leaves resemble those of *Wormwood*, bearing the flowers in a long spike, and having a *rough seed-vessel*.

13. {OAK OF HIERUSALEM.   *Botrys.*
    {OAK OF CAPPADOCIA.   *Ambrosia.*

Unpleasant; having a *serrate leaf* with *stinging prickles*.

14. NETTLE.   *Urtica urens.*

Seed-vessel; bearing *chaffy tufts*, ‖ either that which hath a *roundish leaf*: or that whose leaf is more *oblong and pointed*.

14. {BLITE.   *Blitum.*
    {PRINCES FEATHER, *Amaranthus*.   *Amaranthus.*

Place of Growth; being usually *upon walls*, having *red stalks*, and a rough seed.

16. PELLITORY OF THE WALL.   *Parietaria.*

Littleness; being the least of this kind; ‖ either that which hath *weak stalks, leaning on the ground*, with leaves like those of Time but smaller, bearing the seeds in clusters about the joynts: or that which is of a *woody stalk*, bearing the flowers and seeds at the top of the branches.

17. {RUPTUREWORT.   *Herniaria.*
    {STINKING GROUND-PINE.   *Camphorata.*

Herbs according to their Flowers. Part. II.

II. HERBS OF A COMPOUND FLOWER NOT PAPPOUS.

II. HERBS having a COMPOUND FLOWER NOT PAPPOUS, may be diftinguifhed into fuch whofe flowers are compounded either of

Short hollow ftamina thick fet together in a thrumm, with a circle of leaves: or without fuch a circle, commonly called *Corimbiferous*, being either of

   Undivided leaves; having a

     Radiate flower; whofe limb is

       Yellow; either the

         Greater; and talleft, either that which is the *biggeft of flowers*: or that which hath a *tuberous efculent root*.

Flos folis.
Flos folis Pyramidalis.

1. {SUN-FLOWER.
    HIERUSALEM-HARTICHOKE.

         Leffer; having a *crooked feed*.

Caltha.

     2. MARIGOLD.

       White; either the *greater* and taller, having a *ramous leavy ftalk*: or the *leffer* and lower, having *a naked ftalk*.

Bellis major.
Bellis minor.

3. {GREAT DAISY.
    DAISY.

     Naked Flower; confiderable for having

       A ftrong pleafant fmell; either that which is the *bigger* plant, of a *broad leaf*: or that which is the *leffer* plant, of more *narrow leaves* more deeply indented, whofe flowers grow in an Umbell.

Coftus hortorum.
Ageratum.

4. {ALECOST, *Coftmary*.
    MAUDLIN TANSY.

       Long hoary leaves; either that which is *Odorate*, having a *yellowish flower*, of a dry *ftramy confiftence*, preferving the colour for feveral years after its being gathered: or that which bears a *white flower*, the more common fort of which is not *Odorate*.

Stæchas citrina.
Gnaphalium.

5. {GOLDEN STÆCHAS.
    CUDWEED, *Cottonweed*.

   Divided leaves; having a

     Radiate flower; whofe limb is

       Yellow; confiderable for the *leaves*, being

         More finely divided; either that which *grows* ufually *amongft Corn*: or that which doth commonly grow in *mountainous places*, having leaves like thofe of Fennel.

Chryfanthemum fegetum.
Buphtalmum verum.

6. {CORN MARIGOLD.
    OX-EY.

         Winged leaves; *like* thofe of *Tanfy*.

Flos Africanus.

     7. AFRICAN MARIGOLD.

       White; whofe leaves are

         More finely divided; either that of a *pleafant*: or that of an *unpleafant fent*.

Chamamelum.
Cotula fætida.

8. {CAMOMIL.
    STINKING MAYWEED.

         Lefs finely divided; being of a *ftrong fent*.

Matricaria.

     9. FEAVERFEW.

Chap. IV. *Herbs according to their Flowers.*

{*Undivided*; being long and narrow; ‖ either that whose leaves are indented about the edges: or that whose leaves are smooth, being of a hot taste.

10. {SNEEZEWORT. — *Ptarmica.*
    {TARRAGON. — *Draco herba.*

Naked flower; whose stalks are
{*More woody*; either that whose *leaves* are more *green*: or that whose leaves are generally *hoary* and *white*.

11. {SOUTHERNWOOD. — *Abrotanum mas.*
    {LAVENDER COTTON. — *Abrotanum femina.*

{*Less woody*; either that of a *bitter taste*, and more *pleasant smell*: or that whose *sent* is *not so pleasant*, whose *leaves* are green above and *hoary underneath*.

12. {WORMWOOD. — *Absinthium.*
    {MUGWORT. — *Artemisia.*

{*Bearing* their *flowers* in the fashion of *an Umbell*, having *winged leaves*, ‖ either that which is of a *strong* and not unpleasant *sent*: or that which is *less odorate*.

13. {TANSY. — *Tanacetum.*
    {MILFOIL. — *Millefolium.*

Oblong tubulous leaves; the
{*Greater*; bearing many flowers upon a stalk, ‖ either that whose leaves upon breaking have several little *hairy strings*, the flower made up of tubulous leaves lasciniated at the top: or that of a more *globular flower*, the *root* seeming to have *a piece bitten off*.

14. {SCABIOUS — *Scabiosa.*
    {DIVELS BIT. — *Morsus Diaboli.*

{*Lesser*; bearing but *one flower* upon a stalk, like that of Scabious, ‖ either that of a *round blew flower*, having a leaf like that of the lesser daisy: or that of *grassy leaves* and a *naked stalk*.

15 {BLEW DAISY. — *Globularia.*
   {THRIFT, *Sea Gilly-flower.* — *Caryophyllus marinus.*

{*Oblong flat leaves*; without any thrumm in the middle, bearing blew flowers, ‖ either that which is *smaller* and *annual*: or that which is *larger* and *perennial*.

16. {ENDIVE. — *Endivia.*
    {SUCCORY. — *Cichoreum.*

III. PAR-

86 Herbs according to their Flowers. Part. II.

III. PAPPOUS HERBS.

III. PAPPOUS HERBS, may be distributed into such whose heads are either

Round and Squamous, considerable upon Account of their
- *Leaves*; whether
  - *Prickly*; either that of a *lesser*: or that of a *bigger head used for food.*

Carduus.
Cinara.
1. { THISTLE.
     { HARTICHOKE.

  - *Hoary*; either that whose *flower* is commonly *blew*, of *tubulous jagged leaves*: or that which bears a *purple flower* of *flat leaves*.

Cyanus.
Ptarmica Austriaca.
2. { BLEWBOTTLE.
     { AUSTRIAN SNEEZEWORT.

  - *Serrate*; commonly *winged*, ‖ the *Lesser*: or the *Greater* used in Physick.

Serratula.
Centaurium majus.
3. { SAW-WORT.
     { GREAT CENTORY.

  - *Stalks*; being *dry* and *hard*, bearing usually a *purple flower*; ‖ either that of a more *dark*: or that of a *lighter colour*.

Jacea.
Stæbe.
4. { KNAPWEED.
     { SILVER KNAPWEED.

  - *Seeds*; being more *large*; either that of *White*: or that of *Black feeds*

Carthamus.
Chondrilla crupina.
5. { BASTARD SAFFRON.
     { BEARDED CREEPER.

Plain or flat; whose flower is either
- *Radiate*, or naked.
  - *Terrestrial*; considerable upon account of their
    - *Roots*; being more *large*, bearing *yellow flowers*; ‖ either that of a *lesser leaf*, the *root* of which is counted *poysonous to beasts*: or that of a *larger and longer leaf*, the *root* of which is *odorate and bitter*, and counted *wholsome to men*.

Doronicum.
Helenium.
6. { LEOPARDS-BANE.
     { ELECAMPANE.

  - *Leaves*; being *thick, fatty* and *jagged*, bearing *yellow flowers*; ‖ either that which bears a *thrummy flower*: or that which bears a *radiate flower*.

Senecio.
Jacobæa.
7. { GROUNDSIL.
     { RAGWORT.

  - *Flowers*; as to their
    - *Manner of growth*; in a kind of *Umbel*, or *Tuft*; ‖ either that whose *flowers* are *naked and purplish*: or that whose *flowers* are *radiate* and *yellow*.

Eupatorium cannabinum mas.
Virga aurea.
8. { DUTCH AGRIMONY.
     { GOLDEN ROD.

    - *Colour*; either that which bears *flowers of different colours*, the leaves whereof somewhat resemble the rays of a Starr: or that whose *flowers* are generally *yellow*, the leaves of the plant being *Odorate*.

Aster.
Coniza.
9. { STARWORT.
     { FLEABANE.

Marine;

Chap. IV. *Herbs according to their Flowers.*

⎧ *Marine*; having *long thick leaves*; ‖ either that the *border* of
⎪ whose flower is *Purple* and the *middle* of it *Yellow*: or that of a
⎨ *Yellow flower* and *hard stalks*, the *leaves* being *narrow* and *cut in*
⎪ *at the ends.*
⎪   ⎧ SEA-STARWORT.   *Tripolium.*
⎪ 10.⎨ GOLDEN FLOWER'D SAMPHIRE. *Crithmum chrysanthemum.*
⎪ *Double*; the plants having a *milky juice*, distinguishable by their
⎨ *Heads*; being *smaller*; either that of a more *rugged leaf* used for
⎪   Sallads: or that of a *smoother leaf*, said to sweat out a gumm
⎪   at the joints.
⎪   ⎧ LETTICE.   *Lactuca.*
⎪ 11.⎨ GUMM SUCCORY.   *Chondrilla.*
⎩ *Leaves*; whether

  ⎧ *Jagged*; either that of a *solid stalk*: or that of a *hollow smooth*
  ⎪ *stalk*, the seed of which being ripe, doth with the down
  ⎪ upon it, spread it self into a Sphærical figure.
  ⎪   ⎧ HAWKWEED.   *Hieracium.*
  ⎨ 12.⎨ DANDELION.   *Dens Leonis.*
  ⎪ *Undivided*; ‖ either that whose *leaves* are *long and grassy*, the flow-
  ⎪ er of which being *closed*, doth represent *a goats beard*, whose
  ⎪ *root* is *esculent*: or that whose *leaves* are *round pointed*, *and*
  ⎪ *hairy.*
  ⎪   ⎧ GOATS-BEARD.   *Tragopogon.*
  ⎪ 13.⎨ MOUSE-EAR.   *Pilosella.*
  ⎩ *Resembling* thistles; but not prickly; either that which bears
    larger: or that which bears *lesser* flowers.
       ⎧ SOWTHISTLE.   *Sonchus.*
    14.⎨ NIPPLEWORT.   *Lampsana.*

IV. UMBELLIFEROUS HERBS whose LEAVES are MORE BROAD and less finely cut,

IV. UMBEL-LIFEROUS HERBS OF BROADER LEAVES.

may be distinguished into such as are,

Odorate; and of a strong sent; whether such as is

More pleasant; in such kind of plants as are

More properly belonging to this tribe; to be distinguished upon Account of

Leaves; as to their

Shapes; whether such are are

Of Different shapes in the same plant, the *lower* leaves towards the bottom of the stalk being *rounder* and *broader*, and those upon the stalk more *finely cut* having *Aromatic seeds*; || either that of a *smaller seed*: or that of a more *large seed*, being round and hollow, the leaves of the plant being of less pleasant sent then the seed

Anisum.
1. { ANNIS.
   { CORIANDER.

Coriandrum.

Winged leaves; resembling those of

Parsnip; having the like smell and taft.

Sison.
2. BASTARD STONE PARSLEY.

Fearn; either that which hath a *large black furrowed seed*: or that whose seed is *less, and more slender*, resembling an Oat.

Myrrhis. Cicutaria vulgaris.
3. { SWEET CICELY.
   { WILD CICELY.

Not *winged*; resembling *Parsley*, but being much broader; either that which hath a *large black streaked seed*: or that which is *a taller plant*, having *less leaves* and a *stronger sent*.

Hipposelinum. Levisticum.
4. { ALEXANDERS.
   { LOVAGE.

Colour; whether

Pale green; having large and broad leaves; || either that which hath a *yellow juice*, the *Umbel* of whose flowers is somewhat *spherical*, which dies after bearing seed: or that which is of very near affinity to this in shape and sent, but *not so large*, and *more perennial*.

Angelica. Imperatoria.
5. { ANGELICA.
   { MASTERWORT.

Dark green; being indented; either that whose *seed is broad*: or angular.

Laserpitium. Libanotis Theophrasti. Silermontanum.
6. { LASERWORT.
   { HERB FRANKINCENSE OF THEOPHRASTUS.

Hairy tuft, encompassing the bottom of the stalk.
7. SERMOUNTAIN.

Less properly belonging to this tribe; having *winged leaves*; || either that whose *flowers* are *tubulous*: or that which bears a great *tuft* of *white flowers* of a *sweet sent*.

Valeriana. Ulmaria.
8. { VALERIAN.
   { MEDOW SWEET.

Less

Chap. IV.   Herbs according to their Flowers.

Lefs pleafant;

Leffer; ‖ either that of a *weaker fent,* but *efculent* and of a grateful taft: or that of a *ftronger fent,* growing naturally *in moift places.*

9. ⎰ PARSLEY.   *Petrofelinum.*
   ⎱ SMALLAGE.   *Apium paluftre.*

Larger; of a *rough ftalk,* and *winged leaves.*

10. HERCULES ALL-HEAL.   *Panax Herculeum.*

Not odorate; diftinguifhable by their

Roots; being *efculent;* ‖ either that of a *bigger* root *growing fingle:* or that of a *lefs root growing in clufters.*

11. ⎰ PARSNIP.   *Paftinaca fativa latifol.*
    ⎱ SKIRRET.   *Siferum.*

Leaves; whether

Whole, and fomewhat nervous; ‖ either that whofe leaves are more *round,* the *ftalks growing through them:* or that whofe *leaves* are more *long.*

12. ⎰ THOROUGH WAX.   *Perfoliata.*
    ⎱ HARES-EAR.   *Bupleurum.*

Winged, and *indented;* ‖ either that whofe *root* is of a *hot biting taft:* or that whofe *leaf* is *divided* into *three, five,* or more *segments,* being *long* and *narrow.*

13. ⎰ BURNET SAXIFRAGE.   *Pimpinella faxifraga.*
    ⎱ UMBELLIFEROUS ERINGO.   *Eryngium umbelliferum.*

Of different fhapes in the fame plant; the *lower leaves* being divided like *Parfley,* the *leaves upon the ftalk* being *undivided,* and encompaffing it, bearing a great, black, round feed.

14. CANDY ALEXANDER.   *Smyrnium Creticum.*

Place of growth; being proper to *wet grounds;* ‖ either that whofe leaves are *hairy* and of a *deep green,* bearing a *white flower:* or that whofe *leaves* are *not hairy.*

15. ⎰ COW-PARSNIP.   *Sphondilium.*
    ⎱ WATER-PARSNIP.   *Sium.*

N   V. UM.

Herbs according to their Flowers. Part. II.

V. UMBEL-
LIFEROUS
HERBS OF
FINER
LEAVES.

V. UMBELLIFEROUS HERBS whose LEAVES are more FINE-
LY CUT into narrow segments, may be distinguished into such as are
Odorate; having their leaves divided into
 More long narrow segments; considerable upon account of their
  Leaves; being
   Of a dark green; and small seeds; || either that which is *perennial*,
   of *slender seeds* : or that which is *annual*, of *flat seeds*

Fœniculum.
Anethum.
1. { FENNEL.
     { DILL.

Commonly *divided into three segments at the ends*; || either that
whose *leaves* are more *thin and dry*: or more *thick and succulent*, used for sallade.

Peucedanum.
Crithmum.
2. { HOGS FENNEL.
     { SAMPHIRE.

Seed; being either
 Large and broad; || either that of a *tall stature*, the *segments*
 of whose leaves are somewhat *shorter then those of Fennel*: or
 that whose *root smells like Frankincense*.

Ferula.
*Libanotis Ga-
leni.*
3. { GIANT FENNEL.
     { HERB FRANKINCENSE OF GALEN.

Long and more slender; whether the *Bigger* or the *Less*, of an
Aromatick scent.

Meum.
Ammi.
4. { SPIGNEL.
     { BISHOPSWEED.

Stalk; being *crooked, bending several wayes*,
5. HARTWORT.

*Seseli Massili-
ense.*

More short segments; having
 Rough seeds; || either that whose *root* is *large* and *esculent* : or that
 of a *smaller root*, the Umbels when the flower is faded, resembling a Birds nest by closing or bending inwards towards the top.

*Pastinaca sa-
tiva tenui fol.*
Daucus.
6. { CARRET.
     { WILD CARRET, *Birds-nest*.

Long streaked seeds; || either that which is the *taller plant*, bearing
the *lesser seeds*: or that which is the *lower plant* bearing the *larger
seeds*.

Carum.
Cuminum.
7. { CARROWEY.
     { CUMMIN.

Broad large seeds; or having a *leaf hairy* on the backside, and *reddish*.
8. { ALLHEAL.
     { CHERVIL.

*Panax Ascle-
pium.*
Chærophyllum.

Large hollow stalk; || either that of an *offensive smell* and counted
poisonous : or that which resembles this, growing in watery places.

Cicuta.
*Cicutaria a-
quatica.*
9. { HEMLOCK.
     { WATER HEMLOCK.

Not odorate; growing in
 Dryer places; distinguishable by their
  Roots; having
   Tuberous roots; consisting of *one single tuber*, or of *several*.

*Bulbocasta-
non.*
*Filipendula
vulgaris.*
10. { EARTHNUT.
      { DROPWORT.

Roots

Chap. IV. *Herbs according to their Flowers.* 91

⎧ *Roots of a hot biting taſt*; ‖ either that of a *round dark coloured*
⎨ *seed*: or that of a *broad flat seed*, the root of which hath a yel-
⎩ low purgative juice.
    11. ⎧ SPELLITORY OF SPAIN.   *Pyrethrum.*
        ⎩ SCORCHING FENNEL.   *Thapsia.*
⎡ *Stalks of the Umbel*, being *strong and white*, used for the picking
⎢ of Teeth: to which may be adjoined that other plant, if this
⎣ fail, whose *seeds are prickly.*
    12. ⎧ SPANISH PICKTOOTH.   *Gingidium.*
        ⎩ BASTARD-PARSLEY.   *Caucalis.*
Watery places; of
⎡ *Fibrous roots*; ‖ either that whose leaves have *segments like Fennel*,
⎢ but somewhat *broader*: or that whose *segments* are like those of
⎣ *Carret*, but smooth, and with a *milky juice.*
        ⎧ WATER-MILFOIL.   *Millefolium*
    13. ⎨   *aquaticum.*
        ⎩ MILKY-PARSLEY.   *Thysselinum.*
Tuberous root;
    14. WATER DROPWORT.   *Oenanthe.*

VI. VERTICILLATE FRUTICOSE HERBS, being all of them   VI. VERTI-
odorate, may be distinguished into such whose leaves are either   CILLATE
                                                                                                                                 FRUTI-
⎡ *Larger*; whether   COSE
⎢ ⎧ *Hoary and rough*; of a pleasant taſt and smell.   HERBS,
⎢   1. SAGE.   *Salvia.*
⎢ ⎨ *Smooth*; and of a dark green; ‖ either that whose *leaves* are *cut in*
⎢   *like those of an Oak*, more *long and narrow*: or that whose leaves
⎢   are only *indented* about the edges, being more *short* and *broad.*
⎢   2. ⎧ GERMANDER.   *Chamædrys.*
⎢   ⎩ TREE GERMANDER.   *Teucrium.*
⎣ *Lesser*; whose leaves are either
  ⎡ *Short* and *roundish*; the scent being
  ⎢ ⎧ More *quick* and *pungent*; either the *larger*, having a woolly head:
  ⎢ ⎪   or the *lesser.*
  ⎢ ⎨   ⎧ MASTICK.   *Marum.*
  ⎢ ⎪ 3. ⎩ GOATS MARJORAM.   *Tragoriganum.*
  ⎢ ⎩ More *wild* and *gentle*; having *smaller leaves*, which grow *thicker*
  ⎢   *on the stalk.*
  ⎢   4. THYME.   *Thymus.*
  ⎣ *Long* and *narrow*; whether
    ⎡ *Hoary*; the
    ⎢ ⎧ *Greater*; bearing spikes; ‖ either that of *longer spikes*, being the
    ⎢ ⎪   larger plant: or that of *shorter* thicker spikes.
    ⎢ ⎨   ⎧ LAVENDER.   *Lavendula.*
    ⎢ 5. ⎩ CASSIDONY, *French Lavender, Sticadove.*   *Stæchas.*
    ⎢ ⎩ *Lesser*; whose *leaves* are *indented*, being of a more *dull scent*, bear-
    ⎢   ing small flowers.
    ⎢   6. POLIMOUNTAIN   *Polium mon-*
    ⎣ *Smooth*; ‖ either that whose *leaves* are *softer* and *larger*: or that *tanum.*
      whose *leaves* are *harder* and *less.*
        ⎧ HYSSOP.   *Hyssopus.*
      7. ⎩ WINTER-SAVORY.   *Satureia.*

VII. VERTICILLATE NOT FRUTICOSE HERBS, may be distinguished into such as are

Odorate; considerable for their sent, whether

Pleasant;

The *greater kind*; distinguishable by the

Flowers; growing

More *close and thick* together; ‖ either that which is apt to creep and *spread under ground by the roots*: or that whose leaf hath some *resemblance to* the leaf of *a Nettle*.

1. { MINT.
   { CAT-MINT. } *Mentha. Nepeta.*

More *dispersedly*; at the setting on of the leaves, having shorter and broader leaves; ‖ the former of a *darker green*, and *stronger sent*.

2. { BALM.
   { CALAMINT. } *Melissa. Calamintha.*

Seeds; growing *in a large hollow Cup like an inverted Bell*, having leaves like Balm.

3. ASSYRIAN BALM. *Molucca.*

Scaly heads; the former a *more grateful smell*, and *lesser leaves*.

4. { MARJORAM.
   { WILD MARJORAM, *Organy*. } *Majorana. Origanum.*

Leaves;

Not hoary; ‖ either that whose *leaves* are, *like those of Marjoram*, indented, the *flowers* growing *in looser spikes*: or that whose leaves are *like those of Thyme*, but of a different sent.

5. { BASIL.
   { STONE-BASIL. } *Ocymum. Acinos.*

Hoary; having leaves

Broader; ‖ either that which hath *several scaly heads*, being the *lesser plant*: or that which is the *bigger plant*, whose *flowers* grow *in close rundels*, of a stronger sent.

6. { DITTANY.
   { WHITE HOREHOUND. } *Dictamnus. Marrubium album.*

Narrower; a low plant bearing a yellow flower.

7. GROUND-PINE. *Chamæpitys.*

The *least*; a small creeping plant growing *in watery places*, being of a pungent sent.

8. PENNYROYAL. *Pulegium.*

Not pleasant; distinguishable by the

Sent; being *like that of Garlick*; ‖ either that whose *leaves* are *like* those of *Germander*, growing *in watery places*: or that whose leaves are like those of *Sage*, growing in *wooddy places*.

9. { WATER-GERMANDER.
   { WOOD-SAGE. } *Scordium. Scorodonia.*

Leaf; whether

Rough;

Broad leaf; the *bigger* or the *Lesser*.

10. { CLARY.
    { WILD CLARY. } *Sclarea. Horminum.*

Chap. IV. Herbs according to their Flowers.

Resembling those of Nettle ; the one *narrower* : the other *broader* and *rounder pointed.*

11. {DEAD NETTLE, *Archangel*. *Urtica iners.*
    {BLACK HOREHOUND. *Marrubium nigrum.*

Long ; ‖ either the *taller* larger plant : or the *lesser* plant having not so thick a down upon the leaves.

12. {BASE HOREHOUND. *Stachis.*
    {IRONWORT. *Sideritis.*

Smooth ; with a *round jagged leaf*, of a *dark green*, having a *stiffe stalk*.

13. MOTHERWORT. *Cardiaca.*

Not odorate ; considerable for having

Long narrow leaves ; the *flowers* coming out more *dispersedly*, growing *in watery places* ; ‖ either that whose *leaves* are more *narrow*, and *green* like those of Hyssop : or that whose *leaves* are *less narrow*, the *flowers* standing commonly *two together at the joynts*.

14. {HEDGE HYSSOP. *Gratiola.*
    {HOODED LOOSE STRIFE. *Lysimachia galericulata.*

Spicate flowers ;

The *greater* ; ‖ either that of *oblong green notched leaves* and *short spikes* : or that which is the *fatter plant*, having *longer spikes*, growing *in watery places*, bearing sometimes three leaves at a joint.

15. {BETONY. *Betonica.*
    {PURPLE LOOSE STRIFE. *Lysimachia purpurea.*

The *lesser* ; bearing generally *blew flowers* ; ‖ either that whose *leaves resemble* those of *wild Marjoram* : or that whose *leaves* are like those of the *lesser* Daisy, creeping by *strings*.

16. {SELF-HEAL. *Prunella.*
    {BUGLE. *Bugula.*

No leaves ; but only strings or wires, *growing upon other plants*, from whom (when it is arrived to any bigness) it receives its nourishment, the root in the ground dying.

17. DODDER. *Cuscuta.*

VIII. SPI-

Herbs according to their Flowers. Part. II.

VIII. SPICATE HERBS.

VIII. SPICATE HERBS, may be diftinguifhed into fuch as are
Spinous; having prickly leaves, whether thofe whofe head is
 Oblong; ‖ either that whofe *leaves* do fo *encompafs the ftalks* as to hold the rain water: or that of a *jagged leaf*, whofe *roots* are often *Candied for fweet-meats*.

Dipfacus.
Eryngium.

1. { TEASEL.
     ERINGO.

Round; ‖ either which hath a *refemblance* to *Thiftles*: or to *Teafels*.

Carduus globofus.
Virga Paftoris.

2. { GLOBE THISTLE.
     SHEPHEARDS ROD.

Not fpinous; diftinguifhable by their
 Seeds; being *little burrs*; ‖ either that of a *winged leaf* and *yellow flower*: or that of an *undivided leaf*, bearing a *white flower*.

Agrimonia.
Circæa Lutetiana.

3. { AGRIMONY.
     ENCHANTERS NIGHT-SHADE.

Wingedleaf.

Pimpinella fanguiforba.

4. BURNET.

Trefoil; ‖ either that which hath a *woolly fpike*: or that whofe *feedveffel* doth in the top of it *expend* it felf *into five rays*.

Lagopus.
Trifolium ftellatum.

5. { HARES-FOOT.
     STARR-HEADED TREFOIL.

Long leaves; growing *in wet places*; ‖ either that of a *hot biting taft*: or that which hath a *fairer fpike of flowers*, being of an *acid taft*.

Perficaria.
Potamogeiton anguftifolium.

6. { ARSMART.
     NARROW-LEAVED PONDWEED.

IX. HERBS

Chap. IV. *Herbs according to their Flowers.*

IX. HERBS bearing MANY SEEDS together IN A cluster or BUTTON, may be distinguished according to the
- Leaf; into such as have
  - Winged leaves; ‖ either that whose leaf is *underneath hoary* and of a silver colour: or that whose *leaves* are *broad at the end*, having little *pinnulæ towards the bottom* of them, *bearing a burr.*
    1. {WILD TANSY.
       {AVENS.
  - Fingered leaves; growing from the same point of the foot-stalk; ‖ either *five*, having a flower consisting of *five leaves*: or *seven*, the flower consisting *of four leaves.*
    2. {CINQUEFOIL.
       {TORMENTIL.
  - But *one leaf upon the foot-stalk of the flower*, and but *one flower*; ‖ either that whose *leaves* and *stalks* are generally *more Smooth*: or more *Hairy*, the head after the flower is faded, being covered with long woolly locks.
    3. {ANEMONY, *Wind-flower.*
       {PASCH FLOWER.
- Flowers; whether most commonly
  - *Yellow*; shining as if varnished, bearing their seed in a rough head; ‖ either that whose *flower* doth generally consist *of five round pointed leaves*: or that whose *flower* hath *eight or nine leaves blowing early.*
    4. {CROW-FOOT.
       {PILEWORT.
  - *Red*; having *leaves like those of Camomil.*
    5. ADONIS FLOWER.
- Seed; in a *head of a* round flat *cheese-like figure*; ‖ either that which is
  - Of *rounder leaves*; the *Less* or the *Greater.*
    6. {MALLOW.
       {HOLYHOK.
  - Of *hoary soft leaves*; ‖ either the *less* growing *in Marshes*: or the greater *by the Sea.*
    7. {MARSH MALLOWS.
       {TREE MALLOW.
  - Of *jagged leaves*;
    8. VERVAIN MALLOW.

IX. HERBS BEARING MANY SEEDS IN A BUTTON.

Argentina.
Cariophyllata.

Pentaphyllon.
Tormentilla.

Anemone.
Pulsatilla.

Ranunculus.
Chelidonium minus.

Flos Adonis.

Malva.
Malva hortensis major.

Althæa.
Malva arborea.

Alcea.

Of Herbs considered according to their Seed-vessel.

§. V. HERBS of Perfect flowers *considered according to their Seed-vessels*, may be distinguished into such as have
- *A divided Seed-vessel*; into several distinct cases, which may be called CORNICULATE. I.
- An *entire Seed-vessel*; whether
  - *Siliquous*; containing their seeds in long pods, distinguishable according to their flowers, into
    - *Papillionaceous*; the flower having some resemblance to a Butterfly, as the blooms of Pease or Beans, &c. whether
      - CLIMBERS; such as are generally furnished with Tendrils or Claspers. II.
      - NOT CLIMBERS; being without such Tendrils. III.
    - *Not papillionaceous*; such whose FLOWERS do generally CONSIST OF FOUR LEAVES. IV.
  - *Capsulate*; having shorter seed-vessels, distinguishable into
    - *Pentapetala*; such as bear FLOWERS OF FIVE LEAVES. V.
    - *Tripetala*, and *Tetrapetala*; such as bear FLOWERS OF THREE or FOUR LEAVES. VI.
    - *Monopetala*; such as bear a flower of one intire leaf, whether
      - *Campanulate*; such whose flowers have some resemblance to the figure of a Bell VII.
      - *Not campanulate*; the limbs of whose flowers are divided into several segments, representing so many distinct leaves. VIII.
- BACCIFEROUS; whose seeds are included in a juicy pulpe. IX.

I. HERBS OF CORNICULATE SEED-VESSELS.

I. HERBS OF A CORNICULATE or Horned SEED-VESSEL, may be distinguished into such as are
- *More esteemed for the flower*; having
  - *Bigger seeds*; || either that with a *compound broad leaf*, bearing *the largest flower of any low herb*: or that with a *winged leaf* like Ash, having *black shining seeds*, and a sent like Hops.
    1. { PIONY.
       FRAXINELLA, *Bastard Dittany*. — *Paonia. Fraxinella.*
  - *Lesser seeds*; || either that of a *divided slender leaf*, the *flower* having *a long heel*: or that which hath a *compound leaf*, the *flower bending downwards*, consisting of tubulous parts.
    2. { LARKS-HEEL.
       COLUMBINE. — *Delphinium. Aquilegia.*
- *Less esteemed for the flower*; having
  - *Hooded flowers*; and *roundish jagged leaves*; || either that which is counted *Poison*: or that which is counted an *Antidote*.
    3. { WOLVES BANE.
       WHOLSOM WOLVES BANE. — *Aconitum. Anthora.*
  - *Not hooded flower*; || either that of a *tuberous root*, the *flower* coming out of the *middle of the leaf*, blowing in Winter: or that with a *Trimale*, *Staphis agria.*
    4. { WINTER WOLF-BANE. (*angular seed* of *a biting tast*.
       STAFES-ACRE.
- *Seed-vessel*; like the long bill of a bird; || either that which bears *larger flowers*, more sparsedly set: or that which bears *lesser flowers* (in the fashion of an Umbel. — *Geranium. Scandix.*
    5. { CRANES-BILL.
       VENUS COMB, *Shepheards needle*.

II. PA-

Chap. IV. *Herbs according to their Seed-veſſel.* 97

II. PAPILIONACEOUS CLIMBING HERBS, may be diſtributed into ſuch as do climb; either by   II. PAPI-LIONACE-OUS CLIMBERS.

{ *Twiſting*; having long flat cods, their leaves being ſet by threes.
  1. KIDNEY BEAN, *French bean*, *Ginny bean*.   *Phaſeolus.*
Tendrils; or Claſpers, to be further diſtinguiſhed by their
  { *Seed*; whether
    { *Round*; and eſculent; ‖either that whoſe ſeed is *black*, the *leaves and flowers like thoſe of the common Bean*: or that whoſe ſeed is not black, the *leaves of a lighter green*.
      2. { BEAN OF THE ANTIENTS.   *Faba vete-rum.*
         { PEASE.   *Piſum.*
    Flat; and eſculent, having *hairy winged leaves*; ‖ the *Greater*: or the *Leſs*.
      3. { VETCH.   *Vicia.*
         { LENTIL.   *Lens.*
Cods; being *knotted*, otherwiſe reſembling a Vetch.
    4. BITTER VETCH.   *Orobus.*
Stalks; being *Angular*; ‖either that which bears *one pair of ſmooth leaves upon a foot-ſtalk*: or that whoſe *leaf* is *undivided*, only towards the top, *having two or three ſegments*, bearing a *white flower*.
    5. { CHICKLING.   *Lathyrus.*
       { WINGED WILD PEASE.   *Ochrus.*
Leaves; by pairs encompaſſing the ſtalk, being more *broad at bottom*, and *ſharp pointed*, bearing a *yellow flower*, having black ſhining ſeeds.
    6. YELLOW WILD VETCH.   *Aphaca.*
Manner of bearing the eſculent part under ground; ‖either that which bears its ſeed *both under ground, and above ground*: or that of ſmall *tuberous eſculent roots*, bearing *bright purple flowers*, many together upon a foot-ſtalk.
    7. { UNDERGROUND CHICKLING.   *Arachidna.*
       { PEASE EARTH-NUTS.   *Terra glandes.*

98 Herbs according to their Seed-vessel. Part. II.

III. PAPILIONACEOUS NOT CLIMBING.

III. PAPILIONACEOUS HERBS NOT CLIMBING, may be distinguished into such as have; either

More leaves then three;

Esculent; whether the

Larger; of a *flat seed*; ‖ either that of a *great hollow stalk*, broad leaves of a dark green, the cod lined with a woolly substance, the blossoms being black and white: or that which hath a *fingered leaf*, being from one foot-stalk divided into many segments, bearing a spike of flowers.

Faba.
Lupinus.

1. { BEAN.
     { LUPIN.

Cicer.

Lesser; of a *round seed*, having small winged leaves indented, the cods round and turgid.

2. CHICH PEASE.

Not esculent; to be further distinguished by their

Flowers; growing in thick spikes or tufts. The

Greater; ‖ either that whose *leaves grow like those of Vetch, smooth*, and of a sweet taste, a short crooked cod furrowed on the outside, conteining a double row of seeds: or that whose *leaves are hairy*.

Glaux vulgaris.
Astragalus sylvaticus.

3. { WILD LICCORICE.
     { MILK VETCH.

Lesser; ‖ either that whose *flowers grow in a tuft*, the utmost segment of the leaf being broader then any of the other: or that whose *flowers grow in a spike*, having a leaf divided like Rue.

Anthyllis leguminosa.
Fumaria.

4. { LADIES FINGER.
     { FUMITORY.

Seed vessel; whether

Rough; having winged leaves; ‖ either that whose flowers grow in *thicker spikes*, of a shining red colour, with prickly seeds growing at the end of one another: or that whose flowers grow in more *slender spikes* from the sides of the stalk, having a long thick root.

Hedysarum clypeatum.
Caput gallinaceum.

5. { FRENCH HONNYSUCKLE.
     { COCKS-HEAD, *Sanfoin*.

Smooth; whether such as bear

Crooked cods; and yellow flowers, many together: or *crooked seeds* in the shape of a Horsshooe, the seed vessel being indented on one side.

Securidaca.
Ferrum Equinum.

6. { HATHCET VETCH.
     { HORSSHOOE.

Streight; being *long* and *slender*, of *grassy leaves*, and a bright red flower.

Catanance.

7. CRIMSON GRASS VETCH.

Stalk; being *hairy, stiff and erect*, with leaves consisting of many pairs of Wings; ‖ the latter of which will *contract it self upon the touch*, as if it had sense.

Galega.
Herba viva.

8. { GOATS RUE.
     { SENSITIVE PLANT.

Leaves;

Chap. IV. *Herbs according to their Seed-vessel.* 99

Leaves; which are long and winged, being *small plants*; ‖ either that whose *cods* grow together *like the claws of a bird*: or that with a *spinous seed-vessel*.

  ⎧ BIRDS FOOT.   *Ornithopodi-*
  9. ⎨   *um.*
  ⎩ LAND CALTROPS.   *Tribulus terre-*
                   stris.

Not more then three leaves, distinguishable by their

 Flowers; growing in spikes.
  Trefoil; ‖ either that which bears *long spikes* of yellow flowers, to which succeed round seed-vessels, conteining generally but one seed in each: or that of a *shorter spike*.

    ⎧ MELILOT.   *Melilotus.*
    10. ⎨   *Trifolium pra-*
    ⎩ TREFOIL HONNYSUCKLE.   *tense.*

  Not *Trefoil*; having a *grassy leaf*.
     11. MILKWORT.   *Polygala.*

Seed-vessels;

 Long;
  Crooked; ‖ either that whose *leaves have same resemblance to those of Purslain*, growing by threes, of more slender cods: or that which hath *long smooth undivided leaves*, the *seed-vessel* being *like a Caterpiller*.

    ⎧ SCORPION GRASS.   *Blephinum*
    12. ⎨   *Scorpoides.*
    ⎩ CATERPILLER.   *Scorpoides*
                   bupleurifolia.

  streight; whether
   More long and slender; ‖ either that which hath *little* wings or ears at the bottoms of the leaves: or that which hath *long flat cods*.

    ⎧ LOTUS.   *Lotus.*
    13. ⎨   *Fœnum Grae-*
    ⎩ FŒN GREEK.   *cum.*

   Less long and thicker; having *prickly stalks*, bearing a *large flower* in proportion to the plant.
     14. CAMOCK, *Rest-harrow*.   *Resta bovis.*

 Round; and *Spiral*; ‖ either that which is *smooth*: or that which is *prickly*.

    ⎧ SNAIL TREFOIL.   *Medica cochle-*
    15. ⎨   *ata.*
    ⎩ HEDGHOG TREFOIL.   *Medica Echi-*
                   nata.

O 2   IV. SI-

Herbs according to their Seed-vessel. Part. II.

IV. SILIQUOUS HERBS NOT PAPILIONACEOUS, whose *flowers* consist generally of *four leaves*, may be distinguished by their

Being esteemed for the flower, having

    Shrubby staks; and being of a *pleasant sent*, of a *round flat seed*; || either that of *hoary leaves* : or that whose *leaves are smooth, of a deep green*.

    1. {STOCK GILLY-FLOWER.
       WALL FLOWER.

Oblong seeds; || either that which hath a more *broad jagged leaf* : or that which hath a *sharp indented leaf*, compounded of several together upon one foot-stalk.

    2. {DAMES VIOLET, *Double Rocket*.
       TOOTHWORT.

Seeds wrapt up in down; || either that whose *flower grows* out *from the top of the cod*, which makes it to be called *filius ante patrem* : or that which hath a *broad nervous leaf* with a *milkie juice*, bearing the *flowers* in *a tuft*, having a *large cod* filled with *a silkie substance*.

    3. {CODDED WILLOW HERB, *Codded loose strife*.
       UPRIGHT DOGS-BANE, *silk-grass*.

Being used as Esculent; either their

    Roots; whether such as are commonly eaten

    Boyled; || either that whose *leaves* are more *rough*, the *root* commonly *roundish* : or that whose *leaves* are more *smooth*, the *root oblong*, and of a more *firm substance*.

    4. {TURNIP.
       NAVEW.

Raw; of a *biting tast*, bearing *purplish flowers*, and *long knotted cods*.

    5. RADISH.

Leaves; having

    Succulent leaves; of a *blewish grey*; || either that of a *jagged leaf, yellow flower* : or that of an *undivided leaf*, bearing a *white flower*.

    6. {CABBIDGE, *Colewort*, *Colly-flower*.
       CODDED THOROUGH WAX.

Jagged smooth leaves; || either that which bears *larger flowers* growing more *sparsedly* : or that which bears *less flowers* growing more close together.

    7. {ROCKET.
       WINTER-CRESS.

The *smell and tast of Garlick* : or a *hot biting tast*, bearing large cods, which being ripe are of a red colour.

    8. {SAUCE ALONE, *Jack by the Hedge*.
       GINNY PEPPER.

Seeds; || either that of *short square cods* : or that of *long round cods*.

    9. {MUSTARD.
       CHARLOCK.

Margin notes:

IV. SILIQUOUS NOT PAPILIONACEOUS HERBS.

Leucoium
Keiri.

Hesperis.
Dentaria.

Lysimachia siliquosa
Apocynum rectum Syriacum.

Rapum.
Napus.

Raphanus.

Brassica.
Perfoliata siliquosa.

Eruca.
Barbarea.

Alliaria.
Capsicum.

Sinapi.
Rapistrum.

Leaf;

Chap. IV. *Herbs according to their Seed-vessel.* 101

Leaf; whether
- *Divided*; or *jagged*.
  - *Less finely*; being of a *whitish blew*, and bearing commonly a yellow flower; ‖ either that which is a maritim plant, having a *larger flower*, and *longer cods*: or that which hath a *yellow juice*.
    10. {HORNED POPPY. *Papaver cor-*
        {GREAT CELENDINE. *niculatum.*
                                          Chelidonium
                                          majus.
  - *More finely*; having *slender cods*.
    11. FLIXWEED. *Sophia Chi-*
                   rurgorum,
- *Undivided*; whose leaves are
  - *Smooth* towards the top of the stalk, and rough towards the bottom, bearing *white flowers*; ‖ either the *greater*, having many slender long cods growing thick together on the top of the branches: or the *less*, bearing the cods more dispersedly.
    12. {TOWER MUSTARD. *Turritis.*
        {CODDED MOUSE-EAR. *Pilosella sili-*
                            quosa.
  - *Long*; bearing *yellow flowers*, being tall plants; ‖ either that which hath *narrow dark green leaves, not serrate*: or that whose leaves are more *broad*, of a *pale green* and *serrate*.
    13. {TREACLE WORMSEED. *Camelina*
        {YELLOW ARABIAN MUSTARD. *nigrum.*
                                  Draba lutea.
- *Seed* wrapt up *in down*; having five leaves in the flower; ‖ either that which is counted a *Poyson*: or that which is counted an *Antidote*.
    14. {DOGS-BANE. *Apocynum.*
        {SWALLOW-WORT. *Asclepias.*
- *Growing in watery places*; having winged leaves; ‖ either that which is *esculent* of a biting tast, a *short thick cod*: or that which is in some *esteem for the flower*, bearing more *long and slender cods*, and whitish flowers.
    15. {WATERCRESS. *Nasturtium*
        {CUCKOE FLOWER, *Lady-smock*. *aquaticum,*
                                       Cardamine.

V. CAPSU-

Herbs according to their Seed-vessel. Part II.

V. CAPSULATE HERBS of FIVE LEAVED FLOWERS.

V. CAPSULATE HERBS bearing FLOWERS OF FIVE LEAVES,
Undivided; (may be distinguished into such whose leaves are
Esteemed for the flower; whether such whose flowers grow
Sparsedly; being either of
Sweet sent; and elegant structure, their flowers standing in small cups; ‖ either that of a *larger* leaf and flower: or that whose leaf
1. { GILLYFLOWER. (and flower is *smaller.*
   { PINK.

Caryophillus.
Caryophillus minor.

No considerable sent;
Growing in a cup; ‖ either the *larger,* the leaves of whose flowers are more round pointed: or the *lesser,* having a clammy juice,
2. { CAMPION. (whereby little Flyes are caught.
   { CATCHFLY.

Lychnis.
Muscipula.

Not growing in a cup; a low plant, bearing *shining purple flowers.*
3. VENUS LOOKING-GLASS.

Speculum Veneris.

In an *Umbel* or *Tuft*;
Perennial whether that wch bears flowers of *various colours* on the same tuft: or that whose flowers are commonly of a *bright scarlet.*
4. { LONDON TUFT, Sweet *John,* Sweet *William.*
   { BRISTOW NONSUCH.

Armeria.
Lychnis Chalcedonica.

Annual; whose leaves are of a bitter taft.
5. LESSER CENTAURY.

Centaurium minus.

Not esteemed for the flower; considerable either for their
Manner of growth; whether
Erect; bearing
Red flowers; growing commonly amongst Corn; ‖ either that which bears *small flowers,* of smooth leaves, round seed, an angular cup: * or that which bears *larger flowers,* of a deep red,
6. { COW-BASIL. (hoary leaves, and angular seed.
   { COCKLE. (leaves are

Vaccaria.
Pseudo-melanthium.

Yellow flowers; of a red juice when bruised, whether such whose
Lesser; ‖ either that of a *round stalk:* or that of an *angular*
7. { St. JOHNS-WORT. (stalk.
   { St. PETERS-WORT.

Hypericum.
Ascirum.

Larger; having a *round seed-vessel,* like a berry.
8. TUTSAN, *Park-leaves.*

Androsæmum vulgare.

Procumbent; bearing
White flowers; whose leaves are cut in about the middle; ‖ either that which bears a more *large flower:* or that which bears a *little*
9. { STICHWORT. (*flower* having hairy leaves.
   { COMMON CHICKWEED.

Gramen Leucanthemum.
Alsine myosotis.

Coloured flowers; the latter being spotted on the backside of
10. { BASTARD CHICKWEED. (the leaves.
    { PIMPERNEL.

Alsine.
Anagallis.

Milkie juice; bitter and caustick, of a triangular seed-vessel.
11. SPURGE, *Tithymal.*

Tithymalus.

Large flowers; ‖ either that wch is used for the making of fine linnen, having long narrow leaves, & a round seed vessel, conteining oblong shining seeds: or that with a stiff stalk, having leaves like those of
12. { FLAX, *Linseed.* (*Sallow,* sometimes 3 or 4 at one setting on.
    { YELLOW LOOSE STRIFE.

Linum.
Lysimachia lutea.

Divided leaves; ‖ either that which hath a strong sent, a round seed-vessel, the leaves of a whitish blew colour: or that which bears a large flower of a pale blew, with a circle of leaves under it, having a large seed-
13. { RUE, *Herb of grace.* (vessel, horned at the top.
    { FENNEL FLOWER.

Rute.
Nigella.

VI. CAPSU-

Chap. IV. *Herbs according to their Seed-veſſel.* 103

VI. CAPSULATE HERBS, whoſe flowers conſiſt of three or four leaves, may be diſtinguiſhed into ſuch as are; either of

Three leaves; in the flower, being water plants; ‖ either that which hath long leaves like *Aloes*, with ſharp ſerrate edges: or that whoſe leaf doth in the figure of it reſemble a barbed Arrow.

1. { FRESH WATER SOULDIER.
   { ARROW-HEAD.

VI. CAPSULATE of three or four leaved flowers.

Militaris aizoides.
Sagittaria.

Four leaves; in the flower, to be further diſtinguiſhed by the

Seed-veſſel; whether

Compreſſed;

Larger; and more broad; ‖ either that whoſe leaf is like the leaf of a *Nettle*, the ſeed-veſſel ſhining like *Sattin*: or that of hoary ſtalks

2. { BULBONACH, *Honeſty, Sattin*. (and leaves, being the leſſer.
   { MADWORT OF DIOSCORIDES.

Viola lunaris.
Alyſſon Dioſcoridis.

Leſſer; the former of a biting taſt.

3. { THLASPI.
   { SHEPHEARDS PURSE.

Thlaſpi.
Burſa paſtoris.

Round; of

Larger heads; and flowers being narcotic; ‖ either that of a bitter white juice of which *Opium* is made, with a ſtar-like covering on the top of the ſeed-veſſel: or that whoſe leaf is more finely

4. { POPPY.   (jagged, having a rough ſeed-veſſel.
   { BASTARD POPPY.

Papaver.
Argemone.

Leſſer heads; and flowers, being of a hot biting taſt; ‖ either that wᶜʰ bears a white flower & reddiſh ſeed: or that which bears long narrow leaves upon the ſtalk, and others that are broader, and jagged

5. { GARDEN CRESS. (towards the bottom of the ſtalk.
   { SCIATICA CRESS.

Naſturtium.
Iberis.

Leaf; as to the

Biting taſt; ‖ either that which is a *large plant* of a *juicy ſerrate leaf*, of a light blewiſh green: or that which is a *low ſmall plant*, of jagged leaves, and rough ſeed-veſſel, growing many together, each con-

6. { PEPPER-WORT.   (teining one ſeed.
   { SWINES CRESS.

Lepidium.
Coronopus Ruellii.

Shape; being like thoſe of *Ivy*, the ſtalks being divided into three, and ſo ſubdivided, one ſide of the lower part of the leaf ſtanding

7. BARRENWORT.   (out more then the other.

Epimedium.

Flower; in reſpect of the

Colour; being *yellow*, large plants; ‖ either that whoſe leaves are of a blewiſh green, long and ſmooth, *uſed in dying*: or that whoſe leaves

8. { WOAD.   (are more *narrow* and *indented*.
   { GOLD OF PLEASURE.

Glaſtum.
Myagrum.

Manner of growth; in ſpikes.

Upon the top of the ſtalks; bearing ſmall blew flowers; ‖ either that of leſſer leaves indented: or that of a naked ſtalk, growing by

9. { VERVAIN.   (the ſea ſide.
   { SEA-LAVENDER.

Verbena.
Limonium.

From the ſides of the ſtalks; whether the

Larger; having a flat ſeed-veſſel.
  10. BROOKLIME.

Anagallis aquatica.

Leſſer; being ſmall plants, having compreſſed ſeed-veſſels like thoſe of *Shepheards-purſe*: the latter bearing the *bigger*

11. { SPEEDWELL.   (*flower of a bright blew*.
    { WILD GERMANDER.   VII. CAM-

Veronica.
Chamaedrys ſtruis.

Herbs according to their Seed-vessel. Part. II.

VII. CAMPANULATE

VII. CAMPANULATE HERBS, may be distinguished into such as are

Climbing;

Pomiferous; bearing

Bigger esculent fruit; either such as have

Softer skins or coats; ‖ either that which is the largest, of a waterish taft, having a large seed with a welt about the edges: or that which is of a more rich pleasant taft, with a plain seed not marked in the limb of it.

Pepo.
Melo.
1. { POMPEON, *Quash*.
    { MELON, *Musk-melon*.

Shelly coats; growing to such a hardness as renders them fit to make bottles, &c. ‖ either that which bears commonly a white flower: or that of a yellow flower.

Cucurbita.
Citrullus.
2. { GOURD.
    { CITRUL.

Lesser;

Esculent; of a whitish pulp, and waterish taft.

Cucumis.
3. COWCUMBER.

Purgative; ‖ either that of a figure like a *Pear*, of a bitter juice: or that like a *Cowcumber*, but smaller and rough, the seeds spirting out upon breaking off the stalk.

Colocynthis.
Cucumis asininus.
4. { COLOQUINTIDA.
    { WILD COWCUMBER.

Neither esculent nor purgative; having a leaf like that of a *Vine*, but less, the fruit oblong but very small.

Balsamina mas.
5. MALE BALSOM.

Capsulate; having a short round seed-vessel, and angular seeds, climbing by twining about other plants; ‖ either that which is not purgative: or that which hath a milky juice in the root. A violent purgative.

Convolvulus.
Scammonia Syriaca.
6. { BINDWEED.
    { SCAMMONY.

Erect; considerable for the flower, being either

Greater; ‖ either that whose flower is bigger at the bottom: or that which is less at the bottom.

European;

Viola Mariana.
Trachelium.
7. { COVENTRY BELLS.
    { THROATWORT.

Exotic; ‖ either that which hath flowers of several colours, leaves like those of *Nightshade*, growing by pairs, the branches *alternatim*: or that whose leaves are jagged, having a large thorny seed-vessel.

Mirabile Peruvianum.
Stramonium.
8. { MERVAIL OF PERU.
    { THORN APPLE.

Lesser, ‖ either that which hath

An Esculent root; a long leaf, a blew flower, the edge divided into five points: or that whose root is not esculent.

Rapunculus.
Campanula.
9. { RAMPION.
    { BELL-FLOWER.

A hollow flower; somewhat like the finger of a Glove: the second being of a purgative quality.

Digitalis.
Sesamum.
10. { FOXGLOVE.
     { OYLY PURGING PULSE

A Narcotic quality; ‖ either that which hath large smooth unctuous leaves, but very small seed: or that which hath soft woolly leaves jagged.

Nicotiana.
Hyosciamus.
11 { TOBACCO.
    { HENBANE.

VIII. CAPSU-

Chap. IV. *Herbs according to their Seed-vessel.* 105

VIII. CAPSULATE HERBS NOT CAMPANULATE, having their leaves divided into several segments, may be distinguished into such as have

Naked stalks;
- *Of a rough nervous leaf*; ‖ either that which bears *one flower* upon a stalk which is *bigger*, being divided into *five laciniæ* : or that which bears a *less flower, many together* at the top of the stalk.
  1. {PRIMROSE.
     {PAIGLE, *Cowslip*.
- *Of a thicker smoother leaf*; the *flowers* growing *many together*, standing in a *shorter cup*; ‖ either that which bears the *bigger* : or the *smaller flower*, the leaves being hoary underneath.
  2. {BEARS EAR.
     {BIRDS EY.
- *Of a round indented leaf*;
  3. BEARS EAR SANICLE.

Leavy stalks; whether

Taller plants; considerable for
- *Bearing their flowers in spikes*; the limb of the *flower* being divided into *five segments*, with very *little hose*; ‖ either that whose *leaves* and *stalks* are *hoary* : or that which hath *less leaves*, being *green*.
  4. {MULLEIN.
     {MOTH MULLEIN.
- *Having small duskie flowers*; ‖ either that of a *roundish leaf*, and *weak stalk*, the *flower* being a kind of *Tube*, *with a lip* on one side : or having a *stiff stalk*, a *leaf like a Nettle*, a small *purplish flower*, and a *round seed-vessel*.
  5. {BIRTHWORT.
     {FIGWORT.

Lesser plants; whether such as are

Deciduous; to be further distinguished by their different flowers.
- *Resembling a head* with *a gaping mouth*; having long narrow leaves, the second having *a heel*.
  6. {SNAPDRAGON.
     {TOAD-FLAX.
- *Resembling a helmet* or hood; (or that with *smaller husks*:
  Having creased indented leaves; ‖ either that with *turgid husks* :
  7. {COCKSCOMB.
     {EYBRIGHT.
- *Having broad jagged leaves*; with a *spike of gaping flowers*, being a larger plant : or having *long leaves* jagged about the setting on, with *large seed*.
  8. {BRANK URSIN, *Bears-breech*.
     {COW WHEAT.
- *With heels*; ‖ either that whose *seed* when ripe will *spirt out of the cod*, bearing yellow flowers : or that of a *pale downy leaf*, weak *stalks*, *trailing* on the ground.
  9. {CODDED ARSMART.
     {FEMALE FLUELLIN, *Female Speedwell*.

Ever green; having *weak stalks creeping* on the ground.
  10. PERIWINKLE.

Primula veris.
Paralysis.

Auricula Ursi.
Paralysis montana.

Cortusa.

Verbascum.
Blattaria.

Aristolochia.
Scrophularia.

Antirrhinum.
Linaria.

Crista galli.
Euphrasia.

Branca Ursina.
Melampyrum.

Noli me tangere.
Elatine.

Vinca pervinca.

P   IX. BAC-

Herbs according to their Seed-veſſel. Part. II.

IX. BACCI-
FEROUS
HERBS.

IX. BACCIFEROUS HERBS, may be diſtinguiſhed according to their

Qualities ; into ſuch as are

Eſculent ; either in reſpect of the

Fruit ; being

Moſt pleaſant ; a *Trefoil* propagating by ſtrings or wires.

Fragaria.

1. STRAWBERRY.

Leſs pleaſant ; ‖ either that of a *leaf like Agrimony*, bearing round fruit of a bright red : or that of a *broad hairy rough leaf*, bearing a large fruit almoſt as big as a *Cowcumber*.

Pomum amoris.
Malum inſanum.
Battata.

2. { APPLE OF LOVE.
   { MAD APPLE.

Root ; bearing *winged leaves*, and a *bell flower*.

3. POTATO OF VIRGINIA.

Malignant ; whether ſuch whoſe leaves are more

Simple and undivided ; ‖ either that which hath a *broad leaf*, bearing *black berries* : or that which hath a *more long*, broad, *dark* coloured *leaf*, a great root, bearing great berries on ſingle ſtalks.

Solanum.
Mandragoras.

4. { NIGHTSHADE.
   { MANDRAKE.

Compound ; or made up of many ſegments; ‖ either that which bears *light green berries in a cluſter* : or that which bears *but one leaf* divided into four or five parts, and but *one black berry*.

Aconitum racemoſum.
Herba Paris.

5. { HERB CHRISTOPHER, *Berry bearing Wolves-bane.*
   { HERB TRUE LOVE, *One Berry.*

Manner of growth ; of the

Plants themſelves ; being *Climbers*, whether ſuch as are conſiderable for

Purgativeneſs ; bearing red berries ; ‖ either that of a great *white root*, having leaves like a *Vine*, but more rough : or that of a great *black root*, with leaves like thoſe of *Ivy*.

Bryonia alba.
Bryonia nigra.

6. { WHITE BRIONY.
   { BLACK BRIONY, *Wild Vine, Ladies ſeal.*

Being full of crooked prickles ; having a *long triangular leaf.*

Smilax aſpera.

7. PRICKLY BINDWEED.

Berries ; whether in a

Bladder ; ‖ either that which is a *low plant*, which bears a *red berry* in a *large bladder* : or that whoſe leaves are like *Chickweed*, ramping upon other plants.

Alkakengi.
Cucubalum.
Plinii.

8. { WINTER CHERRY.
   { BERRY BEARING CHICKWEED.

Umbel ; having *winged leaves*, like *Elder*, both for ſhape and ſent.

Ebulum.

9. DANEWORT.

Of Shrubs.

§. VI.

SHRUBS may be distributed into such as are
- *Bacciferous*;
  - *Deciduous*;
    - SPINOUS, or thorny. I.
    - NOT SPINOUS. II.
  - EVERGREEN. III.
  - SILIQUOUS; such as bear their seeds in PODS. IV.
- *Graniferous*; bearing smaller seeds, whether such as are
  - DECIDUOUS. V.
  - EVERGREEN. VI.

1. BACCIFEROUS SPINOUS shrubs of DECIDUOUS leaves, may be distinguished into such as have either
- *Compound* leaves; whether such as may be called
  - *Fingered*; viz. when several proceed from one point, bearing an esculent berry consisting of many little pulpy grains aggregated together in one head; ‖ either that whose *branches* are *erect*, bearing the more pleasant fruit: or that whose branches are *procumbent* and trailing
    1. RASBERRY, *Raspis*.   *Rubus Idæus.*
       BRAMBLE, *Blackberry*.   *Rubus vulgaris.*
  - *Winged*; viz. growing by pairs against one another upon a middle rib; ‖ either that which bears the *more beautiful and sweet flower*: or that whose flower is *less beautiful and sweet*.
    2. ROSE.   *Rosa.*
       BRIER.   *Rosa canina.*
- *Simple leaves*;
  - *Divided* into several segments; ‖ either that which bears a *more juicy esculent berry*, being the *lesser plant*: or that which bears a *drier red berry*, being the *taller plant*.
    3. GOOSBERRY.   *Grossularia.*
       WHITE THORN, *Haw-thorn*.   *Oxyacantha.*
  - *Undivided*; whether
    - *Roundish*; whose fruit is
      - *Esculent*; ‖ either that which produces a *fruit like a small Plum*, black, round, of an acid austere tast, the blossoms coming out before the leaves: or that which bears its *fruits in clusters*, being long slender reddish, of an acid tast.
        4. SLOE-TREE, *Black-thorn*.   *Prunus sylvestris.*
           BARBERRY.   *Berberis.*
      - *Not esculent*; whether
        - *Purgative*; having leaves like those of a *Plum-tree*, bearing black berries *used in dying*.
          5. PURGING THORN.   *Rhamnus Catharticus*
        - *Not purgative*; ‖ either that which hath long, stiffe, slender, sharp thorns, bearing a *fruit resembling a hat*: or that whose berries contein *a long streaked seed*.
          6. CHRISTS THORN.   *Paliurus.*
             BOXTHORN.   *Lycium.*
    - *Long*; and somewhat *hoary*.
      7. BUCKS THORN.   *Rhamnus.*

II. BAC-

Of Shrubs. Part. II

II. BACCIFEROUS DECIDUOUS NOT SPINOUS.

II. BACCIFEROUS Shrubs of DECIDUOUS leaves, NOT SPINOUS, may be diſtributed into ſuch whoſe berries are; either
- Eſculent; bearing their fruit
  - In cluſters; ‖ either that of a rich juice, ſpungy wood, *trailing branches:* or that whoſe leaves are like thoſe of *Gooſberry,* but larger, and erect (*branches.*)

Vitis.
Ribes.

1. { VINE, *Grape, Raiſin.*
   CURRAN.

Vitis Idæa vulgaris.

- Singly; being a *low plant,* of dark green leaves, hollow flowers, ſmall (*fruit.*)
  2. BILBERRY, *Whortle-berry.*

Not eſculent; to be further diſtinguiſhed with reſpect to the Leaf.
- Undivided;
  - Round; conſiderable for the
    - Manner of bearing their fruit; whether
      - In *Umbels;* whoſe leaves are
        - Hoary; underneath; ‖ either that which bears *black berries,* containing one flat ſeed: or that which bears *red berries.*

Viburnum.
Aria.

3. { WAYFARING TREE.
   WHITE BEAM TREE, *Cumberland Hawthorn.*

- Green; having *red twigs,* and a *black fruit,* conteining one kernel.

Cornus fœmina.

4. DOGBERRY TREE.

- In cluſters; having but one grain in a black berry; ‖ either that

Padus Theophraſti.
Mahaleb.

5. { BIRDS CHERRY. (whoſe leaves are *larger:* or *leſſer.*)
   WILD ROCK CHERRY OF AUSTRIA. (leaves are

- Sparſedly; having ſeveral grains in a berry; whether ſuch whoſe Hoary underneath, and *leſs;* ‖ either that of a thicker leaf, bearing a *red berry,* covered with a kind of down: or that other

Chamæmeſpilus.
Dioſpyros.

6. { DWARF MEDLER. (bearing a *black berry.*)
   SWEET WHORT.

- Green and *larger;* like thoſe of *Alder,* but ſmoother, bearing a *black berry,* the inward *bark* being a violent *purgative.*

Alnus nigra baccifera.

7. BERRY BEARING ALDER.

- Flowers; being tubulous and odorate; ‖ either that which is *climb-*

Periclymenum.
Periclymenum rectum.

8. { WOODBINE, *Honyſuckle.* (*ing:* or that which is *erect.*)
   UPRIGHT WOODBINE.

- Taſt of the fruit; being *hot, biting, aromatic,* growing in cluſters, each cluſter coming out on the ſide of the ſtalk, oppoſite to a leaf on

Piper.

9. PEPPER. (the other ſide, being a *Climber.*)

- Long;
  - Purgative; bearing red berries; ‖ either that which ſends out its bloſſoms in winter before the leaves, being of a ſweet ſent: or that whoſe younger branches and berries are quadrangular.

Mezereon.
Enonymus.

10. { MEZEREON.
    SPINDLE TREE.

- Not *purgative;* having ſlender flexile twigs; ‖ either that which bears *black berries in cluſters:* or that which bears *red berries*

Liguſtrum.
Caſſia Poëtarum.

11. { PRIVET. (*more ſparſedly.*)
    SHRUB CASSIA.

- Jagged; ‖ either that which bears a great *round cluſter of white flowers:*

Sambucus Roſea.
Sambucus aquatica.

12. { GELDER ROSE. (or that which bears its *flowers in an Umbel.*)
    WATER ELDER. (*berries.*)

- Compound; bearing a flower like *Jeſſamine* with round black ſhining

Polemonium.

13. YELLOW JESSAMINE. (*ſtalks.*)

- Having no leaf; the *flowers* and *berries* coming out *at the joynts of the*

Tragus.

14. SEA-GRAPE.

III. BAC-

Chap. IV. Of Shrubs.

III. BACCIFEROUS SEMPERVIRENT SHRUBS, may be distribu- **III. BACCI-**
Compound; whether   (ted into such whose leaves are; either **FFROUS SEMPERVI-**
Winged; || either that which is of a *fragrant smell*, bearing *yellow seeds* **RENT**
in black berries: or that which bears *small berries like Mulberries*. **SHRUBS.**

1. { **TRUE BALSOM,** *Balm.*   *Balsamum*
   { **THORNY BURNET.**   *Judaicum.*
                                    Poterium.

Fingered; having several leaves growing from one foot-stalk, bearing
2. **DWARF PALM.**   (the fruit in clusters. *Palma humilis.*

Intire; whether of
Indented edges; bearing
Black berries; || either that whose *leaves* grow *against one another*:
or that whose leaves grow *alternately.*

3. { **PHYLLYRÆA,** *Mock-privet.*   *Philyraea.*
   { **EVERGREEN PRIVET.**   *Alaternus.*

Red berries; || either that of *oblong shining serrate leaves*, bearing
fruit like *Strawberries*, but bigger: or that which bears berries of a
4. { **STRAWBERRY TREE.**   (more *pale yellowish red. Arbutus.*
   { **EVERGREEN THORN.**   *Pyracantha.*

Smooth edges; to be further distinguished by the   (leaves are
Tast; hot and biting, being violent purgers; whether such whose
Broader; of a tough stalk, the leaves towards the bottom being
more long then those of *Bays*, bearing greenish flowers, and black
5. **SPURGE LAUREL.**   (berries, of a very hot tast. *Laureola.*

Narrower; || either that which bears *long pale leaves* and red berries: or that which bears *dark green leaves*, the berries growing
6. { **SPURGE OLIVE.**   (by threes. *Thymalaea.*
   { **WIDOW WAIL.**   (either *Chamalaea tricoccos.*

Flower; as to the manner of its growth, as likewise of the berries;
In the midst of the leaf; whether having
Larger leaves; *not spinous*: the latter of which hath a small leaf
growing out of the middle of another leaf, betwixt which two,
the blossoms and berries do grow.
7. { **LAUREL OF ALEXANDRIA.**   *Laurus Alexandrina.*
   { **HORSE-TONGUE.**   *Hypoglossum.*

Lesser leaves; *spinous*, bearing large red berries.
8. **BUTCHERS BROOM.**   *Ruscus.*

In an Umbel; having a *thick, broad, dark* coloured *leaf*, bearing
early flowers, and said to blossom twice in one year.
9. **WILD BAY.**   *Laurus sinus.*

Leaf; whether
Small, slender; and prickly at the ends, being odorate; || either that
whose leaves and wood, are of a more *pleasant sent*, producing
blewish berries: or that whose sent is *less pleasant*, bearing *black*
10. { **JUNIPER.**   (berries. *Juniperus.*
    { **SAVIN.**   *Sabina.*

Roundish and broad; || either that which is *odorate*: or that whose
flowers grow *in clusters*, bearing *pentagonal fruit* about the big-
11. { **MYRTLE**   (ness of a *Pease. Myrtus.*
    { **MYRTLE SYMACH.**   *Rhus myrtifol.*

Manner of growing; upon other plants; || either that which hath weak
branches, angular shining leaves, *black berries in clusters*, growing
commonly upon other trees or walls: or that which *never grows on*
12. { **IVY.**   (*the ground*, of a paler colour and *transparent berries. Hedera.*
    { **MISSELTO.**   *Viscus.*

IV. SI-

Of Shrubs. Part. II.

IV. SILIQUOUS SHRUBS.

IV. SILIQUOUS SHRUBS, may be diftinguifhed into fuch as are
Deciduous; whether having
  Intire leaves; the
    Greater; being a tall plant, approaching nearer to the magnitude of a Tree, bearing beautiful fpikes of blew flowers.
      1. LILACH, *Pipe-tree*. — *Syringa cæruleo flore.*
    Leffer; either that of a *round leaf*, being a *low plant*, the bud of whofe flower, when pickled, is an efculent fauce, bearing large *white flowers*: or that which is *taller*, bearing *yellow flowers*.
      2. { CAPAR. — *Capparis.*
           { THORNY BROOM. — *Afpalathus.*
  Compound leaves;
    Trefoils; bearing yellow flowers; the *Greater*, or the *leffer*.
      3. { BEAN TREFOIL. — *Laburnum.*
           { SHRUB TREFOIL. — *Cytifus.*
    Winged leaves;
      European; confiderable for having
        A purgative quality; || either that which hath no od leaf at the end: or that which bears its feeds in hollow pods or bladders.
          4. { SENA. — *Sena.*
               { BASTARD SENA. — *Colutea.*
        An efculent root; of a fweet juice.
          5. LICCORICE. — *Glycyrrhiza.*
      Exotic;
        The *Greater*; being thorny, bearing yellow flowers; || either that whofe *leaves* are *fmaller*, the flowers growing in a fphærical clufter, being odorate: or that whofe *leaves* are much *larger*.
          6. { BINDING BEAN TREE. — *Acacia.*
               { LOCUST TREE. — *Acacia Americana.*
        The *Leffer*; confiderable for the falling down of the branches, and clofing of the leaves upon a touch, as if the plant had fenfe.
          7. HUMBLE PLANT. — *Planta humilis.*
Sempervirent; having
  Green twigs; bearing yellow flowers; || either that which hath long flender, fquare, flexile twigs, and long thin cods: or that whofe twigs are more fhort, and ftiffe, and prickly, bearing fhorter cods more full and thick.
    8. { BROOM. — *Genifta.*
         { FURRS. — *Genifta fpinofa.*
  Hoary leaves; || either that which hath *long thorns*, ftanding thick, bearing white flowers fhaped like thofe of *Broom*, having *winged leaves*: or that which is a *Cinquefoil*.
    9. { GOATS THORN. — *Tragacantha.*
         { DORYCNIUM. — *Dorycnium.*

V. GRA-

Chap. IV.   Of Shrubs.

V. GRANIFEROUS DECIDUOUS SHRUBS, may be distinguished into such as are

Erect; to be considered according to their

Flowers; whether such as have

Smaller flowers; in spikes; bearing

Round fruit; like berries; || either that which bears *five leaves* upon a foot-stalk: or whose *seed-vessels are pentagonal*, conteining *small yellow seed*.

1. {CHAST TREE.
   {SPIKED WILLOW OF THEOPHRASTUS. *Agnus castus. Spiræa Theophrasti.*

Seed wrapt up in Down; having very small leaves like those of *Cipres*, and an odorate wood.

2. TAMARISK.   *Tamariscus.*

Larger flowers; whether

Odorate; || either that which hath *weak branches*, whose flowers are of a more *pleasant smell*: or that whose flowers are of a *strong and less pleasant smell*.

3. {JESSAMINE.   *Jasminum.*
   {WHITE PIPE TREE.   *Syringa alba.*

Not odorate; having *leaves like* those of *Marsh mallow*, being *soft and hoary.*

4. SHRUB MALLOW.   *Althæa.*

Odorateness of the leaves; || either that which grows *in fenny places*, bearing *long leaves*, and small *squamous Catkins* : or that which is a *lower plant*, having roundish nervous *leaves*, upon long foot-stalks, bearing *woolly tufts, and seeds like Lentils*.

5. {GALLS.   *Elaeagnus cordi.*
   {RED SUMACH.   *Coccigrea.*

Milkiness of the juice; being a *violent purger*; having *long leaves* of a *pale green colour.*

6. TREE SPURGE.   *Tithymallus arborescens*

Climbers; either by

Twisting; || either that which is a *Trefoil*: or that which hath *winged leaves*, bearing the flowers in a cluster, having *feathery tufts*.

7. {CLEMATIS, *Virgins-bower.*   *Clematis.*
   {TRAVELLERS JOY.   *Viorna vulgi.*

Laying hold on walls or trees by small tendrils; like clawes or fingers.

8. VIRGINIAN CLIMBERS, *Virginian Ivy.*   *Hedera quinquefol. Canadensis.*

VI. GRA-

Of Shrubs. Part. II.

VI. GRANIFEROUS EVERGREEN SHRUBS

Ciſtus.
Nerium.

VI. GRANIFEROUS EVERGREEN SHRUBS, may be diſtinguiſhed into ſuch as are *European*; conſiderable for
  Bearing large flowers; whether that which hath *hoary leaves*, the flower conſiſting of *five leaves*: or that which bears *long ſtiffe leaves of a dark green*.
  1. ⟨HOLY ROSE.
     ⟨OLEANDER, *Roſe-bay*.
  Having *a purging quality*; whether ſuch as have
    Hoary leaves; ‖ either that which hath *ſmall leaves, thick ſet* upon the
    ſtalk, being *hoary underneath*: or that whoſe *leaves* are *bigger, and
    hoary all over*, bearing ſmall flowers in tufts.

Sana munda.
Xarton rair.

  2. ⟨SANA MUNDA.
     ⟨GUTTWORT, *Trouble-belly*.
  Smooth hard dry leaves; bearing a *blew flower like that of Scabious*.

*Alypum mon-
ſpelienſium.*

  3. HERB TERRIBLE.
  Being *odorate*; whether ſuch as have
    Hoary leaves; *verticillate*, having *hooded flowers*; ‖ either that which
    hath *narrow long leaves hoary underneath*: or that which hath
    broader *leaves hoary all over*, bearing yellow gaping flowers.

Roſmarinus.
*Salvia fruti-
coſa.*

  4. ⟨ROSEMARY.
     ⟨SAGE MULLEIN.
  Green leaves; whether that which bears *ſmall flowers* in an *Umbel*:
  or that which bears a *large flower* like that of *Oleander*, yellow and ſpotted.

*Seſeli Æthio-
picum.*
*Ledum Alpi-
num.*

  5. ⟨HARTWORT.
     ⟨SWEET MOUNTAIN ROSE.
  The place of their growth; whether
    Near the Sea; being of a pale colour; ‖ either that whoſe *leaves are
    ſmooth*, bearing *moſſy flowers*, and a *ſmall compreſſed ſeed*: or that of
    winged hoary ſhining leaves, bearing *yellow flowers* in cluſters.

Halimus.
Jovis barba.

  6. ⟨SEA PURSLAIN.
     ⟨SILVER BUSH.
  In barren places; being a low plant, having *ſmall hollow flowers*, and *little leaves*.

Erica.

  7. HEATH.
  Exotic; a *low ſhrub*, the branches ſpreading and growing thick together, which *after being dried* and ſhrunk up, *will* upon being *put into
  warm water dilate* and expend themſelves.

*Roſa Hieri-
cuntina.*

  8. ROSE OF JERICO.

Of Trees.

§. VII.

Trees may be diſtinguiſhed according to their
  Fruit or Seed; being contained either in a
    Fleſhy pulp; whether
      ⟨POMIFEROUS.   I.
      ⟨PRUNIFEROUS. II.
      ⟨BACCIFEROUS. III.
    Hard ſhell;
      ⟨NUCIFEROUS.   IV.
      ⟨GLANDIFEROUS, or CONIFEROUS. V.
    SINGLE TEGUMENTS, or Coverings. VI.
  WOODS OR BARKS. VII.
  GUMMS OR ROSINS. VIII.

L POMI-

Chap. IV.   *Of Trees.*   113

1. **POMIFEROUS TREES**, may be distinguished into such as are   1. POMI-
More properly called Trees; whether   FEROUS
Deciduous; having   TREES.
Visible Blossoms;
Esculent when ripe;
More round; the *tree* spreading more in breadth; both as to the *branches* and *roots* of it, the *fruits* having an outward cavity at each end, in the place of the *blossom* and the *stalk*, and five inward *cavities* lined with *stiffe membranes*, each of which doth
     1. APPLE.   (commonly contein two *kernels*. *Malus.*
Less round; that part of the *fruit* where the *stalk* grows, being more *prominent*; ‖ either that which *rises more in height*: or that which *spreads more in breadth*, being a *lower* and more *crooked* tree, whose *fruit* is covered with a *Down*, being when raw, of an
     2. SPEAR.   (unpleasant taste and sent. *Pirus.*
       QUINCE.   *Malus cydo-*
Not esculent, till rotten;   *nia.*
The greater; ‖ either that *smaller tree*, having *long leaves*, dark green above and white beneath, the *fruit having a wide aperture* in the place of the *blossom*: or that *thorny tree*, whose *leaf* and *fruit* is like a *Hawthorn*, but the *fruit* bigger, and of a pleasant *acidity*.
     3. MEDLAR.   *Mespilus.*
       LAZAROLE.   *Mespilus Aro-*
The lesser; being *tall trees*; ‖ either that of *winged serrate leaves*, bearing a *fruit like a small Pear*: or that of *jagged leaves*, bearing a *lesser fruit in clusters upon long foot-stalks*.   *nia.*
     4. TRUE SERVICE.   *Sorbus.*
       COMMON SERVICE.   *Sorbus termi-*
No visible blossoms; unless (as JOHN BAUHINUS observes) within   *nalis.*
the *fruit*, being a *weak tree*, of *smooth bark*, *large leaves*, divided commonly into *five jags*, whose *fruit* is of an oblong *Pear-like* figure, of a more soft consistence, full of little grains.
     5. FIGG.   *Ficus.*
Sempervirent; or *evergreen*; whose fruit is either
Round; of a
Hard, crustaceous, brittle rine; a *thorny tree*, bearing large beautiful *blossoms*, the *fruit* full of *grains in a red pulp*, with a kind of *Coronet* on the top of the *fruit*, at the place of the *blossom*.
     6. POMEGRANATE.   *Malus Puni-*
Softer rine; the *fruit* as to its colour being of a *deep yellow*; ‖ either   *ca*
that which hath a *quick juice of a grateful acidity*: or that whose
     ORANGE.   (juice is of a *more dull and flat taste*. *Aurantia.*
     7. ADAMS APPLE.   *Pomum Ada-*
Oblong; and *oval*; being of a *pale yellow*; ‖ either the *bigger*, whose   *mi.*
rine is *more thick*, and whose *juice is less acid*: or the *less*, whose rine
     CITRON.   (is *more thin*, and whose *juice is more acid*. *Malus medi-*
     8. LEMMON.   *ca. Limonia.*
Less properly called Trees; bearing *fruits* of some resemblance to *Figgs*; ‖ either that which grows to a great bigness, bearing a pleasant *fruit*, many in a cluster, being *Annual*: or that whose *leaves* grow out of one another, of which those in *Northern Countries* are commonly so
     PLANTAIN TREE.   (small as to be reckoned amongst *Herbs*. *Musa arbor.*
   9. INDIAN FIGG.   Q   II. PRU- *Ficus Indica.*

Of Trees.

II. PRUNIFEROUS TREES.

II. PRUNIFEROUS TREES, may be distinguished into such as are

Not Purgative;

  Deciduous; whose fruits are

    Greater; whose stones are

      Rough; having many deep crooked furrows; ‖ either that whose fruit is *covered with a Down*: or that whose skin is *not downy*.

Malus Persica.
Nuciperfica.

1. { PEACH. *Malacotoon.*
   { NECTARINE.

      Smooth; ‖ either that, which is *sooner ripe*, of a more *dry, solid,* yellow *pulp*: or that of a more *succulent pulp*.

Malus Armeniaca.
Prunus.

2. { APRICOCK.
   { PLUMM.

    Lesser; putting out *blossoms* before *leaves*; ‖ either that which bears a more *round fruit upon a long foot-stalk*: or that which bears a more *oblong fruit upon a shorter foot-stalk.*

Cerasus.
Cornus.

3. { CHERRY.
   { CORNELION.

  Sempervirent: having *stones* with very small *kernels*: ‖ either that which hath *long narrow leaves, hoary underneath,* the *fruit* not esculent till pickled: or that which hath very *long leaves, like those of Reed,* the *fruit* growing in clusters, of a pleasant taste.

Olea.
Palma.

4. { OLIVE.
   { DATE.

Purgative; being sold in *Apothecaries shops*.

  Used sometimes for food; ‖ either that whose *fruit is bigger*: or that which bears a *small black turbinate fruit,* standing *in a little cup,* of a black, sweet, viscid pulp, adhering to the *stone*, which contains three *seeds*.

Myrobalanus.
Sebesten.

5. { MIROBALANE.
   { SEBESTEN.

  Not used for food; ‖ either that whose *fruit* hath some *resemblance to an Olive*: or that which bears a *red fruit,* the *leaf short, round, serrate, of a deep green.*

Zizyphus alba.
Zizyphus sativa.

6. { WHITE JUJUBS.
   { COMMON JUJUBS.

III. BAC-

Chap. IV. *Of Trees.*

III. BACCIFEROUS TREES, may be distinguished into such as are III. BACCI-
- *European* ; (either FEROUS TREES.
  - *Deciduous* ; whose fruit is
    - *Esculent* ; having *broad, roundish, serrate, rough leaves,* bearing a fruit like that of a *Rasberry*, but bigger.
      1. MULBERRY. *Morus.*
    - *Not esculent* ; having
      - *Winged leaves* ; the wood more
        - *Soft* and spungy ; || either that, the younger branches of which are full of *Pith*, bearing the berries in an *Umbel*, being of an ill sent: or that which *bears its berries in a close tuft*, the wood being used for giving a black tincture to *Leather*.
          2. {ELDER. *Sambucus.*
             {SUMACH. *Rhus Sumach.*
        - *Hard* ; || either that which bears its *berries in an Umbel*, being of a red colour and an acid tast: or that which bears a *small, round, oblong fruit, in long clusters,* having many hollow excrescences
          3. {QUICKEN TREE. (like *Bladders*. *Fraxinus bubula.*
             {TURPENTINE TREE. *Terebinthus.*
      - *Single leaves* ; bearing *a small black fruit upon a long foot-stalk,* like that of a *Cherry,* the leaves resembling those of *Nettle*.
        4. NETTLE TREE. *Lotus.*
- *Evergreen* ; considerable for their
  - *Berries* ; whether such as bear
    - *Black berries* ; || either that whose leaves are more *short, odorate, of a deep green,* each berry conteining two seeds: or that whose leaves are more *pale, long, shining and serrate*.
      5. {BAY. *Laurus.*
         {LAUREL. *Laurus cerasus.*
    - *Red berries* ; || either that which hath *small narrow leaves* of a dark green: or that which hath *large shining prickly leaves*.
      6. {YEW. *Taxus.*
         {HOLLY. *Agrifolium.*
    - *Whitish berries* ; having *small round leaves of an ill sent,* a hard close
      7. BOX. (wood of a yellowish colour. *Buxus.*
  - *Gumms* ; || either that which hath *winged leaves, without an od leaf at the end* : or that which hath *long narrow leaves, like those of Iris,* producing a red Gum called *Sanguis draconis*.
    8. {MASTIC TREE. *Lentiscus.*
       {DRAGON TREE. *Draco arbor.*
- *Exotic* ;
  - *Deciduous* ; || either that whose *fruit is Aromatical, being the bottom of the flower,* which when ripe, *grows turgid in the middle* where the seeds are conteined: or that of *winged leaves, serrate, of a deep green,* bearing *white berries in clusters*.
    9. {CLOVE TREE. *Caryophillus aromaticus.*
       {BEDE TREE. *Azedarach.*
  - *Evergreen* ; || either that of an *Aromatic wood* used in Physick, having *leaves like those of a Fig-tree,* but less: or that of *winged leaves, long, narrow, sharp pointed,* bearing berries like those of *Asparagus,* in clu-
    10. {SASSAFRAS. (sters. *Sassafras.*
        {INDIAN MOLLE. *Molle arbor.*

IV. NUCI-

116   *Of Trees.*   Part. II.

IV. NUCI-
FEROUS
TREES.

IV. NUCIFEROUS TREES, may be diftinguifhed into fuch as are;
⎡ *European* ; conteining in one common hufk
⎢ ⎡ *One Nut* ; having a covering that is either
⎢ ⎢ ⎡ *Thick* and pulpy ; having oyly kernels ; ‖ either that which is the
⎢ ⎢ ⎢ larger tree of *winged leaves, odorate,* having a *rugged kernel,* divi-
⎢ ⎢ ⎢ ded into feveral lobes : or that which is a *leffer tree,* having *long*
⎢ ⎢ ⎢ *narrow ferrate leaves,* and *a fmooth kernel.*

Juglans.
Amygdalus.
1. ⎰ WALNUT.
   ⎱ ALMOND.

⎢ ⎢ ⎣ *Thin* husks ; either fuch as are
⎢ ⎢ ⎡ *Wholly encompaffed* ; and covered by their hufks ; whether that of
⎢ ⎢ ⎢ *winged leaves,* having a *white* thin *fhell,* upon which there is ano-
⎢ ⎢ ⎢ ther rugged covering: or that whofe *leaf is like that of a Quince,*
⎢ ⎢ ⎢ green above and white underneath, *the fruit covered with a*
⎢ ⎢ ⎣ *downy husk,* the kernel of a bad taft.

Piftacia.
Styrax.
2. ⎰ PISTACIE, *Fiftic-nut.*
   ⎱ STORAX.

⎢ ⎢ ⎣ *Open at one end* ; being fmaller Trees, of broad indented leaves,
⎢ ⎢   bearing *Catkins* ; ‖ either that of a *larger kernel* and *thinner fhell,*
⎢ ⎢   whofe *husk* is *longer* : or that of a *leffer kernel* and *thicker fhell,*
⎢ ⎢   whofe *husk* is *fhorter.*

Avellana.
Corilus fylve-
ftris.
3. ⎰ FILBERT.
   ⎱ SMALL NUT.

⎢ ⎣ *Several Nuts* ; whofe outward hufk is
⎢ ⎡ *Echinate* and prickly ; ‖ either that which hath *long, fmooth, deeply*
⎢ ⎢ *indented leaves,* the hufk conteining three or four Nuts : or that
⎢ ⎢ which bears a *fhort, roundifh, fhining leaf,* having a fmooth bark,
⎢ ⎣ and Nuts of a triangular figure.

Caftanea.
Fagus.
4. ⎰ CHESNUT.
   ⎱ BEECH.

⎢ ⎣ *Smooth* ; and thin, *in the form of a Bladder* ; being a fmall tree of

Staphylo-den-
dron.
5. BLADDER NUT.   (winged leaves.

⎣ *Exotic* ; conteining in one common hufk
⎡ *One Nut* ; ‖ either that which is *a large tree,* bearing *the largeft Nut of*
⎢ *all that are known,* covered with a thick rine upon the fhell : or that
⎢ which hath a *hard Aromatic kernel,* covered immediately with a yel-
⎢ lowifh *Aromatic husk,* called *Mace,* upon which there is a thin fhell,

Nux mofcha-
ta.
6. ⎰ COCO.   (and upon that a pulpy coat.
   ⎱ NUTMEG.

⎣ *Several Nuts* ; having a covering
⎡ *More thin* ; whofe kernels are ufed for the making of drinks, being
⎢ but fmall trees ; ‖ either that which grows *in fhady moift places,*
⎢ having many kernels together in a hufk : or that which is lefs
⎢ properly called a *Nut,* bearing *a double kernel in a husk,* each of
⎣ them being flat on one fide, and gibbous on the other.

Cacao.
Buna arbor.
7. ⎰ CHOCOLATE.
   ⎱ COFFI.

⎣ *Covered with a woolly fubftance* : or that which befides the outward
    tegument hath likewife *an inward pulp,* wherein *the fruit lies, of the*
    fhape of a Heart, and the bigneffe of a Bean, ufed in Phyfick.

Goffipium.
Anacardium.
8. ⎰ COTTON TREE.
   ⎱ ANACARDIUM.

V. GLAN-

Chap. IV.   Of Trees.

V. GLANDIFEROUS, and CONIFEROUS TREES, may be distinguished into such as are

Glandiferous.
- *Deciduous;* ‖ either that which is a *large tree*, of a *hard lasting wood*, a *rugged bark*, the *leaves waved at the edges*: or that whose *leaves* are *more deeply divided*, bearing *a larger fruit*, standing in great thick rugged cups, used for tanning.
  1. { OAK.   *Quercus.*
     { BITTER OAK.   *Cerrus.*
- *Evergreen;* ‖ either that whose *leaves resemble those of Holly*, being of a dark green above, and white underneath: or that which is very like to this, having a very, *thick, light, porous, deciduous bark.*
  2. { HOLM OAK.   *Ilex.*
     { CORK TREE.   *Suber.*

Coniferous;
- *Deciduous;* bearing small *Cones;* ‖ either that which grows *in watery places*, having *leaves* of a *dark green*, shaped *like those of the Nut-tree*: or that whose leaves are very slender, growing *in tufts*, more thin *at distances*, of a paler colour.
  3. { ALDER.   *Alnus.*
     { LARICH TREE.   *Larix.*
- *Evergreen;* whose *Cones are*
  - *Bigger;* ‖ either that which is a *large tall tree*, bearing *great roundish Cones of smooth scales, standing upwards*, the leaves being small, narrow, and thick set together: or that which bears *long slender leaves, two growing out together from one socket*, the *Cones* consisting of *hard woodly scales*.
     4. { CEDAR.   *Cedrus.*
        { PINE.   *Pinus.*
  - *Lesser;* having
    - *Long leaves;* ‖ either that whose *leaves* encompass and cover the branches, bearing *long Cones hanging downwards*: or that whose leaves grow from each side of the *stalk*, being more flat, like those of *Tew*, green on the upper side, and whitish underneath, furcated at the end, bearing *Cones shorter and thicker*, growing erect.
       5. { MALE FIRR TREE, *Pitch-tree.*   *Abies mas.*
          { FEMALE FIRR TREE.   *Abies fæmina.*
    - *Short leaves;* ‖ either that which grows in a *conical* figure, bearing *small roundish Cones*: or that which hath *compressed branches* of a strong resinous sent, bearing *small Cones encompassed with six scales.*
       6. { CYPRESS.   *Cupressus.*
          { TREE OF LIFE.   *Arbor vitæ.*

VI. TREES

Of Trees. Part. II.

VI. TREES whose Seeds are in SINGLE TEGUMENTS.

VI. TREES bearing their Seeds in SINGLE TEGUMENTS or Coverings, may be distinguished into such whose seeds are conteined in Pods; called *Siliquous trees*; whether such whose *Pods* are

Siliqua arbor.

Larger; being
 Esculent; having *winged leaves*, and *very broad Pods*.
  1. CAROB, St *John's bread*.
 Purgative; ‖ either that which bears a *round, black*, and *very long Pod*, whose pulp is used as a benign purgative: or that which bears a *thick Pod*, having *winged leaves*, and a purgative pulp.

Cassia.
Tamarindus.

 2. ⎰ CASSIA.
  ⎱ TAMARIND.

Arbor Juda.

Lesser; having a *round leaf*, bearing elegant *purple blossoms*, and a *thin Pod*.
 3. JUDAS TREE.

Membranaceous coverings; whether

Foliaceous husks; ‖ either that whose *leaves* are *rough* and indented, having a *rugged bark*: : or that whose *leaf* is somewhat *longer and smoother*, having a *more even bark*.

Ulmus.
Carpinus.

 4. ⎰ ELM.
  ⎱ HORNBEAM.

Alate seed-vessels; or *Keys*; whether such as do generall bear

Fraxinus.

Single Keys; having *winged leaves*, a *smooth bark*, and a *tough wood*.
 5. ASH.

Double Keys; ‖ either that which hath *smaller leaves*, divided into five segments, being a *brittle wood*: or that which hath *broader leaves*, more deeply divided, being a *soft wood*.

Acer minus.
Acer majus.

 6. ⎰ MAPLE.
  ⎱ SYCAMORE.

Catkins; called *Juliferous trees*; whether such as are of

Lesser leaves; ‖ either that which hath *slender reddish twigs*, smooth and *white branches*: or that which bears a *roundish crenate leaf*, upon *very slender foot-stalks*, which makes them apt to shake upon every little breath of wind.

Betula.
Populus tremula.

 7. ⎰ BIRCH.
  ⎱ ASPIN.

Larger leaves; ‖ either that whose leaves are of a *dark green*, like those of *Ivy*, having *a whitish bark*, and growing in watery places: or that whose leaves are *laciniated*, being *of a dark green above, and hoary white underneath*.

Populus nigra.
Populus alba.

 8. ⎰ BLACK POPLAR.
  ⎱ WHITE POPLAR.

Longer leaves; of a soft wood, growing most naturally in moist places; ‖ either that whose leaves are more *dense and compact*, being the *larger tree*: or that which is a *lesse tree*, having a *broader leaf*, and bearing *larger Cat-kins*.

Salix angustifol.
Salix latifol.

 9. ⎰ WILLOW.
  ⎱ SALLOW.

Round Buttons; ‖ either that which hath *broad leaves ending in a point*, being smoother above then underneath, bearing a *sweet blossom*, and a *round fruit* about the bigness of a *Pease*, conteining *one seed*: or that which hath a *divided leaf*, whose *fruit* is *echinate* or *prickly*, conteining *several seeds*

Tilia.
Platanus.

 10. ⎰ LIME TREE.
  ⎱ PLANE TREE.

VII. TREES

Chap. IV.   *Of Trees.*

VII. TREES confidered according to their WOODS or BARKS, may be diftinguifhed into fuch as are principally known and taken notice of for their

Woods; according to their ufes in
  Phyfick; whether fuch as are efteemed
    Cordial; being a hard, heavy, unctuous, Aromatic wood, the grain like that of *Oak.*
      1. ALOE TREE.   *Lignum Aloes.*
    Diaphoretic; of a hot biting taft; ‖ either that which is ufed againft the *Pox:* or that which is commended as an *Antidote* againft the biting of *Serpents.*
      2. { GUAIACUM, *Pockwood*.   *Lignum vitæ.*
        { SNAKEWOOD.   *Lignum colubrinum.*
    Cooling and Aftringent; whether that of a deep red, being hard, heavy, and of a finer grain, having a dull taft and no fent: or that which is yellowifh, of a ftrait courfe grain, and fragrant fmell like *Musk.*
      3. { RED SAUNDERS.   *Santalum rubrum.*
        { YELLOW SAUNDERS.   *Santalum citrinum.*
    Ufeful againft the Stone and difeafes of the Kidneys; ‖ either that which tinges *Water* fo, as to make it in feveral lights to appear of two colours, *blewifh and yellow,* not confiderable for *taft or fmell:* or that which is *yellowifh* in the middle, and *white* on the outfide, having a hottifh taft, and a fent like that of a *white Rofe.*
      4. { LIGNUM NEPHRITICUM.   *Lignum nephriticum.*
        { ROSEWOOD.   *Lignum Rhodinum.*
  Mechanics; whether for
    Dying a red colour; the former being a *hard heavy wood* of a ftrait grain, with *ftreaks of black.*
      5. { BRASIL WOOD.   *Brafilium lignum.*
        { LOG WOOD.
    Fabrile ufes; whether the making of
      Cabinets; being capable of a fhining politure; ‖ either that of a *black colour,* a clofe grain, being very heavy: or that which is *variegated* with *red and white.*
      6. { EBONY.   *Ebenum.*
        { PRINCES WOOD.
    Tubes; for the conveiance of *Water,* being ftreight flender trees, growing to a very great height, having a tuft of branches only at the top, the greateft part of them being *pith,* inclofed in a *fhell* of very *hard wood,* fomewhat refembling a *Rufh,*
      7. CABBIDGE TREE, *Palmetto Royal.*
Barks; or *Rines;* either that which is
  Efculent; being *Aromatic,* and of a fweet taft.
    8. CINNAMON.   *Cinnamomum.*
  Medicinal; ‖ either that which is fo foveraign a remedy for the *cure of Agues,* being of a *dark colour,* no *confiderable taft:* or that which is of *an Afh colour,* and a *hot biting taft,* good againft the *Scurvy.*
    9. { CORTEX FEBRIFUGUS PERUVIANUS, *Jefuits powder.*   *Cortex febrifugus.*
      { CORTEX WINTERANUS.   *Cortex Winteranus.*

VIII. TREES

Of Trees. Part. II.

VI. TREES whose Seeds are in SINGLE TEGUMENTS.

VI. TREES bearing their Seeds in SINGLE TEGUMENTS or Coverings, may be distinguished into such whose seeds are contained in Pods; called *Siliquous trees*; whether such whose *Pods* are

Siliqua arbor.

⎧ Larger; being
⎨ *Esculent*; having *winged leaves*, and *very broad Pods*.
⎪   1. CAROB, *St John's bread*.
⎩ *Purgative*; ‖ either that which bears a *round, black, and very long Pod*, whose pulp is used as a benign purgative: or that which bears a *thick Pod*, having *winged leaves*, and a purgative pulp.

Cassia.
Tamarindus.
2. ⎰ CASSIA.
   ⎱ TAMARIND.

Arbor Juda.

Lesser; having a *round leaf*, bearing elegant *purple blossoms*, and a *thin*
   3. JUDAS TREE.   (*Pod.*
Membranaceous coverings; whether
Foliaceous husks; ‖ either that whose *leaves* are *rough* and indented, having a *rugged bark*: : or that whose *leaf* is somewhat *longer and smoother*, having a *more even bark*.

Ulmus.
Carpinus.
4. ⎰ ELM.
   ⎱ HORNBEAM.

Alate seed-vessels; or *Keys*; whether such as do generall bear

Fraxinus.

⎧ *Single Keys*; having *winged leaves*, a *smooth bark*, and a *tough wood*.
⎨   5. ASH.
⎩ *Double Keys*; ‖ either that which hath *smaller leaves*, divided into five segments, being a *brittle wood*: or that which hath *broader leaves*, more deeply divided, being a *soft wood*.

Acer minus.
Acer majus.
6. ⎰ MAPLE.
   ⎱ SYCAMORE.

Catkins; called *Juliferous trees*; whether such as are of
Lesser leaves; ‖ either that which hath *slender reddish twigs*, smooth and *white branches*: or that which bears a *roundish crenate leaf*, upon *very slender foot-stalks*, which makes them apt to shake upon every little breath of wind.

Betula.
Populus tremula.
7. ⎰ BIRCH.
   ⎱ ASPIN.

Larger leaves; ‖ either that whose leaves are of a *dark green*, like those of *Ivy*, having *a whitish bark*, and growing in watery places: or that whose leaves are *laciniated*, being *of a dark green above, and hoary*

Populus nigra.
Populus alba.
8. ⎰ BLACK POPLAR.   (*white underneath*.
   ⎱ WHITE POPLAR.

Longer leaves; of a soft wood, growing most naturally in moist places; ‖ either that whose leaves are more *dense and compact*, being the *larger tree*: or that which is a *lesse tree*, having a *broader leaf*, and bearing *larger Cat-kins*.

Salix angustifol.
Salix latifol.
9. ⎰ WILLOW.
   ⎱ SALLOW.

Round Buttons; ‖ either that which hath *broad leaves ending in a point*, being smoother above then underneath, bearing a *sweet blossom*, and a *round fruit* about the bignes of a *Pease*, conteining *one seed*: or that which hath a divided *leaf*, whose *fruit* is *echinate* or *prickly*, conteining *severall seeds*.

Tilia.
Platanus.
10. ⎰ LIME TREE.
    ⎱ PLANE TREE.   VII. TREES

Chap. IV. Of Trees.

VII. TREES considered according to their WOODS or BARKS, may be distinguished into such as are principally known and taken notice of for their

- *Woods*; according to their uses in
  - *Physick*; whether such as are esteemed
    - *Cordial*; being a hard, heavy, unctuous, Aromatic wood, the grain like that of *Oak*.
      1. ALOE TREE. — *Lignum Aloes.*
    - *Diaphoretic*; of a hot biting tast; ‖ either that which is used against the *Pox*: or that which is commended as an *Antidote* against the biting of *Serpents*.
      2. { GUAIACUM, *Pockwood*. — *Lignum vitæ.*
         { SNAKEWOOD. — *Lignum colubrinum.*
    - *Cooling and Astringent*; whether that of a deep red, being hard, heavy, and of a finer grain, having a dull tast and no sent: or that which is yellowish, of a strait course grain, and fragrant smell like *Musk*.
      3. { RED SAUNDERS. — *Santalum rubrum.*
         { YELLOW SAUNDERS. — *Santalum citrinum.*
    - *Useful against the Stone and diseases of the Kidneys*; ‖ either that which tinges *Water* so, as to make it in several lights to appear of two colours, *blewish and yellow*, not considerable for *tast or smell*: or that which is *yellowish* in the middle, and *white* on the outside, having a hottish tast, and a sent like that of a *white Rose*.
      4. { LIGNUM NEPHRITICUM. — *Lignum nephriticum.*
         { ROSEWOOD. — *Lignum Rhodium.*
  - *Mechanics*; whether for
    - *Dying a red colour*; the former being a *hard heavy wood* of a strait grain, with *streaks of black*.
      5. { BRASIL WOOD. — *Brasilium lignum.*
         { LOG WOOD.
    - *Fabrile* uses; whether the making of
      - *Cabinets*; being capable of a shining politure; ‖ either that of a *black colour*, a close grain, being very heavy: or that which is *variegated* with *red and white*.
        6. { EBONY. — *Ebenum.*
           { PRINCES WOOD.
      - *Tubes*; for the conveiance of *Water*, being streight slender trees, growing to a very great height, having a tuft of branches only at the top, the greatest part of them being *pith*, inclosed in a *shell* of very *hard wood*, somewhat resembling a *Rush*,
        7. CABBIDGE TREE, *Palmetto Royal.*
- *Barks*; or *Rines*; either that which is
  - *Esculent*; being *Aromatic*, and of a sweet tast.
    8. CINNAMON. — *Cinnamomum.*
  - *Medicinal*; ‖ either that which is so soveraign a remedy for the *cure of Agues*, being of a *dark colour*, *no considerable tast*: or that which is of *an Ash colour*, and *a hot biting tast*, good against the *Scurvy*.
    9. { CORTEX FEBRIFUGUS PERUVIANUS, *Jesuits powder.* — *Cortex febrifugus.*
       { CORTEX WINTERANUS. — *Cortex Winteranus.*

VIII. TREES

Of Trees. Part. II.

VIII. TREES *confidered according to their* **GUMMS** *or* **ROSINS**.

VIII. TREES considered according to their **GUMMS** or **ROSINS**, may be distinguished; either according to their

- *Gums*; whether
  - *Odorate*; being of a *bitter taft*, proceeding from an *exotic thorny Tree.*
    1. **MYRRHE.**
  - *Not odorate*; ‖ either that which proceeds from an *Egyptian thorny tree*: or that which is of a yellowish colour and bitter taft, leaving behind it a kind of sweet rellish, somewhat like *Liccorice.*
    2. { **GUMM ARABICK.**
         SARCOCOLLA
- *Rosins*; whose consistence is more
  - *Solid*; and hard
    - *Odorate*; having a
      - *More pleasant sent*; used for
        - *Suffumigations*; being transparent; having
          - *Lesser grains*; ‖ either that which proceeds from an *Arabian tree*: or that which is of near resemblance to this, proceeding from an *Æthiopian Olive*, of a *whitish colour* mixed with *yellow particles.*
            3. { **FRANKINCENSE,** *Olibanum.*
                 GUM ELEMI.
          - *Bigger grains*; proceeding from an *American tree*, the latter of which is more clear and transparent.
            4. { **GUMMI ANIMÆ.**
                 COPAL.
        - *Perfumes*; ‖ either that which is of a more hard consistence, and more tenacious: or that which is more easily dissolved.
          5. { **CARANNA.**
               BENJAMIN.
      - *Less pleasant sent*; either that which is
        - *More volatile*; white and transparent from several *trees.*
          6. **CAMPHIRE.**
        - *Less volatile*; ‖ either that which is *unctuous and bitterish*, easily growing soft, proceeding from an *exotic thorny tree*: or that which proceeds from a tall *tree like Poplar.*
          7. { **BDELLIUM.**
               TACA MAHACA.
    - *Not odorate*; of a *red tincture*, used in *painting* and *varnishing.*
      8 **LAKE.**
  - *Liquid*; being of a sweet sent; ‖ either that which is of a *more strong smell*: or that which is of a *reddish colour*, used for stopping *defluxions.*
    9. { **LIQUIDAMBRA.**
         BALSAMUM PERUVIANUM.

Myrrha.

Gummi Arabicum. Sarcocolla.

Thus. Gummi Elemi.

Gummi Animæ. Copal.

Caranna. Benzoin.

Camphora.

Bdellium. Taca mahaca.

Lacca.

Liquidambra. Balsamum Peruvianum.

CHAP.

CHAP. V.

I. *Concerning Animals, the general distribution of them.* II. *Of exanguious Animals.* III. *Of Fish.* IV. *Of Birds.* V. *Of Beasts.* VI. *A Digression concerning* Noah's *Ark*.

Sensitive creatures may be distinguished into such as are counted more §. I.
- *Imperfect*; which have something analogous to blood, but are destitute of that red juice commonly so called, being therefore stiled EX-ANGUIOUS, having either no leggs, or more legs then four,
- *Perfect*; whether
  - FISHES, which have no legs, but fins answerable to them, being covered with a naked skin, or with scales, whose proper motion is *swimming*.
  - BIRDS, which have two leggs and two wings, whose bodies are covered with feathers, being oviparous, whose proper motion is *flying*.
  - BEASTS, which are for the most part, four-footed, hairy, and viviparous, excepting only some few which are without feet or hair, and are oviparous.

It may be observed to be amongst these (as it is amongst the other ranks of *Beings*,) that the more perfect kinds are the least numerous. Upon which account, *Insects* being the most minute and imperfect, and some of them (perhaps) of a spontaneous generation, are of the greatest variety, tho by reason of their littleness, the several *species* of them, have not hitherto been sufficiently enumerated or described, by those Authors who have particularly applyed themselves to this study.

There are sundry of these, as likewise of other Animals, which have no *Latin* names, as being unknown to the *Romans*, & there are sundry which have no *English* names, as being strangers to us. And amongst those that have *English* names, some are here described by their usual Appellations in *Latin*, because I knew not at present how to render them properly in *English*: And some there are peculiar to some coasts and rivers, and not commonly known elsewhere, which are hard to be enumerated.

As for *fictitious Animals*, as *Syren*, or *Mermaid*, *Phœnix*, *Griffin*, *Harpy*, *Ruck*, *Centaur*, *Satyr*, &c. there is no provision made for them in these tables, because they may be infinite; and besides, being but bare names, and no more, they may be expressed as *Individuals* are.

Of Exanguious Animals.

§. II. Those kinds of more imperfect Animals, which are destitute of that red juice, commonly called blood, are stiled *Exanguious*; to which may be annexed that general name given to the least kinds of these, viz. *Insect*, from that incisure or resemblance of cutting what is common to most of them in some part of their bodies.

These EXANGUIOUS ANIMALS may be distinguished into
- *Lesser*; usually called *Insects*; whether such whose generation is
  - *Analogous to that of other Animals*; which breed young like themselves, growing from a lesser to a greater magnitude, not being transmutable into any other *Insect*; whether such as have
    - NO FEET OR BUT SIX feet, being WITHOUT WINGS. I.
    - SIX FEET and WINGS, or MORE feet THEN SIX. II.
  - *Anomalous*; whether such as
    - ARE DESIGNED TO A FURTHER TRASMUTATION. III.
    - Have in their production undergone severall *mutations*; being first *Eggs*, then *Maggots* or *Caterpillars*, then *Aurelia*, and then *flying Insects*, which after their first production do not increase in magnitude; whether such as have
      - NAKED WINGS. IV.
      - SHEATHED WINGS. V.
- *Greater*; whether
  - *Hard*; whose *bones* are on their outside; being either
    - CRUSTACEOUS; namely such as are wholly covered with a *tough flexile substance*, having generally eight *legs*, besides a pair of *claws*, and two or more annulated *horns* or *feelers*. VI.
    - TESTACEOUS; of a more *hard and brittle substance*
      - TURBINATED; consisting of a *cone-like cavity*, rouled up in a *spiral*, which beginning at the *Aperture* or *mouth* of them, doth generally proceed from the left hand to the right. VII
      - NOT TURBINATED. VIII.
  - SOFT. IX.

I. INSECTS

Chap. V. *Of Exanguious Animals.*

I. INSECTS of an Analogous generation, having *no feet*, or *but six feet*, being *without wings*, may be diſtributed into thoſe that are *Apoda*; without *feet*.

- *More oblong* and *round*;
  - *Larger*;
    - *More ſlender*; of a *reddiſh* colour, with very *little diſtinction of parts*; ‖ either that which breeds *in the earth*: or that which breeds *in the bodies of children*.
      1. { EARTH WORM. *Vermis.*
         { BELLY WORM. *Lumbricus Inteſtinorum.*
    - *More thick*; ‖ either that which breeds *in watery places*, being *uſed for the drawing of blood*: or that which is covered with a *ſlimy moiſture*, having *four little horns* like *prominencies*, or *feelers*.
      2. { LEECH. *Hirudo.*
         { SNAIL. *Limax.*
  - *Leſſer*; breeding in *Animals*; ‖ either the more *minute*, being ſmall *white Worms*, breeding in the *lower guts of Men*: or the *bigger*, ſticking their *heads* in the *inward membranes of Horſes ſtomachs* or *guts*.
    3. { ASCARIDES.
       { BOTTS.
- *More ſhort* and *flat*; ‖ either that whoſe ſhape doth ſomewhat *reſemble a Flounder*, found both in waters, and in the branches of the *Porus biliaris*, and the *liver* of ſeveral of the *Ruminant kind*: or that of a *Quadrate body*, with a *little trunk* ſtanding out betwixt two *Antennæ*, and ſix *ſtringy ſubſtances behind*, living in the *Sea*.
  4. { FLUKE.
     { ASILUS.

Hexapoda; having *ſix feet*.

- *Terreſtrial*;
  - *Greater*;
    - *More ſlender*; ‖ either that whoſe *body* is ſomewhat *compreſſed*, *ſending out a light* from her *tail*: or that which is of a *whitiſh* colour, more *oblong*, breeding *in Meal*.
      5. { GLOW-WORM. *Cicindela.*
         { MEAL-WORM, *Gentle*. *Tenebrio.*
    - *Leſs ſlender*; ‖ either of a
      - *Darker* colour; being *like a Beetle without wings*, but ſeeming to have ſome little *rudiments of wings*, noted for being apt upon a touch to ſend out a *yellowiſh oyly ſubſtance* from his *joynts*.
        6. PROSCARAB. *Proſcarabæus.*
      - *Lighter* colour; whether that which *reſembles a Locuſt without wings*: or that which is of a *Cheſnut colour*, *flat*, *broad*, *ſoft*, avoiding *light places*.
        7. { FIELD CRICKET. *Brucus.*
           { COCK ROCHES. *Blatta male alata.*
  - *Leſſer*; troubleſome to other *Animals*; ‖ whether that of a *paler colour*: or that of a *dark red*, being *ſalient*.
    8. { LOUSE. *Pediculus.*
       { FLEA. *Pulex.*
- *Aquatic*; having a *compreſſed body*, with an *oblique decuſſation* upon the *back*, and a *long tail*.
  9. WATER SCORPION. *Scorpio aquaticus.*

H. IN-

Of Exanguious Animals.

II. INSECTS winged, or having above six legs.

II. INSECTS of an Analogous generation, having either *wings or more* *Winged*; whether (*legs then six*, may be distributed into such as are *Terrestrial*; whose bodies are

  More oblong;

    Living in open fields, and *feeding on plants*; ‖ either that kind, by the swarms of which whole *Countries* have been sometimes destroyed, having *long hinder legs* for leaping, *making a noise by rubbing their legs against their wings*: or that of *a long slender breast, often holding up the two fore-legs*, which are longer then the other.

Locusta.
Mantis.

1. { LOCUST, *Grashopper*.
    MANTIS.

    Living in holes of the ground, and *houses*; ‖ either that which affects to reside *near Hearths and Ovens*, making a noise like a *Locust*, by the affriction of the *wings*, having the *wings* lying more close to the body: or that whose *fore-legs* are *broad and strong, divided into fingers like those of a Mole*, whereby it is inabled in a very short space (to dig a hole in the ground.

Gryllus.
Gryllo-talpa.

2. { CRICKET.
    FEN-CRICKET, *Evechurr, Churr-worm.*

  More compressed and *broad*; ‖ whether that which hath *broad angular shoulders*, being marked with an *oblique decussation* on the *back*, having *the proboscis reversed under the belly*: or that which is of a *Chesnut colour*, having *large stiff wings, avoiding the light*.

Cimex.
Blatta alata.

3. { CIMEX SILVESTRIS.
    WINGED COCKROCH.

Aquatic; having a *decussation* or kind of *Lozenge*-mark on the *back*; ‖ either that which *runs upon the top of the water*, having *long legs* like those of a *spider*: or that which hath *two long swimming legs* behind, (whereby he *swims in the water*.

Tipula.
Cicada aquatica.

4. { WATER SPIDER.
    CICADA AQUATICA.

Not winged;

  Terrestrial; having

    Eight legs; being *hurtful* to

      Animals; either the

        Larger; whether that which by *drawing out* from *the belly* a *slimy substance*, and working it with the *feet, doth frame a small Web* to catch *Flies*: or that which hath an *oval body*, *two forcipate claws*, *a knotty tail, with a crooked sting at the end of it*.

Aranea.
Scorpius.

5. { SPIDER.
    SCORPION.

      Middle kind; ‖ either that of a *round body, the legs fixed to the neck*, sticking to *Animals* by thrusting the *head* into their *skin*: or that which is of *a dark red colour, a tender skin*, causing a very offensive *stink*, when crushed.

Ricinus.
Cimex.

6. { TICK, *sheep-tick*.
    PUNICE, *Wall-louse*.

      Least kind; ‖ either that which *breeds in corrupted Cheese, fruit, &c.* or that which doth *work it self into the skin of children*.

Syro.
Acaris.

7. { MITE.
    WHEAL WORM.

  Clothes; being of a *silver colour, mealy, oblong, of swift motion*.

Tinea.

8. MOTH.

Fourteen legs; covered with a *scaly armature*, having a *flat belly*, and a *gibbous back*, being apt to roul it self up when touched.

Asellus.

9. SOW, *Ch. eslip, Hog-louse, Wood-louse*.

More

Chap. V. *Of Exanguious Animals.* 125

10. { *More then fourteen feet;* || whether that whose *body* is of a more com-
    SCOLOPENDER.   (pressed: or a more round figure.   *Scolopendra.*
    JULUS.   *Julus.*

11. { *Aquatick*; || whether that which *sticks to Fish*, not much differing from an
    Asellus, but only in respect of the *tail*, which is somewhat broad: or that
    SEA LOUSE,   (whose *back* is more *gibbous*, being apt to *skip*. *Pediculus marinus.*
    SEA FLEA, *Sugg, River Shrimp.*   *Pulex marinus.*

III. INSECTS of an ANOMALOUS generation, designed for a fur-   III. ANO-
ther transmutation, may be distinguished into such as are   MALOUS
  INSECTS.

{ *Apoda*; those that are *without feet*, considered according to the
  General name;
    1. MAGGOT.   *Eula.*
  Particular kinds; whether such as are.
  { *Sharp at both ends*; || either the *bigger*, producing the *savificous kind*:
    or the *lesser*, breeding in the *excrescies of Oaks*, and the *tufts of Bri-
    ars*, and sometimes creeping out of the sides of *Caterpillars*, produ-
    cing a smaller sort of *shining Fly*, many of which are *Seticaudes*.
  2. { BEE MAGGOT, *Grub.*
       SHINING FLY MAGGOT.
  Broad and flat at their tails; || either the *greater*, having *two black
  spots* on the *tail*, the *fore-part* being more slender, with two little
  black *hooks* upon the *head*, by fixing of which, this Insect doth draw
  his *body* forward, from whence *Flesh-flies* proceed: or the *lesser*, with
  3. { GENTILE, (a short erect *tail*, producing *Flies* of the *Wasp* kind.
       WASP-LIKE FLY MAGGOT.

Pedata; having *legs*, whether
{ *Hexapoda*; such as have *six legs*.
  { *Aquatic*; living in the *water*; || whether that which is *naked*, producing
    Dragon-flies: or that which is *in a case with little straws* or sticks ad-
  4. { LIBELLA WORM.   (hering to it, producing *May flies*. *Phryganeum.*
       CADEW, *Straw-worm.*
  Terrestrial; breeding several sorts of *Scarabs*; || whether that which
  is of a strait *figure*: or that whose *tail* is *inverted* under the *belly*.
  5. { STRAIT BEETLE PRODUCING HEXAPOD.
       WHIRL WORM.   *Spondyle.*

More then six legs; considerable according to the
{ *General name*; comprehending all such, as besides three pair of slender crooked *legs*, on the *three first annuli* next the *head*, have two
  or more short thick *legs* behind, and two *appendages* at the *tail*. To
  which may be adjoyned the most principal of those.
  6. { CATERPILLAR.   *Eruca.*
       SILK WORM.   *Bombix.*
  Particular kinds; whether having
  { *Eight feet*; that which in its progressive motion doth first gather
    its *body* up into a *loop*, resting it upon his *hinder feet* and the *ap-
    pendages* of the *tail*, and then thrusting himself forward, or else
  7. { GEOMETRA.   (skipping forward.
       SKIPPING WORM.
  Many feet; amongst which the most common and numerous kind
  have *fourteen feet*; || whether those that are *smooth*: or those that
  8. { SMOOTH CATERPILLAR.   (are *hirsute*.
       PALMER WORM, *Bear worm.*   IV. NA-

Of Exanguious Animals. Part. II.

IV. NAKED WINGED INSECTS, which in their production do undergo several notations, may be distributed into such, whose *wings* are either
- *Membranaceous*; consisting of a *thin transparent film*, being bred of
  - *Apoda*; without feet (*Maggots* or *Worms* that are
    - *Bigger*; (habit and breed, having *four wings*; whether such as are
      - *Favificous*; or making of *Combs*, in which multitudes of them do co-
        - *Beneficial*; by their gathering of *Hony and Wax* from *Plants*; ‖ either that which is of a more *oblong figure*, the males of which (called *Drones*) are without *stings*, being commonly preserved in *Gardens*: or that which is more *short, thick and hairy*, living *Apis. Bombilius.*

          1. $\begin{cases}\text{BEE, }Drone, Hive, Comb. \text{ (more wildly in lesser swarms.)}\\ \text{HUMBLE-BEE.}\end{cases}$

          Hurtful; by their destroying of *fruits, Bees, &c.* being of an *oblong figure*, and a *yellow colour*; ‖ either the *less*, of a *lighter yellow*: or the *greater*, of a *deeper yellow*. *Vespa. Crabro.*

          2. $\begin{cases}\text{WASP.}\\ \text{HORNET.}\end{cases}$

      - *Not favificous*; having (*Wasps.*)
        - *Four wings*; whether, such as in their shapes resemble *Bees* or *Wasps.*

          3. $\begin{cases}\text{BEE-LIKE FLY.}\\ \text{WASP-LIKE FLY.}\end{cases}$

        - *Two wings*; ‖ whether that of a *short thick body*, of various bignesses and *colours*, proceeding from an *oblong round Aurelia*, feeding on *flesh*: or that of a *yellowish colour*, and *longer legs*, feeding in *dung*. *Musca carnaria. Musca stercoraria.*

          4. $\begin{cases}\text{FLESH FLY.}\\ \text{DUNG FLY.}\end{cases}$

    - *Lesser*; living *gregariously*; ‖ either that of an *oblong body*, with a *deep incisure*, having *four wings*, of which there are many that at sometimes are without *wings*: or that of a more *slender body*, a *tuft on the head*, living near *watery places*, having but *two wings*. *Formica. Culex.*

      5. $\begin{cases}\text{ANT, }Emmet, Pismire.\\ \text{GNAT.}\end{cases}$

  - *Pedata*; having *six feet*; whether those of
    - *Broad wings*; ‖ either that which hath a *great head, a long strait proboscis* lying under the *belly*, making a loud noise, by the help of two stiffe *membranes* that are upon his *breast*: or that which hath a near resemblance to a *Butterfly*, in respect of the largeness of the *wings*, but (only they are *not farinaceous* or *erect*). *Cicada. Musca papilionacea.*

      6. $\begin{cases}\text{CICADA.}\\ \text{PAPILIONACEOUS FLY.}\end{cases}$

    - *Narrow wings*; being bred out of the *water*; ‖ either of a *naked hexapod Worm*: or of *one* that lives *in a case*, to which little sticks and straws do adhere. *Libella. Snicauda.*

      7. $\begin{cases}\text{DRAGON FLY, }Bolts-head.\\ \text{MAY FLY.}\end{cases}$

    - *Long legs*; having but *two wings*.

      8. CRANE FLY. *Shepheards fly.*

- *Farinaceous wings*; being covered with a *mealy substance* easily coming off upon a touch, which in the *Microscope* appears to consist of small *downy feathers*, as the most ingenuous Mr. *Hook* hath first discovered; whether such whose *wings* in the usual posture are
  - *Erected*; standing upright upon their *backs*, being of great variety for *colours* and *magnitudes*, distinguishable into these two common kinds, *Papilio. Phalæna.*

    9. $\begin{cases}\text{BUTTERFLY.} \text{ (such as appear }by day,\text{ or }by night.\\ \text{MOTH.} \text{ (strong, and the }tail\text{ more broad.)}\end{cases}$

  - *Compressed*; lying more flat on the *body*, the *wings* being more *short and* *Predatrix.*

    10. HAWK BUTTERFLY.

V. SHEA-

V. SHEATHED WINGED INSECTS, commonly called *Beetles* or *Scarabs*, may be distributed into such, whose coverings are more Thick, *strong and horny*; whether those that are accounted

Horned; having either

One *horn*; the *greater*, the *biggest of this tribe*, the *horn* turning downwards: or the *lesser*, being one of the *smallest of this tribe*, having *Antennæ* on each side of his *snout* or *horn*, which together represent the *Greek* letter ψ, breeding amongst and devouring Corn.
1. { RHINOCEROTE.
     { WEEVILL.

Two horns;

Stiffe, without *joynts*; whether *branched* like those of a *Stagg* : or
2. { STAG BEETLE. (not *branched* like those of a *Bull*.
     { BULL FLY BEETLE.

Limber, and with joints; improperly called *horns*, being *Antennæ* or *feelers*; ‖ either that whose *Antennæ* are very long and reversed over his back : or that which hath *knobbed feelers* not so long.
3. { GOAT-CHAFER.
     { KNOBBED HORN'D BEETLE.

Not horned;

Terrestrial; having

Longer coverings for their *wings*;

The *greater*;

Of a *dark blackish colour*; whether that which is most *common*: or that other of near resemblance to this, having *serrate legs*, using to roul *Dung* into little balls, by working backwards
4. { COMMON BEETLE. (with his *hinder feet*.
     { DUNG BEETLE.

Of a *lighter colour*; ‖ either that of a *russet colour*, living in *Trees*, having a long sharp *tail*, extended beyond the *wings* : or that
5. { DORR, *Grey Beetle*. (of a *shining green*, feeding on *Roses*.
     { GREEN CHAFER.

The *lesser*; ‖ either that of a *long slender body*, frequent about houses, making a noise like the *minute* of a *Watch*, by striking the bottom of *his breast* against his *belly* : or that of a more *short round figure*, living in the *fields*, being either wholly *red*, or
6. { DEATH WATCH. (sometimes spotted with *black*
     { LADY-COW.

Shorter *coverings*; not reaching half the length of their *bodies*, which are long and slender, having forked *tails*, which they turn up in their defence ; ‖ the *greater* which is *black* : or the *less* which
7. { STAPHILINUS. (is of a *reddish colour*
     { EARWIGG.

Aquatic; ‖ either the *greater*, living *under water*, having the *hinder pair of legs longer for swimming*, being said to fly out of the *water* sometimes in the *night* : or the *less* of a *gibbous round shining back*,
8. { GREAT WATER SCARAB. (playing *on the top of the water*.
     { LESS WATER SCARAB.

Thin, *weak and flexile*; of more *oblong bodies*; ‖ either that which is of a *green, gilded, shining colour*, used for *Causticks* : or that which shines
9. { CANTHARIS. (in the night.
     { GLOW WORM FLY.

V. SHEATHED WINGED INSECTS.

Rhinoceros.
Scarabæus nasi-cornis.

Cervus volans.
Buceros.

Capricornus.
Scarabæus Antennis nodosis.

Scarabæus vulgaris.
Scarabæus Pilularis.

Scarabæus Arboreus.

Scarabæus domesticus.
Scarabæus punctatus.

Staphilinus.
Forficula.

Scarabæus aquat. major.
Scarabæus aquat. minor.

Cicindela.

VI. The

Of Exanguious Animals.   Part. II.

VI. CRU-STACEOUS EXANGUI-OUS ANIMALS.

VI. The greater sort of EXANGUIOUS ANIMALS being CRUSTACEOUS, may be distributed into such whose figure is more *oblong*;

The *greater*; having

Naked shells; of a *dark brown colour*; || either that which hath four pair of *legs*, and *two great claws*: or that which hath *no claws*, but five pair of *legs*, the *feelers* somewhat *compressed*, being *thorny on the back*.

Astacus. Locusta marina.
1. { LOBSTER.
     LONG OISTER.

Downy shell; having a *broad head*, with two *short, broad, laminate prominencies* from it, five pair of *legs*, and *no claws*.

Ursus marinus.
2. SEA BEAR.

The *lesser*; living in

Fresh water; *resembling a Lobster*, but much *less*, of a *hard shell*.

Astacus fluviatilis.
3. CRAYFISH, Crevice.

Salt water; having a *thinner shell*, being of a pale flesh colour; || either that of a *sharper tail*, the two *fore-legs* being *hooked* and not *forcipate*: or that which hath a *broader longer tail*, with two purple spots upon it, being the greater.

Squilla. Squilla Mantis.
4. { SHRIMP, *Prawn*.
     SQUILLA MANTIS.

Shells of other Sea Fishes; having besides two *claws*, and two pair of *legs* hanging out of the *shell*, two other pair of soft hairy *legs* within the *shell*.

Cancellus.
5. HERMIT FISH, *Souldier Fish*.

Roundish; comprehending the *Crab-kind*, whose *bodies* are somewhat *compressed*, having generally *shorter tails folded to their bellies*.

The *Greater*; having

Thick, strong, short claws; the latter of which hath *serrate prominencies on the side of the claws*, somewhat resembling the *Comb of a Cock*.

Cancer vulgaris. Cancer Heraclioticus.
6. { COMMON CRABB.
     SEA COCK.

Slender claws; || either that of a *longer body*, having *two horns between his eyes*, being *rough* on the *back* and *red* when alive: or that whose upper *shell* doth *extend beyond his body*, having a *long stiffe tail*.

Cancer majus. Cancer moluccensis.
7. { CANCER MAJUS.
     MOLUCCA CRAB.

The *Lesser*; resembling

A *Common Crab*; but being much less.
8. LITTLE CRABB.

A *Spider*; whether that which is somewhat more *oblong* in the body, having a *long snout*: or that whose *body* is *round*.

Aranea marina. Aranea crustacea.
9. { SEA SPIDER.
     CRUSTACEOUS SPIDER.

VII. TESTA-

Chap. V.   *Of Exanguious Animals.*   129

VII. TESTACEOUS TURBINATED exanguious ANIMALS, may be diſtributed into ſuch as are   *VII. TESTA-CEOUS TURBINA-TED ANI-MALS.*

More properly ſo called; whether ſuch whoſe *ſpiral convolutions*
Do appear on the outſide; being either

Not produced; but equal on both ſides; ‖ either the *Greater*, having ſeveral *Diaphragms perforated*, the *Animal* within ſomewhat reſembling a *Polypus*: or the *Leſs*, being of a *dark red colour*, and found in *freſh water*.

1. ⎨ NAUTILUS.
   ⎩ WATER-SNAIL.

Produced; whether

More ſhort in the *ſpiral production*, conſiderable for having a *Purple juice*; heretofore uſed in *Dying*, the *ſhells* being either *knobbed* or *thorny*; ‖ either that whoſe *ſhell* is very *large and thick*, being the *ſtrongeſt* and *heavieſt of this kind*, having a *long aperture*: or that which hath a *roundiſh aperture*, with a *neb* or beak *at one ſide of it*.

2. ⎨ MUREX.
   ⎩ PURPURA.

Long aperture; ‖ either that whoſe *turbinated part is almoſt plain*, and the *part not turbinated*, *much produced*, ſomewhat like a *Cylinder*: or that which is of a *great bigneſs*, having *ſeven ſtrong furrowed prominencies from one ſide of the aperture*.

3. ⎨ CYLINDROIDES.
   ⎩ APORRHAIS.

Roundiſh aperture; ‖ either that which is more *prominent*, having more *revolutions*: or that which is more *compreſſed*, having *fewer revolutions*, many of them having a *knob* by the *aperture*.

4. ⎨ SEA SNAIL.
   ⎩ NERITES.   *Cochlea.*

More oblong; always ending in a ſharp point, having either a more *Prominent baſe*; ‖ either the *Greater*: or the *Leſſer*.

5. ⎨ BUCCINUM.
   ⎩ TURBO.

Flat baſe; *broad* and *round*, being neareſt to the figure of a *Cone*; the *greater*: or the *leſſer*, whoſe *baſe is leſs flat*.

6. ⎨ TROCHUS.
   ⎩ PERIWINKLE, *Welke*.

Do not appear on the outſide; but are within the ſhell, having long apertures; ‖ either that whoſe *aperture* is more *narrow*, being *furrowed* on either ſide: or that whoſe *aperture* is ſomewhat *wider*, not furrowed on the ſides of it.

7. ⎨ VENUS SHELL.
   ⎩ PERSIAN SHELL.   *Concha Veneris. Concha Perſica.*

Leſs properly ſo called; being of near affinity to the *Univalvs*, the *inſide* having a *pearl-like ſhining colour*, with ſeveral *holes* on one ſide, being at one end on the outſide ſomewhat *turbinated*.

8. SEA EAR.   *Auris marina.*

S   VIII. EXAN-

Of Exanguious Animals. Part. II.

VIII. TESTACEOUS ANIMALS NOT TURBINATED.

VIII. EXANGUIOUS TESTACEOUS ANIMALS NOT TURBINATED, may be diſtributed into ſuch as are

Univalve ; having but one *ſhell* ; whether being

Unmoved ; ſticking faſt to *Rocks* or other things; ‖ whether that whoſe *convexity* doth ſomewhat reſemble a ſhort *obtuſe* angled *cone*, having *no hole* at the *top* : or that which is of an *oblong figure*, ſomewhat *Cylindrical*, fixed at the bottom to the place where firſt it was bred, with (*an aperture at the top.*)

Patella. — 1. { LIMPET.
Balanus. — { CENTER FISH.

Moveable ; ‖ either that of a *Spherical figure* ſomewhat *compreſſed*, full *of prickles*, having one large round *aperture* at the bottom, and another *ſmall aperture* oppoſite to it : or that which is of a more *oblong figure*, a *tender ſhell*, having *two apertures* on the ſame *ſide*.

Echinus. — 2. { BUTTON-FISH.
Echinus ſpatagus. — { MERMAIDS HEAD.

Bivalve ; having two *ſhells* ; whether more

Roundiſh ; ſuch whoſe outſides are

Smooth ; ‖ whether that of a *larger thicker ſhell*, of a *pearl-like ſhining*, whoſe inward part towards the joynt, doth end in a narrow *ſinue* or *cavity* : or that which is *whitiſh* on the *outſide*.

Concha margaritifera. — 3. { MOTHER OF PEARL.
Galades. — { GALADES.

Rough ; ‖ either that whoſe *joynt* is more *narrow*, having no *prominences* in the inſide of it : or that whoſe *joynt* is more *broad*, with *two prominencies* and *two correſpondent cavities* in each *ſhell*.

Oſtrea. — 4. { OYSTER.
Spondylus. — { PONDYL.

Furrowed ; ‖ either the *bigger* ; having one or two *ear-like prominencies* on the *outſide* towards the *joynt* : or the *leſſ*, having no ſuch prominencies.

Pecten. — 5. { SCOLLOP.
Pectunculus. — { COCKLE.

Oblong ; conſiderable for being

Leſſ long ; and neareſt to the *round* kind, being ſmooth, and having *thin ſhells* ; ‖ either the *greater*, of a *flattiſh* and *compreſſed figure* : or the *leſſer*, being ſomewhat of a *triangular figure*, having the edges (*of the ſhell* indented.)

Chama. — 6. { CHAMA.
Tellina. — { TELLINA.

More long ; whether ſuch as are

Of a dark blackiſh colour on the outſide ; ‖ either the *greater*, which from a *joynt* at one end more acute and ſlender, doth grow out to a great length, becoming broad at the other end, having a *ſilk-like ſubſtance* within the *ſhell* : or the *leſſ*, of which one kind hath the *joynt* at the end, and is commonly eaten, the other hath the (*joynt* on the ſide.)

Pinna. — 7. { PINNA.
Muſculus. — { MUSCLE.

Not cloſed exactly in all parts of their ſhells ; ‖ either that which lyes *in holes* in a kind of *marle* at the bottom of the *Sea*, having an *aperture* near the *joynt*, and a *little hook* in the *inſide* : or that which is open at both ends, being the *longeſt* of all the reſt, in proportion to (its bigneſs.)

Pholas. — 8. { PHOLAS.
Solen. — { SHEATH-FISH, *Razor-fiſh*

Growing by a neck to other things ; whoſe *ſhell* conſiſts of *five parts*, commonly (though falſly) ſaid to produce a *Bird*, being of a *triangular figure*.

Bernicla. — 9. BARNICLE.

IX. SOFT

Chap. V. *Of Exanguious Animals.*

IX. SOFT EXANGUIOUS ANIMALS, may be diftributed into such as are

- *More Perfect*; having *mouthes* like the *beaks of Birds*, with *eight ftringy fubftances* about them ferving inftead of *legs*, their *bodies* conteining a *black liquor like Ink*; whether thofe whofe *bodies* are more
  - *Obround*; having
    - No *Antennæ*; or *feelers*, and being *without any bone*; ‖ either the *greateft*, growing to a *vaft magnitude*: or the *lefs*, whofe *legs* are longer in proportion, being of a *fweet fent*.
      1. { POURCONTREL, *Preke, Polypus.*
         SWEET POLYPUS. *Polypus. Bolitana.*
    - *Antennæ*; ‖ either the *greater*, with a great, thick, foft, not *pellucid bone* in the *body*: or the *leffer*, which is without fuch a *bone*, having *fmall roundifh flapps* on either fide of the *body*.
      2. { CUTTLE FISH.
         LESSER CUTTLE. *Sepia, Sepiola Rondeletii.*
  - *Oblong*; ‖ either that of *longer Antennæ* with *triangular flaps*, having a *long pellucid bone refembling a Sword*: or that of *fhorter Antennæ*, having the *triangular flaps* nearer the *tail*, being of a *reddifh colour*.
    3. { SLEVE.
       REDDISH SLEVE. *Loligo. Loligo rubra.*
- *Lefs perfect*; counted *Zoophytes*, as being betwixt *Plants* and *Animals*; whether fuch as have
  - *More diftinction of parts*; ‖ either that which hath fome *refemblance to a Hare*: or that which hath fome *refemblance to a naked black Snail*, without *horns*.
    4. { SEA HARE.
       HOLOTHURIUS. *Lepus. Holothurius.*
  - *Lefs diftinction of parts*;
    - *Pellucid*; being a kind of *Gelly*, roundifh at the top, marked with *reddifh lines* in the *form of a Starr*, or *Rofe*, having feveral kinds of *rays* like *legs*, proceeding from the middle of it.
      5. BLUBBER. *Palmo marinus.*
    - *Not pellucid*; ufually fticking to other things; ‖ either that which is of *various figures*, being covered with *a hard callous skin*, conteining an *efculent pulpy fubftance*: or that which is of a flefhy confiftence, having *no hard skin*, being of various *fhapes* and bigneffes, fome of them ftinging the *hand* upon the touch.
      6. { TETHYA.
         SEA NETTLE. *Tethya. Urtica marina.*

Of Fish.

§. III.   FISH may be diſtributed into ſuch as are
- *Viviparous*; and ſkinned; whoſe figure is either
  - OBLONG and roundiſh.   I.
  - FLAT or thick.   II.
- *Oviparous*; whether ſuch as do generally belong to
  - *Salt water*; to be further diſtinguiſhed by their
    - *Finns on the back*; whether ſuch, the *rays* of whoſe *finns* are
      - *Wholly ſoft* and flexile.   III.
      - *Partly ſoft*, and partly *ſpinous*; having
        - TWO FINNS on the back.   IV.
        - But ONE FINN.   V.
    - *Figure*; whether
      - OBLONG.   VI.
      - FLAT.   VII.
    - CRUSTACEOUS COVERING.   VIII.
  - *Freſh water*; being ſcaly.   IX.

I. VIVIPA-   I. VIVIPAROUS OBLONG FISH, may be diſtributed into ſuch as
ROUS OB-   are
LONG FISH.
- *Cetaceous*; breeding their young within them, having *lungs* and no *gills*, and but *one pair of finns*; ‖ either the *greateſt of all living Creatures*, of which there are ſeveral *ſpecies*, one without *teeth* or a *tube* to caſt *water*, another with *teeth* and ſuch a *tube*, and another with a large long *horn* : or that other *Fiſh* of a *leſs magnitude*, which is *gregarious*, often *appearing above water*.

Balæna.   1. { WHALE.
Delphinus.   { PORPOISE, *Dolphin.*

- *Cartilagineous*; ſaid to *hatch* their young ones within their *bellies*, whoſe mouths are placed under their *noſes*; whether ſuch as are more
  - *Proper to the Sea*; having generally a double *Penis*, *wide mouths*, and five *apertures* on each ſide inſtead of *Gills*; to be further diſtinguiſhed by their having
    - *Long ſnouts* or *prominencies*; ‖ either in the faſhion of a *Saw :* or in the figure of a *ſword*, being without thoſe apertures on the ſide, common to the reſt.

Priſtis.   2. { SAW-FISH.
Xiphias.   { SWORD-FISH.

- *Rows of very ſharp teeth*; ‖ the *Greater :* or the *Leſſer.*

Canis carcha-   3. { SHARKE.
rias.   { GLAUCUS.
Glaucus.

- *Lips rough like a File*, but *without teeth*; ‖ the *Greater :* or the *Leſſer.*

Muſtelus lævis.   4. { HOUND-FISH.
Aſterias.   { SPOTTED HOUND-FISH.

- *Thorns on their backs*; ‖ either *joyning to* the former part of the *Finns :* or obliquely *croſſing the rays of the finn.*

Galeus ſpinax.   5. { THORNBACK DOG.
Centrina.   { HOG-FISH.

The

Chap. V.   *Of Fish.*   133

⎧ *The aperture of their mouths, nearer to their noses* then any of the
⎨ other sorts of *Dog-fish*; and being spotted; ‖ either with *large*
⎩ *black spots*: or with *smaller spots*.
     6. ⎧ GREATER DOG-FISH.   *Catulus ma-*
         ⎩ LESSER DOG-FISH.   *jor.*
⎧ *A head like* the head of *a Crutch*, with the *eyes* at the ends of the   *Catulus mi-*
⎨ *transverse*, growing to a vast bigness: or having a very *long slen-*   *nor.*
⎩ *der tail.*
     7. ⎧ ZYGÆNA.   *Zygæna:*
         ⎩ FOX.   *Vulpecula.*
⎧ *Common to salt and fresh water;* having *gills*, but no *teeth*, their *mouths*
⎨ being placed under their *noses*; ‖ either that whose *body* is *penta-*
⎨ *gonous*, having *five rows of bonny lamins*, not properly *scales*, *four*
⎩ *strings* hanging before the *mouth*: or that which is more *round*.
     8. ⎧ STURGEON.   *Acipenser.*
         ⎩ HUSO.   *Huso.*

II. VIVIPAROUS CARTILAGINEOUS FISH; whose *bodies* are II. VIVIPA-
not long and round, may be distributed into such as are   ROUS FISH
⎧ *Flat* and *broad*; distinguishable by some peculiarity in their parts, as to   NOT LONG
⎨ *Length*; of the   AND
⎨ ⎧ *Tail*; being either   ROUND.
⎨ ⎨ ⎧ *Spinous*; having a *sharp serrated thorn on the tail* counted vene-
⎨ ⎨ ⎨ mous; ‖ either that whose *snout is less* or *more prominent*.
⎨ ⎨ ⎩ 1. ⎧ PASTINACA.   *Pastinaca.*
⎨ ⎨   ⎩ AQUILA.   *Aquila.*
⎨ ⎨ ⎧ *Not spinous*; ‖ either that whose *back is smooth*: or *thorny*.
⎨ ⎨ ⎩ 2. ⎧ FLARE.   *Raia Lævis.*
⎨ ⎩   ⎩ THORNBACK.   *Raia clavata.*
⎨ ⎧ *Snout*; being sharp; ‖ either that whose *body is shorter* in propor-
⎨ ⎨ tion to the breadth: or that whose *body is longer*.
⎨ ⎩ 3. ⎧ RAIA OXYZYNCHOS, *Maid*.
⎨   ⎩ SQUATINO-RAIA.
⎨ ⎧ *Breadth of the head*; having a *thick short tail* in the fashion of a *Bat-*
⎨ ⎨ *tledore*; ‖ either that which hath *five purple spots on the back*: or
⎨ ⎨ that which hath *one round aperture for each gill*, a vast *mouth*, with
⎨ ⎨ *stringy substances* on his *head* and *back*.
⎨ ⎩ 4. ⎧ CRAMP-FISH.   *Torpedo.*
⎨   ⎩ SEA-DIVEL.   *Rana pisca-*
⎨ ⎧ *Situation of the mouth*; which opens *at the end of the snout*, and not *trix.*
⎨ ⎨ underneath, as the rest of this *tribe*, having a more *oblong body*, and
⎨ ⎨ a very *rough skin*, with *finny substances*, standing out from each side
⎨ ⎩ like *wings*.
⎨   5. SCATE, *Angel-fish*.   *Squatina.*
⎩ *Thick and short*; ‖ either that which hath *no tail*, but resembles the *head*
   of a *Fish* cut off, with *one tooth in each jaw*, and *one hole for each gill:*
   or that which is of *a reddish colour* and *spinous*.
     6. ⎧ MOLE.   *Mola.*
         ⎩ LUMP.   *Lumpus.*

                                          III. OVI-

Of Fish. Part. II.

III. OVIPA- III. OVIPAROUS FISH, whose back FINNS are wholly soft and
ROUS FISH *flexile*, may be distinguished into such as have
of FLEXILE
FINNS.
    Three such soft finns on their backs; namely the *Cod-kind*, which use to
    be preserved for humane food by salting; either the
      Shorter and thicker; whether
        Larger; ‖ either that which hath a kind of *beard*: or that of a *black
        coloured back.*

Molva.   1. { COD-FISH, *Keeling.*
Asellus niger.   { COLE-FISH.

        Lesser; ‖ either that which hath a *black spot* on either side: or that
        which is of a *softer body*, having very *small scales*, being *the least* of
        this kind.

Asinum ami-   2. { HADDOCK.
quorum.   { WHITING.
Asellus mollis.

      Longer and more slender; ‖ either that whose *flesh* when salted, looks
      yellow, and is more *brittle*: or that other of near resemblance to this,
      whose *hinder finn seems to be two*, by reason of its rising up higher
      in the further part, tho it be properly but *one*.

Asellus longus.   3. { LING.
Merlucius.   { HAAK, *Poor John.*

    Two soft flexile finns; either the
      Bigger; whether the
        Tunny kind; having very *small scales*, scarce discernable, with seve-
        ral *pinnulæ* both above and below, besides their *finns*, being of a
        shining blew on the *back*, and a *silver colour* on the *belly and sides*;
        the
          Larger; ‖ either that which hath *no streaks* on the *sides*: or that
          which hath *oblique transverse streaks* from *head* to *tail.*

Thynnus.   4. { TUNNY.
Pelamis.   { PELAMIS.

          Lesser; having *oblique transverse streaks* more *undulated.*
Scombrus.   5. MACKEREL.

      Flying fish; having large spotted *finns* like *wings*, with two *long strong
      thorns* behind the *head*: to which may be adjoined for its affinity
      in flying, that other *Fish*, which hath but *one soft finn* on the *back*,
      with *large scales* near his *tail.*

Milvus.   6. { KITE-FISH.
Hirundo Pli-   { SWALLOW-FISH.
nii.

    Least kind; distinguishable by their having
      The lower pair of finns connected; ‖ latter having a *shorter head*, and
      more *tumid jaws.*

Gobius mari-   7. { SEA GUDGEON.
nus.   { PAGANELLUS.

      *The rays of the former finn on the back, rising up much higher then
      the membrane which connects them*; ‖ either that whose former
      pair of *finns* are *connected*: or that which hath a *hole instead
      of gills*, whose *eyes* stand more *close together.*

     8. { JOTO.
        { DRACUNCULUS.

    Little black spots in the figure of Lozenges.
     9. APHUA GOBITES.

One

Chap. V.   *Of Fish.*   135

lOne *soft flexile finn*; diftinguifhable by their
- *Being of the Herring kind*; namely *scaly*, without *teeth*, of a *bright silver colour* on the *belly*, and a *dark shining colour* on the *back*, prefently dying when taken out of the *water*, having generally a *row of sharp prickles* under the *belly*; whether the
  - *Larger*;
    - *More common*; being *gregarious*, fwimming together in great multitudes; || the *greater* : or the *lesser*.
      10. {SHERRING, Sprat.
      {PILCHARD.   *Harengus major. Harengus minor.*
    - *Less common*; being fomewhat *bigger* and *flatter* then a *Herring*, with feveral *black spots* on the *sides*, coming up into *Rivers*.
      11. SHAD.   *Clupea.*
  - *Lesser*; || either that which is more *proper to falt water*, being *long* and *roundish*, having the *upper mandible* much more produced then the other: or that which lives in *Lakes*, being of a *broader figure* then the former.
    12. {ANCHOVY.
    {CHALCIS, *Sarda*.   *Encrasicholus.*
- *Being of the Horn-fish kind*; having a *longer slender body* and a *long snout*; || either that which is more known and *common in Europe*, having one *finn* from the *anus* to the *tail*, and another oppofite on the *back*, the *vertebra* or *back-bone* being of a *green colour* : or that which is here *less common*, belonging to the *West-Indies*, having *no finn upon his tail*.
  13. {NEEDLE-FISH.
  {TOBACCO-PIPE-FISH.   *Acus. Petimbuaba.*
- Having between the *eyes* two *finn-like substances*; and but two or three *rays* in the lower pair of *finns*, with a *row of small teeth*, and a *fang at each end*; || either that which hath upon his *back-finn* a *beautiful spot variegated* with *rundles*; or that whofe *finn* is of an *unequal altitude*.
  14. {BLENNUS.
  {SCORPIOIDES.
- *Wanting the lower pair of finns*; || of a *deep figure*, fomewhat refembling that of a *Turbut* : or being of a *red colour*, with *large scales*, a great *flat head*, fteep from the *eyes* to the *fnout*.
  15. {STROMATEUS, *Callichthys*.
  {NOVACULA.
- Having fome *sharp teeth*; and feveral *other round broad teeth* in the *palate*, the tops of which are commonly fold for *Toad-stones*.
  16. LUPUS MARINUS SCHONFELDII.
- *Breadth or depth downwards*; || either that which hath *two long rays* extending beyond the *tail*, one from the *back*, the other from the *belly* : or that which hath but *one long ray*, like a *Bodkin*, proceeding from the *fin* on the *back*. Both *exotic Fishes*, defcribed by *Margravius*.
  17. {PARU.
  {GUAPERUA.

IV. OVI-

IV. OVIPA- ROUS FISH having one finn SPI- NOUS, and the other FLEXILE.	**IV. OVIPAROUS FISH** having two *finns* on the *back*, whereof the former is *spinous* and stiffe, and the other *soft* and *flexile*, may be distinguished into the

Bigger kind; whose figure is

   Shorter; distinguishable by their

     Having *small scales*; being *square* towards the *tail*, which is *forked*: or else being of a more *deep figure*, with the *rays* of the *fore-finn* very low, the former of them pointing towards the head.

     1. { AMIA, *Leccia Salviani*.
        { GLAUCUS.

     Having the *finns* almost *joyned*; || either that with a little *short beard* under the *chin*, being *undulated obliquely* from the *back* to the *belly* with *blewish* and *yellow streaks*: or that other of a near resemblance to this, only without a *beard*, and of a more *black colour*.

     2. { CORACINUS.
        { UMBRA.

   Longer; having a *large mouth*, with *sharp teeth*; || either that which is *spotted* when young, being very *voracious*: or that other of some resemblance to the former, having *large scales*, an *obtuse angled mouth*, with *streaks* of *black* and *white* from *head* to *tail*.

Mugil.   3. { LUPUS.
        { ENGLISH MULLET.

Lesser kind; whether such as are considerable for

   Having two or three long *prominences* like *fingers* before their lower *finns*; great bonny *heads*, large broad *finns*, called the *Gournet-kind*, to be further distinguished by their

     Colour; Red, or Grey.

Cuculus.   4. { RED GOURNET, *Rochet*.
Hirundo.   { GREY GOURNET.

     Forked snouts; by reason of two *flat prominencies* resembling *horns*; || either that of *shorter*: or that of *longer horns*, the latter of which is covered with large *bonny scales*, with *eight rows of thorns*, the *body octangular*, having but *two fingers*.

Lyra prior
Rondeletii.   5. { TUB-FISH, *Piper*.
        { LYRA ALTERA RONDELETII.

   Being of a *reddish colour*; with two long *prominencies* from the *lower jaw*, esteemed delicate food; || either the *bigger*, whose *scales* are larger and stick faster to the *skin*: or the *lesser*, whose *scales* are less, and apt to come off upon a touch.

Mullus major.   6. { TRUE MULLET.
Mullus minor.   { LESSER MULLET.

The length of their bodies; whether

   Having the *lower mandible longer* then the other, the *finns* on the *back* being at a greater *distance*: or having the *second finn* on the *back* very *small*, with a *wide mouth* like that of *a Serpent*.

     7. { SPHYRÆNA.
        { SAURUS.

Being

⸨ Being of a flattish figure; with *oblique transverse yellowish streaks*, from the *back* to the *belly*, having the *eyes* very near the *mouth*: or being more *roundish*, somewhat of the colour and figure of *Mackerel*, only a *row of prickles* on each side make it to appear quadrangular.

8. { WEAVER, *Dragon-fish*.   *Draco.*
    { TRACHURUS.

Wanting the lower pair of finns; or being of a *reddish colour, without teeth*, having the *scales* edged with short hairy *filaments*, which makes it rough to the touch.

9. { CAPRISCUS.
    { APER.

Having a long slender snout; with a strong movable *serrated thorn*, belonging to the former *finn on the back*, inclining towards the *tail* with *bonny substances* instead of the *lower finns*, the *finns* on the *back* being nearer to the *tail* then in other *Fish*: or having a strong *serrated horn* standing upright *on the head*.

10. { TRUMPET-FISH.   *Scolopax.*
     { MONOCEROS CLUSII.   *Monoceros Clusii.*

Having the mouth and eyes reversed, looking upwards: or having a *great head*, very *wide gills*, and but three *rayes* in the lower pair of *finns*, the *body* being *spotted*.

11. { URANOSCOPUS.
     { SCORPÆNA.

Being of a deep figure, without *scales*, having *on each side a broad black spot*, and long *bristles* rising up above the *rays* of the *finns*.

12. DOREE, *St. Peters fish*.   *Faber.*

Of Fish.

V. OVIPA-
ROUS·FISH
of ONE
FINN, part-
ly STIFF,
and partly
SOFT.

V. **OVIPAROUS FISH** having *one finn* on the *back*, the *rays* of which are *partly stiffe* and *spinous*, and *partly soft* and *flexile*, may be diſtinguiſhed into ſuch whoſe figure is more

⎧ *Broad*; or *deep*; whether
⎨ *European*;
⎩ *Bigger*; diſtinguiſhable by their

COLOURS; whether

Gold colour between the *eyes*, having *round ſharp teeth*, and for the moſt part a *purple ſpot* near the *gills*: or that which is of a like figure to the former, but only without this *gold colour*, being *black* about the *tail*.

Aurata.
Sparus.

1. ⎧ GILT-HEAD, *Sea-bream*.
   ⎩ SPARUS.

Streaked with yellow from *head* to *tail*; ‖ either that whoſe *ſtreaks* are more *obſcure*, being of a *ſhorter body*: or that whoſe *ſtreaks* are *more conſpicuous*, being of a *longer body*.

2. ⎧ CANTHARUS.
   ⎩ SALPA.

Streaked with a dark colour, tranſverſe the back; ‖ either that whoſe *ſtreaks* are *more obſcure*, being of a *ſhorter broader figure*, and having *broad flat teeth*: or that whoſe *ſtreaks* are *more conſpicuous*, being of a *longer body*.

3. ⎧ SARGUS.
   ⎩ MORMYLUS.

Reddiſh; on the *back* and *ſides*; ‖ either the *greater*, having a *dark ſpot* on each ſide near the *head*: or the *leſſer*, being without ſuch a *ſpot*.

4. ⎧ PAGRUS.
   ⎩ RUBELLIO.

Being ſomewhat more produced in their *bodies* then the others of this *deep kind*; ‖ either that which is *black* about the *tail*, having *great eyes*: or that of *a reddiſh colour*, with four remarkable *teeth* in *either jaw*.

5. ⎧ MELANURUS.
   ⎩ DENTEX.

Having the *finn* on the *back* ſo low in the middle, that it ſeems two, with *great heads full of prickles*, counted venemous; ‖ either the *greater*, of a *reddiſh colour*: or the *leſſer*.

Scorpius major.
Scorpius minor.

6. ⎧ GREATER SCORPION-FISH.
   ⎩ LESSER SCORPION-FISH.

Leaſt of theſe *deep fiſhes*, of a *dark colour*, with *large ſcales*, and *long ſtreaks* from *head* to *tail*.

7. CHROMIS.

Indian; deſcribed by *Margravius*; ‖ either that of a *forked tail*, having two *prickles* on the cover of *each gill*: or that which hath *broad ſpots* on either ſide.

8. ⎧ JAGURACA.
   ⎩ ACARA.

Long

Chap. V. *Of Fish.* 139

!*Long*; diftinguifhable by
- *Variety and beauty of colours*; ‖ either the *Greater*, of which there are feveral kinds, the moft beautiful of which, is called *Pavo*, the more dark, *Merula*: or the *Leffer*.

9. { SEA-THRUSH.   *Turdus.*
    { JULIS.

Dark broad ftreaks; croffing the *back*; confiderable for having
- *Heads* variegated with *red* and *blew*; ‖ either the *Greater*: or the *Leffer*, having a black fpot in the middle of the *finn* on his *back*,

10. { SEA PERCH.   *Perca marina.*
     { SACHETTUS.

The lower jaw longer then the upper; ‖ either that which is *without prickles*: or that which hath *two prickles on the cover of the gills*,

11. { PHYCIS.
     { CHAUNA.

A broad black fpot on either fide; or *very great eyes* in proportion to the *body*.

12. { MÆNAS.
     { BOOPS.

VI. OVIPAROUS FISH OF AN OBLONG FIGURE, being generally without *scales*, having *slimy skins*, apt to bend and twist with their *bodies* more then other *Fish*, may be distributed into such as are

European; being either

  Proper to Sea-water;

    Longer;

      Round; whether

        More thick; || either that which hath but *one pair of swimming finns*, and *two little horns*: or that which hath *no swimming finns*, with *four little horns*, and a *sharp snout*, the *skin variegated with yellow*.

1. { CONGER.
   { MURÆNA.

Cungrus.

        More slender; || either that which grows to a very great length, having a *wider* and *longer mouth* then an *Eel*, the *finn* not reaching the *tail*, which is round and not flat: or that which hath one *continued finn* as *Eeles*, with *four stringy prominencies* from the *lower mandible*, less round and long then the former.

Serpens marinus.

2. { SEA SERPENT.
   { OPHIDION PLINII.

      Flat; like a *Ribbon* or *Fillet*; || either the *bigger* of a *reddish colour*, having two pair of *finns*: or the *lesser*, whose *flesh is transparent*, and the *finn* on the *belly* thrice as deep as that on the *back*, having but one pair of *fins*.

3. { TÆNIA MAJOR.
   { TÆNIA MINOR.

    Shorter; || either that with *two finns on the back*, with a kind of *beard*, and instead of the *lower pair of finns*, having *two long stringy substances* cleft at the ends: or that which is of a *smaller magnitude*, having *one pair of swimming finns*, with *a forked tail*, to which the *back finn* is extended.

4. { TINCA MARINA.
   { SAND-EELS.

  Common to salt and fresh water; having a *round aperture for the mouth*, with which they suck their nourishment, and *seven holes* on each side instead of *gills*, being *Cartilagineous*, without *swimming finns*; || either the *Greater*: or the *Lesser*.

Lampetra major.
Lampetra minor.

5. { LAMPREY.
   { LAMPERN.

  Proper to fresh water; considerable for having.

    Two pair of finns; || either that which is the *biggest of this tribe*, having two very long *strings* from the *upper jaw*, and four shorter from the *lower jaw*, onely *one small finn* upon the *back*, and a long one under the *belly*: or that which is *shorter* and *thicker* then an *Eel*, with a *short beard* from his *lower mandible*, having *two finns* on the *back*, the *hinder finn* on the *back* and that under the *belly*, not being *contiguous* to the *tail*, *variegated* in the colour.

Silurus.
Mustela.

6. { SHEAT FISH, *River whale*.
   { EEL POUT.

One

Chap. V.   *Of Fish.*   141

One pair *of finns*;
    7. EEL.   *Anguilla.*
Indian; described by *Imperatus*; ‖ either that with *two long horns reversed* over the *back*: or that which hath a *flatness on his head* and part of his *back*, *in which there are* divers transverse *rimulæ* or chinks.
     8. ⎧SPADA MARINA.
        ⎩REMORA IMPERATI.

    VII. PLAIN or flat FISH, being *oviparous* and *bonny*, both whose   VII. OVI-
eyes are on the same side of the flat, and the *mouth transverse*, swimming   PAROUS
broadwise, are either   PLAIN
                                                                                         FISH.
⎧*Oblong*; and *squamous*;
⎪   *Greater*; having the *mouth* on the *right side of the eyes*; ‖ either
⎪   that which is *not spotted*: or that which *is spotted*.
⎪   ⎧COMMON SOLE.   *Solea.*
⎪   1. ⎩SPOTTED SOLE.   *Solea oculata.*
⎪   *Lesser*; having the *mouth on the left side of the eyes*, having bigger
⎨   *scales*.
⎪   2. POLE.   *Cynoglossus.*
⎪*Quadrate*;
⎪   *Greater*; ‖ either that of a *grey marble* colour, *spinous*, having the
⎪   *eyes on the right side*: or that which hath the *eyes on the left side*,
⎪   being the biggest of this *Tribe*.
⎪   ⎧TURBUT.   *Rhombus.*
⎪   3. ⎩HALIBUT.
⎪*Middle kind*; being of a *dark grey*, and full of *small asperities*.
⎪   4. BRETT.
⎩*Lesser kind*; ‖ either that of a *sandy reddish colour*, without *scales* or
      asperities, having the *eyes on the left side*: or that which is *reddish*,
      squamous, and with *black spots*.
          ⎧PLAIS.   *Passer.*
     5. ⎩FLOUNDER, *Fluke*.   *Passer niger.*

VIII. FISHES

VIII. FISHES OF A HARD CRUSTACEOUS SKIN, may be distributed into such as are for the figure of them, either

- *Spherical*; having two *broad teeth* like those of men; whether
  - *Without thorns*; ‖ either that which hath a more *prominent mouth*, and a *bonny breast*: or that which is encompassed with very *short hairs*, close (set.
    1. { ORBIS SCUTATUS, *Globe-fish*.
       { ORBIS HIRSUTUS.
  - *With thorns*; or *prickles*; ‖ either *streight*: or *hooked*.
    2. { ORBIS MURICATUS.
       { ORBIS ECHINATUS.
- *Angular*; whether such as are more
  - *Perfect*; either
    - *Triangular*; being *variegated* with *angular figures* on the *body*; ‖ either that which is *without horns*: or *with horns*.
      3. { TRIANGULAR FISH.
         { TRIANGULAR FISH HORNED.
    - *Pentagonal*; or of a *five angled figure*, encompassed with *pentagonal*
      4. HOLOSTEUS. (*bonny scales*.
  - *Imperfect*; for which reason they are by some reckoned amongst *Insects*, having *tubes*, with a kind of *valve*, *instead of mouths*; ‖ either that which is more *oblong*, of an *Hexangular* figure to the end of the *finn* on the *back*, and after *quadrangular*: or that whose *body* is of an *Heptangular* figure *in the former part*, and *quadrangular in the hinder part*, being *spinous*, the *head having some resemblance to that of a Horse*.
    5. { ACUS ARISTOTELIS.
       { HIPPOCAMPUS.
- *RADIATE*; in the form of the *Rays* of a *Starr*.
  6. STARR-FISH.

Piscis triangularis.
Piscis triangularis cornutus.

Stella piscis.

IX. SQUAMOUS RIVER FISH, may be distributed into such as are

- *Bigger*; whether (either
  - *Voracious*; whose *scales* are set together either
    - *More loose*; being generally bigger, such as have on their *backs*
      - *One finn*; placed near the *tail*, with *wide mouths*, and *sharp long teeth*, every other of which is moveable.
        1. PIKE, *Jack*, *Pickerel*.
      - *Two finns*; the hindermost of which is *small*, *fleshy* and *without rays*, having generally *teeth*, which may be stiled the *Trout-kind*, comprehending such as are.
        - *Common to fresh and salt water*; ‖ either the *biggest*, of a *reddish flesh*: or the *least*, of a *white flesh*, and *violaceous smell*.
          2. { SALMON.
             { SMELT.
        - *Proper to fresh water*; whether
          - *Spotted*; the *Greater*: or the *Lesser*, living in *Lakes*.
            3. { TROUT.
               { CHARR.
          - *Not spotted*; considerable for being
            - *More round*; ‖ either that which is streaked from *head* to *tail*, having the *finn* on the *back* bigger and broader then in *Trouts*: or that having a *long snout*.
              4. { GRAYLING.
                 { UMBER.

Lucius.

Salmo.
Violacea.

Truita.
Carpio.

Thymallus.
Oxyrynchus.

More

More broad; and *compressed*, of a *small mouth, without teeth*; ‖ the *Greater*, somewhat like a *Herring*: or the *Lesser*.

5. { FARRA.
{ LAVARETTUS.

More close; and *compact*; being generally *less scales* in proportion then the others, having a *wide mouth*, without *teeth*, but *asperities analogous to teeth*, comprehending the *Perch-kind*, of which in sundry *Countries* there are several varieties, distinguishable by their *bigness* or *littleness*, *thickness* or *slenderness*. But the two principal kinds to which the others may be reduced, are ‖ either such as have *two finns* on the *back*, the first *spinous*, and the other *soft*, with transverse *black streaks* on the *side*, being commonly the *bigger*: or but *one finn*, which is partly *spinous*, and partly *soft*, being of a *yellowish colour*, and commonly

6. { PERCH.   (*lesser*. *Perca*.
{ RUFFE.   *Perca aurata*.

Not voracious; comprehending the *Carp-kind*, wch have *one finn* on the *back*, *no teeth* in their *mouth*, but only in the *orifice* of their *stomacks*, over which *teeth* there is a kind of *stone* or *bone*, for the most part of a *triangular figure*, by affriction against which, they grind their food; *Bigger*; comprehending such as delight more in   (whether the *Standing waters*; ‖ either that whose *scales* are *larger*, and *more loose*, the *first ray* of the *finn* being strong and serrate, having *four stringy prominencies from the upper lip*: or that whose *scales* are *less* and *more compact*, being very *slimy*, of a *greenish colour*, the lower pair of *finns* in the *male* being more thick and fleshy.

7. { CARPE.   *Cyprinus*.
{ TENCH.   *Tinca*.

Running waters; whether such as are more
Thick and round; ‖ either that which hath *four stringy prominencies* resembling *a beard*: or that which hath *a great head*.

8. { BARBLE.   *Barbus*.
{ CHUB, *Chevin*.   *Capito*.

Broad and deep; ‖ either the *most broad*: or that which is *less broad*, having commonly *red eyes and finns*.

9. { BREAM.   *Abramis*.
{ ROCHE.   *Rubellio*.

Lesser; floating usually towards the *top* of the *water*; ‖ either that which is more thick, of some resemblance to a little *Chub*: or that

10. { DARE, *Dace*.   (which is more compressed and thin, *Leuciscus*.
{ BLEAK, *Blea*.   *Alburnus*.

Least kind of River Fishes; whether such as live more towards the *Lower parts of the water*, near the *ground*: either such as have on the *back One finn*, with a kind of *beard* on the *mouth*; ‖ the *greater*: or the *lesser*.

11. { GUDGEON.   *Gobio*.
{ LOACH, *Groundling*. *Gobius barbatus*.

Two finns; with a *large broad head*.

12. BULL-HEAD, *Millers-Thumb, Gull*.   *Gobio Capitatus*.

Upper parts of the water; or near *banks*; ‖ either that which hath but *one finn* on the *back*, being smooth: or that which hath *two finns*, being prickly, having *three strong prickles* on either side, and a kind of

13. { MINNOW.   (Armature consisting of *four* or *five Lamina* *Phoxinus*.
{ BANSTICLE, *Stickleback*.   *Pungitius*.

Of Birds.

§ IV. BIRDS may be diftinguifhed by their ufual place of living, their food, bignefs, fhape, ufe and other qualities, into
- *Terreftrial*; living chiefly on *dry land*; whether
  - CARNIVOROUS; feeding chiefly on *Flefh*. I.
  - PHYTIVOROUS; feeding on *Vegetables*; whether
    - Of *fhort round wings*; lefs fit for flight. II.
    - Of *long wings*, and fwifter flight; having their *Bills*; either more
      - LONG AND SLENDER; comprehending the *Pidgeon* and *Thrufh-kind*, III.
      - SHORT AND THICK; comprehending the *Bunting* and *Sparrow-kind*. IV.
  - *Infectivorous*; feeding chiefly on *Infects*; (tho feveral of them do likewife fometimes feed on *Seeds*) having *flender ftreight bills* to thruft into holes, for the pecking out of *Infects*; whether the
    - GREATER KIND. V.
    - LEAST KIND. VI.
- *Aquatic*; living either
  - About and NEAR WATERY PLACES. VII.
  - *In waters*; whether
    - FISSIPEDES; having the *toes of their feet* divided. VIII.
    - PALMIPEDES; having the *toes of their feet* united by a membrane. IX.

I. CARNIVOROUS BIRDS.

I. CARNIVOROUS BIRDS, may be diftinguifhed into fuch as are either
- *Rapacious*; living upon the prey of other *Animals*, having *hooked beaks and talons*, amongft which the *females* are generally more large ftrong and fierce.
  - *Diurnal*; preying in the day time.
    - The bigger and *ftronger kind*; noted either for *quick Sight*, or *Sent*; the latter of which is by *Gefner* diftinguifhed from the former, that the *beak* of it, doth not grow crooked immediately from the root, but only at the end or tip of it.
      - 1. { FAGLE. *Aquila.*
           { VULTUR. *Vultur.*
    - The *middle kind*; being either made ufe of and *trained up by Men* for the catching of other *Birds*, of which there are great varieties, diftinguifhable by their manner of *flight, bignefs, fhape, the Birds they prey upon*, &c. or fuch others as are of near affinity to thefe, but *not* commonly *ufed to this purpofe.*
      - 2. { HAWK. *Accipiter.*
           { KITE, *Buzzard, Glede*, *Milvus.*

| !*The least kind*; the former having *prominent nostrils*, being well known by his *voice*: the other with a *processus on the outside of the upper mandible*.

3. {CUCKOO.   *Cuculus.*
   {BUTCHER BIRD.   *Lanius.*

Nocturnal; preying in the night, having *broad faces*, and *great eyes*; ‖ of which, some have *tufts of feathers* standing out *like* long ears, or *horns*: others being *without such tufts*.

4. {OWL HORNED.   *Bubo cornutus.*
   {OWL NOT HORNED.   *Bubo non cornutus.*

Semirapacious; feeding commonly either on *Carrion*, or other things, and more *seldome on living Animals*.

The *Crow-kind*; having a *bill* somewhat large and strait; ‖ amongst which, those that are most common with us, are of a deep *black* colour, in their bodies

The *bigger kind*; Greater: or Less.

5. {RAVEN.   *Corvus.*
   {CROW.   *Cornix.*

The *lesser kind*; having a mixture of *dark brown with black*: or being wholly *black on the body*, with *red bill and legs*.

6. {DAW.   *Monedula.*
   {CHOUGH.   *Coracias.*

The *Parret-kind*; of *hooked bills*, having *two toes before*, and *two behind*, considerable for the variety of *beautiful colours*, and the *imitation of speech*; ‖ the *Greater*: or the *Less*.

7. {PARRET.   *Psittacus.*
   {PARAQUETO.   *Psittacus minor.*

The *Py-kind*; of a *chattering voice*, having *many notes*; ‖ either *pyed with black and white*, *with a long train*: or having *some of the smaller feathers on each wing, variegated with blew and black*.

8. {MAGPY, *Py*.   *Pica caudata.*
   {JAY.   *Pica glandaria.*

The *Woodpecker-kind*; climbing upon *trees* and *walls*, in order to which they are furnished with *strong feathers in their train*, to support them in *climbing* and *pecking*; ‖ of which there are various *species*, reducible to these two kinds; such as have a very *long tongue*, with *two claws behind* and *two before*: or such as have *shorter tongues*, and but *one toe behind*.

9. {WOODPECKER OF LONG TONGUES.   *Picus martius.*
   {WOODPECKER OF SHORTER TONGUES.

That kind of *Eagle*, which is
- Of a *dark yellow* colour, having *legs feathered* down to the *foot* — called *Chrysaetos*.
- *Black* all over, excepting a *white spot* between the *shoulders* on the *back*. — *Melanaetus*.
- With a *ring* of *white* on his *tail*. — *Pygargus*.
- *Osprey.* Feeding on *Fish*. — *Ossifragus*.

That kind of *Vulture* noted for
- *Percnopteros.* Having his *head* and part of *neck bare of feathers* — called *Bald Vulture*.
- *Vultur Borticus. Ald.* Being of a *Chesnut colour*, and *feathered* down to the *toes*. — *Chesnut coloured Vulture*.
- *Vultur aureus.* Being of a *yellowish colour*, very great, having some of the *feathers* of the *wing*, three foot long. — *Golden Vulture*.

Hawks are usually distinguished into such are
- *Short winged*; having their *wings* considerably shorter then their *trains*, of which there are usually reckoned three kinds.
  - *Accipiter Palumbarius.* The biggest of this kind — called Fem. *Goshawk*, Male *Tarcell*.
  - *Accipiter fringillarius.* The lesser of this kind; either having
    - *Transverse streaks* of yellow. — F. *Sparrowhawk*, M. *Musket*.
    - *Tinnunculus.* *Oblong streaks*. — *Kestril*.
- *Long winged*; having their *wings* equal to, if not longer then their *trains*, of which there are usually reckoned these six kinds, noted for
  - *Jerfalco.* A *whitish colour*, but *spotted on the back* with black spots. — F. *Gerfalcon*, M. *Jerkin*.
  - *Falco montanus.* Having a *fastigiated* or rising *head*, being of an *ash colour*. — *Mountain Falcon*.
  - *Falco.* A *thick head* and *flat*, a *short neck*, and striking with the *breast*. — F. *Falcon*, M. *Tarcel*.
  - *Lanarius.* Having a *blewish bill* and *legs*. — F. *Lanner*, M. *Lanneret*.
  - *Subbuteo.* Having a *white spot behind his eyes* on each side. — *Hobby*.
  - *Æsalon.* Being the *least* of all *Hawks*. — F. *Merlin*, M. *Jack-Merlin*.

Kites may be distinguished into such as are noted for
- *Milvus.* Having a very *forked Train*. — *Common Kite*.
- *Buteo Triorchis.* Being or seeming *bald on the head*, having a *round train*, feeding on *young Rabbets*. — *Common Buzzard*.
- *Anatario.* Feeding on *Fish*. — *Bald Buzzard*.
- *Pygargus minor.* Being of a *white* or *ash colour*, with a *white streak* on the *Train*. — *Ring-tail*.

Lanius or *Butcher bird*, is of three several kinds, noted either for being
- Of a *reddish colour* on the back, the most common somewhat bigger then a *Sparrow*. — called *Lanius vulgaris*.
- *Particoloured*, of the same bigness with the former.
- *Ash-coloured*, about the bigness of a *Blackbird*. — *Lanius cinereus major*.

Owls horned are of three kinds, namely such as are noted for being
- Of the bigness of an *Eagle*, feathered down *to the toes*. — *Bubo*.
- Of the bigness of a *tame Dove*. — *Otus, Asio*.
- Of the bigness of a *Misle bird*, with a single *feather* on each side for a *horn*. — *Scops*.

Owls

Chap. V.   Of Birds.   147

Owls not horned, are of five kinds, namely such as are noted for

Having a *border of feathers about the face*, the *legs feathered* and *toes hairy*, about the bigness of a *Pidgeon*.	called	Our common white Owl, living in Barns. *Aluco.*
Having a *ring of* white *feathers about each eye*, a white bill, hairy legs and feet.		*Ulula Aldrovandi.*
Being of a *darker colour*, living in *Ivy-bushes*.		Our common field Owl. *Strix Aldrovandi.*
Being like a *Cuckoo*, having a *short small bill*, but a *wide mouth*.		Goat-sucker. *Caprimulgus.*
Being the *least of all*, not bigger then a *Black-bird*.		*Noctua.*

Crows are usually distinguished into three kinds, namely that which is

Carnivorous,	called	Crow.
Frugivorous, of a black colour; *gregarious*, building their nests together.		Rook. *Cornix frugiv.*
Frugivorous, party coloured; black and cinereous.		Roiston Crow. *Cornix Cinera*

To the *Py-kind*, those other *birds* may be reduced which are noted for having

The *wings* and *head* of a bright *azure*.	called	Roller *Argentoratensis.*
A *dark* colour spotted with *white*.		*Caryocatastes.*
A tuft of *feathers* on his *head*.		*Garrulus Bohemicus.*
A *bill* bigger then his *whole body*.		Toucan.
A *large bill*, with a kind of *horn reversed* upon the *bill*.		*Rhinoceros.*
Two long strings like the small naked stemm of a *feather* reaching from the *back* beyond the *train*, and strong *legs* and *claws*.		Bird of Paradise. *Manucodiata.*

These three last *exotic Birds* are not perhaps so proper to this tribe, but I know not at present how to reduce them better.

To the first sort of the *Woodpecker-kind*, those *Birds* may be reduced which are noted for

Being *Greater*; of a *Greenish colour*, and a *black spot* on the *head* of the *male*.	called	Woodspite. *Picus Martius viridis.*
Black colour, excepting a *red spot* upon the *head* of the *Cock*.		Hickwall. *Picus maximus niger.*
Being of a *lesser magnitude*, about the *bigness* of a *Black-bird*, variegated with *black* and *white*, with a *red spot* on the *head* of the *Cock*.		Witwall, Hibo. *Picus varius.*
Holding the *head* on one side, somewhat bigger then a *Sparrow*, of a *brownish colour*.		Wry-neck. *Jynx, Torquilla.*

To the second sort of the *Woodpecker-kind*, those other *Birds* may be reduced, which are noted for

An *Ash colour*, being about the bigness of a *Sparrow*.	called	Nuthatch. *Sitta.*
A *long slender bill*, being about the bigness of a *Sparrow*.		Wall-creeper. *Picus muralis.*
A *long slender bill*, being a little bigger then a *Wren*.		Ox-eye-creeper. *Certhia.*
Being about the same colour and bigness as a *Lark*, and noted for climbing upon *Reeds*.		Reed-Sparrow. *Junco.*
A *greenish colour*, and less.		Lesser Reed-Sparrow. *Cornix varia.*

V 2   II. PHY-

Of Birds. Part. II.

II. PHYTIVOROUS BIRDS OF SHORT WINGS, less fit for flight; may be distinguished into such as are

Flying; such as can bear up their *bodies* (tho with some difficulty) by the motion of their *wings*, for some considerable time and space, having generally *shorter bills*, being *pulveratricious*, of whitish flesh, most proper for food, having *gizzards* (i.e.) *strong musculous stomacks*, laying many *Eggs*, called the *Poultry-kind*.

Domestic;

Gallus.   The *most common*; having *the train compressed upwards*.
1. COCK, Hen, *Capon, Chicken, Pullet, Poultry.*
   Less common; having an elegant *train*, which is sometimes turned up and spread, and *spurs* on the *legs*; ‖ either that whose *colours are more elegant and beautiful*, having a *tuft on the head*: or that which is *less beautiful*.

Pavo.
Gallo-pavo.   2. { PEACOCK.
              { TURKY.

Wild; either the

Bigger kind;
Living chiefly in woods; the former being distinguishable by having *a long train wherein the feathers do gradually increase towards the middle*: the other, by being *feathered on the legs*.

Phasianus.   3. { PHEASANT.
               { ATTAGEN.
Living in open fields; having *no heel* or *back claw*; ‖ either the greater, being about the bigness of a *Turky*: or the less, being about the bigness of a *Pheasant*.

Otis.   4. { BUSTARD.
           { ANAS CAMPESTRIS BELLONII.
Being serrate on each side of the *claws*, and hairy to the *toes*; ‖ either the bigger, feeding usually on *fine leaves*: or the less, feeding on *Heath*, of a black colour, the *feathers* of the *train* reversed sidewayes.

Urogallus.   5. { COCK OF THE WOOD.
Tetrao.   { HEATH COCK, Grous, Pout.

Middle kind; of a *short train*, to be further distinguished by their
Reddish Breasts; with the figure of a *Horshooe*: or having a *red bill* (*and legs*.)

Perdix.   6. { PARTRIDGE.
Perdix rubra. { RED PARTRIDGE.

Hairy legs; ‖ either that which hath *a black spot under the bill*: or that which is wholly *white excepting some black on the train*, being hairy to the very *nails* or *claws*, living on the *Alps*.

Gallina Corylorum.   7. { HAZLE HEN.
                        { LAGOPUS.

Least poultry-kind; ‖ either that which hath a *short train*, *a small back toe*: or that which is *of a deep body compressed upwards*, having longer *legs*, with a bill more like *a Water-hen*.

Coturnix.   8. { QUAILE.
Rallus.   { RAILE.

Not flying; being the biggest of all *Birds*; the one *having only two*, and the other *three claws*.

Struthio-camelus.   9. { ESTRICH.
Emeu.   { CASSAWARE, *Emew.*

III. PHY-

Chap. V.   *Of Birds.*   149

III. **PHYTIVOROUS BIRDS OF LONG WINGS**, and swifter in III. **PHY-**
flight, having their *bills* more *long* and slender, may be distinguished into **TIVOROUS**
Pidgeon-kind; laying but *two Eggs*. The   (the **LONG**
  Bigger; whether the *most common* and *domestic*, of great variety of **WINGS.**
    colours, *living in houses*: or that which *lives in woods*, of an *ash co-*
    lour, having a *ring* of *white* about the *neck*.
    1. { **PIDGEON,** *Dove.*   *Columba.*
       { **RING-DOVE,** *Queest.*   *Palumbus tor-*
  Lesser; ‖ either that which hath a *reddish breast*: or that which is ge-   *quatus.*
    nerally *marked on* each side of *the neck with azure and black*, except
    some that are wholly *white*, being *the least of this kind*.
    2. { **STOCK-DOVE.**   *Oenas, Vinago.*
       { **TURTLE.**   *Turtur.*

Thrush-kind; of a *lesser* magnitude then *Pidgeons*, and *longer trains* in proportion to their *wings*, laying *more Eggs* then *two*, being generally *bacci-*
  Speckled on the breast;   (*vorous.*
    Canorous considerable for having the *bill*
      More round; being of a *dunnish green* on the *back*, feeding on
        Missle berries; ‖ the *Greater*: or the *Lesser*.
      3. { **MISSLE-BIRD,** *Shreight.*   *Turdus visci-*
        { **THRUSH,** *Throstle, Mavis, Song-Thrush.*   *vorus.*
      More flat; spotted either with *whitish*, or *reddish spots*: the latter *Turdus.*
        of which hath likewise a *reddish tail*
      4. { **STARE,** *Starling.*   *Sturnus,*
        { **MERULA SAXATILIS,** *Ruticilla major.*
  Not Canorous; being *Birds of passage*, coming only in *Winter*; the
    Greater: or the *Lesser*.
    5. { **FELDEFARE.**   *Turdus pila-*
       { **REDWING,** *Swinepipe.*   *ris.*
  Not speckled on the breast;   *Turdus ilia-*
    Less beautiful for their colours;   *cus.*
      Canorous; ‖ either that which is *more black*, with *yellow bills* and
        legs: or *less black*, having some *dark shining blew* on the *back*,
        being somewhat waved on the *breast*.
      6. { **BLACKBIRD.**   *Merula;*
        { **PASSER SOLITARIUS.**
    Not canorous; ‖ either that which hath on the *breast* an *Area* of
      white: or that which is of an *ash colour*.
      7. { **MERULA TORQUATA.**
        { **MERULA MONTANA.**
  More beautiful for their colours;
    The Greater; ‖ either that which hath a *reddish bill*, the *wings* and
      train black, the rest of the *body* bright *yellow*: or that which
      hath a long *black bill*, a long *crest of feathers upon the head*, tipped
      with *black*, with transverse streaks of *black* and *white* upon the
      8. { **GALBULA.**   (*wings.*
        { **HOOP.**   *Upupa.*
    The Lesser; having the *three foremost toes joyned together to the first*
      joynt, without any *membrane*, the *outmost* and *middle toe*, *to the*
      second joynt; ‖ either the *bigger*, having a *Bill* somewhat *crooked*: *Apiaster, Ish-*
      9. { **BEE-EATER.**   (the *lesser*, having a *strait* strong *bill.* *rope;*
        { **KING-FISHER,** *Alcyon.*   V. **PHY-**   *Ispida.*

Of Birds.   Part. II.

IV. PHYTIVOROUS BIRDS OF SHORT THICK BILLS.

Emberiza alba Gesneri
Alauda congener.
Cuchryamus Bellonii.
Citrinella Hortulanus.

IV. PHYTIVOROUS BIRDS OF SHORT, THICK, strong BILLS, being generally *Granivorous*, may be distinguished into such as do belong either to the

- *Bunting-kind*; having a *hard knob in the pallate* of the mouth.
  - The *bigger*; being *Canorous*.
    1. BUNTING.
  - The *Lesser*; not esteemed for singing; ‖ either that of a *yellowish body*: or that which is *yellow about the throat*.
    2. { YELLOW-HAMMER.
         HORTULANE.

Passer.
Passer montanus.

- *Sparrow-kind*; without such a *knob* in the *mouth*.
  - *Not canorous*;
    - The *more common and lesser kind*; living either *about houses*: or *in mountains*, having a *reddish head*.
      3. { SPARROW.
           MOUNTAIN SPARROW.
    - The *less common and greater kind*; with a bigger *stronger bill* then the other, to break the *stones* of *fruits* for their *kernels*; ‖ either that without a *crest*: or that with *one*.
      4. { COCOTHRAUSTES.
           COCOTHRAUSTES CRISTATUS INDICUS.
  - *Canorous*;
    - *Bigger*; ‖ either that with a *great head* and a *red breast*: or that with a *cross bill*, the upper and lower part crossing each other towards the middle, said to sing in *Winter*

Rubicilla.
Loxia.

      5. { BULL-FINCH, *Alpe, Nope*.
           SHELL-APPLE, *Cross-bill*.

    - *Lesser*; considerable for their different colours; being either
      - *Greenish*; the *Bigger*: or *Lesser*.

Chloris.
Passer Cauarius.

      6. { GREENFINCH.
           CANARY BIRD.

      - *Brownish*;
        - The *Bigger*; ‖ either that whose *breast* is of a *dilute red*: or that which is *variegated with black on the head*.

Fringilla,
Monte-fringilla.

      7. { CHAFFINCH.
           BRAMBLE, *Brambling*.

        - The *Lesser*; *not red* about the *bill*: or *red* about the *bill*.

Linaria.
Linaria rubra.

      8. { LINNET.
           RED LINNET.

V. IN-

Chap. V.   *Of Birds.*   151

V. INSECTIVOROUS the GREATER, may be diftinguiſhed in- *V.INSECTI-*
to ſuch as are of   *VOROUS.*
                                                               GREATER.

Swifter flight; comprehending the *Swallow-kind*, of *long wings, forked trains, ſhort legs,* being much upon the wing, *Birds of paſſage,*
coming in *Summer.*

  The greater; *building in Chymneys*, variegated with *black* and *white,*
  having a *red ſpot* on the *breaſt* : or *building in Churches,* of a *blackiſh colour*, very *ſhort feet,* the *biggeſt of this kind.*
       { SWALLOW.   *Hirundo.*
  1. { SWIFT, *Martlet, Church-Martin.*   *Hirundo apes.*

  The leſſer; *building about houſes*, of a *white rump,* and *feathered down
  to the toes* : or *building in banks,* with a *broad ſpot on the breaſt.*
       { MARTIN.   *Martis.*
  2. { SAND-MARTIN, *Shore-bird.*   *Hirundo ripa-
                                                            ria.*

Slower flight;

  Canorous; confiderable for

    Singing in the night; being of a *dark reddiſh colour.*
       3. NIGHTINGALE.   *Lufcinia.*

    Having a long heel; the *greater* : or the *leſs,* living in *watery places.*
       { LARK.   *Alauda.*
    4. { TIT-LARK.   *Alauda pra-
                                                          tenſis.*

    Having a red breaſt; or a *red train.*
       { ROBIN REDBREAST, *Ruddock.*   *Rubecula.*
    5. { REDSTART.   *Ruticilla.*

  Not Canorous; confiderable for

    The delicacy and *fatneſs of their fleſh*; ‖ *living* either *amongſt Figs,* of
    which there are ſeveral varieties, the moſt common and beſt
    known, being from his *black head* called *Atricapilla* : or *living in
    holes of the ground,* and having a *white rump.*
       { BECCAFIGO.   *Ficedula.*
    3. { WHEAT-EAR.   *Oenanthe.*

    Having a long train, and *frequently moving it*; ‖ either the *more
    common one,* which is *black and white* : or that which is *leſs com-
    mon*, of a *yellow colour.*
       { WAGTAIL.   *Motacilla.*
    7. { YELLOW WAGTAIL.   *Motacilla fla-
                                                          va.*

    Living; ‖ either upon *ſtony places or open Heaths* : or that which
    creeps in *hedges*, having the *back* like that of a *common Sparrow,*
    the *breaſt* of a *Lead colour,* with a *black bill.*
       { STONE SMICH.   *Muſcicapa
    4. { HEDGE SPARROW.   tertia Aldro-
                                                          vandi.
                                                          Curruca.*

VI. The

VI. The LEAST kind of INSECTIVOROUS BIRDS, may be distributed into such as are

VI. LEAST INSECTIVOROUS BIRDS.

Canorous; whether of a
- *Greenish colour* in the *body*; to be further distinguished by the colour of the
  - *Head*; ‖ either that of a *black*: or that of a *yellow head*.
    1. { LIGURINUS.
       { SERINUS.
  - *Neck*; being of an *ash colour*.
    2. CITRINELLA.
- *Passer Troglodytes.* *Brownish colour*; and spotted, the *train* more erect.
    3. WREN.

Not Canorous; being either
- *Greenish*; considerable for
  - *Having a tuft of yellow, or red feathers upon the head*: or being in other respects of the same shape with this, but only wanting such a *tuft*.
    4. { REGULUS CRISTATUS.
       { REGULUS NON CRISTATUS.
  - *Making a humming noise*; of which there are several varieties not yet sufficiently described.
    5. HUMMING BIRD.

Trochilus.

Variegated with *black* and *white*;
- *Fringillago.* The bigger; with a broad *black spot down the breast*;
    6. GREAT TITMOUSE.
- The lesser; considerable for having
  - A *blewish head*: or a *black head*.
    - *Parus Carulus.*
    - *Parus ater.* 7. { TITMOUSE.
                      { COLEMOUSE.
  - A *long train*: or a *Tuft on the head*.
    - *Parus caudatus.*
    - *Parus Cristatus.* 8. { LONG TAILED TIT.
                           { CRESTED TIT.

VII. AQUA-

Chap. V.   Of Beasts.   153

VII. **AQUATIC BIRDS** living about and NEAR WET PLACES, having *longer legs*, and *long slender bills* for their more convenient going and fetching up their food in such places, may be distinguished into

 The *Plover-kind*; whose *bills are about one inch and a quarter long*.
  The *bigger*; having
   A *tuft on the head*; being in the *body* and *wings* of a *dark* and *white* colour.
    1. LAPWING, *Puet*.   *Vanellus.*
   No tuft; ‖ either that of a *greenish* colour, wanting a *back claw*: or that of a grey colour with a very *small back claw*.
    2. { GREEN PLOVER.   *Pluvialis viridis.*
     { GREY PLOVER.   *Pluvialis cinerea.*
  The *lesser*; being *without any back claw*: ‖ either that of a *greyish* colour, caught by imitation: or that which hath a *black fillet* about the *eyes*, and a *forked train*.
    3. { DOTTEREL.   *Morinellus.*
     { SEA LARK.   *Charadrios.*

 The *Redshank-kind*; whose *bills are about two inches long*.
  The *bigger*; considerable for
   Having a *red bill and legs*: or for having a kind of *ruffe about the neck* of the *males*, of great variety of colours, being *pugnacious*.
    4. { REDSHANK.   *Hæmatopus.*
     { RUFFE.   *Avis pugnax.*
   Being *mixed of black and white*; ‖ whether the *greater*, having *transverse streaks of black and white on the train*: or the *lesser*, having only the *exterior feathers of the train white*.
    5. { TRINGA MAJOR.
     { TRINGA MINOR.
  The *lesser*; having *white bellies*; ‖ either that whose *back* is *grey*: or that of a *dark brown* colour.
    6. { KNOT.
     { STINT.

 The *Woodcock-kind*; whose *bills are about three inches long*; whether having
  Strait bills;
   Frequenting fresh waters; of a *fulvous* colour *spotted*; ‖ the *greater*: or the *less*; the *male* of which latter is much *less*, and of a shorter bill then the *female*.
    7. { WOODCOCK.   *Scolopax.*
     { SNIPE.   *Gallinago minor.*
   Frequenting salt waters; ‖ either that of a *black and white colour*, with *red bill and legs*, wanting a *Postica*: or that of a *grey colour*, having a *Postica*.
    8. { SEA PY   *Hæmatopus Bellonii.*
     { GODWIT.   *Fedoa.*
  Crooked bills; ‖ either that of a *grey colour*: or that whose *feathers* are of an elegant *scarlet*, excepting the *wings*, which are *black*.
    9. { CURLEW.   *Arquata.*
     { GUARA BRASILEANA.

Of Birds. Part. II

VIII. AQUATIC FISSIPEDES.

VIII. AQUATIC BIRDS, *living* much *in the water*, being FISSIPEDES. ∥ may be diftinguifhed into fuch as are,

Not *fwimming*; but *wading*; comprehending the *Crane-kind*, having long necks and legs, long and ftrong bills; whether

Sharp pointed bills; either fuch whofe *necks* are

Longer; confiderable for

Building in *Fenny places*; being *hairy on the head*, having the *windpipe* reverfed in the form of the Letter **s**, and being *Herbivorous*: or *building on Houfes* and *Chymneys*, of a *black and white colour*, with *red legs and bill*, making a noife by the *collifion* of the *beak*, being *Pifcivorous*.

Grus.
Ciconia.

1. { CRANE.
    { STORK.

Having a thicker bill; fomewhat crooked and fhorter then the others of this *tribe*, with *fcarlet* coloured *wings*; or having a *tuft of briftles on the head*.

2. { PHÆNICOPTER.
    { GRUS BALEARICA.

Being of *an afh colour*, having a *tuft of feathers* ftanding out *behind the head*, *building on trees*; being *Pifcivorous*, with one *blind gut*; ∥ either the *greater*: or the *leffer*.

Ardea.

3. { HEARN.
    { ARDEA CINEREA MINOR.

Being of *a white colour*; in other refpects like the former; the greater: or the *leffer*.

Ardea alba major.
Ardea alba minor.

4. { GREATER WHITE HEARN.
    { LESSER WHITE HEARN.

Shorter neck; ∥ either that which is *fulvous* and *fpotted*, being *Pifcivorous*, having *one blind gut*: or that which is *white* with a *red bill*.

Ardea ftellaris.
Ardea Brafilica.

5. { BITTOUR.
    { BRASILEAN BITTOUR.

Broad and round pointed bill; like a *Spoon*, *Pifcivorous*, of a *white colour*.

Platea.

6. SHOVELAR, *Spoon-bill*.

Swimming; either

The *Diving-kind*; being much under water, and *finn-footed*, viz. with a *membrane* ftanding off on each fide of the *toes*, having *downy feathers*, and wanting a *train*; ∥ either the *greater*, having a *longer bill*: or the *leffer*, having a *fhorter bill*.

Colymbus major.
Colymbus minor.

7. { GREAT DIDAPPER, *Dabchick*.
    { LITTLE DIDAPPER.

The *More-hen-kind*; whofe *bodies* are fomewhat compreffed fidewayes; whether

Finn-footed; having a *membrane* of *Scollopt edges* on each fide of the *toes*, a *bald head*, being of *a black colour*.

Fulica.

8. COOT.

Not *finn-footed*; ∥ either the *greater*, which hath a little *red baldnefs*: or the *leffer*, having a long *red bill*.

Gallinula.

9. { MOOR-HEN, *Water-hen*.
    { GALLINULA SERICA.

IX. AQUA-

Chap. V.   Of Birds.   155

IX. AQUATIC PALMIPEDE Birds, whose *toes* are joyned together with a *membrane*, may be distinguished into such whose *bills* are either

Flat and *blunt*; being *Herbivorous*.

The *greater*; ‖ either the *biggest* of a *white colour*, having *black legs*: or the *lesser*, the *males* of which are commonly *white*.

1. { SWAN, *Cygnet*.
   { GOOSE, *Gander, Gosling*.

Cygnus.
Anser.

The *middle kind*; ‖ either the *bigger*, of a beautiful colour, the *head* of a *dark green*, the *body white*, with large spots of *orange colour*: or the *lesser*, having *reddish legs*.

2. { SHELDRAKE.
   { DRAKE, *Duck*.

Anas.

The *least kind*; ‖ either the *bigger*, having the *bill* and *legs* of a *lead colour*: or the *lesser*, being from the *eyes* to the hinder part of the *head* of a *greenish colour*.

3. { WIDGIN.
   { TEALE.

Penelope.
Querquedula.

Sharp; being generally *Piscivorous*.

The *Solan-goose kind*; having the *four toes joyned together*; ‖ whether *White*; ‖ either that which hath a *long bill*, *hooked* at the end, laying but *one Egg*: or having a *great bag under the bill*.

4. { SOLAN-GOOSE.
   { PELLICAN.

Onocrotalos.

Black; the *greater*, used for *catching of Fish*: or the *lesser*.

5. { CORMORANT.
   { SHAGG.

Corvus marinus.
Graculus palmipes.

The *Puffin-kind*; *frequenting desart Islands, wanting a posticâ, going upright, laying but one Egg*; whether such as build their nests *Within the ground*; in holes; ‖ either that which is *more common in Europe*, having the *top of the head*, the *back*, *wings and train* of a *black colour*, the rest *white*, the *bill* somewhat compressed upwards, short, of a triangular figure, and *red* at the point: to which may be adjoyned that *American Bird*, of a like shape to this, but *bigger*.

6. { PUFFIN.
   { PENGUIN.

Anas arctica Clusii.
Penguin.

On the ground; chiefly rocky places, making their nests together; ‖ either that with a *compressed black bill*, *hooked at the end*, having a *white line on either side*: or that of a *longer bill*, *less sharp*, not *hooked*.

7. { RAZOR-BILL.
   { GUILLAM.

Alca Wormii.
Lomvia.

The *Diving-kind*; being much under water, having *round serrate bills*, *hooked at the end*; ‖ either that which is *variegated with black and white*: or that which is of a *cinereous colour on the back*, with a *red head*, and a *tuft upon it*.

8. { DIVER.
   { DUNN DIVER.

Mergus.
Mergus cirratus.

The *Gull kind*, being *much upon the wing as Swallows*, commonly of an *ash colour*; ‖ either the *bigger*: or the *lesser*, having *red bill* and *legs*, with a *forked train*.

9. { GULL, *Sea-mew*.
   { SEA SWALLOW, *Scray*.

Larus.
Hirundo marina.

X 2   Besides

Besides the common sort of *Swans*, there is a wild kind, called *Hooper*, having the *wind-pipe* going down to the bottom of the *breast-bone*, and then reversed upwards in the figure of the Letter *S*.

Besides the common *Goose*, there are several sorts of *wild ones*, whereof one is *black* from the *breast* to the middle of the *belly*, called *Brant Goose, Bernicla*, or *Brenta*.

To the *Widgeon-kind* may be reduced that other *fowl*, about the same bigness, the two middle *feathers* of whose *train* do extend to a great length, called *Sea-Pheasant, Anas cauda acuta*.

To the *Teal-kind* should be reduced that other *fowl*, of the like shape and bigness, but being *white* where the other is *green*, called *Gargane*.

To the *Gull-kind*, doth belong that other *Bird*, of a long slender *bill* bending upwards, called *Avogetta recurvi rostra*.

Of Beasts.

Q. V. BEASTS, may be distinguished by their several shapes, properties, uses, food, their tameness or wildness, &c. into such as are either
- *Viviparous*; producing living young.
  - WHOLE FOOTED, the *soles* of whose *feet* are undivided, being used chiefly for *Carriage*. I.
  - CLOVEN FOOTED. II.
  - *Clawed*, or *multifidous*; the end of whose *feet* is branched out into *toes*; whether
    - NOT RAPACIOUS. III.
    - RAPACIOUS; living upon the prey of other *Animals*; having generally *six short pointed* incisores, or *cutting teeth*, and *two long fangs* to hold their prey; whether the
      - CAT-KIND; having a *roundish head*. IV.
      - DOG-KIND; whose *heads* are *more oblong*. V.
- OVIPAROUS; breeding *Eggs*. VI.

I. WHOLE FOOTED BEASTS.

Equus.

I. WHOLE FOOTED BEASTS, may be distinguished into such as
- *Solid hard hoofs*; considerable for (are either of
  - *Swiftness* and *comeliness*; being *used for riding*.
    1. HORSE, *Mare, Gelding, Nag, Palfrey, Steed, Courser, Gennet, Stallion, Colt, Fole, Filly, Neigh, Grooms, Ostler*.
  - *Slowness* and *strength* in *bearing burdens*; having *long ears*; ‖ either the more *simple* kind : or that *mungrel* generation begotten on a

Asinus.
Mulus.

2. ASSE, Bray. (*Mare*.
   MULE.

Lev. 11. 4. 26.
- *Softer feet*; having some resemblance to the
  - *Cloven footed-kind*; by reason of the upper part of the *hoof* being divided, being *ruminant*, having a *long slender neck*, with one or two *bunches* on the *back*.

Camelus.
3. CAMEL, *Dromedary*.
- *Multifidous kind*; having little *prominencies* at the end of the *feet*, representing *toes*, being of the *greatest magnitude* amongst all other *beasts*, used for the carriage and draught of great weights, and more particularly esteemed for the *tusks*.

Elephas.
4. ELEPHANT, *Ivory*.   II. CLOVEN

Chap. V.   *Of Beasts.*   157

II. **CLOVEN FOOTED BEASTS,** may be distributed into such as II. CLOVEN
Horned and Ruminant; having *two horns*.   (are FOOTED
                                                              BEASTS.
  Hollow; not branched nor deciduous, being common both to the *males*
  and *females*, useful to *men* both living and dead; whether the
    Bigger; being useful both by their *labour and flesh*;
      1. KINE, *Bull, Cow, Ox, Calf, Heifer, Bullock, Steer, Beef, Veal,* Bos.
         Runt, bellow, low, Heard, Cowheard.
    Lesser; being useful either in respect of the *Fleece and Flesh* : or *Hair
      and Flesh.*
         ⎧SHEEP, *Ram, Ewe, Lamb, Weather, Mutton, Bleat, Fold, Flock,* Ovis.
      2. ⎨GOAT, *Kid.*   (*Shepheard.* Capir.
  Solid; branched, deciduous, being proper only to the *males*; whe-
    ther the
    Bigger kind; ‖ either that of the *highest stature*, having *horns* with-
      out *brow-antlers*, of a *short stemm*, and then spreading out into
      breadth, branched at the edges: or that of a *lower stature*, ha-
      ving round, long, branched *horns*.
         ⎧ELKE.   Alcis.
      3. ⎨STAGG, *Hart, Hind, Red Deer, Venison.*   Cervus.
    Middle kind; whose horns become broad towards the ends; ‖ ei-
      ther that of *lesser horns*, not used for labour: or that which hath
      the *largest horns* in proportion to that *body*, of any other *Deer*, with
      a double branched *brow-antler*, being in the *Northern Countries*
      used for the *drawing of Sleds.*
         ⎧BUCK, *Doe, Fawn, Pricket, Sorel, Sore, Fallow Deer, Venison.* Dama.
      4. ⎨REIN-DEER, *Tarandu.*   Rangifer.
    Least kind; having a *short, round, branched horn.*
      5. ROE-BUCK, *Roe.*   Capreolus.
  Horned but not ruminant; having but one *horn*, placed on the *nose*, be-
    ing a *beast* of great bigness, covered with a kind of *Armature*, and
    counted untamable.
      6. RHINOCEROT.   Rhinoceros.
  Ruminant but not horned; being useful to *men* only, when living, for
    carriage of burdens, having the *longest neck* of any other *Animal*
    (if there be really any such *Beast*.)
      7. CAMELOPARD, *Giraffa.*   Camelopardus.
  Neither horned nor ruminant; useful only when dead, for its flesh.
      8. HOG, *Swine, Bore, Sow, Pig, Porket, Barrow, Shoot, Pork, Ba-* Porcus.
         con, Brawn. Grunt.

Amongst those that belong to the *Bovinum genus*, there are several
sorts described by *Authors* distinguished by their having either
    A *Beard*;   ⎫   ⎧*Urus.*
    A *Bunch on the back*;   ⎬ stiled ⎨*Bisons.*
    Horns reflected about the ears. ⎬   ⎨*Bonasus.*
    Broad, flat, rugged horns; ⎭   ⎩*Buffalus.*

Besides the more common kinds of *Sheep*, there are others mentioned
by *Authors*, and described to have
    Streight wreathed horns. ⎫ called ⎧ *Ovis Strepsiceros.*
    Great thick tails.   ⎭   ⎩ *Broad tailed Sheep.*
                                                                Amongst

Amongſt thoſe that belong to the *Goat-kind*, beſides the more vulgar ſort, there are others whoſe *horns* are either

Ibex. Angular and knobbed. ⎫ called ⎧ *Stone Buck.*
Gimpſe Rupi- Small and round; being hooked at the end. ⎬ ⎨ *Shamois.*
capra. Streight and wreathed. ⎭ ⎩ *Antilope.*
Gazel.

III. CLAW- III. CLAWED Beaſts NOT RAPACIOUS, may be diſtinguiſhed
ED NOT into ſuch as are either
RAPACI-
OUS.

Man-like; having *faces* and *ears* ſomewhat reſembling thoſe of *Men*, with only four broad *inciſores*, or *cutting teeth*, and two ſhort *eye-teeth*, not longer then the other, their *fore-feet* being generally like *hands*, with *thumbs*, going upon their *heels*; whether the

Bigger kind; ‖ either that which hath a *ſhort tail*: or that which hath *no*
Papio. ⎧ BABOON, Drill. (*tail.*
Simia. 1. ⎨ APE, *Jackanapes.*

Leſſer kind; having a *long tail*, and being *very nimble*: to which may be adjoined, for its affinity to this kind in reſpect of the *face*, that *beaſt* which is the *ſloweſt* of all others, having but three *toes* on each *foot*, feeding on *leaves*, having a *blind gut* joyned to the *upper orifice of his ſtomack*, being probably *ruminant*.

Cercopithecus. ⎧ MONKEY, *Marmoſit.*
Ignavus. 2. ⎨ SLOTH, *Haut, Ay.*

Hare-kind; having two long *teeth* in the *lower jaw* before, and two others oppoſite to thoſe (tho not quite ſo long) in the *upper jaw*, moſt of which are counted *ruminant*, becauſe when they have by the help of their *inciſores* filled their *mouths* with meat, they after chew it over
Levit. 11. again with their *Molares* or *grinders*, but they are not properly *ruminant*, becauſe they have but one *ſtomach*, out of which they do not fetch up their food being once ſwallowed.

Theſe may be diſtinguiſhed into the

Bigger kind; whether ſuch as are covered with
 Hair; living either
  Above ground; being of all others the *moſt fearful*.
Lepus. 3. HARE, *Leveret.*
  Under ground; ‖ either that with *long ears* and a *ſhort tail*: or that with *ſhort ears* and a *long tail*, being ſaid to ſleep all the *Winter*.
Cuniculus. ⎧ CONNY, *Rabbet.*
Mus Alpinus. 4. ⎨ MARMOTTO.

Quills; ‖ either the *bigger*: or the *leſſer* kind.
Hiſtrix. ⎧ PORCUPINE.
Echinus. 5. ⎨ HEDGHOG.

Middle kind; ‖ either that which *lives* in *Trees*, with a *ſpreading* buſhy *tail*: or that which *lives on the ground*, with a *ſhort tail*, and *courſe hair*, having only *three toes* on a *foot*.
Sciurus. ⎧ SQUIRREL.
 6. ⎨ GINNY PIG.

Leaſt kind; living commonly, either
 In houſes; being *miſchievous* to *Corn*; ‖ the *greater*: or *leſſer* kind
Sorex. ⎧ RAT.
Mus domeſti- 7. ⎨ MOUSE.
cus.
 Abroad, under ground; having ſmall *eyes*, and broad *feet like hands*, being not ſo properly belonging to this *tribe*, but of near affinity to it.
Talpa. 8. MOLE. Beſides

Chap. V.   Of Beasts.   159

Besides the common *Rat* there are others having
Flat tails, their *hinder feet* being *palmipedes*, ⎱cal⎰ ⎧*Water-rat*, *Musk-rat*. *Mus Norva-*
Short tails, and *spotted skins*.   ⎰   ⎱led⎱ *Leming*.   *gicus.*

Besides the more common sort of *Mice* there are others
Of *long snouts*, counted venemous.   ⎫   ⎧*Field-mouse, Sheew-mouse.* *Mus araneus.*
Of a *sandy colour*, a *spreading tail*,   ⎬called⎨*Dormouse.*   *Mus Avella-*
   sleeping much.   ⎪   ⎪   *narum.*
Having *wings*, upon which there are   ⎬   ⎨*Batt, Flittermouse.*   *Vespertilio.*
   four *claws* instead of *feet*, the only ⎪   ⎩
   flying *beast*.   ⎭

IV. RAPACIOUS Beasts of the CAT-KIND, may be distributed **IV. RAPA-**
into such, whose *bodies* are in proportion to their *legs*, either **CIOUS**
                                                                    CAT-KIND.
  Less long; having generally two *Claviculæ* or *canel-bones*, by which
    they are inabled to strike or cuff with their *fore-feet*, and to climb,
    being able to sheath their *claws*; whether the
    Bigger; considerable for
      Boldness and courage; being the chief of all *wild beasts*: or for *slow-*
       ness and *sluggishness*, going upon the *heels*.
      1. ⎰LION-*ess, Whelp, roar.*   *Leo.*
        ⎱BEARE, *Cub.*   *Ursus.*
      Spottedness; ‖ either with *Rundles*: or with *Streaks*.
      2. ⎰TYGER.   *Tigris.*
        ⎱PARD, *Panther, Leopard.*   *Pardus.*
      Quick sightedness;
      3. OUNCE, *Lynx.*   *Lynx.*
    Lesser; ‖ either that *Domestic Animal*, the *Enemy* to *Mice*: or that *wild*
     fierce creature, of some resemblance to this, producing *Civet*.
      4. ⎰CAT, *Kitling, Kitten, Mew.*   *Catus.*
        ⎱CIVET-CAT.   *Zibetta.*
  More long; namely such as by the length of their *bodies*, and shortness of
    their *legs*, are fitted to creep and wind themselves into holes, for the
    catching of their prey. The *Verminous-kind*; whether such as are
    Terrestrial; of a
      Courser furr; being noxious to *Rabbets*; ‖ either that which is fre-
       quently *trained up by Men for the catching of Connies*: or that
       which is of a *stinking savour*.
      5. ⎰FERRET.
        ⎱POLECAT, *Fitchew.*   *Viverra.*
      Finer furr; whether the   *Putorius.*
      Bigger; being commonly *white under the throat*.
      6. MARTIN, *Sable, Gennet.*   *Martes.*
      Lesser; ‖ either that which is *wholly white, excepting a black spot on*
       the tail: or that whose *belly is white*, the tip of the *tail black*, the
       back of a *light dun*.
      7. ⎰STOAT, *Ermine.*
        ⎱WEESLE.   *Mustela.*
    Amphibious; ‖ either that of a *finer furr*, having a *broad, thick, scaly*
     tail: or that of a *courser furr*.
      8. ⎰CASTOR, *Beaver.*   *Castor.*
        ⎱OTTER.   *Lutra.*

As

160   *Of Beasts.*   Part. II.

As for that mongrel generation, which many Authors describe, as being begotten betwixt a *Pard* and a *Lioness*, being therefore called *Leopard*, as likewise that other *Beast*, commonly described by the name of *Gulo* or *Jerf*, and that other named *Hyæna*. There is reason to doubt, whether there be any such *species* of *Animals*, distinct from those here enumerated: Tho the belief of these (as of several other fictitious things) hath been propagated by *Orators*, upon account of their fitness to be made use of in the way of similitude.

V. RAPA-CIOUS DOG-KIND.

V. RAPACIOUS Beasts of the DOG-Kind, may be distinguished into such as are either

European;
  Terrestrial; whether

Canis.
Lupus.

(*Bigger*; ‖ either that which is noted for *tameness* and *docility*: or for *wildness* and *enmity to Sheep*.

1. { DOG, *Bitch, Puppy, Whelp. Bark, bay, yelp.*
    WOLF, *Howle.*

Lesser; living usually in holes within the ground; ‖ either that which is noted for *subtilty*, having a *bushy tail*: or that which is noted for *tenacity in biting*, being esteemed commonly (tho falsly) to have the *legs* on the *left side* shorter then the other.

Vulpes.
Taxus.

2. { FOX.
   BADGER, *Grey, Brock.*

Amphibious; whether the *Bigger*, Being *less hairy*, having *great tusks*: or the *lesser*, being *more hairy*.

Phocæ.

3. { MORSE, *Sea-horse.*
   SEAL, *Sea-calf.*

Exotic; being noted for

Gregariousness; going in great troops, and being said to assist the *Lion* in hunting.

Lupus aureus.

4. JACKALL.

Long snout, and *feeding on Ants*, and sometimes on *roots*; ‖ either that of a *hairy*: or that of a *crustaceous covering*.

Tamandua.
Tatu.

5. { ANT-BEARE.
   ARMADILLO.

A bag under the belly; wherein the *young ones* are received, being apt to hang by the *tail*, having a mixed resemblance both to an *Ape* and a *Fox*.

Simivulpes.

6. CARAGUYA.

Amongst the several *species* of *Animals*, there is not any of greater variety in respect of accidental differences, then that of *Dogs*, which being the most familiar and *domestick Beast*, hath therefore several names assigned to it according to these differences, which are derived either from the *Countries* in which they are originally bred, and from which they are brought to other places, as *England, Ireland, Iceland, Ginny, &c.* or their bigness or littleness, or from their shape, colour, hairiness, &c. But they are chiefly distinguishable from those uses which men imploy them about, either in respect of

Delight;

Chap. V.   *Of Beasts.*   161

{*Delight*; LAP-DOGS.
{*Companying*; when they serve only to follow us up and down. CURRS.
{*Custody* of places or things; MASTIFS.
{*Hunting*; either by
  {*Sight*; GASE-HOUNDS.
  Smell; whether for
    {*Birds*; SPANIELS
      {*Terrestrial*; LAND SPANIELS.
      {*Aquatic*; WATER SPANIELS.
    {*Beasts*; of a
      {*Greater* kind; HOUNDS.
      {*Lesser* kind; BEAGLES.
  Swiftness; and running after
    {*Greater Beasts*; GREYHOUNDS.
    {*Lesser Beasts*; LURCHERS.
{*Play*; TUMBLERS.

VI. OVIPAROUS BEASTS; may be distinguished by their different ways of progressive motion; whether   VI. OVIPA-
ROUS
BEASTS.

{*Gradient*; having *four feet*, the figure of their *bodies* being either more
  {*Broad*; whose outward covering is
    {*Crustaceous*; || belonging either to the *Land*: or to the *Water*.
       1. {TORTOISE, *Land-tortoise*.   *Testudo.*
          {TURTLE, *Sea-tortoise*.   *Testudo mari-
na.*
    {*Skinny*; || either that which is not *poisonous*: or that which is counted
       2. {FROG, *Tadpole, croke*.   (*poisonous.*   *Rana.*
          {TOAD, *Tadpole*.   *Bufo.*
  {*Oblong*; whose *bodies* and *tails* are more produced; whether the
    {*Greatest kind*; being skinned and scaly; || either the *larger*: or the
    lesser, the latter of which is described to have a *dew-lap* under the
       3. {CROCODILE, *Allegator, Cayman, Leviathan*.   (*throat.* *Crocodilus.*
          {SENEMBI, *Iguana*.
    {*Middle kind*; || either that which is *most common* in other *Countries*,
    and of greatest varieties: or that which hath *two toes behind* in
    each *foot*, with *prominencies* upon the *head* like *ears*, being said
    (tho falsly) to feed only upon *air*.
       4. {LIZARD.   *Lacerta.*
          {CHAMELION.   *Chamaleo.*
    {*Least kind*; || either that of a *brownish* colour with *yellow spots*: or
    that of a more *dark colour*, having a broad tail for swimming. *Salamandra*
       5. {LAND SALAMANDER, *Land Eft, Newt*.   *terrestris.*
          {WATER SALAMANDER, *Eft, Newt*.   *Salamandra
aquatica.*
{*Creeping*; being without *feet*, and of round oblong *bodies*; whether the
  {*Bigger kind*;
     6. SERPENT, *Hiss*.   *Serpens.*
  {*Middle kind*; || either that which is *not poisonous*: or that which is
    counted *poisonous*, having two long, hollow, moveable *teeth*, hatch-
    ing the *Eggs* within its *body*.
     7. {SNAKE, *Hiss*.   *Navis tor-
quata.*
       {VIPER, *Adder, Aspe*.   *Vipera.*
  {*Least kind*; commonly esteemed *blind* and *poisonous*.
     8. SLOW WORM.   Y   That *Cæcilia.*

That kind of *Animal* which is commonly called a *Dragon*, and described to be a kind of *Serpent* with wings and feet (if there ever were any such thing) might possibly be some monstrous production, but there is reason to believe that there is no such standing *species* in nature.

Besides the common kind of *Frogs*, there is another distinct sort, called the *Green frog*, feeding on leaves, having blunt broad toes.

Besides the more usual sorts of *Lizards*, there are others described, as having some distinct peculiarity in respect of

	called	
Bigger magnitude, and greenness of colour. Blunt broad toes.		The green *Lizard*. The *Facetane* Lizard.
Thicker body, having a tail annulated with scales.		*Cordylus*.
Slender body and small feet, resembling a *Slow worm*.		*Chalcidica*, Lizard.
Small head, and lesser scales.		*Scinke*.

§. VI. Having now dispatched the enumeration and description of the several species of Animals, I shall here take leave for a short digression, wherein I would recommend this, as a thing worthy to be observed, namely, that great difference which there is betwixt those opinions and apprehensions which are occasioned by a more general and confused view of things, and those which proceed from a more distinct consideration of them as they are reduced into order.

He that looks upon the Starrs, as they are confusedly scattered up and down in the Firmament, will think them to be (as they are sometimes stiled) innumerable, of so vast a multitude, as not to be determined to any set number: but when all these Starrs are distinctly reduced into particular constellations, and described by their several places, magnitudes and names, it appears, that of those that are visible to the naked eye, there are but few more then a thousand in the whole Firmament, and but a little more then half so many to be seen at once in any Hemisphere, taking in the minuter kinds of them, even to six degrees of magnitude. It is so likewise in other things: He that should put the Question, how many sorts of beasts, or birds, &c. there are in the world, would be answered, even by such as are otherwise knowing and learned men, that there are so many hundreds of them, as could not be enumerated; whereas upon a distinct inquiry into all such as are yet known, and have been described by credible Authors, it will appear that they are much fewer then is commonly imagined, not a hundred sorts of Beasts, nor two hundred of Birds.

From this prejudice it is, that some hereticks of old, and some Atheistical scoffers in these later times, having taken the advantage of raising objections, (such as they think unanswerable) against the truth and authority of Scripture, particularly as to the description which is given by *Moses*, concerning *Noah*'s Ark, *Gen.* 6. 15. where the dimensions of it are let down to be three hundred cubits in length, fifty in breadth, and thirty in height, which being compared with the things it was to contein, it seemed to them upon a general view, (and they confidently affirmed accordingly) that it was utterly impossible for this Ark to hold so vast a multitude of Animals, with a whole years provision of food for each of them.   This

This objection seemed so considerable, both to some of the ancient Fathers, and of our later Divines, who were otherwise learned and judicious men, but less versed in Philosophy and Mathematicks, that they have been put to miserable shifts for the solving of it. *Origen*, and Saint *Austin*, and several other considerable Authors, do for the avoiding of this difficulty affirm, that *Moses* being skilled in all the learning of the *Ægyptians*, doth by the measure of cubits, here applyed to the Ark, understand the *Ægyptian Geometrical cubit*, each of which (say they) did contein six of the *vulgar cubits*, namely, nine foot. But this doth upon several accounts seem very unreasonable, because it doth not appear, that there was any such measure amongst the *Ægyptians* or *Jews*, styled the *Geometrical cubit*: And if there were, yet there is no particular reason, why this sense should be applyed to the word cubit here, rather then in other places. It is said of *Goliah*, that his height was six cubits and a span, which being understood of the *Geometrical cubit*, will make him fifty four foot high, and consequently his head must be about nine foot in the height or diameter of it, which must needs be too heavy for *David* to carry. [1 Sam.17.4.]

Others not satisfied with this solution, think they have found a better answer, by asserting that the stature of mankind being considerably larger in the first ages of the world, therefore the measure of the cubit must be larger likewise, and perhaps double to now what it is, which will much inlarge the capacity of the *Ark*. But neither will this afford any reasonable satisfaction. For if they will suppose men to be of a much bigger stature then, 'tis but reasonable that the like should be supposed of other animals also; in which case this answer amounts to nothing.

Others will have the sacred cubit to be here intended, which is said to be a hands breadth longer then the civil cubit, *Ezech.*43.13. But there is not any reason or necessity for this. And 'tis generally believed, that the sacred cubit was used only in the measure of sacred Structures, as the Tabernacle and Temple.

This seeming difficulty is much better solved by *Joh. Buteo* in the Tract *de Arca Noe*, wherein supposing the cubit to be the same with what we now call a foot and a half, he proves Mathematically that there was a sufficient capacity in the *Ark*, for the conteining all those things it was designed for. But because there are some things liable to exception in the Philosophical part of that discourse, particularly in his enumeration of the species of Animals, several of which are fabulous, some not distinct species, others that are true species being left out; therefore I conceive it may not be improper in this place to offer another account of those things.

It is plain in the description which *Moses* gives of the *Ark*, that it was divided into three stories, each of them of ten cubits or fifteen foot high, besides one cubit allowed for the declivity of the roof in the upper story. And 'tis agreed upon as most probable, that the lower story was assigned to contein all the species of beasts, the middle story for their food, and the upper story, in one part of it, for the birds and their food, and the other part for *Noah*, his family and utensils.

Now it may clearly be made out, that each of these stories was of a sufficient capacity for the conteining all those things to which they are assigned.

For the more diſtinct clearing up of this, I ſhall firſt lay down ſeveral tables of the divers ſpecies of beaſts that were to be received into the Ark, according to the different kinds of food, wherewith they are uſually nouriſhed, conteining both the number appointed for each of them, namely, the clean by ſevens, and the unclean by pairs, together with a conjecture (for the greater facility of the calculation) what proportion each of them may bear, either to a Beef, or a Sheep, or a Wolf; and then what kind of room may be allotted to the making of ſufficient Stalls for their reception.

Beaſts feeding on Hay.			Beaſts feeding on Fruits, Roots and Inſects.			Carnivorous Beaſts		
Number. Name.	Proportion to Beeves.	Breadth of Stalls. feet	Number. Name	Proportion to Sheep.	Breadth of the Stalls. feet	Number. Name	Proportion to Wolves.	Breadth of their Stalls. feet
2 Horſe	3	20	2 Hog	4		2 Lion	4	10
2 Aſſe	2	12	2 Baboon	2		2 Beare	4	10
2 Camel	4	20	2 Ape	2		2 Tigre	3	8
2 Elephant	8	36	2 Monky			2 Pard	3	8
7 Bull	7	40	2 Sloth			2 Ounce	2	6
7 Urus	7	40	2 Porcupine	7	20	2 Cat	2	6
7 Biſons	7	40	2 Hedghog			2 Civet-cat		
7 Bonaſus	7	40	2 Squirril			2 Ferret		
7 Buffalo	7	40	2 Ginny pig			2 Polecat		
7 Sheep	1		2 Ant-bear	2		2 Martin		
7 Stepciſeros	1	30	2 Armadilla	2		2 Stoat	3	6
7 Broad-tail	1		2 Tortoiſe	2		2 Weeſle		
7 Goat	1			—	—	2 Caſtor		
7 Stone-buck	1	30		21	20	2 Otter		
7 Shamois	1					2 Dog	2	6
7 Antilope	1					2 Wolf	2	6
7 Elke	7	30				2 Fox		
7 Hart	4	30				2 Badger	2	6
7 Buck	3	20				2 Jackall		
7 Rein-deer	3	20				2 Caraguya		
7 Roe	2	36						
2 Rhinocerot	8							
2 Camelopard	6	30						
2 Hare	2 Sheep							
2 Rabbet								
2 Marmotto								
	92	514					27	72

In this enumeration I do not mention the Mule, becauſe 'tis a mungrel production, and not to be rekoned as a diſtinct ſpecies. And tho it be moſt probable, that the ſeveral varieties of Beeves, namely that which is ſtiled *Urus*, *Biſons*, *Bonaſus* and *Buffalo*, and thoſe other varieties reckoned ed under *Sheep* and *Goats*, be not distinct species from *Bull*, *Sheep*, and and *Goat*; There being much less difference betwixt these, then there is betwixt several Dogs: And it being known by experience, what various changes are frequently occasioned in the same species by several countries, diets, and other accidents: Yet I have *ex abundanti* to prevent all cavilling, allowed them to be distinct species, and each of them to be clean Beasts, and consequently such as were to be received in by sevens. As for the *Morse, Seale, Turtle,* or *Sea-Tortoise, Crocodile, Senembi,* These are usually described to be such kind of *Animals* as can abide in the water, and therefore I have not taken them into the Ark, tho if that were necessary, there would be room enough for them, as will shortly appear. The *Serpentine-kind, Snake, Viper, Slow-worm, Lizard, Frog, Toad,* might have sufficient space for their reception, and for their nourishment, in the Drein or Sink of the *Ark*, which was probably three or four foot under the floor for the standings of the Beasts. As for those lesser Beasts, *Rat Mouse, Mole,* as likewise for the several species of Insects, there can be no reason to question, but that these may find sufficient room in several parts of the *Ark*, without having any particular Stalls appointed for them.

Tho it seem most probable, that before the *Flood*, both Men, Beasts and Birds did feed only upon Vegetables, as may appear from that place, Gen. 1.29,30. *And God said, Behold I have given you every herb bearing seed which is upon the face of all the earth, and every tree in which is the fruit of a tree yelding seed, to you it shall be for meat. And to every beast of the earth, and to every fowl of the air, and to every thing that creepeth upon the earth, wherein there is life, I have given every green herb for meat,* compared with *chap.* 9.3. Where after the *Flood*, when the productions of the Earth were become of less efficacy and vigor, and consequently less fit for nourishment, God saith to *Noah, Every moving thing that liveth, shall be meat for you, even as the green herb have I given you all things.* Yet because this proof is not so very cogent to convince a captious Adversary, but that he may still be apt to question, whether the Rapacious kinds of Beasts and Birds, who in the natural frame of their parts are peculiarly fitted for the catching and devouring of their prey, did ever feed upon herbs and fruits; Therefore to prevent such Cavils, I shall be content to suppose that those *Animals* which are now *Predatory* were so from the begining: upon which, it will be necessary to enquire, what kind of food might be proper and sufficient for them, during their abode in the *Ark*. Now 'tis commonly known, that the *ruminant kind* are most usually the prey for the *rapacious kind* of beasts.

It appeares by the foregoing tables, that the beasts of the *rapacious carnivorous kinds*, to be brought into the *Ark* by pairs, were but forty in all, or twenty pairs, which upon a fair calculation are supposed equivalent, as to the bulk of their bodies and their food, unto twenty seven *Wolves*; but for greater certainty, let them be supposed equall to thirty *Wolves*: and let it be further supposed, that six *Wolves* will every day devour a whole *Sheep*, which all Men will readily grant to be more then sufficient for their necessary sustenance: According to this computation, five *Sheep* must be allotted to be devoured for food each day of the year, which amounts in the whole to 1825.

Upon these suppositions there must be convenient room in the lower story

story of the *Ark* to contein the forementioned sorts of beasts which were to be preserved for the propagating of their kinds, besides 1825. *Sheep*, which were to be taken in as food for the *rapacious Beasts*.

And tho there might seem no just ground of exception, if these beasts should be stow'd close together, as is now usual in Ships, when they are to be transported for any long voyage; yet I shall not take any such advantage, but afford them such fair Stalls or Cabins as may be abundantly sufficient for them in any kind of posture, either standing, or lying, or turning themselves, as likewise to receive all the dung that should proceed from them for a whole year.

And that the *Ark* was of a sufficient capacity for these purposes, will appear from the following *Diagram*. In which there is a partition at each end of the *Ark*, marked A A, of fifteen foot wide, and the breadth of the *Ark* being seventy five foot; these partitions must contein in them five *Areas* of fifteen foot square, and an *Area* of five foot square, being sufficient to contein four *Sheep*, therefore one of fifteen foot square must be capable of thirty six *Sheep*; Allowing one of these *Areas* at each end for stairs, there will eight of them remain, (viz. four at each end) to be reckoned upon for the conteining of *Sheep*; which eight will be capable of receiving 288 *Sheep*.

Besides these partitions, at the end there are five several passages marked B B, of seven foot wide for the more convenient access to the several Stalls; the four *Areas* on the side marked C C, designed for Stalls, are each of them eighteen foot wide, and about two hundred foot long. And the two middle *Areas* marked D D, are each of them twenty five foot wide, and about two hundred foot long.

Supposing the two middle *Areas* to be designed for *Sheep*; an *Area* of twenty five foot square must be capable of a hundred, and there being sixteen of these, they must be capable of 1600 *Sheep*, which being added to the former number of 288 will make 1888. somewhat more then 1825 the number assigned for those that were to be taken in for food.

The four side *Areas* marked C C, being each of them eighteen foot wide, and two hundred foot long, will be more then sufficient to contein the several beasts which were to be preserved for the propagating of their kind; for which in the foregoing Tables their is allotted to the length of their Stalls only six hundred and six foot, besides the largeness of the Stalls allotted to each of them. So that there will be near upon two hundred foot overplus, for the reception of any other beasts, not yet enumerated or discovered.

As for that fashion of the *Keel* of Ships now in use, whereby they are fitted for passage through the Waters, and to endure the motion of the Waves: This would not have been convenient for the business here designed; The *Ark* being intended only for a kind of *Float* to swim above water, the flatness of its bottom, did render it much more capacious for the reception of those many living Creatures, which were to be conteined in it. And tho towards the end of the Flood when it began to abate, God is said to *Make a wind to pass over the Earth, whereby the waters were asswaged*, Gen. 8. 1. Yet 'tis not likely that in the time of the deluge, when the whole Earth was overflowed, that there should be any such rough and boisterous winds as might endanger a Vessel of this Figure; such winds usually proceeding from dry Land.

From

Chap. V. Noahs Ark.

From hence it may be evident, that there ~~is sufficient~~ room in the

~~...y of the Ark~~, rather then to find sufficient room for those several species of *Animals* already known. But because it may be reasonably presumed, that there are several other species of beasts and birds, especially in the undiscovered parts of the world, besides those here enumerated, therefore 'tis but reasonable to suppose the *Ark* to be of a bigger capacity, then
what

God is said to *Make a wind to pass over the Earth, whereby the waters were asswaged*, Gen. 8.1. Yet 'tis not likely that in the time of the deluge, when the whole Earth was overflowed, that there should be any such rough and boisterous winds as might endanger a Vessel of this Figure; such winds usually proceeding from dry Land.

From

Chap. V. *Noahs Ark.*

From hence it may be evident, that there was sufficient room in the lower story for the convenient reception of all the sorts of beasts that are yet known, and probably for those other kinds that are yet unknown to these parts of the World.

The next thing to be cleared up, is the capacity of the second story for conteining a years provision of food. In order to which 'tis to be observed, that the several beasts feeding on hay, were before upon a fair calculation supposed equal to ninety two *Beeves*: but to prevent all kind of Cavils which may be made at the proportioning of them, let them be as a hundred, besides the 1825. *sheep* taken in for food. But now because these are to be devoured by five *per diem*, therefore the years provision to be made for them, is to be reckoned but as for half that number, *viz.* 912. These being divided by seven to bring them unto a proportion with the *Beeves*, will amount to 180, which added to the former hundred make 280, suppose three hundred. So then according to this supposition, there must be sufficient provision of hay in the second story to sustein three hundred *Beeves* for a whole year.

Now 'tis observed (saith *Buteo*) by *Columella*, who was very well versed in the experiments of Husbandry, that thirty or forty pound of hay is ordinarily sufficient for an *Ox* for one day, reckoning twelve ounces in the pound. But we will suppose forty of our pounds. And 'tis asserted by *Buteo* upon his own tryal and experience, that a solid cubit of dryed hay, compressed, as it uses to be, when it hath lain any considerable time in Mows or Reeks, doth weigh about forty pound; so that for three hundred *Beeves* for a whole year there must be 109500. such cubits of hay, (*i.e.*) 365. multiplied by 300. Now the second story being ten cubits high, three hundred long, and fifty broad, must contein 150000. solid cubits, which is more by 40500. then what is necessary for so much compressed hay; and will allow space enough both for any kind of beams and pillars necessary for the fabric, as likewise for other repositories, for such fruits, roots, grain or seed, as may be proper for the nourishment of any of the other *Animals*. And likewise for such convenient passages and apertures in the floor as might be necessary for the putting down of the hay to the Stalls in the lower story. From which it is manifest that the second story was sufficiently capacious of all those things designed for it.

And then as for the third story; there can be no colour of doubt, but that one half of it will be abundantly sufficient for all the species of birds, tho they should be twice as many as are enumerated in the foregoing tables, together with food sufficient for their sustenance, because they are generally but of small bulk, and may easily be kept in several partitions or Cages over one another. Nor is there any reason to question, but that the other half would afford space enough both for *Noah's* family and utensils.

Upon the whole matter, it doth of the two, appear more difficult to assign a sufficient number and bulk of necessary things, to answer the capacity of the *Ark*, rather then to find sufficient room for those several species of *Animals* already known. But because it may be reasonably presumed, that there are several other species of beasts and birds, especially in the undiscovered parts of the world, besides those here enumerated, therefore 'tis but reasonable to suppose the *Ark* to be of a bigger capacity, then what

what may be sufficient for the things already known, and upon this account it may be asserted, that if such persons who are most expert in Philosophy or Mathematicks, were now to assign the proportions of a Vessel that might be sutable to the ends here proposed, they could not (all things considered) find out any more accommodate to these purposes, then those here mentioned.

From what hath been said it may appear, that the measure and capacity of the *Ark*, which some Atheistical irreligious men make use of, as an argument against the Scripture, ought rather to be esteemed a most rational confirmation of the truth and divine authority of it. Especially if it be well considered, that in those first and ruder ages of the World, when men were less versed in Arts and Philosophy, and therefore probably more obnoxious to vulgar prejudices then now they are, yet the capacity and proportions of the *Ark* are so well adjusted to the things it was to contein; whereas if it had been a meer humane invention, 'tis most probable, that it would have been contrived according to those wild apprehensions, which (as I said before) do naturally arise from a more confused and general view of things, as much *too big*, as now such men are apt to think it too little, for those ends and purposes to which it was designed.

CHAP. VI.

The Parts of Animate Bodies; whether I. *More* Peculiar, *or* II. *More* General.

§. I:
PECULIAR
PARTS of
Animate Bodies.

UNder this Head of PECULIAR PARTS of *Animate* Bodies are comprehended all the Parts that belong to the whole kind of *Plants*: But as to *Animals*, it contains onely such as are peculiar to some of them, not common to all. And these are comprehended with the others under the same Head, because I could not otherwise place them conveniently to my purpose. They are distinguishable by their relation to

Plants; as being
{ LASTING PARTS. I.
 ANNUAL PARTS. II.
 KINDS OF FRUIT. III.
Animals; belonging chiefly unto
{ SWIMMING *Animals*. IV.
 FLYING *Animals*. V.
 GOING *Animals*. VI.

I. By

Chap. VI. *Parts peculiar.* 169

I. By LASTING PARTS of *Plants* are meant *such as* do usually continue during the *life* of the Plant, and are not renewed every year. And because the chief of these is styled WOOD, therefore may that be here adjoyned by way of affinity. These are distinguishable by their Fabric and Consistence, together with their Position and Shape; being either more

I. LASTING PARTS of Plants.

- *Hard* and Solid; considered *according to the*
  - *Position; as to the*
    - *Earth*, wherein Plants do grow; being either
      - *Within it*; to which may be *adjoyned* those *parts* in the body of the Plant *which have* some *analogy* to Roots.
        - 1. { ROOT, *Radical, radicate, eradicate.*
             KNOT, *Knurle, Knag.*
      - *Without it*; the upright part above ground; ‖ either the *greater*, upon, and from which the branches do grow: or the *lesser*, growing up from the same root.
        - 2. { STOCK, *Stem, Trunk, Body, Stalk, Stub, Stump.*
             SUCKER, *Shoot.*
    - *Plant it self, shooting from the Stem* of it; ‖ whether *greater* and *spread*: or *less*, and *pointed*, being common likewise to *Fishes, &c.*
      - 3. { BRANCH, *Sprig, Sion, young Shoot, Graft, Bough, Arm* of a Tree, *Slip, Lop.*
           THORN, *Prickle, Spinous.*
  - *Shape* and Figure; ‖ more *cylindrical* and *stiff*: or more *taper* and *flexile*.
    - 4. { STICK, *Staff, Stake, Cudgel, Scepter, Mace, Crosier, Virg, Leading-staff, Truncheon, Battoon, Rest, Scatch, Crutch, Helve, Perch, Tally.*
         WAND; *Twig, Rod, Switch, Pole.*
- *Soft.*
  - *Not dissolvable;* ‖ *outward*: or *inward.*
    - 5. { RINDE, *Bark, Pill.*
         PITH.
  - *Dissolvable*, by *Water*, or by *Fire*; being ‖ either of an *aqueous*: or an *unctuous* nature.
    - 6. { GUM.
         RESIN.
- *Liquid*; of a ‖ more *watery*: or more *unctuous* consistence.
  - 7. { JUICE, *Sap, Succulent.*
       BALSAM.

170   *Parts peculiar.*   Part. II.

II. ANNU-
AL parts of
Plants.

II. By ANNUAL *Parts* are meant such as are renewed every year; which are either

More principal; *those parts whereby Plants do propagate their kinds.*
- *Antecedent to the Seed*; either that most tender part of a Plant, considerable for its beauty and colour, *adhering to the first rudiments of the Seed:* or that which is answerable to this in Willows and Nut-trees, *&c.*

   1. { FLOWER, *Blossom, Bloom, blown, Nosegay, Posey.*
       { CATKIN, *Palm.*

The Seed it self; *in respect of* the
- *Parts* belonging to it, and *encompassing it*; || either the most
  - *Soft* and *succulent*; *betwixt* the outward *Skin* and the inward *Seed vessel*: or the most *hard crustaceous* part *containing the Seed.*

   2. { PULP.
       { STONE, *Shell.*

- *Thin part for Covering*: or *Oblong, for Defence.*

   3. { HUSK, *Hull, Shell, Skin, Chaff, Boled.*
       { BEARD.

Aggregate of Fruit or Seed; of a Figure || more *gross* and *confused:* or more *narrow, oblong,* and *taper.*

   4. { CLUSTER, *Bunch, Pannicle.*
       { EAR, *Spike, Spire, Bent.*

Less principal; to be further distinguished by the Figure, in respect of
- *Thickness* or *Thinness*; either such as are more *thick*, namely *the first little swellings* in the growth of a Plant, or of the parts of it: or such as are more *thin*, namely those *laminated parts*, belonging either to Plants themselves, or to their flowers.

   5. { SPROUT, *Bud, shoot, burgeon, pullulate, repullulate, germinate, put forth, spring forth.*
       { LEAF, *Foliage, Blade.*

Length; whether such as are
- *Proper to the Flower*; the *greater*, standing up singly in the middle of the flower: or the *lesser*, being small threddy filaments within the flower, whereof there are usually many together.

   6. { STILE.
       { STAMEN, *tuft.*

- *Common to other parts of the plant*; || either those small stemms, upon which *flowers* and *leaves* do grow: or those kinds of *thready shoots*, by which climbing *Plants* do take hold of and *twist about* the *things* that stand next to them

   7. { STALK, *Footstalk, shank.*
       { TENDREL, *Clasper.*

Hollowness; *conteining* within it, either || *the leaves of the flower:* or the *fruit.*

   8. { CUP, *Perianthium.*
       { PERICARPIUM.

Chap. VI. *Parts peculiar.* 171

III. By FRUITS are meant thofe more Succulent parts of Plants, which are either the *Receptacles of Seed*, or elfe the *Seeds themfelves*; to which may be adjoyned, by way of affinity, the general name denoting the EXCRESCENCES of Plants, as Galls are of Oken leaves, &c.

III. Kinds of FRUITS.

Fruits may be diftinguifhed into fuch as are

Receptacles of Seed.
- *Eaten* commonly *by men*; whofe eatable part is *covered with* a
  - *Soft Skin.*
    - *Without Stones*; being generally a larger fruit.
      1. APPLE, *Pomiferous.*
    - *With Stones*; ‖ either the *greater* kind, conteining one fingle ftone encompaffed with an efculent pulp: or the *lefs*, growing either in Clufters, or difperfedly on Trees, Shrubs and Herbs, conteining generally feveral fmall feeds or ftones in the pulp or hufk of it.
      2. { PLUM, *Pruin, Pruniferous.*
           BERRY, *Bacciferous.*
  - *Hard Shell*; namely that kind of fruit, whofe only efculent part is inclofed in a hard covering.
      3. NUT, *Nuciferous.*
- *Not eaten* commonly *by men, but by beafts.*
  - *Confifting of one* only *Seed, in a Seed-veffel*; ‖ *roundifh*: or *flat-figured.*
      4. { MAST, *Acorn, Pannage.*
           KEY.
  - *Conteining feveral Seeds*; being ‖ more *folid*: or *hollow.*
      5. { CONE, *Apple.*
           COD, *Huek, Pod, Shell, fhale, filiquous.*

Seed; ‖ being the *moft minute kind* of Fruit, whereby Plants propagate their Kinds; or the *Inmoft parts* of Seeds.
      6. { GRAIN, *Corn, Kern.*
           KERNEL.

The *Peculiar* parts of Animals here enumerated are faid to be fuch as belong *chiefly*, not only, *to the feveral* kinds of *Swimming, Flying, Going Animals*; becaufe there are fome under each Head that belong alfo to other Animals. So *Spawn* and *Cruft* belong *to Infects*, and fome *Beafts*, as well as to *Fifh*. So Trunk or *Probofcis*, and *Egg* do belong to fome *Going Animals*, as well as to *Flying*. So doth *Embryo to a Bat* and all *Viviparous Fifh*, as well as to *Going Animals*. But thefe Parts are more commonly and generally found amongft thofe Kinds under which they are lifted.

Z 2 IV. Thofe

IV. Parts peculiar to SWIMMING ANIMALS.

IV. Those *Parts peculiar* chiefly to SWIMMING ANIMALS, to which Custom hath ascribed distinct names, do serve either *for* their
Outward Covering; with respect to different Magnitudes.
- *Lesser*; being *a Thin lamin.*
  1. SCALE.
- *Greater*; || *opening usually upon* a *Joint,* as in Oisters, *&c.* or an *entire* Armature, *without* such *opening,* as in Lobsters, *&c.*
  2. { SHELL, *Testaceous.*
     { CRUST-*aceous, Shell.*

Respiration; those *Opening* parts *on the sides of the Head*, which are thought to supply the place of Lungs.
  3. GILL.

Progressive motion; serving either to
- *Direct this motion*; by feeling such objects as lye in the way, being long prominencies, standing off from the head, common to several Insects.
  4. FEELERS, *Horns, Antennæ.*
- *Assist in this motion*; whether of
  - *Swimming*; as in most kinds of skinned and scaly fish.
    - *Internal*; a thin membrane filled with air, by the help of which Fishes poise themselves in the water.
      5. SWIMMING BLADDER.
    - *External*; || either those *thin broad* substances, standing off from the body of the Fish: or those *long slender* parts belonging to these
      6. { FINN.
         { RAY, *Radius, Pinnula.*
  - *Going*; as in crustaceous exanguious Animals.
    7. CLAW.

Procreation; belonging either *to the* || *Males*: or *Females.*
  8. { MILT, *Soft row.*
     { SPAWN, *Hard row.*

V. The

Chap. VI.   Parts peculiar.   173

V. The *Parts peculiar* TO FLYING ANIMALS are either
Not fleshy; such as serve *for*
- *Outward covering*, which is done by small *oblong bodies*, *with hair-like branches* growing from both sides of them, the bottom of which is a kind of a *hollow Cylinder* like a reed.
  1. { FEATHER, *Plume, callow, fledge, pluck.*
     { QUILL.
- *Progressive motion*; which in such kind of Creatures is twofold.
  - *Flying*; which is done by those *parts fastned on the shoulders, by the motion of which they strike the Air:* These are generally an aggregate of Feathers; but in Bats and Flies of a Skinny consistence. To which may be adjoyned that aggregate of *hindermost Feathers, whereby they steer themselves* in their Flight.
    2. { WING.
       { TRAIN, *Tail.*
  - *Going*; by a *Foot with* several *Toes* ‖ *divided:* or *united by* some *film* for their better help in Swimming.
    3. { TALON, *Pounce, Claw, Clutch.*
       { FLAT FOOT, *Palmipede.*
- *Feeding* and *Fighting*; ‖ the *mouth* of a Bird: or a kind of *hollow tube* through which some things suck their nourishment.
  4. { BEAK, *Bill.*
     { TRUNK, *Proboscis, Snout.*
- *Fighting onely*; of a *sharp* figure; ‖ either *on the side of the Leg:* or *in the Tail*, counted poisonous.
  5. { SPUR.
     { STING, *Prickle.*
- *Procreation*; ‖ a *roundish body covered with a Shell:* or a *yellowish case containing a Maggot*, which is transmuted into a Moth or Butterfly.
  6. { EGG, *Nit, Flyblow.*
     { CHRYSALITE, *Aurelia.*

Fleshy; belonging to the
- *Fore-part*; and placed either ‖ *on the top of the head:* or *under the Jaw.*
  7. { COMB, *Crest.*
     { GILL, *Wattle.*
- *Hinder-part*; ‖ either that *Protuberance about the end of the Back-bone:* or that *Cavity* or *Glandule* in it *containing* an unctuous *substance for* the *suppling of the Feathers.*
  8. { RUMP.
     { OIL-BOX.

VI. The

VI. Parts peculiar TO GOING ANIMALS.

VI. The *Parts peculiar* belonging TO GOING ANIMALS are such as serve *for*

Outward covering; considerable according to the

More general name; denoting a small *oblong flexile body*, *growing Plant-like out of the skin*: or *Aggregates of these, growing thick together and curled.*

1. { HAIR.
     WOOL.

Particular kinds; ‖ either a more *big* and *stiff* kind of *hair*: or the more *small* and *softer* kinds of *hairy substances*, sometimes ascribed to Feathers.

2. { BRISTLE·
     DOWN, *Lint.*

Aggregates; more proper to *Hair*: or to *Wool.*

3. { FURR, *Ermin, Minivor*, &c. *Timber.*
     FLEECE, *Flu.*

Hairy parts; ‖ *on* the Chin or *Face*: or *on* the *Neck.*

4. { BEARD, *Mustach, Whisker.*
     MANE, *Crest.*

Progressive motion; whether ‖ *in whole* or *cloven-footed Animals*: or *in multifidous* or *clawed Animals.*

5. { HOOF.
     NAIL, *Claw.*

Fighting; the *foremost* part serving for offence *against greater Animals*: or the *hindermost* part serving for defence *against Insects.*

6. { HORN, *Head, goring.*
     TAIL, *Scut, Dock, Crupper, Single* of *Deer.*

Procreation; the *young in the Womb* before its birth: or the *bag wherein it is* contained.

7. { EMBRYO, *Child* in the Womb.
     SECUNDINE, *After-birth.*

Of GENERAL PARTS.

§. II. **B**Y GENERAL PARTS of *Animals* are meant such as are more *common to the whole kind*, or at *least* the more perfect kinds, as *Beasts and Men*; there being *several* parts enumerated under this head, as Milk, Marrow, Bone, Gristle, Tooth, Dug, Rib, Navel, all under the fifth Difference, and some under the sixth, which are *not common to all sorts of Insects, Fishes,* and *Birds.* These are distinguishable into

Homogeneous.
{ CONTAINED. I.
  CONTAINING. II.

Heterogeneus.
External.
{ HEAD. III.
  TRUNK. IV.
  LIMM. V.
INTERNAL. VI.

I. CON-

Chap. VI. *Parts general.* 175

I. CONTAINED HOMOGENEOUS PARTS are such kind of fluid Bodies as are distinguishable by their various Consistences and Uses, and not by any difference of Shape or Figure; because, being liquid, they have no Shape of their own, but must be contained *termino alieno.* They are either more

Thin and Aerial.
  1. SPIRIT-*uous.*
Liquid and Fluid; being either
  More limpid; and of an aqueous transparency, || for *diluting* and attenuating the Humors: or a prepared Juice for *nourishing* the several parts.
  2. { SERUM, *Whey.*
     { SUCCUS NUTRITIUS.
  More opacous and thick.
  Not generally diffused; being *useful* either *for*
    Nutrition; || a whitish humor in the Mesentery *extracted from the food before Sanguification:* or *receiving a farther digestion in the breasts* for the nourishment of the Fœtus.
  3. { CHYLE.
     { MILK, *Cream, Beestings, milch, Dairy.*
  Generation; || *common to both Sexes:* to which may be adjoyned that excrementitious moisture *proper to some Females.*
  4. { SPERM, *Seed, seminal.*
     { MENSTRUA, *Courses.*
  Diffused through the whole, and mixed together in one Mass; considered either according to the
    General name; denoting that *red juice* in the bodies of the more perfect Animals.
  5. BLOUD, *Crimson.*
    Particular kinds; of which this whole mass is said to consist, commonly stiled the four *Humors*, and according to the old Theory, esteemed to be either
      Hot; and || *moist*: or *dry.*
  6. { BLOUD, *Sanguin.*
     { CHOLER, *Gall.*
      Cold; and || *moist*: or *dry.*
  7. { PHLEGM, *pituitous.*
     { MELANCHOLY, *Choler adust.*
More consistent; || *in the Head*, the organ of the inward Senses: or *in the Cavity of the Bones*, for the moistning of them.
  8. { BRAIN.
     { MARROW, *medullary.*

II. CON-

II. CONTAINING HOMOGENEOUS PARTS

II. CONTAINING HOMOGENEOUS PARTS are distinguishable by their Qualities of Hardness and Softness, or by their Figures and Uses; being either *of a*

- *More hard Consistence*;
  - *For strengthning of the Fabric*; ‖ either the *most hard* and dry: or *less hard*; both devoid of Sense
    - 1. { BONE, *Skull*.
         GRISTLE, *Cartilage*.
  - *For uniting of the Bones and Muscles*; ‖ either *oblong*: or *the extremity of the Muscle* affixed to the part which is to be moved.
    - 2. { LIGAMENT.
         TENDON.
- *More soft Consistence*; being either
  - *Thin and broad*; *for covering of* ‖ the *outward parts*: or the *inward parts*.
    - 3. { SKIN, *Cuticle, Fell, Hide, Pelt, Slough, flay, excoriate, gall*.
         MEMBRANE, *Film, Pannicle, Tunicle, Skin, Pericardium, Pericranium, Peritonæum*.
  - *Oblong and narrow*;
    - *Hollow*; *for conveyance of the Bloud* ‖ *to the Heart*: or *from the Heart*.
      - 4. { VEIN, *Venal*.
           ARTERY -*all*.
    - *Solid*; for conveyance of the Spirits, *serving for Sense*: or those *small hair-like bodies* of which the Muscles consist.
      - 5. { NERVE, *Sinew*.
           FIBRE, *Grain, Filament*.
  - *Crass*; of no determinate Figure; *useful for*
    - *Motion*; according to the name, ‖ *more general*: or *particular*.
      - 6. { FLESH, *Parenchyma, carnal, Carnosity, incarnate*.
           MUSCLE, *Brawn*.
    - *Preserving from Heat and Cold*: or the *Percolation of some humors*.
      - 7. { FAT, *Suet, Tallow*.
           GLANDULE, *Kernel, Emunctory, Almond, Bur, Sweet-bread, Nut*.

V. The

Chap. VII.   *Parts general.*   177

III. Amongst *External containing Heterogeneous parts*, that which is the III. Of the *chief*, being the Seat and Residence of the Soul, is the HEAD: To which HEAD. may be opposed the other part styled BODY, *Carcass*.

The parts of the Head are either
- *More general*; || either *the fore-part less hairy:* or *the hinder-part more hairy*.
  - 1. { FACE, *Visage, Aspect, Countenance, Favour, Look, Mine, Physiognomy, Feature, Vizzard, Mask*.
       PATE, *Scalp, Noddle, Sconce, Scull, Brain-pan*.
- *More particular* parts of the Head and Face are either
  - *More properly Organical*; for
    - *Sense*; whether such parts as are
      - *External*; used for
        - *Seeing,* or *Hearing*.
          - 2. { EY, *Ocular, optic, see, view, look, kenn, behold, gaze, pore*.
               EAR, *Lug, bear, hearken, auricular*.
        - *Tasting,* or *Smelling*: ∥ either that Scissure of the Face through which we breath and receive our nourishment: or that hollow prominence, through which we breath and smell.
          - 3. { MOUTH, *Chaps, muzzle, oral, devour*.
               NOSE, *Snowt, Nostril, smell*.
      - *Internal*; used for
        - *Tasting, Speaking,* or *Eating*;
          - *Convex*; ∥ either that *of a soft Fleshy substance*, whereof there is but one: or that *of a most hard and dry consistence*, whereof there are many.
            - 4. { TONGUE, *lick*.
                 TOOTH, *Fang, Tusk, bite, gnaw, nibble, Holders, Grinders*.
          - *Concave*; either *the upper inward part of the Mouth:* or *the open passage through the Neck,* into the middle region of the Body.
            - 5. { PALATE, *Roof*.
                 THROAT, *guttural, jugular*.
  - *Less properly Organical*; but contributing to the making up the Fabric of the Face; distinguishable by their various Positions into
    - *Upper* and *fore-right*; ∥ *Extremity of the Face:* or *Protuberance over the Eye*.
      - 6. { FOREHEAD, *Brow, Front*.
           EY-BROW.
    - *Lateral*; ∥ *towards the middle:* or *towards the upper parts*.
      - 7. { CHEEK, *Jole*.
           TEMPLES.
    - *Lower*;
      - *Fore-right*; ∥ either the upper and lower *Extremity of* that Scissure which makes *the Mouth:* or the *Extremity of the Face*.
        - 8. { LIP.
             CHIN.
      - *Lateral*;
        - 9. { JAW, *Chap, Mandible, Jole*.
             PLACE OF TONSILLÆ.

A a   IV. By

IV. Of the TRUNK.

IV. By TRUNK is meant the middle part of *the Body*, considered *abstractly from Head and Limms*. The *Parts of the Trunk* are distinguishable by their various Positions, being either

Upper; towards the top of the Trunk.
- *Not determined* to fore or hinder part, but common to both; ‖ the *Stem-like of the Head*: or the *upper Convexity of Breast and Back*.
  1. { NECK, *Nape, Dulap.*
     { SHOULDER, *Scapulary.*
- *Determined* to the
  - *Fore-part*; ‖ more *general*: or more *specially* the glandulous part designed for milk *in females*.
    2. { BREAST, *Pectoral, Bosom.*
       { DUG, *Udder, Teat, Nipple, Pap, Breast.*
  - *Hinder part*; more *general*: or more *specially* the *Bones* of it.
    3. { BACK.
       { VERTEBRA, *Spondyl, spinal, Chine.*

Middle.
- *Hinder-part*; ‖ the *direct* Muscles: or *transverse* Bones.
  4. { LOIN, *Chine.*
     { RIB.
- *Side-part*; ‖ more *general*: or more *specially the lower* part of it.
  5. { SIDE, *Lateral, collateral.*
     { FLANK, *Rand.*
- *Fore-part*; more *general*: or more *specially* the concave *middle* part of it.
  6. { BELLY, *Paunch, Pannel, Peritonæum.*
     { NAVEL, *Umbilical.*

Lower;
- *Fore part*; the *concave* part ‖ *between the belly and thighs*: or seat of the Privities *between the thighs*.
  7. { GROIN.
     { SHARE, *Twist.*
- *Hinder-part*; ‖ more *general*: or *specially* the *Cavity*.
  8. { BUTTOCK, *Breech, Haunch, Ham.*
     { FUNDAMENT, *Dock.*

V. By

Chap. VII.   *Parts general.*   179

V. By LIMM or *Member* is meant any special *part designed for Action*, **V.** Of the *moveable upon*, and distinguishable by its *Joints*: for which reason the LIMMS. word JOINT may be annexed to it by way of affinity, one being the thing moved, and the other the thing upon which the motion is made.

They are either

Upper Limm.
- *Innermost*: or next to the Trunk, *with its Joint.*
  1. { ARM. / SHOULDER.
- *Middlemost.*
  2. { CUBIT. / ELBOW, *Pinion.*
- *Outermost.*
  3. { HAND -*le, wield, Manual, manage, Palm, Fist, Clutch, Grasp; Haft, Hilt, Glove.* / WRIST.

Lower Limm.
- *Innermost*: or next to the Trunk.
  4. { THIGH, *Hip, Ham, Haunch, Pestle.* / HUCKLE.
- *Middlemost.*
  5. { SHANK, *Leg, Shin, Calf.* / KNEE.
- *Outermost.*
  6. { FOOT, *Hock, Trotter, tread, trample, stamp, Instep.* / HEEL, *Calcitrate, kick, Pastern.*

Common both *to upper and lower* Limm; the Joints of which may be distinguished by the order of first, second, or third: or innermost, middlemost, or outermost.

  7. { FINGER, *Toe, Thumb.* / KNUCKLE.

Parts general.

IV. Of the TRUNK.

IV. By TRUNK is meant the middle part of *the Body*, considered *abstractly from Head and Limms*. The *Parts of the Trunk* are distinguishable by their various Positions, being either

Upper; towards the top of the Trunk.
- Not *determined* to fore or hinder part, but common to both; ‖ the *Stem-like of the Head*: or the *upper Convexity of Breast and Back*.
  1. { NECK, *Nape, Dulap.*
     { SHOULDER, *Scapulary.*
- *Determined* to the
  - *Fore-part*; ‖ more *general*: or more *specially* the glandulous part designed for milk *in females*.
    2. { BREAST, *Pectoral, Bosom.*
       { DUG, *Udder, Teat, Nipple, Pap, Breast.*
  - *Hinder part*; more *general*: or more *specially* the *Bones* of it.
    3. { BACK.
       { VERTEBRA, *Spondyl, spinal, Chine.*

Middle.
- *Hinder-part*; ‖ the *direct* Muscles: or *transverse* Bones.
  4. { LOIN, *Chine.*
     { RIB.
- *Side-part*; ‖ more *general*: or more *specially the lower* part of it.
  5. { SIDE, *Lateral, collateral.*
     { FLANK, *Rand.*
- *Fore-part*; more *general*: or more *specially* the concave *middle* part of it.
  6. { BELLY, *Paunch, Pannel, Peritonæum.*
     { NAVEL, *Umbilical.*

Lower;
- *Fore part*; the *concave* part ‖ *between the belly and thighs*: or seat of the Privities *between the thighs*.
  7. { GROIN.
     { SHARE, *Twist.*
- *Hinder-part*; ‖ more *general*: or *specially the Cavity.*
  8. { BUTTOCK, *Breech, Haunch, Ham.*
     { FUNDAMENT, *Dock.*

V. By

Chap. VII.   *Parts general.*   179

V. By LIMM or *Member* is meant any special *part designed for Action,* **V. Of the** *moveable upon,* and distinguishable by its *Joints:* for which reason the **LIMMS.** word JOINT may be annexed to it by way of affinity, one being the thing moved, and the other the thing upon which the motion is made.

They are either

Upper Limm.
- *Innermost:* or next to the Trunk, *with its Joint.*
  1. { ARM.
       SHOULDER.
- *Middlemost.*
  2. { CUBIT.
       ELBOW, *Pinion.*
- *Outermost.*
  3. { HAND-*le, wield, Manual, manage, Palm, Fist, Clutch, Grasp, Haft, Hilt, Glove.*
       WRIST.

Lower Limm.
- *Innermost:* or next to the Trunk.
  4. { THIGH, *Hip, Ham, Haunch, Pestle.*
       HUCKLE.
- *Middlemost.*
  5. { SHANK, *Leg, Shin, Calf.*
       KNEE.
- *Outermost.*
  6. { FOOT, *Hock, Trotter, tread, trample, stamp, Instep.*
       HEEL, *Calcitrate, kick, Pastern.*

Common both *to upper and lower* Limm; the Joints of which may be distinguished by the order of first, second, or third: or innermost, middlemost, or outermost.

7. { FINGER, *Toe, Thumb.*
     KNUCKLE.

Parts general. Part. II.

VI. Of the INWARDS.

VI. *Containing Heterogeneous Internal parts,* called INWARDS, *Entrails, Bowels. Foy, Pluck, Purtenance, Umbels, Haſtlet, Garbage, Giblets,* reckoning from the uppermoſt, may be diſtinguiſhed by their Order, Shape and Uſes, into

Upper ; towards the Summity of the Body.
  Hollow and oblong ; *for the conveyance of* the || *Nouriſhment :* or of the Breath.
  1. { GULLET.
     { WIND-PIPE, *Rough Artery, Weaſand.*
  Maſſie and more ſolid ; within the Breaſt; *for* || *Bloud-making :* or Breathing.
  2. { HEART, *Cordial, Core, Pericardium.*
     { LUNGS, *Lights.*
  Thin and broad ; *for partition* || *tranſverſe,* betwixt the upper and lower Belly : or *direct,* betwixt the Lobes of the Lungs.
  3. { DIAPHRAGM, *Midriff.*
     { MEDIASTINE.

Lower ; diſtinguiſhable
  Both by their Shapes and Uſes.
  Hollow ; || *wide, but not long,* for containing and digeſting of Food : *long, but not wide,* for conveying of the Food and Excrement.
  4. { STOMACH, *Maw, Paunch, Ventricle, Craw, Crop, Gorge, Pouch, Gizzard, Tripe.*
     { GUT, *Entrails, Bowels, Garbage, Chitterling, Colon.*
  Maſſie and ſolid ; *for ſeparating of* || *Choler :* or of *Melancholy.*
  5. { LIVER, *Hepatic.*
     { SPLEEN, *Milt.*
  Thin and broad, by which the Guts are || *connected :* or *covered.*
  6. { MESENTERY.
     { CAUL, *Kell.*
  By their Uſes alone, as being *for,*
  Separating the Urine : or *containing the Urine or the Gall.*
  7. { KIDNEY, *Reins.*
     { BLADDER, *Veſicle.*
  Generation ; denoting || the *parts for Generation :* or *the Glandules for preparing the Sperm.*
  8. { PRIVITIES, *Genitals, Pizzle, Tard, Fore-skin, Prepuce.*
     { TESTICLE, *Stone, geld, ſpay, Eunuch.*
  Conception in Females, namely, the part containing the Fœtus.
  9. WOMB, *Mother, Matrix, hyſterical, uterine.*

CHAP.

CHAP. VII.

Concerning the Predicament of Quantity, viz. I. Magnitude. II. Space; *and* III. Measure.

The chief *notions* belonging to the Predicament of *Quantity* are reducible to these general Heads;
{ MAGNITUDE.
  SPACE.
  MEASURE.

Of MAGNITUDE.

The word MAGNITUDE is intended to signifie all the notions of *continued Quantity*: to which may be adjoyned by way of affinity the word EXTENSION, by which is meant that kind of Quantity whereby a thing is said to have *partem extra partem*, one part out of another, being the same thing with the former under another Consideration.

§. I.

Magnitudes are distinguishable according to their
{ DIMENSIONS. I.
  MUTUAL RELATIONS to one another. II.
  AFFECTIONS, in respect *of Figure*; whether
  { SIMPLE. III.
    Compound; either
    { LINEARY. IV.
      PLANARY. V.
      SOLIDARY. VI.

As for *Oration*, which is enumerated in the usual Systems as one of the Species of Quantity; that is now by common consent acknowledged to be very *improperly stiled Quantity*; and therefore it is left out here, and referred to another place.

I. That kind of *Quantity whereby the Magnitude of Bodies is to be measured*, is called DIMENSION. To which may be adjoined upon account of Affinity, That notion of *Quantity, whereby a thing is capable of being separated into several parts*, DIVISION, *distribute, part*.

I. DIMENSION.

Dimensions are of a four-fold difference.

The *least of Magnitudes*, so styled by those who write *de Indivisibilibus*, as being in their account infinitely little.

1. POINT, *Prick, Tittle, Punctilio, Ace, Jot, Whit*.

The *second* kind, *described by the flux of a point*, or composed of infinite such points, is styled.

2. LINE, *delineate, rule*.

The *third*, *described by the draught of a line*, or composed of infinite such lines.

3. SUPERFICIES, *Plain, Surface*. To which may be annexed, that more particular notion of *Superficies*, called AREA, *Plot, Bed, Page*.

The *fourth*, *described by the lifting up a Superficies*, or composed of infinite Superficies.

4. SOLID, *Body, Bulk*.

By these may be express'd those Algebraical notions of *Absolute, Lineary, Quadratic, Cubic*; and so, continuing this Table, *Quadrato-Quadratic, Quadrato-Cubic, Cubo-Cubic, Quadrato-Cubo-Cubic*, &c. as far as one pleases.

II. The

II. MUTU- AL RELA- TIONS-	II. The MUTUAL RELATIONS of one Dimension to another are either of

Point to line; as being either in ‖ *the midst* : or *extremities* of it.
 1. {CENTER.
   POLE, *Zenith*, *Nadyr*.

Point to Lines, or *Line to Plains*; which do mutually ‖ either *meet* : or *intersect*.
 2. {VERTEX.
   INTERSECTION, *Cut*.

Line to Plain; or *Plain to Solid*.
 Angular; being ‖ either in the *midst* : or the *extremities* of it.
  3. {DIAGONAL.
    SIDE.
 Round; being either
  Extern; ‖ *touching* : or *cutting* it.
   4. {TANGENT.
     SECANT.
  Intern;
   Central; ‖ either more general, passing *from side to side* : or particularly that which passes from *Pole to Pole*.
    5. {DIAMETER, *Ray*.
      AXIS.
   Not central; ‖ either *from Periphery to Diameter* : or *from Periphery to Periphery*.
    6. {SINE.
      CHORD.

Line to Line, *Plain to Plain*, or *Solid to Solid* ; having
 Bare respect to one another in regard of
  Distance; ‖ either being *æquidistant* : or else *removing farther* : or *approaching nearer*.
   7. {PARALLEL.
     {DIVERGING, *Reclining*.
      CONVERGING, *inclining*.
  Position; making an *Angle*, *oblique* : or *right* : or *parallel*.
   8. {OBLIQUE, *a-skue*, *a-slope*, *awry*, *Declivity*, *shelving*, *flaunt*, *splay*, *skue*, *slope*, *wry*, *steep*, *incline*, *lean*, *glance*, *swagg*, *a-squint*, *leer*.
     DIRECT, *Erect*, *upright*, *perpendicular*, *advance*, *precipitate*, *headlong*, *down-right*, *up an end*, *set up*, *prick up*.
     TRANSVERSE, *Cross*, *overthwart*, *thwart*, *traverse*, *point-blank*.
 Mutual Contact ¶ ‖ either *returning from the other* : or *cutting through the other*.
   9. {REFLECTED, *Bound*, *rebound*, *recoil*, *repercussion*, *reverberate*, *rebuff*.
     REFRACTED.

III. To

Chap. VII.   *Magnitude.*   183

III. To the *Affections of Magnitudes*, in respect of more SIMPLE FIGURE, may be adjoyned the general notion of FIGURE, *shape, Feature, Fashion, Form, Frame, Scheme, Lineament, the Make, well set,* or *proportioned, transform, transfigure, deface, disfigure.*

III. SIMPLE FIGURE.

These Affections may be distinguished into such as belong

Onely to Lines drawn from point to point; || *the nearest way:* or *not the nearest way*
1. { STRAIGHTNESS, *Right, direct, point-blank.*
   { CROOKEDNESS, *Curve, a-wry, hooked, bow, bend, wry, embow, winding, indirect, fetch a compass.*

To lines and Plains; whether considered
  Absolutely; in
    General; *contained within* || *one line*, whose every part is equally distant from the same Center: or *three or more lines*, whose extremities touch one another.
2. { CIRCLE, *Periphery, Circumference, environ, encircle, surround, Ring, Rundle, Epicycle.*
   { ANGLE, *Corner, Coyn, Nook, Elbow, Polygon.*
  Special; of the Angular, || *whether of ninety degrees:* or *more:* or *less.*
    { RIGHT ANGLE.
3. { OBTUSE, *blunt, dull.*
    { ACUTE, *sharp, keen, whet.*
  Respectively; in Bodies whose superficies is composed || either *all of straight lines:* or *of lines bending in the midst, outward:* or *inward.*
    { PLAIN, *level, flat, even.*
4. { CONVEX, *prominent, gibbous, protuberant, turgid, embowed.*
    { CONCAVE, *Hollow, Cavity, Pit, Hole.*

To Plains or Solids, of
  Simple Figure; whose superficies is || *Circular:* or *Angular of equal sides.*
5. { SPHERE, *Orb, Globe, Ball, Bullet, Round, Bullet, Pomander, Pommel, Bede*
   { CUBE, *Dy.*
  Mixed Figures; described either by the
    Lifting up || *of a Circle:* or *of an Angular plain.*
6. { CYLINDER, *Bar, Column, Cann, Cannon, Role.*
   { PRISM, *Bar, Wedge.*
  Laying on, *in progression from a Point, infinite Plains* || *circular:* or *angular.*
7. { CONE, *Taper, Spire, Steeple, Shaft, Pinnacle.*
   { PYRAMID, *Spire, Steeple, Shaft, Pinnacle, Obelisk.*

To Lines, or Plains, or Solids; denoting either
  The different Sections of a Cone, being cut || either *parallel to the sides of it:* or *besides the Parallel* either way.
8. { PARABOLA -*icall.*
   { HYPERBOLE.
   { ELLIPSIS, *oval.*
  The revolution of a Line about || a *Cone:* or *Cylinder.*
9. { SPIRAL, *serpentine, turbinated, wreath, coyling, worm.*
   { HELIX, *Winding.*

IV. COM-

IV. Compound Figures LINEARY.

IV. COMPOUND FIGURES of Magnitude LINEARY by unclosed Lines, are either

More *Simple*; by

One Line; whether ||*solid*: or *hollow*.
1. {PIN, *Gad, Nail, Peg, Tag, Tack, Tenter. Needle, Probe.*
   {HOLE, *Hollow, Pore, Vent, Meash, Orifice, Meuse, punch, perforate, run thorough.*

Two lines;

The end of one meeting with the end of the other; || either *convex:* or *concave.*

Sharp;
2. {TOOTH, *Cusp, Point, Neb, Scrag, Tine, Tenon, Cog, ingrail,* indented.
   {NOTCH, *Nick, Nock, crenated, Gap, hatcht, inveck, indented.*

Blunt.
3. {PROTUBERANCE, *Prominence, Process, Stud, Bofs, Excrescence, Gibbous, Crump, Bunch, Knob, Rub, jutting, rising, tuberous, standing out, stick out, goggle, copped, turgid, Brow, Hillock, Knob, Knot, Node, Cragg, Scrag, Lobe, gorbellied, heave, swell, strut.*
   {DENT, *Dimple, Sinking, Dock, Crease, indent, Hole, Pit.*

The *end* of one with the *midst* of the other *meeting:* or the *midst* of one with the *midst* of the other *cutting.*

4. {FIGURE of the letter T, *Crutch.*
   {CROSS, *Decussation, athwart, Turn-stile.*

Three Lines; at

Several points making Angles; either || *on the same side:* or *on diverse sides.*
5. {STAPLE.
   {WINDLE.

The *same point* ||*meeting,* or *cutting;* which is applicable likewise to more lines then three.
6. {TUFT, *Lock, Tassel, Tresses, Thrum, Hassock, Nap, Rug, Fringe.*
   {ASTERISC.

More *Compounded;*

Distinctly;

Pin || with *versatil Pin:* or with *versatil Lamin.*
7. {WHIP, *Flail, Scourge.*
   {FLAG, *Fane, Banroll, Penon.*

Pin || with *Tooth* or *Protuberance,* &c. or with *Notch* or *Dent.*
8. {HOOK, *Crook, Clasp, Hasp, Tatches, Flook, Tenter, Cramp-iron.*
   {FORK, *Prong, horned.*

Mixedly, with some kind of Alternation; || either with *Protuberance* and *Dent:* or with *Staple* and its *reverse.*
9. {UNDULATED, *waved, winding.*
   {CRENATED, *Battlement.*

Chap. VII. *Magnitude.* 185

·V. *Compound Figures* of Magnitude PLANARY, expressible by closed Lines, may be distinguished into such as do either
Comprehend Superficies.
  Straight; either of three : or of four Angles.
  1. { TRIANGLE.
     { SQUARE, *Quadrangle, Quadrate, Diamond figure, Rhomb-oid, Lozenge, Parallellogram.*
  Curve; either ‖ *Round :* or *Oblong.*
  2. { RING, *Ferule, Hoop, Annulet, Collet, Rundle, Rowel.*
     { LOOP, *Button-hole, Eye, Link, Noose, Halter.*
  Mixed; being either ‖ *part of a Ring* with one straight : or *a whole Ring* with several Diameters.
  3. { BOW.
     { WHEEL.
Consist in being Superficies; as the precedent Figures fluxed into breadth. So the *Flux of a*
  Pin : or a *Hole,* do make
  4. { LAMIN, *Flake, Leaf, Board, Plank, Lath, Plate, Schedule, Scrole, Sheet, Wafer, Cake, Leam, Flap, Label, Coit.*
     { CHINK, *Crevise, Fissure, Cleft, Crack, Cranny, Chap, Flaw, Rift, Split, Slit, Loop-hole, cleave, spring a leak.*
  The FIGURE *T* or *Cross* and *Asterisc,* do make
  5. { TRESSEL, *Table.*
     { PINION, *Nut.*
  Cusp : or *Notch,* do make.
  6. { EDG, *sharp.*
     { GUTTER, *Chamfer.*
  Protuberance : and *Dent.*
  7. { RIDGE, *Bank, Dam, Bridg, Edg, Ledg.*
     { FURROW, *Ditch, Dike, Kennel, Channel, Foss, Trench, Dock, Drein, Cut, Dimple, Rivel, Shrivel, Wrinkle, rumple, pucker, Pleit.*
  Staple and *Windle*
  8. { FORM.
     { STEP, *Grees.*
  Square and *Ring.*
  9. { TUBE SQUARE.
     { TUBE ROUND, or *Pipe, Spout, Trunck, Tunnel.*

V. Compound Figures PLANARY.

VI. *Compound Figures* of Magnitude *Solidary*, may be diſtinguiſhed into ſuch as are either

Intern; denoting the inner parts of a Magnitude to be ‖ either *full of ſmall Cavities*: or to be *one great Cavity*: or to have *no Cavity*.
1. { POROUSNESS, *Spunginess, fungous, ſinking, hollow.*
   { HOLLOWNESS, *Cavity, concave, Grot, Cave, Den.*
   { MASSINESS, *ſolid, Bulk.*

Extern; compounded either of

Sphere or *Cube, with* ‖ *Cylinder*: or with *Cone.*
2. { BOTTLE, *Button, Bolt-head.*
   { PIN, *beaded.*

Cylinder or *Priſm*, with

Diverſe Figures; whether ‖ *Cube and Pyramid*: or *Cone and Pyramid.*
3. { PEDESTAL.
   { TURRET or *Tent, Tower, Pinnacle.*

Another of the ſame kind; either ‖*perpendicular*: or *tranſverſe.*
4. { GUDGEON.
   { MALLET.

Gone with Cone; having ‖ *Baſe to Baſe*: or *Vertex to Vertex.*
5. { BUOY FIGURE.
   { HOUR-GLASS FIGURE.

Elliptic; repreſenting the figure of a Sphere cruſhed, ‖either *about the midſt by a Hoop*: or *at the ends by two oppoſite Plains.*
6. { OVAL, *Elliptical.*
   { BOWL.

Spirals: or *Helixes.*
7. { BOTTOM, *Clue, glomerate, wind about.*
   { SKEIN, *Hanke, Reel.*

Of SPACE.

§. II. THe word SPACE, *Scope, Room, Compaſs, Interim, Interval,* (according to the common uſe of it) is a name importing the more general notion of that wherein any thing is contained or done;

Comprehending both { *Time.*
{ *Place.*
{ *Situation.*

I. By TIME, *Tract, Tide, Proceſs, Opportunity, Seaſon, Continuance,* is
meant continued ſucceſſive Quantity, having for its common term, IN-
STANT, *Moment, Trice, Nick.*

This is diſtinguiſhable according to the

Simple differences of it.
1. { PRESENT, *at this time, now, immediately, inſtantly, current, ready.*
   { PAST, *expired, former, fore-going, ago, already, even now, heretofore, gone, over, out, a-late, erewhile, long ſince.*
   { FUTURE, *time to come, after-time, hereafter, preſently, anon,
   by and by, ſhortly, ſtraitway, ere long, henceforth, proceſs of time,
   after a long while.*

Mixed

186

Chap. VII.   *Space.*   187

I. *Mixed* relations of it.
  Comparative ; betwixt
    The *Exiſtings of ſeveral things*; whether ||*both together in the ſame time*:
    or whether in *diverſe times*, ſo that one is *before* or *after* the other.
      2. { SIMULTANEOUS, *of the ſame time, Synchroniſm, contemporary,*
                compatible, conſiſt, together, concomitant.
            DISTANT, { PRECEDING, *antecedent, former, foregoing, previ-*
                ous, Priority, before, take place, get the ſtart, Predeceſ-
                ſor, premiſe.
                SUCCEEDING, *latter, Poſteriority, ſuccedaneous,*
                hinder, follow, go after, Succeſſor.
    The *Conſiderations* of the *ſame thing* at *ſeveral times* ; whether
      Paſt ; || *little :* or *much.*
        3. { NEWNESS, *Renovation, innovate, renew, anew, Neoteric, Neo-*
            phyte, novel, Novice, Puny, modern, freſh, upſtart, green, late,
            laſt, a little while ago.
           OLDNESS, *ancient, Antiquity, priſtin, ſenior, ſtale, inveterate,*
            of long ſtanding, yore, obſolete, out of date, a long while ago.
      Future ; ||*little :* or *much*
        4. { SOONNESS, *ſudden, early, rath, betimes, forthwith, ſhortly, pre-*
            ſently, eftſoon, quickly, in a trice, out of hand, imminent, immedi-
            ate, incontinent, inſtant, ready, anticipate, accelerate, put on, rid
            way, in the turning of a hand, twinckling of an eye, timely, ſpee-
            dily, in haſt, after a little time.
          LATENESS, *tardy, laſt, adjourn, defer, delay, put off, out of date, di-*
            latory, procraſtinate, prolong, prerogue, protract, reſpite, retard, after
            (a long while, far in the day.
  Abſolute ;
    Particular ;
      Determinate ; expreſſing || *at what time* a thing was: or *from whence*
        5. { DATE.   (it is to be reckoned.
           EPOCHA, *Hegira.*
      Indeterminate ; expreſſing only the
        Continuing of it ; || *a great :* or *little* time.
          6. { PERMANENCY, *laſting, abiding, continuing, durable, ſtay,*
              remain, perſevere, enduring, inceſſant, indelible, perennial,
              tedious, hold out, of ſtanding.
           TRANSITORINESS, *fading, flitting, frail, glance, tranſient,*
              temporary, ſhort, for a ſpirt, for a little while, quickly gone.
        Recurring of it ; || *many :* or *few* times.
          7. { FREQUENCY, *often, ever and anon, thick◼e, common,*
              recourſe, reſort.
           SELDOMNESS, *rare, ſcarce, ſtrange, unuſual, thin, deſuetude.*
  Univerſal ;
    Collective ; when a thing *continues* || throughout *the whole time :*
    or only *ſome intermediate parts* of it.
      8. { PERPETUITY, *continual, inceſſant, ſtill, at all times, alwayes.*
          AT TIMES, *temporary, by ſnatches, by fits, bout, ever and anon,*
          now and then, reſpit, ſometimes.
    Diſtributive ; when a thing exiſts || in *every part of time :* or *not*
    in any part of it.
      9. { EVERNESS, *Eternity, endleſs, for ever and ever, always.*
          NEVERNESS.   B b 2   II. The

II. PLACE. II. The Space wherein any thing is contained, is called PLACE, *Room, local, standing, station, precinct, set, put, position, lay, dispose, pitch, plant Guns, dislocate, Prospect.*

It is distinguishable, as the former, according to the more
- *Simple* differences of it; denoting that place; ‖ *wherein* we are: or *out of which* we are.
    1. { PRESENCE, *face to face, at hand, here, hand to hand, confront, ready, residence.*
       { ABSENCE, *Mich, away, non-residence.*
- *Mixed* relations of it.
    - *Comparative*; betwixt the
        - *Existence of several things;* ‖ whether *both together in the same place:* or *in divers places.*
            2. { CONTIGUITY, *touch, contact, hit, joyn, close, grazing.*
               { DISTANCE, *off, keep off, bear off, stave off, way off, set farther, stand away.*
        - *Consideration of Distance or Place* interposed, according to the differences of ‖ *Little :* or *Much.*
            3. { NEARNESS, *Vicinity, Propinquity, Proximity, nigh, next, close, adjacent, adjoyn, neighbour, imminent, impendent, immediate, ready at hand, accost, draw on, approach, at, by, hard-by, besides, hithermost.*
               { REMOTENESS, *far, farther, aloof, wide of, distant, outmost, ultimate, great way off.*
    - *Absolute*;
        - *Particular.*
            - *Determinate;* expressing what is the particular *place* ‖ *to which a thing belongs :* or *whence it began.*
                4. { HOME, *Scene.*
                   { RISE, *Source, Country, Original, Spring, Root.*
            - *Indeterminate;* expressing only
                - The *taking up of* ‖ *a great :* or *little* place.
                    5. { AMPLENESS, *spacious, large, burly, wide, vast.*
                       { NARROWNESS, *close, scantness, strictness, restrained.*
                - The *occurring* in ‖ *many :* or *few places.*
                    6. { OBVIOUSNESS, *common, rife, thick.*
                       { RARENESS, *seldom, scarce, thin.*
    - *Universal.*
        - *Collective;* when a thing is continued ‖ throughout the *whole place :* or is only in *some parts* of it.
            7. { CONTINUANCE, *produce, subsist, along, close.*
               { DISCONTINUANCE, *by coasts, sparsim, cease, pause, respit, leak off, intermit, interrupt.*
        - *Distributive;* when a thing is in ‖ *every place :* or *none.*
            8. { UBIQUITY, *Omnipresence.*
               { NULLIBIETY.

Chap. VII.   Space.   189

III. The mixed Notion made up of *Position* and *Place*, or the Application of the parts of a Body to the parts of Place, respectively, is styled SITUATION, *Seat, set, site, lying, standing, pitch, plant, position, placing*; to which may be annexed, by way of affinity, that respect of the imaginary face of a thing towards some other thing or place, called VERGENCY, *tending, leaning, inclining, banker, toward, upon that hand, Rhombe.*
These are either more

III. SITUATION.

General; respecting ‖ the *Universe*: or the *four chief terms of it*.
1. { EAST *Orient.*
    { WEST, *Occidental.*
2. { NORTH, *Septentrional, Arctic.*
    { SOUTH, *Meridional, Antarctic.*

Special; with relation to the several parts of any thing, consider'd as a
Line; the *interjacent* part: or those which are most remote from each other.
3. { MIDDLE, *Intermediate, Mean, Core, Heart, Wast, main body, Noon, between both, Interim, Interval.*
    { EXTREME, *Term,* { END, *final, last, extremity, ultimate, surcease, last, end, utter,* { *terminate, expire, in fine.* *utmost.* { BEGINNING, *First.*

Superficies; the outmost parts of which, being considered either with relation to *the thing it self*: or some *other thing* to which it is adjoyned, is commonly styled
4. { SIDE, *Flank, Wing, Cheek, lateral, collateral, Limb, Rim, Brink, Brink, Edge-wise, Hem, Ridg, Skirt, List, Selvage, Welt, Gard, Eaves, Battlement.*
    { MARGIN, *Limit, Marches, Border, Verge, Meer, Bound, Term, Front-ier, Land-mark, adjacent, abutt, confine, Purliew.*

Body;
In *general*; either as to such parts as are
Higher: or *Lower*.
5. { UPPER-SIDE, *Ridge, above, vertical.*
    { UNDER-SIDE, *lower, neather, bottom.*
Within: or *Without*.
6. { IN-SIDE, *internal, intrinsecal, inward, inner, inmost, intestine,*
    { OUT-SIDE, *external, extrinsecal, outward, outmost, utter, utmost, Surface, superficial, exterior, ambient.*

Living Bodies; specially men, with relation either to
The *Head*: or *Foot*.
7. { TOP, *Tip, Head, Crown, Upper end, Knap, Apex, Vertical, Chapiter.*
    { BOTTOM, *Base, Lower end, Pedestal, Foot, Sole.*
The *Face*: or *Back*.
8. { FORE-PART, *Front, Frontispiece, Prow, Van-tguard, Vanward, foreward.*
    { HINDER-PART, *Back, Rere, rereward, endorse, last, Poop, Posterior,*
The *right hand*: or *left hand*.
9. { RIGHT SIDE, *Dexter, Starrbord.*
    { LEFT SIDE, *sinister, Larrbord.*

Of

Of MEASURE.

§. III. MEASURE.

THose several *relations of Quantity, whereby men* use *to judge of* the *Multitude or Greatness* of things, are styled by the name of MEASURE, *Dimension, mete, survey, Rule*; to which the relative term of PROPORTION, *Portion, Rate, Tax, Size, Scantling, Pittance, Share, Dose, Mess, Symetry, Analogy, commensurate, dispense, allot, adapt,* is of some Affinity, signifying an *equality* or similitude of *the respects that several things* or quantities *have to one another.* They are distinguishable into such as respect either

- MULTITUDE. I.
- MAGNITUDE. II.
- GRAVITY. III.
- VALOR. IV.
- *Duration.*
  - More GENERALLY CONSIDERED. V.
  - As RESTRAINED TO LIVING CREATURES. VI.

I. MULTITUDE.

I. To the *Measure* whereby we judge *of the* MULTITUDE of things may be annexed NUMBER, *enumerate, reckon, compute, muster, count, re-count, Tale, tell, Arithmetic, Cyphering.* If the way of Numeration were now to be stated, it would seem *more convenient* to determine the first *Period* or Stand at the number *Eight*, and *not* at *Ten*; because the way of Dichotomy or Bipartition being the most natural and easie kind of Division, that Number is capable of this down to an Unite, and according to this should be the several denominations of all other kinds of Measures, whether of Capacity, Gravity, Valor, Duration. So eight Farthings would make a Peny, eight Pence a Shilling, eight Shillings an Angel, eight Angels a Pound. So eight Grains should make a Scruple, eight Scruples a Dram, eight Drams an Ounce, eight Ounces a Pound, *&c.* But because general *custom* hath already agreed upon *the decimal way,* therefore I shall not insist upon the change of it.

The different degrees of Number generally received, are these.

1. ONE, *Ace, Unite, Once, First, Imprimis, Single.*
2. TWO, *a Couple, a Brace, a Pair, a Yoke, Second-ly, Twice, Double, Twofold, Bipartite.*
3. THREE, *a Leash, Ternary, Trey, Third-ly, Tertian, Thrice, Treble, Threefold, Tripartite, Trine-ity.*
4. FOUR, *Fourth-ly, Quartan, Quaternion, Fourfold, Quadruple, Quadrupartite, Quartile.*
5. FIVE, *Fifth-ly, Quintuple, Fivefold.*
6. SIX, *Sixth-ly, Sixfold, Sextuple, Sextile, Senary.*
7. SEVEN, *Seventh-ly, Septuple, Sevenfold.*
8. EIGHT, *Eighth-ly, Octuple, Eightfold.*
9. NINE, *Ninth-ly, Ninefold.*

How other numbers besides these here enumerated may be expressed both in *writing* and *speech,* see hereafter, Chap.

II. Measures

Chap. VII.   Measure.   191

II. Measures of *Magnitude* do comprehend both those of Length, and of Superficies or Area, together with those of Solidity; both comprehended in that which is adjoyned, *viz.* the word CAPACITY, *hold, contain*. The several Nations of the World do not more differ in their Languages, then in the various kinds and proportions of these Measures. And it is not without great difficulty, that the Measures observed by all those different Nations who traffick together, are reduced to that which is commonly known and received by any one of them; which labour would be much abbreviated, if they were all of them fixed to any one certain Standard. To which purpose, it were most desirable to find out some *natural Standard*, or *universal Measure*, which hath been esteemed by Learned men as one of the *desiderata* in Philosophy. If this could be done in *Longitude*, the other Measures might be easily fixed from thence.

II. MAGNITUDE.

This was heretofore aimed at and endeavoured after in all those various Measures, derived from natural things, though none of them do sufficiently answer this end. As for that of a *Barly corn*, which is made the common ground and original of the rest, the *magnitude* and *weight* of it may be so various in several times and places, as will render it incapable of serving for this purpose; which is true likewise of those other Measures, an *Inch, Palm, Span, Cubit, Fathom, a Foot, Pace*; &c. none of which can be determined to any sufficient certainty.

Some have conceived that this might be better done by subdividing a *Degree upon the Earth*: But there would be so much difficulty and uncertainty in this way as would render it unpracticable. Others have thought, it might be derived from the *Quick-silver experiment*: But the unequal gravity and thickness of the *Atmosphere*, together with the various tempers of Air in several places and seasons, would expose that also to much uncertainty.

The most probable way for the effecting of this, is that which was first suggested by Doctor *Christopher Wren*, namely, by *Vibration of a Pendulum*: Time it self being a natural Measure, depending upon a revolution of the *Heaven* or the *Earth*, which is supposed to be every-where equal and uniform. If any way could be found out to make Longitude commensurable to Time, this might be the foundation of a *natural Standard*. In order to which,

Let there be a solid Ball exactly round, of some of the heaviest metals: Let there be a String to hang it upon, the smallest, limberest, and least subject to retch: Let this Ball be suspended by this String, being extended to such a length, that the space of every Vibration may be equal to a second Minute of time, the String being, by frequent trials, either lengthned or shortned, till it attain to this equality: These Vibrations should be the smallest, that can last a sufficient space of time, to afford a considerable number of them, either 6, or 500 at least; for which end, its passing an arch of five or six degrees at the first, may be sufficient. The *Pendulum* being so ordered as to have every one of its Vibrations equal to a second minute of time, which is to be adjusted with much care and exactness; then measure the length of this String, from its place of suspension to the Centre of the Ball; which Measure must be taken as it hangs free in its perpendicular posture, and not otherwise, because of stretching: which being done, there are given these two Lengths, *viz.* of the *String*, and of the *Radius* of the Ball, to which a third Proportional must be found out;

which

which must be, as the length of the String from the point of Suspension to the Centre of the Ball is to the Radius of the Ball, so must the said Radius be to this third: which being so found, let two fifths of this third Proportional be set off from the Centre downwards, and that will give the Measure desired. And this (according to the discovery and observation of those two excellent persons, the Lord Viscount *Brouncker*, President of the Royal Society, and *Mon. Huygens*, a worthy Member of it) will prove to be 38 *Rhinland* Inches, or (which is all one) 39 Inches and a quarter, according to our *London* Standard.

Let this Length therefore be called the *Standard*; let one Tenth of it be called a *Foot*; one Tenth of a Foot, an *Inch*; one Tenth of an Inch, a *Line*. And so upward, Ten Standards should be a *Pearch*; Ten Pearches, a *Furlong*; Ten Furlongs, a *Mile*; Ten Miles, a *League*, &c.

And so for Measures of *Capacity*: The *cubical* content of this Standard may be called the *Bushel*: the Tenth part of the Bushel, the *Peck*; the Tenth part of a Peck, a *Quart*; and the Tenth of that, a *Pint*, &c. And so for as many other Measures upwards as shall be thought expedient for use.

As for Measures of *Weight*; Let this cubical content of distilled Rainwater be the *Hundred*; the Tenth part of that, a *Stone*; the Tenth part of a Stone, a *Pound*; the Tenth of a Pound, an *Ounce*; the Tenth of an Ounce, a *Dram*; the Tenth of a Dram, a *Scruple*; the Tenth of a Scruple, a *Grain*, &c. And so upwards; Ten of these cubical Measures may be called a *Thousand*, and Ten of these Thousand may be called a *Tun*, &c.

As for the Measures of *Mony*, 'tis requisite that they should be determined by the different Quantities of those two natural Metals which are the most usual materials of it, viz. *Gold* and *Silver*, considered in their Purity without any *allay*. A Cube of this Standard of either of these Metals may be styled a *Thousand* or a *Talent* of each; the Tenth part of this weight, a *Hundred*; the Tenth of a Hundred, a *Pound*; the Tenth of a Pound, an *Angel*; the Tenth of an Angel, a *Shilling*; the Tenth of a Shilling, a *Peny*; the Tenth of a Peny, a *Farthing*.

I mention these particulars, not out of any hope or expectation that the World will ever make use of them, but only to shew the possibility of reducing all Measures to one determined certainty.

These measures of MAGNITUDE (to which may be annexed the Notion of CONTENT) may be reduced to these Heads.

1. Line.
2. INCH.
3. FOOT.
4. STANDARD.
5. PEARCH.
6. FURLONG.
7. MILE.
8. LEAGUE.
9. DEGREE.

Each of which is *applicable* either *to Longitude, Area,* or *Bulk*: the last of which comprehends the Measures of Capacity.

III. GRAVITY. III. Measures of GRAVITY (to which may be annexed for affinity the *thing by which Gravity is measured*, styled WEIGHT, *Poize, counterpoise, Plummet,*) may be distributed into these kinds.

1. GRAIN.
2. SCRUPLE.
3. DRAM.
4. OUNCE.
5. POUND.
6. STONE
7. HUNDRED.
8. THOUSAND.
9. TUN.

IV. The

Chap. VII.   *Measure.*   193

IV. The Gradual differences of that common Measure of the VA- iv. VALOR.
LUATION or *worth of all vendible things* (to which may be adjoyned
that which is used *as this common Measure,* ftyled MONY, *Cash, Coin,
Bank, Treasure, pecuniary, Mint, Stamp, Medal, Counter, Purse,*) may be di-
ftinguished into

  1 FARTHING, *Dodkin.*   5 POUND.
  2 PENY.   6 HUNDRED.
  3 SHILLING.   7 THOUSAND.
  4 ANGEL.

V. Unto the Measure of TIME may be adjoyned for its affinity the v. TIME.
word which fignifies the Permanency of any thing in its exiftence, from
its beginning to its end, DURATION, *abide, continue, perfift, endure,
hold out, laft long, perfevere, everlafting, furvive.*

Time is ufually diftributed by the Revolution of the heavenly Bodies,
or rather of the Earth and Moon, into fuch Spaces as are required to a
revolution of the

⎰*Earth in its Orb;* according to the
⎱ *Whole*
   1. YEAR, *Twelvemonth, Anniverfary, Annual, Biennial,* &c.
  Parts; confiderable as being the *proper feafons for the*
   Growth and *ripening* of Vegetables.
  2. ⎰SPRING, *Vernal.*
    ⎱SUMMER.
   Decaying of Vegetables, according to ‖ a *leffer :* or *greater degree.*
  3. ⎰AUTUMN, *Fall of the Leaf, Harveft.*
    ⎱WINTER, *Hybernal, hyemal.*
Moon in its own proper courfe *about the Earth :* to which may be ad-
joyned the ufual name given to the *fourth part of this.*
  4. ⎰MONTH, *Menftrual.*
    ⎱WEEK, *Sennight, Fortnight.*
Earth about its Axis; according to the
⎰*Whole*
⎱ 5. DAY NATURAL, *Quotidian.*
Parts;
 Greater;
  Time while the Sun continues ‖ *above :* or *below* the Horizon.
  6. ⎰DAY ARTIFICIAL, *Diurnal.*
    ⎱NIGHT, *Nocturnal, Pernoctation, lodge.*
  Part of the day artificial, ‖ *former :* or *later.*
  7. ⎰MORNING, *Mattins, early, dawning, betimes.*
    ⎱AFTERNOON, *Evening.*
 Leffer parts of time; being each of them ‖ the 24th part *of a natu-
ral day,* called an Hour : or the 6oth part *of an hour.*
  8. ⎰HOUR, *Horary.*
    ⎱MINUTE.

VI. AGE.

VI. Life-time, or the AGE of LIVING Creatures, (as particularly applied to Men, to which there is something answerable in other Animals; to which may be adjoyned the word SECULUM, *Age, Estate, Generation,*) is, according to common use, distinguished by such Terms as do denote the gradual differences of it.

1. The *first and most imperfect State*, when ‖ *destitute of the use of reason:* or *having but little use of it.* comprehending the two first ten years.
   - INFANCY, *Babe, Child, Cub.*
   - CHILDHOOD, *Boy, Girl, Wench, green years.*

2. The *less imperfect Age, subject to the sway of Passions*; ‖ either *more,* or *less,* containing the third and fourth ten years.
   - ADOLESCENCY, *adult, Lad, Springal, Stripling, Youth, Lass, Damosel, Wench.*
   - YOUTH, *Juvenile, Younker.*

3. The *perfect Age as to the Body:* or *the declining Age of the Body, but most perfect for the Mind,* styled *vergens ætas,* or the Age of Wisdom; the former comprehending the space betwixt the 40th and the 50th, and the latter containing the space betwixt the 50th and the 60th (year.
   - MANHOOD, *virile, middle age.*
   - DECLINING AGE, *elderly.*

4. The *last and most imperfect Age,* by reason of the decay of Vigor, which commonly happens both in *Body* and *Mind,* ‖ either according to the *first and better part of it:* or the *last and worst part* of this State, reaching from the 60th to the 70th, and from thence for the (time after.
   - OLD AGE.
   - DECREPIDNESS, *Crone.*

CHAP. VIII.

Concerning the Predicament of Quality; *the several Genus's belonging to it, namely,* I. Natural Power. II. Habit. III. Manners. IV. Sensible quality. V. Disease; *with the various Differences and Species under each of these.*

WHether many of those things now called *Quality,* be not reducible to Motion and Figure, and the Situation of the parts of Bodies, is a question which I shall not at present consider. 'Tis sufficient that the particulars here specified are most commonly known and apprehended under that notion as they are here represented, and are still like to be called by the same names, whatever new Theory may be found out of the causes of them.

The several Genus's under this Predicament are such kinds of Qualities as are either
- *Internal;* whether
  - *Innate;* NATURAL POWER.
  - *Superinduced;* considered more
    - *Generally;* styled by the common name of HABIT.
    - *Specially;* with respect to the customary Actions of men considered
- *External;* denoting either (as voluntary MANNERS.
  - Those more general affections of bodies which are the objects of SENSIBLE QUALITY. (sense.
  - Those special impotencies of living bodies, whereby they are disabled SICKNESS. (for their natural functions.

As

Chap. VIII.   *Natural Power.*   195

As for *Figure*, which by the common Theory is reduced under this Predicament, that, being a Qualification or *Modification of Quantity*, may more properly be referred thither.

Of NATURAL POWER.

THose kinds of *Natural* innate *Qualities, whereby things are rendred able or unable to act or resist*, according to their peculiar natures, are styled
{ NATURAL POWERS, *Faculty, Capacity, Endowment, Talent, Gift, Ability, Strength, Energy, Force, Virtue, may, can.*
{ IMPOTENCIES, *Disability, Incapacity, invalid, unable, weak, infirm, lame, dead.*

§. 1.

These Natural Powers may be distributed into such as are
{ More *particular*; viz. the Faculties that are
  { RATIONAL. I.
  { *Sensitive.*
  { INWARD. II.
  { OUTWARD. III.
{ More *general*; being either
  { SPIRITUAL. IV.
  { *Corporeal*; *relating to the good of* the
    { INDIVIDUUM. V.
    { SPECIES. VI.

I. Those *Faculties whereby we are inabled to apprehend and compare the general natures of things* as to Truth and Falshood, Good and Evil, *and to demean our selves accordingly* towards them, are styled
{ RATIONAL, *Reasonable, Ratiocination.*
{ IRRATIONAL, *Unreasonable, brutish.*

I. RATIONAL FACULTIES.

These may be distinguished into
{ *Apprehensive*; whereby we are rendred able or unable to
  Know and apprehend knowable things, Generals as well as Particulars, respecting in them Truth and Falshood.
  1. { UNDERSTANDING, *Intellect, Mind, mental, apprehend, comprehend, perceive, conceive, reach, resent, Sentiment.*
     { IDIOTICALNESS, being as a *natural Fool, Changeling, Innocent*
  Compound and compare Notions together, so as to make a right estimate of things and consequences.
  2. { JUDGMENT, *Judicious.*
     { INJUDICIOUSNESS, *simple, silly.*
  Apply general Principles *to particular cases*, being a kind of practical Judgment or Memory relating to matters of Duty.
  3. { CONSCIENCE.
     { UNCONSCIONABLENESS, *Searedness, Profligateness, moral, Insensibility.*
{ *Motive*; whereby we do rationally *follow* any thing *as good*, or *fly it as evil:* or *being without any such motion.*
  4. { WILL, *Desire, List, Option, Vote, Wish, Mind, Pleasure, covet, voluntary.*
     { LISTLESNESS, *no mind to.*

Cc 2   II. INTER-

II. INTERNAL SENSES are so styled, because they belong to the *interiour parts*, and are conversant about internal and *absent* as well as *present* things. Whether there be any such real Faculties in the Soul as are mentioned under this and the preceding Head, is not here to be debated. 'Tis sufficient that common experience doth acquaint us with such various operations of the Mind, and that general custom hath agreed upon such names for the expressing of them.

These are likewise distinguishable into

Apprehensive; whereby we are rendred *able* or *unable for the*
- *Receiving of impressions from the outward Senses.*
  1. { COMMON SENSE, *perceive, discern, apprehend, Sentiment, resent, conceive, discover, find.*
     STUPOR, *Numness, amaze, astonish, narcotic, amuze, asleep, set on edge.*
- *Compounding and comparing* what is communicated from the outward Senses.
  2. { PHANSIE, *Imagination, Conceit, fantastical, capricious, Phantasm.*
     DOTAGE, *Delirium, Dizzard, Sot, besot.*
- *Retaining* such impressions.
  3. { MEMORY, *recollect, re-call, commemorate, remember, call or come to mind, put in mind, suggest, record, recount, con over, getting by heart, by rote, without book, at ones fingers ends, memorable, memorial, memorandum, mindful.*
     FORGETFULNESS, *Oblivion, Unmindfulness, overslip.*

Motive; whereby, in order to our own Conservation, *we follow or fly* what is by the judgment of the Senses represented as *good or evil*.
  4. { APPETITE, *Desire, Inclination, Concupiscence, Stomach, Longing, Lust, having a mind to.*
     LOATHING, *fulsome, nauseate, glut, cloy, go against, queasie, squeamish, wambling, qualm, detest.*

III. EXTERNAL SENSES are so styled, because they reside in the exteriour parts of the body, and do apprehend only external present things; which common opinion hath determined to the number of Five:

Commodious (amongst which some are said to be
- *For Discipline*; *whereby we discern*
  - *Light and Colour.*
    1. { SIGHT, *Vision, View, ken, Optic, descry, discern, espie, spie, peep, prie, see, perceive, look upon, behold, Glimpse, Spectacle, Spectator, Inspection, Revise, Prospect, first blush, visible, conspicuous.*
       BLINDNESS, *Dimness, dark, poreblind, put out ones eyes.*
  - *Sounds.*
    2. { HEARING, *attend, hearken, listen, give ear, audible.*
       DEAFNESS, *surd.*
- *For the trial of* our Food *at a distance.*
  3. SMELL, *Odor, Savour, Sent, Pomander, Perfume.*
- *Necessary for* the
  - *Immediate trial of* our Food.
    4. TAST, *Gust, Savour, Relish, Smack, Smatch, Tang, toothsom.*
  - *Perception of tangible things.*
    5. { TOUCH, *feel, contact, tactile, palpable, grope.*
       NUMNESS, *Stupor, dead, torpid, asleep.*

Though common Language have not affixed particular names to the *impotencies* of some of these, yet they ought *to be provided for* as well as the rest.

IV. Those

Chap. VIII.   *Natural Power.*   197

IV. Those natural *Habitudes of the Soul* or *Spirit which render it fit or unfit for its* proper *functions*, are styled by that general name of TEM-PER *-ature, -ament, Disposition, Spirit, Genius, Fancy, Humor, Vein, Quality, Condition, Constitution, Nature.* IV. TEMPERS OF SPIRIT.

These may be distinguished into such as are more

- *General;* chiefly of *moral disposition,* denoting ‖ the *goodness:* or *badness* of it.
  1. { INGENUITY, *Good nature, Candor, candid, free, liberal, clear.*
     { DISINGENUITY, *Ill nature, Perverseness, thwart, cross, froward, untoward, wayward, awkward, refractory, untractable, wilful, stubborn, sullen, dogged, sturdy, stiff, restiff.*

- *Particular;* as to
  - *Action;* denoting
    - *Ability,* or *disability;* aptitude, or ineptitude for it.
      2. { SPRIGHTLINESS, *Wit, Vivacity, ingenious, brisk, lively, quick, acute, sharp, debonair, mercurial, pregnant, presentness of mind.*
         { DULNESS, *Stupidity, gross witted, hard-headed, torpid, soft, thick, heavy, dazle, dolt, Block-head, Logger-head, Dunce, Sot, indocil, dreaming.*
    - *Attention:* or *levity of mind* in it.
      3. { SERIOUSNESS, *earnest, grave, sober, staid, sad, substantial, solemn.*
         { WANTONNESS, *lightness, airy, playward, gamesom, dallying, sportful, trifling, lascivious, giddy, petulant, skittish, toying, Ramp, Gigg, Rigg, Gambol*
    - *Aptitude* or *Ineptitude to moderate* the
      - *Irascible appetite.*
        4. { GENTLENESS, *Tameness, Mildness, Meekness, Lenity, break, reclaim, tame, come to hand.*
           { FIERCENESS, *Wildness, Haggard, Savage, barbarous, curstness, surly, eager, furious, dire, fell, grim, rough, source, keen, untamed.*
      - *Concupiscible appetite.*
        5. { OPPOSITE TO RAPACITY, *not rapacious.*
           { RAPACITY, *ravenous, voracious, greedy, Harpy, devour, preying.*
    - *Ability* or *disability to attempt or resist difficulties.*
      6. { STOUTNESS, *Boldness, manful, redoubted, daring, sturdy, strenuous.*
         { LAZINESS, *sluggish, lither, lurden, Drone, dull, soft.*
  - *Action* and *Passion,* denoting an *ability* or *disability* to *endure* and hold out both in *acting* and *suffering.*
    7. { HARDINESS, *Tolerance, strenuous, robust, stout, sturdy, industrious, painful.*
       { NICENESS, *Softness, Tenderness, Delicateness, Curiosity, fine, squeamish, effeminate, finical, dainty.*

V. Those

V. TEMPERS OF BODY FOR THE INDIVIDUUM.

V. Those CORPOREAL HABITUDES, whereby things are rendred *able or unable* to *act or resist for the* good of the INDIVIDUUM, are usually styled by those general names of *Temper, Complexion, Frame, State, Constitution, Disposition, Nature.*

These are distinguishable into such as concern,

The just *number of the parts;* ∥ *having all :* or *wanting some.*

1. { WHOLENESS, Intireness, perfect, safe and sound, tite, consolidate, of one piece.
    MUTILOUSNESS, maimed, mangle, lame, lopped, crippled.

The *nature* of the whole or parts; being either

Negative or *Positive* of

Corruption.

2. { SOUNDNESS, Sanity, Healthiness, hail, heal, whole, clearness.
    ROTTENNESS, Putridness, Corruption, purulent, tainted, unsound, moulder, festered, addle, Matter, rankle, suppurate, putrefie, Carrion

Trouble to the sense of Feeling.

3. { INDOLENCE, Ease, lenitive, relaxation, clearness, lighten.
    PAIN, Ach, smart, ail, anguish, grief, ill at ease, sore, pang, thro, torment, torture, ake, excruciate, twing, twitch, fret, gripe, gird, racking.

Positive or *Negative;*

General; relating to the state of the body, ∥ *good :* or *ill.*

4. { VIGOR, Vivacity, thriving, vegetous, flourishing, lusty, lively, sprightly, florid, quick, fresh, in heart, in good plight, in proof, pert, smart, crank, sturdy, revive.
    DECAYING, consume, wear, wast, drooping, fading, out of heart, flagging, languish, break, fail, going down, fall away, bring down or low, decline, impair, quail, abate, molder, pine, wither, perish, spend, corrupt.

Special; respecting the

Plight of the fleshy parts, ∥ *full :* or *sparing.*

5. { FATNESS, plump, pampered, burly, corpulent, gross, foggy, pursie, battle.
    LEANNESS, macilent, meagre, Starveling, flue, poor, bare, spare, thin, lank, gaunt, Rascal, scraggy, ghastly, pine, emaciate, fall away, Carrion, skin and bone.

Figure and colour of the external parts, ∥ *right :* or *wrong.*

6. { BEAUTY -fulness, Handsomness, Pulchritude, Comeliness, Elegance, Decency, fair, goodly, well-favoured, seemly, polite, quaint, pretty, graceful, lovely, personable.
    DEFORMITY, unhandsome, ill-favoured, ugly, uncomely, misbecoming, indecorum, absurd, unseemly, misshapen, foul, squalid, Hagg, deface, disfigure.

Ability, or *disability for Action or Passion.*

7. { STRENGTH, Force, Might, Validity, Puissance, robust, strenuous, stout, sturdy, in heart, main, corroborate, fortifie, recruit.
    WEAKNESS, Feebleness, Debility, Imbecillity, Infirmity, disabled, faint, languid, dead, frail, out of heart, heartless, flagging, invalid, small, bring down or low, enervate, decline, enfeeble.

Chap. VIII.   *Natural Power.*   199

Aptitude or *ineptitude for Motion,*
In a place.

8. { AGILITY, *Nimbleneſs, Activity, Lightneſs, Volubility, quick, dexterous, Mercurial, reſtive, handy, man of his hands.*
LUMPISHNESS, *Unweildineſs, dulneſs, groſs, heavy, purſie, Lob, Lubber, Slugg, Lozel.*

To a place.

9. { SWIFTNESS, *Fleetneſs, Celerity, Speed, faſt, apace, ſodain, quick, rapid, hurry, accelerate, haſten, curſory, hy, expedite, run, ſend, whisk, poſt.*
SLOWNESS, *Heavineſs, ſlackneſs, dull, Slug, tardy, leiſurely, ſoftly, dilatory, retard, foreſlow, delay, Lob, Lubber, lumpiſh, Lurdan, torpid, unwieldy, gingerly.*

VI. *Such corporeal Habitudes as do concern the Propagation of the Species, do refer either to the*   **VI. TEMPERS FOR PROPAGATION OF THE SPECIES.**

Kinds of things apt for Propagation, *according to the General name.*

1. SEX, *Kind, Gender, Epicene, Hermaphrodite.*

Particular diſtribution into || *more, or leſs noble.*

2. { MALE, *maſculine, Buck, Bore, Dog, Gib, Cock, Milter, He.*
FEMALE, *feminine, Doe, Sow, Bitch, Hen, Spawner, She.*

Diſpoſition of things || *for, or againſt Propagation.*

3. { FRUITFULNESS, *fertile -ity, fœcund, prolifical, fructifie, rank, produce fruit.*
BARRENNESS, *Sterility, Unfruitfulneſs, infertile, blaſting, blite.*

State of things generated, when they || *have attained the perfection they ought to have : or elſe are in a ſtate of imperfection, by reaſon of exceſs,* or *defect.*

4. { RIPENESS, *Maturity, mellow, Precocity, ſtale, hatch.*
OVER-RIPENESS, *fading, decaying, withering.*
UNRIPENESS, *immature, green.*

Of

Of HABIT.

§. II. Such *superinduced Qualities*, whether infused or acquired, *whereby the natural Faculties are perfected*, and rendred more ready and vigorous in the exercise of their several Acts, according to the *more* or *less* perfect Degrees of them, are styled by the name of

⎧ HABIT, *Endowment, enure, qualifie, Gift, Talent.*
⎨
⎩ DISPOSITION, *Propensity, Proclivity, Promptitude, Proneness, Inclination, readiness, given to, addiction, fitness, aptitude.*

To the more general consideration of Habit may appertain

⎧ Those *States* or Conditions of life which either reward or enable men
⎪ for vertuous Actions; comprehending the
⎪   ⎧ ENDS OR REWARD OF VERTUE. I.
⎪   ⎨
⎪   ⎩ INSTRUMENTS OF VERTUE. II.
⎨ Those *Qualifications*, which, though they are not properly Vertues, yet
⎪ do prepare for, and dispose unto, and, in other respects, circumstan-
⎪ tiate Vertue it self, both in the *Habit* and *Operations* of it, and are
⎪ therefore styled AFFECTIONS OF VERTUE, either
⎪   ⎧ INTELLECTUAL. III.
⎪   ⎨
⎪   ⎩ MORAL. IV.
⎪ The *Kinds of* vertuous Habits, whether
⎩   ⎧ INFUSED, both Intellectual and Moral. V.
    ⎨
    ⎩ ACQUIRED INTELLECTUAL. VI.

I. REWARDS OF VERTUE.

I. Those things which are *due to the merit of* ‖ *Vertue* or *Vice*, are styled
⎧ REWARD, *Guerdon, Meed, Prize, Recompence.*
⎨
⎩ PUNISHMENT, *Penalty, Penance, Judgment, Plague, Vengeance, inflict, suffer, impunity, scotfree.*

These may be distinguished into such as are either more

⎧ *General*; viz. that state wherein a thing injoys as much perfection as it
⎪ is capable of.
⎪   ⎧ HAPPINESS. *Felicity, Bliss, Blessedness, Beatitude, good, weal, welfare.*
⎪ 1.⎨
⎪   ⎩ MISERY, *Unhappiness, Infelicity, Extremity, Calamity, Woe, Distress, Disaster, Affliction, Tribulation, Trouble, Plague, Judgment, Caitiff, Wretch, poor, pitiful, deplorable.*
⎨ *Particular*; relating to the reward of
⎪   ⎧ *Moral* Vertue; in the enjoyment of those things that conduce to our
⎪   ⎪ *bene esse*.
⎪   ⎨ *External*;
⎪   ⎪   ⎧ PROSPERITY, *flourishing, thriving, auspicious, fortunate, hap-*
⎪   ⎪ 3.⎨ *py, good luck, success, speed.*
⎩   ⎩   ⎩ ADVERSITY, *Affliction, distress, tribulation, cross, disaster, infelicity, suffering, persecution, duress, fall, pressure, mischance, mishap, misadventure, misfortune, unfortunate, unluckie, unprosperous, inauspicious, sinister, dismal, ill luck,* or *success.*

Internal,

Chap. VIII.   Habit.   201

        ⎩ *Internal*; ‖ *quiet*, or *disquiet* of the Affections.
3. ⎧ CONTENTATION, *Tranquillity, Contentment, Serenity, Hearts-*
   ⎨ *ease, Equanimity, Sedateness, Rest, be satisfied, acquiesce.*
   ⎩ ANXIETY, *Discontent, thought taking, dump, trouble, anguish, disquiet, vexation, perplexity, streight, pinch.*
    ⎩ *Christian* Vertues and Graces; consisting in an everlasting Vision and Fruition of God.
4. ⎧ SALVATION, *Beatifical Vision, Heaven, Glory.*
   ⎨ DAMNATION, *Condemnation, Hell, perdition.*

II. The INSTRUMENTS OF VERTUE, commonly styled the **II. INSTRU-**
Goods of Fortune, requisite to the due exercise of the Acts of many Ver- **MENTS OF**
tues, and one kind of Reward belonging to it, do concern either **VERTUE.**

  ⎧ *Our Persons*, and the being at our own disposal.
1. ⎧ LIBERTY, *Freedom, at large, deliver, release, inlarge, set free, rid, dispatch, ransom, redeem, manumise, emancipate, give one his head, scope, arbitrary, undetermin'd, unconfined, may, may chuse:*
   ⎩ RESTRAINT, *confine, streighten, repress.*

  Our Possessions; being either ‖ *sufficient*, or *insufficient*, for our occasions and conveniencies, according to that rank and station wherein we are placed.
2. ⎧ RICHES, *Wealth, Opulence, Pelf, Means, Fortunes, Estate, thrive, Treasure, make, enrich, worth, well to pass.*
   ⎩ POVERTY, *Necessity, Penury, Indigence, Need, Want, poor, empoverish, ruine.*

The sutableness of the things which we have or do, and that satisfaction which we receive by them.
3. ⎧ PLEASURE, *Delight, Delectation, Enjoyment.*
   ⎩ UNPLEASANTNESS, *Grief, Trouble, displeasing.*

Our Names, and the esteem we have amongst good men.
4. ⎧ REPUTATION, *Credit, Countenance, Applause, Name, Honour, Vogue, report, Fame, redoubted, of Note, Glory, Renown, well-sounding.*
   ⎩ INFAMY, *Disgrace, discredit, dishonour, disparage, defame, discountenance, shame, ignominy, Stein, Blot, Blemish, Slur, inglorious, illiberal, ignoble, notorious, ill reflexion, or sound, or name.*

Our *Degrees*, and the quality of our Conditions in relation to others; being either considerably above them, or below them.
5. ⎧ DIGNITY, *Promotion, Preferment, Advancement, Honour, Worship, Greatness, State, Port, Title, preeminence, upper-hand, High place, raise, exalt, illustrious.*
   ⎩ MEANNESS, *Lowness, Obscurity, Baseness, Vileness, ignoble, plain, abase, debase, degrade, Abjectness.*

  ⎩ Our *Ability* to protect our selves and others from injury, which is the usual result or consequent of the rest.
6. ⎧ POWER -*full, Potent-ate, Greatness, Interest, Strength, Might, Puissance, Mastery, Prevalence, Predominance, over-sway, rule -the rost, bear a stroke.*
   ⎩ IMPOTENCE, *weak, inconsiderable.*

Habit. Part. II.

III. AFFECTIONS OF INTELLECTUAL VERTUE.

III. AFFECTIONS of INTELLECTUAL VERTUE, may be diſtinguiſhed by their reference to thoſe two Faculties in the

Rational Soul, imployed for the gaining of Knowledge, viz.

- *Invention;* which is || *rightly,* or *wrongly* diſpoſed by
  1. { SAGACITY, *Perſpicacity, Sharpneſs, Subtilty, Dexterity, Wit, clear, quick, acute, ſearching, piercing, docil, towardly, apt, prompt.*
     DULNESS, *Stupidity, Heavineſs, groſs-witted, indocil, dreaming, Dolt, Dunce, Blockhead.*
- *Judgment;* which is || *well diſpoſed,* by ſuch a temper of mind as doth incline a man to aſſent unto things upon ſuch evidence as is in it ſelf ſufficient: or *ill diſpoſed,* by ſuch a temper as inclines a man either *to aſſent* unto things upon ſuch evidence as is *inſufficient,* or *not to aſſent* upon ſuch as is *ſufficient.*
  2. { FAITH, *Docility, Teachableneſs, Towardlineſs, Aptneſs.*
     CREDULITY, *Eaſineſs, light* or *raſh of belief, facil.*
     INCREDULITY, *Unteachableneſs, Untowardlineſs, Scepticalneſs, Scrupulouſneſs, Unbelief.*

Senſitive Soul, which are apt to hinder us from Knowledge.

- *Phancy;* which is || *well,* or *ill* diſpoſed by
  3. { SOBRIETY, *diſcreet, grave, ſerious, ſtaid, ſteddy, ſettled, ſage.*
     CONCEITEDNESS, *Affectation, Singularity, fantaſtical, vagary, wild, light, airy, giddy, freakiſh, whimſical, hair-brain'd, brain-ſick, Humoriſt, Opiniaſter.*
- *Appetite;* which is fitly regulated by our being concerned for any Truth according to a due meaſure; and not either *more* or *leſs* then the *evidence* and *importance* of it, doth require.
  4. { MODERATION, *Temper, Meaſure, Gentle-neſs, qualifie, reduce to reaſon.*
     SLIGHTNESS, *Slackneſs, negligence, remiſneſs, Neutrality, frigid, cold, indifferent, unconcerned, ſlatering, ſuperficial, curſory, overly, perfunctory, faint.*
     FIERCENESS, *Fanaticalneſs, vehemence, violence, eagerneſs, earneſt, furious, heady, immoderate, dogmatical, Opiniaſter, boiſterous, rough, ſour, keen.*

IV. AFFECTIONS OF MORAL AND HOMILETICAL VERTUE.

IV. The *Affections* of MORAL and HOMILETICAL *Vertues,* do concern either

The Temper and Frame *of our Minds,* as to their due

- *Attention;*
- *For any kind of Advantage,* or Expedient.
  1. { CONSIDERATION, *Adviſedneſs, deliberate, ruminate, forecaſt, of* or *on purpoſe.*
     CUNCTATION, *Loitering, Delay, ſlack, trifling, linger, lag, while off, drive off, put off.*
     RASHNESS, *Haſtineſs, Temerity, heady, hair-brain'd, fool-hardy, curſory, headlong, precipitate, unadviſed, incogitancy, inconſiderateneſs, preſumption.*

Againſt

Against any kind of Evil, Danger or Impediment.

2. ⎧ HEEDFULNESS, *Warineß, Care, Canteloufneß, Watchfulneß, Attention, Intention, Caution, minding; circumspection, chary, vigilant, cautious, shie, advised, aware, beware, intend, look to or about, see to, take heed, be thoughtful, take thought, take warning, narrow-*
⎨ CARKING, *Solicitude, Anxiety, over-thoughtful.* (ly.
⎩ CARELESNESS, *Heedlesneß, incogitancie, negligence, flattering, slightneß, lightneß, supineneß, inconsiderate, oscitation, overly, perfunctory, superficial, secure, unwary, retchless, cursory, idle, slothful, sluggardly, slubbering, diffolute, uncircumspect, hand over head, not regard, overslip.*

Freedom and Readineß of our *Faculties* about any thing.

3. ⎧ ALACRITY, *Chearfulneß, readineß, forwardneß, with all ones heart, with a good will, free; glad, promptneß, propensity, rather.*
⎩ GRUDGING, *maunder, murmure, mutter, repine, regret, querulous, go against, with an ill will.*

Reality of our Intentions, sutable to our outward Pretences.

4. ⎧ SINCERITY, *Uprightneß, reality, cordialneß, heartineß, downright, honest, plain, simple, unfeigned, sound, clear, uncorrupt.*
⎩ HYPOCRISIE, *Diffimulation, double tongue or heart, hollow-hearted, feigning, false, counterfeit, sophistical, pretend.*

The *Vigorousneß of our Endeavours* in the prosecution of fitting means.

5. ⎧ DILIGENCE, *Affiduity, Sedulity, Industry, Attention, Care, Labour, Study, instant, elaborate, ply, bestir, stickle, lay about him, earnest, indefatigable, take pains.*
⎨ DOUBLE-DILIGENCE, *overdoing, busie, pragmatical, fain, medling.*
⎩ SLOTH, *Idleneß, lazineß, carelesneß, lither, loose, retchleß, dreaming, Drone, Sluggard, Truant, loiter.*

The *Universality* required to vertuous Actions, in respect of the *Object.*

6. ⎰ INTEGRITY, *Honesty, intire, equal, impartial, incorrupt, upright.*
⎱ PARTIALITY, *unequal, making a difference, accepting of persons.*

Time of continuance.

7. ⎧ CONSTANCY, *Perseverance, Stability, Steadineß, stedfast, firm, fixed, sure, certain, resolute, inflexible, unchangeable, abide, persist, hold out, stand out, stay by, stick to, unwearied, indefatigable.*
⎨ PERTINACY, *Obstinacy, Contumacy, pervicacious, peremptory, stiff, wilful, inexorable, inflexible.*
⎩ LIGHTNESS, *Inconstancy, fickleneß, levity, instability, mutability, uncertain, unsteddy, unstable, unstedfast, unsettled, unstaid, wavering, divers, dodging, shittle, shuttle, flippery, variable, mutable, changeable, trifling, giddy, freakish, paltring, fast and loose.*

D d 2   V. Those

V. INFUSED HABITS.

V. Those are styled INFUSED HABITS, to which the Divine favour and assistance is required after a more especial manner; which are therefore styled by the general name of GRACE, *Gift.*

To which may be opposed UNGRACIOUSNESS, *Impiety, graceless, ungodly, carnal, wicked, sinful.*

These are either

General; consisting in

- *A change of mind* from evil to good.
  1. { REPENTANCE, *Penitence, compunction, relent, remorse, contrition, rue, return, reclaim, renew, regeneration, penance.*
     IMPENITENCE, *Obdurateness, Hard-heartedness.*

- *An habitual frame of mind*, whereby we are fitted for vertuous actions, and more especially for the Duties of Religion.
  2. { HOLINESS, *Sanctity, Godliness, Piety, Devotion, Righteousness, Sanctification, sacred, Pureness.*
     UNHOLINESS, *Wickedness, Iniquity, Impiety, Ungodliness, Prophaneness, Corruption, Sin, Miscreant, graceless, Caitiffe.*

- *An inlargement of Soul*, to desire and endeavour public general good, and taking it off from being immersed in narrow selfish designs.
  3. { SELF-DENIAL, *Christian Magnanimity, Generosity, Public-spiritedness, Greatness of mind, Resignation.*
     SELFISHNESS, *Narrowness, Pedanticalness, Littleness of mind, Worldling.*

Particular; styled *Theological Vertues*; respecting

- *Truth and Falshood*; a readiness to yield an effectual assent unto revealed Truths upon such grounds as their natures are capable of, and such as are sufficient to prevail with any such prudent teachable man as is free from any affected Captiousness.
  4. { FAITH, *Belief, Believer, Creed.*
     INFIDELITY, *Unbelief, Miscreant.*

Good and Evil.

- *Future*; being an acquiescence of the mind in the expectation of such Promises as are revealed.
  5. { HOPE, *Trust, Affiance, Reliance, Recumbency.*
     DESPAIR, *Despondency, out of heart, forlorn, hopeless, past hope, deadness of heart.*

- *General*; wishing well, and endeavouring to be helpful and serviceable unto all, according to the due proportion we are obliged to by natural or revealed Light.
  6. { CHARITY, *Love.*
     UNCHARITABLENESS, *Maliciousness.*

VI. Those

Chap. VIII. Habit.

VI. Those are styled ACQUIRED INTELLECTUAL HABITS which may be gotten by Industry, and tend to the perfecting of the Mind or Understanding. They are distinguishable by their

- Objects; being either
  - Speculative; furnishing the mind with due Notions and conceptions concerning the Nature of things, their Causes, Differences, Relations and Dependencies.
    1. { SCIENCE, *Knowledge, Skill, Theory, Learning, Insight.*
       { CURIOSITY.
       { IGNORANCE, *rude, untaught.*
  - Active; denoting Skill in men and business, whereby we are inabled to judge what is fit and convenient, according to various cases and circumstances.
    2. { WISDOM, *Prudence, Discretion, Sapience, wise, sage, politic.*
       { CRAFT, *Cunning, Subtilty, Shiness, Policy, Device, Quirk, Sleight, Fetch, Wile, Trick, sly, shrewd, Knave, Shark, Shift, come over one, over reach.*
       { FOLLY, *Fool-ishness, Simplicity, Silly-ness, Imprudence, Indiscretion, witless, unwise, absurd, shallow, Noddy, Ninny, Sot, infatuate, Foppery.*
  - Effective; implying Skill in those several Operations and Works which concern Humane life.
    3. { ART, *Skill, Dexterity, Craft, Cunning, Insight, Knack, expert, well-seen in, good at, artificial, Workman, Artist.*
       { UNSKILFULNESS, *bungling, blundering, botching, fumbling, cobling, slubber, smatter, ignorant, silly, rude, gross, jejune, inexpert, inartificial, awkward, Freshman, Novice.*
- The manner of acquiring them; whether by
  - Our own Observation, and repeated Trials.
    4. { EXPERIENCE, *Practice, Exercise, Knowledge, conversant, versed, expert, Experiment, Empyric.*
       { INEXPERIENCE, *inexpert, raw, to seek, Puny, Novice, Freshman, unversed.*
  - The Teaching of others, either || *vivâ voce,* or *ex scriptis.*
    5. { LEARNING, *Literature, Scholarship, scholastic, Liberal Science, Skill, indoctinate.*
       { UNLEARNEDNESS, *illiterate, unlettered, rude, simple.*

Of

Of MANNERS.

§. III. *T*He *Customary* and habitual *Actions* of men *considered as voluntary*, and as they are capable of Good or Evil, Reward or Punishment, are styled by the name of MANNERS, *Ethic, Moral-ity*.

To which may be adjoyned the general name of such *customary Actions* as are *mutual betwixt man and man*, styled CONVERSATION, *Carriage, Demeanour, Comportment, homiletical, Communication, lead, life, living, sociable, behave*.

The Vertues belonging to these do comprehend all those Habits which concern the regulating both of our *Wills* and *Affections*, and of our *Conversations*. They are distinguishable by the Faculties which they moderate, and the Objects they are conversant about, into such as do more immediately concern the regulating of our

{ *Wills and Affections*, and that Rectitude of mind which we are obliged unto with reference to our selves, *considered more separately*, according to those principal parts of which we consist, *viz.* Soul and Body, Reason and sense, together with the things we possess, being either
 { More GENERAL. I.
 { More *Particular*, relating to
   { Our BODIES. II.
   { Our ESTATES or DIGNITIES. III.

Conversations, or the right Demeanour of our selves *considered as Members of Society*, in our converse with others; the due managing of the common Affairs and Businesses of life, according to the relations wherein we stand towards those whom we are to deal with. These are commonly called *Homiletical* Vertues; being either
 { More GENERAL and Common. IV.
 { More *Particular*, towards
   { SUPERIORS. V.
   { INFERIORS. VI.

I. VERTUE. I. Those kind of *Moral habits* which serve for the *regulating of our Wills and Affections more General*, are commonly styled by the name of VERTUE, *Honesty, Probity, Righteousness, brave*; denoting such Habits whereby we are inclined and inabled to observe a due Mediocrity in our Actions. To this is properly opposed the notion of VICE, *Sin, Crime, Dishonesty, Trespass, Transgression, Fault, Failing, Infirmity, Oversight, wicked, Improbity, Turpitude, unrighteous, unjust, bad, naught, vile, base, loose, evil, ill, corrupt, venial, heinous, debauched, lewd, lawless, licencious, foul, flagitious, enormous, profligate, Miscreant, Ruffian, Caitiff, Villain, Rakehell, Libertine, defile, pollute.* These may be distinguished into such as relate to the Inclination of our Minds, either

{ *In Debitis*; in such things as are due from us
 { By *Law*;
1. { JUSTICE, *Righteous-ness, right, square dealing, upright dealing.*
   { IN*JUSTICE*, *Unrighteousness, Wrong.*
     { RIGOUR, *rigid, extreme, severity, overstrict.*
     { REMISSION, *Over-sparing.*

Right

Chap. VIII.	*Manners.*	207

Right Reason.
More *general*; respecting our Actions towards others, in such cases as the Law-giver (could he have foreseen) would have provided for; whereby a man is willing to recede from his own strict right, & the utmost extremities of things, and to take the most amicable way in the accommodating of Differences, supplying that by right Reason which is not provided for in the words of the written Law.

2. { EQUITY, *Moderation, reasonable, conscionable, Chancery, fair dealing, in reason.* (*unequal.*
   { SUMMUM JUS, *Rigidness, sourness, unreasonableness, iniquity,*

More *particular*; in *our Thoughts* concerning other *mens* words or actions, being ready to interpret every thing in the best sense, when there is no evident reason to the contrary.

3. { CANDOR, *fair, ingenuous, candid, fair dealing.*
   { CENSORIOUSNESS, *Sinister suspicion, captiousness, controling,* (*carping, find fault.*

In Gratuitis; respecting chiefly the
Benefactor; being either
More *general*; denoting ‖ a *propension of mind to do good* to others, together with *external actions* sutable thereto.

4. { GOODNESS, *Benignity, benevolence, beneficence, kindness, good turn, beholding, gratifie.*
   { MISCHIEVOUSNESS, *Maleficence, ill turn.*

More *particular*; respecting such as are in a state of misery.

5. { MERCY, *tender-hearted, pitiful, propitious, soft.*
   { CRUELTY, *Immanity, inhumane, hard-hearted, pittiless, savage, dire, truculent, barbarous.*

Beneficiary; namely, a propension of mind to put a just esteem upon the Favours we receive, and to take all occasions of acknowledging and requiting them.

6. { GRATITUDE, *Thank-fulness, give or render thanks.*
   { INGRATITUDE, *Unthankfulness, ingrateful.*

In arduis; whether things
Hard to be done; whereby we are made duly resolute against all such difficulties either of Fear or Discouragement as may hinder us in our duty.

7. { FORTITUDE, *Valour, Courage, Manhood, Prowess, Puissance, stout, redoubted, undaunted, bold, daring, valiant, resolute, in heart, of spirit, manly, manful, sturdy.*
   { RASHNESS, *Temerity, fool-hardiness, audacity, desperate, heady, hair-brain'd, boisterous, precipitate.*
   { COWARDISE, *timorous, faint-hearted, fearful, soft, Craven, Dastard, Poltron, Recreant, out of heart, to flinch, to cow.*

Hard to be suffered; in respect of
Pain.

8. { PATIENCE, *Long-suffering, forbearance, abide, bear, brook, endure, sustein, tolerate, weather it out.*
   { OBSTINACY, *stubborn, sturdy, peremptory.*
   { SOFTNESS, *Tenderness, Impatience, relent, mollifie.*

Provocation to Anger and Revenge, in which we are to observe a due Mediocrity.

9. { MEEKNESS, *Mildness, long-suffering, gentleness, clemency, lenity,*
   { LENTITUDE, *Stupor, Insensibility.* (*calm, put up.*
   { RASH ANGER, *curst, hasty, pettish, peevish, snappish, testy.*

H. The

II. Vertues relating to our BODIES.

II. The more *special* Vertues for the regulating of our Wills and Affections in things relating to our BODIES, whose Object is *Jucundum* or *Utile*, are either.

Of a more *large extent*; denoting an Ability to withstand all such temptations of allurement whereby we may be hindred in our Duty.

1. { TEMPERANCE.
    SENSUALITY, *Voluptuousness, Intemperance, debauched, dissolute, effeminate, Epicure.*

Of a *lesser extent*; concerning the Moderating of our natural Appetites towards things which concern the Preservation of the

Individuum; either

More *necessary*; as in

Meats.

2. { ABSTINENCE, *abstemiousness, fasting.*
    MACERATION.
    GLUTTONY, *Surfeit, voracity, gormandizing, pampering, ravenous, sated, Gully-gut.*

Drinks.

3. { SOBRIETY, *Abstemiousness.*
    DRUNKENNESS, *Sot, besot, inebriate, heady, intoxicate, fox, carouse, overtaken, whittled, fuddled, tipsie, Tipler, Soaker, Pot-companion, Toss-pot.*

Sleep.

4. { VIGILANCE, *Watchfulness.*
    SLUGGARDLINESS, *Sloth, Drowziness, Sleepiness.*

Less *necessary*; which concern

Refreshments from Labour.

5. { MODERATENESS IN RECREATION.
    IMMODERATENESS IN RECREATION.

External Decorum and Ornament.

6. { CLEANLINESS, *Neatness, smugg, terse.*
    NICENESS, *Finicalness, Delicateness, Daintiness, Curiosity, dapper.*
    SLOVENLINESS, *Uncleanness, Nastiness, sordid, filthy, squalid, foul, Sloven, Slut, slubber.*

Species; as *Venery.*

7. { CHASTITY, *Continence, Honesty.*
    UNCHASTITY, *Incontinence, Wantonness, lascivious, unclean, obscene, ribaldry, bawdy, lewd, light, dishonest, corrupt, defile, deflowr, incest, rape, ravish, viciate.*

III. Vertues

Chap. VIII. Manners.

III. Vertues relating to the due moderating of our Affections towards the things which concern our ESTATES and DIGNITIES, whose Object is *Profit* or *Esteem*, may be distinguished into such as do more particularly concern *Estates* and Possessions; being either,

More *general*; denoting a *Mediocrity* about getting, or keeping, or spending.

1. { LIBERALITY, *Bounty, Munificence, open-handed, free, generous, frank, large.*
   { PRODIGALITY, *Profuseness, wastful, lavish, riotous, embezil, lash out, Havock, run out.*
   { COVETOUSNESS, *Avarice, Worldliness.*

More *special*; in

Getting.

2. { PROVIDENCE.
   { SCRAPING, *Rapacity, greedy, craving, griping, ravenous, ring, near.*
   { SLATERING, *Improvidence.*

Keeping.

3. { FRUGALITY, *Parcimony, thriftiness, good husbandry, saving, sparing, near.*
   { PENURIOUSNESS, *crib, hard, close-fisted, hide-bound, over-thrifty, tenacity, pinching, pinch-peny, Churle, Niggard, Miser, close, near.*
   { SQUANDRING, *flying-out, ill-husbandry, unthriftiness, spend-thrift, wast, embezzil, mis-spend.*

Spending; distinguished by its Objects; either

The Public.

4. { GENEROSITY, *Magnificence, Bounty, Grandeur, stately, pompous, sumptuous, brave, noble, heroic.*
   { RIOTOUSNESS, *Profuseness, Luxuriousness, blade-it, debauch, Roister.*
   { SORDIDNESS, *Baseness, unworthy, penurious.*

The Poor; relieving the wants of others.

5. { ALMSGIVING, *Charity, Dole, Alms, relieve, Pensioner, Bedes-man, Eleemosynary, Hospital.*
   { CHURLISHNESS, *uncharitable, rough, Niggard.*

Strangers.

6. { HOSPITALITY, *harbour, entertain, treat, open-house.*
   { INHOSPITABLENESS.

Dignities and Esteem; in respect of the

Avoiding or suffering of Disgrace.

7. { MODESTY, *Bashfulness.*
   { SHEEPISHNESS, *shamefacedness, over-bashful, sneaking, softness.*
   { IMPUDENCE, *shamelesness, Audacity, saucy, immodest.*

Seeking or bearing of Honour; as putting a *just value* upon things, (having but a little esteem for little things,) as likewise upon himself, and his own merits; and *not* either

Less then he ought.

8. { MAGNANIMITY, *brave, noble, heroic, generous, greatness of mind.*
   { INSOLENCE, *arrogance, haughtines, presumption, vaunting, vaporing.*
   { PUSILLANIMITY, *Baseness, sordid, pedantical.*

More then he ought.

9. { MODESTY.
   { ABJECTNESS, *sneaking, narrowness and littleness of mind, base.*
   { AMBITION, *Presumption, High-mindedness, Vain-glory, Arrogance, aspire, overweening, Rodomohtade, affectation of Empire.*

IV. HOMILETICAL COMMON Vertues.

IV. HOMILETICAL Vertues more COMMON, are such vertuous habits as are required in men of all degrees and conditions for the regulating of their mutual Conversations. Not that the other Vertues before specified, are not likewise necessary to this end: but that they do not so directly and immediately tend to it as these others do which are styled HOMILETICAL. To which may be opposed INSOCIABLENESS, *Barbarism*.

These are distinguishable into such as render our Conversation; either *Profitable* to each other: which may be considered according to the

Matter; such as tend to the preservation of

Truth; either in our

Declarations or Assertions.

1. {VERACITY, *Truth*.
   LYING, *Leasing, forge, fib, flam, false, perjury.* { OVER-SAYING, *Hyperbole, Boasting, Ostentation, vapor, crack, brag, vaunt, swagger, Rodomontade.*
   UNDER-SAYING, *Detraction, Diminution, disparage, traduce, depreciate.* }

Obligations or Promises.

2. {FIDELITY, *trusty, true, loyal.*
   UNFAITHFULNESS. { OFFICIOUSNESS, *Fawning.*
   TREACHERY, *perfidious, false, faithless, unfaithful, untrusty, disloyal, Recreant, Traitor, Ambodexter, betray, falter, undermine, prevaricate.* }

Peace.

3. {PEACEABLENESS, *Quietness, Concord, Accord, Agreement, Union, appease, atone, pacifie, reconcile, compose, take up, compromize, still, calm, set at peace, part a fray.*
   UNPEACEABLENESS. { TAMENESS.
   CONTENTIOUSNESS, *Strife, Dissension, Discord, Variance, Controversie, Difference, Broils, Contest, Combustion, Debate, Division, Bickering, litigious, quarrel, wrangle, clash, jarr, brabble, jangle, Garboil, Odds, Brangling, Conflict, Squabble, Brawling, Cavilling, captious, Incendiary, Barreter, Bowtefew, Shrew, Scold.* }

Manner; such as regulate our Carriage with a due respect of

Things; in

Saying what is fit to be said.

4. {FRANKNESS, *Freeness, plain, open-hearted.*
   { TOO MUCH OPENNESS, *Tell-tale, Blab.*
   RESERVEDNESS, *shy, nice, coy, demure, staunch, wary, close.* }

Concealing what is fit to be concealed.

5. {TACITURNITY, *staunch, close, still, counsel-keeping, secrecy, silence.*
   LOQUACITY, *Babbling, Garrulity, talkative, babble, blab, chatter, gabbling, tattle, prate-itle.* }

Persons; in observing a just Decorum.

6. {GRAVITY, *seriousness, sober, demure, sage, stayed, earnest, settled, solid.*
   VANITY, {FORMALNESS, *Coxcomb, fond, foppish.*
   LIGHTNESS, *flashy, Freak, Levity, Petulance.* }

Pleasant

Chap. VIII.   Manners.   211

pleasant to each other; serving to regulate

Our *Outward carriage* towards others, both Actions and Speeches, as to a Facility for Converse, together with our desires and endeavours by all honest wayes to please others, and care not to offend them.

7. { COURTESY, *Comity, mannerlineß, civility, affability, kindneß, humanity, gentle, fair, humane, benign, tractable, smooth.*
    { FAWNING, *Assentation, Adulation, obsequious, smooth, glavering, gloze, cogg, cajole, curry favour, collogue, wheedle, crouch, creeping, scraping, flatter, sooth, clawing, Blandishment, Parasite, Sycophant, Claw-back.*
    { MOROSENESS, *curst, crabbed, cynical, froward, churlish, uncivil, boisterous, rude, sullen, surly, unmannerly, hard to please, humorsome, rough, harsh, sour, testy, snappish, dogged, currish, waspish, tetchy, wayward, peevish, pettish.*

Our *Words and Speeches*; either in

More serious debates; making due allowances to others, affording them just liberty.

8. { COMPLACENCY, *Civility, smooth, soft, popular;*
    { ASSENTATION, *Flattery, glozing, soothing, fawning, mealy-mouth'd, trencher-friend.*
    { MAGISTERIALNESS, *Arrogance, Imperiousneß, Lordlineß, masterly, pedantical, rough, over-bear, Roister.*

Less serious matters; by such honest mirth whereby Conversation is to be sweetned.

9. { URBANITY, *Facetiousneß, Raillery, Drollery, jocular, jocund, merry, Conceit, Jest, Squib, Clinch, Quibble, Wagg.*
    { SCURRILITY, *Buffoonry, Abusiveneß, Pasquil, Zany, Vice.*
    { RUSTICITY, *Clownishneß, boisterous, blunt, barbarous, rough, rude, Kerne, home-bred, Slouch, uncivil, unmannerly, dirty.*

E e 2   V. HOMI-

Manners. Part. II.

V. HOMIL. VERT. towards SUPERIOURS.

V. HOMILETICAL VERTUES whereby we are to regulate our Demeanour towards our SUPERIOURS, may be distinguished into such as are

More general; denoting the Habit of behaving our selves as we ought towards all in a superiour relation.

1. { DUTIFULNESS, *submissive*.
   { UNDUTIFULNESS, *sturdiness, stiff, untoward, untractable.*

More special; *ex parte*

Subjecti; as *Inferiours*, and at a distance from them.

2. { HUMILITY, *Lowliness, abase, humble, gentle, submission, demissness.*
   { PRIDE, *Haughtiness, Loftiness, high-minded, Lordly, elate, stately, perk, self-conceit, arrogance, magisterialness, presumption, overween, puff up, look big.*

Objecti; as to *Superiours* in

Place.

3. { REVERENCE, *Honour, regard, respect, veneration, awe, dread, Worship.*
   { IRREVERENCE, *Petulance, Sauciness, malapert, perk, presumptuous.*

Gifts.

4. { RESPECT, *Grace, Honour, deference, civility, esteem, observe, veil to.*
   { DISREPECT, *Dishonour, neglect, slighting, undervaluing, disregard, vilifie.*

Authority;

General.

5. { SUBJECTION, *Homage, Loyalty, Allegiance, at ones command, serve under.*
   { REBELLION.

Special; as

Governing.

6. { LOYALTY, *Allegiance, Fealty, Homage.*
   { TREACHERY, *betray, Traitor, disloyal.*

Commanding.

7. { OBEDIENCE, *obsequious, observant, pliable, submissive, tractable, towardly, Conformity, follow, serve, be subject to.*
   { DISOBEDIENCE, *Contumacy, Obstinacy, refractory, self-willed, unruly, untoward, transgress, trespass, break, violate, take head, stiff-necked, wilful, masterless, restive.*

Punishing; submitting to Justice, and suing for Mercy, or *contr*.

8. { SUBMISSION, *give place to, give way, yield, resign, surrender, at discretion of.*
   { CONTUMACY, *Obstinacy, Self-will, stubborn, sullen, stiff, untractable, wayward, stout, stiff-necked, refractory.*

VI. HOMI-

Chap. VIII.   Manners.   213

VI. HOMILETICAL VERTUES whereby we are to regulate our Demeanour *towards* our INFERIORS, may be distinguished into such as are

More general.
1. { GRACIOUSNESS, *Favour, Indulgence, gentle, kind, mild, serene, soft, benign, propitious.*
    { HARSHNESS, *Ruggedness, sourness, roughness.*

More particular; ex parte

Subjecti; in respect of our *Superiority*, from which we are ready upon occasion to yield and stoop down.
2. { CONDESCENSION, *deign, vouchsafe, bear with, suffer.*
   { INSOLENCE, *Magisterialness, imperiousness, roughness, strictness, stately, domineer, insult, swagger, Roister, Ruffian.*

Objecti; as to *Inferiors*, in

Place or Gifts.
3. { AFFABILITY, *Courtesie, gentleness, facil, fair, demeanour.*
   { SUPERCILIOUSNESS, *roughness, stern, sour, scornful, stately, surly, arrogant.*

Authority; in

General; ‖ *preserving* such in their *just rights,* or *invading of them.*
4. { PROTECTION, *shelter, defence, guard, patronage, refuge.*
   { TYRANNY.

Special; as

Governing.
5. { GOOD GOVERNANCE, *Discipline, Regiment.*
   { MALE-ADMINISTRATION, *misgoverning, ill governance.*

Commanding.
6. { REASONABLENESS.
   { UNREASONABLENESS.

Punishing when one ought.
7. { SEVERITY, *strict.*
   { FONDNESS, *Indulgence, cocker, dote, make much of, tender, chary.*

Remitting, when there is just occasion.
8. { CLEMENCY, *Gentleness, favourableness, lenity, mildness.*
   { AUSTERITY, *stern, strict, inflexible, asperity, rigor, stiff, rigid, harsh, sharp, tart, rough, crabbed.*

Though several of the Vertues and Vices enumerated under this and the former Head, may be ascribed sometimes to persons in other capacities; yet they do primarily and originally appertain to the Relations of *Superiours* and *Inferiours*.

Of SENSIBLE QUALITY.

§. IV. BY SENSIBLE QUALITY is meant such kind of Quality as falls under our outward Senses, or the Affections of Bodies considered as they are the Objects of Sense: To which may be opposed the Notion of OCCULT QUALITY. These do relate either to the
- *Eye* and things visible.
  - {*Primary*, LIGHT. I.
  - {*Secondary*, COLOUR. II.
- *Ear*, SOUND. III.
- TAST and SMELL. IV.
- *Touch*; viz. such Qualities as are more
  - {ACTIVE. V.
  - {PASSIVE. VI.

In this distribution of Sensible Qualities, those that are *Visible* and *Tangible* are, both because of their Number and Variety, each of them reduced under double Differences. Whereas those that belong to the Senses of *Tast* and *Smell* are, for the contrary reason, contracted under one. The gradual Differences belonging to every one of these are so very numerous, that no Language doth, or indeed can, provide for them; but we are fain to denominate each of them from that subject in which it is most commonly found and known. And, for the farther help of the common defect of Languages as to such things, I have in the following Tables (where it could conveniently be done) reduced things to double Opposites, which, with the addition of the transcendental points of *Augmentative* and *Diminutive*, will much facilitate the expression of the several degrees of these things.

I. LIGHT.

I. That is styled PRIMARY VISIBLE, by the help of which we are inabled to see other things; being Inherent chiefly either in
- *The Air*; according to the more
  - *General Nature* of it; denoting the *intermediate* or *extremes*, the latter of which is properly a total Privation.
    1. {TWILIGHT, *Dawning.*
       {LIGHT, *Lux, lightsome, illuminate, enlighten, glimmer, glimpse, flash.*
       {DARKNESS, *gloomy, close, dim, duskie, Eclipse, obscure, sad, swart, brown.*
  - *Particular Kind* or Degree; the Opposite to which doth suppose some secondary Light.
    2. {LIGHT, *Lumen, lucid, Luminary, irradiate, Sunshine.*
       {SHADOW, *Shade, Umbrage, adumbrate, Screen, Canopy, Curtain.*
- *The Superficies of solid Bodies*; from which a *strong* or *weak* reflexion is styled.
    3. {BRIGHTNESS, *Lustre, splendor, refulgence, glister, glitter, dazling, shine, coruscation, clear, fair, orient, polite, gloss, resplendent, illustrious, furbish, polish, burnish, irradiate.*
       {DIMNESS, *gloomy, cloudy, blink.*

Chap. VIII.   Sensible Quality..   215

The Bulk and Solidity of Bodies; according to their ‖ *capacity*, or *incapacity* of conveying *Light*.

4. {*TRANSPARENCY, Perspicuity, pellucid, diaphanous, clear, thin*:
    OPACITY, Thick.

Both the Superficies and Bulk of Bodies; signifying ‖ *a freedom from*: or *liableness unto*, any *single* or *interspersed impediment*.

5. {*CLEARNESS, fair, immaculate, unspotted, clarifie*.
    SPOTTEDNESS, Blemish, Blot, Blur, Mote, Mole, Freckle, Speck, Stain, Soil.

II. *Secondary Visible* Qualities, are by a general name styled CO-
LOURS, *Tincture, Hue, Complexion, Stain, Tinge*; by which are meant
those *various Appearances in the Superficies of Bodies which do* more immediately *affect the Eye*.   II. CO-LOUR.

They are distinguishable into those that are more
simple; and counted either
  (*Primary*; whether ‖ the *intermediate*, or the *two extremes*.
1. {*GRAYNESS, Freez, grisly, hoary, russet*.
    {*WHITENESS, blank, blanch, bleach*.
    {*BLACKNESS, sable, sad, swart, brown, Negro*.
  (*Secondary*; most considerable according to their order in the Rainbow: the usual Colour of
  Bloud: or of *Gold*.
2. {*REDNESS, Crimson, Vermilion, Scarlet, Stammel, ruddy, Murrey, Gules*.
    {*YELLOWNESS, Sallow, Tawny*.
  Vegetables: or the appearing Colour of the *Heavens*.
3. {*GREENNESS, Verdure*.
    {*BLEWNESS, Azure, Watchet*.
  Juice of the Fish *Murex*.
4. PURPLE.
Mixed; according to the more
  General names.
5. {*VARIEGATEDNESS, motly, pyed, particoloured, divers colours, embroider, inlay*.
    CHANGEABLENESS.
Particular kinds; being made either by
  Points: or *Lines*:
6. {*SPECKLEDNESS, Freckled*.
    STRIATEDNESS, brindled, streaked, striped.
  Roundles, or *Squares*,
7. {*DAPPLEDNESS*.
    CHECQUEREDNESS.

III. Sensible

Senfible Quality. Part. II.

III. SOUND. III. Senfible Quality perceptible by the Ear, together with the Privation of it, is ftyled by the name of

{ SOUND, *Noife, refound, Report, Coil, Rout, Racket, blow, loud, dinn, quetch, Echo, Euphony.* To which may be adjoyned thofe natural words (*fiditia d fono*) *bounce, buz, chatter, chink, clack, clap, clafh, clatter, click, clink, crafh, crufh, ferk, hum, hifs, jar, jingle, jerk, knock, rattle, ruffle, rumble, ruftle, clutter, lafh, pipe, ring, fcream, fhriek, fnap, fqueak, fquall, roar, thump, toot, twang, thwack, tinkle, wheez, whimper, whip, whine, whiftle, yell.*

SILENCE, *Stilnefs, hufh, bold ones peace, mum, tacit, quafh, quiet, whift, 'ft.*

The feveral Notions belonging to this Head, to which different names are afligned, do concern either the

- *Caufes of it;* confidered
  - *Formally;* according to which feveral Sounds are made; either by an *intermediate*, or a *ftronger* and quicker: or *weaker* and flower percuflion of the Air.
    1. { MEAN, *Tenor, Counter-tenor.*
         ACUTE, *fhrill, Treble, Canto.*
         GRAVE, *low, Bafe, deep*
  - *Materially;* when it is made by things
    - *Metalline*, or other folid brittle bodies; either || *clear:* or *interrupted* by fome difcontinuity of the parts.
    2. { RINGING, *jingle, tinkle, Bell, tole, chime, Peal, Knell.*
         JARRING, *Clattering.*
    - *Animal;* being either.
      - More *general* to the more *perfect Animals:* or to *Man.*
    3. { VOICE, *vocal, call, cry, invocate, Tone.*
         ARTICULATE. *Voice, fpeak, eloqution, pronounce,*
      - More *fpecial*, and peculiar to fome brute Creatures; which may likewife be imitated with artificial Inftruments, by the forcible compreflion of Air through a rimule: or through an equable concavity.
    4. { HISSING, *Whizzing.*
         WHISTLING.
- *Relations;* as a
  - *Single perfect Sound:* or near *half more* or *lefs* then fuch a Sound.
    5. { NOTE, *Tone, Key.*
         SHARP.
         FLAT.
  - *Perfect Series of Notes:* or *aggregate of fuch Series.*
    6. { TUNE, *Leffon, Chime, Ayre, Strain.*
         CONSORT.
- *Affections;* either of
  - *Single Notes;* being either || *full* and *perfect:* or *impedite* and *imperfect.*
    7. { CLEARNESS, *fhrill.*
         HOARSNESS, *Harfhnefs.*
  - *Notes together;* in refpect of their || *agreement:* or *difagreement.*
    8. { CONCORD, *Symphony.*
         DISCORD, *Diffonance, untunable*
  - *Tunes together;* in refpect of their || *agreement:* or *difagreement.*
    9. { HARMONY, *Melody, Mufic.*
         JANGLING, *Tintamar.*

IV. The

Chap. VIII. *Sensible Quality.* 217

IV. The *Sensible Qualities* belonging to the TAST and SMELL, are of so near affinity, that several Languages do assign to them the same names. **IV. TAST and SMELL.**

They are distinguishable into the

More *general* and extreme, as to the ‖ *agreeableness:* or *disagreeableness* of them to the Palate or Nose.

1. { SWEETNESS, *Pleasant, luscious, toothsom, fragrant, odoriferous, Perfume.*
    UNSAVOURINESS, *Stink, Stench, fœtid, noisom, fulsom, rank.*

More *special* and middle; from

Thin and *warm* matter, like that of Oil or Butter: or that of Pepper.

2. { FATTINESS, *Oily, unctuous, gross, greasie.*
    ACRIMONIOUSNESS, *biting, keen, cutting.*

Cooling and *constringing* matter, like that in Green fruit: or in Galls.

3. { AUSTERENESS, *Harshness, sowr, tart.*
    ACERBITY, *Astringency, styptic.*

Penetrating vellicating matter, like that of Vinegar and Limons: or that of Aloes and Wormwood.

4. { ACIDITY, *sharpness, eager, hard.*
    BITTERNESS.

Matter of a *moderate consistency*: apt to corrode by its siccity.

5. { SALTISHNESS, *saline, brackish, briny, seasoned.*
    FRESHNESS, *unsalted, flashy.*

The *vividness*: or decay of the Spirits in any thing.

6. { FRESHNESS, *Smartness, brisk, quick, lively, spirituous.*
    DEADNESS, *vapid, decayed, insipid, wearish, flashy.*

The *beginning*: or farther degree of *Putrefaction.*

7. { MUSTINESS, *Moldiness, vinewed, fusty.*
    ROTTENNESS, *addle, putrid.*

F f V. *Tactile*

V. ACTIVE TACTILE QUALITIES.

V. *Tactile Qualities* more ACTIVE are commonly distinguished by their being

- *Primary,* from whence the others proceed; being either ‖ the *intermediate :* or the *extremes* of that Quality, whereby
  - *Homogeneous* or *Heterogeneous* things are congregated, or separated.
    1. { TEMPERATENESS, *Warmness, Tepidness, lukewarm.*
       { HEAT, *hot, sultry, ardent, torrid, fervent, swelter, inflame, scald, Parch, Scorch.*
       { COLDNESS, *bleak, piercing, biting, chill, cool, frigid, refrigerate.*
  - A Body is easily ‖ bounded by itself: or conformed to any other Body, wherein it may be contained.
    2. { MOISTNESS, *dank, damp.*
       { WETNESS, *Humidity, liquid, mash, slabber, daggle.*
       { DRINESS, *Siccity, exsiccate, arid, sear, parch.*
- *Secondary,* such as are derived from the first; referring either to
  - The *Texture of parts,* as to ‖ *nearer :* or *farther distance.*
    3. { CLOSENESS, *shrink, Constipation, consolidate, compact.*
       { DENSITY, *Crassitude, Thickness, Condense-ation, thronged, pressed.*
       { RARITY, *Thinness, attenuate, rare-ifie.*
  - *Inclination to Motion* ‖ *downwards :* or *upwards.*
    4. { WEIGHTINESS, *massie.*
       { GRAVITY, *Ponderousness, Heaviness, lumpish, weighing, pressing down.*
       { LEVITY, *Lightness.*
  - *Aptitude* or *Ineptitude to Motion.*
    - *Common to Liquids* and *Solids.*
      5. { CONSISTENCY, *congeal, stand.*
         { HARDNESS, *indurate, callous, brawny.*
         { FLUIDITY, *liquid, flow, dissolve.*
    - *Proper to Solids.*
      6. { FLEXIBLENESS, *Pliableness, pliant, bend, bow, stoop.*
         { LIMBERNESS, *supple, lank, lith, ling, gentle, pliant, pliable, slack, flagging.*
         { STIFNESS, *stark, tite, rigid, harsh, inflexible.*

VI. *Tactile Qualities* more PASSIVE, are distinguishable by their denoting either the

- *Giving way to :* or *resisting of the Touch.*
  1. { YIELDINGNESS, *give place.*
     { SOFTNESS, *Tenderness, mollifie, relent, give.*
     { HARDNESS, *obdurate, indurate, callous.*
- *Fabric of Bodies,* as to their
  - *Superficies ;* being ‖ *more :* or *less plain.*
    2. { EVENNESS, *plain, level.*
       { SMOOTHNESS, *Sleekness, glibbery, slippery, terse, polite, polish, burnish, Calender.*
       { ROUGHNESS, *Asperity, Ruggedness; uneven, harsh, ruffle, rumple, puckered, cragged.*

Bulk,

| ⎧ Bulk, being in its self, or in its parts, of ‖ an *indifferent :* or of a greater or *smaller* magnitude.
| ⎨ ⎧ ORDINARINESS, of the most usual and common size.
| 3. ⎨ COURSNESS, *gross, thick.*
| ⎩ FINENESS, *Tenuity, Subtilty, thin, attenuate.*
Adhesion of parts, in
⎧ *Fluids:*
| ⎧ SLIMINESS, *mucilaginous, roping.*
| 4. ⎨ CLAMMINESS, *viscous, adhering, stick to, cling, cleaving, glutinous,* Bird-lime.
| ⎩ UNCTUOUSNESS, *Slipperiness, Lubricity, glib.*
⎩ *Solids.*
| ⎧ FIRMNESS, *Fastness.*
| 5. ⎨ TOUGHNESS, *ductile, malleable.*
| ⎩ BRITTLENESS, *Friableness, crisp, short, frail, fragil.*
Ineptitude or aptitude to Local motion, chiefly in Solids.
| 6. ⎧ STEDDINESS, *establish, stability.*
| ⎨ FASTNESS, *Fixedness, Firmness, stedfast, wistly, set, settle, clenching, Rivet, stick in.*
| ⎩ LOOSENESS, *slease, Slackness, unfastned, unfixed, unsteddy, unstedfast, unsetiled, Luxation.*

Of SICKNESS.

THose kind of *Impotencies* of the Body, as to its natural Functions, which are usually accompanied with Pain, are styled by the common name of SICKNESS, *Disease, ill, Malady, Relapse, unhealthy, unwholsom, crazy, Distemper, Indisposition, ail,* Fit, *mortality, taken with,* Spittle.

To which is opposed HEALTH, *Sanity, Soundness, heal, incurable, wholsom, recover, safe and sound, well, clear, how do you.*

The principal Notions referring to this Head may be distinguished into such as signifie either
⎧ The more general CAUSES OF DISEASE. I.
⎨
⎩ The *Diseases themselves;* whether
⎧ *Common* to the whole Body, and the various parts of it, in respect of
⎨ DISTEMPERS. II.
⎩ TUMORS. III.
Peculiar to some parts; either the
⎧ HEAD, or ARISING THENCE. IV.
⎨ MIDDLE REGION, the Breast, or its parts. V.
⎩ LOWER BELLY or Bowels. VI.

Besides the Diseases enumerated in the following Tables, there are divers others not here provided for, because they may be otherwise sufficiently expressed: As for instance, those that belong to the *Appetite,* may be exprest by the notes of *Excess, Defect, Depravation.*

And thus likewise may it be with those other Functions of *Concoction, Sanguification, Nutrition, Augmentation,* &c.

Those that belong to the Organical parts, in respect of any Imperfection as to their just Number, Magnitude, Conformation, Site, Connexion, &c. may also be otherwise sufficiently expressed.

I. GENERAL CAUSES OF DISEASE

I. The GENERAL CAUSES OF DISEASE, may be distinguished into such as are either

Extrinsecal, and without the body; whether from

   Other bodies of a malignant dangerous quality, ‖ either spreading their efficacy by insensible *Effluvia*: or such as being taken in a small quantity, prove *destructive* to life.

1. { CONTAGION, *Infection, taint, catching, run, spread, diffuse.*
    POISON, *Venom, envenom, virulent.*

Violent motion; causing either ‖ a *dissolution of continuity*: or too great a *pressure upon the parts*, when the skin is not cut.

2. { WOUND, *Hurt, Sore, vulnerary, cut, break ones head, Scarr.*
    BRUISE, *Contusion, crush, batter, shatter.*

Intrinsecal; with relation to the

Humors; whether ‖ as *to the error of Excess*: or *bad disposition.*

3. { PLETHORA, *Fulness.*
    CACOCHYMIA, *Ill humors.*

Qualities; ‖ according to the *general name*, denoting Excess or Defect: or *that particular Indisposition* which is most frequent, namely, too much Heat.

4. { DISTEMPER.
    INFLAMMATION.

Parts and *Vessels*; with respect to the

Stopping, or *blowing* of them up.

5. { OBSTRUCTION, *Oppilation.*
    INFLATION, *puffed up, flatulent, windy.*

Putrefying, of them; considered according to the usual

Antecedent, or Cause; ‖ a *Collection of putrid matter.*

6. ABSCESSUS, *Aposteme.*

Consequent, or Effect; in relation to the

Aperture or Cavity made by the Corrosion of this putrid matter; being either ‖ *roundish*, or *oblong.*

7. { ULCER, *Sore, Botch, Canker.*
    FISTULA.

Defect of animal spirits, whereby Sense and Motion is to be communicated, so as a part becomes cadaverous and mortified, according to a ‖ *lesser*: or *greater* degree.

8. { GANGRENE.
    SPHACELUS.

Chap. VIII. Sickness. 221

II. Diseases belonging to the whole Body, or the various parts of it, in respect of DISTEMPER, are distinguishable into such as do arise either **II. DISTEMPERS of Body.**
From some putrid matter, causing a preternatural heat; being either
- Not *infectious*; seated in the
  - Humors; whether ‖ *continuing* : or *intermitting*, according to certain seasons.
    - 1. { FEVER, *Calenture*.
         AGUE, *quotidian, tertian, quartan*.
  - *Habit of the Body*, which is usually accompanied by *a wasting away of the parts*.
    - 2. { HECTIC.
         CONSUMPTION, *tabid*.
- *Infectious*; by
  - *Effluvia*; being usually accompanied with
    - *Spots in the skin*, ‖ according to a *lesser* : or *greater* degree of danger.
      - 3. { MALIGNANT FEVER, *Spotted fever, Purples*.
           PLAGUE, *Pestilence, Pest, pestiferous, pestilential, the Sickness, Murrain*.
    - *Breakings out in the skin*.
      - *More dangerous*; according to degrees *greater* : or *lesser*.
        - 4. { POX.
             MEASLES.
      - *Less dangerous*; accompanied with pain of *itching* and *burning*, from *bilious matter*; ‖ either that which doth usually overspread the whole body: or that which is commonly only in some parts, being apt to diffuse it self gradually, being accompanied with *redness* and *scurfiness*.
        - 5. { ITCH, *Mange*.
             TETTER, *Ring-worm, Shingles*.
    - *Roughness in the skin*.
      - 6. { LEPROSIE, *Lazar, Leper*.
           SCURF, *Morphew, Scald*.
  - *Contact in Venery*.
    - 7. LUES VENEREA, *French-pox*.
- From *some humor not in it self corrupted*, but by its superfluity *distending* the inward *membranes* of the Bones, the Muscles or Nerves: or *discolouring by Redness*, and heating the outward skin; being a thin light matter that may be easily discussed.
  - 8. { GOUT, *Arthritis*.
       ERYSIPELAS, *St. Anthony's fire*.

III. Those

III. TU-MORS.	III. Those Diseases by which the parts are swelled and distended beyond their due proportion, are styled TUMORS, *Rising, swell, turgid, node.*

These may be distinguished into such Tumors as are either in the
- Cuticle, or upper skin, *with little or no pain*; being ‖ *small collections* of watery matter hindered from transpiring: to which may be adjoyned that which is *subsequent upon the drying of this* and such other putrid matter, causing a roughness upon the skin with little exulceration.
  1. { PUSTULE, *Wheal, Whelk, Pimple, Push, Sty.*
     { SCAB.
- Skin it self *and Flesh.*
  - With purulent matter.
    - Not *poisonous*: either ‖ *of a bigger magnitude*, and apt to pass from one part to another, of more difficult cure: or *of a lesser magnitude*, more frequent, and less dangerous.
      2. { KING'S EVIL, *Scrophula, Struma.*
         { BOIL, *Blain, Sore, Whitlow, Ancome.*
    - *Poisonous* and corroding; being either ‖ *hard and unequal*, discolouring the skin by paleness or blackness, with Veins about it resembling the Leg of a Crab, and exceeding difficult in the Cure: or else a *collection of thick putrid bloud* violently hot, with fretting and malignity.
      3. { CANCER, *Wolf.*
         { CARBUNCLE, *Sore, Plague-sore.*
  - Without purulent matter.
    - Not *discolouring the skin*; whether of a
      - Bigger *magnitude*; either ‖ *soft*: or *hard.*
        4. { WEN.
           { SCIRRHUS.
      - Lesser *magnitude*; being kinds of Plants rooted ‖ *in the skin:* or *below it.*
        5. { WART
           { CORN.
    - *Discolouring the skin* with redness, and occasioned by Cold.
      6. CHILDBLANE. *Kibe.*
- Veins or *Arteries* immoderately distended.
  7. { VARIX.
     { ANEURISMA.
- Tendons.
  8. GANGLION, *Spavin.*

IV. THE

Chap. VIII.   *Sickness.*

IV. The DISEASES belonging to the HEAD, or NERVES, or arising thence, may be distinguished into such as relate more
Immediately to the *Brain* it self, the seat and organ of the principal Faculties; either in regard of its
- *Substance*; when it is indisposed for the
  - *More principal* and noble Faculties; either by ‖ *some hot Vapour* or Humour diffused: or from *some particular Hurt* or Inflammation, causing a depravation of the Intellectuals, Fancy and Memory; either ‖ *with a Fever,* or *without.*
    1. ⎨ FRENSY, *Delirium, frantic, light-headed, phrenetic.*
       ⎩ MADNESS, *out of ones wits, raving, distraction, besides ones self, wood, brain-sick, crack-brained, crazed, lunatic.*
  - *Less principal* Faculties; by the
    - *Superfluity* of cold pituitous matter, causing ‖ *excessive drowsiness*: or by crass crude vapours rising from the stomach, working a kind of *Suffocation in sleeping* by a sense of weight upon the Breast.
      2. ⎨ VETERNUS, *Sopor.*
         ⎩ EPHIALTES, *Night-mare, Incubus.*
    - *Corruption* of some crass phlegmatic humor, either ‖ *in the Brain, causing much drowsiness and deliration*: or *in the Arteries which should convey the spirits to the Brain, causing first a giddiness, and then an abolition of Sense and Motion.*
      3. ⎨ LETHARGY.
         ⎩ APOPLEXY.
    - *Defluxion* of Humours (which are sometimes salt or sharp) either ‖ *on the Lungs*: or *other parts of the Body, Limms,* or *Joynts.*
      4. ⎨ CATARRH, *Distillation, Rheum, Defluxion.*
         ⎩ RHEUMATISM.
- *Ventricles*; ‖ *when any hot Vapour doth agitate and disturb the motion of the spirits,* so as objects seem to turn round: or *when any cold phlegmatic humour doth obstruct their motion, causing a privation of Sense, with convulsive motions in several parts.*
  5. ⎨ VERTIGO, *Giddiness, Swimming in the head, Dizziness, Scotomy.*
     ⎩ EPILEPSY, *Falling-sickness.*

Mediately to the
- *Nerves*; which may be either
  - *Obstructed*; whether ‖ the *greater Nerves, and for a longer continuance*: or *the lesser Branches, for a shorter space,* whereby Sense and Motion is hindered.
    6. ⎨ PALSIE, *paralytic.*
       ⎩ NUMNESS, *Stupor, asleep.*
  - *Contracted more generally*: or *distended in some particular part.*
    7. ⎨ CONVULSION.
       ⎩ CRAMP, *stitch.*
  - *Oppressed with superfluous moisture,* causing an unequal growth of the parts, specially the Head and Joints.
    8. RICKETS, *Rachitis.*
- *Throat*; by such an inward Swelling and Inflammation as doth hinder Swallowing and Respiration.
    9. SQUINANCY, *Quinsie.*

V. The

V. DISEA-
SES of the
MIDDLE
REGION.

V. *The Diseases* belonging to the MIDDLE REGION and its parts, may refer either to the

Lungs; in their being

Obstructed by some crass phlegmatic matter adhering to the sides of the Pipes, from whence follows

Too frequent Respiration.

 1. SHORTNESS OF BREATH, *Anhelatio, Panting, Pursiness.*

Difficulty of Breathing, according to ‖ a *lesser,* or *greater degree:* by the latter of which men cannot fetch their breath, unless in an upright (posture.

 2. { ASTHMA, *Tissick, broken-winded, wheeze.*
    { ORTHOPNOEA.

Ulcerated, and by degrees putrefying; from whence sometimes doth proceed *much purulent matter to fill up the cavity of the Thorax:*

 3. { CONSUMPTION, *Phthisis.*
    { EMPYEMA.

Heart; by some noxious vapours or humours, which do either

Provoke to too frequent and vehement motion for the freeing it self from them,

 4. PALPITATION.

Hinder the motion of it; according to ‖ a *lesser:* or *greater* degree.

 5. { FAINTING, *Failing, languish, Qualm.*
    { SWOUNING, *Swound, Leipothymia.*

Side; from some Inflammation within the Membranes covering the inside of the Ribs, causing difficulty of breathing, and provocation to coughing, upon which great pain follows, accompanied with a Fever.

 6. PLEURISIE.

VI. DISEA-
SES of the
BOWELS.

VI. *Diseases* belonging to the LOWER BELLY or Bowels, may be distinguished into such as do concern the

Stomach; by sharp humors corroding the mouth of it, causing sometimes Fainting and cold Sweats.

 1. CARDIALGIA, *Heart-burning.*

Liver and Gall; being caused by some impotence in them for the doing of their Functions, in not digesting & distributing the humors belonging to them; causing either ‖ *Paleness of colour, Faintness, Indisposition to stir:* or *Yellowness and Swarthiness of colour, accompanied with faintness and nauseousness.*

 2. { GREEN-SICKNESS, *Cachexie.*
    { JAUNDISE, *Yellow-jaundise, Black-jaundise.*

Stomach and Liver, and other Bowels jointly; which, being defective in the works of Concoction and Distribution, do occasion *a superfluity of serous matter distending the skin of the belly and other parts of the body, accompanied with some wind:* and sometimes *a windy vapour, accompanied with some watery humors, stretching the belly.*

 3. { DROPSY, *hydropical.*
    { TYMPANY.

Spleen; by its dispersing *four and feculent humors:* or *noxious vapors,* into other parts of the body; the former of which is usually accompanied with faintness, weariness, looseness of teeth, spots on the body, and specially on the legs.

 4. { SCURVY, *Scorbute.*
    { HYPOCHONDRIACAL VAPOURS, *Splenetic.*

Guts;

Guts; ‖ from *some sharp humor that corrodes, or vapor that distends the Colon*: or *from some hardned excrement, or some other like matter, stopping the Ilia or smaller Guts.*
5. { COLIC, *Belly-ach.*
   { ILIAC PASSION.

Faculties of excretion; whether by
Stool; either as to the *excess* of this: or the *voiding of blond.*
6. { DIARRHÆA, *Lax, Looseness, Flux.*
   { DISENTERY, *Bloody flix.*
Urine; either by some stony concretion in the Kidneys or Bladder: or a continual involuntary urining by drops.
7. { STONE.
   { STRANGURY.

Lower part of the belly or *Scrotum*; ‖ *by a breach of the internal Membranes, or too much distention of it, or by superfluity of waterish or windy matter*: or *in the Veins about the Fundament.*
8. { RUPTURE, *Hernia, Burst, Broken-belly.*
   { HÆMORROIDS, *Piles.*

Mother or *Womb*; by ‖ causing *convulsive motions*: or *stopping of the Breath.*
9. { HYSTERICAL PASSION, *Mother.*
   { SUFFOCATION.

CHAP. IX.

Concerning the Predicament of Action; *the several kinds of it.* I. Spiritual. II. Corporeal. III. Motion. IV. Operation.

NExt to the Predicament of Quality may succeed that of *Action*; the several kinds of which may be distributed into such as have for their Agent a
{ *Spirit*, or spiritual faculty, called SPIRITUAL ACTION.
{ *Body*, or material substance, respecting chiefly either the
  { Actions of Animate bodies, called here CORPOREAL ACTION.
  { Passage of bodies from one place to another, styled MOTION.
  { Sundry kinds of works, about which men of several callings use to imploy themselves, styled OPERATION.

SPIRITUAL ACTION.

THe Genus of SPIRITUAL ACTIONS, may be distributed into such as do belong either *to*
{ GOD. I.
{ *The Soul,* with reference to the
  { *Understanding.*
    { SPECULATIVE. II.
    { PRACTICAL. III.
  { WILL. IV.
  { *Fancy* or *Appetite*; the Actions of which are styled *Affections* or Passions, and may be distinguished into such as are either more
    { SIMPLE. V.
    { MIXED. VI.

§. I.

G g   I. By

1. ACTIONS OF GOD. I. By ACTIONS OF GOD in this place, are meant only his *transient* Actions, which are terminated in the Creatures. As for his *immanent* Actions, because we can frame no other conceptions of these but such as are sutable to the acts of our own minds, therefore *may they be* sufficiently *expressed by those that follow* in the next Differences. These *transient* Acts here enumerated, do *primarily belong to the Divine Nature*; though some of them may *in a secondary manner*, and by way of allusion and participation, be sometimes ascribed *to other things*: To which may be annexed upon the account of Affinity the general name of those Actions which do exceed all Natural power, MIRACLE, *Wonder, supernatural.*

These are distinguishable into such as do concern either the

Putting of things into their *first being*: or *reducing them to nothing.*

1. { CREATION, *Making, Creator, Creature,*
    { ANNIHILATION, *Annul, disannul, abolish, extinguish, bring to nought,*
    Government or disposal of things; (*call-in, cancel, put out.*)

  More general; whereby he doth most *freely* and *wisely* take care of, and provide for all things: To which may be opposed by some Analogy such a necessary Concatenation and *unalterable order* amongst things *as doth not admit* of any *liberty*: or *such a blind contingency of things as excludes all wisdom*, expressed usually by the words,

2. { PROVIDENCE, *Fore-sight, Fore-cast.*
    { FATE, *Destiny.*
    { FORTUNE, *Chance, Accident, Venture, Adventure, casual, Hap, Luck, Hazard, fortuitous, a Hit, peradventure, perhaps.*

  More special; belonging either to

  Animate Creatures; by

  Contributing to their || *well*: or *ill* being.

3. { BLESSING, *Beatitude, Benediction.*
    { CURSING, *accurse, ban, Malediction, Execration.*

  Continuing them in their particular kinds of Being: or *depriving* them of it.

4. { PRESERVATION, *Conservation, Protection, Keeping, maintain, save, Saviour, shelter, guard, keep, cherish.*
    { DESTRUCTION, *Perdition, Confusion, Bane, Devastation, Loss, pernicious, subvert, undoe, ruine, confound, extirpate, abolish, bring to naught, stroy, destroy, cast away, perish, cut off, waste, consume, dissolve, exterminate, extinguish, fall, gone.*

  Keeping or *taking* them *from any evil* felt or feared: or *leaving them to it.*

5. { DELIVERANCE, *Rescue, Save-iour, Salvation, free, quit, rid, clear, exempt.*
    { DERELICTION, *destitute, forlorn, deserting, give up, relinquish, cast off, deliver up, forsake, leave, forgo.*

  Rational Creatures; as to their

  Minds; by *discovering* to them, or *impressing* upon them, in an extraordinary way, such *Truths* or *Inclinations* as humane industry could not of it self attain to.

6. { REVELATION, *open, disclose, discover, Vision, Enthusiasm, Fanatic, Oracle.*
    { INSPIRATION, *infuse.*

  States; by *delivering them from* a condition of servitude & *misery.*

7. REDEMPTION, *deliver, save, ransom, rescue.*

Chap. IX.   *Spiritual Action.*   227

II. ACTIONS of the UNDERSTANDING and Judgment SPECULA-   II. SPE-
TIVE, *Contemplation, Theory,* are such as do *concern the* various *exercise of our*   CULA-
Understandings about the *Truth* and *Falshood* of things, with respect either to   TIVE A-
Understanding ; being either   (the   CTIONS of the Under-
- *Preparative* ; in the *first Objectization* of a thing : or the *reflexive Thought*   standing.
  about it, together with what else one knows of that kind.
  1. { THINKING, *Cogitation, bethink, deem, imagin, esteem, Conceit, Notion, Thought-ful, pensive, mind it, suggest, put in ones head,*
       MEDITATING, *Study, considering, cast about in ones mind, muse, contemplate, Elucubration, think, fore think, premeditate, ponder, extempore.*
- *Operative* ; in ‖ the comparing of things *to find out* what is *Truth :* or the *Thought resulting* from such comparison.
  2. { INQUISITION, *Examination, Search, Scrutiny, exploration, investigate, Disquisition, seek, discuss, hunt, canvase, cast water, Quest, Inquest.*
       DISCOVERY, *detect, find, perceive, sift out, pick out, Invention, excogi-*
Judgment ;   *(tate, Author, Inventor, tell, inkling, 'tis out.*
- *Primary* ; in *judging* such discovery ‖ *agreeable* to *Truth :* or *disagreeable.*
  - *More general.*
    3. { ASSENT, *Consent, accord, agree, concurr, allow, acknowledge, yield, suffrage, Voice, Vote, of the same mind, think good.*
         DISSENT, *differ, disagree, of another mind, Discord.*
  - *More special* ; according to its arguments ; as
    - *Proceeding from Causes*
      - *Extrinsecal* ; *Testimony* ‖ *sufficient :* or *insufficient.*
        4. { BELIEVING, *Credit, credible, Faith, Trust.*
             DISBELIEVING, *Discredit, incredible, Distrust.*
      - *Intrinsecal* in the thing it self ; that it is ‖ *conclusive :* or *not so conclusive but that it may be otherwise.*
        5. { KNOWING, *Cognition, conscious, wist, witting, aware, privy, Intelligence, learn, inform, acquaint, cognizance, notice, inkling prescience, omniscient.*
             DOUBTING, *misdoubt, mistrust, distrust, suspence, hanging staggering, hesitate, pendulous, dubious, ambiguous, at a stand, stick at, Quandary, Scruple, Sceptic, uncertain, Apocryphal, 'tis a question.*
    - *Productive* of these *Effects* in ‖ *higher,* or *lower* degrees.
      6. { CERTAINTY, *Assurance, sure, evince, convince, demonstrate, evidence, undoubted, out of doubt, without doubt, doubtless, infallible.*
           OPINION, *Conceit, Judgment, Sentiment, Mind, Tenet, think, suppose, surmise, ween, overween, unanimous, likely, probable, prejudice, apprehend, fancy, repute, deem, Verdict, Sentence, shoot ones bolt.*
- *Secondary* ; *judging* of Truth found, as to the
  - *Consequence* of it, in respect of other things to be concluded from it, or to follow upon it ; in *Thesi :* or *in Hypothesi.*
    7. { REASONING, *Discussing, Arguing, Ratiocination, Logic.*
         CONJECTURING, *Guessing, surmise, divine, mind gives, conceit, Presumption, probable.*
  - *Importance :* or *frivolousness* of it.
    8. { ESTEEMING, *accounting, prizing, valuing, rating, regard, respect, repute, count of, care for, think well of, set by, stand upon, credit, prefer.*
         CONTEMNING, *despising, slighting, undervaluing, disregarding, set at nought, scorn, disdain, abjectness, despicable, vilifie, disesteem, neglect, set light by, make nothing of, I pass not for it, Nickname, pish.*

G g 2   III. ACTI-

Spiritual Action. Part.II

III. PRACTICAL ACTIONS of the Understanding.

III. ACTIONS of the UNDERSTANDING and Judgment PRACTICAL, do concern the enquiry after and taking notice of the Nature of things, *with reference to their Goodness or Fitness to any purpose.* They are distinguishable, as the former, by their respect to the

Understanding; being either

Preparative, in the *first Objectization* of a business: or *the reflexive Thought about it*, together with what else one knows of that kind.

1. { DELIBERATING, *ponder, weigh, forecast.*
   OBSERVING, *advert, animadvert, give ear, attend to, heed, regard, give ones mind to, look to, mark, note, mind, pry, peep, watch, take notice, notable, remarkable, oversee, overlook.*

Operative, in ‖ the *comparing of means* to find which is expedient: or the *Thought resulting* from such comparison.

2. { CONSIDERATION, *revolve, scan, advise, forecast, recognize, premeditate ponder, peruse, study, recount, reflect, review, revise, weigh, bethink, consult, cast in ones mind, retrospection, ruminate.*
   INVENTION, *devising, excogitate, find out, make, Author.*

Judgment;

Primary; in *judging* the thing found to be ‖ *agreeable* to its end: or *disagreeable.*

More general.

3. { APPROVING, *liking, allowing, think good, take well, fancy him, find a Bill, currant.*
   DISAPPROVING, *disliking, disallowing, disavow, mislike, condemn, explode, reprobate.*

More special; according to its motives; as

Proceeding from Causes

Extrinsecal; Warranty ‖ *sufficient* : or *insufficient.*

4. { TRUST, *Confidence, betrust, entrust, rely, repose, enfeoff, recommend, credit, charge, rest upon,*
   DISTRUST, *Mistrust, Diffidence, Suspicion, Surmize, Jealousie, Umbrage, call in question, misgive.*

Intrinsecal in the means it self; ‖ *conclusive* that it is so: or *not so conclusive* but that it may be otherwise.

5. { SATISFACTION, *Content, acquiesce, resolve.*
   SCRUPLE, *Doubt, dissatisfie.*

Productive of these Effects; in ‖ *higher* : or *lower degrees.*

6. { ASSURANCE, *Confidence, sure, certain, resolved, secure, confirm.*
   PERSWASION, *think, believe.*

Secondary; in *judging* of expedients found, ‖ *as to the use of them, how they are to be ordered and managed : or what is like to be the event of them.*

7. { CONTRIVING, *projecting frame, machinate, plot, forecast, cast about, or in ones mind, find a way, devise, Conveyance.*
   EXPECTING, *look for, wait, gaping after, mind gives me, make account, stay for, watch for.*

IV. ACTIONS OF THE WILL.

IV. ACTIONS OF THE WILL. Under this Head are to be considered the *Kinds* of such Actions; *belonging* either *to the*

End as future; comprehending Acts more

Simple;

Imperfect and *diminute*; ‖ *for:* or *against* one thing rather then another.

1. { INCLINATION, *Propensity, Proclivity, Proneness, Forwardness, hankering, having a mind to, Prejudice for, bent, addicted.*
   AVERSION, *Prejudice against, unwillingness, coyness, stand off.*

Impedite

Chap. IX.   Spiritual Action.   229

Impedite and *conditional*; ||*for*: or *against* a thing, if left to it self.

2. { VELLEITY, *Woulding, Wishing, Desire, List, Vote, Will, Mind, Option, rather.*
   { NOLLEITY, *Backwardness, go against, grudge, loth, Regret, Reluctancy, think much, rather not, unwilling, with an ill will.*

Perfect; denoting || *the determining of it self to do*, or *not to do*: or *the taking of farther time to consider.*

3. { PURPOSING, *Intention, Decree, destine, determine, appoint, design, resolve, ordain; mean, nonce, bent, minded, set himself, set ones mind, predestinate, preordain.*
   { DEMURRING, *besitating, hanging, suspence, stick at, Quandary.*

Complicate; towards an object considered as difficult, signifying || the *purpose of doing* it notwithstanding such Difficulties: or *doubting* because of such Difficulties.

4. { RESOLUTION, *Fixedness, determined.*
   { WAVERING, *fluctuate, hanging, suspence, irresolute, staggering.*

Means;

Antecedently; determining what to || *take*: or *leave*.

5. { ELECTION, *chusing, select, Choice, cull, picking, prefer, set aside, Option, Pre-election, predestinate, rather.*
   { REJECTION, *refuse, Preterition, pass by, cast off, cast aside, cast away, reprobate, repudiate, renounce, explode, out-cast*.

Consequently; || *continuing in the purpose* of using such means: or *ceasing such purpose*.

6. { PROSECUTING, *persevere, persist, hold on.*
   { DESISTING, *giving off, leaving, cease, surcease, end, terminate, determin, stay, rest, pause, forbear, withdraw, falter, supersede, break off, go out, give over, lay aside*, or *down*.

End obtained; as to the || *resting* or *not resting* of the Will in it as good.

7. { DELECTATION, *Fruition, Rejoycing, Joy, Gladness, Delight, Comfort, Complacence, Pleasure, Solace, Satisfaction, Content, placid, please, affect, acceptable, delicious, sweet, welcome.*
   { DISPLACENCE, *Sorrow, Grief, Discomfort, unpleasant, irksome, grievous, Offence-ive, Disgust, Dislike, Distast, stomach, unacceptable grating, malecontent.*

Affections; either of the

Will it self in its actings; consisting in || its *having a power* of applying it self to the doing or not doing this or that: or *not having such power*.

8. { LIBERTY, *arbitrary, free, may, may chuse.*
   { DETERMINATION TO ONE, *must, cannot chuse but, limit, Necessity.*

Actions of the Will; denoting || the doing of things according to the *free inclinations of our own minds*: or *the being necessitated by some external impediments* to do any thing *against such inclinations*.

9. { SPONTANEITY, *of ones own accord, freely, willing, voluntary, with a good will, unbidden, gratis, ready.*
   { COACTION, *Compulsion, Constraint, Force, enforce, Violence, unwillingness, maugre, perforce, extort, wrench, wrest, in spight, will or nill, driving, pressing, bear down, over-awe.*

V. *Acti*

V. SIMPLE PASSIONS,

V. *Acts* of the Senſitive part, namely of the *Fancy*, and chiefly of the *Appetite*, whereby the mind is moved and diſturbed with the apprehenſions of things, are ſtyled PASSIONS, *Affection, Perturbation, pathetic.*

Thoſe amongſt theſe are called *more* SIMPLE which conſiſt onely of one ſingle Act. They are diſtinguiſhable into ſuch as concern things under the notion of

1. *New unexpected* ſurprizing: or elſe things *over-common* and too much repeated; without reſpect to the good or evil of them, being chiefly a diſturbance of the Fancy; ſtyled
   - ADMIRATION, *marvel, wonder, amaze, aſtoniſh.*
   - TÆDIUM, *glut, loathing, cloy, dawl, nauſeate.*

Good or *Evil* which we

Wiſh to happen to them.

2. - FAVOUR, *Benevolence, Benignity, Grace, Good will, kind propitious, ingratiate, Favorite, Dilling, Well-wiſher, make much of.*
    - MALIGNITY, *Malice, Spite, Pique, Grudge, Prejudice, Deſpite, Diſcourteſie, Diſfavour, ſiniſter, virulent, malevolent, ill will, ill minded.*

Apprehend to be in them; whether

Abſolute; flowing from ‖ our general apprehenſions *of the Worth* of things, and our need of them: or the *Evil*, and our being hurt by them.

3. - LOVE, *Affection, inamour, dote on, ſmitten, amiable, beſotted, amorous, dear, endear, Darling, Minion, Paramour, well-beloved, Likings, Fancy, Philtre.*
    - HATRED, *Malice, Rancour, Spite, Virulence, odious, abhor, abominate, deteſt, cannot endure, Grudge, Pique, Heart-burning, cankered, exulcerate.*

Relative to different notions *concerning*

Both Good and Evil; conſidered as

Preſent.

4. - MIRTH, *Glee, Solace, Chearfulneſs, Sport, blithe, bliſſom, buxom, frolick, jolly, jocund, jovial, merry, exhilarate, glad, crank, debonair, comical, pleaſant, ſanguin, Jubile.*
    - GRIEF, *Sadneſs, Sorrow, Melancholy, Heavineſs, doleful, deplorable, diſconſolate, bitter, penſive, dejected, tragical, ruful, amort, moan, bemoan, wail, bewail, lament, Dump, caſt down, vex, trouble, cut, take on, whimper, pule, woe, agony, anguiſh, mourn, Plaint, Cry, take heavily.*

Abſent and *poſſible.*

5. - DESIRE, *Affection, covet, crave, fain, long for, luſt, greedy, Inclination to, hankering, wiſh, Concupiſcence, eager, earneſt, importunate, thirſt after, have a mind to.*
    - AVERSATION, *Antipathy, Regret, Reluctancy, Diſtaſt, irkſom, eſchew, ſhun, avoid, abhor, loath, execrate, cannot endure, or abide,*

Abſent

Chap. IX.   *Spiritual Action.*   231

Absent and *probable*; *as to*
The nature of the Act.

6.
- HOPE, *Trust, Recumbency, Affiance, Rely.*
- FEAR, *Awe, Dread, Terrour, Horrour, Consternation, hideous, dismal, afraid, agast, formidable, horrible, terrible, fright, fray, terrifie, scare, startle, daunt, deterr, dismay, amate, appale, dare not, terrible, Bugbear, Hobgoblin.*

The *greater:* or *lesser* degree of this Probability.

7.
- CONFIDENCE, *Affiance, Trust, build upon, rest upon, rely, repose, secure, pert, in heart, dare, presume, take to.*
- DIFFIDENCE, *Suspicion, Jealousie, Mistrust, Distrust, out of heart, faint-hearted, cast down, heartless, misdoubt, misgive.*

The *issue* and event; which as it is represented to have Difficulties in it ‖ either *superable:* or *insuperable*; so it excites.

8.
- BOLDNESS, *Courage, Audacity, daring, sturdy, hardy, stout, venturous, pert, malapert, embolden, presume.*
- DESPAIR, *Despondency, forlorn, hopeless, dash, cast down, deadness of heart, heartless, past hope.*

Evil alone, or opposition from others, *wherein there is contempt:* to which may be annexed by way of affinity (though it be not properly a simple Passion) that particular *desire of making such actions* whereby others have been injurious to us, to become *hurtful to themselves*, so as they may be sensible of it.

9.
- ANGER, *Ire, Passion-ate, Wrath, Sharpness, Rage, Outrage, Pett, Choler, Gall, fume, storm, fret, pelt, chafe, vex, take on, inflame, kindle, irritate, inrage, exasperate, incense, provoke, move, sullen, hasty, furious, outragious, mad, look big, placable, appease, stomack, Animosity, heart-burning, irascible, rough, hot, curst, snappish, snarle, snuffle.*
- REVENGE, *avenge, Vengeance, vindictive, wreak.*

VI. MIXED

VI. MIXED PASSIONS, are such as do not consist of any single Act, but are made up of more then one, to be distinguished by the Object they are conversant about, and by the Simple Passions of which they consist, into such

VI. MIXED PASSIONS.

Determined either to Good or Evil; with respect to (as are

The particular interest of *Repute*; being conversant *about*

Good, which we apprehend to be in it self *honourable* and worthy, implying ‖ *Confidence and Love* in the promoting of it: or *Confidence and Joy* in the owning of it.

1. { ZEAL, *ardent, Devotion, earnest, fervent, hot, warm, intent, eager, Zelot.*
    GLORYING, *Triumph, Exultation, boast, brag, Bravado, Rodomontado, Thrasonical, crack, crow, vapor, vaunt, Ostentation, swagger, vainglory, flourishing, take a pride.*

Evil, which we apprehend to be in it self *dishonourable* and unworthy: implying ‖ a mixture of *Hatred and Aversation* against the committing of it: or *Sorrow and Diffidence* for the committing of it.

2. { SCORN, *set light by, slight, despise, contemn.*
    SHAME, *faced-full-less, abash, bashful, ashamed, out of countenance, confound, quash, dash, Impudence, Turpitude, put to shame.*

The more general interests belonging to

Our selves; respecting either

Good that is *dear to us*, implying a ‖ mixture of *Love, Anger,* and *Hope*, that we may excel others in it: or a mixture of *Love, Anger,* and *Fear*, lest we should by others be deprived of it.

3. { EMULATION, *vy, strive, struggle.*
    JEALOUSIE, *suspicion, surmize.*

Evil; whether as done

By our selves; being either ‖ a mixture of *Sorrow* and *Fear* upon dissatisfaction in having committed it: or *Sorrow* and *Desire*, as wishing it had not been committed.

4. { REMORSE, *Compunction, Contrition, relent, beshrew, trouble of*
    REPENTANCE, *Penitence, rue.* (*mind.*

By others; ‖ either *a vile thing by any person*, or *any evil by a vile person*; implying a mixture of *Anger* and *Hatred*: or of *Anger* and *Aversa-*

5. { INDIGNATION, *Scorn, dudgeon, fume, murmure.* (*tion.*
    DISDAIN, *Scorn.*

Others; in respect of the

Good befalling them, (as we think) ‖ *worthily*, or *unworthily*; implying a mixture of *Love* and *Joy*: or *Hate* and *Grief.*

6. { JOY FOR THE GOOD OF OTHERS, *Gratulation, congratulate, Sympathy.*
    ENVY, *Spite-full, invidious, grudge, repine, malign.*

Evil befalling them, (as we think) ‖ *worthily*, or *unworthily*; implying a mixture of *Hate* and *Joy*: or of *Love* and *Grief.*

7. { ἘΠΙΧΑΙΡΕΚΑΚΊΑ, *Joy for the evil of others.*
    PITTY, *Compassion, commiserate, condole, relent, ruthful, tender, woful, yeann, Bowels, bemoan, bewail, lament, deplore, Sympathy, fellow-feeling.*

Indetermined either as to Good or Evil, but concerning both consisting in a distraction of the Mind by a *conflict of any two contrary Passions*: to which may be opposed (though not so proper to this place) the *transport* of the Mind, being wholly possess'd *with one Passion*: styled

8. { AGONY.
    EXTASIE, *Transport, Amazement, Consternation, Maze, Traunce, Rupture, ravish, astonish, extatical.*

COR-

Chap. IX.   *Corporeal Action.*   233

CORPOREAL ACTION.

BY CORPOREAL ACTIONS are meant such Actions *whose Agent is a* ♂ II.
Body or Material substance. They are distinguishable into such as are
More peculiar to Living creatures; either more
- *Absolute*; belonging to
  - VEGETATIVES. I.
  - SENSITIVES. II.
  - RATIONALS. III.
- *Relative* to the
  - Outward SIGNS OF PASSION. IV.
  - GENERAL Notions belonging to DEMEANOUR. V.
Common with them to other things, to which by Analogy they are ascribed, the different kinds of GESTURE. VI.

I. *Corporeal* ACTIONS belonging chiefly to VEGETATIVE Bodies, may be distinguished into such as are either.   I. ACTIONS VEGETATIVE.

Primary and more general; denoting the *making*: or *unmaking* of a thing; the *motion towards a new form*: or *from the precedent form*; styled
1. { GENERATION, *get, beget, procreate, propagate, breeding, engender, Generation.*
   { CORRUPTION, *Dissolution, consumption.*   (*sis.*

Secondary and more particular; relating unto the
- *Conveying*, or *receiving in that first matter which is to be formed into an animate Body.*
  2. { IMPREGNATION, *beget, pregnant, breeding, teeming, conceived, get with child, big, great with child,* or *egg.*
     { CONCEPTION, *with child, Superfetation.*   (*soon.*
- *Bringing forth* what hath been thus conceived; either *in due time*: or *too*
  3. { PARTURITION, *Bearing, Birth, Nativity, bringing forth, travail, groning, in labour, lying in, Child-birth, easing, farrowing, kindling, foling, whelping, deliver, Midwife, brought to bed, cry out, lay egg.*
     { ABORTION, *miscarry, Mischance, cast young, Castling, untimely birth, Slink, still-born.*
- *Improvement* of what is thus brought forth; either
  - *Peculiar to the Young*; implying that more then ordinary tenderness to be used towards things in that state, || whether *more general*: or that which is *proper to viviparous Animals.*
    4. { FOTION, *cherishing, foster, foment, brood, Incubation, hatching.*
       { LACTATION, *giving suck, suckle.*
  - *Common to Young and Old*;
    - *Antecedent*; || the *taking in of sutable and sufficient aliment*: or *the fitting of this aliment by fermentation.*
      5. { FEEDING, *living upon, Aliment, Food.*
         { DIGESTING, *Concoction, put over.*
    - *Consequent* from the
      - *Union of the Aliment to the body*: and *its improving* thereby.
        6. { NOURISHING, *Nutrition, maintain, Nutriment.*
           { GROWING, *come up, increase, improve, thrive, Spring, Proficient*
      - *Union*: or *disunion, of* the *Body and Soul.*
        7. { LIVING, *Life, quick, alive, enliven, vivifie, revive, survive, vital, Resurrection.*
           { DYING, *Death, dead-ly, mortal, fatal, dy, decease, depart, expire, give up the ghost, defunct, kill, slay, mortifie, dispatch, Slaughter, Mortality, capital.*

H h   II. *Cor-*

II. AC- 11. *Corporeal* ACTIONS belonging to SENSITIVE Bodies, may be di-
TIONS   stinguished into such as are either
SENSI-
TIVE.   *More principal* and natural; denoting the *kinds of natural Appetite*, toge-
          ther with *such Actions as tend to the satisfying of them*; relating to the
          Preservation of the Individuum, as to the desire of
            Nourishment, for the supply of Decays; and that either by
              Food: or Meat.
              1. { HUNGER, *Appetite, Stomach, eager, greedy, ravenous, Famine,*
                    sharp-set.
                   EATING, *devour, gorging, fall to, Meal, Repast, Refection, Food,*
                    Meat, Aliment, edible, Viands, Victuals, fall to ones Meat.
              Liquor.
              2. { THIRST, *dry.*
                   DRINKING, *Potion, potulent, potable, quaff, soop, soaking, lap, swill,*
                    carouse, sip, tipple, bibble, guzzle, Draught, Drench, Water, Butler,
                    Buttery, Cellar.
            Rest and refreshment after labour and weariness; comprehending the
              Appetite or inclination after this: or *the Satisfaction of such Appetite,*
              consisting in a cessation from all Actions of the outward Senses, by
              a relaxation of the Nerves.
              3. { DROWSINESS, *Heaviness.*
                   SLEEPING, *asleep, dormant, a Nap, lull, Slumber, narcotic, roost.*
            State supposed, belonging to this Appetite, or the Satisfaction of it, de-
              noting the *general Action of the Senses:* or *the working of the Fancy*
              in sleep.
              4. { WAKING, *awake, watch, Reveiles, raise from sleep.*
                   DREAMING.
            Propagation of the Species.
              5. { LUST, *Salacity, Lechery, Venery, Concupiscence, libidinous, carnal,*
                    fleshly, blossom, clicket, proud.
                   COITION, *coupling, gendring, lie with, know carnally, Copulation,*
                    rutting, tread, venery.
          Less principal and preternatural; referring to several affections of the
            Touch, and different kinds of Pain; being either
            Proper to the Skin and outward parts; caused by *an agitation of some*
              thin Vapours stopped in their expiration, which is remedied by *such a*
              kind of affriction with an edge as doth open the Pores, that the Vapors
              may transpire.
              6. { ITCHING.
                   SCRATCHING, *Scraping, clawing, Scalping-iron.*
            Common to other parts; and caused by
              Distention or compression of the parts: or *sharpness of humours.*
              7. { AKING, *Ach.*
                   PRICKING, *Crick, pungent, sharp, stitch.*
              Dissipation of the Spirits in the softer parts by a light touch: or *corro-*
                sion of the membranous parts.
              8. { TICKLING, *Titillation.*
                   SMARTING, *piercing.*
              Obstruction either *in the Nerves or Muscles;* causing || some *vellications in*
                the Nerves: or a *hot pungent pain* in the Muscles.
              9. { TWITCHING, *Vellication, Pinching.*
                   TINGLING.

III. The

Chap. IX. *Corporeal Action.*

III. The *Corporeal* ACTIONS *peculiar to Men*, or the several wayes of *expressing their mental Conceptions*, are either by *Articulate sounds*; considered according to

III. ACTIONS PECULIAR TO MEN.

The *general* name, together with the *privation* of it.

1. { SPEAKING, *talk*, *utter-ance*, *mentioning*, Elocution, *pronounce*, *express*, *deliver*, Prolation, *Spokes-man*, *effable*, *voluble*, *fluent*, *say*, *tell*, *mutter*, *mumble*, *jabber*, *jargon*, *vein*, *Grammar*, *Rhetoric*, *Oratory*, *Eloquence*, *Prolocutor*, *nuncupative*, *by word of mouth*.
   MUTENESS, *dumb*, *speechless*, *silent*, *blank*, *tongue-tied*.

The *defects of speaking*, as to || the *continuity of speech* : or the prolation *of some particular letters*.

2. { STUTTERING, *Stammering*, *falter*, *hammer*.
   LISPING.

The *degrees of loudness* in speaking; either || *without any vocal sound* : or *with much noise*.

3. { WHISPERING, *mutter*, *round in the ear*.
   EXCLAMATION, *Acclamation*, *hollow*, *hoot*, *hoop*, *shout*, *baul*, *clamor*, *cry*, *Lure*, *Out-cry*, *roar*, *screech*, *scream*, *squeak*, *squeal*, *loud*, *lift up ones voice*, *set out ones throat*.

The *particular kinds of speaking*; referring

To *such words as we see before us*; either || *more perfect* : or *imperfect*.

4. { READING, *Lecture*, *Lesson*, *legible*, *peruse*.
   SPELLING.

To the *manner of ordering our voice according to musical Tunes*; either || the *more perfect* : or the *more imperfect attempt*.

5. { SINGING, *Song*, *Ditty*, *Ballad*, *Carol*, *Canticle*, *Lay*, *Ode*, *Madrigal*, *Eclogue*, *canorous*, *Modulation*, *chant*, *Chorister*, *Quire*.
   CHIRPING, *questing*, *quittle*.

The *several relations of speaking*; when we say that to another which we expect should be || *repeated* : or *written* by him.

6. { DICTATING, *prompting*, *suggest*.
   ENDITING.

Figures representing either words or things, and *made* either || *immediately by mens hands* : or *by the impression of Types*.

7. { WRITING, *penning*, *drawing*, *engrossing*, *Hand*, *Manuscript*, *subscribe*, *superscribe*, *inscribe*, *transcribe*, *Postscript*, *interline*, *indorse*, *scrawle*, *scrible*, *rude draught*, *Pen-man*, *Scribe*, *Writer*, *Scrivener*, *Secretary*, *Clerk*, *Note*, *Ticket*, *Docket*, *Short-hand*, *Tachygraphy*, *Brachygraphy*, *Cryptography*, *set ones hand*, *set down*, *take* or *put in writing*, *enter into book*, *write out fair*.
   PRINTING, *Imprint*, *Impression*, *typographical*, *Type*, *Press*, *put in Print*.

IV. SIGNS OF PASSIONS.

IV. The OUTWARD SIGNS OF our inward PASSIONS, are either

More peculiar to some single Passions; as to

Admiration: or *Sating*; *Straining the* ‖ *eyes*: or *the brows*.
1. { STARING.
   { MOVING THE BROWS.

Love: or *Hate*; *expansion*: or *contraction of the Muscles* of the Face.
2. { SMILING, *smirking, sneering, simper*.
   { LOWRING, *powting, scowling, frowning, grinning, look sowre*.

Mirth: or *Sorrow*.
3. { LAUGHING, *deride, ridiculous, giggle, chuckle, tihi, flicker*.
   { WEEPING, *mourn, cry, Tears, wailing, Plaint, bemoan, bewail, lament, blubber, shed tears, whining*.

Desire: or *Aversation*; *scruing the body*: or *wagging the head*.
4. { WRIGLING.
   { MOVING THE HEAD, *Nodd*.

Hope: or *Fear*; expressed either by the
Body or parts of it; being ‖ *moved once and quick*: or *oft and continuedly*: or *deprived of motion*.
5. { STARTING, *flinching*.
   { TREMBLING, *quaking, shaking, shudering, Trepidation, quivering, shiver, quaver, chatter*.
   { RIGOR, *Horrour, Stifness*.

Breath; ‖ emitted *short and quick*: or emitted *slow and long*: or *sucked up suddenly*.
6. { HUFFING, *snuff, puff*.
   { SIGHING, *sobbing*.
   { SUCKING *up the breath, sniff*.

Confidence and *Diffidence*: or *Boldness* and *Despair*; *setting the hands against the sides*: or *heaving up the shoulders*.
7. { KEMBOING.
   { SPANISH SHRUG.

Anger: or *Revenge*; by *emission of the breath*; either ‖ *vocal, but not articulate*: or *articulate, but not distinctly* intelligible.
8. { GRONING.
   { GRUMBLING.

More *common* to several Passions; by *discolouring the countenance* ‖ *with* a greater degree of *Redness* then doth belong to the natural hue; appertaining either to Joy, Love, Desire, but chiefly to *Shame*: or else with *Whiteness*; belonging to those more violent perturbations of Grief, Anger, &c. but chiefly to *Fear*.
9. { BLUSHING, *flush*.
   { PALENESS, *wan, ghastly, pallid, appale*.

V. The

Chap. IX.   *Corporeal Action.*   237

V. The general notions belonging to DEMEANOUR, *Carriage,* **V. DEMEA-**
Comportment, Deportment, Garb, behave, or the manner of our *converfing* **NOUR.**
towards one another in refpect of fuch Corporeal Actions as either
cuftom or common opinion hath put a decency and fitnefs upon, are confiderable; either according to the

{More *general kinds*; denoting

The *endeavour to exprefs our refpect to others,* by ‖ *going to them :* or *ftaying by them or for them.*

1. { VISITING, *go to fee.*
    WAITING, *Attend-ance, ferve, Retinue, Train, Valet, Page, Lac-quey, ftay for, tarry for, tend.*

The *congrefs or meeting of others,* in refpect of ‖ our *applying our felves to them :* or *their receiving or ufing of us.*

2. { ADDRESSING, *accoft.*
    ENTERTAINING, *treat, entreat, ufage, reception, welcome.*

The *kinds of gefture,* or *words, fignifying refpect.*

3. SALUTATION, *careffing, accoft, greet, hail, commendations.*

More *fpecial kinds*; confifting in

Geftures.

At a diftance; by *bowing* of the ‖ *Body :* or *Knees.*

4. { CONGEEING, *cringe, duck, make a leg, crouch.*
    CURCHEEING, *Genuflexion.*

Near; either more

Ruftic.

5. { CLAPPING.
    SHAKING HANDS.

Gentile; by *joyning* of the ‖ *Body :* or *Face.*

6. { EMBRACING, *clafping, clip, coll, grafp, hug, twine.*
    KISSING, *Smack.*

Words; whereby we exprefs

Our ‖ *efteem of others :* or our *bufinefs with them.*

7. { COMPLEMENTING, *Courtlinefs, Careffing.*
    CONFERRING, *commune, parley, talk, treat, fpeak with, Dia-logue.*

Our *good wifhes to others*; either at our ‖ *firft meeting :* or *parting.*

8. { SALVEDICTION, *accoft, greet, hail.*
    VALEDICTION, *adieu, farwell, take leave.*

VI. GESTURE,

VI. GE-
STURE.

VI. GESTURE, *Action, Behaviour, Gesticulation, Mimic*, doth denote such an *Animal action* or motion *as alters the situation* of the whole or parts of the body: To which the word POSTURE, *Position*, may be annexed by way of affinity; signifying the *situation in which such motion is determined.* The several *kinds* of these *Gestures* and *Postures* (which are applicable likewise to inanimate things) do *refer* either *to the weights being incumbent upon something.*

Below it: And these are distinguished *according to* the imaginary progress of that body or the parts of it,

Upward; either more

  Direct.
  1. { RISING, *arise, raise, rouse, ly up, sit up, stand up, rear, elevate, lift up, erect, exalt, Resurrection*
       STANDING, *Station-ary, Footing, Perch, Rampant,*
  Oblique.
    Keeping the height, and
      Inlarging the terms.
      2. { STRETCHING, *retching, extending, Distention, Expansion, produce, sprein, strein, draw out.*
           SPREAD, *square.*
      Narrowing the terms.
      3. { SHRINKING, *contracting, Coarctation, couch, gather up.*
           CRUMPLE, *smudge.*
    Altering the height, by motion of the
      Trunk.
      4. { STOOPING, *crouch, bow, bend, couring.*
           LEANING, *lolling, Recumbency, stay* or *rest upon:*
      Lower Limbs.
        Hipps.
        5. { SITTING, *set, sedentary, seat*
             SATE, *squat.*
        Knees.
        6. { KNEELING, *Genuflexion, fall on knees.*
             ON KNEES.

Downward; either more
  Direct.
  7. { FALLING, *fell, cast down, sink.*
       LYING, *Prostration, groveling, lay, along, all along, flat, level, couch.*
  Oblique.
  8. { TURNING.
       REVERSE, *inverted.*

Above it; whether ||*partly:* or *wholly;* each of which is either motion or rest.
  9. { CLINGING.
       HANGING, *pendent, suspended, dangling.*

MOTION.

Chap. IX.

MOTION.

THat Action whereby things do pass from one place to another is styled §. III. MOTION, *move, remove, stir, wag, shake, quetch, shog, jog, start, jerk, budge, dislodge, flitting, shuffle, shuttle, rummage, agitation, going, passing, transferr, place, make a stirr.*

REST, *Quiet, still, unmoved, repose, sedate, settle, stand, stay, stand or ly still, Requiem, ease, Pause, acquiesce, settle, sit, lodge, lull, Sabbath, dead of the night, take rest.*

By the word *Motion* here is meant Local Motion, which doth always accompany Corporeal Action, upon which account many of the Species under this Head might, if there were convenient room for them, be reckoned under the former; but their places here may serve sufficiently to express and distinguish them. This Local Motion of bodies may be distinguished into

⎧ *Natural.*
⎪ ⎧ Of the *whole*; more
⎪ ⎪ ⎧ *General*, respecting the Kinds of Animal PROGRESSIVE MOTION. I.
⎪ ⎨ ⎨ *Particular*, referring to the VARIOUS NOTIONS OF GOING. II.
⎪ ⎪ ⎩ Of the *parts*; considered
⎪ ⎪ ⎧ More *largely*; as belonging to ANIMAL ACTION IN COMMON. III
⎨ ⎨ As *restrained* to the Acts of
⎪ ⎪ ⎧ PURGATION. IV.
⎪ ⎪ ⎩ ⎨ EXERCISE. V.
⎩ VIOLENT MOTION according to the several kinds of it. VI.

I. Kinds of ANIMAL PROGRESSION, may refer either to   I. ANIMAL PROGRESSION.

⎧ *Beasts*; more ‖*perfect*: or *imperfect.*
⎪ 1. ⎰ GOING, *gressive, a Step, Pace, Gate.*
⎪ ⎱ HALTING, *Cripple, lame, limp, hobble, foundred.*
⎪ *Birds*; in the
⎪ ⎧ *Air*; by the *motion of the wings*: to which may be annexed that other
⎪ ⎪ kind of Motion of the wings whereby Birds use to keep themselves up
⎪ ⎨ in the same place with *little or no Progression.*
⎪ 2. ⎰ FLYING, *fluttering, soar, volatile, towre.*
⎪ ⎱ HOVERING.
⎨ *Water*; either ‖*upon it*: or *into and under it.*
⎪ 3. ⎰ FLOTING.
⎪ ⎱ DIVING, *duck, plunge.*
⎪ *Fish*; either ‖ more generally *within* the water: or more specially *downwards into it.*
⎪ 4. ⎰ SWIMMING, *launch.*
⎪ ⎱ SINKING.
⎪ *Insects*; as
⎪ ⎧ *Grashoppers* and *Fleas, &c.* the more ‖*perfect*: or *imperfect.*
⎪ 5. ⎨ LEAPING, *skipping, jump, frisk, spring, caper, curvet, bound.*
⎪ ⎩ HOPPING.
⎪ *Ants*: or *Worms, &c.*
⎩ 6. ⎰ CREEPING, *crawl, sprawl, reptile.*
   ⎱ WRIGLING, *insinuate, scrue or wind himself in.*

Though each of these Motions do principally belong to such kinds of living Creatures, yet are they not so to be restrained to them but that they may be truly ascribed to others.

H. The

II. MODES OF GOING.

II. The several MODES OF GOING, may be distinguished into *The Self-motion or Ition of Animals;*

On an ordinary Plain or declivity; according to the

Lesser: or greater degrees of Velocity.

1. { WALKING, *Ambulation, Procession, Perambulation, go, wade, Ford, waddle, Lacquey, Path, foot it, trip along.* (man.

   RUNNING, *galloping, Career, Course, Race, start, Goal, outstrip, Foot-*

Different Motion of the four legs; || when either those of one side move together: or when they move cross and diagonally.

2. { AMBLING, *pacing, thorough-paced.*
   TROTTING, *prancing.*

Different Extensions || of the body according to height: or of the legs according to wideness.

3. { STALKING, *jetting, strutt, portly going.*
   STRADLING, *stride, a stride, divaricate.*

Different Modes, whether more || regular: or irregular.

4. { STEDDY.
   STAGGERING, *reeling, Vacillation, Tottering.*

On a very smooth Plain.

5. { SLIDING, *glide, slipping.*
   STUMBLING, *Titubation, blunder, falter, lapse, slip, trip.*

On a difficult Declivity, || upwards: or downwards.

6. { CLIMBING, *clambering, scaling.*
   TUMBLING.

The being carried by something else; on || the Land: or Water.

7. { RIDING, *being horsed or mounted, taking horse, Post-ilion.*
   SAILING, *Navigation, Voiage, launch, take water or ship, embark, waft*

III. MOTIONS OF THE PARTS.

III. *Animal* MOTIONS *belonging to the various parts, are either*

More principal;

Of the Heart originally, and from thence of the Bloud in the Arteries: to which may be adjoyned the Motion of the Guts.

1. { PULSE, *throb, beat.*
   PERISTALTIC.

Of the Lungs, || more general, or the Sound made by some impediment of breathing through the Nose.

2. { RESPIRATION, *breathing, fetch wind, draw breath, take breath.*
   SNORTING, *snoring.*

Less principal; of the

Mouth and Thorax; by the forcible || emission, or attraction of Breath.

3. { BLOWING, *puffing, blast.*
   SUCTION, *supping, sip, soop, drawing, emulgent, snuff up.*

Diaphragm or Stomach; agitated by a convulsive Motion || upwards, or downwards.

4. { SOBBING.
   HICCOUGH, *Tex.*

Jaws; by a

Repeated Motion in the || first, or second preparation of Food.

5. { MASTICATION, *chewing, champ, gnawing, browzing, mumble.*
   RUMINATION, *chewing the cud.*

Single Motion; to which may be annexed that Motion of the musculous parts of the body, caused by some flatulent vapours.

6. { YAWNING, *gape, Uscitation, gasp.*
   PANDICULATION, *retching, stretching.*

[Tongue

| *Tongue*, or *Throat*.
  { LICKING, *lap, flap*.
7. { SWALLOWING, *gulp, ingurgitate, devour, pouch, gobble*.
IV. Those kinds of *Actions* whereby several *Animals* do cast off such *excrementitious parts* IV. PUR-
as are offensive to nature are styled PURGATION, *voiding, evacuating, Excrement, fluxing*: GATION.
to which may be opposed the Notion of *BINDING, costive, styptic, restringent, astringent*.
These Motions may be distinguished by the kinds of parts so amoved; either the more
⎧ *Vaporous* and windy; *from the*
⎪ ⎧ *Head*.
⎪ { 1. SNEEZING, *neeze, Sternutation*.
⎪ ⎩ *Stomach upwards*, or *Guts downwards*.
⎪   { BELCHING, *parbreak; breaking wind upwards*.
⎪ 2. { FARTING, *breaking wind downwards, Scape*.
⎪ *Serous* and *watry*; *from the*
⎪ ⎧ *Whole habit* of the body.
⎪ ⎪   { SWEATING, *Exudation, diaphoretic, sudorific, all in a water*.
⎪ ⎨ 3. { TRANSPIRATION, *breathing, Evaporation, Effluvium, Perspiration*.
⎪ ⎪ *Head*.
⎪ ⎪   { SPITTING, *Salivate-ion, Spittle, bespit, spawl, bespawl, slaver, drivel, Flux*.
⎪ ⎩ 4. { BLOWING THE NOSE, *mucous, Snivel, Snot*.
⎨ *Lungs* and *Chest*.
⎪   { COUGHING.
⎪ 5. { EXCREATION, *haking, hemming*.
⎪ *Greater* or *lesser Veins*.
⎪   { BLEEDING, *opening a Vein, Phlebotomy, let blood, draw blood, Lancet*.
⎪ 6. { SCARIFYING, *lance*.
⎪ *Skin*.
⎪   { BLISTERING, *Vesication, caustic*.
⎪ 7. { CUPPING.
⎩ *Bladder*.
  8. URINING, *piss, make water, hold ones water, stale, diuretic, Diabetes, Dysury*.
Consistent and *gross parts*; from the ∥ *Stomach upwards*, or the *Guts downwards*.
   { VOMITING, *spewing, casting, disgorging, puke, regurgitate, retching*.
   { DUNGING, *purging by siege, going to stool, scour, Draught, Lask, laxative, Looseness,
     muting, soluble, sective, Muck, Ordure, Siege, Stool, Sir-reverence, excrement,
     easment, ease the belly, Jakes, Privy, House of office*.

V. By RECREATION, *Diversion, Pastime, Sport, Exercise*, are meant those several V. RE-
kinds of *Actions* which are used *for divertisement* or *Exercise*: to which may be annexed CREATI-
the word GAME, *Play, Prize*, signifying such kind of *Exercises*, wherein there is an en- ON.
⎧ *Mind*; depending upon   (deavour for *Mastery*. These are either of the
⎪ ⎧ *Chance onely*; according to ∥ the more *general name*: or that particular kind which is
⎪ ⎪ most frequent *by marked Cubes*.
⎪ ⎨   { LOT, *Sortition, Cuts, Ballot, cast* or *draw Lots*.
⎪ ⎪ 1. { DICE, *a Dy, cock-all, rifle*.
⎪ ⎩ *Chance* and *Skill*.
⎨   { CHARTS.
⎪ 2. { TABLES.
⎪ *Skill onely*.
⎪   { CHESS.
⎩ 3. { DRAUGHTS.
⎧ *Body*; in respect of
⎪ ⎧ *The whole*; requiring
⎪ ⎪ ⎧ *Strength* and *Skill*.
⎪ ⎪ ⎪   { BOWLING.
⎪ ⎪ ⎨ 4. { BALLING, *Tennis, Foot ball, Stool-ball, Sto-Ball, Pel-mel*.
⎨ ⎪ ⎪ *Agility* and *Skill*.
⎪ ⎪ ⎪   { DANCING, *Masking, Revels, a Ball, Morice, Mumming*.
⎪ ⎪ ⎩ 5. { VAULTING.
⎪ ⎪ *Strength, Agility* and *Skill*.
⎪ ⎪   { WRESTLING, *grapling, strugling, striving, handy gripes, strike up ones heels*.
⎪ ⎩ 6. { FENCING, *Gladiator, Tilting, Tournament, justling, play at weapon* or *foils*.
⎩ *The Eye*, or *the Ear*.
     { SIGHTS, *Shews, Theatre, Amphitheatre, Pageants, Spectacle*.
  7. { MUSIC, *Serenade, strein, aer, tun., prelude, Waits, Crowd, Fiddle-er, Minstrel,
       play on an Instrument*.

VI. The

VI. VIOLENT MOTION.

VI. The *general kinds* of VIOLENT MOTION, may be distributed according to the effects upon the thing moved, into such as denote

Translation into a new place; comprehending

Motion together; when the *Mover sustains the thing moved:* to which may be annexed By way of affinity that other *Action, by which one thing sustains, or hinders the falling of another.*

1. {
   CARRYING, *bring, convey, bear, serve, import, waft, weare about one, portable, portage, porter, baggage, vehicle, fare, beer, packhorse.*
   BEARING, *supporting, sustain, hold up, prop, shore up, stay up, uphold, carry, stand under, shoulder up, bolster up.*
}

Amotion, when the Mover and Moved do at the beginning cease to be contiguous: or *Admotion,* when the thing moved doth end in a contiguity of something else.   (*coit, sling,*

2. {
   CASTING, *throwing, fling, hurl, project, inject, eject, ding, pelt, toss,*
   CATCHING, *apprehend, lay hold, snatch, lay hands on, grapple, graspe, scamble.*
}

Often returns into the same place; according to ‖ *greater* or *less degrees.*

3. {
   SWINGING, *Vibration, waving, brandish, agitate, exagitate, to and fro, flourish, rock, sway, dangling, pendulous, wield.*
   SHAKING, *Quassation, Concussion, jogging, agitate, dandle, wag, swag, sway, jolt, totter, flutter, shatter, waving.*
}

Some impression from the Mover; according to the more

General name: or that which is from an obtuse hard body.

4. {
   STRIKING, *Percussion, smite, bang, beat, baste, buffet, cuff, dash, bit, swinge, thump, thwack, Blow, Stripe, slap, flap, rap, tap, kick, wince, spurn, bob, box, fillip, whirret, yerke, pummel, punch, rebuff, repercussion, collision, gnash, skittish, interfere, let fly at,*
   KNOCKING, *beating Blow, butt, Mallet, battering, jobbing, Ramm.*
}

Particular kind; by the end of a thing, more ‖ *obtuse,* or *acute.*

5. {
   POUNDING, *braying, Contusion, stamp.*
   PECKING, *Mattock, Pick-ax.*
}

Dissolution of Union in the same body; *according to*

The Stiffness, or *Limberness* of the body wherein it is made.

6. {
   BREAKING, *Fracture, Rupture, burst, Crack, Crash, Squash, Dash, Flaw, Shatter, shiver, crumble.*
   TEARING, *torn, dilacerate, rend, rent, ragged, tattered, flittered, jagged, pull in pieces.*
}

The Figure of the body by which it is made; either ‖ *an edge,* or *a point.*

7. {
   CUTTING, *Incision gash, slash, hack, hew, chop, rip, chip, snip, slice, section, segment, carve, disject, whittle, barb, pare, top, lop, curtail, dock, sharpe, keen, Hatchet, Pole-ax.*
   PRICKING, *stabbing, Goad, pungent, runn in, thrust in, goar.*
}

OPE-

Chap. IX.

OPERATION.

THe sundry kinds of *works about which men* of several Callings use to *imploy themselves*, are usually styled by the name of §. IV.
OPERATION, *Labor-ious, Pains, Travail, Toil, moil, Turmoile, drudg, droil, work, handy-work, Ply, cooperate, take pains, lay about him, PLAT, Sport, lusory, dally.*
These are either
{ More *Common* and general; relating to
  MECHANICAL FACULTIES. I.
  MIXED MECHANICAL Operations. II.
{ More *Particular*; belonging to the providing of
  Food, AGRICULTURE. III.
  Houses, or Utensils, FABRILE Arts IV.
  Clothing, SARTORIAN Trades. V.
  Physic, CHYMICAL, Pharmaceutical Operations. VI.

I. OPERATIONS belonging to the MECHANICAL Faculties, are either such as do refer to the   I. MECHANICAL OPERATIONS.

Lever; for the forcible motion of a thing ‖ *upwards*, or *downwards*.
1. { LIFTING, *heave, hoise, advance, elevate, exalt,* Lever, Crow, Crane.
     DEPRESSING, *strein, stress, weigh down.*

Balance; for ‖ *trial of* the *weight* of things, or the *preponderating of one*
2. { LIBRATING, *balancing.*   (*side*.
     BIASSING, *preponderate.*

Wedge; for the *dividing of hard tough bodies*; to which may be opposed the *thrusting of them close together.*
3. { CLEAVING, *rive, slit, split, Cleft, Chink, Chap, Crevise.*
     COMPRESSING, *crib, gripe, pinching, press, squeezing, straining, wring, nip, twing, throng, crowd, crush, Constipation, bulge.*

Pully; when the mover and moved continue their Contiguity in ‖ *admotion*, or *amotion*.
4. { PULLING, *pluck, tow, tug, lugg, twing, twitch, draw, drag, Draught, bale, Revulsion, vellication, distract.*
     THRUSTING, *push, shove, drive, rush, justle, repell, extrude, intrude, press, throng, crowd, crumm, farce, wedge in, venvue, run at, foin at.*

Wheel; by ‖ *continued turning about,* or *rolling backward or forward*.
5. { VERTIGINATING, *turning round, Revolution, wheeling, Rotation, twirl, whirl, spinn, role round.*
     VOLUTATION, *tumbling, rolling, wallow, welter, rock, trundle, waddle.*

Screw; to which may be adjoyned for some affinity the *action of that concave Instrument used for the projection of water.*
6. { SCREWING, *Winch.*
     SYRINGING, *squirting, spirt, spouting.*

Spring; wherein there is a motion of restitution: to which may be annexed for its affinity the *forcible putting a thing out of its natural tension* and posture.
7. { SPRINGING, *elastical, fillip.*
     BENDING, *bow, warp, crooke.*

I i 2   II. Those

II. MIXED MECHANICAL OPERATIONS.

II. Those are styled MIXED MECHANICAL OPERATIONS, which are not appropriate to any one kind of Art, but are general and common to many. These do concern the

Uniting or seperating of several bodies; considered more
- *Simply.*
  - 1. { BINDING, *gird, Band, Bond, Bundle, Packet, Fardle, sheafe, faggot, tack, lace, swaddle, swathing, trussing, girt, surcingle.*
    LOOSENING, *unbind, undoe, solve, lax, slack, relaxation.*
- *Relatively* to the affections of binding; viz. *fastning of the bond* ‖ *by a knot,* or *confused kinds of knots.*
  - 2. { TYING, *Knot, Node, bracing, buckling, coupling fastning, knit, furling.*
    TANGLING, *entangle, hamper, ravel, perplex, snarled, felter, intricate, involved, Intrigues, extricate, complicate, insnare, Labyrinth.*

Concealing, or *manifesting;* either more
- *Common.*
  - 3. { COVERING, *heal, Veil, shroud, hide, whelm, stop, Canopy, Hood, Lid, palliate, cloake, overlay, overrun, overshadow.*
    UNCOVERING, *open, expose, discover, shew, reveal, naked, unmask, unveil.*
- *Special;* relating to Containing bodies.
  - 4. { SHUTTING, *stop, close, inclosing, immure, exclude, seclude, recluse, obstruct, Wink, fold up, pinn up, sowe up, seal up, corke up, lute up, lock up, put to the door.*
    OPENING, *breaking up, disclose, display, Expansion, gap, Slade, Aperture, unstop, expose, lay or set open.*

Putting of things ‖ *nearer together,* or *farther asunder;* either
- *More general.*
  - 5. { GATHERING, *Collect-ion, assemble, convene, compile, levy, raise men or money, Receiver, rake or scrape together, rally, glean, pick up.*
    SCATTERING, *discuss, disperse, dissipate, sprinkle, strew, insperfion.*
- *More particular;* with reference to the
  - *Capacity of*
    - *Consistent bodies,* and such as are not supposed to be contained.
      - 6. { HEAPING, *accumulate, amass, lay up, stow, pile, Stack, Mow, Cock, Rick, Shock, Drift, Dunghill, mixen.*
        SPREADING, *diffuse, Expansion, display, Suffusion, strew, run, plash, lay cloth.*
    - *Fluid Bodies,* and such as are supposed to be contained in something.
      - 7. { FILLING, *replenish, Repletion, full, plenary, sated, stow, cram, stuff, farse, recruit.*
        EMPTYING, *evacuate, vacant, Vacuity, rid, void, exhaust, Chasm, clear, lanke, lave, draw dry.*
- *Motion* of bodies, chiefly fluids; according to ‖ the *more general* name: or that which is *involuntary, and besides intention.*
  - 8. { POURING, *Effusion, Infusion, gush, guggling, yewer, Tunnel.*
    SPILLING, *shedding, run out, seeth over.*

III OPERA-

Chap. IX.   *Operation.*   245

III. OPERATIONS belonging to AGRICULTURE, do concern either **III. AGRI-**
The *Ground,* or *Land;* in respect of   **CULTURE.**

    Loosning it; either || *by single persons:* or *by the help of drawing Beasts.*
    1. { DIGGING, *delve, break up, spit, spade.*
       { PLOWING, *tilling, breaking up, coulter, share.*
    Breaking the clods, and smoothing the surface.
    2. { HARROWING.
       { ROLLING.
    Helping or directing the Fertility of the ground, by || *adding some new matter,* or *removing the impediments of noxious Plants.*
    3. { MANURING, *cultivate, dunging, marling, soiling, Tilth, culture.*
       { WEEDING.

The *Grane* or *Seed,* chiefly of Herbs; in respect of

    Putting it into the ground, or *taking it off from the ground upon its maturity.*
    4. { SOWING, *seminate.*
       { REAPING, *mowing, Crop, Harvest, Sithe, Sickle, stubble, swarth.*
    Separating of it from || *the straw,* or *lesser husks:*
    5. { THRESHING, *Flail.*
       { WINNOWING, *Fan, Ventilation.*

The *Propagation of Trees* or *Shrubs* chiefly, by

    Putting the Root of the Plant in the ground; to which may be adjoyned *the putting of Grain segregately into the ground,* which is sometimes used for Pulse.
    6. { PLANTING, *implant.*
       { SETTING.
    Joyning a part of one Plant to another; either || *to the top of the body,* or *some branch being cut,* or *to the sides of the body.*
    7. { GRAFTING, *ingraft, Imp.*
       { INOCOLATING.
    Cutting off superfluous Branches; to which may be adjoyned *the cutting down of the whole.*
    8. { PRUNING, *dressing, cutting, coping.*
       { FELLING, *grubb, wood-fall.*

IV. By

IV. FABRILE OPERATIONS, (*Smith, Carpenter, Mason*, &c.) are meant all such kind of works as do primarily concern our Houses or Utensils, whether for necessity, or ornament: to which may be adjoyned those Operations which concern the making of Earthen ware, styled FIGULATORY, *Potter*. These are distinguishable into such as denote

Dissolution of Continuity; either by

Seperating of some thin parts from the surface of a body by rubbing with an edge: or *breaking the body it self into minute parts* by percussion with some obtuse body.

1. { SHAVING, *scraping, raze, razour.*
     CONTUSION, *bruising, pounding, stamping, braying, morter, pestle,*

Dividing from a body some small parts; either ‖ *by affriction upon a stone*, or *with an iron instrument*.

2. { GRINDING, *attrition, Grist, Querne, Mill.*
     FILING, *Raspe.*

Dividing the parts of a body, by cutting it, either ‖ in *roundish cavities*, or *in oblong scissures.*

3. { BORING, *perforate, foraminate, pierce, Bodkin, Dril, Awle, Gimlet, Wimble, Trepann, Awgre.*
     SAWING, *Saw, whipsaw*, &c.

Uniting either of metalline or other bodies *by some third body adhering*.

4. { SODERING, *Cement, luting.*
     GLUING, *cementing, glutinous, conglutinate.*

Shaping of bodies into particular figures; either by *Hammering*, or *melting*.

5. { FORGING.
     CASTING, *melt, founding, fusile, molde.*

Cutting, either ‖ *a solid and bulky*, or *a flat figure.*

6. { CARVING, *Sculpture.*
     GRAVING, *ingrave, etching.*

Compressing of a soft body; or *circumagitating* either a soft: or hard body.

7. { KNEADING, *moulding, plastic.*
     TURNING, *Lath.*

Adorning the surface of the body; either by ‖ *variety of colours*: or adding an *external lustre* to it.

8. { PAINTING, *limn, draw, enamel, fucus, pensil.*
     VARNISHING, *size.*

Chap. IX.   Operation.   247

V. SARTORIAN OPERATIONS do concern either the   V. SARTO-
Preparation of stuffs; by   RIAN OPE-
                                                                 RATIONS.
  Making several vegetable or animal substances into *Thred.*
  1. ⎧ TWISTING, *tortion, wreath, writhing, twine, winding.*
     ⎩ SPINNING, *spinster, Rock, Distaff.*
  Joyning such Threds together into Cloth.
  2. ⎧ WEAVING, *Texture, Contexture, Loom, Web, braid, woven, Hur-*
     ⎨ *dle, Shuttle, Wicker, Matt.*
     ⎩ KNITTING.
  Thickning and *colouring* such Cloth.
  3. ⎧ FULLING, *milling, Fuller.*
     ⎩ DYING, *stain, Tincture, tinge, ingrain.*
  Making of Stuffs *into Vests:* either by
    Uniting necessary, and *cutting off unnecessary* parts.
  4. ⎧ SOWING, *Stitch, Seam-ster, Suture, Welt, Needle, dearn, quilt,*
     ⎨   *draw cloth, rip.*
     ⎩ CLIPPING, *Scissors, shear, shorn, cut.*
  Placing together the parts in ‖ *greater,* or *lesser* plicatures.
  5. ⎧ FOLDING, *wrap, lap, pleit, clinching, clutching, doubling, invelop.*
     ⎩ CURLING, *crisping, frizling, furling.*
  Preserving of such Stuffs or Vests *clean;* common likewise to other
  things.
    By the help of *Water* or *liquor;* either when
      Things are *put into,* and *agitated in the water;* to which may be op-
      posed the *putting upon them other bodies of a more gross consistence;*
      styled
  6. ⎧ WASHING, *scouring, Lotion, rince, Laver, Laundress, gargling.*
     ⎩ SMEARING, *daubing, anoint, ointment, Unction, greaze,*
         chrism; and many with [*be*] as *bespaul, spit, spue, sprinkle.*
    Water is imbibed and communicated to the thing; to which may be
    adjoyned, for its affinity, the *putting of things into liquor, in order*
    to the communicating of some new quality to such liquor.
  7. ⎧ SOAKING, *steeping, embrewing, macerating, watering* Land, &c.
     ⎨   *bathing, imbibe, sinke, sop, brewis, embrew.*
     ⎩ INFUSION *watering* Fish, &c. *macerate, Decoction, impregnate.*
    By external *Motion* of or upon them, ‖ *more,* or *less* violent.
  8. ⎧ RUBBING, *scrape, Friction, Frication, scrub, chafe, Attrition,*
     ⎨   *fret, gall, scowr, taw, grate.*
     ⎩ WIPING, *stroke, terse, handkerchief, towel, napkin.*
    By *Instruments* to seperate those minuter bodies which adhere to the
    superficies.
  9. ⎧ BRUSHING, *sweeping, Beesom, Whisk,* Brush, Broom, Maukin.
     ⎩ COMBING, *carding, currying.*

                                                          VI. By

VI. CHYMICAL OPERATIONS.

VI. By CHYMICAL OPERATIONS are meant such kind of works as tend to the *changing* of bodies, with respect to the *Position and Figure of their minuter parts.* By this, amongst other ends, Medicaments are usually prepared; for which reason, those kind of Operations styled PHARMACEUTICAL, belonging to the Apothecary, may be hereunto annexed.

The Operations belonging to this Head, do concern the changing and preparing of Bodies; either *by*

Instruments, for the reduction of them into minute parts; ‖ by *compression and affriction* betwixt two hard bodies: or *by separating the parts so reduced, through a porous Plain.*

1. ⎧ GRINDING.
   ⎨ SIFTING, *bolting, Sieve, siercing, ranging.*

Liquors; either

Changing the Consistence of bodies; *by reducing* them *into* ‖ a more *liquid:* or a more *dry consistence.*

2. ⎧ DISSOLUTION, *melt, liquefie, dissolve, thaw, fusil, flux, run about.*
   ⎨ COAGULATION, *congealing, Clod, Curd, Gelly, Clot-teted, Gore, Concretion, grumous.*

Dividing hard bodies into minute parts; ‖ *by an acid liquor*, through which such parts are dispersed: or *the sinking down of such parts to the bottom*, by the mixture of some other liquor.

3. ⎧ CORROSION, *eating, fretting, gnawing, caustic.*
   ⎨ PRECIPITATION, *settling.*

Separating of these parts from the liquor; *by passing them through a porous body;* either ‖ *downward:* or *both upward and downward.*

4. ⎧ STRAINING, *Percolation, squeeze, Colender.*
   ⎨ FILTRATION, *filtre.*

Heat; applicable chiefly either to

Liquid bodies; which being kept for some considerable time in a gentle heat, upon this usually follows; either the

Loosning the inward parts of such bodies, so as by agitation they *work one upon another;* styled

5. ⎧ DIGESTION.
   ⎨ FERMENTATION, *work, fret, Leven, Yeast, Barm, Rennet.*

Separating of the finer parts, by raising them up in the form of a Liquor: or *the farther separating of the more spirituous from the watery parts of this liquor.*

6. ⎧ DISTILLATION, *Still, Limbeck, cohobation.*
   ⎨ RECTIFYING.

Hard and solid bodies; either by

Driving away the more watery and volatil parts, *and leaving the more solid:* or *raising the volatil parts in the form of a Salt.*

7. ⎧ CHARRING, *chark, Tinder.*
   ⎨ SUBLIMING, *Sublimation.*

Burning away the combustible parts of a body: or *turning the parts remaining after such burning into a liquor.*

8. ⎧ CALCINATION.
   ⎨ LIXIVIATION, *deliquiate, Lye, Buck.*

CHAP.

CHAP. X.

Concerning Relation more private, namely, I. Oeconomical *or Family Relation, together with the several kinds of things relating to those in that capacity, either as,* II. Possessions; *or,* III. Provisions.

THE *Species of Relation* are the most numerous amongst the Tables of Accidents, by reason of their mixed natures, comprehending both *Substances, Qualities* and *Actions,* as they are circumstantiated by some peculiar respects, according to which they are here considered.

More private Relation may be distinguished into such as denote; either
{ Those Personal respects or Actions, which belong to the first kind of Association of Men into Families; called OECONOMICAL RELATION.
{ Those things which are necessary to the well being of Families, either as
{ POSSESSIONS.
{ PROVISIONS.

OECONOMICAL RELATION.

That respect wherein one man may stand to another, according to the first and most natural kind of association of men into Families, is styled OECONOMICAL RELATION, *Family, Houshold, domestic, menial, House, Home.*

The Notions belonging to this Head, may be distinguished into such as signifie; either
Personal Relations, of
{ CONSANGUINITY. I.   { SUPERIORITY, or Inferiority. III.
{ AFFINITY. II.   { EQUALITY. IV.
Oeconomical Duties referring to *Education;* consisting either in
{ WORDS. V.
{ DEEDS. VI.

I. Those who partake of the same Bloud, are styled *Relations* of CONSANGUINITY, *Kin, kindred, Bloud, House, Stem, Stock.*

These are distinguishable into such as are; either more
General; denoting *such as have* ∥ *preceded, or succeeded.*
1. { PROGENITOR, *Ancestor, Forefather, Extraction, Parentage, Elders, Pedegree, Genealogy.*
   { DESCENDANT, *Lineage, Off-spring, Race, Issue, Progeny, Generation, Posterity, Stock, Breed, Kind, Extraction, Stem, spring from.*
Special; whether
Direct; ∥ *ascending,* or *Descending.*
2. { PARENT, *Sire, Father, Mother, Dam, paternal, maternal, Grandsire,* &c. *Orphan.*
   { CHILD, *Issue, Son, Daughter, Brood, Litter, filial, adopt, Posthume.*
Lateral; either ∥
Ascending, or descending.
3. { UNCLE, *Aunt.*
   { NEPHEW, *Niece.*
Equal.
Immediate; whether ∥ *by both Parents,* or *by one*
4. { BROTHER, *Sister-hood.*
   { HALF BROTHER.
Mediate; either ∥ *Brothers Children,* or *their Descendants.*
5. { FIRST COSIN, *German.*
   { COSIN.

250   *Oeconomical Relation.*   Part. II.

II. AFFINI-TY.
II. Those respects which do either refer unto or arise from a state of Marriage, whereby persons are mutually ingaged to Fidelity and Constancy, are styled Relations of AFFINITY, *Alliance, Kindred.*

These are distinguishable into such as do concern either

That *state preceding* whereby persons are rendred capable of it as to their || *not being married :* or *not having coupled with any other person.*

1. { COELEBS, *Single life, Bachelour, Damosel, Maid.*
    VIRGIN, *Maid.*

The endeavour after Marriage ; wherein, if several persons stand in competition, there doth thence arise this double Relation.

2. { SUTER, *Paramor, Sweet-heart, Mistress, Servant, woo, canvase court,*
    RIVAL, *Corrival, Competitor.*   (*make love.*

The first beginning of this Affiance, by a mutual Promise in order to the consummating of it.

3. BETROTHED, *contracted, spouse, espouse, Affiance, sure.*

The full completing of it by all its Solemnities.

4. MARRIED, *Matrimony, Wed-ding, Match, Mate, nuptial, conjugal, Husband, Wife, Toke-fellow, Spouse, Bride-groom, Bains, Dower, Bygamy, Polygamy, Hymen, Epithalamium.*

The state resulting from a dissolution of it by Death.

5. WIDOWER, *Dowager, Relict, Jointer.*

III. SUPERI-ORITY.
III. Relations of SUPERIORITY, *Betters,* and INFERIORITY, *Underlings,* do originally belong to Families, in which was the first kind of Government, and from thence are derived all the secondary Relations which follow ; respecting either

Minors ; as to their

Souls and Religion.
1. { GODFATHER, *Godmother, Gossip, stand for.*
    GODCHILD.

Bodies ; in respect of || *nourishing :* or *being nourished.*
2. { FOSTERER, *Nurse, educate.*
    NURSLING.

Minds ; || *instructing :* or *being instructed* in any Science or Art.
3. { TEACHER, *Master, Tutor, institute, instruct, inform, indoctrinate, Doctrine, Document, docil, Lecture, Lesson, train, discipline, enter, read to, Rabbi.*
    LEARNER, *Apprentice, Disciple, Pupil, Scholar, Puny, Neophyte, young beginner, Student.*

Estates.
4. { GUARDIAN, *Tutor, Tuition.*
    PUPIL, *Minority, Ward-ship, under-age, non-age.*

Majors or *Minors ;* in respect of

Habitation ; as *supreme :* or *subordinate ;* whether in a relation
More fixed.
5. { MASTER OF THE FAMILY, *House-wife, Good man of the house.*
    DOMESTIC, *of the houshold, menial.*

More occasional.
6. { HOST, *Landlord, boord, tabling, sojourn, entertain, Inn, Hospitality, Inholder.*
    GUEST, *Boorder, Sojourner, quarter, lodge, lie, tabling, at livery.*

Power

Chap. X.   *Oecomomical Relation.*   251

Power to command: or *Duty to obey.*
7. { MASTER, *Lord, Sir, Mistress, Dame, Madam, Lady:*
     SERVANT, *Servitor, Minister, Man, Maid, Handmaid, servile, administer, Hind, Journeyman, Prentice, Waiter, Lacquey, Footman, Page, Livery.*
Benefits || *conferred:* or *received.*
8. { BENEFACTOR, *Courtesie, Kindness, Favour, Service, Good turn, Pleasure, gratifie, oblige, ingage, good office, Patron.*
     BENEFICIARY, *beholding, bound, obliged, ingaged humble Servant.*
General obligation of || *protecting others:* or *being under such Protection.*
9 { PATRON-*age, support, dedicate.*
    DEPENDANT, *Retainer, Cadet, Client, Follower, Retinue, wait.*

IV. Relations of EQUALITY or Fellowship (as was said concerning IV. EQUALIthose of the former Difference.) do originally belong to persons in an TY.
Oeconomical capacity; though they are not in the strictest sense to be
so confined; but they are likewise applicable to persons upon other considerations.
These are founded; either upon
Mutual Love: or *Hatred,* which should be chiefly upon the account of
   Vertue: or Vice.
1. { FRIEND-*ship, Confident, Privado, intimate, all one, being in with, Amity, amicable, befriend, great with, strike in with. kind. attone.*
     ENEMY, *Adversary, Foe, Antagonist, Opposite, Opponent, Feud, Hostility, Odds, Spite, Enmity, being out with, fall out with, adverse party.*
Conversation with others, chiefly upon the account of Pleasure; or *Segregation* from others.
2. { COMPANION, *Compeer, Associate, Fellow. Match, Mate, Consort, Society, Sociable-ness, Comrade, Collegue, Complice, Concomitant, Gossip, associate, accompany, Crew. Gang, keep company with.*
     SOLITARY, *lonesom, a'one, onely, recluse, sole, single, Solitude, by it self, retired, desolate, several, aside.*
Near: or *remote Habitation.*
3. { NEIGHBOUR, *adjacent, vicinity.*
     FOREINER, *Alien, exotic, extraneous, peregrine, outlandish.*
Particular *Knowledge:* or *Ignorance* of others.
4. { ACQUAINTANCE, *Familiar-ity, conversant.*
     STRANGER, *strange, alienate, unacquainted, uncouth, alien.*
Dealings with others.
Joint'y; as one party.
   { 5. PARTNER, *Copartner, Partizan, Sharer, impart, joyn, communicate, Communion, halves, joynt-stock, partake.*
Mutually; as party and party.
   6. CUSTOMER.

K k 2   V. The

Oeconomical Relation. Part. II.

V. EDUCA-
TION ſpeci-
ally relating
to WORDS.

V. The chief Oeconomical Duties (which are likewiſe applicable to other Relations) are thoſe which concern the due Government of perſons in this capacity, chiefly of the inferiour and younger ſort, ſtyled by the general name of EDUCATION, *inſtitute, train, breed, bring up. ſeminary.*

Education Duties conſiſting *in* WORDS do *reſpect* either

A thing to be done, or *forborn* ; expreſſing to others our Deſires, or their Duties.

Simply ; *to perſons*

Inferior ; || *for it :* or *againſt it.*

1. { COMMAND, *require, bid, impoſe, charge, injoyn, exact, appoint, preſcribe, Mandate, Precept, Injunction, Commandment, Imperative, Warrant, will.*
   FORBID. *Prohibit ion, interdict, inhibit, barr, contraband, countermand.*

Equal ; || *for it :* or *againſt it.*

2. { PERSUADE, *exhort, ſuaſory, move, preſs, win, cajole, Motive, Inducement, ductile, exorable, pliable, flexible, draw in, Eloquence.*
   DISSUADE, dehort.

Superior ; || *for it :* or *againſt it.*

3. { INTREAT, *beſeech, pray, deſire, crave, ask, petition, ſupplicate, Poſtulation, invite, implore, Obteſtation, Obſecration, requeſt, ſue, ſupplicate, ſolicit, preſs, urge, inſtant, Importunity, conjure, exorable, inexorable.*
   DEPRECATE.

Argumentatively ; (i.) with reaſons *repreſenting it* chiefly as

Honeſt : or *diſhoneſt.*

4. { ADVISE, *counſel, conſult, wiſh one.*
   WARN, *admoniſh, Monition, advertiſe, Caution, Item, Precaution, premoniſh, notifie, Proviſo, Caveat, forewarn.*

Pleaſant : or *unpleaſant.*

5. { ALLURE, *tempt, tice, entice, till, drill, inveigle, move, draw, lull, lure, lead, tole, train, egg on, win, trepan, bait, ſtale.*
   DETERR, diſhearten, fright.

Profitable : or *hurtful.*

6. { PROMISE.
   THREATEN, *Commination, menace, denounce:*

A thing already done ; expreſſing our || *liking :* or *diſlike* of it ; whether

To themſelves, in their preſence.

7. { COMMEND, *applaud, extoll, magnifie, hem, recommend.*
   REPREHEND, *reprove, rebuke, chide; blame, check, ſnib, quip, rate, rattle, controll, take up, ſhent, find fault, ſhrive, Redargution, culpable, Satyr, ſcold.*

To others, in their abſence.

8. { PRAISE, *Fame, Glory, Renown, Encomium, extol, exalt, laudable, plauſible, applaud commend, Doxology, Panegyric.*
   DISPRAISE, diſcommend.

VI. Occono-

Chap. X.   Oeconomical Relation.   253

VI. Oeconomical *Duties* of EDUCATION consisting chiefly in VI. EDUCA-
DEEDS, may be distinguished into such as are either   TION DEEDS.

Precedent ; signifying the || *assisting* : or *bindring* another *in the*
- *Way of doing*
  1. {DIRECT, steer, guide, lead, govern.
     SEDUCE, tempt, err-or, astray, mislead, deceive, delude, pervert, beguile, debauch, inveigle, Mistake, Oversight, Fallacy, Sophistry, draw in, lead aside, Fools Paradise.
- *Will of doing.*
  2. {INCOURAGE, animate, hearten, comfort, solace, abett, back, cheer, cherish, countenance, set on, stand by, patronize, quicken, excite.
     DISCOURAGE, dishearten, disanimate, weaken, discomfort, baulk, daunt, droop, quail, out of heart, crest-faln, exanimate.

Concomitant ; *supporting against Evil.*
- *Past* : or *present.*
  3. {COMFORT, Consolation, solace.
     DISCOMFORT, disconsolate, uncomfortable.
- *Present, or future* ; whether of
  - *Want* ; either || *in whole* : or *in part.*
    4. {MAINTAIN, sustain, support, find, keep, provide for, Subsistence, Livelihood.
       STIPENDATE, Allowance, Exhibition, Pension, Annuity, Scholarship.
  - *Danger.*
    5. {DEFENDING, standing to or by one, guard, ward, preserve, shelter, protect, save, fence, keep, tutelary.
       DESERTING, leave, destitute, forsake, quit, flinch, relinquish.

Consequent ; relating *to the*
- *Persons* ; || *endeavouring to better them by punishments while there is hope* : or *ceasing to punish them as being past hope.*
  6. {CORRECTING, chastising, discipline, inflict.
     GIVING OVER; leave.
- *Event of such dealings* ; *by making them* || *better* : or *worse.*
  7. {REFORM, reclaiming, mend, convert, correct.
     HARDEN, incorrigible, indurate, obdurate, seared.

OECONO-

OECONOMICAL POSSESSIONS.

§. 11. BY OECONOMICAL POSSESSIONS, *Estate, Goods, Substance, Stock, Ability, Chattels, hold, injoy, seized of, occupy, indow, in hand, enter upon,* are intended such kinds of things as are necessary upon several accounts for the use, preservation, and well-being of a *Family*. And though divers of these things, as *Land, Buildings,* &c. be common as well to Political and Ecclesiastical Bodies, yet do they (as was said before) originally belong to *Families*, to which all other Associations were subsequent, and in which they were founded. To this may be adjoyned that other Notion signifying the benefit accruing to us by our Possessions, styled REVENUE, *Income, Intrado, Patrimony, Rent, Profit, Endowment, Steward, Fee, Vails, Perquisites, the proceed.*

These Possessions do refer either to things

- *Natural*, as LAND. I.
- *Artificial*; whether
  - *Buildings*, considered according to their
    - KINDS. II.
    - Parts.
      - GREATER. III.
      - LESSER. IV.
  - *Things serviceable for*
    - CARRIAGE. V.
    - FURNITURE, *Utensils*. VI.

1. Possessions of LANDS.

I. That part of the *Earth wherein any man hath a propriety*, is styled LAND, *Earth*. And if he commonly resides upon it, 'tis called his DWELLING, *Habitation, Mansion, Home, inhabit, reside, Inmate, Desert, Wilderness, Solitude, abide, settle, stay.*

The several Notions belonging to this, may be distinguished into such as signifie

- Both *Land and Habitation*, || *sufficient for one Family*: or *a small aggregate of such.*
  1. - FARM, *Grange, Mesuage, Tenement, Tenant, Copyhold.*
     - MANOR, *Lordship, Village, Thorp, Homage, Tithing, Liberty.*
- *Land alone*; according to the
  - General name: *or the name denoting a larger extent of it.*
  2. - FIELD, *Grounds, Croft.*
     - FORREST, *Chase, Verderer, Purlieu.*
  - *Particular kinds;* distinguishable *according to their*
    - *Uses*; either for ||
      - *Herbs*: or *Fruit-Trees*.
      3. - GARDEN.
         - ORCHARD, *Nursery.*
      - *Corn*: or *Hay*.
      4. - ARABLE, *tilled Land, ear Land, Fallow, Lay Land.*
         - MEDOW, *Mead.*
      - *Tame Beasts*: or *wild Beasts*.
      5. - PASTURE, *Down, Lawn, Herbage, Hayward, Lease, Panage.*
         - PARK, *Warren, Paddock, Keeper.*
      - *Fish*: or *Fowl*.
      6. - POND, *Stew.*
         - DECOY.

Fewel;

Chap. X.   Possessions.   255

{ *Fewel* ; ‖ *greater* : or *less.*

7. { WOODS, *Sylvan, Thicket, Cops, Grave.*
    HEATH.

Qualities ; being either of

{ *Equal wetness* ; ‖ *from fresh* : or *from salt Water.*

8. { FEN.
    MARSH.

{ *Unequal wetness* ; whereof the excess is either ‖ *on the surface* : or *under the surface,* within the Land.

9. { MOOR, *plashy, slabb.*
    BOGG, *Quagmire, Slough, Fastness.*

II. Those kinds of *Helps* or *Contrivances whereby men preserve the Places of their abode* from the Injuries of Weather, and other Inconveniencies, are styled by the common name of BUILDINGS, *Edifice, Structure, Fabric, erect, Architecture, Superstructure, Substruction.*   II. BUILDINGS.

To which may be opposed the Notion of *buildings decayed,* called RUINS, *dilapidate, demolish, raze, Dissolution, Wrack, Rubble, Rubbish, fall, break, subvert, throw down, lay waste.*

These may be distinguished, according to their Uses, into such as are for

{ *Ordinary habitation* ; whether ‖ *immoveable* : or *moveable.*

1. { HOUSE, *Mansion, Mesuage, Cote, Cottage, Hut, Shed, Hovel, Lodge, Place, domestic, Ining.*
    TENT, *Tabernacle, Pavilion, Booth, Bowre.*

Grandeur : or *Strength.*

2. { PALACE, *Seraglio.*
    CASTLE, *Cittadel.*

Height and beauty ; either *with* ‖ *a flat* : or *sharp top.*

3. { TOWER, *Turret.*
    STEEPLE, *Pinnacle, Shaft, Spire.*

Religious worship ; *for Invocation* or *Preaching* : or *for Sacrifice.*

4. { TEMPLE, *Church, Chappel, Sanctuary, Synagogue, Mosque, Cathedral, Chancel, Quire.*
    ALTAR.

Warmth, Cleanliness or *Health* ; whether *by* ‖ *warm Air* : or *Water.*

5. { STOVE, *Hot-house.*
    BATH, *Stew, Bain, drencht.*

Passage ; either

{ *Above ground* ; ‖ *over the Water* : or *over dry Land.*

6. { BRIDGE, *Pontage.*
    SCAFFOLD, *Stage.*

{ *Upon the ground* ; denoting ‖ *a paved passage betwixt Buildings* : to which may be annexed *the more general term of the passage place.*

7. { STREET, *Piazza, Lane, Ally.*
    WAY, *Rode, Causway, Course, Avenue, convey, egress, Ally, Path, Passage.*

Under ground.

{ *For Persons.*

8. VAULT, *Grott.*

{ *For Water* ; ‖ *useful* : or *superfluous.*

9. { AQUÆDUCT, *Conduit, Water-course.*
    SINK, *Sewer, Kennel.*

III. To

III. Greater parts of BUILDINGS.

III. To the GREATER PARTS OF which BUILDINGS do consist, and into which they may be distributed, may be adjoyned that usual kind of division styled BAY.

These are either

More general; concerning the
- *Main design of the Timber-work*: or *the dividing part*.
  1. { FRAME, *Compages, Skeleton*.
     { PARTITION, *Wall*.
- *Principal places*; whether || *segregate*: or *aggregate*.
  2. { ROOM, *Chamber, Cabbin, Cell, Hall, Parlour*, &c. *Kennel, Sty*;
     { *Stable*, &c. *Lobby, Loft*, &c.
     { APARTMENT.
- *Vacancies or Passages*; || *without*: or *within*.
  3. { COURT, *Yard, Back-side*.
     { ENTRY, *Passage, enter*.

More particular; distinguished according to their Uses and Situations;

- *Support*. (being either for
  - *Intern*.
    - *Lower*; whether || *erect*: or *transverse*.
      4. { FOUNDATION, *Ground-work, Substruction, Base, Bottom, fundamental, underpinning, ground-pinning*.
         { FLOOR, *Ground, Deck, Contignation*.
    - *Higher*; || *erect*: or *transverse*.
      - *Oblong and narrow*.
        5. { PILLAR, *Column, Post, Jambe, Pile, Pilleter*.
           { BEAM, *Sparr, Rafter, Mantle, Transom, Summer*.
      - *Flat*: or *Curve*.
        6. { WALL, *Sepiment, immure, countermure, mural*.
           { ARCH, *Vault, embowed*.
  - *Extern*; || *put to*: or *built to the part which it supports*.
    7. { PROP, *till, support, uphold, stay up, shore up, shoulder up, underprop, under-set*.
       { BUTTRESS.
- *Covering*; whether || *highest*: or *subordinate*.
  8. { ROOF, *Covering, Tilt, Penthouse, Leads, Thatch, Tiling, Slate*,
     { SIELING. (*Shingles*.
- *Warmth*; either || *Simple*: or *with a Tube to it for passage of the Smoke*.
  9. { HEARTH.
     { CHIMNEY, *Tunnel, Mantle*.

IV. Lesser parts of BUILDINGS.

IV. LESSER PARTS OF BUILDINGS are distinguishable into such as are serviceable; either for

- *Passage upwards and downwards*; being either || *immoveable*: or *moveable*.
  1. { STAIRS.
     { LADDER, *Scale*.
- *Passage in and out*; either of || *Persons*: or *fresh Air*; considered according (to the
  - *Whole*.
    2. { DOOR, *Gate, Port-er, Wicket, Postern, Hatch, Porch, Portal*.
       { WINDOW, *Casement, Balcony*.
  - *Parts relating to a Door chiefly, or Window*.
    - *Without it*; || *above*: or *below*.
      3. { THRESHOLD, *Sill, Groundsill*.
         { LINTEL.

Upon

Chap. X.   *Possessions.*   257

  Upon it; *for* the
   Opening and shutting of it.
    More artificial; || *the fixed:* or *loose part.*
   4. { LOCK, *Padlock.*
      KEY.
    More simple; to open || *from within onely:* or *both wayes.*
   5. { BOLT, *Barr, Sparr.*
      LATCH.
   Motion of it; || *concave:* or *convex.*
   6. { HINGE.
      STAPLE; *Hook.*

 V. By CARRIAGE is meant the *Conveyance* of things *from one place to another:* to which may be annexed by way of affinity the Notion of the *Heavy thing to be carried,* BURTHEN, (*Load, lade, onerate, Fare, Fraight, charge, surcharge, Luggage, Lumber, disburthen, exonerate, overcharge, overload.*)   **V.** Things for CARRIAGE.

 The provisions of this kind do *relate to things* considered as
Whole; being used for the Carriage either of Persons or Goods, and moving either

 With Wheels;
  Four Wheels; either || *the more elegant:* or *the more plain.*
  1. { COACH, *Chariot.*
    WAIN, *Waggon.*
  Two Wheels; either || *the more elegant:* or *the more plain.*
  2. { CHARIOT.
    CART; *Carr, Dray, Tumbrel.*
 Without Wheels; being either to be
  Carried between the Movers; either || *the more elegant:* or *the more plain.*
  3. { SEDAN, *Litter.*
    BARROW.
  Drawn along after them.
  4. { SLED.
    WELSH CART.
Parts of the thing upon which the weight is drawn or carried; serving either for
 Fastning to the Animals which draw or carry; used either || *double:* or (*single:*
  5. { SHAFT, *Thills.*
    POLE.
 Motion; being for figure and situation ||
 Round and erect: or *oblong and transverse.*
  6. { WHEEL, *Truckle, Trundle.*
    AXIS, *Spindle.*
 The central: or *semidiametral parts of the Wheel.*
  7. { NAVE.
    SPOKE, *Fellow.*
Furniture of the Animals which draw or carry; either for
 Supporting of || *the Trunc:* or *the Feet of the burthen.*
  8. { SADDLE, *Pack-saddle, Pad, Pannel, Pillion.*
    STIRRUP.
 Directing the Motion; by the || *Head:* or *Sides.*
  9. { BRIDLE, *Rein, Headstall, Curb, Snaffle, Bit.*
    TRACE.

          L l   **VI.** By

VI. FURNI-
TURE.

VI. By FURNITURE (*Utensils, Implements, Houshold-stuff, Moveables, Goods, furnish, fit, provide, procure, ready,*) is meant those *moveable things* of various kinds *requisite to the several uses of a Family.* These are either

More simple, intended chiefly for Action, according to
- The *general name.*
  1. INSTRUMENT, *Implement, Tool.*
- Some *special kinds* of Instruments; ||*for cutting:* or *for knocking.*
  2. { KNIFE, *Razor.*
     { HAMMER, *Sledge, Mallet, malleable, ductile, Beetle, Poleax.*

Less simple, being made up of several parts joyned together; according to
- The *general name:* or *that kind used for the drawing up of water.*
  3. { JUGAMENT, *Frame.*
     { PUMP.
- Some *special kinds;* being used *for*
- *Putting things upon;* being either ||*moveable:* or *fixed.*
  4. { TABLE, *Stall, Dresser, Bord, Cupbord.*
     { SHELF.
- *Sitting upon onely;* to which may be annexed by way of affinity, that other Utensil intended *for the ease and softness of sitting or lying.*
  5. { STOOL, *Seat, Fourm, Bench.*
     { CUSHION, *Pillow, Boulster, Pillion.*
- *Sitting and leaning:* or *sitting and lying upon.*
  6. { CHAIR, *Throne, Settle.*
     { COUCH.
- *Lying and sleeping upon;* to which that may be annexed of the same affinity as in the Fifth.
  7. { BEDSTED, *Settle, Cradle, Testor.*
     { BED, *Pallet, Hammock, Matiress, Nest, Kennel, Litter, Upholster.*

More complicate, by reason of the mixture with Wheels or Screws, &c. according to
- The *general name:* or *that particular kind used for the taking of Animals.*
  8. { MACHIN, *Engine, Frame, Gin.*
     { TRAP, *Gin, Springe, Pitfal, Toyle, Weare, Weele, Buck, Net, In-snare.*
- Some *special kinds;* for ||*grinding of Corn,* &c. or *distinguishing of Hours.*
  9. { MILL, *Querne.*
     { CLOCK, *Watch.*

PROVISIONS.

§. III. Under this Head of PROVISIONS (*Accommodations, Equipage, furnish, provide, procure, purvey,*) are comprehended some of the same kinds of things as under the former, with this peculiar Difference, That several of the particulars under this are more occasional and transient,

and

Chap. X. *Provisions.* 259

and not of such continual usefulness as those under the other. These are distinguishable into *such as*

- *Have particular references*, either to
  - *Food*, as to
    - *The kinds of it.*
      - ORDINARY. I.
      - EXTRAORDINARY. II.
    - *The manner of* PREPARING *it.* III.
  - CLOTHING. IV.
  - VESSELS. V.
- *Are of a* COMMON MIXED Nature. VI.

I. By SUSTENTATION ORDINARY (*Commons, Fare, Cheer, Diet, Meat, Viands, sustenance, Victuals, Manciple, Caterer, Pantry,*) is intended such kind of Food as is usual *for ordinary persons,* and ordinary *times*; either according to the **I. SUSTENTATION ORDINARY.**

- *General name;* whether ||*greater, more stated, constant and usual*: or *less, and more occasional.*
  1. MEAL, *Dinner, Supper, Refectory.*
     REFECTION, *Bait, Bever, Break-fast, Collation, Repast, Nunchion.*
- *Particular kinds;* distinguishable according to the matter; whether
  - *Solid and consistent;* being made either of
    - *Grain or some Vegetable,* ||*baked in a drier substance without any considerable mixture,* of all other the most common and necessary: or else being *made up and mixed with some other eatable substance.*
      2. BREAD, *Loaf, Manchet, Cake, Dough, Bisket, Past, Batch, Pantry, Pantler.*
         PUDDING, *Haggis, Sausage, Dumpling, Link.*
    - *Milk* ||*condensed in the finer part:* or of Milk *coagulated and pressed.*
      3. BUTTER.
         CHEESE.
    - *Animal musculary substance;* either ||*alone:* or *put into some bready substance,* which is likewise capable of some other ingredients.
      4. FLESH.
         PIE, *Pasty, Tart, Custard, Flawn, Past, Pastry, Pastler.*
  - *Liquid;* either for
    - *Eating;* consisting of
      - *Water boiled with some other ingredients,* ||*for the strengthening of it for Food:* or *for the coagulating of it.*
        5. BROTH, *Pottage, Porridge, Caudle, Cullice, Grout, Gruel, Panado, Posset, Ptisane, Frumenty, Hogwash, Potherbe.*
           GELLY, *congeal.*
      - *Fatty juice of several Vegetables, and sometimes of Animals,* eaten with other things, and useful for Medicine; to which may be adjoyned *the watery juice of dressed Flesh.*
        6. OIL.
           GRAVY, *Juice.*
    - *Drinking;* the *infusion of Barly or some other Grain first macerated;* either ||*without Hopps:* or *with Hopps.*
      7. ALE, *Whort, Brew.*
         BEER, *Drink, Whort, Brew.*

L l 2 II. SUSTEN-

II. SUSTENTATION EXTRAORDINARY (*Cates, Delicates, Dainties, Liccorous,*) may be considered according to the

- *General name*; *signifying abundance, variety and delicacy*; either of ‖ more (*substantial Meats:* or of *Sweet-meats.*)
  1. { FEAST, *Gaudy.*
       BANQUET, *Juncket, Sweet-meat, Desert.*

- *Particular kinds*; used for
  - *Eating*; comprehending
    - *Common requisites, for the better relishing of other Food;* to which may be adjoyned *the various mixtures of things, to render them grateful* (*to the Palate.*)
      2. { SAUCE, *Sallet.*
           CONFECTION, *Conserve, Comfit, Sucket.*
    - *Usual ingredients of Sauce*; being either for the Taſt
      - *Sweet*; viz. *the juice of the sweet Cane,* ‖ *concreted:* or *deliquiated or dissolved into a liquor of a thick consistence.*
        3. { SUGAR.
             SYRUP.
      - *Of hot and savory Guſt and Smell.*
        4. SPICE, *Aromatic, Grocery.*
      - *Sour*; ‖ *the juice of Grapes, or infusion of Barly being eager:* or *the juice of Crabs.*
        5. { VINEGAR.
             VERJUICE.
  - *Drinking*; whether more
    - *Natural*; being either ‖ *more simple:* or *the juice* of Fruits, chiefly Grapes: or *other drinks made by mixture.*
      6. { WINE, *Sider, Perry, Stum, Muſt, Vintage, Vintner, Sack, Claret, &c.*
           BEVERAGE, *Syllabub, Mede, Waſſal.*
    - *Artificial, by distillation with fire;* according to ‖ *the more general name:* (or *that particular kind moſt in uſe.*)
      7. { SPIRITS.
           BRANDY.

III. Actions relating to the **PREPARATION OF FOOD** (*dreſſing, crude, raw,*) are either

- *General and antecedaneous*; signifying either ‖ *the killing and dividing of Beaſts for Food:* or *the more common notion of fiting both Fleſh and other proper Materials, in order to their being eaten.*
  1. { BUTCHERING, *Shambles, Slaughterhouse.*
       COOKING, *dreſſing, Kitchin, Scullion, dreſs Meat.*

- *Special and subsequent*; denoting the several kinds of Cookery; either
  - *More principal*; the preparing and dreſſing things.
    - *Wet*; in a ‖ *wider*, or *closer veſſel*; *in a greater,* or *leſſer quantity.*
      2. { BOILING, *Decoction, Seething, sod, Ebullition, parboil, poach.*
           STEWING.
    - *Dry*; ‖ *by holding it to, or turning it about near the Fire:* or *by laying it on a hot Hearth, or in some close heated Cavity.*
      3. { ROASTING, *Toſting, Spit, Broach, Jack.*
           BAKING, *Baker, Oven, Paſtry, Batch.*
    - *Mixed*, part being wet and part dry; either ‖ *in an open broad veſſel:* (or *by laying it on the Fire.*)
      4. { FRYING, *Fricace, Fritter, Steak.*
           BROILING, *Carbonadoing, Grilliade, Gridiron, Raſher.*

  - *Leſs principal*; relating to the
    - *Preparing of it*; by
      - *Cutting,*
        - *Into*; *punctim* or *cæſim*, *pointwise* or *edgewiſe.*
          5. { PINKING, *Pouncing, Pricking.*
               SLASHING, *gaſhing, haſhing, carbonado, jagg.*
        - *Through*;

Chap. X.   Provisions.   261

⎧ ⎧ Through; either in ‖ laminated : or more minute particles.
⎨ 6. ⎨ SLICING, Collop, Hash.
⎩ ⎩ MINCING, shred, chop, cut small.
Application of other things; either ‖ wet : or dry.
  7. ⎧ BASTING, Dripping, sprinkle, Inspersion.
     ⎩ FLOWRING, powdering, corning, spicing.
Mixed, (i.) both cutting and application.
  8. ⎧ STRATIFY, Lair, interlacing, interlard, lay in.
     ⎩ LARD, prick in, stick in, interlarding.
Preserving; either ‖ in wet : or in dry.
  9. ⎧ PICKLING, sousing.   (Mummy.
     ⎩ CONDITING, preserving, embalming, candying, seasoning,

IV. CLOTH-
ING.

IV. Such things as are requisite for the covering of our nakedness, and the preserving of us from the injuries of weather, are styled by the name of CLOTHING, Vest, Apparel, attire, Array, Garment, Raiment, Habit, Garb, Stole, Robe, Weed, accoutred, clad, dight, dressing, make ready, wear, invest, Livery, put on or off, naked, stript, bare, Taylour, Wardrope.

To which may be adjoyned, for its affinity, the usual name of those other things of the like use amongst men upon particular occasions, and more generally required for labouring beasts; ARMAMENT, Harness, Tackle, Array, Habiliment, Trappings, accoutred, Furniture, Traces.

The several particulars under this Head may refer; either to
The matter of which Vests are made; which is either
  Some Animal substance; either of
    Beasts.
      The hairy parts.
        1. ⎧ WOLLEN, Cloth.
           ⎩ HAIRY, Stuff, Sackcloth.
      The Skins of Beasts prepared.
        2. LEATHER, Buff, Cheverel, &c. Tann, Curry.
    Insects, viz. the Silk-worm.
      3. SILK, Mercer, Sattin, Velvet, Plush, Taffety, &c.
  Some Vegetable substance; either ‖ the Rind of Plants, as Hemp, Flax, Nettle, &c. or growing upon Trees,
    4. ⎧ LINEN, Canvase, Lawn, Damask, Diaper, &c.
       ⎩ COTTON, Bombast, Fustian.
The use and fashion; either for
  Ornament onely; being elegantly distinguished with Apertures and
    5. ⎧ LACE, garded, galloon, &c.   (Intercisions.
       ⎩ PURLE.
  Ornament and binding; being a
    Long Lamin; ‖ narrower : or broader.
      6. ⎧ RIBBAND, Fillet, Tape, Favor, Knot, Hairlace.
         ⎩ SCARF, Garter.
    Long Pin; ‖ slenderer : or thicker.
      7. ⎧ THRED, Line, Wire, Yarn, Packthred.
         ⎩ CORD, String, Halter, Rope, Slip, Line, Rein.
    Lamin; specially of Leather : or Loop and Pin.
      8. ⎧ THONG, Latchet, Strap.
         ⎩ BUCKLE.
  Ornament and covering of ‖ the outside : or the inside.
    9. ⎧ FACING.
       ⎩ LINING.   V. Such

V. VES-
SELS.
V. Such kind of *Utensils* as ſerve *to contain* other things, are uſually called VESSELS, *Cask, Receptacle, Pan, Plate,* &c.

Theſe are diſtinguiſhable by their Matter, Shapes and Uſes, into ſuch as ſerve

Keeping and carriage of things; being either (*for the*
- *Pliable to the things they contain*; whether ‖ *more looſe:* or *more cloſe.*
  - 1. { BAG, *Sack, Budget, Pocket, Pouch, Purſe, Sachel, Scrip, Wallet, Poke, Male, Knapſack, Portmantue, Cloak-bag.*
    CASE, *Sheath, Scabbard, Shrine, Covering, Quiver, Tike, Pillowbear.*
- *Stiff*; for
  - *Arids*; being made either of ‖ *bords*: or *twigs*.
    - 2. { BOX, *Cheſt, Trunk, Ark, Coffer, Cabinet, Casket, Bin, Clapper, Cupbord, Hutch, Locker, Safe, Spence, Preſs, Pyx, Coffin, Sumpter, Desk, Flasb, Till, Drawer, Cap-caſe.*
      BASKET, *Flasket, Maund, Frail, Hamper, Pannier, Scuttle, Weel, Dorſer.*
  - *Liquids*; in
    - *Greater quantities*: either ‖ *cloſed at both ends:* or *open at one.*
      - 3. { BARREL, *Cask, Fat, Firkin, Keg, Hogſhead, Kilderkin, Pipe, Tun, Butt, Rundlet, Cooper.*
        TUB, *Bucket, Coul, Vate, Ciſtern, Pale, Piggin.*
    - *Leſs quantities*; whether (Earth, &c.
      - *shallow*; being made either of ‖ *Metal:* or *other materials,* Wood,
        - 4. { DISH, *Platter, Pan, Charger, Voider, Baſon, Laver, Patin, Plate, Porringer, Saucer.*
          TRAY, *Pan, Boul, Trough.*
      - *Deep*; of ‖ *a bigger*: or *leſſer aperture.*
        - 5. { POT, *Flagon, Tankard, Jack, Jar, Pitcher, Jugg, Mugg, Noggin, Poſnet, Urne.*
          BOTTLE, *Crewet, Jugg, Cruſe.*

Dreſſing or boiling of Meat; either ‖ *without:* or *with feet.*
  - 6. { KETTLE, *Caldron, Copper, Furnace.*
    SKILLET, *Pipkin.*

Spending; either by
- *Taking out, the Tube of effuſion:* to which may be adjoyned *the inſtrument*
  - 7. { FAUCET, *Spout.* (*for ſtopping it.*
    TAP, *Spiggot, Stopple.*
- *Receiving in*; whether ‖ *of a roundiſh:* or *oblong Cavity.*
  - 8. { SPOON, *Ladle, Scummer.*
    SCOOP, *Shovel, laving.*
- *Laying on of Meat:* or *pouring out of Drink.*
  - 9. { TRENCHER, *Plate.*
    CUP, *Boul, Goblet, Beaker, Cann, Chalice, Mazer, Glaſs.*

VI. COMMON MIXED MATERIALS.

VI. The laſt Head of COMMON MIXED Materials, muſt be acknowledged to be a very Heterogeneous heap. But the ſeveral particulars under it being very neceſſary in their kinds, and not reducible to any of the other Heads, I am forced to put them together here, not knowing at preſent how to reduce them more properly. They are diſtinguiſhable by their Ends or Uſes; being *ſuch Proviſions as concern*

Food for Cattel; either ‖ *of dried Graſs:* or *dried ſtems of Grain.*
  - 1. { HAY, *Fodder.*
    STRAW, *Fodder, Halm, Litter, Thatch.*

Warmth, and preparing of Food for men.
  - 2. FEWEL, *Firing, Logg, Collier, Woodmonger.*

Giving of Light; being made either ‖ *of the dried Fat of Animals:* or *of Oil.*
  - 3. { CANDLE, *Link, Taper, Torch, Light, Lanthorn.*
    LAMP.

Curing

Curing of Wounds or Sores by outward application, being *a Confection of Medicaments*, which is *sometimes spread upon some Vest matter*.

4. { SALVE, *Unguent, Ointment.*
{ PLASTER, *Cataplasm, Serecloth, Poultis.*

Cleansing or Stiffening of Clothes.

5. { SOPE
{ STARCH.

Communication by Writing; denoting either the

Instrument: or *Liquor to write with.*

6. { PEN.
{ INK.

Matter to write on; considered either ‖ *simply in its nature*: or *as it is compacted in Aggregates.*

7. { PAPER, *Parchment, Vellum, Schedule, Bill-et, Ticket, Stationer.*
{ BOOK, *Volume, Tome, Treatise, Manuel, compile, compose, Library, Tract, Pamphlet, Manuscript, Stationer.*

Ornament; by *representation of* the likeness of *things* ‖ *in plain*: or *in solid.*

8. { PICTURE, *Pourtraiture, Effigies, Draught, Map, Chart, Landscap, Emblem, Image, Projection, Scheme, Diagram, Analem, Arras, Enammell.*
{ IMAGE, *Statue, Puppet, Idol, Coloss, Crucifix.*

CHAP. XI.

Concerning Relation more public, whether I. Civil. II. Judiciary. III. Military. IV. Naval. V. Ecclesiastical.

MOre publick relation may be distributed into such as do concern those several respects, *Actions* and *Things*; belonging either to

{ Several Families associated under Government, CIVIL RELATION.
{ Courts of Judicature, and matters of Law, JUDICIAL RELATION.
{ A state of Warr, MILITARY RELATION.
{ Mens Affairs and Traffique on the Water, NAVAL RELATION.
{ Matters of Religion and Worship, ECCLESIASTICAL RELATION.

CIVIL RELATION.

THat Relation arising from the associating of Families under Government for mutual benefit and defence, is styled *Political* or CIVIL, *Republic, Commonwealth, State, political, secular.* §. I.

To which may be opposed ANARCHY, *Confusion.*

The Notions belonging to this do refer either to

{ *Persons* in a political capacity, considered according to their
{ DEGREES. I.
{ PROFESSIONS or Vocations. II.
{ CONVENTIONS. III.
{ *Things* or businesses, relating to
{ RIGHTS. IV.
{ CONTRACTS for the Alienation of our Rights. V.
{ OBLIGATIONS for the Confirmation of Contracts. VI.

I. Those

Relation Civill. Part.II.

I. DEGREES OF MEN.

1. Those differences whereby men under a Political Relation, are distinguished from one another, according to their several ranks, are styled, DEGREES, *Place, Quality, Rank, Order, Scutcheon, Coat of Arms, Herald.*
To which may be opposed the word PARITY, *Levelling.*
These are either

More general; according to the first common Difference of ‖ *governing,* namely such to whom doth belong the power and care of directing others in their duty, and rewarding or punishing them accordingly: or *governed,* namely such as are under this Power.

1. { MAGISTRATE, *Rector, Governour, Regent, Rule-er, Dominion, Sway, Consul, President, Provost, Warden, Head, Territory, Seigniory, Major, Baylif, Syndic, States, Jurisdiction.*
SUBJECT-*ion, Vassal, submit, Homage, Liegeman, Private person, truckle, Underling.*

More particular; relating to

Kinds of principal Magistrates; which have great variety of Titles in several Countries, not necessary to be distinctly provided for here, excepting onely such as are either; ‖ *Sovereign:* or *Homagers* to some other.

2. { KING, *Sovereign, Emperor, Imperial, Monarch, Queen, regal, royal, Majesty, reign, Kingdom, Lord, Dynasty, Sultan, Cham, Liege Lord, Regent, Realm, Diadem, Crown, Coronation, Scepter, Throne, enthrone, Viceroy.*
PRINCE, *Potentate.*

Orders of Subjects.

Higher.

More general; comprehending the ‖ *greater:* or *lesser Nobility.*

3. { LORD, *Peer, Nobleman, honourable, Patrician, Duke, Marquess, Earl, Count, Viscount, Baron.*
GENTLEMAN, *Gentry, Knight, Esquire, Sir, Madam, Worship-ful, Gentil-ity, Wellborn.*

More special; with relation to the *Degrees in liberal Professions;* either ‖ *perfect:* or *inchoate.*

4. { GRADUATE, *commence, Degree, Doctor, Master, Rabbi.*
CANDIDATE, *Batchelor, Inceptor, canvas, sue, stand for.*

Middle; considered

Aggregately.

5. PEOPLE, *Folk, Commonalty, Community, mean, obscure, ignoble, Plebeian, Populacie, popular, populous.*

Segregately; as they are *Inhabitants* either in ‖*Cities:* or the *Countrey*

6. { CITIZEN, *Free-man, enfranchise, Denizon, Townsman.*
YEOMAN.

Lower sort; considered

Aggregately.

7. RABBLE, *Vulgus, Tag-rag, base.*

Segregately; according to their want of ‖ *Dignity:* or *Wealth.*

8. { VILLAIN, *Varlet, Rascal, Peasant, Boor, servile, Sirrah, Vassal, base.*
BEGGAR, *Rogue, Mendicant, Shake-ragg.*

Conditions of men; as having ‖ a *right to dispose of themselves:* or *not.*

9. { FREE-MAN, *liberal, enfranchise, Burgess.*
SLAVE, *emancipate, manumit, servile, illiberal, Bondman, Bondage, Thraldom, enthrall, enslave, serve, Droyl, Drudge.*

II. That

Chap. XI.   *Civill Relation.*   265

II. That courſe of life about which one is uſually employed, and to **II. PRO-**
which he applies himſelf for the getting of a Subſiſtence, is ſtyled his **FESSIONS.**
PROFESSION, *Vocation, Calling, Trade, Function, Occupation, Courſe of life,*
Craft, Myſtery.

To which may be adjoyned the word denoting the actual Uſe of ſuch
Callings, PRACTICE, *Exerciſe, Uſe, follow, put in ure.*

Theſe may be diſtinguiſhed, into ſuch as are either

More *neceſſary* and beneficial to humane life; whether

Liberal Profeſſions, ſuch as become free and generous men; relating ei-
  Things.   (ther *to*
  Sacred; as ‖ *diſcovered by revelation:* or as the knowledge of
  them is *attainable by nature.*
  1. { DIVINE, *Theology, Clerk, Schoolman.*
       PHILOSOPHER.
  Civil and political; namely, ‖ *the more generally received Laws* and
  Conſtitutions: *or thoſe belonging to a particular Nation.*
  2. { CIVIL LAWYER.
       COMMON LAWYER, *Pettifogger.*
  Natural; with particular *reference to* the *diſeaſes* of mens bodies
  and their *cure;* either ‖ *by direction:* or *by manual operation.*
  3. { PHYSICIAN, *Medicine, Patient, Empiric, Mountebank;*
       Quack-ſalver, Farrier, Leach, Receipt.
       CHIRURGION, *dreſs a wound.*
  Words or language: or *the ornaments of diſcourſe.*
  4. { PHILOLOGER, *Critic.*
       POET *-ry, Poem, Bard, Muſe.*

Illiberal; belonging more peculiarly

To a Town; conſiſting of *Trades* of ‖ *exchange:* or *manufacture.*
  5. { MERCHANT, *Market, Pedler, Huckſter, Badger, Hawker, Regra-*
       ter, Shopkeeper, Traffic, Dealing, Merchandize, Fair, Mart.
       MECHANIC, *Handicraft, Artificer, Manufacture, Artizan,*
       Work houſe.
To the Country; relating to the *moſt ancient* Profeſſions of
  Tilling the ground: or *feeding of Cattel.*
  6. { HUSBANDMAN, *georgic, Hinde, Agriculture, Tillage, Bayliffe.*
       HERDSMAN, *Shepherd, Paſtor, Cow-herd, Hog-herd.*
  Catching of wild Animals.
  7.   HUNTSMAN, *Hunt-er, Fowler, Fiſher, chaſe, trace, courſe, Ve-*
       niſon, Game, Pocher.
Both to Town and Country; for the carriage of things by ‖ *Water:* or
Land.
  8. { MARINER.
       CARRIER, *Ripier, Cargo.*

Not neceſſary; comprehending thoſe ſeveral Profeſſions *which tend to*
the *diverſion* of others; ‖ *by acting or perſonating ſome particular ſtory*
or *Fiction:* or *by amuſing of men by the Agility of body or hand.*
  9. { PLAYER, *Actor, Comedian, Tragedian, Play, Stage, Theatre,*
       Enterlude, Perſonate.
       PRESTIGIATOR, *ſhewer of tricks, juggle, Legerdemain,*
       Hocas pocas, Tumbler, Dancer on the ropes, &c. *Mountebank.*

M m   III. The

Civil Relation. Part. II.

III. CON-
VENTION

III. The several Aggregates of men under Political Government, are usually styled either by that more *general:* or *special* name.

{ CONVENTION, *Assembly, Meeting, Congregation, Convocation, Company, Rendezvous, Concourse, Confluence, Quire, Chapter, Committee, Club, Hall, convene, Conventicle, Sessions, Assize, flock,* or *gather together.*
{ SOCIETY, *Gyld, Gang, Tribe, Clan, Fraternity, Club, Knot, Crew, Fellowship, Company.*

These are either such as have the same

General *inducements*; in respect of

Language and supreme Government; whether ||*primitively:* or *derivatively.*

1. { NATION *-al, epidemical, naturalize, People, Country, vernacular, Patriot.*
   { COLONY, *Plantation.*

Place of Habitation; considered *according to* the

General *name;* denoting such as inhabit || *more dispersedly in the open fields:* or *more close together, usually within fenced places.*

2. { COUNTRY, *rural, rustic, Peasant, Boor, Hinde, Kern, Swain, Clown, Tike.*
   { TOWN, *Burrough.*

Special *kinds;* signifying *all that part of a Nation under the same Subordinate Government;* ||*dwelling more at large:* or *such as dwell close together,* with peculiar Liberties and Priviledges in common amongst them.

3. { PROVINCE, *Circuit.*
   { CITY, *Suburbs, Metropolis, See, Borough, municipal.*

Lowest Government; whether || *with:* or *without Jurisdiction.*

4. { SHIRE, *County, Tribe, District, Riding.*
   { PARISH, *parochial, Parson, Vicar, Thorpe, Village.*

Special *inducements;* for ||

Attendance on Governours: or *advice in the Government.*

5. { COURT *-ier, aulical.*
   { COUNCIL, *Senate, Parliament, Diet, Conclave, Consistory, Sanhedrim, Synod, Committee.*

Education in Learning; either || *of the Adult, with a power to license them for the Liberal professions:* or *onely of Children* or *young beginners.*

6. { UNIVERSITY, *Academy, School.*
   { SCHOOL.

Regulating the affairs of some ||*Trade:* or *Profession;* especially if they cohabit for those ends in a kind of Political family.

7. { CORPORATION, *Gyld, Brotherhood, Fraternity, Company, Society, community, municipal, incorporate.*
   { COLLEGE *-iate, Fellow.*

Driving on of some design; || *in general:* or *with particular reference to the opposing of what is legally established.*

8. { LEAGUE, *Confederacy, Combination, Alliance, Complice, Partisan, Party, side with, joyn, hold together, Pack, compact.*
   { FACTION, *Sect, Juncto, Gang, conspire, side with, combine, Party-zan, Oligarchy.*

IV. The

Chap. XI.   *Civill Relation.*   267

IV. The *things* which in *Justice* or *Equity* do belong to persons, are **IV. RIGHTS.** called RIGHTS, *Title, Interest, Estate, Tenure Holding, Freehold, Gift, Collation, Reversion, Landlord, Paramount, endow, enfeoff.* To which may be adjoyned the word LIBERTIES, denoting whatsoever is *permitted,* or *not forbidden* to them.

These are considerable according to their
- Original; being either
  - Primary and unwritten.
    - *Not voluntary*; but *according to* || *the condition of its first being:* or *common practice and continuance.*
      1. {NATURE.
         CUSTOM, *accustom, Use, Wont, Guise, Fashion, Rite, Usage, usual, currant, common, ordinary, ure, enure, Habit, Practice, Haunt, prescribe, unusual, obsolete, familiar, received, conversant, Habit, manner, course, Hank, Exercise, Prescription, Desuetude.*
    - *Voluntary*; according to the || *choice of the Will:* or *a determined order.*
      2. {SELECTION, *choice.*
         SUCCESSION, *devolve, follow, Place.*
  - Secondary and written.
    - General; whether || *perpetual:* or *temporal.*
      3. {LAW, *Act, Statute, Decree, Sanction, Constitution, Canon, Rule, legal, legitimate, enact, ordain, order, abrogate, repeal, prescribe, Legislator.*
         EDICT, *Ordinance, Proclamation, Order, Breve, Bull, Act, Rule, Sanction, Rescript.*
    - Special; conferring || *Right to have:* or *Right to do.*
      4. {PATENT, *Charter, Brief, Letters Patents, Placard.*
         COMMISSION, *Brief.*
- Parts; consisting in
  - Power over that which is
    - *One's own;* either || *totally:* or *as to the use of it.*
      5. {PROPRIETY, *Concern, Owner, Proprietary.*
         USUS-FRUCTUS.
    - *Another's;* either as to || *his person:* or *his affairs.*
      6. {AUTHORITY, *Power, Dominion, Prefect, President, Head, Provost, Master, Plenipotentiary, authentic, classic, govern, ratifie, Rule, sway, inspection, dispose, Precinct, Territory.*
         OFFICE, *Place, Cure, overlook, officiate, superintend, surveigh, oversight, charge, conduct, Commissary, Prefect, Collegue, Groom.*
  - Liberty; with respect to
    - *Advantages by special Law;* either || *of the supreme Magistrate:* or of *some particular rank of Subjects.*
      7. {PREROGATIVE, *Royalty.*
         PRIVILEGE, *Franchise, enfranchise, freedom, Grace, preeminence.*
    - *Remission* or exemption *from the rigour of a general Law,* in its || *Commanding:* or *prohibiting.*
      8. {DISPENSATION.
         LICENCE, *Permission, Sufferance, Leave, allowance, Faculty, Connivence, Placard, Prattick, let, may, suffer, admit, dispence, Pass-port, Safe conduct, Letters of Mart.*
    - *Punishing:* or *imposing* burthens.
      9. {TOLERATION, *Connivence, suffer, let alone, Quarter.*
         IMMUNITY, *free, Discharge, Exemption, Quarter, scot-free.*

V. The

V. CON-
TRACT.

V. The *mutual negotiating betwixt men* in their ordinary converse with one another is styled CONTRACT, *Commerce, Entercourse, Traffick, Trade, Negotiation:* to which may be annexed for affinity the most general occasion for such Intercourse, namely, the *parting with one thing for the getting of another,* called EXCHANGE, *barter, chaffer, cope, swap, truck, chop, Commutation, Scourfing, Bargain, Match.*

The principal matters belonging to this Head do either refer to

Actions;
  General; whether
    Absolute; *transferring a thing from one to another*; whether ‖ *for his use to whom it is transferred:* or *for his use that transfers.*
      1. {ASSIGNING, *consigning, conveying, resigning, deliver, put over.*
         DEPOSITING, *Trustee, Feoffee, enfeoff, charge, commend, recommend, entrust, commit, Fiduciary, Sequestration.*
    Conditional; ‖ *giving:* or *having right to an Estate after the death of him who disposeth of it.*
      2. {BEQUEATHING, *devising, Legacy, Testament, Will, Executor, Intestate.*
         INHERITING, *Heir, hereditary, Heritage, Patrimony, Fee-simple, Entail, disherit, Hereditament, Portion, Primogeniture.*
  Special; either by
    Parting with: or *procuring propriety* in any thing, upon the consideration *for something else to be taken* or *given* in exchange.
      3. {SELLING, *vent, utter, Ware, Commodity, Sale-able, venal, vendible, staple, put off, retail, afford, handsel, monopoly, make mony of, serve one with.*
         BUYING, *purchase, Cater, Chapman, Customer, engrossing, ransom, redeem, regrate, forestal, interlope, preemption, the refusing.*
    Parting with: or *procuring the temporary use of something* belonging to
      The more general name. (*another*; according to
      4. {LENDING, *Loan, Creditor, prostitute, trust.*   (*given.*
         BORROWING, *take up.*
      The particular kind; relating to some *temporary reward* to be ‖ *taken,* and
      5. {DEMISING, *let, let out, let to farm, lease, Lessor, Landlord, Broker, Rent, Principal, Interest, put to use.*
         HIRING, *farming, backney, mercenary, prostitute, Tenant, Lessee, Lease, Rent, Interest, Use, at livery, Gratis.*
    Bestowing skill or labour about any business: or *compensating of it.*
      6. {EARNING, *Merit, Desert, Meed, Demerit, supererogate.*
         WAGES, *Fee, Salary, Pension, Stipend, Vails, fare, freight, gratis.*

Things; whether more
  Private; to be *exhibited by the*
    Buyer; either ‖ *the whole value:* or *a part of it,* for assurance of the rest.
      7. {PRICE, *Rate, Value, Worth, Ransom, stand in, cost, cheap, dear, precious, sumptuous, rich, inhaunce, depreciate.*
         EARNEST, *Gage, Pledge.*
    Seller; either ‖ *the thing bought:* or *some part,* for security of the whole.
      8. {BARGAIN, *Ware, Commodity.*
         SEISIN, *Livery, install, admit, Entry, inthrone, inaugurate, invest.*
  Publick; towards defraying the *charge of Government*; whether ‖ *ordinary:* or *occasional.*
      9. {TRIBUTE, *Custom, Annates, Gabel, Excise, Toll, Impost, Publicane.*
         TAX, *Rate, Contribution, Collection, assess, Publicane, Subsidy, Tunnage, poundage, pannage, Pole, Collector, Scot, Sesment.*

VI. Those

Chap. XI.   *Civil Relation.*   269

VI. Those several kinds of Assurances which men offer concerning **VI. OBLIGA-**
what they intend to give or do, are styled, OBLIGATIONS, *plight, en-* **TIONS.**
gage, Deed, bind, Bond, Bill, evidence, &c. *undertake for.*
And when such Obligations are reciprocal, they are then called PA-
CTIONS, *Agreement, Compact, Covenant, Bargain, Condition, Indent, Match,*
Stipulation, Sponsion, Warranty, Article, strike up a bargain.
These are either
- *Imperfect*; or degrees towards Contracts more
  - *Remote*; *in the first overtures of a Contract*; whether || *as begun by one*:
    1. { BESPEAKING, *Retain.*   (or *mutual betwixt both.*
       { TREATING, *driving a Bargain, capitulate, chaffer, parley, cheapen,*
       huck, haggle.
  - *Near*; *in proposal of those terms according to which one obliges himself to* ||
    2. { BID, *offer, huck, haggle.*   (*buy*; or *sell.*
       { DEMAND, *cheapen, ask, exact.*
- *Perfect*; either in
  - *Words*;
    - *Spoken.*
      - *Common*; || *ingaging our Veracity*, sometimes *with the addition of*
        such *solemn expressions* as may testifie our reality.
        3. { PROMISE; *Word, Parol, plight, Covenant, League, undertake*
           for, pass ones word.
           { PROTESTATION, *Asseveration, averr, vouch, stand in, Atte-*
           station.
      - *Sacred*; *ingaging our Religion*, and appealing to God *as* || a *Witness*,
        and as a *Judge*, to punish us upon our falshood.   (*Oath.*
        4. { SWEARING, *Oath, deposing, abjure, Perjury, adjure, purge upon*
           { IMPRECATION, *Execration, Malediction, Cursing.*
    - *Written*; attested *with* || our peculiar *name*, or *Mark*: or *Impressing*
      some figure in Wax, or some like matter
      5. { SIGNING, *Obligation, Deed, Evidence, Bill, Indenture, Instru-*
         ment, Writing, Muniment, Conveyance, Policy, subscribe, under
         ones hand, set ones hand.
         { SEALING, *Seal, Signet, Sigil, Bond, specialty.*
- *Security*;
  - *Personal*: whether || *express, by promising for another, and making*
    himself liable to the same Penalty upon the other's failing: or *impli-*
    cit, by speaking in one's behalf.
    6. { SPONSION, *Stipulation, Bail, vouch, undertake for, Surety-ship,*
       Hostage, Security, Warrant, Caution, engage, responsible for.
       { INTERCESSION, *Mediate or, interpose, speak for.*
  - *Real, of ones Goods*; either
    - *Absolute*; *by ingaging for the truth of a Promise* either || *the Goods in*
      specie, or *only his right to them.*
      7. { PAWN, *Pledge, gage, engage.*
         { MORGAGE, *Security, Statute, Caution, engage.*
    - *Relative*; *by ingaging them for the success of a thing contingent*,
      || either *as Principal*, or *as Accessory.*
      8. { WAGER, *Stake, vy, lay, prize.*
         { BET, *Stake, vy, revy.*

JUDI-

JUDICIAL RELATION.

§. II. The several Notions referring to matters of Law and Courts of Judicature, are comprehended under that which is styled JUDICIAL RELATION, *forensical, Court, Hall, extrajudicial.*
These are distinguishable into such as *concern*
- PERSONS. I.
- CAUSES and Actions. II.
- *Faults,*
  - {CAPITAL. III.
  - {NOT CAPITAL. IV.
- *Punishments,*
  - {CAPITAL. V.
  - {NOT CAPITAL. VI.

I. PERSONS. I. PERSONS considerable under this Head of Judicial Relation, may be distinguished into such as are either
- *More principal.*
  - *Persons judging.*
    - *Legally* constituted; || *Principal:* or *Accessory.*
      - 1. { JUDGE, *Chancellour, Commissary, Censor, Moderator, Official, Jury, Inquest, Doom, Sentence, decide, determine, censure, Judicatory, judicial, Court, Bench, Tribunal.*
        ASSESSOR, *Syndic, Bencher, Alderman, Canons, Prebends, Chapter, Fellows, assist, Sides-men.*
    - *Voluntarily* consented to by the parties; || *to determin the Suit :* or *cease the Enmity between them.*
      - 2. { ARBITRATOR, *Umpire, Days-man, comprimize, Referree, award*
        MEDIATOR, *Incercessor, deal-between, intermediate, Mean.*
  - *Persons judged;* whether || *active:* or *passive;* in
    - *Criminals.*
      - 3. { ACCUSER, *Informer, challenge, Endite-ment, charge, attaint, peach, empeach, arraign, tax, lay to ones charge, call in question; Presentment, Bill. prosecute, Promooter.*
        PRISONER, or *reputed Criminal, Delinquent, Malefactor, Defen-* (dant.
    - *Judicials.*
      - 4. { PLAINTIF, *Accuser, complain, blame.*
        DEFENDANT, *Apology, excuse, vindicate.*
- *Less principal; relating* either to the
  - *Judges; for* ||
    - *Writing:* or *saying* publicly.
      - 5. { NOTARY, *Register, Remembrancer, Secretary, Clerk, Scribe,*
        CRIER. (*Protonotary, Rolls, enroll.*
    - *Fetching:* or *keeping.*
      - 6. { PURSEVANT, *Messenger, Catchpole, Serjeant.*
        MARSHAL, *Keeper, Jailour.*
  - *Parties;* || *to advise and speak in behalf of either party:* or *to declare the truth indifferently betwixt both* of them.
    - 7. { ADVOCATE, *Counsel, Pleader, maintain, defend, vindicate, Lawyer, Barrester, Proctor, Clyent.*
      WITNESS, *Evidence attest, testifie, Testimony, Affidavit.*

II. To

Chap. XI.   *Judicial Relation.*   271

II. To the more general words of *Actions* or PROCEEDINGS, *Cau-* II. PRO-
ses, in Judicial Affairs, may be annexed those less general words of SUIT, CEEDINGS.
Controversie, implead, commence, Case, Cause, Action, go to law, wage law, pre-
ferr a Bill, Barrester, Brabble.
  These are either
    Antecedent; on the part of the
      Plaintiff; in ∥ *giving legal notice:* or *seizing on the person or goods of*
        his Adversary.
    1. { CITATION, *Subpœna, Process, call, warn, summon, Sumner, Appa-*
         ritor, Bailiff, Beadle.
         ARREST, *attach, apprehend, distrein, seize, lay hold on, Embargo,*
         Serjeant, Baily, Catchpole, Beadle, Replevy.
      Defendant; ∥ *giving assurance of answering in Court :* or *coming him-*
        self, or by his Substitute, to answer it accordingly.
    2. { BAIL.
         APPEARANCE, *forth-coming.*
    Concomitant.
      Preparatory; by the
        Parties; ∥ *active:* or *passive.*
    3. { ACTION, *Endictment, Bill, Process, arraign, implead, sue, com-*
         mence suit, wage law, Barretor.
         PLEA, *Apology.*
      Judges; in their ∥ *taking notice of and hearing the Cause:* or *making*
        search into the merits of it.
    4. { COGNIZANCE, *Hearing.*
         EXAMINATION, *Trial, sift out, Hearing, Inquisition, interrogate,*
         Scrutiny, scann, view, review, revise, canvase, gage, pumpe out.
    Decisive.
      Common; ∥ *agreeing upon the state of the Question :* or *determining*
        what the merit is.
    5. { JOYNING ISSUE;
         SENTENCING, *Doom, Judgment, Verdict, Censure, Decree, Or-*
         der, adjudge, decide, determin, award, definitive.
      Passive, in the parties; as they are found ∥ *not to have transgressed the*
        Law: or *having transgressed it.*
    6. { INNOCENT, *clear, blameless, harmless, justifie-cation, vindicate,*
         discharge, cleanse, purge, compurgation.
         GUILTY, *nocent, delinquent, peccant, convict, culpable, faulty,*
         tardy, Offender, Transgressor, propitiate, expiate.
      Active, in the Judge; pronouncing the party either ∥ *free from:* or
        obnoxious to Punishment.
    7. { ACQUITTING, *absolving, assoil, clear, discharge, loosing, purging,*
         quit, release.
         CONDEMNING, *cast, damn.*
    Consequent; in the
      Parties, ∥ *expresly declining the Judgment:* or *referring the Cause to*
    8. { PROTESTING.   (*some higher Judicature.*
         APPEALING.
      Judges; by ∥ *inflicting the Punishment :* or *freeing from it.*
    9. { EXECUTING, *inflict, suffer, Executioner, Hangman.*
         PARDONING, *forgiving, remit, release, venial, Indulgence, put up.*
                                                        III. CRIMES

III. CRIMES CAPITAL.

III. CRIMES CAPITAL, (*Enormity, facinorous, criminal, Malefactor,*) such as are or ought to be punished with Death, may be distinguished into such Offences as are more immediately *against*

- *God and Religion*; namely, the ‖ *confederating with evil spirits*; to which may be adjoyned for affinity (though not counted capital) the *pretending to discover secret, and foretel future things by foolish forbidden Arts.*
  - 1. { WITCHCRAFT, *Conjuring, Necromancy, Sorcery, Black-art, Magic, enchant, fascinate, fore-speak, Charm, Spell, Cunning-man.*
    WIZARDING, *Manteia, Divining, Gypsie, Fortune-telling, Soothsaying, Sorcery, Augury, Astrology, Geomancy, Pyromancy, Physiognomy, Cheiromancy, Palmistry, Sigil, Talisman.*
- *Man*; whether;
  - *A public person*, or Magistrate.
    - More *general*; implying ‖ *declared hostility against him*: or *exposing him to his enemies.*
      - 2. { TREASON, *Traitor, betray.*
        CONSPIRACY, *betraying.*
    - More *particular*; ‖ *a forcible opposing of him by Arms*: or *occasioning some illegal tumultuous dissension in the Multitude.*
      - 3. { REBELLION, *Rising, Insurrection, Defection, Revolt, take head.*
        SEDITION, *Commotion, Combustion, Riot, Uproar, Mutiny, Tumult, Hurly-burly, Scuffle, Stirrs, Quoil, Racket, Boute-feu, Incendiary, turbulent.*
  - *Any private person*; according to the
    - *General name*; by which it is called in our English Laws.
      - 4. FELONY.
    - *Particular kinds*; distinguishable by their Objects, as being against
      - *Life*; *by taking it away illegally.*
        - 5. MURTHER, *Assassin-ate, Homicide, Manslaughter, Massacre, Parricide, cut-throat, blood-thirsty.*
      - *Chastity*; by *unnatural coition*, either ‖ *with Beasts*: or *Males.*
        - 6. { BESTIALITY, *Buggery.*
          SODOMY, *Buggery, Catamite.*
      - *Estate*; *with respect to another's.*
        - *Goods*; taking them away either ‖ *openly and forcibly*: or *secretly and by craft.*
          - 7. { ROBBERY, *Rapine, Sacrilege, Thief, Bandito, Pyrate, Pickroon, pillage, take a purse.*
            THEFT, *steal, purloin, lurch, filch, pilfer, nim, surreptitious, Plagiary, Sacrilege, Cut-purse, Pick-pocket, light-fingered, Larceny.*
        - *Habitation*; ‖ *by burning it*: or *breaking into it.*
          - 8. { HOUSE-BURNING, *Incendiary.*
            BURGLARY, *House-breaking.*

IV. Crimes

Chap. XI.   Judicial Relation.   273

IV. Crimes or FAULTS NOT CAPITAL, may be distinguished **IV. FAULTS**
into such as are (*son.* **NOT CAPITAL.**

- *General*; any *action against ones Right, especially with contempt of the Per-*
  1. ⎰ INJURY, *Wrong, Harm, Trespass, Hurt, Grievance, Abuse, Dammage.*
     ⎱ AFFRONT, *Contumely, Outrage, Slur, Despite, Indignity, put a trick on.*
- *Special*; *against*;
  - *Chastity*; whether ‖ *by a single : or a married person.*
    2. ⎧ FORNICATION, *Whore-dom, Courtesan, Concubine, Harlot, Trull,*
       ⎨ *Punk, Leman, Quean, Drab, Strumpet, prostitute, deflour, stuprate,*
       ⎪ *vitiate, wenching, Brothel, Stews, Bawd, Pander.*
       ⎩ ADULTERY, *Concubine.*
  - *Estate*;
    - *General*; ‖ *by unjust getting : or keeping of another's Right.*
      3. ⎰ USURPATION, *incroach, intrench, grow upon, invade, intrude,*
         ⎱ DETENTION, *with-holding, keep back.* (*thrust in.*
    - *Particular, as to the manner of it*; *by abusing*
      - *Skill*; in ‖ *taking advantage of another man's ignorance,* especially in actions of Commerce : or *misusing his own skill in the falsifying of a thing.*
        4. ⎧ FRAUD, *Deceit, Guile, Cozening, Delusion, Collusion, Illusion,*
           ⎪ *dodge, trepan, over-reach, prevaricate, circumvent, go-beyond,*
           ⎨ *impose, gull, beguile, defraud, Imposture, Knave, Rook, Cheat,*
           ⎪ *Shift, Shark, cog, slur, wheedle, come over one, supplant.*
           ⎪ FORGERY, *counterfeit, false, adulterate, sophisticate, coin, de-*
           ⎩ *vise, forge, falsifie, foisting, Interpolation, Impostor, suppositititious, surreptitious.*
      - *Power*; by ‖ *taking advantage of another man's necessity or impotence : or exceeding the allowance of the Law.*
        5. ⎰ OPPRESSION, *Force, Violence, exact, overcharge.*
           ⎱ EXTORTION, *Exaction, Rapine, Rapacity, wresting, wring, griping, ravin, poling, pilling.*
      - *Course of Law*; by endeavouring to corrupt ‖ *the Officers of Justice : or the Witnesses.*
        6. ⎰ BRIBERY, *Corruption, dawbing.*
           ⎱ SUBORNATION.
  - *Good name*; endeavouring to render another
    - *Criminal*; by accusations ‖ *not true* : or *made unlawfully against an absent person.*
      7. ⎰ CALUMNY, *Obloquy, Slander, Aspersion, opprobrious, Detraction,*
         ⎱ *False accusation, carping, belie, defame, disparage, traduce.*
         BACKBITING, *Libel, Tale-bearer, Tell-tale, Whispering, Pick-thank.*
    - *Infamous*; by objecting ‖ *another's failings* : or *our own favours.*
      8. ⎰ REPROCHING, *nip, taunt, scoff, twit, Opprobry, obloquy, tax, traduce.*
         ⎱ UPBRAIDING, *cast in one's teeth, exprobrate, twit.*
    - *Odious* : or *ridiculous.*
      9. ⎰ REVILING, *rail, scold, brawl, Contumely, inveigh, invective, foul-mouthed, Cucking-stool.*
         ⎱ MOCKING, *deride, flout, jeer, scoff, twit, gibe, quip, gird, frump, bob, taunt, wipe, jerk, Sarcasm, Pasquil, Irrision, Illusion, Satyr, Burlesque, play upon.*

N n   V. By

V. PUNISH-
MENTS CA- V. By *Punishment* is meant the evil of Suffering, inflicted for the evil
PITAL. of Doing; to which may be adjoyned the loss or Extinction of a man's
Right in a thing which he formerly injoyed, styled FORFEITURE.

PUNISHMENTS CAPITAL are the various manners of putting men to death in a judicial way, which in several Nations are or have been either

Simple; by
- *Separation of the parts*; ‖ *Head from Body*: or *Member from Member*.
  1. { BEHEADING, *strike off ones head*.
     { QUARTERING, *Dissecting*.
- *Wound*.
  - *At distance*; whether ‖ *from Hand*: or *from Instrument*, as Gun, Bow, &c.
    2. { STONING, *Pelting*.
       { SHOOTING.
  - *At hand*; either by
    - *Weight*; ‖ *of something else*: or *one's own*.
      3. { PRESSING.
         { PRECIPITATING, *throwing or casting headlong*.
    - *Weapon*; ‖ *any way*: or *direct upwards*.
      4. { STABBING.
         { EMPALING.
- *Taking away necessary Diet*: or *giving that which is noxious*.
  5. { STARVING, *famishing*.
     { POISONING, *Venom, envenom, virulent*.
- *Interception of the Air*; at the
  - *Mouth*; distinguished according to the place of the party, ‖ *in the Air*: or *in the Earth*.
    6. { STIFLING, *smoother, suffocate*.
       { BURYING ALIVE.
  - *Water*: or *Fire*.
    7. { DROWNING.
       { BURNING ALIVE.
  - *Throat*; ‖ *by weight of a man's own body*: or *the strength of others*.
    8. { HANGING.
       { STRANGLING, *throttle, choke, suffocate*.

Mixed of wounding and starving; the body being ‖ *erect*: or *lying on a Wheel*.
9. { CRUCIFYING, *Cross*.
   { BREAKING ON THE WHEEL.

VI. PU-

Chap. XI.   *Military Relation.*   275

VI. PUNISHMENTS NOT CAPITAL are distinguished by the **VI. PUNISH-**
things or subjects receiving detriment by them, as being either *of the* **MENTS**
Body; according to the **NOT CA-**
  General name; signifying great pain. **PITAL.**
    1. TORTURE, *Torment, excruciate.*
  Special kinds; by
    Striking; with ‖ *a limber:* or *a stiff Instrument.*
  2. { WHIPPING, *lashing, scourging, leashing, jerk, Rod, slash, Switch,*
       stripe, Beadle.
     { CUDGELLING, *bastinado, baste, swinge, swaddle, shrubb, slapp,*
       thwack.
    Stretching of the limms violently; the body being ‖ laid along for that
    purpose: or *lifted up into the Air.*
  3. { RACK.
     { STRAPPADO.
Liberty; of which one is deprived *by Restraint* ‖
  Into ‖ *a place:* or *instrument for custody.*
  4. { IMPRISONMENT, *Incarceration, Durance, Custody, Ward, clap*
       up, commit, confine, mue, Pound, Pinfold, Gaol our, Counter, Cage,
       Coop, Toleboth, Dungeon, Marshal, release, secure, set fast.
     { BONDS, *Fetters, Gyves, Shackles, Manicles, Pinnion, Chains.*
  Out *of a place* or country; whether ‖ *with allowance of any other:* or *con-*
  finement to one other.
  5. { EXILE, *Banish-ment, exterminate, proscribe, eject, expel, out-lawed.*
     { RELEGATION.
Repute; whether ‖ *more gently:* or *more severely by burning marks in one's*
  6. { INFAMATION, *Ignominy, Pillory.*   (*flesh.*
     { STIGMATIZATION, *Branding, Cauterizing, burning in the hand.*
Estate; whether ‖ *in part:* or *in whole.*   (*Mark.*
  7. { MULCT, *Fine, amerce, sconce.*
     { CONFISCATION, *Forfeiture.*
Dignity and power; by *depriving one of* ‖ *his Degree:* or *his capacity to bear*
  8. { DEGRADING, *deposing, depriving.*   (*Office.*
     { INCAPACITATING, *cashier, disable, discard, depose, disfranchize.*

MILITARY RELATION.

THis Head of MILITARY RELATION, is intended to contain such   §. III.
Notions as concern the various respects and capacities belonging
to a state of War. The *using of the united Force and Arms of many against*
others, is styled WAR-*fare, martial, polemical, Militia, Chivalry.*
  And the *being without mutual opposition* is called Peace.
  The Notions appertaining to this Head, do relate either to *Military*
{ ACTIONS. I.
  EVENTS. II.
  Persons.
  { SEGREGATE. III.
    AGGREGATE. IV.
  Instruments necessary to War, AMMUNITION. V.
  PLACES. VI.

N n 2   I. *Military.*

Military Relation. Part. II.

I. MILITARY ACTIONS.

I. **Military ACTIONS** may be distinguished according to the
General name; denoting the endeavour of ‖ doing hurt: or preserving from hurt.
1. { OFFENDING, Offence-ive, Annoy-ance.
    { DEFENDING, protect, guard, shelter, shrowd, ward, preserve, keep, maintain,
Particular kinds or degrees; whether such as are (make good, tutelary.
Opposite and in several.
  Declaring enmity on the ‖ offensive: or defensive side.
  2. { PROVOKING, challenge, irritate, invite, bait, stir up, dare, vy.
      { DEFYING, dare
  Beginning of actual ‖ offence: or defence.
  3. { ASSAULTING, assail, attaque, invade, encounter, Onset, set upon, charge,
      { Inrode, Rencounter, Incursion, fall on, run upon.
      { RESISTING, withstand, stand against, bear up against, turn head, struggle with, Antiperistasis.
  Endeavouring ‖ to dispossess one of his place: or to frustrate such endeavours;
  Keeping from necessaries: or supplying with necessaries. (either by ‖
  4. { BESIEGING, Siege, beleaguer, beset, block up, hem in, lay siege.
      { RELIEVING, succour, supp'y, help, recruit, reinforce, subsidiary, Ayd.
  Underdigging the Sepiment; either ‖ to make a breach in it: or to hinder
  5. { MINING, undermine, Sapping. (the making of such a breach.
      { COUNTERMINING.
  Entring forcibly to assault the besieged: or going out to assault the besiegers.
  6. { STORMING, assaulting, boarding, attaque, scaling, on-slaught.
      { SALLYING, issue out
Reciprocal and in common; whether by wayes of
Force; viz. the mutual endeavours of corporeal mischief to one another;
General name: or that which is betwixt two. (according to the ‖
  7. { FIGHTING, Combat, Conflict, encounter, cope, bicker, Fray, impugn,
      { DUELLING, Single combat, Champion, List. (scuffle, List.
Special kinds, betwixt numerous parties, according to set order and appointment; either of ‖ some part of the Army: or the whole
  8. { SKIRMISHING, Fray, Velitation, pickeer.
      { BATTELLING, Set fight, Set battel, joyn battel, Shock.
Skill, or some secret art to deceive an Enemy; according to the ‖ general name: or by concealing Souldiers for the sudden surprisal of others.
  9. { STRATAGEM, ensnare, Device, Trick, Train, surprize.
      { AMBUSH, Ambuscado, insidiate, lay wait, lurk, way lay, surprize.

II. MILITARY EVENTS.

II. **Military EVENTS** may be distinguished into such as are either
Of Importance; whom ‖ one keeps as before: or gains from the other: or loses his own; relating to the
Condition usually befalling such as are ‖ equal: or stronger: or weaker.
  1. COMING OFF UPON EQUAL TERMS.
     { VICTOR, overcome, defeat, discomfit, beat, win, vanquish, get the day,
       -the better, -the upper hand, quell, predominant, prevail, subdue,
       suppress, over-bear, -master.
     { OVERTHROWN, subdued, foiled, suppressed, routed, worsted, beaten,
Place of fighting. (defeated, discomfited, brought under.
  2. STAND HIS GROUND.
     { ADVANCE, get ground.
     { RETIRE, retreat, give back, shrink, recede, recoyle.
Country of fighting.
  3. KEEP THE FIELD.
     { PURSUE, chase, course, follow, prosecute, Hue and Cry.
     { FLY, run away, rout, fugitive, take ones heels, put to flight.

Town

Chap. XI.   *Military Relation.*   277

{*Town assaulted.*
4. {HOLD OUT, *make good, maintain, stand out, hold tack.*
   {TAKE, *win.*
   {LOSE, *yield, surrender, Rendition.*
Goods of those that fight.
5. {SAVE ONE'S OWN.
   {BOOTIES, *Forage, Plunder, Pillage, Quarry, Prey, Prize, Free-booter,*
       Letters of Mart, Letters of Reprize.
   {SPOILS, *harras, havock, ravage, rifle, sack, ransack, Wreck, Devastation,*
Persons concerned.   (*Ruin, Wast, depopulate.*
6. {ESCAPE, *evade, scape, eschew, get rid, get quit off, get off, shift away, get*
   {CAPTIVATE, *take prisoner.*   (*clear.*
   {YIELD, *give up, render, surrender, resign, deliver.*
Final issue of the War.
   {SAVE.
7. {CONQUER, *bring under, master, mate, quel, vanquish, repress, suppress,*
       tame subdue, win.
   {SUBMIT, *give up, humble, yield, surrender, come in.*
Of shew on the Victor's side, (for the conquered makes none;) either by
some ‖ *solemn Actions to be publicly performed:* or *Things and Structures*
to remain in memory of the Victory.
8. {TRIUMPH, *exult, crow, exultation, Bonfire.*
   {TROPHEE.

III. *Military* PERSONS (*Souldier, Warrier, Reformado, serve, press,*) *se-*   III. MIL-
gregate, may be distinguished by those several imployments for which they   ITARY PER-
are designed; being either for   SONS SE-
                                                                              GREGATE.
Fighting; ‖ *on foot:* or *on horse-back*
1. {FOOTMAN, *Infantry, Lance-knight.*
   {HORSMAN, *Cavalry, Light-horse, Curasier, Dragoons, Trooper, Reister, Rider*
Signs to the Army; belonging either to ‖ *Foot:* or *Horse.*
Visible.
2. {ENSIGN, *Ancient, Colours, Standard, Pennon, Banner.*
   {CORNET, *Banner, Colours.*
Audible.
3. {DRUMMER, *Drum, Tabor, Tabret.*
   {TRUMPETER, *Trumpet.*
Distributing Orders; ‖ *ordinary, belonging to each aggregate part:* or *extraor-*
4. {SERJEANT.   (*dinary, belonging to the Army.*
   {ADJUTANT
Discovery; either ‖ *of the Country in general:* or *amongst the Enemies.*
5. {SCOUT, *crusing, descry.*
   {SPY, *Emissary, Setter, Intelligence.*
Prevention of danger that might happen either to ‖ *Persons:* or *Places.*
6. {GUARD, *Convoy, custody, keep, ward, keep guard, relieve the guard, Corps*
   {WATCH, *Ward, Corporal.*   (*du guard*
Both Discovery and Prevention; denoting *such a one as* ‖ *stands and examines:*
or *lies on the ground to listen and observe*
7. {SENTINEL, *Sentry,*
   {PERDUE.
Digging: or *other servil works;* denoting such Servants of the Army as fol-
8. {PIONER.   (low the Baggage.
   {CALO, *Pedee, Black guard.*   IV. *Mi-*

IV. Military PERSONS AGGRE-GATE.	**IV.** *Military* PERSONS AGGREGATE (*Party of Souldiers, Forces, disband*) may be diftributed according to fuch different names as do denote either the *Whole*; being an armed Multitude fit to affault or refift, confifting of many

1. ARMY, *Hoft, Forces, Battalia.* (fubordinate divifions.

Parts; according to

{ The *firft* : or the *fecond greateft fubdivifions.*
2. { BRIGADE, *Battalion, Terce.*
   { REGIMENT, *Legion, Tribune, Colonel.*

The *third*: or *fourth fubdivifion*, belonging both to Horfe and Foot:
3. { COMPANY, *Troop, Band, Captain, Centurion.*
   { SQUADRON.

Order and Situation; whether with || *the fide of every one towards the fide of the*
4. { RANK. (*next: or the face of every one towards the back of the next,*
   { FILE, *Roe.*

Ufes and Services for which fuch perfons are defigned; whether ·

{ To *march before the Army*, for clearing of the way : or *to follow after*, for
5. { VANCURRIER. (help and fupply in cafe of neceffity.
   { RESERVE.

{ To *begin the Fight* : or *to ingage in the moft difficult fervices*, being ufually a
6. { FORLORN HOPE. (felected Company.
   { COMMANDED PARTY.

To *take care of* and *defend the Baggage.*
7. TRAIN.

V. AMMUNITION.	**V.** The Provifions neceffary for Offence and Defence are ftyled by the general name of AMMUNITION, *Magazin, charge, difcharge, Arcenal.*

To which may be adjoyned the word BAGGAGE, *Impediments, Luggage, Lumber.*

They are diftinguifhable according to their Shapes, and thofe feveral Ufes for which they are defigned, into fuch as are more

{ *General*; denoting the common names belonging to things of this nature; whe-
1. { WEAPON, *Arms offenfive.* (ther fuch as are || *offenfive*: or *defenfive.*
   { ARMOUR, *defenfive Arms, Mail, Headpiece, Helmet, Scull, Gorget, Gauntlet, Habergeon, &c. Armorer, Armory.*

Special; for

Offence.

Comminus, near hand; being either for

{ *Striking* chiefly; whether || *bruifing :* or *cutting.*
2. { CLUB, *Bat, Batoon, Battle-ax, Mace, Pole-ax, Cudgel.*
   { SWORD, *Scimitar, Hanger, Rapier, Tuck, Ponyard, Stilletto, Dagger, Fauchion, Glave, Cutler.*

Thrufting chiefly; of which the latter is fometimes ufed for *ftriking.*

{ SPIKE, *Spear, Launce, Javelin, run at tilt.*
3. { HALBERT, *Partizan, Trident.*

Eminus, at a diftance; whether

Ancient and lefs artificial; denoting either the

Inftrument giving the force, being of a curved figure and elaftical *power*; to *be held in the hand, either* || *immediately* : or *by the ftock to*
4. { BOW, *fhoot, Archer, Fletcher.* (*which it is fixed.*
   { CROSS-BOW, *fhoot.*

Inftrument or Weapon projected; whether || *immediately out of the hand:*
5. { DART, *Javelin, Harping-iron.* (or *mediately from fomething elfe.*
   { ARROW, *Shaft, Bolt.*

Modern and more artificial, (i.) fire-Arms; denoting either the

Veffels giving the force; according to the name of || *the whole kind :* or of *the bigger kind.* 6. GUN,

Chap. XI.   *Military Relation.*   279

6. {
  GUN, *shoot, Snaphance, Fire-lock, Musket, Carbine, Blunderbuss,*
  Piece, Arquebus, Petronel, Pistol, Dagg, Potgun, play upon.
  ORDNANCE, *Cannon, Artillery, Saker, Minion, Basilisk, Drake,*
  &c. shoot.
}

Utensils; *signifying the thing* || *enkindling:* or *enkindled.*

7. {
  MATCH, *Tinder, Touchwood, Spunk.*
  POWDER, *Gunpowder.*
}

Things discharged; either || *solid:* or *hollow.*

8. {
  BULLET, *Ball, Pellet, Shot.*
  GRANADO, *Petard.*
}

Defence.

9. BUCKLER, *Shield, Target.*

VI. Such kind of Places, together with such kind of Contrivances belonging to them, as relate to a state of War, may be styled MILITARY PLACES or *Works*, (*Munitions, Fortifications, fenced, Hold, dismantle.*)   VI. MILITARY PLACES.

To which may be adjoyned for its affinity the common notion of such things as are used for the fencing of Places; SEPIMENT, *Wall, Pale, Fence.*
These may be distinguished into such as are   (*Enclosure, Fold, Mound.*)

More principal;

Comprehending the Area contained within them.

Greater; in || *Country:* or *Town.*

1. {
  CAMP, *encamp, quarter.*
  GARRISON.
}

Less; more || *independent:* or *dependent.*

2. {
  SCONCE, *Fortress, Platform, Fort.*
  BLOCK-HOUSE, *Fort, Bastion, Strong-hold.*
}

Not comprehending the Area contained within them.   (*Earth.*)

General; denoting a Sepiment || *Ridge-like of Earth:* or *Furrow-like in the*

3. {
  RAMPIER, *Wall, Bulwark, Line, Counterscarf, Mound, Out-work.*
  DITCH, *Dike, Foss, Trench, Mote.*
}

Special; signifying the || *outward:* or *inward Wall.*

4. {
  VAUMURE.
  LINING.
}

Less principal; whether

Parts.

Greater; either *of* || *a round:* or *many-angled figure.*

5. {
  HALF-MOON.
  HORN-WORK.
}

Lesser; either || *angular to defend the sides of a place:* or *the straight sides*   (*to be so defended.*)

6. {
  REDOUBT.
  FLANKER.
}

Accessions; belonging to the

Out-parts; being a *series of* || *great Piles erected:* or *Holes dug in the earth.*

7. {
  PALLISADO.
  FURNACE-HOLE.
}

Entrance; Military Doors || *to shut transverse:* or *to let down ditect.*

8. {
  TURNPIKE.
  PORTCULLIS.
}

Walls; signifying *an erect crenated Margo upon the Walls;* || *either built upon them:* or *made by setting on Baskets filled with earth.*

9. {
  PARAPET.
  GABION.
}

NAVAL

NAVAL RELATION.

§. IV. The Head of *Naval Relation* is intended to comprehend the various Notions and Expressions, belonging to mens affairs and traffick on the
- *Things.* (Waters; respecting either
  - KINDS OF VESSELS used for Passage. I.
  - Parts of *Vessels*; relating to such as serve for
    - Containing; HULL. II.
    - PROGRESSIVE MOTION OR STAYING. III.
    - RIGGING. IV.
  - PERSONS. V.
  - ACTIONS. VI.

KINDS OF VESSELS.

I. The KINDS OF VESSELS which are used for passage on the Waters, are in several Countries of so great variety and names, by reason of their being distinguished by some little accidental Differences, that it will be very difficult for the most expert person to give a sufficient enumeration of them: and therefore I shall in this place distribute them onely according to their various *Magnitudes*, and the *Uses* for which they are designed: according to which they may be distinguished into such as are denoted under the
- *General name*; belonging to the ‖ *lesser*, or *greater kind*.
  1. BOAT, *Oars, Wherry, Sculler, Canoe, Cockboat, Waterman.*
     SHIP, *Pink, Pinnace, Shallop, Sail, Vessel, Navy, Fleet, naval.*
- *Particular kinds*; either
  - *Lesser for the Sea,* or *greater for Rivers.*
    2. KETCH, *Bark, Flyboat.*
       BARGE, *Lighter, Gallyfoist, Brigandine,* &c.
  - *Greater;* being *moved* either *by*
    - *Sails and Oars.*
      3. GALLY.
    - *Sails onely;* and used chiefly *for*
      - *Burthen.*
        4. GALEOT, *Caramosil, Carrack, Caravel.*
      - *Traffick* and Merchandize.
        5. MERCHANT-MAN, *Bottom.*
      - *Fighting.*
        6. MAN OF WAR, *Frigot, Caper, Armada, Privateer.*
      - *Passage.*
        7. PACQUET-BOAT.

II. HULL.

II. By HULL is meant the main Bulk or Body of the Ship, considered abstractly from its Masts and Rigging. The parts of which may be distin-
- *Timbers.* (guished into such as relate to
  - *Fixed at the*
    - *Bottom of the Ship;* lying either ‖ *direct,* or *transverse.*
      1. KEEL.
         RUNG.
    - *End;* either the ‖*former,* or *hinder part.*
      2. STEM, *Prow.*
         STERN, *Poop.*
  - *Moveable upon a Centre* or Hindge; ‖ *for lifting up* the Anchor or any great weight: or *for steering* the Ship.
    3. CAPSTAIN.
       RUDDER, *Helm, Steer.*

‖ *Places*

Chap. XI.   Naval Relation.

Places or rooms.; relating to the
- *Former, or hinder part above.*
  - 4. { FORE-CASTLE.
       { ROUND-HOUSE.
  - *Middle space*; || *betwixt the Main-most and Fore-castle,* or *the rooms built above this towards the Stern.*
    - 5. { WAST.
         { HALF-DECK.

Apertures; in the
- *Floor or Deck,* supplying the office of Doors and Windows; || *greater,* or *lesser.*
  - 6. { HATCHES.
       { SCUTTLE, *Gratings.*
- *Sides*; || *for putting out the Ordnance,* or *for passage of Water from the Deck.*
  - 7. { PORT-HOLE.
       { SCUPPER.

Interstices; betwixt || *the edges of the planks,* or *the side-timbers of the Ship.*
- 8. { SEAM.
     { SPURKET.

Shape or figure of the Hull; with respect to || *the gathering or joyning together of the planks upon the Ship's quarter under water,* or *so much of the Hull as hangs over both ends of the Keel*; styled
- 9. { RAKE OF POST, *Tuck.*
     { RAKE OF STEM.

III. *Parts* of Vessels serving chiefly *for the* **PROGRESSIVE MOTION** or Staying of them, may be distinguished, by the matter of which they consist, into such as are of

Wood; according to the more
- *General names*; denoting such woody parts as are either
  - *Fixed and upright*; or *the upper parts of these, round and prominent.*
    - 1. { MAST.
         { TOP, *Boul.*
  - *Moveable and transverse*; applyed either to the || *top,* or *bottom of the Sail.*
    - 2. { YARD.
         { BOOM.
  - *Separate*; serving for thrusting against || *the Water,* or *the Earth.*
    - 3. { OAR, *row.*
         { POLE.

Particular kinds of Masts; (applicable likewise to Top, Yard, and Sails,) being placed either *in the*
- *Fore-part*; whether || *leaning,* or *upright.*
  - 4. { BOUL-SPRIT.
       { FORE-MAST.
- *Middle,* or *hinder-part.*
  - 5. { MAIN-MAST.
       { MIZZEN-MAST.

Cloth; serving for the
- *Catching and opposing the Wind*; either || *principally,* or *additionally.*
  - 6. { SAIL, *Course.*
       { BONNET, *Drabler.*
- *Distinction of Nations,* or the several *Officers* of a Navy; set up either || *above,* on the *Masts,* or *below,* at the *Stern.*
  - 7. { FLAG.
       { ANCIENT.
- *Ornament and so*; or *used to mark out the Wind's quarter.*
  - 8. { STREAMER.
       { JACK.

Iron; for || *staying and holding the Ship,* or *the fastning of it to other Ships.*
- 9. { ANCHOR, *Kedger.*
     { GRAPPLE.

O o   IV. By

Naval Relation: Part. II.

IV. RIGGING IV. By RIGGING is meant the several kinds of Cordage *belonging to a Ship*; in respect of the
- *Masts*; serving either *for the*
  - *Keeping them upright*; namely, || *that are more declive on either side of the Masts*: or *those that are more transverse.*
    1. { SHROUDS, *Puttocks.*
       { STAYES.
  - *Ascent up to them*; those *smaller ropes which cross the Shrouds as the*
    2. RATLINGS.   (*rounds of a Ladder.*
- *Yards*; serving *for the*
  - *Tying of them*: or *the pulling of them to and fro.*
    3. { PARREL.
       { JEARS.
  - *Squaring or transversing*: or *making them to hang higher or lower.*
    4. { BRACES.
       { LIFTS.
- *Sails*; serving *for the*
  - *Tying of them to the Yards*: or *the pulling them to and fro.*
    5. { ROBINS.
       { SHEATS.
  - *Furling them across*: or *to raise up the bunt or protuberant part of the Sail.*
    6. { BRALE.
       { BUNT-LINE.
  - *Making of them to stand closer by a wind*; being *fastned* either to || *the Clew or corner of the Sail*: or *the middle part of it.*
    7. { TACKS.
       { BOWLINE.
- *Anchor*; according to || *the more general name*: or *the name belonging to*
    8. { CABLE.   (*the lesser kind of such ropes.*
       { HAWSER, *Halser.*

V. NAVAL PERSONS. V. PERSONS belonging to the management of NAVAL Affairs, *Mariners, Seafaring-men*, may be distributed into such whose Charge doth concern the
- *Defence of the Ship* by fighting; either
  - *More principal*; the *Chief*, who in Fight is to make good the Halfdeck: or *his Deputy*, whose place in Fight is the Fore-castle.
    1. { CAPTAIN.
       { LIEUTENANT.
  - *Less principal*; having *the charge of the* ||
  - *Squadrons for the Watch*: or *being to take care for the setting and relieving of the Watch*, and that the Souldiers keep their Arms clean.
    2. { QUARTER-MASTER.
       { CORPORAL.
  - *Ordnance, Shot, Powder,* &c.
    3. GUNNER.
- *Sailing of the Ship,* and the care of its parts and Lading; either
  - *More principal*; whose charge it is to
  - *Direct the course,* and *command all the Sailors*: or *to bring the Ship*
    4. { MASTER.   (*safe to harbour.*
       { PILOT.
  - *Keep account of the Goods,* what is *received* and *delivered.*
    5. { CAPE-MERCHANT.
       { PURSER.
                                                         Preserve

Preserve the Rigging and Tackle and the Long-boat: or *to attend the Skiff with a peculiar gang to go to and fro upon occasion.*

6. { BOATSWAIN.
     COCKSWAIN.

Less principal; serving to

Keep the Decks clean.

7. SWABBER.

Manage the Sails below: or *to ascend for taking in the Top-sails, &c.*

8. { SAILERS, *Mid-ship-men, Skipper.*
     YONKERS, *Fore-mast-men.*

VI. NAVAL ACTIONS may be distinguished into such as are *done* **VI. NAVAL ACTIONS:**

To the Ship; for the

Securing of the Seams betwixt the Planks; either by || *beating in of Okum,* (i.) pieces of old Ropes or hards of Flax : *or putting a list of Canvas along the Seam, and then pouring hot Pitch upon it.*

1. { CALKING.
     PARSLING.

Smoothing the outside; by || *washing or burning off all the filth* with REEDS or Broom; or *smearing over so much of the Ship as is to be in the water* with a mixture of Tallow, Sope and Brimstone, boiled together, to preserve the Calking, and to make the Vessel more slippery for passage.

2. { BROMING, *Breaming.*
     GRAVING.

Defending it against Worms; by || *casing that part of the Hull within water* with Tar and Hair, and then nailing over thin Boards : or *inlarging the Breadth,* by ripping off some of the Planks; and then, having added other Timbers, to put on the Planks again, styled

3. { SHEATHING.
     FURRING.

Varying the Position of a Ship; either || *for the mending of it,* by making it to lie on one side, the better to come at its lower parts: or *for the motion of it,* by so ordering the Lading and Rigging that it may be in the best condition for sailing.

4. { CAREENING.
     TRIMMING.

By the Ship; either

Resting; when 'tis || *staid by the Anchor:* or *laid leaning to one side.*

5. { RIDING AT ANCHOR.
     HULLING.

In motion; either more

Direct; when it || *goes as it should:* or *runs its head in the wind more*

6. { KEEPING A-WIND.   (*or less then it should.*
     GRIPING.
     FALLING TO THE LEEWARD.

Lateral; when it || *doth lean too much on one side:* or *doth turn too much*

7. { HEELING, *feeling.*   (*on each side.*
     ROLLING.

O o 2   ECCLE-

ECCLESIASTICAL RELATION.

§. V. Under this Head of ECCLESIASTICAL RELATION (*Clergy, Spiritual, Church,*) are comprehended the several Notions and respects belonging to a Church-state. By *Church* is meant a Society of men as agreeing in the same kind of inward apprehensions of, and external demeanour towards, the Divine Nature: to which may be opposed the word TEMPORAL, *Civil, Humane, Secular, Lay, Prophane.*

Notions of this kind, may be distinguished into such as do denote

KINDS OF RELIGION. I.
Persons; in regard of their
  ECCLESIASTICAL CALLINGS. II.
  STATES OF RELIGION. III.
Actions; belonging to
  WORSHIP. IV.
  DISCIPLINE. V.
  INSTITUTIONS. VI.

I. RELIGION.
  I. That habit of reverence towards the Divine nature, whereby we are inabled and inclined to serve and worship him after such a manner as we conceive most acceptable to him, is called RELIGION, *Piety, Godliness*. The Privation of which is styled ATHEISM, *Irreligion, Impiety*. Men are distinguished by their kinds of Religion into *such as*

Are wholly without any revelation of the true God and his Worship; but that *knowledge* which *they have* is either
  Simple, from the dictates of mere *Reason*.
    1. NATURAL RELIGION.
  Mixed, and corrupted *with the worship of false gods*.
    2. PAGANISM, *Heathenism, Ethnic, Infidel, Gentil, Painim.*
Have revelations: or pretend to them; whether by
  Moses, in which they rest.
    3. JUDAISM, *Judaical, Jew.*
  Christ and his Apostles, added to Moses.
    4. CHRISTIANITY.
  Mahomet, superadded to the rest.
    5. MAHOMETISM, *Turcism.*

II. Those who apply themselves to the businesses of Religion as their particular *Calling*, may be stiled ECCLESIASTICAL PERSONS, *Clergy, Churchman, spiritual, Hierarchy.*

II. ECCLESIASTICAL PERSONS.

To which may be opposed, TEMPORAL, *Lay-ic, civil, secular, prophane.*

These may be distinguished into such as are

Injoyned; being set apart to some peculiar function in the Church, and by way of office devoted to assist in the duties of Religion, whether such as were in use

Before the Law; being || *the chief Administrators of religious Services, as Masters of Families*: or *such others as then and since were extraordinarily called and gifted to foretell future things.*

1. { PATRIARCH.
    { PROPHET -*ical, divine, prophesie, foretell, presage, prognosticate, Prediction, Seer, Sibyl.*

Under the Law; || *appointed for the principal works of divine Service*: or such as were *subordinate and assistant to them.*

2. { PRIEST.
    { LEVITE -*ical.*

Under the Gospel; being either

Temporary; || *who were first indued with the power of Miracles*, of whom there were onely twelve : or *such others as these took in for their help, to travel up and down for the spreading of Christianity.*

3. { APOSTLES -*ical.*
    { EVANGELISTS -*ical, Gospel.*

Permanent, and to be continued; whether

More principal; denoting *the chief Ecclesiastical Officer* || *of a Province*, with several Cities : or *some particular City and the Territory adjoyning.* (*vince.*

4. { PRIMATE, *Arch bishop, Metropolitan, Mufty, Patriarch, Province.*
    { BISHOP, *Prelate, Ordinary, Episcopal -acy, Suffragan, Superintendent, Pontificial, Diocess, See, Cathedral, Mitre, Crosier, Hierarchy.*

Less principal; such as are || *the chief Officers of particular Parish-churches* : or *others subordinate and assistant to these.*

5. { PRESBYTER, *Priest, Elder, Minister, Incumbent, Curate, Chaplain, Parson.*
    { DEACON, *Minister.*

Not injoyned; but voluntary, to be further distinguished, according to the

General name; denoting those that are under a vow of Poverty, Cœlibate, and obedience to their Superiours, to whom may be adjoyned for affinity, such others as oblige themselves to certain offices with them.

6. { REGULAR, *Religious Person, order, rule.*
    { PENITENTS, *Confraternity, Convert.*

Particular kinds; such as live either || *together in Society* : or *alone by themselves.*

7. { MONK, *Frier-ry, Nunn-ery, Novice, Abbot, Abbess, Abby, Prior-ry, General, Provincial, Gardian, Monastic, Monastery, Minster, Cloister, Covent, Society, Cowle, Father.*
    { HERMIT, *Anchorite, Cell, Recluse.*

III. Persons

III. STATES OF RELIGION.

III. Persons considered according to their several STATES and Conditions in respect OF RELIGION, may be distinguished either by their

- Faith and Judgments; whether ||*true*, or *false*, *as to the essential points of Religion*.
  1. { ORTHODOX, *Believer*.
     { HERETIC *-al, Heresie, Miscreant*.
- Charity to and communion with the body of those that agree in the same Profession: or being the faulty cause of the breach of such Communion.
  2. { CATHOLIC, *Communicant, Communion, Son of the Church*.
     { SCHISMATIC, *Schism-atical, Sect-ary, Recusant, Separate*.
- Suffering upon the account of Religion; being either
  - Great, but not unto Death.
    3. CONFESSOR.
  - Great unto Death. To which may be opposed the *inflicter of sufferings* upon account of Religion.
    4. { MARTYR *-dom*.
       { PERSEQUUTOR.
- Eminent degrees of ||*Religiousness*: or *Irreligiousness*.
  5. { SAINT, *Hero-ical, canonize*.
     { SCANDAL *-ous, profligate, Offence*.
- Former state, in respect of the several terms from which and to which men are *changed*; either ||*from bad to good*: or *from good to bad*.
  6. { CONVERT, *Proselyte, regenerate, reclaim, turn, come over*.
     { APOSTATE, *Back-slider, Renegado, Defection, revolt, draw back, turn, forsake, fall away, relapse, Fugitive, Tergiversation*.

IV. WORSHIP.

IV. That *inward and outward reverence* whereby we acknowledge the Esteem due to the Superiority and Excellency of another, together with the two extremes of this, viz. *Redundant*, when men give this *to such things as they ought not* for the Matter, or *in such a degree as they ought not* for the Measure; and *Deficient*, when men do either *contemn or neglect sacred things* and duties, are styled

- WORSHIP, *Adoration, Veneration, Devotion, devout, Liturgy, Divine service, Mattins, Vespers, Even-song*.
- SUPERSTITION, *Bigot*.
- PROPHANENESS, *Impiety, impious, ungodly*.

The more special *acts of Worship* may be distinguished into such as are more

- Ordinary and constant; whereby we
  - Apply our selves to God; whether more
    - General; whereby we ||*address to him for relief in all our wants and fears*, upon the belief of his infinite Goodness and Power: or making solemn and religious promises to him.
      1. { PRAYER, *Invocation, Collect, Orizon, Oratory, Ejaculation, call upon*.
         { VOW, *Votary, devoted*.

Chap. XI.   *Ecclesiastical Relation.*

⎰ *Special*; whereby we do either ‖
⎱ *Acknowledge our own faults and deserts :* or *intreat his favour and help.*

2. ⎰ CONFESSION, *acknowledge, Shreeve.*
   ⎱ PETITION, *supplicate, sue, beg, Litany, crave, request, Supplyant, Bedes-man, Boon.*

Return our acknowledgements to him for the good things we enjoy ; either ‖ *more general :* or *by Singing.*

3. ⎰ THANKSGIVING, *praise, magnifie, extol, Grace.*
   ⎱ PSALM, *Hymn, Anthem.*

Instruct others publicly, or excite them to religious duties ; either ‖ *in a more continued solemn Discourse :* or *by the asking and answering of Questions* in the plainest manner about the most necessary points of Religion.

4. ⎰ PREACHING, *Homily, Sermon, Postil, Pulpit.*
   ⎱ CATECHISING, *Catechism.*

Occasional; relating unto
⎰ *Solemnities of* ‖ *joy :* or *sadness.*

5. ⎰ FESTIVITY, *Festival, Holy-day, High-day, Sabbath, Jubilee, Wake, genial, good time.*
   ⎱ FASTING, *Humiliation, Ember-week, Lent, Vigil, Eve.*

Ritual Offices observed amongst Christians ; pertaining to
⎰ *Entrance into the state of Wedlock :* or *dissolving of that state.*

6. ⎰ MARRIAGE, *Wedd-ing, Matrimony, nuptial, Bride-groom, Hymen.*
   ⎱ DIVORCE.

Return into the Congregation after Parturition.

7. CHURCHING.

Actual taking upon themselves the Obligation made by their Sponsors in Baptism.

8. CONFIRMATION.

Performing the Rites due to the Dead by putting their bodies ‖ *into the ground :* or *under some Monument, to preserve the memorial of them.*

9. ⎰ BURYING, *interr, Grave, Funeral, Obit, Obsequies, Herse, Sepulture, Church-yard, Charnel-house.*
   ⎱ ENTOMBING, *Tomb, Sepulchre, Monument, Epitaph.*

V. Actions

V. DISCI-
PLINE.

V. Actions relating to Ecclesiastical Authority or DISCIPLINE, do concern the due ordering of the circumstances of Ecclesiastical or Sacred things to the best convenience. The Notions belonging to this Head, do refer either to the work of,

Setting things aside to a peculiar use; according to the
   More general Notion belonging to Things, and Times, and Places, as well as Persons; namely, the ‖ *separating of them from common use:* or *abusing them as being but common.*
      1. { CONSECRATION, *sacred, sanctifie, hallow, devote, dedicate, Holiness.*
         PROPHANATION, *unhallowed, impious, common, Lustration.*
  More particular kind, appropriated to Persons.
      2. { ORDINATION, *Consecration,*
         DEPRIVATION, *depose.*

Regulating of abuses in Ecclesiastical matters; according to the more
  General name.
    3. CENSURE.
  Particular kinds; consisting in a
    Temporary privation of Church-priviledget.
      4. SUSPENSION.
    Permanent, being the highest Ecclesiastical punishment; by a ‖ *cutting off from all Church communion* and privileges: or *the restoring one so cut off.*
      5. { EXCOMMUNICATION, *Anathema, Curse, cut off, separate.*
         ABSOLUTION, *loosing, discharge, assoile, purge, clear, pardon, acquit.*

VI. INSTI-
TUTIONS.

VI. By INSTITUTIONS or *Ordinances* are properly meant such kinds of things or duties as we could not have known or been obliged unto without particular Revelation. These may be distinguished into

Rules for our Instruction in Religion; which, according to the several manners of conveyance, were either ‖ *written:* or *unwritten.*
    1. { SCRIPTURE, *Bible, Word of God, Holy Writ, Text, Testament.*
       TRADITION, *Delivery, Cabala.*

Services to be done; according to the more
  General name; consisting in our *offering or giving* things *unto God.*
    2. OBLATION, *Offering, Offertory.*
  Particular kind, proper to the *times under the Law;* which required the *offering of such things* by Fire *as* were either ‖ *for Food:* or *for Perfume.*
    3. { SACRIFICE, *Victim, Holocaust, Host, Oblation, Hecatombe.*
       INCENSE, *Censor.*

Certain external signs and means for the signifying and conveying of internal spiritual Grace; according to the more
  General name.
    4. SACRAMENT -*al.*
  Particular kinds.
    Under the Law; for the ‖ *initiating:* or *confirming* men in that Religion.
    5. { CIRCUMCISION, *Cutting off the fore-skin.*
       PASSOVER. *Paschal, Easter.*
    Under the Gospel; whether for ‖ *initiating:* or *confirming.*
    6. { BAPTISM, *Christen, Font, Pædobaptism*
       EUCHARIST, *Communion, the Lord's Supper, The Sacrament, Host, Mass, Missal.*

CHAP. XII.

I. *A general Explication of the design of the foregoing Tables.* II. *Particular Instances in the six principal heads of it.* III. *Some things to be noted concerning* Opposites *and* Synonyma. IV. *An enumeration of what kinds of things are not to be particularly provided for in such tables.*

The principal design aimed at in these Tables, is to give a sufficient enumeration of all such things and notions, as are to have names assigned to them, and withall so to contrive these as to their order, that the place of every thing may contribute to a description of the nature of it. Denoting both the *General* and the *Particular head* under which it is placed; and the *Common difference* whereby it is distinguished from other things of the same kind. §. I.

It would indeed be much more convenient and advantageous, if these Tables could be so contrived, that every *difference* amongst the *Predicaments* might have a transcendental denomination, and not depend at all upon a numerical institution. But I much doubt, whether that Theory of things already received, will admit of it; nor doth Language afford convenient terms, by which to express several differences.

It were likewise desirable to a perfect definition of each species, that the *immediate form* which gives the particular essence to every thing might be expressed; but this form being a thing which men do not know, it cannot be expected that it should be described. And therefore in the stead of it, there is reason why men should be content with such a description by *properties* and *circumstances*, as may be sufficient to determine the primary sense of the thing defined.

Of these descriptions I shall here give an instance under each of the six *Principal Heads*. §. II.

The word *Goodness* is a transcendental, one of the General differences of things, or affections of entity, implying a respect to something without it self, namely, to the Will, by agreement to which things are rendered lovely and desirable, as by their disagreement they are rendered hateful and avoidable, which is the opposite notion of *Evil*. TRANSCENDENTAL.

The word *Diamond* doth by its place in the Tables appear to be a Substance, a Stone, a pretious Stone, transparent, colourless, most hard and bright. SUBSTANCE.

The word *Flower* or blossom is one of the peculiar parts, belonging to Plants, an annual part, more principal, antecedent to the seed, considerable for its beauty and colour.

The words *Newness* and *Oldness* do signifie notions belonging to Quantity, to space, to time, and more particularly to time past, according to the degrees of less or greater, as the next pair, *soonness* and *lateness*, doth relate to time future, according to the same degrees of Less or Greater. QUANTITY.

The word *Moderation* is a Quality, a Habit, an Affection of intellectual QUALITY.

P p

lectual virtue, whereby we are concerned for any truth,according to a due meafure, not more or lefs then the evidence and importance of it doth require, to which the notion of *fiercenefs* or *fanaticalnefs* is oppofed as the deficient extreme.

ACTION. The word *Pitty*, doth by its place denote an Action, fpiritual, of the foul in refpect of the Appetite, whofe actions are commonly ftiled Affections or Paffions: 'Tis a mixed Paffion, confifting of Grief and Love, occafioned by fome evil, which (as we think) doth unworthily befall others. As *Envy* doth of Grief and Hate upon account of fome good befalling others (as we think) unworthily.

RELATION. The word *Parent* by the place of it in the Tables, doth denote the thing thereby fignified, to be a Relation, Oeconomical, of Confanguinity, direct afcending; as *Child* is direct defcending.

And thus is it with all thofe other particulars, which are placed either directly or *collaterally*, either by way of *Oppofition* or of *Affinity*.

§. III. Only 'tis here to be noted.

1. That fome of thofe which are placed as *Oppofites*, do not alwayes fall out to be under the fame Predicament or Genus with thofe things to which they are adjoyned; as it muft be in fuch things as are *privatively* oppofed, as *Blindnefs, Deafnefs, Darknefs*, &c. And fo likewife for fome of thofe species which are put in for their *affinity*, as *Point, Center, Pole*, and fuch other things as are not *directly*, but *reductively* only under any predicament.

2. That fome Radixes, befides the *redundant* and *deficient* extremes, have likewife an *Oppofite common*; fo to the word *Juftice*, there is oppofed an *Oppofite common*, *Injuftice*, befides the excefs *Rigor*, and the defect *Remiffion*. So to *Veracity*, the *Oppofite common* is *lying*; which may be either by way of Excefs, *over-faying*, boafting, flattering: or of Defect, *under-faying, detraction*. So to *Equality*, the *Oppofite common* is *Inequality*, imparity, difparity; the excefs of which is *Superiority*, and the defect *Inferiority*. This is natural to all Radixes that have double Oppofites, though inftituted Languages have not provided words to exprefs it.

3. Many of the Synonymous words put to the Radixes, are referred to more heads then one, upon account of their various equivocal acceptions. And befides fuch words or phrafes as are more plainly Synonymous, there is likewife an addition of fuch other, as are either more *immediate* derivations, whether Adjectives, Verbs, Adverbs: or more *mediate*, being by compofition to be made off from thofe Radixes to which they are adjoyned: Of which I fhall give an inftance or two, under each of the fix general Heads.

TRANSCENDENTALS. In the Table of *Tranfcendentals*, T. III. 2. the Radical is GOODNESS, to which thefe other words are adjoyned, *Weal, welfare, right, regular, well, rectifie, better, beft*. Amongft which, the words *Weal, welfare*, are mentioned as *Synonoma*, denoting fuch a ftate of being as is defirable, and are fuppofed to be Subftantives Neuter. *Well-doing* or Good action, is the Subftan. Act. The words *Good, right, regular*, are the *Pofitive* adjectives from the root. *Better, beft*, are the *Comparative* and *Superlative* adjectives. *Well, right*, &c. are the Adverbs. *Rectifie* is good make, and to be expreffed by compofition with the Tranfcendental particle of *Caufe*.

So for the Oppofite to this, EVILNESS to which thefe words are adjoyned,

Chap. XII.   *Fore-going Table.*

joyned, *Ill, bad, naught, wrong, amiss, shrewd, scurvy, lewd, horrid, horrible, corrupt, pravity, deprave, sin, fault, trespass, trangress-ion, Peccadillo, worse.* Amongst which, the words *Badness, pravity,* are Synonymous to the Radicals; and supposed to be Substantives newter. The words *Sin, fault, trespass, trangression,* will be Substan. Act. which being compounded with the Transcendental Particle, *Diminutive* or *Augmentative,* will denote a *Peccadillo* or small fault, or an *Enormity* or heinous crime. The words *Evil, ill, bad, naught, wrong, corrupt,* are Adjectives of this root, and being compounded with the Transcendental Particle of Augmentative, will be of the same importance with those other words, *shrewd, scurvy, lewd, horrid, horrible,* &c. The words *Ill, amiss, wrong, badly, naughtily,* are the Adverbs. The words denoting to *sin, trespass, transgress,* are the Verb. Act. which being compounded with the Transcendental Particle of Cause, will signifie *Corrupt, deprave.*

So in the Tables of *Substance,* Be. II. 1. the Radical is KINE, signifying the *Bovinum genus* ; the other words reduced to it are, *Bull, Cow, Ox, Calf, Heifer, Bullock, Steer, Beef, Veal, Runt, Bellow, Low, Heard, Cowheard,* Some of which are to be made off from this root by compositions with the Transcendental Particles.   SUBSTANCE.

So the Root Kine with the Transcendent. Part.
- Male. — Bull, Bullock, Steere.
- Female. — COW, Heifer, Steeres
- Young. — Calf.
- Voice. — Bellow, Low.
- Dimin. — Runt.
- Aggregate. — Heard.
- Officer. — Cowheard.

will signifie

The rest are to be made off by other Compositions : So *Ox* is untesticled or gelt Bull ; *Beef, Veal,* is the flesh of Kine or Calf.

Be. II. 2 The Radical is SHEEP ; to which are adjoyned the words, *Ram, Yew, Lamb, Weather, Mutton, Bleat, Fold, Flock, Shepheard.* Each of which words are to be made off from this radical, by some kind of compositions.

The word Sheep being compounded with the Transcend. Particle of
- Male. — Ram.
- Female. — Yew.
- Young. — Lamb.
- Voice. — Bleating.
- Sepiment. — Fold, Sheepfold.
- Aggregate. — Flock.
- Officer. — Shepheard.

will signifie

Gelt Ram is *Weather*, Flesh of Sheep is Mutton.

Mag. III. A. the Radical is FIGURE, to which these other words are annexed, viz. *Shape, Feature, Fashion, Form, Frame, Scheme, Lineament, the make, well set or proportioned, transform, transfigure, deface, disfigure.* Amongst which the former words, *Shape, Feature, Fashion, Form, Frame, Scheme, Lineament, the make,* are, according to one of those senses wherein each of them is commonly used, the more mediate *Synonyma*, the rest are to be made off by composition, either with   QUANTITY.

{Transcendental particles of the {Perfective, *well-set* or *proportioned.* word *change, transform, transfigure,* {Corruptive, *defaced, disfigured.*

Sp. I. 1. The Radical is PRESENT, to which is adjoyned, *at this time, now, immediately, instantly, current, ready.* The more immediate *synony-*

ma are, *This time* or *instant*. The words *Current, ready,* are Adjectives. *Now, immediately, instantly,* are the Adverbs of this root.

One of the Opposites to this Radical, is PAST, or *time past* ; to which these other words are put, *Expired, former, foregone, ago, already, even now, heretofore gone, over, out, a-late, erewhile, long since,* which are thus to be made off. The words *Expired, former, foregone, over, out,* are the Adjectives of this root. The words *already, heretofore, out,* are the Adverbs, which being compounded with the Transcendental Particle.

⎧ Augment. ⎫ will sig- ⎧ *A great while ago, long since.*
⎩ Dimin. ⎭ nifie. ⎩ *Even now, a-late, erewhile, a little while ago.*

The other Opposite is FUTURE, to which these words are adjoyned, *Time to come, after time, hereafter, presently, anon, by and by, shortly, straitway, ere long, henceforth, process of time, after a long while.* Amongst which these words or phrases, *Time to come, after time, process of time,* are Synonymous substantives. *Hereafter, henceforth,* are Adverbs, which being compounded with the Transcendental Particle of

⎧ Augment ⎫ will sig- ⎧ *After a long while.*
⎩ Diminut. ⎭ nifie ⎩ *Presently, by and by, anon, shortly, straitway, ere long.*

Sp. II. 3. is the Radical NEARNESS, to which these other words are added, *Vicinity, Propinquity, Proximity, nigh, next, close, adjacent, adjoyn, neighbouring, imminent, impendent, immediate, ready at hand, accost, draw on, approach, at, by, hard by, beside, hithermost.* Amongst which, the words *Vicinity, Propinquity, Proximity,* are Synonymous substantives. *Nigh, close, adjacent, adjoyning, neighbouring, imminent, impendent, immediate, next, hithermost,* are Adjectives. *By, hard by, at, at hand, besides,* are Adverbs. *Approach, accost, draw neer* or *on,* are Verbs.

So for the Opposite to this, REMOTENESS, to which are adjoyned the words, *farr, farther, aloof, wide of, distant, utmost, ultimate, great way off.* Amongst which the words, *far, farther, distant, utmost, ultimate,* are Adjectives. *Aloof, wide of, a great way off,* are Adverbs.

QUALITY. NP. II. 3. the radical word is MEMORY, to which these other words are adjoyned, *Recollect, recal, commemorate, remember, call* or *come to mind, put in mind, suggest, record, recount, con over, getting by heart, by rote, without book, at ones fingers ends, memorable, Memorial, Memorandum, mindful.* Amongst which the words, *Remember, commemorate, record, recount,* are Verbs, which being compounded with the Transc. Particle

⎧ Cause, will signifie *Suggest, put in mind,* or *cause to remember.*
⎨ Endea- ⎫ will sig- ⎧ For the present, *Recal, recollect, call to mind.*
⎩ vour. ⎭ nifie. ⎩ For the future, *Con over, get by heart, by rote,* &c.

Mindful is an Adject. Neut. *Memorable* is an Adj. Pass. Abstr. *Memorandum, Memorial,* is to be compounded with the Transcend. Part. Sign, denoting a Sign for remembrance.

NP. V. 9. the Radical is SWIFTNESS, to which these other words are adjoyned, *Fleetness, Celerity, speed, fast, apace, quick, sudden, rapid, hurry, accelerate, hasten, cursory, hye, expedite, run, scud, whisk, post.* Amongst which the words, *Fleetness, Celerity, Speed,* are Synonymous subst. *Quick, sudden, fast, rapid, expedite, cursory,* are Adj. *Apace, quickly -er,* are Adverbs. *Hye, hasten, run, post, hurry, scud, whisk,* are Verbs. *Accelerate, expedite,* as also *hasten, hurry,* when they denote a Transitive efficiency, are to be expressed by composition with the Transc. Particle of Cause or make.

So for the Opposite to this, SLOWNESS ; to which are adjoyned the

the words, *Heaviness, slackness, dull, slugg, tardy, leasurely, softly, dilatory, retard, foreslow, delay, Lob, Lubber, [...], Lurdan, torpid, unwieldy, gingerly.* The words, *Slackness, heaviness,* are Synonymous substantives. *Dull, sluggish, tardy, lumpish, torpid, unwieldy, dilatory,* are the Adjectives of this root; which being compounded with the Transc. partic. of Person, will be of the same signification with those other words, *Slugg, Lob, Lubber, Lurdan.*

The words, *Slowly, leasurely, softly, gingerly,* are the Adverbs of this Radical. *Retard, foreslow, delay,* are the Verbs.

So Man. I. O. the Radical word is VICE; to which these other words are reduced, *Sin, Crime, Dishonesty, Improbity, Trespass, Transgression, Fault, Failing, Infirmity, oversight, turpitude, unrighteous, unjust, vile, base, loose, evil, ill, bad, naught, corrupt, venial, wicked, heinous, debaucht, lewd, lawless, licentious, fowl, flagitious, enormous, Profligate, Miscreant, Ruffian, Caitiff, Villain, Rakehell, Libertine, defile, pollute,* which are thus to be made off from this root.

The words
Sin, Dishonesty, Improbity, are Subst. N.
Trespass, Transgression, are Substant. Ad. which Substantives being compounded with the Transcendental Particle.
⎰ Augment ⎱ will sig- ⎰ *Crime, Enormity, Turpitude.*
⎱ Dim ⎰ nifie ⎱ *Fault, Infirmity, Failing, Oversight.*
Evill, ill, bad, naught, corrupt, vicious, unrighteous, unjust, are the Adject. Neut. which being compounded with the Transcend. Particle, Augment. will be of the same importance with those other words, *Base, Foul, Lewd, Filthy, debauched, flagitious, Enormious, profligate, heinous, mortall.* If it be compounded with the Transcendental Particle *Dim.* it will signifie *Venial.* If with the Transc. Partic. for Person, it signifies, *Ruffian, Villain, Rake-bell, Libertine, Miscreant, Gaitiffe.*
Corrupt, defile, pollute, debauch, are the Verb compounded with the Transcendental Particle of *Cause,* or Make.

In the Tables of Action. AS. V. 4. O. The Radical is GRIEF; to ACTION; which are adjoyned the words, *Sadness, Sorrow, Melancholy, Heaviness, dolefull, deplorable, disconsolate, bitter, pensive, dejected, tragical, rufull, amort, moan, bemoan, wail, bewail, lament, dump, cast down, vex, trouble, Cutt, take on, whimper, pule, woe, agony, anguish, mourn, cry, take heavily.* Which are thus to be made off from the Root.

⎧ *Sadness, sorrow, Heaviness, Melancholy, Trouble,* are Synonymous Subst. which being compounded with the Transc. Particle Augmentative, will express those other words, *Anguish, woe, Agony.*

Pensive, sad, Heavy, Melancholy, sorrowfull, dejected, disconsolate, cast down, are Adjectives which being compounded as the former, will be of the same importance with those other words, *Dolefull, rufull, bitter, tragical;*

Deplorable, dolefull, may be the Adject. P. Abst.

Moan, bemoan, wail, bewail, lament, mourn, cry, plain, are the Verb of this Root, which in some Acceptions is to be compounded with the Transcendental Particle of Sign.

Take on, take heavily, ⎱ Verbs to be compounded with ⎰ *Augment.*
whimper, pule, whine, ⎰ the Transcendental Particle ⎱ *Dimin.*

Vex, Cut, cast down, are Verbs Active.

⎩ *Dump, all amort,* to be compounded with the Transc. Partic. Impetus.

AC. 1.

AC. I. 7. O. The Radical is DYING; to which these other words are adjoyned, *Death, deadly, mortall, fat*... *ye, decease, depart, expire, give up the ghost, defunct, kill, slay, mortifie, dispatch, slaughter, mortality, Capital*; which are thus to be made off.

Death is Subst. N. *Mortality* is Subst. N. Abst. *Slaughter* is the Subst. compounded with the Particle *Cause.*

Dead, defunct, is Adj N. *Deadly, fatall, mortall, capital,* is Adj. A. Abst.

Dye, decease, depart, expire, give up the Ghost, is the Verb; which being compounded with the Transcendental Particle *Cause* or *make*, will signifie to *Kill, slay, dispatch, mortifie.*

AC. III. 1. The Radical is SPEAKING; to which these words are adjoyned, *Talke, utter-ance, mention, Elocution, pronounce, express, deliver, Prolation, Spokesman, effable, voluble, fluent, say, tell, mutter, mumble, jabber, jargon, Vein, Grammar, Rhetoric, Oratory, Eloquence, Prolocutor, nuncupative, by word of mouth.*

Talking, Telling, Saying, Expressing, Delivering, Mentioning, are Substant. Synonymous to the Radical; which being compounded with the Transc. Particle of *Manner,* will denote the sense of those other words which denote a respect to the mode of speaking, viz. *Elocution, Pronunciation, Utterance, Vien* : And being compounded with the Particle Officer, it signifies, *Proloquutor.* If with the Particle Art, it may denote the several Acts of speaking. So the Art of speaking congruously is *Grammar*; ornately is *Rhetoric, Eloquence*; Perswadingly is *Oratory, Eloquence.* If with the Particle Corruptive, it may signifie, *Muttering, Mumbling, Jabber, Jargon.* The words *Fluency, Volubility,* are the Subst. Abst. Act. with the Particle Perfective. *Nuncupative-ly, by word of mouth,* are the Adj. and Adv. of this root. *Talk, tell, say, utter,* are the Verbs. *Spokesman,* is the pro, or *instead,* speaking person.

AC. III. 7. The Radical is WRITING; to which these other words are annexed, *Penning, Drawing, Engrossing, Hand, Manuscript, subscribe, superscribe, inscribe, transcribe, postscript, interline, indorse, scrawle, scrible, Penman, Scribe, Scrivener, Secretary, Clerk, Note, Ticket, Docket, Shorthand, Tachygraphy, Brachygraphy, Cryptography, set ones hand, set down, take or put in writing, enter into book.*

Which words are thus to be made off from this root. The words *Penning, drawing,* and the Phrases, *set ones hand, take* or *put in writing, enter into book,* are the more immediate *Synonyms* of the Radical. *Hand, Manuscript, draught,* are the Substantive Passive.

The Words			with the Transc. Partic.	
Scribe, Penman, Writer		Adj. Act.		Person
Secretary, Clerk, Scribe				Officer
Scrivener.				Mechanic
Note, Ticket, Docket		Adject. Pas.		Thing
Short-hand, Brachygraphy, Stenography		Subst.		Art of { Short, Speedy, Secret } W
Tachygraphy				
Cryptography				
Engross, write out fair		Verb		Perfective
Scrible, scrawl				Corruptive

Subscribe, superscribe, inscribe, &c. are the Verb, compounded with the Prepositions. *Sub, super, in,* &c.

Chap. XII. *Fore-going Table.* 295

In the Tables of Relation. RO. I. 2. The Radical is PARENT; to RELATION. which are adjoyned the words *Sire, Father, Mother, Damm, paternal, maternal, Grandsire*, &c. *Orphan*, which are thus to be expressed,

Sire, Father } are Parent { Male
Mother, Damm } { Female

Paternal, Maternal, are the Adjectives of Father, Mother; *Grandsire* is Fathers Father, or second Father; *Orphan* is un-parented.

So for the Opposite Radical CHILD; to which these other words are adjoyned, *Issue, Son, Daughter, Brood, Litter, filial, adopt, posthume*, which are thus to be expressed.

{ *Issue, Brood, Litter* } { Kind
{ *Son* } By composition with the { Male
{ *Daughter* } Transcendental Partic. { Female
{ *Adopt* } { Cause

Filial is the Adj. *Posthume* is a Child born after the Parents Death.
RC. I. 2. The Radical is KING; to which these words are adjoyned, *Soveraign, Emperor, Imperial, Monarch, Queen, regall, royal·ty, Majesty, Reign, Kingdom, Lord, Dynasty, Sultan, Cham, Liege Lord, Regent, Realm, Diadem, Crown, Coronation, Scepter, Throne, inthrone, Viceroy.*

Which are thus to be made off. The Radical being a Substantive of the Person, these other words must be Synonymous to it, viz. *Soveraign, Monarch, Emperor, Lord, Liege Lord, Sultan, Cham, Regent.* The word *Emperor* being sometimes used for such a one as hath other Kings under his Dominion, may according to this notion of it, be expressed by composition, with the Transc. Particle of Augmentative. *Queen* by the Particle Fœm. *Majesty, Royalty*, are Subst. Abst. *Regal, royal, Soveraign, Imperial*, are the Adject. N. *Realm, Kingdom*, are the Adj. Pass. with the Particle, Thing. The *Reign* is the Subst. Act. To *Reign* is the Verb. *Viceroy, Regent*, is Adj Act. with Transf. Part. Person and the Preposition *Pro*, or *instead*. *Crown, Diadem*, is Head-Sign of Majesty. *Scepter* is Staff-Sign of Majesty. *Throne* is Royal Seat. *Coronation, inthroning*, is solemnity of King-making, or King-declaring.

By these Instances, it may appear, what course is to be taken, with that great variey of Words, adjoyned to other Radicals.

§. IV.

The things and notions provided for in these Tables, are such only as are of a more *simple* nature; others that are of a more *mixed* and complicated signification, are to be expressed periphrastically, as may be seen in the Dictionary. Such words only, are absolutely necessary for such a design, as are *purely* simple; which if they could be acurately distinguished, would be much fewer then those here enumerated; But for the preventing of frequent and large periphrases, it may be convenient to take in some others that are not purely simple.

There are some kinds of things that are not capable of being provided for in a Character and Language, proposed for Universal use, as namely all such as are appropriated to particular *Places* or *Times*.

I. Such as are peculiar to some particular *place* or Nation, As

1. *Titles of Honour*, Duke, Marquess, Earl, Viscount, Baron, Baronet, Knight, Esquire, &c. Which are to be expressed by the several degrees which they belong to in the *Nobilitas Major*, or *Minor*.

2. *Titles of Office* and Place, as Sheriff, Maior, Bayliff, &c. Master, Warden,

Warden, President, Provost, Principal, Rector, &c. which are all to be expressed by the common notion of *Prefecture*.

3. *Degrees in Professions*, Doctor, Master, Bachelour, Serjeant at Law, Barrister, &c.

4. *Law Terms* of Tenures, Writ, &c. Copyhold, Freehold, Knights-service, &c. *Habeas corpus, nisi prius, Defeasance, Certiorari, Replevin, Supersedeas, Subpæna,* &c.

5. To which may be added the several *terms of Heraldry*, as Fess, Chevron, &c. which are not common to all Nations.

II. Such as are continually altering, according to several ages and *times*, As

1. *Vests and Garments*, to which there are every day new names assigned, according as several fashions do arise.

2. *Kinds of Stuffs*, as Baise, Flannel, Serge, Kersey, Grograin, Tammy, Tabby, Sattin, Plush, Velvet, Tiffany, Lawn, Douless, Canvas, Buckrom, &c. Diaper, Damask, &c. which are to be periphrastically expressed by their matter and figure.

3. *Games* and *Plays*, of which the old ones do continually grow into disuse, and every age produceth new kinds.

4. *Drinks*, The Wines of several Countries, and Grapes, as Malmsey Muskadell, &c. And so for other made Drink, as Tei, Coffi, Chocolate, Rambuze, Syllabub, &c.

5. *Meats*, as several prepared Dishes, Cullace, Bisk, Oglia, &c. The variety of Breads, Bisket, Cracknel, Bunn, Simnel, &c. Several confections, as Marmalade, Codigny, &c. Confections in Physick, as Diascordium, Mithridate, &c.

6. *Tunes* for Musick, or Dauncing, as Coranto, Galliard, Sarabrand, Jig, Pavan, Almain, &c. And so for the various kinds of Musical Instruments, Sackbut, Hauboy, Cornet, Lute, Theorbo, Viol, Cittern, &c.

7. The names of several *Tools* belonging to Trades, which are not the same in all Nations, and are every day multiplyed.

8. To which may be added the names of divers sects, whether Philosophical, Political, or Religious; which are various according to several places and Times, many of them being derived from the names of *Persons*, and therefore not to be provided for in such a Theory of things as is proposed for Universal use. But as any of these may be periphrastically expressed in the *Latin*, or in the Language of any other Nation, which has no one word for them; so may they likewise, with the same facility be described in a Philosophical Character or Language.

PART.

PART. III.

Concerning Natural Grammar.

CHAP. I.

1. *Concerning the several kinds and Parts of Grammar.* 2. *Of Etymology, the general Scheme of Integralls and Particles.* 3. *Of Nouns in general.* 4. *Of Substantives Common, denoting either Things, Actions, or Persons.* 5. *Rules concerning Nouns of Action.* 6. *Of Substantive abstracts.* 7. *Of Adjectives according to the true Philosophical notion of them.* 8. *The true notion of a Verb.* 9. *Of derived Adverbs.* 10. *A general Scheme of the fore-mentioned Derivations.*

§ I.

Having now dispatched the second thing proposed to be treated of, namely, the *Scientifical* part, containing a regular enumeration and description of such things and notions, as are to be known, and to which names are to be assigned, which may be stiled *Vniversal Philosophy*; I proceed in the next place to the *Organcial* part, or an enquiry after such kind of necessary helps, whereby as by instruments we must be assisted in the forming these more simple notions into complex Propositions and Discourses, which may be stiled *Grammar*, containing the Art of Words or Discourse.

Grammar may be distinguisht into two kinds; 1. *Natural*, and *General*; 2. *Instituted* and *Particular*.

1. *Natural* Grammar, (which may likewise be stiled Philosophical, Rational, and Universal) should contain all such Grounds and Rules, as do naturally and necessarily belong to the Philosophy of letters and speech in the *General*.

2. *Instituted* and *Particular* Grammar, doth deliver the rules which are proper and peculiar to any one Language in Particular; as about the Inflexion of words, and the Government of cases, &c. In the *Latin*, *Greek*, &c. and is defined by *Scaliger* to be *scientia loquendi ex usu*. De Causis L. L. Cap. 76.

The first of these only is upon this occasion to be considered. It hath been treated of but by few, which makes our Learned *Verulam* put it among his *Desiderata*; I do not know any more that have purposely written of it, but *Scotus* in his *Grammatica speculativa*, and *Caramuel* in his *Grammatica Audax*, and *Campanella* in his *Grammatica Philosophica*. (As for *Schioppius* his Grammar, of this title, that doth wholly concern the Latin tongue;) Besides which, something hath been occasionally spoken of it, by *Scaliger* in his book *de causis linguæ latinæ*; and by *Vossius* in his *Aristarchus*. But to me it seems, that all these Authors in some measure (though some more then others) were so far prejudiced by the common Theory of the languages they were acquainted with, that they did not sufficiently abstract their rules according

according to Nature. In which I do not hope, that this which is now to be delivered can be faultless; it being very hard, (if not impossible) wholly to escape such prejudices: yet I am apt to think it less erroneous in this respect then the rest.

The parts of Grammar are principally these three.

1. Concerning the *kinds of words*, or those several modes and respects, according to which the names of things may be varied in their Acceptions; being made either derivative *Nouns*, or *Adverbs*; together with their several *inflexions* and *compositions*; which may be stiled *Etymology*.

2. Concerning the *proper union* or right construction of these into *Propositions* or sentences; which is called *Syntax*.

3. Concerning the most convenient *marks* or *sounds* for the expression of such names or words; whether by *writing*, *Orthography*; or by *speech*, *Orthoepy*.

§ II. The first of these concerning the *Doctrine of Words*, may refer either, 1. To the *formal differences* or kinds of them; or, 2. To the *Accidental changes* of them, in respect of *Inflection*, *Derivation*, *Composition*.

Words, according to their *formal differences*, and kinds, may be thus distributed.

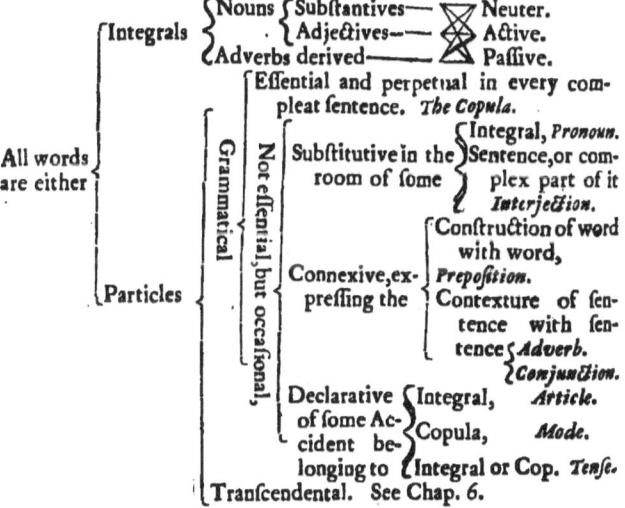

By *Integrals* or Principal words, I mean such as signifie some entire thing or notion: whether the *Ens* or Thing it self, or the *Essence* of a thing, as *Nouns Neuters*, whether concrete or abstract; or the Doing or Suffering of a thing as *Nouns Active* or *Passive*; or the manner and affection of it, as *Derived Adverbs*.

§ III. Those instituted words which men do agree upon for the names and appellations of things, are stiled *Nouns*. Every

Chap. I. *Concerning Natural Grammar.*

Every Noun which in conjunction with a Verb makes a compleat sentence, and signifies simply, and *per modum subsistentis per se*, is called a *Substantive*. That which signifies *per modum Adjuncti*, or *adjacentis alteri*, is called an *Adjective*.

Substantives belong either to one, called *Proper:* or to many, and are therefore styled *Common*.

The former of these are not to be brought under the rules of any science, because Individuals are Infinite; and therefore such *proper names* as pertain each to one only, should be esteemed as so many Articulate voices, to be expressed by such particular vowels and consonants as will make such respective sounds.

§ IV. Noun *Substantives Common* are such names as are assigned to the several kinds or species of things or notions; which, though they are very numerous, yet are they capable of being stated and fixed according to a Philosophical method, as is endeavoured in the fore-going Tables. Concerning which these rules are to be observed.

1. Every Radical word in the Tables is supposed to be a Substantive; though they could not all of them be so expressed, because of the defect of proper words for them in the present Languages; upon which account there is a necessity of expressing some of them by *Adjectives*, and some by an Aggregate of words: but they are all of them to be understood as being simple Substantives.

2. These Radical Substantives may be of various kinds, either 1. Of the *Thing*. 2. Of the *Action* or *Passion*. Or, 3. Of the *Person*, Besides those other kind of Substantives which proceed from these; whether *Abstracts Neuter*, as *Deity*, *Regality*, &c. or such other Abstracts, whether *Active* or *Passive*, as denote a proclivity or capacity, as *Amorousness*, *Amiableness*, &c. which are provided for by the Transcendental Particles.

3. When the Radical is a Noun Substantive of the *Thing*, the most immediate derivations from it, are the Substantives *Active* and *Passive*, to be expressed by the mark of Active or Passive upon the Radical. And the Substantive of the *person*, whether *Agent* or *Patient*, by the Adjective, Active or Passive in the Aorist Tense, with the Transcendental mark of *Person*; So *Dux* and *Calor*, *Light* and *Heat*, are Substantives of the *Thing*; *Illuminatio* and *Calefactio*, Enlightning, Heating, are the Substantives Active, or of the *Action*; *τὸ illuminari, calefieri*, the being Enlightned and Heated are Substantives Passive: or of the *Passion*; *Illuminator, Calefactor*, or *illuminans & calefaciens persona*, the Enlightner and Heater, are Substantives of the *Person* agent; *Illuminatus* and *Calefactus*, the Illuminated or Heated, are Substantives of the *Person* Patient.

4. When the Radical is a Substantive of the *Action*, then the Substantive of the *Person*, is to be expressed as in the former rule; so *Ligatio, Pastio, Salivatio*; Binding, Feeding, Spitting, are Substantives of the *Action*; *Ligator*, *Pastor*, *Salivator*; Binder, Feeder, Spitter, are Substantives of the Agent; and *Ligatus, Pastus, Salivatus*; Bound, Fed, Bespit, are the Substantives of the Patient. And the Substantive of the *Thing* whether Active or Passive, is in this case to be expressed, by the Adjective, Active or Passive in the Aorist Tense, with the Transcendental

scendental mark of *Thing*. So *Ligans res*, a binding thing, is *Ligamentum*, a Bond or String; and *nutriens* or *pascens res*, a nourishing or feeding thing, is *nutrimentum*, food or nourishment; so *ligata res*, a bound thing, is *Ligatum*, a Bundle or Fardle; so *excreta* or *salivata res*, is *Excrementum*, or *Saliva*, Excrement or Spittle.

5. When the Radical is a Substantive of the *Person*, then the Substantive of the Action or Passion (as was said before) are the most immediate derivations from it, and to be expressed by the Mark of Active or Passive upon the Radical; So *Magistratus, Rex, Judex*, &c. *Magistrate, King, Judge*, &c. are Radicals of the Person; The Substantives of Action belonging to each of these, are *Gubernatio, Regnatio, Judicatio, Governing, Reigning, Judging*; And the Substantive of the *Thing* whether *Active* or *Passive*, is to be expressed by the Adjective Active or Passive in the Aorist Tense, with the Transcendental note of *Thing*; So *Gubernans res* a governing thing; *regens res* a reigning thing; and *judicans res* a judging thing, *viz.* A Canon or Rule by which we judge of streight and crooked, right and wrong; So *Gubernata res*, the governed thing, is *Ditio*, Territory, Dominion, Jurisdiction; *Regnata res*, is *Regnum* the Kingdom; *Judicata* res, is *Judicium*, Judgment.

As those names which are assigned to signifie things themselves, and do not denote either Action or Passion, are stiled *Nouns neuter*: so those names which are assigned to signifie the Doing or Suffering of things are stiled *Active* or *Passive*. The same notion which in the *Greek* and *Latin* is expressed by the *Infinitive Mode* Active or Passive, is that which I here intend by the Substantive Active or Passive; and that it may properly be so stiled, I shall endeavour to prove afterwards.

Though every Noun Substantive have not an Active or Passive belonging to it either in the *Greek, Latin, English*, &c. yet according to the Nature and Philosophy of things, whatsoever hath an *Essence*, must likewise have an *Act*; either of *Being* or *becoming*: or of *Doing* or *being done*: or of *making* or *being made*: to *be*, or *do*. And consequently every Radical Substantive which is capable of Action, should have an Active or Passive formed from it, which is commonly called a *Verb*.

As for such things which have not of their own any proper Act of *Doing*, they are not capable of the derivation of Active and Passive, *ob defectum materiæ*; as in the words Stone, Mettle, &c. But the Verbs belonging to such Radicals can be only *Neuter*, denoting the Act of Being or becoming; unless when they are compounded with the Transcendental mark of *Causatio*, which will adde to them a Transitive sense, as Petrifie, Metallifie, &c.

§ V. As for such other Radicals as are capable of Action or Passion, these Rules are to be observed concerning them.

1. More *Generally* these two.

1. Things which according to common acception have belonging to them any one *proper Act of Doing*; their Verbs Actives will denote this Act: For instance, the Verb or Substantive Active of the words *Fire, Water*, &c. is to burn, wet; and so for those Acts of the several parts, *Tongue, Tooth, Mouth, Throat, Foot, Heel*, whose active by this

Rule

Chap. I. *Concerning Natural Grammar.*

Rule will be to *lick, bite, devour, swallow, trample, kick*, and the Active of *Bow, Gun*, is to *shoot* as with a Bow, Gun.

2. Things which have not, according to common acception, any one kind of peculiar Act of Doing appropriate to them; the Actives belonging to such things, will signifie in the General to Act or do according to the nature of such things.

2. More *Particularly* these four.

1. The Actives belonging to such Radicals as are *Substances*, whether Absolute or Relative, do signifie to Act according to the nature of such Substances; so in *absolute* Substances, the Active of *God, Spirit, Man*, will signifie to Act as God, Spirit, Man; and so in *Relative* Substances, the Active of *Father, Judge, Magistrate*, is to Act as a Father, Judge, Magistrate.

2. The Actives of *Quality*, whether Predicamental or Transcendental, do denote the Acts of those *species*, with particular reference to the *differences* under which they are placed; So the Active of *East, West, Obliquity*, &c. being under the difference of *Situation*, must signifie to situate a thing *Easterly, Westerly, Obliquely*. The words of *Line, Surface, Body*, being under the difference of *Dimension*; the Active belonging to them must signifie to Dimensionate as either of these.

The words under the differences of *Figure*, must in their Actives signifie to Figure according to such particular shapes.

Those under the difference of *Time*, the Actives of *Present, Simultaneous, Newness, Oldness, Sooness*, &c. must signifie to Act with such respects of Time.

The Actives of the Differences and Species under *Measure*, should regularly signifie to Measure by *Number, Magnitude, Gravity, Valour, Duration*. The Active of *Inch, Foot, Pace, Fathom*, is to Measure by Inch, Foot, &c. and so for those other Species of *Grane, Drachm*, &c. *Farthing, Penny*, &c.

The Active of *Minute, Hour, Day, Night*, &c. will signifie to continue for such portions or measures of time, according to the sense of the Difference, *Duration*, under which these species are placed.

The Active of *Infancy, Childhood, Adolescency*, &c. may signifie to pass the time of one's Infancy, Childhood, Adolescency, &c.

3. The Active of such Radicals as are *Qualities*, whether Predicamental or Transcendental, signifie to do or deal according to the signification of the said qualities; So the Active of *Fidelity, Severity*, &c. will signifie to deal or Act, *Faithfully, Severely*, &c. The Active of *Goodness, Evilness*, &c. will signifie to Act or Do well or ill, &c.

4. The Active of such Radicals as denote *Actions*, need no other explication but this, that some of them are Active *Absolute*, which in the usual Grammars are stiled *Neuter*; as *Sto, Sedeo, Curro*; others *Transitive*, denoting a transient efficiency; into which latter kind, the former of these may be changed (as was said before) by composition with the Transcendental mark of *Causation*.

There are several English Verbs, which, without admitting any change by Composition or Inflexion, have both a Neuter and a Transitive signification; as *Corrupt, Feed, Starve, Famish, Move, Rest, Hang, Extend, Shrink, Stagger, Stay*, &c. whose sense is to be distinguisht by the construction.

There

There are some Verbs of the same Natural Philosophical Radix, which are yet expressed by different words, as *Laugh, Deride, Weep, Bemoan, must, need, Necessitate,* &c. And the different notion of these and such like Verbs, is not capable of being expressed by the Transcendental point of *causation*: but by placing after them such a Noun Substantive, or Pronoun Substantive, as may denote the object of those several acts. So the word *Laugh*, being put without any Substantive following, doth signifie in the *Neuter* sense the bare act of Laughing; but if the word me or him, &c. doth immediately follow the Verb, then it is to be rendered *deride* or *laugh* at, me, him, &c.

§ VI. Besides those *Concrete* Substantives, which signifie the *Ens* or thing it self, there are other Substantives which denote the *Essence* of things, stiled *Abstracts*. And these may likewise be distinguished into, *Neuter, Active, Passive*.

That is stiled *Neuter* which denotes the naked Essence of a thing, without any inclination to Action or Passion, as *Deity, Regality*.

That is stiled an Abstract *Active*, which implies a proclivity to Action, as *Regnativity, Amativeness*, or *Amorousness*.

That is called *Passive*, which denotes a capacity or fitness for receiving or suffering of Action, as *Regibility, Amiableness*.

Such Radicals as are *Concretes*, are capable (according to the nature of the things denoted by them) to have all these three kinds of Abstracts formed from them. Whereas such Radicals, as are themselves *Abstracts* Neuter, (as namely several of those under the *Genus*'s and Differences of *Quality* and *Action*) are capable only of the two latter kinds to be formed from them.

§ VII. As Noun *Substantives* are the names which are given to things, considered simply, and as *subsisting by themselves*: So Noun *Adjectives* are the names which are given to the *Adjunct natures* of things, the notion of them consisting in this, that they signifie, the subject or thing to which they are ascribed, to have in it something belonging to the nature or quality of those *Adjectives*, which are predicated of it, or limited by it.

And besides this common notion, they do sometimes likewise in the instituted Languages refer to other notions; as, 1. To *aboundance*, so the words populous, pretious, sumptuous, &c. so in *Latin, fluvius piscosus, aquosa regio*. 2. To *likeness*, so the word dogged, currish, waspish, *Seraphicus, Angelicus*, &c. 3. To Possession, so *Domus regia*, a royal house. 4. To the *matter* of which any thing doth consist; so *scutum aheneum*, A brazen shield. But each of these notions may be otherwise more distinctly provided for. The two first by the Transcendental marks of *Augmentative* and *Like*; and the two next by the prepositions of *Possessor* and *Material cause*. And so the true genuine sense of a Noun Adjective will be fixed to consist in this, that it imports this general notion of *Pertaining to*, or *being Affected with*.

Those Adjectives are stiled *Neuters* which do not denote either Action or Passion; as *Calidus, Lucidus*, Hot, Light.

Those are stiled *Active* or *Passive*, which denote the Action or Passion of the Adjunct thing or Essence. And because these according to

the

the common Theory do Participate both of Noun and Verb; therefore are they by Grammarians stiled *Participles*; Active, as *Calefaciens, Illuminans*, Heating, Enlightning: or Passive, *Calefactus, Illuminatus*, Heated, Illuminated.

And as Abstract Substantives, may be formed from the Concrete; so likewise may Adjectives, which are also distinguishable into Neuters Active, Passive.

§ VIII.

That part of speech, which by our Common Grammarians is stiled a *Verb*, (whether Neuter, Active or Passive) ought to have no distinct place amongst Integrals in a Philosophical Grammar; because it is really no other then an *Adjective*, and the *Copula sum* affixed to it or conteined in it: So *Caleo, Calefacio,* ⎰ *Calidus.* Concerning which *Copula, Calefio*, is the same with *sum* ⎱ *Calefaciens.* and the use of it; more ⎱ *Calefactus*. shall be said hereafter.

§ IX.

That kind of word, which is commonly adjoyned to a Verb, to signifie the quality and affection of the Action or Passion, is stiled an *Adverb*; which may be distinguished into *Derived* and *Underived*. The former of these is here particularly intended, and doth generally belong to Languages. The latter is afterwards treated of amongst the Particles.

As every Radical is supposed naturally to have its *Adjective*, so likewise its *Adverb*; and though no Language in use doth admit of so general a derivation of Adverbs, yet the true reason of this is from their imperfection and deficiency; for the Signs ought always to be adequate unto the things or notions to be signified by them.

As *Adjectives* were before distinguished into *Neuter, Active, Passive*, so likewise ought *Adverbs* to be. And as every Adverb is immediately derived from some Adjective, so every kind of Adjective hath some kind of Adverb derived from it.

For the more easie understanding of these things, I shall here adjoyn a general Scheme of the fore-mentioned derivations; wherein I shall be necessitated to form several new words according to common analogy.

§ X.

All Integrals are either.
⎧ Concrete.
⎪ ⎧ Substantive.
⎪ ⎪ ⎰ Neuters. *τὸ calere vel calor. Lucere vel lux.* ⎱ Heat. Light.
⎪ ⎪ ⎨ Active. *Calefactio. A. Illuminatio.* ⎬ Heating. Enlightning.
⎪ ⎪ ⎱ Passive. *Calefactio. P. Illuminari.* ⎰ Being Heated. Enlightned.
⎪ ⎨ Adjective.
⎪ ⎪ ⎰ Neuter. *Calidus. Lucidus.* ⎱ Hot. Light.
⎪ ⎪ ⎨ Active. *Calefaciens. Illuminans.* ⎬ Heating. Enlightning.
⎪ ⎪ ⎱ Passive. *Calefactus. Illuminatus.* ⎰ Heated. Enlightned.
⎪ ⎩ Adverb.
⎪   ⎰ Neuter. *Calidè. Lucidè.* ⎱ Hotly. Lightly.
⎪   ⎨ Active. *Calefacienter. Illuminanter.* ⎬ Heatingly. Illuminatingly.
⎪   ⎱ Passive. *Calefactè. Illuminatè.* ⎰ Heatedly. Illuminatedly.
⎩ Abstract.

Sub-

	Subſtantive.		
	Neuter. *Caloritas. Luciditas.*	⎱	Hotneſs. Lightneſs.
	Active. *Calefactivitas. Illuminativitas.*	⎬	Calefactivity. Illuminativity.
	Paſſive. *Calefactibilitas. Illuminabilitas.*	⎰	Calefactibility. Illuminability.
	Adjective.		
	Neuter. *Caloritativus. Luciditativus.*	⎱	Caloritative. Luciditative.
	Active. *Calefactivus. Illuminativus.*	⎬	Calefactive. Illuminative.
	Paſſive. *Calefactibilis. Illuminabilis.*	⎰	Calefactible. Illuminable.
	Adverb.		
	Neuter. *Caloritativè. Luciditativè.*	⎱	Caloritatively. Luciditatively.
	Active. *Calefactivè. Illuminativè.*	⎬	Calefactively. Illuminatively.
	Paſſive. *Calefactibiliter. Illuminabiliter.*	⎰	Calefactibly. Illuminably.

CHAP. II.

1. *Of Particles in general.* 2. *Of the Copula.* 3. *Of Pronouns more generally.* 4. *More Particularly.* 5. *Of Interjections more generally.* 6. *More Particularly.*

§ I. HAving thus explained what is meant by *Integral* words, which ſignifie entire things and notions, with the ſeveral kinds of them. I proceed in the next place to treat, concerning *Particles*, or leſs principal words, which may be ſaid to conſignifie, ſerving to circumſtantiate and modifie thoſe *Integral* words, with which they are joyned, being ſtiled by the Hebrew Grammarians *Dictiones*.

The words of this kind are exceeding numerous and equivocal in all Languages, and add much to the difficulty of learning them. It being a very hard matter to eſtabliſh the juſt number, of ſuch as in all kinds are neceſſary, and to fix to them their proper ſignifications, which yet ought to be done in a Philoſophical Grammar. I ſhall in this Eſſay, ſelect out of Inſtituted Languages, ſuch of the ſeveral ſorts, as I conceive ſufficient for this purpoſe.

Theſe were before diſtinguiſhed, into ſuch as refer, either to *Grammatical*, or *Tranſcendental* notion.

Thoſe are ſtiled *Grammatical*, which ſuppoſing words to retain their primary ſenſe, do ſerve for the circumſtantiating of them, either by union, abbreviation, inflexion, or ſome other way for the qualifying of their ſignifications or conſtructions.

§ II. The moſt neceſſary amongſt all the reſt, which is eſſential and perpetual in every compleat ſentence, is ſtiled the *Copula*; which ſerves for the uniting of the Subject and Predicate in every Propoſition. The word *Subject* I uſe, as the Logicians do, for all that which goes before the *Copula*; which if it conſiſt of only one word, then it is the ſame which Grammarians call the *Nominative caſe*. By the word *Predicate*, I mean likewiſe all that which follows the Copula in the ſame ſentence, whereof the Adjective (if any ſuch there be) immediately next after the Copula, is commonly incorporated with it in inſtituted Languages, and both together make up that which Grammarians call a *Verb*.

Amongſt

Chap. II.   *Concerning Natural Grammar.*

Amongst those Particles which are not essential and perpetual, but used according to occasion, some are stiled *Substitutive*; because they supply the room either, 1. Of some *Integral* word, as *Pronouns*, or 2. Of some *Sentence* or complex part of it, as *Interjections*.

As Nouns are notes or signs of *things*; so Pronouns are of Nouns; and are therefore called *Pronomina, quasi vice Nominum,* as being placed commonly instead of Nouns. They represent things either

§ III.
Jul. Scalig. de caus. L. L Cap. 127.

1. *Immediately* and in kind, without respect to the names of those things. So when its said, I exhort thee or him : The Pronoun I represent to our thoughts the person speaking, suppose *John*; and the words thee, him, the person spoken to or of, suppose *William* or *Thomas*.

2. *Mediately* by their names, which are either

  1. *Exprest with the Pronoun,* as commonly it happens upon the first intimation or mention of the thing; as *this* or *that* man or book, and in these cases the Pronouns are commonly called *Demonstrative*.

  2. *Supplyed by the Pronouns,* as is usual for Brevities sake, at the repeating of the mention of a thing lately before spoken of; as *he*, *it*, &c. and then the Pronoun is called *Relative*. Examples of both sorts are to be had in the Grammars of Instituted Languages.

More commodiously for our purpose, the Pronouns are to be considered either according to their, 1. *Number*. 2. *Modifications*.

1. As to their *Number*; there are twelve which may be stiled *simple* Pronouns, and three other that are *Compound*.

The Simple Pronouns, for the better convenience of and complyance with the Characters, are reduced into these three combinations; whereof the first and last combinations are single, the other double.

{ I. }	{ This.	That. }	{ Any one. }
{ Thou. }	{ Same.	Another. }	{ Every one. }
{ He. }	{ Certain one.	Some one. }	{ All. }

Of all which it is to be observed, that they are in some kind or other, *Quantitatives*; that is to say, every one of these Pronouns makes the whole Proposition, or at least that part of the Proposition, which is affected with it, according to its own nature, to be either Singular, Indefinite, Particular or Universal.

2. The *Modifications* of Pronouns, whereby they are varied into different significations, are of two kinds.

1. *Possessive,* denoting a relation of Propriety or Possession unto the person or thing spoken of, which is applicable to all Pronouns, as I, Mine; Who, Whose, &c.

2. *Reduplicative,* denoting a particular Emphasis, *whereby* a word is raised and intended in its signification; as I my self, Thou thy self, &c.

Moreover it is to be observ'd, that the Personal Pronouns, and any of the rest being us'd Substantively, are capable of Number and Case; and that all other Pronouns beside the Personal, are capable of Composition with the Transcendentals of Person and Thing, of Place, Time and Manner.

All these Pronouns I have thought fit to represent more largely under four combinations in these following Tables.

R r   The

§ IV. The first Combination of Pronouns denoting the three Persons are *Substantives*, and for their Quantity *singular*, and cannot properly represent any other then Individual beings. I have here adjoyned to them their plurals, for the sake of their Possessives ; *ours, yours, theirs*, which without them cannot be so conveniently expressed.

	Sing. Numb.	Plur. Numb.	
Ego me.	1. *I.* me	We, us.	*Nos.*
Meus.	Poss. My, Mine.	Ours	*Noster.*
Egomet.	Redup. Even I. I my self.	We our selves.	*Nos ipsi, nosmet.*
Ego ipse.	Poss. Red. my own.	Our own.	
Tu te.	I. 2. *THOU.* Thee.	Yee, you.	*Vos.*
Tuus.	P. Thy. Thine.	Yours.	*Vester.*
Tu ipse, temet.	R. Thy self, even thou.	Your selves.	*Vos ipsi, vosmet.*
	P. R. Thy own.	Your own.	
Ille, iste.	3. *HE.* Him. She. Her.	They, them, those.	*Illi.*
Suus, ejus.	P. His. Hers.	Theirs.	*Suus, eorum.*
Ipse, se.	R. He himself, even he.	They themselves. *Illi ipsi, sfee.*	
	P. R. His own, her own.	Their own.	

The second Combination of Pronouns as likewise the rest that follow, are properly *Adjectives*, though by reason of *Ellipsis* they are sometimes used Substantively. The three first of them, *this, that, the same*, are for their Quantities *singulars*, and do denote several relations of *Identity*; The three last, viz. *Another, A certain one, Some one*, are for their Quantities, *singulars* or *Particulars indeterminate*. The first of them implies the Relation of *Diversity*.

Hic.	1. *THIS.*	*THAT.*	*Ille, is, iste.*
Hujus.	P. Belonging to this ⎫ Person.	Belonging to that, it.	*Illius.*
Hic ipse.	R. This very P. T. ⎭ Thing.	That very.	*Ille, ipse.*
Hìc.	Pl. Here.	There.	*Illic, ibi, istic*
Nunc.	T. Now.	Then.	*Tunc.*
Hujusmodi.	M. This manner	That manner.	*Istiusmodi.*
Idem.	II. 2. *THE SAME.*	*ANOTHER*, other, else.	*Alius.*
Ejusdem.	P. Belonging to the same.	Anothers.	*Alterius.*
	R. Self-same.	Wholy or quite ano-	
Ibidem.	Pl.	Elsewhere. (ther.	*Alibi.*
	T.	Otherwhile.	*Alias.*
	M.	Otherwise.	*Aliter.*
Quidam.	3. *A CERTAIN.*	*SOME.*	*Aliquis.*
	P. Belonging to a certain P.T.	Somebodies.	
	P. L. A certain place.	Somewhere.	*Alicubi.*
	T. A certain time.	Some time.	*Aliquando.*
	M. A certain manner.	Some manner.	*Quodammodo.*
		Some wise.	

The

Chap. II. *Concerning Natural Grammar.*

The third Combination of Pronouns are

General or Particular indefinite;

Ullus.   1. *A NT*, ought, ever a.
     P. Any ones, any bodies.
Ullibi, usquam.   Pl. Any where.
Unquam.   T. Any time.
Ullo modo.   M. Any manner.

III. *General distributive;*

Unusquisq;   2. *EVERY ONE.*
     P. Every ones, belonging to, or concerning every one, *Person, Thing.*
     Pl. Every where.
     T. Every time.
     M. Every manner.

General Collective;

Omnis.   3. *ALL.*
     P. Belonging to all, *Persons, Things.*
Ubiq;   Pl. All places.
Semper.   T. Always, all times.
Omnimodo.   M. All manner of ways.

The fourth and last Combination is of the *mixed* or compound Pronouns; so styled, because they are made up of some of the other Pronouns, compounded with the three first and most simple of the *Conjunctions.* The first of them *Quis? WHO?* is the Pronoun *All*, taken in pieces, with an interrogation; For he that enquires who did this, means, doubting of all, did such a one? or such a one? &c. of all them that were capable to do it: but he that doubts only of one, enquires, did he do this? where *Quis* is plainly resolved into a Pronoun incorporated with a *Conjunction Interrogative.* And as for the second of these, *Qui* it is commonly translated *And he.* And the third *Whosoever* is the same as *If any one.* They may be distinguished into,

IV.

1. *Interrogative;*
WHO? which? what?   *Quis?*
P. Whose?   *Cujus?*
Pl. Where?   *Ubi?*
T. When?   *Quando?*
M. How?   *Quomodo?*

2. *Relative;*
WHO, which, that.   *Qui.*
P. Whose.   *Cujus.*
Pl. Where.   *Ubi.*
T. When.   *Quando.*
M. After which manner.   *Quomodo.*

3. *Reduplicative;*
WHOSOEVER, whomsoever, whichsoever, whatsoever.   *Quisquis, Quicunq;*
P. Whosesoever.   *Cujuscunq;*
Pl. Wheresoever   *Ubicunq;*
T. Whensoever.   *Quandocunq;*
M. Howsoever, after what manner soever.   *Quomodo cunq;*

And thus much may serve for stating the number, nature, signification and use of this second kind of Grammatical Particle stiled *Pronoun*.

§ V. Those Substitutive Particles, which serve to supply the room of some sentence or complex part of it, are stiled *Interjections*. These are by some denyed to be words, or any part of distinct speech, but only natural signs of our mental notions, or passions, expressed by such rude incondite sounds, several of which are common with us to Brute Creatures. And as all Nations of men do agree in these kind of natural passions, so likewise do they very much agree in the signs or indications of their *mirth*, *sorrow*, *love*, *hatred*, &c.

Scalig. L. L. Cap. 13.
These kind of Particles are generally expressed by aspirated sounds, *affectum enim notant, & ideo confertus editur spiritus*, because of that affection and vehemence, which is commonly denoted by them.

The kinds of these may be very numerous, according to the various motions and passions of the mind; but those that are of the most frequent and general use, may be reduced under these three combinations, whereof the first only is single, the other two double.

§ VI. The two first Combinations may be stiled *Solitary* and *Passive*, being used by us when we are alone, or not so directly tending to discourse with others, in which the Party speaks as suffering some mutation in himself. They are the result, either of a *surprized*.

I. {
1. *Judgment*, denoting either
  1. *Admiration*. Heigh.
  2. *Doubting* or considering. Hem, Hm, Hy.
  3. *Despising*. Pish, Shy, Tysh.
Affection; moved by the Apprehension of *Good* or *Evil*.
}

II. {
Past;
  1. { *Mirth*. Ha, ha, he.
       Sorrow. Hoi, oh, oh, ah.
Present;
  2. { *Love*, and pity, Ah, alack, alas.
       Hate, and anger, vauh, hau.
Future;
}

Utinam, ò si.
  3. { *Desire*, O, o that.
       Aversation, Phy.

The last Combination may be stiled *Social* and *Active*, being never used by us when we are alone, but immediately tending to discourse with others, in which the party speaks with design to procure some mutation in his Hearers. These may be distinguished into such as are

III. {
Precedaneous to discourse.
  1. { *Exclaiming*. Oh, Soho.
       Silencing. St, Hush.
Beginning of discourse.
  2. { *General*; to dispose the senses of the Hearer.
       { *Bespeaking attention*. Ho, Oh.
         Expressing attention. Ha.
Special; to dispose the Affections of the Hearer by way of
  3. { *Insinuation* or blandishment. Eia, Now.
       Threatning. Væ, Wo.
}

CHAP.

CHAP. III.

§ I. *Of Prepositions in General.* § II. *The particular kinds of them.* § III. *Explication of the four last Combinations of them, relating to* Place, *or* Time.

THose are ſtiled *Connexive* Particles, whoſe proper uſe is to ex- § I.
preſs, either 1. The *Conſtruction of word with word* called *Pre-*
poſition; or 2. The *Contexture of ſentence with ſentence*, called *Adverb*
and *Conjunction*.

Prepoſitions are ſuch Particles, whoſe proper office it is to joyn Integral with Integral on the ſame ſide of the *Copula* ; ſignifying ſome reſpect of *Cauſe, Place, Time*, or other circumſtance either Poſitively or Privatively. Theſe having ſuch a ſubſerviency to Nouns, in reſpect of which, they are by ſome ſtiled *Adnomia*, or *Adnomina* and *Prænomina*, as Adverbs have to Verbs. They are therefore here treated of before Adverbs, whoſe office is chiefly to wait upon Verbs.

There are thirty ſix Prepoſitions or eighteen paires of them, or ſix Combinations, which may, with much leſs equivocalneſs then is found in inſtituted Languages, ſuffice to expreſs thoſe various reſpects, which are to be ſignifyed by the kind of Particle.

The two firſt Combinations of Prepoſitions, do comprehend ſuch § II.
as are uſed to expreſs *Cauſality*, and may be ſtiled *Cauſal*.
The firſt Combination of *Cauſal* Prepoſitions are either,

I. {
  More *General*, denoting either *the Author, Subject, or Poſſeſſor* of any thing; expreſſed in the Latin by the *Genitive* caſe: or the *Formal*, or *Inſtrumental cauſe*, or *Manner of doing*, expreſſed in the Latin by the *Ablative* caſe : Neither of them having any Particle in that Language appointed for them.
  1. { *O F*   Caſ. Gen.
       W I T H, By   Caſ. Abl.
  More *Particular*; denoting either
    The *Efficient*, or the *Final* cauſe.
  2. { *B Y*   Ab. a per.
       F O R   Ob, pro, propter.
    The *Material* cauſe, *ex qua*, or *circa quam*.
  3. { *O U T O F*   Ex, è.
       C O N C E R N I N G, upon.   De, circa.
}

The ſecond Combination of Cauſal Prepoſitions doth contain ſuch as do relate either to the notion of

II. {
  Ideal and *exemplary*, or *Subſtitutive*
  1. { *A C C O R D I N G T O*   Juſter, ſecundum.
       I N S T E A D   Pro, vice.
  Social or circumſtance of ſociety; *Affirmed*, or *Denyed*.
  2. { *W I T H*   Cum,
       W I T H O U T, void of   Sine, abſq;
  Adjuvant and agreement with: or *oppoſing* and enmity againſt
}

FOR

Pro, Contra.	3. { *FOR, on this side.* { *AGAINST, opposite unto.*

The rest of the Prepositions do primarily refer to *Place* and *Situation*; Secondarily to time; And some of them, by way of Analogy, to *Comparison*. Some of these are *Absolutely determined*, either *to Motion*, or *to Rest*, or the *Terminus of motion*. Others are *relatively applicable to both*; Concerning which this rule is to be observed. That those which belong to motion, cannot signifie rest: But those which belong to rest, may likewise signifie motion in the *Terminus*.

The third Combination doth consist of such as respect *space in general* being either

		Absolutely determined to
		Motion; either || of *Coming*, or *Going*
Ad. A.		1. { *TO* { *FROM*
	III.	*Rest*; or the *Terms* of this motions, denoting either; *Nearness* and contiguity: ro *Distance*
Apud. Procul.		2. { *AT* { *OFF*
		Relative both to motion and rest, with respect to the *Intermediate space* betwixt those Terms, either || *Direct*, or *Indirect*.
Trans. Circum.		3. { *OVER* { *ABOUT*

The fourth Combination doth consist of such Prepositions, as respect *Space*, with a particular restriction to the notion of *Containing*, being either

		Absolutely determined to
		Motion; whether of || *Ingress*, or *Egress*
In. Ex.		1. { *INTO* { *OUT OF*
	IV.	*Rest* or the *Terms* of these Motions.
Intra. Extra.		2. { *WITHIN* { *WITHOUT*
		Relative both to Motion and Rest, with respect to the *Intermediate space* either || *Direct* or *Indirect*.
Per. Præter.		4. { *THOROUGH* { *BESIDE*

The fifth Combination doth contain such Prepositions as relate to the *Imaginary parts of a thing*, whether the

		Head or *Feet*, being absolutely determined to
		Motion; either || *Ascent* or *Descent*,
Sursum. Deorsum.		1. { *UPWARDS* { *DOWNWARDS*
	V.	*Rest* or the *Terms* of these motions,
Supra. Infra.		2. { *ABOVE* { *BELOW*
		Face or *Back*, being *Relative* both to Motion and Rest.
Ante. Post.		3. { *BEFORE* { *AFTER*

The sixth Combination doth comprehend such Prepositions as are applicable both to Motion and Rest, relating to the situation of some

Chap. III. Concerning Natural Grammar. 311

some *third thing* spoken of, which the Speaker considers as being

VI.
- *Higher* or *Lower* then that third thing, denoting a contiguity or nearness to it
  1. { *UPON* — Super.
     { *UNDER* — Sub.
- *Nearer* to it, or *Farther* from it
  2. { *ON THIS SIDE* — Citra.
     { *BEYOND* — Ultra.
- In the *intermediate* space unto two other things, or *opposite* to one of them.
  3. { *BETWIXT, between* — Inter
     { *AGAINST, over against.* — Adversùs.

§ III. For the clearer explication of these *Local Prepositions*, I shall refer to this following Diagram. In which by the *Oval Figures* are represented the *Prepositions determined to Motion*, wherein the Acuter part doth point out the tendency of that motion. The *squares* are intended to signifie *rest* or the *Term* of *Motion*. And by the *round figures* are represented such *relative* Prepositions, as may indifferently refer either to *Motion* or *Rest*.

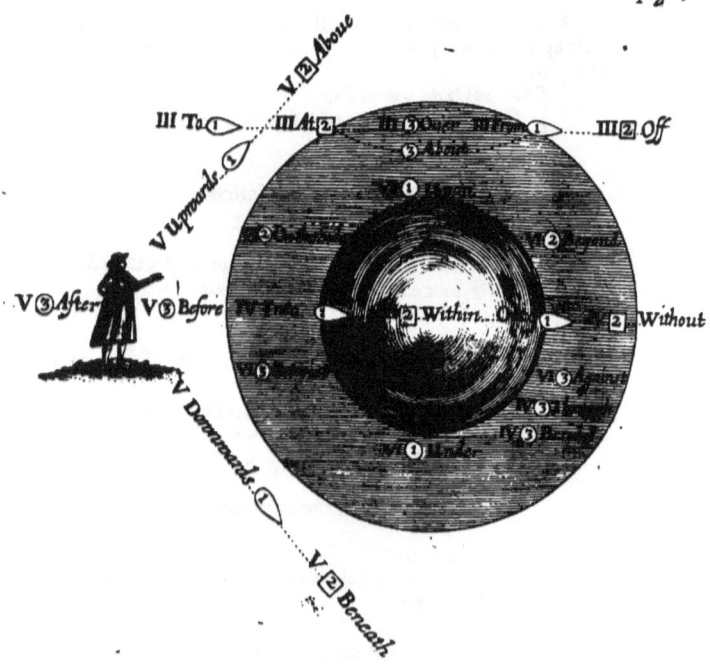

pag. 311.

Some of these Prepositions, *viz. Above, Below, Before, After,* are by common Analogy applicable to signifie *comparison,* which use being generally received, and the words having in them a natural sutableness to this purpose, there is no danger of any ambiguity.

Several of the Prepositions are sometimes used Adverbially, as *Ante, Post, Præter, Contra, Inter, Infra,* &c. which use when it happens, the sense will easily distinguish. The difference between these two parts of speech, *Prepositions* and *Adverbs,* being so nice, that 'tis hard in some cases to distinguish them; upon which 'tis questioned, whether every Preposition as it compounds a Verb, do not put on the nature of an Adverb; and it seems to be so, because it Modifies the Act after the same manner as Adverbs do, as in the words *Præficio, Benefacio,* &c.

CHAP. IV.

I. *Of Adverbs in General.* II. *The Particular kinds of them.* III. *Of Conjunctions.*

§ I.
Chap. 1.
Sect. 8.

THose two kinds of Connexive Particles which serve for the contexture of sentence with sentence, are called *Adverbs* and *Conjunctions.* The first of these are commonly described to be such kind of words as are for the most part adjoyned to Verbs to signifie some kind of Mode or Circumstance, belonging either intrinsecally or extrinsecally to them.

Of *Adverbs derived* from Integrals, enough hath been said in the Chapter of Integrals. The rest of those words which are commonly called *Adverbs,* according to their true Original, are either derived from [a] *Pronouns,* or else they are [b] *Modes of Verbs,* or else they are [c] *Conjunctions;* And some of them may be periphrastically expressed by Radicals. So that according to the true Philosophy of speech, I cannot conceive this kind of words to be properly a distinct part of speech, as they are commonly called. But until they can be distributed into their proper places, I have so far complyed with the Grammars of instituted Languages, as to place them here together, and to branch them under the five following Combinations.

[a] As. So. From. This. That.
[b] Yea. Nay. Perhaps. Truly.
[c] Rather. Than.

§ II.

Whereof the first doth consist of such Adverbs as denote

The manner of our Apprehension of Complex things, or the *nexus* betwixt the several terms of a Proposition; whether more

Ita, immo, maximè.
Non, nequaquam, minimè.

Simple; || *Affirming* or *Denying*
1. { Y E A, I,
   { N A T, not, no,

I. { Mixed; applicable both to Affirmation and Negation; either || *Conjectural* doubtful and contingent: or *Certain* and confident, implying a kind of attestation or something superadded to bare Affirming or Denying.

Fortè, forsan.
Profectò.

2. { P E R H A P S, perchance,
   { T R U L T, indeed, surely, in truth, verily.

Similitude; the former being *Comparative General,* the other the *Redditive* of it.

A S

Chap. IV. Concerning Natural Grammar.

3.	{ A S, *even as* { S O *semblably.*	Ut. Sic.

The second Combination are all of them *Comparative*, either of

II. {
- *Equality*; the latter being the *Redditive* of the former
  - 1. { HOW / SO — Quàm. Tam.
- *Inequality*; according to several degrees.
  - *Greater*;
    - 2. { MORE / MOST — Magis. Maximè.
  - *Lesser*;
    - 3. { LESS / LEAST — Minùs. Minimè.

The third Combination doth consist of such as are; either

III. {
- *Elective*; whether of *Prelation* and preference: or *Preterition* and postponency.
  - 1. { RATHER / THAN — Potiùs. Quàm.
- *Local and Temporal*, implying a respect betwixt something *absent* and *past*; either to ‖ that which is *present*: or to that which is at *distance* and *future*.
  - 2. { YET, *still, hitherto,* / UNTIL — Adhuc, hactenus. Donec.
- *Temporal only*; the former representing *time existing* and present, the other implying a *relation of posteriority* after lapsing and expiring of some time.
  - 3. { WHILST / AT LENGTH — Dum. Tandem.

The fourth Combination doth contein such as denote the Circumstance of

IV. {
- *Society*, ‖ *Affirmed*, or *Denyed*; Conjunction or Exclusion
  - 1. { TOGETHER / ONLY, *alone,* — Unà, simul. Tantùm.
- *Repetition*, or *resemblance and equivalence*
  - 2. { AGAIN / AS IF — Iterum. Quasi.
- *Privation* or *Restitution*; the former signifying the *devesting* a thing of its form; the other the re-investing of it with its precedent form; the first of these hath no Particle that is used simply for it, but only in Composition, both in *Latin* and *English*: the latter we sometimes express in English by *Back*:
  - 3. { UN, *dis.* / RE, *back.* — Un. dis. Re, retro.

The fifth and last Combination doth consist of three single Particles, denoting *Proximity* or nearness; being either

V. {
- *Definite* and determinate; whether
  - *Affirming some little defect* or Imperfection
    - 1. ALMOST, *e'en, well-nigh, towards, within a little of* — Fere.
  - *Denying the utmost perfection*
    - 2. SCARCE, *hardly* — Vix.
- *Indefinite*, and indeterminate *to more or less*, over or under;

Sſ. but

but affirming a nearness to the chief term

Circiter.   3. *THEREABOUTS, under or over.*

§ III.   *Conjunctions* are such Particles as serve for the *joyning* together of *words*, or rather of *sentences*. Of these there may be reckoned these four Combinations, or twelve paires; though all of them be not alike simple and of equal necessity, yet there is none of them without its particular convenience.

The first Combination doth consist of such as are either

                Interrogative, ‖ *Affirmative,* or *Negative.*

An.   1. { *WHETHER TEA?*
Noume.   { *WHETHER NO?*

     I. { *Conjunctive,* ‖ *Affirmative,* or *Negative,*

Et, atq;   2. { *AND*
Nec.   { *NEITHER*

               Conditional, ‖ *Affirmative,* or *Negative,*

Si.   3. { *IF, so that,*
Nisi.   { *UNLESS.*

The second Combination doth contain such as are either

               Approbative, or *Discretive* and *restrictive,*

Equidem.   1. { *INDEED*
Sed.   { *BUT*

    II. { *Concessive,* or *Exceptive*

Etsi.   2. { *ALTHOUGH*
Tamen.   { *YET*

               Disjunctive, ‖ *Definite,* or *Indefinite,*

Vel.   3. { *OR*
Sive.   { *EITHER.*

The third Combination are all of them *Causal;* either

              Adjunctive of the end; whether cause or Event; ‖ *Affirmative* or *Negative,*

Ut.   1. { *THAT, to the end that,*
Ne.   { *LEAST THAT*

    III. { *Ratiocinative,* belonging to the *Antecedent;* whether ‖ that which makes it *follow* the Consequent : or that which may indifferently *precede* or *follow.*

Nam.   2. { *FOR*
Quia.   { *BECAUSE*

             Ratiocinative belonging to the *Consequent;* whether ‖ *interrogative* and indefinite : or *illative,* and demonstrative,

Cur.   3. { *WHY, wherefore, what is the cause or reason,*
Ergo.   { *THEREFORE.*

The last Combination doth consist of such as are either

            Declarative; whether ‖ of the *cause,* or of the *event,*

Quum.   1. { *WHEREAS, seeing that, sith that,*
Exinde.   { *THEREUPON*

    IV. { *Additional,* and transitional, whether ‖ *continuative,* or *suppletive,*

Etiam.   2. { *LIKEWISE, also, together with, moreover,*
Etcæt.   { *AND SO FORTH,* &c.

            Expositive; either ‖ by *Synonyme,* or by *Instance,*

Videlicet,   3. { *TO WIT, viz.*
nempe.   { *FOR EXAMPLE, EX GR.*   The
Exemp. gr.

The three last of these are not properly Particles or single words, but rather the Contractions of several words, they are here added to the rest for greater convenience, partly for compleating the number and filling up the vacancies; and partly in Complyance with the use of most vulgar Languages, when they write contractedly.

CHAP. V.

I. *Of Articles.* II. *Of Modes.* III. *Of Tenses.* IV. *The most distinct way of expressing the differences of Time.*

BEsides these fore-mentioned Particles which may be called more *Absolute*; there are others more *servile* and auxiliary, serving for the fuller expression of some Accident belonging to a word. These were before distinguished into such as do belong either, 1. To an *Integral alone*, as *Articles.* 2. To the *Copula alone*, as the *Modes.* or 3. *Both to Integral and Copula* as the *Tenses.* Each of which are in some Languages taken in, or involved in the inflexion of words: But in others, they are provided for by distinct words to express them. § I.

Articles are usually prefixed before Substantives for the more full and distinct expression of them, they may be distinguished into

Enuntiative, which may be used indifferently before any Substantive, not already possest with the Demonstrative. *A. An.*

Demonstrative, which gives a peculiar Emphasis to its Substantive, and is applyed only to such a Person or Thing, as the hearer knows, or hath reason to know, because of its eminence or some precedent mention of it. *The*

Though these be not absolutely *necessary* to a Language, because the *Latin* is without them; yet are they so *convenient* for the greater distinctness of speech, that upon this account, both the *Hebrew*, *Greek*, *Slavonick*, and most other Languages have them.

To shew in what manner the subject is to be joyned with his Predicate, the *Copula* between them is affected with a Particle, which from the use of it, is called *Modus*, the Manner or *Mode.* § II.

Now the Subject and Predicate may be joyned together either *Simply*, or with some kind of *Limitation*, and accordingly these Modes are either *Primary* or *Secondary*.

The *Primary Modes* are called by *Grammarians Indicative*, and *Imperative*.

When the Matter is declared to be so, or at least when it seems in the speakers power to have it be so, as the bare union of Subject and Predicate would import; then the *Copula* is nakedly expressed without any variation: And this manner of expressing it, is called the *Indicative Mode.*

When it is neither declared to be so, nor seems to be immediatly in the speakers power to have it so; then he can do no more in words but make out the expression of his will to him that hath the thing in his power, namely to his {Superiour / Equal / Inferiour} by {Petition / Perſwaſion / Command} And the manner of theſe affecting the *Copula* (Be it ſo, or *ſive eſſe*, let it be ſo) is called the *Imperative Mode*; of which there are theſe three varieties, very fit to be diſtinctly provided for. As for that other uſe of the *Imperative Mode*, when it ſignifies *Permiſſion*; this may be ſufficiently expreſſed by the *Secondary Mode* of *Liberty*. You may do it.

The *Secondary Modes* are ſuch, as when the *Copula* is affected with any of them, make the ſentence to be (as Logicians call it) a *Modal Propoſition*.

This happens when the Matter in diſcourſe, namely, the being or doing or ſuffering of a thing, is conſidered not *ſimply by it ſelf*, but *gradually in its cauſes* from which it proceeds either *Contingently* or *Neceſſarily*.

Then a thing ſeems to be left as *Contingent*, when the ſpeaker expreſſes only the *Poſſibility* of it, or his own *Liberty* to it.

1. The *Poſſibility* of a thing depends upon the power of its cauſe, and may be expreſſed when {Abſolute / Conditional} by the Particle {CAN / COULD}.

2. The *Liberty* of a thing, depends upon a freedom from all Obſtacles either within or without, and is uſually expreſſed in our Language, when {Abſolute / Conditional} by the Particle {MAY / MIGHT}.

Then a thing ſeems to be of *Neceſſity*, when the ſpeaker expreſſeth the reſolution of his own will, or ſome other obligation upon him from without.

3. The *Inclination of the will* is expreſſed, if {Abſolute / Conditional} by the Particles {WILL / WOULD}.

4. The Neceſſity of a thing, from ſome *external obligation*, whether *Natural* or *Moral* which we call duty, is expreſſed, if {Abſolute / Conditional} by the Particle {MUST, ought, ſhall, / MUST, ought, ſhould}.

§ III. That kind of ſervile Particle which doth belong both to the Integral and the *Copula*, is ſtiled *Tenſe*.

Tho Tenſes in inſtituted Languages are appropriated only to *Verbs*, yet 'tis very plain that according to the true Philoſophy of ſpeech, they ſhould likewiſe be aſcribed to *Subſtantives*; And that this would in many reſpects be a great advantage to Language. As there is *Amatio*, ſo there ſhould be *Amavitio* and *Amaturitio*, &c.

Theſe kind of Auxiliary Particles, ſtiled *Modes* and *Tenſes*, are in the Modern Languages expreſſed by ſuch ſervile words, as do not ſignifie any compleat Act, but rather ſome reſpects and circumſtances belonging to other Acts; and by that means have in them a natural fitneſs to be ſubſervient to the inflexion of other Integral words. So the *Conditional* Modes are ſupplyed by the words *Poſſum* or *Poſſibile*, *Licet*,

Chap. V.   *Concerning Natural Grammar.*   317

Licet, Libet, Volo, Necesse, Oportet, Debeo. And so are the *Tenses*, by those servile words of *Facio, Habeo,* besides the *Copula, sum.*

The Tenses are usually distinguished into

- Present
  - Active. *Do, dost, doth,*
  - Passive. *Am, art, is, are.*
- Past
  - Imperfect
    - Active. *Did, didst,*
    - Passive. *Was, wert, were.*
  - Perfect
    - Active. *Have, hast, hath,*
    - Passive. *Have been, hast been, hath been.*
  - Pluperfect
    - Active. *Had, hadst,*
    - Passive. *Had been, hadst been.*
- Future
  - Active. *Shall, will, shalt, wilt,*
  - Passive. *Shall be, will be: shalt be, wilt be.*

But the most distinct and explicit way of expressing any Proposition, is by affixing these Tenses, both to the *Copula,* and the *Predicate*; the *latter* of which will shew the time of the Action, &c. whether past, present, or future: and the former, the state of the Person or Subject, who doth this Action, whether he { *Has been, Is now, Shall be hereafter.* } either { *Past that Action, Acting in it, Yet to do it.* }

§ IV.

And a Proposition thus expressed, is in the very expressing of it, resolved into its parts of *Subject, Copula,* and *Predicate,* according to these following examples.

I { Have been / Am / Shall be } Hot   { Calui / Caleo / Calebo }

I { Have been / Am / Shall be } having been Hot   { Calebam / Calueram / Caluero }

I { Have been / Am / Shall be } to be hot hereafter   { Fui caliturus / Sum caliturus / Ero caliturus }

I { Have been / Am / Shall be } Heating   { Calefeci / Calefacio, or sum calefaciens / Calefaciam }

I { Have been / Am / Shall be } Having heated   { Calefeceram / Calefaciebam, sum qui calefecit / Calefecero }

I { Have been / Am / Shall be } to Heat hereafter   { Fui calefacturus / Sum Calefacturus / Ero calefacturus }

I { Have been / Am / Shall be } Heated   { Fui Calefactus / Calefio, vel sum calefactus / Calefiam, vel ero calefactus }

I $\begin{cases}\text{Have been}\\ \text{Am}\\ \text{Shall be}\end{cases}$ having been Heated $\begin{cases}\textit{Fueram calefactus}\\ \textit{Calefiebam}\\ \textit{Fuero calefactus}\end{cases}$

I $\begin{cases}\text{Have been}\\ \text{Am}\\ \text{Shall be}\end{cases}$ to be Heated hereafter $\begin{cases}\textit{Fui}\\ \textit{Sum}\\ \textit{Ero}\end{cases}$ *Calefaciendus.*

But if any should conceive this way needless or too laborious, as being too much distant from the manner of Instituted Languages; he may by putting the *Copula* in the place of the Tense, as well express his mind in this, as in any other Instituted Language.

CHAP. VI.

I. *Of Transcendental Particles, The end and use of them.* II. *The usual ways for enlarging the sense of words in Instituted Languages.* III. *The General Heads of Transcendental Particles.*

THose Particles are here stiled *Transcendental,* which do circumstantiate words in respect of some Metaphysical notion; either by enlarging the acception of them to some more general signification, then doth belong to the restrained sense of their places: or denoting a relation to some other Predicament or Genus, under which they are not originally placed.

Whereas in a Philosophical Language, every word ought in strictness to have but one proper sense and acception, to prevent equivocalness; which sense is to be restrained according to that place and relation, which the words have in the Tables: And yet on the other side, it would much promote copiousness and elegancy, if there might be any way so to change and vary the sense of any word, as may with all, leave it free from ambiguity. For this purpose, as likewise for the Abbreviating of Language are these Transcendental notes suggested.

There are two ways used in Instituted Languages, specially in *Latin* for varying the sense of words; either by *Tropes:* or by such a kind of *Composition* as doth *alter the terminations* of them.

1. The sense of a word is varyed by Trope; either in respect of some

Agreement and convenience, which it hath with the word for which it is used; whether more
 General; as in *Metaphore*
 Special; when the
  Whole, whether Universal, Essential, Integral, *is put for* any of the respective *parts,* or contrary wise, *Synecdoche.*
  Subject, Object, Cause, &c. is put for the *Adjunct, Adject, Effect,* &c, or contrary wise, *Metonymy.*
Opposition; when one Opposite is put for the other, *Irony.*

Of

Chap. IV.   *Concerning Natural Grammar.*   319

Of all which there are store of examples in the common books of Rhetorick; And there will be occasion to cite several of them in the following Chapter, amongst the instances that are given of the Transcendental Particles.

Words are varied by changing their Terminations many ways; of which these that follow are some of the Principal in the Latin.

1. *Preparatives* or *Meditatives*; are expressed by the Termination (*urio*) *Scripturio, Esurio, Parturio, Micturio.*

2. *Inceptives*; by the termination (*sco*) *Lucesco, Calesco, Senesco.*

3. *Frequentatives*; by the termination (*ito*) *Clamito, Agito.*

4. *Augmentatives*; by the termination (*osus*) *Aquosus, Fluviosus, Piscosus.*

5. *Diminutives*; by the terminations (*lo, lus, la, lum, aster*) *Cantillo, Scribillo, Libellus, Lapillus, Homunculus, Mercatulus, Vesicula Corpusculum, Corculum, Crepusculum, Surdaster, Medicaster, Grammaticaster.*

6. The Notion of *Segregate*; by the termination (*tim*) *Viritim, Verbatim, Gradatim.*

7. *Power* and *Propensity Active*; by (*ivus, ivitas*) *Activus, Activitas.*

8. *Power* and *Propensity Passive*; by (*ilis, ilitas*) *Possibilis, Possibilitas.*

9. *Cause*; by composition with *Facio, Mortifico, Magnifico, Prolificum,* &c.

10. *Kind*; by (*plex* and *farius* and *genus*) *Simplex, Duplex, Multiplex, Bifarius, Multifarius, Omnigenus, Multigenus.*

11. The notions of *Officer*, and *Tradesman*; whether *Merchant* or *Mechanick* promiscuously, are commonly expressed by the termination (*arius*) which doth originally and properly signifie the notion of *belonging to*, but is thus limited by reason of the words, *Officiarius, Mercator, Faber,* understood.

Apiarius, Armentarius, Caprarius, Equarius, Accipitarius, Librarius, &c.

Lanarius, Linarius, Piscarius, Aviarius, Pomarius, Lactarius, &c. *Arcuarius, Armamentarius, Aurarius, Doliarius,* &c.

12. *Instrument* or *Jugament*; by the termination (*trum*) *Haustrum, Aratrum, Plaustrum, Rastrum,* &c.

13. *Vessel*; by (*bulum*) *Thuribulum, Infundibulum.*

14. *House*; by (*ile, ale, arium*) *Equile, Ovile, Bubile, Caseale, Aviarium, Columbarium, Gallinarium.*

15. *Chamber* or *Room*; by (*ina, arium, terium*) *Officina, Textrina, Tonstrina, Sutrina, Popina, Vestiarium, Carnarium, Apodyterium, Conisterium, Sphæristerium.*

16. *Place in General*; by (*arium, etum*) *Vivarium, Aquarium, Pomarium, Colluviarium, Frutetum, Dumetum, Arundinetum, Ericetum,* &c.

17. *Person* or *Agent*; by the termination (*or*) *Pastor, Fossor, Frondator, Vindemiator, Arator, Messor,* &c.

Now if all other respects and circumstances, which are capable and proper to be expressed by these kind of Particles, were in some such way provided for; this would exceedingly abbreviate the number

of

of words, prevent much circumlocution, contribute to perspicuity and distinctness, and very much promote the elegance and significancy of speech.

What may be the most convenient number of such Transcendental Particles, is not easie to determine; But those mentioned in the eight following Combinations, (though not all of the same extent and comprehensiveness) have each of them some peculiar pretence of being listed under this number.

These may be distributed into such as are more
- *General.*
  - Essential. I.
  - Circumstantial. II.
- *Special,* whether belonging to
  - *Substance.* III.
  - *Quantity.* IV.
  - *Quality.* V.
  - *Action.* VI.
  - *Relation,* with respect to
    - Quality and Action. VII.
    - Affections of Animals. VIII.

The first Combination doth comprehend such *General Essential* respects, as are either

I.
- *Comparative;* denoting *similitude* and resemblance; whether that which consists chiefly || in *words* or in *things*
  - 1. METAPHOR
  - LIKE
- *Positive;* denoting the nature or essence of the subject spoken of, as to those common notions of
  - *General* beings, either || the *common essence,* or *common circumstances*
    - 2. KIND
    - MANNER
  - *Individual* beings, whether || *irrational* or *rational*
    - 3. THING
    - PERSON

The second Combination doth contein such General *Circumstantial* respects as are; either more

II.
- *Absolute;* signifying, *Position* or *Duration*
  - 1. PLACE
  - TIME
- *Relative;* as to
  - *Effecting* or *Representing*
    - 2. CAUSE
    - SIGN
  - *Being* in *conjunction* with others, or *separate* from others
    - 3. AGGREGATE
    - SEGREGATE.

The

Chap. VI.   *Concerning Natural Grammar.*   321

The third Combination doth contain such kind of *Special* respects, belonging to *Substance*, as result from their Application to other Substances, and the uses for which they are designed; namely, for *Enclosure* and service, whether of

III. {
1. { *Places*; or *Things*
SEPIMENT
ARMAMENT

Men; either such coverings as are
2. { *Contiguous* and fitted to their bodies, serving *for defence*, || against *Weather* or *Enemies*
VEST
ARMOUR

More *remote*, according to || the more *General*, or *Special* kind or part
3. { HOUSE
ROOM

The fourth Combination doth comprehend some of those *Special* respects belonging to Corporeal things, which do chiefly concern the *Figure* of them, whether

IV. {
1. { *Shape alone*; *Broad* and *Flat*, or *Slender* and *Long*
LAMIN
PIN

Shape and *Use*
2. { *More Simple*; designed, either for *Operation* or *Containing*
INSTRUMENT
VESSEL

Less simple; whether || such as are not *necessarily designed for motion*, being of a *less complicate* figure; or such as are *designed for motion*, whose figure is *more complicate*
3. { JUGAMENT
MACHIN

The fifth Combination doth contain such kind of Notions as relate to the *Quality* of Things or Persons, whether considered more

V. {
1. { *Abstractly*; either the more *General* Quality, whereby the natural Powers are perfected, or more *special* relating to *Practical* matters
HABIT
ART

Concretely; denoting personal Qualifications, whether
2. { *Degrees* and *Business*; or *Faculty* and *Skill*
OFFICER
ARTIST

3. { *Professions* of *Manufacture* or *Exchange*
MECHANIC
MERCHANT

Tt   The

The sixth Combination doth contain such imperfect servile notions, as belong to *Action* or *Passion*, with respect to the

VI.
- *Ability*, or *Disposition* of a thing
  1. {POWER / APTITUDE}
- *Beginning* or *Repeating* of an Action
  2. {INCEPTIVE / FREQUENTATIVE}
- Application of the Power; whether ‖ in a *common* and *ordinary*, or in some *sudden* and *vehement* degree
  3. {ENDEAVOUR / IMPETUS}

The seventh Combination doth contain such kind of servile *Relative* notions, as are *common* both to *Quality* and *Action*; denoting either the

VII.
- *Measures* and degrees of things
  - *Great* or *Little*
    1. {AUGMENTATIVE / DIMINUTIVE}
  - *Too much*, or *too little*
    2. {EXCESSIVE / DEFECTIVE}
- *Manner* of a Thing or Action, whether ‖ *as it should be*, or *as it should not be*
  3. {PERFECTIVE / CORRUPTIVE}

The eighth and last Combination doth relate to some Affections of Animals, either

VIII.
- *Sounds* made by them, whether ‖ *inarticulate*, or *articulate*
  1. {VOICE / LANGUAGE}
- *Sexes* of them
  2. {MALE / FEMALE}
- The *first* most impotent and *imperfect Age*; to which may be adjoyned, that more general name belonging to any *whole*, which is likewise applicable to inanimate beings.
  3. {YOUNG / PART.}

CHAP.

CHAP. VII.

Instances of the great usefulness of these Transcendental Particles, with directions how they are to be applyed.

FOR the better explaining of what great use and advantage these Particles may be to Language, I shall give some examples severally to each pair of them, according to the order premised: Beginning with the first.

I.

1. {METAPHORICAL
    LIKE

These two are paired together, because of their affinity, each of them denoting an enlargement of the sense of the word; the first *more general*; the other with reference to *similitude*, properly so called.

The note of *Metaphorical* affixed to any Character, will signifie the Metaphor. enlarging the sense of that word, from that strict restrained acception which it had in the Tables, to a more universal comprehensive signification: By this, common Metaphors may be legitimated, retaining their elegancy, and being freed from their ambiguity. So

These words, with this note will signifie

Element	Rudiment, Principle	Shining	Illustrious
Root	Original	Hypocritical	Counterfeit
Way	Means	Banish	Expel
Thick	Gross	Companying	Being together
Thin	Subtle	Strengthen	Fortifie, fence
Streight	Upright	Wrigle in	Insinuate
Crooked	Perverse	Prophesie	Prediction
Obtuse	Dull	Consecrate	Dedicate
Acute	Quick	Suiter	Candidate
Ripe	Perfect	Woo	Canvase
Immature	Imperfect	Rival	Competitor
Fertile	Fruitful as to inventi-	Raise	Prefer, Advance
Barren	Unfruitful (on, &c.		
Beautiful	Decent, Comely		
Deformed	Absurd, Indecent		
Ornate	Elegant, Quaint		
Homely	Rude		
Light	Evident, Plain		
Dark	Mystical, Obscure		

So in the Tables of *Action*; those Acts which are primarily ascribed unto God, as *Preserving, Destroying, Delivering, Forsaking, Blessing, Cursing*, &c. because they may by analogy be applyed to other things, therefore this mark will enlarge their acception. So for those other Acts belonging to the *rational soul*; as, *Thinking, Believing, Knowing, Observing, Expecting, Consenting, Dissenting, Esteeming, Contemning, Willing,*

Tt 2

Willing, Nilling, Fruition, Delectation, Election, Rejection, &c. though they are primarily acts of the Rational Soul; yet becaufe there is fomewhat analogous to them in other Creatures; therefore fuch words with this mark may without ambiguity be ufed in fuch a general fenfe.

So in *Judicial Relation*; *Accufe, Complain, Excufe, Witnefs, Regifter, Citation,* &c. So likewife in *Military Relation*; *Offend, Defend, Provoke, Refift, Befiege, Affault, Skirmifh, Fight, Stratagem, Overcome, Tield, Fly, Purfue, Efcape,* &c. Each of thefe and many other words may by this note (when there is juft occafion to apply it) be made more copious, and yet preferved diftinct in their fignifications.

Like.
The other Particle, *Like,* being affixed to any word, doth denote a varying of the fenfe of that word, upon the Account of fome fimilitude, whether in refpect of *Quality* and difpofition, *Refemblance, effect,* and manner of *doing,* or *outward fhape* and *fituation.*

1. This fimilitude may fometimes refer to the *Quality* and difpofition of a thing; in which fenfe 'tis frequently expreffed in our Englifh Tongue by Adjectives, with the Termination (*ifh*) *Devilifh, Brutifh, Currifh, Wafpifh, Apifh*: and fometimes without it; as *Angelical, Dogged, Cynical, Viperous, Serpentine,* &c. which do not always fignifie according to the ftrict derivation of fuch Adjectives, but do many times denote only a fimilitude.

2. After the fame manner are the feveral varieties of *Colours* to be expreffed, namely, by their refemblance to other things commonly known. So Afhes-like, or *Cineritius,* is *Afh-colour.* So Flefh-like is *Carnation*; Blood-like is *Crimfon*; Lyon-like is *Tawny.* So for thofe other refemblances to the Sky, to Gold, Grafs, Straw. So *Piceus,* or Pitch-like, is a *deep black*; *Coracinus,* or Crow-like, is a *fhining black.* So for Milky, Snowy, Ivory, kinds of White, &c. And thus likewife is it for the variety of *Taftes* and *Smells*; the differences of which are not provided for with diftinct words in any Language, but may this way be fufficiently expreffed; namely, by their likenefs to fuch other things as are commonly known.

3. Sometimes it may refer to fome kind of Refemblance in refpect of *effect,* according to which fenfe thefe words are frequently ufed; *Inflame, Sparkle, Cloud, Exhalation, Fumes, Vapour.*

4. Sometimes to the *manner of doing*; fo to fpeak Infant-like, is to *Jabler*; to graft-like Feathers is to *Impe*; to dart-like water, is to *Spirt, Squirt*; to tremble-like with the voice, is to *Warble, Thrill*; Dog-like crying, is *Whining*; Stealing-like, is *Surreptitious,* &c.

5. This

Chap. VII.   *Concerning Natural Grammar.*   325

5. This Particle is likewise applicable in respect of shape and situation. So

These words with this note		will signifie
Downe	Thistle Downe	
	Lint of Linnen	
	Hoariness of Mold	
Fibre	Grain of Wood	
Apple	Pomander, Pommel	
Bullet	Pellet	
Arme	Arme of Tree, Sea	
Trunc	Hulk of a Ship	
Beake	Stemm of a Ship	
Foot	Pedestal	
Bridge	Bridge of a Musical instrument	
Money	Medal, Counter	

2. { **KIND** I.
     { *MANNER*

The first of these may be compounded with words of *Number*, to make them signifie under the notion of *Multiplicative*, which the Latins express by the Termination (*plex*) *Simplex, Duplex, Multiplex*, &c. And the English by the Termination (*fold*) *Twofold, Threefold, Manifold*. — Kind.

In its composition with other Characters, it will serve to express those words which are used to signifie the general or special *kinds of things*; and being affixed to any of the differences, will make them signifie as a *Genus* or *Species*. It is applicable both to Substantives and Adjectives.

Some of our English words of this sense, are expressed by the Termination (*age*) as *Herbage, Pascuage, Foliage, Vintage, Cordage, Stoage*, &c. that is the kind of Herbs, Pasture, &c.

These words wth this note		will signifie	These words thus marked		will signifie	
People	Populacy, Folk, Commonalty		Bisulc			Cattle
Parent	Parentage		Stag			Red Deer
Child	Off-spring, Progeny, Issue, Brood, Litter		Buck			Fallow Deer
			Hog			Swine
Foot Souldier	Infantry		Domestic bird			Poultry
Horse Sould.	Cavalry		Guns			Artillery

There are several Adjectives likewise expressible this way; as *Multifarious, Homogeneous*, or *Similar, Heterogeneous*, or *Dissimular*, &c.

2. The use of the second Particle is by its composition with Rela- Manner. tive and Quantitative Pronouns, to express such words as these; *Quomodo*, how or after what manner; *Hujusmodi* after this manner; *Ejusmodi* after that manner, &c. It is applicable likewise unto *Adverbia moris, Meatim, Tuatim, Suatim* (i) *Meo, Tuo, Suo More*. The Antients were wont to say, *Canatim, Suatim, Bovatim*, that is, after the manner of Dogs, of Swine, &c. And it is still in use to say *Humanitus*, after the manner of men.

The

The Composition with this Particle may likewise be useful in expressing those words which do in their proper notion contain a reference to the *Mode* of things. So

This mark upon the word		will make it signifie		The words thus marked		will signifie	
	Loqution		Pronunciation		Height		Stature
	Sentence		Eloqution		Feeding		Diet
	Joyning		Phrase, Style		Vest		Garb, Tire
	Using		Connexion		Face		Aspect, Countenance
	Right		Usage		Air		Meen, Visage, Favour
	Good, Well		Tenure		Sound		Weather
	Evil		Right				Tone
			Wrong				

I.

3. { THING / PERSON

Each of these may be compounded with the *Relative* or *Quantitative* Pronouns, serving to distinguish such as refer to *Things*, from those that belong to *Persons. This, That, The same, Another, A certain, Some. Thing* or *Person.*

Thing.   The former of these being affixed to any word in the Tables belonging to the Predicament of Quality, Action, Relation, or to any other word which doth primarily denote a person, will determine the sense of that word to a *Substantive of the Thing*; as it hath been already declared in the Doctrine of Substantives.

This note may be affixed

1. To *Adjectives Neuter.* So

The words { Obscure, Seeming, Prestigiatory, Frivolous } with this mark will signifie { Mystery, Semblance, Trick, Trifle. }

2. To *Adjectives Active*, commonly called Participles Active. So

The words { Nutrient, Medicating, Purging, Binding, Buying } with this mark will signifie { Nutriment or Aliment, Medicament or Medicine, Purge, Bond or String, Price }

3. To *Adjectives* or Participles *Passive*, in the Aorist Tense. So

The words		will signifie		The words		will signifie	
	Created		Creature		Inherited		Inheritance, Patrimony
	Acted		Fact		Seen		Spectacle
	Believed		Fides quæ		Urinated		Urin
	Fancied		Phantasm		Dunged		Dung
	Prophesied		Prophesie		Spit		Spittle
	Tyed		Knot		Seemed		Pretence, Pretext
	Bound		Bundle, Fardle		Drunk		Drink
	Tryed		Experiment		Eaten		Food, Meat
	Weaved		Web		Eleemosynated		Alms

So the Adjectives Passive of the words *Teaching, Learning, Reading, Singing, Selling,* with this affix, will signifie *Doctrine, Lesson, Lecture, Song, Ware.*

The

Chap. VII.   *Concerning Natural Grammar.*

The second of these Particles may refer either to, 1. The *Quality* and relation; or 2. The *Agency*; or 3. The *Patiency* of the Person.

If to the first of these; it must be affixed to an *Adjective Neuter*; if to the second or third, it must be affixed to an *Adjective Active* or *Passive*.

Of the first kind are such examples as these.

The words	will signifie	The words	will signifie
Vile	Rascal, Varlet	Flattering	Parasite
Miserable	Wretch, Caitiff	Facetious	Jester, Wag
Perfidious	Villain, Traytor	Fornicating	Whore, Harlot
Crafty	Knave		Strumpet
Idiotical	Fool, Idiot		Whoremonger
Wandring	Vagrant, Vagabond	Rustic	Boor, Peasant
Licentious	Royster, Blade		Hind, Swain
Uncleanly	Sloven	Military	Souldier
Slow	Lob, Lubber	Ecclesiastic	Clerk, Clergy
Idle	Truant	Secular	Lay
		Proposititious (i) put in substitu-	Attourney, Surrogate
		Aulical (tion	Courtier
		Art	Artizan, Artist
		Nullus	*Nemo*

Of the second are such examples as these.

The words	will signifie	The words	will signifie
Acting	Actor	Conveying	Convoy
Creating	Creator	Vowing	Votary
Farming	Farmer	Giving	Donor
Lending	Creditor	Receiving	Receiver
Owing	Debitor	Beginning	Inceptor, Novice
Pronegotiating	Factor	Travelling	Traveller, Passenger
Beneficencing	Benefactor	Seeing	Spectator
Interpreting	Truch-man	Hearing	Auditor, Hearer

Of the third are such examples as these.

Sent	Messenger
Eleemosynated	Eleemosynary
Beneficenced	Beneficiary
Tryed	Probationer

II.

1. $\begin{cases} PLACE \\ TIME \end{cases}$

This first pair in the second Combination of Transcendental Particles, are of more then ordinary extent and usefulness, because they may be serviceable to compound other words besides Integrals.

The first of them may be Compounded with *Pronouns*, as was shewed before in the doctrine concerning Pronouns; and so serve to express *Adverbs of place*, as in this, that, every, &c. *here, there, every, where.*

Besides which, the Composition with this Particle may be proper to express other names of Places, which are commonly derived, either from,

1. The

1. The things contained in them.
2. The *uses* to which they are designed.
3. The *Relations* by which they are bounded.

Of the first kind are such as these.

The words			will signifie		The words			will signifie	
Metal		Mine			Hops			Hopyard	
Tin		Stannary			Flowers			Garden	
Stone		Quarry			Fire			Hearth	
Deer		Park			Smoke			Chimney	
Conies		Warren			Ship resting			Harbour, Haven, Rode	
Trees		Wood, Grove			Stream			Channel, Kennel	
Shrubs		Coppice						Gutter, Drain	
Fruit-trees		Orchard			Abjectaneous				
Vines		Vineyard.			Water			Sink	

Of the second kind are such examples as these.

The words			will signifie		The words			will signifie	
Ambulation					Dwelling			Mansion, Messuage	
Tectised		Cloyster			Washing			Bath	
High (low		Terrace			Flesh-selling			Shambles	
Baking-hol-		Oven			Publick Spectacle			Theater	
Fire-hollow		Furnace			Deers Lying			Laire	
Protection		Asylum, refuge			Birds Sleeping			Roost	
		Sanctuary, shelter			Ship-making			Dock	
Hiding		Covert			Unshipping			Key, Wharf	
Meeting		Rendezvouz			Wares			Hyth	
Sacrificing		Altar							
Preaching		Pulpit							

Of the third kind are such instances as these.

These words		will signifie	
Authority		Territory, Signiory Jurisdiction, Principality, Dominion	
Kings Authority		Kingdom, Realm	
Tribe		County, Shire	
Academical		Academy, University	
Arch-Bishops ⎫		Province	
Bishops ⎬ Authority		Diocess	
Presbyters ⎭		Parish	

Time.   The second of these Particles, namely, *Time*, may be Compounded

1. With *Numbers*, to make them signifie as *Adverbs Cardinals*; as *Semel, bis, ter*, &c. *Decies, vicies, centies, millies, multoties*, &c. Once, twice, thrice, ten times, twenty times, a hundred times, a thousand times, many times, *&c.*

2. With *Pronouns*, to express Adverbs of time; as in this, that, all, *Now, Then, Alway*, &c.

3. With

Chap. VII.   *Concerning Natural Grammar.*   329

3. With *Integrals*; as in such examples.

These words will signifie
- Festival — Holy time
- Paschal — Easter
- Nativity of Christ — Christmass
- Coming of the Holy Ghost — Whitsuntide
- Grape gathering — Vintage
- Forinsical — Term
- Non-Forinsical — Vacation

II.

2. $\begin{cases} CAUSE, \text{ or make} \\ SIGN. \end{cases}$

When words are in their significations to be more peculiarly deter- Cause. mined to their Transitive efficiency, then is this first note to be affixed. It is frequently in Latin expressed by a Composition with *facio* subjoyned, and sometimes in English by a Composition with (*be*) prefixed; as in the words, *Befool, Besot*, &c.

The instances of this kind do frequently occur, and are very numerous. So

These words will signifie

Know	Acquaint, Advertise	Sit	Set
Certain	Certifie, assure	Lye	Lay
Wonder	Amaze, astonish	Sweat	Sudorific, Diaphoretic
Anger	Provoke, incense		
Fear	Fright, daunt, dismay	Urine	Diuretic
Love	Enamour, endear	Child	Adopt
Shame	Abash	Ignoble	Attaint
Humble	Abase	Free	Enfranchize
Contender	Boutefeu, incendiary	Slave	Enslave
Boldness	Embolden	Money	Mint, coyne
Powerful	Enable	Erre	Seduce
Impotent	Disable	Evil	Deprave, marr
Great	Magnifie, aggravate	Exceed	Cloy
Little	Diminish, abate	Stay	Detain, hold at bay
Healthy	Cure, heal		
Dye	Kill, slay, mortal	Go	Set packing
Live	Enliven, quicken	Bleed	Let blood
Fade	Wear out, consume	Shine	Burnish, polish
Rise	Raise, rouse, start	Manifest	Illustrate, clear
	Flush, spring, unkennel	Sparkle	Strike fire
Fall	Fell, throw down	Lose	Endamage

This mark is applicable both to Substantives and Adjectives, as in *Adoption, Adopting, Adopted, Sudorification, Sudorific*, &c.

V v   The

Sign. The other Transcendental note of *Sign* is adjoined to the former, by reason of some kind of affinity (though somewhat remote) which there is betwixt them. As the former Particle doth import the notion of *efficiency* or making; so doth this of *Representing* or signifying. It is applicable both to Substantives and Adjectives. So

These words will signifie:
- Anchor / Buoy / Arming or incursion pass. / Alarum
- Foot / Footstep, track / Jugam. Invas. / Beacon
- Wound / Scar / Future event / Ominous
- Percussion / Vibex, Black and Blew / Evil / Inauspicious
- Vest service / Livery / Great evil / Portentous
- Wind / Weathercock Fane / Terminal or Limit / Meer, land-mark
- Family, or Nobility / Coat of Arms / To head or hand / Becken
- Regality / Crown / To grief / Lament, deplore, bewail, bemoan
- Magistracy / Mace / To praise / Applaud

II.

3. { AGGREGATE
    { SEGREGATE

Aggregate. The first of these doth denote a multitude in Society, unto which common speech doth needlesly assign several distinct names; whereas the Natural notion is the same in all of them; and therefore such various names may justly be reckoned amongst the redundancies of Language. So

These words will signifie:
- Assessors / Bench / Young Dogs / Litter
- Souldiers / Party / Foxes /
- Travelling Merchants / Caravan / Pigs / Airy
- Waiters / / Hawks / Team
- Ships / Train, retinue / Ducks / Brood
- Military Ships / Navy, Fleet Armado / Chickens Fish / Scour, Fry Scull
- Sheep / Flock / /
- Geese / / Trees / Wood, Grove
- Cows / Heard / Small trees / Coppice
- Deer / / Shrubs / Thicket
- Hoggs / Drove / Ferne / Brake
- Drawing horses / Teame / Hay / Reek, Stack
- Hunting dogs / Pack / Straw / Cock
- Partridge / Covey / Fewel wood / Pile
- Bees / Swarm / Twigs / Bavin

And so likewise may it be for those others words
- Jewels / Carcanet
- Feathers / Plume
- Berries / Cluster, Bunch
- Counters / Set
- Cards / Pack
- Dice / Bale
- Silk, Cloth, &c.

So

Chap. VII. *Concerning Natural Grammar.* 331

So the words Selling, or Hiring, with this mark, will signifie to sell by *whole sale*, and to *hire by the Great*.

The second of these being opposite to the former, will signifie *Segregate* things under the notion of *distribution*; and being segregated, which we commonly express by the words *Each* and *Every*; it is applicable to the *Numbers* to make them *distributives*: *Singuli, Bini, Trini*, &c. Each one, every two, every three, or one by one, by twos, by threes, &c. And so for all other things capable of the like notion. The Latins express it by the Termination (*tim*) as was said before. So

Sigillatim	One by one	*Paulatim*	By little and little
Viritim	Man by man	*Pedetentim*	Foot by Foot
Ostiatim	Door by door	*Gradatim*	By degrees
Verbatim	Word by word	*Seriatim*	By ranks or classes

The English, besides the above-mentioned peculiar way of Phraseology, doth sometimes express this notion by compounding with the Termination (*ly*) as *Hourly, Daily, Weekly, Monthly, Annually*, &c. It is applicable likewise to Nouns of Action, or Verbs. So

These words { Giving / Gathering / Selling / Hiring } will signifie { Distributing, Dispensing / Picking up / Retailing / Hiring by the day }

III.

1. { LAMIN / PIN }

The first pair in the third Combination do properly refer to the *Figure* of things; and the note of these, added to the name of the *matter* of which they consist, will be useful to supply the words for several things.

The former of these doth denote a broad and flat Figure.

These words { Wood / Glass / Paper / Mettal / Lead / Iron supertinu'd } will signifie { Board, Plank / Pane / Leaf, Sheet / Plate / Sheet / Latin }   These words { Fire / Ice, Snow / Pudding fryed / Bread / Staffe } will signifie { Leam / Flake / Pancake / Sippet, Tost, Wafer / Lath }

The second denotes a round and long Figure, and being affixed to *Pin.* the word signifying the matter of it, or the thing about which it is used, it may serve for the expression of several names. So

{ Iron / Wood / Vest / String / Cuspidated } { Nayle / Peg / Pin / Tag / Tine }

Vv 2   INSTRU-

III.
2. $\begin{cases} INSTRUMENT \\ VESSEL \end{cases}$

This pair is intended to signifie the General Names belonging to each of the two principal kinds of *Utensils*.

Instrument. By *Instrument*, is meant such a kind of *Utensil*, as is of a more *simple figure*, and properly designed for *Operation*. This mark is to be affixed to the Character of that particular *Action* or *Operation*, in which such instruments are used; and whereas there may be several kinds of instruments, that may be useful for the same kind of operation; they are to be farther distinguished by their *Matter, Figure, Bigness*, or some other circumstance. So

Their words		will signifie		Their words		will signifie	
Foraminating Little			Shaving		Razor		
Great	Aule, Piercer Drill, Bodkin Gimlet, Wimbel Auger		Filing Sawing Graving Planing		File Saw Graver, stile Plane		
Digging	Spade, Shovel		Contusion		Pestle		
Cuspidate	Pick-ax, Mattock		Painting		Pencil		
Reaping, Great Little	Sythe Syckle		Writing Candle supporting		Pen Candlestick		
Fuel supporting Little Great	Dog, Creeper Andiron, Cobiron		Weaving Clipping		Shuttle Shears		
Striking, Cutting Little Great	Hatchet Axe		Brushing Combing		Brush, Beasom Comb		
Lifting	Leaver		Horary		Dyal		
Weighing	Ballance		Star measure		Astrolabe		
Cleaving	Wedge		Sub-forging		Anvil		
Wheeling	Wheel		Ringing		Bell		
Screwing	Screw		Whipping		Scourge, Rod		
Springing	Spring		Rosting		Spit		
Threshing	Flaile		Vision		Spectacles		
Gathering	Rake		Signifer		Colours, Auntient, Cornet, Banner		
Scattering	Fork						
Cribrating	Sive						

Vessel. Under this second Particle (*Vessel*) are comprehended such kind of simple Utensils, whose proper use is to *contain*; they are distinguishable either

1. By the *things* which *they* are designed to hold and *contain*.
2. By the *operations* and actions *for which* they are *used*.
3. By the *matter* of which they consist, together with their several *figures* and *quantities*.

Chap. VII. *Concerning Natural Grammar.*

Of the first kind are such instances as these. So

The words		will signifie		The words		will signifie	
	Water		Cistern		Wooden		Bowle
	Oyle				Leather		Jack
	Glass		Cruet, Cruce		Pottage		Porringer
	Earth		Jarr		Sauce		Saucer
	Drink				Table fire		Chafing-dish
	Little		Cup, Pot, Chalice		Candle		Lanthorn
	Great		Goblet		Inke		Inke-horn
	Earthen		Pitcher		Urine		Chamber-pot

Of the second are such as these. So

The words		will signifie		The words		will signifie	
	Washing				Melting		Crucible
	Little		Bason		Distilling		Still, Alembick
	Great		Laver		Straining		Colander
	Boyling				Infusion		Tunnel, Funnel
	Little		Skillet		Exfusion		Ewer
	Great		Caldron, Kettle		Contusion		Mortar
			Copper, Furnace		Incense		Censor, Perfu-
	Earthen		Pipkin				mers pot
	Frying		Frying-pan		Baptism		Font

Of the third sort there are such examples as these. So

The words		will signifie	
	Earthen		Pot
	Narrow		Urne
	Broad		Pan
	Wooden		
	Oblong		Trough
	Great		Vatt
	Glassy		Vial

III.
$$3.\begin{cases} JUGAMENT \\ MACHIN \end{cases}$$

This next pair is put to signifie such kind of Utensils as are of a *less simple figure* then the former.

Jugament. The word *Jugament* doth comprehend such kind of forms as are *distensoria longa*; consisting of several distinct parts united by Art, being *more* complex then instrument, and *less* then Machin. The mark of it is to be affixed, either to the name of the *Action* or the *Thing* about which they are used: as in these examples.

The words	will figuifie	The words	will figuifie
Carriage of Persons . Dead Living, by Men Horses	Barrow Bier Sedan Litter	Printing Holding Suspension Extension Feet imprison	Press Pincers Gallows, Gibbet Rack
Traction Plowing Harrowing Winnowing Weaving Beasts Food Bird restraining Fish catching Stream stopping Roling Shadowing	Tumbrel Plow Harrow Fan Loom Rack, Cratch Coop, Pen, Cage Weele Sluce Roler Canopy, umbrella, Screen	Head imprison Neck Sub-foot Broyling Fewel Session Bed Clipping Circle making Wind music	Stocks Pillory Yoke Pattin Gridiron Grate Stoole, Settle Bedstead Cizzars Compass Organ

Machin. By the second are intended such Utensils as are of a *more complicate figure*, being mixed either with Wheels, Scrues, or Pullies, and *designed for motion*. The mark is to be affixed unto the Character of the Action for which they are used. So

The words	will figuifie	The words	will figuifie
Hour Signing Sounding Portatile Grinding Little	Watch Clock Pocket watch Mill Quern	Rosting Up-pulling Holding Compressing Way-measuring	Jack Crane Vice Press Way-wiser

IV.
$$1.\begin{cases} SEPIMENT \\ ARMAMENT \end{cases}$$

Sepiment. The first of these may serve to express and describe those several kinds of things and names which are used for *Enclosure*. So

These words	will figuifie	These words	will figuifie
Wood Lamin Staff or Beam Shrub Earth	Pale Rail Hedge Bank	Water Sheep Military of basket Transverse shutting	Mote Sheepfold Line, outwork, &c. Gabion Barricado

The

Chap. VII. *Concerning Natural Grammar.*

The second mark for *ARMAMENT* or Tackle, will serve to Armament. describe sufficiently several things of that nature, without affording distinct names for them, to be applyed unto the Character of the Action or Part to which it belongs.

These words will signifie:

Horse, cohibiting	Bridle	Horse back	Saddle
instigating	Spur	Rustic	Pannel
Head	Head-stall		Pack-saddle
Mouth	Bitt, Snaffle	Riders foot	Stirrup
Neck	Collar	Leg	Gambado
Tayl	Crupper	Circumligating	Surcingle, girdle
Foot	Horse-shooe	Finger for sowing	Thimble

IV.

2. { VEST
     { ARMOUR

The first of these will help to describe those various names that are given to several sorts of *Garments*, according to the *Parts*, *Things*, or other circumstances most considerable in their use. So

Head	Cap	Breast	Stomacher
Margined	Hat		Bib, Biggin
Low	Bonnet	Arm	Sleeve
Reticulate	Cawl	Hand	Glove
Bishops head	Miter	Woollen	Mitten
Votaries head	Cowl	Belly	Apron
Fore-head Linnen	Frontlet, cross-	Thighs close	Breeches
Face	Mask (cloth	Loose	Petticoat
Chin	Muffler	Leg	Stocken, Hose
Neck	Band	Leather	Boot
Trunc	Doublet	Foot	Shooe
Sub-trunc	Wastcoat	Loose	Slipper
Super-trunc	Jerkin, Coat		Pantofle
Loose super humeral	Hood	Inner	Sock
Inmost Linnen	Shirt, Shift	Upper loose	Cloak
Outmost Linnen	Surplice, Frock	Close	Cassock
Bishops Linnen	Stole	Long loose	Gown
Silk	Rochet	Bed woollen	Blanket
Service facing	Livery	Linnen	Sheet (terpane
Chamber	Hanging	Covering	Coverlet, coun-
Table Woollen	Carpet	Pensil	Curtain
Linnen	Table cloth	shadowing	
		Concealing	Mantle, Veil

The second Particle is designed only for *defensive Armour*, which Armour, bears some Analogy to *Vests*. The note of it may be affixed to the several Parts. So

Head	Helmet, murrion	Hand	Gauntlet
Neck	Head-piece	Leg	Greaves, Jambeaux
	Gorget	Defensive to be	Shield, Buckler
Trunc	Habergeon, Corslat	handed	Target
Breast	Breast-plate		
Back	Back-piece		

HOUSE

IV.
3. { HOUSE / ROOM }

House. The first of these will by its composition serve to express those various names which are given to *Houses*, in reference to the several things or uses they are designed for. So

These words will figure		These words will figure		These words will figure		These words will figure
Corn threshed	Granary, Garner	Publick hospitating	Inn
Not threshed	Barn	Sale of Wine	Tavern
Hogs	Sty	Ale	Ale-house
Dogs	Kennel	Votaries	Abby, Cloister
Horses	Stable		Covent, Monastery
Hawks	Mew	Sick persons	Spittle, Hospital
Pigeons	Dove-cote	Eleemosynated	Alms-house
Bees	Hive	Mad	Bethlehem
Conny	Borough	Idlers	Bridewel
Lions or Bears	Den	Imprisonment	Goal, Prison
Ammunition	Arsenal, Magazine	Forinsic	Hall
		Discipling	School
Bones of dead	Charnel	Fornicat.	Stews, Brothel
Water	Conduit		Bordel

Room. As the former Particle may be useful for the expression of the names of several *Houses*; so will this second for particular *Rooms* or Chambers. So

These words will figure		These words will figure		These words will figure		These words will figure
Conventus	Hall	Cloths	Wardrobe
Eating	Dining room	Clothing	Vestry, dressing-room
Discourse	Parlour		
Sleeping	Bed-chamber, Dormitory	Armory	Armour
		Selling	Shop
Walking	Gallery	Preserving	Repository
Privacy	Closet	Drying	Kill, drying loft
Books	Library		
Meat		Exter. dimin.	Lobby, Anti-chamber
Preparing	Kitchin		
Keeping	Larder, Pantry	Way	Passage, room
		Upper	Loft, Garret
Baking	Pastry	Naval	Cabbin
Potation	Buttery	Bees	Cell
Potus	Cellar	Counsel	
Dunging	Jakes, Privy house of office	Secret	Conclave
		Ecclesiastic	Consistory

HABIT

Chap. VII.   *Concerning Natural Grammar.*

V.
1. {HABIT
   {ART

Each of these are applicable to Nouns. The use of the first Particle, is to denote the *Habitualness* of any such thing whose Radix is not primarily under that Genus of *Habit*. So these words *Rejoycing, Worshipping, Obedient, Disobedience*, &c. with this mark, will be determined to the *Habit* of *Chearfulness, Devotion, Obedience, Contumacy*, &c.

There are many Radical words under other Predicaments, as that of *Action, Love, Zeal, Compassion, Envy*, &c. *Singing, Writing*, &c. That of *Relation*, as *Governing, Bargaining, Thieving, Whordom, Deceiving*, &c. which when they are to be used under the notion of *Habits*, must be marked with this affix.

The chief use of the second Particle, is to supply the place of those several names which are commonly given to *Arts* and *Sciences*. So

These words	will signifie	These words	will signifie
Quantity	Mathematic	Weight	Static
Magnitude	Geometry	Building	Architecture
Number	Arithmetic	Wars	Chivalry
World	Cosmography	Military order	Tactic
Star motion	Astronomy	Swording	Fencing
Land	Geography	Language	Grammar
Times	Cronology	Oration	Oratory
Harmony	Music	Arguing	Logic
Vision	Optic, perspective	Manners	Ethic
		Transcendent	Metaphysic

And so for those other cheating Arts of *Manteia* or *Wizarding*, with which the world always hath been and will be abused. In the naming of these it would be convenient to add the word *Manteia*, the better to distinguish these from such as are *true Arts and Sciences*. So

The Art of	
Star mant.	Astrology
Hand mant.	Chiromancy
Face mant.	Physiognomy
Fire mant.	Pyromancy
Water mant.	Hydromancy

V.
2. $\begin{cases} OFFICER \\ ARTIST \end{cases}$

Though this second pair be not of any great affinity, yet are they here united, upon account, that they both denote personal respects.

Officer. The first of them affixed to any single Character, will signifie the notion of *Prefecture* in any kind of place, imployment, relation; whether *Honourable*, or mean and *Servile*, as the Integral shall denote: But if the Integral be compounded with the Preposition *Pro*, or *Vice*, or instead of, which signifies the notion of *Substitution*, it will then express the *Deputy* or substituted officer; if with the Preposition *Sub* or *Under*, it will then denote the *Inferiour* or subordinate officer of that kind. So

These words will signifie

Navy	Admiral, Vice-admiral	Street	Scavinger
Arms	General, Lieuten-Gen.	Citing	Sumner, Apparitor
Brigade	Major General	Peace	Justice, Constable
Regiment	Colonel, Tribune	Degrees	Herauld
Company	Captain, Centurion	Writing	Secretary, Clerk
Military Provision	Commissary	Speaking	Prolocutor
Ten Souldiers	Corporal, Serjeant	Ante-ambulant Pro-Presbyt.	Usher, Beadle Curate
Tribe	Sheriff, Under-Sheriff	Sub-Presbyt.	Clerk
	Major	Pasture	Hayward
City	Chancellour, Vice-chan.	Sheep	Shepherd
University		Cows	Cow-herd
		Hogs	Hog-herd
College	Master, Warden, President, Provost, Rector, Principal	Deer	Keeper
		Conies	Warrenner
		Hawks	Falconer
		Provision	Steward, Manciple, Caterer
Abby	Abbot, Prior		
Manners	Censor		
Alms	Almner, Subalmner	Meat ordering	Sewer
		Drink	Butler
Accounts	Auditor	Door	Porter
Money	Bursar, Treasurer	Chamber	Chamberlain
		Horse	Groom, Hostler
Revenue	Steward		
Gathering	Collector	Agriculture	Bailiff
Market	Clerk of Market	Arresting	Baily, Beadle, Serjeant, Catchpole
Poor	Overseer		
Temple	Church-warden		
Book	Librarian	Imprisoning	Jailour, Warder
Parturition	Midwife		
Singing	Chorister	Whipping	Beadle
Cleansing		Executing	Executioner
Temple	Sexton	Fornicating	Pander, Bawd

The

Chap. VII. Concerning Natural Grammar.

The other Affix for *ARTIST*, is not of so much use or necessity Artist. as the rest, because it may be sufficiently expressed by those two Particles of Art and Person. It is here put in, because I could not think of any more convenient notion of the like affinity to supply this place. So

These words		will signifie	
	Quantity		Mathematician
	Magnitude		Geometrician
	Number		Arithmetician
	World		Cosmographer
	Star		Astronomer, &c.

V.
3. { *MECHANIC*
   { *MERCHANT*

The last pair in this Combination may properly serve to express those words which are commonly given to Persons from their several Trades and Occupations.

The first, for the Trades of *Manufacture*, according to the several Mechanic. employments or object matters about which such Trades are conversant; some of which will be capable of composition with the Preposition *Sub* or *Under*. So

These words		will signifie		These words		will signifie	
	Stone		Mason		Leather		Tanner
	Wood		Carpenter		Cloth		Clothier
	Metal		Smith		Cloth thickning		Fuller
	Gold		Gold-smith		Vest		Taylor
	Iron		Black-smith				Botcher
	Lead		Plummer		Foot-vest		Shoomaker
	Pewter		Pewterer				Cobler
	Brass		Brasier		Head-vest		Hatter
			Tinker		Hand-vest		Glover
	Gems		Lapidary		Spinning		Spinster
	Statues		Statuary		Sowing		Sempster
			Sculptor		Washing		Laundress
	Painting		Painter		Bed		Upholster
	Musick		Minstrel		Tub		Cooper
			Fidler		Knife		Cutler
	Medicine		Apothecary		Bow		Fletcher
	Printing		Printer		Candle		Chaundler
	Writing		Scrivener		Book		Book-binder
	Cord		Roper				

And so for other particular Trades which belong to other matters, as *Gun, Lock, Clock, Watch*, &c.

Xx 2   The

Merchant. The second for the trades of *Exchange*, many of which were wont in their *English* names to be compounded with the Termination *Monger*; as *Wood-monger*, *Iron-monger*, *Fish-monger*, &c. From the old Latin word *Mango*, which signifies a *Seller*. So

These words		will signifie		These words		will signifie	
	Flesh		Butcher		Linnen		L. Draper
	Cattle		Grasier		Woollen		W. Draper
	Spice		Grosser		Head-vest		Haberdasher
	Wine		Vintner		Old-vest		Broker
	Victuals		Victualer		Silk		Mercer
	Medicament		Drugster		Book		Stationer

VI.

1. {*POWER* or *Ability*
   APTITUDE or *Proneness*.

Betwixt these two there is an evident affinity, both of them being common servile notions, and of very general extent; they are applicable to an *Integral* both *Substantive* and *Adjective*, and capable both of an *Active* and *Passive* sense: Being expressed in Latin by the Termination (*tivus* and *bilis*) and in English by the Termination (*tive* and *ble*) And when the words to which they are affixed are compounded with any Adverb of a Negative or Privative sense, they are by that Adverb made to signifie, *Impotence* or *Ineptitude*, either *Active* or *Passive*.

Though the derivations of *Abstracts* before-mentioned may serve well enough for several of the following instances, yet to prevent the ambiguity that may otherwise happen in some of these derivations, it will be proper to make use of these Particles. We have not actually indeed such variety of words as may be suted to these notions; but this is from the defect of Language, for the things themselves are naturally capable of this kind of inflexion. •

Power. The first of these may signifie either
- Affirmatively
  - Substantive, denoting *Ability*
    - Active, to do, *Sensitiveness*, *Visiveness*
    - Passive, to be done, *Sensibleness*, *Visibleness*
  - Adjective, or *Able*
    - Active, to do, *Sensitive*, *Visive*
    - Passive, to be done, *Sensible*, *Visible*
- Negatively
  - Substantive, denoting *Inability*
    - Active, to do, *Insensitiveness*, *Invisiveness*
    - Passive, to be done, *Insensibleness*, *Invisibility*
  - Adjective, or *Unable*
    - Active, to do, *Insensitive*, *Invisive*
    - Passive, to be done, *Insensible*, *Invisible*

By

Chap. VII.   Concerning Natural Grammar.   341

By this Particle are all these common words to be exprest, *Capable, Effable, Audible, Accessible, Comprehensible, Evitable, Fallible*, &c. which being compounded with the Negative Particle (*in*) will signifie the opposite, as, *Incapable*, &c.

In this sense, to render a man *Unresponsive*, is to *Confound, Poze, Puzzle, Non-plus*. A person *insolutive*, or (as we commonly say) insolvent, is a *Bankrupt*; *Unwalkative*, is a *Cripple*; *Non-surrective*, is *Bedrid*; *Unsatiable*, is *Flue*, &c.

The second of these may likewise signifie, either   *Aptitude.*
- Affirmatively, whether affixed to
  - Substantive, denoting *Aptness*
    - Active, to do, *Amorousness, Credulousness*
    - Passive, to be done, *Amiableness, Credibleness*
  - Adjective, *Apt*
    - Active, to do, *Amorous, Credulous*
    - Passive, to be done, *Amiable, Credible*
- Negatively, whether affixed to a
  - Substantive, *Unaptness*
    - Active, to do, *Unamorousness, Incredulousness*
    - Passive, to be done, *Unamiableness, Incredibleness*
  - Adjective, *Unapt*
    - Active, to do, *Unamourous, Incredulous*
    - Passive, to be done, *Unamiable, Incredible*

There are great variety of Integrals, to which these notes are applicable. So

These words will signifie		These words will signifie	
Motion	Agile, Nimble-ness	Evaporative	Volatile
Fear	Timerous, Terrible	Imitative	Mimical
		Cleanse	Abstersive
Shame	Bashful-ness	Corrode	Corrosive
Anger	Hasty, Touchy, Peevish, Froward, Choleric, Testy, Pettish, Snappish, &c.	Sickness	Crazy
		Sleep	Sickly Drowsie
		Grudge	Querulous
Contention	Captious-ness, Quarrelsom	Kick	Skittish
		Break	Frail Brittle
Contempt	Scornful, Despicable	Correction	Corrigible
Lust	Salacity, Libidinous	Associate	Sociable
		To be found	Obvious
Inventiveness	Sagacity	Inhabit	Habitable
Play	Wanton, Gamesome	Trouble	Troublesom

There are some words in our English Tongue which are used promiscuously, both Actively and Passively; as *Changeable, Mutable, Alterable, Pitiful, Fearful, Mortal*, &c. whereby they are liable to mistake, which may be prevented by these Particles, being duely apply'd either to a *Substantive* or *Adjective*, *Active* or *Passive*, as the sense shall require.

INCEP-

VI.
1. INCEPTIVE
2. FREQUENTATIVE

Inceptive.   The first signifies the *beginning* of Actions or Things; which being a kind of *Mode* or imperfect notion, is therefore fit to be joyned as a *servile* and *auxiliary*. 'Tis commonly expressed in English, by the word *Wax* or *Grow*; And in *Latin* (as was observed before) by the Termination *sco, Senesco, Lucesco, Calesco; Wax old, Wax light, Wax hot,* &c. There are in our Language some peculiar words and phrases, which do only import this notion, and by this mark will be rendred needless and redundant. So

These words will signifie	These words will signifie	These words will signifie	These words will signifie
Fire	Kindle, Tind, Light	Possess	Take Livery and Seisin
Break	Crack	Repent	Relent
Usurp	Encroach	Trade	Set up
Navigate	Take shipping, Launch	Work	Set to work
		Hold	Take hold
Itinerate	Set forth	Effluviate	Tap, Broach
Proceed	Set forward		

So the word Morning, with this note will signifie, *Dawning, Dayspring, Aurora, Diluculum*; And the word day or night, with this mark will signifie, *Crepusculum, Twilight*.

Frequentative.   The second of these doth signifie the repetition or *wontedness* of Actions, which is such a kind of servile notion as the former, and therefore fit to be this way provided for. It is of a very large extent in the use of it, being (as the other notion of inceptive likewise is) applicable to most Verbs; And there are some words in our English which will by this note be rendred needless. So

These words will signifie	These words will signifie	These words will signifie	These words will signifie
Drink	Bibble, Tipple	Demand	Solicit, Dunne
Talk	Babble		
Move in Water	Dabble	Sigh	Sob
Come	Haunt, Resort	Disappear	Twinckle, Glimmer
Repeat	Inculcate	Pull	Vellicate
	Ingeminate	Bite	Gnaw

It may be worthy consideration to enquire, whether the opposite to each of these, *viz. Desinative* and *Raritive* or seldom, ought not to be particularly provided for in this kind.

Chap. VII. *Concerning Natural Grammar.* 343

VI.
3. {ENDEAVOUR
    IMPETUS

Both these may contribute to the Abbreviating of Language, when they are compounded as serviles; there being several distinct words and phrases, which by such composition will be rendred needless, their true notions being sufficiently expressable by the use of these Particles.

The first denotes the Application of a Mans self to the doing of any thing. So *Endeavour.*

These words { Hear, See, Feel, Lift, Catch } will signifie { Listen, Hearken, Attend, Give Ear, Pry, Peep, Grope, Heave, Catch at }

These words { Strike, Strike thrustingly, Obtain, Provide, Sell } will signifie { Strike at, Foine at, Reach after, Purvey, Set to Sale }

The second doth denote the particular fit, or sudden violence of any Action or Thing. So *Impetus.*

These words { Motion, Thrust, Pull, Percussion, Catch, Bite, Exclamation } will signifie { Start, Jerk, Rush, Twitch, Rap, Snatch, Snap, Shout, Squeak, Squeal, Scream, Shreek }

These words { Running, Anger, Melancholy, Flame, Wind, Rain, Battel, Disease } will signifie { Career, Fury, Dump, Flash, Flaw, Gust, Storm, Shock, Fit, Paroxysm }

VII.
1. {AUGMENTATIVE
    DIMINUTIVE

These are of very general comprehensive usefulness in Language.

The former of them doth properly denote Transcendental *Greatness*, both *Extensive* and *Intensive*. When it is applyed to *Bodies*, 'tis of the same import with those usual words, *Great, Huge, Vast, Main*: and is by the Latins often expressed in Adjectives by the Termination (*osus*) whereby they signifie the notion of *Abounding*. *Augmentative.*

When it is applied to *Qualities* or *Actions*, it denotes *Intention of Degrees*, being equivalent with those Articles, *very, much, hard, sore, stark, sound, greatly; Valde, multum, oppido, magnopere, perquam, admodum, vehementer, cumprimis,* &c.

It is applicable likewise by way of Allusion to the *Amplitude, Grandeur,* and eminency of any thing in its kind, which being a general Metaphor, may therefore fitly and safely be this way provided for: As the words *Man, Physician, Merchant,* with the note of *Diminutive* affixed to them, do signifie, meanness and contemptibleness: So the same words with this mark of *Augmentative,* will denote *eminency* and considerableness, being proper to commend and set forth any thing for extraordinariness in its kind.   1. This

344 *Concerning Natural Grammar.* Part III.

1. This mark may be applied to the names of Bodies. So

These words will signifie	These words will signifie	These words will signifie	These words will signifie
Sea	Ocean	Cord	Cable,
Wave	Billow, Surge		Rope
Staffe	Stake, Batt	Dish	Charger
Twig	Pole	Spoon	Ladle
Branch	Bow, Arme of Tree	Hammer Wooden hammer	Sledge Beetle

2. It may be applied to such names as signifie Qualities or Actions.

These words will signifie	These words will signifie	These words will signifie	These words will signifie
Hate	Abhor, Abominate, Detest	Past	Antique, of old
		Oblique	Steep
Fear	Aghast, Hideous, Dread, Terrour,	Vicious	Flagitious, Heinous,
Anger	Rage, Wrath, Fury, Rave,	Hunger	Profligate Greadiness, Eagerness
Grieve	Take on		
Shame	Confusion	Eat	Devour,
Wonder	Astonish Consternation	Drink	Voracious Carouse, Quaff, Swill
Malice	Rancor		
Care	Anxiety, Solicitude	Spit Hot	Spawl Torrid, Swelter, Soultry
Willing	Forward		
Desire	Long for	Pain	Torment, Torture
Known	Notorious	Price	Pretious, Costly, Sumptuous,
Ask	Adjure, Urge		Dear
Labour	Toile, Moile, Drudge	Adorned	Brave, Gallant, Gorgeous, Splendid, Sparke
Endeavour	Bestir, Stickle, Strive, Coil, Ado, Contend	Beat	Swing
Affirm	Averr, Avouch, Vouch	Pull Prove	Tug Demonstrate
Deny	Renounce	Reprove	Rate
Sound	Loudness, Noise	Solemnity	Grandeur
Voice	Clamour, Roar, Cry	Fame	Renown

Diminutive. The second of these being directly opposite to the first, is of like extent and usefulness, and will not need any further explication but only by Instances.

1. 'Tis

Chap. VII.   *Concerning Natural Grammar.*   345

1. 'Tis applicable to bodies and things. So

These words will signifie

Horse	Nag	Chamber	Cell, Cabin
Pike	Pickerell, Jack	Tower	Turret
House	Cottage	Sword	Dagger, Ponyard, Stilletto
Bed	Pallet	Gun	Pistol, Dagg
Door	Wicket	Stream	Brook, Rivulet
Rain	Mizling, drizling	Prominence	Stud
Skin	Tunicle, Cuticle	Foss	Wrinkle
Bladder	Veficle	Script	Ticket, Scrole
Dust	Atome, Mote		Schedule
Branch	Sprig	Piece	Scrap, Crum
Images	Babies, Puppets,		

2. 'Tis applicable to Qualities and Actions. So

These words will signifie

Hot	Tepid, Lukewarm	Drink	Bibb, Sip
Moist	Damp, Dank	Cognition	Hint, inkling, intimation
Light	Glimmering	Doubt	Scruple
Spot	Speck	Sin	Peccadillo, Failing
Wild	Skittish	Vomit	Puke
Gust	Smack, Tang	Burn	Parch, Scorch, Sweal
Sound	Quatch	Boil	Parboil, reare
Skill	Smattering	Play	Dally
Handsome	Pretty	Sleep	Slumber, Nap
Good		Ringing	Jingle, Tinkle
More	A little	Prayer	Ejaculation
Great	Greater	Comment	Gloss, Notes, Annota- (tion
Many	More	Contention	Jarring, Bickering
Price	Cheap	Past	Alate
Move	Wag	Future	Shortly, soon
Stumble	Trip	Oblique	Steep, slope
Halt	Limp	Sum	Driblet
Fight	Fray, Scuffle	Proportion	Pittance, Scantling
Bite	Nibble	Aggregate	Parcel

3. This note may sometimes be applied in a *Metaphorical* sense to signifie contemptibleness or *littleness of value*, as well as *littleness of bulk*. So the word Man with this note may signifie either *Dandiprat, Dwarf, Elf, Zany, Pigmy*; or else *Scrub, Sorry fellow, Companion, Jack*. So the word Physitian with this note, will signifie *Mountebank, Quack-salver, Empyrick:* And the word Merchant being so noted, will signifie *Pedler, Huckster,* &c.

Yy   EXCESSIVE

VII.
2. {EXCESSIVE / DEFECTIVE}

Excess.

These are joyned upon account of opposition, the meaning of each being very obvious.

The former denoting all kind of excess; Particularly, 1. The redundant extreme in all *Qualities*, or Vertues together. 2. With such other notions as bear some kind of *Analogy* or resemblance to these in other things. As likewise, 3. The *Nimiety* of any Quality or Action.

1. Of the first kind are such instances as these. So

These words will figure	These words will figure	These words will figure	will figure
Diligence	Double diligence	Modesty	Abjectness
Consideration	Cunctation	Abstinence	Maceration
Heedfulness	Carking	Cleanliness	Finicalness
Patience	Obstinacy		niceness
Constancy	Pertinacy	Frugality	Penuriousness
Knowledge	Curiosity	Liberality	Prodigality
Prudence	Craft	Magnificence	Luxuriousness
Moderation	Slightness, Neutrality		riotousness
		Courtesie	Fawning
Justice	Rigor	Taciturnity	Shiness
Fortitude	Rashness	Urbanity	Scurrility
Magnanimity	Insolence	Gravity	Formality
Meekness	Lentitude, stupor	Faith	Credulity
		Hope	Presumption

2. Of the second kind, these are some Instances. So

These words	will figure	These words	will figure
Plane	Mountain	Parabola	Hyperbole
Oblique	Direct	Mean	Acute
Present	Past	Ripeness	Over-ripe
Simultaneous	Preceding	Equal	Superior
Flet	Gibbous	Sufficiency	Excess

3. Of the third kind, there are these Instances. So

These words	will figure	These words	will figure
Esteem	Over-value	Long	Tedious, prolix
Opinionate	Over-weene	Old	Stale
Great	Over-grown	Extension	Sprain
Load	Over-charge	Dunging	Scowring
	Surcharge	Soon	Over-soon
Adorned	Gay, Gaudy	Repetition	Battology, Tautology
Sweet	Luscious		
Laugh	Giggle	Baked	Over-baked
Hasten	Precipitate	Boiled	Over-boiled
Chide	Scold	Roasted	Over-roasted

The

Chap. VII.   *Concerning Natural Grammar.*

The mark of *Defect* is in each particular correspondent to the Defect.
former, denoting either

1. The deficient extreme in all kind Acts, Habits, Vertues, as may be seen by the opposites to those before-mentioned.

{ Diligence   { Idleness
{ Consideration { Rashness
{ Heedfulness   { Carelesness

2. Some kind of resemblance to this in other things.

{ Plane   { Valley
{ Oblique { Transverse
{ Present { Future, *&c.*

3. The deficiency of any Action, or the under-doing of a thing.

{ Esteem   { Under-value
{ Opinionate { Under-weene
{ Great   { Not sufficiently big, *&c.*

{ Baked   { Under-baked
{ Boyled { Under-boyled.

VII.
3. { *PERFECTIVE*
   { *CORRUPTIVE*

This pair may be of very general use for all kind of *Actions* and *Things*.

Besides those general notions referring to the measure and *degrees of things* in the two former pairs, it may be requisite to provide the like way for expressing the *manner of them*, as to *Well* or *Ill*; *Right* or *Wrong*; as it should be, as it should not be. The first of these is in many *Greek* words expressed by the composition with εὖ and ὀρθῶς, and Perfective. in *English* by *Well* and *Right*. So

	These words will signifie		These words will signifie
Figured	Well-favoured	Event	Prosper, Succeed, Speed,
Come	Well come		Fortunate,
Advised	Well advised		Lucky,
Healthy	Well in health		Auspicious
Put	Set right		Good plight
Understand	Understand aright	State	Debonair
Use	Use aright	Humour	Euphony
Time	Oportunity,	Voice	Orthography
	Season, Good time	Lettering	Demonstrate
		Prove	

Corruptive. The second of these is sometimes expressed in *English* by composition with those Particles *Dis.* or *Mis.* or *Un.* So

These words		will signifie	These words		will signifie	
	Colour	Dis-colour		Conster		Mis-conster
	Figure	Dis-figure		Use		Mis-use, Abuse
	Place	Dis-place		Lead		Mis-lead, Seduce
	Order	Dis-order		Name		Mis-call, Nic-name
	Proportion	Dis-proportion		Event		Mis-fortune
	Service	Dis-service				Mis-chance
	Temper	Distemper				Mis-hap
	Esteem	Mis-prision				Mis-adventure
	Opinion	Mistake				
	Become	Mis-become				

These words		will signifie
	Timely	Unseasonable, Untimely
	Figured	Unfashioned, Defaced
	Event	Unlucky, Unprosperous, Unhappy, Unfortunate, Unsuccessful, Sinister, Adverse

This mark may likewise serve to express the true notion of several other words, which are not usually thus compounded.

These words		will signifie	These words		will signifie
	Fancy	Caprichious, Freakish, Conceited	Horse		Jade
	Ancestor	Degenerate	Write		Scribble
	Jester	Buffoon	Cut, Carve		Whittle, Hack
	Temper	Humorist	Content		Male-content

VIII.

1. {*VOICE* / *LANGUAGE*}

The first of these will by its composition serve to express those several words which are used for the *Voices* of divers *Animals*: or for the voices that are used in expressing sundry *Actions* or *Affections*. So

These words		will signifie	These words		will signifie
	Lion	Roaring	Sparrow		Chirp
	Horse	Neighing	Hog		Grunting
	Ass	Braying	Dog		Barking
	Bull	Bellowing	anger		Snarling
	Cow	Lowing	Whelp		Yelping
	Sheep	Bleating	Frog		Croking
	Wolf	Howling	Cock		Crowing
		Yelling	Goose		Gaggle
	Hen	Cackle	Owle		Hoot
	Chicken	Peep	Bee		Buz, Hum
	Swallow	Chatter			

This

Chap. VII.   *Concerning Natural Grammar.*   349

This note may likewise be applied to such kind of voices as belong to several affections. So

These words {
 Grudging
 Grief
 Anger
 Contention
 Praise
} will signifie {
 Mutter, grumble, murmur
 Wail, mourn, moan
 Chafe, storm
 Brangle, brawl, wrangle
 Plaudit
}

The second particular is paired with the former for its affinity to Language: it. The proper *use* of it is by its composition with the names or characters of several Countries or Nations, to express the notion of the Languages spoken by them. So the Character or word of *English*, *Spanish*, *French*, *Italian*, *German*, &c. with this affix, will determine these words to the signification of those Tongues or Languages: And the same note affixed to the name of any *Tribe*, may signifie the *Dialect* of it. There seems to be least necessity of this Particle; and it might well be spared, if any more proper could be thought of, to supply the place of it.

VIII.
2. { *MALE*
    FEMALE }

The second pair in this last Combination is for the distinction of such things as have *Sex*. And all those names of *Animals* or *Relations*, which are distinguishable only by their *Sex*, ought not to have any other distinction in their appellations but that of their Sex : So that whereas we say, *Ram*, *Yew*, *Boar*, *Sow*, &c. *Father*, *Mother*, *Son*, *Daughter*, &c. It would be more agreeable to the Philosophy of Speech, if these things were to be expressed a *male sheep*, a *female sheep*, a *male or female swine*; a *male or female Parent or Child*, &c.

These marks are applicable

1. To kinds of *Animals*; of which there are such instances as these.

These words {
 Man
 Lion
 Horse
 Bull
 Stag
 Buck
} will signifie {
 Woman
 Lioness
 Mare
 Cow
 Hind
 Doe
} These words {
 Dog
 Cock
 Drake
 Gander
 Drone
 Milter
} will signifie {
 Bitch
 Hen
 Duck
 Goose
 Bee
 Spawner
}

2. To Relations of Persons; as in these instances. So

The words {
 Brother
 Uncle
 Nephew
 Sutor
 Servant
 Bridegroom
 Husband
 Batchelour
} will signifie {
 Sister
 Aunt
 Niece
 Mistress
 Sweet-heart
 Bride
 Wife
 Maid
} The words {
 Widower
 King
 Lord
 Master
 Man-servant
 Abbot
 Friar
 Sloven
 Whoremonger
} will signifie {
 Widow
 Queen
 Lady
 Mistress, Dame
 Maid-servant
 Abbess
 Nun
 Slut
 Whore, Strumpet
}

YOUNG

VIII.
3. {YOUNG / PART}

Young. By the first of these is meant the young ones or *brood* of any sorts of Animals, for which we have no proper word in *English*. So

These words { Horse, Cow, Deer, Sheep, Goat, Hog, Bear } will signifie { Colt, Foal, Filly; Calf; Fawn; Lamb; Kid; Pig; Cub }

These words { Dog, Cat, Cony, Hare, Hen, Frog, Herring } will signifie { Puppy, Whelp; Kitlin, Chitt; Rabbet; Leveret; Chicken; Tadpole; Sprat }

Part. By the second of these may be expressed such kind of names as do comprehend in them the notion of *Part*, under the several relations of 1. *Situation*. 2. *Proportion*. 3. *Figure* or *Colour*. 4. *Use*.

1. Of the first kind there are such examples as these. So

These words {
Ship { Fore / Hinder }
Army { Fore / Middle / Hinder / Side }
Oration { Fore / Hinder }
} will signifie {
Prow, Beak / Poop, Stern
Van, Vauntguard, Front / Main Battel / Rere, Rereward / Wing
Preamble, Preface, Proem, Prologue / Epilogue, Conclusion
}

2. Of the second are such instances as these.
{ A second / A fourth / A tenth } { Half / Quarter / Tithe, &c. }

And so a fourth part of a Circle is a Quadrant, a sixth part is a Sextant, &c.

3. Of the third kind there are such instances as these.
Hand
   Convex   Back
   Concave   Palm
Leg
   Fore   Shin
   Hinder   Calf
Egge
   White   White
   Yellow   Yolk
   Off-cut   Segment

Chap. VII. *Concerning Natural Grammar.* 351

4. Of the fourth kind there are such examples as these.

These words		will signifie	
Covering			Lid
Stopping			Stopple
To be handed			Handle, Haft, Helve, Hilt
Bell } striking			Clapper
Gun }			Cock
Shoo-fastning			Latchet

It may happen sometimes that two of these Transcendental Particles should concur to the composition of some words: In which case it will be worth consideration, whether it may not be more distinct to express one of them by an *Integral*, and the other by an *Affix*.

It may likewise deserve some farther inquiry, whether some of these Particles here nominated, may not be spared to make room for others more useful; as particularly those servile general notions of

{ Continuing
{ Discontinuing

{ Permitting
{ Hindering

{ Facility
{ Difficulty; as likewise, Flower, Fruits, Disease, &c.

I have been somewhat the longer in treating concerning these Transcendental Particles; because being for the most part *new*, and not all of them used in any one Language, they do thereupon stand in greater need of being more particularly and fully explained and discussed.

I have now done with the first part of *Etymology*; namely, concerning the *formal differences* or kinds of words, whether { Integrals
{ Particles.

CHAP.

CHAP. VIII.

Of the Accidental Difference of words. I. *Inflexion.* II. *Derivation.* III. *Composition.*

THE next thing to be treated of, is concerning the *Accidental Differences* of words; and amongst these

§. I. 1. Concerning the *Inflexion* of them, which doth consist in the several ways of varying the same word to sundry modes of signification. This is not *arbitrary*, as it is used in several Languages; much less should the rules to this purpose, which belong to the Latin, be applied to Vulgar Tongues, to which they are not suited (as many Grammarians use to do) but it ought to be founded upon the Philosophy of speech and such *Natural* grounds, as do necessarily belong to Language.

Integral words are all capable of Inflexion.

1. Noun *Substantives* are inflected in a threefold respect.

1. By *Number*, *Singular* and *Plural*, which being more Intrinsecal to them, ought to be provided for in the Character or word it self, and not by an Affix.

2. By *Gender*, in things that are capable of *Sex*, which are naturally but two, *Masculine* and *Feminine*: These being less Intrinsical to the primary notion of the word, may be more properly expressed by affixes; and then the kind or species of every Animal (abstractedly from the respective Sexes of it) may be signifyed by the Radical word it self, without any sign of Sex, which will prevent much equivocalness.

3. By *Cases*, which is not so essential and natural to Substantives, as to be provided for in the word it self, by varying the Terminations of it; For though this course hath been used in the *Greek* and *Latin*: yet neither do the Oriental Tongues, *Hebrew, Chaldee, Arabick*, &c. nor those Occidental of *French, Italian, Spanish*; nor I think doth any Modern Tongue in the world this way express them.

The true notion of the *Nominative* Case, is that which precedes the Verb, and the *Accusative*, that which follows the Verb; of which in speech that is suited to natural Structure and Syntax, there ought to be no other sign or note then the very order. As for the *Genitive* Case, the proper notion of that, is its following another Substantive *in regimine*: But because the following Substantive is not always governed by that which precedes; as *Urbs Roma, Rhenus Fluvius, Taxus arbor*, &c. therefore 'tis proper to have a Particle or Preposition for it, as our *English* (*Of*) and (*De*) in the *French, Italian, Spanish*, which was treated of before. The *Dative* Case is expressed by the Preposition (*To*) the *Vocative* by the Interjection of bespeaking (*O*) and the *Ablative* Case by such a Preposition as denotes Formal or Instrumental cause, or manner of Doing. So that the true notion of the *Genitive*, *Dative, Ablative* Case, is nothing else but that obliquity in the sence of a Substantive, which is caused and signifyed by some Preposition annexed to it, as the *Vocative* is by an Interjection.

And

Chap. VIII.   *Concerning Natural Grammar.*   353

And besides these three ways of Inflexion, I have shewed before how Substantives are capable likewise of *Active* and *Passive* voice, and of *Tenses*.

Noun *Adjectives* need not have any note to express *Number, Gender, Case*, because in all these they agree with their Substantives; unless such Adjectives as are used Substantively, by reason of their composition with the Transcendental marks of *Person, Thing, Time, Place*, &c. In which case they have the same kinds of Inflexion with Substantives. But there is belonging to them,

1. A transverse Inflexion by *degrees of Comparison*, which may be best denoted by the extrinsical affixes of *more, most ; less, least*.

2. An Inflexion by Voice *Active* and *Passive*, which makes them of the same nature with those words which we call Participles.

3. An Inflexion by *Tenses*. And though usually in the *Latin* there are but two Tenses, viz. *Present* and *Future*, in each voice of the Participle, *Amans, Legens: Amaturus, Lecturus: Amatus, Lectus: Amandus, Legendus:* excepting in some few words, *Sequens, Sequutus, Sequuturus ; Gaudens, Gavisus, Gavisurus:* and of *Cœnatum*, which is used promiscuously both Actively and Passively ; yet this is a defect in the Latin Tongue : For the natural notion doth render Participles as well capable of the Preter Tense ; and accordingly the Greeks have τύπων, τετυφὼς, τύψων, & τυπ]όμυΘ, τετυμμΘ, τυφθησόμυΘ : He that beats, he that hath beaten, he that will beat ; he that is beaten, he that hath been beaten, he that will be beaten. The like would have been in Latin, if the Philosophy of Speech had been as well observed in the Institution of that Language.

Derived Adverbs are capable of Inflexion by *degrees of Comparison*.

Amongst the Particles, there are only two that are capable of Inflexion ; *viz.* the *Copula*, and *Pronouns*.

The *Copula* is inflected by *Mode* and by *Tense* ; which I have sufficiently explained before : Only 'tis here to be noted, that besides those *definite* notions of time past, present, and to come, there is likewise *Tempus Aoristicum*, or *indefinite* time ; and that whenever the Copula is used *in materia necessaria*, it ought to be understood as being indeterminate to any of those differences of time. So for such sayings, *Homo est animal, Deus vivit*, &c. there is no kind of time, whether past, present, or future, wherein these sayings are not equally true ; so that the sense of such sayings is *est, fuit, erit ; vivit, vixit, vivet*. And therefore it would be convenient to make some distinction for expressing this indefinite time. *Chap. 5.*

Pronoun Substantives are inflected by *Number* and *Gender*, and by *Case*, as Noun Substantives are ; besides that kind of improper Inflection, whereby they are made *Possessives* ; which is rather a kind of Derivation, and *reduplicative*, which consists only in the doubling of them for the greater *Emphasis*.

The other Particles are not capable of Inflexion, because they do not denote any *Essence* or *Act*, which is capable of several modes or respects, as Integrals, and two of the Particles do : but only the *Circumstances* or *Modifications* of other words ; and therefore may be stiled indeclinable or invariable.

§ II. As to *Derivation*, there ought naturally to be but one kind of Root, from which the several differences of Integrals should be derived; and this should be a Noun *Substantive* which signifies the *Thing*, or the *Essence*. If it be a Noun Substantive *Neuter;* then the first branches of it are Substantives *Active* and *Passive*; after which succeed the *Adjectives* belonging to each of them, and then the *Adverbs*, which denote the Quality or Manner of being or doing. All which belong to one branch. Another branch is the Substantives *Abstract*, which have the same kind of derivations from them, as the former; as is more distinctly explained before.

Chap. I.
§ XI.

§ III. As to the last accidental difference of words, viz. *Composition*. 'Tis to be noted, that the words of a Philosophical Language should be so suted unto natural notions, that there should be little need of other compositions, besides those by *Prepositions, Adverbs*, and *Transcendental Particles*. But if this were desired for greater elegance and copiousness of Speech, it should be capable of any composition whatsoever, which may be signified in writing by some *Hyphen* or mark of Union, to joyn the words compounded; and in Speech by pronouncing them together as one word, without changing the nature of either. So the word *Idolatry* is *Idol-worship*, &c.

CHAP. IX.

Of the second part of Grammar called Syntax.

AS the first part of Grammar doth treat concerning the nature and differences of particular words: So the second part of Grammar stiled *Syntax*, doth concern the proper way of Union or right Construction of words, into Propositions, or continued Speech. And this may be distinguished into two kinds. 1. That which is *Customary* and figurative: or 2. That which is *Natural* and regular.

1. That structure may be stiled *Customary* and figurative, which is used in the Phraseologies or forms of Speech, peculiar to several Languages, wherein words are put together according to a *Metaphorical* and tralatitious sense of them; as in those Latin Phrases, *Redigere in ordinem*, which signifies, *Privare magistratu*; *E medio tollere*, for *Occidere*. And so for those English Phrases of Breaking a jest, Hedging in a Debt, Taking ones heels and flying away, Being brought to bed, Lying in, Being in Labour or Travail, *&c.* All which ought to be rendred according to the natural sense and meaning intended by those Phrases; which is observed in the regular Translation of any Language. And he that would go about to render such forms of Speech, according to the strict and natural sense of the words, could not reasonably expect to be understood in any other Language.

But besides these kind of *Metaphors* which are peculiar to some Tongues, there are others of a more general use, which may be well enough retained in a Philosophical Language.

2. That

Chap. IX. *Concerning Natural Grammar.*

2. That structure may be called *Regular,* which is according to the natural sense and order of the words.

The General Rule for this order amongst *Integrals* is, That which governs should precede; The Nominative Case before the Verb, and the Accusative after; The Substantive before the Adjective: Only Adjective Pronouns being Particles and affixed, may without inconvenience be put indifferently either before or after. *Derived Adverbs* should follow that which is called the *Verb,* as denoting the quality or manner of the Act.

As for the *Grammatical Particles,* those which serve for the Inflexion or Composition of words should naturally precede; and so likewise should other Adverbs, and Prepositions.

Transcendental Particles are to be joyned in composition at the ends of words, to vary their termination.

Besides the *order* required in Syntax, something ought to be subjoyned concerning the *Quantity* of Vowels or Syllables, together with the several distinctions or *interpunctions* to be observed betwixt words and sentences.

As for that part usually treated of in instituted Grammars, stiled *Prosodia,* concerning the quantity of Vowels, there needs not any thing to be said unto that here; because in a Philosophical Language every Vowel is supposed to be in the writing sufficiently distinguished in this respect; every long Vowel having a note or mark to signifie its prolation.

The expressing of any one syllable in a word, with a little *higher tune,* and *longer time* then others, is to be exprest by an accent; as in the words, Consènt, Contrìve, Compòse, Hàving, Wìsdom, Fòrtune, Pròfit, Pàrentage, Prìvilege, Consìder, Detèrmine, *&c.*

The distinctions to be observed betwixt words and sentences, may refer either to 1. The *time;* or 2. The *manner of pronouncing.*

1. The first concerns those Pauses or *intervals of rest* to be observed in Pronouncing, which were anciently distinguished into three kinds; namely, *Comma, Colon, Period.* The first of these being marked with a point by the middle of the Letter; The second at the top; The last at the bottom. Unto these, later times have added two others; namely, a mark to signifie something intermediate betwixt *Comma* and *Colon,* stiled *Semicolon;* and something more then a *full point,* which is usually exprest by a greater distance betwixt the words, or by a Breach in the line.

The use of these Points is to direct what kind of pause is to be observed, and how the tenor or tone of the voice is either to be continued or to fall.

2. The *manner of pronouncing* words doth sometimes give them a different sense and meaning, and Writing being the Picture or Image of Speech, ought to be adapted unto all the material circumstances of it, and consequently must have some marks to denote these various manners of Pronunciation; which may be sufficiently done by these seven kinds of marks or Interpunctions.

1. *Parenthesis.*

1. *Parenthesis*.
2. *Parathesis*, or Exposition.
3. *Erotesis*, or Interrogation.
4. *Ecphonesis*, Exclamation or wonder.
5. *Emphasis*.
6. *Irony*.
7. *Hyphen*.

1. *Parenthesis* serves for the distinction of such an additional part of a sentence as is not necessary to perfect the sense of it, and is usually expressed in our Western Languages by the inclosing of such words betwixt two curve lines ( )

2. *Parathesis*, or Exposition, is used for distinction of such words as are added by way of explication of something preceding, and is usually expressed by inclosing such words between two angular lines; as [ ]

3. *Erotesis*, or Interrogation, is a kind of Period for the distinction of such sentences as are proposed by way of Question, and is usually thus marked ?

4. *Ecphonesis*, or Wonder and Exclamation, is a note of direction for raising the tone, upon occasion of such words as denote some vehement passion, and is noted thus !

5. *Emphasis* is used for the distinction of such word or words, wherein the force of the sense doth more peculiarly consist, and is usually expressed by putting such words into another kind of Character, as suppose the Italic.

6. *Irony* is for the distinction of the meaning and intention of any words, when they are to be understood by way of Sarcasm or scoff, or in a contrary sense to that which they naturally signifie: And though there be not (for ought I know) any note designed for this in any of the Instituted Languages, yet that is from their deficiency and imperfection: For if the chief force of Ironies do consist in Pronunciation, it will plainly follow, that there ought to be some mark for direction, when things are to be so pronounced.

7. *Hyphen* is a note that signifies the uniting of two syllables or words into one, and may properly be used when two words are to be compounded together: It is usually expressed by two little strokes, thus (-)

CHAP.

CHAP. X.

Of Orthography. I. *Concerning the doctrine of Letters: the Authors who have treated of this Subject.* II. *A brief Table of such simple sounds as can be framed by men.* III. *A further explication of this Table, as to the Organs of Speech, and as to the letters framed by these Organs.*

ORthography is that part of Grammar, which concerns the doctrine § I. of *Letters,* which being the most simple *Elements of Speech,* it ought therefore to be so stated, that there may be a sufficient number of them to express all Articulate sounds, and not more then are necessary to this end. Much consideration is requisite to the right establishment of these; upon which account this subject hath been largely debated, by several Authors of great names and reputation for Learning: Besides those Famous Emperours, *Cajus Cæsar,* and *Octavius Augustus,* who both writ upon this subject: *Varro* likewise, and *Appion,* and *Quintilian,* and *Priscian,* did bestow much pains upon the same enquiry, concerning the just number of *Letters.* And in later times, it hath been treated of with great variety of Opinions, by *Erasmus,* both the *Scaligers, Lipsius, Salmasius, Vossius, Jacobus Matthias, Adolphus Metkerchus, Bernardus Malinchot,* &c. Beside several of our own Country-men, *Sir Thomas Smith, Bullokar, Alexander Gill,* and Doctor *Wallis*; the last of whom, amongst all that I have seen published, seems to me, with greatest Accurateness and subtlety to have considered the Philosophy of Articulate sounds. But besides such (whose considerations upon this subject are made publick) I must not forget to acknowledge the favour and good hap I have had, to peruse from their *private* papers, the distinct Theories of some Dr. *William* other Learned and Ingenious persons, who have with great judgment *Holder,* applyed their thoughts to this enquiry; in each of whose Papers, there are several suggestions that are new, out of the common rode, and very considerable.

Letters may be considered according to their { *Essence* { Names
Order
Accidents { *Affinity*
Figure
Pronunciation }

The *Essence* of Letters doth consist in their *Power* or proper sound, which may be naturally fixed and stated, from the manner of forming them by the instruments of speech; and either is, or should be the same in all Languages.

What variety there is of these, may appear from the Distribution of them into their several kinds, according to the following Table; wherein it is endeavoured and aimed at, to give a rational account of all the simple sounds that are, or can be framed by the mouths of men.

Letters

§ II.

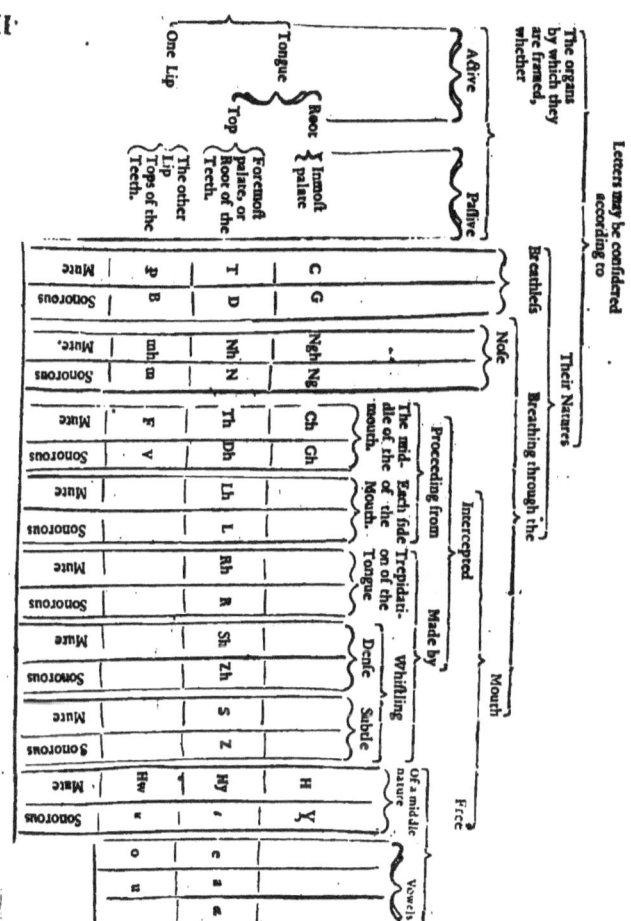

Chap. X. *Concerning Natural Grammar.* 359

§ III.

For the better explication of this Table, there are these two things to be considered : 1. The *Causes* of these Letters. 2. The *Letters* themselves.

1. In the *Causes* of Letters there are observable
- The *Organs* by which they are formed, either more
  - Common ; Lungs, Throat, Mouth, Nose.
  - Peculiar.
    - *Passive*
      - Palate ; according to the { *Inmost* or middle parts / *Foremost*
      - Teeth ; either the
        - Root or inner gums
        - Top
      - Lip { Upper / Lower
    - *Active* ; whether the
      - Tongue ; according to the
        - Root or middle
        - Top
      - Lips
- The *Actions* of these Organs, whether by
  - *Appulse* ; of the
    - Lips ; either
      - To one another
      - To the tops of the teeth
    - Tongue ; in respect of the
      - Top of it ; to the Teeth, { Tops / Roots or gums their
      - Root or middle of it, to the Palate
  - *Trepidation*, or vibration ; either of the
    - Lips
    - Tongue ; whether { Top / Root or middle of it
  - *Percolation* of the breath, between the
    - Lips contracted
    - Tongue ; either the
      - Top of it, applied to { Tops / Roots } of the Teeth
      - Root or middle of it, applied to the *inward palate*.

These I conceive to be all the kinds of Actions and Configurations which the organs are capable of, in order to Speech.

What kind of Letters are framed by these, will appear in the next Table.

All

- All simple letters may be distinguished into such as are; either
  - *Apert* and free, according to degrees
    - *Greater*; stiled most properly *Vowels*, which may be distinguished into
      - *Labial*, being framed by an emission of the breath through the Lips contracted,
        - *Less*. (O)
        - *More*, with the help of the Tongue put into a concave posture long ways, the Whistling or French (U)
      - *Lingual*; the breath being emitted, when the Tongue is put into a posture
        - *More concave*, and removed at some distance from the palate (*a*).
        - *Less concave* or plain, and brought nearer the palate (*a*)
        - Somewhat *convex* towards the palate (*e*)
    - *Lesser*; being either
      - *Sonorous*; of which it may be said, that they do somewhat approach to the nature of Consonants, and are *mediæ potestatis*; because when they are joyned with any Vowel to compose that which we call a Dipthong, they put on the nature of *Consonants*; and when they are not so joyned, but used singly, they retain the nature of *Vowels*, which is the reason why it hath been so much disputed amongst some Learned Men, whether they are to be reckoned amongst *Vowels* or *Consonants*.
      - These may be distinguished into
        - *Labial*; by an emission of the breath through the Lips, more *Contracted* (*v*)
        - *Lingual*; when the breath is emitted betwixt the middle of the Tongue in a more *Convex* posture, and the palate (*s*)
        - *Guttural*; by a free emission of the breath from the Throat (y)
      - *Mute*; When the breath is emitted through the Organs of speech, being in the same position as before: but without voice, to be distinguished as their three preceding correspondents, into
        - *Labial* (*bv*) or (*vh*)
        - *Lingual* (*hi*)
        - *Guttural* (*h*)
  - *Intercepted* and shut; according to degrees
    - *Lesser*; which because they have something Vowelish in them, are therefore by some styled *Semivowels*, being spiritous and breathed, whether
      - *Labial*; being pronounced through the
        - *Mouth*; by
          - *Appulse* of either lip to the opposite teeth, framing
            - V. Sonorous
            - F. Mute
          - *Trepidation* of the Lips, like that sound which is used in the driving of Cows, to which there is a correspondent

dent mute, sometimes used as an Interjection of disdain.

Percolation of the breath, betwixt both the Lips contracted round-wise, which makes the vocal whistling sound, to which likewise there is a correspondent mute whistling: But neither of these two last pairs being of use in Language, they need not therefore have any Marks or Letters assigned to them.

Nose; by an appulse; either of the Lips against one another: or against the top of the { M. Sonorous.
Teeth, framing { HM. Mute.

Lingual; either in respect of the

Top of the Tongue; being pronounced through the

Mouth; by

Appulse, of the top of the Tongue, to the

Top of the Teeth; the breath being emitted through the middle of the Mouth, fra- { Dh sonorous.
ming { Th mute.

Foremost part of the Palate; the breath being emitted through the

Corners of the mouth, { L sonorous.
framing { Hl mute.

Trepidation or Vibration; against the inmost part of of the Palate, { R. sonorous.
framing { HR. mute.

Percolation of the breath; between the top of the the Tongue, and the roots of the Teeth, whether more

Subtle, fra- { Z. sonorous.
ming { S. mute.
Dense, fra- { Zh. sonorous.
ming { Sh. mute.

Nose; by an appulse of the top of the Tongue to the roots of the Teeth, { N. sonorous.
framing { HN. mute.

Root or middle of the Tongue; being pronounced through the

Mouth; by

Appulse; to the inward Palate, { Gh. sonorous.
framing { Ch. mute.

Trepidation; which will frame a sound like the snarling of a dog, to which there is a correspondent mute, like that motion which we make in haaking, not necessary to be provided for by any Letter for Language.

Percolation of the breath between the root of the tongue and the inward palate; to which there is a correspondent mute, which makes a sound like the hissing of a Goose, not necessary to be provided for by any mark assigned to them for Letters.

Nose; by an appulse of the root of the tongue to the inward palate,

palate, fra-⸨NG sonorous.
ming⸩NGH. mute.

Greater; which do most partake of the nature of Consonants, and may be stiled non-spiritous or breathless, to be distinguished according to the active instruments of speech into

Labial; Intercepting of the breath by closure of the Lips, framing ⸨B. sonorous.
⸩P. mute.

Lingual; in respect of the

Top, intercepting the breath, by an appulse to the bottom of the Teeth, fra-⸨D. sonorous.
ming⸩T. mute.

Root; intercepting the breath, by an appulse to the inmost palate; fra-⸨G. sonorous.
ming⸩C, mute.

These I conceive (so far as I can judge at present) to be all the simple sounds that can be framed by the Organs of Speech.

CHAP.

CHAP. XI.
Of Vowels.

THose Letters are called *Vocales*, Vowels, in pronouncing of which by the Instruments of Speech, the breath is freely emitted; and they are therefore stiled *Apert* or open Letters. These may be *distinguished* either, 1. *Formally*, by their several Apertions, and the manner of configuration in the instruments of Speech required to the framing of them, which constitutes the distinct species of Vowels; or 2. *Accidentally*, by the quantity of time required to their prolation, by which the same Vowel is made either *long* or *short*.

There are (I conceive) eight simple different species of Vowels, easily distinguishable, whose powers are commonly used. I cannot deny, but that some other intermediate sounds might be found; but they would, by reason of their proximity to those others, prove of so difficult distinction, as would render them useless; these eight seeming to be the principal and most remarkable periods, amongst the degrees of Apert sounds.

As for the third of the *Labials*, the *u Gallicum*, or *whistling u*, though it cannot be denied to be a distinct simple vowel; yet it is of so laborious and difficult pronunciation to all those Nations amongst whom it is not used (as to the English) especially in the distinction of long and short, and framing of Dipthongs, that though I have enumerated it with the rest, and shall make provision for the expression of it, yet shall I make less use of it, than of the others; and for that reason, not proceed to any further explication of it.

It will be difficult to express the several powers of these Vowels by writing; Pronuntiation being such a thing, *quæ nec scribitur, nec pingitur, nec hauriri eam fas est, nisi vivâ voce*. And therefore the best way for the explaining of them, is by such known words as may be given for the instance of each of them. And as for the figure or writing of those four, which are not commonly esteemed to be distinct species of Vowels, I shall make choice to represent them by such Characters, as may seem least strange. What kind of power or sound that is, which is peculiar to each of these seven Vowels, may be easily understood by these following Instances:

Lipsius de rect. Pronuntiatione L. Lat. cap. 3.

α	Short	Bŏt-*tom*	Fol-*ly*	Fot	Mot	Pol	Rod
	Long	Bought	Fall	Fought		Paule	Rawd
a	Short	Batt	Val-*ley*	Fatt	Mat	Pal	Rad-*ner*
	Long	Bate	Vale	Fate	Mate	Pale	TRade
e	Short	Bett	Fell	Fet	Met	Pell	Red
	Long	Beate	Veale	Feate	Meate	Peale	Reade
i	Short	Bitt	Fill	Fitt	Mit-*ten*	Pill	Rid
	Long	Beete	Feele	Feete	Meete	Peele	Reede
o	Short						
	Long	Bote	Foale	Vote	Mote	Pole	Rode
ꝏ	Short		Full	Fut		Pul	
	Long	Boote	Foole	Foote	Moote	Poole	Roode
y	Short	But	Full	Futt	Mutt-*on*	Pull	Rudd-*er*
	Long						Amongst

A a a 2

Amongst these, the Vowels not commonly owned by us in writing, are these four, α, ι, ȣ, y. But that they are distinct species of Vowels, and have peculiar powers of their own, not expressible by any other Letters, (supposing every Letter (as it ought) to be determined to one particular sound) may sufficiently appear from the above mentioned, and several other Instances. And that those two which are commonly used with us for distinct Vowels; namely, the third and the fifth, *I*, and *U*; as in the words *Light, Lute,* are not simple Vowels, but *Dipthongs,* I shall shew afterwards.

Though the Vowel (*o*) do not admit of any instance in our Language, wherein it is used *short,* nor the Vowel (y) wherein it is used *Long* ; yet there are naturally such differences of these Vowels, as well as of the rest. Suppose a long Vowel to be divided into two parts; as *Bo-ote,* pronounce it then with half the time, and it must make the short Vowel *Bote.* And thus on the contrary, doubling the time of a short Vowel, as By-yt, will render it *Long:* which may serve to explain how these Vowels naturally are capable of being made both long and short; Though by reason of general disuse amongst us, such differences would at first seem somewhat difficult, and not easily distinguishable.

The Vowel (α) is placed first; partly partly in conformity with other Alphabets, and because 'tis the most Apert amongst the *Linguapalatal* Vowels. 'Tis expressed by this Character, because being one of the *Greek* Letters, 'tis more commonly known. 'Tis framed by an emission of the Breath, betwixt the Tongue and the Palate; the tongue being put into a more concave posture, and removed further off from the palate.

The Vowel (*a*) is framed by an emission of the Breath, betwixt the tongue and the concave of the palate; the upper superficies of the tongue being rendered less concave, and at a less distance from the palate.

The Vowel (*e*) is framed by an emission of the Breath, betwixt the tongue and the concave of the palate, the upper superficies of the tongue being brought to some small degree of convexity.

The Vowel (*i*) is expressed by this Character, because 'tis the most simple figure; and therefore doth best suit with the most acute Letters; as likewise, because this Letter, amongst many other Nations is already used and pronounced according to the sound which is here intended. 'Tis framed by an emission of the Breath betwixt the tongue and the concave of the palate, the upper superficies of the tongue being put into a more convex posture, and thrust up near the palate.

The Vowel (*o*) is the first, and most apert of the *Labials*; being framed by an emission of the Breath, betwixt the Lips, a little drawn together and contracted.

The Vowel (ȣ) is the second of the *Labials,* requiring a greater contraction of the Lips. 'Tis expressed by this Character, which is used in Greek for *ȣ* Dipthong; because commonly that Dipthong, as also the French *ou* is pronounced in the sound of this simple Vowel.

The Vowel (y) is wholly *Guttural,* being an emission of the breath from the throat, without any particular motion of the tongue or lips. 'Tis expressed by this Character which is already appropriated by the Welsh for the picture of this sound.

The

Chap. XI. *Concerning Natural Grammar.*

The *difference* betwixt long and short Vowels, should alwaies be *written* as well as pronounced, that is, there should be some Note or Mark to express when a Vowel is to be used *long*.

These eight Letters before enumerated, I conceive to be so many distinct species of Vowels, *formally different* in respect of their *Powers*; and though I cannot at present think of any other besides, yet having formerly, upon new considerations, and suggestions, so often changed my thoughts upon this enquiry, I dare not be dogmatical about it, or assert confidently, that there neither are, nor can be any more: For who knows how many other minute differences of Apertion may be now used, or hereafter found out, by others, which practise and custom may make as easie and distinguishable to them, as these are to us? Besides that the measure of *Apertion* (as is well observed) must be like continued quantity, *divisibilis in infinitum*. Only this (I think) may be safely affirmed, that the establishment of Vowels here mentioned, will serve much better to express all articulate sounds, than can be done by any of the ordinary Alphabets now in use.

I cannot but animadvert here on the by, upon that Argument which *Capellus*, and others do much insist upon, against the Antiquity *De Antiquitate* of the *Hebrew* Points, or Vowels; Because (say they) the making of so *Punctorum, l.1.* many, is an injudicious, and irrational invention, for which there is no real ground; there being in nature, and amongst other Languages, but five distinct Vowels, and not fourteen: And therefore they conclude the Invention of them to be new, and not of any great Antiquity.

To speak freely in this case (without interposing as to the main state of the Question) This Reason doth not seem to be of any force. Though the Conclusion they infer should be true, yet this Argument urged for it, is *false*, both as to the *Consequence*, and *Antecedent*. The *Imperfections* and Defects of any Invention, do rather argue the *Antiquity*, than the *Novelty* of it; there being much time and experience required to the perfecting any invention: And it would rather follow, that because they are *imperfect*, therefore so very much like to be *Ancient*. But besides, the Hebrew Vowels will upon consideration, be found to be a contrivance full of more than ordinary Accurateness, founded upon the Philosophy of Articulate sounds, and may without any force be applied to the number here established: Excepting the French (u).

α { Long א / Short א   a { Long א / Short א   e { Long א / Short א   i { Long א / Short א
o { Long י / Short א   u { Long י / Short א   y { Long / Short א

And though there be no distinct Character for א short, and y long, perhaps that Language as well as the English seldom using such distinction in those sounds; yet is (י) sometimes in that Language used in stead of a short Vowel, and (א) for a long Vowel.

The use of Scheva in the Hebrew, is to direct the joyning of such Consonants together, as would otherwise be of very difficult, pronunciation, and not easily unite, as in the words למוד and סליח, which

should

should be pronounced lmodh and mloch, but because LM and ML, will not of themselves coalesce, therefore is *Schevah* interposed, which being rapidly pronounced (and that probably as our short y) does not seem to make any distinct Syllable.

So that it seems much more colourable to infer the *Novelty* of the Hebrew Points, from the *Accurateness*, than from the injudiciousness of their contrivance.

CHAP. XII.

Of Consonants.

THose Letters are stiled *Consonants*, in the pronouncing of which the Breath is intercepted, by some Collision or Closure, amongst the Instruments of Speech: And for this reason are they stiled *Clausæ Literæ*, as the *Vowels* are *Apertæ*.

The common distinction of these into *Semi-vowels* and *Mutes*, will not upon a strict enquiry be adæquate. And therefore I do rather chuse to distribute them into these three kinds;

1. πνευματώδη, Spiritous, or Breathed.
2. ἡμίπνευα, (if I may use that word) Semi-spiritous, or half Breathed.
3. ἄπνευμάτα, Non-spiritous, or Breathless.

1. By *Spiritous*, or Breathed, are meant such Consonants, as require to the framing of them a more strong emission of the Breath, either through ⎰ Nose.
the ⎱ Mouth.

1. The Consonants which are to be breathed only through the *Nose*, may be again distin- ⎰ 1. Sonorous, as M. N. Ng.
guished into ⎱ 2. Mute, as hm. hn. hng.

Both these kinds, as likewise those that follow through the Mouth, have some imperfect sound of their own, without the joyning of any Vowel with them; though the sonorous only be *Vocal*; and the mute sort are only a kind of Whisper.

By *Sonorous*, are meant, such as require some voice or vocal sound, to the framing of them.

By the *Mutes* of these, are meant other Letters of the same configuration, pronounced with a strong emission of the Breath, without any *Vocal* sound.

(*m*) is *mugitus*, the natural sound of *Lowing*, when the Lips are shut, and the sound proceeds out of the Nose. 'Tis counted of difficult pronunciation in the end of words: For which reason, the Latin Poets cut it off in Verse, when it comes before a Vowel in the next words: And the Greeks do not terminate any word with it.

(N) is *Tinnitus*, when the breath is sent out, the Limbus of the Tongue being fixed towards the Gums, or bottom of the upper Foreteeth. In the pronouncing of this, the breath is emitted only out of the Nose, which makes it differ from (L). 'Tis counted a pleasant and
easie

Chap. XII. *Concerning Natural Grammar.* 367

easie Letter, which may perhaps be the reason why this Letter N, and L, and R, are for the most part, both *in Greek and Latin immutable*, both in Declensions and Conjugations.

(Ng) is framed by an appulse of the Root of the Tongue towards the inner part of the Palat. The sound of it may be continued simple, as well as any other; which makes it evident to be a single letter, and not a compound of n, and g, as we usually write it: Thus the word *Anguis*, in the true spelling of it, should be writ A, ng, G, ʊ, ı, s. The Hebrew y is supposed by divers Authors, but I think groundlesly, to be of this power. I know several things may be said, to render it probable, that the power here intended, may be sufficiently expressed, by a more soft and slight manner of pronouncing the letters N & G compounded together : But I rather incline to reckon it a simple and distinct Letter.

To the Sonorous letters of this kind, there are three *Mutes* of affinity, *hʊ, hn, hng*; which are formed when the breath is emitted through the Instruments of Speech, in the same position respectively as in the former, but without any Vocal Sound. The two first of these are in use amongst the *Welsh* and *Irish*: And the last of them, in the opinion of *Bellarmine*, and some other Grammarians, is rather the true sound of the *Hebrew* y.

2. The Spiritous Consonants to be breathed through the *Mouth*, are likewise of two kinds, { Sonorous, V. Dh. L. R. Z. Zh.
{ Mute, F. Th. hL. hR. S. Sh.

(V) is the same with that which we call V Consonant : 'Tis of the same power which is commonly ascribed to B *asperated*, or rather *incrassated*. So the Western Jews pronounce their Letter (ב) when not Dageshated. And 'tis observed that in Ancient Monuments amongst the Latins, these two Letters have been often put for one another: And that in some words, where the sense hath been very much varied by this change; so *Acerbus* for *Acervus*: *Veneficium* for *Beneficium*. The power of this Letter was first expressed among the Latins by the *Digamma Æolicum*, (Ϝ) (so stiled for its *Figure, not* its *Sound*) which ^{Scaliger de Causis L. L. cap. 28.}

is now the Character for the Letter (F) but had at first the power of the Consonant (V) and was written in *Claudius* his time invertedly, as DIꟻAI, AMPLIAꟻIT. This Letter is framed by a kind of straining or percolation of the Breath, through a Chink between the lower lip and upper teeth, with some kind of *Murmure*. ^{Vossius Gram. lib. I. cap. 15.}

(F) is the correspondent *Mute* to this : 'Tis framed by the same kind of position of the Lip and Teeth, and percolation of the Breath betwixt them, with this only difference, that as the former was with some kind of Vocal Sound, so this is wholly mute. This seems to be such an incrassation of the Letter (P) as (V) is of (B). 'Tis answerable to the Greek (φ). And though several of the Greek words with (φ) are rendred in Latin by Ph, as *Philosophia, Sophista*, &c. yet the *Italians* write *Filosofo, Sofista*, &c. and some other words are so rendred in *Latin*, as φυγη, *fuga*, φημη, *fama*. What that dilutness is, which *Vossius* saith is more proper to F, than to φ, I understand not ; nor is it easie to guess at the meaning of that in *Cicero*, concerning *Fundanius*, and *Phundanius*, unless perhaps it be, as *Lipsius* guesses, of pronouncing it as *Pfhundanius*, or else as *P-hundanius*. ^{ibid.}

(Dh)

(Dh) and its correspondent Mute (Th) are of that power which we commonly ascribe to the Letters D, & T, aspirated or incrassated. And though these two Powers are commonly used by us without any provision for them by distinct Characters, yet our Ancestors the *Saxons* had several Letters to express them. They represented (Dh) by this mark (ð) as in Faðer, Moðer, ðe, ðat, ðen: And (Th) by this mark (þ) as þeif, þick, faiþ. And 'tis most evident that the sounds of them (though we usually confound them, under the same manner of writing) are in themselves very distinguishable, as in these Examples.

Dh.	Th.
Thee, this, there, thence, that, those, though, thou, thy, thine. Father, Mother, Brother, Leather, Weather, Feather. Smooth, Seeth, Wreath, Bequeath.	Think, thine, thigh, thing, thistle, thesis, thankes, thought, throng, thrive, thrust. Doth, death, wrath, length, strength, Loveth, Teacheth, &c.

These Letters are framed by a percolation of the Breath through a kind of Chink betwixt the tongue and upper teeth, the first with some kind of vocal sound, the other wholly mute.

(Gh) and its Correspondent (Ch) are both of them framed by a vibration of the root or middle of the tongue against the Palate, the former being *vocal*, and the other *mute*. They are each of them of difficult pronuntiation: The first is now used by the *Irish*, and was perhaps heretofore intended by the spelling of those English words, *Right, Light, Daughter, Enough, Thorough*, &c. Though this kind of sound be now by disuse lost amongst us, the latter of them (Ch) is now used amongst the Welsh, and was perhaps heretofore intended by the Greek Letter (χ.) Neither of them is easily imitable by any mouth not trained up to the practise of them.

(L) is *Clangor*. 'Tis formed by an appulse of the Tip of the tongue to the Palate, and then forcing out the Breath. 'Tis esteemed *facillima & liquidissima Literarum*; in the pronouncing of which, most Nations do agree.

(Lh) or (hL) the correspondent Mute to this, is much used by the Welch: They seem to form it as the other (L) only by abstaining the voice, and a more forcible emission of the Breath, as is used in all other mute letters of the Spiritous kind.

(R) is *Stridor vel susurrus*: 'Tis called from the snarling of Dogs, *Litera Canina*: 'Tis made by a quick trepidation of the tip of the tongue being vibrated against the palate; for which, they who are disabled, by reason of the natural infirmity of their tongues, which is called Τραυλισμὸς, *Balbuties*, do commonly pronounce in stead of it, the letter (L) which is of a more soft and easie sound. *Demosthenes, Alcibiades, Aristotle, Scaliger*, the Fathers, are said to have laboured under this Infirmity.

(Rh) or (hR) the correspondent mute to this, is made by a forcible emission of the breath, through the instruments of Speech in the same position as for the Letter (R) but without any vocal sound. 'Tis the same with the Greek (ῥ) and much in use amongst the *Welsh*.

(Z)

Chap XII. *Concerning Natural Grammar.* 369

(Z) is by some stiled (*s*) *molle*. 'Tis properly the *Greek* (ζ) and the *Hebrew* (ז). 'Tis framed by an appulse of the tongue towards the upper Teeth or Gums, and then forcing out the breath from betwixt the tongue and the upper teeth, with a vocal sound, which makes a more dense kind of *hissing*, mixed with some kind of *murmur, apumq; susurro persimilem*: 'Tis of the same affinity with S, as B with P, D with T, and G with C. That double Letter in the Hebrew (צ) which is by some accounted equivalent to this, is of a quite different power, as were easie to illustrate by several examples.

(*S*) the correspondent *mute* (though it be commonly reckoned for a semivowel) is framed as the former, but without any vocal sound. 'Tis stiled *Sibilus*. The power of it is the natural sound of *Hissing*; for which reason 'tis called *Litera Serpentina*. The *Hebrews* have two Characters for this Letter, besides two others for its Allies. Among the *Persians* all words that signifie *Grandeur* and Magnificence, are said to be terminated with it: Though others condemn it for a harsh, unpleasing, quarelling Letter. *Messala Corvinus*, a great man, and a famous Orator among the Romans, is said to have writ a particular Treatise against this Letter, much esteemed of amongst learned men. And *Pindar* likewise writ an *Ode* against it, *versus ἀσίγμος*, wherein there was no word that had any *s* in it. The disability of pronouncing this Letter, is called *Blæsitas, Lisping*, when 'tis corruptly sounded like (*th*).

(Zh) the sonorous Consonant, and (Sh) its correspondent mute, are framed by a percolation of the breath, betwixt the tongue rendered concave, and the teeth both upper and lower: The first being *vocal*, the other *mute*. Though they are not provided for commonly by distinct and simple Characters, yet are they distinct and simple letters; both of them facil and common: The first amongst the French, who express it by *I*, as in the word *Iean*, &c. and is easily imitable by us: And though the other did once cost 42000 men *Judges* 12. 6. their lives, for not being able to pronounce it, yet is it of common use with many Nations.

2. By *Semispiritous* or half breathed Consonants, are meant such as are accompanied with some kind of vocal murmure, as B, D, G. whereas

3. Those are stiled *non-spiritous* or breathless, which are wholly mute; as, P, T, C.

(*B* and *P*) are framed when the breath is intercepted by the closure of the Lips; the first of them being more soft, with some kind of murmure, the other more hard and wholly mute.

(*D* and *T*) are commonly framed, by an appulse or collision of the top of the tongue against the teeth, or upper gums; the first being more soft and gentle, with some kind of murmure, the other wholly mute.

(*G* and *C*) are framed more *inwardly*, by an interception of the breath towards the throat, by the middle or root of the tongue, with such a kind of difference between them, as there is betwixt the two former pairs.

Bbb CHAP.

CHAP. XIII.

Of Compound Letters, whether Vowels, Consonants,

Besides these simple Letters before enumerated, there are others commonly used, which may be {Vowels. / Consonants. stiled Compound, both

The Compound Vowels are called commonly *Dipthongs*, or *Tripthongs*, or *Bissona* in Latin; but because the signification of those words may as well agree with double Consonants, therefore others would have them stiled *Bivocales*, or *Trivocales*. *Jacobus Matthiæ* in his Treatise *de Literis*, and our learned *Gataker*, in a particular Discourse to this purpose, do earnestly contend that there are no such things as Dipthongs. Their principal Arguments depend upon this Supposition, That (ı and ʋ) (which are necessary Ingredients to the framing of all usual Dipthongs) are Consonants, the same with y and w. Others would have them to be of a middle nature, betwixt Vowels and Consonants; according to which Opinion I have already described them: From whence the Reason is clear, why these Vowels concur to the making of Dipthongs, because being the most *contract* of Vowels (as is also the Vowel (y) of which more hereafter) They do therefore approach very near to the nature of *Literæ clausæ*, or Consonants; there being no Transition amongst these, either from one another, or to the other intermediate sounds, without such a kind of motion amongst the Instruments of speech, by reason of these different *Apertions*, as doth somewhat resemble that kind of Collision required to the framing of Consonants.

Several Languages use several kinds of these Dipthongs, but how many there are in nature, may be easily collected by the former division of Vowels (supposing that to be according to nature) One of these two Vowels ı or ʋ must be an ingredient into all usual Dipthongs, either as {Preposed. / Subjoyned.

1. These Vowels ı and ʋ may be *preposed* in this mixture before each of the other; in which case they will have the same power that we commonly ascribe to y and w, and will frame these twelve Dipthongs.

ıα	yall, yawne	ʋα	wall
ıa	yate yarrow	ʋa	wale
ıe	yet yellow	ʋe	well
ıo	yoke	ʋo	woe
ıu		ʋu	
ıy	young	ʋy	wunn, worse.

2. They

Chap. XIII. *Concerning Natural Grammar.* 371

2. They may be *subjoyned* to each of the other; as in these Instances:

aͮ	boy	aʊ	aw
aͥ	Ay	aʊ	
eͥ		eʊ	hew
oͥ		oʊ	
uͥ		uʊ	
yͥ	our English (i) in bite	yʊ	owr, owle.

3. They may be both preposed and subjoyned to themselves and to one another.

ıı	yee	ıʊ	you
ʊʊ	woo	ʊı	wee

As for the other intermediate Vowels being preposed before one another, they will not afford any coalescing sounds that are easily distinguishable. E being preposed before α, a, o, y, will scarce be distinguished from ıα, ıa, ıo, ıy. A, before E, will be but as ā, before α, o, u, it will not coalesce into a plain sound. The same likewise may be said of the other Vowels, α, o. So that of this kind the whole number is twenty four. And this I conceive to be a sufficient enumeration of the natural Dipthongs.

I cannot deny but that other Dipthongs may be made by the mixture of the Vowel (y) which were perhaps in use amongst the Jews, and exprest by (y) But being now, as I think, generally disused amongst other Nations, and for that reason very difficult to be pronounced, I shall not therefore take any further notice of them.

When two Vowels are put together by way of Dipthoug, so as to coalesce in one Syllable, 'tis necessary that there should be some Note or Mark in their Characters, to signifie their conjunction, as is usual in some of the *Greek* and *Latin* Dipthongs; as ᾳ, ᾳ, ᾱͅ, œ, æ. Otherwise there can be no certainty, whether the word be to be pronounced as a *Monosyllable*, or *Dissyllable*, as in D-u-el, Duel. Sw-et, Swet.

'Tis a common Assertion amongst Grammarians, *Priscian*, *Quintilian*, and others, That no one syllable can consist of three Vowels, and consequently that there can be no *Tripthongs*; which I conceive to be founded upon the former mistake; namely, that ı and ʊ are to be used as Consonants: For 'tis evident, that each of these may coalesce with every one of the first Dipthongs, as ıaʊ, yaw, ʊaı, way, ıeʊ yew, ʊyı, in wile, wight, qui, &c.

The compound Consonants are usually distinguished into such as are {Asperated. Double.

1. Those are stiled aspirated, which seem to be mixed with (H) and are usually so written; as θ, φ, χ, ʋ. But in propriety of speech, if aspiration be defined to be an impetus of Breathing, then these Consonants cannot so fitly be said to be *aspirated*, but rather *incrassated* by

Bbb 2 com-

compression of the breath in framing of them. Though not only the *European* Nations do at this present express them by this mixture of (H,) but it was likewise the opinion of the *Antients*, as may appear; because before those Letters θ, φ, χ, were invented by *Palamedes*, the *Grecians* were wont to express the power of them, by adding the aspiration H, to τ, π, κ. Yet 'tis very plain, that each of these Consonants esteemed to be aspirated, are *simple* Letters; because in the prolation of them, the same sound doth still continue, and therefore they ought not to be reckoned amongst the mixed Letters.

Vossius de Gram. cap. 16.

2. *Double Consonants* are such as are compounded of some of the other Letters, and for the *Compendium* of writing, are in several Languages expressed by *single Characters*, and reckoned in the *Alphabet* as if they were distinct species of *simple Letters*. Such are in the Latin Alphabet Q, X, and the double Letter Z, whose power is the same as DS. or TS. To which *Claudius Cæsar* would have added an *Antisigma* in this form (Ↄ) which should have had the power of the Greek ψ, or PS.

Scaliger de de Causis L. L. cap. 21.

As for the Letter Q, 'Tis commonly granted to be a Compound of C and U; for which reason, in many ancient Books, the Letter V was not written after Q, as being involved in it; so *qis, qa, qid*. But what kind of V this should be, is much debated. Some would have it to be the *Consonant*, against which *Joseph Scaliger* argues, that then it would not be pronounceable, being of near affinity to F, *qfis*, for *quis*. But upon consideration, it will be found to be the Letter *u* coalescing into a Dipthong with the subsequent Vowel, *cuam*, being the same with *quam*.

Vossius Gram. cap. 27.

Diatribe de varia literarum pronuntiatione.

What the true Original is of (J) Consonant, and that power which we give to (Ch) in the words *Charity, Cheese, Chosen, Chink,* &c. is a question men have much differed about. 'Tis evident that neither of them are single Letters, because in the prolation of them, we do not end with the same sound with which we begin. As for that Conjecture, that I Consonant may be expressed by dzy, dzyindzyer, Ginger, dzyudzy, Judge *a* or else that this sound is compounded of the Consonants dy, as *dyoy* for *joy; dyentle, gentle, lodying* for *lodging*. And so for the power that we ascribe to Ch, that it may be sufficiently expressed by Ty, as *ortyard*, for *Orchard, rityes*, for *riches* : These I think need not any particular refutation. It seems to be plain, that J Consonant is a Compound of D, and Zh; and Ch of T, and Sh.

Alex. Gyll, Gram. cap. 1.

Dr Wallis Gram.

As for the other three Consonants, that are reckoned in the common Alphabet, K, W, Y, enough hath been said to prove them unnecessary. If C be used alwaies in its proper power (as every Letter ought) then K must needs be superfluous; and therefore the *Welsh* who use C only for one kind of sound, have no K. And as for the Letters W, Y, their power is the same with that of the Vowels *u*, and *i*, as will evidently appear when they are rapidly pronounced before any other Vowel by way of *Dipthong*, so as to make but one Syllable; *u̯wee* warr warr, *i̯sim* swim, *i̯es* yes, *i̯oke* yoke, *i̯uth* youth. The words young and younker being originally of the Dutch, are by them written junk junker.

And as for the Aspirations, wheele, where, when, &c. our Forefathers the *Saxons*, did antiently prefix the Aspirations before the vowels;

els; as hʉl, hʉer, hʉen, which will in pronunciation be of the very same sound and power, wherein these words are now used, and therefore is more natural and proper than the common way of writing.

According to this establishment, the simple Letters will be thirty four, whereof eight are Vowels, and twenty six Consonants, besides twenty four Dipthongs.

The Greek Letters are said to have been at first only 16; namely, A, B, Γ, Δ, Ε, Ι, Κ, Λ, Μ, Ν, Ο, Π, Ρ, Σ, Τ, Υ. To which *Palamedes* is said to have added the three Aspirates Θ, Φ, Χ. *Epicharmus* the *Sicilian* the double Letters Z, Ξ, Ψ. and *Simonides* the two long Vowels η and ω. Notwithstanding which, that Alphabet is still in several respects defective. *Vossius de Gram. cap.18.*

What *Theodorus Bibliander* suggests in his Tract *de ratione communi omnium Linguarum*, that all sounds both articulate, and inarticulate, may sufficiently be expressed by 13 Letters, and an Aspiration, *viz.* the five ordinary Vowels, & B, G, D, L, M, N, R, S, is so very irrational, that I cannot think it needs any particular confutation.

As for those other new Alphabets that are proposed by Sir *Thomas Smith, Bulloker, Alex. Gill*, they do none of them give a just enumeration of the simple Elements of speech, but what by the mixture of long and short Vowels, which do not differ specifically, together with the insertion of double Letters, they do too much increase the number of them. Besides that some other Letters are left out and omitted.

According to this establishment of Letters, if the *Lords Prayer* or *Creed* were to be written according to our present pronunciation of it, they should be each of them thus Lettered.

The Lords Prayer.

Ɏʉr fådher hʉitsh art in héven, halloëd bi dhyi nåm, dhyi cingdym cym, dhyi ʉill bi dyn, in erth az it iz in héven, giv ys dhis dai yʉr daili bred, and fᴂrgív ys yʉr trespassez az ʉi fᴂrgív dhem dhat trespass against ys, and léd ys nat intʉ temptasiᴂn, byt deliver ys frᴂm ivil, far dhyn iz dhe cingdim, dhe pyʉer and dhe glari, far ever and ever, Amen.

The Creed.

Ɏi bilív in Gᴂd dhe fådher ᴂlmyiti måker ᴂf héven and erth, and in Dzhesys Cryist hiz onli syn yʉr Lᴂrd, hʉ ʉaz cᴂnséved byi dhe holi Gost, bᴂrn ᴂf dhe Virgin Mȧri, syffered ynder Pᴂnsiys Pyilat, ʉaz crʉsifiëd ded and byriëd. Hi desſended intʉ hel, dhe thyrd dai hi rosʻagain frᴂm dhe ded. Hi assended intʉ héven, hʉer hi sitteth at dhe ryit hand ᴂf Gᴂd dhe fådher, frᴂm hʉènſ hi shᴂl cym tʉ dzhydzh dhe cʉic and dhe ded. Ɏi bilív in dhe holi Gost, dhe holi catholic tshyrtsh, dhe cᴂmmʉniʉn ᴂf Saints, dhe fᴂrgivnes ᴂf sinz, de resyrrecsion ᴂf dhe bady, and lyif everlasting. Amen.

Thus much may suffice, concerning the *Forms, Essences,* or *Powers* of the several Letters. CHAP.

CHAP. XIV.

Of the Accidents of Letters. 1. *Their Names.* 2. *Their Order.* 3. *Their Affinities and Opposition.* 4. *Their Figure, with a twofold Instance of a more regular Character for the Letters, the latter of which may be stiled* Natural. 5. *Of Pronunciation.* 6. *Of the several letters disused by several Nations.*

Something ought briefly to be added concerning the Accidents of Letters, *viz.* their 1. Names. 2. Order. 3. Affinity. 4. Figure. 5. Pronunciation.

§ I. *Names.*
1. Of their *Names*. Letters being of themselves the most simple Elements of Speech, ought therefore to be expressed by the most simple names, and such as do signifie their several *Powers*: In which respect, the *Roman* Alphabet used in these Western parts of the world, hath an advantage above other learned Languages, wherein the Vowels are no otherwise named than by their own sounds, as A, not *Aleph* or *Alpha*; much less have they distinct names for long and short Vowels, as *Kamets*, *Kametscatuph*, &c. And those which they reckon as the two kinds of Consonants, *Semi-vowels* and *Mutes*, are likewise distinguished in their very Names. The Vowels being preposed in those which they call *Semi-vowels*, el, em, en, ar, and subjoyned in the Mutes, be, ce, de, ge, pe, te.

As for the other Letters before mentioned, which have a Right to be put in the Alphabet, they may be thus named: The sonorous ones, Eng, EV, Edh, Egh, EZ, EZh. The Mute ones, Hme, Hne, Hnge, Fe, The, Che, HLE, HRE, SE, She.

§ II. *Order.*
2. The most proper and natural *Order* of the Letters, I conceive to be the same in which they have been before treated of. *Vowels* should be reckoned up by themselves, as being a distinct kind, and *first*, both for their priority in *Nature*, *Necessity*, and *Dignity*. If the order of these were to be regulated from the Instruments of speech, then u, o, v, should be first, as being *Labial*, and *a*, a, e, i, next, as *Lingual*, or *Linguapalatal*, and y last, as being *Guttural*. *Scaliger* would have A and O to be acknowledged for the first Vowels, as being *Soni amplissimi.* The next E, I, as being of a middle sound, and the last U, as being *soni obscurissimi.* That which to me seems the most proper Method, is to reckon them up according to their degrees of Apertion: Only in conformity with the common Alphabets, I begin with the Linguals, *æ*, a, e, i, o, v, u, y.

De causis Ling. Lat. cap. 38.

Amongst the Consonants, the *Sonorous* should precede, as approaching nearest to the nature of Vowels. And amongst them, if those that are breathed through the *Nose* do precede, M must be the first, as being *Labial*; N next, as being *Dental*; and then NG, as being *Linguapalatal*. Next, those that are breathed through the *Mouth*, according to this order, V, Dh, Gh, L, R, Z, Zh. The first being *Labial*, the next *Dental*, the others *Lingua-dental,* or *Lingua-palatal.* Next should

should follow the Spiritous Consonants that are *Mutes*; and first those pronounced through the *Nose*, HM, HN, HNG, then those pronounced through the *Mouth*, F, TH, CH, hl, hr, S, Sh. Then the semi-spiritous Consonants, B, D, G. And lastly, the non-spiritous, or breathless Consonants, P, T, C.

3. The Affinity of Vowels each to other is not difficult to determine, a and a of a middle sound, e and 1 of a more acute, o and u of a more grave tone. If they were to be opposed to one another, this distribution would be most natural, (α i) (a o) (e u) (v u) and so *vice versa*, (i α) (o a) (u e) (u v.) § 3. *Affinity.*

The Affinity amongst the Consonants most obvious is this, (M, HM) (N, HN,) (NG, HNG,) (V, F,) (Dh, Th,) (Gh, Ch,) (L, HL,) (R, HR,) (Z, S,) (Zb, Sh,) (BP) (DT) (GC.)

4. Though all Nations do or should agree in the same power and sound of the Letters, yet they differ very much in those *Figures* and Characters, whereby they represent them in writing according to those divers Alphabets that are received in the world: Amongst which, though some are much more convenient than others, yet none of them seem contrived upon a Philosophical ground. In the framing of such a Literal Character, these Conditions ought to be observed. § 4. *Figure.*

1. They should be the most simple and facil, and yet elegant and comely as to the shape of them.

2. They must be sufficiently distinguished from one another.

3. There should be some kind of sutableness, or correspondency of the figure to the nature and kind of the Letters which they express.

It is not either necessary or convenient in the framing of a Language to make use of all the Letters belonging to the Alphabet; but 'tis sufficient that such only be made choice of, as are most easie and pleasant in the pronunciation and sound of them. But though it be not needful to introduce all the Letters into the common use of a Language, yet it is most necessary that some way should be provided for representing the powers of all the simple Letters, because without this, there can be no way to express the *proper names* used in several Languages, whether of Places, or Persons, &c. as *England, London, Oxford, John, Mary*, &c. There being frequent occasion in discourse to mention the names of such *Individuals*: And these being nothing else but such words or sounds as men have agreed upon to signifie such particular places or persons, must therefore be expressed by such Letters as make up these sounds. And though this real Character here treated of (as it is made effable) may serve for most of them, yet because there are several others not this way provided for, therefore may it be proper to offer some distinct Alphabet of Letters. Of which, I had provided several Instances and Examples agreeable to the Rules above mentioned. But I shall at present (because I would not too much digress) set down only two; which to me seem considerable in their several kinds. The former being more facil and *simple*, the other more *complicate*; but with this advantage, that it hath in the shape of it some resemblance to that Configuration which there is in the Organs of speech upon the framing of several Letters. Upon which account it may deserve the name of a *Natural Character* of the Letters.

The Letters according to the first design, are represented in the following Table, consisting of 31 Ranks and 15 Columnes.

pag. 376.

	1	2	3	4	5	6	7	8	9	10	11	12	13	14	15
1			a	a	e	o	u	y		a	a	e	o	u	y
2			ꝗ	o|	o|	ꝗ	ɗ	ɗ		｜º	｜o	｜o	｜ᵖ	｜ᵖ	｜ᵇ
3	h	｜	ꝗ	ᑯ	ᑯ	ꝗ	ꝗ	ꝗ	H	ꝑ	ᵱ	ᵬ	ꝑ	ꝑ	ᵬ
4	w	｜	ꝗ	ᑯ	ᑯ	ꝗ	ꝗ	ꝗ	W	ꝑ	ꝑ	ᵬ	ꝑ	ꝑ	ᵬ
5	y	｜	ꝗ	ᑯ	ᑯ	ꝗ	ꝗ	ꝗ	Y	ꝑ	ᵱ	ᵬ	ꝑ	ꝑ	ᵬ
6	b	ꝗ	ꝗ	ꝗ	ꝗ	ꝗ	ꝗ	ꝗ	B	ꝑ	ꝑ	ᵬ	ꝑ	ꝑ	ᵬ
7	p	ꝑ	ꝑ	ꝑ	ꝑ	ꝑ	ꝑ	ꝑ	P	ꝑ	ꝑ	ᵬ	ꝑ	ꝑ	ᵬ
8	v	ꝗ	ꝗ	ꝗ	ꝗ	ꝗ	ꝗ	ꝗ	V	ꝑ	ꝑ	ᵬ	ꝑ	ꝑ	ᵬ
9	f	ꝑ	ꝑ	ꝑ	ꝑ	ꝑ	ꝑ	ꝑ	F	ꝑ	ꝑ	ᵬ	ꝑ	ꝑ	ᵬ
10	d	ꝗ	ꝗ	ꝗ	ꝗ	ꝗ	ꝗ	ꝗ	D	ꝑ	ꝑ	ᵬ	ꝑ	ꝑ	ᵬ
11	t	L	L	L	L	L	L	L	T	L	L	L	L	L	L
12	dh	ꝗ	ꝗ	ꝗ	ꝗ	ꝗ	ꝗ	ꝗ	Dh	ꝑ	ꝑ	ᵬ	ꝑ	ꝑ	ᵬ
13	th	L	L	L	L	L	L	L	Th	L	L	L	L	L	L
14	g	T	T	T	T	T	T	T	G	T	T	T	T	T	T
15	c	L	L	L	L	L	L	L	C	L	L	L	L	L	L
16	gh	T	T	T	T	T	T	T	Gh	T	T	T	T	T	T
17	ch	L	L	L	L	L	L	L	Ch	L	L	L	L	L	L
18	z	Ƨ	Ƨ	Ƨ	Ƨ	Ƨ	Ƨ	Ƨ	Z	Ƨ	Ƨ	Ƨ	Ƨ	Ƨ	Ƨ
19	s	ſ	ſ	ſ	ſ	ſ	ſ	ſ	S	ſ	ſ	ſ	ſ	ſ	ſ
20	zh	Ƨ	Ƨ	Ƨ	Ƨ	Ƨ	Ƨ	Ƨ	Zh	Ƨ	Ƨ	Ƨ	Ƨ	Ƨ	Ƨ
21	sh	ʃ	ʃ	ʃ	ʃ	ʃ	ʃ	ʃ	Sh	ʃ	ʃ	ʃ	ʃ	ʃ	ʃ
22	l	)	)	)	)	)	)	)	L	)	)	)	)	)	)
23	hl	L	L	L	L	L	L	L	hL	L	L	L	L	L	L
24	r	(	(	(	(	(	(	(	R	(	(	(	(	(	(
25	hr	(	(	(	(	(	(	(	hR	(	(	(	(	(	(
26	m	ꝗ	ꝗ	ꝗ	ꝗ	ꝗ	ꝗ	ꝗ	M	ꝑ	ꝑ	ꝑ	ꝑ	ꝑ	ꝑ
27	hm	ꝗ	ꝗ	ꝗ	ꝗ	ꝗ	ꝗ	ꝗ	hM	ꝑ	ꝑ	ꝑ	ꝑ	ꝑ	ꝑ
28	n	J	J	J	J	J	J	J	N	J	J	J	J	J	J
29	hn	J	J	J	J	J	J	J	hN	J	J	J	J	J	J
30	ng	U	U	U	U	U	U	U	Ng	U	U	U	U	U	U
31	hng	U	U	U	U	U	U	U	hNg	U	U	U	U	U	U

Chap. XIV. *Concerning Natural Grammar.*

The first Rank doth contain the Characters for the six more *simple* Vowels, both prepofed and fubjoyned according to a threefold place, at the top, the middle, and the bottom of the Character, the former three being meer *Rounds*, the other *Hooks*. Thofe of a *middle power*, becaufe they are neceffary Ingredients to the making of all the ufual Dipthongs, therefore have they a larger Character affigned to them, to which any of the other Vowels may be affixed, when they are to coalefce into Dipthongs. And though the Letter Y be properly (as it is reckoned) one of thofe that are *mediæ poteſtatis*, and may be compounded into a Dipthong with any of the other Vowels, yet becaufe it is not now (for ought I know) made ufe of to this purpofe, in any of thofe Languages that are commonly known and ufed amongſt us; therefore is it at prefent reckoned only amongſt the Vowels.

The fecond Columne (befides the marks for thofe three Letters H, ᵹ, i,) doth contain likewife the Characters for all the Confonants, according to their feveral affinities; where the *Non ſpiritous* Confonants are expreſſed by *ſtraight lines*, the *Spiritous* Confonants of affinity to them being diſtinguiſhed by a little hook affixed at one end. The other Confonants by *curve* lines, with the like diſtinction for their correſpondent Mutes. The reſt of the Ranks and Columnes conſiſting of mixed Letters, either the mixtures of the Vowels with H, ᵹ, or I, or elſe the incorporating the Character for each of the ſix Vowels with that of the Confonant, the Vowel being prepofed in the 3,4,5,6,7,8. Columnes, and fubjoined in the other.

As for the Characters that ferve for Interpunction, the *Comma* may be expreſſed by a ſmall, ſtreight, oblique line (,) The *Semicolon, Colon* and *Period,* may continue as they are now uſed by moſt of the *Europeans*; there being nothing in their figure, of any fuch near refemblance to the other Characters, as may make them liable to miſtake. And ſo likewife may thoſe other Notes, which ſerve to diſtinguiſh the various manners of Pronuntiation, whether Explication [ ] Interrogation ? Wonder ! Irony ¡   only the two curve Lines for Parentheſis ( ) being here uſed for the Letters L, and R, may be fupplied by thefe [ ]

At the bottom of this Table there is an Inſtance of the Lords Prayer, being lettered ſutably to our prefent pronuntiation of it.

The Letters according to the fecond defign may be thus contrived;

Chap. XIV. *Concerning Natural Grammar.*

The first Columne doth contain the Vowels, as they are distinguished into

- *Labial*; being framed by an emission of the Breath through the Lips, whether
  - *Less contracted*; O.
  - *More contracted*, and somewhat compressed
    - *Downwards*, ʊ.
    - *Upwards*, U.
- *Lingual*; the Tongue being put into a posture
  - *More concave*; and removed, at some distance from the Palate, α.
  - *Less concave*; or plain, and brought nearer to the Palate, a.
  - *Somewhat convex*, towards the Palate, e.
  - *More convex*, i.
- *Guttural*, Y.

The other Columnes do contain the Consonants, as they are distinguished into

- *Labial*; whether such as are
  - *Breathless*; { Sonorous } { B. }
               { Mute   } { P. }
  - *Breathing*; through the
    - *Mouth*; { Sonorous } { V. }
              { Mute   } { F. }
    - *Nose*; { Sonorous } { M. }
              { Mute   } { HM. }
- *Lingual*; either in respect of the
  - *Top* of the Tongue, whether such as are
    - *Breathless*; { Sonorous } { D }
                   { Mute   } { T }
    - *Breathing*, through the
      - *Mouth*; by
        - *Appulse*, of the top of the Tongue to the
          - *Top of the Teeth*, the breath being emitted through the midst of the { Sonorous } { Dh }
            mouth, { Mute } { Th }
          - *Foremost part of the Palate*, the breath being emitted through the corners { Sonorous } { L }
            of the mouth { Mute } { HL. }
        - *Trepidation* or Vibration, against the inward part of the
          Palate, { Sonorous } { R. }
                  { Mute   } { HR. }
        - *Percolation* of the Breath betwixt the top of the Tongue and the roots of the Teeth, whether more
          - *Subtle*, { Sonorous } { Z. }
                     { Mute   } { S. }
          - *Dense*, { Sonorous } { Zh. }
                     { Mute   } { Sh. }
      - *Nose*; by appulse of the top of the Tongue to the Root of the

Ccc 2 Teeth,

Teeth, { Sonorous { N. } Mute { HN. }

Root or middle of the Tongue appulsed to the Inward Palate, whether such as are

{ Breathless; { Sonorous { G. } Mute { C. }
{ Breathing; through the
{ Mouth, { Sonorous { GH. } Mute { CH. }
{ Nose, { Sonorous { NG. } Mute { HNG. }

Unto each of the Letters represented by a Face, there is adjoyned a lesser Figure, consisting only of the chief out-lines representing the Organs of speech.

The *Labials* are represented by two curve Figures for the Lips. The *Linguals* by the Figure of the Tongue, according to its various application; either of the *Top* or *Root*, to the several parts of the *Palate*, or of the *Teeth*.

The *Sonorous* Consonants, of each kind, are distinguished from the *Mutes*, by the addition of (˘) to represent the motion of the Epiglottis, by which sound is made.

The *Breathing* or Spiritous Consonants are represented by a longer *undulated Line*, passing through the *Mouth* in some of them, either betwixt the *Lips*, in F, V. or between the *Tongue* and *Palate*, in Dh, Th, Gh, Ch, R, HR. In the two last of which, the top of the Tongue is divided, to represent that Trepidation or Vibration, in the framing of these Letters. Or by the sides of the Tongue in L, HL. Or betwixt *the Top of the Tongue and the Teeth*, in Z, S, Zh, Sh. In the two last of which, the undulated Line is doubled, to represent that more *dense Percolation* of breath, used in the framing of those Letters.

Those that are breathed through the *Nose*, have this undulated line above the Palate, as in M, HM, N, HN, NG, HNG.

I propose these only as being natural Pictures of the Letters, without any Design of common use, for which they are less fit, by reason of their being so complicated.

§ 5. Pronunciation.

§ 5. Though each of the Letters have their distinct powers naturally fixed, yet that difference which there is in the various manner of *Pronunciation*, doth somewhat alter the Sound of them. And there are no two Nations in the world that do exactly agree in the same way of pronouncing any one Language (suppose the *Latin*) Amongst persons of the same Nation, some pronounce more *fully* and *strongly*, others more *slightly*, some more *flatly*, others more *broadly*, others more *mincingly*. And in the hearing of forreign Languages, we are apt to think, that none of the Letters we are acquainted with, can frame such strange sounds as they seem to make: But this doth principally proceed from the several modes of Pronunciation; the variety of which may well enough consist with the distinct power of the Letters. 'Tis obvious to any one to observe, what great difference there will be in the same words, when spoken *slowly* and *treatably*, and when tumbled out in a *rapid precipitate* manner. And this is one kind of difference in the pronunciation of several Nations; The *Spaniards* and

Itali-

Chap. XIV. *Concerning Natural Grammar.* 381

Italians pronouncing more *slowly* and *Majestically*, the *French* more *volubly* and *hastily*, the *English* in a middle way betwixt both. Another different mode of Pronunciation betwixt several Nations, may be in regard of *strength* and *distinctness* of pronouncing, which will specially appear in those kind of Letters which do most abound in a Language. Some pronounce more deeply *Guttural*, as the *Welsh*, and the Eastern people, the *Hebrews*, and *Arabians*, &c. Others seem to thrust their words more *forwards*, towards the *outward* parts of the mouth, as the *English*; others more *inward* towards the palate, as the *French*; some speak with stronger collisions, and more vehement aspirations, as the *Northern* people generally, by reason of their abundance of spirits and inward heat; others more *lightly* and *softly*, as the *Southern* Nations, their internal spirits being more weak, by reason of the outward heat.
Prolegomena in Biblia Polyglot.

One principal Reason of the various sounds in the pronunciation of several Languages doth depend upon the nature of those Letters, of which they do chiefly consist and are framed. Upon which account, the *Greek*, which abounds in Vowels and Dipthongs, is more smooth. And though the *Latin* have fewer Vowels, yet it is so equally mixed with them, as to be rendred facil and pleasant; whereas the *Hebrew* doth abound in some harsh Consonants, *Aspirations* and *Gutturals*.

I cannot here omit the Censure which an ingenious person gives concerning the difference of many of our *European* Languages, in respect of their pronunciation. The *Italian* (saith he) is in pronunciation, pleasant, but without Sinews, as a still flowing water; the *French* delicate, but inward and nice, like a woman that dares scarce open her mouth, for fear of marring her Countenance. The *Spanish*, Majestical, but withal somewhat terrible and fulsom, by the too much affectation of the Letter O. The *Dutch* manly, but withal harsh and quarrelsom. Whereas our *English* (saith he) hath what is comely and Euphonical in each of these, without any of their Inconveniences. 'Tis usual for men to be most favourable towards the Language unto which they have been most accustomed. 'Tis likely that Forreigners may be as apt to complain of several Defects in our Language as we are of theirs.
R. C. of Anthony in Cambd. Remains.

That which doth generally seem most difficult to Strangers in our English Tongue, is the pronouncing of certain Aspirations (as they are stiled) very frequently and familiarly used amongst us, but hardly imitable by others, though these are but few; these five words (as it is said) comprehending all of them. *What think the chosen Judges?* Which a little practise might overcome.

It were desirable in a new invented Language, to make use chiefly of such Letters and Syllables, as are of general practise, and universally facil in Pronunciation: But the custom of several Nations is so exceeding various in this respect, that 'tis very difficult to find out what these are; most of the Letters being disused, and not acknowledged for Letters, in several Countries.
§ 6.

(α) is frequently used by other Nations, but not owned with a distinct Character by the English. (Nations.

(a) is frequently used by us Englishmen, but not so much by other

(e) is generally received, but very ambiguously pronounced.

(i) is

Purchas. lib. 5. cap. 9.   (i) is not owned by us for a distinct Vowel, though we frequently use the power of it. And the *Mexicans* are said not to use the Letter (y) which is the same with this (as was shewed before.)

By Walton Introduction.   (o) is not in the Armenian Alphabet, nor do the *Syrians* own it, but use (u) or (aw) instead of it. Some of the Ancient Cities in *Italy*,

Idem Proleg. 13. 5.   those of the *Umbri* and *Tusci* did not use this Vowel, but *u* instead of it, (saith *Priscian*.)

(ж) according to the true power of it, is not owned by us, nor by many other Nations with a distinct Character.

(y) is scarce acknowledged by any Nation except the Welsh.

(ü) is (I think) proper to the *French*, and used by none else.

(M and N) are so general, that I have not yet met with an Account of any Nation by whom they are not used.

(NG) is not owned for a Letter by any, except perhaps the Hebrews.

(V) is not pronounced by the *Mexicans*, *Arabians*, *Persians*, *Saxons*.

(Dh) seems difficult to most Nations, though frequently used by us Englishmen.

(Gh) is not any where, except amongst the *Irish*.

* *Vincent le Blanc. Part 3. 16.*
† *Alex. Rhodes Dission. Anim. cap. 1.*
‖ *De recta scriptione Linguæ Anglicanæ.*

(L) is not used by the * *Brasileans*, nor the men of † *Japan*. Many of the *Italians*, especially the *Florentines*, do seem to dislike this Letter, though others stile it the sweetest of all the rest, saith ‖ Sir *Thomas Smith*.

(R) is not used by the *Mexicans*, *Brasileans*, or the men of *China*, (say several of the same Authors) The *Americans* near *New-England*, pronounce neither L, nor R; but use N instead of both; pronouncing *Nobstan* for *Lobstan*.

Alex. Rhodes ibid.   (Z) is not owned for a Letter by the Inhabitants of *CochinChina*.

(Zh) is not owned for a distinct Letter, either by us *English*, or almost any other,

(HM, HN, HNG) are not, for ought I know) owned by any, excepting only the *Welsh* and *Irish*, and the last perhaps by the *Jews*.

(F) is not pronounced by the *Brasileans*.

(Th) seems difficult to many Nations, and is owned by very few, to be a distinct Letter.

(Ch) is not used by any (for ought I can find) except the *Grecians* and the *Welsh*.

(HL) is almost proper to the *Welsh*, and scarce used by others.

(HR) though frequent amongst the *Grecians*, yet is rarely used by others.

Purchas. lib. 5. cap. 9.   (S) is not used by the *Mexicans*.

(Sh) That this was not universal among the *Jews*, may appear by the Scripture Story of *Shiboleth*, nor is it either in the *Greek* or *Latin*.

Idem l. 10. c. 3.
Item. vol. 5. c. 18. Sect. 6.
Vossius de Gr. cap. 27.

(B) is not pronounced by the men of *China* or *Japan*.

(D) is not used amongst the Inhabitants of *China*.

(G) is not pronounced by the *Mexicans*.

(P) is not acknowledged in the *Arabick*, nor was this used amongst the *Jews* before the Invention of Points.

(T) is not used by the Inhabitants of *Japan*.

(C)

Chap. XIV. *Concerning Natural Grammar.*

(C) as reſtrained to the power of K, is for ought I know, of general uſe.

'Tis not improbable but that there may be a difficulty and difuſe of every one of theſe Letters in ſeveral Nations of the world; upon which account it is excuſable, if in the framing of a Language, it be propoſed to make uſe of all the Letters, without any particular choice of ſome, and ſecluſion of others. Or if any be excluded, they ought in reaſon to be ſuch, as ſeem moſt difficult to thoſe, amongſt whom this Language hath its firſt Riſe and Original. And ſuch others ſhould be moſt frequently uſed, as are generally eſteemed moſt eaſie and pleaſant.

Theſe 34 Letters before enumerated, will ſuffice to expreſs all thoſe articulate ſounds, which are commonly known and uſed in theſe parts of the World. I dare not be over-peremptory in aſſerting that theſe are all the *Articulate Sounds*, which either are, or can be in Nature; it being perhaps as impoſſible to reckon up all ſuch, as to determine the juſt number of *Colours* or *Taſts*: But I think that theſe are all the principal Heads of them, and that as much may be done by theſe (if not more) as by any other Alphabet now known.

PART

PART IV.

Concerning a Real Character, and a Philosophical Language.

CHAP. I.

The Proposal of one kind of Real Character (amongst many others which might be offered) both for the Integrals, whether Genus's, Differences or Species, together with the Derivations and Inflexions belonging to them, as likewise for all the several kinds of Particles.

THe next Enquiry should be, what kind of *Character* or Language may be fixed upon, as most convenient for the expression of all those Particulars above mentioned, belonging to the Philosophy of *Speech*; in order to which it may seem, that the first Enquiry should be concerning *Language*; Because *Writing* is but the figure of *Articulate sound*, and therefore subsequent to it: But though it be true, that men did first *speak* before they did *write*, and consequently *writing* is but the figure of *Speech*, and therefore in order of *time* subsequent to it; yet in order of *Nature* there is no priority between these: But *voice* and *sounds* may be as well assigned to Figure, as *Figures* may be to *Sounds*. And I do the rather begin with treating concerning a common *Character* or *Letter*, because this will conduce more to that great end of *Facility*, whereby (as I first proposed) men are to be invited to the Learning of it. To proceed from the *Language* to the Character, would require the learning of both; which being of greater difficulty, than to learn one alone, is not therefore so sutable to that intention of ingaging men by the *Facility* of it. And because men that do retain their several Tongues, may yet communicate by a *Real Character*, which shall be legible in all Languages; therefore I conceive it most proper to treat of this in the first place, and shall afterwards shew how this Character may be made *effable*, in a distinct Language.

All Characters signifie either *Naturally*, or by *Institution*. Natural *Characters* are either the Pictures of things, or some other *Symbolical*

Representations of them, the framing and applying of which, though it were in some degree feasible, as to the general *kinds* of things; yet in most of the *particular species*, it would be very *difficult*, and in some perhaps *impossible*. It were exceeding desirable that the *Names* of things might consist of such *Sounds*, as should bear in them some Analogy to their *Natures*; and the Figure or Character of these Names should bear some proper resemblance to those *Sounds*, that men might easily guess at the sence or meaning of any name or word, upon the first *hearing* or *sight* of it. But how this can be done in all the particular species of things, I understand not; and therefore shall take it for granted, that this Character must be by *Institution*. In the framing of which, there are these four properties to be endeavoured after.

1. They should be most simple and easie for the Figure, to be described by one *Ductus* of the pen, or at the most by two.

2. They must be sufficiently distinguishable from one another to prevent mistake.

3. They ought to be comely and graceful for the shape of them to the eye.

4. They should be *Methodical*, Those of the same common nature, having some kind of sutableness and correspondence with one another; All which qualifications would be very advantageous, both for *Understanding*, *Memory* and *Use*.

Those Characters must represent either
- Integrals
  - Radicals.
  - Derivations.
  - Inflections.
- Particles
  - Grammatical.
  - Transcendental.

The first thing to be enquired after, is to find out fitting Marks for the common Genus's or Heads in the former Tables of Integrals, which are there reduced to the number of forty. It were not difficult to offer several Varieties of these Marks or Generical Characters, with their different Advantages and Conveniences; to which purpose I had prepared sundry kinds of them, which I once thought to have inserted here: but upon further consideration, I shall mention only one of them, which I have chosen out of the rest, as seeming to me to be in all respects the most convenient amongst them.

Chap. I. *Concerning a Real Character.* 387

Transcend. { General	Animals { Exanguious	Action { Spiritual
Rel. mixed	Fish	Corporeal
Rel. of Action	Bird	Motion
Discourse	Beast	Operation
God	Parts { Peculiar	
World	General	Relation { Oecon.
Element	Quantity { Magnitude	Possef.
Stone	Space	Provis.
Metal	Measure	Civil
Herb confid. accord. to the { Leaf	Quality { Power Nat.	Judicial
Flower	Habit	Military
Seed-vessel	Manners	Naval
Shrub	Quality sensible	Eccles.
Tree	Disease	

The Differences are to be affixed unto that end which is on the left side of the Character, according to this order;

1 2 3 4 5 6 7 8 9

The Species should be affixed at the other end of the Character according to the like order.

1 2 3 4 5 6 7 8 9

And whereas several of the Species of Vegetables and Animals, do according to this present constitution, amount to more than Nine, in such cases the number of them is to be distributed into two or three Nines, which may be distinguished from one another by doubling the stroke in some one or more parts of the Character; as suppose after this manner, ⸺ ⸺. If the first and most simple Character be made use of, the Species that are affixed to it, will belong to the first combination of *Nine*; if the other, they will belong according to the order of them, unto the second Combination.

Those Radicals which are paired to others uppon account of *Opposition*, may be expressed by a Loop, or (o) at the left end of the Character, after this manner, o⸺

Those that are paired upon the account of *Affinity*, are to be expressed by the like Mark at the other end of the Character, thus, ⸺o

The double Opposites of *Excess* or *Defect*, are to be described by the Transcendental points, denoting *Excess* or *Defect*, to be placed over the Character, as shall be shewed after.

Ddd 2 *Adje-*

Adjectives should be expressed by a *Hook* at the right end of the Character in ⎰ Genus's or Differences, thus —◡
⎱ Species —◡ —◡

Adverbs (being very near of kin to adjectives) may be expressed by a *Loop* in the same ⎰ Genus's and Diff. —○
place. In ⎱ Species —○ —○

Abstracts may be expressed by a *Hook* at the left end of the Character. In ⎰ Genus's ◡—
⎱ Differences and Species ◡— ◡—

The *Active* and *Passive* voice may be expressed, one of them by a *Hook*, and the other by a *Loop*, at the left end of the Character, after this manner, in ⎡ Genus's ⎰ Active ◡—
⎢ ⎱ Passive ○—
⎣ Differences or Species ⎰ Active ◡— ◡—
⎱ Passive ○— ○—

The *Plural Number* may be expressed by a hook at the right end of the Character, after this manner, in ⎰ Genus's and Differences —◡
⎱ Species —ᶜ —◡

The Characters of the *Particles* should each of them be of a less figure, and capable of being varied to a threefold place. The *Grammatical Particles*, being applied to the sides of the Character, and the *Transcendental Particles* to the top of it.

These *Grammatical Particles* are here contrived to such a kind of distinct sutableness, so as each of the several kinds of them, hath a several kind of Character assigned to them.

1. The *Copula*, by the mark of (°)

2. *Pronouns*, by Points. (·· ·· ··)

3. *Interjections* by upright Lines streight or hooked, (ı ŋ ɹ ɹ ʋ)

4. *Prepositions*, by small curved Figures ⎰ ᴜ ᴧ ⊃ ⊂ ⎱
⎰ ᴡ ᴍ ᴈ ᴇ ⎱
⎱ ᴡ ᴍ ⊂ ⊃ ⎰

5. *Adverbs*, by a right angled Character ⎰ ⌐ ⌐ ⌐ ⌐
⎱ ⊤ ⊥ ⊣ ⊢
+

6. *Conjunctions* by an acute angled Character ⎰ ᴠ ᴧ ⟩ ⟨
⎱ ⋎ ⋏ ⟩ ⟨

7. *Articles* by two oblique Lines to be placed ⎰ \ \
towards the top of the Character ⎱ / /

8. *Modes*

Chap. I. _Concerning a Real Character._

8. _Modes_ by circular Figures } ⁂
 mixed } ⁂

9. _Tenses_ by a small streight transverse Line (-)

Amongst these _Grammatical Particles_ the first six are more principal and absolute, _viz._

1. The _Copula_, being the Verb _sum_, according to a threefold difference of time.

     | Have been, hast been, hath been.
   o | Am, art, is, are.
     | Shall be.

2. _Pronouns._ { I, Thou, He } { We, Ye, They } { This, That, The same, Another, A certain, Some body }

      { Any, Every, All } { Who? Which. Whosoever. }

If one of these Pronouns, suppose (·) be placed at the side of the Character before it, — it signifies the first Person (_I_,) If at the middle, — it signifies the second person (_Thou._) If at the bottom, — it signifies the third person (_He._) And if they are thus affixed after a Character that signifies _Action_, they will then denote the Accusative Case, Me, Thee, Him. so ˙○⸺ is, _I love him._

If any of the Pronouns are to be rendered in their _Possessive_ sence, this is to be expressed by a little curve Line under them, as (˘˘) So ˘— is My, or Mine, (⌒—) is Ours, (˘—) is Thy or Thine, (˸—is His, And (˷—) is Theirs.

The _Reduplicative_ Notion of Pronouns may most naturally be expressed by a doubling of their Character with a _Fulcrum_ or _Arrectarius_ interposed. So |˙| is I me, that is, I my self. ·|· is Thou thee, Thou thy self. ·|· He him, He himself. And so for the _Possessives_ that are reduplicative ̍|̍ Mine mine, that is, My own, _&c._

And whereas several of the Pronouns were before said to be applicable both unto Place, Time, and Manner, this ought to be expressed in writing by the help of an _Arrectarius_, with the Transcendental Marks of Pl. T. M. So ˙|is, Which place. Thus ˙| is, What place, or Where? ̍| is, What time, or When? ̍| is, What manner, or How?

Interjections may be thus expressed;

{ Admiring, Doubting, Despising } { Love, Hatred, Mirth, Sorrow, Desire, Aversation }

     { Exclamation, Silence, Bespeaking, Expressing attention, Insinuation, Threatning }

The

The Marks for Prepositions may be thus applied;

$$\left\}\begin{matrix}\text{Of, With}\\ \text{By, For}\\ \text{Out of, Concerning}\end{matrix}\right\} \quad \sim \left\{\begin{matrix}\text{According, Instead}\\ \text{With, Without}\\ \text{For, Against}\end{matrix}\right\}c$$

$$\sim\left\{\begin{matrix}\text{To, At}\\ \text{From, Off}\\ \text{Over, About}\end{matrix}\right\}m$$

$$3\left\{\begin{matrix}\text{Into, In}\\ \text{Out of, Without}\\ \text{Thorough, Beside}\end{matrix}\right\}\varepsilon \quad \sim\left\{\begin{matrix}\text{Upwards, Above}\\ \text{Downwards, Below}\\ \text{Before, Behind}\end{matrix}\right\}\sim$$

$$2\left\{\begin{matrix}\text{Upon, Under}\\ \text{On this side, Beyond}\\ \text{Betwixt, Against}\end{matrix}\right\}s$$

The Marks for *Adverbs* may be thus applied;

$$\prec\left\{\begin{matrix}\text{Yea, Nay}\\ \text{Perhaps, Truly}\\ \text{As, So}\end{matrix}\right\}L \quad \neg\left\{\begin{matrix}\text{How, So}\\ \text{More, Most}\\ \text{Less, Least}\end{matrix}\right\}r \quad \blacktriangle\left\{\begin{matrix}\text{Rather, Than}\\ \text{Yet, Until}\\ \text{Whilst, At length}\end{matrix}\right\}\tau$$

$$\dashv\left\{\begin{matrix}\text{Together, Only}\\ \text{Again, As if}\\ \text{Un, Re}\end{matrix}\right\}\vdash \quad +\left\{\begin{matrix}\text{Almost.}\\ \text{Scarce.}\\ \text{Thereabout.}\end{matrix}\right.$$

The Marks for *Conjunctions* may be thus applied;

$$v\left\{\begin{matrix}\text{Whether yea, Whether no}\\ \text{And, Neither}\\ \text{If, Unless}\end{matrix}\right\}\lambda \quad \succ\left\{\begin{matrix}\text{Indeed, But}\\ \text{Although, Notwithstanding}\\ \text{Or, Either}\end{matrix}\right\}\prec$$

$$y\left\{\begin{matrix}\text{That, Least that}\\ \text{For, Because}\\ \text{Wherefore, Therefore}\end{matrix}\right\}\lambda \quad \lambda\left\{\begin{matrix}\text{Whereas, Thereupon}\\ \text{Also, \&c.}\\ \text{viz. e.g.}\end{matrix}\right\}\lambda$$

The other three kinds of Particles are more servile and auxiliary. The *Articles* may be expressed (as was said before) by two oblique Lines to be placed towards the top of the Character $\left\{\begin{matrix}\text{A}\\ \text{The}\end{matrix}\right.$

The Mark for the *Imperative* Mood, according as it is applied to several places of the Character, may express the mode of
· {Petition
· {Persuasion
· {Command

The

Chap. I.   *Concerning a Real Character.*   391

The Secondary Moods may have their Marks thus applied to them ;

$$\left\{\begin{array}{l}\text{Power}\\ \text{Liberty}\\ \text{Will}\\ \text{Necessity}\end{array}\right.\left\{\begin{array}{l}\text{Can}\\ \text{Could}\end{array}\right.\;\left\{\begin{array}{l}\text{May}\\ \text{Might}\end{array}\right.\;\left\{\begin{array}{l}\text{Will}\\ \text{Would}\end{array}\right.\;\left\{\begin{array}{l}\text{Must, shall}\\ \text{Must, should}\end{array}\right.$$

Several of these Secondary Modes, will according to their places, towards the top, middle, and bottom of the Character, comprehend in them the several differences of time; so ' is I would have writ.

The Marke for the Tenses, Past, Present, and Future, may be thus applied ; ⎡ Have been, hast been, hath been.
⎨ Am, art, is.
⎣ Shall be.

The Transcendental Marks to be put in three places over the head of the Character, may be thus applied ;

{ Metaphor } { Kind }   { Thing }   { Place } { Cause }   { Aggregate }
{ Like   } { Manner } { Person }   { Time } { Sign }   { Segregate }

{ Lamin } { Instrument } { Jugament }   { Sepiment } { Vest   } { House   }
{ Pinn } { Vessell   } { Machin   }   { Armament } { Armour } { Chamber }

{ Habit } { Officer } { Mechanic }   { Ability   } { Inceptive   } { Endeavor }
{ Art   } { Artist } { Merchant }   { Proneness } { Frequentative } { Impetus }

{ Augmentative } { Excess } { Perfective }   { Voice   } { Male   } { Young }
{ Diminutive   } { Defect } { Corruptive }   { Language } { Female } { Part }

Whereas there is somewhat peculiar in the nature of *Numbers*, distinct from any of the other Heads, by reason of their great multitude, and various kinds ; It may seem therefore necessary to offer some more particular directions for the expression of them, both as to the Numbers themselves, and as to the Grammatical Variations of them.

Numbers are usually expressed in Writing either by *words at length*, or by *Figures*.

The Character here proposed under the first difference of Measure, is that which doth answer to the writing of Numbers in *words at length*,

And

And because the Species enumerated under that difference, are but nine, for the nine Digits; therefore will it be convenient in the first place, to explain the manner how all other numbers above nine, are to be expressed in this Character; which may be done by affixing some of these four Marks, (   ) put after the Character, closer to the Body of it than ordinary, to denote those round Numbers, Ten, Hundred, Thousand, Million.

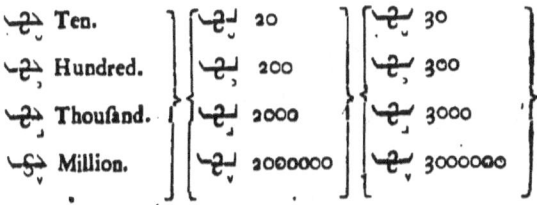

But because those common Figures now in use, borrowed from the *Arabians*, are so generally known, and a kind of Universal Character already received; therefore it may be most convenient still to retain the use of them, as being much better fitted for all the Arithmetical Operations, of *Addition, Subtraction, Multiplication* and *Division*, &c. than either that Numerical Character mentioned before, or the way of Numeration by Letters, or any other way that I can think of.

As for those Variations of which Numbers are capable, and according to which Grammarians do commonly distinguish them, they may be thus expressed.

1. Those which are called *Cardinal Numbers*, One, Two, Three,&c. are the Radical Numbers themselves.

2. *Ordinals*, as First, second, third, &c. are *Adjectives Neuter*. Firstly, secondly, thirdly, &c. are the *Adverbs Neuter*.

3. *Distributives* may be exprest by the *Substantive Neuter*, with the Transcendental Mark of *Segregate*, the Substantive it self being put for one sort of Distributive in the *singular* Number, as sing. 3. (segr. will denote three, one by one; or for another sort of Distributive, being put in the *plural* number, as plural 3.(segr. will signifie by threes, or three by three.

4. *Collectives* may be exprest by the *Substantive Neuter*, with the Adverb *together* before it, with the transcendental Mark of Aggregate over it, as together-three, or three (Aggr. is a ternary, a leash, &c.

5. *Multiplying* a Number may be expressed by the *Active* of it, as *a*. three is trebling, and *being multiplied* by the *Passive* of it, as *p*. three being trebled.

6. *Dividing* a Number into parts, may be exprest by the *Active* with the transcendental Mark (*Part*. as *a.* three (part) is dividing into 3 parts, or active tripartition. *Being divided* into parts, may be expressed by the *Passive* with the mark of *part*; as *p*. three (part) is being divided into 3 parts, or passive tripartition. If this Division be into *equal* parts, one may express it by adding the Adverb *equally*.

7. A

Chap. I.   *Concerning a Real Character.*   393

7. A *Fraction* may be exprest ; If it be the Aliquot part of a Number, by the *Adjective Neuter,* with the Transcendental Mark of *Part*; as adj. three (part) a third part, and it may be written thus, 3)1 ; If it be not the Aliquot part of a Number, it may be exprest by both the Numbers which are to be considered in it, as three sevenths may be called a seventh part of three, and it may be written thus, 7)3.

8. A *Ration* may be exprest likewise by both the Numbers which are to be considered in it, in speaking thus ; as three to seven, in writing ⁷⁄₃.

9. Number of *Species* or *Sorts,* may be exprest by the Number with the Transcendental Mark of (kind) as threefold, 3 (kind.

10. Number of *Times* or *Places* likewise, by the Transcendental Marks of *Time* or *Place* respectively, as once, twice, &c.

in one { time / place } in two { times / places } in three { times / places } &c.

11. *Abstract* Numbers, as Unity, Duality, Trinity, may be exprest by adding the Mark of Abstract upon the Character.

If the Question be how these Grammatical Variations may be contrived in the use of the ordinary Figures for Number, this may be done by affixing such variations upon a Transverse Line over the head of the Figure, So 1. 2. 3. will be the Adjective, first, second, and third, &c. So 1. 2. 3 will be the Adverb, Firstly, secondly, thirdly, So 2. 3. 4. will be twofold, threefold, fourfold, &c So 1. 2. 3. &c. will be once, twice, thrice, &c.

The Characters that serve for Interpunction, may be thus contrived ;

Comma ,

Colon .

Period ,

Those other Notes to distinguish the various manners of Pronuntiation may be Charactered after this manner ;

Hyphen

Parenthesis ( )

Explication [ ]

Interrogation ?

Wonder !

Irony \

Eee   These

These Marks having not any such near resemblance to the other *Real Characters*, appointed either for Integrals or Particles, need not therefore be changed,

The Note for *Emphasis*, may be expressed either by a reduplication of the Characters, if it consist in one word; or by some variety in the shape of the Characters, if it consist in several words, as is usual in that way of printing Words in an *Italic* Letter

The meaning of these things will appear more plainly by an Example: To which purpose I shall set down the Lords Prayer, and the Creed written in this Character, which I shall afterwards explain and resolve according to the forementioned Rules.

CHAP.

CHAP. II.

Instances of this Real Character in the Lords Prayer and the Creed.

For the better explaining of what hath been before delivered concerning a Real Character, it will be necessary to give some Example and Instance of it, which I shall do in the *Lords Prayer* and the *Creed*: First setting each of them down after such a manner as they are ordinarily to be written. Then the Characters at a greater distance from one another, for the more convenient figuring and inter lining of them. And lastly, a Particular Explication of each Character out of the Philosophical Tables, with a Verbal Interpretation of them in the Margin.

The Lords Prayer.

1 2 3 4 5 6 7 8 9 10 11
Our Parent who art in Heaven, Thy Name be Hallowed, Thy

12 13 14 15 16 17 18 19 20 21 22 23 24 25 26
Kingdome come, Thy Will be done, so in Earth as in Heaven, Give

27 28 29 30 31 32 33 34 35 36 37 38 39 40 41 42 43
to us on this day our bread expedient and forgive us our trespasses as

44 45 46 47 48 49 50 51 52 53 54 55 56 57 58
we forgive them who trespass against us, and lead us not into

59 60 61 62 63 64 65 66 67 68 69 70
temptation, but deliver us from evil, for the Kingdome and the

71 72 73 74 75 76 77 78 79 80.
Power and the Glory is thine, for ever and ever, Amen. So be it.

Our

1. (⌒|) The first Particle being expressed by Points, doth denote the thing thereby signified to be a *Pronoun*: And whereas there are two Points placed level, towards the upper side of the Character, they must therefore (according to the Directions premised) signifie the first Person Plural Number, *viz. We*. And because there is a curve Line under these Points, that denotes this Pronoun to be here used *Possessively*, and consequently to signifie *Our*.

Parent

2. (⫞⊥) This next Character being of a bigger proportion, must therefore represent some *Integral* Notion. The Genus of it, *viz.* (⊥) is appointed to signifie *Oeconomical Relation*. And whereas the Transverse Line at the end towards the left hand, hath an affix, making an acute Angle, with the upper side of the Line, therefore doth it refer to the first Difference of that Genus, which according to the Tables, is relation of Consanguinity: And there being an Affix making a right Angle at the other end of the same Line, therefore doth it signifie the second Species under this Difference, *viz. Direct ascending*, by which the Notion of *Parent* is defined. And this being originally a Noun of Person, doth not the need therefore Transc. Note of Person to be affixed to it. If it were to be rendred Father in the strictest sense, it would be necessary that the Transcendental Note of *Male* should be joyned to it, being a little hook on the top, over the middle of the Character, after this manner (⫞⊥). The word Father in the most Philosophical and proper sense of it, denoting a *Male Parent*. And because the word Parent is not here used according to the strictest sense, but Metaphorically; therefore might the Transcendental Note of *Metaphor*, be put over the head of it; after this manner, (⫞⊥). But this being such a Metaphor as is generally received in other Languages, therefore there will be no necessity of using this mark.

Who

3. (∵|) This Character consisting of Points, must therefore denote a *Pronoun*; and because it consists of three Points, therefore must it denote one of the *Compound* Pronouns, and being placed towards the middle of the Character, therefore must it signifie *Who* personal, or *Which* real.

Art

4. (○|) This Particle, being a small Round, doth therefore denote the *Copula*, and being placed towards the middle of the Character, it must therefore signifie the present tense of it, *Am, art, is, are*, and being joyned with a Noun of the second person, is therefore in English to be rendered (*Art*.)

In

5. (ᶜ|) This Particle being of a curved figure, must therefore refer to Prepositions. And by the shape of it, it must belong to one of the Opposites in the fourth Combination of Prepositions, and by the place of it, being towards the upper end of the Character, it is determined to the Preposition (*In*.)

Heaven

6. (⊢) This Generical Character is assigned to signifie *World*, the right angled affix on the left side, denoting the second Difference under that Genus, namely *Heaven*, which is defined to import either

Chap. I. *Concerning a Real Character.*

a place or state of the greatest perfection and happiness; and because there is no affix at the other end, therefore doth it signifie the Difference it self, and not any Species.

7. (⌣|) This Particle, for the Reason before mentioned (*Numb.* 1.) is a possessive Pronoun, for its consisting of a single Point, it must be of the singular number; and for its place towards the middle of the Character, it must relate to the second Person, *viz. Thy*, or *Thine*. — Thy

8. (∠⌒) The Genus denoted by this Character is *Transcendental General*; the affix to the end on the left side, doth signifie the first Difference under that Genus, *viz.* the Kinds of Things and Notions, or those essential Communities wherein the things of different natures do agree. The affix at the other end of the same Line, making an obtuse angle with the lower side of it, doth signifie the fourth Species under that Difference, *viz. Name*; which according to its primary sense is described to be the word assigned for the signifying any thing or notion. — Name

9. (⁸|) This Particle is appointed to signifie that which is called the Imperative Mode by way of Petition, or *May it be*, or we pray that it may be. — May it be

10. (⌒ᴗ⌒) This Generical Character doth signifie *Ecclesiastical Relation*: The affix making a right angle with the under part of the Genus, doth denote the fifth Difference, which refers to *Discipline*, or the due ordering of the Circumstances of Ecclesiastical or sacred things to the best advantage; under which the first Species denoted by the acute Angle on the other end and side, doth signifie the more general notion of separating things from their Commonness, and setting them apart by way of Honour to a more peculiar use, which is called Consecrating or *Hallowing*. By the Loop on the affix for the Difference, is signified the *Passive Voice*; and by the Hook on the other affix, the notion of *Adjective*. — Hallowed

11. (⌣|) as *Numb.* 7. — Thy

12. (2ʃ⌐) This Generical Character doth signifie *Civil* or Political *Relation*. The affix on the left side, doth signifie the first Difference under that Genus which is *Degrees of Persons*. The affix on the Species side, doth refer to the second Species, which is *King*, defined to be the most principal and absolute amongst the kinds of Magistrates. The Hook at the end of the Difference affix doth signifie Action: So that the proper notion expressed by this Character is *Regnation*, or τὸ *regnare*, which is the Substantive of *Action*, as King is of Person. — Regnation, or τὸ regnare

13. (⁸|) as *Numb.* 9. — May it be

14. (⌒ᴗ⌒) The Genus denoted by this Character is *Transcendental Action*; the affix on the Difference side, making an acute Angle with the lower side, doth signifie the sixth Difference, which according to the Tables doth refer to *Ition*, going, or passing; the affix on the Species — coming

cies fide, being the firſt, doth according to the Tables, refer to the word *Coming*, which is deſcribed to be motion to a place nearer to us: The Hook on the Difference doth ſignifie *Active voice*, and the Hook on the other affix, the notion of *Adjective*, viz. *Coming*.

Thy   15. (↙|) as *Numb*. 7.

Will   16. (⏚↵) This Genericall Character doth ſignifie the firſt Genus in Quality, which according to the Tables is *Natural Power*. The affix for the Difference, making an acute Angle, with the upper ſide of the Genus, muſt ſignifie *Rational Faculty*. The affix on the Species ſide, making an obtuſe Angle with the lower ſide, muſt ſignifie the fourth Species, which is that Faculty we call *Will*, whereby we do rationally follow after that which is good, and fly what is evil. The hook on the left ſide upon the Difference affix, denotes the *Active voice*. So that the proper Signification of this Character is *Volition*, or τὸ *velle*.

May it be   17. (ᵉ|) as *Numb*. 9.

Done   18. (⌒↳) The ſame Genericall Character with *Numb*. 14. denoting *Tranſcendental Action*. The obtuſe angle on the left ſide ſignifies the third Difference, viz. *General Actions relating to Buſineſs*. The acute Angle at the other end, ſignifies the ſixth Species, viz. the doing or effecting what we undertake and deſign, which we call *performing* or *accompliſhing*; the Loop at the end of the Difference doth denote the *Paſſive voice*, and the Hook upon the other affix, the notion of *Adjective*; ſo that this Character ſignifies the *Adjective Paſſive*, of perform, viz. *performed* or *done*.

So   19. (⌐|) This Character being a right angled Particle, doth denote ſome *Adverb*; and by its ſhape it appears to be one of the Oppoſites in the firſt Combination, and by its place towards the lower end of the Character, it is determined to the Particle (*So*.)

In   20. (ᵉ|) as *numb*. 5.

Earth   21. (⊢⊣) The ſame Genericall Character as *numb*. 6. ſignifying *World*, the affix making a right Angle, doth denote the ſecond difference under that *Genus*, namely, the *Celeſtial* parts of it in general, amongſt which, this Globe of Sea and Land whereon we live, is reckoned as the ſeventh Species, denoted by the affix at the other end.

As   22. (⌐|) This Particle being oppoſite to that *numb*. 19. ſignifying *So*, muſt therefore ſignifie *As*, the one being the *Redditive* of the other.

In   23. (ᵉ|) as *numb*. 5.

Heaven   24. (⊢⊣) as *numb*. 6.

Maiſt thou be   25. (ᵇ|) The ſame as *numb*. 9. but being here joyned with a word Active of the ſecond Perſon, it muſt be rendered in Engliſh, *Maiſt thou be*.

26.

Chap. II. *Concerning a Real Character.*

26. (⸺) The Genus of this Character is the same with *number* Giving. 14, & 18. denoting *Transcendental Action*; The affix on the left hand, making an obtuse Angle with the lower side of the Genus, doth therefore signifie the fourth Difference, which concerns Actions relating to *Commerce:* and the affix at the other end making such an obtuse angle, doth therefore signifie the fourth Species, which according to the Tables, is *Giving*, described to be the parting with something to another, to which we our selves have a right. The Hook at the end of the Difference affix, doth signifie *Active*, and the other, *Adjective*, viz. *Giving*.

27. (⸺) This Particle, by the figure of it, must signifie a Preposition of the third Combination, and by its place at the upper side of the Character, it is determined to signifie the Preposition (*To.*) To.

28. (⸺) This Particle consisting of Points, doth therefore denote Us. a *Pronoun*; and because there are two Points placed in a Level towards the top of the Character, therefore must it signifie the first Person plural, as *numb*. 1. And coming after a Verb, it is to be rendered in English as we do the Accusative Case, (*Us.*)

29. (⸺) as *numb*. 5. In

30. (⸺) This Pronoun particle consisting of two points placed obliquely from the bottom towards the top, doth therefore signifie one of the *Relative* Pronouns; and being placed at the top of the Character, it must signifie (*This.*) This

31. (⸺) This Generical Character is appointed to signifie the Day Genus of *Measure*. The affix on the left hand, making a right angle with the lower side of the Line, signifies the fifth Difference, which is Measure of *Time*. The affix at the other end, making the like angle, doth denote the fifth Species, *viz. Day Natural*, which is described to be the time of the Suns motion from any one Meridian to the same again.

32. (⸺) as *numb.* 1. Our

33. (⸺) This Character is appointed to signifie the Genus of *Oeco-* Bread *nomical Provisions*, of which, the first Difference denoted by the affix on the left hand, doth refer to *Sustentation ordinary*, and the first Species at the other end, doth refer to such kind of ordinary food as is of a more solid consistence, made of Grain, or some other Vegetable baked, without any considerable mixture, being of all other kinds of Food most necessary and common, which is *Bread*.

34. (⸺) The Genus of this Character doth signifie *Transcenden-* Expedient *tal General*, as before, N. 8. The affix on the left hand being the fifth, doth denote the *Differences of things relating to means*; where the seventh Species, denoted by the affix at the other end, doth signifie that kind of usefulness, which may probably promote the end, which we call *Expediency*; and because the Hook at the end of the Species affix doth denote *adjective*; therefore this Character must signifie *expedient*.

35.

And	35. (˙∣) The Particle reprefented by an acute angled figure, muſt therefore refer to *Conjunctions*. By the poſition of the Angle downwards, and by the ſituation of it towards the middle of the Character, it muſt denote the Conjunction, *And*.
Maiſt thou be	36. (⁸∣) as *numb*. 9.
Forgiving	37. (∽⚬⸝) The Genus of this Character doth ſignifie *Judicial Relation*. The affix on the Difference ſide, making a right angle with the upper ſide of the Genus, doth therefore ſignifie the ſecond Difference, *viz. Judicial Actions*. The affix for the Species being the ninth, doth ſignifie that kind of *Forinſic Action*, which is *conſequent with reſpect to the Judges*, inflicting the puniſhment or freeing from it; the firſt of which is *executing*, to which is oppoſed (ſignified in the Character by the Loop on the left hand) *Pardoning*, or forgiving. The Hook upon the affix for the Difference, denoting the *Active voice*, and that upon the other affix, the *Adjective*.
To	38. (⁀∣) as *numb*. 27.
Us	39. (∣ʺ) as *numb*. 28.
Our	40. (˘∣) as *numb*. 1.
Treſpaſſes	41. (∽⌣‿) The ſame Generical Character as *numb*. 8, & 34. ſignifying *Tranſcendental General*. The obtuſe angle on the left ſide doth ſignifie the third Difference, *viz*. the more *common and abſolute Differences of things*. The affix at the other end, making a right Angle with the upper ſide, doth ſignifie the ſecond Species, namely, that Difference of things which doth include a reſpect to the Will, as to their agreement or diſagreement with that Faculty, whereby they are rendered deſirable, or avoydable; which we call *Goodneſs* or *Evilneſs*. The Loop towards the left hand, at the joyning of the Affix, doth denote the Oppoſite in the Tables, namely, *Evilneſs*: The Hook at the other end of the ſame Affix, doth ſignifie the *Active* voice; and the hook on the other ſide, the *Plural Number*: So that the true importance of this Character muſt be *evil actions*, which is the ſame with that which we ſtile *Treſpaſſes*.
As	42. (ˌ∣) as *numb*. 19.
We	43. (¨∣) as *numb*. 24.
Are	44. (o∣) as *numb*. 4. But being here uſed with a word of the plural number, it muſt be rendered *Are*.
Forgiving	45. (∽⚬⸝) as *numb*. 37.
To	46. (⁀∣) as *numb*. 27,
Them	47. (∣..) This Particle Pronoun conſiſting of two points placed level, muſt ſignifie the Plural Number of one of the Perſonal Pronouns, and being at the lower end of the Character, it muſt ſignifie *They*, and coming after the Verb, it muſt be rendered *Them*.
Who	48. (·∣) as *numb*. 3.

Chap. II.   *Concerning a Real Character.*   401

49. (°|) as *numb.* 44. But being here placed towards the upper part of the Character, it muſt ſignifie the Copula in the Preter Tenſe, *Have been*.   Have been

50. (◌⌣◌) The ſame Radical as *numb.* 41. Only the Hook on the Species affix, is on that ſide which ſignifies the notion of *Adjective*, viz. *Tranſgreſſing*.   Tranſgreſſing

51. (₁|) This Particle doth by its figure appear to be one of the oppoſite Prepoſitions of the ſecond Combination, and by its poſition towards the bottom of the Character; it is determined to (*Againſt*.)   Againſt

52. (|″) as *Numb.* 24.   Us

53. (ᵛ|) as *Numb.* 31.   And

54. (°⁺|) This Particle by the figure of it, muſt be one of the Oppoſites of the firſt Combination of *Adverbs*, and by the place of it, it muſt be the Negative Particle *No*, or *Not*.   Not

55. (°|) as *Numb.* 9.

56. (ʊ⌐) The ſame Generical Character as *Numb.* 14, 18. 26. ſignifying *Tranſcendental Action*, The Difference on the left hand, being the ſame as *Numb.* 14. Namely, the ſixth, denoting *Itiou*; where the fifth Species ſignified by the right angled affix at the other end, doth by the Tables ſignifie *Leading*, which is deſcribed to be the cauſing of another thing to come after. The Hook on the Difference affix, doth ſignifie *Active*, and the other Hook *Adjective*. viz. *Leading*.   Maiſt thou be Leading

57. (|″) as *Numb.* 28.   Us

58. (³|) This Particle by the place and ſhape of it, muſt be oppoſite to that, *Numb.* 5. And conſequently, according to the Tables, muſt ſignifie (*Into*.)   Into

59. (⌒ₚ) The Generical Character the ſame with that, N. 14, 18, 26, 56. The right Angle on the left ſide denoting the ſecond Difference, *viz.* General Relations of Actions Comparate: The right Angle at the other end and ſide, ſignifying the fifth Species, which in the Tables, is *Comparing*; to which is adjoyned by way of Affinity (ſighified by the Loop) the Notion of *Trying*, or the Examining of things, for the diſtinguiſhing of their Truth and Goodneſs. And becauſe this is in it ſelf of an indifferent nature, and conſequently not to be deprecated; therefore the true Notion of it in this place, muſt be confined to ſuch kind of Temptations or Trials as may be hurtful, which is expreſſed by the Tranſcendental Particle of *Corruptive*, ſet on the top of the Character towards the right hand.   Temptation

60. (°|) This Particle by the figure of it, muſt denote a *Conjunction*, and an Oppoſite belonging to the ſecond Combination, and by the place of it towards the upper end of the Character, it is determined to the *Conjunction*, (*But*.)   But

Fff   61.

402   *Concerning a Real Character.*   Part IV.

Maift thou be
61. (⁵|) as *Numb.* 9.

Delivering
62. (22₁) This Generical Character doth fignifie *Spiritual Action*, under which the firft Difference denoted by the acute Angle on the left fide, doth refer to the Actions of God, (*i. e.*) fuch kind of Actions as do primarily belong to the Divine Nature; though fome of them may in a fecondary manner, and by way of participation be afcribed to other things. The right Angle made by the other affix, doth denote the fifth Species, which is defined to be the keeping or taking one from any kind of evil; which we call *Delivering*. The Hooks upon each affix (as hath been often faid before) muft denote *Active*, and *Adjective*.

Us.
63. (|`) as *Numb.* 24.

From
64. (ᴗ|) A Prepofition of the third Combination, and by its place at the middle of the Character, it is determined to the Prepofition *From*.

Evil
65. (ᴗᴗ) The fame Radical Character as *Numb*, 41, 50. The little upright ftroke on the top towards the right hand, being the Tranfcendental Note of *Thing*.

For
66. (ɣ|) This Particle, by the fhape of it, muft be a Conjunction of the third Combination, and by the pofition of it about the middle of the Character, it muft be the Caufal Particle *For*, or *Becaufe*.

The
67. (´|) This oblique ftroke towards the top is appointed to fignifie one of the Articles fubfervient to Subftantives; and becaufe the obliquity of it, is from the bottom upwards towards the right hand, therefore doth it denote the Demonftrative Article *The*.

Regnation, or
to regnare.
68. (2ᔕ|) as *Numb.* 12.

And
69. (ɣ|) as *Numb.* 35.

The
70. (´|) as *Numb.* 67.

Power
71. (ᒻᴛᴛ) This Generical Character doth fignifie *Habit*; the right angle on the left fide, denoting the fecond Difference, which comprehends the Inftruments of Virtue, commonly ftiled the *Goods of Fortune*: the right angle at the other end, fignifying the fifth Species, which is *Power*, defcribed to confift in an ability to protect our felves and others from Injury.

And
72. (ɣ|) as *Numb.* 35.

The
73. (´|) as *Numb.* 67.

Glory
74. (ᒻᴛᴛ̈) The fame Character, both as to the Genus and Difference with *Numb.* 71. The affix towards the right hand fignifying the fecond Species, which is *Reputation*, which by the tranfcendental mark of *Augmentative* over the Character towards the right hand, doth import the Notion of *Glory*, *viz.* the greateft kind and degree of Reputation.

75.

Chap. II.   Concerning a Real Character.

75. (o|) as *Numb.* 4.   Is

76. (⌐|) as *Numb.* 7.   Thine

77. (⌐∠). This Generical Character, doth signifie the Genus of *Every*
Space. The acute angle on the left side to the top, doth denote the
first Difference, which is *Time*. The other affix signifies the ninth species under this Difference, which is *Everness*. The Loop at the end
of this affix denotes the word to be used *adverbially*; so that the sense
of it must be the same which we express by that phrase, *For ever and
ever*.

78. ( ) The word *Amen* in the Literal Character.   Amen

79. (,|) as *Numb.* 19.   So

80. (*|) as *Numb.* 9.   May it be.

Ff 2   The

The Creed.

[Script characters]

```
 1 2  3       4          5      6 7 8    9    10   11
```
I believe in God the Father Almighty Maker of Heaven and

```
 12   13  14    15       16 17  18  19 20      21  22
```
of Earth, and in Jesus Christ his Son only our Lord, who was

```
  23   24 25    26      27  28 29   30      31       32
```
conceived by the Holy Ghost, born of the Virgin Mary, suffered

```
 33       34        35 36    37 38   39     40 41  42
```
under Pontius Pilate, was crucified, dead, and buried, he descended

```
 43  44  45 46 47 48  49 50 51 52  53  54    55    56 57 58
```
into hell, he did rise from the dead in the day third, He ascended

```
 59   60    61 62  63 64 65   66 67    68       69         70
```
into heaven, where he sitteth at the right hand of God the Father,

```
 71  72   73  74 75  76 77   78 79  80    81 82 83  84 85 86
```
from whence he shall come to judge the Quick and the dead. I believe

```
        87     88  89    90    91    92     93      94
```
in the Holy Ghost, the Church holy Catholick, the Communion of

```
 95 96    97      98 99  100 101 102   103 104 105   106 107
```
Saints, the forgiveness of sins, the resurrection of the body, and the

```
 108    109
```
life everlasting.

1. (`|`) This Particle being a single point, must denote one of the demonstrative Pronouns in the singular Number: And by its place towards the upper end of the Character, and before the Verb, the Nominative Case of the first Person, *viz. I.*   I

2. (`o|`) This Particle being a Round, must signifie the *Copula*, and being placed towards the middle, and joyned with the Nominative case of the first person, it must be rendered (*Am.*)   Am

3. (`⌐⌐⌐`) This Generical Character is appointed to signifie the Genus of *Habit*. The affix on the left hand making a right angle with the lower side, doth signifie the fifth Difference under that Genus, which according to the Tables, is *Infused Habit.* The other affix making an obtuse angle, doth signifie the fourth Species, *viz. Faith*; which is defined to consist in a readiness of mind to yield an effectual assent (without any affected captiousness) unto revealed Truths, upon such Grounds as their natures are capable of, and such as are in themselves sufficient to prevail with a prudent teachable man. The Hook upon the Difference denotes the *Active* voice, and the hook upon the Species, the *Adjective*, viz. *Believing.*   Believing

The Word *Believe* being of an equivocal sense, may likewise be expressed by the Genus of *Spiritual Action*, the second difference, relating to the Acts of the *Speculative Judgment*, and the affinis of the second Species, which is *Believing*, described to be an assent to any thing as truth upon the credit of others by whom it is related. But I rather chuse the former, as being more proper to this place.

4. (`∠`) A streight Line being the most simple, is put for the Character of *God*. The acute angle on the left side doth denote the first Person of the Blessed Trinity, namely, *God the Father*; which by following the Verb, is supposed to be in the *Object* case. And this may better express the true notion of *Credo in Deum*, than by using the Preposition *In*, as the sense of that Particle is determined in the foregoing Tables.   God the Father

5. (`,—⌐`) This Character doth by the two strokes denoting an Hyphen, appear to be a *Compound.* The two Points denote a Pronoun of the third Combination, and by the place of them at the bottom, they must signifie the *Universal Collective*, viz. *All.* The Integral Character with which this is compounded, is the Genus of *Natural Power.* The Hook at the end signifies the Grammatical notion of *Adjective.* So that this compound Character may be rendered All-powerful, Omnipotent, or *Almighty.*   Almighty

6. (`(|`) This Particle doth signifie the *Demonstrative* Article *The.*   The

7. (`(|`) This Particle being a small transverse Line placed at the side, must denote one of the *Tenses*, and being placed towards the upper part, it must signifie the Preter Tense.   Having been

8. (`⊇`) The Genus of this Character is appointed to signifie *Spiritual*   Creating person

ritual Action, or the Action of a Spirit, or Spiritual Faculty. The affix on the left, and that likewise on the right side, making acute angles with the upper side, must therefore signifie the first difference under that Genus which refers to *Actions of God*, and the first Species of that Difference, namely, *Creation*; which is defined to be, the putting of things into their first being. The hook at the end of the Difference affix, doth signifie *Active*, and the other *Adjective*. The transcendental mark, of a little flat Line on the top towards the right hand, doth denote *Person*; so that this Character with the precedent affixes, doth properly signifie, *the having been Creating Person*.

Of

9. (˙|) This Particle doth by its figure appear to be one of the Prepositions of the first Combination, and by its position towards the top of the Character, it is determined to be the first of them, which in *Latin* and *Greek*, is expressed by the *Genitive* case, and in *English* by the Particle *Of*.

Heaven.

10. (+—) The Genus of this Character signifies *World*. The affix on the left side denoting the second Difference, is *Heaven*.

And

11. (v|) This Particle, by the shape of it, appears to be a Conjunction of the first combination, and by the position of it towards the middle of the Character, it must be the second of them, *viz.* the *Conjunction Affirmative*, namely, *And*.

Of

12. (˙|) as *Numb*. 9.

Earth

13. (+—+) The same Character as to Genus and difference with *Numb*. 10. The affix for the Species making an acute Angle, and passing below the middle line, doth denote the seventh Species, which according to the Tables, is this Globe of Sea and Land.

And

14. (v|) as *Numb*. 11.

Jesus Christ

15. (—) The same Generical Character as *Numb*. 4. The right Angle denoting the second Person in the Blessed Trinity, *viz. Jesus Christ*.

His

16. (.|) This Particle being a single point, must denote one of the *Demonstrative Pronouns* in the singular number; and by its place towards the bottom of the Character, it must signifie the third Person, or *He*; and being made possessive by the curve line under it, it must be rendered *His*.

Son

17. (∝⊃) The Genus of this Character doth denote *Oeconomical Relation*. By the acute angle on the left side, is signified the first Difference, which is Relation of *Consanguinity*. By the right angle at the other end, is denoted the second Species, which is described to be *Direct Ascending*, namely, *Parent*; to which is opposed *Direct Descending*, namely, *Child*, which opposition is denoted by the Loop on the left side of the Character.

Only

18. (ᴐ⊃) The same Genus with the former, the fourth Difference,

rence, denoting Relations of *Equality*; the second Species signifying that particular Relation which is founded upon our *Conversing* with others, namely, *Companion*. To which the opposite (signified by the Loop at the joyning of the difference affix) is being in a state of *Segregation* from others. The hook upon the Species affix, denoting Adjective, viz. Alone, or *Only*.

19. (⁰|) These two Points standing level, must signifie one of the Demonstrative Pronouns, in the *Plural number*. By the place of them towards the upper side of the Character, they must denote the first Person, *We*; which being by the curve line rendered *Possessive*, must signifie *Our*. — Our

20. (⌐⌐) The Genus of this Character is assigned to signifie *Civil Relation*; of which the first difference doth denote *Degrees of Persons*. The second Species signifying the *supreme* Magistrate, to whom others owe Subjection and Obedience, viz. King, Lord, *Soveraign*. — Soveraign

21. (·|) This Particle consisting of three Points, must therefore signifie one of the Compound Pronouns. By the position of it towards the middle of the Character, it denotes the second of them, to be rendered *Who*, when we speak of a *Person*: and *Which*, when we speak of a *Thing*. — Who

22. (°|) The Copula, as *Numb*. 2. but being here placed towards the top of the Character, it must be rendered in the Preter tense, viz. *Hath been*, or *Was*. — Was

23. (⌐⌐) The Genus of this Character is assigned to *Corporeal Action*. The acute angle on the left side, denoting the first Difference, namely, such corporeal actions as belong primarily to *Vegetative* and living bodies. The right angle at the other end, signifies the second Species, which in the Tables is *Impregnation*; to which the Word *Conception* is adjoyned by way of Affinity, signified by the Loop on the right side. The Loop on the Difference affix, signifying the *Passive* voice; and the Hook upon the Species affix, *Adjective*. — Conceived

24. (·|) This Particle, by the figure and position of it, must be the second in the first combination of *Prepositions*, relating to the *Efficient Cause*, which we render *By*. — By

25. (·|) as *Numb*. 6. — The

26. (⌐⌐) The same Genus with numb. 4, and 15. The obtuse angle signifying the third Person of the Blessed Trinity, viz. Holy Ghost. — Holy Ghost

27. (⌐⌐) The same Genus and Difference as numb. 23. The affix towards the right hand making an obtuse angle with the upper side must signifie the third Species, which is *Parturition*, or bringing forth. The Loop at the end of the difference affix, denoting *Passive* voice, and the Hook on the other side, *Adjective*; viz. *Borne*. — Borne

28. (·|) This Particle, by the figure and position of it, doth appear — Of

pear to be the third of the first combination of Prepositions, relating to the *Material Cause, ex qua* (*Of*)

The
29. ('|) as numb. 6.

Virgin
30. (⤵) The same Genus as numb. 17, & 18. The affix towards the left hand, denoting the second Difference, which is Relation of *Affinity*; the other affix denoting the first Species, *viz.* that preceding state, whereby persons are rendered capable of Marriage, namely, *Celibate*, to which the notion of *Virgin* is joyned as an affinis (denoted by the Loop on the right side) described to be one that hath not coupled with any other.

Mary
31. (ꜩCI) The name *Mari* in the Literal Character, as being a proper name.

Capitally punished
32. (ᴄ⸺ᴏ) The Genus of this Character doth belong to *Judicial* Relation; the difference affix being the fifth, must denote *Capital punishment*; the Loop upon the Difference affix signifying *Passive*, and the hook upon the other affix, *Adjective*.

Under
33. ('|) This Particle, by the figure and position of it, must be the first Opposite in the sixth combination of Prepositions, namely, *Under*.

Pontius Pilate
34. (ꜩL S/S IJꜩ) These being proper Names, are to be expressed only by a Literal Character, according to our English pronunciation.

Was
35. (°|) as numb. 22.

Crucified
36. (ᴄ⸺ᴏ᷉) The same Genus and Difference with numb. 31. Under which *Crucifying* is reckoned as the ninth Species. The Loop on the Difference affix doth denote the notion of *Passive* voice; and the Hook at the other end, the notion of *Adjective*, *Crucified*.

Dead
37. (◡⤳) The same Genus and Difference with numb. 23, & 27. signifying such corporeal Actions as do primarily belong to Vegetatives. The affix on the right side, making an acute angle with the upper part of the transverse, and passing below it, doth signifie the seventh Species, which is *Living*; to which *Dying* is opposed. And that the Opposite is here intended, may appear by the Loop at the joyning of the Difference affix; the hook on the Species affix signifying *Adjective*.

And
38. (v|) as numb. 11.

Buried
39. (ᴄ⸺ᴏ) The Genus of this Character is assigned to Ecclesiastical Relation; the fourth Difference comprehending the more common Actions belonging to Religion: the affix at the other end, being a thorough stroke, and making an obtuse angle to the upper side, must denote the ninth Species, which is *Burying*, described in the Tables to be one of those Ritual Offices consisting in performance of the Rites due to the dead, by putting their Bodies into the Ground. The Loop

Chap. II. *Concerning a Real Character.*

Loop on the Difference affix, doth signifie (as before) *Passive*, and the other Hook *Adjective*.

40. (.|) A Pronoun of the third person, singular number, *viz.* He *He*.

41. (°|) as numb. 22. Was

42. ("᠂ ↶") This appears by the Hyphen, to be a compound Descending Character. The Particle in this composition, doth by the figure and position, denote the Opposite to the first of the fifth Combination of Prepositions, *viz. Downward.* The Genus of the Integral Character, is *Transcendental Action.* The affix on the left side, making an acute angle with the bottom of the Line, doth denote the sixth Difference, which is *Ition,* or the passing of things from one place or state to another; and because there is no affix at the other end, therefore this Character must denote the Difference it self. The Hooks on each side, do signifie *Active* and *Adjective.*

43. (³|) This Particle doth by the figure and position of it, appear Into to be the first of the fourth Combination of Prepositions, and consequently to signifie *Into.*

44. (d┼) This Character is the same for Genus and Difference with numb. 10. which doth there signifie *Heaven;* and whereas here there Hell is a Loop at the joyning of the Difference affix; therefore must it denote that which is opposite to the former; namely, *Hell.* This Clause might perhaps be more properly expressed thus; *He became in the state, or he passed into the Invisible place, of the having died persons.*

45. (.|) as numb. 40. He

46. (°|) as numb. 22. Was

47. (↶) The same Genus with numb. 23, 27, & 37. Denoting *Corporeal Action.* The acute angle on the left side, doth denote the Rising sixth Difference, which is *Gesture;* namely, such animal motion whereby the situation of the Whole or Parts is altered. The acute angle at the other end to the upper side, doth denote the first Species, which is motion upwards direct; namely, *Rising.* The Hooks on each affix denote *Active* and *Adjective.*

48. (⌐|) This Particle, by the figure and position of it, must be the From second of the third combination of *Prepositions, viz. From.*

49. ('|) as numb. 6. The

50. (┐|) as numb. 7. Having been

51. (↶) This Character is in all respects the same with numb. 37. Dead persons Excepting only, that there is another hook upon the Species affix to signifie *Plural Number,* together with the transcendental Note of *Person* at the top of the Character towards the right hand, which makes the importance of this Character, with the two preceding Particles to be, *The having died Persons.*

Ggg 52.

On	52. (ᵉ|) Though this Prepofition be properly *local*, fignifying *in*, as being oppofite to numb. 43. Yet it is applicable, as the others of the fame kind are, to *Time*; in which cafe it may be rendered *On*.
The	53. (ʹ|) as numb. 6.
Day	54. (┤├) The Character is the Genus of *Meafure*. The affix both on the left and right fide, denote the fifth Difference, which is Meafure of *Time*, and the fifth Species, which is *Day Natural*.
Third	55. (⌐ʹ) The fame Genus with the former, denoting *Meafure*. The Difference affix making an acute angle with the upper fide of the tranfverfe, doth denote the firft Difference, which refers to *Number*. The obtufe angle at the other end of the tranfverfe, denoting the third Species, which according to the Tables, is the number *Three*. The Hook on this affix, fhews this Word to be ufed *adjectively*, viz. *Third*.
He	56. (.|) as numb. 40.
Was	57. (°|) as numb. 22.
Afcending	58. (",⌐⌐) Such a Compound as numb. 42. Only the Prepofition here, being the firft of the fifth Combination, muft fignifie *Upwards*; and confequently, as the numb. 42. did fignifie *Defcending*: fo this muft be the Oppofite to it; namely, *Afcending*.
Into	59. (³|) as numb. 43.
Heaven	60. (┤┼) as numb. 10.
In	61. (ᵉ|) as numb. 52.
Which place	62. (⋅⋅|) A Compound of the Pronoun *Which*, and the tranfcendental Mark of Place, viz. *Which place*.
He	63. (.|) as numb. 4.
Is	64. (o|) The Copula in the prefent tenfe, which being applied to the third Perfon fingular, muft be rendered (*is*.)
Sitting	65. (⌐⌐) The fame Character, both as to Genus and Difference, with that, numb. 47. The fpecies affix making a right angle with the bottom of the tranfverfe, muft denote the fifth Species; namely, fitting; the hook upon this affix, fignifying the notion of *Adjective*.
At	66. (ʹ|) This Particle, by the figure and pofition of it, doth appear to be the firft Oppofite in the third combination of Prepofitions, and to fignifie *At*.
The	67. (ʹ|) as numb. 6.
Right hand	68. (⌐⌐) The Genus of *Space*. The obtufe angle on the left fide, denoting

Chap. II.   *Concerning a Real Character.*   411

denoting the third Difference under that Genus; namely, *Situation*: the oblique line at the other end of the transverse, passing by both sides of it, doth denote the ninth Species under that Difference, viz. Right Side, or *Right Hand*.

69. (⌐|) as numb. 9. — Of

70. (⌐) as numb. 4. — God the Father

71. (⌐|) as numb. 48. — From

72. (⌐•) as numb. 62. — Which place

73. (.|) as numb. 40. — He

74. (₀|) The Copula in the Future tense, signifying, *Shall be*. — Shall be

75. (⌐) The Genus of transcendental Action, the sixth Difference, as before, numb. 42, 58. The first Species, viz. *Come*. The hooks on each affix, denoting *Active*, *Adjective*, viz. *Coming*. — Coming

76. (⌐|) This Particle, by the figure and position of it, doth appear to be the second opposite in the first combination, and to signifie a respect to the final Causes in Latin, *ob*, *propter*, in English, *For*. — For

77. (⌐) The Genus of *Judicial Relation*. The first Difference, which is Forinsic Persons; and the first Species, which is *Judge*. The hook upon the difference affix, denotes this to be a Noun of Action, viz. Judication, or *Judging*. — Judging

78. ('|) as numb. 6. — The

79. (⌐) as numb. 51. Only, there wants the Note of Opposite; so that as that signified dead persons, this must signifie living persons. — Quick

80. (•|) as numb. 11. — And

81. ('|) as numb. 6. — The

82. (⌐|) as numb. 7. — Having

83. (⌐) as numb. 51. — Died persons

84. (˙|) as numb. 1. — I

85. (o|) as numb. 2. — Am

86. (⌐) as numb. 3. — Believing

87. (⎯) as numb. 6. — The Holy Ghost

88. ('|) as numb. 26. — The

89. (⌐) The Genus of *Ecclesiastical Relation*; the transcendental mark — Church

Ggg 2

mark over it, denoting *Aggregate*, which is the proper notion of *Church*.

Holy

90. (☧) The same Genus and Difference, as numb. 3. Denoting *Infused Habit*; the second Species being *Holiness*, described to be that habitual frame, whereby one is fitted for virtuous actions; more especially for the duties of Religion: the hook upon the Species affix, denoting the Notion of *Adjective*, viz. Holy.

Universal

91. (☧) The Genus of this Character is assigned to signifie *Transcendental Relation mixed*; the obtuse angle at each end, must denote the third difference, and the third species: the third difference under that Genus, containing such transcendental relations as concern *Number*. The third species, being that more distinct relation of *one Indeterminate*, or *All*, viz. *Particularity*, or *Universality*. The Loop at the joyning of the difference affix, denoting an Opposite, doth determine the Character to the second of these: And the Hook at the end of the species affix, doth make it signifie as an *Adjective*, viz, *Universal, Catholick*.

The

92. (`|) as numb. 6.

Communion

93. (☧) The Genus of Ecclesiastical Relation, as numb. 89. The third Difference, concerning *states of Religion*; the second species, *Catholick*, or *Communicant*, which is described to be one that is in a state of Charity with the body of those that agree in the same profession: the *Abstract* of which, denoted by the hook upon the difference affix, is *Communion*.

Of

94. ("|) as numb. 9.

Saints

95. (☧) The same Genus and difference, as numb. 93. The fifth species denoting such as are *eminently religious*; the hook upon the species affix, signifying the *Plural Number*, viz. *Saints*.

The

96. (`|) as numb. 6.

Being forgiven

97. (☧) The Genus of *Judicial Relation*, as numb. 77. The second difference denoting *Judicial Actions*. The ninth species signifying that kind of Judicial Action, which concerns the *inflicting of punishment*, or *freeing from it*, *Executing*, or *Pardoning*. The Loop, at the joyning of the difference affix, denotes this to be an Opposite, viz. Pardoning or *Forgiving*. The Loop upon the top of this affix, signifies the passive voice, viz. the *being forgiven*.

Of

98. ("|) as numb. 9.

Sins

99. (☧) The Genus of *Transcendental General*; the third difference respecting the more common and absolute differences of things; the second species denoting that difference of things, which doth include a respect to the Will, as to the agreement or disagreement of things with that Faculty, stiled *Goodness* or *Evilness*. The Loop towards the left hand, at the joyning of the affix, denoting *opposite*, viz.
Evil-

Chap. II.   *Concerning a Real Character.*   413

Evilness; the hook at the other end of the same affix, doth signifie the *Active* voice; and the hook upon the other affix, doth denote the *plural number*: So that the meaning of this Character, must be *evil actions*, the same as Trespasses, or *Sins*.

100. (´|) as numb. 6.   The

101. (|) The mark of Future tense.   Future

102. (, ⌐⌐⌐) A compound Character. The Particle, doth by the figure and the position of it, appear to be the third Opposite in the fourth Combination of Adverbs, which is *Re*, denoting *Restitution* to what was before. The Integral Character signifies *Life*; as numb. 79.   Relife, or living again

103. (˝|) as numb. 9.   Of

104. (´|) as numb. 9.   The

105. (○┼) The same Genus as numb. 10. signifying *World*. The first difference under that Genus, being *Spirit*. The Opposite to which, denoted by the Loop at the joyning of the Affix, is *Body*.   Body

106. (v|) as numb. 11.   And

107. (´|) as numb. 6.   The

108. (|) as numb. 101.   Future

109. (⌐⌐⌐) The same Integral as 102.   Life

110. (, ⌐⌐⌐) A compound with the Pronoun *All*, as numb. 5. The Genus of the Integral being the same with numb. 54, 55. doth denote *Measure*; the fifth difference of which, doth signifie measure of time, to which the word *Duration* is adjoyned by way of Affinity, signified by the Loop at the right side, where the hook denotes *Adjective*: So that the true sense of this Character, is *All-during*, or *Everlasting*.   Everlasting

I forbear any other Examples out of *Aristotle, Euclid, Tully, Terence,* which I once thought to have subjoyned; because if what hath been already delivered, be sufficiently understood, it will appear easie enough to render any thing out of those Authors, in this Character.

I shall only add concerning the Character here proposed, that besides the *Facility, Comliness* and *Distinctness* of it, containing a Description of what is to be expressed by it, both as to the nature of the things, and the Grammatical Variation of the words; 'tis likewise a much *shorter* way of writing, than that by Letters: and by the great Variety which it is capable of, would afford the surest way for *Cryptography* or *secret* Writing.

CHAP.

CHAP. III.

How this Real Character may be made effable in a distinct Language, and what kind of Letters or Syllables may be conveniently assigned to each Character.

BY what hath been already delivered, it may sufficiently appear, how any thing or Notion, which falls under humane Discourse, may be expressed by such a Character as shall be legible to men of all Nations and Languages.

I come now to shew how this Universal *Character* may be made effable in a distinct *Language*: The unfolding of which (supposing what hath been said about the Character and Grammar, to be well understood) will need but little time and pains.

The Qualifications desirable in a *Language*, should have some analogy and proportion to those before mentioned concerning a *Character* or way of *Writing*; Namely,

1. The words of it should be *brief*, not exceeding two or three Syllables; the Particles consisting but of one Syllable.
2. They should be *plain* and *facil* to be taught and learnt.
3. They should be *sufficiently distinguishable* from one another, to prevent mistake and equivocalness; and withal *significant* and *copious*, answerable to the conceipts of our mind.
4. They should be *Euphonical*, of a pleasant and graceful sound.
5. They should be *Methodical*; those of an agreeable or opposite sense, having somewhat correspondent in the sounds of them. The order to be observed in the assigning of Letters and Sounds to these Characters, must be after the same manner with the Method before made use of, in treating concerning these Characters: Beginning first with *Integrals*, according to their several Varieties, and then proceeding to the *Particles*.

The *Integrals* may be considered, either as they are *Radicals*, placed in the Tables, either more *direct*, whether *Genus*, *Difference*, or *Species*; or else *Laterally*, either by way of *Affinity* or *Opposition*.

And next to the Words or Sounds appointed for each of these Radicals, it is to be considered, by what kind of Changes or Varieties, the several *Derivations* and *Inflections* may be expressed.

The first thing to be stated in such an Institution, is to assign several Letters and sounds for the 40 *Genus*'s. It were not difficult to offer great variety of these; but to pitch upon that which upon all accounts would be the best, will require so much consideration, and practise, and so many Trials as I cannot pretend unto.

That

Chap. III. Concerning a Real Character. 415

That which at present seems most convenient to me, is this;

Transcend.				Parts			Action			Relation	
	General	Bα	Animals	Exanguious	Zα		Spiritual	Cα		Oecon.	Co
	Rel. mixed	Ba		Fish	Za		Corporeal	Ca		Possef.	Cy
	Rel. of Action	Be		Bird	Ze		Motion	Ce		Provis.	Sα
	Discourse	Bi		Beast	Zi		Operation	Ci		Civil	Sa
	God	Dα		Peculiar	Pα					Judicial	Se
	World	Da		General	Pa					Military	Si
	Element	De	Quantity	Magnitude	Pe					Naval	So
	Stone	Di		Space	Pi					Ecclef.	Sy
	Metal	Do		Measure	Po						
Herb consid. accord. to the	Leaf	Gα	Quality	Power Nat.	Tα						
	Flower	Ga		Habit	Ta						
	Seed-vessel	Ge		Manners	Te						
	Shrub	Gi		Quality sensible	Ti						
	Tree	Go		Disease	To						

The *Differences* under each of these *Genus's*, may be expressed by these Consonants B, D, G, P, T, C, Z, S, N.
in this order; 1 2 3 4 5 6 7 8 9.

The *Species* may be expressed by putting one of the seven Vowels after the Consonant, for the Difference; to which may be added (to make up the number) two of the Dipthongs, according to this order
$\begin{cases} α, & a, & e, & i, & o, & υ, & y, & yi, & yυ. \\ 1 & 2 & 3 & 4 & 5 & 6 & 7 & 8 & 9. \end{cases}$

For instance, If (De) signifie *Element*, then (Deb) must signifie the first difference; which (according to the Tables) is *Fire*: and (Debα) will denote the first Species, which is *Flame*. (Det) will be the fifth difference under that Genus, which is, *Appearing Meteor*; (Detα) the first Species, viz. *Rainbow*; (Deta) the second, viz. *Halo*.

Thus, if (Ti) signifie the Genus of *Sensible Quality*, then (Tid) must denote the second difference, which comprehends Colours; and (Tida) must signifie the second Species under that difference, viz. *Redness*: (Tide) the third Species, which is *Greenness*, &c.

Thus likewise, if (Be) be put for the Genus of *Transcendental Relation of Action*, then (Bec) must denote the sixth difference, which is *Ition*; and (Becυ) will signifie the sixth Species, which is *Following*.

As for those Species under Plants and Animals, which do exceed the number of Nine, they may be expressed by adding the Letters *L*, or *R*, after the first Consonant, to denote the second or third of such Combinations. Thus, if Gαde be *Tulip*, viz. the third Species in the first Nine, then Glαde must signifie *Ramson*, viz. the third in the second Nine, or the twelfth Species under that Difference. So if Zana be *Salmon*, viz. the second species in the first Nine, then Zlana must signifie *Gudgeon*, viz. the second in the second Nine; or the eleventh Species under that Difference.

It

It must be granted, that there is one inconvenience in this Contrivance for the supernumerary Species, namely, that according to this way of expressing them, they are scarce capable of the derivation of Adjective: But this is more tolerable, because in such matters, where this will happen, there is no necessary occasion for this derivation.

Those Radicals which are joyned to others by way of *Affinity*, may be expressed; 1. In *Monosyllables*, by repeating the Radical Vowel before the Consonant. For example, if (De) signifies *Element*, then (Ede) must signifie that which is joyned to it by way of affinity, *viz.* Meteor. If (Di) be *Stone*, then (Idi) will signifie *Concretions*, &c. 2. In *Dyssyllables*, by repeating the second Radical Consonant after the last Vowel: Thus, if (Dade) be *Planet*, (Daded) will signifie *Comet*. If (Dego) be *Ice*, (Degog) will signifie *Snow*, &c.

Those Radicals which are paired together upon the account of *single Opposition*, may be expressed,

1. In *Monosyllables*, by putting the *opposite Vowel* before the first Consonant, according to that order of Opposition before set down;

namely, of $\begin{Bmatrix} \alpha \\ a \\ e \end{Bmatrix}$ to $\begin{Bmatrix} 1 \\ o \\ \upsilon \end{Bmatrix}$ or y.

Thus, if (Dα) be put to signifie *God*, then (idα) must signifie that which is opposed, namely, *Idol*. If (Dab) be *Spirit*, (odab) will be *Body*. If (Dad) be *Heaven*, (odad) will signifie *Hell*.

2. In *Dyssyllables*, by adding the Letter (S) to the last Vowel: Thus if (Pida) be *Presence*, (Pidas) will be *Absence*. If (Tadʊ) be *Power*, then (Tadʊs) will be *Impotence*.

As for those *double Opposites* by way of *Excess* or *Defect*, which sometimes occur, as they are to be represented in writing by the Transcendental Points of *Excess* or *Defect*, on the top of the Character, so are they to be expressed in speaking by those Syllables appointed to these Characters, which must be added to the termination of the word: Thus if (Teba) be *Justice*, (Tebas) will signifie the *Opposite Common*; namely, *Injustice*: And (Teballa) the Opposite by way of Excess; namely, *Rigor*, and (Teballo) the Opposite by way of Defect, *viz.* Remission.

   Tepα *Veracity.*
   Tepαs *Lying.*
   Tepαlla *Over-saying.*
   Tepαllo *Under-saying, Detracting.*

Adjectives should be expressed by changing the first radical Consonant, according to this establishment;

   $\begin{Bmatrix} B, D, G, P, T, C, Z, S, N. \\ V, Dʊ, Gʊ, F, Tʊ, Cʊ, Zh, Sh, Ng. \end{Bmatrix}$

Thus,

Chap. IV.   Concerning a Real Character.   417

Thus, if, {Dα / De / Do} do signifie {God / Element / Stone} then {Dᴙα / Dᴙe / Dᴙo} must fi-gnifie {Divine / Elementary / Stony.}

Adverbs may be expressed by turning the first Radical Vowel into a Dipthong. So Dαɩ is *Divinely*. (Syɩb) is *Religiously*. (Syɩgas) is *Schismatically*.

Abstracts may be expressed, 1. In *Monosyllables* of the Genus, by adding the Letter (r) after the first Radical Vowel. So Dαr is *Deity* or *Divinity*.
In *Monosyllables* of the *Difference*, and *Dissyllables* of the *Species*, by changing the second Radical Character Consonant thus;

{B, D, G, P, T, C, Z, S, N.
 V, Dh, Dzh, F, Th, Tsh, Zh, Sh, Ng.}

The Letters Dzh, and Tsh, being the same power which we Englishmen give to the Letters G, and Ch, in the words *Ginger*, and *Charity*. Thus
(Bαd) is *Cause*; (Bαdh) is *Causality*.
(Saba) is *King*, (Sava) is *Regality* or *Majesty*.

There are only two things noted in the Character belonging to the *Inflection* of words; namely,

1. The *Active* and *Passive* voice, to be expressed by the Letters L, and N, after the first Vowel: thus (Sαlbə) is *Regnation*; and (Sαmbə) is τὸ *regnari*.

2. The Plural Number in *Substantives*, which is sometimes likewise affixed to Adjectives, when they are used substantively, by reason of any transcendental Mark joyned to them. And this may be done by prolonging the first Vowel, which upon all other occasions, is to be pronounced as being short. But because it will be difficult to prolong this Vowel in Monosyllables of the Genus, when no Consonant doth follow; therefore in this case it may be proper to add the Vowel ᴙ to the Radical Vowel. So if Dα be *God*, Dαᴙ will be *Gods*.

According to this establishment, every Radical Genus, Difference and Species, may be expressed by such words as are facil and pleasant. Those words that are most harsh and difficult, will happen amongst such of the Derivations as are seldom used; as in some of the Active or Passive Adverbs, and in some of the Abstracts.

By these Instances it will be easie to understand all the rest.

The Particles may be expressed either by simple Vowels or Dipthongs, or by some of those Monosyllables, not used for any of the Genus's or Differences.

Amongst the Grammatical Particles, the more principal are, the *Copula*, *Pronouns*, *Interjections*, *Prepositions*, *Adverbs*, *Conjunctions*.

Hhh   1. The

1. The *Copula*, or Verb *Sum*, according to its threefold place in the Character, may be expressed by these Dipthongs
{ oɩ ɩa.
  oɩ ɩa.
  oɩ ɩe. }

2. The *Pronouns*, according to their several kinds, may be expressed by these Vowels and Dipthongs;

·	α	··	αɩ	:	ɩ	·	o	:	αʊ	ʋ	oɩ.
·	a	··	aɩ	:	ʊ	·	y	:	aʊ		ʊʊ.
·	e	··	eɩ	:	yɩ	·	yʊ	:	eʊ	ʋ	ɩɩ

Possessive Pronouns by prefixing (H.) *Reduplicative*, by interposing (L.) So Hα is *mine*, Hαlα is *my own*.

3. The *Interjections*, being Natural sounds themselves, need not have any assigned to the Characters of them, than what are General. So

ɩ { Heigh
    Hm, Hu.
    Pish, Shu, Tush } ɔ { Ah, alack, alas.   Vauh, Hau.
                            Ha, ha, he.   Hoi, ah, oh.
                            O, O that.   Phy. } r

ʋ { Oh, soho.   St, hush, mum, whift.
    Ho, oh.   Ha.
    Eja, now.   Væ, wo. } ɩ

4. The *Prepositions* may be expressed by Monosyllables framed of L, and R; after this manner.

ʋ { Lα, Li.   { Rα, Rɩ.   { Lαl, Lil   { Rαl, Ril
    La, Lo.   > Ra, Ro.   ϻ { Lal, Lol ϻ Ral, Rol } ɛ
    Le, Lʊ. }   Re, Rʊ. }   Lel, Lʊl }   Rel, Rʊl }

        ϻ { Lαr, Lir   { Rαr, Rir
            Lar, Lor ϻ ɩ { Rar, Ror } s
            Ler, Lʊr }   { Rer, Rʊr }

5. *Adverbs* may be expressed by Monosyllables, with the initial Letter M. after this manner;

ʋ { Mα, Mi   { Mαl, Mil   { Mαr, Mir   { Mαs, Mis   { My.
    Ma, Mo ϻ { Mal, Mol } r { Mar, Mor } r { Mas, Mos } ϻ { Myɩ.
    Me, Mʊ } { Mel, Mʊl } { Mer, Mʊr } { Mes, Mʊs }   { Myʊ

6. *Conjunctions* may be expressed by Monosyllables, with the Initial Letter N, after this manner;

ʋ { Nα, Ni   { Nαl, Nil   { Nαr, Nir   { Nαs, Nis
    Na, No ϻ { Nal, Nol } r { Nar, Nor } r { Nas, Nos } ϻ
    Ne, Nʊ } { Nel, Nʊl } { Ner, Nʊr } { Nes, Nʊs }

Chap. III. *Concerning a Real Character.* 419

The more servile Particles are of three kinds; *Articles, Modes, Tenses.*

1. The *Articles* being but two, may be thus expressed, { ˋ el. / ɑl. }

2. The *Imperative Mode*, according to its threefold difference of *Petition, Perswasion, Command,* may be expressed by these Dipthongs, ɩo, ɩʊ, ɩy.

The *Secondary Modes*, by Dipthongs or Tripthongs, according to their differences of *Absolute* or *Conditional.* So the Mode of

{ Power
Liberty
Will
Necessity } whether *Absolute* or *Conditional*, is to be expressed by { ʊɑ, ʊɑl.
ʊa, ʊal.
ʊe, ʊel.
ʊo, ʊol. }

3. The *Tenses, Past, Present,* and *Future,* may be expressed by these Dipthongs, ʊl, ʊy, ʊyl.

The *Transcendental* Particles, to be added by way of Composition in the termination of words, may be expressed by these Syllables,

{ iɑ, Ia, Ie
Iʊ, Io, Iy } { ʊɑ, ʊa, ʊe
ʊl, ʊo, ʊy } { Mɑ, Ma, Me
Ml, Mo, Mʊ } { Mɑl, Mal, Mel
Mil, Mol, Mʊl }

{ Nɑ, Na, Ne
Nl, No, Nʊ } { Nɑl, Nal, Nel
Nil, Nol, Nʊl } { Lɑ, la, le
Ll, Lo, Lʊ } { Rɑ, Ra, Re
Rl, Ro, Rʊ }

In which Constitution, the Marks made use of before, either for *Prepositions, Adverbs,* or *Conjunctions,* have the same Syllables assigned to them.

It is here to be noted, that as *Numbers* are provided for in *writing,* by distinct Characters from the rest, so should they likewise have some sutable provision in *speaking.* And because there are two waies before suggested for the expression of Numbers by *writing,* namely, either by *words at length,* or by *Figures,* there should therefore be some provision answerable to each of these for *speaking.*

1. The *Words at length* for the nine Digits, are to be made off from the Tables after the same manner as all other Species are; and as for the other Numbers above this, *viz.* Ten, Hundred, Thousand, Million, they may be expressed by adding the Letters L, R, M, N. after the last Vowel; according to these Examples:

Hhh 2   Pobɑl.

Pobαl 10.	Pobal 20.	Pobel 30.
Pobαr 100.	Pobar 200.	Pober 300.
Pobαm 1000.	Pobam 2000.	Pobem 3000.
Pobαn 1000000	Poban 2000000.	Poben 3000000, &c.

| Pobαm | Pobʊr | Pobʊl | Pobʊ. |
| One thousand | Six hundred | Sixty | Six. |

Arithmet.
Pract. cap. 17.

2. The *Figures* of Numbers, may be most conveniently expressed in *Speech*, in that way suggested by *Herrigon*; namely, by assigning one Vowel or Dipthong, and one Consonant to each of the Digits, suppose after this manner,

$$\begin{cases} 1, & 2, & 3, & 4, & 5, & 6, & 7, & 8, & 9, & 0. \\ α, & a, & e, & i, & o, & ʊ, & y, & iʊ, & yi, & yʊ. \\ b, & d, & g, & p, & t, & c, & l, & m, & n, & r. \end{cases}$$

According to which constitution, a word of so many Letters, may serve to express a number of so many places. Thus either of these words, αcʊc, αʊcʊ, bʊcʊ, will signifie 1666; which is as much a *better* and *briefer* way for the expressing of these numbers in *speech*, as that other is for writing, betwixt *Figures* and *Words at length*.

The Grammatical Variations belonging to Number, whether *Derivations* or *Inflexions*, may for the nine Digits be framed according to common Analogy. For greater Numbers, it may be convenient to prefix the Difference denoting number in general; namely, Pob before the word, for any Particular; as suppose αcʊc be the word for the number, let it be made $\begin{cases} Pobαcʊc \\ Pobαcʊl \end{cases}$ for the *Cardinal* Number $\begin{cases} 1666 \\ 1667 \end{cases}$

then $\begin{cases} Fobαcʊc \\ Fobαcʊl \end{cases}$ will be the *Ordinal*, or Adjective Neuter, denoting the $\begin{cases} 1666^{th} \\ 1667^{th} \end{cases}$ &c.

By what hath been said, it is easie to conceive, how this Character may be made effable as to all the *Species* of things, together with their *Derivations* and *Inflexions*. As for *Individuals*, I have shewed before, how the names of them are to be expressed by a Literal Character.

But these things will more distinctly appear by instance of something written in this Language: In Order to which, I shall offer an Example of it in the Lords Prayer and the Creed.

CHAP.

CHAP. IV.

An Instance of the Philosophical Language, both in the Lords Prayer and the Creed. A Comparison of the Language here proposed, with fifty others, as to the Facility and Euphonicalness of it.

AS I have before given Instances of the Real Character, so I shall here in the like method, set down the same Instances for the Philosophical Language. I shall be more brief in the particular explication of each Word; because that was sufficiently done before, in treating concerning the Character.

The Lords Prayer.

Hai coba ʊʊ ia ril dad, ha babi ıo ſʊymta, ha ſalba ıo velca, ha talbi ıo vemgʊ, mʊ ril dady me ril dad ıo velpi ral ati ril i poto hai ſaba vaty, na ıo ſʊeldyʊi lal ai hai balgas me ai ia ſʊeldyʊs lal ei ʊʊ ia valgas rʊ ai na mi ıo velco ai, ral bedodlʊ nil ıo cʊalbo ai lal vagasie, nor al ſalba, na al tado, na al tadala ia ha piʊbyʊ ꝙ mʊ ıo.

1	2	3	4	5	6	7	8	9	10	11
Hai	coba	ʊʊ	ia	ril	dad,	ha	babi	ıo	ſʊymta	ha
Our	Father	who	art	in	Heaven,	Thy	Name	be	Hallowed,	Thy

12	13	14	15	16	17	18	19	20	21	22	23	24	25	26
ſalba	ıo	velca,	ha	talbi	ıo	vemgʊ,	mʊ	ril	dady	me	ril	dad,	ıo	velpi
Kingdome	come,		Thy	Will	be	done,	so	in	Earth	as	in	Heaven,	Give	

27	28	29	30	31	32	33	34	35	36	37	38	39	40	41
ral	ai	ril	i poto	hai	ſaba	vaty,	na	ıo	ſʊeldiʊs	lal	ai	hai	balgas	
to us	on this	day	our	bread	expedient	and	forgive		to us		our	trespaſſes		

42	43	44	45	46	47	48	49	50	51	52	53	54	55	56	57	58
me	ai	ia	ſʊeldyʊs	lal	ei	ʊʊ	ia	valgas rʊ	ai,	na	mi	ıo	velco	ai	ral	
as	we	forgive	them	who	trespaſs		against	us,		and	lead	us	not	into		

59	60	61	62	63	64	65	66	67	68	69	70	71	72
bedodlʊ	nil	ɩo	cʊɑlbo	aɩ	lal	vɑgaɩɩe	nor	ɑl	ſalba	na	ɑl	tado,	na
temptation	but		deliver us from evil				for the Kingdom, & the power, and

73	74	75	76	77	78	79	80.
ɑl	tadalɑ	ɩo	ha	pɩʊbyʊ			
the Glory	is thine,		for ever and ever.		Amen.	So be it.	

Our	1. (Hɑi) This Dipthong (ɑi) is aſſigned to ſignifie the firſt Perſon plural amongſt the Pronouns, *viz. We.* The Letter *h* prefixed to it, doth denote that Pronoun to be uſed poſſeſſively, *viz. Our.*
Parent	2. (Coba) Co doth denote the Genus of *Oeconomical Relation*; the Letter (b) ſignifying the firſt difference under that Genus, which is Relation of Conſanguinity; the Vowel (a) the ſecond Species, which is *Direct aſcending*; namely, *Parent.*
Who	3. (ʊʊ) This Dipthong is appointed to ſignifie the ſecond of the compound Pronouns, *Who*, perſonal; or *Which*, Real.
Art	4. (ia) This dipthong is appointed to ſignifie the preſent tenſe of the Copula (*eſt*) and being ſpoken of the ſecond perſon, is to be rendered *Art.*
In	5. (ril) is a *Prepoſition*, the firſt Oppoſite of the fourth combination; and therefore muſt ſignifie (*in*.)
Heaven	6. (dad) The Syllable (da) is appointed to ſignifie the Genus of *World*; the addition of the Letter (d) doth denote the ſecond difference under that Genus, which is *Heaven.*
Thy	7. (ha) The Vowel (a) is aſſigned to ſignifie a Pronoun of the ſingular number, and ſecond perſon. The Letter (h) before it, doth denote it to be underſtood poſſeſſively, and to ſignifie (*Thy*) or (*Thine.*)
Name	8. (bɑbi) The Syllable (bɑ) doth denote the Genus of *Tranſcendental General.* The Letter (b) doth denote the firſt difference, and the Vowel (i) the fourth Species, which is *Name.*
May it be	9. (ɩo) This Dipthong is appointed to ſignifie that kind of *Imperative Mode* (as it is commonly ſtiled) which is by way of Petition; the ſenſe of it being, *I pray that it may be.*
Hallowed	10. (Sʊymtɑ (Sy) is put for the Genus of *Eccleſiaſtical Relation.* The Conſonant (t) for the fifth difference, and the Vowel (a) for the firſt ſpecies, which according to the tables, is, *Conſecration*, or *Hallowing.* The Addition of the Vowel (ʊ) to (S) doth ſignifie the notion of *Adjective*; and the addition of the Letter (m) at the end of the firſt

Chap. IV. *Concerning a Philosophical Language.*

first Syllable, signifies the *Passive* voice, viz. *Hallowed*.

11. (ha.) as numb. 7.   *Thy*

12. (Salba) (Sa) is *Civil Relation*; (b) denotes the first difference, *Kingdom or Regnation* which is degrees of persons; and (a) is the second species, which, according to the tables, is *King*; the addition of (l) to the first Syllable, doth denote a word of *Action*, viz. *Regnation*.

13. (lo) as numb. 9.   *May it be*

14. (Velcα) (Be) is the Genus of *transcendental action*; (c) denotes the sixth difference under that Genus, and (α) the first species, which signifies *Coming*: the turning of (b) into (v) denotes this word to be an *Adjective*, and the Letter (L) to be an Active. *Coming*.

15. (ha) as numb. 7.   *Thy*

16. (tαlbi) (tα) doth denote the Genus of *Natural Power*, (b) the *Will or volition* first difference, and (l) the fourth Species; namely, *Will*: the Letter (l) denoting a Noun of Action, viz. *Volition*.

17. (lo) as numb. 10.   *May it be*

18. (vemgȣ) (be) is the Genus of *Transcendental Action*; (g) denotes the third difference, and (ȣ) the sixth species; which is, *Performing*, or Accomplishing: the change of (b into v) denoting this word to be an *Adjective*, and (m) *Passive*, *Performed*. *Done or accomplished*

19. (mȣ) This Monosyllable with (m) must denote an Adverb, and *So*. the last opposite of the first Combination; which is, *So*.

20. (ril) as numb. 5.   *In*

21. (dady) (da) is the Genus of *World*, (d) is the second difference, which is *Heaven*; the Vowel y signifying the seventh species under that difference, which is this *Earth*, or the Globe of Land and Sea, whereon we inhabit. *Earth*

22. (me) Paired with numb. 19. and therefore must signifie, *As As*.

23. (ril) as numb. 5.   *In*

24. (dad) as numb. 6.   *Heaven*

25. (lo) The same Particle as numb. 9. But being here joyned *Maist thou be* with a word active, and relating to the second person, it must be rendered, *Maist thou be*.

26. (velpi) (be) is Transcendental Action (p) the fourth difference, and (i) the fourth species, which is *Giving*: b changed into v, denoting adjective, and (l) active. *Giving*.

To	27. (lαl) A Preposition of the first Combination, signifying *To*.
Us	28. (αι) A Pronoun, first person, plural number; namely, *We*, or *Us*.
In	29. (ril) as numb. 5.
This	30. (ı) The first of the relative Pronouns, signifying *This*.
Day	31. (poto) po is the Genus of Measure, (t) the fifth difference, and (o) the fifth species, which is *Day*.
Our	32. (hαι) as numb. 1.
Bread	33. (Sαba) Sα denotes the Genus of *Oeconomical Provisions*, (b) the first difference, and (a) the second species, which is *Bread*.
Expedient	34. (Vαty) (bα) is the Genus of *Transcendental General*, (t) the fifth difference, y the seventh species; the change of *b* into *v*, denotes this Word to be an *Adjective*, and to signifie *Expedient*.
And	35. (Na) A Conjunction, the second of the first Combination, *viz. And*.
Maist thou be	36. (ιo) as numb. 25.
Forgiving	37. (Sᴕeldyᴕs) Se is the Genus of Judicial Relation *d*, the second difference, yᴕ the ninth species, which is *Forgiving*: ᴕ joyned to the first Consonant, signifying the notion of *Adjective*, and *l*, of *Active*, (*s*) the Opposite.
To	38. (lαl) as numb. 27.
Us	39. (αι) as numb. 28.
Our	40. (hαι) as numb. 1.
Trespasses or Male-actions	41. (bάlgas) (bα) the Genus of transcendental general, (g) the third difference, (a) the second species, (s) at the end, denoting the word hereby signified, to be placed in the Tables as an Opposite, and the Letter (l) in the first syllable, signifying the *Active* voice, and the prolonging of the first Vowel, exprest by the Accent over it, denoting the *Plural Number*.
As	42. (Me) as numb. 22.
We	43. (αι) as numb. 28.
Are	44. (ιa) as numb. 4. But being here adjoyned to a word of the first Person *Plural*, it must be rendered, *Are*.
Forgiving	45. (Sᴕeldyᴕs) as numb. 37.
To	46. (lαl) as numb. 27.
Them	47. (eι) A Pronoun, third person, plural number, *They*, or *Them*.

48.

Chap. IV. *Concerning a Philosophical Language.* 425

38. (ʊʊ) as numb. 3. — Who

49. (ια) the preter tense of the Copula. — Have been

50. (Vαlgas) as numb. 41. Only that was a substantive of Action, and of the plural number, denoted by the length of the first Radical Vowel; whereas this is an *Adjective*, signified by (v.) — Transgressing

51. (ιʊ) A Preposition being the last Opposite of the second Combination; and therefore must signifie, *Against*. — Against

52. (αι) as numb. 28. — Us.

53. (na) as numb. 35. — And

54. (mi) An Adverb, the first Opposite of the first combination, signifying *No*, or *Not*. — Not

55. (ιo) as numb. 25. — Maist thou be

56. (Velco) (be) is the Genus of *Transcendental Action*. (c) denotes the sixth difference, and (o) the fifth species, which is *Leading*; the Letters (v) and (l) signifying: *Adjective. Active*. — Leading

57. (αι) as numb. 28. — Us

58. (ral) a Preposition, the first of the fourth Combination; and therefore must signifie, *Into*. — Into

59. (bedodlʊ) (be) is *transcendental action*, (d) denotes the second difference, (o) the fifth species, which is *Trying*; the second (d) doth denote this word to be joyned in the Tables as an affinis: the last syllable (lʊ) signifies the transcendental particle *Corruptive*, which in composition, must denote the worst sense of a word, and here it must signifie such temptation or trial sas ought not to be. — Temptation

60. (ril) a Conjunction, the first oppofite of the second combination, signifying, *But*. — But

61. (io) as numb. 25. — Maist thou be

62. (cʊαlbo) (cα) is the Genus of *Spiritual Action*, (b) signifies the first difference, and (o) the fifth species, which is, *Delivering*; the Letters ʊ and *l* signifying *Adjective Active*. — Delivering

63. (αι) as numb. 28. — Us

64. (lal) a Preposition, the second of the third combination; and therefore must signifie, *From*. — From

65. (vαgasie) as numb. 41. Only the *b* is turned into *v*, to denote *Adjective*, and the (l) is here left out, which signifies action, and the transcendental Particle (ie) is here added, to denote *Evil thing*. — Evil

66. (nor) a Conjunction, the second Opposite in the third combination, signifying, *For*. — For

Iii 67.

The	67. (αl) The demonstrative Article, *viz. The.*
Kingdom	68. (Salba) as numb. 12.
And	69. (na) as numb. 35.
The	70. (αl) as numb. 68.
Power	71. (tado) (ta) is the Genus of *Habit*, (d) is the second difference, and (o) the fifth species, which is *Power.*
And	72. (na) as numb. 35.
The	73. (αl) as numb. 68.
Glory	74. (Tadalα) (tad) is the same Genus and Difference with numb. 72. the second (a) denoting the second species, which is Reputation or Fame; the last syllable (lα) being added to the termination, doth signifie the first of the seventh combination, amongst transcendental notions, *viz. Augmentative,* the highest kind or degree of Reputation, which is, *Glory.*
Is	75. (ɩa) as numb. 4. But being here applied to the third person, and singular number, is to be rendered *Is.*
Thine	76. (ha) as numb. 11.
Everlastingly	77. (Pɩȣbyȣ) (Pɩ) doth denote the Genus of *Space*, (b) the first difference, (yȣ) the ninth species, which is (Everness,) the adding of the Vowel (ȣ) to make a Dipthong with the first Vowel, signifies the word to be an Adverb, *Everlastingly.*
Amen	78. (ꝗu) the word *Amen* in the Literal Character.
So	79. (mȣ) as numb. 19.
May it be.	80. (ɩo) as numb. 9.

The

Chap. IV. Concerning a Philosophical Language.

The Creed.

α ɩa tʋalti daƀ eʋιʋα,αl ʋι cʋalbαιʋ la dad na la dady, na dαd he cobas cʋopas hαɩ ſaba, ʋʋ ɩα cʋambab la αl Dαg, cʋambe le αl codαd ᴘƇ/ , ſʋemt rir ᴘȽ S/S I)ƎȴI , ɩα ſʋemtyʋ, cʋabyɩ, na ſʋympyʋ, e ɩa lir-velc rαl odad, e ɩα cʋalcα lal αl ʋι cʋabyſιʋ, ril αl poto fobe, e ɩα lαr-velc ral dad, ril ʋʋ-ʋα e ɩa cʋalco lil αl pigyʋ la daƀ, lal ʋʋ-ʋα e ie velcα lo ſelba αl cʋabyιʋ na αl ʋι cʋabyſιʋ. α ɩa tʋalti Dαg, αl ſyʋe tʋata vages, αl ſydzha la ſygo αl ſemdy la baſgas αl ʋyι mʋɩ-calby la αl odab na αl ʋyι caby eʋ-yſyt.

```
                    ͡          ͡       -       ͡       ͡       ͡
 1 2 3         4         5      6 7  8    9     10    11
α ɩa tʋalti   daƀ     eʋιʋα    αl ʋι cʋalbαιʋ la  dad    na
I am believing God  the Father Almighty Maker of Heaven and

    ͡           ͡     ͡        ͡   ͡    ͡      ͡
 12  13  14     15       16 17  18      19  20     21     22
 la  dady na    dαd          he cobas cʋopas hαɩ ſaba  ʋʋ    ɩα
 of  Earth, and in Jeſus Chriſt his Son only our Lord, who was

  ͡        ͡          ͡         ͡                 ͡
 23   24  25       26     27 28  29     30     31       32
 cʋambab la αl     Dαg    cʋambe le αl  codαd           ſʋemt
 conceived by the Holy Ghoſt, born of the Virgin Mary, ſuffered

                      ͡      ͡        ͡         ͡
   33    34       35   36     37 38    39    40 41    42
  rir  ᴘȽS/S I)ƎȴI,   ɩα   ſʋemtyʋ cʋaby na ſʋympyʋ e ɩα lir-velc
  under Pontius Pilate, was crucified, dead, and buried, he deſcended

     ͡              ͡            ͡         ͡         ͡
 43 44  45 46 47 48 49 50 51    52 53 54   55  56 57
 rαl odad e ɩα cʋalcα lal αl ʋι cʋabyſιʋ ril αl poto fobe, e ɩα
 into hell, he did riſe from the dead   in the day third, He was

   ͡               ͡      ͡                ͡      ͡
  58    59  60 61 62 63 64 65    66 67    68   69   70
  lαr-velc ral dad, ril ʋʋ-ʋα e ɩa cʋalco lil αl pigyʋ la  Daƀ
  aſcending into heaven, in which place he is ſitting at the right hand of God the Father
```

Iii 2

| 71 | 72 | 73 | 74 | 75 | 76 77 | 78 79 | 80 | 81 82 | 83 | 84 85 86 |

lal ƻƻ·ƻɑ e   ie velcɑ lo felbɑ ɑl cƻabyiƻ na ɑl ƻl cƻabyfiƻɑ ta
from whence he shall come to judge the Quick and the dead. I am

| | | 87 | 88 | 89 | 90 | 91 | 92 | 93 | 94 |

tƻalti Dɑg   ɑl fy·ƻe tƻata vages ɑl fydzha   la
believing in the Holy Ghost, the Church holy Catholick, the Communion of

| | 95 96 | 97 | 98 99 | 100 101 102 | 103 104 105 | 106 107 |

fygo ɑl femdY   la baſgas al ƻyɪ mƻɪ·calby lɑ ɑl odab   na ɑl
Saints, the forgiveness of sins, the resurrection of the body, and the

108 109 110

ƻyɪ caby cƻ·yfyt.

life everlasting.

I — 1. (ɑ) a Pronoun of the first person, and singular number, *I*.

Am — 2. (ɪa.) The copula, *est*, in the present tense, which being used with the first person, doth signifie *Am*.

Believing — 3. (tƻalti) (ta) denotes the Genus of *Habit*; the fifth difference, *i*, the fourth species, which is Faith; the adding of ƻ to t, denotes the word to be an adjective, and the Letter *l* signifies the active voice, *Believing*.

God the Father — 4. (Dɑb) The Monosyllable Dɑ is appointed to signifie *God*, or the divine nature; the addition of the Consonant *b*, will denote the first person in the Blessed Trinity.

Almighty — 5. (eƻtƻɑ) A Compound of a Particle, and an Integral, the Particle being a dipthong, appointed to signifie *All*. The Syllable tɑ, denoting the Genus of *Power*; the addition of ƻ, makes it to be an adjective, *viz. potent*, or *powerful*.

The — 6. (ɑl) the demonstrative Article, *The*.

Having been — (ƻɪ) the sign of the preter tense.

Creating person — 8. (tƻalbɑiƻ) (cɑ) is the Genus of spiritual action (b) denotes the first difference, and ɑ the first species, which is *Creation*; the addition of ƻ to c, signifies adjective, and the Letter (l) active; the last dipthong (iƻ) denotes the transcendental composition of *Person*. So that this word with the two preceding Particles, does import, *the having Created Person*.   9. (lɑ)

Chap. IV. *Concerning a Philosophical Language.* 429

9. (lα) the first Preposition, signifying *Of*. Of

10. (dad) (da) the Genus of *World*, and (d) the second difference, Heaven. which is *Heaven*.

11. (na) the second Conjunction of the first Combination, signify- And ing *And*.

12. (lα) as numb. 9. Of

13. (dady) The same Genus and difference, as numb. 10. The Earth Vowel Y signifying the seventh species, which is, *This Earth*.

14. (na) as numb. 11. And

15. (dαd) the second person of the Blessed Trinity. Jesus Christ

16. (he) the Vowel *e* signifies a Pronoun of the third person, and His singular number, the Letter *b* prefixt, shews it to be used possessively, for *His*.

17. (cobas) the syllable (co) is assigned to the Genus of *Oeconomi-* Son *cal Relation*, the Letter (b) to the first difference, and the Vowel (a) for the second species, the Letter (s) denoting the word hereby signified, to be an Opposite, *viz. Son*.

18. (cбopas) the same Genus as the former (p) signifying the fourth difference, and (a) the second species, and the Letter (ъ) an Opposite, Only *viz. Alone*, or *Only*.

19. (hαs) A Pronoun, first person possessive, plural number. Our

20. (Saba) (Sa) the Genus of Civil Relation, (b) the first difference, *viz*. Degrees of persons, (a) the second species, which is *Sove-* Soveraign *reign*, or *Lord*, to whom we owe Obedience, or subjection.

21. (ъъ) the second of the compound Pronouns, signifying *Who*, or *Which*. Who

22. (ια) The Copula *Est*, in the preter tense. Was

23. (cъambab) (ca) is the Genus of corporeal action, (b) the first Conceived difference, and (a) the second species; the adding of the second Radical Consonant (b,) denotes this word to be adjoyned in the tables, by way of affinity, and consequently to signifie Conception, (ъ) signifying *Adjective*, and (m) *Passive*.

24. (lα) the second Preposition in the first Combination, (*By*) By

25. (αl) as numb. 6. The

26. (Dαg) the third Person in the Blessed Trinity. Holy Ghost

27. (cъambe) the same Genus and Difference with numb. 23. (e) Borne signifying the third species, which is Parturition (ъ) denoting *Adjective*, and (m) *Passive*.

28.

Of	28. (le) the third Prepofition in the firft Combination, relating to the Material Caufe, *of*.
The	29. (αl) as numb. 6. *The*
Virgin	30. (codαd) the fyllable (co) as was faid before, is affigned to *Oeconomical Relation*, (d) is the fecond difference, and (α) is the firft fpecies; the repeating of the fecond Radical Confonant at the end, makes this word to denote fomething adjoyned by way of Affinity, *viz. Virgin*.
Mary	31. ( ) the name Mari in the literal Character.
Capitally punifhed	32. (ſƃemt) the fyllable (fe) is for Judicial Relation, the Letter (t) is the fifth difference, *viz. Capital punifhment*, (ƃ) is *Adjective*, and (m) *Paffive*,
Under	33. (rir) A Prepofition, the firft oppofite of the fixth Combination, *viz. Under*.
Pontius Pilate	34. (ᚠᛚ ʃ/ſ ⸝⸝)ꝺ) the name Pontius Pilate, in the Literal Character.
Was	35. (ıα) as numb. 22.
Crucified	36. (ſƃemtyƃ) the fame Genus and Difference as numb. 32. the laft Dipthong (yƃ) denoting the ninth difference, which is *Crucifying*, the firft (ƃ) being the mark for *Adjective*, and the Letter (m) for *Paffive*.
Dead	37. (cƃabys) the fame as to genus and difference, with numb. 23, & 27. the Vowel (y) fignifying the feventh fpecies, the Letter (s) an oppofite, and the vowel (ƃ) *adjective*.
And	38. (Na) as numb. 11.
Buried	39. (lƃympyƃ) The fyllable (fy) is *Ecclefiaftical Relation*, (p) the fourth difference, and (yƃ) the ninth fpecies, which is *Burial*; the firft (ƃ) being the fign of *adjective*, and (m) of *paffive*.
He	40. (e) Pronoun of the third perfon, fingular number, *viz. He*.
Was	41. (ıα) as numb. 22.
Defcending	42. (lir-velc) This word is a Compound, the firft fyllable (lir) is a Prepofition, the firft oppofite of the fifth Combination, fignifying *downwards*; (be) is the Genus of *tranfcendental action*, the Letter (c) the fixth difference, which is *Ition*, (ƃ) the *adjective*, and (l) the *active*, *Down-going*, or *Defcending*.
Into	43. (rαl) a Prepofition, the firft of the fourth Combination, fignifying *Into*.

Chap. IV. *Concerning a Philosophical Language.* 413

44. (odαd) (dα) is the Genus of *World*, (d) is the second diffe- Hell
rence, which is *Heaven*, the vowel (o) which is opposite to (a) being
prefixt, denotes this to be the word opposite to Heaven, *viz. Hell.*

45. (e) as numb. 40. *He.* He

46. (ια) as numb. 22. Hath been

47. (cϑalcα) (cα) is *Corporeal Action*, (c) is the sixth difference, Rising
and (α) the first species, *viz. Rise*, (ϑ) the *adjective*, and (l) the
active.

48. (lal) a Preposition, the second of the third Combination, From
From.

49. (αl) as numb. 6. *The.* The

50. (ϑi) as numb. 7. Having been

51. (cϑabysiϑ) The same radical word with numb. 41. the Dip- Dying persons
thong (iϑ) being a transcendental composition, denoting *Person*.

52. (ril) a Preposition, the first opposite of the fourth Combinati- On
on, signifying *In*.

53. (αl) as numb. 6. The

54. (Poto) the syllable (po) doth stand for the Genus of *Measure*, Day
(t) the fifth Difference, and (o) the fifth Species, which is *Day*.

55. (ſobe) The same Genus as the former, (b) the first Diffe- Third
rence, relating to *Number*, (e) the third Species, the turning *p* into *ſ*,
signifying *adjective*, viz. *Third*.

56. (e) as numb. 40. He

57. (ια) as numb. 22. Was

58. (lα˛velc) a Compound as numb. 42. Only the Prepositi- Ascending
on here, being the first of the fifth Combination, must signifie *Upwards*;
and the word *Ascending*.

59. (rαl) as numb. 43. Into

60. (dad) as numb. 10. Heaven

61. (ril) as numb. 52. In

62. (ϑϑ˛ϑα) A Compound of the Pronoun *Which*, and the transcen- Which place
dental Mark of Place.

63. (e) as numb 40. He

64. (ια) as numb. 2. But being here spoken of a third Person in
the singular number, must be rendered. (*is*.)

65.

Sitting	65. (cʊalco) The same Genus and Difference as numb. 47. (o) being the fifth Difference, which is *sitting*, (ʊ) *adjective*, and (l) *active*.
At	66. (lil) a Preposition, the first Opposite in the third combination, signifying *At*.
The	67. (α l) as numb. 6.
Right hand	68. (pigyʊ) (pi) is the Genus of *Space*, (g) the third Difference, and (yʊ) the ninth species, which is *Right hand*.
Of	69. (lα) as numb. 9.
God the Father	70. (Dαb) as numb. 4.
From	71. (lal) a Preposition, the second of the third Combination, signifying *From*,
Which place	72. (ʊδɾʊα) as numb. 70.
He	73. (e) as numb. 45.
Shall be	74. (ie) the Copula in the future tense, *shall be*.
Coming	75. (velcα) *be* is the Genus of *transcendental Action*, *c* the sixth difference, and α the first species, which is *Come*, the turning of *b* into *v*, denoting *adjective*, and *l Active*.
For	76. (lo) a Preposition, the second opposite of the first Combination, viz. *For*.
Judging	77. (Selbα) (Se) is Judicial relation *b* the first difference, and α the first species, which is *Judge*; the Letter *l* signifies a Noun of action, viz. *Judging*, or *Judication*.
The	78. (α l) as numb. 6.
Quick	79. (cʊabyiʊ) ca is the Genus of *corporeal action*, *b* the first difference, and y the seventh species, which is *Life*, the vowel ʊ signifying adjective, viz. *Living*, ιʊ being the transcendental composition for *Person*.
And	80. (na) as numb. 11.
The	81. (αl) as numb. 6.
Having	82. (ʊ) as numb. 7.
Died persons	83. (cʊabyGʊ) as numb. 51.
I	84. (α) as numb. 1.
Am	85. (ia) as numb. 2.
Believing	86. (tʊalti) as numb. 3.
The Holy Ghost	87. (Dαg) as numb. 27.
The Church	88. (αl) as numb. 6.
	89. (fyˑʊe) the syllable *fy* is put for the Genus of *Ecclesiastical Relation*,

… Chap. IV. *Concerning a Philosophical Language.* 433

lation, the Dipthong (ʮe) being the transcendental for *Aggregate.*

90. (tʮata) Ta is the Genus of *Habit*, *t* the fifth difference, and *a* the second species, which is *Holiness*; the addition of (ʮ) to the first Radical, doth signifie the word to be an *adjective,* viz. *Holy.* — Holy

91. (vages) (ba) is the Genus of *Transcendental Relation mixed,* *g* the third difference, and *e* the third species, (s) the note of opposite, ʮ the sign of *adjective,* viz. *Universal.* — Universal

92. (αl) as numb. 6. — The

93. (Sydzha) Sy the Genus of Ecclesiastical Relation, *g* the third difference, *a* the second species, which is *Communicant,* or *Catholic*; the turning of *g* into the same power that we give to J consonant, signifies this word to be an Abstract, viz. *Communion.* — Communion

94. (lα) as numb. 9. — Of

95. (Sygo) Sy is Ecclesiastical Relation, *g* the third difference, *o* the fifth species, which is *Saint,* the prolonging of the first Vowel denotes the plural number. — Saints

96. (αl) as numb. 6. — The

97. (semdy) Se is the Genus of *Judicial Relation,* *d* the second difference, and *y* the seventh species, which is *Remission,* or *Forgiveness,* *m* denotes the passive voice. — Being forgiven

98. (lα) as numb. 9. — Of

99. (bαlgas) bα is *transcendental general,* *g* the third difference, *a* the second species, *s* denotes an opposite, *l* a Noun of action, and the prolonging of the first Radical Vowel, the *plural* number. — Sins

100. (αl) as numb. 6. — The

101. (ʮyι) the Future Tense. — Future

102. (mʮs-calby) a compound, the Particle mʮs signifying *re,* or *again,* (caby) being before rendered *Life,* *l* denoting *Active.* — Relife, or living again

103. (lα) as numb. 9. — Of

104. (αl) as numb. 6. — The

105. (odab) Da is the *World,* dab is *Spirit,* to which is opposed *Body,* signified by prefixing the Vowel *o,* which is opposite to *a.* — Body

106. (na) as numb. 11. — And

107. (αl) as numb. 6. — The

108. (ʮyι) as numb. 101. — Future

109. (caby) the same Radical as numb. 37, and 102. Only this is not an Opposite, nor an Adjective. — Life

Kkk 110.

everlasting 110. (eʊ,yfyt) (eʊ) is all, as numb. 5. (py) is the Genus of Measure, (t) the fifth difference, which is measure of time, the affinis to which, (here denoted, by prepoſing the Radical Vowel y) is Duration, *p* being turned into *f*, ſignifies Adjective, *i. e. All-during*, or *Everlaſting*.

I am ſenſible that this Contrivance for the Language is not ordered (as to the facility and pleaſantneſs of the ſound) to ſo good an advantage as it might have been upon further conſideration and practiſe: But as it is, I think it may (even in theſe reſpects) come into compariſon with any of the Languages now known. For the better trial of which, I ſhall give ſeveral Inſtances of the Lords Prayer, as it is rendred in fifty ſeveral Languages, and written in our common Letter; moſt of which, I have taken out of *Geſner*, *Mithridates*, and *Megiſerus* his *Specimen*, as they have collected and lettered them to my hands. For the reſt, I am beholding to other Books, and the aſſiſtance of ſome particular Friends.

English

Chap. IV. Concerning a Philosophical Language. 435

English	1. Our father who art in heaven	Hallowed be thy Name
Hebrew	2. Abinu shebbashamaim	Iikkadesch schemocha
Arabic	3. Yā Abánallādi phissamawati.	Yatakaddasu smoca
Syriac	4. Abun dbashmajo	Nethkadesh shmoch
Æthiop	5. Abúna xabasharatjath	Yithkádash shimácha
Greek	6. Páter hemōn ho en tois ouranois	Hagiasthētō tò onoma sou
Copti	7. Peniot etchennipheoui	Mareftoubaṇe pecran
Latin	8. Pater noster qui es in cœlis	Sanctificetur nomen tuum
Spanish	9. Padre nuestro que estas en loscielos	Sanctificato sea el tu nombre
Portuguese	10. Padre nosso que stas nos ceos	Sanctificado seja o teu nome
French	11. Nostre pere qui es és cieulx	Ton nom soit sanctifie
Italian	12. Padre nostro che sei ne' cieli	Sia sanctificato il nome tuo
Friulian	13. Pari nestri ch'ees in cijl	See santificaat la to nom
Sardinian of the City	14. Pare nostre che ses en loscels	Sia sanctificat lo nom teu
Sardinian of the Countrey	15. Babu uostru sughale ses in foschelus	Santufiada su nomine tuo
Grysons	16. Bab nos quel tii ist in eschil	Santifichio sala ilgtes num
Germ. ancient	17. Pater unser du ta himel bist	Diu namo werde geheyliget
Germ. modern	18. Unser Vatter der du bist im Himmel	Geheyliget werde dein nahm
Old Saxon	19. Uren fader thic arth in heofnas	Sic gehaigud thin noma
Dutch	20. Onse vader die in den hemelin (zijt	Uwen naem werde geheylight
Danish	21. Vader vor du som est i himmelen	Heillige vorde dit naffn	Megiserus
Island	22. Vader tor sun ert ai himmum	helgist bitt nam ti	
Lappian	23. Isa meidhen joko oleth taju ahilla	Puitettu elkohon sun nimets	M.
Suedish	24. Fadher war som est i himlom	helghat werde titt namps	M.
Gothic	25. Itta unsar thu in Himmina	ethnai name thein	M.
Carnish	26. Ozha nash kir si v' nebesih	Posvezhenu bodi iime tvoie	M.
Dalmatian	27. Otfoe nas koyi-yessna nebissih	Szvetisse gyme tvoye	
Hungarian	28. Miattynack ki vagy mennyegbe	Megh stentel teffek ax te newed.	
Croatian	29. Ozhe nash ishe esina nebesih	Svetise jme tuoe	M.
Servian	30. Otze nash ishe jesi v' nebesih	Posvetise jme twoje	M.
Walachian	31. Tatal nostru cinerestsi in cerin	Sfincinschase numelle ten	M.
Bohemian	32. Otozie nass genz syna nebesich	Ozwiet se meno twe	Gesnerus
Lusatian	33. Wosch nasch Kensch sy nanebebu	Wss weschone bushy me twove	M.
Polonian	34. Ocziecz nasch ktory jestosz wniebye	Swyecz sie gymye twa	G.
Lituanian	35. Tewe musu kursey esi danguy	Szwenkis wardas tawo	
Livonian	36. Abes muus kas tu es eek sckan debbesis	Schweritz tows waarcz	M.
Russian	37. Oche nash Izghae yease nanæbæsægh	Da sueatesa Ima tuoæ	
Tartarian	38. Atcha wyzom khy hokta sen algusch	Ludor senug adongkel suom	M.
Turkish	39. Babamoz hanghe gugtesson	Chudufs olsum sjenungh adum	M.
Armenian	40. Hair mer or iercins des	Surb eglizzi anun cho	M.
Persian	41. Ai pader makeh dar osman	Pāk bashoud nām tou	
Chinish	42. Ngŏ tèm fŭ' chè tsay thien	Ngŏ tèm yŭen id niûn chim xim	
Welsh	43. Ein Tad yr hwn wyt yn y nefoedd	Sancteiddier dy enw	
Irish	44. Bir nathir araigh air nin	Nabz tar hanimti	Megiserus
Biscan	45. Gure aita cerua tan aicena	Sanctifica bedi hiretcena	
Frisian	46. Wsa haita, derstu biste yne hymil	Dyn name wird heillig	M.
Madagascar	47. Impoey entsica itay hanautaugh and angbitsl	Inghatamen heffiahots	
Poconchi	48. Catat tazah bilcat	Aki nim ta incahbraxih	
NewEngland	49. Noshun kesukquot	Quittiana tamunach kooweshunk	
Philos. Language	51. Hai coba wι ι2 ril dad	Ha babi ιo suymtα	

52. Ÿr fádher höitsh art in Hålloed bι dhyı nám
héven:

Kkk 2

	Language	Thy Kingdom come	Thy Will be done
	English	1. Thy Kingdome come	Thy Will be done
	Hebrew	2. Tabo malcutecha.	Teaſah rezonecha
	Arabic	3. Táti malachtoca	Tacuno mashiároca
	Syriac	4. Thithe malcuthoch	Nehue zebionoch
	Æthiop	5. Thymtſa mangyſtcha	Yichún phachádacha
	Greek	6. Elthéto he Baſilei a ſou	Genethéto tò thelemá ſou
	Copti	7. Mareſinje tecme touro	Netebnacmareſſhopi
	Latin	8. Adveniat regnum tuum	Fiat Voluntas tua
	Spaniſh	9. Venga el tu reyno	Fagaſe tu voluntad
	Porteguese	10. Venna à nos ò teu reyno	Seja ferta à tua voluntade
	French	11. Ton royaume advenie	Ta volunte ſoit faite
	Italian	12. Venga il regno tua	Si a fatta la volunta tua
	Friulian	13. Vigna lu to ream	See fatta la too voluntat
	Sardinian of the City	14. Venga lo regne teu	Faſaſe la voluntat tua
	Sardinian of the Countrey	15. Bengiad ſu rennu tuo	Faciadſi ſa voluntade tua
	Gryſons	16. Ilgtes ariginam uigna ter nus	La thia uoeglia d' uainta
	Germ. ancient	17. Din riche chome	Din wille geſcehe
	Germ. modern	18. Dein Reich komme	Dein Will geſchehe
	Old Saxon	19. To cymeth thin ryc	Sic thin Willa ſue
	Dutch	20. Uw Coninckrijcke kome	Uwen Wille geſchiede
Megiſerus.	Daniſh	21. Til komme dit Rige	Worde din Wilie
M.	Iſland	22. Komi tit riche	Uerdi tinn Vile
M.	Lappian	23. Tulkohon ſun waleakunta.	Si oſkohon ſun tahioſt
M.	Suediſh	24. Till homme titt rike	Skee tin Wille
	Gothic	25. Uimai thiudinaſſus theins	Werthe Willga theins
M.	Carniſh	26. Pridi k' nam krayleſtvu tvoie	S' idiſe volia tvoia
	Dalmatian	27. Pridi kralyeſs tvo tvoze	Eudi volya tvoya
M	Hungarian	28. Jujonel az te orſſagod	Legyen te akaratod
	Croatian	29. Pridi ceſa raſtvo tvuoe	Budi volia tvoja
M.	Servian	30. Pridi Kraileſtvo tuoie	Budi volia tuoia
M.	Walachian	31. Scuie imparacia ta	Suſe fie voia ta
Geſnerus.	Bohemian	32. Przid kralowſtwi twe	Bud wule twa
M.	Luſatian	33. Poſhiſh knam kraileſtwo twoio	Softany woli twoia
G.	Polonian	34. Przydzy twa krolleſtwo	Dandz wolya twa
M.	Lituanian	35. Ateyk karaliſte tawo	Buk wala tawo
	Livonian	36. Enack mums tows walſtibe	Tows praatz buska
M.	Ruſſian	37. Da predet Tzaazſtuia tuba	Da booder Volya tuoya
M.	Tartarian	38. Chanluchong bel ſun ſenung arkchueg.	Alei gier dauk
	Turkiſh	39. Gelſon ſenung memlechetun	Olſum ſhénung iſtred gunh
M.	Armenian	40. Ecefzza archaiuthai cho	Eglizzin camch cho
	Perſian	41. Bayaid padſhah tou	Shoud howáſt tou
	Chiniſh	42. Ál gúé lín	Ni chì chím him
	Welſh	43. Deued dy deyrnas	Bid dy ewyllys
M.	Iriſh	44. Tigiuh da riatiathe	Deantur da hoilaamhuoil
	Biſcan	45. Et hez betti hire rehuma	Eguin beti hire hazantatea
	Friſian	46. Dyn ryck to komme	Dyn Wille moet ſchan
	Madagaſcar	47. Uahoi jachanau hoant aminay	Fiteiannau hoofaitzangh
M.	Poconchi	48. Jtthauri inchalita pan cana	Haba intaniuita
	NewEngland	49. peyaumoowtch kukketaſſootamoonk	Kuttenantamoonk
	Philoſ. Language	50. Ha ſalba ιo velca	Ha talbi ιo vemgv
		51. Dbyl cingdym cym.	Dhyi ɣil bi dyn

Chap. IV. Concerning a Philosophical Language.

English	1. In earth as it is in Heaven	Give us this day our daily bread	
Hebrew	2. Ci baschamaim u baarez	Lachmenu temidi ten lanu hajom	
Arabic	3. Camà phissamai wa ala'l ardi	Chùbzana'lladi lil gadi shtinaol yaum	
Syriac	4. Aikano dbashmajo hocano oph barao	Havlan lachmo dsunkonan jaumomo	
Æthiop.	5. Bachama bashamai wabamdyrni	Shishajana zalalà ylathanà habanà yom	
Greek	6. Hôs en ouranô kai epi tes ges	Ton arton hemôn ton epiousion dos hemin semeron	
Copti	7. Phredichentphenembi jenpicahi	Penuiki strasti meisnawphou	
Latin	8. Sicut in cœlo sic etiam in terra	Panem nostrum quotidianum da nobis hodie	
Spanish	9. Assy en el cielo, como en la tierra	Nuestro pan cotidiano dad le a nosotros oy	
Portuguese	10. Assi nos ceos, come na terra	O pao no sso de cadadia dano lo oie nesto dia	
French	11. Ainsi en la terre, comme au cieulx	Nostre pain quotidiain donne nous aviourdhuy	
Italian	12. Si come in cielo cosi in terra	Dacci hoggi il nostro pane quotidiano	
Friulian	13. Sice'in cijl et in tierra	Da nus hu'el nestri pan cotidian	
Sardinian of the City	14. Axicom en lo cel i en la terra	Lo pa nostre cotidia dona anosaltres hui	
Sardinian of the Countrey	15. Comenti in chelo et in sa terra	Su pane nostru dognidedie duna anosateros hoc	
Grysons	16. In terra sco la so in eschil	Do a nus nos paun boutz & in miinchia di	
German ancient	17. In erde also in Himels	Unser tagolicha biot cib uns hinto	
Germ. modern	18. Auf erden, wie im Himmel	Unser taglich biot gib uns heut	
Old Saxon	19. Is in heofnas and in eorthe	Uren hlaf ofer wirtlic sel us to dæg	
Dutch	20. Geliijck in den hemel oockop der aerden	Ons daghelijcks biot gheeft ons heden	
Danish	21. Saa paa jorden som hand er i himmelen	Giff os i dag vort daglige Biod	
Islelandish	22. Suoma ai himme so ai pood	Burt vort dagligt geb tu os i dag	Megiserus
Lappism	23. Sowin tai tahissa ngnman' palla jaiwane	Mewhen joka paiwen leipa mehslen tana	M.
Swedish	24. Sa som i himmelen saock pa jordenne	Wart daglight biod giff oss idagh	M.
Gothic	25. Sue in himmina gah ana arte	Hlaef unsarana thana senteinan gif uns himmadaga	M.
Carnish	26. Kakor nanebi taku nasemlij	Kruh nash usak dainii dai nam dones	M.
Dalmatian	27. Kako na nebu tako i na zemlyi	Kruh nas sivagdanyni day nam danas	M.
Hungarian	28. Mi keben menyben azon kepen it ez se old ounis	Mi kenyerunk, & minden nappas adgyad neke unh	M.
Croatian	29. Jako na niebesih j tako nasemlij	Hlib nash usag danni dai nam danas	M.
Servian	30. Kako vnebi i takos nasemlij	Hlib nash usak danii dai nam danas	M.
Walachian	31. Cum in cerin asa prepo mortu	Puine noa de tote zilelle dene nobe astazi	Gesnerus
Bohemian	32. Yakona nebi tak y na zemi	Chleb nash wezdeysii dey nam dnes	M.
Lusatian	33. Takhak nanebu tak heu nasemu	Klib nasch schidni day nam thensa	G.
Polonian	34. Yako wniebi y na zemi	Chlieb nasch pow schedny day nam day say	
Livonian	35. Kayp and dangaus teyp ir andziames	Donos musu wisu dienu dok mumus szedien	
Livonian	36. Kasch kan debbes ta wursan summes	Musse deaistche mayse duth mums schodeen	M.
Russian	37. Yaco na nebesoe Jnazemlee	Ghlab nash nasou schneei dazgd nam dnas	
Tartarian	38. Achtaver visungundaluch	Ot mak chu musen vougon	M.
Turkish	39. Nicse gugthe ule gyrde	Echame gumozi hergun on vere bize buzun	M.
Armenian	40. Orpes jercins en jercri	Zhazt mer hanapazord tue mez assur	M.
Persian	41. hamzienànkeh dar osmân niz dar zamin	Bedih marab amrouz nân kefaf rouz mara	
Chinish	42. Tu ty su sim thyan	Ngh teng awdng nul kja jàu ngh ngh zid jong lcark	
Welsh	43. Er y ddaiar, megis y mae yn y ne-fodd	Dyroi ni heddyw ein bara bennyddiol	
Irish	44. Air nimh agis air thalamht	Ar nara latk dhuill tabhair dhuin a nioshh	Megiserus
Biscan	45. Cerban be cala lurrean ere	Gure eguneco ogula igue eguin	
Frisian	46. Opt yttrick as yne hymil	Ons deillix bre jonws jub. d	
Madagascar	47. In tanetona and anghiesi	Mahon mehohanzu anrou aniou abinathane anesica	
Poconchi	48. Pahuis bach a cal be intan tazah	Chaye suna tahuimen ka quih v. i.	
New England	49. Ken nach obbasie neane kesukqut	Asummeetsuongash Aeeulukoki th as in sueaan peupsu aesukoh	
Philos. Language	50. Me ril dady me ril dad	Io velpi ral as ril pota i hai saba vaty
	51. In erth az it is in héven	Giv ys dhis dai y'r daili bred	

438   *Concerning a Philosophical Language.*   Part IV

	English	1. And forgive us our trespasses	As we forgive them that trespass against us
	Hebrew	2. Uslach lanu eth cobothenu	Caascher anachnu solechim lebaale chobotheenu
	Arabic	3. Waghphir lanâ mâ aleina	Camà nàghphiro nahnu limàn lanà alcibi
	Syriac	4. Vashbuk lan chaubain	Aikano doph chanan shbakan lchaibeian
	Æthiop	5. Hydyg lanà abashana	Hai kai hemà ophitemen toà à ophileteà hemòn
	Greek	6. Kai aphes hemin tà ophilemata hemòn	Twchobol nostro
	Copti	7. Onobchanieteron nanebolmphretitio	Sicut & nos remittimus debitoribus nostris
	Latin	8. Et remitte nobis debita nostra	Assi como nosotros perdonamos à nuestros deudores
	Spanish	9. Y perdona nos nuestras deudas	Assi como nos perdoamos aos nossos devidores
	Porteguese	10. E perdoa nos sonnoras nossas dividas	Comme nous pardonnons a ceulx qui nous ont offenses
	French	11. Et pardonne nous noz faultes	Si come noi perdoniamo à debitori nostri
	Italian	12. Es perdonaci i nostri debiti	Sicu noo perduin agl nestris debitoors
	Friulian	13. Et perdonni nus glu nestris debiz	Axicom l nosaltres dexiam als deutoris nostres
	Sardinian of the City.	14. I dexia anosaltres losdeutres nostres	
	Sardinian of the Countrey.	15. Et lassa anosateros is debitus nostris	Comente e nosateros a isdebitores nostros
	Grysons	16. Parduna à nus nos dbits	Sco aua sain à nos dbitaduors
	German ancient	17. Unde unsere scultze belasuns	Als zuch wer belasendt unteren schuldigen
	Germ. modern	18. Und bergib uns unsre schuld	Als wir auch bergeben unsern schuldigen
	Old Saxon	19. And forget us scylta urna	Sut we forgeten scyldgum urum
	Dutch	20. Ende bergheeft ons onse schulden	Gtlijck dock wy bergheven onsen schuldenaren
Megiserus.	Danish	21. Oc forlad os vor skyld	Som wi forlade voos skyldener
M.	Isleland	22. Og bergeb oz skulden bozn	Suosem vi bergebem sku thun bozn
M.	Lappian	23. ja anna anteize meiden synbia	Ruin moe annaman bastahan rickosstien
M.	Suedish	24. Och forlat oss wara skuld	Salom ock wy forlate them os skyldigh aro
M.	Gothic	24. Gab aflet uns thatei sculansoigaima	Sua sue gab weis afletam thaim sculans unsarim
M.	Carnish	26. inu odpusti nam dulge nashe	Kakor tudimi odpustimo dushnikom nashim
	Dalmatian.	27. Jud pusci naam duge nase	Kako i my odpuschyamo duznikom nashim
M	Hungarian	28. Es bochasdmegh neck eunkaz mi vetkezynketmi	Kepen meg bochasunk ellen wuck vetettehnek
M.	Croatian	29. Jodpusti nam dlgi nashe	Jaco she imi odpushshaamo dlshnikom nashim
M.	Servian	30. Jodpusti nam duge nashe	Kako imi otpushkaamo dushnikom nashim
Gesnerus.	Walachian	31. Sunc jerta gresalelle nostre	Cum sonei jerta me grysidor nostri
M.	Bohemian	32. Y odpust nám nasse winy	Yako y my odpusstiam nassim winikom
G.	Lusatian	33. Awoday nam wyni nashe	Ack my wodawamij winikum nostim
	polonian	34. A odpuscz nam uyny nascha	Yako y my odpuscsamy winowaytzom nashzy
M.	Lituanian	35. Ir atlayisk mums musu kaltes	Kayp ir mes atlaydziam sawiemus kaltiemus
	Livonian	36. Pammiate mums musse grake	ka mes pammart musse partadveken
M.	Russian	37. Jo staue nam dolghij nasha	Yaco Inwge Ofstuwslayem dolzgnecom nashim
M.	Tartarian	38. Kai visum ja sachen	Alen bisdacha saielhe ein hisum jasoch namalin
M.	Turkish	39. Hem bassa bize borsligomozi	Nycse binde ballarunborse tigleremozi
	Armenian	40. Eu thogl mez zpaartis mer	Orpes eu mech thoglumch meroxt partapanax
	Persian	41. Wodar kedsar mara konàhan ma	Chonankeh mà niz mikedsarim ormingneza
	Chinish	42. uul myan ong-o tsi ay	Zin ugò ise sa toà ngò isi oy tsit
	Welsh	43. A maddeu i ni ein dyledion	Fel y maddeuwn nit i'n dyledwyr
M.	Irish	44. Agis math duin dairfhiacha amunti	Agis mathum bid ure feathu muim
	Biscan	45. Eta quitta jettrague gure còztac	Nola gutre guec calsuntey quittatzeu baitra negu
M.	Frisian	46. In berieb vos vos schriben	As vy beyr vos schylbairs
	Madagascar	47. amanhanan mangbasaca banagota antsica	Tomaysai manghasana bata antotananontitay
	Poconchi	48. Nachach ta camac	he sncaopachycquicmaezim acquital chi quih
	New England	49. Kab ahquontamatinneau nummatcheseongash	Neane matchenuke qutagig mia quantzinummoneg
	Philos. Language	51. na so sueldys lal as has balgas	ze as sa sueldys lal es us valges rs as
		52. and ſɑrgiv ys y'ɛr trespaſez	az ʋs ſɑrgiv ðhem dhat trespaſs againſt ys.

Chap. IV. Concerning a Philosophical Language.

English	1. And lead us not into temptation,	But deliver us from evil, Amen.	
Hebrew	2. Veal tebienu lenissajon,	Ella Hazzilénu mera, Amen.	
Arabic	3. Walâ túdkilná hagiârib,	Lakin nagjinnâ minnash shirriri.	
Syriac	4. Ulotalaan Inesiuno	Elo pazzan men vishó. Amin.	
Æthiop	5. Waïthabyana wysh tha manshúthi,	Alá adychnana balhhánana ymkúlu ychûl·	
Greek	6. Καὶ μὴ ἰσενεγκῇς ἡμᾶς εἰς πειρασμόν,	Ἀλλὰ ῥῦσαι ἡμᾶς ἀπὸ τοῦ πονηροῦ, Amen.	
Copti	7. Ouo omper tenechou epirasmos,	Alla nah menebalch enpipethmou.	
Latin	8. Et ne nos inducas in tentationem,	Sed libera nos à malo, Amen.	
Spanish	9. Y no nos dexes caër en la tentation,	Nas libra nos de mal, Amen.	
Portuguese	10. E nao nos dexes cahir in tentacao,	Mas libra nos do mal. Amen.	
French	11. Et ne nous induy point en tentation,	Mais deliure nous de mal, Amen.	
Italian	12. Et non c' indurre in tentatione,	Ma liberaci dal male. Amen.	
Friulian	13. E no nus menas in tentation,	Mà libora nus dal mal.	
Sardinian of the City.	14. I no nos iuduescas en la tentatio,	Mas liura nos del mal.	
Sardinian of the Countrey.	15. E no nos portis in sa tentatione.	Impero libera nos da su male.	
Grysons	16. Nun ens mener in mel aprouaimaint.	Dimpersemaing spendra nus da ruots mels	
German ancient	17. And in chozunga nit leitest du unsich	An belose unsich sone ubele	
Germ. modern	18. Und führe uns nicht in versuchung	Sondern erlose uns vom bösen	
Old Saxon	19. And no inlead usth in custnung	Ok gefrig urich from ife	
Dutch	20. Ende en leydtons niet i verweer-kinghe.	Maer verlost ons van den bosen.	
Danish	21. Oc leed os icke vdi friskelse	Men frels os fra ont.	Megiserus. M.
Isleland	22. Int leide os e hi breizlut	Hellbur byelsa os ver illu	M.
Lappian	23. Ja ale sata met ta kin saugen	Mutra paassa meite pahasta	M.
Saedish	24. Och inleedh oss ickei frestelse	Uchan freis oss ifram onto	M.
Gothic	25. Gah ni briggees uns in frastub	Ak lauzii uns af thamma oblin.	M.
Carnish	26. Inu neupelai nas v' iskushno	Tamazh reshi nass od flega	M.
Dalmatian	27. Ine naash uvediu-napasst	Da oslobodi naas od asila.	
Hungarian	28. Es ne vigy mynket az kesertet	Ben de stabaditz megh minket azgonosztul	M.
Croatian	29. Ine isbavi nas od nepriashni		
Servian	30. Ine vauedi nas v' napast	Dais bavi nas od sla	M.
Walachian	31. Sunu ne duce prenoi in Kale deispirra	Sune men tu jaste preroi de ren.	N.
Bohemian	32. Y ne uwod nasz do pokussenii	Ale zbaw nas od zleho.	Gesne us.
Lusatian	33. Neweshi nass dospi towana	A le wimoshi nas wot slego, Amen.	M.
Polonian	34. Nyewodz nasz napokul chenye	Alye zbaw nasz od zlego,	G.
Lituanian	35. Ir newesk musu ing pagúndynima	Bet giaf bekmus nog pikro, Amen.	
Livonian	36. Ne wedde mums louna badeckle	Pet passatza mums nuwusse loune	M.
Russian	37. Ineuedi nas spapast	No Jzbaue nas ot looczuaho, Ameen.	
Tatarian	38. Datcha koima visu suman acha	Illa garta visenn gemandam.	M.
Turkish	39. Hem yedma bizege heneme	De churtule bizy jaramazdan.	M.
Armenian	40. Eu mi tanir zmezi phorzuthai	Ail pharceai zmez i zara.	M.
Persian	41. Wodar azmaish minadar mara	Leikan halats kon mára az sharir, Amin.	
Chinish	42. Teú' pu ngô chiň chi eu iu' dedú caan	Náj kyeta ngô ju' chin' ò.	
Welsh	43. Ac nac arwain ni i brofedigaeth	Either gwared ni rhag drwg, Amen.	
Irish	44. Agis na triaic astoch un anau sen	Ic sar sino ole, Amen.	M.
Biscen	45. Eta egçai zala sar eraci tentatio-netan	Baina belibça gaitzac gaich totic.	
Frisian	46. In lied ws nact in versleking	Din fry ws bin it quad.	M.
Madagascar	47. Aman hanau aca mahatetsanay abin sherseuesse ratsl	Feha hanau metesahahanay tabin haratsian abi.	
Poconchi	48. Macoacana chipan catacchibi	Conteçara china unche tsiri, Amen.	
New England	49. Ahque tagkompagumainnean en quetchhuaonganit	Webe pohquohwussinean wutch machitut, Amen.	
Philos. Language	50. Na mi ſo velco as ral bedodl⸱	Nil ſo cualbo as lal vagasie, Amen.	

51. And léd ys nαt intʊ temp-tαſiαn, Byt deliver ys frαm ivil,

It would be convenient, that every one of these Instances should be Philosophically Lettered, according to the true pronunciation used in each Language; but this being a thing of too great difficulty, I do not attempt it. 'Tis probable that the doing of this, would make most strange Languages seem more harsh and uncouth, than now they do; as appears by that Instance of the English, this way written, which I have subjoyned in the last place, for the more accurate comparing it with the Philosophical Language.

In the comparing of these Languages, it may be granted that some few words of each Language may seem preferrible to others in this: But take it altogether, and in the whole, and it may at least stand in competition with the best of them, as to its facility and pleasantness. 'Tis most likely, that the generality of Readers will be apt in the comparing of these Instances, to give the precedence to those Languages they are acquainted with. I should desire no more from them, but that they would be content to permit this new Language to come in the next place, which would be a sufficient testimony for it.

But then for the *Philosophy* of this Language, it hath many great advantages above any other. Every *Word* being a description of the thing signified by it; Every *Letter* being significant, either as to the *Nature* of the *Thing*, or the *Grammatical Variations* of the *Word*, which cannot be said of any of the rest; besides the constant Analogy observed in all kind of *Derivations* and *Inflexions*.

CHAP.

CHAP. V.

Directions for the more easie Learning of this Character and Language, together with a brief Table containing the Radicals, both Integrals and Particles; together with the Character and Language by which each of these is to be exprest.

IF any Man shall think it worth his time and pains to learn this Character; the most facil and natural order to be observed in this, will be, to begin with the 40 common Heads or *Genus*'s, which should be learnt out of that General Scheme, Part II. Chap. I. where there is expressed some reason of their order; the understanding of which will much facilitate the fixing of them in the memory.

Next to these, he may proceed to the *Differences* belonging to each *Genus*, which though they are in the Character expressed by that numerical institution of First, Second, and Third, &c. yet are they to be committed to memory from their real significations. So the First, Second, and Third differences under the *Genus* of *Beast*, are to be learned and remembred, not as First, Second, and Third, &c. but as *Whole-footed, Cloven-footed*, and *Clawed*, &c. (not Rapacious, Rapacious Dog-kind, Rapacious Cat-kind) and *Oviparous*. Thus when we see any of the differences belonging to *Measure*, we are not to name them by their numerical order of 1, 2, 3, 4, 5, 6, but by the things which they denote, as Measure of *Multitude, Magnitude, Gravity, Valour, Duration, Age*. And to this end all the differences are to be learned out of the larger Tables, where there is some reason to be seen for the order of most of them.

Next to these, the several *Species* are to be learned, belonging to each *Difference*, at least so many of them as are like most frequently to occur in discourse. As for the various kinds of *Meteors, Stones, Herbs, Shrubs, Trees, Exanguious Animals, Fishes, Birds, Beasts*, and the kinds of *Diseases*, though they are to be provided for in the Tables, that they may be written when there shall be occasion for the mention of them; yet 'tis not ordinarily necessary to commit them all to memory, because those who are most expert in any Language, may not yet be able to remember all the names of such things. But as for such *Species* as are fit to be remembred, they are to be learned out of the first and larger Tables, where they are each of them described and determined, as to their primary significations, and some reason is attempted of their number and order, the understanding of which will make them more easily remembred.

After these the Particles are to be learned, which should be likewise out of the first Tables, where the meaning of them is described and determined.

But for the better helping of the memory in cases of doubt or forgetfulnefs, it may be proper to have recourfe to the Synopfis here adjoined, by which it is eafie at the firft or fecond view to find out the true place of any *Integral* or *Particle*, together with the Derivations and Inflexions belonging to the Radicals.

'Tis here to be noted concerning this briefer Scheme or Table, that in feveral of the *Genus*'s pertaining to Subftance, there are only fome few of the firft Species or Pairs of them mentioned under each difference as inftances; the reft being to be fought for in the larger Table. Thofe that are paired by way of oppofition, are put in a diftinct Character.

The firft Part, and the former half of the fecond, do contain a Philofophical Dictionary for all Integral, Radical words: The remaining Part doth contain all the Particles neceffary to Speech, befides a Summary of the whole Grammar, with reference both to the Character and Language; which I conceive to be fo plainly fet down, as not to need any particular explication.

But now becaufe there is no more general inclination amongft perfons of all Ages and Qualities, then that of Gaming, which Men can continue at for a long time with much pleafure, and are leaft apt to be weary of: Therefore the reducing of the Learning of this Character to a Game, may be a fpecial help and furtherance to it. In order to which it were not difficult to fhew, how it might be brought into feveral Games, like to thofe either at Dice or Cards. Of the former of which I had once thought to have given an inftance, with relation to the Particles, by which it would be eafie to underftand how the like might be done for all the reft: But upon fecond thoughts I do at prefent forbear it.

CHAP.

exprest. And, which is another great incongruity, as to the indistinctness of those which are thus provided for; neither are all *words*

(not ———————— may as conveniently be in like manner expreſt. And, which is another great incongruity, as to the indiſtinctneſs of thoſe which are thus provided for; neither are all *words*

of

conveniently be in like manner ..., which is another great incongruity, as to the indistinctness of those which are thus provided for; neither are all *words* of

may as conveniently be in like manner exprest. Some, which is another great incongruity, as to the indistinctness of those which are thus provided for; neither are all *words*

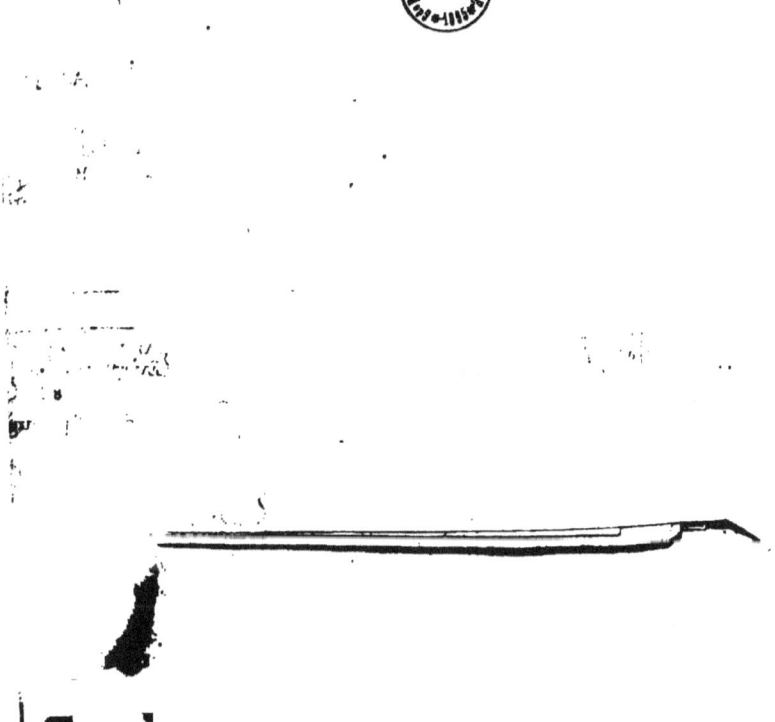

CHAP. VI.

The Appendix, containing a comparison betwixt this Natural Philosophical Grammar, and that of other instituted Languages, particularly the Latin, in respect of the multitude of unnecessary Rules, and of Anomalisms. Concerning the China Character. The several Attempts and Proposals made by others towards a new kind of Character, and Language. The advantage in respect of Facility, which this Philosophical Language hath above the Latin.

HAving thus briefly laid the Foundations of a *Philosophical Grammar*; I am in the next place to shew the many great advantages both for *significancy, perspicuity, brevity*, and consequently *facility*, which a Character or Language founded upon these Rules, must needs have above any other way of communication, now commonly known or used. And because the *Latin* doth in these parts of the world supply the place of a Common Tongue, therefore I shall chiefly insist upon the comparison with that.

1. As for the first part of Latin Grammar concerning *Orthography*, it will be needless here to speak any thing further to this, having before mentioned the imperfections of that Alphabet; the *redundancy* of it in some respects, and the *deficiency* of it in others; the incongruity of giving several powers to the same Letters, &c. which particulars are further manifested by what hath been delivered concerning natural Orthography.

As to the other parts of the Latin Grammar $\left\{\begin{matrix}\textit{Etymol.}\\\textit{Syntax.}\end{matrix}\right.$ I shall endeavour to prove that they do exceedingly abound with unnecessary *Rules*, besides a vast multitude of *Anomalisms* and exceptions, which must needs render it exceedingly perplexed and difficult to the Learner.

2. In the second part concerning *Etymology*. 1. There is a great imperfection as to the *just number* and *true sense* of Radical words.

1. In some respects *too many*, by reason of the *Synonima's* which do very much abound in it.

2. In other respects *too few*. There is a common word for the notion of *Parent*, abstracted from either Sex, *Father* or *Mother*. And so for *Child, Liber*. But none for the relation of *Brother, Sister, Husband*, and *Wife, Uncle, Aunt, Nephew, Niece*, &c. And so for the names of several Plants, and Living Creatures of every kind, which no Dictionary doth sufficiently express. And though the *Latin* doth provide for some of those notions expressed by the Transcendental Particles, yet is not their number sufficient, there being several others (not provided for) which may as conveniently be in like manner exprest. And, which is another great incongruity, as to the indistinctness of those which are thus provided for; neither are all *words*

of the like *notion* expressible by such *terminations*, nor doth the same *termination* always express the same *notion*.

3. The words of it are exceeding *Æquivocal*, scarce one amongst them which hath not divers significations, either *absolutely*, or *in phrase*, or *both ways*; from which Homonimy, those Particles which occur most frequently in discourse are not free, *ut, pro*, &c.

2. There are many improper and preternatural Rules concerning *Inflexion*.

1. As to Noun *Substantives*, both in respect of { *Genders, Cases, Declensions.*

1. In respect of *Genders*, which are needlesly multiplyed, there being but two in nature; nothing properly having *Gender* but what hath *Sex*. That which is called the *Neuter*, doth by its very name signifie that it is no *Gender*; and besides these *Genders* are irrationally applyed.

1. Things that have *no Sex* are expressed by words,
{ Masculine, *Gladius, Arcus*,
  Fœminine. *Vagina, Sagitta.*

2. Things that have *Sex* are denoted, 1. Sometimes by words of the *Neuter* Gender, *Scortum, Amasium*, &c. 2. Those words whose significations are common to Male and Female, are sometimes rendred only in the *Masculine* Gender, as *Fur, Latro, Homicida*, &c. and sometimes only in the *Fæminine*, as *Proles, Soboles*, &c. and sometimes only in the *Neuter*, as *Animal, Mancipium*, &c. 3. Many words which signifie the same thing, and are Synonimous, are yet used in several Genders { *Appetitus, Aviditas, Desiderium.* { *Sermo, Oratio.* { *Domus, Domicilium.* { *Crinis, Coma.* { *Capillus, Cæsaries*, &c.

He that would see more of this kind, may consult *Nonius Marcellus, de indiscretis generibus*: Where he reckons up abundance of words, which according to Ancient Authors, were used both in the *Masculine, Fæminine*, and *Neuter* Gender.

2. In respect of *Cases*, which are not so conveniently exprest by varying Nouns with Terminations, which is the Latin way as by placing them in the natural order of Construction and Affixing Prepositions to them (as was said before.)

3. In respect of *Declensions*, of which the Latin hath five, which add no small difficulty and trouble to the learning of that Language: Now if the expression of Cases by varying the Termination be unnecessary and inconvenient, these are much more so; because they are but several ways of varying such Cases.

2. As to Noun *Adjectives*, neither *Number*, nor *Gender*, nor *Case*, nor *Declension* do naturally pertain to them; but they are sufficiently qualified in all those respects by the *Substantives* to which they belong: As for their inflexion by *degrees of comparison*, which is proper to them; 'tis not so natural that these should be expressed in the *Terminations* of the words, as by *Auxiliary Particles*. The Adverbs of *more*, and *most*, *less*, and *least*, being upon other accounts necessary, and sufficient to express this notion in *Adjectives*, therefore the other way must needs be superfluous. Which is likewise applicable

cable unto the comparison of *Particiles*, and *derived Adverbs*.

3. As to *Verbs*, there are very many unnecessary Rules concerning their { *Kinds*, *Inflexion*, } in respect of { *Conjugations*, *Number*, *Persons and Tense in the Termination*, *Modes*, *Gerunds*, *Supines*. }

1. For their *Kinds*; 'tis not according to the Philosophy of speech to distinguish *Verbs* into *Active*, *Passive*, *Neuter*, *Deponent*, and *Common*, or into *Personal*, and *Impersonal*.

1. Those sorts of Verbs which they call *Active*, *Passive*, *Neuter*, and which are properly to be expressed by the Verb *Sum*, and the Adjective { *Active*, *Passive*, *Neuter*, } are all the distinct kinds of Verbs.

2. As for those that are stiled *Deponents* and *Common*, they are acknowledged to be but irregularities and kinds of *exceptions* from the common rule of *Verbs*.

3. All Verbs are naturally capable of *Persons*, though in some Verbs the Latin doth not admit this, 'Tis proper to say, I ought, I am ashamed, *&c.* as well as *Oportet*, *Pudet*. Scaliger de causis L.L. cap. 124.

2. As to the inflexion of Verbs.

1. The several *Conjugations*, of which there are four in Latin, are such a preternatural incumbrance, as *Declensions* are in *Nouns*, being but several ways of varying those Terminations or Cases of the Verb, which in themselves are needless and troublesome.

2. *Number* doth not naturally belong to Verbs, but only *quia Verbum à nomine dependet*, as *Scaliger* speaks; upon which account it might as well have *Gender* too, as it is in the *Hebrew*, *Syriack*, *Chaldee*, *Arabick*, *Æthiopick*, which yet we account very superfluous and improper. Ibid. cap. 151.

3. The expression of the *Persons* and *Tenses* by the Terminations of the words, is both unnecessary and improper, because there is in other respects a necessity of using those *Pronouns* by which these *Persons* are expressed. And supposing that a man must therefore learn *Ego*, *Tu*, *Ille*, *Nos*, *Vos*, *Illi*. It would much facilitate and contract Grammatical Rules, if the Verbs themselves might remain invariable. The same may likewise be said of Tenses, which may properly be expressed by auxiliary Particles.

3. For *Modes*, (to say nothing of the distribution of them, which is quite irrational) the expression of the *Optative* and *Subjective* is most naturally made out by Auxiliary Particles. That which is called the *Infinitive Mode*, should according to the true Analogy of that speech be stiled a *Participle Substantive*.

There hath been formerly much dispute amongst some Learned Men, whether the notion called the *Infinitive Mode*, ought to be reduced according to the Philosophy of speech. Some would have it to be the prime and principal Verb, as signifying more directly the notion of *Action*; and then the other varieties of the Verb, should be but the Inflexions of this. Others question whether the *Infinitive Mode*

Mode be a Verb or no, becaufe in the Greek it receives Articles as a Noun. *Scaliger* in the ſtating of this queſtion, concludes it to be a Verb; becauſe it ſignifies with Time, but will not allow it to be a *Mode*; becauſe it is without *Perſon* or *Number*. To which *Voſſius* adds, that though it be not *Modus actu*, yet it is *Modus in potentia*, becauſe it is reſolveable into other Modes. *e.g. Lator me veniſſe*, (i.) *quod venerim*. And ſo are other Modes reſolveable into this, *Eſt miſerorum ut malevolentes ſint & invideant*, (i.) *malè velle & invidere bonis.*

^{De cauſis L. L. Cap. 117.}

^{De Analogia lib. 3. cap. 8.}

^{Plaut, Capt.}

All which difficulties will be moſt clearly ſtated by aſſerting it to be a *Subſtantive Participle*. For which this reaſon is to be given; becauſe it hath all the ſigns both of a Noun Subſtantive and a Verb.

The Properties or *Criteria* whereby a Subſtantive is to be known are theſe four;

1. That it is capable of the Articles *A*, or *The*, to be prefixed before it, which is ordinary in the Greek for the *Infinitive Mode*, and doth well enough agree to the natural notion of it in other Languages.

2. 'Tis capable of that kind of Obliquity by prefixing Prepoſitions, which is commonly ſtiled variation by *Caſes*. The *Gerunds* in *di, do, dum*, being in the true notion of them, but the *Caſes* of that which we call the *Infinitive Mode*.

3. It may be joined in conſtruction with *Adjectives* or *Pronouns Poſſeſſive*.

4. 'Tis capable of *Number* in the natural notion of it, though it be not ſo uſed in Languages; the words *Actiones* and *Lectiones*, being but the Plural number of *Agere, Legere*.

The ſigns or Properties whereby a Verb may be known, are theſe three;

1. In our Engliſh tongue the Particle (*To*) may be prefixed before it.

2. It ſignifies with time.

3. It hath two voices, *Active* and *Paſſive*.

And therefore being both a *Subſtantive*, and a *Verb*, it ſhould according to the Theory of the Latin be ſtiled a *Participle Subſtantive*. To which may be added, that it is in the true notion of it, frequently reſolveable into a Noun Subſtantive, as in theſe Inſtances. *Virtus eſt vitium fugere*, (i.) *Fuga vitii eſt virtus. Magis paratus ſervire quam imperare.* (i.) *ſervituti quam imperio. Dignus Amari.* (i.) *Amore.*

As for the *Imperative Mode*, that is in this reſpect defective, becauſe it makes no diſtinct Proviſion for thoſe different notions to be expreſſed by it, *viz. Petition, Perſwaſion, Command.*

^{Voſſius de Analog. Lib. 3. cap. 9. and 11.}

5. *Gerunds* and *Supines* are unneceſſary inflexions of Verbs, the notion of them being expreſſible by the *Infinitive Mode*, whoſe Caſes they are. *Venio Spectatum* (i.) *Spectare. Turpe dictu* (i.) *dici. Caeſar venit ad oppugnandum urbem* (i.) *oppugnare*. And ſometimes by a Noun that ſignifies Action. *Defeſſus ambulando* (i.) *ambulatione*.

^{De Lingua Latina, Lib. 5.}

I cannot here omit the mentioning of what *Varro* hath obſerved, that the inflexions of a Verb through its ſeveral voices of *Active, Paſſive*, together with *Modes, Tenſes*, &c. amount to about *five hundred* ſeveral Caſes of inflexion. Now there being four diſtinct ways of *conjugating* Verbs, theſe variations may upon that account be reckoned to be *two thouſand*, the learning of which (though all
Verbs

Verbs were *regular*) would be no small labour and difficulty. But then consider the vast multitude of *Anomalisms* and exceptions in the inflexions of Verbs, and that will more than double this difficulty and labour.

2. As to the *derivation* of Latin words; whereas the Radix should according to *Philosophy* be only a *Noun Substantive*, 'tis here sometimes a *Verb*, a *Participle*, an *Adverb*, a *Preposition*, which is unnatural and improper! And then besides, there is no certain Analogy amongst these; à *Scribo*, *Scriptor*; but they do not say, à *Bibo*, *Biptor*, but *Bibax*, &c.

3. The Rules of *Composition* are not fixed to any certain Analogy. 'Tis *Ænobarbus*, not *Ænibarbus*, and yet they say, *Magniloquus*, not *Magnoloquus*. The same Prepositions, when in Composition, do sometimes *encrease* and augment the force of the word,

as in { *Infractus*, *Incavus*, *Incurvus*.
per | *Perfidelis*, *Perfruor*.
de { *Deamo*, *Demiror*.
ex | *Exclamo*, *Exaggero*.
dis { *Discupio*.

Again, the same Prepositions do sometimes in Composition import a denial or privation of the sense of the word.

in { *Indoctus*, *Improbus*.
per | *Perfidus*, *Pervicax*.
de { *Demens*.
ex | *Excors*, *Exanguis*.
dis { *Diffido*.

So the Particle *re* doth in Composition sometimes signifie *repetition*, as *retego*; and sometimes *privation*, as *revelo*, than which nothing can be more irrational and incongruous.

Unnecessary Rules in the Latin Syntax.

That is called *figurative* and irregular *Syntax*, which customary use, and not any natural propriety doth make significative; wherein there are some words always either *redundant*, or *deficient*, or *transposed*, or *changed*, from their proper notion. These *Phraseologies* are to be accounted an imperfection of Language, and one degree added to the curse of the confusion; because they do exceedingly encrease the difficulty of Learning Tongues, and do not adde to the brevity or perspicuity of expression, but rather cumber and darken it with ambiguities.

The regular *Syntax* of the Latin doth consist in { *Concord*,
{ *Regimen*.

1. *Concord* is the agreement of several words in some accidents and circumstances; as betwixt, 1. *Substantives* and *Adjectives*. 2. *Two Substantives*. 3. *Substantives* and *Verbs*. 4. *Antecedent* and *Relative*. Concerning which there are so many difficult perplexed Rules, as are

enough

enough to tire out and difcourage any young Learner, moft of them being founded upon fuch principles as are not natural to the Philofophy of fpeech.

3. The *Regimen* of words doth concern their government of others in refpect of {*Cafe*, *Mode*.

1. There are a great multitude of Rules that concern *Subftantives*, *Adjectives*, *Pronouns*, in reference to their governing of the *Genitive*, *Dative*, *Accufative*, *Ablative* Cafe.

2. So for *Verbs*, that fome of them muft govern the *Nominative*, others the *Genitive*, others the *Dative*, others the *Accufative*, and others the *Ablative* Cafe; fome promifcuoufly both {*Genitive*, *Accufative*,

{*Genitive*, {*Accufative*, Befides the feveral Rules concerning thofe *Ablative*, *Ablative*. divers Cafes which may precede the *Infinitive Mode*; fome words requiring a *Nominative*, others a *Dative*, others an *Accufative*. To which may be added thofe various Rules about *Gerunds*, *Supines*, *Participles*, in reference to the feveral Cafes, *Genitive*, *Accufative*, *Ablative*, governed by them.

3. There are feveral Rules that concern the Regimen of *Adverbs*, both as to {*Cafes*, Nomin. Gen. Dat. Accuf. Ablat. *Modes*, Indicat. Imperat. Optat. Subjunct.

4. Other Rules refer to the Regimen of *Prepofitions*, fome of which govern the *Accufative*, others the *Ablative* Cafe, and fome both.

5. Other Rules refer to the Regimen of *Conjunctions*, both as to *Cafes* and *Modes*.

6. Others to *Interjections*, divers of which are faid to govern the *Nominative*, *Dative*, *Accufative*, *Vocative* Cafe.

Befide thefe for Syntax, there is a great multitude of Rules in the Latin *Profodia*, about the *Accenting* and *quantity* of words: whereof fome are *General*, referring to the nature of Letters and Syllables; others more particular, concerning the firft or middle Syllables in any word, amongft which there is no certain and conftant Analogy: They fay, *Hectgrem*, & *Pratōrem*.

It cannot be denyed but that all thefe Rules are neceffary to the *Latin* Tongue; but this argues the imperfection of that Language, that it fhould ftand in need of fuch and fo many Rules as have no foundation in the *Philofophy of fpeech*. I am not ignorant that our Learned *Verulam*, fpeaking concerning the inflexions ufed in the more *Ancient* Languages by Cafes, Modes, Tenfes, *&c.* in which the *modern* Languages are very fparing, fupplying them by *auxiliary particles*; from thence infers, *ingenia priorum feculorum noftris fuiffe multo acutiora & fubtiliora*. But with reverence to the judgment of that incomparable Man, though it muft be granted, that the Language being fo, there was great wit in reducing the inflexions of words to fuch Rules of Art; yet if thefe Rules be not *neceffary* to Language, and according to *nature*, but that words may fignifie fufficiently and in fome refpects better without them, then there is greater judgment fhewed in laying them afide, or framing a Language without them.

De Augment. Scient. lib. 6. cap. 1.

If all thefe Rules were *general* and *conftant*, yet the multitude and variety

Chap. VI. *Concerning a Philosophical Language.* 449

variety of them would adde much difficulty to the *Latin*: But now the exceptions and *Anomalisms* to these Rules are so very numerous, that there is much more pains required for the remembring of them, than of the Rules themselves; insomuch that many eminent Grammarians have written against *Analogy*, both in Greek and Latin.

I shall offer a very brief view of them.

As to the inflexions of Nouns in respect,

1. Of *Number*; there are abundance of *Substantives*, whose sence and signification is naturally capable of both *Numbers*; some of which want a *singular*, others a *plural* number.   *Vossius de Anal. Lib. 1. Cap. 39. ad Cap. 44.*

2. In respect of *Gender*; the Rules to discover the Genders of words by their Terminations, are not without multitude of exceptions. There are divers words that are of one *Gender* in the *singular*, and another in the *plural* number. *Tartarus, Tartara. Locus, Loci, & Loca. Carbasus, Carbasa. Supellex, Supellectilia. Cœlum, Cœli. Epulum, Epulæ,* &c.

3. In respect of *Cases*; some words abound in Cases. *Avaritia, Avarities. Araneus, Aranea. Antidotus, Antidotum,* &c. Others have no Cases, and are stiled *Aclita*, or *Aptota*; as *Sinapi, Pondo, Nequam, Cornu, Quatuor, Quinq; Sex, Septem, Octo, Novem, Decem, Viginti, Triginta,* &c. *Centum, Mille,* &c. Others called *Monoptota*, have but one oblique Case, which in some is the *Genitive*, as *Hujusmodi, Ejusmodi*; in others an *Accusative*, as *Inficias*; in others the *Ablative, Promptu, Jussu, Injussu,* &c. Other Nouns have but two Cases, and are therefore stiled *Diptota*, as *Necesse, Necessum; Suppetiæ, & Suppetias*. And there are divers others that are *Triptota, Tetraptota, Pentaptota*.   *Vossius de Anal. Lib. 1. Cap. 47. 48. Lib. 2. à 1º ad vicesimum caput.*

4. In respect of *Declensions*; the Terminations of the Cases both in the singular and plural number in divers Declensions are not without many exceptions, as *Musis, Filiabus,* &c. Some words are of several Declensions, as *Pascha, Paschæ. Paschatis.*

2. As to the *inflexions* of *Adjectives* by the degrees of comparison; there are many words which signifie quality, and are naturally capable of *increase*, and *decrease*, and consequently of this inflexion, which are yet exempted from it: So *Cicur, Opimus, Claudus, Egenus, Almus,* &c.   *Ibid. Lib. 2. Cap. 22.*

Some want only a *Positive*, as *Prior Primus, Ulterior Ultimus*: Others a *Comparative*, as *Novus Novissimus, Falsus Falsissimus, Pius Piissimus*. Others a *Superlative*, as *Juvenis Junior, Senex, Senior,* &c. Besides that those which are inflected through all degrees, have several irregularities in the manner of it; *Similis Simillimus*, not *Similissimus. Bonus, Malus, Magnus, Parvus.*

3. As to the inflexion of *Verbs*; many Verbs of the *Active* voice are sometimes used in a *Passive* signification, and several others of the *Passive* voice used *Actively*. The exceptions about the *Conjugations* of Verbs, especially those referring to the *præter tense* and *supines*, are so exceeding numerous, that it is not easie to recite them: Some are wholly without them, others have them without any Analogy; as *Fleo Flevi, Sero Sevi, Fero Tuli. Ubi à Dissimilibus Similia, à Similibus Dissimilia.*   *Ibid. Cap.3. 5. Ibid. à Cap. 19. ad Cap.47.*

M m m   Some-

Sometimes divers Verbs have the same *Præter tense*, as
Cresco, } *Crevi,* *Luceo,* } *Luxi.* *Fulgeo,* } *Fulsi,* &c.
Cerno, *Lugeo,* *Fulceo,*

And so for Supines,
Cresco, } *Cretum.* *Pando,* } *Passum.* *Vinco,* } *Victum,* &c.
Cerno, *Patior,* *Vivo,*

Some Verbs are of several conjugations, *aggero* *ras,* } *Dico* *Dicas,* } &c.
ris, *Dicis,*

Some are of none of the four conjugations; as *Sum, Volo, Fio, Eo,* &c. Others are defective in respect of Modes and Tenses; as *Aio, Ave, Dari, Fari, Forem,* &c.

Those particular Terminations which signifie a Verb to be *Inchoative, Frequentative, Diminutive,* are not without many exceptions.

As for the several Anomalisms in *Syntax,* referring either to *Concord* or *Regimen*; they are so exceeding numerous, that it would be too tedious to recite them: And they may be seen in every Grammar.

Adde to these the several exceptions in the Rules of *Prosodia,* about the right *accenting* and *quantity* of words.

And from all these particulars put together, it is sufficiently evident that there may be very many and great advantages in a Philosophical Language, above that of the Latin Tongue; especially in these two respects, that this hath { *no unnecessary Rules,* { *no Exceptions.*

As for the *China* Character and Language so much talked of in the world, if it be rightly represented by those that have lived in that Country, and pretend to understand the Language, there are many considerable faults in it, which make it come far short of the advantages which may be in such a Philosophical Language as is here designed.

<small>Trigaltius Hist. Sinensis, Lib. 1. Cap. 5. Semedo Hist. of China, Part 1. Cap. 5.</small>

1. The *multitude* of Characters and Words, of which there are about 80000. others say 120000. and of these a man must have in readiness about eight or ten thousand before he is to be counted one that can write the Character, or judged fit to express his mind by it.

2. These Characters are strangely complicated and difficult as to the *Figure* of them, as may sufficiently appear by the following instance of the Lords Prayer in this Character: The Manuscript of which, together with a Catechism in the *China* Character and Language, was communicated to me by that Ingenious, and Inquisitive Person, Mr. *Lodowick*; in which there was both the Creed and Ten Commandments, with several Questions and Answers about the Principles of Christian Religion: The Language being writ on one side of the Character in our common Letters, and a verbal Translation in Latin on the other side. I did purpose out of this to have inserted the Lords Prayer as it was in that Copy; in order to which I procured a Cut to be made of the Character: but this Manuscript being destroyed in the late Fire, and not knowing where to procure a supply of it, I am necessitated to offer the Characters without the Verbal Interpretations of them. Their way of reading is known to be from the top or the right side downwards.

Ngò

Chap. VI. *Concerning a Philosophical Language.* 451

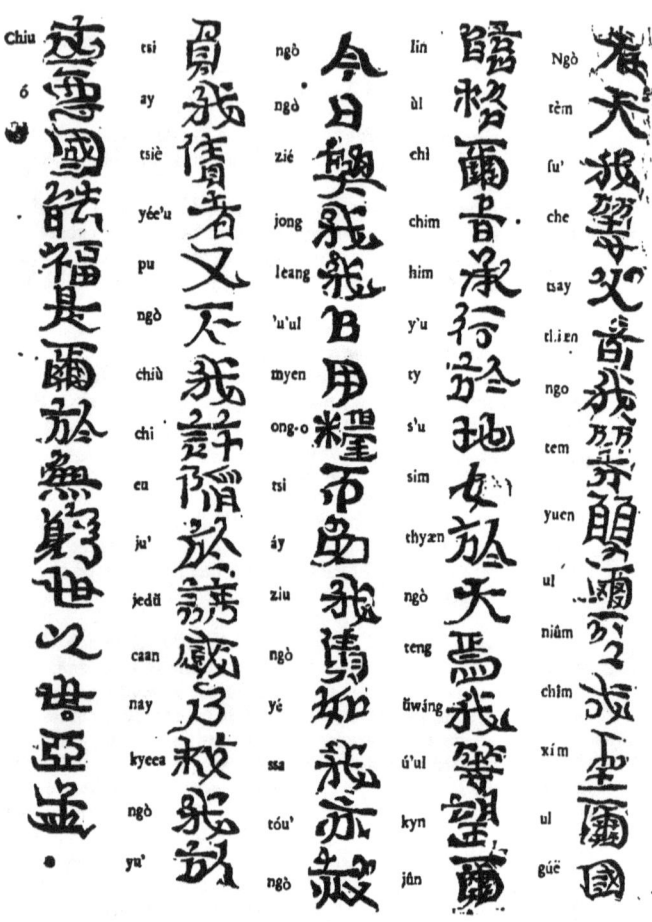

Besides the difficulty and perplexedness of these Characters, there doth not seem to be any kind of Analogy (so far as I am able to judge) betwixt the shape of the Characters, and the things represented by them, as to the Affinity or Opposition betwixt them, nor any tolerable provision for necessary derivations.

3. To this may be added the great *Æquivocalness* of the Language, every word having divers significations, some of them no less than twenty or thirty several sences; upon which account *Alvarez Semedo* affirms it to be more difficult than any other Language in the World.

> Theoph. Spizelius de Re literaria Sinensium, lately Published 1661. Sect. 6. Histor. Chinæ, Part 2. Cap. 2.

4. The *difficulty* of *pronouncing* it, every Syllable (as this of *Ko*) hath no less than ten several ways of pronunciation, as saith of Author; and it hath more than thirty several significations in the *Anamitish* Language, as *Alexander Rhodes* observes in his *Dictionary*. Such various Accents they are necessitated to make use of, as other people cannot imitate. The Syllable *Ba*, according to its various Accents, hath six several sences, of no kind of affinity or nearness to one another. And the most expert Men among themselves are not able so exactly to distinguish in pronunciation, without using several attempts and repetitions to explain what they mean; or sometime by making the Figure of the Character they would express with their Fingers in the Air, or upon a Wall, or Table.

> Lingua Anamitica, cap. 2.

5. Though in some particulars they seem to found their Character upon the *Philosophy of things*, yet 'tis not so in others. The Character put for a precious Stone (saith *Semedo*) must be used with additions to it for several kinds of *Gems*, as *Pearls*, &c. So the Character for any kind of *Tree*, must have joined to it, the Character for *Wood*; and the letter that signifies *Metals*, must be annexed to the Character of *Iron*, *Copper*, *Steel*, &c. The meeting with which passage, was no small satisfaction to me, in reference to that way which I had before pitched upon for the most natural expression of things. But this (saith he) is no constant Rule amongst them. It should seem to be observed only in some few *species* of nature which are most obvious, there being reason to doubt whether they had any such general Theory of Philosophy, as might serve for all other things and notions.

> Hist. Part 1. Cap. 6.

In this it is to be acknowledged that they have a great advantage above the Latin, because their words are not declined by Terminations, but by Particles, which makes their Grammar much more easie than that of the Latin.

> Ibid.

To this I might adde something concerning the advantage of this Philosophical way, above those attempts towards a Universal Character which have been made by others. That of *Marks* or Letters by *Cicero*; that of *numbers* by an Ingenious Country-man of our own, followed since by *Beckerus*, and by *Athanasius Kircher*; together with that other attempt towards an Universal Language, by *Philip Labbé*. All which are in this one respect defective, because they are not Philosophical; upon which account they are much more difficult, and less distinct.

> Mr. Beck of Ipswich.

These things being premised concerning the many *needless Rules*, and great variety of *exceptions* in the Latin; it will not be very difficult to make a comparison betwixt that, and the Character and Language here proposed.

For the right estimating of the difficulty which there is in the Learning of any Language, these two things are to be enquired into.
1. The

Chap. VI. *Concerning a Philosophical Language.* 453

1. The *multitude of words*. And 2. The *Grammatical Rules* belonging to such a Language.

1. As to the first of these, *Hermannus Hugo* asserts that no Language hath so few as 100000 words; and *Varro* is frequently quoted by divers Learned Men, as if he affirmed that there are in the *Latin* no less than *five hundred thousand*. But upon enquiry into the scope of that place they relate to, it will appear that he doth not there design to give an account of the just number of words in the *Latin*, but only to shew the great variety which is made by the *Inflexion* and *Composition* of *Verbs* : To which purpose the first thing he lays down is, That there are about one thousand Radical Verbs in the *Latin*. And then Secondly, That every Verb in the Declensions of it, hath about five hundred several varieties or Cases of Inflexion, which make up the number of five hundred thousand. And then Thirdly, He supposeth each of these to be compounded with nine Prepositions, as for instance, the word *Cessit, Recessit, Accessit, Abscessit, Incessit, Excessit, Successit, Decessit, Concessit, Processit* ; this will raise the whole number to *five millions* : in which account he reckons only the Cases and Compositions of Verbs, and takes no notice of the Particles of speech, nor such other words as are not radically Verbs, which are very numerous.

De origine Scribendi, Cap. 4. Bp Walton, Davies, Boxhornius.

Of all other Languages, the *Greek* is looked upon to be one of the most copious; the Radixes of which are esteemed to be about 3244. But then it doth exceedingly abound in *Composition*, in which the *Latin* Tongue being more sparing, must therefore upon that account have more Radicals. What the particular number of these may be, is not easie to determine; because Learned Men do not agree about many of them, whether they are *Radicals*, or *Derivatives*. They may be by moderate computation estimated to be about *ten thousand*, most of which are either *absolutely*, or in phrase, or *both ways* equivocal. *Notavi ex Varrone, Nonnio & Festo, non extare vocabulum apud Latinos quod plures significationes non habet*, saith *Campanella*. Many of them have no less than twenty distinct significations, and some more. Now for every several sense, we may justly reckon so many several words, which will much augment the former number. But suppose them only to treble it, and then the *Latin words* are to be reckoned thirty thousand.

Grammat. Philosoph. Lib. 1. Cap. 1.

2. Now for the *Latin Grammar*, it doth in the common way of Teaching take up several of our first years, not without great toyl and vexation of the mind, under the hard tyranny of the School, before we arrive to a tolerable skill in it. And this is chiefly occasioned from that great multitude of such Rules as are not necessary to the Philosophy of speech, together with the *Anomalisms* and exceptions that belong to them; the difficulty of which may well be computed equal to the pains of Learning one third part of the words; according to which the labour required to the attaining of the *Latin*, may be estimated equal to the pains of Learning forty thousand words.

Now in the way here proposed, the words necessary for communication are not three thousand, and those so ordered by the help of natural method, that they may be more easily learned and remembred

bred than a thousand words otherwise disposed of; upon which account they may be reckoned but as one thousand. And as for such Rules as are natural to Grammar, they were not charged in the former account, and therefore are not to be allowed for here.

So that by this it appears, that in point of easiness betwixt this and the Latin, there is the proportion of one to forty; that is, a man of an ordinary capacity may more easily learn to express himself this way in one Month, than he can by the Latin in forty Months.

This I take to be a kind of Demonstration *à Priori*; and for an Argument *à Posteriori*, namely, from Experiment. Though I have not as yet had opportunity of making any tryals, yet I doubt not, but that one of a good Capacity and Memory, may in one Months space attain to a good readiness of expressing his mind this way, either in the *Character* or *Language*.

FINIS.

AN ALPHABETICAL DICTIONARY,

Wherein all

ENGLISH WORDS

According to their

VARIOUS SIGNIFICATIONS,

Are either referred to their Places in the

PHILOSOPHICAL TABLES,

Or explained by such Words as are in those

TABLES.

LONDON,
Printed by J. M. for *Samuel Gellibrand* and
John Martin, 1668.

AN ADVERTISEMENT TO THE READER.

FOr the better underſtanding of the References in the following Dictionary, the Reader is deſired to take notice, that the Abbreviations therein uſed, are thus to be explained;

A.	Affinis.	Ha.	Habit	(er
a.	active	HF.	Herb ⎫ conſidered ⎧ Flow-
AC.	Action Corporeal	HL.	Herb ⎬ according ⎨ Leafe
adj.	adjective	HS.	Herb ⎭ to the ⎩ (Seed-
Adv.	Adverb underived			(veſſel
adv.	adverb derived	(inc.	inceptive	
(aggr.	aggregate	(imp.	impetus, or fit	
(apt	aptitude, or proneneſs.	(inſtr.	inſtrument	
AS.	Action Spiritual	Int.	Interjection	
(arm.	armament	(jug.	jugament	
(aug.	augmentative			
		(lam.	lamin	
Be.	Beaſt			
Bi.	Bird	(mach	machin.	
		Mag.	Magnitude	
Conj.	Conjunction	Man.	Manners	
(corr.	corruptive	Mea.	Meaſure	
		(mech	mechanic	
D.	Deficient extreme	(merc.	merchant	
D.	Diſcourſe	Met.	Metal	
(def.	defective	Mo.	Motion	
(dim.	diminutive			
		NP.	Natural Power	
E.	Exceeding extreme			
El.	Element	O.	Operation	
(end.	endeavour	O.	Oppoſite	
Ex.	Exanguious	(off.	Officer	
(ex.	exceſſive			
		p.	paſſive	
(fem.	female	(perf.	perfective	
Fi.	Fiſh	PG.	Parts General	
(freq.	frequentative	Po.	Poſſeſſions	
		(pot.	Power, or ability	
G.	God	PP.	Parts Peculiar	

Pr.

To the Reader.

Pr.	Provisions	(segr.	segregate
Pre.	Preposition	Sh.	Shrub
Pro.	Pronoun	Sp.	Space
		sp.	specially
Q.	Quality sensible	St.	Stone
RC.	Relation Civil	T. or TG.	Transcend. General
RE.	Relation Ecclesiastical	TA.	Transcendental Action
RJ.	Relation Judicial	TM.	Transcendental Mixed
RM.	Relation Military	Tr.	Tree
RN.	Relation Naval		
RO.	Relation Oeconomical	v.	verb
S.	Sickness	W.	World

The Literal Figures, as I, II, V, &c. denote the order of the Differences under each Genus; and the other Figures, the order of the the Species under each Difference. So the word *sheep* in the Dictionary is marked Be. II. 3. The meaning of which is, That the thing signified by that word is described in the Philosophical Tables under the Genus of BEAST, the second difference, and the second Species. And *Goat* is Be. II. 2. A. (*i.e.*) 'tis joyned as an Affinis to the same Species.

The Design of the Philosophical Tables is to enumerate and describe all kinds of *Things* and *Notions*: And the Design of this Dictionary, is to reckon up and explain all kinds of *words*, or *names* of things.

And that the Reader may the better understand the usefulness of having all words set down according to their different Acceptions, and by what kind of Analogy they come to be used in such various sences (which is one of the particular advantages of this Dictionary) I shall here select out of it one particular Instance, for each of these several kinds of words, *viz.* a *Substantive*, an *Adjective*, a *Verb*, a *Particle*; by which it will be easie to understand any of the rest.

So the word *CORRUPTION*, according to that Notion of it which is

Primary and proper, doth denote the *Being*, or *Making* of a *thing*, *evil*, or *worse*, whether by
- *Admixtion* with that which is bad, and then it is of the same importance with the word *Defiling*.
- *Privation*, as to a thing
  - *Being*, so corruption is *destroying*.
  - *Usefulness*, so corruption is *spoiling*.

Secondary, as applied to things
- *Natural*, so Corruption will denote according to the Degree of it, either *Infection*, or *Decay*, or *Putrefaction*.
- *Moral*, whether more
  - *General*, so it denotes the Evilness of the mind or manners, *Unholiness*, *Viciousness*.
  - *Special*, so 'tis peculiarly applied to *Unchastity* and *Bribery*.

So the word CLEAR, may fignifie either
- *Entire of it felf*; fo clearly is *wholly*.
- *Not mingled with others*; fo Clear is *Simple*.
- fpecially not with worfe; fo Clear is *Pure*.
- *Being free from impediments*, or not being hindered from
  - *Being, doing, or receiving*, which [notion of Clear may be often expreft by the Tranfcendental mark of Perfective. There may be Inftances of it given in every Genus; as particularly,
    - *Quality*, whether
      - *Natural Power*, fo a clear fight or underftanding is a good f. or u. It is applied to the
        - *Mind*, as a *clear Wit*, or *Spirit*.
        - *Body*, fo we fay one is clear of ficknefs or pain, has a clear skin, *&c.*
      - *Habit*, as a *clear Reputation*, that is a good R.
        - fp. Sagacity and Sincerity are thus called Clearnefs.
      - *Manners*, as *Clear Dealing*, that is Candor or Franknefs.
      - *Senfible Quality*.
        - *Vifible*, as *clear weather*, or sky or water, *&c.*
        - *Audible*, as *clear found*.
      - *Sicknefs*, as *clear of any difeafe* (i. e.) not Infected, or not Difeafed.
    - *Relation*.
      - *Civil*, as a *Clear Eftate*.
      - *Judicial*, as *Clear of any Crime*.
      - *Military*, as *Clear Coaft*.
      - *Ecclefiaftic*, as *Clear of any Cenfure*.
  - *Being Done*, fo Clear is *Eafie*, or not difficult; *Being Known*, fo Clear is *Plain* or manifeft; *Being come to*, or *Paffed through*, fo Clear is *Acceffible*, or *Paffable*, or *Empty*.

So the word DELIVER, according to its primary fenee, is the motion (Met.) or the paffing of a thing, or of the Poffeffion of it, or of the Power over it, from one to another. It is commonly ufed in relation either to the
- *fubject*, or thing deliver'd, whether
  - *Things*; fo Deliver may fignifie *Depofiting*, *Paying*, *Refigning*.
  - *Words*, as to the
    - *Matter*, whether concerning
      - *Fact*, fo Delivering is *Narration*
      - *Doctrine*, fo Delivering is *Teaching*
    - *Manner*, whether
      - *Immediately* by
        - *Mouth*, fo to deliver, is to *fpeak*,
        - *Pen*, fo to deliver, is to *write*
      - *Mediately*, fo Delivering is *Tradition*
- *Terms* of this motion, either *from* a

- Better condition *to a worse*, being used
  - *Passively*, so Delivering is *Dereliction*
  - *Actively*, whether
    - *Involuntary*, so Delivering is *yielding*
    - *Voluntary*, so Delivering is *Betraying*
- *Worse* condition *to a better*.
  - *Temporal*, whether by way of
    - *Prevention*, so Delivering is *Preserving*, or *Causing to escape*.
    - *Remedy*, from
      - *Captivity*, so to deliver, is to *Uncaptivate*.
      - *Bondage*, so to deliver, is to *Unslave*.
      - *Prison*, so to deliver, is to *Unimprison*.
      - *Danger of Child-birth*, so to deliver, is the Active of *Parturition*.
  - *Eternal*, so delivering is *Redemption*.

So the Particle BY, is sometimes used in the sence of an
- *Integral*, signifying the notion of *Digression* or *Accessory*, as *on the by*; and is of the same importance with such kind of Negatives, as not *principal*, not *pertinent*, not *public*, not *ordinary*; as a *By-way*: And sometimes 'tis used to denote a common speech implying something of contempt, as a *By-word*.
- *Preposition*
  - *Causal*,
    - Efficient, *By such an Author.*
    - Instrumental, *Slain by the sword.*
    - Final, or end, *By reason of, &c.*
  - Local or Temporal, being sometimes used in that same sence with those other Prepositions.
    - *Before*, as, By God, (*i.*) before God.
    - *At*, as, Come by, (*i.*) obtain, or come at.
    - *In*, as, by day, (*i.*) in the day time.
    - *Through*, as, by such a street, (*i.*) through such a street.
    - *Besides*, as, by the mark, (*i.*) besides.
- *Adverbs* denoting the Circumstance of Nearness, whether
  - *Local*. So By, or hard by, is near such a *Place*.
  - *Temporal*. So By and by, is nearness in *Time*, signifying future (dim.)

Besides

To the Reader.

Besides those Phraseologies wherein the Particle is used to signifie the *Manner* of things, as, *By the By, By the Great, By Retail, By it self*, &c. Which Phrases are to be expressed by the Adverbs Neuter of *Digression, Aggregate, Segregate, Solitary*, &c. So those Forms of Speech, *By course, By the day*, or *day by day, By degrees, By turns, House by House, Year by Year*, &c. are to be expressed by the Adverbs of *Course, Day, Degree, Turn, House, Year*, with the Transcendental Note of Segregate.

The Alphabetical DICTIONARY.

A B

A Article, 1.
   Abandon. T A. II. 2, O.
Abase.
  [a. Lowness,] TM. II, 4, O.
  [a. Meanness,] Ha. II, 5. O.
  [a. Humility,] Man. V. 2.
Abash, [a. Shame.] AS. VI. 2. A.
Abate
  [a. Little,] TM. I. 1. D.
  [a. Diminution,] TM. I. 7. D.
  [a. Remission,] TM. I. 8. D.
  [a. Subduction,] TM. VI. 7.
Abbat, [Abby's Officer.]
Abbie, [Colledge of Monks.]
Abbreviate, [a. Brevity,] TM. II. 1, O,
  [a. Epitome,] D. V. 6.
Abbridge, [a. Abbreviate.]
Abdicate, TA. I. 3, O.
Abecedarian, [Learner of elements,] D. I.
Abed, [in bed,] brought, [adj. pret. parturition.]
Abet,
  [v. Accessary,] TM. IV. 4. O.
  [v. Incourage,] RO. VI. 2.
  [a. Help.] T. II. 5.
Abhor,
  [v. Hate, AS. V. 3. O. (augm.)
  [v. Aversation, AS. V. 5. O. (augm.)]
Abide.
  [continue.]
  [v. Duration,] Mea. V. A.
  [v. Permanent,] Sp. I, 6.
  [v. Constancy,] Ha. IV. 7.
  [v. stay] TA. VI. O.
  [dwell] Po. I. A.
  suffer.
  [v. Passion,] T. I. 7. O.
  [v. Patience,] Man. I. 8.
Abject.
  [Mean,] Ha. II. 5. O. (augm.)
  [Contemptible,] AS. II. 8. O. (augm.)
  excess of modesty, Man. III. 9. E.
Ability.
  [Potentialness] T. III. 5. O.
  [Nat. Power] NP. per tot.
  [Possessions] Po.
Abjure, [Swear, RC. VI. 4. (against.]
Ablatum, TM. VI. 7.
Able, [adj. Ability.]
Abode, vid. *Abide.*
Abolish.
  [a. Nothing] T. I. 1. O.
  [Annihilate] AS. I. 1. Q.
  [Destroy] AS. I. 4. O.
  —*Law* [v. Law (un.]
  —*Act* [v. Act (un.]

A B

Abominate.
  [v. Hate] AS. V. 3. O. (aug.)
  [Aversation] AS. V. 5. O. (aug.)
Aboord [into, or in Ship.]
Abortion, AC. I. 3. O.
Above, Prep. V. 1. O.
  [adv. Upper] Sp. III, 5.
  [More then, &c.]
Abound, v. TM. I. 2. E.
  [v. Redundance,] TM. I. 3. E.
About, 'as round'—Prep. III. 3. O.
  [more or less] Adv. V. 3.
  [concerning] Prep. I. 3. O.
Abroad, [out of] Prep. IV. 2.
  [without] Prep. IV. 2. O.
  [in public] adv. TM. V. 4.
Abrogate [un-law.] RC. IV. 3.
Abrupt.
  [confused] TM. V. 2. O.
  [sp. ended   confused-
   discontinued   ly.]
Absence, Sp. II. 1. O.
Absolving.
  [Acquitting,] RJ. II. 7.
  [un-excommunicate,] RE. V. 5.
Absolute.
  [perfect] T. III. 9.
  op. to dependent, TM. IV. 3. O.
  op. to relative, T. I. 8. O.
Absolution, vid. *Absolve.*
Abstein, TA. V. 6. O.
  [v. Abstinence] Man. II. 2.
Abstemious, [adj. Abstinence,] Man. II. 2.
  sp. from Wine.
Abstersive, adj.
  [a. purgation (dim.]
  [a. purity] TM. V. 6.
Abstinence, TA. V. 6. O.
  vertue, Man. II. 2.
Abstract, D. II. 2.
  [epitome] D. V. 7.
Abstruse.
  [obscure] D. III. 9. O.
  [concealed] TA. I. 8. O.
Absurd.
  [foolish] HA. VI. 2. D.
  [not congruous] T. V. 5.
Abundance, TM. I. 2. E.
Abuse, [Use, TA. V. 6. (corr.)]
  [speak Injuriously] RJ. IV. 1.
Abusiveness.
  [proneness to abuse.]
  [scurrility] Man. IV. 9. E.
Abutt [v. Margin,] Sp. III. 4. A.
Abysse [Deep] TM. II. 3. (aug.)
Academy, RC. III. 6.
Acara, Fi. V. 8. A.
Accelerate.
  [a. Swift] NP. V. 9.
  [a. Soon] Sp. I. 4.

A C

Accent, D. I. 9.
Accept, TA. IV. 4. A.
Acceptable.
  [adj. p. Accept,] TA. IV. 4. A.
  sp. [apt.]
  [delighting] AS. IV. 7.
Acception of a word.
  [meaning] D. II. A.
Access.
  [v. Come] TA. VI. 1.
  [power   a
   leave   of   to come.]
   opportunity   p
Accessary, TM. IV. 4. O.
Accident.
  op. to Subst. T. I. 5. O.
  [adj. Contingent] T. V. 8. O. (thing.)
  [adj. Fortune] AS. I. 2. D. (thing.)
  sp. Event. TA. V.
Acclamation. AC. III. 3. O.
  [Exclamation through Joy of Praise]
Accommodate.
  [a. Congruous, T. V. 6. (make)
  [a. Means] T. II. 6. O.
  [a. Provision] Pr.
Accompany.
  [v. Companion] RO. IV. 2.
  [v. Being, T. I. 1.   with or
  [v. Going, TA. VI.   together]
Accomplish.
  [a. Perfect] T. III. 9. (make)
  [Perform] TA. III. 6.
  [Finish] TA. III. 7.
Accord.
  [a. Assent] AS. II. 3.
  [a. Congruous] T. V. 5.
  Of one—
  [with simultaneous Spontaneity]
  Of ones own—
  [adv. Spontaneous,] AS. IV. 9
According.
  [adv. Congruous,] T. V. 5.
  —*as,* Adv. I. 3.
  —*to,* Prep. II. 1.
Accordingly, Adv. I. 3. O.
Accost.
  [a. Near] Sp. II. 5.
  [Address] AC. V. 2.
  [Salute] AC. V. 3.
Accompting.
  [Reckoning] TA. IV. 6.
  [Esteeming] AS. II. 8.
Accoutred.
  [Clothed] Pr. IV.
  [Armamented] Pr. IV. A.
Accrue.
  [p. Effect] T. II. O.
  [v. Event] TA. V.

A a 2   Accu-

AC — AD — AD

Accumulate, [a. Heap] O. II. 6.
Accurate. adj. Perfect. T. III. 9.
Accurse [Curse] AS. I. 3. O.
Accuse.
  [as Informer] R J. I. 3.
  [as Plaintiff] R J. I. 4.
  —*falsly*, a. Calumny. R J. IV. 7.
Accustom. a. Custom. RC.IV. 1.A.
  —*to doe*, &c. *a. do*, &c. (frequent)
Ace.
  [One,] Mea. II. 1.
  [Point] Mag. I. 1.
Acerbity. Q. IV. 3. A.
Ach [Pain] N P. V. 3. O.
Achieve.
  [a. Perfect] T. III. 9.
  [Perform] TA. III. 6.
  [a. Action] T. 1. 7.
Acid. Q. IV. 4.
Acknowledge.
  [Assent] AS. II. 3.
  [Concession] D. VI. 3.A.
  [Confess] D. VI. 9.
Aconite. (Wooly's-bane)
  Winter. FS. I. 3.
Acorn [Mast of the Oke.]
Acquaint. [Know (make)]
Acquaintance. RO. IV. 4.
Acquiesce.
  [v. Rest.] Mo. O.
  [v. Content] Ha. I. 3.
Acquire.
  [Obtain] TA. V. 1.
  [Gain] TA. V. 2.
Acquitting.
  —*of debt*. TA. IV. 9.
  —*of guilt*. R J. II. 7.
Acre. [Area of 160 Pole square.]
Acrimony. Q. IV. 2. O.
Act.
  [Action] T. I. 7.
  [Chapter] (as an act in a Play) D. III. 3. .
  [Law] RC. IV. 3.
  [Edict] R C. IV. 3. A.
  [real existence] T. III. 5.
  to—a. Action.
  —*in a Play*. RC. III. 9.
Action. T. 1. 7.
Spiritual—AS
  —*of God*. AS. I.
  —*of the Speculative Understanding*. AS. II.
  —*of the Practical Understanding*. AS. III.
  —*of the Will*. AS. IV.
Corporeal—AC.
  —*of Vegetative*. AC. I.
  —*of Sensitive*. AC. II.
  —*of Man*. AC. III.
  [Gesture] AC. VI. A.
  Judicial—R J. II.
  [Suit] R J. II. A.
Active.
  [adj. Action (apt.)]
  [adj. Business, (apt.)]
  [adj. Nimbleness] N P. V. 8.
Actual. T. III. 5.
Acus Aristotelis, Fi. VIII. 5.
Acute.
  Sharp. [adj. cut, (apt)]
  —*angle*. Mag. III. 3. O.

[Intense] T M. I. 8. E.
[Sprightly] N P. IV. 2.
—*Sound*. Q. III. 1. E.
[Sagacious] Ha. III. 1.
Adage D. V. 1. A.
Adamant [Diamond] St. IV. 1.
Adapt.
  [a. Proportion (perf.)]
  [a. Congruous.]
Add.
  [*to*——}
  together——} put.]
  [adj. Sum (make)]
  [adj. Aggregate, (make)]
  [Find   } Sum
  [reckon } Aggregate]
Adder, [Viper] Be. VI. 7. A.
  —*s Bit*. Ex. IV. 7.
  —*s Tongue*. H L. I. 9. A.
Addict.
  [Cuting } Hammer— } of Barrel
            Instrument } (mech.)
Addict. [v. Incline { naturally }
                      { habitually }]
Addition. T M. VI. 6. vid. *Add*.
Addle [Putrid] N P. V. 2.
Address. A C. V. 2.
Adequate. adj. Equality. T M. I. 5.
Adhere. T A. II. 2.
Adherent, [adj. a. TA. II. 2.]
  [Accessary] TM. IV. 4. O.
Adjacent.
  [Margining] Sp. III. 4. A.
  [Near] Sp. II. 3.
Adjective. D. II. 3. O.
Adieu, [Valediction.] AC. V. 8. O.
Adjoin.
  [Join] TA. II. 1.
  [Margin] Sp. III. 4. A.
  [Near] Sp. II. 3.
Adjourn.
  [discontinue till a set day]
  [a. Late. Sp. I. 4. O.] by discontinuing. T M. III.
Adjudge to—a. Sentence. R J. II. 5. A.
Adjunct. T. VI. 1. O.
Adjure.
  [a. Swear] R C. VI. 4. (make)
  [Entreat   } for God's sake.
  Command }
Adjust.
  [a. Equal] T M. I. 5. (make)
  [a. Congruous] T. V. 5. (make)
  [Balance] TA. IV. 6. A.
Adjutant. R M. III. 4. A.
Adjuvant. T. II. 5.
Administer.
  [Serve]
  [Yield] TA. IV. 1.
  [Give] TA. IV. 4.
Administration, [Vice-Executorship to—sentenced.]
  Male—Man. VI. 5.
Admiral, [Navy (Officer.)]
Admiring. A S. V. L
Admit.
  [Permit] (p. to enter.)
  [Concession] D. VI. 3. A.
  [Allow of]
Admonish, Warn. RO. V. 4. A.

Adolescence. Me. VI. 2.
Adonis-flower. H F. IX. 5.
Adoe, [Endeavour.] T A. III. 4.
Adopt, [instead-a. child, RO.I. 2. O. (make)
Adore, [worship.] RE. IV.
Adorn, [a. ornate.] T M. V. 5.
Advance.
  [go forward] R M. II. 2. E.
  [a. Direct. Mag.II.8.E.(make)
  [a. Lift] O. I. 1. A.
  [a. Upper] Sp. III. 5.
  [a. Superiority
  [a. High] T M.   } TM.I.5.E.
  II. 4.   } RO.III.
  [Prefer. [a. Dignity.] M. II. 5.
Advantage.
  [Superiority] T M. 1. 5. E.
  [Gain] TA. V. 2.
  [Occasion] T. II. 4. A.
Advent, [to-Coming.] TA. VI. 1.
Adventitious.
             { Intention } Sp.
  [besides] { Expectation } Ca-
             { tion.   } sual.]
  [Accessory] TM. IV. 4. O.
Adventure.
  [Contingency] T. V. 7. O.
  [Fortune] AS. I. 2. D.
  [Essay] TA. III. 4. A.
  [Danger] T. V. 3. O.
  [Out-sent, adj. Commerce (thing)
  At-[without fear of the event.]
Adverb.
  [Derived. D. II. 4.
  Underived. D. II. 9.
Adverse.
  [Opposite] T. VI. 8. O.
  [Contrary] T. V. 5. O.
  [Enemy] RO. IV. 1. O.
  [Adversity] Ha. I. 2. O.
Adversary, [Enemy] RO. IV. 1. O.
Adversity. Ha. I. 2. O.
Advert, [observe] AS. III. 1. A.
Advertise.
  [Know, AS. II. 5. (make)
  [Warn] RO. V. 4. A.
Advise.
  Giving—[a. Advice.] RO.V. 4.
  Taking—[p. Advice.] RO.V. 4.
Advised. [adj. p. Advice.]
  [adj. Considerate] Ha. IV. 1.
  [adj. Heedful] Ha. IV. 2.
Adulation, [Fawning] Man. IV. 7. E.
Adult, [adj. Adolescence.] Me. VI. 2.
Adulterate, [Forgery] R J. IV. 4. A.
Adultery. R J. IV. 2. A.
Adumbrate, [a. Shadow.] Q. I. 2. O.
Advocate.
  [Pleader] R J. I. 7.
  [Mediator] R J. I. 2. A.
Advowson, [Right R C. IV. of future giving Presbyters (place)]
Adust. [adj. p. preter. Fire.]
Afar. [adv. Remote.] Sp. II. 3. O.
Affable. [adj. Man. VI. 3.]
                              [adj.

AG | AL | AL

[adj. Courtefie] Man. IV. 7.
Affair.
[adj. p. fut. Do (thing)
[Bufinefs] TA. III.
[Thing] T. I. 2.
Affect.
[v. Affectation.]
[v. Affection.]
[Delight] AS. IV. 7.
Affectation., [Conceitednefs.]
HA. III. 3. O.
—of *Empire* [Ambition.]
MA. III. 9. D.
Affection.
Paffion, AS. V. & AS. VI.
[Defire] AS. V. 4.
[Love] AS. V. 2.
Affiance.
[Betrothing] RO. II. 3.
[Confidence] AS. V. 6.
Affidavit, [Sworn Teftimony.]
R J. I. 7. A.
Affinity. RO. II.
Affirming, D. VI. 2.
Affix [to { faften.
             { Put.]
Afflict, [a. Adverfity,] Ha. I. 2. O.
Affluence, [Abundance.] TM. II. 2. F.
Afford, [permit to have.]
[Yield] TA. IV. 1.
[Grant] D. VI. 3. A.
[Give] TA. IV. 4.
[Sell] RC. V. 3.
Affraid, [adj. Fear.] AS. V. 5. O.
Affront, RJ. IV. 1. A.
Afresh.
{ New. Sp. I. 3.
[adv. { Repeated. TA. II. 6.
[again] Adv. IV. 2.
After.
[op. to before]
[behind] Prep. V. 3. O.
[adv. Pofterior]
[adv. Follow]
[According to]
As by patern. Prep. II. 1.
[adv. Congruous to]
—*Birth*, [fecundine.] PP. VI. 7. A.
—*Noon*, [after—adj. noon. (time.
—*Time*, [adj. Future.] Sp. I. 1. D. (Time.)
Again. Adv. IV. 2.
[adv. p repeating.] TA. II. 6.
Againft. Prep. II 3. O.
*Over—*Prep. VI. 3. O.
Agaric, [Fungus of Larix-tree.]
Agaft, [adj. Fear. AS. V. 5. O. (augm.]
Agat. St. II. 1. A.
Age.
[Life-time] Mea. VI.
of what—[adj. preter. Age, how many years?]
under—[of Pupillar age.]
of full—[Un-pupilled by Age]
[adj. præt. Adolefcence.]
middle-[Manhood.] Me. VI. 3.
*Declining—*Mea. VI. 3. A
*Old—*Mea. VI. 4.

*Decrepit—*Mea. VI. 4. A.
[Generation] Mea. VI. A.
Agent.
[adj. a. Action. (perfon)
[pro—adj. Bufinefs, TA. III.
{ (Officer.)
{ (Perfon.)
Aggravate.
[a. Great] TM. I. 1. E.
[a. Intenfion] TM. I. 8. E.
Aggregate. TM. III. 6. O.
Agility.
Nimble, NP. V. 8.
[Swift] NP. V. 9.
Agitate
[Move] Mo. (freq.)
[Drive] TA. VI. 5. O.
[Swing] Mo. VI. 3.
[a. vice-bufinefs. TA. III.
Aglet, [round Lamin. (dim.)
Agnus-Caftus. Sh. I. 6. A.
Agoe, [adv. Paft.] Sp. f. 1. E.
Agony, AS. VI. 8.
{ Grief
{ Anger } (Impetus.)
Agree.
[v. Congruous] T. V. 5.
[a. Contract] RC. V.
—*to*
[Confent] AS. II. 3.
[Grant] D. VI. 3. O.
—*together*, V. Man. IV. 3.
Agreeable.
[Congruous] T. V. 5.
[Expedient.] T. V. 6.
Agriculture. O. III.
Agrimony, HF. VIII. 3.
*Dutch—*HF. III. 8.
Aground { on earth
           { contiguous to the
Ague, S. II. 1. A. (earth.)
                    { Love.
Ab, Interject. fp. { Sorrow.
                    { Defire.
                    { Infinuation.
Ay, [adv. Ever.] Sp. I. 1.
Aid, [Adjuvant.] T. II. 5.
Ail.
[v. Paffion] T. I. 7. O.
[v. Import.] NP. V. O.
[v. Want] TA. I. 5. O.
Aim.
[Object] T. VI. 2.
[End] T. II. 6.
Air, El. II.
Ethereal, El. II. 1.
—*of face*, [Figure, (modus)
           { Tune.]
Wood, [Maple tuberous (augm.)
—*to—abroad*, [put in the Air.]
Airy.
[adj. Air.]
[Wanton] NP. IV. 3. O.
[Conceited] Ha. III. 3. O.
—*of Hawks.* { Younglings
             (aggreg.) of Hawks.
Ake, AC. II. 7.
Akorn, [Maft of the Oke.]
Alabafter, St. II. 1.
Alacrity, Ha. IV. 3.
Alarm.

[Arming (fign)
[Affaulting (fign)]
Alafs, Interject. II. 1.
Alate, [Paft. Sp. I. 1. E. (dim.)
Alaternus, Sh. IV. 4.
Albeit, [Although.] Conj. II. 2.
Alchimy, [Chimic.] O. VI.
Alcoran, [Scripture of Mahometans.]
Alcyon [King-fifher.] Bi. III. 9.
Alder, Tr. V. 3.
Berry bearing, —Sh. II. 7.
Alderman, [Affeffor of Corporation (Officer.)
Ale, Pr. I. 7.
Ale-coft, HF. II. 4.
Ale-hoof, [Ground-Ivy] HL. VI. 11.
Ale-houfe, [adj. Selling (houfe) of Ale.]
Alembick, [adj. Diftillation (veffel.)
Alexander, HF. IV. 4.
Algebra, [adj. Invention (art) in quantity (Science.)
Alien, [Foreiner.] RO. IV. 3. O.
Alienate, Po. O. (felf.)
[un—a. Proprietary from him.
[a. Stranger] RO. IV. 4. O.
Alight.
[un—{ Ride]
     { Sit]
Down-go] TA. VI.
Alike.
[adv. Like.] TM. V. 1.
[adv. Equal] TM. I. 5.
Aliment, [adj. Nutrition. AC. I. 6. (thing)
Alimony, [Proportioned (thing) for Provifions.]
Alifanders, HF. IV. 4.
Alive, [adj. AC. I. 7.]
—*Cole*, [n. adj. Fire cole.]
Alkakengi, [Winter-cherry.]
HS. IX. 8.
Alkanet, HL. IX. 2.
All, Pron. V. 3.
at—[adv. Any.]
—*be it*
—*though* } Conj. II. 2.
—*one*, [Equal.] TM. I. 5.
—*ready*, vid. *Already.*
—*together*,
[adv. Total] TM. VI.
[adv. Aggregate] TM. III. 6. O.
[adv. Perfect] TM. III. 9.
—*waies* { in } { all (times)
         { adv.}
Sp. in all times when it ought to be.]
Allay.
[a. Remifs] TM. I. 8. D.
[a. Little] TM. I. 1. D.
[v. more-remifs, &c.]
Allege.
[a. Argumentation.]
[a. Quotation.]
Allegiance.
[Loyalty] Man. V. 6.
[Duty of Subjection.]
Allegory, [continued Trope,] fp. Metaphor.]
Alley. A a a 2 Nar-

AL — AM — AN

{ Street }
[narrow { Way }
{ Area }
All-heal, H F. V. 8.
Hercules—H F.IV. 10.
Alligator [Crocodile] Be. VI. 3.
Ally, vid. *Alliance*.
Alliance.
 [League] RC. III. 8.
 [Affinity] RO. II.
Alloy { Stiffen
 { un-price } by mixture]
Allot, [Appoint { Measure
 { Proportion }]
Allow.
 [Appoint] { Measure
 [Permit] {p.} { Proportion
 [Stipendiate] RO. VI. 4. A.
 [Give] TA. IV. 4.
 [Yield] TA. IV. 1.
 [Grant] D. VI. 3. A.
 [Approve] AS. III. 3.
 [Consent] AS. II. 3.
Allowance.
 [appointed] { Measure
 [Permitted] { Proportion
 [Stipend] RO. VI. 4. A.
 [Maintenance] RO. VI. 4.
Allude, [a. Allusion.] D. IV. 9. A.
Allure. RO. V. 5.
Allusion. D. IV. 9. A.
Almanack, [adj. Year-book, of pl. Series of Daies, of every Month.]
Almes, [adj. p. Almsgiving (thing) —giving.
 the Virtue, Man. III. 5.
 the Act, [a. Almsgiving.] Man. III. 1.
Almicantar, W. VI. 7. A.
Almighty, [all-adj. Power.] Ha. II. 6.
Almner, [Alms (officer)
Almond.
 Tree, Tr. IV. 1. A.
 Fruit, Tr. IV. 1. A. (Fruit)
 [Glandule] PG. II. 7.
 Place of them, PG. III. 9. A.
Almost. Adv. V. 1.
Aloe.
 Herb, HL. VIII. 1. A.
 Tree, Tr. VIII. 1.
Aloft [Adv. High.] TM. II. 4.
Alone.
 [Solitary] RO. IV. 2. O.
 [Only] Adv. IV. 1. O.
Along.
 [on this side] Prep. VI. 2.
 [beside] Prep. V. 3. O.
 [adv. p. continue.]
 all— [adv. Lying] AC. VI. 7. A.
Aloof [adv. Remote.] Sp. II. 3. O.
Aloud [adv. Sound. Q. III. (aug.)
Alpe [Bullfinch] Bi. III. 5.
Alphabet { Series } of Letters.
 { Catalogue }
Already.
 [having been before]
 [adv. preter. Past.] Sp. I. 1. E.
 [which is now]
 [before this time]
Also. Conj. IV. 1.

Altar, Sacrificing (place.) Po. II. 4. A.
Alter, [Change.] TA. II. 6. A.
Altercation, [Contentiousness.] Man. IV. 3; D.
Alternation, [Turn.] T. VI. 7.
Althæa, HF. IX. 7.
Altitude, [Height.] T M. II. 4.
Alum. St. V. 2.
Am.
 [v. Being] T. I. 1.
 Copula.
Amain, [adv. Intension.] T M. I. 8. E.
Amalgama, Mingle with Quick-filver.
Amaranthus. [Princes Feather] HF. I. 15. A.
Amass, [a. Heap.] Q. II. 6.
Amate, [a. Fear.] AS. V. 6. O.
Amaze.
 [a. Extasie] AS. VI. 8. A.
 [a. Stupor] NP. II. 1. O.
 with admiration, AS. V. 1.
Ambages, [about—Wandring Speeches.]
Ambassage.
 [Political RC.Sending]TA.VI.4.
Amber. St. II. 8. A.
 —gris. St. V. 9.
Ambient.
 [about the outside]Sp.III.6.O.
 [adj. Periphery]
Ambiguous, [adj. p. abst. Doubt.]
 [adj. Equivocation.]
Ambition, Man. III. 9. E.
Ambling, Mo.II.2.
Ambodexter.
 [using equally all his hands.]
 [seeming of all parties.]
Ambulatory, [adj Walk] Mo.II.1
Ambush, BM. I. 9. A.
Amen [it } Imper. { Being
 } { Copula.]
Amend, [v. Better.] TM. I. 9. E.
 make—s [v. compens.] TA. II. 7. A.
Amerce, [Mulct] R J. VI. 7.
Amethyst, St. IV. 6.
Amia. Fi. V. 1.
Amiable [adj. p. Love (abstr.]
Amicable, [adj. a. Friend.] RO. IV. 1
Amiss. adv.
 [adv. } Evil.] T. III, 2 O,
 { Err.] TA. III. 8.
 Trance. (corruptive)
Amity, [a.Friend.RO.IV.1(abst.)
Ammi, [Bishops-weed.] HF. V. 4. A.
Ammunition, RM. V.
Amomum.
Among, [betwixt.] Prep. VI. 3.
Amorous, [adj.a Love. AS. V. 3. (Abstr.)
Amort, [adj. Grief. AS. V. 4. O. (impetus)
Amount, [p. Sum.] TM. VI. 6. A
Amphibious, [Inhabiting Land and Water.]
Amphiboly, [Doubtfulness of sense.]

Amphitheatre, [Round building for Shews.]
Ample.
 Wide, Sp. II. 5.
 [Great] TM. I. 1. E.
 [Broad] TM. II. 2.
Ampliation. D. IV. 2. O.
Amplifie, a. D. IV. 2. O.
Amulet, [adj. a. Physitian (thing) with—adj. p. carry (abstr.) adj. hang at neck, &c.]
An. Article. I.
Anabaptist, [Rebaptizing Schismatic.]
Anacardium. Tr. IV. 8. A.
Anagram, [Play of changing the orders of Letters.]
Analem, [Representing (thing) by lines; sp. of the Sphere imaginary.]
Analogy, [Proportion.] Me. O.
Analysis, [Artificial Segregation.]
Anarchy. RC. O.
Anas Campestris Bellonii. Bi. II. 4. A.
Anatheme, [Excommunication.] RE. V. 5.
Anatomy.
 Cutting up, [Segregation by cutting.]
 Body cut up, [Body segregated by cutting.]
Ancestor, [Progenitor.] RO. L. 1.
Anchor. RN. III. 9.
Anchorite, [Hermit. RE. II. 7. A. circumseptimented.]
Anchove. Fi. III. 12.
Ancient.
 [adj. Old] Sp. I. 3. O.
 [adj. Old-age.] Mea. VI. 4.
 [Ensign] RM. III. 2.
 —of Ship. RN. III. 7. A.
Anckle, [Protuberant end of the Leg-bone.]
Ancome, [Porous bile.]
And, Conj. I. 2.
Andiron. [Fewel-supporting (Instrument.]
Anemony, HF. IX. 3.
Aneuresma. S. III. 8. A.
Anew.
 [adv. } New. Sp. I. 3.
 } Repeat.TA. II. 6.
 [again] Adv. IV. 2.
Angel.
 [Spirit] W. I. 2.
 Good—W. I. 2.
 Bad—W. I. 2. O.
 In money, Mea. IV. 4.
 Fish, [Scate] Fi. II. 5.
Angelica. HF. IV. 5.
Anger. AS. V. 9.
 vitions—Man. I. 9. D.
Angle. Mag. III. 2. O.
 right—Mag. III. 3.
 obtuse—Mag. III. 3; E.
 acute—Mag. III. 3. D.
 to—[Hunt Fish with Wand and Line.]
Anguish.
 [Anxiety.] Ha. I. 3. O.
 [Pain] NP. V. 3. O. (augm.)
 [Grief]

AN | AP | AP

[Grief] AS. V. 4. O. (augm.)
[Trouble] TA. V. 9. O. (aug.)
Angular, [adj. Angle.] Mag. III. 2. O.
Any.
  the particular, Pron. II. 3. O.
  the Indefinite, Pron. III. 1.
  —*whither*, [to any (place)
  —*where*, [in any (place.)
Animadversion, [Observation.] AS. III. 1. A.
Animal. W. V. 4.
Animate parts of the world. W.V. 1. O. —[Encourage] RO. VI. 2.
Animosity {old } anger.]
  {perverse}
Aniseed. HF. IV. 1.
Ankle, vid. *Anckle.*
Annals, [adj. Year (segr.)] History
Annats [Tribute out of the Years Revenue.]
Annex, [to- joyn] TA. II. 1.
Annihilate. AS. I. 1. O.
Anniversary. [adj. Year (segr.) sp. Solemnity.]
Annoy.
  [a. Hurt] T. V. 1. O.
  [a. Trouble] TA. V. 9. O.
Annotations, [Comment.] D. V. 6. D.
Annual, [adj. Year (segreg.)]
Annuity.
  [adj. year (segr.)] {Paiment.
  {Rent.}
  {Stipend.}
Annull.
  [a. Nothing] T. I. 1. O.
  [Annihilate] AS. I. 1. O.
  [un-do]
Annulet, Mag. V. 2. (dim.)
Annunciation, [Narration] D. V. 3.
Anoint, [smear] O. V. 6. A.
Anomalous.
  [not- (adj. p.) Rule] D. IV. 5.
  [exorbitant]
Anon, [Adv. Futur. Sp. I, 1. O.]
Anonymous, [not- (adj. p.) name.] T. I. 4.
Another. Pron. V. I. & diff. T. III.
Answer. D. VI. 1. O.
  —*able.*
  [adj. Congruity] T. V. 5.
  [adj. Fut. Reckoning] TA. IV. 6.
Ant. EX. IV. 5.
  —*bear,* Be. V. 5.
Antagonist.
  [Enemy] RO. IV. 1. O,
  [Contrary] T. V. 5. O.
  [Oppofite] T. VI. 8. O.
Antarctic.
  —*Circle.* W. VI. 5. O.
  —*Pole.* [adj. South pole.]
Antecedent, [Preceding.] Sp. I. 2. E.
Antedate, [before- a. date.] Sp. I. 5.
Anthem. RE. IV. 2. A.
St. *Anthony's fire,* [Eryfipelas.] S. II. 7. A.

Antic, [Old] {Corrupt.}
  Sp. I. 3. O. {Manner.}
Antichrift, G. 2. O.
Anticipate.
  [Prevent] TA. III. 9.
  [v. Soon] Sp. I. 4. E.
Antidote, [adj. againft- poyson (thing.)
Antilope, [goat (kind) having ftraight wreathed horns.]
Antimony, Met. III. 2.
Antipathy, [natural Averfation.] AS. V. 5. O.
Antiperiftafis, [Refiftance of contrary quality.]
Antipodes, [Over againft- fited in the remoteft parts of the Globe diametrically oppofite]
Antiquary, [Learned (Artift) in Old (things.)
Antiquated, [Annull'd by being un-cuftom'd.]
Antique, vid. *Antic.*
Antiquity.
  [Oldnefs] Sp. I. 3. O.
  [Old-age] Me. VI. 4.
Antithefis, [Oppofition.] T. VI. 8. O. (thing)
Antitype, [typed. T. II. 3. A.
Anvil, [the Iron (fupporting (Inftr.) of the hammered (thing.)
Anxiety, HA. I. 3. O.
Apace, [adv. Swift.] NP. V. 9.
Apart.
  [adv. Segregate] TM. III. 6.
  Transf. (Segreg.)
Ape. Be. III. 1. A.
Aper, Fi. IV. 9. A.
Aphorifm.
  [brief Rule] D. IV. 5.
  [Authentic sentence] D. III. 1. A.
Aphua gobites. Fi. III. 9.
Apocryphal, [doubtfully authoriz'd.]
Apologue.
  [Fictitious example]
  [Inftructive Fiction]
Apology, [Plea.] R J. II. 3. A.
Apophthegm, [wife Sentence.]
Apoplexy. S. IV. 3. A.
Aporrhais. EX. VII. 3. A.
Apoftafie. RE. III. 6. O.
Apoftem. S. I. 6. A.
Apoftle. RE. II. 3.
Apothecary. O. VI. A.
Appale.
  [a. Pale. AC. IV. 9. O.]
  [a. Fear. AS. V. 6. O.]
Apparel. Pr. IV.
Apparence.
  [feeming] TA. I. 9. A.
  —*at Law.* R J. II. 2. A.
  [ens apparens] T. I. 2. O.
Apparent.
  [adj. Seeming] TA. I. 9. A.
  [adj. Manifest] TA. I. 9.
Apparition, [p. See of Spirits..
Apparitor, [adj. a. Citation, R J. II. 1. (Officer.)
Appartment. Po. III. 2. A.

Appeal. R J. II. 8. A.
Appear.
  [v. as Thing] T. I. 2. O.
  [v. Manifeft] TA. I. 9.
  [v. Seeming] TA. I. 9. O.
  [—*Judicially*] R J. II. 2. A.
Appearing Meteor. El. V.
Appeafe, [un-— a. Anger] AS. V. 9.
Appendage, [adj. Acceffary. (thing.) TM. IV. 4. O.
Appertein, [v. Pertinence.] TM. IV. 5.
Appetite. NP. II. 4.
Applaud.
  {Commend. RO. V. 7. (fign.)
  {Praife. RO. V. 8. (augm.)
Apple.
  Tree, Tr. I. 1.
  Fruit, PP. III. 1.
  Thorn.— HS. VII. 7. A.
  —*of Love.* HS. IX. 2.
  Adams,— Tr. I. 7. A.
  Mad— HS. IX. 2. A.
  —*of the Eye* [Black (part) of the Eye.
Apply. TA. II. 3.
  [Together-joyn] TA. I. 1.
Appoint.
  [Intend] AS. IV. 3.
  [Defign] TA. III. 1.
  [a. Command] RO. V. 1.
Appofite
  {Congruous. T. V. 5.
  {Pertinent. TM. IV. 5.
Apprehend.
  [understand] NP. L. 1.
  [a. common Senfe] NP. II. 1.
  [a. Opinion] AS. II. 6. O.
  [arreft] R J. II. 1. A.
Apprentice.
  [Learner. RO. {Merchant.}
  III. 3. O   {Mechanic.}
Approch, [v. Near.] Sp. II. 3.
Approbation. AS. III. 3.
Appropriate. TA. I. 2.
  [a. Proper, T M. IV. 6. (make)
Approve. AS. III. 3.
Appurtenance.
  [Pertinent] TM. IV. 5.
  [Acceffory] TM. IV. 4. O.
Apricock. Tr. II. 2.
April, [the fourth Month.]
Apron, [hanging (Veft) before the Belly.]
Apt.
  Transf. (abftr.)
  [adj. Congruous] T. V. 5.
  [adj p. Difpofition] HA. O.
Aptitude.
  [Congruity] T. III. 5.
  [Sagacity] Ha. III. 1.
  [Alacrity]
  [Difciple (abftr.)
Aquarius, [11th. of the 12 parts of the Zodiac.]
Aqueduct. Po. II. 8. A.
Aquila, Fi. II. 1. A.
Aquofity, [Water (abftr.)]
Arable, Po I. 4.
Aray.   [Cloath]

AR

[Cloath] Pr. IV.
[Order] TM. V. 2.
Arbalist, [adj. a. Crosbow. RM. V. 4. A. (person)
Arbitrary, [adj. Liberty.] AS. IV. 8.
Arbitrator. R] I. 2.
Arbitrement, v. R] I. 2.
Arbor [Room of Trees.]
Arbutus, [Strawberry Tree] Sh. III. 4.
Arch [Principal.]
  an Arch, Po. III. 6. A.
  —*of Circle*, [part of adj. Circle-line.]
Archangel, [Principal Angel.]
  dead Nettle, HF. VIII. 10.
Archbishop, [Primat.] RE. II. 4.
Archdeacon, [Bishops Substitute.]
Archer, [adj. a. Bow. RM. V. 4. (person.)
Architecture, [a. Buildings. (Art.)
Architrave, [Chief beam.]
Archives, [Store (place) of old Writings.]
Arctic, [adj. North.]
  —*Circle*, W. VI. 5.
  —*Pole*, [adj. North pole.]
Ardent,
  [adj. Fire] El. I.
  [adj. Heat, Q. V. 1. E. (aug.]
  [adj. Zeal] AS. VI. 1.
Area, [Surface.] Mag. I. 3.
Argent, [of Silver Colour.]
Argue. v. D. IV. 6.
Argument,
  [Matter] T. II. 7.
  [Object] T. VI. 2.
  [adj. a. Argumentation, D. IV. 8. (thing.)
Arid, [Dry.] Q. V. 2. D.
Aries, [first of the 12 parts of the Zodiac.]
Aright,
  Transc. (Perf.)
  [adv. Good] T. III. 2.
Arise. AC. VI. 1.
  as Sun [above- adj. Horizon (incept.)
  as Hill [upward- Oblique.] Mag. II. 8.
Aristocracy, [Government by the Nobles.]
Aristolochy, [Birth-wort.]
Arithmetic, [Numbring (art)]
Ark, [Box.] Pr. V. 2.
Arm.
  —*of Man*, PG. V. 1.
  —*of the Sea*. [Bay.]
  —*of a Tree*, [Branch.] PP. I. 3.
  to—[Arms.]
Armada, [Army of Ships.]
Armadillo, Be. V. 5. A.
Armament. Pr. IV. 2.
Army, RM. IV. 1.
Armor, Arms defensive, RM. V. 1. A.
Armorer, [Arms (mechanic.)]
Armory, [Arms (place.)]
Arms,
  offensive [Weapons] RM. V. I.
  defensive. RM. V. 1. A.

AS

man at—— [armed (pst) Horse-man.]
  as in a Scutcheon [adj. Degree RG. I. (sign) picture.]
Aromatic. [adj. Spice.] Pr. II. 4.
Arquebus, [RM. V. 6. (augm.)]
Array, vid. Aray.
Arraign, [a. Bill.] R] II. 3.
Arrant, [Genuin.] T. III. 4.
Arras, [Room (vest) weaved picture (like.)]
Arrear, [Residue Debt.]
Arrest R] II. 1. A.
Arrive, [to- come.] TA. VI. 1.
Arrogance,
  [Pride] Man. V. 2. O.
  Magisterialness [Man. IV. 8. D.
  Superciliousness [Man. VI. 3. O.
Arrogate, [Claim.] TA. I. 3.
Arrow. RM. V. 5. A.
  —*head*. HS. VI. 1. A.
Arse, [Buttock.] PG. IV. 6.
Arsenal, [Ammunition (place.)]
Arsenick. St. VI. 4. A.
Arsmart. HF. VIII. 6.
  codded—HS. VIII. 9.
Art. Ha VI. 2.
Artemisia, [Mugwort.] HF. II. 2. A.
Artery. PG. IL 4. A.
  rough—[Wind-pipe] PG. VI. 1. A.
Artichoke. HF. III. 1. A.
Article.
  [Section] D. III. 2. A.
  [Pact] RC. VI. A.
  [adj. Accusation, R J. I. 3. (thing)
  as, A. Th. D. II. 8. A.
Articulate. III. 3. A.
Artificer. RC. II. 5. A.
Artificial.
  [adj. Art] Ha. VI. 3.
  [Factitious] T. III. 7. O.
Artillery, [Ordnance.] RM. V. 6. A. (aggreg.)
Artist, [adj. Art. Ha. VI. 3. (person.)
Artizan. RC. II. 5. A.
As,
  opp. to So, Adv. I. 3.
  —{ Ear
  —{ Long }—
  —{ Much
  .So { far } { far
      long } how { long
      much } { much
  —*for*, [concerning] Prep. I. 3. O.
  —*for example*, [ex. gr.] Con. IV. 3. O.
  —*if*
  —*it were*] Adv. III. 2. O.
  —*though*]
  where—
  for—*much*—{ Conj. IV. 1.
  whilst] adv. III. 1.
Asarabacca HL. V. 6.
Ascarides. Ex. I. 3.
Ascend, [upward. Prep. V. 1. Ition. TA. 6.]
Ascertain, [v. Certain. AS. II. 5.

AS

A. (make.)
Ascribe,
  [a. Predicate] D. II. 8. O.
  [Claim] TA. I. 3.
Ash. Tr. VI. 5.
  —*colour*, [adj. ashes. El. IV. 3. (colour.)
Ashamed, [adj. Shame.] AS. VI. 2. A.
Ashes. El. IV. 3.
Ashore, [on- shore]
Aside.
  [adv. { Separation] TA. II. 1. O
        { Solitary] RO. IV. 2. O.
        { Rejection] AS. IV. 5. O.
  Lay—*or* { 5. O.
  cast— { Desist] AS. IV. 6. O.
         { Intermit]
Asilus. Ex. I. 4. A.
Ask,
  { Enquire [a. Question.] D. VI. 1.
  Require { Necessary }
          { Expedient } make]
  Entreat] RO. V. 3.
  Beg, [a. Begger.] RC. I. 8. A.
  Demand.
  as price, RC. VI. 2. O.
  as due, TA. IV. 2. A.
  [Command] RO. V. 1.
Askew, [adj. Oblique] Mag. II. 8.
Asleep, [adj. Sleep,]AC. II. 3. O.
  numb'd, [adj. p. Stupor], NP. II. 1. O.
Aslope, [Oblique] Mag. II. 8.
Asp.
  Serpent, [Viper] Be. VI. 7. A.
  Tree, [White poplar] Tr. VI. 7. A.
Asparagus. HL. IX. 6.
Aspect, [Face, PG. III. 1. (manner)
Asperity,
  [roughness] Q. VI. 2. D.
  austereness] Man. VI. 8. O.
Aspersion, [Calumny] R] IV. 7.
Asphodel, [Kings-spear] HL. V. 1.
Aspiration, [Respiration. Mo. III. 2. (Impetus.)
Aspire [a. Ambition.] Man. III. 9. E.
Asquint, [Oblique (corrupt) Vision (manner)
Ass Be. I. 2.
Assa foetida, [the gum of Lazar-wort.]
Assay,
  [Essay] TA. III. 4. A.
  Endeavour] TA. III. 4.
Assail, [Assault.] RM. I. 3.
Assassin, [a. Murther, RL III. 4. sp. under pretence of Religion.]
Assault, RM. I. 3.
Assemble, [a. Convention.] RC. III.
Assent. AS. II. 3.
Assentation, [Fawning.] Man. IV. 8. E.
Assertion, [Affirmation.] D. VI. 2.
Assess,
  [a. Tax] RC. V. 9. O.
  [Impose, adv. Proportion.]
  Assessor.

AT

Assessor.
—in Judgment, RJ. I. 1. A.
—of Taxes, [v. Assess (Officer)
Asseveration, [Affirmation. D. VI. 2. (augm.)
Assiduity, [Diligence.] Ha. IV. 5.
Assign.
Transfer right. RC. V. 1.
[Design] TA. III. 1.
Assimilate, [a. Likeness. TM. V. 1. (make)
Assist.
[v Adjuvant] T. II. 5.
[v. Assessor] RJ. I. 1. A.
Assize.
Judgment [adj. Shire, Judicial Convention.]
[adj. { Law Authority } Measure]
Associate, [a. Companion. RO. IV. 2. (make)
Assoil, [Absolve.] RJ. II. 7.
Assume.
{ to—— together- } take] TA. I. 4.
Assure.
[v. Certain] AS. II. 6.
[v. Assurance] AS. II. 6.
Asswage, [v. Remission.] TM. I. 8. D.
Asterisk. Mag. IV. 6. A.
Asthma, S. V. 2.
Astonish.
[a. Wonder, (augm.) AS. V. 1. (make)
[a. Extasie. AS. VI. 8. A. (make)
[Stupifie with { Wonder. Fear. }]
Astray.
[adj. { Err } TA. III. 8. Wander } TA. VI. 3. A.
Astride, [adj. Stride. Mo. I]. 3. O.
Astringent.
—in Virtue, [Binding.] Mo. IV. O.
in Tast, [Austere] Q. IV. 3.
Astrolabe, [Star-measuring (Instr.]
Astrology, [Conjecturing (Art) by the stars.]
Astronomy, Measuring (Art) of Heavenly (things)
Asunder.
[adv. Segregate] TM. III. 6.
[adv. Separate] TA. II. 1. O.
At.
[Near, augm.] Prep. III. 1. O.
[In] Prep. IV. 1. O.
—all.
[in any { Thing. Manner. }
—{ last length } Adv. III. 3. O.
—{ last least most } adv. { last. least. most. }
—once { adv. One. in one (time with one blow, &c.
Atchieve.
[a. Action] T. I. 7.
[Perform] TA. III. 6.

AV

[a. Perfect. T. III. 9. (make)]
Atheism. RE. I. O.
Atmosphere. El. II. 1. A.
[Sphere of Vapors.]
Atom, [Indivisible body (dim.)
Atone.
[un-Enemy RO. IV. 1. O. (make)
[a. Friend, RO. IV. 1. (make)
Attac.
[Beesiege] RM. I. 4.
[Assault] RM. I. 3. A.
Attach, [Arrest] RJ. II. 2.
Attagen. Bi. II. 3. A.
Attein. [Obtein] TA. V. 1.
Atteint.
[a. Accuser] RJ. I. 3.
[un-a. Noble. RC. I. 3. (make)
Attempt, [Essay] TA. III. 4. A.
Attend.
[Continue expecting]
[Wait] AC. V. 1. A.
Hearken [Hear (endeavor]
—unto, [a. Observe.] AS. III. 1. A.
Attention, vid. *Attend.*
{ Heedfulness } Ha. IV. 2.
{ Diligence } Ha. IV. 5.
Attenuate [a. Rarity. Q. V. 3. D. (make)
Attest.
[a. witness] RJ. I. 7. A.
[a. Protestation]
Attire, [Clothing.] Pr. 4.
Attorney, [for—businessing (person] sp. Lawyer.]
Attract, [to—draw.]
Attribute, [Predicate.] D. II. 8. O.
Attrition.
[Rubbing] O. V. 8.
[Grinding]
upon a body, O. IV. 2.
between bodies, O. VI. 1.
[Decay, NP. V. 4. O. by use.]
Avail.
[a. Adjuvant] T. II. 5.
[a. Profit] T. V. 1.
Avant, [un—Imperat. Ition.] TA. VI.
Avarice, [Covetousness] Man. III. 1. D.
Audacity, [Boldness.] AS. V. 8.
Audible, [adj. p. Hear (apt.)
—Quality. Q. III.
Audience.
[Hearing]
[Convention for Hearing.]
[Hearers (Aggreg.)
Audit, [Convention for reckoning.]
to—[a. reckon.] TA. IV. 2.
Auditor.
Hearer [hearing (person]
Accountant [reckoning. TA. IV. 6. (Officer]
Auditory, vid. *Audience.*
Avenge, [Revenge.] AS. V. 9. A.
Avens. HF. IX. 1. A.
Avenue, [to—way.]
Averr, [Affirm D. VI. 2. (augm.)

AW

Aversation. AS. V. 5. O.
Aversion. AS. IV. 1. O.
Avert, [from-turn.] TA. VI. 2. O.
Auger, [great Boring. O. IV. 3. (Instr.)
Augment, [increase]
{ Great Intense } (make)
{ more Great more Intense } (make)
Avoid. TA. VI. 7. O.
[a. Aversation] AS. V. 5. O.
Avouch, [Affirm solemnly.]
Avow, [Affirm solemnly.]
Aurelia, [Chrysolite.] PP. V. 6. A.
Auricular, [adj. Ear.]
Auspicious, [Prosperous.] Ha. I. 2.
Austerity.
Tast. Q. IV. 3.
Vice, Man. VI. 8. O.
Authentic, [adj. Authority.] RC. IV. 6.
Author.
[Efficient] T. II. 1.
[adj. a. preter.Invention.]AS. III. 2. O.
Authority.
[Right] RC. IV. 6.
[Testimony] sp. Credible.]
Autumn. Me. V. 3.
Auxiliary, [Adjuvant.] T. II. 5.
Aw.
[Fear] AS. V. 6. O.
[Reverence] Man. V. 3.
—full, [adj. Fearing (apt.)
Away.
[From] Prep. III. 2.
[Off] Prep. III. 2. A.
[Absent] Sp. II. 1. O.
[From—Imper. Go.] TA. VI. 1. O.
—with, [Off] Prep. III. 2. O. sp. with an Imperative.]
Fling.
[From—go { Hastily. Angrily. }
Stand—[Be more distant.]
Awake, [adj. AC. II. 4.
to—[un-sleep.]
Award, [Sentence.] RJ. II. 5. A. sp. of Arbitrators.]
Aware.
[Before-knowing]
[adj. Heedfulness] Ha. IV. 2.
Awkward.
[not { Skilful. Agil. }
[Perverse] NP. IV. 1. O.
Awle, [adj. Iron (dim.) boring (Instr.)
Awry.
[Oblique] Mag. II. 8.
[Crooked] Mag. III. 1. O.
[adj. Err] TA. III. 8.
Ax, [Carpenters (Instr.) for to cut strikingly.]

Battle-

BA

Battle- ⎧ Club. ⎫
Pole— ⎨ Cutting ⎧ RM.V. 2. ⎫ ⎬
Pick— ⎩ ⎩ Hammer. ⎭ ⎭
— [hammer for pecking.]
Axiom.
[adj. p. Authority Sentence]
D. III. 1. A.
[Rule] D. IV. 5.
Axis ⎫
Axle-tree. ⎬
—of Globe. Mag. II. 5. A.
—of Cart. Po. V. 6. A.
Ay, [Sloth] Be. III. 2. A.
Azimuth. W. VI. 4. A.
Azure. [Blew.] Q. II. 3. A.
—Stone. St. II. 3. A.

B

BAbble, [a. Loquacity.] Man IV. 5. D.
Babe, [adj. Infancy (person.] Me. VI. 1.
Baby, [Factitious Man. (dim.)]
Bable, [adj. Vanity. T. IV. 5. (thing)
Baboon, Ee. III. 1.
Bachelor, [adj. Cœlibat. RO. II. 1. (person)
—of Arts, [having the first Academical degree.]
—s Button, [Campion.] HS. V. 2.
Back.
Noun.
—of Body.
[Hinder part] Sp. III. 8. O.
—of Animal, PG. IV. 3.
Adverb.
[Un] Adv. IV. 3.
[Re] Adv. IV. 3. O.
—to the ⎧ Place ⎫
same ⎨ Person ⎬ again
⎩ Condition ⎭
Preposition.
[From] Prep. III. 2.
to— one.
[a. Accessory] TM. IV. 4. O.
[Incourage] RO. VI. 2.
[a. Adjuvant] T. II. 5.
give— [Retire] RM. II. 2. D.
Keep— ⎧ Abstein ⎫ TA. V. 6.
Keep one-- ⎨ Detein ⎬ (O.
[a. Cohibit] T. II. 2. O.
[a. Hinder] T. II. 5. O.
—door.
[adj. hinder-part door]
door of the hinder part of the house.]
—friend, [Conceal'd Enemy.]
Backbite. R]. IV. 9.
Back-slide, [a. Apostate.] RE. III. 6. O.
Backward.
[adj. Backwardness]
⎧ toward- ⎫ the hinder part]
⎩ to —— ⎭
Backwardness.
[Aversation] AS. V. 5. O.
[Nolleity] AS. IV. 1. O. (dim.)
Bacon, [Condited Hogs-flesh.]

BA

Bad, [Evil.] T. III. 2. O.
Badge, [Sign] T. VI. 5.
Badger.
Beast, Ec. V. 2. A.
[Merchant] (corr.) of Corn]
Bag, Pr. V. 1.
cloak—[behind-riding bag.]
—pipe, Musical (Instr.) of Pipes and Bag.]
Baggage, [Carried (things) adj. a. hinder (apt)
[utensils of the Army.] RM. V. A.
Bay.
—tree, Tr. III. 5.
Rose—[Oleander] Sh. VI. 1. A.
Wild—Sh. III. 9.
—colour, [Chesnut colour.]
brown— [black. Q. II. 1. O.
(dim) adj. Chesnut colour.]
—in Water, [Transverse bank.]
—of Sea. W. IV. 4.
—of Building. Po. III. A.
—windows, [Prominent windows.]
to—at [against-a. Dog (voice)]
Bail. R] II. 2.
Baily.
Bailiff.
Magistrate [adj. Town (officer.)]
Serjeant [adj. ⎧ Citation ⎫
⎨ Arresting ⎬ (Officer.)
⎩ Servant. ⎭ [adj. Agriculture (Officer.)
Bain, [Bath.] Po. II. 5. A.
Bait, [Sustenance.] Pr. I. (sp. adj. Hunting.]
to—
[Refresh] TA. V. 8. sp. with Sustenance in journey.]
[Allure] RO. V. 5 sp. with Sustenance.
as Hook or Trap, [make adj. allure (apt.)]
[Provoke] RM. I. 2.
Bake. Pr. III. 5. A.
—er, [Baking ⎧ (Officer.) ⎫
⎩ (Mechanic.) ⎭
Balad, [Plebeian Song.]
Balance, [adj. librating O. I. 2. (jug.)
[Librating] O. I. 2.
[Equal the weight]
[a. Equal (make)]
Even Accounts TA. IV. 2. A.
Balast, [Weight, un- adj. a. roll (apt)
Balcony, [Prominent doored window.]
Bald.
[Un-hair'd]
[not-ornate]
[not-congruous]
Bale.
[Heap. ⎫
[Aggregate ⎬ together-bound.]
Balk.

BA

—of Earth, [Area not ploughed.]
to—
[Omit] TA. III. 8. A.
[Discourage] RO. VI. 2. A.
Ball.
Balling. Mo. V. 4. A. (Instr.)
Sphere [Mag. III. 5. sp. (dim.)
Convention for dancing]
Balloting, [a. Suffrage (sign) with Balls.]
Balm.
Herb. HF. VII. 2.
Assyrian—HF. VII. 3.
Juice. PP. L. 7. A.
Balsam.
Plant.
Male—HS. VII. 5.
True—HS. III. 5.
Juice. PP. I. 7. A.
Balsamum. Peruvianum. Tr. VIII. 9. A.
Ban.
[Curse] AS. I. 3. O.
—role, [Flag.] Mag. IV. 7. A.
Band.
[adj. a. Binde (thing)
[Obligation] RC. VI.
[writing Obligatory] RC. VI. 5.
[Company] RM. IV. 3.
Band, [Cast alternly.]
sp. various waies]
Bandito.
⎧ Proscribed ⎫
⎨ Military robbing ⎬ (person.)
Bandog, [Dog tied for Guard.]
Bane.
[Destruction] AS. I. 4. O.
rats—[Arsenic] St. VI. 4. A.
Banes.
[Promulgation of fut. Marriage]
Bang, [Strike.] Mo. VI. 4.
Banish, [a. Exile.] R] VI. 1.
Bank.
[Oblong, more-high (part)
[Ridge] Mag. V. 7.
[Shore] W. IV. 6.
[Shelf] W. III. 5. A.
[Series] TM. III. 7.
—of Mony, [Mony (Aggr.) sp. to be lett (segreg.)]
Banker, [adj ⎧ (person ⎫ of
demising ⎨ (Merchant ⎬ Money.)
Banket. Pr. II. 1. A.
Bankrout, [adj. failing (person ⎫
⎧ Declared ⎫ not-so-
[Debtor ⎨ sentenced ⎬ lutive]
Banner.
⎧ Ensign. RM. ⎫
[adj. ⎨ III. 2. ⎬ (thing)
⎩ Cornet. RM. ⎭
III. 2. A.
Banquet. Pr. II. 1. A.
Banstickle. Fi. IX. 13. A.
Baptism. RE. VI. 5.
Bar.
[Bolt] Po. IV. 5.
—of, &c.
⎧ Cylinder, Mag. III. 5. ⎫ of
⎨ Prism. Mag. III. 6. A. ⎬ &c.
adj.

BA | BA | BE

[adj. Impedient (thing)]
[adj. Pleading]RJ.I.7.(place)
to—
[a. Impedient] T. II. 5. O.
[a. Forbid] RO. V. 1. O.
Barb.
[Back-diverging Chips]
to—the Hair.
[a. Figure (Perf.) by cutting.]
sp. the beard.
Barbarism. Man. IV. O.
Barbarous.
[adj. Barbarism] Man. IV. O.
[adj. Rusticity] Man. IV. 9. D.
[adj. Fierceness] NP. IV. 4. O.
[adj. Cruelty] Man. I. 5. O.
Barber, [Hair cutting (Mechanic.)]
Barbery. Sh. I. 4. A.
Barbel. Fi. IX. 8.
Bard, [Old (manner) Poet.]
Bare.
[not-clothed]
[Lean] NP. V. 5. O.
[Scarce] TM. I. 2. D.
to—
[un-clothe]
Bargain.
Contract. RC. V.
Thing dealt for, RC. V. 8.
Barge. RN. I. 2.
Bark.
[Rinde] PP. I. 5.
[Ship] RN. I. 2. A.
to—
Peel [un-rinde.]
Yelp, as a { Dog.
{ Fox.
to { a. Dog (voice)
{ a. Fox (voice)
Barly. HL. II. 3.
wild—HL. III. 4. A.
Barm.
[adj. a. ferment (thing) of Beer.
Barn, [House for Straw.]
Barnacle.
Fish. Ex. VIII. 9.
Instrument [Nose Compressing (instr.)]
Baron.
[Noble (person.)]
sp. of the fifth degree downward]
—of Exchequer, [Judge of Court for King's Revenue.]
Baronet, [Gentleman of the first Degree.]
Barrel.
Vessel, Pr. V. 3.
Measure. Me. II. 4.
Barrenness. NP. VI. 3. O.
Barreter, [Contentious (person) adj. a. Suit. RJ. II. A. (apt)
Barricado, [Transvers shutting (sepiment)]
Barriers, [Sepimented end of Race (place)]
Barrister, [Pleading Lawyer.]
Barrow,
[un-testicled Hog]

Jugament. Po. V. 3. A.
Barter, [Exchange.] RC. V. A.
Base.
Subst.
—of Column, [Bottom.] Sp. III. 7. O.
—in Song, [Grave] Q. III. 1. D.
Adj.
[Low] TM. II. 4. O.
[Ignoble]
[Rabble] RC. I. 7.
[Villain] RC. I. 8.
[Spurious] T. III. 4. O.
[Vitious] Man. I. O.
[Pusillanimous] Man. III. 8. D.
[Sordid] Man. III. 4. D.
Bashfull.
adj. { Shame (habit)] AS. VI. 2. A.
{ Abjectness] Man. III. 9. E.
Basil. HF. VII. 5.
Stone—HF. VII. 5. A.
Cow—HS. V. 6.
Basilisk.
[Serpent killing by seeing]
[Great Ordnance]
Basket. Pr. V. 2. A.
Bason. [Dish. Pr. V. 4. deep.]
Bass. [Bed. Po. VI. 7. A. of rushes.]
Bastard.
[Spurious] T. III. 4. O.
[begot of Parents not together-married.]
Baste.
[Whip] RJ. VI. 2.
[Cudgel] RJ. VI. 2. A.
Moisten. Pr. III. 7.
Baston.
{ Staff.] PP. I. 4.
{ Club.] RM. V. 2.
Bastonade, [Cudgelling.] RJ. VI. 2. A.
Bat.
[Club] RM. V. 2.
Bird *flying-Mouse* (kind.)
—fowling, [Hunting Birds by Night.]
Batch, [Bread. (Aggreg.)
sp. in-one (time) baking.]
Bath Po. II. 5. A.
—ing, [Soking] O. III. 5. O.
Battaglia, [ordered Army.]
Battel.
Part of Army.
Action. RM. I. 8. A.
—ax.
[Cutting { Club]
{ Hammer]
Batter, [Bruise by { Striking.]
{ Knocking.]
a—y, [Assault with Cannon.]
Battle, [adj. Fatt.] NP. V. 5.
to—[Score for Diet (segreg.]
Battle-door, [Lamia (Instr.) for striking.]
Battlements.
Figure. Mag. IV. 9. A.
[Margin (sepiment) of the Roof.]

Bavin, [together bound (aggreg.) of Twigs.]
Bawd, [adj. Fornication (Merchant.)]
Bawdy, [adj. Unchast.] Mm. II. 7. O.
Bawl, [Exclaim.] AC. III. 3. O.
Bdellium. Tr. VIII. 7.
Beach. Sh. IV. 2. A.
Beacon, [adj. Fire (sign) of p. invaded.]
Bead.
[Sphere }
[Cube } (dim) perforated.]
—s-man.
[for praying (person)]
[adj. p. Almes (person)]
Bede-tree, Tr. III. 9. A.
Beadle.
Before-walking (Officer)
[adj. a. Citation (Officer)
[Arresting RJ. II. 7. A. (Officer.)
{ Whipping (Officer)
Beagle.
[Dog (dim) hunting Beasts by smell.
Beak.
—of a Bird. PP. V. 4.
—of a Ship.
Beaker, [Cylinder (manner) Cup.]
Beam.
—of an house. Po. III. 5. A.
—of a Cart, [Pole] Pr. V. 4. A.
—of Balance, [Transverse (part, of B.)]
Weavers—Transverse line of Wood.]
—of the Sun, [Line of Light.]
Meteor. El. I. 4.
Beam-tree.
White—Sh. II. 3. A.
Bean. HS. III. 3.
French—
Ginny—— } HS. II. 1.
Kidney—
—of the Ancients. HS. II. 2.
binding-tree. Sh. IV. 6.
—tresoile. Sh. H. 7. A.
Bear. v. Be. IV. 1. A.
—foot.
Sea—Ex. VI. 2.
—breech [bank ursin] HS. VIII. 8
—ear. HS. VIII. 2.
—Sanicle. HS. VIII. 3.
Bear, v.
Support. Mo. VI. 1. A.
[Carry] Mo. VI. 1.
[Parturition] AC. I. 3.
Suffer.
[a Passion] T. I. 7. O.
[a. Patience] Man. I. 8.
—down.
[Fall (make)]
[Compel to grant]
—off.
[adj. a. distant (endeavour)]
[Suffer (endeavour)
Bbb

BE | BE | BE

—out.
[adj. a. Safety (make)]
—up against
[Continue Suffering]
[Continue Resisting]
—with.
[a. Patience] Man. L. 8.
[a. Condescention] Man. VI. 3.
(Company (Companion
Respect v. Respect
— Sway   Sway
Witness   Witness
—ones self, [a. Demeanour.]
Beard.
—of Animal. PP. VI. 4.
—of Corn. PP. II. 3. A.
Bearded Creeper. HF. III. 5.
Beast Be.
Beastly, [adj. a. Beast. (Metaph.]
Beat.
[Knock] Mo. VI. 4. A.
[Strike] Mo. VI. 4.
[Overcome]
—back.
[back- { Drive }
         { Put. }
        { Striking. }
by { Fighting. }
—the Price. AC. VI. 1. A.
Beatitude.
[Happiness] Ha. I. 1.
[p. Blessing] AS. I. 3.
Beaver. [Castor] Be. IV. 8.
Beauty. NP. V. 6.
Becalm. [Quiet.] TA. V. 9.
Because. Conj. III. 2. O.
Bescattge. Bi. V. 6.
Beckon. [v. Head (sign)]
Becometh.
Transf. (Inceptive)
is done [is, adj. p. Action.]
is made.
  [is, adj. p. Efficient]
  [is Effect] T. II. O.
  [is Event] TA. V.
  [is decent] T. V. 2.
Bed.
Houshold-stuff. Po. V. 7. A.
—sted. Po. V. 7.
—rid, [not-adj. rise (pot.)
       out of—]
—of Earth, [Superficies.]
Mag. I. 3.
Ladies Bedstraw. HL. IX. 6. A.
Bedaub, [a. Defilement.] TM. V. 6. O.
Bedding, [adj. Bed. (things)]
Bedewed, [adj. p. Dew. (make)]
Bedlam, [Prison of mad (persons.]
Bee. Ex. IV. 1.
humble. Ex. IV. 1. A.
—like fly. Ex. IV. 3.
—eater. Bi. III. 9.
—flower, [orchis] HL. IV. 8.
to—
[v. Being] T. I. 1.
Copula.
Beech. Tr. IV. 4. A.
Beef, [Beev's flesh.]
Beeing. T. I. 1.

as—[as] Adv. I. 3.
Beer.
[Drink] Pr. I. 7. A.
[adj. Carrying (jug.) for dead bodies.]
Beestings.
[Milk of adv. new adj. preter. parturition.]
Beet. HF. I. 10.
Beetle.
[Insect] Ex. V.
Common—Ex. V. 4.
Dung—Ex. V. 4. A.
Knobbed horned—Ex. V. 3. A.
Instrument [wooden Mallet (augm.]
Befal [v. Event.] TA. V.
Befool, [a. Fool. (make)]
Before.
—in place. Prep. V. 3
—in comparison, [more then.]
—in time, [adv. Preceding] Sp. I. 2. E.
—hand.
         { Gained } TA. V. 2.
[Ha-   { Prepared } TA. III. 2.
ving   { Prevented } TA. III. 9.
Beg.
[a. Begger] RC. I. 8. A.
[Entreat. RO. V. 3. (augm.]
—ger. RC. I. 8. A.
Beget.
[a. Generation] AC. I. 1.
[a. Efficient] T. II. 1.
Begin. TA. III. 5.
Transf. (Incep.)
Beginning. Sp. III. 3. D.
Beguile, [a. Fraud.] RJ. IV. 4.
Behave.
[a. Conversation] Man. A.
[a. Demeanour] AC. V.
[a. Gesture] AC. VI.
Behead. RJ. V. 1.
Behind. Prep. V. 3. O.
[Hinder part] Sp. III. 8. O.
left—
{ Staying } TA. VI. O.
{ Remaining }
[Residue] TM. VI. 7. O.
—in Arrears, [Debtor.] TA. IV. 7. O.
[Inferior] TM. I. 5. D.
—hand, { Lost } TA. V. 2. O.
[having { not-prepared }
        { been Prevented }
Behold.
[a. { Eye }
    { See }
    { Observe }
Beholding.
[Beneficiary] RO. III. 8. D.
[Owing thanks]
Behove.
[v. Expedient] T. V. 6.
it—ed, &c.
[&c ought] Mood II. 2.
—full, [Expedient.] T. V. 6.
Bel, [adj. Ringing. Q. III. 2. (Instr.]
—fry, [adj. Convention (place) for adj.) a. Ringing (persons.]

—flower. HF. VII. 9. A.
Belching. Mo. IV. 2.
Beldame, [Old (corr.) man. (form.]
Beleaguer, [Besiege] RM. I. 4.
Belye, [a. Calumny.] RJ. IV. 7.
Believe. AS. II. 4.
Easiness to— [Credulity.]
Ha. III. 2. E.
Belly. PG. IV. 6.
—Worm. Ex. I. 1. A.
Bellis, [Daisie] HF. II. 3. A.
Bellow, [a. Bull (voice)
Bellows, [adj. a. Wind (Instr.]
Bellwine, [adj. Beast (Metaph.]
Belong, [v. Pertinence.] TM. IV. 5.
Beloved, [adj. p. Love.] AS. V. 2.
Below.
[Beneath] Prep. V. 2. O.
[Inferior] TM. I. 5. D.
Belt, [to-binding (Armament) Sword]
Bemoning.
{ with } { Sorrow (sign)
{ for   } sp. With Voice.]
Bench.
[long fixed Seat]
[adj. Judg. (place)] RJ. I. 1.
[Assessors, (aggr.] RJ. I. 1. A.
Bencher, [Assessor in College of Relation Judicial (person.]
Bend. O. I. 7. A.
[adj. a. Crooked] Mag. III. 1. O.
[Shrink] AC. VI. 3.
[be crumpled] AC. VI. 3. A.
[p. Oblique] Mag. II. 8.
—ones self, [together-fold.] O. V. 5.
Beneath.
[Inferior] TM. I. 5. D.
[Below] Prep. V. 2. O.
Benediction, [Blessing.] AS. I. 3.
Benefactor. RO. III. 8.
Beneficence.
Vertue, [Goodness] Man. L. 4.
Action, [a. Benefactor.]
Beneficial, [a. Benefactor.]
Beneficiary. RO. III. 8. O.
Benefit, [adj. a. Benefactor (thing)
Benevolence, [Favour] AS. V. 9.
Benjamin. Tr. VIII. 5. A.
Benighted.
Benignity.
[Favour] AS. V. 9.
[Courtesie] Man. IV. 7.
[Gratiousness] Man. VI. 1.
Bent. [adj p. bend.]
[adj. pret. purposing] AS. IV. 3.
—of Grass, [Ear] PP. II. 4. A.
Benum. [a. Stupor.] NP. II. 1. O.
Bequeath. RC. V. 2.
Beray, [a. Defile.] TM. V. 6. O.
Berbery. Sh. III. 4.
Bereave, [a. Privative.] T. III. 3. O.
Berry. PP. III. 2. A.

BE | BE | BI

one—[Herb true love] HS. IX. 5, A.
Beseech, [Entreat.] RO. V. 3, humbly.]
Beseeging. RM. I. 41
Beseem, [adj. Decency.]
Beset.
  [About-gard]
  [Besiege] RM. I. 4.
Beshrew.
  [a. remorse.]
  [a. Velleity] { Miscarrying, Event (corr.) }
Beside.
  [Near] Prep. IV. 3. O.
  [not { to, at, &c. }
  —the mark,
    { Erring, Wandring } from]
  —himself, [Mad.]
  [Also] Conj. IV. 2.
Redundant.
Besmear, [Defile.] TM. V. 6. O.
Besom, [adj. sweeping (instr.)]
Besot.
  [a. Dotage.] NP. II. 2. O. (make)
  (sp. with { Love, Excess, Drunkenness. }
Bespawl.
  [Defile with upon-spitting.]
Bespeak. RC. VI. 1.
Besprinkle, [Wet (make) with Drops.]
Bespue.
  [Defile with upon-spuing.]
Best, [most-good.] T. III. 2.
  —part. TM. VI. 1.
  doe ones—[most-endeavour.] TA. III. 4.
Bestiality. RJ. III. 6.
Bestir.
  [Move (aug.)] Mo.
  [Endeavour] TA. III. 4.
  [Diligence] Ha. IV. 5.
Bestow.
  [Give] TA. IV. 4.
  [Disburse] TA. IV. 5.
  [Spend]
Bet. RC. VI. 8. A.
Betake.
  [to-Ition] TA. VI.
  sp. for Safety.]
Bethink.
  Cogitation, AS. II. 1.
  [Consider] AS. III. 2.
Betide, [v. Event.] TA. V.
Betime.
  [adv. Soon] Sp. I. 4.
  [adv. Morn] Mc. V. 7.
Betoken, [before-sign | T. VI. 5.
Betony. AF. VII. 15.
Betraying.
  Evil.
    [a. Treachery] Man. V. 2. D.
    [a. Perfidiousness] Man. V. 6. O.
    [a. Treason] RJ. III. 2.
  Indiff.
    [Shewing] TA. I. 8.
    [Manifesting] TA. I. 9.

Betrothed,] RO. II. 3.
Better, [more-good.] TM. I. 6. E.
  [Victory.] RM. H. 1.
  [Superiority] TM. I. 5. E.
  Ones—r. RO. III.
Between. Prep. VI. 3.
  —themselves.
    [Privately] adv. TM. V. 4.
  —Both.
    [Middle.] SP. IN. 3.
    [Indifferent.]
Bever.
  [Refection] Pr. I. 1. A.
  Beast, [Castor.]
  Hat, [Head (vest) of Fur of Bever.]
  Armour, [For-head (Armor.]
Beverage. Pr. II. 6. A.
Bevy. [Aggreg.]
Bewail.
  [for-grief (sign)
  sp. with Exclaiming.]
Beware.
  [adj. a. Heedfulness] Ha. IV. 2.
  [a. Aversation] AS. V. 4. O.
Bewitch. RJ. III. 1.
Bewray.
  [Shew] TA. I. 8.
  [Manifest] TA. I. 9.
Beyond. Prep. VI 2. O.
  [Superior] TM. I. 5. E.
Bezoar.
  [Contra-poison
  sp. Stone of the Persian Goat.]
By.
  the—[Digression] D. V. 9. A.
  Adjective.
  [adj. Digression] D. V. 9. A.
  [adj. Accessory.] TM. IV. 9. O.
  —word, (accessary (thing)
  of common discourse)
  sp. with contempt.]
  [not-adj. { Principal, Pertinent, Public, Ordinary. }
Preposition.
Efficient, Pre, I. 2.
Instrument. Pre. I, 1. A.
End.
  —reason of. Pre. I. 2. A.
  { Local, Temporal, before }
  —God.
  [at]
  come—[obtein] TA. V. 1.
  [in]
  —day.
  [through]
  [beside]
  [Adverb]
Local { nigh.]
Temporal
  —and { Nearly after, adv. future (dim.) }
Manner.

{ the by, great, retail, it self } Adverb [by { Digression g. (1.) [Aggregate, r. (1.) [Segregate, it s. (1.) [Solitary.] }
Segregation.
  { course, the day, degrees, turns } { c, d, d, t } [Segr.]
  Day] { day [d.], House } { house [h.], Year } { year [y.]
Bib.
  a—[Child's breast (vest]
  to—[Drink, AC. II. 2. A. (freq.)
Bible, [Book of Scripture.]
Bicker.
  [a. Fight, RM I. 7. (dim.)
  [a. Contention. Man, IV. 3. D.
Bid.
  [Command] RO. V. 1.
  Invite [Intreat to come.]
  —Banes } publish { b. fur.
  —Festival } { f. fur
  —Battel } { b.
  —Defiance } Offer { d.
  —Money } { m.
  —Prayer, [Exhort to togetherpray.]
  —Price. RC. VI. 2.
Biennial.
  { During, Returning after } 2 years}
Big.
  [Great] TM. I. 1. E.
  —with Child, [adj. p. Great through having been impregnated.]
to look { angrily. AS. V. 8. proudly.] Man. V. (s. O.
Bigamy, [Having together-two Marrieds.]
Biggin, [adj. Linnen Head (vest.]
Bilberry. Sh. II. 2.
Bile. S. III. 3. A.
Bill.
  —of Bird, [Beak.] PP. V. 4
  Hook, [Cutting-hook.]
  Scroll, [Lamin of Paper,]
  [Catalogue] TM. III. 7. A.
  [Accusation, &c.] RJ, II. 3.
  [Obligation.] RC. VI. 5.
  —of Exchange, [Bill for Exch.] RC. V. A.
Billet.
  —of Paper, [adj. Paper (Lamin.]
  Appointment for Lodging]
  —of Wood, [Stick (aug.)] sp. for Fuel.]
Billow, [Wave.] W. IV. 1. E.
Bin.
  [Box, Pr. V. 2.

Bbb 2   sp.

BI | BL | BL

sp. for Bread.]
Binde.
 [Ty] O. II. 1.
 [a. Bonds] RJ. VI. 4. A.
 make Coſtive [a. binding] Mo. IV. O,
 [Oblige] v. RC. VI.
 —by Script. RC. VI. 5.
 —a Book ,][a. Mechanic—]
Bindweed. HS. VIII. 6.
 Sea—HL. VI. 13. A.
 black—HF. I. 3. A.
 prickly—HS. IX. 7.
Biographer, [a. Hiſtory (perſon) of Lives.]
Bipartite, [divided into two parts.]
Birch. Tr. VI. 7.
Bird. Bi.
 —lime, (Viſcous (thing) for taking Birds.]
 —'s-Cherry. Sh. II. 8.
 —'s-Ey. HS. VIII. 2. A.
 —'s-Foot. HS. III. 9.
 —'s-neſt. HL. V. 7.
 HF. V. 6. A.]
Birt, [Turbut.] Fi. V. 2.
Birth.
 Extraction, [p. Progenitor.] RO. I. 1.
 Nativity, [p. Parturition.] AC. L. 3.
 Bearing, [a. Parturition.]
 that is born, [adj. p. Parturition.] AC. I. 3.
 after—[Secundine] PP. VI. 7. A.
 —wort. AS. VIII. 5.
Biſhop. RE. II. 4. A.
 —'s-weed. HF. V. 4. A.
Bisket.
 [Bread bak'd for duration]
 [dried, Bread (Lamin)]
Biſmute. Mer. III. 3.
Biſons, [Bull (kind) having a bunch on the back]
Biſſextile, [Excedent fourth year.]
Biſtort. [Snakeweed] HL. VII. 9.
Bit.
 [piece] from-broken (part)]
 —of Bridle, [Horſe-reſtreining (Armament)]
Bitch, [Dog. Be. III. 1. (fem.)
Biting.
 as with Teeth, [a. Tooth.]
 —in, [un-ſpeak (endeavour.]
 as in Taſt or Smell [a. Acrimonious]
Bitter.
 —in Taſte. Q. IV. 3. O.
 [Auſtere] Man. VI. 8 O.
 Doleful, [adj. a. Grief, AS. V. 3. O. (cauſe)
Bittour. Bi. VIII. 5.
Braſileen—Bi. VIII. 5. A.
Bitumen. St. V. 8.
Blab.
 [adj. a. Loquacity] Man. IV. 5. O.
Black. Q. II. 1. D.

—art, [Witchcraft.] RJ. III. 1.
—berry, [Berry of Bramble.]
—bird. Bi. III. 6.
—and blew, [Blew Black.]
 as Bruiſe (ſign)
Bladder. PG. VI. 7. A.
 ſwimming—PP. IV. 5.
 —ſtut. Tr. IV. 7. A.
Blade, [Lamin.] Mag. V. 4.
 —of Plant, [Leaf] PP. II. 5. A.
 One—HM. VI. 22.
 Twy—HM. VI. 22. A.
 —of Shoulder, [Flat bone of Shoulder.]
 to—it [a. Riotouſneſs.]
Blain [Boil] S. III. 3. A.
 —worm
Blame, [Impute fault.]
 —leſs, [Innocent.] RJ. II. 6.
Blanch, [a. White.] Q. II. 1. E.
Blandiſhment, [a. Fawning.] Man. IV. 7. E.
Blank.
 [White.] Q. II. 1. E.
 [not upon-written] AC. III. 7.
 a—
 to—[a. Mute.] AC. III. 1. O.
Blanket.
 [woollen {Covering (thing.)
                Bed (veſt.)
Blaspheme.
 [Speak {Evil } {God.}
         {Injury} of {Prin-
                     (ces.)
Blaſt.
 [Decay. NP. IV. 4. O. (make.)
 Vapor. El. VI. 5.
 [Blowing. Mo. III. 3. {(impe-
 [Wind. El. II. 4.   {tus.)
Blatta fœtida. In. III. 4. A.
Blaze.
 [a. Flame.] El. I. 1.
 [adj. a. Public.] TM. V. 4.
Blazing-ſtar, [Comet] El. I. 2.
Blazon.
 [adj. a. Public. (make)
 [a. Deſcription adj. Degree (ſign)
Blea, [Bleak] Fi. IX. 10. A.
Bleach, [open to the {Wind.
                      {Sun.
 ſp. for white (make)
Bleak.
 [Piercing Cold]
 Fiſh. F. IX. 10. A.
Bleared, [Diſeaſed by Inflammation of the Membrans.]
Bleat. a.
 {Sheep }
 {Goat } (voice.)
Bleed.
 [a. Bloud] PG. I. 5.
 Phlebotomy. Mo. IV. 6.
Blemiſh, [a. Spotted.] Q. I. 5. O.
Blend, [Mix] T. III. 8. O.
Blenn. Fi. III. 14.
Bleſſedneſs, [Happineſs.] Ha. I. 1.
Bleſſing. AS. I. 3.
Blew. Q. II. 3. A.
 —bottle. HF. III. 2.
Blight.
 Vapor. El. VI. 5.

Decay. NP. V. 4. O.
Blind. NP. I. 1. O.
 a—[Falſe pretence]
Blink.
 [Dim] Q. I. 3. O.
 [Tremble with the Eye-lids]
Bliſs, [Happineſs.] Ha. I. 1.
Bliſſom, [a. Luſt.]
 ſp. of Sheep.]
Bliſter. Mo. IV. 7.
Blite. HF. I. 14.
Blitheneſs, [Mirth.] AS. V. 3.
Block.
 [Stock] PP. I. 2.
 —of Wood, [Thick piece—]
 —head, [Dull] Ha. III. 1. O.
 —houſe, RM. VI. 2. A.
 to—up, [Beſiege. RM. I. 4. remotely.]
Blood, vide Bloud.
Bloom, [Flower.] PP. II. 1.
Bloſſom, [Flower.] PP. II. 1.
Blot, [adj. a. Spot. Q. I. 5. O. (thing.)
 —out.
 {Deſtroy}
 {Null   } {Writing.]
Blote.
 {a. Swell   } with
 {a. Condite (dim.) } Smoke]
Bloud,
 Proper.
 Red juice of perfect Animals. PG. I. 5.
 One of the four humors. PG. I. 6.
 —bound, [Dog. adj. hunt (apt) men by ſent.]
 —ſhot, [Spotted with Bloud within the Tunicle.]
 —ſtone, [Cornelian.]
 —thirſty {Mur-
 [adj. a. {ther. } (apt)
          {Kill. }
 —wort. HA. II. 10.
 let—a. Mo. IV. 6.
 Deſcendent (kinde)
 [Conſanguinity] RO. I.
 of the whole [adj. Conſang. by both Parents.]
 of the half- [adj. Conſang. by one Parent.]
 [Murther] RJ. III. 4.
Bloudy Flix.
 [Dyſentery] S. VI. 6. A.
Blow
 a—
 [Stroke] Mo. VI. 4.
 [Knock] Mo. VI. 4. A.
 to—
 [a. Breath] Mo. III. 3.
 [a. Winde]
 —an Horn, [a. Sound.] Q. III (make)
 —one's Noſe. Mo. IV. 4. A.
 [a. Flower] PP. II. 1.
Blubber.
 Fiſh. Ex. IX. 5.
 [Fat of Whale.]
 to—
 [wet with weeping]
Blunder.
 [adj.

BO

[adj. Unskilful] Ha. VI. 3.
[adj. Stumble. Mo. II. 3. A.
(freq.)
[Confused (make)
Blunt.
[Dull] NP. IV. 2. O.
[Rustic.] Man. IV. 9. D.
[not-adj. a. Cutt (apt.)
[Obtuse.]
Blur.
[a. Spot. Q. I. 5. O. (freq.)
Blush. AC. IV. 9.
at first—{appearance.}
p. See.}
Bluster, [a. Winde violently.]
Boar, vid. *Bore.*
Board.
Plank, [adj. Wood (Lamin.)
Entertainment, [v. Hoste]
RO IV. 5.
—*er,* [Guest.] RO. IV. 5. O.
to—*a Ship,* [into-goe.]
sp. by Storm.
Boast.
[Glorying] AS. VI. 1. O.
[Oversaying] Man. IV. 1. E.
Boat. RN. I. 1.
—*Swain.* RN. V. 6.
Bob.
[Strike (dim.) with hand.
[Mock (dim.)
Bode [before {Shew}
{Sign}
Body.
Op. to Spirit. W. I. O.
[Solid] Mag. I. 4.
Op. to Head. PG. III. O.
[Trunk.] PG. IV.
—*of Tree,* [Stock] PP. I. 2.
—*of Army,* [adj. Middle
(part)
Bodkin, [adj. Boring(Instr.)Cqne]
Bog. Po. I. 9. A.
Boy, [adj. Childhood (male)
Boil. Pr. III. 2.
à—S. III. 3. A.
Boisterous, {Tempest]W.VI.7.A
[adj. {Fierceness}
{Stoutness, (corr.)
Boldness
Temper, [Stoutness.] NP.
IV. 6.
Affection, AS. V. 8.
Virtue,[Fortitude]Man.I.7.
Bole, [Lump.] TM. VI. 4.
—*armoniac.*
Bolled, [adj. Husk.]
Bolster, [Red (dim.)
sp. for the Head]
—*up.*
[Bear] Mo. VI. 1. A.
[Encourage] RO. VI. 2.
Bolt,
Ear. Po. IV. 5.
prisoners—[Pin of fetters]
[obtuse Arrow.]
to shoot ones—
[Declare ones Opinion.]
thunder,—[pibble (kind)
—*upright,* [adj. Direct.]
to—*Meal.*

BO

[Sift, m.—through{Bag.}
{Linnen
{Sive.}
Bond.
[Obligation] RC. VI. 5.
—*s.* R I. VI. 4. A.
Bondage, [Slave. (abstr.)]
Bondman, [Slave.] RO. III.
6. O.
Bone. PG. II. 1.
Bone-fire, [Fire{built for Joy.}
{adj. Festival.}
Bon-grace, [Shadowing (Vest)
for the Forehead.]
Bonnet {Low} Head (vest.)
{Flat}
—*of Sail.* RN. III. 6. A.
Book.
aggr. of Leaves. Pr. VI. 7. O.
without—[adv. Memory]
—*binder,* [adj. Book (Mechanic)
—*seller,* [adj. Book (Merchant)
agg. of Chapters. D. III. 3. A.
Boom.
[Stick]
[Pole]
[Beam]
[Tree]
—*of Sail.* RN. III. 2.
—*on Shore,* [Direct beam for
flat (signe)
Boon, [adj. p. Petition. (thing)
Boope. Fi. V. 12. A.
Boot.
[adj. Leather. (vest) for Leg
and Foot]
[Vantage] TM. VI. 2. A.
what boots it? {Profit?}
[*what doth it*] {Help?}
Fire—{
Gate—{Materials permitted for {s.}
Plough.—{ {p.}
Booth, [Tent.] Po. II. 1. A.
Booty. RM. II. 5. E.
make—*of,* [Take for—]
Borage. HA. II. 9.
Borax, [Chrysocolla.] St. V. 6. A.
Bord, vid. *Board.*
Bordell, [adj. Fornication(house)
Border, [Margin.] Sp. III. 4. A.
Bore, [Hog. Be. II. 4. (male)
to—O. IV. 3.
Born, [adj. p. Parturition.]
Borne, [adj. p. Bear]
Borough,
[Town] RC. III. 2. A.
[City] RC. III. 3. A.
Borrow. RC. V. 4. O.
Bosom.
Space betwixt Clothes and
Breast.]
{Space between the Dugs.
Boss,{Protuberance} Mag.
IV. 3.
Botanic, [adj. Herb (Science.)
Botargo, [Condited Spawn of
Mullet.]
Botch.
[Swoln Ulcer]

BO

[Piece unskilful-{Mend}
ly joined to {Fill}
to—[v. Unskilfulness] Ha.
VI. 3. O.
Both.
—*this and that,* [and—]
—*waies,* [All—]
Botrys. HP. VI. 12.
Bots, Ex. I. 3. A.
Bottle.
[Pot with narrow mouth]
Figure. Mag. VI. 2.
—*nose,* [adj. Protuberance
(augm.)—]
—*flower.* HP. I. 7.
blew—
—*of hay,*[about-tied(aggr.)-]
Bottom.
Lowest part. Sp. III. 7. O.
—*of the Heart,* [Inmost(part)-]
[Foundation] Po. III. 4.
—*of Thread,* Mag. VI. 7.
[Ship.]
Bouget, [Bag (dim.)
sp. adj. Leather.]
Bough [Branch] PP. I. 3;
Bought, [adj. p. Buy.]
Boule.
Figure. Mag. VI. 6. A.
[adj. Bouling (Instr.) Mo. V. 4.
Bounce.
{Knock}
{Sound} (Impetus)
Bound.
[adj. p. Bind]
[Beholding]
[Beneficiary]RO. III. 8. O.
[Owing thanks]
[Limit]
[Common, Margin]Sp.III.
4. A.
(Place.)
[adj. End{Thing.}
{Sign.}
[Motion, adj. Reflexion.]
Bounty, [Liberality.] Man. III. 1.
Bourn, [River (dim.)
Bout, [Course.]
Boutefeu, [a. {Contention}
{Sedition}
Bow. (make.)
[Bend] O. I. 7. A.
[a. Crooked. Mag. III. 1. O.
(make.)
—*outward,* [a. Convex
(make)
—*inward,* [a. Concave
(make)
Bowe. (make)
Weapon RM. V. 4.
Cross—RM. V. 4. A.
Figure. Mag. V. 3.
rain— El. V. 1,
saddle—[Convex (part) of
the Saddle.]
Bowell, [Gutt.] PG. VI. 4. A.
Bower.
[adj. a. Shadow (thing)]
[Tent of Leaves and Branches.]
Ladies—Sh. II. 2. A.
Virgin—HM. I. 7. A.
Bowl. Mag. VI. 6. A.

to—

BR

to—Mo. V. 4.
Bowle, [Wide Cup.]
Bowline. RN. IV. 7. A.
Bowsprit. RN. III. 4.
Bowyer, [adj. Bow (Mechanic.]
Box.
  Tree. Tr. III. 7.
  Chest. Pr. V. 2.
  Stroke, [Striking with flat hand.]
Brabble, [Contention in words.] sp. about Contracts.]
Brace.
  Buckle, [Together-ty.]
  Couple, [Together-two.]
  —of a Ship. RN. IV. 4.
Bracelet, [Ornament of the Wrist.]
Brach, [Dog (fem.)]
Brachygraphy, [Short-Writing(art)]
Bracket, [Up-bearing piece.]
Brackishness. Q. V. 5.
Brag. AS. VI. 1. O.
Bragget, [Ale made with Spice.]
Bray.
  [Pound] No. VI. 5.
  Voice.
  [a { Ass
      { Elephant } (voice.)
      { &c.
Braid, [Weave with fingers.]
Brail. RN. IV. 6.
Brain. PG. I. 8.
  —pan, [Bone that conteins the Brain.]
  —sick.
  [adj. s. fancy { Excess }
                { Disease }
  [Mad, (dim)
  hair—[adj. Ha. IV. 1. D.]
Brake.
  [Aggr. of Fern] HL. I. 4.
  [Breaking { Juga- { Flax
   ment) for { { Hemp
Bramble. Sh. I. 1. A.
Brambling. Bi. VI. 7. A.
Bran, [Courser (Part) of ground Corn.]
Branch. PP. I. 3.
Brand.
  fire—[Fire wood.]
  Mark [Stigmatization (sign]
  to— [Stigmatize]RJ.VI.6.A
Brandy. Pr. II. 7. A.
Brandish, [Swing.] Mo. VI. 3.
Brangle, [a. Contention (voice)]
Brank, [Buck-wheat] HF. I. 3.
Brank Ursin. HS, VIII. 8.
Brant goose, [black headed goose (kind.)]
Brasil. Tr. VII. 5.
Brass. Met. II. 1.
Bravado, [Glorying (impet.) of his a. fut. Action.]
Brave.
  Heroic. [adj. Virtue. (aug.)]
  Noble. [adj. Generosity.]
  Gawdy. [adj. Ornate, (aug.]
Brawl, [a. Contention (voice.)]
Brawn.
  [hard { Muscle }
         { Fleshy (part) }]

BR

[Bore's flesh soused.]
Braze, [adj.p.Superficies(make) with Brass.]
Brazier, [Brass (Mechanic.)]
Breach. vid. Break.
Bread.
  white—[fine—]
  brown—[course—]
  sweet—[principal Glandule.]
Breadth. TM. II. 2.
Break, discontinue the parts, adv. impetus.
Break.
  Proper. Mo. VI. 6.
  —ones neck, RJ. V. 3. A.
  —on the Wheel RJ. V. 9. A.
  [Tear] Mo. VI. 6. A.
  —one's belly, [-one's peritonæum.]
  —one's winde [·one's diaphragm.]
  [adj. p. Asthma. (make)]
  [Violate] TA. III. 6. O.
  —Covenant ⎫
  —Law   ⎬ violate { c. }
  —Oath   ⎭   { l. }
  —Promise   { o. }
Discontinue, [adj. p. TM. III. (make.)]
  —Company ⎫   { c. }
  —Course ⎬ discont. { c. }
  —Custom ⎭
  [Reclaim]
  —an Horse, [un- adj. fierce (make.)]
  [Cease]
  —fast, [Cease to—]
  —up, as { Convention
           { Ill weather
           { &c.
[Cease confusedly.]
  [Fail] TA. IV. 8. O.
  —State
  [Decay]
  —with { Age   { decay
         { Sorrow with { Age.
                        { Sorrow }
  [Ruine]
  —one's heart.
  —one's winde, [a. Perish.]
  —Superficies.
  —out in botches. [Discont. the skin with, &c.
  [Wound]
  —one's head. [Wound the skin of—]
  [Plow] [Dig.] &c.
  —up land.
  [Open]
  —one's minde.
  —up a letter.
  [Appear]
  —out as { Fire.
           { Light.
           { Sickness.
  [a. Impetus]
  —a Jeft [a. Jeft. (imp.)]
  —in, [In-ition. (imp.)]
  —open, [a. Open. (imp.)]
  —out, [Out-ition. (imp.)]

BR

—winde, [a. Wind. (imp.)]
—upward. Mo. IV. 2.
—downward. Mo. IV. 2. A.
Breakfast, [adj. Morning refection.]
Bream. Fi. IX. 9.
  Sea—[Gilt-head] Fi. V. 1.
Breast, vid. Brest.
Breath.
  [adj. p. Respiration. Mo. III. 2. (thing.)
  Sucking up the —AC. IV. 6. A.
  [Air]
  [Fume]
  [Vapor]
  —ing.
  [Respiration.] Mo. III. 2.
  —sweat, [Sweat (remiss.)]
Breech. PG. IV. 6.
  —es, [Vest for the lower (part) of Trunk.]
Bear's—HM. IV. 2. A.
Breed.
  Ingender, [a. Generation.]
  [p. Impregnate]
  [Educate] RO. VI.
  { Kind
  { Race
  [descendent { (aggreg.)
              { (kind)
Bref.
  Adj.
  [Shortness] TM. II. 1. O.
  [p. Epitome] D. V. 7.
  Subst.
  [Edist]
  [Commission] RC. IV. 4. A.
Breese.
  Insect
  Gentle Wind, El. VI. 6.
Brest. PG. IV. 2.
  [Dugg] PG. IV. 2. A.
  —plate, [adj. Brest (armor)]
Bret. Fi. VII. 3. A.
Breviary, [Epitome.] D. V. 7.
Breviature.
  [Shortning]
  [Shrinking]
Brevity, [Shortness.] TM. II. 1. O.
Brew.
  { Beer } (make)
  { Ale }
  [Mingle] T. III. 8. O.
Brewes, [Lamins of Bread steeped.]
  sp. in Fat of boiled meat.]
Bribe. RJ. IV. 6.
Brick. St. I. 1. A.
Bride, [adj. present Marriage (fem.)]
  —groom, [adj. pres. Marriage (male.)]
  —maid, [Companion (fem.) of the Bridegroom.]
  —man, [Companion (male) of the Bride.]
Bridal,[adj. Marriage Solemnity.]
Bridewell, [Public. adj. Correction (house.)]

Bridge.

BR | BR | BU

Bridge. Po. II. 6.
—of Lute, [Ridge supporting the Strings.]
—of Nose, [Prominent Gristle.]
Bridle. Po. V. 9.
to—[a. Cohibit.] T. II. 2. O.
Brier. Sh. I. 2. A.
Brigade. RM. IV. 2.
Brigandine.
[Coat of Male.]
[Ship adj. a. Booty (apt.)]
Brightness. Q. I. 3.
Brim [Margin.] Sp. III. 4. O.
Brimstone. St. V. 4.
Brine, [Salt dissolv'd.]
—y taste, [Saltishness.] Q. IV. 5.
Bring, [Cause to with- { go. come.
Bring, [with- { go. (make.) come. (make.)
[to- { carry. drive. lead. }
go to—[fetch.] TA. VI. 4. A.
[Cause,] [Cause to { be. go. come.
—down.
[adj. a. { Low Inferior } (make) under]
[diminish] TM. I. 7. O.
[weaken] NP. V. 7. O.
—forth.
[a. Parturition.] AC. I. 3.
—low.
[diminish] TM. I. 7. O.
[decay]
—to nought.
[adj. p. ruine (make.)]
[a. destroy] AS. I. 4. O.
[annihilate.] AS. I. 1. O.
—to pass.
[a. Cause] T. II.
[a. Efficient.] T. II. 1.
—under.
[overcome] RM. II. 1. E.
[conquer] RM. II. 7. E.
—up.
[begin] TA. III. 3.
[educate] RO. VI.
[with- { go. come.
—on the way.
[accompany in Travel (incept.)]
—to bed.
[assist in parturition.]
—word, [Narration.]
Brink, [Margin.] SP. III. 4. O.
Briony.
white—HS. IX. 6.
black—HS. IX. 6. A.
Brisk, [Sprightly.] NP. IV. 2.
Bristle, PP. VI. 2.
to—
[a. direct (make) one's Bristles.]
Bristow Non-such. HS. V. 4. A.

Brittleness. Q. VI. 5. D.
Broach, [adj. Roasting (instr.)]
to—
[a. un-barrel (incept.)]
Broad, [adj. Breadth.]
Speak
[Plain corr.]
[pronounce Rurally]
sp. opening (augm.) one's mouth.]
[a. openness.]
—awake, [Perfectly—]
Brock, [Badger.] Be. V. 2. A.
Brocket, [Hart (male) of the second year.]
Broil. Pr. III. 4. A.
Broils.
[Contentions] Man. IV. 3. D.
[Troubles] TA. V. 9. O.
Broken-winded, [adj. p. Asthma.]
Broker.
[Substitute (Merc.)]
[Merchant of old things]
Brooch, [Gemmed Ornament.]
Brood.
[Children (aggr.)]
[Aggregate (young)]
to—
[a. Fotion by over-sitting]
Brook, [River (dim.)]
—lime. HS. VI. 10.
garden—HL. VIII. 5. A.
to—[adj. a. Patience.] Man. I. 8.
Broom. Sh. IV. 8.
butchers—Sh. III. 8.
thorny—Sh. IV. 2. A.
—Rape. HL. V. 8.
a—[Brushing (instr.)]
—ing. RN. VI. 2.
Broth. Pr. I. 5.
Brothel [Fornication (house.)]
Brother. RO. I. 4.
half—RO. I. 4. A.
—in Law, [Brother by Affinity.]
—hood.
[Brother (abstr.)]
[Corporation] AC. III. 7.
Brow, [Forehead.] PG. III. 6.
Moving the—AC. IV. 1. O.
—of an Hill. [Protuberance.] Mag. IV. 3.
Brown
[Dark (dim.)]
[Black (dim.)]
Browzing.
[Mastication] Mo. III. 5.
sp. of Boughs.]
Bruise.
[Contusion] O. IV. 1. A.
Hurt. S. I. 1. A.
Brunt, [Impetus.] T. VI. 6. A.
Brush.
[Branch. PP. I. 3. (dim.)]
Instrument.
[Brushing (instr.) clothes.]
[Painting (instr.)]
to—O. V. 9.
Brute.
[Animal] W. V. 3.
[Rumor] D. V. 3.
Bruitsh.

[adj. Beast (like)]
[adj. Irrational]
Bubble. El. III. 1. A.
Buccinum. Ex. VII. 5.
Buck.
[Deer] Be. II. 4.
sp. adult (Male.)
—of Clothes.
[Clothes (aggr.) for washing by Lixiviation.]
—for fishing, [adj. take (mach.) of Fish.]
—s borne. HL. VIII. 2. A.
—s thorne. Sh. I. 7.
—mast, [Mast of Beech.]
—weed.
—wheat. HA. V. 5. A.
Bucket.
[Tub, adj. p. carry (apt) by handle.]
Buckle. Pr. IV. 8. A.
Buckler. RM. V. 9.
Buckram, [Canvas stiffened.]
Buckfom, [adj. Vigor face (manner.)]
Bud, [Sprout.] PP. II. 5.
Budge.
to—[Move (dim.)]
Budget [Bag (dim.) sp. adj Leather.]
Buff, [adj. Leather (Arms.)]
sp. of Buffals Skin limber.]
Buffel, [Bull (kind) having flat ragged horns.]
Buffet, [Strike with hand together-folded.]
Buffoon, [adj. Scurrility (person.)]
Bug. In. II. 1. A.
Bugbear, [adj. a Fear, (apt.) adj. Fiction (thing.)]
Buggery. AJ. III. 5. A.
Bugle.
[adj. Glass-bead]
[Horn (dim.) for sounding]
Herb. HF. VII. 16. A.
Bugloss. HL. IX. 1. A.
Vipers—HL. IX. 2. A.
Wall—
Buying. AC. V. 3. O.
Build.
—ing. Po. II.
Greater parts of—Po. III.
Lesser parts of—Po IV.
—upon, [Be confident of.]
Bul, vid. **Bull.**
Bulboc astanum.
Bulbonach. HS. VI. 2.
Bulbous, HL. IV.
Bulfinch. Bi. IV. 3.
Bulge, [Mar, by in-crashing.]
Bulk [Massiness]
[Solid] Mag. I. 4.
[Total] TM. VI.
[Aggregate] TM. III. 6. Q.
Bull.
[Beast, Be. II. 1. (male)]
Writing, [Edict.] RC. IV. 3. O.
sp. of Pope.]
—Beetle. Ex. V. 2. A.
—finch. Bi. IV. 5.
—head, [Miller's thumb.] Fi. IX. 12.
—rush

BU | BU | CA

—*rush*, [Great (kind) rush.]
Ballace, [Plum of Black-thorn.]
Bullet. RM. V. 8.
Bullion { Gold / Silver } [not-coin'd]
Bullock, [Bull, Be. II. 1. (dim.)
Bulwark, [Rampier.] RM. VI. 3.
Bumbaft.
 [adj. Cotton stuffing (thing)
 [not-necessary (thing) in-
 thrusted.]
 [affected words]
Bunch.
 [Protuberance] Mag. IV. 3.
 [Cluster] PP. II. 4.
 [Aggregate] adj. TM. III. 6. O.
 (thing.)
 sp. together-tied.]
Bundle, [adj. aggregate. TM. III.
 6. O. (thing.)
 sp. together-tied.]
Bung.
 [Upper Orifice of the Barrel]
 sp. for Infusion.]
Bungling, [Unskilfulness.] Ha. VI.
 3. O.
Bunting. Bi. IV. 1.
Bunt-line. RN. IV. 6. A.
Buoy.
 Figure. Mag. VI. 5.
 [Anchor, (sign)
Bur,
 [Principal Glandule]
 —*of the Ear*, [Lower Protube-
 rance
 —*of Dock*, [Ear] PP. II.
 λ
Butter—HL. VI. 1. A.
 —*read*. ML. III. 15. A.
 Great—HL. VI. 1.
 Little—HL. VI. 2. A.
Burden,
 —*of a Song*, [Repeated verse]
 Load. Po. V. A.
 to—[adj. a. Heavy (make)
 upon, &c.]
Burgeon, [Sprout] PP. II. 5.
Burgess { Magistrate / Free-man } of a Town.]
Burglary. RJ. III. 8. A.
Bury, RE. IV. 8.
 —*alive*. RJ. V. 6. A.
Burl, [Pick the knots and motes out of Cloth.]
Burlesque.
 [Facetious imitation (corr.)
 [Mocking imitation of Poem.]
Burly.
 [adj. Ample.] Sp. II. 5.
 [adj. Fat. (augm.)
Burnet. HF. VIII 4.
 Thorny—Sh. III. 1. A.
Burning.
 Proper, [adj. a. Fire.] El. 1.
 house—RJ. III. 7.
 —*alive*. RJ. V. 7. A.
 —*in the hand*, [Stigmat.] RJ. VI. 6.
 —*Lance*, [Dart] El. I. 4. A.
 [Improper]
 [Rosting (Exc.)
 —*Fever*. S. II. 1.

Sun—[adj. p. Colouring
 (corr.) by the Sun.]
Burnish { Smooth / Brighten } by rubbing.]
Burrage. HL. IX. 1.
Burrow, [Hole in the Earth.]
 Cony—[Cony's (house.)
Burser, (adj. disbursing (off.)
Burst, vid. *Break*.
 —*Cow*, [Blain-worm.]
Burstenness, [hernia.]
Burt. [Turbut.] Fi. V. 2.
Bush { Shrubs / Hairs } (aggr.)
 Silver—Sh. VI. 6. A.
Bushel [8 Gallons.]
Busie.
 [adj. a. Business]
 [adj. a. Double diligence.] Ha. IV. 5. E.
 —*body*, [adj. a. Diligence
 (corr.)
Business.
 Employment, TA. III.
 [adj. a. Troubling (thing)]
Busk, Lanin for Woman's
 breast (vest.)
Buskin, [Vest until middle of
 leg.]
Bustard. Bi. II. 4.
But.
 Conjunction.
 but, Conj. II. 2. O.
 —[indeed] Conj. II. 2. as,
 but lately, &c.
 —[onely] Adv. IV. 1. O.
 —*that*, [unless.] Conj. I. 3. O.
 —*yet*.
 [notwithstanding] Conj. II. 2. O.
 Preposition.
 [beside] Prep. IV. 3. O.
But
 [thick extremity]
 sp. of Stock.]
 [Barrel (augm.)
 [measure]
 [Mark]
 [Bank at-adj. p. shoot (apt.)
 [Sign, adj. p. aim (apt.)
 to—
 [knock thrusting]
 sp. with Forehead.]
Butcher, [Butchering (Mechanic.]
 —*ing*. Pr. III. 1.
 —*bird*. Bi. I. 3. A.
 —*'s broom*. Sh. IV. 5. A.
Butler, [adj. Provisions (Officer)
 for adj. p. drink (thing.)
Butter. Pr. I. 3.
 —*milk*, [Milk after Butter (make.)
 —*fly*. Ex. IV. 9.
 Hawke—Ex. IV. 10.
 —*bur*. HL. VI. 1. A.
 —*wort*. HL. VI.
Buttery, [adj. Drinking (room.)
Buttock. PG. IV. 9.
Button. Mag. VI. 2.
 —*hole*. Mag. V. 2. A.

—*Fish*. Ex. VIII. 2.
Batchelor's—[Campion] HS. V. 2.
Buttress. Po, III. 7. A.
Buxom.
Buz, [a. Bee (voice.)
Buzzard, [Kite] Bi. I. 2. A.
bald—[White-headed—]

C

C Abala, [Tradition.] RE. VI. 1. A.
Cabbage. HS. IV. 6.
 —*Tree*. Tr. VII, 8.
Cabbin, [Chamber (dim.)
 sp. in a Ship.]
Cabinet.
 [Box { precious (ed / most esteem- } things)
Cable. RN. IV. 8.
Cacao. [Chocolate] Tr. IV. 7.
Cackle, [a. Hen (voice.)
Cacochymia. S. I. 3. A.
Cade.
 [Lamb educated in house.]
Cadence, [adj. Concluding
 Sound.]
Cadet, [Dependent.]
Cadew. Ex. III. 4. A.
Cage.
 [Imprisonment (room.)
 sp. for Birds.]
Cayman [Crocodile] Ee. VI. 3.
Cajole.
 [perswade by { Craft. / Flattering.}
Caitiff.
 { Wicked / Miserable } (augm.)
Cake, [Flat bread.]
Calaminaris. St. II. 7. A.
Calamint. HF. VII. 2. A.
Calamity, [Misery.]
Calcine. O. VI. 8.
Calculate, [Reckon.] TA. IV. 6.
Calendar, [adj. Year-book of
 Series of daies of every month.]
Calender, [a. smoothness] sp. of
 Cloth.
 —*a*—[adj. calendring (mech.)
Calends, [First day of the
 month.]
Calenture, [Fever (augm.)
Calf,
 Beast.
 [Bull, Be. II. 1. (young.)
 —*'s snout*. [Snap-dragon.]
 HS. VIII. 6.
 [Hart (male) of the first year.]
 Sea—[Seal.] Ee. V. 3. A.
 —*of the Leg*.
 [Protuberance behind the Leg.]
 [Hinder Muscles of the Leg.]
Calif. [Successor of *Mahomet*.]
Call. RN. VI. 1.

Call

CA | CA | CA

Call.
  [a. Voice]
  [a. Name]
  [Summon
  —*to mind*, [re-a. memory.]
  —*to witness*, [a. Witness (make.)]
  —*in*,
    [un-public]
    [a. annihilation]
  —*upon*, [Invocate.]
  —*ing*, Profession.]
Callous.
  [Hard { skin. / Muscle.}]
Callow.
  [Downy]
  [not-feathered]
Calm. El. VI. 6. A.
  [adj. Peaceableness]
  [adj. Meekness]
Calo. RM. III. 8. A.
Caltrops.
  Iron (instr.) having four points most distant from each other.
  land—HS. III. 9 A.
  water—HL. VII. 8. A.
Calumny. RJ. IV. 7.
Cambuge, [Concrete juice purgative.]
Camel. Be. I. 3.
  —*'s Hay.* HL. III. 11. A.
Camelopard, [Giraffa.] Be. II. 7.
Camerade.
  [adj. Chamber Companion]
Cammock, [Rest-harrow.] HS. III. 14.
Camomil. HF. II. 8.
Camp. RM. VI. 1.
  —*master*, [adj. Camp. (Officer.]
Campania, [Plain.]
  [Summers war.]
Camphire, Tree. Tr. VIII. 6.
  Gum. [Gum of Camphire tree.]
Campion. HS. III. 2.
Can.
  Active.
    [adj. Potentialness]
    [adj. Natural Power]
    [adj. Power.]
  Pass.
    [adj. Possibility.]
  • [May] Mod. I. 1.
  a—[Footless Cup]
Canary.
  —*bird.* Bi. IV. 6. A.
  —*grass.* HL III. 1.
  —*wine*, [Wine of the Canaries.]
Cancel.
  [a. Annihilation]
  [a. Spoil]
  [un—]
Cancer.
  Ulcer. S. III. 4.
  Constellation, [Star (aggr.) call'd the Crab.]
  Sign [the fourth of the twelve parts of the Zodiac.]
  tropic of—W VI. 5.

Cancer Majus. Ex. VI. 7.
Candy, [Condite with Sugar.]
  —*Alexander.* HF. IV. 13.
Candid. [adj. Candor.]
Candidate. RC. I. 4. A.
Candle. Pr. VI. 3.
  —*stick*, [Supporting (vess.) for Candle.]
Candor. Man. I. 3.
Cane. HL. III. 13.
Canel.
  —*bone*, [Bone next to the Weasand.]
  —*tree*, [Cinamon] Tr. VIII. 8.
Canibal, [adj. Eating (person) of men.]
Canis.
  —*major*, [Stars (aggr) called Greater Dog.]
  —*minor*, [Stars (aggr.) called Lesser Dog.]
Canker.
  [Ulcer], sp. within the mouth.]
  [Rust] Met. IV. 5. sp. of Brass.]
  Worm, [Caterpillar.]
Cankered, [adj. p Canker.]
  —*stomach*.
  [Old { Wrath / Hatred.}]
Cannibal, [adj. Eating (person) of men.]
Canons.
  —*of breeches*, &c. [Hollow Cylinders—]
  —*of a Cathedral*, [Assessors of the Bishop.]
  Rules, [adj. RE. Laws.]
  [Ordnance] RM. VI. 5. A.
Canonize.
  { Make / Sentence } one a Saint]
  { Declare
Canoo, [Boat of one Tree.]
Canopy, [over-adj. Head.]
  adj. { Shadowing / Covering } (thing.)
Canorous, [adj. a. Sing. (apt.)]
Cantharides. Ex. V. 9.
Cantharus. Fi. V. 2.
Canticle, [adj. p Sing (thing.)]
  sp. Little, &c.
Cantle, [Fragment.] TM. VI. 5. A.
Canto, [Treble (part) of a Song.]
Cantonize, [Divide into little Governments.]
Canvas, [Linnen of Hemp.]
  —*ing.*
  { a. Suter / Contend } or suffrages.]
  [Examin (augm.)]
Cap.
  [adj Head (vest]
  sp. Congruous to the Head]
  —*case*, [Box (dim)
  to—[un-vest the Head.]
  [Wooden (jug.) fastning
  { Top-mast } to the Mast]
  { Flag-staff

—*a pe*, [from head to foot]
—*Verses*, [Play at repeating Verses.]
Capable.
  [adj. a. Receive (pot.)]
  [adj. Subject
  [adj. Passion } (pot)
Capacity.
  { Subject / Receive / Passion } (pot.)
Caparison, [adj. Ornat. (armam.) of Saddle.]
Cape.
  —*of Cloke*, [adj. p. fold (Lamin.)]
  [Promontory] W. III. 4.
  —*Merchant.* RN, V, 5.
Caper.
  [Leap]
  sp. with trembling (like) of the Leggs.]
  Fruit. Sh. IV. 1.
Capital.
  [Private man of War]
  [Ship prædatory.]
Capital.
  [adj. Head.]
  [adj. a. Dy (apt.)]
  crime, [cr. punishable with dying (make)]
  [Cheef] TM IV 4.
Capitulate, [Treat about Conditions.]
Capon, [un-testicled Cock.]
Capra saltans. El. I. 5
Caprichious, [Fantastic] (corr.
Capricorn, [Tenth of the 12 parts of the Zodiac]
  tropic of—W VI 5.
Capriscus. Fi. IV. 9.
Capstain. RN. II. 3.
Captain.
  —*of Foot*, [adj. Company (Officer.)]
  —*of Horse*, [adj. Troop (Offi.)]
  —*of a Ship.* RN. V. 1.
Captious.
  [Censorious]
  [prone to { be displeased / dispute / quarrel }]
Captivate. RM. II. 6 E.
Captive, [adj. p. Captivate (person.)]
Caput Mort [Sediment remaining of distilled (thing)]
Car, [Cart.]
Caract, [Eighteenth part of a Dram.]
Caraguia. Be. V. 6.
Caramosel. RN. I. 4.
Caranna. Tr. VIII. 5.
Caravan, [Travelling (aggr.) of Merchants.]
Caravel, [Ship (augm.)]
Caraway. HF. V. 7.
Carbine, [Gun (augm.) of Horseman.]
Carbonado, [Broil'd adj. flashing] Pr. III. 5.
Carbuncle.
  Sore. S. III. 4. A.
    Ccc   Gem.

CA

Gem, [Ruby (augm.)]
Card
playing—[adj. Card. Mo. V. 2. (Inftr.]
  playing at—s [Mo. V. 2.
Geographic—[Defcription by picture.]
to—wool.
  [Un-intangle by Comb] O. V. 9. A.
  [Prepare for Spinning by Combing]
Cardamom.
Cardialgia. S. VI. 1.
Cardinal, [Principal.]
  [Chief, Clergy of Rome]
  —points, [Eaſt, Weſt, North, and South]
Care, [Thinking (augm.]
Carefulneſs.
  [Heedfulneſs] Ha. IV. 2.
  ſp. with { Trouble.
             Affliction. }
  [Diligence]
Careleſneſs.
  [Heedleſneſs] Ha. IV. 2. D.
  [Sloth]
Careſſing, [a. Seem. (ſign) love (augm]
Cargo, [Catalogue of Ships merchandize.]
Carine. RN. VI. 4.
Cark. Ha. IV. 2. E.
Carkanet, [Jewel (aggr.)
Carkaſs, [Dead body.]
  of a Fowl, [Trunk.]
Carnal.
  [adj. Fleſh]
  [Natural]
  [Worldly]
  [adj. Luſt]
  [Ungracious]
Carnation, [adj. Fleſh-colour.]
Cernoſity, [Fleſh abſtr.]
  a—[Excrefcence, adj. Fleſh.]
Carob. Tr. VI. 1.
Caroll, [Joyful Song.]
Carowſe [Drink (aug.]
Carp. Fi. IX. 7.
to—
  [Calumniate words]
  [Except contentiouſly.]
Carpenter.
  [adj. Houſe faber]
  [adj. Wood (Mechanic.]
Carpet.
  [Wool- { Ornament { for len { Veſt { Table.]
Carract, [Eighteenth part of a Dram.]
Carraway. HF. V. 7.
Carreer, [Running (imp.)]
Carret. HF. V. 6.
  wilde—HF. V. 6. A.
Carry.
  Go ſupporting. Mo. VI. 1.
  er.—RC. II. 8. A.
  Inſtruments for—ing. Pe. V.
  [a. Demeanour]
  [a. Converſe]
  [Support] Mo. VI. 1. A.
Carriage.

CA

  [adj. p. Carry (thing)
  [adj. a. Carry (manner)
  [Demeanour] AC. V.
  [Converſe] Man. A.
Carrick. RN. I. 4.
Carrion.
  [Dead body] ſp. putrid.]
  [Lean (augm.]
Cart. Po. V. 2. A.
  welſh—Po. V. 4. A.
Cartilage, [Griſtle.] PG. II. I. A.
Carve. O. IV. 6.
  —meat:
  { Unjoint
    Segregate } the Limbs.]
    Diſtribute
Carvel.
Caſe.
  Condition of dubitable Event
  [Condition] T. II. 4.
  [State.] T. VI. 4.
  [Doubtful (thing)
  [Queſtion]
  [adj. p. { Doubt
            Queſtion } (thing)]
  [State ſp. of Queſtion.]
  —of Conſcience, [Moral Queſtion]
  in Law.
  [Queſtionable Action (kinde.]
  [Cauſe of Suit]
  [Suppoſition] D. VI. 3.
  in—[If]
  in no—[Not redupl.]
  put—[imp. Suppoſe.]
  [Event] TA. V.
  [ſp. { Doubtful
         Suppoſed }]
  Veſſel. Pr. V. 1. A.
  —of a word.
  { Obliquity { of termina-
    Change   { tion.]
Caſement, [Door of Window.]
Caſh, [Preſent Mony.]
  —keeper, [Private Mony (Officer.]
Caſhire.
  [un-a. Souldier (make) penally.]
  [a. Incapacitating] ſp. a. Souldier.]
Caſk, [Veſſel] Pr. V.
  ſp. Barrel.] Pr. V. 3.
Casket.
  [Veſſel (dim.]
  [Box for precious (things.)]
Caſſaware. Bi. II. 9. A.
Caſſia. Tr. VI. 2.
  Shrub—Sh. II. 11. A.
Caſſidony. HF. VI. 5. A.
Caſſock, [Upper cloſe (veſt.)]
Caſt.
  adj. p. Motion (make.)
  ſp. Impetuouſly.
  & ſp. from { Contiguity
               p. Support } of its
               Capacity. } ver.
  throwing, Mo. VI. 2.
  as Metal. O. IV. 5. A.
  as Guilty, [Condemn.]
  as Nauſeous, [Vomit]

CA

  —about.
  { Think   } AS. II. 1.
  { Conſider   } AS. III. 2.
  { Contrive   } AS. III. 7.
  —away, vid.—off.
  —down, [down-caſt.]
  { Sorrowful
    Deſpondent } (make.)
  —in ones mind, vid.—about.
  —in ones teeth, [Upbraid.] RJ. IV. 8. A.
  —into { a. Form   { ſp. by
          a. Figure } caſting.]
  —into Sleep, [adj. a. Sleeping (make.)
  —off.
  [a. Reject] AS..V. 5. O.
  [a. Abdicate] TA. I. 3. O.
  [a. Abandon] TA. II. 2. O.
  [a. Dereliction] AS. I 5. O.
  —up.
  —into heap, [a. Heap.]
  —into ſum, [a. Sum.]
  —clothes, [not-fut. uſed cl.]
  —dice, [a. Dice.]
  —lots, [a. Lots]
  —skin.
  [adj. a. Let go. Ta. I. 6. O—]
  [adj. a. Change. TA. II. 6. O—]
  —water.
  [a. Inquiſition. RJ, II, 2.—]
  [a, Try. RJ. II. 4. A—]
  —Young, [a. Abortion.]
Caſtle. Po. II. 2. A.
Caſtor. Be. IV. 8.
Caſtrate, [Un-adj. a. teſticle (make.)
Caſtrel, vid. Keſtrel.
Caſual, [adj. Fortune. AS. I. 2. D.]
Caſuiſt.
  [Teacher of moral Doctrines.]
  [Solver of moral Doubts]
Cat. Be. IV. 4.
  Civet—Be. IV. 4. A.
  —mint.
  —s-tail. HL. II. 3. A.
Catalogue. TM. III. 7. A.
Catamite, [adj. p. Sodomy (perſon.]
Cataplaſm [Plaſter.] Pro. VI. 4. A.
Cataract, [Direct fall of River.]
  —in the eye, [Opacous (thing) in the water of the Eye.]
Catarrh. S. IV. 4.
Cataſtrophe, [adj. a. Altering Concluſion.]
  ſp. Altering to worſe.]
Catch.
  [adj. p. Reſt (make)
  ſp. Impetuouſly.
  & ſp. in its Comprehenſion.
  Catch, Mo. VI. 2. O.
  [Arreſt] RJ. II. 1. A.
  —poll, [Arreſting (Officer)
  [Purſevant] RJ, I. 6.
  [Obtain]
  as Fire, [a. Fire (imp.)
  as Infection, [p. Contagion.]
  [Take] TA. I. 4.

—at

CA

—at,
{ desire
{ endeavour } to { get }
{ offer } to { take }
{ Catch }
[Overtake] TA. VI. 6. A.
—*fly*. HS. V. 2. A.
Cafe. [Pr. II. (thing)]
Catechizing. RE. IV. 3. A.
Category, [Predicament.] TA.
Categorical, [absolute]
Cater, [Buy provisions.]
Caterpiller. Ex. III 6.
Flower, HS. III. 12. A.
Cathedral, [Temple of Bishop's (place.)]
Catholic. RE. III. 2.
Catmint. HF. VII. 1. A.
Cattel, [Beasts]
sp. Cloven footed.]
Cavalry.
[Horsemen { (kind
[a.— { (aggreg.
Caudle, [Broth of Egg, Wine, &c.]
Cave, [Cavity in the Earth.]
{ Room
[Under-ground { House
{ Hole
(aug.)
Caveare, [Condited spawn of Sturgeons.]
Caveat, [Caution (sign.]
Cavern, vid. *Cave*.
Caught, [adj. p. Catch.]
Cavill.
{ Objection } Contentious }
{ Dispute } (corr.)
Cavity, [Hollowness.] Mag. VI. 1. E.
Caul. PG. VI. 6. A.
—*for the head*, [adj. Net (figure.) head (vest.]
Cauldron, [Kettle (aug.]
Cause.
Proper. T. II.
[Efficient] T. II. 1.
[Impulsive] T. II. 2.
[Occasion] T. II. 4.
[End] T. II. 6.
In discourse.
[Reason]
[adj. a. Argumentation (thing)]
In Law.
[Cause of Suit]
[Suit] R]. II. A.
[Proceeding]R]. II.
Causey,
[Factitious way]
[Way pav'd with Stones]
Caustic { a. Burning } Medi-
{ a. Corroding } cine.]
Cautelousness, [Heedfulness.] Ha. IV. 2.
Canterizing, [Stigmatize.] R]. VI. 6. A.
Caution [a Heedfulness.]
—*money*, [Stipulatory-money before-paid.]
Cautiousness, [Heedfulness.] Ha. IV. 2.
Cease { Discontinue.
{ Desist.]

CE

Cecily, vid. *Ciceley*.
Cedar. Tr. V. 4.
Cell, [Room (dim.]
Regular's (toom)
Celandine. HS IV. 10. A.
Celebrate, [a. Solemnity]
Celebs. RO. II. 1.
Celerity.
[Swiftness] NP. V. 9.
[Dispatch] TA. III. 5.
Celestial, [adj. Heaven.] W. II.
Celibate, [Celebs (abstr.]
Cellar, [adj. Store (room) for adj. p. Drink (thing.]
Cement, [Glue of Stones.]
Censer, [adj. Burning (vessel) of Incense.]
Censor, [Judge] sp. of manners.]
Censorious. Man. I. 3. O.
Censure,[a.— { Judge.
{ Sentence.]
—*ecclesiastic*. RE. V. 3.
Centaur, [adj. Fiction Horseman.]
Center. Mag. II. 1.
Center-fish. Ex. VIII. 1. A.f
Centon, [adj. aggregate (thing) of divers fragments]
Centory.
Greater—HF. III. 3 A.
Lesser—HS. V. 5.
Century, 100.
Centurion, [adj. Company (Officer.]
Cerecloth, [Plaster'd cloth.]
Ceremony, [Circumstance] sp. solemn.]
Certain.
[Sure] adj. AS. II. 6.
—*ly*. Adv. I. 2, O.
[Manifest]
[Some] Pron. II. 3.
Certainty. AS. II. 6.
Certifie.
[adj. Certainty (make]
[adj. a. Know (make]
Ceruse. Met. IV. 5. A.
Cess (tax)
Sp.according to his proportion]
Cessation { Discontinue.
{ Desist.
Chaff { Recrement } of winnow-
{ Husks } ed Grain
Chafe. [Heat by rubbing.]
[Rub] O. V. 8.
[Heat] Q. V. 1. E.
—*ing-dish*, [adj. Table (vessel) for Fire.]
Stomach, [adj. Angry (aug.]
Chafer.
[Bay Scarab]
Goat—Ex. V. 3.
Green—Ex. V. 5. A.
Chaffer.
[Treat concerning the Price]
[Exchange]
Chaffinch. Bi. IV. 7.
Chain, [Cord { Binding.
of Loops for { Ornament.]
Chair. Po. VI. 6.

CH

Chalcedony. St. V. 6.
Chalcis. Fi. III. 12. A.
Chaldron, [36. Bushels.]
Chalenge.
[Claim]
[Provoke]
[Accuse]
Chalice, [Footed drinking { vessel.]
Chalk. St. VI. 1.
Chama. Ex. VIII. 6.
Chamaecyparissus.
Chamber, [Room]
sp. Sleeping (room)
Chamberlein.
[adj. Chamber (Off.]
[adj. City mony (Off.]
Chameleon. Be. VI. 4. A.
Chamfer, [Gutter (freq.)
Chamomil. HF. II. 8.
Champ, [Mastication]
Champain, [Plain.] W. III. 1. E.
Champion, [Instead-fighting (person.]
Chance, [Fortune.]
Chancel, [Chief adj. Temple (Room.]
Chancellor, [Judge of Equity.]
Chancery, [Court of Equity.]
Chandler, [Candle { Mech.
{ Merch.
Chanel. W. IV. 5. A.
Change.
[Alter] TA. I. 1. O.
Mutation, TA. II 6. A.
—*of the Moon*.
[Time when the Moon ends one Course, and begins another]
[Exchange]
Changeable.
Mutable, [adj. Change (apt.]
Of divers Colours. Q. II. 5. A.
Changeling.
[Instead-put]
[Idiot]
Channa. Fi. V. 11. A.
Chant, [Sing.]
Chanter, [Chief Singer.]
Chantry, [Ecclesiastical singing (place.)]
Chaos, [Unformed matter.]
Chap.
[Chink] Mag. V. 4. O.
—*of mouth*.
[Jaw]
sp. Bone of it.]
Chape, [End (arm.) of the Swords case.]
Chaplain { Domestic } Presby-
{ Private } ter.]
Chaplet, [Wreath of Flowers for the head.]
Chapman, [adj. a. Buying (person.]
Chappel, [Temple { (dim.
{ accessory.]
Chapter.
—*of book*. D. III. 3.
—*of Cathedral*.
[Bishop's Assessors (aggr.]
[Their Convention]

[And

[And Convention-house.]
—of Pillar, [Top of Column.]
Character. D. I. 1. A.
  [Description]
Charcole, [Cole made by charking.]
Chare, [Business (dim.]
  [Instead-business.]
Charge.
  Proper [Load] Po. V. A.
  —a Gun.
    [adj. p. Ammunition (make)]
  In Oeconomic.
    [Command]
  In Civil sense.
    [Trust]
    have—of, Be intrusted with.
    [Office]
    Cost, [Expence]
  In Judicial.
    [Accuse]
      Lay to one's— [a. Accuser.]
  In Military.
    [Assault]
Charger, [Dish (aug.) for Esculents.]
Chary.
  [adj. Indulgence]
  [Heedful for]
  [Loth that it should suffer]
Chariot. Po. V. 2.
Charity. Ha. V. 6.
Chark. O. VI. 7.
Charleswain, [Stars (aggr.) called, &c.]
Charlock. HS. IV. 9. A.
Charm { Witch } with words.
       { Wizard }
Charnel, [Room for dead bodies.]
Charr. Fi. IX. 3. A.
Charring. O. VI. 7.
Charter, [Patent]
  sp. For grant of Privilege]
Chase.
  [Treey Country]
  sp. for Deer.
  [Forrest] Po, I, 2, A.
  to—
    [Hunt]
    [Drive]
    [Pursue]
Chasm, [Emptiness.]
  —in the Skie. El. V. 5.
Chast, [adj. Chastity.]
  —tree. Sh. V. 1.
Chastise, [Correct.]
Chatt, [Loquacity.]
Chattels, [Goods not inheritable.]
Chatter.
  with ones Tongue.
  as Birds.
    { a. Swallow } voice]
    { a. Pie   }
  [Prate]
  with ones Teeth.
    [Tremble——]
    sp. with Sound (aug.]

Cheap.
  [adj. { Price } (dim.)]
         { Value }
  [Sorry] TM. I. 4. D.
Cheapen, [Treat concerning the price.]
Cheat, [Fraud.]
Check,
  [Interrupt Motion]
  [Hinder]
  [Cohibit]
  [Reprove]
Checker, vid. Exchequer.
  —'d with Colours. Q. II. 7.
Cheef, [Principal.]
Cheek. PG. III. 7.
  [Side] Sp. III. 4.
Cheer.
  Diet, [Quantity of Food.]
  [Face (manner]
  to—
    [Encourage.]
    [Merry (make.]
    [Cheerful (make.]
Cheerfulness, [Alacrity.] Ha. IV. 2.
Cheese. Pro. I. 3. A.
Cheeslip, [Sow.] Ex. II. 9.
Cheesrunning [Ladies bedstraw] HL. IX. 6. A.
Cherish.
  [a. Fotion] AC. I. 4.
  [Preserve indulgently]
Cherry. Tr. II. 3.
  Birds—Sh. II. 5.
  Winter—HS. IX. 8.
  Wildrock-of Austria. Sh. II. 5. A.
Cherub.
  [Angel]
  [image of Angel]
Cheruil. HF. V. 8. A.
Chesil.
  [Prism. for { Cutting }]
              { Carving }
Chess-playing. Mo. V. 5.
Chest.
  [Box] Pr. V. 2.
  of the Body.
  [Trunk]
    sp. the Cavity of it.]
Chestnut. Tr. IV. 4.
Cheverel, [Leather of Gote's skin.]
Cheveron, [Tooth (like) lines.]
Chevin, [Chub.] Fi. IX. 8. A.
Chew, [Mastication.]
  —the Cud, [Re-masticate.]
Chibbol, [Young Onion.]
Chickling. HS. II. 5.
  under-ground—HS. II. 7.
Chick, [Hen (young.]
  —weed. HS. V. 9. A.
  Bastard—HS. V. 10.
  berry bearing—HS. IX. 8. A.
Chide, [Reprove angrily.]
Chill, [Cold (dim]
Chilblain. S. III. 7.
Child,
  By Relation.
    Natural. RO. I. 2. O.
    to be with—[to have conceived.]

—in the womb, [Embryo.]
—birth, [Parturition]
—bed, [the Bed in which adj. a. pret. Parturition lies.]
  in—[adj. a. pret. Parturition.]
  ' Adventitious.
  Foster——RO. III 2. O.
  God——RO. III. 1. O.
  Ward——RO. III. 4. O.
  By Age.
    [Infant]
    Boy.
Childhood.
  [Infancy] Mea. VI. 1.
  Boy's age, Mea. VI. 1. A.
Childish, [adj. Child (like.]
Childless, [Not-parent.]
Chime.
  [Tune with the Bells]
  [Ring melodiously]
Chimera, [adj. Fiction (thing.]
Chimist. [O. VI. (mech.]
Chimny. Po. III. 9. A.
Chin. PG. III. 8. A.
China, [root of an Indian climbing plant.]
Chine, [Bone of the Back.]
Chin-cough, [adj. a. pret. Duration (aug.) Cough.]
Chink, Chap. Mag. V. 4. O.
Chip. TM. VI. 3.
  to—
    [Cut into Chips.]
    [From-cut the outside.]
Chiromancy, [Wizarding by the sight of hand.]
Chirp.
  dim. Singing. AC. III. 5. A.
  Voice of Birds, [a. Sparrow (voice)]
Chirurgeon. [adj. RC. III 2. (person)]
Chit, [Cat (young]
Chitterling, [Smallest guts.]
Chivalry, [War (art.]
  sp. adj. Horseman.]
Chives, vid. Cive.
Chocolate. Tr. IV. 7.
Choice.
  Subst.
    [Election] RC. IV. 2.
    [Diversity]
    [Many of { Kinds.}]
    divers   { Valors.}
  Adject.
    [Excellent]
Choke, [Strangle.] RC. V. 8.
Choler. PG. I. 6. A.
  —adust, [melancholy]
Cholerick.
  [adj. Choler]
  [adj. Anger (apt.]
Choose, [a. Election.]
  As to do. AS. IV. 5.
  As to Office. RC. IV. 2.
  may—[is adj. Liberty.]
  cannot—but, [is adj. p. Determination.]
Chop,
  [Mince.]

CI | CI | CL

[Mince] Pr. III. 6. A.
—*ing knife*, [Mincing (inst.)
—*ing block*,
  [Supporting (inst.) for the chopped (thing.)
  [Cut by striking]
—*of mutton*.
  [From-cut (part)—]
  [sp adj. Proportion.]
—*in*, [Come sudden.]
  [Exchange]
Chord. Mag. II. 6, A.
Chorister, [adj. Singing (Off.)]
Chorus.
  [together-Singers (Aggr.)]
  [Players together-speaking (aggr.)]
Chough. Bi. I. 6. A.
Chrism, [Anointing.]
Chrift. G. II.
Christen, [Baptize.]
Christendom, [World of Christians,]
Christianity. RE. I. 4.
Christmas, [Festival (time) of Christ's birth.]
—*day*, [Festival day of Christ's birth.]
Chromis. Fi. V. 7.
Chronicle.
  [Relation of things done according to the Series of times.]
Chronology.
  [History of times.]
  [Computing (art) of times]
Chrysocol, [Borax]
Chrysolite. PP. V. 6. A.
Chub. Fi. IX. 8. A.
Chuckle, [Laugh (augm.]
  [sp. Inwardly.]
Church.
  Society, [RE. (aggr.)]
  Temple. Po. II. 4.
  —*warden*, [adj. Temple (Off.)]
  —*yard*, [Court of Temple]
Churching. RE. IV. 6.
Churl, [adj. Churlishness (person.)]
Churlishness.
  [Rusticity] Man. IV. 9. D.
  [Moroseness] Man. IV. 7. D.
  op. to Alms. Man. III. 5. D.
  [Roughness]
Churn, [Motion (freq.) vicissitudinary.]
Chur-worm. [Fen-Cricket.] Ex. II. 2. A.
Chyle. PG. I. 3.
Chymic Operation. O. VI.
Cicada. Ex. IV. 6.
  —*aquatica*. Ex. II. 4. A.
Cicely.
  Sweet—HF. IV. 3.
  wi d—HF. IV. 3. A.
Cicutaria.
Cider, [Wine of Apples.]
Cimex. [Punice] Ex. II. 6. A.
  —*silvestris*. Ex. II. 3.
Cinders, [Fiery ashes]

—*of Sea-cole*, [Charred remainders—]
Cinnabar. Met. III. 5.
Cinnamon. Tr. VII. 8.
Cinqfoil. HF. IX. 2.
Cipher.
  [adj. Number (sign) Character.]
  [Character]
  [Secret Character]
  [Number]
  to—[adj. a. Number (art.)]
  [Nothing (sign) Character.]
Cypres, [Transparent Linnen.]
  —Tr. V. 6.
Circle. Mag. III. 2.
  By which the World is divided. W. VI.
Circuit.
  [Region]
  [Margin of Circle]
Circular, [adj. Circle.]
Circulate, [About-going]
Circumcision. RE. VI. 5.
Circumference, [Circle about-adj. Margin.]
Circumflex, [Long sounding.]
Circumlocution, [Express by many words.]
  [Paraphrase] D. V. 5. A.
Circumscribe, [About—a. compass.]
Circumspect, [Cautious.]
Circumstance. T. VI. 3.
Circumvent, [a. Fraud.]
Cistern, [a. Keeping (vessel) for Water.]
Citadel, [Castle.] Po. II. 2.
Citation.
  Summons RJ. II. 2.
  [Quotation] D. IV. 9.
Citerior. Sp. II. 2. E.
City. RC. III. 3. A.
Citizen. RC. I. 6.
Citrine, [adj. Citron colour.]
Citrinella. Bi. VI. 2.
Citron. Tr. L 8.
Citrull. HS. VII. 2. A.
Cittern, [Little musical (instr.) having brass strings.]
Cirsium. Sh. II. 6. A.
Cive. HL. IV. 10. A.
Civet, [Sweat of the Civet Cat.]
  —*Cat*. Be. IV. 4. A.
Civil.
  [adj. Civility]
  [adj. City]
  [adj. Civil relation]
  —*Relation*. RC.
  —*Lawyer*. RC. II. 2.
  —*War*.
    [War between {Nation. men of the Commonsame wealth.]
Civility.
  [Courtesie] Man. IV. 7.
  [Complaisance] Man. IV. 8.
Clack, [Knock (freq.) sound.]
  a—[adj. Knock (machin.)]

Clad, [Clothed]
Clay. El. IV. 4.
Claim. TA. I. 3.
Clamber, {adv. Difficult.}
  {[Climbe (corr.)]
Clamminess. Q. VI. 4. E.
Clamor, [Exclaim] AC. III. 3. O.
Clancular, [Secret.]
Clandestine, [Secret.]
Clap. AC. V. 5.
  —*up*.
    [Finish adv. sudden]
    [Imprison]
    sp. suddenly.
  —*of thunder*, {sound (imp.) of th.}
Clapboard, {Oaken (lamins) for lining Rooms.}
Clapper.
  [Box] Pr. V. 2.
  Instrument, [Striking (part) of ringing (instr.)]
Claret, [Red French Wine]
Clary. HF. VII. 10.
  Wild—HF. VII. 10. A.
Clarifie.
  [Separating the course (parts.)]
  [a. Clear (make.)]
Clash.
  [against-Strike]
  [sp. reciprocally.]
  [a. Contention]
Clasp.
  [Hook]
  [Embrace]
Clasper, [Tendril.] PP. II. 7. A.
Class, [Series.]
Classic, [Authentic.]
Clatter, [Jarring.]
Clause. D. III. 1.
Claw.
  as of man, [Nail.]
  a—*back*, [Fawner.]
  as of Beast. PP. VI. 5. A.
  as of Bird. PP. V. 3.
  as of Shell-fish. PP. IV. 7.
  to—[Scratch]
Clean.
  [Pure] TM. V. 5.
Quite and— {perfectly Totally}
Cleanliness. Man. II. 6.
Cleanse.
  [Clean (make.)]
  [a. Innocent (make.)]
  [Vndefiled (make.)]
  [Un a. guilty (make.)]
Clear.
  Entire of it self.
  —*ly*. [Wholly.]
  Not mingled with other, [Simple.]
  sp. not with worse.
  [Pure]
  [Not hinder'd {being from {doing Receiving}
  E.g. in any genus, as of (perf.)
  Quality or Relation
  NP.

CL

—*understanding*, [Und. (perf.]
—*sight*, [Sight (perf.]
as to Mind.
 [Ingenuous]
 [Sprightly]
as to the Body.
 [Sound]
 [Indolent]
 [Beautiful]
Ha.
—*repute*, [Rep. (perf.]
sp. [Sagacious]
 [Sincere]
Man.
 [Candid]
 [Frank]
Quality.
Visible.
 [Lightsom]
—*weather*. El. VI. 1.
 [Bright]
 [Transparent]
 Unspotted. Q. I. 5.
Audible.
—*sound*. Q. III. 7.
RC. [Not in Debt] TA. IV. 9.
R]. [Not in Guilt] R]. II. 7.
RM. [Not in War] RM. II. 7.
RE [Not under Censure] RE.
 V. 5. O.
S. [Not {Infected.}{Diseased.}]
Not hinder'd from being done.
 [Easie]
Not hinder'd from being known.
 [Plain]
 [Manifest]
Not hinderd {Come to.}{Pass'd through.} from being
 [Accessible]
 [Empty]
 [Passable]
Cleaver.
 [Cleaving (instr.]
 [Knife (augm.) to strike with]
Cleavers. [goose-gra's] HL. IX.
 9. A.
Cleaving.
Sticking.
 [a. Clammy]
 [Adhering]
Chapping, [apj. p. Chink.]
as with a Wedge. O. I. 3.
Cloven-footed.
Cleer, vid. Clear.
Cleft.
 [Chink] Mag. V. 4. O.
 [adj. p. Cleave]
Clematis. Sh. V. 7.
Clemency. Man. VI. 8.
Clergy. RE. II.
Clerk, [adj. {Church-}{Writing} {Officer.}]
 [adj. Clergy (person]
 [adj Church (off.]
 —*of Church*, [Minister's subordinate (officer.]
 [adj. Writing (offic]
 —*of Exchequer.*
 —*of Rolls.*
 Gentleman's—

CL

—*of Market*, [adj. Market (off.]
Clew, [Bottom.]
Click, [a. Sound as Watch.]
Clicket, [Lust.]
 sp. of Rabbets.]
Client, .
 [Dependent]
 [adj. p. Advocate (person]
Cliff. W. III. 3. A.
Climacteric, [adj. a. Altering (apt.) seventh year.]
Climate, [adj. p. Latitude (place) of 13 hours, 13 and a half, &c]
Climbe. Mo. II. 5.
Climber of Virginia. Sh. V. 8.
Clinch.
—*a Nail*, [Fix it by {re-knocking}{folding} {the point}{of it.}]
—*ones Fist*, [Fold the hand.]
a—[Urbanity (endeavor) by similitude of words.]
Cling. AC. VI. 9.
Clink, [a. Sound as Chains.]
Clip.
 [Cut] O. V. 4. A.
 [Embrace]
Clock, Po. VI. 6. A.
 what is it of—[what hour is it according to the—]
Clod, [Lump.]
Clog, [Hinder.]
Cloy.
 [adj. p. Excess (make]
 [adj. a. Nauseate with abundance.]
Cloister.
 [House of Monks]
 [Roofed walking (place]
Cloke, [Wide outer (Vest]
to—
 [Cover]
 [Pretence]
 [Conceal]
Cloke-bag, [Sack to be tied behind the Saddle.]
Closeness, Nearness impeditive of Penetration.
 Nearness
 of thing to thing.
 [Nearness]
 [Contiguity]
 [Continuity]
 of the parts of a thing.
 The Extremes.
 [Narrowness]
 The Middle parts.
 Closeness, Q. V. 3.
 [Denseness] Q. V. 3. E.
 Impeditive to the
 Surface.
 to close.
 [adj. Hide.]
 [adj. Conceal]
 Periphery.
 to close,
 [adj. a. Sepiment]
 a Close.
 [adj. p. Sepiment (place]
 Top.
 to close.

CL

with its own.
 [adj. Shut]
 [adj. p. Whole] as a Wound.
with mothers.
 [adj. Cover]
 Side.
 to close.
 [Together-join]
 [Together-fold] as a Letter.
 End.
 to close, [adj. a. Finish.]
Of Penetration; by
 Ey, [Darkness] as of weather.
 Ear, [Silence.]
 Reservedness.
 Hand, &c.
 [Fastness]
 [Penuriousness]
Closet, Room (dim.) for privacy]
Clot.
—*bird.*
—*burr.*
Cloth.
Stuff for Clothing [adj. Clothing thing]
 Cotton—Pr. IV. 4. A.
 Hair—Pr. IV. 4. A.
 Linnen—Pr. IV. 4.
 Woollen—Pro. IV. 1.
—*worker*, [adj. cloth (Mechanic.]
Clothe.
 [make Cloth]
 put on [adj. p. Clothing (make]
Clothing. Pr. IV.
Clottered, [Coagulated]
Cloud. El. III. 2.
Clove.
—*of Garlick*, [Bulb of the root]
—*tree*. Tr. III. 9.
Cloun, vid. Clown.
Clout.
 [Fragment of Cloth]
 [adj. Mending (thing]
to—
 [Mend]
 [Strengthen] by addition.]
Clown.
 [adj. Country (corr.]
 [adj. Rusticity (person]
 —*ishness*, [Rusticity.]
Clu, [Bottom.] Mag. VI. 7.
Club.
 Weapon, RM. V. 2.
 [Society.]
Cluck, as a Hen.
 [Calling (voice]
Clung.
 [adj. a. preter. Cling]
 [together-adhering]
Cluster. PP. II. 4.
 [adj. aggregate (thing]
Clutch.
 [Talon. PP. V. 3. (Aggreg.]
 [Hand] PG. V. 3. Holding.
 TA. V. 5. (augm.]
to—

CO

to—
[Shrink] AC. V. 5. O.
[Together-fold] O. III. 5.
[Hold (corr.)]
Clutter.
[Confused {Motion}{Sound}]
Clyster, [Medicinal drink for fundament.]
Coach. Po. V. 1.
—*man,* [Coach (Officer.)]
—*box,* [Seat of Coach (Officer.)]
Coaction. AS. IV. 9. O.
Coadjutor, [With-helper.]
Coagulating. O. VI. 2. A.
Coalition [a. p.] {Uniting.}
Coarctation.
[together-joyning (augm.)]
[Shrinking]
Coast.
Quarter, [Country near.]
Sea. coast, [nigh- adj. Sea Country.]
to— [Travail (end.) by conjecture.]
Coat.
Garment, [Outward close (vest.)]
—*of Male,* [Woven (like) armour.]
—*of Arms,* {Nobility}{Gentility} (sign.
Cottage, [Rustic house (dim.)]
Cobble.
[Mend, (corr.)]
[a. Unskilful] Ha. VI. 3. O.
Cob-iron, [Supporting (instr.) for Spit.]
Cobler, [Mending (mech.) of Leather (vest) for foot.]
Cobweb, [Spider's woven (thing)]
Cock.
[Male] [sp. bird]
[Bird, Bi. II. 1. (male)
—*'s comb.* HS. VIII. 7.
—*'s head.* HS. III. 5. A.
heath— Bi. II. 5. A.
—*of the wood.* Bi. II. 5.
Exanguious.
Sea— Ex. VI. 6. A.
—*Roches.* Ex. I. 7. A.
winged— Ex. II. 3. A.
Instrument,
—*of Dial,* [Pin—]
—*of Gun-lock,* [adj. a. Fire (machin.)]
—*for Water,* [Lock of Pipe.]
Weather— [Winde (sign) instrument.]
—*of Hay,* [Heap—]
—*boat,* [Boat (dim.]
—*swain.* RN. V. 6. A.
Cockall, [Dicing with heel-bones.]
Cockatrice, [Serpent killing by Sight.]
Cocker, [adj. a. Fondness.] Man. VI. 7. D.
Cocket, [Writing of Tribute

CO

(off.) for {impore}{export} of wares]
Cockle.
Fish. Ex. VIII. 5. A.
Herb. HS. V. 6. A.
Cockrel, [Hen (male) (young.)]
Coco. Tr. IV. 6.
Cocothraustes. Bi. IV. 4.
—*Cristatus.* Bi. IV. 4. A.
Cod.
Fish. Fi. III. 1.
—*of Plant.* PP. III. 5. A.
—*of Animal,* [Testicles (vessel.)]
—*piece,* [adj. Privities (vest.)]
Codicil, [Added writing.]
Coequal, [Equal.]
Coerce, [Cohibit.]
Coessential, [Of the same Essence.]
Coetaneous, [Together in Age.]
Coeternal, [Together-eternal.]
Coexistent, [Together-existent.]
Coffee. Tr. IV. 7. A.
Coffer, [Chest.]
—*er,* [Keeping (off.) of Treasure.]
Coffi. Tr. IV. 7. A.
Coffin.
[Receiving (vessel)]
[Box for dead body]
Cog.
—*of Mill,* [Tooth of wheel.]
to—
[Fawn.]
[a. Fraud.]
Cogitation, [Thinking]
Cognation of things. T. VI. 8.
Cognisance,
[Acknowledging]
of Cause. R. II 4.
Badge, [Service (sign.)]
Coheir, [Together-heir.]
Coherent.
[Together {Sticking.}{Joining.}]
[adj. Congruity]
Cohibitive cause. T. II. 2. O.
Cohobation, [Repeated Distillation.]
Cohort, [Troop.]
Coy, [adj. Aversation (apt.)]
Coif, [Close adj. head (vest.)]
Coil, [Confused {Motion.}{Sound.}]
to—a rope, [a. Spiral.]
Coin.
—*of a Wall,* [Corner—]
[Mony]
to—
[a. Mony (make)]
[a. Print (sp. in Metal)]
[a. Fiction]
[a. Forgery]
Coincident, [Together-adj. Event]
Coistrel, [adj. Adolescence (male.)]
Coit. [Lamin. adj. p. cast (apt.)]
Coition. AC. II. 5. A.
Colander, [adj. Streining (vessel.)]

CO

Cold.
—*to sense.* Q. V. 1. D.
[Remiss]
a— [Disease from cold]
Cole.
Live—[Fired fuel (Part)]
Dead—[un-fired fuel (part)]
Sea—St. VI. 3. A.
—*black,* [Black (augm.)]
Cole-rake. Instr.
Cole-mouse. Bi. VI. 7. A.
Cole-wort, [Cabbage.] HS. IV. 6.
Co'et, {Concave (place}{Gem (place} of Ring.
Colic S. VI. 5.
Coll, [Embrace.]
Collar, [Environing (armam.) for neck.]
Collateral.
[of the same Series]
[Accessary]
Collation,
[Giving]
[Right of giving]
[Refection, Pr. I. 1. A.]
[Comparing. TA. II. 5.]
Collect, [adj. Epitome prayer.]
Collection.
[a. Gathering]
[adj. p. Gathering (thing.)]
Collective.
[Together-gathering]
[adj. Aggregate]
Collector, [adj. a. {Person.}{Officer.}] Gathering
College. RC. III. 7 A.
sp. of Scholars.
Collegue.
Companion
adj p. Leag.
[Together adj. p. Colledg.]
Collier, [Fuel {Officer.}{(mech.}{(mere.}]
Colli-flower, [Cabbage]
Collision.
[Together {striking.}{Reciprocal}]
Collogue, [Fawn.]
Collop.
[Chip]
[Slice]
Colloquy, [Together-discourse.]
Collusion, [Agreeing to cheat.]
Colon.
[adj. Fundament Gut.]
Period. D. I. 6.
Co'onel, [Regiment (Off.)]
Colony. RC. III. 1. A.
Coloquintida. HS. VII. 4.
Color. Q. II.
[Pretext]
—*s* [adj. {Ensign}{Cornet} (thing)]
Coloss, [Image (augm.)]
Colt {Horse}{Ass} (young)
—*s-foot.* HL. VI. 1.
mountain— [Horse foot] HL. VI. 3.
Columbine. HS. I. 2. A.
Column, [Pillar Poss. III. 5.]
Colure, [Meridian through Tropics.]

Comb.

CL

—*understanding*, [Und. (perf.)
—*a sight*, [Sight (perf.)
as to Mind.
  [Ingenuous]
  [Sprightly]
as to the Body.
  [Sound]
  [Indolent]
  [Beautiful]
He.
—*repute*, [Rep. (perf.)
sp. [Sagacious]
  [Sincere]
Man.
  [Candid]
  [Frank]
Quality.
Visible.
  [Lightsom]
—*weather*. El. VI. 1.
  [Bright]
  [Transparent]
Unspotted. Q. I. 5.
Audible.
—*sound*. Q. III. 7.
RC. [Not in Debt] TA. IV. 9.
RJ. [Not in Guilt] RJ. IL 7.
RM. [Not in War] RM. 4. 7.
RE [Not under Censure] RE. V. 5. O.
S. [Not {Infected.} {Diseased.}
Not hinder'd from being done.
  [Easie]
Not hinder'd from being known.
  [Plain]
  [Manifest]
Not hinderd { Come to. .
from being { Pass'd through.
  [Accessible]
  [Empty]
  [Passable]
Cleaver.
  [Cleaving (instr.)
  [Knife (augm.) to strike with]
Cleavers. [goose-grass] HL. IX. 9. A.
Cleaving.
Sticking.
  [a. Clammy]
  [Adhering]
Chapping, [apj. p. Chink.]
as with a Wedge. O. I. 3.
Cloven-footed.
Cleer, vid. *Clear*.
Cleft.
  [Chink] Mag. V. 4. O.
  [adj. p. Cleave]
Clematis. Sh. V. 7.
Clemency. Man. VI. 8.
Clergy. RE. II.
Clerk-[adj. {Church-} {Writing} {Offi-cer.}
  [adj. Clergy (person)
  [adj. Church (off.)
  —*of Church*, [Minister's subordinate (officer.)
  [adj. Writing (offic)]
  —*of Exchequer*.
  —*of Rolls*.
Gentleman's—

CL

—*of Market*. [adj. Market (off.)]
Clew, [Bottom.]
Click, [a. Sound as Watch.]
Clicket, [Lust.]
sp. of Rabbets.]
Client, .
  [Dependent]
  [adj. p. Advocate (person)
Cliff. W. III. 3. A.
Climatleric, [adj. a. Altering (apt.) seventh year.]
Climate, [adj. p. Latitude (place) of 13 hours, 13 and a half, &c]
Climbe. Mo. II. 5.
Climber of Virginia. Sh. V. 8.
Clinch.
  —*a Nail*, [Fix it by { re-knocking } the point { folding } of it.]
  —*ones Fist*, [Fold the hand.]
  a—[Urbanity (endeavor) by similitude of words.]
Cling. AC. VI. 9.
Clink, [a. Sound as Chains.]
Clip.
  [Cut] O. V. 4. A.
  [Embrace]
Clock, Fo. VI. 6. A.
  what is it of—[what hour is it according to the——]
Clod, [Lump.]
Clog, [Hinder.]
Cloy.
  [adj. p. Excess (make)
  [adj. a. Nauseate with abundance.]
Cloister.
  [House of Monks]
  [Roofed walking (place)
Cloke, [Wide outer (Vest)
to—
  [Cover]
  [Pretence]
  [Conceal]
Cloke-bag, [Sack to be tied behind the Saddle.]
Closeness, Nearness impeditive of Penetration.
  Nearness
  of thing to thing.
    [Nearness]
    [Contiguity]
    [Continuity]
  of the parts of a thing.
  The Extremes.
    [Narrowness]
  The Middle parts.
  Closeness, Q. V. 3.
    [Denseness] Q. V. 3. E.
  Impeditive as to the Surface.
  to close.
    [adj. Hide.]
    [adj. Conceal]
  Periphery.
  to close,
    [adj. a. Sepiment]
  a Close.
    [adj. p. Sepiment (place)
  Top.
  to close.

CL

with its own.!
  [adj. Shut]
  [adj. p. Whole] as a Wound.
with smothers.
  [adj. Cover]
Side.
to close.
  [Together-join]
  [Together-fold] as a Letter.
End.
to close, [adj. a. Finish.]
Of Penetration; by
Ey, [Darkness] as of weather.
Ear, [Silence.]
Reservedness.
Hand, &c.
  [Fastness]
  [Penuriousness]
Closet, Room (dim.) for privacy.]
Clot.
  —*bird*.
  —*burr*.
Cloth.
Stuff for Clothing [adj. Clothing thing]
  Cotton—Pr. IV. 4. A.
  Hair—Pr. IV. 1. A.
  Linnen—Pr. IV. 4.
  Woollen—Pro. IV. 1.
  —*worker*, [adj. cloth (Mechanic.)
Clothe.
  [make Cloth]
  put on [adj. p. Clothing (make)
Clothing. Pr. IV.
Clottered, [Coagulated]
Cloud. El. III. 2.
Clove.
  —*of Garlick*, [Balb of the root.]
  —*tree*. Tr. III. 9.
Clown, vid. *Clown*.
Clout.
  [Fragment of Cloth]
  [adj. Mending (thing)];
to—
  [Mend {by addition.}]
  [Strengthen]
Clown.
  [adj. Country (corr.)
  [adj. Rusticity (person)
  —*ishness*, [Rusticity.]
Clu, [Bottom.] Mag. VI. 7.
Club.
  Weapon, RM. V. 2.
  [Society.]
Cluck, as a Hen.
  [Calling (voice)
Clung.
  [adj. a. preter. Cling]
  [together-adhering]
Cluster. PP. II. 4.
  [adj. aggregate (thing)
Clutch.
  [Talon. PP. V. 3. (Aggreg.)
  [Hand] PG. V. 3. Holding.
  TA. V. 5. (augm.)

to—

CO

to—
[Shrink] AC. V. 5. O.
[Together-fold] O. III. 5.
[Hold (corr.]
Clutter.
[Confused {Motion} {Sound}]
Clyster, [Medicinal drink for fundament.]
Coach. PO. V. 1.
—*man*, [Coach (Officer.)]
—*box*, [Seat of Coach (Officer.)]
Coaction. AS. IV. 9. O.
Coadjutor, [With-helper.]
Coagulating. O. VI. 2. A.
Coalition [a. p.] {Uniting.}
Coarctation.
[together-joyning (augm.)]
[Shrinking]
Coast.
Quarter, [Country near.]
Sea. coast, [nigh- adj. Sea Country.]
to—[Travail (end.) by conjecture.]
Coat.
Garment, [Outward close (vest.)]
—*of Male*, [Woven (like) armour.]
—*of Arms*, {Nobility Gentility} (sign.)
Cottage, [Rustic house (dim.)]
Cobble.
[Mend, (corr.)]
[a. Unskilful] Ha. VI. 3. O.
Cob-iron, [Supporting (instr.) for Spit.]
Cobler, [Mending (mech.) of Leather (vest) for foot.]
Cobweb, [Spider's woven (thing)]
Cock.
[Male] [sp. bird]
[Bird. Bi. II. 1. (male)
—*'s comb.* HS. VIII. 7.
—*'s head.* HS. III. 5. A.
heath—Bi. II. 5. A.
—*of the wood.* Bi. II. 5.
Exanguious.
Sea—Ex. VI. 6. A.
—*Rocher.* Ex. I. 7. A.
winged—Ex. II. 3. A.
Instrument,
—*of Dial*, [Pin—]
—*of Gun-lock*, [adj. a. Fire (machin.)]
—*for Water*, [Lock of Pipe.]
Weather—[Winde (sign) instrument.]
—*of Hay*, [Heap—]
—*boat*, [Boat (dim.)]
—*swain.* RN. V. 6. A.
Cockall, [Dicing with heel-bones.]
Cockatrice, [Serpent killing by Sight.]
Cocker, [adj. a. Fondness.] Man. VI. 7. D.
Cocket, [Writing of Tribute

CO

(off.) for {impore export} of wares]
Cockle.
Fish. Ex. VIII. 5. A.
Herb. HS. V. 6. A.
Cockrel, [Hen (male) (young.)]
Coco. Tr. IV. 6.
Cocobrauftes. Bi. IV. 4.
—*Cristatus.* Bi. IV. 4. A.
Cod.
Fish. Fi. III. 1.
—*of Plant.* PP. III. 5, A.
—*of Animal*, [Testicles (vessel.)]
—*piece*, [adj. Privities (vest.)]
Codicil, [Added writing.]
Coequal, [Equal.]
Coerce, [Cohibit.]
Coessential, [Of the same Essence.]
Coetaneous, [Together in Age.]
Coeternal, [Together-eternal.]
Coexistent, [Together-existent.]
Coffee. Tr. IV. 7. A.
Coffer, [Chest.]
—*er*, [Keeping (off.) of Treasure.]
Coffi. Tr. IV. 7. A.
Coffin.
[Receiving (vessel)]
[Box for dead body]
Cog.
—*of Mill*, [Tooth of wheel.]
to—
[Fawn.]
[a. Fraud.]
Cogitation, [Thinking]
Cognation of things. T. VI. 8.
Cognisance.
[Acknow'edging]
of Cause. R'. II 4.
Badge, [Service (sign.)]
Coheir, [Together-heir.]
Coherent.
[Together {Sticking.} {Joining.}]
[adj. Congruity]
Cohibitive cause. T. II. 2. O.
Cohobation, [Repeated Distillation.]
Cohort, [Troop.]
Coy, [adj. Aversation (apt.)]
Coif, [Close adj. head (vest.)]
Coil, [Confused {Motion. Sound}]
to—*a rope*, [a. Spiral.]
Coin.
—*of a Wall*, [Corner——]
[Mony]
to—
[a. Mony (make)]
[a. Print] (sp. in Metal)
[a. Fiction]
[a. Forgery]
Coincident, [Together- adj. Event]
Coistrel, [adj. Adolescence (male.)]
Coit, [Lamin. adj. p. cast (apt.)]
Coition. AC. II. 5. A.
Colander, [adj. Streining (vessel.)]

CO

Cold.
—*to sense.* Q. V. 1. D.
[Remiss]
a—[Disease from cold]
Cole.
Live—[Fired fuel (Part)]
Dead—[un-fired fuel (part)]
Sea—St. VI. 3. A.
—*black*, [Black (augm.)]
Cole-rake, instr.
Cole-mouse. Bi. VI. 7. A.
Cole-wort, [Cabbage.] HS. IV. 6.
Co'et, {Concave (place Gem (place} {of Ring.}
Colic S. VI. 5.
Coil, [Embrace.]
Collar, [Environing (armam.) for neck.]
Collateral.
[of the same Series]
[Accessary]
Collation.
[Giving]
[Right of giving]
Refection. Pr. I. 1. A.
Comparing. TA. II. 5.
Collect, [adj. Epitome prayer.]
Collection.
[a. Gathering]
[adj. p. Gathering (thing.)]
Collective.
[Together-gathering]
[adj. Aggregate]
Collector, [adj. a. {Person. Officer.} Gathering]
College. RC. III. 7. A.
sp. of Schollars
Collegue.
[Companion]
[adj. p. Leag.]
[Together adj. p. Colledg.]
Collier, [Fuel {Officer. (mech.) (merc.}]
Colli-flower, [Cabbage]
Collision.
[Together {Reciprocal} striking.]
Collogue, [Fawn.]
Collop.
[Chip]
[Slice]
Colloquy, [Together-discourse.]
Collusion, [Agreeing to cheat.]
Colon.
[adj. Fundament Gut.]
Period. D. I. 6.
Co'onel, [Regiment (Off.)]
Colony. RC. III. 1. A.
Coloquintida. HS. VII. 4.
Color. Q. II.
[Pretext]
—*s* [adj. {Ensign Cornet} (thing)]
Coloss, [Image (augm.)]
Colt {Horse Ass} (young)
—*s-foot.* HL. VI. 1.
mountain-[Horse foot] HL. VI. 3.
Columbine. HS. I. 2. A.
Co'umn, [Pillar Poss. III. 5.]
Colure, [Meridian through Tropics.]
Comb.

CO

Comb.
  [Combing (inftr.)]
  to—O. V. 9. A.
Creft. PP. V. 7.
Cox——
  Herb.
  [adj. Folly (perfon)]
  [adj. Formalnefs, Man. IV. 6. E. (perfon)]
Hony—[Bees Chambers (aggr.)]
Combat, [Fighting.]
Comber.
  [Burthen]
  [Trouble]
  [Hinder.]
Combine.
  [Together-a, {join.] league.] [action.]}
Combuftion.
  [Burning.]
  [Contention]
  [Sedition.]
Come.
  Motion {toward} {to} TA. VI. 1.
  fp. from a remoter term to a nearer.
  —about, [Turn.]
  —after, [Follow.]
  —again, [Return.]
  —at {a thing, [Obtain.]} {a perfon, [Affault.]}
  —back, [Return.]
  —by, [Obtain.]
  —forth.
  [become {vifible.}{known.}]
  [be manifefted]
  —forward {Proceed.}{p. Increafe.}
  —in, [Submit.]
  —off, [p. Event.]
  —upon equal terms. RM. II. 1.
  —Victor. RM. II. 1. E.
  —Lofer. RM. II. 1. D.
  —on, [Proceed.]
  —over, {P. Convert.}
  —a perfon, {a. Craft.}{a' Fraud.}
  —out.
  [become {vifible.}{known.}]
  [be manifefted.]
  —to {v. Event.}{p. Sum.}
  —to good, [v. Event. (perf.)]
  —to hand, [v. Event——]
  —to light, {p. Manifeft.}{p. Public.}
  —to Minde, [adj. p. Memory.]
  —to nought, {(corr.)}{[v. Event] nothing.]}
  —to pafs, [v. Event.]
  —to felf, [Return to former Condition.]
  —up, {Become}{Grow} vifible.]
  —upon, [Affault.]
  —with, [Bring.]
Being.
  [future.]

to——[adj. future.]
  [near.]
  [prefent.]
  (inc.)
  [adv. End.]
  —fhort [v. Defect adv. End.]
  —to, [p. Sum adv. End.]
  [adv. Total.]
  —to, [p. Total.]
Being the Effect.
  —of it, [Be the Effect——]
Being the Event.
  Vide fupra.
  Appearing.
  Forth—ing, [adj. fut. Appear.]
  Parturition.
Comedy, [Play with merry Conclufion.]
Comely.
  [Decent]
  [Handfom]
Comet. W. II. 3. A.
  Meteor. El. I. 2.
Comfet, [adj. p. Confection (thing) with Sugar.]
Comfort. RO. VI. 3.
Comfrey. HL. IX. 4.
Comical.
  [adj. Comedy]
  [adj. Mirth]
Comity, [Courtefie.] Man. IV. 7.
Comma. D. I. 5.
Command.
  v. Precept. RO. V. 1.
  [a. Mafter]
  [a. Magiftrate]
  at ones— {Command} by {adj. p.} {Govern} one.]
  a commanded Party. RM. IV. 6.
Commander.
  [Commanding {Perfon.}{Off.}]
  [adj. Wood (inftr.) for indriving Columns]
Commemorate
  [Re-a. memory (make.)]
  [a. Memory folemnly.]
Commence.
  [Begin]
  [Take a Degree] {Doctor.}{Mafter.}
  [Be made—
  —an Action, [a. Action.]
  RJ. II. O.
Commend.
  [Praife.]
  —to felf. RO. V. 7.
  —to others. RO. V. 8.
Entruft, [Depofit]
  [Speak ones {Salutations to} {remembrance} (another.)]
Commendations.
  To do ones-- {Speak ones Love.} {Be Meffenger of ones Salutation.} {Infiead-falute.}
  Letters o-{Praife.}{a. Truft (make.)}
Commenfurate, [Together-pro-

portioned.]
Comment. D. V. 6.
  —ary. D. V. 6.
Commerce. TA. IV.
Commination, [Threat.] RO. V. 6. O.
Commiferate, [a. Pity.] AS. VI. 7. O.
Commiffary, [Officer.]
  Ecclefiaftic, [Inftead-Judge Ecclef.]
  Military, [adj. Provifions (off.)]
Commiffion. RC. IV. 4. A.
  —er, [Commiffion'd (perfon.)]
Commit.
  [Doe]
  fp. as Fault.]
  [Entruft]
  as Prifoner, [a. Imprifonment.]
Committee, [Authorized perfons (aggr.)]
  [Council (dim.)]
Commixtion.
  [Mixture]
  [Together-mixture]
Commodious.
  [Congruous]
  [Convenient]
  [Profitable]
Commodity.
  [Convenience]
  [Profit]
  [Ware]
Common.
  [adj. {All}{Every}{Many}]
  Op. to Proper. TM. IV. 6. O
  [Public.] TM. V. 4.
  [adj. People]
  —wealth.
  [adj. RC. (thing)]
  [Common Profperity.]
  [Government by the People.]
  [Obvious]
  [Frequent]
  [Ufual]
  [Not-confecrated]
Commonalty, [People (kind)]
Commons, [not-Lords.]
  —of Victual.
  [Proportioned {Food.}{Provifions}]
  —for Cattel.
  [Common {Pafture}]
  [Peoples]
Commotion.
  [Motion]
  [Sedition]
  [Trouble]
Commune, [Confer.] AC. V. 7. A.
Communicate.
  [Common (make)]
  [Partnerfhip (make)]
  [Known (make)]
Communication.
  [Converfation]
  [Conference] AC. V. 7. A.
  [Dif-

CO | CO | CO

[Discourse.]
Communion.
[Together- { Union. } { Partnership. }]
[Lord's Supper.] RE. VI. 6. A.
Community, [Common (kinde)]
Commutation.
[Commerce]
[Exchange]
Compact.
[Together-join (augm.)]
[Close (augm.)]
[Agreement]
[Together-league]
[Covenant]
Company.
[Together { Being Going Travelling }]
[Companion (abst.)]
[adj. aggregate (thing)]
[adj. Multitude (aggr.)]
[Society]
[Convention]
[Corporation]
of Souldiers. RM. IV. 2.
To—[Together- { Be Go Travel }]
Companion.
Fellow. RO. IV. 2.
[Accessary (person)]
[Urbane (person)]
[Sorry (person)]
Compare. TA. II. 5.
In Comparison of, [Being compared with]
Compass.
[About-goe]
[Goe about the out-side]
fetch—[Go, adv. Curve]
[About-sepiment]
[v. Circle]
Mariners—
[Box to direct Navigation.]
[adj. Magnet { (Jug.) (Vess.) }]
Pair of—[Writing (instr.) of Circles.]
[Comprehend]
[Obtain]
—of a year, &c. [Space—&c.]
Compassion, [Pity] TA. VI. 7. O.
Compatible { agreeing.
[Together- adj. Congruous.]
Compeer.
[Like]
[Companion]
Compell, [a. Coaction]
Compellation, [a. Name.]
Compendium.
[adj. Shortness]
[adj. p. Epitome]
Compendium.
[Epitome]
[Short method]
Compensate. TA. II. 7. A.
Competent, [Sufficient.]
Competitor, [Rival.]
Compile.

[Compound]
[a. Book (make)]
Complacence.
[Delight] AS. IV. 7.
Vertue. Man. IV. 8.
Complain.
[Grief (sign)]
[a. Accuser]
Complaisance. Man. IV. 8.
Complementing. AC. V. 7.
Complete.
[Perfect]
[adj. p. Finishing]
Complexion.
[Aggregate]
[Composition]
[Temper]
[Colour of Face]
Complie.
[v. Congruity]
[Follow]
[Imitate]
[Please by v. Congruity.]
Complicated, { aggregated intangled [Together Mingled. }]
Complices.
[Together-leagued (persons)]
[Companions]
[Accessories]
Comportment.
[Gesture]
[Demeanor]
[Conversation (manner)]
Compose.
[Together-put]
—{ Book, [a. Book } (make Verse, [a. Verse]
[a. Order (perf.)]
[Un-confused (make)]
[adj. a. Agree (make)]
[a. Quiet]
Compound.
[Together { put join }]
[Make of many parts]
[a. Mixture]
[Covenant to pay Less than ones debt.]
Comprehend.
a. Capacity. TA. II. 4.
[Understand { All Perfectly Totally }]
Compression. O. I. 3. O.
Comprize, vid. Comprehend.
Compromise, [together-submit to Arbitration]
Compulsion, [Coaction]
Compunction.
[Remorse]
[Repentance (inc.)]
Compurgation.
[a. Innocent by witness]
Computation.
[Account]
[Numbring]
Con-over, [again-say (freq.) for remembring.]
Concatenation, [Together-chaining.]
Concave. Mag. III. 4. D.

Conceal. TA. I. 8. O.
Conceit.
[Fancy]
[Opinion]
[Witty saying]
Conceitedness. Ha. III. 3. D.
Conceiving.
[a. Common sense]
[a. Fancy]
[a. Understanding]
[a. Thought]
——with young. AC. I. 2. A.
Concentre, { together- adv. Same } centre
Conception. AC. I. 2. A.
Concern, [v. { Proper. Profitable. }]
Concerning.
[Pertinent]
[Of]
Concession. D. VI. 3. A.
Conciliator, [Reconciler.]
Concise, [adj. Shortness.]
Concitation, [Impulsion.]
Conclave. { Chamber (sp. Secret.) [Council }]
Conclude.
[End]
[Finish]
[Determine]
[v. Inference]
Concoct, [a. Digestion.]
Concomitant.
[adj. Simultaneity]
[Together-being]
Concord.
[Agreeing]
Symphony. Q. III. 8.
Concordance, [Catalog. { words for finding of } things]
Concorporate, { a. Body [Together- a. Corporation }]
Concourse.
[Together-coming (augm.)]
[Convention (augm.)]
Concrete.
[Coagulate]
op. to Abstract. D. II. 2. O.
Concubine.
{ Appropriated Whore] in-stead-Wife]
Concupiscence.
[Appetite]
[Desire]
[Lust]
[Nature (corr.)]
[Original Sin]
Concur.
[Meet]
[Together { be agree come }]
Concussion, [Shaking.]
Condemn.
Sentence. RJ. II. 7. O.
[Blame]
[Disapprove]
Condense, [dense.]
Condescend.
[a. Man. VI. 2.]
[Permit]

Ddd · Con-

CO

Condescension. Man. VI. 2.
Condign [Worthy]
Conditing. Pr. III. 9. A.
Condition. T. II. 4.
  [Quality]
  [Disposition]
  Capacity. TA. II. 4.
  [State]
  [Supposition]
  [Covenant]
Condole, [Together-grieve]
Conduce, [a. Help.]
Conduct.
  [Leading] TA. VI. 5.
  [a. Officer]
  Safe—[Licence of safe going]
Conduit, [Aqueduct] Po. II. 8. A.
Cone. Mag. III. 7.
  Fruit. PP. III. 5.
Confection. Pr. II. 2. A.
Confederacy, [League] RC. III. 8.
Confer.
  [Give] TA. IV. 4.
  [Compare.] TA. II. 5.
  Discourse together. AC. V. 7. A.
Confess.
  [Acknowledge]
    anothers praise.
    our own.
      { Sin. RE. IV. 2.
      { Error. D. VI. 9.
Confessor.
  adj. Hear- { (Person
    ing   { (Officer } for
      confession of Sins.
  Sufferer for Religion. RE. III. 3.
Confidence.
  Affection. AS. V. 7.
  [Assuredness] AS. III. 6.
Confident, [adj. Confidence.]
  ones— { adj. a. counsel
  [ones { adj. p. trust } friend]
Confine.
  [a. Finite]
  [a. Cohibit] TA. II. 2. O.
  [a. Imprisonment]
Confines, [Margining Countries]
Confirm.
  [Strengthen]
  [sp. More-strengthen.]
  [More-assure]
  [a. Witness.]
  —*ation.* D. VI. 6. A.
  —*Ecclesiastic.* RE. IV. 8.
Confiscation. RJ. VI. 7. A.
Conflict.
  [Fight] RM. L 7.
  [a. Contention]
Confluence { Coming (aug.
  [Together- { Convention
Conform.
  [adv. Congruous-do]
  [So-do]
  [a. Obedience]
Confound.
  [adj. p. Confused (make]
  [Mingle]

CO

  [adj. p. Shame (make]
  Posing] D. VI. 8.
  [Destroy] AS. I. 4. O.
Confraternity,
  [Colledge]
  [Corporation]
  [Penitents, (aggr.] RE.II.6.A.
Confront, [a. Opposite present]
Confused, [adj. Confusion.]
Confusion.
  Disorder, TM. V. 2. O.
  [Shame (augm.]
  [Destruction] AS. I. 4. O.
Confutation. D. VI. 7.
Confute, [a. Confutation.]
Congeal.
  [a. Coagulate]
  [a. { Gelly }(make]
       { Ice   }
Congee. AC. V. 4.
Conger. Fi. VI. 1.
Conglutinate, [together- { glue]
                             { join]
Congratulate, [a. Joy for good of others.] AS. VI. 6
Congregation, [Convention]
Congruous, [adj. T. V. 5.]
Conic [adj. Cone.]
Conie. Be. III. 4.
Conjecture.
  —*ing.* AS. II. 7. A.
Conjugal, [adj. Marriage]
Conjugate. [Together-derived]
Conjugation, [Forming (manner) of endings of Verbs]
Conjunction.
  [Joining]
  Particle. D. II. 9. A.
  —*of Planets* [neerness]
Conjure.
  [a. Witchcraft]
  [a. Entreat (augm.]
Conjurer, [a. Witchcraft (person.]
Connexion, [Joyning (manner]
Connive.
  [Tolerate secretly]
  [Not hinder]
  [Not-punish]
Conquer. RM. II. 7. E.
Consanguinity. RO. I.
Conscience. NP. I. 3.
  Stupidity of—NP. I. 3. O.
Consciencious, [adj. Conscience (perf.]
Conscionable.
  [According to Conscience]
  [adj. Equity]
Conscious.
  [Knowing]
  [Together-knowing]
  [Accessory]
Consecration. RE. V. I.
  —*of Bishop,* [a. Bishop (make]
Consectary { Additional]
  [Inference { Accessory]
Consent. AS. II. 3.
  with one—[Together-Adv. IV. 1. consenting]
Consequence.
  [Illation]

CO

  [Importance]
  sp. Future]
Consequent, [Inference]
Conserve.
  [Confection] Pr. II. 2. A.
  to—
  [Preserve]
  [Confect]
  —*ation.* AS. I. 4.
Consider.
  Think. AS. III. 2.
  [Compensate] TA. II. 7. A.
  —*ing.* AS. III. 2.
  —*that;* [Whereas] Con. IV. 1.
Considerable, [Important.]
Considerateness. Ha. IV. 1.
Consideration.
  [Impulsive]
  [Respect]
  [Compensation]
Consign, [Assign] RC. V. 1.
Consist.
  [adj. p. Simultaneous]
  [Agree]
  —*ence.*
  Tactil Quality. Q. V. 5.
Consistory.
  { Council
  { Council (place
  sp. Ecclesiastic.]
  sp. Of Bishops.]
Consolation, [Comfort]
Consolidate.
  [a. Wholeness]
  [a. Closeness]
Consonant.
  [Congruous]
  Letter. D. I. 2. A.
Consort.
  [Companion]
  [Harmony]
  —*of Music.* Q. III. 6. A.
Conspicuous,
  [adj. p. See (apt.]
  [adj. Manifest (augm.]
Conspire, [a. Faction]
Constable, [Subordinate adj. a. peace (Off.]
Constancy. Ha. IV. 7.
Constellation, [Stars (aggr.]
Consternation.
  Fear (augm.]
  [Extasie]
  [sp. through Fear.]
Constipation.
  [Together-thrusting]
  [a. Close]
Constitute.
  [a. Cause]
  [a. Efficient]
Constitution.
  [a. Efficient]
  [Appointment]
  [Law]
  [Edict]
  [Mixture]
  [Disposition]
  [Temper of mind] NP. IV.
  [Temper of body] NP. V.
Constrain, [a. Coaction]
Construction.
  [a. Effi-

CO

[a. Efficient]
[a. Interpret]
Conful, [Magistrate of City.]
Confult.
[Together- {Confider / Counfel}]
[Ask / Take} advice]
Confume, vid. *Confumption*.
Confummate.
[a. Perfect]
[a. Finifh]
Confumption.
[a. Decay (make)]
[Diminifh]
[Spoil]
[Deftroy]
[Corruption]
Difeafe. S. II. 2. A.
—of the Lungs. S. V. 3.
Contact.
[Touch]
[Contiguity]
Contagion. S. I. 1.
Contaminate, [Defile.]
Contein.
[Comprehend] TA. II. 4.
[Keep chaft]
Contemn. AS. II. 8. O.
Contemplate, [Meditate.] AS. II. 1. A.
Contemporary, [adj. Simultaneity.]
Contemptible, [adj. p. Contempt (apt.)]
Contend, [a. Contention.]
Content.
[Capacity]
[Contentation] Ha. I. 3.
[Satisfaction] AS. III. 5.
Contentation. Ha. I. 3.
Contentioufnefs. Man IV. 3 D.
Conteft, [Contention in words]
Contexture, {Weaving / Together— Joining}
Contignation, [Together joining of Floors.]
Contiguity. Sp. II. 1.
Continence, [Chaftity]
Continent.
[adj. Chaftity]
Land. W. III. 2.
Contingent. T. V. 7. O.
Continue.
[a. Permanence]
[a. Duration]
[Stay]
—*ed*
—*Quantity*. TM. II.
Continual.
[Permanent]
[Perpetual]
Continuance.
—*of Place.* Sp. II. 7.
—*of Time*, [Permanence.]
In—*of Time.*
[After much Time]
[At length]
Contrabanded, [Forbidden to be imported.]
Contract.
[Together-draw]

CO

[Bargain] RC. V.
[Betroth]
[Obtain]
—*a difeafe*, [adj. p. Difeafe.]
Contradiction. D. VI. 4. A.
Contradictory, [adj. Contradiction]
Contrary. T. V. 5. O.
Contribution.
[Giving]
fp. Proportionable]
[p. Free.]
[Tax]
Contrition, [Remorfe]
Contrive. AS. III. 7.
Controle.
[Obferve / Cenfure} Faults]
[Reprehend]
[Cohibit]
—*er*, [adj. Cohibiting (Off.]
Controverfie.
[Difpute]
[Suit]
Contumacy.
Conftancy (Exc.) Ha. IV. 7. E.
op. to Obedience Man. V. 8. D.
Contumely, [Affront.]
Contufion O. IV. 1. A.
[Bruife] S. I. 1. A.
Convey.
[v. Way]
[Lead]
[Carry]
[Send]
—*ance.*
[Carriage]
[Sending]
[Contrivement]
[Alienating Writing]
Convene.
[a. Citation]
[v. Convention]
Convenience.
Agreeablenefs. T. IV. O.
[Congruity]
[Expedience]
Convenient.
[Congruous]
[Expedient]
Conventicle, [Secret Convention (corr.)]
Convention. RC. III.
Converging. Mag. II. 7. D.
Converfant.
[adj. Converfation]
[Accuftomed]
[Expert]
Converfation. Man. A.
Qualification for—Man. IV.
Convert.
[Turn (make)]
[Apply]
[Profelyte] RE. III. 6.
[Penitent] RE. II. 6. A.
[Reform] RO. VI. 7.
Convex. Mag. III. 4. E.
Conviction. D. VI. 8. A.
—*by Law*, [Prove Guilty.]
Convocation, [Convention Ecclefiaftic.]

CO

Convoy, [Travelling Guard.]
Convulfion, S. IV. 7.
Cook, [Cookery (mech.]
—*ery.* Pr. III. 1. A.
Cool, [Cold (dim.)]
[a. Cold]
Coop, [Prifon of Parallel Sticks]
to—
[Imprifon]
[Environ]
Cooper, [adj. Barrel (mec.)]
Cooperate, [Together-operate]
Coordinate, {Height / [Of equal} Degree]
Coot. Bi. VIII. 8.
Copal. Tr. VIII. 4 A.
Copartner.
[Partner]
[Acceffary]
Cope.
[Change]
[Fight]
[Prune]
Prieft's—
Copy.
Original. T. II. 3
Set a—[a. T. II. 3.]
Tranfcript. T. II. 3. O.
—*out.* [a. T. II. 3. O.]
—*hold* [Eftate / Tenement} for life]
Copious, [Abundant]
Copped.
[Sharp topped]
[adj. p. Point]
Copper.
Metal. Met. I. 4.
[Kettle]
Copperas, [Vitriol.] St. V. 2, A.
Coppis, [Place of Trees (dim.)]
Copula. D. II. 6.
Copulation, [Coition.]
Copulative, [Joining.]
Coracinus. Fi. IV. 2.
Coral. Se. II. 6.
Cord. Pr. IV. 7. A.
Cordage, [Cord (kind)]
Cordial.
[adj. Heart]
[Heart-ftrengthning Medicin]
[adj. Sincerity.]
Cordylus [Lizard (kind) having a tail annulated with fcales.]
Core.
[Heart (like) part]
[Middle (part)]
[fp. Hardeft part]
Coriander. HF. IV. 1. A.
Cork.
Tree. Tr. V. 3. A.
[Wood of Cork Tree]
[Stopple of Cork-wood]
Cormorant. Bi. IX. 5.
Corn.
[Plant for adj. Bread]
Standing—[Not-reaped]
—*field*, [Field of—]
—*flagg.* HL. IV. 6. A.
[Seed for Bread]
[Grain] PP. III. 6.
—*on the Toe.* S. III. 6. A.

[Pow

CO

[Powder] TM. VI. 4. A.
 To—[a. Powder] Pr. III. 7. A.
  sp. with Salt.]
Cornel-tree. Tr. II. 3. A.
Cornelian, [Sardius] St. III. 3.
Corner.
 [Angle] Mag. III. 2. A.
 [Tooth] Mag. IV. 2.
 [Notch] Mag. IV. 2. O.
 —of the eye, [Dent—]
 [adj. Hiding (place]
Cornet.
 Enfign, RM. III. 2. A.
 Mufic, [Bafs pipe.]
Corollary, [Inference additional.]
Coronation, [Solemnity of a King (make.]
Coroner, [Enquiring (Off.) of Murther.]
Coronet, [Head-environing, Nobility-fign, Ornament.]
Corporal, [adj. Body]
 —of Souldiers, [Subordinate, adj. Watch (Off.]
 —of a Ship RN. V. 2. A.
Corporation. RC. III. 7.
Corporeal [adj. W. I. Op.]
Corps, [Body.]
 —du gard, [Gard (aggr.]
Corpulent.
 [Having great Body]
 [Fat (augm.]
Correct.
 End or Effect.
 General.
  [Repair] TA. II. 9.
  [a. Right]
  [Mend] TM. I. 9. E.
 Moral.
  [Reform] RO. VI. 7.
 Means or Inftrument.
 Words.
  [Reprehend] RO. V. 7. O.
 Deeds.
  [Punifh] Ha. I. O.
  Chaftife. RO. VI. 6.
Correlative, [Together-relative.]
Correfpond.
 [a. Congruity]
 [a. Reciprocation]
 [adv. Re- { Congruity }
 ciprocal { Friendfhip }
  { Known (make) }
Corrival, [Rival]
Corroborate.
 [Strengthen]
 [Confirm]
Corrode. O. VI. 3.
Corrofive, [adj. a. Corroding (apt.]
Corruption.
 General, { [a. Evil] T. III. 2. O.
  { [a. Worfe] TM. I. 9. D.
 By Admixtion.
  [Defiling] TM. V. 6. O.
 By Privation.
  Of its Being.
   [Destruction] AS. I. 4. O.
  Of its Ufefulnefs.
   [Spoiling] TA. II. 9. O.

CO

Natural.
 [Infection] S. I. 1.
 [Decay] NP. V. 4. O.
 [Putrefaction] NP. V. 2. O.
Moral.
 General.
  [Unholinefs] Ha. V. 2. O.
  [Vice] Man. I. 1. O.
 Special.
  [Unchaftnefs] Man. II. 7. O.
  [Bribery] RJ. IV. 6.
Corflet.
 [adj. Trunk (armour]
 [Pike-man]
Cortex.
 —febrifugus Peruvianus, Tr. VII. 9.
 —Winterianus. Tr. VII. 9. A.
Corufcation.
 [Flame (imp.]
 [Brightnefs]
 fp. Trembling (like.]
Cofmography, [Science of the World.]
Coft.
 [Expence]
 [Price]
Coftard, [Apple.]
Coftive, [adj. p. Binding.]
Coftly, [adj. Coft (augm.]
Coftmary, [Ale-coft.] HF. II. 4.
Cottage, [Houfe (dim.]
Cotton.
 —tree. Tr. IV. 8.
 —cloth. Pr. IV. 4. A.
 —weed [Cudweed] HF. II. 5. A
Couch.
 [Contrive together]
 [adj. a. Proftrate.]
 fp. Shrinking]
 [a—>Po. VI. 6. A.
 —weed, [Dogs grafs] HL. III. 5. A
Covenant, [Paction.]
Covent, [Houfe of Monks.]
Coventry Bell. HS. VII. 7.
Cover, [un-feen (make.]
 Put over. O. II. 3.
 [a. Clothing] Pr. IV.
 —a book, [a. Book (mech.]
 [a. Coition] AC. II. 5. A.
 [Un-feen (make]
 [Conceal]
Coverlet, { Veft }
 [Upper { Covering } of Bed.]
  { Hiding }
Coverts, { Protection } (place.]
  { Defence }
Coverture, [Protection.]
Covet, [a. Defire.]
Covetoufnefs. Man. III. 1. D.
Cough. Mo. IV. 5.
Covie, [Birds (aggr.]
Coul.
 [Tub]
 Monk's—[—head (veft.]
Could, [Mood. II. 1.]
Coulter, [a. Ploughing iron (inft.]
Council. RC. III. 5. A.
Counfel, [Advife.] RO. V. 4.
 keep—[a. Taciturnity.]
Count.
 Earl, [Third degree of Nobility.]

CO

to—
 [Efteem]
 [Reckon] TA. IV. 6.
 [a. Sum]
Countenance { (Habit.]
 [Face { (Manner.]
 out of—[not knowing which way to look.]
 [Pofed]
 [Afhamed]
to—
 [Encourage]
 [adj. p. Reputation (make)
Counter.
 [Mony (like) of bafe Metal]
 [Prifon for { Offenders (dim.]
  { Debtors (dim.]
 [adv. Contrary.]
 —bond, [Bond for indemnifying Surety.]
 —charge, [Accufe adv. Reciprocation.]
Counterfeit.
 [a. Likenefs]
 [Imitate]
 fp. Fraudulently.]
 [a. feem (make]
 [a. Feign]
 [a. Forge]
 [a. Hypocrifie]
Countermand, [Command contrary.]
Countermine. RM. I. 5. O.
Countermure, [Oppofite wall.]
Counterpane, { Upper (veft) for
Counterpart, { Example.] (bed)
 [Other { Copy.]
Counterpoint, [Congruous part in Mufic,]
Counterpoife, [Oppofitely weigh]
Counterpoifon, [Medicin againft poifon.]
Counter-fcarf, [Oppofite Rampier,]
Counter-tenor, [High Mean]
Countervail, [Compenfate equally.]
Countefs, [Earl (fem.]
County, [Shire,]
Country.
 op. to Town. RC. III. 2.
 [Region] W. III. A.
 ones own—— [Ones Nation (place)
Country-man, vid. Country.
Couple.
 [Together-two]
 fp. Join'd.]
 [Necks—join- { Bonds.]
  ing { Armam.]
 [Unite]
 [Join-two]
 [a. Coition]
Courage, [Fortitude.]
Courier, [Meffenger for difpatch.]
Courfe.
 Subft.
  [Way]
  Water—[Stream]
  [Journey]
  [Running]

[Hunt-

CR

[Hunting]
[Pursuit]
[Order]
[Series]
first—[—dishes (aggr.]
[Turn]
[Sail]
[Custom]
words of—[adj Custome words]
[Manner]
—*of life* { Doing } (manner. Living }
Adj. [Profession]
Grofs. Q. VI. 3. D.
[Sorry.] TM. I. 4. D.
Courser.
[adj. p. ride (apt) horfe]
[Horfe for running]
Courfes, [Menftruum.] PG. I. 4. A.
Court.
—*yard.* Po. III. 3.
[King's Family] RC. III. 5.
[King's Houfe]
[Judgment (place)
[Judicial Convention]
—*daies,* [Daies of judicial Convention.]
to—[a. Suitor]
Courteoin, [adj. Courtefie.]
Courtefan. [Common Whore]
Courtefie.
Vertue.
[Civility] Man. IV. 7.
[Affability] Man. VI. 2.
Thing, [adj. a. Benefactor (thing)
Salutation. AC. V. 4. A.
Courtier.
[King's domeftic.]
[adj. { Courtefie (augm.)} Complement (perfon)
Courtlinefs, [Complement (abftr.]
Courtfhip, [Converfe adj. Complement (augm.)]
Coufen. RO. I. 5. A.
first—RO. I. 5.
to—[a. Fraud]
Cow, [Bull. Ee. II. 1. (fem.]
—*with Calf,* [Pregnant Cow.]
—*heard,* [adj. Cow (Off.]
to—[a. Coward (make.]
Cowardife. Man. I. 7. D.
Cowcumber. HS. VII. 3.
wild—HS. VII. 4. A.
Cowring, [Stooping]
Cowflip, HS. VIII. 1. A.
Cow wheat. HS. VIII. 8. A.
Coxcomb, [adj. Man. IV. 6. E. (perfon.]
Crab.
—*fifh.* Ex. VI. 6.
Molucca—Ex. VI. 7. A.
Little—Ex. VI. 4.
—*loufe,* [Crab (like)—]
—*tree,* [Sour Apple-tree.]
Fruit, [Sour Apple.]
Crabbed.
[Auftere face (manner)
[Morofe]

CR

[Difficult]
Crack,
[Break]
fp. Incept.]
[Chink]
[Sound as of Breaking]
[Brag]
—*brain'd,* [Mad (dim.]
Crackle, [Sound (freq.) of breaking (inc.]
Cradle.
[Bedftead (dim.) adj. p. Volutation (apt.]
Crafifh. Ex. VI. 3.
Craft.
Cunning. Ha. VI. 2. E.
[Mechanic (art.]
Crag, [Rough { Rock.] (augm. { Rocky hill.]
Cram, [Fill(augm.] fp. by thrufting.]
Cramp. S. IV. 7. A.
—*fifh,* [Torpedo.] Fi. II. 4.
—*iron,* [Iron hooks for joining.]
Crane.
Bird. Bi. VIII. 1.
—*fly.* Ex. IV. 8.
—*'s bill.* HS. I. 5.
Machin, [Great lifting (machin.]
Crank.
[Vigorous]
[adj. Mirth]
Cranny, [Chink.]
Crafh,
[Break.]
[Sound of breaking]
[Fit]
Craffitude,
[Thicknefs] TM. II. 5.
[Denfity] Q. V. 3. E.
[Courfenefs]
Cratch, [Veffel in which Ox feeds.]
Crave.
[a. Defire]
[Entreat]
[Petition]
Craven, [Coward.]
Cravingnefs, { Covetoufnefs } Scrapingnefs]
Craw, [Stomach] fp. of Bird.]
Crawling, { Creeping } Mo. I. 6. Wriggling }
Craze, [Bruife.] fp. the Superficies.]
Crazy, [adj. Sicknefs (apt.]
Creak, [Acute found of folid bodies mutually rubbing.]
Cream, [Beft Part.] fp. of Milk.]
Create.
Proper. AS. I. 1.
[a. Efficient]
Creature, [adj. p. Create (thing)
Credence, [Belief]
Credible, [adj. p. Believe (pot.]
Credit.
[Believe] AS. II. 4.
[Efteem] AS. II. 8.

CR

[Reputation] Ha. II. 4.
[Truft.] AS. III. 4.
Creditor. TA. IV. 7.
Creduity. Ha. III. 2. E.
—*in Religion.* Ha. V. 4. E.
Creed, [Epitome of adj. p. ought-believe (things.) fp. in Chriftianity.]
Creek, [Bay (dim.]
Creep.
Crawl. M6. I. 6.
[Wriggle] Mo. I. 6. A.
as Ivy, [Grow contiguous.] [a. Fawning]
—*in,* [Get in { Secretly.] Gradually.]
Crefcent, [Increafing.] fp. Moon.]
Creffes.
garden.—HS. VI. 5.
Indian—HL. VI. 12.
Sciatica—HS. VI. 5. A.
Swines—HS. VI. 6. A.
Water—HS. IV. 15.
Winter—HS. IV. 7. A.
Crefcet.
Supporting (jug.) for boiling veff.]
—*light,* [Not-cover'd Lantern.]
Creft.
[Comb] PP. V. 7.
————*fallen,* [Difcouraged (augm.]
————*of Helmet,* [Comb (like)—]
————*of Arms,* [The Gentry (fign) upon the head (armour.]
[Mane] PP. VI. 4. A.
Crevis
[Chink]
[Crafifh]
Crew, [Companions (aggr.]
Crewet, [adj. Glafs-pot (dim.]
Cry.
[Grief]
[Weep] AC. IV. 3. O.
Vocal.
[Exclaim] AC. III. 3.
—*out,* [a. Parturition (inc.]
—*out* { Accufe } publicupon { Blame } ly.
—*mercy,* [Entreat for pardon.]
—*quittance,* [compenfate]
Proclaim, [a. Cryer.]
Crib.
Pinch]
[Penurious (perfon)
[Oxe's Eating (place)
Crick, [Pricking] AC. II. 7. fp. through Cold]
Cricket. Ex. II. 2.
Fen—[Eve-churr.] Ex. II. 2. A.
Crier. RJ. I. 5. A.
Crime. RJ. III.
—*not-capital.* RJ. IV.
Crimfon, [Red adj. blood (like.]
Cringe, Congee { (augm.) (freq.)

Crip-

CR　　　CR　　　CU

Cripple, [adj. p. Impotence in Limbs.]
Crisis, [adj.] (time) Judgment (sign)
Crisping, [Curling.] O. V. 5. A.
Critic, [Judger of words]
Critical, [adj.] Judge (apt.)
Crochet, vid. Crotchet.
Crocodile. Be. VI. 3.
Crocus. HL. IV. 7. A.
Croft, [Field (dim.)]
Croke.
[a. {Toad, Raven} (voice)]
As the Bowels, [Sound through wind enclofed.]
Crone, [adj. Decrepit perfon.]
Crook.
[adj. Crookednefs (thing) Mag. III. 1. O.
[Hook]
[Saddle of fticks curved upward.]
to—
[adj. a. Bend]
[adj. p crooked (make)]
[Hook (make)]
Crookednefs. Mag. III. 1. O.
Crop.
—of Bird, [firft Stomach—]
—of Corn, [adj. p. Heap (aggr.)—]
to—{Off—pluck.
tear.
break.}
Crofier, [adj. Bifhop's Staff.]
Crofs.
Figure or Site.
[Oblique] Mag. II. 8.
[Tranfverfe] Mag. II. 8. D.
—cloth, [adj. Tranfverfe forehead drefs.]
to—a River, [To go over a River.]
Decuffated. Mag. IV. 4. A.
—of wood, &c.
[adj. Crucifying (jug) —&c.]
sp. adj. Crofs (fig.)
[Image of adj. Crucifying (jug.)]
to—himfelf, [To a. Crofs (fign) upon—]
—bow. RM. V. 4. A.
—way, [adj. Crofs-way]
Quality.
tranfcendent.
[Contrary]
[Oppofite]
moral.
[Perverfe]
[Contentious]
[Morofe]
[Difobedient]
Event (corr.) [adverfity] of action.
to—[Fruftrate.]
of inftrument.
to—[Spoil]
sp. with tranfverfe line.]
Crofsbill. Bi. IV. 5. A.

Crofswort. HL. IX. 8. A.
Crotchet.
[Hook (dim.)]
[adj. Mufic Letter]
[Invention (corr.)]
[a. Craft (dim.)]
Crouch.
[Stoop] AC. VI. 4.
sp. Adoration (fign.)
[Fawn]
Croud.
Throng, [Together-thrufted (aggr.)]
Fiddle, [Mufic (inftr.) adj. ftrike]
P. {found} with Bow
Crow.
Bird. Bi. I. 5. A.
—'s foot. HF. IX. 4.
Inftrument, [adj. iron adj. lifting (inftr.)]
to—
[a. Cock (voice)]
[a. Triumph (voice)]
[a. Boaft (corr.)]
Crown.
Diadem, [Head-environing Kingfhip (fign) Ornament]
—of the head, [Top—]
—imperial. HL. IV. 1.
Mony, [5 shillings (aggr.)]
Crucible, [Veffel for melting of metals by Fire.]
Crucifie. R. V. 8.
Crucifix, [Image of Chrift crucified.]
Crude, [not prepared {boil'd Pr. III. digefted O.]
Cruelty. Man. I. 5. D.
Cruet, [Small Glafs (veff.) for oil, &c.]
Crum, [Powder]
—of bread, [adj. Infide (part)—]
Crumble, [Crums (make.)]
Crump, [Sinew-contracted.]
—foot, [Shrunk—]
—shoulder, [Prominent—]
Crumpled. HC. VI. 3. A.
Crupper.
[Rump]
[Hinder ftay of Saddle]
[adj. Rump (armain.)]
Crufe.
[Bottle (dim.) of Glafs.]
to—[a. Scout.]
sp. for Booty.]
Crufhing, [Bruifing.]
sp. by Compreffion.]
Cruft.
—of Shel-fifh. PP. IV. 2. A.
—of Bread, [Out-fide—]
sp. Hard.]
Cruftaceous [adj. PP. IV. 2. A.]
Crutch.
[fig. T] Mag. IV. 4.
Staff of lame (perfon)
Cryptography, [Secret writing (art.)]
Cryftal. St. II. 4.
Cu.
[Sign]

[Beginning (fign)]
[Foot (armam.) for Ox]
Cub {Bear (young.)
Fox (dim.)}
Cube. Mag. III. 5. O.
Cubeb.
Cubit.
Limb. PG. V. 2.
Meafure, [Length from Elbow to fingers top.]
Cucking-ftool, [adj. a. Diving (jug.) of Scolds.]
Cuckold, [Husband of Adulterefs]
Cuckoo. Bi. I. 3.
—flower. HS. IV. 15. A.
Cuckquean, [Wife of Adulterer]
Cucumber. HS. VII. 3.
Cud, [Upper Stomach.]
chew the— [Again-mafticate, adj. p. pret. Swallowed (thing.)]
Cudgel.
[Staff]
[Club (dim.)]
[Cudgelling (inftr.)]
—ing. RM. VI. 2. A.
Cudwort. HF. II. 5. A.
Cuff, [Ornament for Handwrift.]
to— [Strike with folded hand.]
Cuirafe. [adj. Trunk (armor.)]
Cull, [Elect] sp. to have.]
Cullis, [1 roth of Poultry.]
Culpable, [Blame [adj. p. Reprehend] (apt.)]
Cultivate, [Manure.]
Culture, [Manure.]
Culver, [Pigeon]
Culverin, [Great Ordnance (kind)]
Cumber.
[a. Earthen]
[a. Trouble]
[a. Hinder]
Cummin. HF. V. 7. A.
Cunctation. Ha. IV. 1. E.
Cunny. Be. III. 4.
Cunning.
[Art]
[Craft]
Cup. Pr. V. 9. A.
—bearer. [adj. Cup (Off.)]
—of a flower. PP. II. 8.
to—Mo. IV. 7. A.
Cupboard {Table sp. for
Box Cups}
Cur, [Dog of ignoble breed, good only to accompany.]
Curafier, [Armed (pert.) Horfeman.]
Curate, {adj. Parifh
Subordinate Prieft
Inftead-}
Curb.
[Cohibiting (part) of Bridle]
[Cohibiting (augm.) Bridle]
to—[Cohibit]
Curdle, [Coagulate.]
Cure, [Re health]
—of Souls, [Officerfhip for Souls.]
Curiofity.
[Per-

CU | CU | DA

[Perfection]
[Excellence]
[Beauty (augm.)]
[Diligence (augm.)]
op. to Science. Ha. VI. 1. E.
[Niceness] Man. II. 6. E.
[Intemperance. Man. II. O,
as to { Ornaments
{ Dainties }
Curlew. Bi. VIII. 9.
Curling. O. V. 5. A.
Curr, vid. Cur.
Currants. Sh. I. 1. A.
Current.
Subst.
[Stream]
Adj.
[Genuine]
[Perfect]
[Approved]
[Adj. Custom] RC. IV. 1. A.
[Common] TM. IV. 6. A.
[Ordinary] TM. V. 3.
Year — [—present]
Curry.
[Comb] O. V. 9. O.
sp. Horse.
—*combe,* [adj. Combing (inst.) for Horse.]
[Prepare Leather.]
—*favour.*
[Fawn for—]
[Endeavour (corr.) for—]
Currish [Dog (like.)]
Curse.
Action of God. AS. I. 3. O.
Action of man.
[Excommunicate]
[Imprecate]
Curst. AC. V. 4. A.
Cursory.
[Swift]
[Rash]
[Slight]
Curst.
[Execrable]
[Fierce] NP. IV. 4. O.
[Angry] Man. I. 9. D.
[Morose]
Curtain.
[Shadowing (vest) before-
adj. hang (apt)
sp. about Bed.]
Curtal.
[Off-cut Tail]
[adj. a. Brevity]
Curtesan, [Common adj. Fornicator (fem.)]
Curtle-ax, [Short Sword.]
Curve, [Crooked.] Mag. III. 1. O.
Curvet, [Go leaping.]
Cushion. Po. VI. 5. A.
Cusp, [Point.] Mag. IV. 2.
Custard, [Pie of Milk and Eggs.]
Custody. (&c.)
[Keeping]
[Garding]
[Imprisonment]
Custom.
Use. RC. IV. I. A.
[Habit]
[Manners]

[Tribute upon Merchandize.]
—*er.*
In buying or selling. RO. IV. 6.
Cut.
Discontinue,
sp. by edged (thing) interpos'd.
Body, sp. Consistent. Mo. VI. 7.
Earth.
[Dig]
water—[Furrow for—]
[Plough]
Stone, &c.
[Carve]
[Grave]
Plant.
[Fell]
[Prune]
Animal.
[Wound]
horse—*s* [-wounds himself.]
[Un—a. Testicle]
Parts excrementitious.
[Pare]
[Shave]
[Clip]
Flesh, &c.
[Mince]
[Chip]
[Slice]
[Slash]
Plain or Line, [a. Intersection.]
Room, [a. Partition]
—*a caper,* [Leap with Leggs trembling (like.)]
Hurt.
Sense.
—*ing,* { [Acrimonious.]
{ [Intense]
Minde.
[a. Grief]
[a. Anger] (augm.)
Estate, [a. Fraud.]
Diminish.
[a. Short]
[Dispatch]
Separate.
—*off,* [a. Separate.]
[Excommunicate.]
[Destroy.]
—*purse,* [Thief]
—*throat,* [Murtherer.]
[Lot]
Cuticle, [Skin. PG. II. 3. outermost.]
Cutler.
[Sword (mech.)]
[Fabrile (mech.) of cutting (instr.)
Cutter, { [Robber.]
{ [Swaggerer]
Cuttle-fish Ex. IX. 2.
Lesser—Ex. IX. 2. A.
Cycle.
—*of Sun,* [Revolution of 28 years, in which the Dominical Letter returns to be the same.]
—*of Moon,* [Revolution of 19 years, in which the same

Lunations return.]
Cygnet, [Swan (young.)]
Cylinder. Mag. III. 6.
Cylindroides. Ex. VII. 3.
Cymbal, [Round brazen Music (instr.)]
Cynical.
[adj. Dog (like.)]
[Morose]
Cypress. Tr. V. 6.

D.

*D*Abble, [Move (freq.) in wet (thing.)]
Dabchick [Lydapper] Bi. VIII. 7.
Dace. Fi. IX. 10.
Daffadil. HL. IV. 4.
Dag, [Gun (dim.)]
Dagger, [Short Sword (dim.)]
Daggle, [adj. a. Durt (dim.)
sp. the Margin.]
Day.
24 hours. Mea. V. 5.
holy—[adj. Festivity.]
to— [In this—]
Time of Light. Mea. V. 6.
—*break,* [Day (inc.)]
—*time,* [Day (time.)]
bread—[adj. { Perfect }
{ Manifest } ..]
far—[Late in the —]
[Victory] RM. II. 1. E.
Days-man, [Arbitrator.]
Daily, [adj. daies (segr.)]
Dainty, [Nice]
—*s,* [Sustenance extraordinary.] Pr. II.
Dairy.
[adj. Milk (kind.)]
[adj. Milk (room.)]
Dale, [Valley.]
Dally.
[Playing] O. O.
[a. Fondness] Man. VI. 7. O.
[a. Wanton] NP. IV. 3. O.
[Protract] TA. III. 5. O.
Dam.
[Parent (fem.)]
{ Impedient }
{ adj. Stay (make } ridge)
to— { adj. a. Impedi- } with
up { a. Stay (ent } ridge)
Dame, { adj. Noble }
{ adj Gentle } fem.
Mistris, [Master (fem.)]
Dammage.
[Loss]
[Hurt]
Dammask, [Fine Linnen of Damascus.]
to— [a. Damascus (manner.)]
Damn.
as God—Ha. I. 4. O.
as man—[Condemn.]
Damnifie, [a. Dammage.]
Damsel, [Young Celebs (fem.)]
Damp.
Subst.
—*fiery*

DA

—*fiery.* El. I. 7.
—*watery.* El. II. 5. A.
Adj [Moist] Q. V. 2. (dim.)
Damsin, [Plum adj. Damascus]
Dancing. Mo. V. 5.
Dandelion. HF. III. 12. A.
Dandiprat, [Little (dim.) man.]
Dandle, [Shaking (dim.) in ones arms.]
Dandruf, [Scurf of the head.]
Danewort. HS. IX. 9.
Danger. T. V. 3. O.
Dangle, [Hang swinging.]
Dank, [Moist] Q. V. 2.
Dapper, [Little nimble]
Dapple. Q. II. 7. A.
Dare.
 Fish [Dase] Fi. IX. 10.
 Venture.
  [adj. Fortitude]
  [adj. Bold] AS. V. 8.
 —*not,* [Fear]
 [Challenge] RM. I. 2.
 —*larks,* [a. Fear (make.)]
Darkness.
 to the Sight. Q. I. 1. D.
 to the Understanding. D. III. 9. O.
Darling, [Most beloved]
Darn, [Sow knitting (like.)]
Darnel. HL. III. 5.
Dart. RM. V. 5.
 Meteor. El. I. 4. A.
Dase. Fi. IX. 10.
Dash.
 Action.
  [Motion (imp.)]
  sp. Fluid against hard.]
  or Hard against fluid.
  [Cast] Mo. VI. 2.
  [Strike] Mo. VI. 4.
  [Write (imp.)]
  [Mixture]
  sp. with worse.]
 Effect.
  [a. Fall]
  [a. Hurt]
  [Break]
  [Scatter parts (dim.)]
  [Spoil]
  [Destroy]
  [adj. {Shame / Despair} (make)]
Dastard, [a. Coward.]
Date.
 Fruit. Tr. II. 4. A.
 Time. Sp. I. 5.
 out of- [Old / Late] (exc.)
Daub, vid. *Dawb.*
Daucus, [Wild Carret]
Daughter, [Child (fem.)]
 —*in Law.*
 [Child (fem.) by Affinity.]
 [Husband's / Wife's] Daughter]
 [Sons Wife]
Daunt.
 [Fear (make)]
 [Discourage]
Daw. Bi. I. 6.
Dawb.

DE

[Plastering]
[Smearing]
[Defiling by Smearing]
[Bribing]
Dawl, [Dull with weariness.]
Dawning, [Morning (incept.)]
Day. HF. II. 3. A.
 great—HF. III. 3.
 blew—HF. II. 14.
Dayse, [a. Dull with Light (exc.)]
Deacon. RE. II. 5. A.
Dead {deprived / Wanting} {Being. Power. Action.}
—Being.
 [adj. pret. Dying]
 —*pay,* [pay of the]
 —*place,* [place Dead.]
 [Not-adj. living]
—Power.
 Natural [Impotent]
 Sense.
  [num'd]
  [extasied] sp. with fear.
  —*asleep* {Dead (like) through}
  —*drunk*
   {Sleep / Drunkenness}
 Vigor, [Dull]
 Strength, [Weak.]
 Transcendent, [Remiss.]
—Action.
 Motion.
  —*water,* [adj. Pool—]
  Affecting the Sense.
   Sight.
   —*Colour,* [Remiss.—]
   Hearing.
   —*of the night,* [Quiet (time)—]
   Taste / Smell} Q. IV. 6. O.
   Feeling.
   —*cole,* [Unfired—]
   —*wall,* [adj. Yielding Q. VI. 1.—]
   —*nettle,* [Archangel]
Deadly.
 [adj. Dying (make)]
 [Not-adj. p. end (pot.) until death]
Deafness. NP. III. 2. O.
Deal.
 do [adj. Action]
  [a. Conversation]
  [a. Business] sp. (merc.)
  —*between,* [a. Mediator.]
 distribute, [Give (segr.)]

 [Quantity]
 [Fir board]
Dean.
 [Chief of Bishop's Assessors]
 [College (Off.)]
Dear.
 [adj. p. Love (augm.)]
 [adj. Price (augm.)]
Dearn, [Sow knitting (like.)]
Dearth, [Scarcity.] TM. L. 2. D.
Death.

DE

Proper. AC. I. 7. O.
Put to-
 [adj. a. Die (make)]
 [a. Punishment capital]
[Cessation]
[Decay]
Death-watch. Ex. V. 6.
Debarr, [a. Impediment.]
Debase, [a. {lowness / meanness} (make)]
Debate.
 [a. Contention]
 [a. Dispute]
Debauch {Vice / Sensuality / Riotousness} (make)
 [adj.
Debilitate, [a. Weakness.]
Deboist, adj. {Vice / Sensuality / Riotousness}
Debonair.
 [adj. Temper. NP. II. (perf.)]
 [Sprightly]
 [Merry]
Debt. TA. IV. 7. O.
Decad, [Ten]
Decalogue, [the Ten Commands of God.]
Decaying. NP. V. 4. O.
Decease. AC. I. 7. O.
Deceive.
 [a. Fraud]
 [a. Error (make)]
 [Frustrating]
 sp. ones Expectation]
 [doe {Beside- / Contra-} {expectation.}]
December, [Twelfth month.]
Decent. T. V. 2.
Deception, vid. *Deceive:*
Decide.
 [a. Sentence]
 [Finish]
 sp. Suit]
Decimation, [Tenthing]
Decipher.
 {interpret / Explain / read} [obscure Characters.]
 [Un-conceal]
Deck, [Floor of Ship.]
 to—[a. Ornate (make.)]
Declaim, [a. Oration {for. / against.}]
Declare.
 [Interpret]
 [Shewing]
 [a. Manifest]
 [a. Public]
 —*for,* [Own publicly.]
Declension, [Changing (manner of the ends of Nouns)]
Decline.
 [a. Diverge]
 —*ing Dial,* [Erect Plain whose Surface is not situated toward North or South.]
 [Avoid]
 [Decay]
 —*ing age.* Mea. VI. 3. A.
 —*a Noune,* [a. Declension.]

De-

DE — DE — DE

Declivity.
[Obliqueness]
sp. Downward verging]
Decoction.
[Boiling]
[Boil'd (thing)]
sp. Infusion]
Decoy. Po. I. 6. A.
Decorum, [Decency]
Decrease, [Diminish]
Decree.
[Purpose]
[Sentence]
[Edict]
Decrement.
[Diminution]
[Loss]
Decrepit, [adj. p. Stooping.]
sp. with Age.
—age. Mea. VI. 4. A.
Decretal, [adj. Decree.]
Decuple, [Ten-fold]
Decussation, [Crossing] Mag. IV. 4. A.
Dedicate.
As to God, [Consecrate.] RE, V. 1.
As to Man, ⎰Honour
[Give to the ⎱Patronage of—]
Deduce, [a. Illation.]
Deduct, [a. Ablatum.]
Deed.
[Action.] T. I. 7.
in very— [Truly]
[Writing] RC. VI. 5.
Deem.
[a. Opinion]
[a. Thought]
Deep, whose bottom is far from
Natural. (its top.
as the whole.
deep. [adj. TM. II. 3.]
the—[Sea]
thick. [adj. TM. II. 5.]
Six—[Six in file]
as a part.
[adj. Inward]
—colour, [Dark (dim.)—]
—Sound. Q. III. 1. D.
—Notion ⎰[hidden]
⎱[obscure]
[adj. under]
[adj. bottom]
Transcendental, [adj. Intense]
—sleep, [Sleep (int.)]
Deer.
fallow—Be. II. 4.
red—Be. II. 3.
Deface.
[Un- a. Figure]
[Spoil]
[a. Deform]
[Destroy]
Defalk, [a. Ablatum]
Defame.
[adj. Infamy (make)]
[a. Calumny]
Default, [Defect]
—of appearance, [Not appearance.]
Defeat.

[n..tration]
Overthrow]
Defecation..
[a. Pure (make)
Un-worst part.]
Defect. TM. I. 3. D.
Defection.
[Apostasie]
[Rebellion]
Defence, vid. Defend.
Defend.
Oppose. RM. I. 1. O.
Protection. RO. VI. 5.
[a. Prisoner] RJ. I. 3. O.
[a. Defendent] RJ. I. 4. O.
[a. Advocate] RJ. I. 7.
Defendent. RJ. I. 4. O.
Defensive, [adj. Defend.]
—arms. RM. V. 1. A.
Defer.
[a. Late (make)]
—before Action, [Respite]
—in Action, [Protract.]
Deference, [Respect.]
Defy. RM. I. 2. O.
Deficient. TM. I. 3. D.
Defile. TM. V. 6. O.
[a. Vice.]
[adj. Vice (make)
a. Unchast]
Define.
[a. Definition]
[a. Sentence]
Definite.
[Finite]
[Express]
Definition. D. IV. 3.
Definitive.
[Express]
[adj. a. Sentence]
[adj. Finishing]
Deflour, [a. Fornication]
Defluxion.
[Distilling]
[Catarrh]
Deformity. NP. V. 6. O.
Defray.
[Disburse]
[Pay]
Defraud, [a. Fraud]
Defunct, [adj. a. pret. Dying.]
Degenerate..
[Not-ancestor (like)]
[Spurious]
Degrade. RJ VI. 8.
Degree. T. VI. 6.
—of person. RC. I.
—in University, [Graduate (thing)]
Measure. Mea. I. 9.
Dehort. [Dissuade]
Deject.
[Down-cast]
[a. Sorrow]
[a. Despair]
Deify, [a. God (make)]
Deign, [a. Condescension.]
Deity, [God (abstr.)]
Delay.
[a. ⎰Late ⎱(make)
⎰Slow ⎱
disposition, [Cunctation]

—before Action, [Respite]
—in Action [Protract]
Delectation. AS. IV. 7.
Delegate.
[adj. p. Substitute (person)
⎧Put⎫
[Instead—⎨Sent⎬ ⎧per-⎫
⎩Judging⎭ ⎩son.⎭
Deliberate. AS. III. 1.
—ness.
[Considerateness] Ha. IV. 1.
[Slowness] NP. V. 9. O.
Deliberation, vid. Deliberate.
with— ⎰[Considerately]
⎱[Slowly]
Delicate.
[adj. a. Delight (apt.)]
[adj. Pr. II.]
Tender, [adj. NP. IV. 7. O.]
[Over-neat] Man. II. 6. E.
—s, [adj. Pr. II. (thing)]
Delicious, ⎰Delectation
⎱[adj. Pleasure ⎰(aug.)
Delight. AS. IV. 7.
Delineate.
[a. Line]
[a. Description. D. IV. 3.]
sp. by Lines]
Delinquent.
[Guilty]
[Prisoner]
Delirium.
[Dotage] NP. II. 2. O.
[Frenzy] S. IV. 1.
Deliver, [Motion (met.) of
the ⎰Possession of ⎱a thing]
⎩Power over⎭
from one person to another.]
—things. TA. IV. 13.
as Intrusting, [Deposite]
as Paying, [Pay]
as Disclaiming, [Resign]
—words ⎰Fact, [Narration]
of ⎱Doctrin, [a. Teacher]
—immediately.
—by Mouth, [Speak]
—by Pen, [Write.]
—mediately, [Tradition]
RE. VI. 1. A.
—from better to worse]
passively.
[Dereliction] AS. I. 5. O.
Actively.
Involuntary, [Yielding]
Voluntary, [Betraying]
—from worse to better]
Temporal, [AS I. 5.]
Preventing.
[Preserve]
[a. Escape]
Remedying.
[Un-captivate]
[Un-slave]
[Un-imprison]
[a. Parturition]
To be—ed, [Parturition]
Eternal, [Redemption.] AS. I. 7.
Delve, [Dig.]
Delude, [Deceive.]
Deluge, [Over-flowing.]
E e e   *Delusion,*

DE

Delusion, vid. *Delude*.
Demand.
—to know, [a. Question.]
—to have. TA. IV. 2. O.
—as Price. RC. VI. 2. A.
Demean.
[Land which the Lord of the Manor uses.]
[a. Demeanour]
Demeanour. AC. V.
Demerit.
[Worthy (abstr.)]
[Earning]
Demi, [Half]
Demi-cannon.
Demi-god, [God (dim.)]
Demi-lance.
Demise. RC. V. 5.
Demiss.
[Low]
[Humble]
[Abject]
Democracy, [Government by the People.]
Demolish [a. Ruin.]
Demon, [Spirit] [sp. Devil]
Demoniac, [Inhabited by Devils.]
Demonstrate.
[Shew]
[a. Certain by Argument]
Demur.
Hesitate. AS. IV. 3. O.
[Ask more for considering time before answering.] (ing.)
Demure.
[Grave]
[Formal]
Den, [Cavity under-ground adj.]
Lion's &c. — Lion's &c. (house)
Deny, D. VI. 2. O.
self—Ha. V. 3.
Denisen, [Admitted member of Nation, Corporation.] (on)
Denominate, [adj. p. Name (make.)]
Denote, [a. Meaning.]
Denounce.
[Publish]
[Threaten]
Density. Q. V. 3. E.
Dent: Mag. IV. 3. O.
Dentex. Fi. V. 5. A.
Dentifrice, [Teeth-cleansing thing.]
sp. Powder.]
Deodand, [adj. p. ought Almsgiving (thing)]
Depart.
[Go] TA. VI. 1. O.
[From-go]
[Die]
Dependent.
Op. to Absolute. TM. IV. 3. O.
Op. to Patron. RO. III. 5. O.
Deplorable.
[adj. a. Grief (ape]
[adj. Misery (augm.)]
Deplorate, [adj. p. Despair.]

DE

Deplore.
[Sorrow (aug.) for]
[Shew sorrow (aug.) for]
Depopulate, [Un-people.]
Deportation, [Carrying into Exile]
Deportment, [Demeanour]
Depose.
[Down Put Lay]
[a. Privative]
—from Dignity, [Degrade]
—from Office, [Incapacitate]
—from Orders, [Deprive]
[Swear] (sp. before Magistrate)
Deposite. RC. V. 1. A.
Deprave, [a. Evil make.]
Deprecate. RO. V. 3. A.
Depreciate.
[Un-a. valor]
[Diminish the worth]
Depression.
Down-forcing. O. I. 1. O.
[Shallowness] TM. II. 3. O.
Deprive.
[a. Privative]
—of Possession, [Un-possess.]
—of orders. RE. V. 2. O.
Depth, vid. *Deep*. TM. II. 3.
Depuration.
[a. Pureness]
[Un-- a. Scum a. Sediment]
Deputy, [adj. Substitute (person)]
Dereliction.
[Abandoning] TA. II. 2. O.
—to Evil. AS. I. 5. O.
Deride, [Mock.] RJ. IV. 9. A.
Derision, [Mocking.] RJ. IV. 9. A.
Derive, [a. Derivative]
Derivative. TM. IV. 1. O.
Derogate.
[From-take]
[Diminish]
sp. Praise.
Reputation
Descant, [a. Paraphrase.]
Descend, [Down-ition.]
Descendent. RO. I. 1. O.
Descent.
[Down-ition.]
as of Ground, [Down-obliquity]
[Descendent. RO. I. 1. O. (abstr.)]
[Extraction]
Descry.
[See (inc.)]
[Finde by Sight]
sp. From far.]
Describe, [a. Description.]
Description. D. IV. 3. A.
Desert.
Merit.
[adj. Worthy { thing abstr.}]
[adj. p. Earn (thing.)]
Wilderness.
[Not-inhabited]
[Not-inhabitable country]

DE

[Banket] Fr. II. 1. A.
to—[Forsake]
Desertion [Forsaking]
Deserve.
[a. Worthy]
[a. Earn]
Designing.
Internal. TA. III. 1.
External [Appoint]
Desire.
In Affection. AS. V. 5.
In Words. [Intreat] RO. V. 3.
Desist. AS. IV. 6. O.
Desk,
[Supporting (jug.) for Book]
[Box to write upon]
Desolate.
[Solitary (augm.)]
[Not-inhabited]
[adj. Grief (augm.)]
Despair.
Affection. AS. V. 8. O.
Sin. Ha. V. 5. O.
Desperate.
[adj. p. Despair.]
[Rash (augm.)]
Desperation.
Affection. AS. V. 8. O.
Sin. Ha. V. 5. O.
Despicable.
[adj. p. Contempt (apt]
[Sorry]
Despise, [Contemn]
Despite.
[Contempt]
[Malignity]
[Done (thing) for to anger one.]
[Affront]
Despondency, {(inc.) Despair, (dim.)}
Destine.
[a. Purpose]
[a. Fate.]
Destiny, [Fate].
Destitute.
[adj. Defect]
[adj. p. Forsake]
Destroy, [a. Destruction]
Destruction.
Action of God. AS. I. 4. A.
[Spoiling]
Desuetude, [Un- a. custom.]
Detect.
[Discover]
[Un-conceal]
[Manifest]
Detein.
[Hold]
—*unjustly*. RJ. IV. 3. A.
[Stay (make)]
Determine.
[Finish]
[a. Desist]
—the Liberty of the Will. AS. IV. 8. O.
—by ones own [a. Purpose] AS. IV. 3.
—by anothers [Sentence] RJ. II. 5. A.
Deterre. RO. V. 5. O.
Detest.
[Loath

DI

[Loath (augm.)]
[Hate (augm.)]
Detract.
  [a. Ablatum]
  [p. From Reputation.]
  [Under-say] Man. IV. 1. D.
  [Calumny]
Detriment.
  [Loss]
  [Diminishing]
Devastation.
  [Destruction]
  [Spoiling]
Devest, { un-a. clothe}
Deviate, { a. privativeness }
  [Wander]
  [Err]
Devil. W. I. 2. O.
  —'s bit. HF. II. 13. A.
  —'s dirt, [adj. Vitriol earth]
  —'s milk, [Spurge.] HS. V. 2.
Devilish, [adj. Devil.]
Devise.
  [Invent]
  [Contrive]
  By Will, [Bequeath]
  [Feign]
  [Forge]
  a—
  [adj. Craft (thing)]
  [Stratagem]
  [Poly]
Devoir.
  [Endeavour]
  [Duty]
Devolve.
  [Successive { to— { Putting]
  [Final }   { Ition]
Devoted.
  [adj. p. Vow]
  [Consecrated]
  [adj. Zeal]
Devotion.
  [Worship (hab.)]
  [Zeal]
Devour.
  [a. Ravenous. NP. IV. 5. O.]
  [a. Glutton]
  [Eat { up all greedily}]
Devout, [adj. Devotion.]
Dew. El. III. 3. A.
  —claw, [adj. Heel-claw.]
  —grass, [Grass (kinde) a. Seed (apt) millet (like)]
  —lap, [Loose skin of the neck.]
Dexterity.
  [Agility]
  [Art. (perf.)]
Die.
  [v. Death.] vid. Death.
  a. Colour. O. V. 3. A.
  a—[adj. Dicing (instr.)]
Diabetes, [Disease of Pissing (exc.)]
Diabolical, [adj. Devil. W. I. 2. O.]
Diadem, [Head-environing King (sign) Ornament.]
Diagonal. Ma. II. 3.

DI

Diagram, [Lined { figure.}
                { picture.}]
Dial.
  [Time-shewing (instr.)]
  [p. By shadow.]
Dialect, [Language (manner.)]
Dialogue, { Discourse } al-
          { Conference } tern.]
Diameter. Ma. II. 5.
Diamond.
  Stone. St. IV. 1.
  Figure, [Square]
  p. of not-right Angles.]
Diaper, [Linen]
Diaphanous, [Transparent]
Diaphoretic, [adj. a. Sweat (make)]
Diaphragm. PG. VI. 3.
Diary, [Narration of days (segr.)]
Diarrhæa. S. VI. 6.
Dibble, [adj. Setting (instr.)]
Dicacity, [Loquacity.]
Dice, [adj. Mo. V. 1. A. (instr.)]
  to play at—Mo. V. 1. A.
  —ore.
Dichotomy, [Division into two.]
Dicker, [Ten skins of Leather.]
Dictate. AC. III. 6.
Dictator, [Chief adj. Authority (Off.)]
Dictionary, [Book for words.]
Didapper, [Dabchick] Bi. VIII. 7.
Diet.
  [adj. Dying (art.)]
  —'s weed. HF. I. 11.
Diet.
  [Regulated victual (manner) Council] RJ. III. 5. A.
Differ, [v. Difference.]
Difference.
  Proper. T. IV.
  [Diversity] T. III.
  [Dissent]
  [a. Contention]
  making a—
  [Distinction]
  [Partiality]
Difficult. T. V. 4. O.
Diffident. AS. V. 7. O.
Diffuse.
  [Spread]
  [Infect]
Dig. O. III. 1.
Digest.
  Natural. AC. I. 5. A.
  Chymic. O. VI. 5.
  [a. Order]
Dight.
  [Clothing]
  [Adorning]
Digit.
  [Inch]
  [Inch (like)]
Dignifie, [a. Dignity.]
Dignity.
  [Worthiness] T. IV. 6.
  High degree. Ha. II. 5.
Digression. D. V. 9. A.
Dike.
  [Ditch]
  [Gutter]
  [Furrow]

DI

Dil. HF. V. 1. A.
Dilacerate, [Tear]
Dilapidate.
  [Ruin]
  [Suffer to decay]
Dilate.
  [a. Breadth]
  [a. Ampliation]
Dilatory, [adj. Delay]
Dilemma, [Argument adj. a. retort (apt.) against both answers]
Diligence. Ha. IV. 5.
  Double—Ha. IV. 5. E.
Dilling, [adj. p. Favour (aug.)]
Dilucidate, [Interpret.]
Dilute, [Remiss.]
Dim.
  [Blind (dim.)]
  [Dark (dim.)]
  —ness.
  [Sight { Corr. }
         { Dim. }]
  op. to brightness. Q. I. 3. O
Dimension. Ma I.
  [a. Measure.]
Diminishing.
  [a. Little TM. I. 1. D.]
  [v. Remission. TM. I. 8. D.]
  [a. Few. TM. III. 1. D.]
  [More- a. little. T. I. 7. D.]
  [More- a. remiss]
  [More- a. few]
Diminutive, [adj. Littleness.]
Dimple.
  [Furrow (dim.)]
  [Dent (dim.)]
Din, [Sound (augm.)]
Dine, [adj. Noon-meal.]
Ding, [Cast.]
Dinner, [Dine.]
Dint, [Impetus.]
Diocess, [Bishop's { Precinct }
                   { (Place) }]
Dip { into- } adj. a. Water.]
    { under- }
Diphthong. D. I. 3. A.
Dire.
  [Fierce]
  [Cruel]
Direct.
  [Straight] Ma. III. 1.
  Upright. Ma. II. 8. E.
  to—RO. VI. 1.
Dirge, [Prayer for the Dead]
Dirt. El. IV. 2.
Disable.
  [Un- a. able (make.)]
  [a. Impotence]
  [a. Weakness]
  [Incapacitate]
Disabuse.
  [Un- a. wrong (make)]
Disadvantage.
  [Hindrance]
  [Loss]
  [Hurt]
Disagree.
  [Dissent]
  [Unpeaceable]
Disallow, [Disapprove.] AS. III. 5. O.
Disanimate, [Discourage.]

Eee2   Dis-

DI

Disannul.
　[Annihilate]
　[Spoil]
Disappoint.
　[Un appoint]
　[Frustrate]
Disapprove. AS. III. 3. O.
Disarm.
　[Un-armour]
　[Take away Arms]
Disaster, [Adversity]
Disavow.
　[Disapprove]
　[Deny]
　[abdicate]
Disband, [Un-RM IV.]
Disbelieve. AS. II. 4. O.
Disburse. TA. IV. 5.
Disburthen, [Unlode]
Discamp, [Un- a. camp.]
Discard.
　[Out-put Cards]
　[Incapacitate]
Discern { See ? the dif-
　　　　 { Seen (make ? ference]
　[See]
　[a. Common sense]
　[a. Difference]
Discharge.
　[Unlode]
　—a Gun, [Un- adj. p. ammunition (make)—]
　[Un-oblige]
　From Duty.
　　[Perform]
　　[a. Immunity]
　From Debt.
　　[Pay]
　　[Acquit]
　From Guilt.
　　[a. Innocent]
　　[Acquit]
　　[Absolve]
Disciple, [Learner.] RO. III. 3.
Discipline.
　[a. Teacher]
　[Good Government] Man. VI. 5.
　Church—RE. V.
　[Correction]
Disclaim, [Abdicate]
Disclose.
　[Un-conceal]
　[Reveal] AS. I. 6.
　[Un-cover] O. II. 3. O.
　[Shew] TA. I. 8.
　[Open] O. II. 4. O.
Discolour, [a. Colour (corr.]
Discomfit, [Overthrow.]
Discomfort. RO. VI. 3. O.
Discommend, [Dispraise.]
Discommodity.
　[Inconvenience]
　[Hurt]
Disconsolate.
　[adj. Discomfort]
　[adj. Grief (augm.]
Discontent.
　[Not-content]
　[adj. Anxiety]
Discontinue, [a. Discontinued.]

DI

　[Leave　　}
　[Absent　 } for some while.]
　[Un-a. custom]
　—ed.
　—Quantity. TM. III.
　—in Place, Here and there. Sp. II. 7. O.
　—in Time, Now and then. Sp. I. 7. O.
Disconvenient, [Inconvenient]
Discord.
　[Not-congruity]
　—in Music. Q III. 8. O.
　[Dissent]
　　[a. Unpeaceableness]
　　[a. Contention]
Discover. AS. II. 2. A.
　[Un-conceal]
　[Reveal]
　[Perceive (inc.]
　[Uncover]
　[Shew]
Discountenance, [Un-a. reputation.]
Discourage. RO. VI. 2. O.
Discourse.
　Elements of— D. I.
　Words—D. II.
　Complex parts of—
　　Grammatical. D. III.
　　Logical. D. IV.
　　Mixed. D. V.
　Modes of—D. VI.
Discourtesie.
　[a. Courtesie. Man. IV. 7. O.]
　[a. Malignity. AS. V. 2. O.]
Discredit.
　[Disbelieve]
　[Infamy]
Discreet.
　[Prudent] Ha. VI. 2.
　[Grave] Man. IV. 6.
　[Sober] Ha. III. 3.
Discrepant, [Different]
Discretion, vid. Discreet.
　at the—of, [To be disposed according to the will of]
Discriminate.
　[a. Difference]
　[a. Distinction]
Discuss.
　Off——　　}
　Apart——　}[shake]
　Scatter]
　[Inquisition]
　sp. by Disputing.]
Disdein. AS. VI. 5. A.
Disease. S.
　to—
　　[a. Disease]
　　[a. Pain]
　　[Trouble]
Disengage.
　[Un-oblige]
　[Un-entangle]
Disentangle, [Un-entangle]
Disesteem, [Esteem (corr.]
Disfavour, [Un-favour.]
Disfigure.
　[a. Figure (corr.]
　[a. Deformity]
Disfranchise, [Un-privilege]

DI

Disfurnish, [Un-furnish.]
Disgorge, [Vomit.]
Disgrace, [Infamy.]
Disguise, [Un- a. seem (make]
Disgust, [Displicence.]
Dish.
　Vessel. Pr. V. 4.
　Chasing—[adj. Table (vess.] for Fire.
　—Clout, Linen for cleansing Dishes.]
　—washer, [Wagtail.] Bi. III. 8. A.
　—of meat, (Meat (aggr.] sp. dished.]
Dishearten, [Discourage]
Dishevel'd, [adj. p. Confusion.] sp. Hairs.]
Dishonest.
　[adj. Vice]
　[Unchast]
Dishonour.
　[Infamy]
　[Disrespect]
Disimbarque { Go   } out of
　　　　　　 { Take } Ship.]
Disinchant, [Un- a. Witchcraft.]
Disingenuity, NP. IV. 1. O.
Disinherit, [Un-inherit (make)]
Disjoin, [Un-join]
Disjoint, [Un-joint]
Disjunctive, [adj. Separate]
Dislike.
　[Disapprove]
　[Displicence]
Dislocate.
　[Un-place]
　[Place (corr.]
Dislodge, [Remove out of his Lodging.]
Disloyal. Man. V. 6. O.
Dismay, [a. Fear (make]
Dismal, [adj. Adversity (augm.]
Dismantle, [Un-fortifie.]
Dismember.
　[Separate Member from Member.]
　[Tear]
Dismiss.
　[Send away]
　[Permit to depart]
Dismount.
　[Un-a. ride]
　[Un-a. jugament]
Disobedience. Man. V. 7. D.
Disobey, [a. Man. V. 7. D.]
Disoblige.
　[Un-a. oblige]
　[Un-a. friend]
Disorder.
　[Confusion]
　[Un-a. Series]
　[Irregularity]
Disown, [Abdicate]
Disparage.
　[a. Infamy]
　[a. Calumny]
Disparity, [Unequality]
Dispark, [Un- a. Park (make]
Dispatch, [Doe soon and perfectly.]
　[Doe]

[Per-

DI | DI | DI

[Perform]
—soon.
Haften. TA. III. 5.
—perfectly.
{ Finish
Send away
Deliver
a. Free (make
Deftroy
Kill }
Dispend. TA. V. 3.
Dispense.
{ Give
a. Segregate
a. Proportion
{ Give } adv. Pro-
a. Segregate } portion
Relax from Law. RC.
IV. 8.
Licence. RC.IV.8.A.
Dispensatory, [Book of Pharmaceutical Compositions (manner.]
Dispeople, [a. empty of Dwellers.]
Disperse, [Scatter]
Displace, [Un-place]
Display.
[Un-fold]
[Open]
Displant.
[Un-plant]
[Remove]
Displease. AS. IV. 7. O.
Displeasure, [Displeasing]
to doe one a——
doe { adj. displicent
(thing)
adj. hurt (thing) }
Dispose, [a. Disposition.]
Disposition.
[Quality] T. I. 6. A.
Natural.
[Temperament]
—of the Mind. NP. IV.
—of the Body.
resp. Individ. NP. V.
resp. Species. NP. VI.
Actual.
[Inclination] AS.IV.1.
[Habit] (inc.) Ha. A.
[Habit] Ha.
{ Action.] T. I. 7.
Cause] T. II. }
a. Authority]
Appoint]
Prepare]
a. Efficient]
Give]
a. Segregate]
a. Order]
a. Series]
a. Place]
Dispossess, [Un- adj. a. possess make.]
Dispraise. RO. V. 8. O.
Disprofit.
adj. Hurtful (thing)
[Loss]
Disproportion.
Proportion (corr.]
Unequality]
Disprove.

[Against-prove]
[Confute]
Dispute, [a. Argumentation.]
Disquiet.
[Anxiety]
[Trouble]
Disquisition, [Inquisition]
[p. by Argument.]
Disrank.
[Un-a. rank]
[Un-a. Series]
[Un-a. Order]
Disregard, [Not-esteeming]
Disrespect. Man. V. 4. D.
Dissatisfie, { [Not-
[Un- } Satisfie]
Dissect.
[Separate by cutting]
Cut (segr.]
Disseize, [Un-a. possess (make]
Dissemble.
Conceal]
a. Hypocrisie]
Dissention, [a. Contention]
Dissenting. AS. II. 3. O.
Dissertation, [Book argumentative.]
Disservice.
Service (corr.]
Impedient (thing]
Dissever.
[Separate]
a. Segregate]
Dissimular, [Unlike.]
Dissimulation, [Hypocrisie.]
Dissipate, [Scatter.]
Dissolve.
a. Loose Q. VI. 6. D.
a. Fluid Q. V. 5. D.
Melt. O. VI. 2.
[Separate]
[Un-convention]
[Destroy]
Corruption]
a. Ruine]
Dissolute.
Careless]
Sensual]
Dissolution, vid. Dissolve.
Dissonant, [Different]
[p. in sound.]
Dissuade. RO. V. 2. O.
Dissyllable, [Of 2 Syllables]
Distaff, [Staff of spinning (machin.]
—thistle.
Distance.
—of time. Sp. I. 2. O.
—of place. Sp. II. 2. O.
Distast.
[Tast (corr.]
Aversation]
Displicence]
Distemper. S. I. 4.
[Temper (corr.]
Sickliness. S. I. 4.
Distension, [Stretching.]
Distich, [Two Verses.]
Distillation.
Rheum, [Disease of dropping (dim.]
Chymic. O. VI. 6.

Distinct.
[adj. p. distinction (perf.]
[Differenced]
[Separated]
[Ordered (perf.]
[Plain]
Distinction. D. IV. 1.
Distinguish.
a. Distinction]
a. Difference]
[Separate]
a. Period]
a. Order (perf.]
a. Plain.]
a. Judge]
sp. (segr.]
Distortion,
[Twisting]
a. Place (corr.]
a. Deformity]
Distract.
[Pull several waies]
Separate]
Divide]
a. Waver (make]
Mad]
Distrein, [Arrest]
sp. Goods.]
Distress.
[Adversity]
Trouble (aug.]
Arresting] sp. of Goods.
Goods arrested]
Distribute.
Give
Deliver } (segr.]
a. Division]
a. Partition.]
a. Kind
a. Part } (segr.]
a. Segregate]
District.
[Region]
Government (place]
Distrust.
In the Judgment. AS. III. 4. O.
In the Affection, [Diffidence]
Disturb.
[Molest] TA. V. 9. O.
a. Impedient] T. II. 5. O.
Disunite.
[Un-unite]
[Separate]
Disuse.
[Un- a. custom]
[Discontinue { Use]
Custom]]
Ditch.
[Furrow]
[Gutter]
Ditt ander. HF. VII. 6.
Dittany. HF. VII. 6.
bastard—[Fraxinella] HS. I. A.
Ditty, [Words adj. p. sing. (apt.]
Divaricate.
[Straddle (make]
Separate]
Dive. Mo. I. 3. A.
Divel, vid. Devil.

Diver.

DI | DO | DO

Diver. Bi. IX. 8.
— *dunn*— Bi. IX. 8. A.
Diverging. Ma. II. 7. E.
Diverse.
  Various. T. IH.
  Manifold, [Many (kind)]
  [Unlike] TM. V 1. O.
  [Light] adj. Ha. IV. 7. D.
  [Morose] adj. Man. IV. 7. D.
Diversifie, [a. Diversity]
Diversion, [Beside-turn]
  [Digression]
  [Recreation]
Diversity. T. III.
Divide, vid. Division.
Dividend, [adj. p. Divisor (thing)]
Divine, [adj. God]
  a—[adj. RC. II. 1. (person)]
  —'s profession. RC. II. 1.
  to—
  [Wizarding,] RJ. III. 1. A.
  [Conjecturing] AS. II. 7.
Divinity
  [God. (abst.)]
  [RC. II. 1. (Science)]
Division.
  Into kinds.
    Exactly. D. IV. 4.
    Not exactly. D. IV. 4. A.
  Into parts.
    [a. Part]
    [a. Segregate]
  Into Parties.
    [Un-a. Society]
    [a. Contention]
  Into Places.
    [a. Separation]
    [a. Distance]
  In Arithmetic, [a. Divisor.]
  In Music, [a. Paraphrase tune]
Divisor. TM. VI. 9.
Divorce. RE. IV. 5.
Diuretic, [adj. a. Urining (make)]
Diurnal, [adj. Day]
  a—[adj. Narration (thing) of News]
Divulge, [a. Public (make)]
Dizzard, [adj. Doting (person)]
Dizzy, [adj. Giddy. S. IV. 5.]
Do, vid. Doe.
Do, [Buck. Ee. II. 4. (fem.)]
Docil.
  [adj. Learn (apt.)]
  [adj. Sagacity]
Dock.
  [Lent] Man. IV. 3. O.
  For Shipping.
    [Haven (dim.)]
    [adj. Building (place) for Ships.]
  In the posteriors, [Dent—]
  [Tail] PP. VI. 6. A.
  to—
    [Off-cut the Tail]
    [a. Short]
  Herb. HF. I. 1. A.
  but—
    great.— HL. VI. 2.
    little.—HL. VI. 2. A.

Docket, [Accessory writing.]
Doctor, [Highest Graduate]
Doctrine, [Taught (thing)]
Document
  [Thing to be Learn'd.]
  [Thing to be Observ'd.]
Dodder. HF. VII. 19.
Dodge, [a. Lightness.] Ha. IV 7. D.
Dodkin, [Least Mony.]
Doe.
  [a. pres.]
  How—you? [How are you?]
  sp. in Health.]
  [a Action]
     Business]
  Have to—with,
    [a. Business]
    [a. Commerce] with]
  a—[Deer (fem.)]
Doings { Action
             Preparation }
Dog.
  Beast. Ee. V. 1.
  —'s bane. HS. IV. 14.
  upright. HS. IV. 8.
  —berry. Sh. II. 4.
  —'s grass. HL. III. 5. A.
  —'s tongue. HL. IX. 4. A.
  —'s tooth. HL. V. 2.
  [Andiron] [Supporting (jug.) for fuel]
  to—[Follow privately]
  —Fish.
  Greater. Fi. I. 6.
  Lesser. Fi. I. 6. A.
  Star.
    [Star call'd the—]
    [Star (aggr.) call'd, &c.]
  —daies, [Daies in which the Sun rises with the Dog-star.]
Dagged.
  [Perverse]
  [Morose]
Doggrel, [Sorry.]
Dogmatical [Fierce] Ha. III. 4. D.
Dole, [adj. p. Alms (thing)]
  —full, adj. Grief]
Dolor.
  [Grief]
  [Pain]
Dolphin. Fi. I. 1. A.
Dolt, [Dull. Ha. III. 1. O. (person)]
Domestic.
  [adj. House]
  [adj. RO.]
  adj. Family. RO. III. 5. O.
Domineer, [a. Insolence.]
Dominion.
  [Power]
  [Authority]
Donation, [Giving]
Donative, [adj. p. Give.]
Done, [adj. p. Action.]
  I have—[I am adj. pret.
     { Action,
       Finishing.]
Donor, [adj. a. Give (person)]
Doom.
  [a. Judge]

[a. Sentence]
Door. Po. IV. 2.
  —keeper, [Guard at door]
  within—s [Within the house]
  without—s, [Without the house]
Dor, [Beetle] Ex. V. 5.
Doree. Fi. IV. 12.
Dormant.
  [Sleeping]
  [Not- { acting
          shewn }]
  a—[Beam]
Dormouse.
  [Mouse (kind)] { (int.)
                   adj. sleeping (apt.) }
Dorser, [Basket.] sp. to be carried on the back.
Dorter, [adj. Sleeping (room)]
Dorychnium. Sh. IV. 9. A.
Dose, [Proportion sp. of Medicine]
Dotage, NP. II. 2. O.
Dotal, [adj. Dowry.]
Dotard, [adj. Doting (person)]
Tree.
Dote, [a. Dotage.]
  —on, [a. Love (exc.)]
Dotterel. Bi. VII. 3.
Double. [Two (kind.)]
  —diligence. Ha. IV. 5. E.
  —leaf, [Twy-blade.]
  —tongue, [Horse tongue.]
  —tongue,
  —heart } Hypocrisie.]
  to—
    [a. Double]
    as Hare, [Back-goe in the same way.]
Doublet.
  [Close (vest) for upper part of the trunk.]
  [Counterfeit gem]
Doublings of vest, [Foldings—]
Doubt. AS. II. 5. O.
  —full, [adj. p. Doubt (apt.)]
  —less, [adv. Certain]
Doucet.
  —of Deer.
Dove, [Pidgeon] Bi. III. 1.
  Ring—Bi. III. 1. A.
  Stock—Bi. III. 2.
Doughty, [Valiant]
Douzen, [Twelve.]
Dowager, [Widow]
Dowe.
  [Bread not baked]
  —baked, [Scarce baked]
  [adj. p. Future bread]
Dower, [Wife's revenue.]
Down.
  [Downward vergent]
  [Toward- { Underside.
             Bottom. }]
  Prep. V. 2.
    { Bear—   b.)
      Break—   b.)
      Go—   } Down g.)
      Pull—   p.)
  Sit—[Sit]
  —look { Downward } look]
         { Guilty }
                          —right.

DR

—*right.*
 [adj. Perpendicular]
 [adj. Sincere]
 —*Stream* [With the Stream.]
 [Decay]
[Hill]
 [Sheep pasture]
Mols or Hair, PP. VI. 2. A.
Dowry, [Wife's estate]
Doxy, [adj. a. Fornication (fem.)]
Doxology, [Sentence of praise]
Drab, { Wicked } Woman.
       { Unchast }
Draco volans, El. I. 4.
Dracunculus, Fi. III. 8. A.
Draffe.
 [Meat for Swine]
 [Worst part]
 [adj. a. Defilement (thing)]
Drag, [Pull.] O. I. 4.
 sp. { Behinde } t.
      { After   }
—*net.* [Net (instr.) for fishing, adj. p. draw (ape.)]
Draggle-tail, [Slut.]
Dragon.
 Fish.
 Insect.
—*fly,* Ex. IV. 7.
 Plant.
—*tree,* Tr. III. 8. A.
—*wort,* HL. V. 9.
—*'s bloud.*
 [Juice of —Tree]
 biting—[Tarragon.]
 Snap—HS. VIII. 6.
 Fire—El. I. 4.
—*'s head,* [Intersection point of Ecliptic by Planet toward adj. a. North.]
—*'s tail,* [Intersection point of Ecliptic by Planet toward adj. a. South.]
Dray, [Cart.]
Drain, [Trench for water.]
 to— [Un- a. water]
Drake.
 Bird, [Duck (male.)]
 Gun, [Least Ordnance.]
 Fire—El. I. 4.
Dram, Mea. III. 3.
Draper, [adj. Cloth (merch.)]
Draught.
 [Drawing]
 [Drawn (thing)]
 [Exemplar]
 [Picture]
 Ships—[Depth of Ship under water.]
 Jakes, [Dunging (room)]
 game of—s. Mo. V. 3. A.
Draw, { a. Move   }
      { a. Move (end   }
      { toward   }
      {   to   } it felf.
 Corporeal.
  { Pull } O. I. 4.
  { Pull (end) }
 —*cart*
 —*net* } [Lead pulling—]
  [Lift]
 —*bridge,* [Lift by pulling.]

DR

—*plants,* [Un a. root, &c.]
—*water,* [Lift, &c.]
 Ship—s, [—is deep in the water.]
 Take into it felf.
 [Breathe] Mo. III. 2.
 [Suck up breath] AS. IV. 6. D.
 [Snuf]
—*after,* [Hunt by Smell.]
 [Suck] Mo. III. 3. O.
 [Drink] AS. II. 2. O.
 Take out of { another }
             { it's place. }
—*blood,* [a. Bleed]
—*lots,* [a. Lot.]
—*mony.* { out-take— }
—*purse,* { Un-sheath.]
—*sword,*
—*tooth,* [Out-pull.]
—*wine.*
 Virtual.
 [a. Exhalation]
 Metonym. Effect by Motion.
—*of the Fingers.*
 —*mony* [Tell—]
—*of the Needle.*
 —*cloth*
—*of Pen or Pencil.*
 —*a Copy.*
 —*a Picture.*
 —* } writing,* [a. Writing.]
 —*up }
 —*dry,* [Empt. (perf.)]
 —*fowl,* [Un-a. gutt]
 —*out.*
  [Extend]
  [Protract]
 Transcendental.
  Cause.
  —*blood,* [a. Bleed]
  [Occasion]
  [Impulsive]
  [Persuade]
  [Entice]
  [Lead]
  [Seduce]
  [Obtein]
 Beginning.
  —*back.*
  [Retreat
   Apostasie } (inc.)
  —*near* } (near (inc.)
  —*on*
  —*to an issue,* [Finish (inc.)]
 Drawer.
  [adj. Draw'ng (person)]
  [Box (dim.) to be out-pull'd and in-thrust]
 Drawers, [Inner thigh (vest.)]
 Dread, [Fear]
  sp. (augm.)
 Dream, [adj. p. AC. II. 4. A. (thing)]
  —*ing.* AC. II. 4. A.
  —*ness,* { [Dulness] }
           { [Sloth]   }
 Dregs.
  [Worst part] TM. VI. 1. O.
  [Sediment] TM. VI. 3. O.
 Drench.
  [Medicinal drink]

DR

 to—
 [Drink (make) by pouring into the mouth]
 [Bathe]
Dress.
 [Prepare]
 —*meat,* { a. Butchery }
          { a. Cookery }
 [Cleanse]
 —*a Horse.*
  { a. Clothe }
  { a. Ornate }
  { Prune   }
  { a. Surgery }
Dresser, [Cook's table.]
Dry.
 Arid. adj. Q. V. 2. D.
 [Thirsty] adj. AC. II. 2.
 [Penurious] adj. Man. III. 3. E.
 [Reserv'd] adj. Man. IV. 4. D.
 —*jest.*
  [adv. concealed a. Urbanity.]
Driblet.
 [Sum (dim.)]
 [Part (dim.)]
Drift.
 [Driving]
 —*of Snow* [Heap of —together blown]
 go a— [Be driven]
 [End]
Drill.
 to—
 [bore]
 [Entice]
 a—[Boaring (instr.)]
 [Baboon] Be. III. 1.
Drink, [adj. p. drinking (thing)]
 —*ing.* AC. II. 2. A.
 a—[Refection]
Drip.
 [a. Drop]
 [Baste]
 —*ing.*
 [adj. basting (thing)]
Drive, { from   }
 move { before } it felf.
 Contiguous, [Thrust.]
 sp. with knocking]
 Not contiguous. TA. VI. 5. A.
 —*away,* [From—]
 —*back,* [a. Retire (make)]
 —*bees,* [a Move B.]
 —*out,* [Out—]
 The Ship—s, [The Ship is driven.]
 sp. when the Anchor lets —*go.*
Metaphor.
 [Coaction] AS. IV. 9. O.
 —*off,* [Protract.]
 Metonym. [Scatter.]
Drivel, [Dropping Spittle.]
 to—[Let go the Spittle out of ones mouth.]
Drizzle, [Rain drops (dim.)]
Droil.
 [a. Operation (augm.)]
 [Servant, adj. a. operation (aug.)]

Droll,

DU

Troll, [a. Urbanity.]
Tromedary, [Camel.] Be. I. 3.
Drone.
  [Bee (male)]
  [Idle (person)]
Droop.
  [a. Decay]
  [p. Discouragement (inc.)]
Drop. El. II. 1.
Dropsie. S. VI. 3.
Dropwort. HF. V. 10. A.
  water—HF. V. 14.
Dross, [worst part.]
  [p. of Metal]
Drove, [adj. p. drive (aggr.)
  sp. of Cattel.]
Drover, [Cattel-driving (person)]
Drought, vid. *Dry*.
Drown.
  Kill. RJ. V. 7.
  [Cover with water]
Drowzy. AC. II. 3.
Drudge, [a. Operation (augm.)
  sp. Servant.]
Drug.
  [adj. O. VI. A. (thing)
  [adj. Sorry (thing)]
Druggist, [Merchant of unprepared medicinal (things)]
Drum, [adj. Drummer (instr.)
  —*of the Ear*, [Drum (like.)]
  —*mer*. RM. III. 3.
Drunk, [adj. a. Drunkenness]
  —*ard*, [adj. Drunkenness (person)]
  —*enness*. Man. II. 3. D.
Due. T. IV. 3.
  [adj. Debtor (thing)]
Dub.
  [Knock]
  sp. with Fist.]
Dubious, [adj. Doubt.]
Duchess, [Duke (fem.)
Duchy, [Duke's (place.)]
Duck. Bi. IX 2. A.
  —*'s meat*. HL. I. 10.
to—
  [Bow the head] as Duck.
  [Congee (augm.)
  [Dive
  —*and Drake* [Reflect (freq) from the Water.]
Ductil.
  [adj. p. figure (apt.) by hammering.]
  [adj. p. Persuade (apt.)]
Dudgeon.
  [Indignation]
  [Root of Box.]
  —*dagger*, [Short Sword whose handle is of the root of Box.]
Duel. RM. I. 7. A.
Dug. PG. IV. 2. A.
Duke, [Noble-man of highest degree.]
Dull, [Obtuse.]
  Op. to { (Sprightly. NP. IV. 2. O. Strenuous [Lazy] Nimble [Lumpish] Swift [Slow] }

EA

Op. to Sagacity. Ha. III. 1. O.
Blunt, [Not adj. a. Cut (apt.)
  [Remiss]
Dulcimer, Musical (instr.)
Dumb.
  [Mute] AC. III. 1. O.
  [Not-speaking]
Dump.
  [Meditation (int.)
  [Anxiety (imp.)
  [Grief (imp.)]
Dun, [Colour of { Mouse.] &c. }
to— [Come and demand (freq.)]
Dunce, [Dull. Ha. III. 1. O. (person.)
  —*down*, [Cat's tail.]
Dung, [adj. p. Dung (thing.)]
  —*fly*. Ex. IV. 4. A.
  to—Mo. IV. 9. A.
  —*land*, [Manure with Dung]
Dungeon [Dark prison]
Duplicate, [Correspondent type]
Durable, [Permanent]
Durance, [Imprisonment]
Duration. Mea. V. A.
Dure, [v. Duration]
  —*ing my stay*, [While I stay]
Duress, [Affliction of body.]
Durt. El. IV. 2.
Dyrty.
  [adj. Durt.]
  [Rustic]
Dusk, [Dark (dim.)]
Dust.
  Earth. El. IV. 1.
  [Powder] TM. VI. 4. A.
  Pin—[Powder of filed pins]
  Saw—[Powder of sawed (thing)]
Duty, [Due (thing.)]
Dutifulness. Man. V. 1.
Dwarf, [adj. Little.]
  sp. (person.)
  —*elder*, [Danes-wort.]
Dwell. Po. I. A.
Dynasty, [Series { Kinde.] of Governours Nation.] of one Family.}]
Dysentery. S. VI. 6. A.
Dysury, [Disease of pissing (def.)]

E.

E Ach, [Every (segr.)]
  —*other*, [Every one reciprocally.]
Eager.
  [Fierce] Ha. III. 4. D.
  [Desirous (int.)
  [Hungry] AC. II. 1.
  [Acid] Q. IV. 4.
  [Intense]
Eagle. Bi. I. 1.
Eaglet, [Eagle (young)]
Ean, [a. Parturition.
  sp. as Sheep.]

EC

Ear.
  —*of Animal*. PG. III. 2. A.
  give— { [Hear Observe } (end.)]
  —*of Pot*, [adj. Hand (part)
  —*of Plant*. PP. II. 4. A.
to—
  as Corn, [To grow up to an Ear.]
  —*land*, [a. Arable.]
  Sea—Ex. VII. 8.
Earwig. Ex. V. 7. A.
Earl, [Noble man of third Degree.]
Early.
  [Soon]
  [adj. Morning Mea. V. 7.]
Earn. RC. V. 6.
Earnest.
  Adj.
  [Serious]
  [Intense]
  [Diligent]
  [Zealous]
  Subst. Pledge. RC. V. 7. A.
  in—[Truly.]
Earth.
  Globe of—W. II. 7.
  Element of—El. IV.
  —*nut*. HF. V. 10.
  —*quake*. El. II. 5.
  —*worm*. Ex. I. 1.
  to—[into-a. Earth]
Earthen Vessel, [adj. O. IV. A. (vess.)]
Ease.
  [Indolence]
  —*the Belly*,
    [a. Dung]
  [Rest]
  [Leisure]
Easement.
  [a. Indolence]
  [Dunging]
  [adj. Dunging (place)]
Easie.
  [adj. Easiness]
  —*to &c*. [adj. &c. (apt.)]
Easiness.
  Facility. T. V. 4.
  [Plainness] D. III. 9.
  [Credulity]
  —*to*, &c. [&c. (apt.)]
East. Sp. III. 1.
Easter, [Passover (time.)]
Eat.
  Feed. AC. II. 1. A.
  [Corrode] O. VI. 3.
Eaves, [Margin of Roof.]
  —*dropper*, [Concealed (person) hearing (end)]
Eb.
  [Down-tide]
  [a. Low]
Ebony. Tr. VIII. 6.
Ebullition, [Bubbling]
Eccentric.
Ecclesiastic, [adj. RE.]
  —*Relation*. RE.
  —*Officers*. RE. II.
  —*Discipline* RE. V.
  —*Institutions*. RE. VI.

Echo,

EI

Echo, [Reflex found.]
Eclipse, [Obscuring by interposition.]
sp. of { Sun. { Moon.]
Eclipticк, W. VI. 3.
Eclog, [pastoral dialog. Song.]
Edacity, [Gluttony.]
Eddy, [Re-flow.]
Edge.
 [Margin] Sp. III, 4. O.
 [Ridge] Mag. V. 6.
 [Cutting (apt.]
 Set ones teeth on — [Stupifie ——]
 —wise, [adv. Side.]
Edible, [adj. p. Eat (abstr.]
Edict, RC. IV. 3. A.
Edifie.
 [a. Building]
 [a. Bettering]
Edifice, [Building,] Po. II.
Edition, [a. Public. (make.]
Education, [a. Nurse.]
 —words, RO. V.
 —deeds. RO. VI.
Eel. Fi. VI. 7.
 sand —Fi. VI. 4. A.
 —pout Fi. VI. 6. A.
Effable, [adj. p. Speak (abstr.]
Effect, T. II. O.
 to this — [—end]
 of no— [adj. Fruitrate]
 to— [Efficient.]
 to take — [Event (perf.]
Effectual, [adj. a. Efficient(apt.]
Effeminate, [Woman (like.]
 [Tender] NP. IV. 7. O.
 [Nice] Man. II. 6. E.
Efficacy, [a. Efficient (abstr.]
Efficient, T. II. 1.
Effigies, [Picture.]
Effluvium, [adj. p. Exhalation (thing.]
Effort, [Endeavour (imp.]
Effusion, { Out— { Forth.. } pouring]
Efsisoon, (At times,] Sp. I. 8. O.
Egges. PP. V. 6.
 with Egge, [Impregnated with Egge.]
 to —[a. Impulsive]
Eglantine, [Rose (kind.]
Egregious, [Excellent.]
Egress.
 [Going out]
 [Way out]
Egret, [Eagle (kind.]
Egyptian, [Wandring wizard.]
Eie, vid. Ey.
Ejaculation, [Prayer (dim.]
 sp. Sudden.]
Eject.
 [Out-cast]
 [Un-&c.]
Eight. Mea. II. 8.
 —teen.
 —ty.
 —hundred, &c.
Either.
 [Any of the two]
 [Or]

EM

Eke, [Also]
Eke out, { Lengthen } by Addition. { Enlarge }
Elaborate, [adj. p. Diligence.]
Elate, [adj. Insolence.]
Elaterium, [concrete juyce of the wild Cowcumber.]
Elbow. PG. V. 2. A.
 [Angle]
Elder.
 [More-old]
 [Priest]
 [Fore-father]
 Tree. Tr. III. 2.
 water—Sh. II. 12. A.
Elecampane, HF. III. 6. A.
Elect.
 —to do. AS. IV. 5.
 —to Office, &c. RC. IV. 2.
Electuary, [Moist consistent medicinal mixture.]
Eleemosynary, [adj. Alms.]
Elegancy.
 [Beauty]
 [Ornateness]
Elegy, [adj. Grief verse (aggr.]
Element. El.
 [Principles]
 —of Discourse. D. I.
Elephant. Be. I. 4.
Elevate, [Lift.]
 —ion of the Pole.
Eleven.
Elf, [Little sorry (thing.]
Eligible, [adj. p. Elect. (apt.]
Elixir, [Best part.]
 sp. adj. Chymic.]
Elk. Be. II. 3.
Ell, [Three foot and 9 inches]
Ellipsis. Mag. III. 8. D.
Elm. Tr. VI. 4.
Elocution, { Speaking } (Manner.] { Articulation }
 sp. Artificial.]
Eloquence, { Ornately.] { Speaking(art) } Persuasively.]
Else.
 [adv. Other]
 [Beside]
 —where, [In other place.]
Elucidate, [Interpret.]
Elude, { avoid } { frustrate }
Elucubrate, [Diligent study.]
Emaciate, [adj. Lean (make.]
Emanation, [Out-flowing.]
Emancipate, [Un-slave.]
Embalm, [Preserve by Conditing.]
Embark, [Into-go.]
 sp. Into Ship.]
Embassador, [adj. RC. sent (Officer.]
Embellish, [a. Ornate (make.]
Ember-week, [Fasting week for Ordination.]
 [adj. Ordination (time.]
Embers, [Fired ashes.]
Embezil, [a. Prodigality.]
Emblem, [Signifying picture.]
 sp. Moral.]
Embody, [a. Body.]

EN

Embolden, [a. Bold (make.]
Emboss, [Adorn with protuberances.]
Embowed, [Arched.]
Embowel, [Un-bowel.]
Embrace. AC. V. 6.
Embrew, [Soke.]
Embroider, [Variegate by sowing.]
Embryon. PP. VI. 7.
Emendation.
 [Mending]
 [Repairing]
Emergent.
 [adj. Event]
 [adj. p. Occasion]
Emerod.
 Stone. St. IV. 4.
 [Vein in the Fundament]
 —s [Tumors about those veins.—]
Emew, [Cassaware.] Bi. II. 9. A
Eminence, [Excellence.]
Emissary.
 [Sent (person]
 [Spy]
Emission, [Out-sending.]
Emmet, [Ant.] Ex. IV. 5.
Emolument, [Profit.]
Empair.
 [a. Worse]
 [Marring]
Empale, R. V. 4. A.
Empannel, [a. Catalog.]
Empeach, [a. Accuser.]
Emperor, [King (augm.]
Emphasis. D. I. 8.
Empire.
 [King (place)]
 [King (abstr.]
Empiric, [Physitian (cort.]
Employ.
 [a. Business TA. III.]
 [Use. TA. V. 6.]
Empoverish, [a. Poverty (make.]
Empress, [Emperor (fem.]
Emptying. O. II. 7. O.
Empyema. S. V. 3. A.
Emry. St. I. 7. A.
Emulation. AS. VI. 3.
Emulgent, [adj. Sucking.]
Emulsion, [Milk (like) Medicine.]
Emunctory, [Glandule] PG. II 7. A.
Enable, [a. Able (make.]
Enact, [a. Law (make.]
Enamel, [Paint with melted Colours.]
Enamored, [adj. a. Love.]
Encamp, [a. Camp.]
Enchant, [a. Witch with words.]
Encircle, [About-a. circle.]
Encline.
 [a. Oblique]
 [a. Vergency]
 [adj. p Disposition] AS. IV. 1.
Enclose.
 [Shut]
 [Contein]
Enclosure.
 [a. Enclosing]
 [Fence]

EN | EN | EP

[Fence]
Encomium, [Praise.]
[adj. a. Praise Oration.]
Encompass, [about- { Ition. } Putting.]
Encounter.
[Assault mutual]
[Meeting]
Encourage. RO. VI. 2.
Encrease. TM. I. 7.
Encroach { (inc.)
[Usurpation { (dim.)
Encumber.
[Hinder { sp with confused
[Trouble { multitude.]
End.
Part.
[Extreme]
[Top]
[Bottom]
—less.
[Eternal]
[Infinite]
Cause. T. II. 6.
to the—that. Conj. III. 1.
Action.
[Desist]
[Finish]
[Event]
Endamage.
[a. Loss (make)]
[a. Hurt]
Endanger, [a. Dangerous]
Endeavour. TA. III. 4.
Endite.
[a. Word]
sp. Writing.] AC. III. 6. A.
[Accuse]
sp. by Writing] RJ. II. 3. A.
Endive. HF. II. 16.
Endorse, [Write on the backside.]
Endowment.
[Quality]
sp. NP.
[Habit]
[Revenue.]
Endue, [v. Quality,]
Endure.
Suffer.
[v. Passion]
[v. Patience]
cannot—[a. Aversation]
last, [a. Duration.]
Enemy. RO. IV. 1. O.
Energy.
[Efficient { Faculty
{ Act]
Enervate, [a. Weakness. NP. V. 7. O.]
Enfeeble, [a. Weakness. NP. V. 7. O.]
Enfeof.
[a. Right]
[Deposit] RC. V. 1. A.
Enflame.
[a. Flame]
[a. Heat (exc.)]
Enforce, [Coaction.]
Enfranchise, [a. Privilege.]
Engage.

[a. Obligation]
[a. Sponsion]
[a. Pawn]
[a. Morgage]
[a. Debtor (make)]
[p. Business (make)]
Engender, [Generation]
Engine, [Machin]
English.
Engraft, [Graft]
Engrave, [Grave] O. IV. 6. A.
Engross.
—writing, [Write (perf.)]
—commodities.
[Buy all]
[Appropriate] TA. I. 2.
Enhaunce.
[a. Intension]
sp. the price.]
Enigmatical, [Obscured with Figures.]
Enjoying.
Fruition. TA. V. 7.
[Possession]
Enjoyn, [Command]
Enlarge, [Large (make)]
[Ampliation] D. IV. 2. O.
[More- a. large (make)]
[Increase] TM. I. 7. E.
Enlighten, [a. Light.]
Enmity, [Enemy (abstr.)]
Ennoble, [a. Noble (make.)]
Enormity.
[Wrong (int.)]
[Vice (abstr.)]
[Crime (augm.)]
Enough, [Sufficiency.]
—and to spare, [Abundance.]
Enquiring, [a. Inquisition.]
Enrage, [adj. a. Anger (make.)]
Enrich, [adj. a. Rich (make)]
Enroll.
[a. Catalog.]
[a. Register.]
Ensign.
[Sign]
Colours. RM. III. 2.
Ensnare.
[Intangle } { by craft]
[Take } { by Stratagem]
Enstall.
[a. Seizin solemnly]
sp. in Seat.]
Ensue.
[Follow]
[Event]
Entail, [a. Inherit (make) adv. Series.]
Entangle. O. II. 2. A.
Enter.
[Into- { go
{ Put]
[Direct]
[Begin] TA. III. 3.
[a. Teacher (inc.)]
—in a b● [Write—]
—into bond, [adj. p. bond.]
—upon.
[Possession (inc.)]
[Seizing]
Enterchangeable, [adj. Reciprocation.]

Entercourse.
[Reciprocal { Passage
{ Converse
{ Business]
Enterfeir, [Strike reciprocally.]
sp. with Heels or Ankles.]
Enterlace.
[Between-put]
[Stratifie]
Enterline, [Write between the lines.]
Enterlude, [Player (thing.)]
Entermeddle, [a. Business.]
Entermingle, [adj. a. Mixt (make.)]
Enterprize, [Essay.]
Enterr, [Bury]
Entertain.
[Receive]
[a. Host]
Treat. AC. V. 2. A.
Enthrall, [a. Slave (make.)]
Enthrone, [a. Seizin solemnly]
sp. in King (place.)]
Enthusiasm, [Counterfeited Inspiration.]
Enthymem. D. IV. 7. A.
Entice, [Allure.]
Entire.
[Total] TM. VI.
[Whole] NP. V. 1.
[adj. Integrity. Ha. IV. 6.]
Entity, [Being (abst.)]
Entitle, [p. Right (make)]
[a. Name.]
Entomb. RE. IV. 9.
Entrals, [Gutts.] PG. VI. 4. A.
Entrance, [a. Enter.]
Entrap, [Take.]
sp. in Machin.]
Entreat.
Pray. RO. V. 3.
[Entertain] AC. V. 2. A.
Entrench.
[a. Ditch (make)]
[Usurp]
Entry.
[Entring (place)]
—into house, &c. Po. III. 3. A.
Entrust.
[Deposit]
[Instead-p-right (make)]
Envenom, [Poisoned (make.)]
Envy. AS. VI. 6. O.
Environ.
[About { be
{ put]
Enumerate, [a. Number]
Enunciation, [Proposition.]
Enure, [a. Custom.]
Enwrap, [Ir.-wrap.]
Eolipyle, [adj. a. Winde (vessel) by Rarefaction.]
Epact, [Difference between Solar and Lunar year.]
Ephemerides, [Book of adj. daies (thing.)]
Ephialtes. S. IV. 2. A.
Epicen, [Of both Sexes.]
Epicure, [adj. Sensuality (person.)]

ER

Epicycle, [Accessory Circle.]
  sp. Whose Center is within the Circumference of another Circle.
Epidemical, [adj. Nation.]
Epigram, [Short Poem.]
Epilepsie. S. IV. 5. A.
Epilog. D. V. 8. O.
Epiphany, [Festival of the Star's apparition].
Episcopal, [adj. Bishop.]
Epistle. D. V. 2. A.
Epitaph, [Writing on Tomb.]
Epithalamium, [adj. Marriage-song.]
Epithet, [Adjunct word]
Epitomy. D. V. 7.
Epoch. Sp. I. 5. A.
Equal. adj. TM. I. 5.
  Relation of—s. RO. IV.
  Coming off upon—terms. RM. II. 1.
Equality. TM. I. 5.
  [Equity]
Equanimity.
  [Equity]
  [Content] Ha. I. 3.
Equator. W. VL 2.
Equilateral, [Having its sides equal.]
Equinoctial.
  —time, [Time of equal night and day]
  —Circle, [Equator]
Equipollent.
  [Of equal { Power } { Efficacy }]
Equippage, [Furniture (manner.)]
Equitable, [adj. Equity.]
Equity. Man. I. 2.
Equivalent TM. I. 6.
Equivocation. D. IV. 1. O.
Equor. W IV. 1.
Er, vid. *Err.*
Eradicate, [Un-root]
Ere.
  [Before]
  —long, [Future (dim.)]
  —while.
    [At some time] Sp. I. 8.
    Lately, [adv. past (dim.)]
  Rather then]
Erect.
  [a. Direct. Ma. II. 8. E.]
  [a. Build. Po. II.]
Eringo. HF. VIII. 1. A.
  *Umbelliferous—*HF. IV. 12. A.
Ermin.
  Beast, [Stoate] Be. IV. 7.
  Fur, [Fur of Ermin]
Err. TA. III. 8.
Errant.
  [Genuine]
  [Wandring]
  [Sent (thing) sp. entrusted.]
Erroneous.
  [adj. Err]
  [False]
Eruption, [Out-breaking.]
Erysipelas. S. VII. A.
Escape.
  Avoid being taken RM. II. 6.
  [Pass not observed]
Escheat.
  [To-{ event } { confiscation }]
Eschew.
  [Avoid]
  [Aversation]
Especial, [Principal]
Espy, { Spy } { See }
Espouse, [a. Spouse]
Esquire, [Gentleman of the middle rank]
Essay. TA. III. 4. A.
Essence.
  [Being (abstr.)]
  [Best part extracted by Distillation.]
Essential.
  [adj. Being]
  [adj. Importance]
Essoin.
  [Excuse for not appearing.]
Establish.
  [adj. Steddy make]
  [Confirm]
Estate.
  [State]
  [Condition]
  [Age]
  [Degree]
  sp. of { Nobleness } { Gentility }
  [Dignity]
  [Revenues (aggr.)]
  [Right]
  [Possession]
Esteem.
  [Think]
  [Judge]
  Value. AS. II. 8.
  [Respect]
Estimation, [Esteem]
Estival, [adj. Summer.]
Estrange, [Alienate.]
Estreat.
Estridge. Bi. II. 9.
Estuate.
  [Move vehemently.]
Etching, [Graving with corroding moist (thing.)]
Eternal, [adj. Everness]
Eternity, [Everness]
Ether. El. II. 1.
Ethic, [adj. Manners (art.)]
Ethiopian, [adj. Black (person.)]
Ethnic, [Pagan]
Etymology.
  [Derivation of words]
  [Derivation (art.)]
Evacuate.
  [a. Empty.]
  [a. Purge.]
Evade.
  [Avoid]
  [Escape]
Evangelist. RE. II. 3.
Evaporate, [Out-vapor.]
Evasion, [Evading]
Eucharist. RE. VI. 6. A.

EV

Eve.
  [Before-day]
  sp. before Festival]
Evechurr. Ex. II. 2. A.
Even.
  Adj.
    [Equal]
    [Of the same { Quantity } { Number } { Strength }]
    Quitts, [Having compensated]
    op. to Odd. TM. III. 5.
    [Plain] Q. VI. 2.
    [Self.]
  Adv.
    [Yea]
    Expletive.
    —as, [As.] adv. I. 3.
    —now
    [Now]
    [Adv. past (dim.)]
Evening. Mea. V. 7. O.
Even-song, [adj. Evening worship.]
Event.
  End. TA. V.
  [Effect] T. II. O.
  —of War. RM. II.
Ever.
  All times. Sp. I. 9.
  —for—[adj. sp. I. 9.]
  —since, [From that (time.)]
  —lasting, [adj. Sp. I. 9.]
  Life—lasting, [Gnaphalium.]
  Some times.
  —and anon.
    [Frequently]
    [At times.] Sp. II. 8. O.
  or—[Before that]
Every,
  —one, Pron. III. 2.
  —where, [In every Place.]
  —whit, [adv. Total.]
Evet, [Salamander] Be. VI. 5.
Evict.
  [Prove]
  [Convince]
Evidence,
  Adj. Manifest.
  [Plainness]
  [Certainty] sp. manifest]
  [Probation] D. VL 6.
  [Testimony]
  [Writing.] RC. VI. 5.
Evil. T. III. 2. O.
  —at ease, [Not indolent]
  *King's—*S. III. 3.
Evince, [Prove]
  sp. Plainly.]
Eunuch, [Un-testicled (person)]
Euphony, [Sound (perf.)]
Euphorbium, [Concrete juice of a
Ew.   (plant.)
  —tree. Tr. III. 6.
  —sheep [Sheep (fem.)]
Ewer, [Vessel for pouring water on hands]
Exact.
  Adj.
    [adj. Rigor.]
                              [adj.

EX

to [adj. Perfect]

___

[a. Rigor]
[Demand } Unmercifully]
 { The utmost]
[a. Oppression]
Exaggerate.
 [a. Great]
 [a. Intension]
 [add Provocation]
 [More-angry (make]
Exagitate.
 [Swing]
 [Vex (endeavour]
Exa't.
 [Lift]
 [Praise (augm.]
 [adj. a. Dignity (make]
Examine.
 [Inquisition] AS. II. 2.
 [a. Question]
 [Trial] TA. II. 5. A.
 Judicially. RJ. II. 4. A.
Example.
 [Exemplar]
 Instance. D. IV. 8. A.
 as for— [e. g.] Conj. IV. 3. O.
Exanguious Animal. Ex.
Exanimate.
 [Discourage (augm.]
Exasperate.
 [a. Intension]
 [More-angry (make]
Exauthorize, [a. Un-authority.]
Exceed.
 [Excell]
 [Abound]
 [Augment]
 [Intense]
 [v. Excess]
Excel.
 [v. Excellent]
 [v. Superior]
 [v. victory]
 —*lent.* TM. I. 4. E.
Except.
 Adv.
 [Beside]
 [Unless]
 —*ion.*
 [Exemption]
 —*to rule.* D. IV. 5. O.
 take—[Be displeased]
Excess.
 Too-much. TM. I. 3. E.
 Vitious. Man. II. E.
 [Gluttony]
 [Drunkenness]
Exchange.
 Bartering. RC. V. A.
 [Merchant's Convention (place.]
Exchequer, [Court of Chief Magistrate's revenue.]
Excise, [Tax upon vendibles.]
Excite, [Impulse.]
Exclaim AC. III. 3. O.
Exclude.
 [Out-shut]
 [Exempt] TA. II. 4.
 [Except]

EX

Exclusive, [Excluding the extreams]
Excogitate, [Invent]
Excommunicate. RE. V. 5.
Excoriate, [Un-skin.]
Excreation. Mo. IV. 5. A.
Excrement.
 [Out-purged (thing.]
 [adj. dunged (thing.]
Excrescence.
 [Out-growing gibbous (thing]
 Fruit-like. PP. III. A.
Excruciate, [Torture.]
Excursion.
 [Out-running]
 [Digression]
Excuse, [Defendent (thing.]
Execrable, [adj. p. Ought aversation. (augm.]
Execration.
 [Cursing]
 [Renounce with Cursing]
Execution, [Performing.]
 —*of Sentence in Law.* RJ. II. 9.
 —*Capital.* RJ. V.
 —*not Capital.* RJ. VI.
 —*er*, [adj. Execution (Off.]
Executor, [Intrusted (person) with Will.]
Exemplar. T. II. 3.
Exemplifie.
 [Give { Copy]
  { Instance]
Exempt. TA. II. 4. O.
 [a. Immunity]
Exercise.
 [Practise]
 [Doe]
 [Custom to doe]
 [a. Experience]
 [Use]
 [a. Motion]
 [a. Recreation]
Exercitation, vid. *Exercise.*
Exhalation. Met. II. 2.
 [Vapor] Met. II. 2. A.
 [Fume] Met. II. 3.
Exhaust.
 [Out-draw]
 [Empty]
Exhibit.
 [Represent]
 [Offer]
 [Give]
Exhibition, [adj. p. Stipend (thing.]
Exhilerate, [a. Mirth.] AS. V. 4.
Exhort, [Perswade] RO. V. 2.
Exhortation, [a. Perswade.]
Exiccation, [a. Driness.] Q. V. 2. D.
Exigent.
 [Occasion] T. II. 4. A.
 [Expediency] T. V. 6.
 [Need]
Exile. RJ. VI. 5.
Eximious, [adj. Excellent.] T. I. 4. E.
Existence, [Being. T. I. 1. (abstr.]

EX

[p. Actual.]
Exonerate, [Un-lode.]
Exorable, [adj. p. Entreat (abstr.]
Exorbitance. TM. V. 4. O.
Exorcist, [Un- adj. a. Devil (Off.]
Exotic, [adj. Forein] RO. IV. 3.
Expansion.
 [Stretching]
 [Spreading]
 [Opening]
Expatiate, [Walk abroad.]
Expell. AS. III. 7. A.
Expedient. T. V. 6.
 an—[Means] T. II. 6. A.
Expedition.
 [Dispatching] TA. III. 5.
 [Travel] TA. VI. 3.
 sp. Military,
Expel, [Out-drive.] TA. VI. 5. A.
Expence, [adj. p. Spend (thing.]
Expend.
 [Spend]
 [Disburse]
Experience.
 [Essay] TA. III. 4. A.
 Habit. Ha. VI. 4.
Experiment.
 [a. Experience (end]
 [adj. p. Essay (thing.]
Expert, [adj. Experience.]
Expiate.
 [Satisfie for Guilt.]
 [Un- a. Guilty (make]
 sp. by Sacrifice.]
Expire.
 [Die]
 [End]
 time—*d*, { ended.]
  { Time past.]
Explain, [Plain (make.]
Explicate, [Plain (make.]
Explicit, [Express] D. III. 8.
Explode.
 [Disapprove (augm.]
 [Reject disgracefully]
Exploit.
 [Action (augm.]
 [adj. p. Perform (thing.]
Exploration.
 [Inquisition] AS. II. 2.
 sp. by Essay.]
Expose.
 [Out-put]
 [Un-cover]
 [adj. p. Danger (make]
Exposition.
 [a. Plain]
 [Interpretation]
Expostulate.
 [Ask accusingly]
 [Complain]
Expound.
 [a. Plain]
 [Interpretation]
Express. D. III. 8.
 —*ion*, [Speech (manner.]
Exprobrate, [Upbraid.] RJ. IV. 8. A.

Expul-

EX — FA — FA

EX

Expulsion, vid. *Expel.*
Expunge, [Un-write.]
Exquisite, [adj. Perfectness.]
Extant.
  [adj. Being]
  [Actual]
  [Adj. p. See (abstr.)]
  [Public.]
Extasie. AS. VI. 8. A.
Extempore, [Without premeditation.]
Extend, [Stretch.]
Extension. Ma. A.
  Posture, [Stretch]
Extent. Ma. A.
Extenuate.
  [adj. a. Little.]
  [adj. a. Thin]
  [Excuse in part]
Exterior, [adj. Out-side.]
Exterminate, [Exile.] Sp.
External, [adj. Out-side.] III. 6. O.
Extinguish.
  [Un-fire]
  [Annihilate]
Extirpate.
  [Un-root]
  [Destroy]
Extoll.
  [Praise (augm)]
Extort, [From-gain violently]
  —*ion.* RJ. IV. 5. A.
Extract.
  [Out-bring]
  [From-proceed (make)
  sp. by Chymic operation.]
  —*an—*
  [Copy]
  [Epitome]
  —*ion* [adj. Descendent (kind) RO. I. 1. O.
Extrajudicial, [Not-judicial]
Extraneous, [adj. Foreiner]
Extraordinary, adj. TM. V. 3. O.
Extravagant.
  [Exorbitant]
  [Impertinent]
  [adj. Digression]
Extream.
  op. to Middle. Sp. III. 3. O.
  op. to Mediocrity. T. I. 2. O.
  [Excessive]
  Utmost [Most-adj. greatness.]
  [Rigid] Man. I. 1. E.
  [Defective]
Extremity.
  [End] Sp. III. 3. O.
  [Misery]
  [Trouble (aug.)]
Extricate, [Un-tangle.]
Extrinsecal, [adj. Out-side.]
Extrusion, [Out-thrusting.]
Exuberant, [Abundance.] TM. I. 2. E.
Exudation, [Out-sweating.]
Exulcerate, [adj. p. Ulcer (make)]
Exultation, [Triumph.]
Ey.
  Member. PG. III. 2.

FA.

blear   ⎫   ⎧*fore*
goggle ⎬ *-ed*⎨*prominent* ⎬ 2.
pink   ⎭   ⎩*little* (dim.
  Apple of the—[adj. Black (thing) of the Ey.]
  —*brow.* PG. III. 6. A.
  —*lid*, [adj. a. Cover (thing) of the Ey.]
  —*service*, [Seeming (end.) to serve]
  —*bright.* HS. VIII. 7. A.
  [Loop.] Mag. V. 2. A.

F.

F*Able.*
  [adj. p. Fiction narration]
  [Lie]
Fabric, [Building.]
Fabrile Operation. O. IV.
Fabulous, [adj. Fiction.]
Face.
  Subst.
  Member. PG. III. 1.
  make—s, [Change Face (manner)]
  [Presence]
  to—
  —*as Person*, &c. [Over against stand]
  —*as Garment*, Pr. IV. 9.
  —*about*, [Turn.]
  —*out a ly.,* ⎧ impudently.⎫
  [ɪ Ly ⎨ pertinaciously.⎬]
Facetiousness, [Urbanity.]
Facil.
  [Easie]
  [Credulous]
  [Affable]
Facilitate, [a. Easiness.]
Facinorous, [Crime (augm.)]
Fact. [Done (thing.)]
Faction. BC. III. 8. A.
Factious, ⎰Faction ⎱ (apt.)
  [adj. ⎱Sedition⎰
Factitious. T. III. 7. O.
Factor, [Instead-Merchant]
Faculty.
  [Natural Power]
  [Licence]
Fade.
  [p. Transitoriness]
  [v. Decay]
Fag, [End (corr.)]
Fagot, [Sticks (aggr.) together-bound.]
Fail.
  [p. Frustrate] TA. V. 1. O.
  [Miscarry] TA. III. 7. O.
  [Omit] TA. III. 8. A.
  [Defect]
  [Faint]
  Insolvent. TA. IV. 8. O.
Fain.
  [Fiction]
  [a. Seem]
  [a. Hypocrisie]
I would—have it, [I desire

FA

  (augm.)]
Faint.
  —*ing.* S. V. 5.
  [Weary]
  [Weak]
  [Remiss]
  [Slight]
  —*hearted.*
  [Coward]
  [Diffident]
Fair.
Adj.
  [Beautiful]
  [Clean]
  [Clear]
  —*dealing.*
  [Equity]
  [Candor]
  —*demeanour.*
  [Courtesie]
  [Affability]
  —*way*, [Not-durty—]
  —*Weather*, [Wea-⎰rainy.
     ther not ⎱cloudy.]
  —*wind*, [Prosperous—]
Subst.
  Mart, [Convention for Commerce.]
  —*ing*, [Given (thing) at Fair.]
Fairy, [Feign'd man (like) Devil.]
Faith.
  [Belief]
  —*rational.* Ha. III. 2.
  —*religious.* Ha. V. 4.
  —*full.*
  [adj. Fidelity.]
  [adj. Ha. V. 4.]
  —*less.*
  [Perfidious]
  [Not-adj. Faith]
Falchion, [Short crooked Sword]
Falcon, Hawk (kind.)
Falconer, [adj. Hawk (Off.)]
Falling.
  Motion proper.
    (Down-fall.)
  —*down*, ⎰Navigate with the
      ⎱Stream.
  —*in*, [Come (imp.)]
  —*with*, [Together-come (imp.)]
    sp. in Fight.]
  —*off*, [Go (imp.)]
  —*on*, [Assault.]
  —*to*
  —*Leeward.* RN. VI. 6. D.
  Motion metaph.
  Begin.
  —*in band with*, [Begin.]
  —*to ones meat*, [Eat (inc.)]
  Event.
  sp. adj. Fortune.
  —*in love with.*
  —*out*, [Event.]
  —*with one*, [Un-friend.]
  —*from higher to lower.*
  —*ing.*
  —*on knees.* AC. VI. 6.
  —*all along.* AC. VI. 7.

—*in*

FA

—en.
—on knees. AC. VI. 6. A.
—all along. AC. VI. 7. A.
—ing Star. El. I. 2. A.
water—s, [a. More-low (inc.)
wood—s, [w. adj. p. Felling]
—from greater to less, [Diminish.]
Flesh—s.
—Hair—s.
—Leaf—s.
—of the Leaf, [Autumn.]
Price—s.
Water—s, [p. Shallow.]
Wind—s, [p. Diminish.]
—from better to worse.
{ Sin.
{ Apostasie }
[Adversity]
[Sickness]
—ing Sickness, [Epilepsie] S. IV. 5. A.
—ing back. [Again sickning.]
[Destruction]
Fallacy, [adj. a. Erring (apt.) Argument.]
Fallible, [adj. Err. (pot.)]
Fallow, [Not-plow'd.]
to—[First plowing]
—deer. Be. II. 4.
False.
Untrue. [adj. T. III. 1. O.]
[ly]
[Wrong]
[Spurious]
[Forged]
[Treacherous]
Falshood. T. III. 1. O.
Falsifie, [a. False.]
Falter, vid. *Faulter*.
Fame.
[Common { Narration } Rumor.]
[Common { Praise (augm.) Reputation }]
Family.
[œconomic relation] RO.
[Kin] RO. I.
[Houshold] [House (aggr.)]
Familiar.
[adj. Acquaintance]
[adj. Custom]
—Spirit, [—devil.]
Famin.
[Food (def.)]
[Want of food]
[Hunger]
Famish, [Starve.]
Famous, [adj. p. Fame.]
Fan, [adj. a. Winde (jug.)]
—for Corn. [adj. winnowing (jug.)]
Fanaticalness.
[Pretending Enthusiasms]
[Fierceness in Religion (cor.)]
Fancy.
Faculty. NP. II. 2.
[adj.] Fancy representation]
[Irrational (imp.)]

FA

[Disposition { (imp.) { (corr.) }
[Opinion]
{ sp. (corr.) }
(Approbation)
(Delectation)
(Love)
Fane, [Index (instr.) of winde.]
Fang, [Long tooth.]
Fantasie. NP. II. 2.
Fantasm, [Fancied (thing.)]
Fantastic.
[adj. Fancy (corr.)]
{ Indulging } fancy.]
{ Following }
[Conceitedness]
Far.
[adj. Distance]
[Remote]
—into
[Deep into]
[Averse]
[Much]
—day
[Much day being past]
[Late]
as—as, [Until]
so—as, [So much as]
Farce, vid. *Farse*.
[Mixture of into—thrusted (things.)]
[Pudding of mixt (things)]
[Scurril Comedy (corr.)]
Farcy, Disease.
Fard. [Paint]
Fardle, [Aggregated (thing) sp. by p. tied.]
Fare.
Diet. Pr. I.
[Event]
—well [I. valediction.]
[Carriage]
sp. by Water.]
[Carried { (aggr.) { (persons) }
[Wages for Carriage]
[Tower for direction of Navigators.]
Farm. Po, I. 1.
take to—[Hiring]
let to—[Demising]
Farra. Fi. IX. 5.
Farrier, [Physitian for horses.]
Farrow, [a. Parturition.] sp. of Swine.
Farse, {Fill. { By into-thrusting } (Corr.) }
Fart. Mo. IV. 2. A.
Farther, vid. *Further*.
[More-far]
—most. Sp. II. 2. D.
[More]
[Also]
Farthest, vid. *Furthest*.
[Most-far]
[Last]
[Most]
Farthing. Mea. IV. 1.
Fascinate, [a. Witchcraft.] sp. By look.]
Fashion.
[Figure]

FA

[Manner]
[Custom] sp. Common]
—of Clothes, [Figure of Clothes.]
sp. Commonly accustomed.]
Fashions, Disease of Horse.
Fast.
Adj.
Fixed. Q. VI. 6. E.
—and loose, Light. [adj. Ha. IV. 7. D.]
—asleep [asleep]
hold [hold (int.)]
—ty [tie]
Firm. Q. VI. 5.
[Swift] NP. V. 9.
Subst. [Absteining from feeding.]
Religious. RE. IV. 5. O.
Fasten.
[Fast (make)]
[Tie]
[Bite]
Fastness, [Place inaccessible.] sp. through bogs.]
Fastidious.
[adj. a. { nauseate } { contemn } (apt.) { scorn }]
Fat.
—of Animal. PG. II. 7.
—Constitution. NP. V. 5.
—Tast or Smell. Q. IV. 2.
[Vessel] vid. *Vat*.
Fate. AS. I. 2. E.
Fatal.
[adj. Fate (abstr.)]
[adj. a' Death.]
Father.
Parent. RO. I. 2. (male.)
—monk RE. II. 7.
—ly, [adj. Father.]
—less, [Un-fathered.]
—in law, [Father by Affinity.]
fore-[Progenitor.] RO. I. 1.
Foster—RO. III. 2.
God—RO. III. 1.
God the—G. I.
Fathom [6. Foot.]
Fatigue, [a. Weariness (thing.)]
Faucet. Pr. V. 7. A.
Fauchion, [Broad short (sword.)]
Faucon, vid. *Falcon*.
Fault.
[Defect (corr.)]
[Evil action]
—capital. R J. III.
—not capital. R J. IV.
finde—
[a. Censoriousness]
[Reprehend]
[Blame]
Faulter.
[Stammer]
[Stumble]
[Err]
[Fail]

Desist

FE — FE — FI

{Defift
Omit } { timorously.
Forfake } { unfaithful-
ly.]
Faulty,
[adj. Fault]
[adj. Wrong]
Faun, vid. Fawn.
Favor.
Affection. AS. V. 2.
[Favor (fign)
fp. Ornament.
fp. Riband.]
Countenance.
[Face { (manner)
(fig.)]
Favorite, [adj. p. Favor (perfon.]
Fautor, [adj. a. Favor (perfon.]
Fawn.
[Affentation] Man. IV. 7. E.
fp. By gefture.]
[Buck. Be. II. 4. (young)
Fealty,
[Fidelity]
[Fidelity (fign)]
Fear. AS. V. 6. O.
for—[Left that]
Fearfulnefs,
Timidity, [Fear (apt.]
Terriblenefs, [a. Fear (apt.]
Fearn. HL. I. 4.
Oake—HL. I. 4. A.
Feaft.
Thing, Pr. II. 1.
Time, [Feftival]
Feat.
[Fact (Done (thing)
[Handfome (dim.]
Feather.
Single. PP. V. 1.
Plume [Feathers (aggr.) for Ornament.]
Feature, [Figure (man.)
fp. Of face.]
February, [Second mouth.]
Fecible.
[adj. p. doe (pot.]
[Poffible]
Feculent, [adj. Sediment.]
Fecundity, [Fruitfulnefs.]
Fee.
[Revenue} fp. of Office.]
[Wages]
[Stipend]
—fimple.
{ Hereditary } right]
{ Abfolute }
—farm.
[Inheritance obnoxious to Rent.]
Feeblenefs, [Weaknefs.]
Feed. AC. I. 5.
—upon, [Be fed with.]
Feeling.
Senfe. NP. III. 5.
—for, [For-fearch by—]
[Suffering]
fellow—[Compaffion]
—Feelers. PP. IV. 4.
Fein, vid. Fain
Fel.
[Feirce] NP. IV. 4. O.

to—[a. Fall]
fp. With ftriking,]
—trees, &c. O. III. 8. A.
a—[Skin]
fp. With fleece.]
—monger.
[Skin { (Mech.]
(Mer.]
—wort, [Gentian] HL. VII. 6.
Fellow.
[Like]
{ Equal]
[adj. RO. IV. (perfon)
[Companion.]
The—of it, [The other congruous to it.]
—worker, [Together—]
—of Colledge, [Affeffor of adj. Colledge (off.]
[Sorry (perfon.]
[Spoke.] Po. V. 7. A.
Fellowship.
[Fellow (abftr.]
[Society]
[Communion]
Felon.
[adj. Felony (perfon)
[Apoftem at the root of the nail]
Felony. RJ. III. 4.
Felt.
[adj. p. Feel]
[Head (veft) woollen with broad margin]
to—[a. Cloth (make) by kneading]
Felter, [Entangle.]
Female } NP. VI. 2. O.
Feminine }
Fen. Po. I. 8.
Fence,
[Enclofure]
[Fortifie]
[Defend]
Exercife. Mo. V. 6. A.
Fenecreek, HS., III. 13. A.
Fennel. HF. V. 1.
Hogs—HF. V. 2.
Gyant—HF. V. 3.
Scorching—HF. V. 11. A.
—flower. HS. V. 13. A.
Feudary.
Feoff, vid. Enfeoff.
Fermenting. O. VI. 5. A.
Fern, vid. Fearn.
Ferret. Be. IV. 5.
to—[Search (int.]
—out, [Out-drive (int.]
—filk,
Ferry.
[Boat for travelling over River]
[Boating (place) over River.]
Fertility, [Fruitfulnefs.]
Fervent,
[Hot (augm.]
[Zealous]
Ferule.
Stone, [Together-coagulated Gravel,]
Metalline, [Ring (fig.) lamin.]

Wood, [adj. Cudgelling (inftrum,)for hand']
Fefcu, [Pin (inftr.) for fhewing the Letters.]
Feft, [Tranfverfe lamin (fig.) in the middle of the Scutcheon,]
Fefter, Putrefie.
Feftival, [adj. Feftivity (time.]
Feftivity. RE. IV. 5.
Fetch.
to—TA. VI. 4. A.
—breath, [In-take—].
—out, [Caufe to come out.]
—up, [Overtake.]
a—
[Invention]
[Craftied (thing)
Fetid, [Stinking.]
Fetter, [Bonds for Legs.]
Feud, [Old enmity.]
Fever. S. II. 2.
malignant—S. II. 3.
Feuerfew. HF. II. 9.
Fewel, vid. Fuel.
Fewnefs. TM. III. 1. O.
Fy. Interj. II. 3. O.
Fib, [Lie (dim.]
Fibre. PG. II. 5 A.
Ficklenefs, [Lightnefs.] Ha. IV. 7. D.
Fiction. T. I. 3. A.
Fiddle, [Mufic (inftr.) ftringed]
—ftick, [Bow for Mufic (inftr.]
—ing,
[a. Mufic with inftrument.]
[a. Vanity]
Fidelity. Man. IV. 2.
Fidge, [Vain ition (freq.]
Fiduciary, [adj. Depofit (perfon.]
Field.
[Grounds,] Po. I. 2.
Keep the—RM. II, 3.
Win the—RM. II. 1. E.
Quit the—RM. II. 3. D.
Fieldfare. Bi. III. 5.
Fiend. W. I. 2. O.
Fierce: NP. IV. 4. O.
Wilde, [adj. NP. IV. 4. O.]
op. to Moderate, [adj. Ha. III. 4. D.]
op. to Meek, [adj. Man. I. 9. D.]
Fife, [Mufical Pipe.]
Fifteen.
Fifty.
Fig. Tr. I. 5.
Indian—Tr. I. 9 A.
—wort. HS. VIII. 5. A.
Fight. RM. I. 7.
Figment, [adj. Fiction (thing.]
Figulation. O. IV. A.
Figure.
Shape. Mag III. A.
Scheme { line
pictur'd } (fig.)
Rhetorical. D. III. 7. A.
Fil. O. II. 7.
Filament, [Fibre.]

Filberd

FI

Filberd. Tr. IV. 3.
Filch, [Theft (dim.]
File.
  —*ing.* O. IV. 2. A.
  a—
    Instrument, [adj. filing (inftr.]
    As of Souldiers. RM. IV. 4. A.
Filial, [adj. Son.]
Filipendula, [Dropwort.]
Fill. O. II. 7.
Fillet.
  [Riband]
  fp. adj. Linen.]
  —of Beaſt.
  —of Pillar, [Square (part.]
Filly, [young horſe (fem.]
Fillip, [Strike with the nail of the finger ſpringingly.]
Film, [Thin Membrane.] PG. II. 3. A
Filthy.
  [adj. a. Defile (abſtr.]
  [adj. Slovenlineſs (augm.]
  a—deal, [Much (corr.]
Filtring. O. VI. 4. A.
Fin. PP. IV. 6.
Final, [adj. End.]
Finch.
  Chaff—Bi. IV. 7.
  Bul—Bi. IV. 5.
  Gold—Bi.
  Green—Bi. IV. 6.
Finde.
  —by Seeking. TA. I. 7. O.
  Perceive, [a. Common ſenſe.]
    { Diſcover.] AS. II. 2. A.
    { Invent.] AS. III. 2.A.
    { Contrive.] AS. III. 7.
  —*by Experience.*
    [Diſcover by Eſſaying.]
    [a. Experience]. Ha. VI. 4.
  —*the Bill,* [Approve the Bill.]
  —*Fault.*
    [a. Cenſoriouſneſs]
    [Blame]
    [Reprehend]
  —*without ſeeking.*
    [a. Fortune to { ſee,] { have,] { &c.]
  [Obtein] TA. V. 1.
  [Maintein] RO. V.)
Fine.
  Adj.
    [Simple.]
    —*force,* [Simple. I.]
    [Pure] [adj. TM. V. 6.]
    [Refined]
    [Un-adj. p. { Worſt part.] { Sediment.]
    [Thin.] [adj. TM. II. 5. O.]
    —*linen,* [Thin (augm.]—]
    [Soft] [adj. Man. I. 8. D.]
    [Tender] [adj. NP. IV. 7. O.]
    [Nice.] [adj. Mah. II. 6. E.]
    [adj. a. Dainties (apt.]
    [adj. Ornateneſs]
    [Craſty.]

FI

Subſt.
  [Mulct] R]. VI, 7.
  in— [In the End.]
Finger. PG. V. 7.
  Fore—[Second—]
  Middle—[Third—]
  Ring—[Fourth—]
  Little—[Fifth—]
  at ones—*s end,* [adv. Memory (perf.]
  light—'*d,* [adj. Theft (apt.]
  —*fern.*
  Ladies—HS. III. 4.
Finical.
  Nice, [adj. Man. II. 6. E.]
  [Conceited. adj. Ha. III. O.]
Finiſh. TA. III. 7.
Finite. T. III. 6.
Fir.
  male—Tr. V. 5.
  female—Tr. V. 5. A.
Fire.
  Proper. El. I.
  bone—[Fire } Joy.]
    built for } Triumph.]
  light—[Flame—]
  wild—[Confection of Powder, adj. a. Fire (apt.]
  —*works.*
  —*brand.*
  —{ *Fork* { F. } { *Shovel* { Sh. } [for—]
  —*lock.*
Meteor.
  —*drake.* El. I. 4.
  licking—El. I. 6. A.
Diſeaſe.
  St. Anthonie's—[Eryſipelas.]
Fireſtone, [Marchaſite] St. I. 3. A.
Firing, [Fuell.]
Firkin.
  [Barrel (dim.]
  Meaſure.
Firm.
  Faſt, [adj. Q. VI. 5.]
  —*land,* [Continent.] W. III. 2.
  Conſtant, [adj. Ha. IV. 7.]
Firmament.
  [Starry heaven] W. II.
  [Ether] El. II. 1.
Firſt.
  In Number, [adj. Mea. II. 1.]
  In Dignity. [Principal.]
Fiſcal, [adj. Exchequer.]
Fiſgig.
Fiſh. Fi.
  —*hook,* [Hook for—]
  —*monger,* [adj. Fiſh (merc.]
  —*pond.* Po. I. 6.
  to—
    [Hunt Fiſh]
    [a. Confeſs (end]
Fiſherman, [Hunting (artiſt of Fiſh.]
Fisk. [Mo. II. (corr.]
Fiſt, [Hand { Folded.] { Contracted.]
Fiſtic, [Piſtach.]
Fiſtula. S. I. 7. A.
Fit.

FL

[adj. Congruity. T. V. 5.]
{ proportion'd]
[Congruouſly { diſpoſed]
         { prepared]
         { furniſhed]
Opportune [adj. Time (perf.]
[Decent]
[Expedient]
a—T. VI. 6. A.
—*of ſickneſs,* [a. Sickneſs.]
—*of the mother.* S. VI. 7.
to—[a. Fit.]
—*with the like,* [Compenſate.]
Fitch, vid. *Vetch.*
Fitcher, Mo. II. (freq.]
  croſs—
Fitchew, [Polecat.] Be. IV. 5. A.
Fitting, vid. Fit. adj.
Five. Mea. II. 5.
  —*hundred, &c.*
Fixed.
  Faſt, [adj. Q. VI. 6. E.]
  [Not adj. p. move (apt.]
  Obſerving (int.]
Flag.
  Figure. Mag. IV. 7. A.
  —*of a Ship.* RN. III. 7.
  —*Ship.*
  [Sedge.]
  —*flower,* [Iris.]
  to—
    [Be weak]
    [Decay]
    [Be limber]
  ſp. Through { Weakneſs.] { Decay.]
  [Hang adv. limber]
Flagitious, [Vitious (augm.]
Flagon, [Cylindrical pot.]
Flagrant.
  [Intenſe]
  [Manifeſt]
Flay, [Un-skin.]
Flail, [adj. a. Threſhing (inſtr.]
Flake, [Lamina.]
Flam, [Ly.]
Flame. El. I. 1.
Flank.
  Side.
  —*of Animal.* PG. IV. 5. A.
  to—[a. Side.]
Flanker. RM. VI. 6. A.
Flap.
  vid. Flag.
  [Strike]
  ſp. with Lamin.]
  a——[adj. Limber (lam.]
  ſp. Hanging.]
  flie—[Flap to drive away Flies.]
  Throat—Cover (thing) of the rough Artery.]
Flaſh.
  [Impetus.]
  —*of fire,* [Flame (imp.]
  —*of water,* [Stream (imp.]
  —*y.*
  Taſte.
    Wateriſh, [adj. Water (like.]
    [Freſh]

FL   FL   FL

[Fresh] Q. IV. 5. O.
Discourse, [Light.] Man. IV. 6. D.
Flask.
  [Box for Gunpowder.]
  [Carriage for Ordnance.]
Flasket, [Long Basket without Lid.]
Flat.
  Corpor.
    [Plain] W. III. 1.
  [adj. Lamin]
    {Shallow} TM. II. 3. O.
    {Low} TM. II. 4. O.
  [adj. Lying] AC. VI. 7. O.
  —*foot.* PP. V. 3. A.
  Transcendent
    [Manifest]
    Absolute, [adj. T. I. 8. O.]
    [Sorry. TM. I. 4. D.]
  a—
    —*in the Sea,* [Shallow (place) in the Sea.]
    —*in Music.* Q. III. 5. D.
Flattery.
  [Fawning]
  [Asseveration]
Flatulent, [adj. a. {Wind Inflation} (make)
Flaunt, [adj p. Ornate (exc.)
Flaw.
  [Break {dim. Outside.}
  [Notch]
  [Bruise]
  [Spot]
  —*of wind,* [Wind (imp.)]
Flawn, [Py of Milk and Eggs.]
Flax. HS. V. 12.
  Toad's—
Flea, Ex. I. 8. A.
  —*bane.* HF. III 9. A.
  —*wort.* HL. VII. 4. A.
  Sea—Ex. II. 2. A.
  to—— [Un-skin.]
Fleam.
  Vid. *Phlegm.*
  [adj. Phlebotomy (instr.)]
Fled, [adj. pret. Flie.]
Fledge, [Feathered.]
Flee, vid. *Fly.*
Fleece. PP. VI. 3.
  to— [Un-fleece.]
Fleet, [Swift]
  to—vid. *Flit.*
  a—Navy, [Ships (aggr.)]
Flegmatic, adj. *Phlegm.*
Flesh. PG. II. 6.
  —*ly* vid. *Carnal.*
    {Natural}
    {Worldly}
  [adj. Lust] AC. II. 5.
  —*y,*
    [adj. Flesh]
    [Having much Flesh]
  to—*one,* [Encourage.]
Fletcher, [adj. Bow (mech.)]
Flew.
  [adj. pret. Flie.]
  Vid. *Flu.*
Flexible.

[adj. Q. V. 6.]
[adj. p. Persuade (apt.]
Fly.
  As Bird. Mo. I. 2.
  As routed. RM. II. 3. D.
  —*out.*
    [a Excess]
    [a. Squander]
  Let—
    [Shoot]
    [Strike at]
  a—[Flying Insect]
  Crane—Ex. IV. 8.
  Dung—Ex. IV. 4. A.
  Flesh—Ex. IV. 4.
  Shepherd's—[Crane-fly.]
  Spanish—[Cantharides] Ex. V. 9.
  Catch—HS. V. 2. A.
  —*boat.*
Flicker, vid. *Flutter.*
Flight, vid. *Fly.*
Flinch.
  [Start] AC. IV. 5.
  {intermit} {timorously}
  {forsake} {unfaithfully}
  {abandon} {cowardly}
Fling.
  [Cast] Mo. VI. 2.
  —*away,* [Away-goe suddenly.]
  Kick, [Strike with the heel.]
Flint. St. I. 3.
Flirt.
  [Impetus]
  [Woman (corr.)]
Flit.
  [Remove]
  [Depart]
  [Transitory]
Flitch, [Half the Trunk and Limms.
  sp. of a Hogg.]
Flitter, [Torn fragment.]
  —*mouse,* [Bat.]
Flittern.
Flix, [Disease of Dunging (exc.)]
  bloody—[Disentery]
  —*weed.* HS. IV. 11.
Flock.
  Aggregate.
  —*together,* [a. Convention]
  —*of Wool.*
  [Course part of—]
  [Curls of Fleece.]
Flook, [Barb of Anchor.]
Floor. Po. III. 4. A.
Florid.
  [adj. {Beauty} {Vigor}]
  [adj. {Flourishing} {Ornament}]
Flosculous.
  [adj. Flower]
  [adj. Ornateness]
Flote. Mo. I. 3.
  a—[Boat (like) of together tied timber.]
Floud.
  [River]
  [Water (exc.)]

[Inundation]
—*gate.*
  [Door for floud]
  [Gate to in-shut water]
Flounder. Fi. VII. 4. A.
Flour.
  [Best part] TM. VI. 1.
  sp. of ground corn.]
  Blossom. PP. II. 1.
  —*gentle.*
  our *Ladie's*—
  —*de luce,* [Iris]
  —*bulbous.* HL. IV. 6.
  —*tuberous.* HL. V. 3. A.
  to—
    [a. Powder] Pr. III. 7. A.
    a. Blossom. PP. II. 1.
Flourish.
  [a. Flour]
  {a. Vigor.}
  {a. Prosper}
  {Discourse ornately}
  {Boast}
  Prelude, [Preparatory Music.]
  [Vibrate]
Flout, [Mock.]
  —*cream.*
Flow.
  [a. River]
  —*ing tide,* [Upward-tide.]
  [Abound]
Flower, vid *Flour.*
Flu, [Not-adj. p. fat (pot.)]
  the—*of a rabbet,* [-Fleece—]
Fluctuate.
  [a. Wave]
  [Waver] AS. IV. 4. O.
Fluellin. HS. VIII. 9. A.
Fluent.
  [abounding]
  [adj. Discourse (apt.)]
Fluidness. Q. V. 5. D.
Fluke. Ex. I. 4.
Flung. [adj. pret. Fling.]
Flurt, vid. *Flirt.*
Flush.
  [Abundance]
  [Mellow]
  [Blush (like)]
  [Wholly of the same colour]
Flute, [pipe]
  sp. Musical.
Flutter, [Fly (end.)]
  [Shake (freq.) the wings.]
Flux.
  vid. *Flix;*
  [Streaming]
  to—
    [Melt]
    [Purge]
    sp. by Salivation.]
Fluxion.
  [Flowing]
  [Fluxing]
Foe, [Enemy]
Fodder {Hay Straw} {Eatable.}
Fog, [Thick mist.]
  —*gy,* [Fat (exc.)]
Foil.

Ggg   [Over-

FO   FO   FO

[Overthrow (dim.)]
[Accessory beauty]
sp. by {Worse} com-
    {Contrary} par'd
    with it.]
Play at —*s*, [Fence with blunt Weapons.]
Foin, [Prick (end) by thrusting (imp.)]
Foist.
to—
  [adv. Silent. Mo. IV. 2. A.]
[Forge]
    {secretly.}
—*in* [Add{ fraudulently.}
    {forgingly.}]
Gally——{Predatory Ship
    (dim.)}
Fold.
Pleit. O. V. 5.
[Shut]
Sheep—[Sepiment for Sh.]
Fole, [Horse (young.)]
to—[Parturition
  sp. of Mare.]
Foliage, [Leaf (aggr.)
  sp. Factitious.]
Folio, [Biggest book (figure.)]
Folk,
  [Person (kinde)]
  [Man (aggr.)]
Folly. Ha. VI. 2. D.
Follow.
Go after. TA. VI. 6.
As Enemy.
  {Persue}
  {Hunt}
As dependent. RO. III. 5. O.
  [Wait] AC. V. 1. A.
  {Obey}
  {Imitate}
  {Practise}
  {Be diligent about}
As consequent [p. Inference.]
As Successor, [Succeed.]
Fome, [Bubbles (aggr.)]
Foment,
  [a. Fotion]
  [Supple by soking]
  sp. In hot (remiss.)
Fondness.
Indulgence. Man. VI. 7. D.
[Vainness] Man. IV. 6. O.
[Folly] Ha. VI 2. D.
Font, [adj. Baptism (vessel)]
Food.
  [Feeding (thing)]
  [Nourishing (thing)]
Fool.
[adj. Folly (person)]
—*hardy*, [Rash,] Man. I. 7. E.
natural—[adj. NP. L I. O.
(person.)]
to—*one*, [a. Fraud.]
to—*with one*, [a. Wantonness.]
Foolishness, [Folly.]
Foord,
[Shallow (part) of River]
sp. over-adj. p. travel (pot.)
Foot.
—*of Animal*. PG. V. 6.

—*ball*, [Play of Striking Ball
  with Foot.]
  [Ball for play by, &c.]
—*cloth*.
—*man*, [adj. Running (apt)
  Servant]
—*souldier*. RM. III. 1.
—*stall*, [adj. Foot (armam.]
—*step*, [Foot (sign.)]
—*stool*, [Foot-supporting
  (armam.)]
by—[By Foot (sign.)]
Crump—*ed*, [Shrunk—ed.]
Flat—*ed*. PP. V. 3. A.
Splay—*ed*, [Divergingly—
  ed.]
to—*it*, [Travel on his
  Feet.]
—*of Cup*
—*of Pillar* {[Foot like—]}
Measure.
—*of Length*. Mea. I. 3.
—*of Verse* [Verse (part.)]
Footing,
[a. Foot (place)]
Foppery.
    {T. IV. 5. O.
[Vanity]{M. IV. 6. O.
[Folly] Ha. VI. 2. D.
For,
Prep.
[Because of] Prep. I. 2. A.
if it had not been—[Unless it
  had been—]
[Concerning] Prep. I. 3. O.
as—*me* [—me]
let him—*me*, [Let him—
  me.]
[Instead of] Prep. II. 1. A.
  op. to Against.]
Adv.
—*a time*, [adv. Transitory.]
—*ever*, [adv. Ever.]
Conj.
[Because] Conj. III. 2.
—*all that*, [Notwithstanding]
  Conj. II. 2. A.
—*fear*, [Left that.] Conj.
  III. 1. O.
—*as much as*, [Whereas.]
  Conj. IV. 1.
—*Example*, [e.g.] Conj.IV.
  3. O.
Forage.
[Provisions]
  sp. for Horses.]
[Booty]
to—
[Goe forth to bring in Provisions.]
[a. Booty]
Forbear.
  {Abstein}
  {Omit}
  {Desist}
  {Spare}
  {a. Patience}
Forbid. RO. V. 1. O.
God—
[Let God {Prevent}
  {Hinder}]
[Be it not that]

Force.
  {Coaction}
  {Violence}
  {Strength}
  {Ability}
  {Efficientness}
  {Importance}
of—[adv. Necessity]
—*s*. RM. IV.
Forcer.
[adj. a. Force {Person}
  {Instr.}]
Fore.
[Before]
[adv. Preventing]
Fore-appoint, [Before-appoint.]
Fore-arm, [Before-arm.]
Fore-cast.
        {Consider}
[Before {Contrive}
[Providence] Man. III. 2.
Fore-castle. RN. II. 4.
Fore-conceiv'd,
  [Before-conceived]
  [Meditated]
Fore-deem.
  {Before
  {Preventingly}judge.]
Fore-door, [adj. Forepart-door.]
Fore-father RO. I. 1.
Fore-foot, [adj. Forepart-foot.]
Fore-front, [Fore-part]
Fore-going, [Preceding]
Fore-hand.
  [Fore-part]
  [Prevent]
Fore-head. PG. III. 6.
Fore-judge.
  {Before——}judge]
  {Preventingly—}
Fore-know, [Before-know.]
Fore-land. W. III. 4.
Fore-man, {First} {person.}
  {Principal}{son.}
Fore-mast. RN. III. 4. A
Fore-noon, [Preceding part of the
  day.]
Fore-ordain, [Before-ordain.]
Fore-part. Sp. III. 8.
Fore-run.
[Before—{Go}
      {Run}
[a. Van-currier]
Fore-sail, [Mizzen-sail.]
Fore-see, [Before-{See}
        {Know}]
Fore-shew, [Before-shew.]
Fore-sight.
  [Fore-seeing]
  [Providence]
Fore-skin, [adj. Forepart-skin.]
Fore-sleeve, [Sleeve from the
  elbow to the wrist.]
  [adj. cubit (vest)]
Fore-slow.
  [a. Slow]
  [Protract]
  [Hinder]
Fore-speak,
  [Before-speak of]
  [Witch with words]
Fore-stall.
                Before-

FO   FO   FR

{ Before ———
{ Preventingly— } buy]
Fore-teeth, [adj. Forepart-
teeth.]
Fore-tell, [Before-tell.]
[a. Prophet]
Fore-think, { Think }
[Before- { Meditate]
Fore-thought, { adj. a. pret.
{ adj. p. } Fore-think.]
Fore-token, [Before a. Sign.]
Fore-top, [adj. Forepart-hair.]
sp. Above the Fore-head.]
Fore-warn, [Before-warn.]
Forfeit.
[un-adj. p. right]
[Lose right]
[sp. Penally.]
[Lose by confiscation]
Forge.
to—
Fabricate. O. IV. 5.
Falsifie. RJ. IV. 4. A.
Feign, [adj. a. Fiction.]
a—[Fabri- { (room) } of adj.
cating { (place) } Iron
(mech.)
Forget, [a, NP. II. 3. O]
—fulness. NP. II. 3. O.
Forgive.
As Crime. RJ. II. 2. O.
As Debt. TA. IV. 9 O.
Forgo, [Be un-adj. p. Possession of]
Voluntarily, [Let go.] TA. I. 6, O.
Begin to be so, [p. Dereliction.]
Continue so, [Abandon.]
Unvoluntarily, [Lose.]
Fork.
Figure. Mag. IV. 8. A.
Instrument, [adj. Fork (instr.]
pitch—[Preparing (instr.) of Hay.]
Forlorn.
[adj. p. Destruction]
[adj. p. Despair.]
[adj. p. Dereliction.]
—hope. RM. IV. 6. A.
Form.
Cause. T. II. 7. A.
[Manner]
set—[Determined expression (manner.]
[Figure]
[Hare's { (Bed)
{ (Place)]
Seat. Mag. V. 8.
Formal.
—cause. T. II. 7. A.
[adj. Formality]
Formality.
[Form, (manner.]
Vice. Man. IV. 6. E.
Former.
[Preceding]
—ly, [adv. Preceding (time.]
[Past]
Formidable, [adj p. Fear (abstr.]
Formost, [First.]
Formulary.

[Set-form]
[Epitome]
Fornication. RJ. IV. 2.
Forrage, vid. Farage.
Forrain, [adj. RO. IV. 3. O.]
—er. RO. IV. 3. O.
Forrest. Po. I. 2. A.
—er, [adj. Forrest (Off.]
Forsake.
As God, [Dereliction.]
As Man, [Desertion.]
— the Right, [Abdicate.]
—the Possession, [Forgo.]
—his Religion, [Apostasie.]
Forsooth.
Truly. Adv. I. 2. O.
Ironic. Int. I. 3.
Forswear.
Abjure.
[Against-swear]
{ [Deny]
{ [Renounce] } with Oath.]
[Swear false]
Fort. [Sconse.] RM. VI. 2.
Forth.
[Out of] Prep. IV. 2.
[Without] Prep. IV. 2. A.
[Public]
—coming.
[Forth- adj. p. bring (pot.]
[Ready to be brought forth]
—with, [Soon]
Fortie.
Fortifie.
[Strengthen]
[adj. a. RM. VI.]
Fortitude. Man. I. 7.
Fortress, [Sconse.]
Fortuitous, vid. Casual.
Fortunateness.
[adj. Fortune (perf.]
[adj. Prosperity]
Fortune. AS. I. 2. D.
—teller, [Before-telling (person) of events]
to—[adj. p. Event]
Forward.
[adj. Forepart]
{ adj. Alacrity]
{ adj. Incline (augm.]
{ Prepared }
adj. p.—{ Begin } (perf.]
{ adj. pret. Proceed]
to—
{ adj. a. Adjuvant]
{ Proceed (make]
{ Dispatch]
egg—[a. Impulsive.]
{ Ition adj. a. fore-
going—{ part]
{ Proceed]
Foss.
[Furrow]
[Ditch]
Fosset. Pr. V. 7. A.
Foster.
[Nurse]
—father. RO. III. 2.
—child. RO. III. 2. O.
—brother, [Together-foster-child.]
[Fotion]

[Educate]
Fotion. AC. I. 4.
Fought, vid. Fight.
Foul.
[adj. p. Defilement]
[Deformed]
[Vitious]
[Slovenly]
[Sordid]
a—deal, [Much (corr.]
[Birds]
to—
[a. Foul (make]
[Hunt Birds]
Found.
{ adj. p. }
{ pret. } find]
to—
[a. Foundation.]
[Cast] O. IV. 5.
Foundation. Po. III. 4.
Founder.
[adj. a. Found { (person)
{ (Mech.)]
to—
[a. Impotent in going (apt.]
[Un-make adj. going (apt.]
Foundling, [adj. p. find (person.]
Fountain. W. IV. 3. A.
Four. Mea. II. 4.
—fold, [four]
—score, [Eighty.]
—square, [Square.] Mag. V. 1. A.
Fourm, vid. Form.
Fowl, vid. Foul.
Fox.
Beast. Be. V. 2.
—Fish. Fi. I. 7. A.
—glove. HS. VII. 10.
—tail. HL. III. 2.
[a. Drunkenness]
Fraction, [Breaking]
Fracture, [Breaking]
Fragment. TM. VI. 5. A.
Fragrant, [Sweet] Q. IV. 1.
Fray.
[Skirmish]
[Fight (dim.]
to—adj. a. Fear (make.]
Fraight.
[Burthen] sp. for Ship]
[Wages for Carriage]
Frail.
[Brittle] Q. VI. 5. D.
[Transitory]
a—[Spherical Basket]
sp. of Rushes.]
Frame.
—of Building. Po. III. 1.
Figure.
in—[adj. p. Order (perf.]
out of—[adj. p. Confusion]
{ Machin.]
{ Jugament.]
to—
[a. Efficient]
[Feign]
[Contrive]
[a. Build]
[v. Congruity]
Franchise, [privilege.]   Frank.

FR | FR | FU

Frank. Man. IV. 4.
Frankincense.
  Tree. Tr. VIII. 3.
  [Resin of Frankincense-tree]
Frantic, [Mad.] S. IV. 1.
Fraternity, [Corporation.]
Fraud. R], IV. 4.
Fraudulent, [ad. Fraud.]
Fraught.
  [Loaded]
  [Full]
Fraxinella. HS. I. 1. A.
Freak.
  [adj. Conceitedness (thing]
  [adj. Lightness (thing]
Freckle, [Spot (dim.) yellow.]
Free.
  [adj. Liberty { Ha. II. 1. / AS. IV. 8.
  [not. { Prisoner / Slave]
  [adj. p. Deliver] AS. I. 5.
  —from, [Without.]
  [adj. Spontaneity] AS. IV. 9.
  [adj. Alacrity]
  [Not-recompensed]
  [Liberal]
Frank [adj. Man. IV. 4.]
  —booter, [adj. a. Booty (person.]
  —bold, [Right not-rented.]
  —man.
    [Not-villain]
    [Citizen]
  [adj. { Immunity } person. / Privilege }
Freedom.
  [Liberty]
  [Ingenuity]
  [Immunity]
  [Privilege]
Free-Mason, [adj. Free-stone (mech.)]
Free-stone, St. I. 1.
Freez.
  Colour, [Gray.]
  Cloth, [Napt (augm.]
  to—[a. { Frost / Ice }]
Freight, vid. Fraught.
Frenzy. S. IV. 1.
Frequent. Sp. I. 7.
  to—[To come (freq.]
Fresh.
  [New]
  —air, [Breez.]
  —man.
    [New-comer]
    [Unexpert (person]
  [adj. Vigor]
  —taste. Q. IV. 6.
  Un-salted. Q. IV. 5. O.
  a—[adv. Repeating] Adv. IV. 2.
Fresh water souldier. HS. VI. 1.
Fret.
  [Rub] O. V. 8.
  —of musical instrument.
    [Under-touching (apt.]
    transverse (thing.]
  [Corrode] O. VI. 3.
  Wine—s.

Un-skin }
  by { rubbing }
  { Pain } corrosion }
  —Work, { Spirally,
    [Graving } &c.
  Vex, [a. Anger.]
Fretum. W. IV. 5.
Fry.
  [Children (aggr.]
  sp. Of Fish.]
  to——Pr. III. 4.
Fricase, [adj. p. Fry (thing.]
Frication,
Friction, } Rubbing.]
Friday, [The sixth day of the Week.]
Friend. RO. IV. 1.
  a—ship, [adj. Benefactor (thing.]
Frier, [Monk] RE. II. 7.
  Friars cowl.
    Broad leaved—HL. V. 10.
    Narrow leaved—HL. V. 10. A.
Frigat [Man of War.]
Fright, [adj. a. Fear (make.]
Frigid.
  [Cold]
  [Slight]
Frigot, [Man of War.]
Fringe, [Tufted line.]
Frippery, [adj. Sorry (thing.]
Frisk, [Leap { Nimble.] / (freq.]
Fritter, [Fried pudding (like.]
Frittillary. HL. IV. 3. A.
Frivolousness, [Vanity.] T. IV. 5. O.
Frize, vid. Freez;
Frizle, [Curl (augm.]
Fro.
  Prep. vid. From.
  to and—[Forward and Backward.]
  a—[Man (fem.]
Frock, [Upper vest of Horse (Off.]
Frog. BE. VI. 2.
Frolic, [adj. Mirth.]
From. Prep. III. 2.
  —henceforth.
  [From this time]
  [At all times after this]
Front.
  [Forehead]
  [Forepart]
Frontier, [Margin.]
Frontispice, [Forepart]
Frontlet, [Forehead (vest.]
Frost. El. III. 4.
  —nail, [Nail. un-adj. a. slide (apt.]
Froth, [Bubble (aggr.]
Frowardness.
  [Disingeniousness]
  [Moroseness]
Frown. AC. IV. 2. O.
Frozen, [adj. p. Freez.]
Fructifie, [adj. a. Fruitful.]
Frugality. Man. III. 3.
Fruit. PP. III.
  { Effect]
  { Event]
  { Profit]

—fulness NP. VI. 3.
  —less, { Unprofitable.] / Vain.]
Fruiterer, [Fruit (merch.]
Fruition, [Enjoying.] TA. V. 7.
Frumenty, [Pottage of Wheat.]
Frump, [Mock (dim.]
Frustrate. TA. V. 1. O.
Fucus, [Paint]
  sp. for the Face.]
Fuddle, [a. Drunkenness.]
Fuel. Pr. VI. 2.
Fugitive.
  [Flying]
  [Apostate]
Ful.
  [adj. p. Fill]
  [Whole]
  [Sufficient]
  [Perfect]
  —moon, [Moon in the midst of her month]
  to—Cloth. O. V. 3.
Fulfil.
  [Perform]
  [Finish]
Fuliginous, [adj. Soot.] El. IV. 3. A.
Fuller, [Fulling (mech.]
Fulsom.
  [Sweet, exc.]
  [Nauseative] NP. II. 4. O.
Fumaria, [Hollow-root.]
Fumble, [a. Hand (corr.]
Fume.
  [Smoak]
  [Exhalation]
  [Indignation]
Fumigation, [Smoking.]
Fumitory. HS. III. 4. A.
Function.
  [Calling]
  [Action in ones Calling]
Fundament. PG. IV. 8. A.
Fundamental.
  [adj. Foundation]
  [Chief]
Funeral, [adj. Burial.]
  sp. the Solemnity.]
Fungus, [Porous.]
Funnel, Cone { (vessel) for / [adj.   through-/ pouring.]
Fur. PP. VI. 3.
  to—RN. VI. 3. A.
Furbish, [a. Bright (make.]
Fury, [Anger (augm.]
  the—es, [Devils (fem.]
Furious.
  [adj. Anger (augm.]
  [Fierce (augm.]
Furling, [Tying loose.]
Furlong. Mea. I. 6.
Furnace.
  [Concave (place) to build Fire
  [Kettle (aug.] (in.]
  —hole in Fortification. RM. VI. 7. A.
Furnish TA. III. 2. A.
Furniture, [adj. Furnishing
  [Provisions] (thing]
  [Tackle.]
  [Uten-

GA

[Utenfils]
Furrier, [adj. Fur {mech. / merch.}]
Furrow. Mag. V. 7. O.
Further, vid. Farther.
— more, [Also.]
to — [adj. a. Adjuvant]
Furtheft, vid. Fartheft.
Furz, [Sh. IV. 8. A.
Fufe, [Cone notched spirally.]
Fufil.
  [Notched]
  [adj. p. Caft]
  [Meltable]
Fufty, [Mufty.] Q. IV. 7.
Fuftian.
  [Courfe Cotton-cloth]
  [Sorry mixt (thing)]
Fuftick.
Future. Sp. L. 1. D.
Fuzbal. HL. I. 2. A.

G.

Gabardin, [Sorry (garment,]
Gabble, [a. Loquacity not intelligible.]
Gabel, [Tribute.]
Gabion. RM. VI. 9. A.
Gable-end, [End of roof.]
Gad.
  [Pin]
  —bee.
  to — [Wander]
Gag, [a. Gaping (inftr.]
Gage.
  [Pledge]
  [Effay]
  to — [Examin] {Depth / Capacity}
Gaggle [Goofe (voice.]
Gay, [adj. p. Ornatenefs (exc.]
Gain.
  Lucre. TA. V. 2.
  [Obtain]
  [Increafe]
Gain-fay.
  [Againft-fay]
  [Deny]
  [Contradict]
Galades. Ex. VIII. 3. A.
Galangal. HL. III. 12.
Galaxy.
Galbanum, [Concrete juice of Gyant Fennel.]
Galbula. Bi. III. 8.
Gale.
  gentle—El. VI. 6.
  ftiff—El. VI. 7.
Galeafs.
Galeot. RN. I. 4.
Galingale. HL. III. 12.
Gall.
  [Choler]
  [Bladder of—]
  Excrefcence of Oke. PP. III. O.
  to —
    {Un-skin / Hurt / Anger}

GA

  fp. by {Rubbing / Wearing.}
Gallant.
  [Ornate (augm.]
  [Excellent]
Galley. RN. I. 3.
  —foift.
  —pot
Gallery, [adj. p. walking (room.]
Gallimaufry, [Confufed mixture.]
Gallinula ferica. Bi. VIII. 9. A.
Gallion.
Galliot. RN. I. 4.
Galloche, [Outermoft foot (veft.]
Gallon.
Galloon. Lace.
Gallop, [Run.]
Gallows, [Jugament for hanging.]
Galls. Sh. V. 5.
Gambado, [Leg (arm.) for riding.]
Gambol.
  [a. Activity]
  fp. with Legs.]
  {Wanton / Vain} (thing)
Game.
  Play. Mo. V. A.
  —fter, [Game (mech.]
  [Hunting.]
  —fome, [Wanton.]
Gammon, [Leg of Hog.]
  fp. Smok'd.]
Ganch, [Precipitating on hooks.]
Gander, [Goofe (male.]
Gang.
  [Society]
  [Faction]
Ganglion. S. III. 9.
Gangrel, [Long (corr.]
Gangrene. S. I. 8.
Gantlet, [Armor for the hand.]
Gantlope.
Gap, [Notch.]
Gape.
  [Open (augm.]
  fp. the mouth.]
  —after, {(augm.) / (earneftly.)}
  [Expect]
  [Yawning]
  [Chafm]
Garb, [Manner.]
  fp. of {Garments. / Demeanor.}
Garbage.
  [Entrails]
  [Worft part]
Garble, [Un- a. worft-part.]
  fp. Spice.]
Garboil.
  [Contention]
  [Trouble]
Gard.
  —of Souldiers. RM. III. 6.
  to — {Defend / Protect / Safe (make.)}
  Princes— {Servants / Officers} for {fafety.}

GE

  —of veftment, [Margin ftrengthned.]
  fp. with Lace.]
Garden. Po. I. 3.
Gardian. RO. III 4.
  [Monks (off]
Gargane, [White headed Teale (kind.]
Gargarifm, [Gargling.]
Gargle, [Gullet.]
  to — [Wafh] {Gullet. / the top of the Wind-pipe.}
Garifh, [adj. p. Ornate (exc.]
Garland, [Head-environing, Joyfign ornament.]
Garlick. HL. IV. 11.
Garment, [adj. Clothing (thing.]
Garner, [adj. a. Keeping (room) for Corn.]
Garnifh, [adj. a. Ornate.]
Garret, [Higheft (room.]
Garrifon. RM. VI. 1. A.
Garrulity, [Loquacity.]
Garter.
  [Ribband for Leg]
  [Binding (veft.]
Gafh, [Slafh.] Pr. III. 5. A.
Gafp, [Gape for breath.]
Gaftly, [adj. a. Fear (make.]
  [Pale] AC. IV. 9. O. (exc.]
Gate.
  [Dore] Poff. IV. 2.
  [Going (manner) Mo. I. 1.
Gather.
  [a. Aggregate]
  [a. Convention]
  Collect. O. II. 5.
  —as Curd, [Coagulate.]
  —as Fruits, [Take F.]
  —as Wind, [adj. p. wind.]
  [Contract]
  —up his Gown, &c. [Lift contracted.]
Calv's — [Cal'vs PG. VI.]
Gaud.
  [Mock]
  Vain, [adj. T. IV. 5. O. (thing.]
  —y.
  [Ornate (exc.]
  [Feaft]
Gavelkind, [Diftribution of Inheritance equally.]
Gaul, vid. Gall.
Gaunch, [Precipitate on hooks.]
Gaunt, [Lean (augm.]
Gauntlet, [adj. Hand (arm.]
Gaze, [Look intently.]
  —bound, [Dog hunting by Sight.]
Gazel, [Antilope.]
Gazet, [adj. Narration (thing) of News.]
Gear, [Thing (corr.]
Geefe, [Goofe plural.]
Geld, vid. Gueld.
Gelder rofe, [Sh. II. 12.]
Gelly. Pr. I. 5. A.
Gem. St. III.
Gemini {Conftellation / Twelfth part} {of the Zodiac.}
  [Third]
Gender, [Sex.]
  to —

GE

to—[a. Generation.]
Genealogy, [Catalogue of Ancestors.]
General.
 Op. to Special. TM. III. 4.
 [adj. Genus]
 [All]
 [Common]
 [Total.]
 [Universal]
 a—[Army (Off.)]
 [Monks chief (Off.)]
Generation.
 Begetting AC. I. 1.
 [Descendent (aggr.) RO. I. 1. O.
 [Age] Mea. VI. O.]
Generative facu'ty. NP. VI.
Generousness. Man. III. 4.
Genesis, [Generation.]
Genet, [Spanish Horse.]
 [Martin]
Genial, [Festival.]
Genitals, [Privities.] PG. VI. 8.
Genius.
 [Temper of mind]
 [Disposition]
 good—[Proper Angel]
 evil—[Proper Devil]
Gentian. HL. VII. 6.
 Dwarfe—HL. VII. 6. A.
Gentil.
 [Pagan]
 [Maggot] Ex. I. 5. A.
Gentile, [adj. Gentleman]
Gentle. T. V. 5.
 [Tame] NP. IV. 4.
 [Courteous]
 [Clement]
 [Gracious]
 [Affable]
 [Easie]
 [Remiss]
 —man. RC. I. 3. A.
 —woman. RC. I. 3. A. (fem.
 [Maggot]
Gentry. RC. I. { [kind.]
 3. A.   { (aggr.)
Genuflexion.
 [Bending knee] AC. VI. 6.
 [Kneeling] AC. VI. 6. A.
Gennin. T. III. 4.
Genus, [Kind.] T. I.
Geography, [Science of the World.]
Geomancy, [Wizarding by the Earth.]
Geometra. Ex. III. 7.
Geometry. [Science of Magnitude.]
Georgic, [adj. Agriculture.]
German.
 Cosin—RO. I. 5.
Germander. HF. VI. 2.
 Tree—HF. VI. 2. A.
 water—HF. VII. 9.
 wild—HS. VI. 11. A.
Germinate, [v. Sprout.] PP. II. 5.
Gerund, [Case of Participle Substantive.]
Gesses, [Foot-bonds for Hawk.]

GI

Gesticulation, { (augm.)
 [Gesturing] { (exc.)
Gesture. AC. VI.
Get.
 [Gain] TA. V. 2.
 [Obtain] TA. V. 1.
 [Obtain to { be]
           { doe]
 —before { Obtain to be before.
         { Prevent.
 —by Heart, [Obtain to remember]
 —out.
 —from person, [Obtain to be out, &c.]
 —a nail, [Pull out a nail.]
 —with childe, [Impregnate]
 —Children, [Generate ch.]
 —clear, { Obtain to be freed.
         { Escape]
 —gone, [From-goe.] TA. VI. 1. O.
 —rid of, [Obtain to be freed from.]
 [Mineral.] St. VI. 3.
Gewgaw, [adj. Vanity. T. IV. 5. O. (thing.)]
Ghess, [Conjecture.]
Ghost, [Spirit.]
 give up the—[Dy.]
 holy—G. III.
 —root.
Giant, [Great (augm.) person.]
Gib, [Cat (male.)]
Gibberish, [Speech not-intelligible.]
Gibbet, [adj. hanging (jug.) with one stem.]
Gibbous, [adj. Protuberance.]
Gibe, [Mock.]
Giblets, [Entrals.] PG. VI. sp. Edible.]
Giddy.
 [adj. Vertigo]
 [adj. Fancy (corr.)]
 [Wanton]
 [Conceited]
 [adj. Light] Ha. IV. 7. O.
Giddiness, [Vertigo.]
Gift.
 [adj. Give (thing)]
 —of God.
 spiritual. Ha. V.
Gig.
 [Cone adj. horn to be vertiginated with whipping.]
 [Whimzy]
 [adj. Conceitedness (thing.)]
Gigantic, [Great { (augm.)
                 { (exc.)
Giggle, [Laugh { (freq.)
               { (exc.)
Gigglet, [adj. Laugh (apt.)]
Gild, [Colour with Gold.]
Gilden-pole.
Gill.
 —of Bird. PP. V. 7. A.
 —of Fish. PP. IV. 3.
Gilliflower. HS. V. 1.

GL

Sea——HF. II. 14. A.
Stock—HS. IV. 1.
Wall—HS. IV. 1. A.
Gilt-head. Fi. V. 1.
Gimlet, [Little-boring (instr.)]
Gimmal, [Factitious joynt.]
Gimp, [Shamois]
Gin.
 [Machin]
 [Trap]
Ginger, [Root of an Indian Iris of a hot biting taste.]
 —ly { Gently } without
     { Slowly } noise.]
Gingle.
 [Ringing (dim.)]
 [Affect sound of Words]
Ginny.
 —hen, [adj. Ginny-hen.]
 —pig, Be. III. 6. A.
Gipsie.
Giraffa. Be. II. 7.
Gird, vid. Guird.
Girdle, vid. Guirdle.
Girl, [Child (fem.)]
Girn, vid. Grin.
Girt, vid. Gurt.
Gith, [Nigella]
Gittern, vid. Guittern.
Give.
 —back, [Retire]
 —over.
 [Desist]
 [Abandon]
 Correct no more. RO. VI. 6. O.
 —up.
 [Yield]
 [Submit]
 —alms, [a. Alms.]
 —ear.
 [Hear (end.)]
 [Observe with Ear]
 —law, [a. Law.]
 —name, [a. Name.]
 —ones { mind } to, adj. p. Disposition
       { self } { (augm.)
 —oath.
 [Swear (make)]
 [Oblige by oath]
 —place.
 —way.
 —to understand, [a. Know (make.)]
 mind—'s me.
 [I conjecture]
 [I expect]
 table—s.
 weather—s.
Gives, [Bonds for legs]
Gizzard, [Second musculous stomach of Bird.]
Glad.
 [adj. Mirth]
 [adj. Alacrity]
 [adj. Delectation]
Gladden.
Glade, [Open (place) through a Wood.]
Gladiator, [adj. Fencing (person.)]

Gladio-

GL · GO · GO

Gladiolus, [Corn-flagg]
Glaive, [Long Sword.]
Glance.
 [Oblique (imp.)]
 {a. Ey
 {a.Object} (imp.)
 sp. adv. {Accessory.
 {Digression.
 [Allusion (dim.)]
 witty—[Urbane (dim.)]
Glandule. PG. II. 7. A.
Glans. [Mast.] PP. III. 4.
Glass. St. II. 4. A.
 drinking—[adj. Glass-cup.]
 looking—[Face-shewing (instr.) by reflexion.]
 —*wort.* HL. VIII. 7.
 [Splendor]
Glaucus. Fi. I. 3. A.
 Fi. IV. 1. A.
Glave, [Long Sword.]
Glavering, [Fawning]
Glaze.
 [a, Glass,
 [To {Shut {with
 {Wall {Glass.]
 [a, brightness]
Glazier, [adj. a. Glass (mech.)]
Glean, [Ga-{left (things.)
 ther the {scattered Ears.]
Glebe, [Land.] sp. Priest's.]
Glede, [Kite.] Bi. I. 2. A.
Glee.
 [Mirth]
 [adj. Mirth Song]
Gleek.
 [Three]
 [Play]
Glib.
 [Smooth] Q. VI. 2. E.
 [Slippery]
Glide, [Kite.] Bi. L 2. A.
 to——[Slide] Mo. II. 4.
Glimmer, [Trembling light (imp.)]
Glimps, {Sud- {Light
 {den {Sight} (dim.)
Glistering, [Trembling (like) brightness.]
Glitter, [Bright]
Globe, [Sphere] Mag. III. 5.
 —*fish.* Fi. VIII. 1.
Gloomy.
 [Cloudy]
 [Dark (dim.)]
 [Dim] Q I. 3. A.
Glory, {Public {Praise.
 {Universal {Reputati-
 (on.
 to—AS. VI. 1. A.
Glorifie, [a. Glory.]
Gloss.
 [Comment (dim.)]
 [Brightness (dim.)]
Glote, [Look obliquely.]
Glove, [adj. Hand (vest,)]
 Fox—HS. VII. 10.
Glow.
 [Be hot]
 [Shine {white
 {fire-like]
 —*worm*, Ex. I. 5.

—*fly.* Ex. V. 9. A.
Glaze, [Assentation]
Glue, [adj. Gluing (thing.)]
 —*ing.* O. IV. 4. A.
 —*y*, [Clammy (augm.)]
Glut.
 [Fill {(sugm.)
 {(exc.)
 [Loathe (make) with abundance]
Glutinous.
 [adj. Glue]
 [Clammy]
Gluttony. Man. II. 1. E.
Glyster, [Medicinal drink for the Fundament.]
Gnash.
 [Together-strike
 [noise (make) with} teeth.]
Gnat. Ex. IV. 5. A.
 —*snapper.*
Gnaw.
 [Mastication]
 [Bite (end]
 [Corrode]
Gnomon, [Hour-shewing pin.]
Go.
 Proper.
 [Ition] TA. VI.
 —of Animal. Mo. I.
 sp. On legs. Mo. II.
 —on toes, [Stalk.] Mo. II. 3.
 [Walk] Mo. II. 1.
 Depart. TA. VI. 1. O.
 Figurate.
 [Move]
 [Event]
 —*about,* [Endeavour (inc.)]
 —*about*
 —*in hand with* } [Begin]
 —*after,* [v. Succeed.]
 —*against me.*
 {I a. Nolleity]
 {I grudge it]
 {I loath it]
 {I nauseate it]
 —*astray,* [Err]
 —*back,* [Retire]
 —*ward* [v. Worse]
 —*before,* [v. Precede]
 —*beyond one.*
 [Superior]
 [Defraud]
 —*down,* [a. Downward.]
 —*forward,* [Proceed.]
 —*on,* [Proceed]
 —*out,* [Cease.]
 —*quick,* [a. Quick,]
 —*through with it,* [Finish.]
 —*to.* Int.
 —*up,* [a. Upward.]
Goad, [Long pricking (instr.) to drive with.]
Goal.
 [adj. p. Object (place)]
 sp. of Race.
 [End] T. II. 6.
Goat. Be. II. 2. A.
 —*'s beard.* HF. III. 13.
 —*Chafer.* Ex. V. 3.
 —*sucker,* [Owle of a short

small Bill, and wide mouth.]
 —*'s thorn.*
 skipping——El. I. 5.
Gobbet.
 [Lump]
 [Fragment]
Gobble, [Swallow greedily.]
Gobius marinus. Fi. III. 7.
Goblet, [Cup (augm.)]
Goblin, [Devil (like) fiction]
God. G.
 —*head,* [God (abstr.)]
 Assion of—AS. I.
 —*the Father.* G. I.
 —*the Son.* G. II.
 —*the Holy Ghost.* G. III.
God-child, RO. III. 1. O.
God-father. RO. III. 1.
God-mother. RO. III. 1. (fem.)
Godless, [Ungodly.]
Godliness.
 [Holiness]
 [Religion (perf.)]
 [Worship (perf.)]
Godwit. Bi. VII. 8. A.
Goggle-eyed, [Protuberantly eyed.]
Gold. Met. I. 1.
 —*mine.* [—(place)]
 —*oar* {Crude
 {not-prepared} &.
 —*smith,* [&. {mech.
 {merch.]
 —*of Pleasure.* HS. VI. 8. A.
 —*en locks.*
 —*rod,* HF. III. 8. A.
Gome, [Grease black'd by agitation.]
Gone.
 [adj. {p.
 {a. pret.} go]
 [adj. Excess]
 [Spoil'd]
 [Destroy'd]
Good.
 Proper. T. III. 2.
 {Profitable
 {Sufficient
 {Convenient}
 [Perfect]
 [Happy]
 —*against,* [Medicinal against]
 —*at,* [adj. Art in.]
 —*for,* [Profitable to.]
 —*face.*
 [Face (perf.)]
 [Handsom]
 —*fellow.*
 —*luck,* [Prosperity.]
 —*man of the House,* [Master of the Family.]
 —*success,* [Event (perf.)]
 —*turn,* [adj. Benefactor (thing.)]
 —*will,* [Favor.]
 make—
 [Perform]
 [Repair]
 [Compensate]
 find } [Approve]
 think }
Goodly, [Handsom.]
Goodness. Man. I. 4.

GR

Goods.
 [Possessions]
 [Houshold-stuff]
Googe. Bi. IX. 1. A.
Goose. Bi. IX. 1. A.
 green—[young—]
 stubble—[autumnal—]
 Soland—Bi. IX. 4.
 —*berry.* Sh. I. 3.
 —*foot.* HF. I. 9. A.
 —*grass.* HL. IX. 9. A.
 —*nest.* (ed.)
Gorbellied, [Protuberantly bellied]
Gore, { Congealed }
 { Coagulated } blood.
 { Gellied }
 to—[Prick (augm.)
 sp. with Horn.]
Gorge.
 [Gullet]
 [Stomach
 sp. of Bird.]
 to—
 [Feed]
 [Fill]
Gorgeous, [Or- (augm.)
 namented (exc.)]
Gorget.
 [adj. Neck (armor)]
 [Linen (vest) for shoulder]
Gors, [Furz.]
Gosling, [Goose (young.)]
Gospel, [adj. Evangelist (thing.)]
Goshawk, [Biggest long winged Hawk.]
Gossip.
 [Child's Godfather]
 [Companion for mirth]
 —*ing,* [Women's Convention for mirth.]
Govern.
 [v. Magistrate]
 [Authority]
 [Direction]
 good—*ance.* Man. VI. 4.
 ill—*ance.* Man. VI. 5. O.
Governor, [adj. Govern(person.)]
Gougeon. Fi. IX. 11.
Gourd. HS. VII. 2.
Gourmandize
 [v. Gluttony]
 [Eat gluttonously]
Gournet
 Red—Fi. IV. 4.
 Grey—Fi. IV. 4. A.
Gout. S. II. 7.
Gown, [Loose long (vest)]
Gozling, [Goose (young.)]
Grace.
 { Favour }
 { Respect }
 { a. Graciousness }
 { Privilege }
 { Elegance }
 { Ornament }
 Infused habit. Ha. V.
 —*less,* [Ungracious]
 —{ Before } meat.
 { After }
 [Thanksgiving] RE. IV.
Gracious,
 [adj. p. Favour]

—*ness.* Man. VI. 1.
Gradation, [Degree (segr.)]
Gradual, [adj. Degree.]
Graduate. RC. I. 4.
Graffing, O. III. 7.
Gray, Q. II. 1.
 Hoary, [White (inc.) with age.]
 a—[Badger] Be. V. 2. A.
Grayhound, [Dog-hunting beast by swiftness.]
Grayling. Fi. IX. 4.
Grain.
 Corn. PP. III. 6.
 —*s,* [Infused Corns of Malt.]
 Weight. Mea. III. 1.
 [Berry
 sp. of Spice.]
 —*s of Paradise,* [Cardamoms.]
 in—[Died with Alkermes]
 [Powder] TM. VI. 4. A.
 —*of Leather,* [Crenated Superficies]
 —*of wood,* [Fibres—]
Gramercy, [Thanks (augm.)]
Grammar, [Art of speaking properly]
 —*parts of discourse.* D. III.
Grammarian, [adj. Grammar (artist.)]
Granado. RM. V. 8.
Granary, [adj. Grain (room.)]
Granat-pome. Tr. I. 6.
Grand, [Great]
Grandame, [Grandmother]
Grandchild, [Child's Child]
Grandeur.
 [Solemnity (augm.)]
 { Generosity }
 { Magnanimity }
Grandfather, [Parent's Parent (male)]
Grandmother, [Parent's Parent (fem.)]
Grandsire, [Parent's Parent (male.)]
Grange, [Farm]
Grant.
 [Concession]
 [Yield]
 [Give.]
Grape,
 [Berry of Vine.]
 Shrub. Sh. II. 1.
 Sea—Sh. II. 14.
Graphical, [figured (perf.)]
 { Plain }
 { Express }
Grapple. RN. III. 9. A.
 to—
 [Catch with hands]
 [Wrestle]
Grasp.
 [About-hand]
 [Embrace]
Grass. W. V. 3. A.
 Cotton—HL. III. 14. A.
 Crested—HL. III. 6.
 Dogs—HL. III. 5. A.
 Feather—HL. III. 14

Finger—HL. III. 8. A.
Goose—HL. IX. 9. A.
Hairy—HL. III. 9. A
Knot—HF. I. 4.
Medow—HL. III. 10.
Oate—HL. III. 8.
Pearle — }
Quaking — } HL. III. 9.
Scorpion—HS. III. 12.
Scurvy—HL. VI. 13
Silk—HS. IV. 3. A.
—*of Parnassus.* HL. VI. 7. A.
—*hopper,* [Locust] Ex. II. 1.
Grate.
 a—
 [Squares (plain)]
 [Fewel (jug.) of parallel pins (augm.) Net (like)]
 to—
 [Rub]
 { Powder } with rubbing.
 { Un-skin }
 [a. Displeasing]
Grateful, [adj. Gratitude.]
Gratifie.
 [Merit thanks]
 [a. Benefactor]
 [a. Complaisance]
Gratings, [adj. Net (fig.)]
 Scuttle.
Gratis.
 [Not-hired]
 [Without wages]
Gratitude, Man. I. 6.
Gratuity, [Gift]
Gratulate, AS. VI. 6.
Grave.
 —Disposition. NP. IV. 3.
 —Converse. Man. IV. 6.
 [Old (like)]
 —Sound. Q. III. 1. D.
 —*ing* { O. IV. 6. A.
 { RN. VI. 2. A.
 a—[Burial (room)
Gravel. St. I. 8. A.
 to—[make not adj. a. travel (abstr.)]
Gravy, Pt. I. 6. A.
Gravity,
 Weight. Q. V. 4. E.
 [Seriousness] NP. IV. 3.
 Discreet carriage. Man. IV. 6.
Graze.
 [Eat Grass]
 —*ier,* [Merchant of fat Cattel.]
 [Touch with reflecting.]
Great.
 [Soft fat]
 [Worst parts of fat]
Great.
 adj. Magnitude. TM. I. 1. E.
 —*with Child,* [adj. p. impregnate.]
 —*with one,* [Familiar (aug.)]
 how—[Of what magnitude]
 the—[Total-work to be done]
 [adj. { Dignity }
 { Power }]
 [Transc. { augm. }
 { Intense }]

—*many,*

GR | GR | GU

—*many*, [Many (augm.)]
Greave, [Leg-armor.]
Greaze, [Smear with fat.]
Greazy, [Fatty]
Greedy.
{ Hungry (corr.)
{ Ravenous }
{ Desire (augm.)
{ Scraping } Man. III. 2. E.
Greef.
  Sorrow. AS. V. 4. O.
  op. to Pleasure. Ha. II. 2.
  op. to Ease. NP. V. 3.
Green.
  —color'd. Q. II. 3.
  —*Chafer*. Ex. V. 5. A.
  —*finch*. Bi. IV. 6.
  —*sickness*. S. VI. 2.
  { Unripe
  { New }
  —*cheese*, [New cheese.]
  —*wound*, [New w.]
  [adj. Childe]
  —*goose*, [Young—]
  —*fish*.
Grees.
  [Hog (young)]
  [Step]
Greet.
  [Salute]
  [Gravel]
Greeve.
  [a. Grief]
  [a. Displicence]
Greevance.
  [adj. Displicence]
  [Injury]
Greevous.
  [adj. a. Grieve (abstr.)]
  [Unpleasant]
Grice.
  [Hog (young)]
Gridiron, [adj. Broiling (jug.)]
Griffon, [Fiction]
Grig, [Marsh-eele.]
Grilliade, [Broil'd (thing)]
Grim.
  { Fierce   } Face
  { Frighting } (manner)
  [Austere]
  —*the Collier*, [Hieracium.]
Grin, [Snare.]
to—
  [Lowr dog (like)]
  [Shew the teeth angrily]
Grind.
  —*ing*.
  —Fabrile. O. IV. 2.
  —Chymic. O. VI. 1.
  —*ers*, [Inmost teeth]
Griping.
  [Grasping]
  { Distention }
  { Compression }
  [Pain by—, &c.]
  Scraping. Man. III. 2. E.
  —*of a Ship*. RN. VI. 6. E.
Grist, [adj. p. Grinde (thing)]
Gristle. PG. II. 1. A.
Grit, [Sand]
Grizly.
  [Gray]

[Grim]
Groat, [Four pence]
Groats, [Oatmeal]
Grocer, [Spice (merc.)]
Grograin, [Stuff of grain (augm.)]
Groin. PG. IV. 7.
Gromel. HL. IX. 5.
Groning.
  Voice. AC. IV. 8.
  [Parturition]
Groom, [Horse (Off.)]
  —*of the Chamber*, [Chamber(Off.)]
Grope, [Search by feeling]
Gross.
  { Thick
  { Great }
  { Course
  { Lumpish }
  { Fat
  { Dull }
  { Unskilfull }
  a—[12 dozen]
  the —[Total]
Grot,   { Cavity }
         { Subterrane Room }
Grotes, [Course Oatmeal]
Grove,   { (aggr.)
         { (place) }
  [Trees
Groveling, [Lying] AC. VI. 7. A.
Ground.
  { Earth
  { Field. Po. I. 2.
  stand ones—RM. II. 2.
  get—RM. II. 2. E.
  loose—RM. II. 2. D.
  —*Ivy*
  —*work*, [Foundation]
  [Foundation]
  [Cause] sp. Impulsive]
  [Element]
  [Sediment]
Ground, [adj. p. Grinde]
Groundling, [Loach] Fi. IX. 11. A.
Ground-pine. HF. VII. 7.
  stinking—HF. I. 17. A.
Groundsil.
  [Threshold]
  Herb. HF. III. 7.
Grow. Bi. II. 5. A.
Grout.
  { Thick
  { Consistent } broth]
  [Millet.] HL. II. 6. A.
Grout-head, [Having a great head.]
Grow.
  adj. Accretion. AC. I. 6. A.
  —*forth*, [—into being visible.]
  —*to the* { ribs—
            { or, &c. }
  [Be continued by growth to, &c.]
  [adj. Vegetation]
  Become, { Effect
          { Be Event }
          { sp. (incept.)
          { Begin { be }
          { to { be made }
  —*in years*
  —*old*   } [Old (inc.)]

{ *kind*, [Unkind
—*out* { (inc.)
of { *use*, [Un-custom
      { (inc.) }
[Increase
sp. adv. degree.]
         { Usurp
—*upon* { Get
         { Increase
                  Gradually.]
Growth, [Growing.]
Grub.
  [Maggot]
  [Worm of a Fly]
to—[Un-root]
Grudge.
  [Nolleity]
  op. to Alacrity. Ha. IV. 3. D.
  [Malignity]
  an old—[Old hatred]
  —*of a disease*, [Impetus(dim.)]
Gruel. [Broth of Corn.]
Grumble. AC. IV. 8. A.
Grummel. HL. IX. 5.
Grumous.
  [adj. Lump
  [Coagulated]
Grunsil. HF. III. 7.
Grunt, [a. Hog (voice)]
Grus Balearica. Bi. VIII. 2. A.
Gryffin.
Guaiacum. Tr. VII. 2.
Guapurua. Fi. III. 17. A.
Guara Brasileana. Bi. VII. 9. A.
Guard, vid. Gard,
Gubbins.
Gudgeon.
  Fish. Fi. IX. 11.
  Figure. Mag. VI. 4.
Gueld, [Un-testicle.]
Guelding, [Untesticled horse]
Guerdon, [Reward]
Guess, [Conjecture]
Guest. RQ. III. 9. O.
Gugaw, [adj. Vanity (thing)]
Guggle, [Pouring (like) sound]
Guide.
  [Direct]
  [Lead]
  [Govern]
Guidon, [Commander's Staff]
Guild.
  [Corporation]
  —*hall*, [Convention (place) of Corporation.]
to—[Colour with Gold]
Guile, [Fraud]
Guillam. Bi. IX. 7. A.
Guilt.
  [Guilty (abstr.)
  [Guilded]
  —*head*. Fi. V. 1.
Guilty, [adj. RJ. II. 6. O.]
Guinny.
  —*hen*, [Hen of Guinny]
  —*pig*. Be. III. 6. A.
Guird.
  [Bind about]
  [Twinge]
  [Mock]
Guirdle, [About-binding (arm.)]
Guirl, [Child (fem.)]
                    Hhh   Guirt:

HA | HA | HA

Guirt.
 [Guirded]
 [Compass]
 Horse-[—Girdle]
Guise.
 { Manner }
 { Custom }
 [adj. Custom (manner)]
Guittar.
Guittern.
Gulch, [Short fat (augm.)]
Gules, [Red]
Gulf.
 [Bay]
 [Whirl-pool]
Gull.
 Fish, [Miller's-thumb] Fi. IX. 12.
 Bird. Bi, IX. 9.
 [Goose (young)]
 [Young (person) adj. p. fraud (apt.)]
 to—[a. Fraud]
Gullet.
 Weasand. PG. VI. 1.
 [Stream (dim.)]
Gulligut, [Glutton]
Gulp, [Swallow (imp.)]
Gum.
 —of tree. PP. I, 6.
 —Ammoniac, [Concrete juice of Giant Fennel]
 —Anima. Tr. VIII. 4.
 —Arabic. Tr. VIII. 2.
 —Dragon, [Gum of Goat's thorn.]
 —Elemi. Tr. VIII. 3.
 the—s, [Parenchyma of the Teeth.]
Gummy, [Stuff
 (p. with p. Gumming.]
Gun RM. V. 6.
 —ner. RN. V. 3.
 —powder. RM. V. 7. A.
Gurgions, [Worst part of Meal.]
Gurnard, vid. Gournet.
Gush, [a. River (imp.)]
Gusset, [Quadrangular (thing) to be between-sow'd]
Gust.
 Sense. NP. III. 4.
 Quality. Q. III.
 —of wind [Wind (imp.)]
Gutt. PG. VI. 4. A.
 —wort. Sh, VI. 2. A.
Gutter. Mag. V. 6. O.
Guttural, [adj. Throat]
Guzzle, [Drink (augm.)]
Gypsie, [Wandring wizard]
Gyrfalcon, [Hawk for Herons]

H.

Haak. Fi. III. 3. A.
Haberdasher.
 —of Hats, [Merchant of head (vest.)]
 —of small wares.
Haberdin.
Habergeon, [Armor for trunk]
Habiliment, [Armament]

Habit, { Quality } { adj. cu- }
 { Condition } { stom. }
 Quality. Ha.
 of the mind.
 Infused, Ha. V.
 Acqui- { Intellectual. Ha. VI.
 red. { Moral. Man.I.
 of the body, [Temperament of the body.]
 of Clothes, [Clothes (manner)]
 [Condition]
 [Custom]
Habitable, [adj. p. Dwelling. (abstr.)]
Habitation, [Dwelling.]
Habitual, [adj. Habit.]
Habitude, [Relation.]
Hack, Cut, {p. } { corr. }
 { (ruggedly) }
Hackney, [Hired (freq.)]
Had.
 [Was, pret.]
 [pret. Have]
Haddock, Fi, III. 2.
Haft, [adj. p. Hand (part.)]
Hag, [Old deformed woman.]
Haggard, [Wilde.]
 (p. Hawk.]
Haggess, [Pudding of Flesh minced.]
Haggle, { Treat } {p. cor.}
 { Commerce }
Hay. Pr. VI, 1.
 [Net]
Hail.
 Meteor. El. III. 5.
 Sound. NP. V. 2.
 to—[Salute]
Haillard, [Rope for hoising the mizzen Sail.]
Hair. PP. VI, 1.
 —Cloth. Pr. IV. 1. A.
 —Lace, [Ribband for binding the hair of the head.]
 —brain'd, [Conceited.]
 —y river weed. HL. I. 10. A.
Maiden—
Haiward, [adj. Pasture (Off.]
Hake, [Spit (end) out of the Throte.]
Halbard. RM. V. 3. A.
Halcyon, [King-fisher.]
 —daies.
 [adj. Calm—]
 [adj. Peace—]
Hale, [Pull]
Half.
 go—[Equal partner.]
 —moon, Fortification. RM. VI. 5.
Halibut. Fi. VII. 5.
Halimus. Sh. VI. 6.
Hall.
 [First room (augm.)]
 [adj. Convention (room)]
 [Civil convention]
 —day, [Day of Convention.]
Hallow.
 [Consecrate]
 [Exclaim]

Halm, [Straw.]
 sp. of Pease.]
Halo. El. V. 2.
Halser, [adj. Ship- adj. drawing (arm.)]
Halt. Mo. I. 1. A.
 make a—[Stay]
Halter, [Cord with Loop in the end (part)]
 [adj. Hanging (arm.)]
 [adj. Neck-bonds]
Ham, [Hollow (part) behind the Knee.]
Hamlet, [Houses (agg.)]
Hammer. Po. VI. 2. A.
 to ————
 [a. Hammer]
 [a. Speak (manner) difficultly.]
Hammock, [Hanging bed]
Hamper, [Basket (augm.)]
 To————[Tangle]
Hanch, [Breech.] PG, IV, 6.
Hand. PG. V. 3.
 —basket, [B. adj. p. carry (apt.) in hand.]
 —breadth, [Measure of h. b.]
 —full, [Capacity of the hand.]
 —gun,
 —kerchief, & { (dim.) adj. p.
 —mill, { use (apt.) with
 —saw, { f. hand.)
 —vice, v.
 —kerchief, [adj. wiping (linen)
 —maid, [Servant (fem.)]
 —over head, [adv Carelesness.]
 —to—[adj, Contiguous (pot.)
 { Present]
 at — { Near]
 at no—[Not, not]
 before—[adv. Preventing.]
 by ————
 from—to mouth, [adv. Necessary (segr.)
 in— { Present }
 { Possessed }
 in—with { adj. pret. Begin }
 { Endeavouring }
 bear in— { Seem } make]
 { Believe }
 go in—with, [Begin.]
 take in—[Undertake]
 in the turning of an—[While one could turn his—]
 out of—[Soon (augm.)
 come to— { To-event }
 { Be tame }
 get the—of one, [a. Victory]
 left — } { side]
 right— { r }
 Set ones—to { Sign }
 { Assist }
 under — { Inferior }
 { Secret }
 under ones—[Signed by one]
 upper—[Victory]
 on both—s, { parts }
 { Sides }
 man of his—s, [Nimble]

lay

HA

Lay—s on, [Arrest]
shake—s, AC. V. 5. A.
—*of a* { Pin } { for shewing
clock, { Finger } { the hour.
—*at Cards,* [adj. p. event adj. a. Card (things)
Handy, { Nimble.
{ adj. Operation (apt.)
—*craft,* [adj. Mechanic (art.)
—*gripes,* { Contiguously fighting.
{ Wreſtling
—*work,* [Work { of hands. } { own. }
Handle.
a— [adj. p. hand { thing } { part }
to—
{ a. Hand
{ Feel
{ a. Object (make)
{ Speak
{ Discourse } of.]
{ Write
{ Entertain
{ Treat
{ Use

Handſel, [First { ſelling } { uſing }]
Handſome.
[Decent]
[Beautiful]
Hang.
Poſture. AC. VI. 9. A.
—*by,* [Acceſſory]
—*down ones head,* [a. downward the head]
—*together,* [Together-adhere.]
—*up,* [a Hang]
—*ing of the bill,* [Declivity.]
Puniſhment. RJ. V. 8.
—*man,* [Execution (mec.)]
Being { Doubting
in ſuſ- { Demurring
pence. { Wavering
As a { Clothe { the
room, { Line { walls]
Hanger.
[Short crooked Sword]
[Loop for tying the Sword]
pot— [Iron (inſtr.) for hanging pot.]
Hank.
—*of thread,* [Skein—]
[Haunt]
Hanker, { Vergency }
{ Incline }
Hanſe, [Corporation]
Hap.
[Fortune]
[Contingence]
[Event]
Happen, [v. Hap]
Happy, [adj. Happineſs]
—*neſs.* Ha. I. 1.
—*ly,* [adj. Fortune]
Harang, [Oration]
Harbinger, [Before-going (Off.) for preparing entertainment]
Harbour.

HA

[adj. Hoſpitality (place.)]
[Port] W. II. 5.
Hard.
{ op. to Fluid. O. V. 5. E.
{ op. to Yielding. Q. VI. 1. D.
op. to Eaſie, [Difficult]
—*to be underſtood,* [Obſcure]
—*headed,* [Dull]
—*to be pleaſed,* [Moroſe]
—*to give,* [Penurious]
—*to* { forgive.
{ repent.
—*hearted,* { Cruel.
{ Impenitent.
—*drink,* [Sowr'd.]
—*ly,* [Scarce.]
—*by,* [adj. Near.]
to follow—[Follow (augm.)]
Harden.
[Hard (make)]
Incorrigible. RO. VI. 7. O.
Hardy.
Diſpoſition. NP. IV. 7.
Affection, [Bold.]
Vertue, [Valiant.]
fool—[Raſh.]
Hare.
Beaſt. Be. III. 3.
—*brain'd,* [Raſh]
—*lipp'd,* [Cloven-lipp'd]
—*'s foot.* HF. VIII. 5.
—*'s ear.* HF. IV. 14. A.
Sea—Ex. IX. 4.
Harken, [Hear (end.)]
Harlot, [adj. Fornication (fem.)]
Harm, [Hurt]
—*leſs,* { Innocent.
{ Not adj. p. Hurt]
Harmony. Q. III. 9.
—*in ſound.* Q. III. 9.
Harneſs, [Armament]
Harp, [Muſic (inſtr.) hollow arch with ſtrings.]
—*ing iron,* [Barbed dart]
Harpie, [Ravenous (perſon)]
Harpſichord.
Harquebuſs, [Foot-mans gun (augm.)]
Harras, { Booty
{ Spoil }
Harrow, [adj. Harrowing (inſtr.)]
—*ing.* O. III. 2.
Harſh.
In general, [Unpleaſant.]
To Senſe { Auſtere
{ Hoarſe
{ Rough
{ Stiff
To Manners { Moroſe
{ Man. VI. 1. D.
{ Auſtere
Hart. Be. II. 3. A.
—*'s tongue.* HL. I. 8. A.
—*wort* { HF. Y. 5.
{ Sh. VI. 5.
Hartichoak, HF. III. 1. A.
Hieruſalem—HF. II. 1. A.
Harveſt, [Reaping]
—*time,* [Autumn]
Haſh, [Sliced fleſh]

HE

Haſlet, [Inwards]
Haſp, [Hook]
Haſſock, [Tuft]
ſp. of Ruſhes.]
Haſt, [Haveſt]
Haſte.
ſp. through Buſineſs.]
in—
[Swiftneſs]
to—en { Diſpatch (augm.)
{ v. Soon }
Haſty.
[Sudden]
[Raſh]
[adj. a. Anger (apt.)]
Hat, [adj. head (veſt) with broad margin]
Hatch.
[Half door]
—*of a ſhip.* RN. II. 6.
to—
—*eggs.*
[Ripen eggs by Fotion]
[a. Parturition
—*flax.*
—*hilt,* [Notch (freq.]
Hatchet, [adj. a. Cut (inſtr.) by ſtriking.]
Hate. AS. V. 3. O.
Have.
[Pret.]
[TA. I. 6.]
—*ing,* { adj. Have
{ Scraping
Haven, W. II. 5.
Haver.
Haughty, [adj. Pride]
Haunch, [Breech] PG. IV. 6.
Haunt, [adj. Cuſtom (place)]
Havock, [Spoil]
Haunt. Be. III. 2. A.
Haw, [Berry.]
—*in the eye,* [Spot—]
—*thorn,* [White—] Sh. I. 3. A.
Cumberland—[White Beam-tree] Sh. II. 3. A.
Hawk, Bi. I. 2.
—*fiſh.* Haak.
—*weed.* HF. III. 12.
Hawker, [Merchant (corr.)]
Hawſer. RN. IV. 8. A.
Hazard, [Danger]
—*at Tennis.*
Hazy. El. VI. 1. O.
Hazle.
—*ben.* Bi. II. 7.
—*nut,* [Small-nut. (Tr. III. 1.)
—*wort.*
He, Pron. I. 3.
Head. PG. III.
Proper.
ſhake the—AC. IV. 4. A.
give one his—[adj. a. Liberty (make.)]
take a—[a. Liberty]
Top.
[Horns]
nail—[N. top]
Forepart.
—*of a barrel,* [adj. Forepart circle (plain)—]

HE

all a—[All to the fore-part.]
Root.
—of an onyon, [Bulbous root—]
Protuberant (part.)
—land, [Promontory.]
Fountain.
Conduit }
River } [Fountain]
Chief.
[Magistrate]
to—{v. Commander.}
Summe.
draw to a—
Heady.
[Rash]
[Fierce]
[adj. a. Drunkenness (apt.)]
[Fuming (augm.)]
Headlines.
Headlong.
[with Head first]
[adj. p. precipitate]
Direct
[Rash]
Head-piece.
[Head]
[adj. Head (armor)]
Headstall, [Head (arm.)]
Headstrong.
[Rash]
[Fierce]
[Not adj. p. Perswade (apt.)]
Heal.
[a. Sound (make)]
[Cover]
Health.
op. to Sickness. S. O.
op. to Rottenness. NP. V. 2.
[Remembrance in drinking]
Heap. O. II. 6.
Hear.
Sense. NP. III. 2.
—judicially, { Cognizance }
{ Trial }
—say, [Rumor]
Heart.
Proper. PG. VI. 2.
—burning, [Cardialgia]
S. VI. 1.
—spoon.
next ones—[First { dying
{ eating
{ &c.
sp. in the Morning]
—sleave.
[Contentment]
Herb [Parsly] HL. V.
5. A.
[Middle]
[Best (part)]
{ Strength }
{ Vigor }
in—[adj. Vigor]
out of—[adj. Weakness]
[Courage]
in—[adj. Courage]
out of—{ Cowardly }
{ adj. Diffidence }
{ Discouraged }
[Affection]

HE

sweet—[Suitor]
with all ones—[adv. Alacrity]
—burning { anger }
{ Old { Hatred }
by—[adv. Memory]
Hearten, [Encourage]
Hearth. Po. III. 9.
Hearty.
{ Heart }
[adj.] { Sincere }
{ Willing }
{ Courage }
Heartless.
[Weak]
[Diffidens]
[Formal]
Heat.
Proper. Q. V. 1. E.
[Anger]
[Zeal]
Heath.
Plant. Sh. VI. 7.
Place. Po. I. 7. A.
Heathcock. Bi. II. 5. A.
Heathen, [Pagan]
Heave.
{ Lift (end) }
{ Protuberant (make) }
sp by Up-thrusting.
Heaven. W. II.
Heavy.
[adj. Gravity]
[Dull]
[Lumpish]
[Drowsy]
[adj. Grief]
Hecatomb, [Sacrifice of 100 Beasts]
Hectic, [adj. Habit]
—fever. S. II. 1.
Hedge.
[Sepiment of Branches, &c.]
—clerk, [Sorry C.]
to—in a debt, [Sure (make) d.]
Hedgehog. Be. III. 5. A.
—trefoile. HS. III. 15. A.
Hedge-sparrow. Bi. V. 8. A.
Heed.
[Observe]
[Be cautious]
—fulness. Ha. IV. 2.
—lesness. Ha. IV. 2. D.
Heel. PG. V. 6. A.
—line of a Ship. RN. VI. 7.
Hegira, [Mahometan's Epocha.]
Hey-net.
Heifer, [Cow adj. youth]
Heigh. Int. I. 1.
Height. TM. II. 4.
Heinous, { adj. Vicious (augm.) }
{ adj. Displicence }
{ (augm.) }
Heir, [adj. Inheriting (person.)]
Held { pret. }
{ adj. p. } [hold]
Helebore.
white—HL. VII. 1.
bastard—[Helleborine]
Helleborine. HL. VII. 1. A.
Helical figure. Mag. III. 9. A.

HE

Heliotrope. HL. IX. 5. A.
Hell. W. II. O.
Helm, [adj. p. hand (part) of Rudder.]
Helmet, [Armor for (head.)]
Help.
[a. Adjuvant]
[a. Relieve]
[a. Remedy]
—one to a thing, [Furnish]
Helve, [Staff of Hatchet]
Hem.
Int. I. 2.
to—
[Hake]
[a. Acclamation]
[Margent]
—in
[About { Sepiment }
{ Inviron }
Hemicycle, [Half circle]
Hemisphere.
Hemlock. HF. V. 9.
water—HF. V. 9. A.
Hemorrhoid. S. VI. 8. A.
Hemp. HF. I. 5.
Hen, [Bird (fem.)]
Henbane. HS. VII. 11. A.
Hence.
[From this place]
[imp. Go]
[Away]
—forth, { From } this time]
{ After }
Hep, vid. Hip.
Hepatic, [adj. Liver.]
Hepatica.
Herald, [adj. Degrees (Off.)]
Herb. W. V. 3.
Considered according to their
—Leaf. HL.
—Flower. HF.
—Seed-vessel. HS.
—Christopher. HS. IX. 5.
—Frankincense of Galen. HF. V. 3. A.
—of Theophrastus. HF. IV. 6. A.
—of Grace, [Rue] HS. V. 13.
—Terrible. Sh. VI. 3.
—True love. HS. IX. 5. A.
—two pence, [mony-wort] HL. VI. 11. A.
[Leaf]
Herbage, [Pasture]
Herbal, [Book concerning Herbs.]
Herbalist, [Herb (artist)]
Herd, [aggregate (thing)]
—'s man. RC. II. 6.
Here.
[In this place]
[adj. Present]
—and there { some } pla-
{ In } divers } ces]
—of, [Of this]
Hereafter.
[After this time]
[adv. Future]
Hereditament, [adj. p. Inherit (thing)]
Hereditary, [adj. Inheriting.]
Heresie.

HI · HO · HO

Hereſie. RE. III. 1. O.
Heretic, [adj. Hereſie (perſon)]
Heretofore.
 [Before this time]
 [adv. Paſt]
Hericano, [Whirlwind (augm.)]
Hering, vid. Herring.
Heritage, [adj. p. Inherit (thing)]
Hermaphrodite, [Of all Sexes.]
Hermit. RE. II. 7. A.
Hermit fiſh. Ex VI. 5.
Hermodactyl, [Root of an exotic Colchicum]
Hernia. S. VI. 8.
Hero.
 [Excellent in virtue]
 [adj. Magnanimity (perſon)]
Heroical, [adj. Hero.]
Heron. Bi. VIII. 3.
 Great white—Bi. VIII. 4.
 Little white—Bi. VIII. 4. A.
 —'s bill. Herb.
Herring. Fi. III. 10.
 red— {Dry {ſalted} b.
       {   {ſmoked}
 white—[Moiſt ſaked]
Herſe, [Box of dead body.]
Heſitate, {Doubt}
          {Demur}
Heteroclite, [Irregular.]
Heterodox, [Not-orthodox]
Heterogeneous, [Of diverſe kinds.]
Hew.
 [Colour]
 [Cut ſtriking]
 rough—[Cut rough.]
Hy, {Haſten.}
    {Diſpatch.}
Hickcough. Mo. III. 4. A.
Hickwall, [Woodpecker] Bi. I. 9.
Hide.
 [Skin]
 —bound.
 [Diſeaſe of ſkin cleaving to the fleſh.]
 [Penurious]
to— {Conceal}
     {Cover}
Hideous, [adj. a. Fear (apt.)]
Hierarchy, [Eccleſiaſtical Magiſtracy.]
Hiero- {Sacred} {Sculpture}
glyphic, {Secret} {Paint}
High.
 Tall, [adj. TM-II. 4. O.]
 [Deep]
 —ſhoes, [Shoes to the ankle.]
 —water, [Deep overflowing tide]
 [Much]
 {Tranſcendent (augm.)}
 —winds, [Winds (augm.)]
 [Ample]
 —forehead, [Ample 6]
 [Public]
 —way, [Public w.]
 {adj. Dignity}
 {Excellent}

—day, [Feſtival d.]]
 [Principal]
 —prieſt, [Primate of P.]
 —minded {Proud}
          {Ambitious}
 [Until]
 breaſt—[Until the br.]
Hill. W. III. 1. E.
Hillock, [Protuberance]
Hilt, [adj. hand (part) of Sword.]
Him.
 Pron. I. 3.
 —ſelf, [Him him.]
Hinde.
 [Hart] Be. II. 3. A. (fem.)
 [adj. Agriculture ſervant]
Hinder.
 —part. Sp. III. 8. O.
 —moſt.
 [adj. Hinder part]
 [Succeeding]
to—
 [a. Impedient]
 [a. Trouble]
 [a. Loſs]
Hinge. Po. IV. 6.
 [Entrails]
Hint, {Expreſſion} {(dim.)}
      {Narration} {(ob-
                    (ſcure)
Hip.
 [Thigh] PG. V. 4.
 [Berry of the wild Roſe]
Hippocampus. Fi. VIII. 5. A.
Hippocras, [adj. p. Spice wine.]
Hire, [Hiring (thing.)]
 —ing. RC. V. 5. O.
His.
 [adj. Pron. I. 5.]
 —own, [Pron. redup.]
Hiſs. Q III. 4.
Hiſtory, [Narration]
Hit.
 [a. Contiguity]
 [a. Strike]
 [a. Fortune]
Hither. {To} {this place.}
        {Till}
 —moſt, [Neareſt]
 —ſide, Sp. II. 2. E.
 —to, {To} {this} {place.}
      {Till}   {time}
 —ward, [Toward this place]
Hive, [Bees (houſe)]
Hm. Int. I. 2.
Ho.
 Int. III. 1.
 no—[No cohibition.]
 not—[For not- a. Providence for.]
Hoar-froſt, [Rime] El. III. 5. A.
Hoary.
 —with Froſt. [White—]
 —with Age. [Gray—]
 —with mustineſs, [Moſſie—]
Hoarſeneſs. Q. III. 8. O.
Hoaſt, vid. Hoſt.
Hob, [adj. Ruſticity (perſon)]
Hobby.
 Horſe, [Ambling horſe (dim
 —horſe [Horſe (like) ſtuff.]

Hawk, [Hawk for Larks.]
Hobble, [Run lame (like.)]
Hobgoblin, [adj. a. Fear (apt.)]
 adj. p. Fiction (thing)]
Hoboy.
Hock, [Foot.]
Hocus-pocus, [Preſtigiator.]
Hod, [adj. Po. V. (jug.)]
Hodge-podge, [Mixture (corr.)]
Hog.
 Proper. Be. II. 8.
 —'s bread.
 —'s fennel.
 —fiſh. Fi. I. 5. A.
 —louſe, [Sow]
 —'s head {Barrel (augm.)}
          {Meaſure [36 gallons.]}
 —ſheep.
Hoiſe, [Lift]
Hold.
 Not let go. TA. I. 6.
 —faſt, [Hold (augm.)]
 [Contain]
 —water, [c. w.]
 {Have}
 {Poſſeſs}
 {Right (manner.)}
 [Eſteem]
 —blameleſs, [Eſteem b.]
 [Continue]
 —at a bay, [a. Stay]
 —back,
 —in, {Cohibit.}
 —off.
 —out, [Continue permanent.]
 —a town. RM. II. 4.
 —ones peace, [a. Silence.]
 [together, [Continue leagued]
 up, [Support.]
 [Expletive]
 [counſel, [Together adviſe]
 [Not looſe]
 [Abſtain
 —ones breath, [Not-breath]
 —ones hand {Abſtain}
             {Omit}
 —ones water, [Not- a. Urine]
the—
 —of a Ship, [Loweſt room (augm.)—]
 lay {—} {Catch}
 take {—} {Arreſt.}
Strong— RM. VI.
Holder.
 [adj. Holding (perſon)]
 [Longeſt tooth]
Hole.
 Through. Mag. IV. 1. O.
 [Not through {Dent}
               {Cavity}
 lurking— [adj. Hiding-place.]
Holy, [adj. Holineſs.]
 —day, [adj. Feſtiviey-day]
 —ghoſt. G. III.
Holineſs.
 Habit. Hs. V. 2.

[P

HO   HO   HU

[p. Confecration]
Holly.
—*oke.* HF. IX. 6. A.
—*tree.* Tr. III. 6. A.
Sea—[Eringo]
Hollow.
Empty, [adj. Mag. VI. 1. E.]
—*hearted,* [adj. Hypocrifie.]
[Concave]
—*eyed,* [Deep-eyed]
As Spunge, [adj. Poroufnefs.]
Holm, [Holly]
—*oke.*
Holoftens. Fl. VIII. 4.
Holothyrinm. Ex. IX. 4. A.
Holpen, [adj. p. Help.]
Homage, { Duty / Acknowledgment } of Subjection
Home, [Dwelling (place) Sp. II. 4.
—*bred,* [Rufticly educated]
come fhort— { finally.
[a. Defect } of home.]
hit him { Strike / a. Contiguity } (augm.) (perf.)
Homelinefs.
Not ornate. TM. V. 5. O.
[Rufticity]
Homicide, [Man-killing]
Homiletical, [adj. Converfation]
—*Vertue.*
—*Common.* Man. IV.
—*Belonging to Superiors.* Man. V.
—*Belonging to Inferiors.* Man. VI.
Homily, adj. p. preaching (thing)
[p. Commanded.]
Homogeneal, [Of the fame kinde.]
Homonymy. D. IV. 1. O.
Honefty.
[Vertue]
[Chaftity]
[Integrity]
Flower, [Bulbonach] HS VI. 1.
Hony.
—*apple,* [Sweet apple (kind)
—*comb,* [Bees (rooms)
—*dew,* [adj. Hony dew]
—*moon,* [Firft month after Marriage]
—*fuckle,* [Woodbine] Sh. II. 8.
French-*fuckle.* HS. III. 5.
Trefoil. HS. III. 10. A.
—*wort.* HL. IX. 3. A.
Honour.
[Reputation]
[Dignity]
[Refpect (augm.)]
—*able.*
[adj. Honour (abftr.)]
[adj. Nobility.]
Honourary, [adj. Honour (fign)]

Hood, [adj. Cover (veft)]
—for head, [Face-covering head (veft.)]
—*wink,* [Cover the eyes.]
Token of Degree, [Loofe adj. fhoulder (veft.)]
Hoof. PP. VI. 5.
to—[Un-hoof]
Hook. Mag. IV. 8.
By—or by crook, [By right or wrong.]
—*ed,* [Curve.]
Hoop, [Ring { of Wood. (augm.) { Iron, &c.]
Bird. Bi. III. 8. A.
Hooper, [Wild fwan] Bi. IX. 1.
Hooping, [Acute exclamation.]
Hoord, [Lay up] TA. V. 4.
Hooting, vid. *Hooping.*
Hop.
Plant. HF. I. 5. A.
[Leaping] Mo. I. 5.
—*on one leg.* Mo. I. 5. A.
Hope.
Affection. AS. 5. 6.
paft—[adj. { a. / p. Defpair.]
Grace. Ha. V. 5.
Hopelefs, [adj. { a. / p. Defpair.]
Hopper.
Horary, [adj. Hour.]
Horde, [Lay up] Ta. V. 4.
Horehound.
Bafe—HF. VII. 2.
Black—HF. VII. 11. A.
White—HF. VII. 6. A.
Horinet, [Mould] HL. L 1. A.
Horizon. W. VI. 1.
Horn.
Proper. PP. VI. 6.
[Angle]
—*owl.* Bi. I. 4.
—*work.* RM. VI. 5. A.
Horn-beam. Tr. VI. 4. A.
Hornet. Ex. IV. 2. A.
Horofcope.
Horrible, { adj. a. Fear
Horrid, { Evil (augm.)
Horror.
[Fear (augm.)]
[Rigor through Fear]
Horfe. Be. I. 1. fp. (male)
to—
—*a man,* [Ride (make.)] fp. on Horfe.]
—*a Mare,* [a. Coition with Mare.]
on—*back,* [On horfe]
—*cloth,* [Horfe's veft]
—*courfer,* [Horfe (Merc.)]
—*foal,* [Young horfe (male)]
—*leach,* [Phyfician for Horfe]
Infect. Ex. I. 2.
—*litter,* [Sedan adj. p. carried between Horfes.]
—*man.*
[Rider]
Souldier. RM. III. 1. A.
—*beef.* HL. VI. 5.
—*tail.* HL. IX. 7.

—*tongue.* Sh. III. 7. A.
—*fly.*
—*mint.*
—*radifh.*
—*fhooe.* HS. III. 6. A.
Sea—[Morfe] Be. V. 3.
Wooden—[Horfe (like) jugement.]
Hortulane. Li. IV. 2. A.
Hofe.
[Leg (veft)]
[Breeches]
Hofier, [adj. Hofe (merc.)]
Hofpitable, [adj. Hofpitality.]
Hofpital { Sick / Poor } men's houfe.]
Hofpitality. Man. III. 6.
Hoftage, [adj. Pledge (perfon)]
Hofte.
[adj. Eucharift bread]
[Army]
op. to Gueft. RO. III. 9.
to—[a. Gueft]
Hoftility, [Enemy (abftr.)]
Hoftler, [Horfe (Off.)]
Hoftry, [adj. Hofte (houfe)]
Hot, [adj. { Heat / Zeal }]
—*houfe,* [Stove]
Hotchpotch, [Mixture (corr.)]
Hovel, [Houfe (dim.) fp. not walled.]
Hovering. Mo. I. 2. A.
Hough, vid. *Hoof,* [Lower joint of hinder Leg.]
Howl [adj. Weeping (voice.)]
Houlet, [Owl.]
Hound, [Dog hunting wild beafts by fmell.]
—*fifh.* Fl. I. 4.
fpotted—Fl. I. 4. A.
—*'s tongue.* HL. IX. 4. A.
Hour. Mea, V. 8.
—*glafs.* Mag. VI. 5. A.
Houfe.
Building. Po. II. 1.
—*breaking.* RJ. III. 8. A.
—*burning.* RJ. III. 8.
to—[a. Houfe]
—*ed,* [Poffeffing houfes.]
[Family]
[Kindred]
Houfhold, [Together-adj. houfe (aggr.)]
—*bread,* [Courfe bread]
—*ftuff,* [Utenfils.]
Houfe-keeping, [Family-office.]
Houfleek, HL. VIII. 1.
Hout, [Exclamation.]
fp. a. Mocking.]
How.
[In what manner]
—*then,* [-therefore.]
op. to So. Adv. II. 1.
Howbeit, [Although]
Howfoever, [How, how.]
Hu, [Colour.]
Hu and cry, [Purfuit fucceffive]
Huck, [Treat, { (augm.) / (corr.) }]
Hucklebone. PG. V. 4. A.
Huckfter, [Merchant (corr.)]
Huddle.

HU | JA | JE

Huddle, { Gather } { (corr.) }
{ Heap } { confu- (sedly.) }
Huffing. AC. IV. 6.
Hug, [Embrace]
Huge, [Great (augm.)]
Hugger-mugger, [Secret (corr.)]
Hul.
— *of a Ship.* RN. II.
— *ing.* } RN. VI. 5. A.
— *lying at* }
— *of Corn,* [Husk]
Hulch, [Protuberance]
Hulk, [Trunk]
Hulver, [Holly]
Hum.
  [Indistinct noise]
  [Bees (voice)]
  [Approve (voice)]
Humane.
  [adj. Man]
— *learn-* { Worldly } { Scien-
  ing, { Lay } { ces.]
  [Courteous]
Humble.
— *ness.* Man. V. 2.
— *bee.* Ex. IV. 1. A.
— *plant.* Sh. IV. 7.
  { Low }
to — { Humble } (make)
  { Submit }
Humid, [Moist]
Humiliation { a. Humility.}
  { Fasting.]
Humility. Man. V. 2.
Humming bird. Bi. VL 5.
Humor.
  Liquor, [adj. a. Moistness (thing)]
  Temper of mind.
  [a. Complacence (end.)]
  [a. Conceitedness]
Humorist.
  [Conceited]
  { Seeming of divers dispositions }
— *physician.*
Humorous, [adj. Humor (corr.)]
Humorsome, [Morose]
Hundred.
  Weight. Mea. III. 7.
— *pound in mony.* Mea. IV. 6.
Hung, { pret. } hang]
  { adj. p. }
Hunger. AC. II. 1.
Hunt.
  [a. Hunts-man]
— *'s man.* RC. II. 7.
— *'s up.*
Hurdle, [adj. p. Weave (thing) of sticks.]
Hurl, [Cast]
Hurlbat, [Club adj. p. cast (apt.)]
Hurlyburly, [Confusion sp. Seditious]
Hurry.
  { Swift } { imp.]
  { Dispatch }
  sp. with Confusion.]
Hurt.
  [a. Hurtful.]
— *full.* T. IV. 1. O.

[a. Injury]
[a. Loss]
[a. Wound]
Hurtleberry, vid. *Whirtle.*
Husband,
  [adj. Married (male.)]
to — [a. Frugal.]
  good — [Frugal (person)]
  ill — [adj. Squandring (person)]
— *man.* RC. II, 6. A.
Husbandry.
  Profession RC. H. 6. A.
  Work, [Agriculture]
  good — [Frugality]
  ill — [Squandring]
Hush, [adj. Silence]
Husk. PP. II. 3.
Huso. Fi. I. 8. A.
Huswife.
  [Mistress of the house]
  [Frugal (fem.)]
Hut, [House (dim.) sp. of Boughs.]
Hutch, [Box.]
Huzz, (a. Bee (voice.)]
Hyacinth. HL. IV. 4. A.
  Indian.— HL. V. 5.
Hybernal, [adj. Winter.]
Hydra, [adj. Water-serpent.]
Hydrography, [Water's science.]
Hydropic, [adj. Dropsie.]
Hyena.
Hymen, [Marriage.]
Hymn. RE. IV. 2. A.
Hyperbole.
  Mathemat. Mag. III. 8. E.
  Rhetor. [fig. of Expression (exc.)]
Hyphen. D, I. 4. A.
Hypochondriac. S. VI. 4. A.
Hypocrisie. Ha. IV. 4. O.
Hypotenuse, [Side over against the right Angle.]
Hypothesis, [Supposition.]
Hypothetic, [adj. Supposition.]
Hyssop. HF. VI. 7.
  Hedge — HF. VII. 14.
Hysterical, [adj. Womb.] PG. VI. 9.
  Disease. S. VI. 9.
Hysteron proteron.

I.

I. Pron. I. 1.
Jabber, { Child (like.) }
  [Pronounce { Imperfectly }
  { Indistinctly]
Jacinth, vid. *Hyacinth.*
Jack.
  { Sorry person] sp. (male.)
  { Man (corr.)
— *anapes,* vid. *Ape.*
— *Daw,* vid. *Daw.*
  Fish. [Pike] Fi. IX. 1.
— *of the Hedge,* [Alliaria]
— *with a lantern.* El. I. 6.
— *of a Ship.* RN. III. 9. A.

[adj. Back (armor)
leathern — [leathern Pot] Pr. V. 5.
— *to turn spit,* [Vertiginating (machin) of rosting (instr.)]
Jackall. Be. V. 4.
Jacket, [Short loose (vest) for Trunk.]
Jade, [Sorry sp. Horse.]
Jag, { Slash } margin.]
  { Torn }
Jaguraca. Fi. V. 8.
Jay. Bi. I. 8. A.
Jail, [adj. Prison (place.)]
— *er.* [adj. Prison (Off.)]
Jakes, [a. Dunging (room.)]
— *farmer,* [Emptying (mech.) of Jakes.]
Jamb, [adj. Side column.]
St. *James-wort.*
Jangle. Q. III. 9. O.
  [a. Contention]
Jannock, [Flat bread of Oats.]
January, [First month]
Jar.
  [Earthen pot for Oil]
  Sound. Q. III. 2. A.
  [a. Contention]
Jargon, [a. Fiction Language.]
Jasmin. vid. *Jessamin.*
Jasper. St. II. 3.
Javelin, [Dart.]
Jaundies. S. VI. 2. A.
Jaunt, [Going (augm.)]
Jaw. PG. III. 9.
Ice. El. III. 4.
Idea. T. II. 3.
Identity. T. III. O.
Idiom, [Property of Language.]
Idiot. NP. I. 1. O. (corr.)
Idle.
  [adj. Sloth]
  [Negligent]
  [Not-busie]
  [Not-pertinent]
Idol, { Picture } adj. p. Worship
  { Image } (person)
Idolatry, [Worship { of Picture } { Image }]
Jealousie. AS. VI. 3. A.]
Jeat. St. VI. 2.
Jeer, [Mock]
Jejune, [adj. Scarcity of.]
Jelly. Pr. I. 5. A.
Jennet, [Spanish nimble horse.]
Jeopardy, [Danger]
Jerfalcon.
Jerk.
  [a. Motion (imp.)]
  [Whip] RM. VI. 2.
Jerkin, [Short loose (vest) for Trunk.]
Jessamin. Sh. V. 3.
Yellow — Sh. II. 13.
Jesses, [Foot-bands for Hawks]
Jest.
  [Not-serious]
  [adj. Urbanity (thing)]

IL | IM | IM

Jesuits powder, [Cortex febrifugus Peruv.] Tr. VII. 9.
Jet. St. VI. 3.
  [adv. proud (like) going (manner)]
Jew. RE. I. 3. (person)
  —*'s-ear*, [Fungus of Elder.]
Jewel.
  [Gem]
  [Gemms (aggr.)]
  [Precious (thing)]
Jewry, [Dwelling (place) of Jews.]
If.
  —*not*, [Unless.]
  —*it had not been for*, &c. [Without, &c.]
  as— Adv. IV. 2. O.
Ignis fatuus. El. T. 6.
  —*lambens.* El. I. 6. A.
Ignoble.
  [Not-noble]
  [adj Mean (augm.)]
Ignominy.
  [Infamy]
  [Infamation]
Ignorance.
  Natural. NP. I. 1. O.
  op. to Science. Ha. VI. 1. D.
  op. to Art. Ha. VI. 3. D.
Iguana, [Senembi] Be. VI. 3. A.
Jig,
  [Walk wantonly]
  [Trick.]
Jill.
  { Sorry (fem.)
    Woman (corr.) }
  [Half pint]
Jingle.
  [Ringing (dim.)]
  [Affectation of sounds of words.]
Iland. W. III. 2. O.
Iliac-passion. S. VI. 5. A.
Ill.
  adj.
    [Evil]
    [Sick]
  —*at ease* { Pained
    Not-indolent }
  —*favoured*, [Deformed]
  —*man*, [Vicious man]
  —*name*, [Infamy]
  —*will*, [Malignity]
  with an—*will*, [adv. Nolleity]
  adv.
    [adv. Evil]
    [adv. Difficult]
Illation. D. IV. 6. A.
Illegal, { Not—
  Against- } adj. Law]
Illegitimate, { Begotten not-adv. Law.]
  Spurious. }
Illiberal, [Not- adj. Reputation.]
Illiterate. Ha. VI. 4. D.
Illuminate, [a. Light.]
Illusion.
  [Deceit]
  [Mocking]

[Diabolical Apparition]
Illustrate, [a. Plain (make)]
Illustrious.
  [Bright]
  [Noble]
  [adj. Dignity]
Image. Pr. VI. 8. A.
  Whether { painted
    graven
    carv'd } im.
    molded
    molten
  Statue, [Solid Image]
Imagin.
  [a. Fansie]
  [Think]
  [Invent]
Imbargo, [Arrest of { Ships. Wares. }]
Imbark, [Into- a. Ship.]
Imbase, { Depreciate by mixture.
  Defile. }
Imbattel, [a. Order for Battel.]
Imbaulm, [Condite]
Imbecillity, [Weakness]
Imbellish, [a. Ornate.]
Imbezil, { Spoil
  a. Prodigal }
Imbibe, { Drink
  Soke }
Imbolden, { a. Boldness.
  Encourage }
Imboss, [Adorn with Protuberances.]
Imbroider, [Variegate by sowing.]
Imbrue, [Soke]
Imbue, [adj. p. Quality (make)]
Imburse, [Receive into purse.]
Imitate. TA. II. 8. A.
Immaculate, [Clear.]
Immanent, [adj. Action adv. inside.]
Immanity, [Cruelty (augm.)]
Immatureness. NP. VI. 4. D.
Immediate. TM. IV. 2.
  [Next]
  [Soon]
Immense, { Infinite.
  Great (augm.) }
Immerse, [Into- ition.]
Imminent, { Near.
  Soon. }
Immoderate.
  [adj. Excess.]
  [Fierce] Ha. III. 4. E.
Immodest, { Not——
  Against— } modest
Immortal.
  [Not- adj. die (abstr.)]
  [adj. Ever.]
Immoveable. [Not moveable.]
Immunity. RC. IV. 9. A.
Immure, { Sepiment with
  Shut up } walls.
Immutable. [Not- adj. p. alter (abstr.)]
Imp, { Graft.
  Lengthen by Grafting }
Impair, [a. Worse.]

Impale. RJ. V. 4. A.
  [Sepiment with Pales]
Impannel, [a. Catalogue.] sp. Names.]
Imparity.
  [Inequality]
  [Oddness]
Impark, [a. Park (make)]
Impart.
  [adj. Partner (make)]
  [a. Narration]
Impartial, [Not-partial (pot.)]
Impassible, [Not- adj. suffer (pot.)]
Impatience. Man. I. 8. O.
Impeach, [Accuse.]
Impedient. T. II. 5. O.
Impediment, [adj. a. Impedient (thing.)]
Impell, [a. Impulsive]
Impendent, [Over-hanging]
Impenetrable, [Not-adj. p. pierce (abstr.)]
Impenitence. Ha. V. 1. O.
Imperative, [adj. a. Command (manner.)]
Imperceptible, [Not- adj. p. common sense (pot.)]
Imperfect. T. III. 9. O.
Imperial, [adj. King]
  Crown—
Imperiousness.
  [Insolence]
  [Magisterialness]
Impertinency. TM. IV. 5. O.
Impetrate, [Obtain sp. by Entreaty.]
Impetuous, [adj. Impetus]
Impetus. T. VI. 6. A.
Impiety.
  [Gracelessness]
  [Atheism]
  [Prophaneness]
Implacable,
  [Not un- adj. p. anger (abstr.)]
  [adv. Pertinaciously angry.]
Implant, [In-plant]
Implead, [a. Sute.]
Implements, [Utensils]
Imply, { Comprehend
  Infer } { by consequence }
Implicit.
  [Comprehended] TA. II. 4.
  [Understood] D. III. 8. O.
  —*faith*, [a. Belief (abstr.) with ignorance of the things to be believed.]
Imploy.
  [Business]
  [Use]
Implore, { (augm.)
  Intreat } humbly
Import.
  [In-carry]
  [Meaning]
  [Importance]
Importance. T. IV. 5.
Importune, [Intreat (augm.)]
Importunate, { Desire
  [adj. Entreat } (aug.)
Impose.
  [Upon

IM · IN · IN

[Upon-put]
[Injoin]
[a. Fraud]
Impoffible. T. IV. 4. O.
Impoft, [Tax of imported things]
Impofthume, [Apofteme]
Impofture.
 [Deceit]
 [Forgery]
 [Fraud]
Impotence.
 op. to Natural power. NP. O.
 op. to Acquired power. Ha. II 6. O.
 [Not-coition (apt.)]
Impotent.
 [adj. Impotence]
 [adj. p. Paffion (exc.)]
Impoverifh, [adj. Poverty (make)]
Impound, [Imprifon in Pound.]
Imprecate. RC. VI. 4. A.
Impregnable, [Not-takeable.]
Impregnation.
 Getting with Child. AC. I. 2.
 [Infufion] O. V. 7. A.
Imprefs.
 [Print]
 [Appropriate fentence]
Impreffion.
 [Influence]
 [During effect]
 [a. Printing]
 [Sign]
Imprimis, [adv. Firft.]
Imprint.
 [Print]
 [Ieave fign]
Imprifonment. RJ. VI. 4.
Improbable, [Not- { true (like) / proveable / opinable }]
Improove.
 [Mend]
 [Increafe]
 [a. Better]
 [Ufe (perf.)]
Improper.
 [Not-proper]
 [Spurious]
 [Figurate]
Impropriation, [Inheritance of Prieft's revenue.]
Improvidence. Man. III. 2. D.
Imprudence. Ha. VI. 2. D.
Impudence, Man. III. 7. D.
Impugn.
 [Fight]
 [a. Oppofition]
 [a. Objection]
Impulfe, [a. T. II. 2. (abftr.)]
 —ive caufe. T. II. 2.
Impunity, [Not- p. punifhment.]
Impure, Defiled]
Impute, { Claim / Predicate]

In.
 Reft. Prep. IV. 1. O.
 —to. Prep. IV. 1.
 —as much as, [Whereas] Conj. IV. 1.
 [Engaged]
 [Friends]
 Motion, [Into] Prep. IV. 1.
 drive— } Into— { drive
 drop—   { drop]
 —pieces, [Into pieces.]
Inability, [Impotence]
Inacceffible, [Not- adj. p. come (abftr.)]
Inamiffable, [Not- adj. p. lofe (abftr.)]
Inamour, [adj. a. Love (make)]
Inanimate, [Not- adj. life]
Inaugurate, [Admiffion adv. folemnity]
Inaufpicious, [adj. Adverfity (fign)]
Inbred, [In-natural]
Incamp, [a. Camp]
Incapacitating.
 Punifhment. RJ. VI. 8. A.
Incapacity, [Impotence]
Incarnate, [adj. p. Flefh]
 to— [a. Flefh]
 As a wound healing, [Again-flefh.]
Incendiary.
 [Houfe-burner] adj. RJ. III. 7. (perfon]
 [adj. a. Contention (make]
Intenfe. RE. VI. 3.
 to— [adj. Anger (make]
Incentive, [Impulfive]
Inceptor.
 [adj. Begin (perfon)]
 [Candidate]
Inceffant, [Permanent]
Inceft, [Unchaftity with Kin.]
Inch. Mea. I. 2.
Inchant, [a. Witch by words]
Inchoate, [adj. p. begin]
Incident.
 { adj. Contingency
 { adj. p. Event }
Incifion, [Cutting]
Incite, [a. Impulfive]
Incivility, [Rufticity]
Inclination.
 [Down-obliquing its fuperficies].
 —towards, [Vergency] Sp. III. A.
 [Difpofition]
 —of the will. AS. IV. 1.
 —of the affection.
  [Favor] AS. V. 2.
Inclofe.
 [In-fepiment]
 [Shut]
 [Comprehend]
Include, [Comprehend]
Inclufive, [Comprehending the Extremes.]
Incogitancy.

[Not-thinking]
 [Heedlefnefs]
Incombuftible, [Not- adj. p. burn (pot.)]
Income, [Revenue]
Incommenfu- / Meafure
rable, [Not: Propor- } (pot.)
with- adj. p. tion
Incommodi. { profitable
ous, [Not- { convenient]
Incommunicable, [Not-communicable]
Incomparable.
 [Moft excellent]
 [Not- { adj. p. Like / adj. p. Equal } (pot)]
Incompatible.
 [Not- { adj. p. Join / adj. p. Si- / multaneous. }]
Incompetent, [Not-competent]
Incomprehenfible, [Not- adj. p. know (pot.) totally.]
Incongruous, [adj. Contrariety]
Inconfiderate, [Carelefs]
Inconfiftent, [Not- adj. p. Simultaneity (pot.)]
Inconftancy. Ha. IV. 7. D.
Incontinent, [Unchaft]
 —ly. [Soon (augm.]
Inconvenient. T. V. 5. O.
Incorporate, [Join into one body.]
Incorporeal, [Not- adj. body]
Incorrigible.
 [Not- adj. p. better (pot.) by Correction]
 [adj. p. Harden (apt.]
Incorruptible, [Not- adj. p. corruption (pot.)]
Incounter.
 [Meet]
 [Fight]
Incourage. RO. VI. 2.
Incraffate, [adj. a. Thick]
Increafe.
 TM. I. 7. E.
 [Great] TM. I. 1. E,
 [v. { Intenfe] TM. I. 8. E.
  { More-Great, &c.]
 [Many] TM. III. 1.
 [Abundant] TM. I. 2. E.
Incredible, [Not- adj. p. believe (pot.)]
Incredulous. Ha. III. 2. D.
Increment, [Increafe]
Incroach, [Ufurp]
Incubus, [Ephialtes] S. IV. 2. A.
Inculcate, [Repeat (freq.]
Inculpable, [Not- adj. p. blame (pot.]
Incumbent.
 [Church (Off.)]
 fp. Parifh Prieft]
 —on, [Pertinent to]
Incumber, { Hinder } fp. with
 { Trouble } confufed multitude]
Incurable, [Not re- adj. p. foundnefs (pot.]

In-

IN IN IN

Incurr, { adj. p. Object }
{ adj. p. Dangerous }
Incursion, [Assault]
Indammage, { Loss }
{ (a.) Hurt }
Indanger, [a. Dangerous]
Indebt, [a. Debt]
Indecent. T. V. 2. O.
Indeclinable, [Not- adj. p. decline (pot.)]
Indecorum, [adj. Indecency (thing.)]
Indeed.
 [Truly] Adv. I. 2. A.
 [adv. Thing]
Indeer, [adj. p. Love (make)]
Indefatigable, [Not-adj. p. weary (pot.)]
Indefinite.
 [Not- distinct]
 [Not-limited]
Indeleble, [Not-deleble]
Indemnifie, [Preserve from adj. p. hurt]
Indemnity, [Not- p. Hurt]
Indent.
 [a. { Notch }
 { Dent } (line)]
 [a. Paction]
Indentures, [Bonds of reciprocal Obligation]
Independent, [Absolute] TM.IV. 3
Indeterminate, [Infinite] T. II. 6. O.
Indevour. TA. III. 4.
Index.
 [Sign]
 [Catalogue]
Indication, [a. Sign]
Indiction, [Space of 15 years]
Indifferent.
 { Great and little. TM. I. 1. }
 Between { Excellent and sorry. TM.I.4. }
 { Intense and remiss.] TM.I. 8 }
 [Not-unlawful] T. V. 1. A.
 [adj. Moderation]
 [Not- { adj. zeal }
 { party }]
Indigent.
 [Poor]
 [Deficient]
 [Wanting]
Indigestion, [Not-digesting]
Indign, [Unworthy]
Indignation. AS. VI. 5.
Indignity, { Disgraceful injury }
{ Affront }
Indirect.
 [Not-straight]
 [Wrong]
Indiscretion, [Folly]
Indisposition.
 [Disposition (corr.)]
 [Not-health]
Indissoluble, [Not- adj. p. loosing (pot.)]
Indistinct.
 [Not-distinct]

Confused]
Individual, [Singular.]
Indivisible, [Not- adj. p. divide (pot.)]
Indocil, { Dull. Ha. III. 1. O. }
{ Not-adj. p. learn (apt.) }
Indoctrinate { a. Teacher }
{ a. Learning }
Indolence. NP. V. 3.
Indorse, [Write on the hind-part]
Indow.
 [Give]
 [p. permanently.]
 [adj. a. Possessions (make)]
Indue, [adj. a. Quality.]
Inducement.
 [adj. Impulsive (thing)]
 [adj. Persuading (thing)]
Induction. D. IV. 8.
—— into a Benefice.
Indulgence.
 [Graciousness]
 [Fondness]
Pope's— [P. Pardon]
Indurate, [a. Hard (make)]
Industry, [Diligence]
Inebriate, [adj. p. Drunkenness (make)]
Ineffable, [Not- adj. p. speak (pot.)]
Inequality. T. I. 5. O.
Inestimable, [Not adj. p. value (pot.)]
Inevitable, [Not- adj. p. avoid (pot.)]
Inexcusable, [Not- adj. p. excuse (pot.)]
Inexhaustible, [Not-adj. p. emptying (pot.)]
Inexorable, [Not-adj.p. { Intreat }
{ Persuade }]
Inexperience. Ha. VI. 4. D.
Inexpiable, [Not Un-adj. p. guilty (pot.)]
Inexplicable, [Not- adj. p. plain (pot.)]
Inextricable, [Not Un- adj. p. tangle (pot.)]
Infallible, [Not- adj. erre (pot.)]
Infamation. RJ. VI. 6.
Infamy. Ha. II. 4. O.
Infancy. Mea. VI. I.
Infantry.
 [Footmen] RM. III. 1. (kind)
Infatuate, [adj. a. Folly (make)]
Infect. S. I. 1.
Infeeble, [adj. a. Weakness (make.)]
Infelicity, [Adversity]
Inseoff.
 [Assign]
 [Deposite]
Infer, [a. Inference.]
Inference. D. IV. 6. A.
Inferiority.
 op. to Equality. TM. I. 5. D.
 Relation of—RO. III. O.
Infernal, [adj. Hell] W. II. O.
Infertile, [Barren]

Infest, [Trouble]
Infidel, [adj. Infidelity (person)]
Infidelity. Ha. V. 4. O.
Infinite. T. III. 6. O.
Infirm, [Weak]
Infix, [In-fix]
Inflame.
 [a. Flame (make)]
 [a. Worse (make)]
Inflamation. S. I. 4. A.
Inflate, [Swell with Wind]
Inflation. S. I. 5. A.
Inflexibleness.
 [Not- adj. p. bend (pot.)]
 [Stiffness]
 { Constancy }
 { Pertinacy }
Inflict.
 [a. Action]
 [p. adv. Punishment]
 [Execute]
Influence.
 { Efficiency }
 { Effectivity }
 [p. Secret]
 [p. of Heavenly bodies]
Infold, [In-fold]
Inforce, [a. Coaction]
Inform.
 [Tell]
 [p. Privately]
 [Teach]
 [Accuse]
Infortunate, { adj. Fortune (corr.) }
{ Adverse }
Infringe, [Violate]
Infuse.
 [Steep] O. V. 7. O.
 [Inspire]
 —— ed habit. Ha. V.
Ingage, [Oblige]
Ingeminate [Repeat (freq.)]
Ingender, [a. Generation]
Ingenious, { adj. Fancy (perf.) }
{ Sprightly }
Ingenuous. NP. IV. 1.
Ingestion, [in-putting]
Ingle.
Inglorious, [Not- adj. p. reputation]
Ingot, [Lump (dim.)]
 [p. of Fined metal]
Ingraft. O. III. 7.
Ingrail, [a. Tooth Mag. IV. 2. (line.)]
Ingratiate, [adj. p. Favor (make)]
Ingratitude. Man. I. 6. D.
Ingredient.
 [Simple (part) of Composition]
 [adj. a. Compounding (thing)]
Ingress.
 [Into-goe]
 [License of into-going]
Ingross.
 [Write (perf.)]
 [Buy all]
Ingulf, [a. Whirl-pool]
Ingurgitate, [In-swallow (aug)]
Inhabit, [Dwell]

Inherent.

Inherent.
 In-being]
 [*Adjunct*]
Inherit. RC. V. 2. A.
Inhesion.
 [*In-being*]
 [*Adjunct* (abstr.)]
Inhibit.
 [*Forbid*]
 [*Cohibit*]
Inholder, [Common Host]
Inhospitable. Man. III, 6. D.
Inhumane.
 {Not-
 {Against-}adj. Man]
 [Cruel } (ringe)
Inject, [Into-cast.] sp. with Sy.
Inimitable, [Not-adj. p. imitate (pot.)
Injoy. TA. V. 7.
Injoyn, [Command]
Iniquity.
 op. to Equity. Man. I. 2.
 [Unholiness]
Initiate, {Begin.
 {Admit.}
Injudiciousness. NP. I. 2. O.
Injunction, [Command]
Injury. R]. IV. 1.
Injustice. Man. I. 1. O.
Ink. Pr. VI. 6. A.
 —*born,* [adj. p. carry (apt.) Vessel for Ink.]
Inkling.
 {Discovery } (dim.)
 {Narration } {obscure}
 {Expression}
Inlay, [Variegate the superficies with in-put (things.)]
Inlarge, vid. *Enlarge.*
Inlighten, [a. Light.]
Inmate, [Subordinate dweller.]
Inmost. [Most-adj. inside.]
Inn, [Common Host (place)]
 —*keeper,* [Common Host]
 to—*Corn,* [Into- a. house Corn.]
Innate, [In-natural]
Innavigable. [Not- adj. p. navigation (pot.)]
Inner, [adj. Inside]
Innocent.
 op. to Guilty. R]. II. 6.
 [Harmless]
 {Idiot
 {Infant }
Innovate.
 [a. New]
 [Begin a Custom]
Innoxious.
 [Not-hurtful]
 [Innocent]
Innumerable, [Not- adj. p. number (pot.)]
Inoculate. O. III. 7. A.
Inofficious, [Not- adj. complaisance.]
In-ordinate, {Wrong}
 {Irregular}
Inquest, [adj. a. {Off.}
 Inquisition {agg.}
Inquination, [Defilement]

Inquire, [a. Inquisition]
Inquisition. AS. II. 2.
 [Examine]
 [Ask]
Inrich, [adj. Riches (make]
Inrode, [Assault Country]
Inroll, [In- a. catalogue]
Insatiable, [Not-adj. p. suffice (pot.)
Inscribe, [On-write]
Inscription, [Name]
Inscrutable, [Not- adj. p. find (pot.)
Insculption, [On-carving.]
Insect. [Exang. (dim.)
Insensible, [Not-adj. p. sense (pot.)
Inseparable, [not- adj. p. separate (pot.)
Insert, {add.}
 {In { put. }
Inside. Sp. III. 6.
Insidiate.
 [a. Ambush]
 [a. Snare]
Insidious.
 [adj. Ambush]
Insight.
 [Into-seeing]
 [Science]
 [Art.]
Insinuate.
 [Into-wriggle]
 [Flatter.]
Insipid, [Not- adj. p. taste (pot.)
Insist, [Upon-stay]
Insociable.
 op. to Homiletic Virtue, [adj. Man. IV. O.]
 {Not-
 {Against } adj. Society]
Insolent.
 op. to Magnanimity. Man. III. 8. E.
 op. to Condescension. Man. VI. 2. D.
Insoluble, [Not- adj. p. loosing (pot.)
Insomuch, [So.] Adv. II. 1. O.
Inspection.
 [Seeing]
 [Oversight]
Inspersion.
 [On- {sprinkling}
 {scattering}
Inspiration of God. AS. I. 6. A.
Instable, [adj. Lightness.] Hab. IV. 7. D.
Install.
 [Admit solemnly]
 [Consecrate]
Instance.
 [Example]
 [Earnest intreaty]
Instant. Sp. I. O.
 [Near]
 —*ly,* { Soon
 adv. { Diligently } augm.]
Instauration, { newing, }
 { (Re- { mending. }
Instep, [Convex of foot-joint.]
Instigation. [Impulsion]

Instill, [In-drop]
Instinct, [Na- { disposition.
 tural { impulsion.]
Institute, [a. Institution.]
Institutes.
 [Commands]
 [Ordinances]
Institution.
 [Instruction]
 [Ordinance]
 —*religious.* RE. VI.
Instruction.
 [Know (make]
 [a. Teacher]
 —*s.*
 [Directive precepts]
Instrument.
 Cause. T. II. 1. A.
 —*of Virtue.* Ha. II.
 —*mechanical.* Po. VI. 1.
 —*of Music,* [adj. Music, (instr.
 —*written,* [Bond.]
 [Substitute]
 Transc. (instr.)
Insufficient.
 [Not-sufficient]
 [Defective]
Insular, [adj. Island]
Insult, [a. Insolence.]
Insuperable, [Not-adj. p. overcome (pot.)
Insupportable, [Not-adj.p.support (pot.)
Insurrection.
 [Sedition]
 [Rebellion (inc.]
Intail, vid. *Entail.*
Intangle, [Tangle]
Integer, [Whole] sp. Number;]
Integral, [Whole]
 —*word.* D. II. 1.
Integrity. Ha. IV. 6.
Intellect. NP. I. 1.
Intelligence.
 [Knowledge]
 [Narration]
 sp. Private.]
Intemperance.
 [Sensuality] Man. II. 1. D.
 [Excess]
Intend.
 [Purpose]
 [Heed]
 [a. Intense (make]
Intenseness. TM. I. 8. E.
Intent.
 [Purpose]
 [End]
Intentive.
 [Heedfull]
 [Seriously } dispos'd to]
 [Earnestly
Intercalation, [Between-putting.
Intercede. RC. VI. 6. A.
Intercept.
 [Take in-coming]
 [Not-seen (make) by between-being]
Intercession. RC. VI. 6. A.
Interchangeable, [Reciprocal.]

IN   IN   JO

Intercourſe, [Commerce]
Intercurrent, [Between- adj. ition.]
Interdict, [Forbid]
Intereſt.
  [Concernment]
  [adj. Pertinent]
  [Proper profit]
  [Right]
  Uſury, [Rent of mony]
Interfere, [Strike mutually.]
  ſp. { Hurt } by ſtrik. m.}
    { Hinder }
Interjacent, [Between-being]
Interjection. D. II. 7. A.
Interim, [Between-ſpace.]
Interior, [adj. Inſide]
Interlace.
  [Mingle]
  [Stratifie]
Interlard, [a. Stratifie
Interline.
  [Between a. line.]
  [a. Stratifie]
Interlocution.
Interlope, [a. Prevent
  ſp. in Buying.]
Interlude, [Stage-play]
Intermeddle.
  [With-mingle]
  [Between a. buſineſs.]
Intermediate.
  [Middle]
  [Mediator]
Intermingle, [a. Mixture]
Intermit, [adj. p. Diſcontinue (make]
Intermix, [a. Mixture.]
Internal, [adj. Inſide]
Interpellation.
  [adj. p. Diſcontinue (make) diſcourſe by between-ſpeaking.]
Interpolation.
  [Between-put]
  ſp. adj. p. Forgery (thing]
Interpoſe.
  [Between-put]
  [a. Interceſſion]
Interpretation. D. V. 4.
Interpunction. D. I. 4.
Interr, [Bury]
Interreign, [Between-time of two a. Kings.]
Interrogation, [Queſtion]
Interrogatory, [adj. p. Queſtion (thing.]
Interrupt.
  [adj. p. Diſcontinue (make]
  [Hinder]
Interſection. Ma. II. 2. A.
Interval, [Between-ſpace]
Intervene, [Between- a. event]
Inteſtate, [Not- adj. a. preter. bequeathing.]
Inteſtine, [adj. Inſide]
Inthrall, [a Slave (make]
Inthroning, [On-ſeating]
  ſp. for Admiſſion (ſign]
Intice, [Allure]
Intimate.

[a. Narra- { conceldedly]
tion { obſcurely]
—*friend,* [Friend (augm.]
Intire.
  [Total]
  [Whole]
  [adj. Integrity]
Intitle.
  [adj. Right (make]
  [Name]
Into, Prep. IV. 1.
Intolerable.
  [Not- { ſuffer } pot.]
  adj. p. { Permit }
Intoxicate.
  [a. Fume (augm.]
  [adj. p. Drunkenneſs (make]
Intractable, [Perverſe]
Intrada, [Revenue]
Intralls. PG. VI.
Intrap, [a. Trap]
Intreat.
  [Pray] RO. V. 3.
  [Entertain]
Intrench, [a. Trench]
Intricate.
  [Tangle]
  [a. Difficult (make]
Intrigue.
  [adj. p. Concealed (thing]
  [adj. Obſcure (thing]
Intrinſecal, [adj. Inſide.]
Introduction.
  [In-bringing]
  [Prologue]
Intrude, [Into-thruſt.]
Intruſt.
  [Inſtead- a. right]
  [Depoſite]
Intuition. [Seeing.]
  ſp. diſtinct.]
Invade.
  [Aſſault]
  [Uſurp]
Invalid.
  [Impotent]
  [Weak]
  [Defective]
Invaſion.
Inveck, [a. Notch (line]
Invective, [adj. Reviling (thing]
Inveigh, [a. Revile]
Inveigle, [Allure]
  ſp. to Evil.]
Invelop, [a. Wrap]
Invenomed, [adj. p. Poiſon]
Inventing. AS. III. 2. A.
Inventory, [Catalogue]
  ſp. of Poſſeſſions.]
Invert.
  [Turn] AC. VI. 8.
  ſp. adv. Contrary.]
  [Retort]
Inveſt, [a. Admiſſion ſolemnly.]
Inveſtigation, [Inquiſition]
Inveterate, [Old]
Invincible, [Not- adj. p. overcome (pot.]
Inviolable, [Not- adj. p. violate (pot.]
Inviron, [About-margin]
Inviſible, [Not- adj. p. ſee (pot.]
Invite.

[Intreat to come]
[Provoke]
Inundation, [Overflowing]
Invocate.
  [Call]
  [Pray]
Involve, { Comprehend }
      { Intmgle }
Involuntary, [Not- adj. p. will.]
Invulnerable, [Not- adj. p. wound (pot.]
Inward, [adj. Inſide]
—*s.* PG. VI.
Job.
  [Operation (dim.]
  [Knock (dim.]
Job's tears. HL. III. 7. A.
Jocular, [adj. Urbanity]
Jocund.
  [adj. Mirth]
  [adj. Urbanity]
Jog.
  { a. Motion } (imp.
  { a. Shaking }
be——ing, [From-go] TA. VI. 1. O.
St. John's-wort, HS. V. 7.
St. John's Breed, [Carob] Tr. VI. 1.
Poor John, [Haak] Fi. III. 3. A
Joy.
  [Mirth] AS. V. 3.
  —*for good of others.* AS. VI. 6.
  —*for evil of others.* AS. VI. 7.
  to——joy one of, &c. [Congratulate one for. &c.]
Join.
  Together-put. TA. II. 1.
  [a. Nearneſs]
  [a. Contiguity]
  [a. Continuity]
  [Aſſociate]
  [a. Partner]
  [a. League]
—*battel,* [a. Battel.]
—*company,* { fit, travel,
  [With- { &c.]
—*er,* [adj. Fabrile (mech.) of wooden Utenſils.]
Joint.
  [adj. p. Join]
  ——*ly,* [Together.]
  Limm. PG. V.
  [Knitting]
  out of——[Having its Joint unplaced.]
  to——[Cut the Joints.]
Jointure, [Widow's Revenue.]
Jole, [Head.]
  ſp. Cheek.]
Jolly, [adj. Mirth.]
Jolt, [Shake (imp.]
  ſp. by Leaping (like.]
Jot.
  { Point
  { Little (thing]
Jove, vid. *Jupiter.*
Jovial, [adj. Mirth.]
Journal, [Narration of daily things.]

Journey,

IT

Joourney, [Travel]
—*man*, [Hired { (mech.]
  subordinate { (merc.]
Iotas. Fi. III. 8.
Irascible, [adj. Angry (apt.]
Ire, [Anger]
Iris, { HL. IV. 6.
      { HL. V. 3. A.
Irksome.
  [adj. Displicence (augm.]
  [adj. Aversation (augm.]
Iron. Met. I. 6.
  —*monger*, [adj. Iron (mer.]
  —*wort*. HF. VII. 2. A.
Irony. D. I. 8. A.
Irradiation, [adj. Bright (make]
Irrational. NP. I. O.
Irreconcileable, [Not re-adj. p.
  Friend (pot.]
Irrefragable { adj. p. deny }
             { Not- adj. p. confute }
                                (pot.]
Irregularity. TM. V. 4. A.
Irreligious. [Atheistical.]
Irremissible, [Not- adj. p. forgive (pot.]
Irreparable.
  [Not-adj. P. { compensate }
               { amend }
                        (pot.]
Irresolute, [adj. Wavering]
Irreverence. Man. V. 3. D.
Irrevocable.
  [Not { again-adj. p. get }
       { back-adj. p. call }
                        (pot.]
Irrision, [Mocking]
Irritate, { Provoke }
           { a. Impulsive }
Irruption, [Violent into-ition]
Is, { a. Being }
     { Copula }
Ischury, [Disease of not-adj. a.
  Urin (pot.]
Ise. El. III. 4.
Isicle, [Frozen drop.]
Ising-glass, [Selenites]
Issue, [Out-goe.]
  [a. Stream (dim.]
  [Sally]
        { Children (aggr.
          RO. I. 2 O.]
Off-spring, { Descendents
          { (aggr.) RO. I.
          1. O.]
[Event]
  —*at Law*. RJ. II. 5.
  to joyn—adj. p. Issue
    (make]
Isthmus. W. III. 3.
It. Pron. I. 3.
Itch. AC. II. 6.
  Disease. S. III. 2.
Item.
  [adj. p. { Reckon }
           { Add } (thing]
          { Admonition (dim.]
          { Narration (dim.]
Iterate, [Repeat]
Itinerant, [adj. a. Travel]
Itinerary, [adj. Travel]
Ition. TA. VI.

JU

Jubile.
  [adj. Festivity-year.]
  [Mirth (augm.]
Jucca. HL. V. 4. A.
Judaism. RE. I. 3.
Judas-tree. Tr. VI. 3.
Judge. RJ. I. 1.
Judgement.
  Faculty. NP. I. 2.
  [Opinion]
  [R]. (thing]
  [Sentence]
         { Punishment from
  —*of God*,{ God.]
         { Cursing. AS. I.
                      3, O.
Judicatory, [adj. R.]
           sp. Place.]
Judicial Relation. RJ.
  Persons in—RI. I.
  Proceedings in—RJ. II.
Judicious, [adj. Judgment
  (perf.]
Jug, [Narrow-neck'd pot.]
     sp. of Earth.]
Jugament. Po. VI. 3.
Juggle, [a. Prestigiator]
Juggler. RC. III. 9. A.
Jugular, [adj. Throat]
Ivy. Sh. III. 12.
  ground—HL. VI. 11.
  Virginian—Sh. V. 8.
Juice. PP. I. 7.
Jujub, Common. Tr. II. 6.
  white—Tr. II. 6. A.
Julap, [Cooling Potion]
July, [Seventh month]
Julis. Fi. V. 9. A.
Julus. Ex. II. 19. A.
Jumble, [a. Confused.]
Jump, [Leap (imp.]
Juncto, [Faction]
Juncture, [Present state of
  things.]
June, [Sixth month]
Juniper. Sh. III. 10.
Junket, [adj. Banquet (thing]
Ivory,   { horn }
  [Elephant's{ tooth]
Jupiter. W. II. 4. A.
Jury, [Equals sworn to judge.]
             { Judges }
Jurisdiction,{ Magistrates}
                      (place.]
Just.
  [adj. Justice]
  [adj. Perfection]
  —*temper*. TM. I. 8.
  —*so*.{ All so.]
        { So so.]
  to—[Game of mutual assaulting with Spears.]
Justice, Man. I. 1.
  —*of Peace*, [adj. Justice
    (Off.]
Justifie.
  [a. { Just }
      { Innocent }
      { Pronounce } { Just }
      { Declare } { Innocent }
Justle, [Thrust (imp.]

KA

         { Shoulders,}
sp. with { Elbows.}
         { &c.}
Jut out, [a. Protuberant.]
Juvenile, [adj. Youth.]

K.

Kalend, [First day of the
  month.]
Kalendar, [Book of months]
Kank, [Muscovia glass.]
Katkin. PP. II. 1. A.
Kecks, [Hollow stalk.]
Kedger, [Anchor (dim.]
Keel. RN. II. 1.
Keeling. Fish.
Keen.
  [adj. a. Cut (apt.]
  [Acrimonious]
  [Intense]
Keep.
In Good.
  [Preserve]
  [Maintain]
Out of Evil.
  Hurtful, [Deliver.]
  Dangerous, [Defend.]
  [a. Permanent]
In Quantity.
  —*at a stay*. TM. I. 9.
In Quality.
  —*dry* {[a. perma-}{ dr.]
  —*warm*,{ manent   }{ w.]
In Place, [Stay.]
          { a. Permanent}
  —*close*,{ Stay   }
                  close.]
              { a. Per-} { in}
  —*one's bed*,{ nent } {one's}
              { Stay   } { bed.]
  —*ones ground*. RM. II. 2.
  —*the field*. RM. II. 3.
  —*the town*. RM. II. 4.
In Possession.
  [Hold] TA. I. 6.
  Not lose. TA. V. 5.
  [Not change]
  —*one's course*.
  —*a wind*. RN. VI. 5.
  [Not violate]
  —*command*, { } { com.]
  —*promise*, {Perform}{ pro.]
  —*word*, {   } { word.]
  —*holy-day* { } { h. d.]
  —*away from*,{ be}
             [Absent{ make]
  —*back*, {   }{Cohibit.]
  —*in*,   {   }
  —*off*. {Be   }{distant}
          {Make }
  —*to it*, {[v. Per-} { doing,}
            { manent } { &c.]
                        { restrain}
  —*under*,[v. Permanent]{ ing,}
                        { subjecting.]
  —*company*, {a. companion.}
              {together-go.]
  —*counsel*, [a. Taciturnity]
  —*house*, [a. RO. III. 5.]

KI KN LA

—*a good house,* [a. RO. III. 5. liberally.]
—*silence,* [a. Silence.]
—*watch,* [a. Guard.]
Keeper.
{ Keeping
{ Guarding } (Off.)
[Park (Off.)]
Keg.
[Barrel (dim.)]
Measure.
Key.
—of door. Po. IV. 4. A.
—of Music, [Principal note]
Fruit. PP. III. 4. A.
[Haven]
Kell. PG. VI. 6. A.
Kemb, vid. Comb.
Kemboing the arms. AC. IV. 7.
Ken, [See]
  [p. From remote (place.)]
Kennel.
[Bed]
[Room]
[Sink]
[Receptacle of filth]
[Gutter for filth]
Kerchief, [adj. Linen (vest) for head.]
Kern.
[Grain]
[adj. Rusticity (person)]
Kernel.
Fruit. PP. III. 6. A.
[Glandule] PP. II. 7. A.
Kersy.
Kestrel, [Hovering Hawk]
Ketch. RN. I. 2. A.
Kettle. Pr. V. 6.
Kibe, [Chilblane.] S. III. 7.
Kick, [Strike { foot
  with { heel]
Kid, [Goat] Be. II. 2. A.
    (young)
to——as Pease. [a. PP. III. 5. A.]
Kidney. PG. VI. 7.
Kil.
a—[Arched fire (place)]
to—[a. dy (make)]
Kilderkin, [Barrel (dim.)]
Kin.
[Consanguinity] RO. I.
[Affinity] RO. II.
Kine. Be. II. 1.
Kinde.
Genus. T. I.
[Species] T. I. A.
a—of, &c.
out of—{ worse { its ancestors
than { it hath been.]
[Sex]
[Manner]
[adj. Kindness]
—*ly,* { eat— { taste (perf.)
       { rip'n— { rip'n (perf.)
Kindeness.
[Favour]
[Courtesie]
[Graciousness]

Kindle.
[a. Fire (inc.)]
[a. Anger (inc.)]
Kindred.
[Consanguinity] RO. I.
[Affinity] RO. II.
King.
Monarch. RC. I. 2.
—*dom,* [King (place)]
—*'s evil,* S. III. 3.
—*at arms,* [Principal Herald.]
—*fisher,* Bi. III. 9. A.
—*spear,* [Asphodel] HL. V. 1.
Kiss. AC. V. 6. A.
Kitchin, [adj. Cookery (room.)]
Kite Bi. I. 2. A.
—*fish.* Fi. III. 6.
Kitlin, [Cat (young)]
Knack, [adj. vanity (thing)]
Knag, [Knurl] PP. I. 1. A.
Knap, [Top] {p. tufted.]
—*sack,* [adj. Travel (bag.)]
—*weed.* HF. III. 4.
Silver—HF. III. 4. A.
Knave.
{ adj. Crafty
{ adj. a. Cheat } (person)
Kneading. O. IV. 7.
Knee. PG. V. 5. A.
—*pan,* [Bone defending the Knee-joint.]
being on his—*s.* AC. VI. 6. A.
Kneel. AC. VI. 6.
Knell, [Ringing for pret. dying (sign.)]
Knife. Po. VI. 2.
Knight, [Gentleman of highest degree.]
Knit.
—*knot,* { bind.]
        { tie.]
—*stockings,* O. V. 2. A.
Knob, [adj. Protuberance (thing)]
Knock. Mo. VI. 4. A.
Knoll.
[Hill (dim.)]
[adj. Protuberance (thing)]
Knop, [adj. Protuberance (thing)]
{p. tufted.]
Knot.
[adj. p. Knit (part)]
[Ribbands (aggr.) tied for ornament]
—*in garden,* [Area figur'd for ornament]
Crew, [adj. aggregate]
{p. corr.)
—*of a tree.* PP. I. 1. A.
—*in grass,* [joint (like—).]
—*grass.* HF. I. 4.
Bird. Bi. VII. 6.
[Difficulty]
to—
[a. Bud]
[a. Coagulate]
Know.
—*mentally.* AS. II. 5.
—*carnally,* [Coition.]
to be known { Claim.]
of, { Confess.]

Knowledge, [Knowing]
[Science.] Ha. VI. 1.
[Experience.] Ha. VI. 4.
Knuckle. PG. V. 7. A.
Knurl, [Knot] PP. I. 1. A.

L.

[Abel, [Lamin.]
{p. of skin upon—p. writing (apt.)
{p. Accessory.]
Labor.
[Operation]
[Endeavor (augm.)]
[Diligence]
to be in—
[a. Parturition]
[adj. p. Pain by Parturition]
Laborer, [adj. Operation (person.)]
Laborious.
Labyrinth, [Build- { tangle
ind adj. a. { Wander } (apt.)
Lac, [Wax of Ants.]
Lace. Pr. IV. 5.
to—[a. Face with Lace.]
to—*together,* [Together-bind. {p. with Lace.]
Laceration, [Tearing]
Lack.
[Not-have]
[Scarcity]
[Defect]
[Want]
Lacky, [adj. a. Foot-servant]
Laconism, [Brief sentencing (manner.)]
Lactation. AC. I. 4. A.
Lad, [adj. Adolescence (person.)]
Ladanum, [Concrete exudation of the holy rose]
Ladder. Po. IV. 1. A.
Lade, [a. Burden.]
—*ing,* [adj. Burden-(thing)]
Lady.
{ adj. Noble
{ adj. Gentle } (fem.)
—*cow.* Ex. V. 6. A.
—*laces,* [Striped grass] HF. IX. 6. A.
—*'s Bedstraw.* HF. IX. 6. A.
—*'s Bower.*
—*'s Glove.* HL. IX. 2.
—*'s Mantle.* HL. VI. 9. A.
—*'s Milk,* [White Thistle]
—*'s Seal,* [Black Briony]
—*'s Slipper.*
—*'s Smock,* HS. IV. 15. A.
—*'s Thistle.* [White Th.]
Ladle, [Spoon (augm.)]
Lag.
[Protract]
Lagopus. Bi. II. 7. A.
Lay.
[Pasture, [adj. lying (make.)]
Condi-

LA

{ Condition } (put)
{ Place }
—about him, { a. Operation }
 (augm.] { a. Diligence }
—aside,
 [a. Defift]
 [Un- a. Officer (make)
—down, [Defift]
—on, [On-put]
 { Take (end }
—out for { Get (end }
 { Disburse for }
—to one's charge, [a. Accuse.]
—to ones Wrift, [Apply]
—together, [a. Summe]
—up. TA. V. 4.
—land, [a. Reft from plowing.]
—a cloth, { Put } on
 { Spread } table.]
—egg, [a. Parturition]
| foundation, [a. Foundation.]
—hands on, }{ Catch
—hold on, }{ Arreft
—level, [a. Level (make)
—open, [a. Open (make)
—fiege to, [Befiege]
—wager, [a. Wager]
—wait, [a. Ambufh]
a—
—land, [adj. Reft land]
—man, [adj. RE. O. (perfon.]
[Song]
[Wagering]
{ Rank }
{ Courfe }
Laic, [Temporal]
Laire,
 [Deer's lying (place]
 Stratifie]
Lake. W. IV. 2. A.
 Tree. Tr. VIII. 8.
Lamb, [Sheep] Be.II. 2. (young)
to— [v. Parturition]
Lame.
 [Mutilated]
 [adj. Halt (apt.]
Lament.
 [Grief, { augm.]
 { fign }
Lamin. Mag. V. 4.
Lamm, [adj. Cudgelling]
Lamp. Pr. VI. 3. A.
Lamprey.
 Fifh. Fi. VI. 5.
 Difeafe.
Lamprill. Fi. VI. 5. A.
Lanar, { Woolly } feathered
 { Soft } Hawk.]
—et, [Lanar (male.]
Lance.
 [Short Pike]
Burning— [Dart.] El. I. 4. A.
 Scarifie]
to— { Cut]
 Open by cutting]
Lancea ardens, ['Dart.] El. I. 4. A.
Lance-knight, [Foot-fouldier]

LA

Lanceprefado,[adj. Military(Off.) over 10.]
Lancet, vid. Launcet.
Lanch, [a. Navigation (inc,)
Land.
 [Earth]
 [Field] Po. I.
  arable—Po I. 4.
 [Countrey] RC. III. 2.
—loper, [adj. Wander (perfon.]
—mark, [adj. Margin (fign.]
to { Come } on fhore.]
 { Bring }
Landlord
 { adj. pret. Demifing }(per-
 { adj. p. Right } fon of) House.]
 Land.]
[Hoft]
Landrefs, [adj. { (mech.]
 Wafhing { fem.]
Landskip, [Picture of Countrey.]
Lane, [Narrow { Street]
 adj. Travel { place.]
by— [Not ufual—]
Language. D. A.
 good, } g. } Difcourfe (manill. } ill. } ner.]
Languid, [adj. Weaknefs.]
Languifh, [Decay]
Lank, { Lean }
 { Empty }
 { Limber }
Lantern, [adj Candle (room.]
Lap.
—of gar-{ Corner } of
 ment, { Margin } Veft.]
 [Space upon the knees]
—dog, [Little Dog kept one-ly for delight.]
—of ear,
to—
 as a Dog, [Drink by licking.]
—up warm, { Fold } for
 { Clothe } warmth.]
Lapidary, [adj. Gem (merc.]
Lapfe.
 { Stumble (dim.]
 { Fall]
 [Lofe by omiffion]
Lapwing, Bi. VII. 3.
Larboard [Left fide]
Larceny, [Theft.]
Larch-tree. Tr. V. 3. A.
Lard, [Fat of Swine]
to— Pr. III. 8.
—er, [adj. Flefh (room.]
Large.
 { Ample]
 { Broad]
 { Great]
 [Abundant]
 [Liberal]
at— [Not-{ cohibited]
 { imprifon'd]
 [adj. Liberty]
Largefs, [Gift (augm.]

LA

Larix tree. Tr. V. 3. A.
Lark, Bi. V. 4.
 Sea—Bi. VII. 3. A.
 Tit—Bi. V. 4. A.
—'s heel. HS. I. 2.
Lafciviousnefs.
 [Wantonnefs]
 [Unchaftnefs]
Lafh, [Whip]
 { Irregularity]
to—out, [a.{ Excefs]
 { Prodigality]
Laferwort. HF. IV. 6.
Lask, [adj. Excefs dunging (apt.]
Lafs, [adj. Adolefcence (fem.]
Laffitude, [p. Weary (abftr.]
Laft.
 { New]
 [Moft. { Late]
 { Remoteft]
 { Hindermoft]
 { adj. Finifhing]
 { End]
a—[Exemplar]
 fp. for Foot veft]
to— { v. Duration]
 { v. Permanent]
Latch. Po. IV. 5. A.
—et, [Thong]
 fp. for Foot veft.]
Late.
op. to Old. Sp. I. 3.
op. to Soon. Sp. I, 4. O.
Latent,{ Concealed]
 { Hid]
Lath, [Lamin fp. of Wood]
Lathe, [adj. Turning (jug.]
Latin, [Language of Romans]
Latitude.
 { Breadth]
 [Diftance from the Equator]
Latter, { Succeeding]
Lattin, [adj. Iron (Lamin) tim'd.]
Lattis, [Oblique Croffes
 { plain.]
Laverentus. Fi. IX. 5. A.
Laudable, [adj. p. Praife (apt.]
Lave, [Empty by out-fcooping.]
Lavender. HF. VI. 5.
 French—[Caffidony] HF. VI. 5. A.
 Sea—HS. VI. 9. A.
—Cotton. HF. II. 10. A.
Laver, [adj. Wafhing (veffel]
Laugh. AC. IV. 3.
 { Contemning.]
—to fcorn, { —{ Mocking.]
 { Laugh }
Lavifh, [Prodigal]
Launce, vid. Lance.
Launch, [a. Swim (inc.]
 fp. Ship.]
Laundrefs, [adj. a. Wafhing (mech.]
Laurel. Tr. III. 5. A.
 Alexandrian—Sh. III. 7.
Law, RC. IV. 3.
—of

LE

—of nature. RC. VI. 2.
—positive. RC. VI. 3.
Civil—[Roman Law]
Father in —— [Father by affinity.]
go to—[a. Suit.]
—day, [a. Cause-day.]
—full. T. V. 1.
—less { Licencious.]
       { Without Law.]
Lawyer.
  Civil—RC. II. 2.
  Common—RC. II. 2. A.
Lawn.
  { Linnen fine (augm.]
  { Treey pasture.]
Lax.
  [Tied (dim.]
  [Loose]
Laxative, [adj. a. Dung (apt.]
Lazer, [adj. Leprosie (person.]
Lazerole. Tr. I. 3. A.
Lazy.
  op. to Stout. NP. IV. 6. O.
  [adj. Sloth]
Lazul stone. St. II. 3. A.
Leach.
  [Physitian]
Lead. Met. I. 5.
  Black—Met. III. 6.
  Red—
  White—[Ceruse] Met. IV. 6.
  —s of house, [Leaden roof
  —wort   of—]
Leade.
  Go before. TA. VI. 5.
  [Begin]
  [Direct]
  [Allure]
  -ing case, [Example] D. IV. 8.
         [Leade (corr.]
  -aside, { Err. (make.]
          { Seduce.]
  -life, { a. Conversation]
        { a. Life]
Leaf.
  —of Plant. PP. II. 5. A.
  —of Paper, [Lamin.]
  —of Fat, [Fat next the ribs.]
    [sp. of Hogs.]
  —of Gold, [Lamin—]
League.
  Confederacy. RC. III. 8.
  Measure. Mea. I. 8.
Leaguer, [Siege.]
Leak.
  [Into-receive water]
  spring a— [into-receive (inc.)
    water.]
Leam, [Lamin of flame.]
Leaning.
  Posture. AC. VI. 4. A.
  [Obliquing]
         ——toward, [Vergency]
Leanness. NP. V. 5. O.
Leap.
  —ing. AC. I. 5.
    [a. Coition]
  —year, [Year of 366 days.]
Learn, { a. Learner]
       { Know (inc.]

LE

—er. RO. III. 3. O.
—ing. Ha. VI. 5.
Lease.
  [Obligation of hire]
  [Pasture]
  to——
  let a— [Demise by Obligation of hire]
  Glean, [Gather the left ears.]
  Ly, [a. Man. IV. 1.
Leash.
  [Three]
  [Dog-couple]
  [Whip]
Least, [Most-little]
  at— { adv. Most-little]
       { Not less]
  —that. Conj. III. 1. O.
Leasure. TA. III. O.
  —ly, { Slow.]
        { adj. Degrees (segr.]
Leather. Pr. IV. 2.
Leave.
  [License]
  Take ones—[a. Valediction]
  to—
    { Not take. TA. I. 4. O.
    { Abandon
    [a. Residue]
    { a. Dereliction]
    { a. Desertion]
    { Give over]
    { Omit]
    { Desist]
Leaven, [adj. a. Ferment (thing)
  sp. of Bread.]
Leaver, [adj. Lifting (instr.]
Lechery, [adj. Lust (apt.]
Leccia Salviani.-Fi. IV. 1.
Lecture, { Read (thing)
         [adj. p. { Teacher]
Ledge, [Transverse protuberant (thing.]
Lee.
  [Sediment]
  [Cover'd from wind]
  Fall to Leeward. RN. VI 6. D.
Leech. Ex. I. 2.
  Vid. Leach.
Leek. HL. IV. 9. A.
  House—[Sedum]
Leer, [Look { obliquely]
             { deceitfully]
Leese, [Lose]
Leet, [Law-day]
Left.
  { pret.
  { adj. p. } Leave.
  [Residue] TM. VI. 7. O.
  Sinister. Sp. III. 9. O.
Leg, [Shank] PG. V. 5.
  —of Mutton, [Thigh of sheep.]
  to make a leg, [a. Congee.]
Legacy, [adj. p. Bequeathing (thing.]
Legal, [adj. Law]
Legate, [Public adj. p. send (person.]

· LE

Legend, [Fabulous Narration.]
Legerdemain, [adj. Prestigiator (thing.]
Legible, [adj. p. read (pot.]
Legion, [Regiment.]
Legislative, [adj. a. Law (make.]
Legitimate, { adj. Law.]
             { Genuine.]
  to——[Un- a Bastard.]
Legumen, [Pulse.]
Leman, [adj. Fornication (fem.]
Lemon. Tr. I. 8. A.
Lend. RC. V. 4.
Length. TM. II. 1.
  at— [After all this] Adv. III. 3. O.
Lengthen, { a. Length.]
          { Protract.]
Lenity, { Clemency.]
        { Meekness.]
Lenitive, { Un-- adj. Pain (apt]
          { adj. a. Indolence (apt.]
Lent.
  { pret.
  { adj. p. } Lend.]
  [adj. Fasting (time.]
Lentils. HS. II. 3. A.
Lentisk, [Mastic-tree]
Lentitude, [Excess of Meekness]
Man, I. 9, E.
Leo, [Fifth of the 12. parts of the Zodiac.]
Leopard. Be. IV. 2. A.
  —s bane. HF. III. 6.
Leper, [adj. Leprosie (person.]
Leprosie. S. II. 5.
Less, [More-little.]
Lessee, [adj. a. Hire (person.]
Lessen, [Diminish.]
Lesson, [adj. p. { Read
                 { Teacher]
Lessor, [adj. a. Demising (person.]
                              (thing.]
Let
  { Licence]
  { Permit]
  -alone, [Not hinder.]
  -bloud, { a. Bleeding.]
          { Cause
  -down, { Help. } to descend]
          { Suffer }
  -go. TA. I. 6. O.
  -in, { Suffer to { in- } go]
  -out, {   { out-}
  -pass, }
  -slip, } [Omit.]
  [Impediment.]
  [Demise.]
Lethargy. S. IV. 3.
Letter.
  [Element.] D. I. 1.
  [Epistle]
  [Bond]
  s patents, [Patent.]
Lettice. HF. III. 11.
  Lambs—
Level.
  { Lying]
  { Plain]
  { Equal]
  { Smooth]

[Plain-

LI

[Plainnefs-trying (inftr.]
Aim, { Towards } direct.]
{ Againft. }
op. to Degrees of perfons.
RC. I. O.
Leven, vid. *Leaven*.
Leveret, [Hare (young.)]
Leviathan, [Crocodile] Be. IV. 3.
Levy, [Gather.]
Levite. RE. II, 2, A.
Levity.
Tactil quality. Q. V. 4. D.
Inconftancy. Ha. IV, 9. D.
Vainnefs. Man. IV. 6. D,
Lewd.
[Evil (augm.)]
[Vicious (augm.)]
[Unchaft]
Lexicon, [Catalogue of interpreted words.]
Ly
[v. Situation]
—*near* } to, [v. Near.]
—*next* }
(v. Proftrate.) AC. VI. 7. A.
{ a. Gueft. } RO. III, 6. A.
{ a. Permanent. } Sp, I, 6.
—*down*. AC. VI. 7. A.
(Be all the
—*from home*, night
{ a Gueft
{ (from home.)
—*in child-* { Shut up }
bed, [Be { In bed } after
                    (parturition.)
—*in wait*, [a. Ambufh]
—*together*, [to-} a. Coition]
gether- a.} a. Bed]
—*under*, { Under-ly }
{ adj. p. Subject }
—*up*, [Rife]
—*with*, [With- { a. Coition. }
{ a. Bed. }
—*bedrid*, [Be un-adj. a. Rife
(pot.) by ficknefs.]
—*hid*, [adj. p. Conceal.]
—*open*, [adj. p. Opening.]
—*ftill*, [adj. Reft.]
[a. Lying] Man, IV. 1. O.
tell a— [a. Man. IV. 1. O.

a—
[a. Lying]
Ly [adj. a. Lixiviation [thing]
Lyingnefs. Man. IV. 1. O.
Liable, [adj. p. Object (pot.)]
Lib, [Un- a. Tefticle]
Libbard, [Leopard.]
Libel, [adj. Book (dim.)
fp. Backbiting.]
Libella worm. Ex. III. 5.
Liberal.
[adj. Free-man]
—*Science*, [Learning] Ha.
VI, 4.
[adj. Liberality]
Liberality. Man. III. 1.
Liberty. RC. IV. A.
—*of converfe*, [Franknefs]
—*of will*, AS. IV. 8.
at— { adj. Liberty }
{ Un- adj. p. { Slave.}
{ Impri-
fonment.]

LI

Libertin, [Not-cohibited adj.
Vice (perfon)]
Libidinous, [adj. a. Luft (apt.)]
Libra, [Seventh part of the Zodiac]
                    (Houfe.)
Library, [adj. Books { Room. }
                    (aggr.)
Libration. O. I. 2.
Lice, [pl. Lowfe]
—*bane*.
Licence. RC. IV. 8. A.
Licentioufnefs.
[Liberty, { exc. }
{ corr. }
[Not cohibited Vice (abftr.)]
Lick. Mo. III, 7.
—*ing fire*. El. I. 6. A.
Licorice. Sh. IV. 5.
wild—HS. III. 3.
Licourous, [Intemperate in banquetting]
Lid, [adj. Covering (inftr.)]
ey—[Covering (part) of the
Ey.]
Liege, [adj. Law]
—*lord*. [Proper King]
—*man*, [Proper Subject]
Lieger.
{ Refident }
{ Ordinary } Embaffadour]
Lieu, [Subftitute (abftr.)]
in—*of*. Prep. II. 1. A.
Lieutenant, [adj. { perfon }
Subftitute { Off. }
—*of a fhip*. RN. V. 1. A.
Life.
[Living-abftr.]
to the—[Living (like)]
Tree of—Sh. IV. 6. A..
—*everlafting*, [Gnaphalium]
—*time*. Mea. VI.
—*of Cicero*, [Narration of
&c.]
Of—*and death*, [adj. Capital]
[Vigour]
Lift.
Move upward. O I. 1.
[Exalt, { a. High. }
{ a. Higher. }
—*up ones voice*, [Exclaim.]
—*of a Ship*. RN. IV. 4. A.
Ligament. PG. II. 2.
Light.
Subft.
Primary—Q. I. 1. E.
Secondary—Q. I. 2.
[Brightnefs]
[adj. a. Light (inftr.)]
as Candle, &c.
to—*a fire*, { a. Fire (inc.)]
[adj. Lightnefs]
—*nefs*.
op. to Heavinefs. Q. V.
4. D.
—*headed*, [Vertiginous]
[Agility]
—*horfe*, [adj. Warhorfe.]

LI

[Serioufnefs. NP. IV.
3. O.
Conftancy. Ha. IV.
7. D.
op. to Gravity. Man. IV.
6. D.
Chaftity. Man. II.
7. D.
[Eafinefs]
—*of belief*, [Credulity]
[Frivoloufnefs]
[Remiffenefs]
make—*of*, [Contemn]
to—
{ Defcend }
as Bird { Settle on feet}
—*from horfe*, [Defcend—]
Happen [a. Event]
—*on*, [Happen to find]
Lighten.
[a. Light]
[Un- a. { Burden }
{ Pain }
[a. Lightning]
Lightening. El. I. 3.
Lighter, [Boat for burden (aug.)]
Lights, [Lungs] PG. VI. 2. A.
Lightfome, [adj. Light.]
Lignum Aloes.
Lignum Nephriticum, Tr.
VII. 4.
Lignum Rhodium.
Ligurinus. Bi. VI. 1.
Like.
[adj. Likenefs]
—*as*, [As]
—*wife*, [adv. Like]
[adj. Equality]
—*for*— { Compenfate }
I—*it*, { Approve }
{ [I { Love } it.]
{ Probable }
Likely, { True (like) }
Likenefs. TM. V. 1.
Liking.
{ Condition }
{ State }
{ Approbation}
{ Love }
Lilach. Sh. IV. 1.
Lilly. HL. IV. 2.
day—HL. V. 3.
water—HL. VI, 4.
—*of the valley*, HL. VII. 7. A.
Limb.
[Joint]
[Part]
Limbeck, [Veffel for hot diftilling.]
Limbernefs. Q. V. 6. E.
Limbus, [Margin]
Lime. El. IV. 5.
Bird—[Glue catch
to { entangle }
{ Birds. }
fp. Prepared juice of Mifleto]
—*hound*.
—*tree*. Tr. VI. 10.
Limit.
{ Sign }
[Finiting { Thing }
{ Place }
Kkk Side]

LI · LO · LO

{ Side]
{ Margin]
to—
[a. { Limitation]
     { Determination]
     { pohibit]
[Apoint precisely]
Limitation. D. IV. 2.
Limn, [Paint with Water-colours.]
Limon.
Limp, [Halt]
Limpet. Ex. VIII. 1.
Linage, [Descendents (aggr.] RO. I. 1. O.
Linchpin.
Linden tree.
Line.
  Dimension. Mag. I. 1.
  —of writing.
  the—[Equator] W. VI. 1.
  Measure. Mea. I. 1.
  [Thred]
  Fishing—[String of hairs for fishing]
  plumb—[String for measuring.]
  [Series]
  to—Pr. IV. 9. A.
  to—*one Fortification with another*, RM. VI. 4. A.
  —*a hedge with*, [Within garrison with Series of]
  [a. Coition] sp. of Dog.]
Lineal, [adj. Line.]
Lineament, [Figure]
Ling.
  Fish. Fi. III. 3.
  [Heath]
Linger, [Protract]
  [Delay]
Linguist, [adj. Language (artist.)]
Lingwort.
Link.
  [Candle of pitch'd Tow]
  [Loop]
  to—*toge* { Knit]
  ther { Joyn]
  [Sausage]
Linnen. Pr. IV. 4.
  —*draper*, [adj. Linnen (merc.)]
Linnet. Bi. IV. 8.
  Red—Bi. IV. 8. A.
Linseed, [Seed of Flax]
Linsey-woolsey.
  [Woven (thing) of Linnen and Woollen]
  [Mixture (corr.)]
Lint, [Down { Shaving } of (like) { Scraping } Linnen]
Lintel. Po. IV. 3. A.
Lion. Be. IV. 1.
  —*s tooth*, [Dandelion]
Lip. PG. III. 8.
Liquid, [adj. Moistness] Q. V. 2.
Liquid amber. Tr. VIII. 9.
Liquor, [adj. a. { Moistness (thing) { Wet]
Lisping. AC. III. 2. A.

List.
  [Catalogue]
  —*of cloth*, [Margin]
  the—*s*, [Combate (place as he—*eth*, [as he willeth]
Listen,
  [Hear (end]
  [Observe with Ear]
Listlesness. NP. I. 4. O.
Litany, [Brief vicissitudinary Prayers]
Literal, [adj. Letter]
Literature, [Learning] Ha. VI. 4.
Litharge. Met. IV. 1.
Litheness, [Limberness] Q. V. 6. E.
Lither.
  { Lazy]
  { Idle]
  { Slow]
Litigious, [adj. Contentious]
Litter.
  Birth [Children (aggr.) of one parturition.]
  Straw [Bed for Horse]
  horse—[Sedan to be carried between Horses]
Little. TM. I. 1. D.
  by—and—[adv. Degrees (dim.)]
  —*ones*, [Young children]
Liturgy, [Pub- { Manner } of lic { Form } Worship]
Live.
  Proper. AC. I. 7.
  [Be]
  —*in exile*[Be banisht]
  [Feed]
  —*upon*, [Feed upon]
  [a. Conversation]
Lively, { Sprightliness]
  [adj. { Vigour]
  —*hood*, { Maintenance]
Live-long.
  [Total]
  [Orpine]
Liver.
  [adj. Living (person)]
  Part. PG. V. 5.
  —*wort*. HL. I. 3. A.
  Noble—[Hepatica]
Livery.
  [adj. Service (sign) garment]
  [Delivering] TA. IV. 5. sp. of possession.]
  —*and seisin.* RC. V. 8. A.
  Horse at—[H. at hired guesting]
Living.
  Vid. *Live.*
  [Maintenance]
Lixiviation. O. VI. 8.
Lizard. Be. VI. 4.
Lo, [Imp. Look.]
Loach. Fi. IX. 11. A.
Loaf, [Bread]
Loath, [adj. Nolleity]
Loathe.
  op. to Appetite. NP. II. 4. O.

[Aversation] AS. V. 5. O.
[Being cloy'd] AS. V. 1. O.
Loathsom, [Loathed (apt.)]
Lob, [adj. Lumpish (person] sp. Great.]
Lobby, [Outer room (dim.)]
Lobe, [Protuberant (part]
Lobster. Ex. VI. 1.
Local, [adj. Place.]
Loch.
  Fish. Fi. IX. 11. A.
  [adj. p. Lick (apt.) Medicin]
Lock.
  [adj. Shutting (jug.)]
  —*on door*, &c. Po. IV. 4.
  —*on a River*, [Water-course-narrowing (jug.)]
  [Tuft]
  —*of Hair.*
  —*of Wool.*
Locker, [Chest]
Locomotion, [Motion from place to place.]
Locust. Ex. II. 1.
  —*tree.* Sh. IV. 6. A.
Lode.
  [Burden]
  to—O. VI. 7.
  [Leading]
  —*star*, { adj. Pole } Star.]
         { Directing }
  —*stone.* St. II. 7.
Lodge.
  [v. Night]
  [a. Rest]
  sp. by night]
  [a. Guest]
  a—[House (dim.)]
Loft, [Upper room]
Lofty.
  [High (augm.)]
  [Proud]
Log.
  { Thick wood]
  { Part of trunk]
  sp. for Fuel.]
  —*line*, [Way-measuring line]
  sp. of Mariners.]
Logarithm.
Loggerhead.
  [Great (corr.) head]
  [Dull (augm.)]
Logic, [adj. a. Reason (art.)]
  —*parts of Discourse.* D. IV.
  chop—[Dispute (corr.)]
Logistic, [adj. a. Computation (art.)]
Logwood. Tr. VII. 5. A.
Lohoch, [Medicament to be lick'd]
Loial. Man. V. 6.
Loin. PC. IV. 4.
Loiter.
  [a. Cunctation]
  [a. Slattering time]
Lolling, [a. Lean (corr.)]
Lome, [Mortar]
London tuft. HS. V. 4.
Lone, [Lending]
Lonesome, [Solitary]
Long.

LO — LO — MA

{ a. Length]
{ a. Duration]
—suffer-{ Meekness]
ing, { Patience]
—time, [Permanent (aug.)]
to—{ a. Desire } (augm.)
    { a. Appetite }
Long Oyster. Ex. VI. 1. A.
Longevi-{ Long life]
ty, { Permanence (aug.)]
Longitude.
[Length]
[Distance from first Merid.]
Looby, [Great (corr.) person]
Look.
[a. Ey]
Face, { State
       { Manner]
to—[a. Ey]
—about, [a. Heedfulness]
—for, [Expect]
—on, [a. Ey]
—to, { a. Heedfulness]
      { a. Observing]
Looking-glass, [Sight-reflecting (instr.)]
Loom, [adj. Weaving (jug.)]
Loop. Mag. V. 2. A.
—hole, [Chink]
Loose.
Not-fixt. Q. VI. 6. D.
[Not cohibited]
[Irregular]
[Remiss]
[Negligent]
[Careless]
[Vicious]
—in one's body. [Diarrhæa.] S. VI. 6.
to—
Unty. O. II. 1. O.
[Absolve] RE. V. 5. O.
Loosestrife.
codded—HS. IV. 3.
hooded—HF. VII. 14. A.
purple—HF. VII. 15. A.
yellow—HS. V. 12. A.
Looverhole, [Open place in the roof.]
Lop, { Off-cut branches]
     { Un-branch]
Loquacity. Man. VI. 5. D.
Lord.
[Baron] RC. I. 3.
[Master] RO. III. 7.
Lordan, [Lazy (person)]
Lordly.
[adj. Lord (like)]
{ Proud]
{ Magisterial]
Lordship.
[Lord (abstr.)]
Mannour. Po. I. 1. A.
Lose.
op. to gain. TA. V. 2. O.
op. to hold, [Let go]
op. to keep. TA. V. 5. O.
as Garrison. RM. II. 4. D.
Loft.
[adj. p. Lose]
[adj. p. Destruction]
Lot, [adj. a. Mo. V. 1. (thing)
to cast—s Mo. V. 1.

Lothe, vid. Loathe.
Lotion, [Washing]
Lattery.
Lotus. HS. III. 13.
Lovage. HF. IV. 4. A.
Loud, vid. Lowd.
Love.
Affection. AS. V. 3.
in—[adj. Love (augm.)]
make—[a. Suitour]
Apple of—
[Charity]
Lovely, [adj. p. Love (apt.)]
Lour. AC. IV. 2. O.
Lout, [adj. Rusticity (person)]
to—AC. IV. 2. O.
Low, [a. Cow (voice)]
Lowbell, { Extasie }
[Bell to { Hunt }
         { Birds]
Lowd, [adj. Sound (augm.)]
Lowe.
[adj. TM. II. 4. O.]
        { Inferiority]
[adj. { Meanness]
        { Under-part]
[adj. { Bottom]
—water, { Shallow w.]
         { Down-tide]
—sound, [Grave s.]
Lowermost, [Most-lowe]
Lowly, [Humble]
Lowre. AC. IV. 2. O.
Lowse. Ex. I. 8.
—wort.
Hog—[Sow]
Sea—Ex. II. 11.
Wall—[Punice]
Lowt, vid. Lout.
Lozange, [Quadrat whose opposite Angles are equal, but not right.]
Lozell, { [Great lumpish (person]
Lubber, {
Lubricity.
[Unctuousness]
Lucid, [adj. Light]
Luck. { Fortune]
      { Event]
sp. Prosperous.]
Good—[Prosperity]
Ill—[Adversity]
Lucre, [Gain]
Lucubration, [adj. { Study]
right   { Work]
Lug, [Ear (corr.) Sad-worm.]
to—[Pull]
Luggage.
[Burden.] Poss. V. O.
[Impediment] T. II. 5. O.
[Utensils (corr.)]
[Baggage] RM. V. O.
Lugubrious, [adj. Grief]
Lukewarm.
[Neither hot nor cold]
[Temperate]
Lull, [Allure to rest]
—asleep, [a. Sleep]
Lumber, vid. Luggage.
Luminary, [adj. a. Light (thing)]
Lump. TM. VI. 4.
—fish. Fi. II. 6. A.

Lumpish. NP. V. 8. O.
Lunar, [adj. Moon]
Lunatic, [Mad] sp. monthly]
Lunchion, [Fragment (augm.)]
Lungs. PG. VI. 2. A.
Lungwort.
Lupin. HS. III. 1. A.
Everlasting—
Lupus. Fi. IV. 3.
—marinus Schonfeldii. Fi. III. 16.
Lurch, [a. Theft]
—er, [Dog hunting lesser beasts by swiftness.]
Lure.
[adj Alluring (thing)]
[a. Exclaiming]
Lurk.
[Lie concealed]
[a. Ambush]
Luscious, [Sweet (exc.)]
Lust.
{ Appetite]
{ Desire]
sp. of Coition. AC. II. 5.
Lusty, [adj. Vigor.]
Luster, [Space of 5 years]
Lustration, [Un-prophane]
sp. by Sacrifice.]
Lustre, [Brightness]
Lute, [Music (instr.) of gutstrings to be struck with fingers.]
to—{ Shut
    { Joyn } by sodering]
Luxation, [a. Loose] Q. VI. 6. D.
Luxury. Man. III. 4. E.
Luxuriant, [adj. Excess]
Luxuriousness, [Riotousness.]
Man. III. 4. E.
Lynx, [Ounce] Be. IV. 3.
Lyra altera Rondeletii. Fi. IV. 5. A;
Lyric, [Verse for song.]

M

Macarone.
[Pudding (like) of Almonds, &c.]
[Confused Mixture]
Mace.
Staff, [Magistracy (sign) club.
Spice, [Husk of Nutmeg]
Reed—HL III. 15.
Maccapà, [Hyphen] D. I. 4. A.
Macerate.
{ Infuse]
{ Soke]
Pine. Man. II. 2. E.
Machin. Po. VI. 8.
Machinate.
[a. Machin]
{ Design]
{ Contrive]
Macilent, [Lean]
Mackerel. Fi. III. 5.

MA | MA | MA

Mad.
—*nefs.* S. IV. 1. A.
 [Frenzy] S. IV. 1.
 [Anger (augm.]
—*wort.* HS. VI. 2. A.
Madder. HL. IX. 8.
baſtard—HL. IX. 9.
Made.
 { pret. } {Make]
 { adj. p. }
—*by art,* [Factitious] T. III
 7. O.
Madrigal, [Song adj. Shepherd.]
Mænas. Fi. V. 12.
Magazine, [Ammunition { (Houſe) (Room)
Maggot. Ex. III. 1.
Bee—Ex. III. 2.
Waſp fly—Ex. III. 3. A.
Magic.
 [Science of obſcure Natural (things)]
 [Witchcraft]
Magiſterialneſs. Man. IV. 8. D.
Magiſtrate. RC. I. 1.
Magnanimity. Man. III. 8.
Magnet. St. II. 7.
Magnifie, { a. Greatneſs.]
 { a. Praiſe (augm.]
Magnificence, [Generoſity] Man. III. 4.
Magnitude. Mag.
Magpy. Bi. I. 8.
Mahometaniſm. RE. I. 5.
May.
 [Fifth Month.]
—*fly.* Ex. IV. 7. A.
—*weed.* HF. II. 8. A.
 [Have { Ability } { Liberty }
Maid.
 [Virgin]
 [Servant (fem.]
 Fiſh, [Ray] Fi. II. 9.
 Mer— [Man (like) Fiſh.]
—*en hair.*
 black—HL. I. 5. A.
 Engliſh black—HL. I. 7.
 white—HL. I. 5.
Majeſty, [King (abſtr.]
Majeſtic, [adj. King (like]
Mail, [Woven (like) armour]
Maim, [a. Mutilation]
Main.
 [Great]
—*land,* [Continent]
—*ſea,* [Ocean]
—*maſt.* RN. III. 5.
 [Principal]
—*battel,* [Middle b.]
—*chance,* { Stock }
 [Chief { Concernment]
 [Intenſe]
—*ſtrength,* [Strength (augm.]
Maintain.
Keep RO. VI. 4.
 [Defend] RO. VI. 5.
Juſtifie, [a. Advocate]
Major.
 [Greater]

[Un- adj. p. Pupil (apt.]
Serjeant— [adj. Regiment (Off.) that gives orders]
Major, [Chief Town (Off.]
Maix, [Indian Bread-corn] HL II. 2.
Make,
 the—[Figure]
 to—
 { a. Cauſe }
 { a. Efficient }
 { Create }
 { Change into }
 { Invent }
 { Feign }
 [Enrich]
 [Prepare]
—*a bed,* [Prepare a bed]
 [Eſteem]
—*account,* [Eſteem]
—*way,* [Prepare way]
—*much.*
 [Eſteem much].
 { Indulge }
 { Favour (ſign)
—*nothing of,* [Contemn]
 [Sell for]
—*money of,* [Sell for money.]
—*the moſt,* [Sell to the moſt-bidder.]
—*better,* { Better }
—*fire,* { Fire } (make]
—*good.*
 { Compenſate }
 { Repair }
 { Defend }
 { Hold out }
—*his ground.* RM. II. 2.
—*haſt,* [Diſpatch]
—*a league,* [League (make]
—*out,* [Plain (make]
—*ready,* { Prepare } { Clothe }
—*reckoning,* [Expect]
—*as if,* [Seem (make]
—*ſale,* [Tell]
—*ſhew,* [Seem (make]
—*ſhift,* [Obtain difficultly]
—*a ſtand,* [Stand]
—*a ſtir,* [Stir]
—*a verſe,* { a. Verſe } { Reconcile }
—*up,* [a. { Repair } { Perfect }
—*uſe of,* [Uſe]
Malady, [Diſeaſe]
Mal-adminiſtration. Man. VI. 5. O.
Malapert.
 [Ill-tutor'd]
 [Irreverent]
 [Bold (corr.]
Male.
—*ſex.* NP. VI. 2.
 [Riding-bag]
Coat of— [Woven (like) armour]
Malecontents, [Not-content]
Malediction, [Curſing.] AS. I. 3. O.
Malefactor.

[adj. a. pret. Evil (perſon.]
 [adj. Criminal (perſon]
Maleficence, [Miſchievouſneſs]
Malevolence, [Malignity] AS. V. 2. O.
Malice, { Malignity } { Hatred } {ſp. old]
Malign.
 [a. Malignity]
 [a. Envy]
Malignant fever. S. II. 3.
Malignity. AS. V. 2. O.
Mall, [Mallet (augm.]
—*to*— [Beat (augm.]
Mallard. [Duck (male]
Malleable, [adj. p. Knocking (pot.]
Mallet, [Wooden hammer]
—*Feigning.* Mag. VI. 4. A.
Mallow. HF. IX. 6.
Marſh—HF. IX. 7.
Shrub—Sh. V. 4.
Tree—HF. IX. 7. A.
Vervain—HF. IX. 8.
Malmſey, [Wine of Malvaſia]
Malt, [adj. p. pret. Fermenting Barley]
Mammock.
 [Lump]
 [Fragment]
Man.
 Kind. W. V. 5.
 Sex, [Man (male]
 [Servant (male]
 If a— [If any one]
 Cheſs— [adj. Cheſs (Inſtr.]
—*of war.* RN. I. 6.
Manacles, [Bonds for the hands.]
Manage, [a. { Buſineſs } { Uſing } { Governing }
Manchet, [Bread of Flowr.]
Manciple, [Buying (Off.) of Victual (things.]
Mandate, [Command ſp. Sent.]
Mandible, [Bone of the jaw.]
Mandilion, [Looſe upper veſt]
Mandrake. HS. IX. 4. A.
Mane. PP. VI. 4. A.
Maner, vid. *Manner.*
Manfull, { adj Manhood } { Stout }
Mange, [Itch]
Manger, [Horſes provender (veſs.]
Mangy, [adj. Itch]
Mangle.
 [Mutilate]
 [a. Fragment (ſegr.]
Manhood.
 [Valour]
 Age. Mez. VI. 3.
Many, [adj. Multitude]
Manifeſt. TA. I. 9.
Manifeſto, [Public Declaration]
Manifold, [adj. Multitude (kind]
Manly.
 [Man (like]
 [Stout]

[adj.

MA

[adj. Fortitude]
Manna, El. III. 6.
Manna fold in fhops, [Concrete Exudation from the wild Afh.]
Manner.
 [Mode,] T. V.
 In a — { Almoft / Thereabout }
 in fome — [adv. fome]
 of what — [What manner]
 [Quality]
 [State]
 [Cuftom]
Mannerly, [Civility]
 [adj. { Civility / Refpect }]
Manners.
 [Civility]
 [Refpect]
Mannifh,
 [Man (like)]
 [Familiar (apt.) with man]
Manfion.
 { Staying / Dwelling } (place)
 [Houfe]
Manflaughter, [Man-killing]
Mantel, [Beam of Chimney]
Mantle.
 [Garment to caft about one]
 [Upper loofe veft]
 to — [a. Froth]
Mantis. Ex. II. 1. A.
Manual.
 [adj. Hand]
 [Book (dim.]
Manucodiata. Py (kind)
Manuduction, [Leading]
Manufacture, [adj. p. Mechanic (thing)]
Manumife.
 [Un-villain]
 [Un-flave]
Manuring.
 [Agriculture] O. III.
 Soiling, O. iii. 3.
Manufcript, [Written Book]
Map, [Picture of Country]
Maple. Tr. VI. 6.
Mar, vid: *Marr.*
Marble. St. II. 1.
March.
 [Third Month]
 to — [Travel] fp. as Souldier.
 — *es,* [adj. Margin country]
Marchant, vid. *Merchant.*
Marchafite. St. I. 3. A.
Marchionefs, [Marquefs (fem.]
Marchpane, [adj. Pr. II. Bread]
Mare, [Horfe (fem.]
 Night — [Ephialtes] S. IV. 2. A.
Margin. Sp. III. 4. A.
Mary, vid: *Marry.*
Marigold. HF. II. 2.
 African — HF. II. 7.
 Corn — HF. II. 6.
 marfh — HL. VI. 4. A.
Marine, [adj. Sea]
Mariner.
 Navigator. RC. II. 8.

MA

 [Seaman] RN. V.
Marjoram. HF. VII. 4.
 Goates — HF. VI. 3. A.
 wild — HF. VII. 4. A.
Marifh. Po. I. 8. A.
Maritim, [adj. Sea]
Mark.
 [Sign]
 Brand, [Stigmatization (fign)]
 Boundary, [Margin (fign)]
 Goal, { adj. p. (place) / Object (thing) }
 Weight, [8 Ounces]
 Money, [13 s. — 4 d.]
 to —
 [a. Sign]
 [Stigmatize]
 [Obferve]
Market, [a. Merchant]
 — *place,* [adj. Merchant (place)]
Marl, [Chalky clay for manuring]
Marlin.
Marmalet. [adj. Pr. II. (thing) of boil'd Quince.]
Marmofit, [Monkey (dim.]
Marmotto. Be, III. 4. A.
Marquefs.
 [adj. Limit (Off.]
 [Next the higheft Noble. man.]
Marring. TM. I. 9. D.
Marry. RE. IV. 6.
 — *ed.* RO. II. 4.
Marrow. PG. I. 8. A.
Mars. W. II. 5.
Marfhal.
 Prevoft — RC. I. 6. A.
 to — [a. Order]
Mart, [Convention for Merchandife]
 Letters of — [Licence of naval predation]
Martagon. HL. IV. 2. A.
Martern, [Fur of Marten]
Martial, [adj. War. RM.]
Martin. Be. IV. 6.
 Bi. V. 2.
 fand — Bi. V. 3. A.
Martingal, [Horfe (arm.) down-holding head]
Martlet, [Swift] Bi. V. 1. A.
Martyr. RE. III. 4.
Martyrology, [Hiftory of Martyrs.]
Marvel, vid. *Mervail.*
Mafcarade, [Antick dance of difguifed (perfons]
Mafculine, [adj. Male]
Mafh, [Mixture]
 fp. of moift confiftence]
 fp. made by Maftication.]
Mafk, [Dance of difguifed (perfons.]
 — *for face,* [adj. Conceal veft for face]
Mafon, { Stone / Wall } (mech.]
 [adj.]
Mafs.

MA

 { Great / Total } [Body]
 [Lump]
 [Eucharift]
Maffacre, { Promifcuous / General } killing]
Maffy,
 [adj. Mafs]
 [Weighty] Q. V. 4.
 [adj. Maflinefs]
 — *nefs.* Mag. VI. 1. D.
Maft.
 Fruit. PP. III. 4.
 — *of fhip.* RN. III. 2.
 Fore — RN. III. 4. A.
 Main — RN. III. 5.
 Middle — RN. III. 5. A.
 Top —
Mafter.
 [adj. { Authority / Power } (perfon)]
 — *of fervant.* RO. III. 7.
 — *of family.* RO. III. 5.
 — *of a fhip.* RN. V. 4.
 — [Teacher] RO. III. 3.
 — *of art,* [Graduate in the arts]
 [Chief]
 — *beam,* { Principal } b.
 — *piece,* { Principal } p.
 to —
 [Get the power over]
 [Conquer]
 [Cohibit]
 [Govern]
Mafter- { Difobedience }
lefs, { Licencious }
Mafterly, [Magifterial]
Mafterwort. HF. IV. 5. A.
Maftic, [Gum of the Maftic-tree]
 — *tree.* Tr. III. 8.
Maftication. Mo. III. 5.
Maftive, [Dog kept for watch]
Mat, [Woven Rufhes (thing) of { Straw]
 — *weed.* HL III. 4.
Match.
 [Equal]
 [Companion]
 [Contract]
 [Paction]
 [Marriage]
 [adj. p. Brimftone (inftr.) for a. fire.]
 — *for Gun.* RM. V. 7.
Mate.
 [Companion]
 [Married]
 [Conqueft]
Material.
 [adj. Matter]
 [Pertinent]
 [Important]
Maternal, [adj. Mother]
Mathematic, [Quantity (Science)]
Matriculate,
 [a. Catalogue]
 [Admit into Univerfity]
Matrimony, [Marriage] RE. IV. 6.
Matrix,

ME

Matrix, [Womb] PG. VI. 9.
Matron.
  { Married } (fem.)
  { Grave }
  [Houſholder (fem.)]
Matter.
  Material cauſe. T. II. 7.
  { Subject }
  { Object }
  { Thing }
  { Buſineſs }
  makes no—[Is not important]
  [Bloud rotted in the fleſh]
Mattins, [Morning worſhip]
Mattock, [adj. Mallet (fig.) pecking (inſtr.)]
Mattreſs, [Bed ſtiffen'd with ſowing (augm.)]
Maturity, { Ripeneſs }
  { Perfection }
Maugre.
  [In enmity of]
  [adv. Coaction]
Mavis, [Thruſh] Bi. III. 3. A.
Maukin.
  [adj. Man (like) engine]
  [Oven-ſweeping (inſtr.)]
Maul, vid. *Mall.*
Maund, [Basket]
Maunder, [Grudging (voice)]
Maw, [Stomach] PG. VI. 4.
Maxim, [Rule]
Maze.
  [Extaſie]
  { Structure } full of { Windings }
  { Place } perplex { Turnings }
Mazer, [Cup (augm.)]
Me, [I accuſat.]
Mead.
  [Medow]
  [Wine of honey]
Meagre, [Lean]
Meal.
  [Ground corn]
  Eating. Pr. I. 1.
  —worm. Ex. I. 5. A.
Mean.
  [adj. Mediocrity]
  [Low] adj. Ha. II. 5, O,
  Plebeian, [adj. People (kinde)]
  a—
  [Mediator]
  [Between—ſpace]
  —among ſounds. Q. III. 1.
  —s. T. II. 6. A.
  [Riches]
  —ing.
  Signification. D. II. A.
  [Purpoſe]
Meaſure.
  Proper. Mea.
  —of Magnitude. Mea. I.
  —of Number. Mea. II.
  —of Gravity. Mea. III.
  —of Valour. Mea. IV.
  —of Time. Mea. V.
  [Moderation]
Meaſh, [Hole.]

ME

Meat.
  [Suſtentation]
  [p. Eating (thing)]
  Sweet—s Pr. II.
  White—s [Meats of milk]
Meazles. S. II. 4. A.
Mechanic.
  —work. O. I.
  —profeſſion. RC. II. 5. A.
Mechoacan.
Medal.
  [Ancient money]
  [Money (like)]
Meddle.
  [Mingle]
  { Action }
  { Buſineſs }
  [a. Diligence (corr.)]
  —with, [a. Object.]
Mediaſtine. PG. V. 3. A.
Mediateneſs. TM. IV. 2. O.
Mediator. RJ. I. 2. A.
Medicine, [adj. a. Medicating (thing)]
Mediocrity. TM. I. 2.
Meditate. AS. II. 1. A.
Medle, vid. *Meddle.*
Medley, [Mixture]
Medler. Tr. I. 5.
Medow. Po. I. 4. A.
  —sweet. HF. IV. 8. A.
Mee, [I accuſat.]
Meed, { Earning }
  { Reward }
Meekneſs. Man. I. 9.
Meer.
  [Simple]
  [Lake (augm.)]
  [Limit (ſign)]
Meet.
  [Congruous]
  [Expedient]
  to—
  Come together. TA. VI. 7.
  [a. Convention]
  —with, [Compenſate.]
Meeter. D. III. 5.
Megrim.
Melancholy.
  Humour. PG. I. 7. A.
  [Grief] ſp. (Habit)
Melampus, Fi. V. 5.
Meldew, [Honey-dew]
Melilot. HS. III. 10.
Melliſluum, [Sweet]
Mellow, [Ripe (augm.)]
Melody, [Harmony]
Melon. HS. VII. 1. A.
Melt, [Diſſolve] O. VI. 2.
Member.
  [Limb]
  [Part]
Membrane. PG. II. 3. A.
Memorable, [adj. p. Memory (apt.)]
Memorandum, [adj. p. ought memory (thing)]
Memory. NP. II. 3.
Memorial, [adj. a. Memory (ſign)]
Menace, [Threaten.]
Mend.

ME

  [Repair]
  [Better] TM. I. 9. E.
Mendacity, [Lyingneſs]
Mendicant, [Begging]
Menial, [Domestic]
Menſtruum. PG. I. 4. A.
Ment, vid. *Mint.*
Mental, [adj. Mind]
Mention.
  [of-ſpeaking]
  [a. Expreſs]
Mercenary, [adj. p. Hire (perſon,)]
Mercer, [adj. Silk Pr. IV. 3. (merc.)]
Merchandiſe, [adj. p. Merchant (thing)]
Merchant.
  Profeſſion. RC. II. 5.
  —ſhip. RN. I. 5.
Mercy. Man. I. 5.
Mercury.
  Planet. W. II. 6.
  Metall. Met. III. 1.
  Herb. HF. I. 6.
  childing—HF. I. 6. A.
  Dogs—HF. I. 7.
  Engliſh—HF. I. 8.
Mercurial.
  [adj. Mercury]
  { Nimble }
  { Sprightly }
Meridian. W. VI. 4.
Meridional, [adj. South]
Merit.
  [Earning]
  [Worthy (thing)]
Merlin, [Hawk for Finches]
Mermaid.
  Mermaid's head. Ex. VIII. 2. A.
Merry, { Mirth }
  { Urbanity }
Mervail, [a. Admiration]
  —of Peru. HS. VII. 8.
Merula.
  —montana. Bi. III. 7. A.
  —ſaxatilis. Bi. III. 4.
  —torquata. Bi. III. 7.
Mes, vid. *Meſs.*
Meſentery. PG. VI. 6.
Meſh, [Hole]
Meſlin, [Mingled corn]
Meſs, [Proportioned part]
  [p. of Meat.]
Meſſage, [Word ſent]
Meſſenger, { (perſon)
  { Sent (Off.)
Meſſias, [Anointed (perſon)]
Meſſuage.
  [Houſe]
  [Farm]
Metall. Met.
  Natural—Met. I.
  Factitious—Met. II.
  Imperfect—Met. III.
Metamorphoſis, [Altering] ſp. of kinde]
Metaphor.
Metaphyſic, [Science of Tranſcendents.]
Mete, [Meaſure]

Metemp-

MI MI MI

Metempsychosis.
Meteor. El. A.
Metheglin, [Wine of honey]
Method, [Order]
Metonymy.
Metrical, [adj. Meeter.]
Metropolitan.
   [adj. Principal]
   [Primate]
Mew. Bi. IX. 9.
Mezereon. Sh. II. 10.
My.
Mich.
   [a. Absent]
   [a. Conceal]
   [a. Penuriousness]
Microcosm, [World (dim.)]
Microscope, [Glass for seeing little (things)]
Mid, [Middle]
Middle. Sp. III. 3.
Mid if. PG. VI. 3.
Midwife, { Parturition [Off.]
          [mech.]
Might, { Strength
        Power }
     (Mod. Cond.)
—*y,* [adj. { Strength
           Power } (aug.)
Milch, [adj. a. Milk]
Mildness.
   { Gentleness
     Meekness
     Graciousness
     Clemency }
   [Not-austereness]
Mile. Mea. I. 7.
Military { Relation. RM.
   Persons { Segregate. RM. III.
           Aggregate. RM. IV.
   Action. RM. I.
   Events. RM. II.
   Ammunition. RM. V.
   Places. RM. VI.
Militia. [RM. (thing)]
Milk. PG. I. 3. A.
  —*wort.* HS. III. 11.
Mill. Po. VI. 9.
Millefoil. HF. II. 12.
  water—HF. V. 13.
  horned—HL. IX. 7. A.
Millers-thumb. Fi. IX. 12.
Millet. HL. II. 6. A.
  Indian—HL. II. 6.
Million, [1000000]
Milt, [Spleen] PP. IV. 5. A.
  —*wort,* [Spleenwort] HL. 17. A.
  Sperme of male fishes. PP. IV. 8.
Milter, [Fish (male)]
Mimic.
   [adj. Player]
   [adj. a. imitate]
   sp. with gesture (corr.)
Mince. Pr. III. 6. A.
  —*ing* { Wanton } (dim.)
  gate { Conceited } gesture (mode)
Mind.

   [Soul] W. I. 6.
   Rational—NP. I.
   [Understanding]
    [Thought] sp. (freq.)
    [Opinion]
    [Observing]
    (a. Heedfulness)
   cast in one's—[Consider]
   [Will]
    [Inclination]
    [Velleity]
    [Purpose]
   fully—*ed,* [adj. pret. Resolution]
   high—*ed,* [Proud]
   ill—{ Ill-purposing]
   ed, { adj. Malignity]
   well—*ed,* [Well affectioned]
   set one's—[a. Purpose]
   Sensitive internal.
   [Fancy]
   [Memory]
   call to—[a. Memory]
   put in—[a. Memory (make)]
   [Appetite]
   [Desire]
   have a—*to,* [a. Desire,]
Mindfull, [adj. Memory]
Mine.
   [adj. *I*]
   [Metal (place)]
   [Face (manner)]
   to—RM. I. 5.
Mineral. W. V. 1.
Minew, vid. Minnow.
Mingle, [a. Mixture]
Minion.
   [Love (augm.)]
   [Ordnance (kind)]
Minister.
   [Servant]
   [Clergyman]
   [Presbyter]
   to—
   [Serve]
   [a. Adjuvant]
   [Give to]
Miniver, [Fur of { Squirrels } belonging to { Weasels } flies.
Minks, [adj. Conceitedness (fem)]
Minnow. Fi. IX. 13.
Minority, { Pupillary
          [Age { Not-virile]
Minster, { College
      [Monks } House]
Minstrel, [adj. Music (mech.)]
Mint.
   Herb. HF. VII. 1.
   Cat—HF. VII. 1. A.
   [Place of a. Money (mech.)]
   to—
   [a. Money (make)]
   [a. Fiction]
Minute.
   [Small (dim.)]
   —*of time.* Mea. V. 8. A.
Miracle.
Mire, [Dirt]
   Quag—[Bog]
Mirobalan. Tr. II. 5.
Mirrour.

   [Looking-glass]
   [adj. Excelling (thing)]
Mirth. AS. V. 4.
Mis, vid. Miss.
Misadventure.
   [Fortune (corr.)]
   [Adversity]
Misapply, [Apply (corr.)]
Misbecome, [Indecent]
Misbegot, [Begot not in marriage]
Misbehave, [Demeanor (corr.)]
Misbelief, [Belief (corr.)]
Miscall, [Name (corr.)]
Miscarry. TA. III. 7.
  —*with child,* [a. Abortion]
Miscellany, [adj. Mixture]
Mischance,
   { Event (corr.)
     adj. Adversity (thing)
   [Abortion]
Mischief.
   [a. Mischievousness]
   [Hurt]
Mischievousness. Man. I. 4. D.
Misconstrue.
   [Understand (corr.)]
   [Interpret (corr.)]
Miscreant.
   [Believer (corr.)]
   [Heretic]
   [Unholy (person)]
Misdeed, [Ill deed]
Misdemeanour, [Demeanour (corr.)]
Misdoing, [Action (corr.)]
Misdoubt.
   [Suspect]
   [Distrust]
Miser, [Penurious (person)]
Misery. Ha. I. 1. O.
Misfortune.
   [Fortune (corr.)]
   [a. Adversity]
Misgive, [Doubt (make)]
Misgovern, [Govern (corr.)]
Mishap.
   [Fortune (corr.)]
   [a. Adversity]
Misinter- { Understand
  pret. { Interpret } (corr.)
Mislead.
   [Lead (corr.)]
   [Seduce]
Mislike, [Disapprove]
Misname, { wrong
        [Name (corr.)
Misplace, { wrong
        [Place (corr.)
Misprision, [Suspition]
Misreckon, [Reckon (corr.)]
Miss.
   [Err]
   [Omit]
   [Want]
   [Discover want]
Missal, [Mass-book]
Misshapen.
   [Figur'd (corr.)]
   [Deformed]
Mission, [Sending]
Missive, [Sent (thing)]

Misspend,

MO | MO | MO

Mispend, [Spend (corr.)]
Miss. El. III. 2. A.
Mistake.
 { Wrong }
 { Errour }
 [Opinion (corr.)]
Mistle-thrush. Bi. III. 3.
Mistleto. Sh. III. 12. A.
Mistress.
 [Master (fem.)]
 [Suitor'd (fem.)]
Mistrust.
 [Doubt]
 [Distrust]
 [Suspition]
Misuse, [Use (corr.)]
Mite.
 Insect. Ex. II. 7.
 Money.
Miter, [adj. Bishop (sign) head vest.]
Mitigate.
 [Diminish]
 [a. Remiss]
 [Un-anger]
Mittens, [Woollen hand (vest)]
Mix, [a. Mixture]
Mixen.
 [Dunghill]
 [Heap of Dung]
Mixture. T. III. 8. O.
Mixen-mast. RN. III. 3. A.
Mizzle. El. VI. 2.
Mobility.
 [Motion (abstr.)]
 [Unconstancy]
Mock.
 Scoff. RJ. IV. 9. A.
 [Deceive]
Mode of thing. T. VI.
Model.
 [Description by lines]
 [Example (dim.)]
 [Epitome]
Moderation.
 [Mediocrity]
 —in opinions, Ha. III. 4.
 —in recreations, Man. II. 5.
 { Govern }
 { Cohibit }
Moderator, [Judge]
Modern, [New]
Modesty.
 —about disgraces. Man. III. 7.
 —about honours. Man. III. 9.
Modicum, [Little]
Modulation, [Warbling]
Moil.
 [Operation (augm.)]
 [a. Defilement]
Moistness. Q. V. 3.
Moity, [Half]
Mold, vid. *Mould.*
Mole.
 [Bank factitious]
 [Spot]
 Beast. Be. III. 8.
 Fish. Fi. II. 6.
Molest, [Troubling] TA. V. 9. O.
 Indian Molle. Tr. III. 10. A.
Mollifie, [a. Soft]

Molten { Melted }
         { Cast }
Moly. HL. IV. II. A.
Moment.
 —of time, [Instant]
 [Importance]
Monarch, [Sole King]
Monastery, { College }
             { Monk's House }
Monastical, [adj. Monk]
Mone, { (sign) }
        { (voice) }
 [Grief]
Money. Mea. IV. A.
 —wort. HL. VI. 11. A.
Moneth. Mea. V. 4.
Mongrel.
 [Of mingled extraction]
 [Spurious]
Monition [Warning]
Monk. RE. II. 7.
Monky. Be. IV. 4. A.
Monoceros Clusii. Fi. IV. 10. A.
Mono- { Privilege of sole }
poly { Appropria-ted } (selling)
Monosyllable, [Of one syllable]
Monster, [Beside-natural (thing)]
Month. Mea. V. 4.
Monument.
 [adj. a. Memory (sign)]
 [Tomb]
Mood.
 [Manner] T. VI.
 [Disposition]
Moon.
 Planet. W. II. 8.
 New—[—Beginning her monethly course]
 appearing—[—(like) Meteor.]
 —wort. HL. I. 9.
 Half— Fortification. RM. VI. 5.
Moor.
 Man, [Tawny man].
 Land. To. I. 9.
 —hen. Bi. VIII. 9.
 to—a ship.
Moot, [Discourse on Law-case.]
Moral, [adj. Manners]
 —Philosophy, [Ph. concerning manners.]
 a—[Signification belonging to manners]
Moralize, [Apply to manners]
More.
 [Superiour]
 Adv. II. 2.
 —over, [Also]
Morfew, [Disease of Scurf on the skin]
Morgage. RC. VI. 7.
Mormylus. Fi. V. 3. A.
Morning. Mea. V. 7.
Moroseness. Man. IV. 7. D.
Morris, [a. Moor's dance]
Morrow.
 [Day { Next after }
       { following }]
 Good——[adj. Morning salutation.]

Morse. Be. V. 3.
Morsel, [Fragment] sp. off-bitten.
Mortal.
 [adj. Dying (pot.)]
 [adj. a. Dying (apt.)]
 [Capital]
 —ity.
 [Dying { (pot.) }
         { (apt.) }]
 [Killing infection]
Mortar.
 For building. El. IV. 4. A.
 [adj. Contusion (vess.)]
Mortifie.
 [a. Death]
 [a. Repentance]
Mortise, [Hole in beam.] sp. in side of it.
Mortmain.
Mortuary, [Payment for the dead.]
Mosaic work.
Mosque, [Temple] sp. of Mahometans.
Moss. HL. I. 3.
Most.
 Adv. II. 2. A.
 for the—part, [adv. Most]
 [Chiefly]
Mote.
 [Ditch (augm.)]
 Atom, [Powder (dim.)]
Moth, { Ex. II. 8. }
        { Ex. IV. 9. A. }
 —mullein. HS. VIII. 4. A.
Mother.
 [Parent (fem.)]
 —tongue, [Language of one's own nation]
 —of pearl. Ex. VIII. 3.
 [Womb] PG. VI. 9.
 [Disease] S. VI. 7.
 —wort. HF. VII. 13.
 [Sediment]
Motion.
 [Locomotion] Mo.
 —of Animals Progressive. No. I.
 —of the parts of Animals. Mo. III.
 *Violent—*Mo. VI.
 [Inclination] AS. IV. 1.
Motive.
 [adj. Move (apt.)]
 [Impulsive]
Motley, [Variegated]
Motto, [Appropriated sentence] D. III. 1. A.
Move.
 [a. Motion]
 —the brows. AC. IV. 1. A.
 the head. AC. IV. 4. A.
 [Offer] TA. IV. 2.
 [a. Impulsive]
 [Perswade]
 [Allure]
 [Angry (make)]
Moveable, [adj. p. Mo- { (pot.) }
                          { (apt.) }]
 —s, [Utensils]
Mould.
 [Earth]

MU · MU · MY

[Earth]
Type} sp. convex}
Casting (vess.} of melted
Figuring (vess.} bodies}
— of the head, [Dent of the upper part of the head]
to — {a. Knead
     {a. Type}
Moulder.
[p. Powder by putrefaction]
— away, [Decay]
Mouldiness. HL. I. 1. A.
[Mustiness]
[Down (like) rottenness]
Moulter, [Un-feathered (make)]
Mound.
[Sepiment]
[Bank]
[Rampire]
Mount.
[Mountain]
[Factitious hill]
to — [Ascend]
— a horse, [Ascend upon a horse]
ill — } _ed {Riding (perf.)
well — }   {on horse (corr.)
— a cannon, [Lift a cannon to his carriage]
Mountain. W. III. 1. E.
Mountebank.
{Wandring } Physician}
{Juggling }
Mourn.
[Shew grief]
[Grief (sign) sp. with (voice)]
in— ing, [adj. p. Vest adv. grief (sign)]
Mouse. Be. III. 7. A.
Dor— [adj. a. sleep (apt.) Mouse (kind)]
Field — [Long snouted venomous mouse (kind)]
Flitter — [Bat]
— ear. HF. III. 13. A.
— tail. HL. III. 16.
codded — HS. IV. 12. A.
Mouth.
Proper. PG. III. 3.
— full, [adj. Mouth capacity]
foul —'d.
[Speaking (apt) indecent (things)]
[Reviling (apt.)]
mealy —'d, [not- adj. reproof (apt.)]
Orifice [Mouth (like)]
[Entry]
to — [a. Reviling]
Mouthy, [adj. Reviling (apt.)]
Mow.
[Heap] sp. of Corn.]
[Mock (sp. with face (manner)]
Mowe, [Reap]
Mue.
[a. Imprisonment]
— feathers, [Let go f.]
Much.
{Great
{Many}
as — [Equal]
for so — as Conj. IV. 1.
make — of, [a. Courtesie

(augm.)
too — [Excessive]
very — [Abundant]
[Transc. {augm.
         {intent.}
Mucilaginous, [Slimy]
Muck.
Mucus.
{Dung
{Snivel}
[Excrement]
Mucketer, [adj. Wiping (thing)]
Mud, [Macerated durt]
Muff, [Tube for warming the hands]
Muffle, [Conceal (vest) sp. face]
Muffler, [Mouth (vest)]
Mufty, [Mahometan chief Primate]
Mug, [Pot for drink]
Mugwort. HF. II. 11. A.
Mulberry. Tr. III. 1.
Mule. Be. I. 2. A.
— fearne. HL. I. 8.
Muletier, [adj. Mule (Off.)]
Mullein. HS. VIII. 4.
moth — HS. VIII. 4. A.
Sage — Sh. VI. 4. A.
Muller. Fi. IV. 6.
English — Fi. IV. 3. A.
Lesser — Fi. IV. 6. A.
Mult. RJ. VI. 7.
Multifarious, [Many (kind)]
Multifidous beasts.
— of the biggest sort. Be. III.
— of the middle sort. Be. IV.
— of the least sort. Be V.
Multiply.
{a. Many
{Increase}
[a. Multiplier]
Multiplicity, [Variety]
Multiplier. TM. VI. 8.
Multitude. TM. III. 1.
Mum.
[Beer in which husks of Walnuts are infused]
[st] Inter]. III. 1. O.
— ing, [Dance {Silents
         of {Disguised}]
Mumble.
[Mastication (corr.)]
{Voice
{Speak} confusedly}
Mummy, [Gum (like) embalmed flesh (sp. of Man)]
Mump, [Move (corr.) the mouth]
Mumps, [Disease swelling of the chaps]
Munday, [Second day of the week]
Mundane, [adj. World]
Municipal, {City
              {adj. Corporation}
Munificence, [Liberality] sp. in gifts]
Muniment, [Deed] RJ. VI. 5.
Munition.
[Fortification]
[Ammunition]
Muræna. Fi. VI. 1. .
Mural, [adj. Wall]

Murder. RJ. III. 4.
Murex. Ex. VII. 2.
            {Grudging
Murmur, {Discontent } sp.
            {Indignation} (voice)
Murr, [Disease of hoarseness through cold distillation]
Murrain, {Disease infecti-
             {Plague (ous } of
Murry, {Dark red} (beasts)
           {Rust colour}
Murrion, [Head (armour.)]
Murther. RJ. III. 5.
Muscle. PG. II. 6. A.
Fish. Ex. VIII. 7. A.
Musculous, [adj. Muscle]
Muse.
[a. Verse (art.)]
[Feign'd Goddess of verse (art)]
[Hole through hedge]
to — [Meditate]
Mushrom. HL. I. 1.
Music.
Sound. Mo. V. 7. A. [Harmony]
Art. Mo. V. 7. A. (art.)
Musk, [Sweet (thing) of Muskcat]
— cat. Herb.
Muskadell.
Musket.
Hawk, [Sparhawk (male)]
Gun, [Footman's gun (augm.)]
Mussle, vid. **Muscle.**
Must.
Mood of Necessity
[Determination] AS. IV. 8.
[Necessity] T. V. 7.
[Wine not yet fermented]
Mustaches, [Upper beard]
Mustard.
Common. HS. IV. 9.
[Sauce of Mustard]
Tower — HS. IV. 12.
Yellow Arabian — HS. IV. 13. A.
Muster.
[adj. a. Number]
[Catalogue] adj. a. TN. III. 7. O.
Mustiness. Q. IV. 7.
Mutable.
[adj. Alter (apt)]
[Light] Ha. IV. 7. D.
Muteness. AC. III. 1. O.
Muting, [Dunging]
Mutilous, NP. V. 1. O.
Mutiny, [Sedition]
              {indistinctly
Mutter, [Speak{confusedly
              {grudgingly}
Mutton, [Flesh of sheep]
Mutual, [Reciprocal]
Muzzle.
[Bonds of mouth]
[a. Silence (make)]
Myriad, [10000]
Myrrh. Tr. VIII. 1.
Myrtle. Sh. III. 11.
— Symach. Sh. III. 11. A.
Mystery.
{Obscure
{Concealed} (thing)
[Trade]
Mythology, [Interpretation of feigned Narrations.]

N.

N *Adir*, [Under- adj. Horizon pole]
Nag, [Gelded horse (dim.)]
Nay, [Not]
— *say* — [Deny]
Nail.
— *of Animal.* PP. VI. 5. A.
{ Iron } pin to be driven in
{ Brass } by knocking
Naked, { Not- } { clothed }
{ Un- } { covered }
Name.
Word. T. l. 4.
— *ly*, Conj. IV. 3.
— *nick*— [Name (corr.)]
[Reputation]
Nap.
[Tufted superficies]
[Sleep (fit)]
Nape, [Hinder part of the neck]
Naphew. HS. IV. 4. A.
Naphtha. St. V. 5. A.
Napkin, [Linen for wiping]
Nappy.
Narcissus, [Daffadil] HL. IV. 4.
Narcotic.
[adj. a. Sleep]
[adj. A. Stupor]
Nard.
Narration. D. V. 3.
Narrow.
op. to Ample, [adj.Sp.II.5.O.]
op. to Broad, [adj.TM.II.2.O]
— *ly*, [adv. Heedfulness]
Nastiness, [Slovenliness (augm.)]
Nation. RC. III. 1.
Native, [adj. Birth]
Nativity.
[Birth]
[Birth (time)]
Natural.
[adj. T. III. 7.]
— *ly*, [adv. Spontaneity]
— *power.* NP.
— *fool*, [adj. Idiot (person)]
Naturalist, [adj. Nature (artist)]
Naturalize, [a. Nation]
Nature.
[Natural (abstr.)]
Law of — RC. IV. 1.
[Temper { Mind }]
[of { Body }]
[Disposition]
Naval, [adj. Ship.]
Nave.
— *of a Church*, [Greatest Temple (room)]
— *of cart, &c.* Po. V. 7.
Navel. PG. IV. 6. A.
— *wort.* HL. VIII. 6.
Sea— HL I. 11. A.
Navew. HS. IV. 4. A.
Naught.
[Nothing]

come to— [Be annihilated]
set at— [Contemn]
[Evil]
— *for*, [Hurtful to.]
Navy.
[Ships (aggr.)]
[Army of ships]
Navigation, [Sailing]
Nauseate, [a. AS. V. 1. O.
Nauseousness, [Lothing] NP. II. 4. O.
Nautic, [adj. Ship.]
Nautilus. Ex. VII. 1.
Neap-tide, [Shallowest tide]
Neast, vid. *Nest.*
Neat.
Beast. Be. II. 1.
[adj. Neatness]
— *ness.*
[Pureness]
[Cleanliness]
[Decentness (augm)]
[Ornateness]
Neb, [Tooth] Mag. IV. 2.
Nebulous, [adj. Mist.]
Necessary, [adj. Necessity]
Necessity.
Proper. T. V. 7.
[Want]
[Poverty]
[Determination]
Necessitous, [Needy.]
Neck. PG. IV. 1.
— *of land*, [Isthmus]
Necromancy, [Witchcraft by the dead]
Nectar, [Drink of the feigned Gods]
Nectarine. Tr. II. 1. A.
Neece, [Nephew (fem.)]
Need, [Want] sp. of necessaries]
— *must — s*, [Must (augm.)]
Needfulness.
[Necessity]
[Expedience]
Needles, [Poverty]
Needle, [Sowing pin]
— *fish.* Fi. III. 13. (p.Magnet)
Marine's — [adj. iron pin. adj.
Shepherds — [Venus combe] HF. I. 5. A.
Needless, [Abundant]
Neer.
{ adj. } { neerness]
{ adv. }
well — [Almost]
[Beside]
— *ness.*
Nighness. Sp. II. 3.
[Frugality]
[Penuriousness]
Neeze, [Sneez]
Neezing-wort, [White Hellebore] HL. VII. 1.
Nefarious, [Vicious (augm.)]
Negation. D. VI. 2. O.
{ Negligence }
Neglect, [a. { Omission }
{ Contemning }]
Negligence. Ha. IV. 5. D.
Negotiate.
[a. Business]

[a. Commerce]
Negro, [Black man]
Neigh, [a. Horse (voice)]
Neighbour. RO. IV. 3.
[Neer] sp. dwelling]
Neither.
[None of the two]
[Nor]
Neophyte, [New Disciple]
Neoteric, New [adj. Sp. I. 3. O.
Nep, [Cat-mint]
Nephew. RO. I. 3. O.
Nerites. Ex. VII. 4. A.
Nerve. PG. II. 5.
Nest, { Room } sp. of bird]
{ Bed }
Nestling, [Bird (young) taken out of the nest]
Net, [Squares(plain) of the thred] sp. for hunting]
Nether.
[More-low]
[Inferiour]
— *most*, [Most low]
Nettle. HF. I. 14.
dead — [Archangel] HF. VII. 11.
— *tree*, [Lotus] Tr. III. 4.
Sea — Ex. IX. 6. A.
Never. Sp. I. 9. O.
— *so much*, [How much soever]
— *the less.* Conj. II. 2. O.
Neuter, [Of no Faction],
Neutrality.
[Slightness] Ha. III. 4. E.
[Being of no Faction]
New. Sp. I. 3.
— *of the Moon*, [Beginning of Moon's monethly course]
— *s*, [New Narration]
Newt, [Lizard] Be. VI. 5.
Next.
[Most near]
[Preceding]
[Following]
[Immediate]
Nibble, [Gnaw (dim.)]
Niceness.
op. to Hardiness. NP. IV. 7. O.
Over-cleanliness. Man, II. 6. E.
Niche, [Dent]
Nick, [Notch]
— *name*, [Name (corr.) sp. adj. Contempt]
in the — [In the instant of time (perf.)]
to —
Niess, [Hawk]
Nigella. HS. V. 13. A.
Niggard, [Penurious (person]
Nigh, [Near]
Night. Mea. V. 6. O.
— *crow.*
— *mare*, [Ephialtes]
— *shade.* HS. IX. 4.
Enchant— *ress* — HF. VIII. 3. A.
Nightingale. Bi. V. 3.
Nightly, [adj. Night (segr.)]
Nilling.

NP.

NO

NP. I. 4. O.
AS. IV. O.
Nim, [a. Theft (dim.)]
Nimbleness, [Agility] NP. V. 8.
Nimis, [Excess]
Nine. Mea. II. 9.
—*ty*,
—*hundred*, &c.
Ninny, [Fool]
Nip.
 [Pinch between the tops of the fingers]
 [Bite (dim.)]
 [Mock (dim.)]
Nipple, [Protuberance (dim.) of Dug.]
—*wort*, HF. III. 14. A.
Nit, [Egg of Louse]
Nitre. St. V. 1. A.
No.
 [None]
 [adj. Nothing]
 [Not any]
—*body*, [No man]
—*where*, [Sp. II. 8. O.]
 [Not]
Nobility, [Lord (abstr.)]
Noble, adj. Lord. RC. I. 3.
 Money [6 s. — 8 d.]
Nocent, { Guilty
          { Hurtful }
Nock, [Notch]
Nocturnal, [adj. Night]
Nod, [Move the head] AC. IV. 4. A.
Noddy, [Fool]
Noddle, [Hinder part of the head]
Node.
 [Protuberance]
 [Tumour]
Noggin, [Pot (augm.) for drink.]
Noise.
 [Sound (augm.)]
 [Rumour (augm.)]
Noisom.
 [Hurtful]
 [adj. Molesting (apt.)]
Nolleity. AS. IV. 2. O.
Nomenclator.
 [Teacher of Names]
 [Dictionary]
Nominate.
 [a. Name]
 [Appoint]
Nonage, [Pupillary age]
Nonce, [Purpose]
None, [adj. Nothing]
Nones, [Days of the moneth next after the first]
Nonplus, [Posing] D. VI. 8.
Non-resident, [Not dwelling]
Nonsuch, [Campion]
Nonsuited, [adj. p. Desist plain-tiffing]
Nook, [Angle]
Noon, [Mid-day]
Noose, [Loop (sp. of snare)]
Nope, [Bulfinch] Bi. IV. 5.
Nor, Conj. I. 4. O.
North. Sp. II. 2.
Nose. PG. III. 3. A.

NU

Nosegay, [Flowers (aggr.)]
Nostril, [Hole of the nose]
Not. Adv. I. 1. O.
—*withstanding*. Conj. II. 2. O.
—*if*—[Unless]
—*to*—
—*Sheep*.
Notable.
 [Extraordinary]
 [Excellent]
Notary. R]. I. 5.
Notation, [Derivation of word.]
Notch. Mag. IV. 2. O.
Note.
 [Sign]
 [Character]
 [Comment (dim.)]
 Tone. Q. III. 5.
 [Extraordinariness]
—*of*—[Extraordinary]
—*to*—[Observe]
Nothing. T. I. 1. O.
Notice.
 { Knowledge
 { Warning }
give — { Known (make)
        { Warn }
take — { Observe
        { Shew to know }
Notifie, { Known (make)
          { Warn }
Notion. T. I. 3.
Notorious.
 [Extraordinary]
 [Manifest]
 [Publicly known]
Novacula. Fi. III. 15. A.
Nevel, [New]
—*a*—[New narration]
Novelty, [Newness]
November, [Eleventh moneth]
Nought, vid. *Naught*.
Novice.
 [New Disciple]
 [Not-expert]
Noun.
 [Name]
 [Integral]
Nourish.
 [Nutrition] AC. I. 6.
 [Feeding]
Now, [At this time]
—*a days*, [In these times]
—*and then*, [At some times]
Noxious, [Hurtful]
Nuisance, [Hurtful (thing)]
Nullity, [Frustration]
Number. Mea. II. A.
Numerous, [adj. Multitude]
Numness.
 Impotence. NP. III. 5. O.
 Disease. S. IV. 6. A.
Nun, [Monke (fem.)]
 Bird, [Titmouse]
Nunchion, [Refection in the afternoon]
Nuncupative, [Spoken]
Nuptial, [adj. Marriage]
Nurse, RO. III. 2. (fem.)
—*child*. RO. III. 2. O.
Nursery.
 [Children (aggr.)]

OB

 [Young trees (aggr.)]
Nusance, [Hurtful (thing)]
Nut.
 Fruit. PP. III. 3.
 Bladder—Tr. IV. 5.
 Chest—Tr. IV. 4.
 earth—HF. V. 10.
 Pistic—[Pistach] Tr. IV. 2.
 Hazle—} Tr. IV. 3. A.
 Small— }
 Wall—Tr. IV. 1.
—*cracker*, [Nut-breaking (jug.)]
—*of a bow*, [Retaining (jug.) of the string.]
—*of the thigh*, [Fat Glandule of the—]
Nut-hatch. Bi. I. 9. A.
Nutmeg, [Fruit of the Nutmeg-tree.]
—*tree*. Tr. IV. 6. A.
Nutriment, [adj. Nourishing (thing.)]
Nutrition. AC. I. 6.
Nymph, [Feign'd } Woods.]
         Goddess of } Rivers, &c.]

O

OAr.
—*of ship*. RN. III. 3.
—*of metal*, [Crude m.]
Oath. RC. VI. 4.
Oats. HL II. 4.
Obdurate.
 [Hard]
 [Impenitent]
Obedience. Man. V. 9.
Obey, [a. Obedience]
Obelisk, [Round Pyramid]
Object. T. VI. 2.
Objection. D. VI. 5.
Obit, [Funeral solemnity]
Oblation. RE. VI. 2.
Obligation. RC. VI. 5.
 Written. RC. VI. 5.
Oblique. Ma. II. 8.
Obliterate, [Un-write]
Oblivion, [Forgetfulness]
Oblong, [More long than broad]
Obloquy, [Reproch]
Obnoxious, [adj. p. Object (apt.)]
Obnubilate.
 [a. Cloud]
 [Darken]
Obscene, [Unchast]
Obscure.
 [Dark]
 op. to Plain. D. III. 9.
 Plebeian, [adj. People(kind)]
Obsecration, [Intreating (augm.)]
Obsequies, [Solemnity of burial.]
Obsequious, [adj. Obedience (augm.)]
Observe.
 Mark. AS. III. 1. A.
 [Perform]
 [a. Respect]

Lll 2   *Obser-*

OB

Observant.
 [adj. Respect]
 [adj. Obedience]
Obsolete, [Unaccustom'd]
Obstacle, [adj. Impedient (thing]
Obstetrication, [Assisting Parturition]
Obstinate.
 Patience (exc.) Man. I. 8. E.
 Constancy (exc.) Ha. IV. 7. E.
Obstruction.
 [Hindering]
 [Stopping up]
 Disease. S. I. 4.
Obtain. TA. V. 1.
Obtestation, [Entreating (augm.]
Obtrude, [thrust]
 [On― part]
Obtuse, [Blunt]
 ―angle. Mag. III. 3. E.
Obvious. Sp. II. 6.
Obumbration, [Shadowing]
Occasion. T. II. 4. A.
Occidental, [adj. West]
Occult, [adj. p. Conceal]
Occupation.
 [Business]
 [Profession]
Occupy.
 [a. Business]
 [a. Possession]
Occur.
 [p. Event]
 [Meet]
Ocean. W. IV. 2.
Ockam, [Tow for calking of Ships.]
Octave, [Eighth day after]
Octavo, [Third figure of books]
October, [Tenth moneth]
Ocular, [adj. Ey] PG. III. 2.
Odd ends, [Residue]
Odds, [Superiority
 {Enemies]
 at―{a. Contention]
Ode, [Song]
Odious.
 op. to Evenness. TM. III. 5. O.
 [Extraordinariness]
Odor, [Smell]
Odoriferous, [Sweet]
Ods, vid. *Odds.*
Oeconomic. RO.
Oecumenical.
 [adj. World]
 [Universal]
Of.
 Genitive. Prep. I. 1.
 [By.] Prep. I. 2.
 [Concerning] Prep. I. 3. A.
 out―Prep. I. 3.
 South―[S. from]
Of.
 [Distant]
 Prep. III. 2. A.
 Cut―{from.{a.}
 Drive―{ d.}

OL

Offal, [Worst part] TM. VI. 1. O.
 sp. adj. Residue.
Offend.
 {Displease]
 {Hurt]
 [Sin]
 ―in fighting. RM. I, 1.
Offensive.
 [Displeasing]
 [Hurtful]
Offer.
 ―to do. TA. III. 3. A.
 ―to give. TA. IV. 2.
 [Bid]
 [Give to God
 {a. Oblation
 {a. Sacrifice
 {a. Incense]
Offertory, [a. Oblation]
Office.
 Trust. RC. IV. 6. A.
 [Employment] TA. III.
 good―[Benefit]
 house of―[adj. {house
 Dunging { room]
Officer, [adj. Office (person]
 Ecclesiastical―RE. II.
Official, [Ecclesiastical Judge]
Officious. Man. IV. 2. E.
 [adj. Complaisance]
Offspring, [Descendents (aggr.] RO. I. 1. O.
Often, [adv. Frequent]
Oh, Interj.
Oil Pr. I. 6.
 ―box of a Bird. PP. V. 8. A.
 ―of corn, [Beard―]
Oilet, [Hole] sp. for Button]
Ointment.
 [adj. Anointing (thing]
 [Salve]
Oister. Ex. VIII. 4.
 ―weed. HL. I. 13. A.
Okam, [Tow for calking of Ships]
Oke. Tr. V. 1.
 bitter―Tr. V. I. A.
 holme―Tr. V. 2.
 Holy―HF. IX. 6. A.
 Scarlet―[Holm]
 ―fearn. HL. I, 4. A.
 ―of Cappadocia. HF. I. 13. A.
 ―of Jerusalem. HF. I. 13.
Oker.
 Yellow―St. VI. 2.
 Red―St. VI. 2. A.
Old.
 [adj. Age]
 how―[of what age]
 ―age. Mea. VI. 4.
 [Decrepit] adj. Mea. VI. 4. A.
 op. to New. Sp. I. 3. A.
 ―clothes, [Decayed c.]
 ―fashion, [Unaccustom'd f.]
 ―souldier, [Experienc'd s.]
 ―time, [T. past (augm.]
Oleander. Sh. VI. 1.
Olibanum, [Frankincense] Tr. VIII. 5.

OP

Oligarchy, [Government by a Faction]
Olive. Tr. II. 4.
Ominous, [Before-signing]
Omitting. TA. III. 8. A.
Omnipotency, [All-mightiness]
Omnipresence, [adv. Ubiquity presence]
Omniscient. [All-knowing]
On.
 ―the contrary, [adv. contrary]
 ―fire, [adj. p. Fire]
 [Toward {left } hand,
 ―the {right }
 [Towards―]
 {Concerning]
 {In] [In
 agree―[Agree{Concerning]
 [Forward]
 come―[Proceed]
 fight―[Prosecute fighting.]
 hold―[Prosecute]
 set―{a. Assault
 {To] {a. Impulsive]
 happen―[H. to.]
 [Upon] Prep. VI. 1.
Once.
 [One (time]
 [In past time]
 all at―[Together. all]
One.
 Proper. Mea. II. 1.
 ―by―[adv. Segregateness]
 ―another, [adv. Reciprocation]
 ―for another, [Compensation]
 ―with another, {Mixture
 [adv. {Confusedness]
 [Any] Pron. III. 1.
 some―Pron. II. 3 A.
 certain―Pron. II. 3.
 [Onely] RO. IV. 2. O.
 [The same]
 all―{Equal]
 {Alike]
 One blade. HL. VII. 5.
Onely. Adv. IV. 1. O.
 [Alone] RO. IV. 2. O.
Onerate, [Lode] O. VI. 7.
Onion. HL. IV. 9.
Onset, [Assault]
Onslaught. [Storming]
Onyx. St. II. 4.
Opacity. Q. I. 4. O.
Opal-stone. St. III. 1.
Open.
 ―ing.
 {Unshut. O. II. 2. O.
 {Uncover. O. II. 3. O.
 {Unfold, [Spread]
 {Un- adj. p. Seal (make]
 {Un adj. p. Impedient (make]
 {Un- adj. p. Obstruction (make]
 {Un-conceal {Reveal]
 {Manifest]
 {Un-adj. Publicness (make.]
 Un-

OR — OR — OV

Un-obscure, [a. Plain]
Un-implicit, [a. Express]
[adj. p. Opening]
—*air*, [Clear air]
—*handed*, [Liberal]
—*hearted*,
Frank, [adj. Man. IV.4.]
In excess, [adj. Min. IV. 4. E]
—*house*, [Hospitality for all comers.]
—*war*, [Manifested war]
—*weather*, { cloudy | W. not { frosty }
Operation.
Mechanic. O. I.
in General. O. II.
in Agriculture. O. III.
in Fabrile. O. IV.
in Sartorian. O. V.
in Chymic. O. VI.
in Pharmaceutic. O. VI. A.
[a. Efficient]
Ophidion Plinii. Fi. VI. 4. A.
Opiniastre.
[Conceited]
{ Wilful }
{ Obstinate }
Opinion. AS. II. 6. O.
Opium, [Soporative juice of Poppy]
Opopanax, [Gummy juice of the root of Hercules Allheel]
Oppilation, [Obstruction] S. I. 5.
Opponent, [adj. Opposition (person)]
Opportunity.
{ Time (perf.) }
{ Occasion (time) }
{ adj. Congruity (time) }
Oppose, [a. Opposition]
Opposition. T. VI. 8. O.
—*of proposition*. D. VI. 4.
in—[distant ½ of a great Circle]
Oppression. RJ. IV. 5.
Opprobry, [Reproch]
Oppugn, [Oppose]
Optic.
[adj. Seeing]
[Seeing (art)]
Optimacy, [Government by the chief (persons)]
Option.
{ Choice }
{ Wish }
Opulent.
{ Rich }
{ Abundant }
Or, Conj. II. 3.
—*elses*, [adv. Other]
Oracle, [adj. p. Speaking revelation]
Orage. HF. I. 9.
Oral, [adj. Mouth]
Orange. Tr. I. 7. A.
Oration. D. V. 2.
Orator, { Oration } [adj. { Entreaty } (person)]
Oratory.
[Oration (art.)]

[Prayer (place)]
Orb.
[Sphere]
—*Imaginary*. W. VI. A.
Orbicular, [adj. Sphere]
Orbis.
—*Echinatus*. Fi. VIII. 2. A.
—*birsutus*. Fi. VIII. 1. A.
—*maricatus*. Fi. VIII. 2.
—*scutatus*. Fi. VIII. 1.
Orchard. Po. I. 3. A.
Orchis. HL. IV. 8.
Ordain.
[Appoint]
{ a. Ordinance }
{ a. Ordination }
Order. TM. V. 2.
Method. TM. V. 2.
[Government]
[Decree]
—*ly*,
[adj. Order (perf.)]
[adj. Manners Homiletic]
[adj. a. Subjection]
Orders.
[plur. Order]
[adj. Ordination (thing)]
Ordinance.
[Decree]
[Law]
[Edict]
[Institution] RE. VI.
Cannon, &c. RM. V. 6. A.
Ordinary.
Usual. TM. V. 3.
Between course and fine. Q. VI. 3.
[Bishop]
Ordination. RE. V. 2.
Ordure.
[Dung]
[Filth]
Ore, [Metal not yet prepared]
O're, [Over]
Organ, [Instrument] Musical.
Organy, [Wild Marjoram] HF. VII. 4. A.
Oriens.
[East]
[Bright]
Orifice, { Hole } { Mouth (like) }
Origany. HF. VII. 4. A.
Original.
{ Primitive }
{ First }
{ Beginning }
{ Rise }
—*copy*, [Exemplar]
Orizon, [Prayer]
Ornament, [adj. a. Ornateness (thing)]
Ornateness. TM. V. 6.
Orphan, [Un-parented]
Orpiment. St. VI. 4.
Orpin. HL. VIII. 2.
Orrage. HF. I 9.
Ort, [Fragment adj. Residue]
Orthodox. RE. III. 1.
Orthography, [a. Letter (perf.)]
Orthopnoea. S. V. 2. A.

Oscitation.
{ Yawning }
{ Carelesness }
Osmund.
Ospry, [Bone-breaking Eagle]
Ostentation.
[Over-saying]
[Glorying]
Ostler, [Common horse (Off.)]
Ostrich. Bi. II. 9.
Otes. HL. II. 4.
Othe. RC. VI. 4.
Other.
{ adj. Diversity }
{ Pron. II. 2. O. }
—*wise*, [adv. Other]
—*whiles*, [In some (times)
—*where*, [In other (places)
every,—[Every second]
the—[The rest]
Otter. Be. IV. 8. A.
Oval. Mag. VI. 6.
Ouch, [Ornament of gemms]
Oven, [adj. a. Baking (place)]
Over.
[adj. Superiority]
[adj. { Power } { Authority }]
[adj. { Abundance } { Excess }]
—*bold*, [B. (Exc.)]
—*much*, [Excess]
{ adv. Vantage }
{ Besides }
—*and above*.
more—[Also]
[Above] Prep. V. 1.
—*thwart*. Prep. III. 5.
[Throughout] Prep. IV. 3.
—*again*, [Through it again]
all—[Through all]
all is—[All is past]
give—[Desist]
read—
[Beyond] Prep. VI. 2. A.
—*against*. Prep. VI. 3. O.
Overawe.
[a. Fear (make)]
[Coaction by fear]
Overbear.
[a. Submit (make)]
[a. Magisterialness]
Overbid, { More then }
{ Bid { (exc.) }
Overbold, [Bold (exc.)]
Overburden, [Burden (exc.)]
Overbuy, [Buy dear (exc.)]
Overcast, { Cover } { shadow }
Overcatch.
Overcharge, [Burden (exc.)]
Overcome, [a. Victory]
Overfill, [Fill (exc.)]
Overflow.
[Over-flow]
[v. Abundance]
Overglut, [Glut (exc.)]
Overgone, [pret. Gone (exc.)]
Overgrow.
[Grow { more than, &c. } { (exc.) }]
[Cover by growing]

Over-

OV   OU   PA

Overhasty, [Hasty (exc.]
Overbear, { adv. Concealed hear }
Overheavy, [Heavy (exc.]
Overlay.
  [Cover (exc.]
  [Kill by covering]
Overly, { Slightness }
  { adv. Sloth }
Overload, [Load (exc.]
Overlong, [Long (exc.]
Overlook.
  { a. By another's doing
    Observe the { doing
      thing   { done }
  [Look too high]
  [adv. Omitting]
Overmaster, [a. Victory]
Overmatch, [a. Superiour]
Overmeasure, [Excess]
Overmuch, [Excess]
Overpass.
  [Omit]
  [Excel]
Overplus.
  [Redundant (thing)]
  [Vantage]
  [Residue]
Overrate, [Tax more than proportion]
Overreach, { Overtake } { a. Fraud }
Overreckon, [Reckon (exc.]
Overripe. NP. VI. 4. E.
Overrule.
  [v. Superiour] RO. III.
  { Yield (make } sp. by Authority }
  [Overcome]
Overrun.
  [Fill (exc.]
  [Cover with multitude]
Oversaying. Man. IV. 1. E.
Oversee, [a. Oversight]
Overshadow, [Cover with shadow]
Overshoot, { shoot }
  [Beyond { go }
  —*himself*, [a. Excess]
Oversight.
  [Office.] sp. of observing what others do in their offices]
  [Errour]
Overskip.
  { Omit
  { Lose } sp. by neglect.]
Overslip.
  { Omit
  { Neglect
  { Forget }
Overspread, [Over-spread]
Overt, [Manifest]
Overtake. TA. VI. 6. A.
  —*n with wine*, [p. Drunkenness—]
Overthrow, { a. Transverse { (make }
  { a. Victory }
  to receive an— RM. II. 1. D.
Overthwart, { Transverse } { Prep. III. 3. }

Overtoil, [Toil (exc.]
Overture, { adj. p. Offer }
  { sp. Proposition }
Overturn, [a. Transverse]
Overvalue, [Value (exc.]
Overween, [a. Arrogance]
Overweigh, [Weigh more than]
Overweight, [More than weight]
Overwhelm, [Cover (augm.]
Ought.
  { v. Dueness }
  { Mood of duty }
  [Any thing]
Ounce.
  Weight. Mea. III. 4.
  Beast. Be. IV. 3.
Our, [adj. plur. Pron. I. 1.]
Out.
  Material. Prep. I. 3.
  Local.
  Of Motion. Prep. IV. 2.
  get— [Obtain]
    { sp. to be without }
  scrape—
  Of Rest. Prep. IV. 2. A.
  all is—
  { Past
  { Finisht
  { Spent
  { Extinct
  { Discovered
  { Public }
  the secret is—
  he is— [He erreth]
  they are— [They are enemies]
  —*of date*, { custom'd }
    { Un- { auxoritied }
  —*of doors*, [Without d.]
  —*of doubt*, [Without d.]
  —*of fashion*, [Un-custom'd]
  —*of frame*, [Confused]
  —*of hand*, adv. Sudden
  —*of heart*, [Discouraged]
  —*of joynt*, [Un-joynted]
  —*of kinde*, [Degenerous]
  —*of order*, [Confused]
  —*of patience*, [Vn-patienced]
  —*of sight*, [Not-visible]
  —*of use*, [Not-used]
  —*of wits*, [Mad]
  —*upon*. { 1. O.
    Int. II. { 3. O.
Outcast.
  [Rejected]
  [Banished]
Outcry, [Exclamation]
Outgo.
  { Go { faster
    { beyond }
  { v. Superiority }
Outlandish, [adj. Foreiner]
Outlaw'd.
  { Un-adj. Suit- (pot.]
  { Proscribed }
Outlet, [Out-ition (place)]
Outlive, { longer than
  { Live } after }
Outmost, [Most adj. outside]
Outpass, [a. Superiority]
Outrage, [Injury (augm.]
Outragious, [adj. Excess (augm.]

  { sp. in Anger }
Outside. Sp. III. 6. O.
Outstand, [a. Duration after]
Outstrip, [Run faster than]
Outward, [adj. Outside]
Outwork.
  [adj. Outside. RM. VI.]
  [Rampier] RM. VI. 3.
Owe.
  as Debt, [a. Debtor]
  as Duty, [a. Dueness]
Owl. Horned. Bi. I. 4.
  Not Horned. Bi. I. 4. A.
Own.
  my— [adj. I, adj. I.]
  one's——*man*, { Rational (perf.) }
  —*er*, { adj. Propriety (person.)
  to— { Appropriate
    { Claim }
Owze. W. III. 7. A.
Owzle, [Black bird]
Ox, Bull. Be. II. 1. [untestisled]
Oxey.
  Herb. HF. II. 6. A.
  Bird. [Woodpecker (kind)] Bi. I. 9. A.
Ozier, [Sallow] Tr. VI. 9. A.

P.

PAce.
  [Mode of going] Mo. II.
  [Step]
  [Five foot]
  [Degree of swiftness]
  [Measure in dancing]
  —*ing*, [Ambling] Mo. II. 2.
Pacifie, { a. Peaceable { (make }
  { Un-anger }
Pack, Aggregate. TM. III. 8.
  sp. together tied]
  —*horse*, [H. for carriage of pack]
  —*saddle*, [S. for carriage of pack]
  —*thred*, [Course thred for tying]
  to— { a. Aggregate by together tying }
    { Heap and bind }
  —*away*, [Depart with one's goods]
  —*cards*, [Order C. fraudulently]
  —*Jury*, [Chuse partially a Jury]
  to let—*ing*, [Depart (make)]
Packet, [Aggregate (dim.)]
  sp. together tied]
  —*boat*. RN. I. 8.
Passion. RC. VI. A.
Pad.
  [Saddle (dim.)]
  —*nag*, [adj. p. Riding (apt.)] horse]
  —*lock*, [adj. p. Hanging (apt.)]

Paddle

PA | PA | PA

Paddle, [Spade (like) staff]
—*to*— [a. Hand (freq.) sp. in water.]
Paddock.
  [Frog]
  [Park (dim.)]
Pædobaptism, [Baptism of Infants.]
Paganellus. Fi. III. 7. A.
Paganism. RE. I. 2.
Page.
  [Servant for waiting]
  —*of pa-* { Side } of paper, { Area } per
Pageant, [Arch for sights]
Pagrus. Fi. V. 4.
Pay, [adj. a. Paying (thing)]
  —*master*, [adj. Paying (Off.)]
  put out of—
  Souldiers—[S. hire]
  —*ing.* TA. IV. 8.
  [Compensating]
Paigle. HS. VIII. 1. A.
Pail, [Tub (dim) with handle]
Pain.
  [a. Punishment]
  op. to Ease. NP. V. 3. O.
  [a. Torture] RJ. VI. 1.
  [Aking, &c.] AC. II. 7.
  op. to Pleasure, [a. Unpleasantness.]
  [Grief]
—*s*, { a. Operation }
     { a. Diligence }
—*fulness*, { Pain } (apt.)
           { a. Pains }
Painim, [adj. Paganism (person.]
Painting. O. IV. 8.
Pair.
  [Equal]
  [Companion]
  [Two]
  [Aggregate (thing)]
  —*of bellows*, [B.]
  —*of cards* [Suit of c.]
Palace. Po. II. 2.
Palate.
  Roof. PG. III. 5.
  [Taste]
Palatine, [adj. Palace]
Pale.
  —*ness.* AC. IV. 9. A.
  a—[Lamin] sp. of wood]
Pales, [Sepiment of Lamins erect.]
Palinody, [Recanting] D. VI. 9. A.
Palisado. RM. VI. 7.
Pall.
Pallet, [Bed (dim.) to be laid on the floor.]
Palliate, { Seem (make) }
           { Cover (corr.) }
Palm.
  —*of hand*, [Concave (part)]
  Tree, [Date]
  dwarfe—Sh. III. 2.
  [Catkin] PP. II. 1. A.
Palmer.
  [Pilgrim]
  —*worm*, [Caterpillar]

Palmetto royal [Cabbidg tree] Tr. VII. 7.
Palmistry, [Wizarding by inspection of the hand.]
Palpable.
  [adj. p. Feeling (apt.)]
  [Manifest (augm.)]
Palpitation. S. V. 4.
Palsy. S. IV. 6.
Palter, { Sloth }
         { a. Lightness }
Paltry, [Sorry]
Pamper, [a. Fat (augm.)]
Pamphlet, [Sorry book (dim.)]
Pan, [Shallow wide (vess.) sp. earthen]
  Brain—[Concave bone covering the brain]
  Knee—[Convex bone covering the knee]
  Warming- [adj. Warming (vess.)]
  Frying-[adj. Frying (vess.)]
  —*cake*, [Fry'd Pudding (Lamin.)]
Panade, [Broth of boil'd bread]
Panage, [Feeding for hogs under the deciduous trees.]
Panch.
  { Stomach }
  { Belly }
  [Earthen Tray]
Pander, [adj. Fornication (merc.)]
Pandiculation. Mo. III. 6. A.
Pane, [Lamin]
Panegyric, [adj. a. Praise oration]
Panel.
  [Lamin (dim.)]
  [Catalogue of names]
  [Saddle for burdens]
  —*of Hawk*, [Belly—]
Pang, [Impetus] sp. pain (imp.)
Panic.
  [Corn] HL. II. 5.
  —*grass.* HL. III. 1. A.
  —*fear*, [Causeless universal f.]
Panier, [Basket] sp. for carriage on horse.]
Pannage, [Tax on cloth]
Pannicle, [Membrane]
Pannier, vid. *Panier.*
Pansy. HL. VI. 5. A.
Pant. S. V. 1.
Panther, [Pard] Be. IV. 2. A.
Pantler, [adj. Bread (Off.)]
Pantofle, [Loose foot (vest)]
Pantry, { Bread }
         { adj. Victual } (room)
Pap.
  [Water adj. p. consistence with bread.]
  —*of an apple*, [adj. p. consistence pulp—]
  [Dug]
Papal, [adj. Pope]
Paper.
  Reed.
  Factitious. Pr. VI. 7.
Papilionaceous fly. Ex. IV. 6. A.

Papist, [Of the Pope's faction]
Parable, [Tralatitious Narration]
Parabola. Mag. III. 8.
Parade, [a. Preparation]
Paradise, [Pleasure (place)]
  Bird of—
  Fools—[De-{ Hope }]
           { ceiving } { Delight }
Paradox, [Against common opinion]
Paragon, [Excellent]
Paragraph, [Section]
Parallax, [Difference between the true place and the seeming.]
Parallel. Mag. II. 7.
Parallels. W. VI. 7.
Parallelogram, [Quadrangle, whose opposite sides are parallels]
Paralogism, [Syllogism (corr.)]
Paralytic, [adj. Palsy] S. IV. 6.
Paramour, { Suitor }
            { Lover } sp. (corr.)
Paramount, [adv. Chief adj. right]
Parapet. RM. VI. 9.
Paraphrase. D. V. 1. A.
Paraqueto. Bi. I. 7. A.
Paraselene. El. V. 3. A.
Parasite, [Flatterer] sp. for victuals.
Parathesis. D. I. 7. A.
Parboil, [Boil (dim.)]
Parbreak, [Vomit]
Parcel, { Part }
         { Aggregate (dim.) }
  —*to*— [a. Segregate]
Parch, [Dry (exc.) with hearing.]
Parchment, [Paper of skin]
Parcimony, [Frugality]
Parcity, [Sparingness]
Pard. Be. IV. 2. A.
Pardon. RE. II. 9.
  —*fault.*
  [Absolution]
  —*debt.* TA. IV. 9. A.
Pare, [From-{ Superficies }
             { cut } { Extremity }]
Parelius. El. V. 3.
Parenchyma, [Flesh] PG. II. 6.
Parent. RO. I. 2.
  —*age*, [Parent (kind)]
Parenthesis. D. I. 7.
Parget, [Plastering]
Parish. RC. III. 4. A.
Parity.
  [Equalness]
  [Evenness]
  Levelling. RC. I. O.
Park. Po. I. 5. A.
  —*leaves*, [Tutsan] HS. V. 8.
Parlament, [National Council]
Parly, { Confer }
        { Treat }
Parlour, [adj. Discourse (room)]
Parching. RN. VI. 1. A.
Parochial, [adj. Parish]
Parole, { Word }
         { Promise }

Paroxysm,

PA | PA | PA

Paroxyfm, [Impetus]
Parrhefs, [Franknefs]
Parricide, [Murder of near kin]
Parrot. Bi. I. 7.
Parfimony, [Frugality]
Parfly. HF. IV. 9.
  Baftard—HF. V. 12. A.
  milky—HF. V. 13 A.
  Stone—HF. IV. 2.
Parfnip. HF. IV. 2.
  Cow—HF. IV. 15.
  Water—HF. IV. 15. A.
Parfon, { [adj. Parifh-Priest] Poffeffor of Prieft's revenue]
Part.
  Portion } TM. VI. O.
  Member
  B.ft—TN. VI. 1.
  Worft—TM. VI. 1. O.
  { Perfon }
  { Faction }
  { Intereft }
  for my—[Con- { Perfon } cerning my { Intereft }
  { Concerning }
  for the moft— [a. { moft perfons } { adv. Moft }]
  on all:—s, [By { Perfons } all { Factions }]
  take one's—[Affift, &c]
  { Quality }
  { Action }
  { Duty }
  one of excellent—s, [—Qualities]
  good } of him { g. } action
  ill } { i. }
  to take in { good— } [Ac- } { ill— } cept { perf.] } { corr.]
to——
  { Divifion }
  [a. { Partition }
  { Segregatenefs } ·
  { Open }
  [a. { Separate }
  [Depart]
  —*a fray*, [Un- a. { Contention } { Fight }
Partake. { Partner } [a. { Acceffory]
Party.
  { Perfon }
  { Faction }
  [Aggregate]
  —*of souldiers*.
  a commanded—RM. IV. 6.
  —*colour'd*, [adv. Variety colour'd]
  —*per pale*, [Alternly]
  [Acceffory]
Partiality, Ha. II. 6. O.
Participate, { Partner } [a. { Acceffory]
Participle. D. II. 3. A.
Particle; [Part (dim.)]
  Word. D. II. 1. A.
Particular,
  op. to Univerfal, [adj. TM. III. 3.]

op. to General. [adj. TM. III. 4.
  a—[Catalogue]
  —*ize*, { Induction } { Example]
Partifan.
  [Partaker]
  [Halbert]
Partition.
  —in a building. Po. III. 1. A.
  —in difcourfe. D. IV. 4. A.
Partner. RO. IV. 5.
Partridge. Bi. II. 6.
  red—Bi. II. 6. A.
Parturition. AC. I. 3.
Paru. Fi. III. 17.
Pafch, [Paffover]
  —*flower*, [Pulfatilla] HF. IX. 3. A.
Pafchal, [adj. Paffover]
Pafquil, [adj. Mocking writing]
Pafs.
  { Ition }
  { Coming }
  [a. { Going }
  { Proceeding }
  { Travelling }
  { Befide }
  fp. { Over }
  { Beyond }
  { Omit }
  —*by* { Not-obferve }
  —*over*, { a. Omiffion } { a. Tranfition }
  —*one's* { life, [Live] } { word, [Promife] }
  —*as bell*, [a. Dying (fign)]
  [a. Paft]
  —*away*.
  —*one's right*, [Alienate]
  —*the time*.
  bring { Effect } *to*— { Perform }
  come to—[adj. p. Event]
  let it——
  I will—[I will defift]
  { Suffice }
  { Exceed }
  { Excell }
  I—not for it, [I efteem it not]
  a——
  { way } fp. over river
  { State }
  brought to that——
  Venue, { Thruft (imp.) } { Prick (end) }
  [Written Licence for travelling]
Paffable, [Indifferent] TM. I. 4.
Paffage.
  { Going }
  { way }
  { Entry }
  { Fare }
  —*boat*.
  [Tranfaction] ·
  [Claufe]
Paffenger, [adj. Travelling (perfon)]
Paffer folitarius. Bi. III. 6. A.
Paffion.

Suffering. T. I. 7. O.
Affection. AS. V. [fp. Anger]
Corp. action fign into it. AC. IV.
Paffive, [adj. Paffion]
Paffover. RE. VI. 5. A.
Pafs-port, [Written Licence of travelling]
Paft, [adj. Paft time]
  —*time*. Sp. I. 1. E.
Pafte.
  [Raw bread]
  [Glue of ground corn]
Pafteler, [adj. a. Py (mech)]
Paftern, [Cavity of the heel]
Pafty, [Py (augm.)]
Paftime.
  { Recreation }
  { Mirth }
Paftinaca. Fi. II. 1.
Paftor.
  { Shepherd }
  { Prieft }
Paftry.
  [adj. Store-room for adj. py (things)]
  [a. py (art.)]
Pafture. Po. I. 5.
Pat, [Congruous]
Patch, [Fragment]
  to——[Repair with fragments]
  —*with*, [a. Fraud]
Pate. PG. III. 1. A.
Patent. RC. IV. 4.
Paternal, [adj. Father]
Paternity, [Father (abftr.)]
Path, [adj. p. pret. Walk (place)]
Pathetic, [adj. a. Paffion (apt.)]
Patible quality, Q.
Patience.
  Vertue. Man. I. 8.
  Herb.
Patient.
  [adj. { Paffion } { Patience }
  a—[adj. p. Phyfician (perfon)]
Patin, { Wide fhallow difh } { Cover of cup }
Patriarch.
  Before Chrift. RE. II. 1.
  [Primate]
Patrician, [Noble]
Patrimony, [adj. p. Inherit (thing)]
Patriot, { Lover } { Benefactor } of one's Nation.]
  { of Dependent. RO. III. 9.
Patron, { of Slave, [Mafter] } { of Church-living, [adj. Giving (pot.)] }
Patronage, [a. Patron]
Patronize.
  [a. Patron]
  [Protect]
Patronymic, [adj. Family (name)]

Pat-

P A

Pattern.
 [Example]
 [Type]
Pattin, vid. *Patin.*
 [Under-adj. foot (jug.)]
Paucity, [Fewness]
Pave, [a. Floor] sp. with stones]
Pavement, [adj. Stone-floor]
Pavillion [Tent (augm.)]
Paw, [Multifidous foot]
Pawn. RC. VI. 7.
Pawnage, vid. *Panage.*
Pawnch, { Belly } PG. IV. 6.
 { Guts (aggr.) }
to— { Un-a. bowel }
 { Discontinue }
Pawse, { Rest }
 a—[Period]
Peace. RM. O.
 —ableness. Man. IV. 3.
 to hold one's— [a. { Taciturnity }
 { Silence }]

Peach. Tr. II. 1.
to—[Accuse]
Peacock, [Bi. II. 2. sp. (male)]
Peahen, [Peacock (fem.)]
Peal, [Tunable ringing]
Pear. Tr. I. 2.
Peasant, { Rustic } (person)
 { Villain }
Pease. HS. II. 2. A.
 *Chich—*HS. III. 2.
 *Winged wild—*HS. II. 5. A.
 —Earth-nuts. HS. II. 7. A.
Peasecod, [Cod of Pease]
Peccadillo, [Sin (dim.)]
Peccant, { adj. a. Sin }
 { Guilty }
Peck, [Two gallons]
 to— Mo. VI. 5. A.
Pectoral, [adj. Breast]
Peculiar, [Proper]
Pecuniary, [adj. Money]
Pedal.
Pedant, { Teacher (corr.) of children }
 { adj. Pusillanimity (person) }
Pedee. RM. III. 8. A.
Pedegree, [Series of Ancestors]
Pedestal. Mag. V. 3.
Pedler, [Wandring Merchant (corr.)]
Pedling, { Sorry (dim.) }
 { Little (corr.) }
Pedobaptism, [Baptism of Infants]
Peeble, St. I. 2.
Peece.
 [Part]
 { Chip }
 { Fragment }
 —meal, [adv. Part (segr.)]
 all to—, [In parts]
 [Total]
 of one. { Entire }
 { Continued }
 [Gun]
 [20 s.]
 to—[Repair]
 sp. by adding fragment]

P E

—together, [Together-joyn]
Peel, vid. *Pill.*
 Bakers—[Staff with Latum at the end]
Peep.
 —of day, [Day (inc.)]
 to—
 [See (end) secretly]
 [Cry as Bird (young)]
Peer.
 [Equal]
 —less, [Not adj. p. Equal (pot.)]
 [Nobleman]
 [Factitious bark]
Peevishness, [Moroseness]
Peg, [Pin] sp. for fastning]
Peiony. HS. I. 1.
Pelamis. Fi. III. 4. A.
Pelf, [Riches (corr.)]
Pelican. Bi. IX. 8. A.
Pellet, [Bullet (like)]
Pellitory.
 —of Spain. HF. V. 11.
 —of the wall. HF. I. 16.
Pellucid, [Transparent]
Pelmel.
 [Game of striking bowl (dim.) through a hole]
 [adv. { Mixture }
 { Confusion }]
Pelt.
 Sheeps—[Sh. skin]
 Shepherds—[Sh. vest.]
 to—
 [Chafe]
 [Cast stones]
Pen.
 [Coop]
 [adj. Writing (instr.)]
 -man, [adj. Writing (person) (Off.)]
 -knife, [K. for pens]
 to— { Sepiment }
 { Write }
Penal, [adj. Punishment]
Penalty, [Punishment]
Penance.
 [Punishment]
 [Repentance]
Pence, [plur. Penny]
Pencil, [adj. Painting (instr.)]
Pendant.
 [p. Hanging thing]
 [Flag]
Pendu- { adj. a. Swing }
lous, { Doubtful }
 [Into—
Penetrate, { Through- } sition }
 Out—
Penguin. Bi. IX. 6. A.
Penile. W. III. 4. O.
Penitent, [adj. Repentance]
Penner, [adj. { Pen (vess) }
 { Writing (person) }]
Penny. Mea. IV. 2.
—father, [Penurious (person)]
—worth, [Price (manner)]
Pennyroyal. HF. VII. 8.
Pennywort.

P E

*Wall—*HL. VIII. 6.
Pennon, [Flag (dim.)]
Pension, [adj. a. Stipendiating (thing)]
 —er, [adj. p. Stipendiated (person)]
Pensive, [adj. { Grief }
 { Thinking } (apt.)]
Pent, [adj. p. Sepiment]
Pentagon, [Figure with five angles]
Pentecost, [Festival for descension of the Holy Ghost]
Penthouse, [Protuberant margin of roof.]
Penuriousness.
 op. to Liberality. Man. III. 3. E.
 op. to Magnificence, [Sordidness.]
Penury.
 Poverty
 Want.
People.
 [Nation]
 *Common—*RC. I. 5.
 to— { Fill } with men }
 { Furnish }
Pepper. Sh. II. 9
 —wort. HS. VI. 6.
 *Ginny—*HS. IV. 8. A.
 *Wall—*HL. VIII. 5. A.
Peradventure, [adv. { Fortune }
 { Contingence }]
Perambu- { About— } walk-
lation, { Through- } ing.]
Perce, vid. *Pierce.*
Perceive.
 { a. Sense }
 { See. } sp. inc.]
 { Understand }
Perceptible, [adj. p. Perceive (pot.)]
Perch.
 [Transverse stick]
 to—[Sit upon a stick]
 Measure. Mea. I. 5.
 Fish. Fi. IX 6.
 *Sea—*Fi. V. 10.
Percolation, [Straining] O. VI. 4.
Percussion, [Striking]
Perdition, { Destruction }
 { Loss }
Perdue. RM. III. 7. A.
Peregrination, [Travelling]
 sp. foreign]
Peregrine, [adj. Foreiner]
Peremp- { Absolute }
tory, { Obstinate }
Perennial, [During through the year]
Perfect. T. III. 9.
 [Finished]
 [adj. Integrity]
 [adj. { Art }
 { Experience }]
Perfidiousness, [Treachery]
Perforate.
 [a. Hole (make)]
 [Through-bore]
Perforce, [adj. Coaction]

M m m *Per-*

PA

Paroxyſm, [Impetus]
Parrheſy, [Frankneſs]
Parricide, [Murder of near kin]
Parrot. Bi. I. 7.
Parſimony, [Frugality]
Parſly. HF. IV. 9.
— *Baſtard* — HF. V. 12. A.
— *milky* — HF. V. 13 A.
— *Stone* — HF. IV. 2.
Parſnip. HF. IV. 2.
— *Cow* — HF. IV. 15.
— *Water* — HF. IV. 15. A.
Parſon, { [adj. Pariſh-Prieſt] / Poſſeſſor of Prieſt's revenue }
Part.
  Portion } TM. VI. O.
  Member }
  B. ſt — TM. VI. 1.
  Worſt — TM. VI. 1. O.
  { Perſon }
  { Faction }
  { Intereſt }
  for my — [Con-{ Perſon } cerning my { Intereſt }
  for the moſt — { Concerning / moſt perſons / adv. Moſt }
  on all: — s, [By { Perſons } / all { Factions }]
  take one's — [Aſſiſt, &c]
  { Quality }
  { Action }
  { Duty }
  one of excellent — s, [—Qualities]
  good } *of him* { g. } *acti*-
  ill } { i. } *on*
  to take in { *good*- } { [Ac-
             { *ill*— } cept { perſ. }
                           { corr. }
to —
  { Division }
  [a. { Partition }
  { Segregateneſs }
  [a. { Open }
  { Separate }
  [Depart]
  — *a fray*, [Un-a. { Contention } / Fight }]
Partake. { Partner }
  { [a. Acceſſory] }
Party.
  { Perſon }
  { Faction }
  [Aggregate]
  — *of ſouldiers*.
  a commanded — RM. IV. 6.
  — *colour'd*, [adv. Variety colour'd]
  — *per pale*, [Alternly]
  [Acceſſory]
Partiality, Ha. II. 6. O.
Participate, { Partner }
  { [a. Acceſſory] }
Participle. D. II. 3. A.
Particle; [Part (dim.]
  Word. D. II. 1. A.
Particular.
  op. to Univerſal, [adj. TM. III. 3.]

op. to General. [adj. TM. III. 4.
  a — [Catalogue]
  — *ize*, { Induction }
            { [a. Example] }
Partiſan.
  [Partaker]
  [Halbert]
Partition.
  — *in a building*. Po. III. 1. A.
  — *in diſcourſe*. D. IV. 4. A.
Partner. RO. IV. 5.
Partridge. Bi. II. 6.
  — *red* — Bi. II. 6. A.
Parturition. AC. I. 3.
Paru. Fi. III. 17.
Paſch, [Paſſover]
  — *flower*, [Puſſatilla] HF. IX. 3. A.
Paſchal, [adj. Paſſover]
Paſquil, [adj. Mocking writing]
Paſs.
  { Ition }
  { Coming }
  [a. { Going }
  { Proceeding }
  { Travelling }
  ſp. { Beſide }
  { Over }
  { Beyond }
  — *by* { Omit }
  { Not-obſerve }
  — *over*, { a. Omiſſion }
  { a. Tranſition }
  — *one's* { *life*, [Live] }
  { *word*, [Promiſe] }
  — *as bell*, [a. Dying (ſign)
  [a. Paſt]
  — *away*.
  — *one's right*, [Alienate]
  — *the time*.
  bring { Effect }
  to — { Perform }
  come to — [adj. p. Event]
  let it —
  I will — [I will deſiſt]
  { Suffice }
  { Exceed }
  { Excell }
  I — *not for it*, [I eſteem it not]
  a —
  { way } ſp. over river }
  { State }
  brought to that — —
  Venue, { Thruſt (imp.) }
  { Prick (end) }
  [Written Licence for travelling]
Paſſable, [Indifferent] TM. I. 4.
Paſſage.
  { Going }
  { way }
  { Entry }
  { Fare }
  — *boat*.
  [Tranſaction]
  Clauſe
Paſſenger, [adj. Travelling (perſon)]
Paſſer ſolitarius. Bi. III. 6. A.
Paſſion.

Suffering. T. I. 7. O.
Affection. AS. V. [ſp. Anger]
Corp. action ſign into it. AC. IV.
Paſſive, [adj. Paſſion]
Paſſover. RE. VI. 5. A.
Paſs-port, [Written Licence of travelling]
Paſt, [adj. Paſt time]
  — *time*. Sp. I. 1. E.
Paſte.
  [Raw bread]
  [Glue of ground corn]
Paſteler, [adj. a. Py (mech)]
Paſtern, [Cavity of the heel]
Paſty, [Py (augm.)]
Paſtime.
  { Recreation }
  { Mirth }
Paſtinaca. Fi. II. 1.
Paſtor.
  { Shepherd }
  { Prieſt }
Paſtry.
  [adj. Store-room for adj. py (things)]
  [a. py (art.)]
Paſture. Po. I. 5.
Pat, [Congruous]
Patch, [Fragment]
  to — [Repair with fragments]
  — *with*, [a. Fraud]
Pate. PG. III. 1. A.
Patent. RC. IV. 4.
Paternal, [adj. Father]
Paternity, [Father (abſtr.)]
Path, [adj. p. pret. Walk (place)]
Pathetic, [adj. a. Paſſion (apt.)]
Paſible quality. Q.
Patience.
  Virtue. Man. I. 8.
  Herb.
Patient.
  [adj. { Paſſion }
  { Patience }]
  a — [adj. p. Phyſician (perſon)]
Patin, { Wide ſhallow diſh }
  { Cover of cup }
Patriarch.
  Before Chriſt. RE. II. 1.
  [Primate]
Patrician, [Noble]
Patrimony, [adj. p. Inherit (thing)]
Patriot, { Lover } of one's Nation. }
  { Benefactor }
Patron, { of Dependent. RO. III. 9. }
  { of Slave, [Maſter] }
  { of Church-living, [adj. Giving (pot.)] }
Patronage, [a. Patron]
Patronize.
  [a. Patron]
  [Protect]
Patronymic, [adj. Family (name)]

Pat-

PA

Pattern.
[Example]
[Type]
Pattin, vid. *Patin.*
[Under-adj. foot (jug.]
Paucity, [Fewness]
Pave, [a. Floor] sp. with stones]
Pavement, [adj. Stone-floor]
Pavillion [Tent (augm.]
Paw, [Multifidous foot]
Pawn. RC. VI. 7.
Pawnage, vid. *Panage.*
Paunch, { Belly } PG. IV. 6.
{ Guts (aggr.]
to—[Un-a. bowel]
Pawse, { Discontinue }
{ Rest }
a—[Period]
Peace. RM. O.
—*ableness.* Man. IV. 3.
to hold one's—[a. { Taciturnity }]
{ Silence }
Peach. Tr. II. 1.
to—[Accuse]
Peacock, [Bi. II. 2. sp. (male)
Peahen, [Peacock (fem.]
Peal, [Tunable ringing]
Pear. Tr. I. 2.
Peasant, { Rustic } (person)
{ Villain }
Pease. HS. II. 2. A.
Chich—HS. III. 2.
Winged wild—HS. II. 5. A.
—*Earth-nuts.* HS. II. 7. A.
Peasecod, [Cod of Pease]
Peccadillo, [Sin (dim.]
Peccant, { adj. a. Sin }
{ Guilty }
Peck, [Two gallons]
to—Mo. VI. 5. A.
Pectoral, [adj. Breast]
Peculiar, [Proper]
Pecuniary, [adj. Money]
Pedal.
Pedant, { Teacher (corr.) of children }
{ adj. Pusillanimity (person) }
Pedee. RM. III. 8. A.
Pedegree, [Series of Ancestors]
Pedestal. Mag. V. 3.
Pedler, [Wandring Merchant (corr.]
Pedling, { Sorry (dim.] }
{ Little (corr.] }
Pedobaptism, [Baptism of Infants]
Peeble. St. I. 2.
Peece.
[Part]
{ Chip }
{ Fragment }
—*meal,* [adv. Part (fegr.]
all to—*t,* [In parts]
[Total]
of one— { Entire }
{ Continued }
[Gun]
[20 s.]
to—[Repair]
sp. by adding fragment]

PE

—*together,* [Together-joyn]
Peel, vid. *Pill.*
Bakers—[Staff with Lattin at the end]
Peep.
—*of day,* [Day (inc.]
to—
[See (end) secretly]
[Cry as Bird (young]
Peer.
[Equal]
—*less,* [Not adj. p. Equal (pot.]
[Nobleman]
[Factitious bank]
Peevishness, [Moroseness]
Peg, [Pin sp. for fastning]
Peiony. HS. I. 1.
Pelamis. Fi. III. 4. A.
Pelf, [Riches (corr.]
Pelican. Bi. IX. 4. A.
Pellet. [Bullet (like]
Pellitory.
—*of Spain.* HF. V. 11.
—*of the wall.* HF. I. 16.
Pellucid, [Transparent]
Pelmel.
[Game of striking bowl (dim. through a hole]
[adv. { Mixture }]
{ Confusion }
Pelt.
Sheeps—[Sh. skin]
Shepherds—[Sh. vest.]
to—
[Chafe]
[Cast stones]
Pen.
[Coop]
[adj. Writing (instr.]
-*man,* [adj. Wri- { (person) }]
ting { (Off.] }
-*knife,* [K. for pens]
to— { Sepiment }
{ Write }
Penal, [adj. Punishment]
Penalty, [Punishment]
Penance.
[Punishment]
[Repentance]
Pence, [plur. Penny]
Pencil, [adj. Painting (instr.]
Pendant.
[p. Hanging thing]
[Flag]
Pendu- { adj. a. Swing }
lous, { Doubtful }
[Into—
Penetrate, { Through- } ition]
[Out—
Penguin. Bi. IX. 6. A.
Penisle. W. III. 4. O.
Penitent, [adj. Repentance]
Penner, [adj. { Pen (vess) }]
{ Writing (person) }
Penny. Mea. IV. 2.
—*father,* [Penurious (person]
—*worth,* [Price (manner]
Pennyroyal. HF. VII. 8.
Pennywort.

PE

Wall—HL. VIII. 6.
Pennon, [Flag (dim.]
Pension, [adj. a. Stipendiating (thing)
—*er,* [adj. p. Stipendiated (person)
Pensive, [adj. { Grief } (apt.]
{ Thinking }
Pent, [adj. p. Sepiment]
Pentagon, [Figure with five angles]
Pentecost, [Festival for descension of the Holy Ghost]
Penthouse, [Protuberant margin of roof.]
Penuriousness,
op. to Liberality. Man. III. 3. E.
op. to Magnificence, [Sordidness.]
Penury,
Poverty
Want.
People.
[Nation]
Common—RC. I. 5.
to— { Fill } with men]
{ Furnish }
Pepper. Sh. II. 9
—*wort.* HS. VI. 6.
Ginny—HS. IV. 8. A.
Wall—HL VIII. 5. A.
Peradventure, [adv. { Fortune }]
{ Contingence }
Perambu- { About— } { walk- }
lation, { Through- } { ing]
Perce, vid. *Pierce.*
Perceive.
{ a. Sense }
{ See. } { sp. inc.]
{ Understand }
Perceptible, [adj. p. Perceive (pot.]
Perch.
[Transverse stick]
to—[Sit upon a stick]
Measure. Mea. I. 5.
Fish. Fi. IX. 6.
Sea—Fi. V. 10.
Percolation, [Straining] O. VI. 4.
Percussion, [Striking]
Perdition, { Destruction }
{ Loss }
Perdue. RM. III. 7. A.
Peregrination, [Travelling]
sp. forein]
Peregrine, [adj. Foreiner]
Peremp- { Absolute }
tory, { Obstinate]
Perennial, [During through the year]
Perfect. T. III. 9.
[Finished]
[adj. Integrity]
[adj. { Art }]
{ Experience }
Perfidiousness, [Treachery]
Perforate.
{ a. Hole (make]
{ Through-bore }
Perforce, [adj. Coaction]

PE | PE | PI

Perform. TA. III. 6.
Perfume, [adj. a. Sweetneſs (thing)]
Perfunctory
  [Slight]
  [Heedleſs]
  [Negligent]
Perhaps, [adv. { Fortune, Contingence }]
  Adv. I. 2.
Periacantha. Sh. IV. 5.
Periambium, [Cup] PP. II. 8.
Pericardium, [Skin about the heart]
Pericarpium. PP. II. 8. A.
Pericranium, [Skin about the skull]
Peril, [Danger] T. V. 1. O.
Perinæum, [Under-privities (part)]
Period.
  [a Ceaſing]
  [End]
  [Sentence] D. III. 1. A.
  Point. D. I. 6. A.
  Interpunction. D. I. 4.
Periodical, [Returning at certain times]
Periphery, { Line about the extremity, Circle } Mag. III. 2.
Periphraſis, [Paraphraſe] D. V. 5. A
Periplaca. Sh. I. 7. A.
Periſh, { Decay, p. Deſtruction }
Periſtaltic motion. Mo. III. 1. A.
Peritonæum, [Membrane of the belly]
Perjury, [Swearing a Lie]
Perriwig, [Factitious hair (aggr.)]
Periwinkle.
  Shrub. HS. VIII. 10.
  Fiſh. Ex. VII. 6. A.
Perk, [Proudly lift himſelf]
Perl.
  Gem. St. III. 2.
  Mother of—[Shell of the adj. a. Perl-oyſter]
  —*in the ey*, [Perl (like) ſpot in the ey]
Permanent, [adj. Sp. I. 6.]
Permit.
  [Not-forbid]
  [Not-hinder]
  [Yielding] TA. IV. 1.
  [a. Licence]
Permutation, [Change]
Pernicious, [adj. a. Deſtruction]
Pernoctation [a. Night]
Peroration, [Concluſion of oration]
Perpendicular, [Direct]
Perpetrate.
  [Doe]
  [Perform]
Perpetual. Sp. I. 8.
Perpetuity
Perplex, [Tangle]
  —*ity*,
  [Tangling (apt.) difficulty]
  [Anxiety]

Perqui. { Neceſſary, }
ſite, { Expedient }
  —*s*, [adj. Event profits]
Perry, [Wine of Pears]
Perriwig, [Factitious hair (aggr.)]
Perſecute.
  [Purſue]
  [Afflict]
  For Religion. RE. III. 4. O.
Perſeverance, [Conſtancy]
Perſevere, a. Conſtancy
Perſian ſhell. Ex. VII. 7. A.
Perſiſt, { Conſtancy, a. Duration }
Perſly, vid. *Parſly.*
Perſon. T. I. 4. A.
  —*, Judicial.* RJ. I.
  —*Military.* RM. III.
  Degrees of——RC. I.
Perſonable, [Figured (perf.)]
Perſonage, { Perſon, Perſon (manner) }
Perſonal preſence. Sp. II. 1.
Perſonate, [Imitate as Player]
Perſpective, [Seeing (art.)]
Perſpicacity, [Sagacity]
Perſpicuity, [Plainneſs]
Perſpiration, [Tranſpiration]
Perſuade. RO. V. 2.
Perſuaſion. AS. III. 6. A.
Pert.
  { Sprightly }
  { Vigorous }
  { Confident }
Pertein, vid. *Pertinence.*
Pertinacy. Ha. IV. 7. E.
Pertinence. TM. IV. 5.
Perturbation.
  { Moleſting } ſp. by affecti-
  { Confuſion } on (augm.)
Perverſeneſs. NP. IV. 1. O.
Pervert.
  [Seduce]
  [Wreſt]
Pervicacy. [Pertinacy]
Peruſe, { Through-, All- } conſider]
Perwinkle, vid. *Periwinkle.*
Peſant, { Ruſtic (perſon), Villain }
Peſt, [Plague]
Peſter, [Moleſt] ſp. (freq.)
Peſtife- { adj. a. Plague }
rous, { Hurtful (augm.) }
Peſtilence, [Plague] S. II. 3. A.
Peſtle, [Braying (inſtr.) Cylindrical (fig.)]
  —*of Pork*, [Thigh—]
Pet, [Anger (imp.)]
Petard, [Ordnance (like) machin for breaking gate]
St. Peters fiſh, [Doree] Fi. IV. 12.
St. Peter's wort. HS. V. 7. A.
Petition.
  [Entreaty]
  Religious. RE. IV. 2. A.
Petrifie, [a. Stone (make)]
Petronel, [Horſeman's gun]
Petty, { Little, Sorry }
Petticoat, [Looſe thigh (veſt)]
Pettifogger, [Lawyer (corr.)]

Pettiſhneſs, [Moroſeneſs]
Petulance, [Impudent wantonneſs]
Pew, [About-ſepimented ſeat]
Pewter. Met. II. 2.
Phantaſy, [Fancy]
Phantaſm, [Seeming (thing) to fancy (corr.)]
Phantaſtic, { adj. a. Fancy (corr.), Conceited }
Pharmaceutical operation. O. VI. A
Phænicopter. Bi. VIII. 2.
Phenix.
Pheſant. Bi. II. 3.
Phyllyrea. Sh. III. 3.
Philologer. RC. II. 4.
Philoſopher. RC. I. 1. A.
Philtre, [adj. a. Love (make) medicin]
Phlebotomy. Mo. IV. 6.
Phlegm. PG. I. 6.
Pholas. Ex. VIII. 8.
Phraſe, { Sentence (manner), Inſtead-word }
Phrenetic, [adj. Frenzy]
Phylactery, [Written (lam.) to be worn]
Phyſic, [adj. a. Phyſician (thing)]
Phyſician. RC. II. 3.
Phyſiognomy.
  Face (manner)
  [Wizarding by inſpection of the face.]
Phyſis. Fi. V. 11.
Py.
  Proviſion. Pr. I. 4. A.
  Bird.
    Mag—Bi. I. 8.
    Sea—[Sea-mew] Bi. VII. 8.
Piacular, [That ought to be expiated by ſacrifice]
Piazza, [About-houſed Area.]
Pibble. St. I. 4.
Pick.
  [Peck]
  [Pluck]
  [Open]
  —*a lock.*
  [Diſcover]
  —*out.*
  —*a ſecret.*
  [Chuſe]
  —*out*, [a. Election]
  [Gather]
  —*up.*
  [Gain]
  —*out of one*, [Gain from one]
  —*a quarrel*, [Obtain (end) an occaſion of q.]
  —*a thank*, [Obtain (end) thanks (ſp. by accuſing)]
  [Pilfer]
  —*Pocket*, { a. Theft [p.], out of [p.] }
  —*Purſe*,
  [Cleanſe]
    a bone, { b. }
    one's ear, [Cleanſe] { e. }
    one's teeth, { t. }
Pickax

PI

Pickax, [adj. a. Pecking hammer]
Picked, [adj. p. Tooth] Mag. IV. 2.
Pickeer, [a. Skirmish]
Pickerel, [Pike (dim.)]
Pickeroon, [adj. a. Bootying ship.]
Pickle, [adj. a. Pickling (things)]
  [State (corr.)]
Pickling. Pr. III. 9.
Pickrel, [Pike (dim)]
Picture. Pr. VI. 8.
Pied, [Variegated]
Pierce,
  Into—{ ition }
  { thrusting }
  [Boring]
  —*a vessel*, [Broach a v.]
  —*ing* { Pricking }
  pain, { Smarting }
  —*er*, [Boring (instr.)]
Piety,
  to God, [Religion (hab.)]
  to Parents, [Gratitude]
Pig, [Hog (young) Be. II. 4.
  Ginny—Be. III. 6. A.
  —*of lead*, [Cast (thing) of Lead.]
Pigeon. Bi. III. 1.
Piggin, [Tub (dim.)]
Pike.
  [Spear] RM. V. 3.
  Fish. Fi. IX. 1.
Pilchard Fi. III. 10. A.
Pile,
  [Post]
  [Heap]
  [Emrod]
  —*wort.* HF. IX. 4. A.
Pilfer, [a. Theft (dim.)]
Pilgrim, [Vow'd traveller for Religion.]
Pill,
  [Ball (dim.)]
  [Rinde]
  to—
  { Strip, { rinde }
  { Un-a. { clothe }
  [Rob]
Pillage.
  [Robbery]
  [Booty]
Pillar. Po. III. 5.
Pillaster, [Pillar (dim.)]
Pillion, [Woman's riding cushion]
Pillory, [Imprisoning (jug.) for head and hands]
Pillow, [Cushion for the head]
  —*beer*, [Case of Pillow]
Pilot. RN. V. 4. A.
Pimpernel. HS. V. 10. A.
Pimple, [Pustule] S. III. 1.
Pin.
  Figure.
  —*without head.* Mag. IV. 1.
  —*with head.* Mag. VI. 2. A.
  —*fish.* Fi. VI. 2. A.
  —*and web*, [Suffusion in the ey.]

PI

—*fold*, [Imprisoning (sep.) for beasts.]
to— { Bolt }
  { Shut }
—*a house*, [Under-fill the foundation]
Pincer, [adj. Pinching (jug.)]
Pinch.
  [a Compression]
  as pain, [Twitch]
  [a. Narrow (make)
  —*penny*, [Penurious (person)]
  [a. Anxiety]
Pine. Tr. V. 4. A.
  —*apple*, [Nut of the Pine tree]
  to—{ Decaying }
  { a. { Lean (augm.) }
Pink,
  Flower. HS. V. 1. A.
  [Ship (dim.)]
  to—Pr. III. 5.
  —*eyed*, [Narrow ey]
Pinna. Ex. VIII. 7.
Pinnace, [Ship (dim.)]
Pinnacle, [Turret for ornament]
Pinnion.
  Figure. Mag. V. 5. A.
  —*of wing*, [Elbow—]
  to—[a. Bonds for the arms]
Pinte.
Pioneer. RM. III. 8.
Piony. HS. I. 1.
Pious, [adj. Piety]
Pip.
  [Point]
  [Disease]
Pipe.
  [Tube]
  Square. Mag. V. 9.
  Round. Mag. V. 9. A.
  [Barrel]
  Measure.
  Wind—PG. VI. 1. A.
  —*tree.* Sh. IV. 1.
  White—Sh. V. 3. A.
  to—{ Music with pipe }
  { a. { Acuteness }
Piper, [Tub-fish] Fi. IV. 5.
Pipkin, [Earthen (dim.) adj. boiling (vess.)]
Pippin.
Pique, { Malignity }
  { Hatred } (sp. secret)
Pirate, [adj. Sea-robber.]
Pisces, [Last of the 12 parts of the Zodiac.]
Piscis triangularis. Fi. VIII. 3.
  —*Cornutus.* Fi. VIII. 3. A.
Pish, [Int. { Contempt }
  { Aversation }]
Pismire, [Ant] Ex. IV. 5.
Pissing. Mo. IV. 8.
Pistach. Tr. IV. 2.
Pistol.
  [adj. Hand-gun (dim.)]
  Money.
Pit, [Dent]
  Arm—[Concave (part) under the arm]

PL

—*fall*, [Concave (place) in the earth for catching birds]
Pitch.
  [Height]
  —*of a hill*, [Obliquity (inc.)—]
  [Tar boyled to a consistence]
  to—
  [Smear with Pitch]
  { Camp, } Place { c. }
  { Net, } Direct { n. }
  { Tent, } Fix { t. }
  •—*a floor*, [a. Floor with stones]
Pitcher, [Earthen pot.]
Pitchfork, [Fork]
Piteous, vid. *Pittiful*.
Pith. PP. I. 5. A.
Pithy.
  [adj. { Pith }
  { Importance }]
Pittance, { Part }
  { Proportion } (dim.)
Pitty. AS. IV. 7. O.
Pittiful, { a. }
  [adj. { p. { Pitty (apt.) }
Pittiless.
  [Not-adj. a. Pitty]
  [Cruel]
Pituitons, [adj. Phlegm.]
Pizzle, [Genital (male)]
Placable, [Un- adj. p. anger (apt.)]
Placard, { Patent }
  { Edict }
Place.
  Proper. Sp. II.
  [Situation]
  —*Military.* RM. VI.
  [House (augment.)]
  [Order]
  [Dignity]
  [Degree] RC. I.
  [Office]
  [Stead]
  to— { a. Place }
  { Put }
  chuse in ones's—
  [a. { Substitute } (make)
  { Successor }
  give—{ Yield } Superiority
  take—{ Take } (sign)
Placid, [Meek]
Plagiary,
  [Stealer { Men }
  of { Writings }]
Plague.
  [Pestilence] S. II. 3 A.
  [Adversity (augm.)]
  to—{ Afflict }
  { Punish }
Play.
  op. to Work. O. A.
  —*fellow*, [Companion in play.]
  —*with*, [Together-play]
  { Imitate }
  { a. Action }
  —*fast and loose*, [a. Lightness.]

N n n 2 —*ibe*

—the { Coward, Fool, Hypocrite, [a. Truant, Wanton, 9.	{ C. F. H. T. W.	sp. by { Carving] Moulding]

—er. RC. II. 9.
Stage— [adj. p. Player (thing)
{ a. Recreation} Mo. V.
{ a. Game} Mo. V. A.
—at a game, [a. Game]
—at Dice, &c. [a. Dice, &c.]
—at single Rapier, &c. [a. Fence at f. &c.]
—upon an instrument, [a. Music.]
—upon a man, [a. Mock a man.]
—upon with guns, [a. Gun]
Plaice. Fi. VII. 4.
Plain.
{ Plain. Mag. III. 4.
{ Even.] Q. VI. 2.
{ Champain. W. III. 1.
Carpenter's—— [adj. a. Even (instr.)
{ Not-obscure. D. III. 9.
{ Manifest] TA. I. 9.
{ Simple]
{ Mean]
{ Homely}
{ Sincere]
{ Frank]
Plaint, [Complaint]
Plaintiff. RJ. I. 4.
Plais. Fi. VII. 4.
Plaister, vid. Plaster.
Plait, vid. Pleit.
Plancher, [Room for fatting of Boar]
Plane. Tr. VI. 10. A.
—— [adj. a. Even (instr.)
Planet. W. II. 3.
—struck.
Planisphere, [Picture of sphere in plain]
Plank, [Thick adj. wood (lamin]
to— [a. Floor with wood (lamin]
Plant. W. V. 2.
to— O. III. 6.
—guns, [Place guns on bank]
—a Country, [a. Colony]
—off oot, [Bottom——]
Plaintain.
Herb. HL. VII. 2.
Sea— HL. VII. 4.
Tree. Tr. I. 9.
Plantation.
[Planting]
[Colony] RC. III. 1. A.
Plash, [Spread boughs]
—of water, [Lake (dim.]
—), [adj. Lake dim.]
Plaster.
Medecin. Pr. VI. 4. A.
Morter. El. IV. 5. A.
—er, [adj. Morter (mech.]
Plastic, [Figuring (art.]

Plat, vid. Pleit.
Plate.
[Lamin] sp. Metall (lam.]
[Vessel] sp. of Silver or Gold]
[Shallow dish]
Platform.
{ Exemplar]
{ Description by lines]
{ Sconce]
Platter, [Shallow dish (augm.]
Plaudite { Praise
{ Joy } (voice)
Plausible, [adj. p. Praise (apt]
Plea. RJ. II. 3. A.
Pleader. RJ. I. 7.
Pleasant. T. IV. 2.
[adj. a. Delectation (apt.]
[adj. Mirth]
[adj. Urbanity]
Pleasing.
[Delectation]
[Appearing]
Pleasure. Ha. II. 3.
[Delectation]
[Will]
at one's— [According to ones will]
to—one, [a. { Benefactor]
{ Complacence]
Plebeian, [adj. People (kinde]
Pledge, [Pawn]
to—one, [Answer in drinking]
Pleit { Fold in wrinkles]
{ Weave with the fingers]
Plenary, { Full]
{ Totall]
{ Perfect]
Plenipotentiary, [Perfectly authorized]
Plenty, [Abundance]
Pleonasm, [Abounding (manner) of sentence]
Plethory. S. I. 3.
Pleurisie. S. V. 6.
Ply, { Diligence]
{ a. Operation]
Pliable { { Limberness]
Pliant, } [adj. { a. Obedience (apt.]
{ p. Persuasion (apt.]
Plight, [Oblige]
[State]
in good— [adj. Vigour]
Plot.
{ Area]
{ Description by lines]
[Design]
Plover.
green— Bi. VII. 2.
grey— Bi. VII. 2. A.
Plow, [adj. Plowing (jug.]
—ing. O. III. 1. A.
Pluck { Pull]
{ Draw]
—a Bird, [Un a. feather]
Sheeps— [Sh. PG. VI.]

Plug, (Wooden adj. stopping (thing)
Plum. PP. III. 2.
—tree. Tr. II. 2. A.
Plumb, [Perpendicular]
—rule, { Perpendicularness} mea-
{ Transverseness} ring (instr.]
Plume, [Feather] PP. V. 1.
[Feathers (aggr.) for ornament]
to— { Un- a. Feather]
{ a. Order (perf.) the feathers]
Plummer, [adj. Lead (mech.]
Plummet, [Weight (dim.]
Carpenter's—— [Weight for measuring perpendicularness.]
Plump.
[Fat]
[Convex (perf.) with fatness]
Plunder, [Booty]
Plunge, { Dive (make)
{ Difficulty (imp.]
Plural, [adj. Plurality]
—ity. TM. III. 2. O.
Pluss, [Silk adj. p. superficies with long tuft]
Pocbe.
[Hunt (corr.]
—egg, [a. Consistence by boiling] sp. unshelled]
Pock.
Small— S. II. 4.
—hole, [Concave Pox (sign]
French— S. II. 6.
—wood [Guaiacum] Tr. VII. 2.
Pocket, [adj. Garment (bag]
Pod, [Cod] PP. III. 5. A.
Poem, [adj. p. Poet (thing]
Poet. RC. II. 4. A.
Poetry, [adj. Poet (art.]
Poinard, [adj. Pricking (apt.) sword (dim.]
Point.
Tittle. Mag. I. 1.
—blank, [Transverse]
Full— [Period]
[Instant]
[of death.
[Tooth] Mag. IV. 2.
—in the compass, [A two and thirtieth part of the circle.]
—in Tables, [A four and twentieth part of the Area.]
—of land, [Promontory]
[Cord (dim.]
[Part]
in every—
it is a—of
[State]
'tis come to that—
[Proposition]
[Case]
[Question]
—in controversie.

P O

to—
 [a. Point]
 [Shew with finger]
 [Distinguish with Period]
Poise.
 [Try the gravity]
 [Weigh equally]
Poisoning. RS. V. 5. A.
Poke, [Bag]
Pole, vid. Poll.
 [Staff (augm.]
 —*ax,* [Cutting {Club, Hammer}]
 —*of Cart.* Po. V. 5. A.
 —*of a ship.* RN. III. 3. A.
 —*of a globe.* Mag. II. 1. A.
Measure. Mea. I. 3.
Polecat. Be. IV. 5.
Polemic {RM.}
 [adj. Disputation]
Policy.
 [Wisdom]
 [Government]
 Civil—[adj. RC. (art.]
 —*of assurance,* [Bond against loss]
Polipus. Ex. IX. 1.
 *sweet—*Ex. IX. 1. A.
Polish.
 [a. Smooth]
 [Brighten]
Polite, {Beautiful, Adorn'd}
Political Relation. RC.
Poll, vid. Pole.
 [Hinder part of the neck]
 by the—[adv. Persons (segr.]
 to—
 [Cut (perf.) the hair]
 [a. Tax]
 {Oppress, Impoverish by taxes}
Pollard.
 [Deer (male) adj. pret. let go his horns]
 [Lopped tree]
Pollute, [Defile]
Poltron, [Coward]
Polygamy, [Having many wives]
Polygon, [Having many angles]
Polymountain. HF. VI. 6.
Polypody. HL. I. 6.
Polysyllable, [Having many syllables]
Poman—Sphear {of perfumes, Apple (like)}
Pomecitron, [Apple of the Citron-tree]
Pomegranat.
 —*tree.* Tr. I. 6.
Pomel, [adj. Sphear (part]
 to—[Beat]
Pomp, [Solemnity]
Pompholyx. Met. IV. 2. A.
Pompion. HS. VII. 1.
Pompous, {Solemnity (augm.] nefs, Magnificence}
Pond, [Lake. W. IV. 7. A. (dim.]
 —*weed.* HL. VII. 8.
 narrow leaved— HF. VIII. 6. A.

P O

*Fish—*Po. I. 6.
Ponder.
 [Deliberate]
 [Meditate]
 [Consider]
Ponderousness, [Heaviness]
Poniard, vid. Poinard.
Pontage, [Tax for bridge]
Pontifical.
 [adj. {Bishop, Primate}]
Pool. W. IV. 7. A.
Poop, [Hinder part of ship]
Poor.
 [adj. Poverty]
 Needy, [adj. wanting]
 [Lean]
 [Little]
 [Sorry]
 [adj. p. Pitty (apt.]
 —*ness,* [Poverty]
 [Bladder]
Pop, {Sound of breaking of bladder}
 —*gun,* [Gun (like) Tube]
Pope.
 [Father]
 [Bishop] [sp. of Rome]
Popinjay, [Parrot]
Poplar
 *black—*Tr. VI. 8.
 *white—*Tr. VI. 8. A.
Poppet, [Statue (dim.]
Poppy. HS. VI. 4.
 *bastard—*HS. VI. 4. A.
 *burned—*HS. IV. 10.
Populace, [People (kind)]
Popular.
 [adj. People]
 [Beloved by the people]
Populous, [adj. p. People (aug.]
Porcellane.
 Herb. HL. VIII. 3.
 Vessel.
Porch, [adj. Door (room.]
Porcupine. Be. III 5.
Pore. Mag. VI. 1.
 —*blind.*
 to—{near, Look fixedly}
Pork, [Hog's flesh]
Porker, [Young hog]
Porphyry, [Reddish Marble]
Porpoiss. Fi. l. 1. A.
Porrage, vid. Pottage.
Porringer, vid. Pottinger.
Port.
 [Haven]
 [Gate]
 —*hole.* RN. II. 7.
 [adj. out-side Dignity]
Portable, [adj. p. {pot. Carry, apt.}]
Portage, [Payment for carriage]
Portal, [Door (room]
Portcullis. RM. VI. 8. A.
Portentous, [Fore-signing some evil (augm.]
Porter, [adj. Door (Off.]
 [Bearer]
Porthole. RN. II. 7.

P O

Portion.
 [Part]
 [adj. Proportion (part]
 Wife's—[W. part of the Inheritance]
Portmanteau, [adj. Riding-bag]
Portray, {a. Description, a. Picture}
Portsale, [Public sale]
Pose.
 [Try] [sp. by questions]
 Non-plus. D. VI. 8.
Posie, {Flowers (aggr.], Sentence upon-written}
Position.
 [Proposition]
 [Affirmation]
 [Site]
 [Posture]
Positive. T. III. 3.
Posture, [Posture]
Posnet, [Standing pot with a handle]
Possess, {Have, Hold, a. Possession}
 —*ion.* Po.
 Prescription, [Custom of possession]
 take—(Possess (inc.]
Posset, [Broth of coagulated milk]
Possibility. T. IV, 4.
Post.
 [Wooden column]
 [Swift] {Carrier, Messenger}
 ride—[Ride on divers horses successively]
 to—[adv. Swiftness (ition.]
 [sp. Riding]
 [Publish by writing on column]
 —*accounts,* [Write the summes in {page, another book}]
Post-date, [Date after pret. writing]
Posteriority, [Succeeding (abstr.]
Posterity, [Descendents (aggr.] RO. 1. 1. O.
Postern, [adj. Hinder-part (door]
Posthumous, [Born after Father's death]
Postil, [adj. p. Preaching (thing]
Postilion, [Before-riding (person]
Postpone, [Less esteem]
Postscript, {After-written, Under- (thing)}
Postulation, [Demand]
Posture. AC. VI. A.
Pot. Pr. V. 5.
 —*companions,* [adj. a. Drunkenness c.]
 —*hangers,* [adj. a. Hanging (jug.) for pot.]
 —*herb,* [H. for broth]
 —*lid,* [adj. Covering (thing) for pot.]

—*shred*

PR

—*sberd*, [Fragment of earthen vess.]
Potable, [adj. p. Drink (apt.)]
Potato. HS. IX. 3.
Potent, [adj. Power]
Potentate, { Powerful (person) / Prince }
Potential, T. III. 5. O.
Potgun, [Gun (like) Tube]
Potion, [Potable (thing) sp. Medicinal]
Potsherd, [Fragment of earthen vess.]
Pottage, [Broth]
Potter, [adj. O. IV. A. (mech.)]
Pottinger, [Dish for broth]
Pottle, [Two quarts]
Potulent, [adj. p. Drink (apt.)]
Pouch.
[Bag (dim.)]
[Stomach]
to—[Swallow]
Pouder. TM. VI. 4. A.
gun—RM. V. 7. A.
to—
[a. Pouder-(make)]
Sprinkle. Pr. III. 7. A.
sp. with salt]
Poverty. Ha. II. 2. O.
Poult, [Grouse]
Poultice, [Soft plaster]
Poultry, [Cock Bi. II. 1. (kinde)]
Pounce, [Claw of bird]
to—[Pink]
Pound.
Weight. Mea. III. 5.
Money. Mea. IV. 5.
Pinfold, [Imprisoning (sep.) for beasts.]
to—
[Imprison]
[Bray with Cylinder] Mo. VI. 3.
Poun- { Tax } adv. Pound
dage, { Payment } (segr.)
Pourcontrel. Ex. IX. 1.
Pouring. O. II 8.
Pourtraiture, [Picture]
Pout, [Angry mouth (manner)]
to—AC. IV. 2. O.
Eel—Fi. VI. 6. A.
[Heathcock] Bi. II. 5.
Power.
Natural—NP.
{ Might } Ha. II. 6.
{ Authority }
—*full*, [adj. a. Power]
in one's—[adj. p. Power]
Pox.
French—S. II. 6.
Small—S. II. 4.
Practice. RC. II. A.
—*Law*
—*Physic* } RC. II. A. { L. }
[Action] { P. }
[Endeavour]
[Essay]
[Exercise]
—*ed*, [Expert]
Pragmaticalness, [Diligent (corr.)]
Pray. RE. IV. 1.

PR

Prayer, [adj. RE. IV. 1. (thing)]
Praise. RO. V. 8.
Prance, { Go proudly }
{ Trot }
Prank,
[Extraordinary action]
to—
[a. Ornate (make)]
Prate, [a. Loquacity]
Pratic, [Licence to trade]
Prattle, [a. Loquacity]
Pravity, [Evil (abstr.)]
Prawn, [Shrimp] Ex. VI. 4.
Preach. RE. IV. 4.
Preamble, [Prologue]
Prebendary, [AT- { Cathedral
tellor of { Collegiate
{ Church }
Precaution, [Warning]
Precedence. Sp, I. 2. E.
Precedent.
[Exemplar]
[Preceding]
Precellence, [Excellence]
Precept, [Command]
Precinct, [Authority (place)]
Precious, [adj. Price (augm.)]
—*stone*, [Gem]
Precipice, [Steep (place)]
Precipitate.
Chymic. O. VI. 3. A.
Capital punishment. RJ. V. 3. A.
[Hast (exc.)]
[a. Rashness]
Precise.
{ Perfect
{ Regular } (augm.)
[Scrupulous]
Precocity, [Soon (exc.) Ripeness.
Precognition, [Before-knowing]
Precontract, [Before-contract]
Predatory, [adj. a. Booty]
Predecessor, [adj. Preceding (person)]
Predestinate, { determine }
{ Before { appoint }
Predicable, [adj. p. Predicate (apt.)]
Predicament. TA.
Predicate, D. II. 5. A.
Predication, [a. Predicate]
Prediction, { Before-telling }
{ Prophecy }
Predominant, { More powerful }
{ adj. a. Victory }
Pre-election. [Rather-chusing]
Pre-eminence.
{ Superiority }
{ Excellence }
{ Dignity }
{ Privilege }
Preemp- { Before- }
tion, { † first- } buying.
Preexistence, [Before-actualness]
Preface, [Prologue]
Prefect, [adj. { Autho- } (per-
{ rity } son)
{ Office }

PR

{ Authority }
—*ure*, { Office }
Prefer.
{ More- } { esteem }
{ Before- } { chuse }
—*person*, { Dignity }
[adj. a. { Power }
—*bill*, [adj. a. Bill]
Prefigure, [Before adj. a. type]
Prefix, [Before- } Fasten }
adj. a. } Appoint }
Pregnant, { Full
{ Important }
Prey, [Booty]
Prejudice, [Before-opinion (corr.)]
—*ial*, { Hurtful }
{ Impedient }
Prejudicate, { a. Sentence }
{ Before- { Condemn }
Preke, [Pourcontrel] Ex. IX. 1.
Prelate, [Bishop] RE. II. 4. A.
Prelude, [adj. Preparation play]
Premeditate, [Before-meditate]
Premise, { put }
{ Before- } suppose }
Premonish, [Before-warn]
Premunire, [Forfeiture of goods and liberty]
Prentice { (merc.) }
[Disciple { (mech.) }
Preoccupation, [Before-possess]
Preordain, [Before-ordain]
Prepare. TA. III. 2.
—*food*. Pr. III.
Preponderate, [More-weigh]
Preposition. D. II. 8.
Preposterous, [Against-order'd]
Prepuce, [Skin to be cut off in Circumcision]
Prerogative. RC. IV. 7.
Presage, [Before-sign]
Presbyter. RE. II. 5. A.
Prescience, [Before-knowing]
Prescribe.
[Before-appoint]
—*by Law*, [a. Law]
—*by Custom*, [a. Right (make) by pret. custom]
presence.
—*in place*. Sp. II. 1.
—*chamber*, [Room for King's presence]
—*in time*. Sp. I. 1.
[Sprightliness]
Present, [adj. Presence]
to—
[Represent]
[Accuse]
a—[Gift]
Pre- { Right of giving } { Priest's
tation { Giving of } { (place)
{ right }
Presently, { adv. Present }
{ adv. Future (dim.) }
{ Keep }
Preserv, { Defend }
{ Condite }
Action of God. AS. I. 4.

Pre-

PR PR PR

Preservative, [adj. a. Preserve (thing)]
President.
  [Prefect]
  [Example]
Press.
  [Thrusting]
  [a. Compression]
  —*to death*. RJ. V. 3.
Printer's— [adj. a. Printing (jug.)]
Wine—[adj. Wine (jug.)]
  [a. { Dense / Fast / Hard / Heavy } make]
  [a. { Necessity / Coaction }]
  —*souldiers*, [a. Souldier (make) by coaction]
  [a. { Persuade / Intreat } (augm.)]

Throng, [Dense { Multitude / Aggregate }]
—*for* { Apparel / Books } [Box—]
Pressure, { Pressing / Necessity / Affliction }
Prest, [Ready]
Prestigiator. RC. II. 9. A.
Presume.
  [a. { Boldness / Confidence }]
  [a. Hope (corr.)]
Presumption.
  [Presuming]
  [Strong argument]
  sp. , Conjectural]
Presumptuousness.
  [Hope (corr.)]
  [Rashness]
  { Irreverence / Arrogance }
Presuppose, [Before-suppose]
Pretence.
  { Seeming / Feigned } cause]
Pretend.
  [Seem (make)]
  [Dissemble]
Preterition, [Omission]
Pretermit, [Omit]
Pretext.
  { Seeming / Feigned } cause]
Pretty.
  [Handsom (dim.)]
  [adj. Mediocrity]
Prevail.
  [a. { Superior / Victory }]
  [Obtain]
Prevarication.
  [Betraying by pleading]
  { Deceit- / ful, } { Action / Speech }
Prevent. TA. III. 9.
Previous, { Preceding / [adj. Preparation] }

Pry, { See (end) / a. Spy }
Priapism. Disease.
Price. RC. V. 7.
Prick.
  [Point]
  Mark, [adj. p. Object (thing)]
  { Tooth } Mag. IV. 2.
  { Prickle, [Thorn] PP. I. 3. A.
  —*ing*. Mo. VI. 7. A.
  —*pain*. AC. II. 7. A.
  —*forward*, { a. Impulsion, five }
  —*in*, [a. Plant]
  up, [a. Direct]
  —*wood*. Sh. I. 4. A.
Pricket, [Buck. Be. II. 6. of the second year.]
Prickle, [Thorn] PP, I, 3, A.]
Pride. Man. V. 2. D.
Priest.
  Jewish—RE. II. 2,
  Christian—RE. II. 5.
Primary, [Chief]
Primate. RE. II. 4.
Prime, { First / Chief }
Primitive. TM. IV. 1.
Primogeniture, [First birth (abstr.)]
Primrose. HS. VIII. 1.
Prince. RC. I. 2. A.
  [King's Son]
  —*'s feather*. HF. I. 15. A.
  —*'s wood*. Tr. VII. 6. A.
Principal.
  [Chief]
  [Governour]
  [Money { demised / disbursed }]
  —*ness*. TM. IV. 4.
Principality. [Government (place)]
Principle.
  [Cause]
  [Rule]
  [Element]
Print.
  [Mark]
  [Impression]
  —*ing*. AC. III. 7. A.
Prior, [Abby (Off.)]
Priority. [Preceding (abstr.)]
Prism. Mag. III. 6. O.
Prison, [Imprisonment (place)]
Prisoner. Reputed Criminal. R. I. 3. O.
  [adj. p. Imprison (person)]
Pristin, { Former / Old }
Privado, [Friend (augm.)]
Private.
  op. to Public, [adj. TM. V. 5. O.
  [Concealed]
  —*man*, [Not-magistrate]
Privateer, [Private man of war.]
Privation, [a. Privative]
Privative. T. III. 3. O.
Privet. Sh. II. 11.
  Ever-green—Sh. III. 3. A.

Mock—Sh. III. 3.
Privy.
  [Knowing]
  [Accessory]
  [Hidden]
  [Secret]
  —*parts*. PG. VI. 8.
Jakes, [Dunging (room)]
Privilege. RC. IV. 7. A.
  —*ed place*, [p. Immunity (place)]
Privities. PG. VI. 8,
Prize.
  [Booty]
  [Reward of victory]
  { Fighting / Gaming } sp. for wager]
  to—
  [a. { Price / Value }]
  [Esteem]
Probable, { Opinion / [adj. Probation] } (apt.)
Probation. D. VI. 6.
  —*er*, [adj. p. Essaying (person)]
Probe, [Depth measure (pin)]
Problem, { Proposition / Question } to be disputed]
Proboscis, [Trunk] PP. V. 4. A.
Proceed. TA. VI. 1.
  —*from*, [adj. p. { Cause / Birth / Being } from]
  —*ings*, [Series of actions]
  —*Judicial*. RJ. II.
  —*the*— { Gain / Revenue }
Process.
  [a. Proceeding]
  [Series]
  —*of a bone*, [Protuberant (part)]
  —*of time*, { Some / After } { much } time]
  —*in Law*, [Citation sp. written]
Procession.
  [Proceeding]
  [Solemn about-walking]
Proclaim, [Publish] sp. solemnly]
Proclamation, { Publishing / Edict }
Proclivity, [Inclinableness]
Procrastinate, { Delay / Protract } sp. till next day.]
Procreate, [Generate]
Proctor.
  [Substitute]
  [Advocate]
Procuration.
  [adj. Proctor (make) sp. writing]
  [Procuring]
Procure.
  [Cause]
  [Furnish]
  [Obtain]
Prodigality. Man. III. 1. E.

Pro.

PR

—*sherd*, [Fragment of earthen vess.]
Potable, [adj. p. Drink (apt.]
Potato. HS. IX. 3.
Potent, [adj. Power]
Potentate, { Powerful (person) / Prince }
Potential, T. III. 5. O.
Potgun, [Gun (like) Tube]
Potion, [Potable (thing)] {p. Medicinal}
Potsherd, [Fragment of earthen vess.]
Pottage, [Broth]
Potter, [adj. O. IV. A. (mech.]
Pottinger, [Dish for broth]
Pottle, [Two quarts]
Potulent, [adj. p. Drink (apt.]
Pouch.
  [Bag (dim.)]
  [Stomach]
  to——[Swallow]
Powder. TM. VI. 4. A.
gun—RM. V. 7. A.
to——
  [a. Powder-(make)]
  Sprinkle. Pr. III. 7. A.
  {p. with salt}
Poverty. Ha. II. 2. O.
Poult, [Grouse]
Poultice, [Soft plaster]
Poultry, [Cock Bi. II. 1. (kinde)]
Pounce, [Claw of bird]
to—[Pink]
Pound.
  Weight. Mea. III. 5.
  Money. Mea. IV. 5.
  Pinfold, [Imprisoning (sep.) for beasts.]
to—
  [Imprison]
  [Bray with Cylinder] Mo. VI. 5.
Poun- { Tax } *adv*. Pound
dage, { Payment } (segr.)
Pourcontrel. Ex. IX. 1.
Pouring. O. II 8.
Pourtraiture, [Picture]
Pout, [Angry mouth (manner)]
to—AC. IV. 2. O.
Eel—Fi. VI. 6. A.
  [Heathcock] Bi. II. 5.
Power.
  Natural—NP.
  { Might } Ha. II. 6.
  { Authority }
  —*full*, [adj. a. Power]
  in one's—[adj. p. Power]
Pox.
  French——S. II. 6.
  Small—S. II. 4.
Practice. RC. II. A.
  —*Law* } RC. II. A. { L.
  —*Physic* } { P. }
  { Action }
  { Endeavour }
  { Essay }
  { Exercise }
  —*ed*, [Expert]
Pragmaticalness, [Diligent (corr.)]
Pray. RE. IV. 1.

PR

Prayer, [adj. RE. IV. 1. (thing)]
Praise. RO. V. 8.
Prance, { Go proudly } { Trot }
Prank.
  [Extraordinary action]
to—
  [a. Ornate (make)]
Prate, [a. Loquacity]
Pratic, [Licence to trade]
Prattle, [a. Loquacity]
Pravity, [Evil (abstr.)]
Prawn, [Shrimp] Ex. VI. 4.
Preach. RE. IV. 4.
Preamble, [Prologue]
Prebendary, [At- { Cathedral } tessor of { Collegiate } Church]
Precaution, [Warning]
Precedence. Sp. I. 2. E.
Precedent.
  [Exemplar]
  [Preceding]
Precellence, [Excellence]
Precept, [Command]
Precinct, [Authority (place)]
Precious, [adj. Price (augm.)]
—*stone*, [Gem]
Precipice, [Steep (place)]
Precipitate.
  Chymic. O. VI. 3. A.
  Capital punishment. RJ. V. 3. A.
  [Hast (exc.)]
  [a. Rashness]
Precise.
  { Perfect }
  { Regular } (augm.)
  { Scrupulous }
Precocity, [Soon (exc.) Ripeness]
Precognition, [Before-knowing]
Precontract, [Before-contract]
Predatory, [adj. a. Booty]
Predecessor, [adj. Preceding (person)]
Predestinate, { determine } [Before- { appoint }]
Predicable, [adj. p. Predicate (apt.)]
Predicament. TA.
Predicate, D. II. 5. A.
Predication, [a. Predicate]
Prediction, { Before-telling } { Prophecy }
Predominant, { More-powerful } { adj. a. Victory }
Pre-election, [Rather-chusing]
Pre-eminence.
  { Superiority }
  { Excellence }
  { Dignity }
  { Privilege }
Preemp- { Before- } *buying*.
tion, { first }
Preexistence, [Before-actualness]
Preface, [Prologue]
Prefect, [adj. { Authority } (person) { Office }]

PR

—*ure*, { Authority } { Office }
Prefer.
  { More- } { esteem }
  { Before- } { chuse }
  —*person*, { Dignity }
  { adj. a. Power }
  —*bill*, [adj. a. Bill]
Prefigure, [Before adj. a. type]
Prefix, [Before- { Fasten } adj. a. { Appoint }]
Pregnant, { Full } { Important }
Prey, [Booty]
Prejudice, [Before-opinion (corr.)]
—*ial*, { Hurtful } { Impedient }
Prejudicate, { a. Sentence } [Before- { Condemn }]
Preke, [Pourcontrel] Ex. IX. 1.
Prelate, [Bishop] RE. II. 4. A.
Prelude, [adj. Preparation play]
Premeditate, [Before-meditate]
Premise, { put }
[Before- { suppose }]
Premonish, [Before-warn]
Premunire, [Forfeiture of goods and liberty]
Prentice { merc. }
  [Disciple { mech. }]
Preoccupation, [Before-possess]
Preordain, [Before-ordain]
Prepare. TA. III. 2.
—*food*. Pr. III.
Preponderate, [More-weigh]
Preposition. D. II. 8.
Preposterous, [Against-order'd]
Prepuce, [Skin to be cut off in Circumcision]
Prerogative. RC. IV. 7.
Presage, [Before-sign]
Presbyter. RE. II. 5. A.
Prescience, [Before-knowing]
Prescribe.
  [Before-appoint]
  —*by Law*, [a. Law]
  —*by Custom*, [a. Right (make) by pret. custom]
Presence.
  —*in place*. Sp. II. 1.
  —*chamber*, [Room for King's presence]
  —*in time*. Sp. I. 1.
  [Sprightliness]
Present, [adj. Presence]
to—
  [Represent]
  [Accuse]
a—[Gift]
Pre- { Right of giving } Priest's
sentation { Giving of right } (place)
Presently { adv. Present } { adv. Future (dim.) }
Preserv, { Keep } { Defend } { Condite }
Action of God. AS. L 4.

Pre-

PR   PR   PR

Preservative, [adj. a. Preserve (thing)]
President.
  [Prefect]
  [Example]
Press.
  { Thrusting }
  { a, Compression }
  —*to death*. RJ. V. 3.
  Printer's— [adj. a. Printing (jug.)]
  Wine—[adj. Wine (jug.)]
  [a. { Dense, Fast, Hard, Heavy } make].
  [a. { Necessity, Coaction }]
  —*souldiers*, [a. Souldier (make) by coaction]
  [a. { Perswade, Intreat } (augm.)]

Throng, [Dense { Multitude, Aggregate, Chief }]
  —*for* { Apparel, Books } [Box—]
Pressure, { Pressing, Necessity, Affliction }
Prest, [Ready]
Prestigiator. RC. II. 9. A.
Presume.
  [a. { Boldness, Confidence }]
  [a. Hope (corr.)]
Presumption.
  { Presuming, Strong argument } sp. Conjectural.
Presumptuousness.
  [Hope (corr.)]
  [Rashness]
  { Irreverence, Arrogance }
Presuppose, [Before-suppose]
Pretence.
  { Seeming, Feigned } cause]
Pretend.
  [Seem (make)]
  [Dissemble]
Preterition, [Omission]
Pretermit, [Omit]
Pretext.
  { Seeming, Feigned } cause]
Pretty.
  [Handsom (dim.)]
  [adj. Mediocrity]
Prevail.
  [a. { Superiour, Victory }]
  [Obtain]
Prevarication.
  [Betraying by pleading]
  [Deceit- { Action, ful } Speech]
Prevent. TA. III. 9.
Previous, { Preceding, [adj. Preparation] }

Pry, { See (end), a. Spy }
Priapism. Disease.
Price. RC. V. 7.
Prick.
  [Point]
  Mark, [adj. p. Object (thing)]
  { Tooth } Mag. IV. 2.
  { Prickle, [Thorn] PP. I. 3. A.
  —*ing*. Mo. VI. 7. A.
  —*pain*. AC. II. 7. A.
  —*forward*, { a. Impul-
  —*on*, } sive
  —*in*, [a. Plant]
  up, [a. Direct]
  —*wood*. Sh. I. 4. A.
Pricket, [Buck. Be. II. 6. of the second year.]
Prickle, [Thorn] PP. I, 3, A.]
Pride. Man. V. 2. D.
Priest.
  Jewish—RE. II. 2.
  Christian—RE. II. 5.
Primary, { First, Chief }
Primate. RE. II. 4.
Prime, { First, Chief }
Primitive. TM. IV. 1.
Primogeniture, [First birth (abstr.)]
Primrose. HS. VIII. 1.
Prince. RC. I. 2. A.
  [King's Son]
  —*'s feather*. HF. I. 15. A.
  —*'s wood*. Tr. VII. 6. A.
Principal.
  [Chief]
  [Governour]
  [Money { demised, disbursed }]
  —*ness*. TM. IV. 4.
Principality. [Government (place)]
Principle.
  [Cause]
  [Rule]
  [Element]
Print.
  [Mark]
  [Impression]
  —*ing*. AC. III. 7. A.
Prior, [Abby (Off.)]
Priority. [Preceding (abstr.)]
Prism. Mag. III. 6. O.
Prison, [Imprisonment (place)]
Prisoner. Reputed Criminal. R]. I. 3. O.
  [adj. p. Imprison (person)]
Pristin, { Former, Old }
Privado, [Friend (augm.)]
Private.
  op. to Public, [adj. TM. V. 5. O.
  [Concealed]
  —*man*, [Not-magistrate]
Privateer, [Private man of war.]
Privation, [a. Privative]
Privative. T. III. 3. O.
Privet. Sh. II. 11.
  Ever-green—Sh. III. 3. A.

Mock—Sh. III. 3.
Privy.
  [Knowing]
  [Accessory]
  [Hidden]
  [Secret]
  —*parts*. PG. VI. 8.
  Jakes, [Dunging (room)]
Privilege. RC. IV. 7. A.
  —*ed place*, [p. Immunity (place)]
Privities. PG. VI. 8.
Prize.
  [Booty]
  [Reward of victory]
  { Fighting, Gaming } sp. for wager]
  —*to*—
  [a. { Price, Value }]
  [Esteem]
Probable, { Opinion, [adj. Probation] } (apt.)
Probation. D. VI. 6.
  —*er*, [adj. p. Essaying (person)]
Probe, [Depth measure (pin)]
Problem, { Proposition, Question } to be disputed
Proboscis, [Trunk] PP. V. 4. A.
Proceed. TA. VI. 2,
  —*from*, [adj. p. { Cause, Birth, Being } from]
  —*ings*, [Series of actions.]
  —*Judicial*. RJ. II.
  the— { Gain, Revenue }
Process.
  [a. Proceeding]
  [Series]
  —*of a bone*, [Protuberant (part)]
  —*of time*, { some, After } much } time]
  —*in Law*, [Citation] sp. written]
Procession.
  [Proceeding]
  [Solemn about-walking]
Proclaim, [Publish] sp. solemnly]
Proclama- { Publishing, tion } Edict
Proclivity, [Inclinableness]
Procra- { Delay, stinate } Protract } sp. till next day.
Procreate, [Generate]
Proctor.
  [Substitute]
  [Advocate]
Procuration.
  [adj. Proctor (make) sp. writing]
  [Procuring]
Procure.
  [Cause]
  [Furnish]
  [Obtain]
Prodigality. Man. III. 1. E.

Pro-

PR

Pro- { Preter-natural } (thing)
digy, { Extraordinary }
sp. before-signing a. adversity]
Prodigious.
 [adj. Prodigy]
 [Great (augm.)]
Produce.
 [Out-take] sp. from concealing (place.)
 [a. Cause]
 —fruit, [a. Fruit]
 —by Multiplication, [a. Product]
 [Known (make)]
 { Extend }
 { Long (make) }
 { Continue }
Product. TM. VI. 8. O.
Proem, [Prologue]
Profane.
 Irreligious, [adj. RE. IV. D.]
 [Not-consecrated]
 to—, RE. V. 1. O.
Profess [a. Profession]
 —ion
 [Acknowledgment]
 Calling. RC. II.
Proffer, [Offer]
Proficient, [adj. Profit]
Profit.
 [adj. Profitable (thing)]
 [Gain]
 [Revenue]
 —able. T. IV. 1.
 to—[a. Profit]
 —in learning, [Increase—]
Profligate.
 [Driven away]
 [Vicious (augm.)]
Profound.
 [Deep]
 [Obscure]
Profundity.
 [Depth]
 [Obscureness]
Profuse, { Prodigal }
 { Squandering }
Progeny, [Descen- { (kinde) }
 dents { (aggr.) }
Progenitor. RO. I. 1.
Prognosticate.
 [Before- { know }
  { tell }]
Progress.
 [Proceeding]
 [Journey]
 [Increase]
 —ion,
 [Proceeding]
 —of Animals. Mo. I.
 { Continuing }
 { Joyning }
Prohibit.
 [Forbid]
 [Hinder]
Projecting.
 [Designing]
 [Contriving]
Projection.
 ——Chymic, [a. Factitious Gold]

PR

—of sphere, [Repressing it upon a Plain]
Prolation, [Articulation]
Prole, [Wander seeking]
Prolifical, [Fruitful]
Prolix, [Long (augm.)]
 [Ample]
Prolocutor, [adj. Speaking (Off.)]
 sp. { First }
  { Chief } Speaker]
Prologue. D. V. 8.
Prolong.
 [Lengthen]
 [Delay]
Prominent, [Protuberant]
Promiscu- { Mixed }
 ous, { Confused }
Promise. RO. V. 6.
 —to God, [Vow]
 —in contract. RO. VI. 3.
 —for another, [Stipulate]
 Espouse. RO. II. 3.
Promontory. W. III. 4.
Promoter, [adj. Accusing (Off.)]
Promote.
 [a. Help]
 [a. Dignity]
Prompt.
 [adj. { Dispatch }
  { Alacrity }]
 [adj. p. Disciple (apt.)]
 [adj. Sagacity]
 to—[Dictate secretly]
Promptuary, [adj. Laying-up (place)]
Promulgate, [Publish]
Prone, { Disposition }
 [adj. p. { Inclination }]
Prong, [adj. Pricking (apt.)]
 Fork]
Pronoun. D. II. 7.
Pronounce, [v. Articulate]
Proof..
 [Probation)]
 [Essaying]
 of—[adj. p. Essaying]
 in—[Fat]
Prove.
 { Probation }
 { Confirmation }
 [Essay]
 [Become]
Prop. Po. III. 7.
Propagate, [v. Multitude (kind)]
 { Alacrity }
Propensity, { Inclination (apt.) }
Proper.
 op. to Common. [adj. TM. IV. 6.]
 op. to Figurate [adj. D. III. 6.]
 [Tall]
Property,
 [Proper (thing)]
 [Propriety]
Prophane.
 Irreligious, [adj. RE. IV. D.]
 [Not-consecrated]
 to—RE. V. 1. O.
Prophesie, [a. Prophet]
Prophet. RE. II. 1. A.
Propinquity, [Nearness]

PR

Propitiation, { Un-enemy }
 { Un-guilty }
 { Un-anger }
 sp. by Sacrifice]
Propitious, [adj. Favour]
Proportion. Mea. A.
 —Arithmetical, [Equality of differences]
 well—ed, [Figured (perf.)]
Propose.
 [a. Proposition]
 [Offer]
Proposition. D. V. 1.
Propound, vid. Propose.
Proprietary, [Proper owner]
Propriety. RC. IV. 5.
Prorogue, [a. Stay till another time]
Proscarab. Ex I. 6.
Proscribe, [Pub- { Command }
 lish { Permission }
  to kill]
Prose. D. III. 4.
Prosecute. AS. IV. 6.
 —judicially, [Continue adj. a. Accuser]
Proselyte, [Convert]
Prosodia, [Measuring (art) of quantities of syllables]
Prospect, [adj. p. See { Place }
  { Area }]
 —ive glass, { Glass (instr.) for seeing remote (things) }
Prosperity. Ha. I. 2.
Prostitute, [adj. p. object (make) adv. common]
 sp. to a. Unchastness]
 a—[Common a. unchast (fem)]
Prostrate, [Lying] AC. VI. 7. O.
Prosyllogism, [Preceding Syllogism.]
Protect. Man. VI. 4.
 [Conservation]
 [Defending]
Protest. RC. VI. 3. A.
 ——against. R]. II. 8.
Protono- { First }
 tary, { Chief } notary]
Proto- { First }
 type, { Chief } type.]
protract. TA. III. 5. O.
Protuberance. Mag. IV. 3.
Proud, [adj. Pride]
 —bitch, [adj. Coition (apt) b.]
Prove, vid. Proove.
Provender, [Corn for horses]
Proverb, [Adage]
Provide.
 [a. Providence]
 [Furnish]
 -for, [a. Heedfulness against]
 { Conditionally }
 —ed that, { that. }
  { If. }
Providence.
 —of God. AS. I. 2.
 —of Man. Man. III. 2.
Providents, [adj. a. Providence]
Province. RC. III. 3.
 —Ecclesiastical, [Primate's (place)]
Provincial, [adj. Province]

a—

PU

—[Chief (Off.) of a Province]
Provision,
  [a. Providence]
  Necessaries. Pr.
Proviso, [adv. Condition]
Provoke,
  as— { Cause
       { Impulsive
  [Angry (make]
  Challenge: RM. I. 2.
Provost, { Authority } (person)
          { Office }
Prow, [Fore-part of a ship]
Prowess, [a. Fortitude]
Proxy, [Substituted (person)]
Proximity, [Nearness]
Prudence, [Wisdom.]
Prune.
  [Plum]
  to—O. III. 8.
Prunel.
Pſalm. RE. IV. 3. A.
Pſalter, [Book of Psalms]
Priſan, [Broth of Barley
         ſp. Medicinal.]
Publican, [adj. Tax (Off.]
Publicneſs. TM. V. 5.
Publiſh, [a. Publicness (make]
Pucker, [Un- a. Evenness by
         ſhrinking]
Puck-fiſt, [Fuzball] HL. I. 2. A.
Pudding. Pr. I. 2. A.
  —*graſs,* [Penny-royal]
Puddle, [Stagnum] W. IV.
         7. A.
  [Durty water]
  to—[a. Durty (make]
Puet, [Lapwing] Bi. VII. 1.
Puff.
  { Wind   } (imp.)
  { Breath }
  [Swell] ſp. with wind] S. I.
         5. A.
  —*up,* [a. Proud (make]
Puffin. Bi. IX. 6.
Pug, [Monkey]
Puiſſance, [Power]
Puke, [Vomit]
Pulchritude, [Beauty]
Pule, [Acute grief (voice]
Pull. O. I. 4. ſp. looking toward
       the object.] ſp. without ſuc-
       ceſs]
  —*bird,* [Un- a. feather b.]
  —*down,* { Diminiſh
           { Weaken
  —*in pieces,* [Tear into frag-
       ments]
Pullein, [Cock Bi. { (kinde
                    { (aggr.)
       II. 1.]
Pullet, [Young hen]
Pully, [adj. O. I. 3. (jug.)]
Pullulate, [Sprout (inc.]
Pulp.
Pulpit, [Preaching (place]
Pulſe.
  Motion. Mo. III. 1.
  [Legumen]
  only purging—HS. VII. 10. A.
Pulverize, [a. Powder
         (make]

PU

Pumice. St. I. 7.
Pump. Po. VI. 3. A.
  Shoe, [limber-bottom'd adj.
         foot (veſt.]
  to—*out,* [Know (end) by
         queſtioning]
Pumpion.
Punaiſe, [Wall-louſe] Ex. II.
         6. A.
Punch, [Thruſt (imp.]
  [adj. p. Hole (make) by ſtri-
         king]
  [Drink of Brandy and Wa-
         ter]
Punctilio, [Point (dim.)]
Punctual, [Perfect]
Pungent, [Pricking
           { New] ſp. Learner
Puny, { Unexpert]
Puniſhment. Ha. I. O.
  —*Capital,* RJ. V.
  —*not Capital.* RJ. VI.
Punk, [adj. Unchaſt (fem.]
Pupil. RO. III. 4. O.
Puppet, [Image (dim.) of man]
Puppy, [Dog. Be. III, 1. (young,]
Purblind, [Not-adj. a. See (pot.
         remote (things)]
Purchaſe, [Buy]
Pure.
  [Simple]
  [Clean]
  —*neſs.* TM. V. 7.
  [Holy]
Purgation. Mo. IV.
  vid. Purge.
Purgatory, [Puniſhment (place)
         for purging from ſin)]
Purge.
  Evacuation. Mo. IV.
  [Dunging] ſp. by Phyſic]
  [Cleanſe]
  [Pure (make]
  Expiating [Unguilty (make]
         [Abſolving]
  —*upon oath,* [Swear (make)
         innocence]
  a—[a. Dunging medecin.]
Purifie, [a. Pure (make]
Purity, vid. Pureneſs.
Purle.
  of lace. Pr. IV. 3. A.
  [Mixture of drinks] ſp. with
         wormwood.]
Purloin, [a. Theft]
Purliew, [Margin of Forreſt]
P urple.
  Fifth. Fi. Ex. VII. 2. A.
  Colour. Q. II. 4.
  —*s,* [adj. a. Purple fever]
Purport, [Meaning]
Purpoſe.
  Intention. AS. IV. 3.
  [Deſign]
  full—[Reſolution]
  beſide the—[Impertinent]
  of—} [adv. { Deſign]
  on—}   { Confederate]
  tothe—} [adv. { Congruous
               { Pertinent
               { Perfect]

PU

to no— { Fruſtration]
         { Frivolous]
  [adv. Frivolous]
to what—[For what end]
Purpura. Ex. VII. 2. A.
Purſe, [Bag for money]
  —*er.* RN. V. 5. A.
  —*net,* [Net bag (like]
  Shepherd's—
Purſevant. RJ. I. 6.
Purſy, { Aſthmatical]
        { Fat (corr.)
Purſlane. HL. VIII. 3.
  —*tree,* [Halimus] Sh. VI. 6.
Purſue, [Follow]
  —*ing.* RM. II. 3. E.
purvey, [Provide]
purulent, [Mattery]
puſh.
  Tumor (dim. S. III. 1.
  to—[Thruſt (imp.]
Puſillanimity. Man. III. 8. D.
Puſs, [Cat]
Puſtule. S. III. 1.
Put.
  { Proper. TA. I. 1.
  { a. Place]
  [a. Cauſe]
  —*away,* [Abdicate]
  —*back,* [Retire (make]
  —*by,* [a. Fruſtration]
  —*down,* [Un- a. { Power
                   { Authority
                   { Office]
  —*forth.*
  { Publiſh]
  { Pullulate]
  Un- a. { Authority
         { Power
         { Office]
  —*in,* [a. Inſide]
  —*bail,* [a. Stipulation]
  —*a box,* [Into a box]
  —*execution,* [a. Execute]
  —*fear,* [a. Fear (make]
  —*one's head,* [a. Think
         (make]
  —*hope,* [a. Hope (make]
  —*mind,* [a. Remember
         (make]
  —*order,* [a. Order]
  —*practice,* [a. Practice]
  —*print,* [a. Print]
  —*remembrance,* [a. Memory
         (make]
  —*writing,* [a. Write]
  —*off,* { Delay
         { Sell]
  —*ones clothes,* [Un- a. clothe]
  —*on,* { Haſten
         { a. Impulſive]
  —*one's clothes,* [a. clothe]
  —*over,* { Digeſtion
          { a. Aſſign]
  —*out,* { Quench
         { Annihilate]
         { Publiſh]
  —*of doors,* [a. Exile]
  —*of office,* [Un- a. Office]
  —*of order,* [a. Confuſion]
  —*one's* { a. Blindneſs]
  eyes, { Un- a. Eye]

Nnn

QU

(Adde)
(Apply)
—to { Arbitrator (make)
(Shut)
—be done, { [Appoint s d.]
—be kept, { to be { k.]
{ a. Dy]
—death, { a. Capital punish.
ment]
—flight, [a. Fly (make)]
—shame, [a. Shame]
—shift, } [a. Difficulty]
—it,
—sword, [a. Sword]
—venture, [a. Essay]
—use, [a. Usury]
—together, [Together-put]
—up.
—a bare, [a. Motion h.]
—petition, [a. Petition]
—sword, [a. Sheath s.]
—wrong, [Not-revenge w.]
—upon, [a. Impulsive]
—case, [Suppose]
—an end to, [a. End]
—trick on, [a. Affront]
[a. Mock]
Putrefaction, [Rottenness]
Putrefie, [a. Rotten (make)]
Putrid, [Rotten]
Puttock, [Kite (kinde)]
Puzzle, [Pose]
Pygmy, [Man (dim.)]
Pyramid. Mag. III. 7. O.
Pyromancy, [Wizarding by inspection of fire]
Pyx, [Box]

Q

Quackfalver, [Physician (corr.)]
Quadrangle, [Four-angled Area.]
Quadrant, [The fourth part of a Circle]
Quadrate, [Square] Mag. V. I. A.
Quadrature, [Squaring]
Quadripartite, [Divided into four parts]
Quadruple, [Fourfold]
Quaff, [Drink (augm.)]
Quagmire, [Bog]
Quail. Bi. II. 8.
to—[adj. p. Discouragement]
Quaint,
{ Beautiful
{ Ornate } (augm.)
{ Perfect
Quake, [Tremble]
{ Quality]
Qualifie, [a. { Moderate]
{ Quiet]
Qualifica- { Quality]
tion. { Condition]
Quality. T. I. 6. A.
Transcendental Relation of—
TM. V.

QU

Sensible. Q.
Visible—Q. I.
Audible—Q. III.
Belonging to Tast or Smell.
Q. IV.
Tactile { more Active. Q. V.
{ more Passive. Q. VI.
[Disposition]
{ Habit]
{ Manners]
{ State]
{ Degree]
Qualm.
{ Nauseousness } (imp.)
{ Fainting
Quandary.
{ Doubt]
{ Musing]
Quantity, T. I. 6.
{ in General. TM. I
{ Continued. TM. II.
Relation of { Discontinued. TM. III.
Quarrel, [a. Contention]
—of glass, [adj. Glass (lam.)]
Quarry.
[Stones (place)]
[Booty]
Quart.
Quartan, [Ague returning every fourth day]
Quarter.
[Fourth part]
—of the Moon, [The fourth part of her monethly course]
—of corn.
—of timber, [The fourth part of a tree cut long-wise]
—staff.
—of Mutton, [The fourth part of the body of sheep]
to—[Cut into quarters]
Capital punishment. RJ. V. I. A.
[Coast]
[a. Guest]
—master. RN. V. 2.
[Immunity from killing]
Quartile, [Distance of ¼ of great Circle.]
Quarto, [Second figure of book]
Quash, { Shame
{ a. } (make)
{ Despair
Herb, [Pompion] HS. VII. I.
Quave, [Tremble]
[p. as bog]
Quaver.
[Tremble]
[Modulation]
Quean, [adj. Unchaft (fem.)]
Queasy, [adj. Nauseousness (apt.)]
Queen, { King (fem.)
{ King's Wife]
Queest, [Ringdove] Bi. III. 1.
Quell, [a. Conquer]
Quench, [Un-a fire]
—thirst, [Un-thirst]
Querister, [adj. Singing (Off.)]
Quern. [Grinding mill.]

QU

Querulous, { Grudge
[adj. a. { Complain } (apt.)
Quest, [Seeking]
[Sworn adj. searching (Off.)]
Question. D. VI. 1.
to call { Accuse (inc.)
in— { Suspected (make)
'tis a— { doubted
['Tis a { disputed } (thing)
Quetch, { Motion
{ Noise } (dim.)
Quibble, [a. Urbanity in found of words]
Quick.
[Alive]
{ Sprightly]
{ Vegete]
—of apprehension, [adj. Sagacity]
{ Nimble]
{ Swift]
{ Soon
{ Transitory } (augm.)
[adj. Dispatch]
—sands. W. III. 7.
—set, [Growing sepiment]
—silver. Met. III. 1.
Quicken, [a. Quick]
Quicken-tree. Tr. III. 3.
Quiddity, [Being (abstr.)]
Quiet.
op. to Motion. Mo. O.
[adj. Silence]
[Peaceable]
op. to Molest. TA. V. 9.
[Without care]
Quill. PP. V. 1. A.
[Pin] sp. concave
Quillet, [a. Frivolousness (dim.)]
Quilt.
[Satiate]
[Stiffen with sowing]
Quince. Tr. I. 2. A.
Quintal, [100 pound]
Quintessence, [Best part]
sp. extracted Chimically]
Quintin.
Quipp, [Se- { Scoff]
cret { Reproof]
Quire.
—of Church, [Chief Temple (part)]
—of people, [Singers (aggr.)]
—of paper, [Four and twenty sheets]
Quirk, [Little frivolous (thing)]
Quit.
to be—with, [adj a. pret. Compensate]
{ Acquit]
to— { Absolve]
{ Forsake]
Quitch, [Dogs grass] HL. III. 5. A.
Quite, [adv. Total]
—and clean. [adv. Total]
Quittance, [adj. Acquitting (thing) sp. writing]
Quiver, [Case for arrows]
to—[Tremble]
{ Confused noise]
Quoil, { Endeavour (augm.)
Quoit,

RA

Quoit, [adj. p. cast (apt) stone (lamin.]
Quotation. D. IV. 9.
Quoth, [Saith]
Quotidian, [adj. Days (regr.]
Quotient. Number TM. VI. 9.

R.

R Abbet, [Cony] Be. III. 4.
Rabbin, [Jew- { Teacher } ish { Graduate }
Rabble. RC. I. 7.
Race.
 [a. Running]
 [adj. Running (place]
 [Series]
 [Descendents (aggr.] RO. I. 1. O.
to— [Spoil] vid. Raze.
Rack.
 [Jugament of parallel pins (augm.]
 —for horse, &c. [Rack for Hay]
 —for spit, [Spit-supporting (jug.]
 —for torment, [adj. RJ. VI. 3. (jug.]
 —bone. PG. IV. 3.
to—
 [Extend violently]
 Torment. RJ. VI. 3.
 —wine, [Separate it from the Lees]
Racket.
 [adj. Net (instr.) for a balling]
 [Tumult]
Radiation, [a. Shining adv. line (figure]
Radical, [adj. Root]
Radicate. [a. Root]
Radish. HS. IV. 5.
Raff, [Worst part]
Raft, [Ship (like) of together-tied Timbers]
Rafter, [Wooden column (dim.]
Rag, [Off-torn fragment]
 —stone. St. I, 2.
 —wort: HF. III. 7.
Rage.
 [Violence (augm.]
 sp. of anger
Ragged, [adj. p. Rough] sp. by tearing]
Raya Oxyrinchos, Fi. II. 3.
Ray.
 Fish. Maide.
 [Half diameter]
 Beam [Line of light]
 [Leaf of metal]
 —in battel, [adj. p. Order for battel]
 —of a Fish. PP. IV. 6, A.
Ray-weed, [Darnel]
Rail.
 [Bar]
 Bird. Bi. II. 8. A.

to— [Revile]
Raillery, [a. Urbanity]
Raiment, [Clothing]
Rain.
 Water. El. III. 3.
 —bow. El. V. 1.
Raise.
 { Life }
 { Rise (make) }
 —Devils, [Appear (make)D.]
 —from sleep, [Waken]
 —siege, [Un- a. siege]
 —up, [Up-raise]
 [High (make)]
 [a. Dignity]
 [a. Cause]
 —a bank, [a. Bank (make)]
 —men, } Gather—
 —money, }
 —war, [War (make]
 [a. { Intension } sp. { Augmentation } more.]
 —one's voice, [More-a. voice]
Raisin, [Dried grape]
Rake, [Staples (line)]
 —of a ship. RN. II. 9. A.
 [adj. Staples (line) together adj. gathering (instr.]
 —hell, [Vicious (augm.) person]
to—
 [Gather with Rake]
 —up together, [Gather as with Rake]
 [a. Pain adv. scratching (like]
Rally, { a. gather }
Again- { a. order }
Ram.
 [Sheep. Be. II. 2. (male]
 [Stinking adv. Goat (like]
to— { Dense }
 [a. { Fast }
 sp. by down-knocking]
 —Into, [Into-ram]
 —mer, } Dense
 { a. Fast } (instr.]
 sp. by knocking]
Ramage.
Ramp, [Leap]
 —ant, [Standing on the hinder legs]
 a— [Wanton adj. a. Rusticity (fem.]
Rampier. RM. VI. 3.
Rampion. HS. VII. 7.
Ramson. HL. IV. 12.
 mountain—HL. IV. 12. A.
Rana piscatrix, [Toad-fish]
Rancour, [Hatred (augm.] sp. old]
Rand.
 —of beef, [Flank——]
 —of leather, [Long (part—]
Random, [Wandering]
 —shot, [Not-aimed]
Range.
 [Sift]
 [a. Order]
 { Wander }
 { About-v. journey }
Rank.
 [Excessive]

[Leafed (exc.]
[Rammish]
[Genuine (corr.]

[Order]
[Series]
[Line]
op. to File. RM. IV. 4.
[Degree]
sp. of person] RJ. I.
Rankle, [Rot]
Ransack.
 [Booty]
 [Search (augm.]
Ransom, [Price { slaving } for un- { captivating }]
to— [Un- { slave } sp. with a. { captive } price]
Rap, [Little striking (imp.]
Rapacity.
 Greediness. NP. IV. 5.
 [Scraping] Man. III. 2, E.
Rape.
 [Wild Turnip]
 [Force]
 [Forcible stupration]
Rapid, [Swift (augm.]
Rapier, [Sword adj. pricking (apt.]
Rapine, [a. Scrapingness { violence } sp. by { extortion }]
Rapture, [Extasie]
Rare, [adj.] Rarity]
 [Thin]
 [Seldom]
 [Excellent]
Rarifie, [a. Q. V. 3. D.]
Rarity.
 [Seldomness] Sp. II. 6. O.
 [Excellence]
 Tactil quality. Q. V. 3. D.
Rasbury. Sh. I. 1.
Rascal.
 [Lean]
 [Sorry]
Rasher, [Broil'd (lamin]
Rashness.
 op. to Fortitude. Man. I. 7. E.
 op. to Confiderate. Ha. IV. 1. D.
Rasp, [adj. Filing (instr.) adj. teeth (plain]
Raspis. Sh. I. 1.
Rat. Be. III. 7.
 —'s bane, [Arsenic]
Rate.
 [Proportion]
 [Price]
 [Tax]
 [Chide]
Rathe.
 [Soon]
 [Early]
Rather, [More]
 sp. More-willingly]
 I had—more { will }
 { I { before } { chuse }
Ratifie.
 [a. Authority]
 [Confirm]
Ratiocination.

RA

[a. Rational]
[Discourse]
Rational. [adj. NP. I.]
—*Power.* NP. I.
—*Soul.* W. I. 6.
Rattle, [adj. Rattling (inftr.]
Rattling.
  [Noise by mutual striking of solids (dim.)]
  [Reproving, augm.]
  —*of ship.* RN. IV. 2.
Ravage, [a. Booty]
Rave. S. IV. I. A.
Ravel, [Tangle]
  [a. Confusion]
Ravelin.
Raven.
  Bird. Bi. L 5.
  to—
  [a. Rapacity]
  [a. {Scrapingness}
       {Extortion}]
  [a. Booty]
Raving. S. IV. I. A.
Ravish.
  {Take
   Stuprate} violently]
  [a. Extasie]
Raw.
  [Un-skinn'd]
  Not-cook'd. adj. Pr. III. O.
  [Not-digested]
  [Unexpert]
Raze.
  [a. Ruine]
  [a. {Destruction}
      {Spoiling}
  sp. by shaving]
Razor.
  [Shaving (inftr.)]
  [Knife for shaving]
  Fish. Ex. VIII. 8. A.
  Bird
  —*bill.* Bi. IX. 7.
  Re. Ad. III. 3. A.
Reach.
  [Extend] AC. VI. 2.
  —*out.*
  [Extend one's arm]
  [Deliver with extended arm]
  {a. Pandiculation}
  {Vomit (end)}
  [v. Continuance until]
  {Take
   Obtain}
  —*after*, [Take (end)]
  [Understand]
  —*of a river*, (curve (part) of stream)
  [End]
  [Design]
Reachless.
  [Careless]
  [Idle]
Read. AC. III. 4.
  —*ing*, [Learning] Ha. VI. 4.
  —*r*, [a. Teacher]
Ready.
  [Present]

RE

{Soon}
{Near}
{Easie}
{Willing}
{Inclined}
[adj. Alacrity]
{Prepared
 Furnish'd
 Clothed}
[Dispatch'd]
—*to dy*, [Almost adj. fut. dying]
Readmit, [Again-admit]
Reality.
  [Thing (abstr.)]
  [Sincerity]
Realm, [King's (place)]
Ream, [Twenty quires]
Reap. O. III. 4. A.
Rear.
  [Raise]
  [a. Direct (make)]
Reason.
  [Cause] sp. {Impulsive}
              {Final}
  [Argument]
  Faculty. NP. I.
  {Moderation}
  {Equity}
  by—of. Prep. I. 2. O.
  in—[adv. Equity]
  out of—[Excessively]
  to—
  —*in one's mind.*
  {Discourse}
  {Dispute}
  —*for*, [a. Probation (end)]
  —*against*, [Confute (end)]
Reasonable, [adj. {Reason}
                    {Mediocrity}]
  —*government.* Man. VI. 6.
Reassemble, [Again-assemble]
Reave, [Un-knit]
Rebaptize, [Again-baptize]
Rebate, [Diminish adv. proportion]
Rebeck.
Rebellion.
  Vice. Man. V. 5. D.
  Crime. RJ. III. 3.
Rebound, [Leap reflexly]
Rebuff, [Back-striking]
Rebuild, [Again-build]
Rebuke, [Reprove]
Rebus, [Express-{Name
  on (manner) of {Sentence by picture]
Recall, {Back-call}
          {Recant}
Recantation. D. VI. 9. A.
Recapitulate, [Repeat the sum]
Recede.
  [Back-go]
  [Retire]
Receit.
  [Receiving]
  [Direction of Physic]
  [adj. Acquitting (thing)]
Receive.

RE

Proper. TA. IV. 3. O.
[Accept]
[Entertain]
—*er.*
[adj. Receiving (person)]
[adj. Gathering (Off.)]
—*ed*, {adj. p. Receive}
       {Customary}
Receptacle.
  {Receiving} {(thing)}
  {Containing} {(vess.)}
Reception, [Receiving]
Recess.
  [Receding]
  [adj. Concealing (place)]
Rech, vid. *Reach.*
Recidivation, [Relapse]
Reciprocation. T. VI. 7. O.
Recite.
  [Repeat]
  [Again-say]
  [a. Narration]
Reckon.
  [Esteem]
  [a. Number]
  [Account] TA. IV. 6.
  —*up*, [a. Number]
  {Number (exc.)}
  over—{Account too-much}
  the—ing, [adj. p. ought pay (thing)]
Reclaim.
  [a. Gentle (make)]
  [Turn]
  —*from errors*, [Convert]
  —*from vice*, [Repent (make)]
Recline, [Down-oblique the superficies]
Recluse.
  [Shut up]
  [Solitary]
Recognize.
  [Consider again]
  [Acknowledge]
Recognizance, [Bond acknowledged before Magistrate]
Recoil.
  [Reflect]
  [Retire]
Recommend.
  [Offer]
  [Entrust]
  sp. adv. Commending]
Recompence.
  [Compensate]
  [Reward]
Reconcile.
  [Un-a. {Enemy}
         {Contention}]
  [a. Peace (make)]
Reconquer, [Back-conquer]
Record.
  [a. Memory]
  [a. Notary]
  take—[a. Notary (make)]
  —*er.*
  {Notary} RJ. I. 5.
  {Judge affistant to the City (Off.)}
  [adj. Music pipe]
Recover.
   [Back

RE

[Back-come]
[Again-{obtain/Gain}]
[Possess again]
[Repair]
[Again- v. Healthy]
Recount.
[a. Narration]
[Consider]
Recourse, [To-coming]
sp. often
Recreant, [Perfidious]
sp. through Cowardise
Recreation. Mo. V.
Moderateness in it. Man. II. 5.
Immoderateness in it. Man. II. 5. D.
Recrement, [Worst part]
—of Metals. Met. IV.
Recriminate, [Retort accusation]
Recruit, {strengthen/fill}
[Again-]
Rect.
op. to Curve.
—angle, [Square having four right angles.]
Rectifying, [a. Right (make)]
Chymical—O. VI. 6. A.
Rector, [Governour]
Recumbency, {Leaning/Trust}
Recusant.
[adj. Refusing (person)]
[Schismatic]
Red. Q. II. 2.
—breast. Bi. V. 5.
—lead, [Cinnabar]
—start. Bi. V. 5. A.
Redargution, [Reproof]
Redbreast. Bi. V. 5.
Redeem.
Action of God. AS. I. 7.
[Back-buy]
[Buy liberty]
[Un-captivate]
[Un- a. slave]
Redeliver, [Back-deliver]
Redemand, [Back-demand]
Redemption, [Redeeming] AS. I. 7.
Redolent, [Sweet]
Redouble, {a. Double/Repeat}
Redoubt. RM. VI. 6.
—ed, {Excellent/sp. in Reputation/sp. for Fortitude}
Redound, {a. Event/Remedy}
Redress, {Amendment}
Redshank. Bi. VII. 4.
Redstart. Bi. V. 5. A.
Redwing. Bi. III. 5. A.
Reduce.
{Cause/Make}
{Again-make}
[Bring back]
Redundant.
[adj. Excess]
[Superfluous]

RE

Reduplicate.
[a. Double]
[Repeat]
Reed. HL. III. 7.
Burr—HL. III. 15. A.
flowring—HL. V. 4.
sweet smelling—HL. III. 11.
—mace. HL. III. 15.
Re-edifie, [Again-build]
Reek.
[Heap]
[Vapour]
Reel.
[Stagger] Mo. II. 4, O.
[a. Skein]
a—[adj. a.] {instr./jug.}
Skein
Re-entry, {Again-/Back .. entry}
Re-esta-{Again-/back—} {esta-/blish/blish}
Refection.
[Refreshment]
Feeding. Pr. I. 1. A.
Refectory, [adj. meal (place)]
Refell, [Confute]
Refer.
[a. Relation]
[a. Arbitrator (make)]
Reference, [a. Arbitrator (make)]
Refine.
[a. Pure (make)]
[Un- a. sediment]
Reflect, [a. Mag. II. 9.]
[Look back]
[Again-consider]
Reflecti-{Reflecting/a. Reputation (corr.)}
on,
Reflux, [Ebbing]
Reform. RO. VI. 7.
Reformado, [adj. pret. Military Off.]
Refracted. Mag. II. 9. A.
Refractoriness.
[Perverseness]
[Contumacy]
Refrain, [Abstain]
Refrane, [Proverb]
Refresh.
op. to weariness. TA. V. 8.
[Mend]
[Renew]
Refrigerate, [Cool]
Refuge, [To-flying] sp. for safety
Place, [adj. {Safe/Protection}] (place)
Refulgent, [Shining]
Refund. TA. IV. 5. A.
Refuse.
[Denying]
[Rejecting]
[Abdicating]
[Power of first buying]
The—[Worst part]
Refute, [Confute]
Regal, [adj. King]
Regard.
[a. Relation]
in that—[Therefore] Conj. III. 3. A.

RE

in—of. Pron. I. 2.
[Esteem]
[Respect]
[Observe]
—less, [Careless]
Regene-{Again beget/rate,} a. Ha. V.
Regent, [Instead-King]
Regiment.
[Government]
[Militia]
as a—of souldiers. RM. IV 2. A.
Region, [Country] W. III. A.
—of the air, [Part]
Register, [Notary]
Regrate, [Buy to sell (corr.)]
Regress, [Again-come]
Regret.
[Grudging]
[Nolleity]
[Aversation]
Regular. RE. II. 6.
Regularity. TM. V. 4.
Regulate, [a. Rule]
Regulus Cristatus. Bi. VI. 4.
—non cristatus. Bi. VI. 4. A.
Rehearse.
[Repeat]
[Again-say]
[a. Narration]
Reject. AS. IV. 5. O.
[Abdicate]
Reign.
[a. King]
[King's (time)]
Reimbark, [Into a. ship again]
Reimburse, [Pay]
Rein.
Horse——[adj. Cohibiting (arm)]
[Cord of Bridle]
[Kidney] PG. VI. 7.
Running of the—[Flux]
Reindeer. Be. II. 4. A.
Reinforce, [Again-strengthen]
Reinvest, [Again-invest]
Rejoyce, [v. Joy]
Rejoynder, [Again-answer]
Reister, [Horseman]
Reiterate, [Repeat]
Relapse, {Again—/Back—} fall
[Again-sicken]
[a. Apostasie]
Relate.
[a. Relation]
[Tell]
[Pertain to]
Relation. T. I. 8.
—Oeconomic. RO.
—of Consanguinity. RO. I.
—of Affinity. RO. II.
—of Superiority and Inferiority. RO. III.
—of Equality. RO. IV.
—Civil. RC.
—Judicial. RJ.
—Military. RM.
—Naval. RN.
—Ecclesiastic. RE.
[Narration]

[Re-

RA

[a. Rational]
[Discourse]
Rational. [adj. NP. I.]
—Power. NP. I.
—Soul. W. I, 6.
Rattle, [adj. Rattling (inftr.)]
Rattling.
 [Noife by mutual ftriking of
 folids (dim.)]
 [Reproving, augm.]
 —of ship. RN. IV. 2.
Ravage, [a. Booty]
Rave. S. IV. 1. A.
Ravel, [Tangle]
 [a. Confufion]
Ravelin.
Raven.
 Bird. Bi. L 5
 to —
  [a. Rapacity]
  { Scrapingnefs }
  [a. { Extortion }]
  [a. Booty]
Raving. S. IV. 1. A.
Ravish.
 { Take }
 { Stuprate } violently]
 [a. Extafie]
Raw.
 [Un-skinn'd]
 Not-cook'd. adj. Pr. III. O.
 [Not-digefted]
 [Unexpert]
Raze.
 [a. Ruine]
 [a. { Deftruction }]
 { Spoiling }
 fp. by fhaving]
Razor.
 [Shaving (inftr.)]
 [Knife for fhaving]
 Fifh. Ex. VIII. 8. A.
 Bird
 —bill. Bi. IX. 7.
Re. Ad. III. 3. A.
Reach.
 [Extend] AC. VI. 2.
 —out.
  [Extend one's arm]
  [Deliver with extended
  arm]
 { a. Pandiculation }
 { Vomit (end) }
 [v. Continuance until]
 { Take }
 { Obtain }
 —after, [Take (end)]
 [Underftand]
 —
  —of a river, (curve (part)
  of ftream)
  { End }
  { Defign }
Reachlefs.
 [Carelefs]
 [Idle]
Read. AC. III. 4.
 —ing, [Learning] Ha.
  VI. 4.
 —r, [a. Teacher]
Ready.
 [Prefent]

RE

{ Soon }
{ Near }
{ Eafie }
{ Willing }
{ Inclined }
[adj. Alacrity]
{ Prepared }
{ Furnifh'd }
{ Clothed }
[Difpatch'd]
—to dy, [Almoft adj. fut.
 dying]
Readmit, [Again-admit]
Reality.
 [Thing (abftr.)]
 [Sincerity]
Realm, [King's (place)]
Ream, [Twenty quires]
Reap. O. III. 4. A.
Rear.
 [Raife]
 [a. Direct (make)]
Reafon.
      { Impulfive }
 [Caufe (fp. { Final }]
 [Argument]
 Faculty. NP. I.
 { Moderation }
 { Equity }
 by—of. Prep. I. 2. O.
 in—[adv. Equity]
 out of—[Exceffively]
 to—
  —in one's mind.
  { Difcourfe }
  { Difpute }
  —for, [a. Probation
   (end)
  —againft, [Confute
   (end)
          { Reafon }
 Reafonable, [adj. { Mediocri-
          { ty }
  —government. Man. VI. 6.
 Reaffemble, [Again-affemble]
 Reave, [Un-knit]
 Rebaptize, [Again-baptize]
 Rebate, [Diminifh adv. propor-
  tion]
 Rebeck.
 Rebellion.
  Vice. Man. V. 5. D.
  Crime. RJ. III. 3.
 Rebound, [Leap reflexly]
 Rebuff, [Back-ftriking]
 Rebuild, [Again-build]
 Rebuke, [Reprove]
 Rebus, [Expreffi- { Name }
  on (manner) of { Sentence }
           { by picture }
 Recall, { Back-call }
     { Recant }
 Recantation. D. VI. 9. A.
 Recapitulate, [Repeat the fum]
 Recede.
  [Back-go]
  [Retire]
 Receit.
  [Receiving]
  [Direction of Phyfic]
  [adj. Acquitting (thing)]
 Receive.

RE

Proper. TA. IV. 3. O.
 [Accept]
 [Entertain]
—er.
 [adj. Receiving (perfon)]
 [adj. Gathering (Off.)]
 —ed, { adj. p. Receive }
      { Cuftomary }
Receptacle.
 { Receiving } { (thing) }
 { Containing } { (vefs.) }
Reception, [Receiving]
Recefs.
 [Receding]
 [adj. Concealing (place)]
Rech, vid. Reach.
Recidivation, [Relapfe]
Reciprocation. T. VI. 7. O.
Recite.
 [Repeat]
 [Again-fay]
 [a. Narration]
Reckon.
 [Efteem]
 [a. Number]
 [Account.] TA. IV. 6.
  —up, [a. Number]
      { Number (exc.) }
  over—{ Account too-
      { much }
  the—ing, [adj. p. ought pay
   (thing)]
Reclaim.
 [a. Gentle (make)]
 [Turn]
 —from errour, [Convert]
 —from vice, [Repent (make)]
Recline, [Down-oblique the fu-
 perficies]
Reclufe.
 [Shut up]
 [Solitary]
Recognize.
 [Confider again]
 [Acknowledge]
Recognizance, [Bond acknow-
 ledged before Magiftrate]
Recoil.
 [Reflect]
 [Retire]
Recommend.
 [Offer]
 [Entruft]
 fp. adv. Commending.
Recompence.
 [Compenfate]
 [Reward]
Reconcile.
         { Enemy }
 [Un-a. { Contention }]
 [a. Peace (make)]
Reconquer, [Back-conquer]
Record.
 [a. Memory]
 [a. Notary]
 take to—[a. Notary (make)]
 —er.
  { Notary } RJ. I. 5.
  { Judge affiftant to the City
   (Off.) }
  [adj. Mufic pipe]
Recover.
    [Back

RE

[Back-come]
[Again-] { obtain }
[Gain] { Repeat }
[Poſſeſs again]
[Repair]
[Again- v. Healthy]
Recount.
 [a. Narration]
 [Conſider]
Recourſe, [To-coming]
 ſp. often
Recreant, [Perfidious]
 ſp. through Cowardiſe]
Recreation. Mo. V.
 Moderateneſs in it. Man. II. 5.
 Immoderateneſs in it. Man. II. 5. D.
Recrement, [Worſt part]
 —of Metals. Met. IV.
Recriminate, [Retort accuſation]
Recruit, { ſtrengthen }
 [Again-] { fill }
Rect.
 op. to Curve.
 —angle, [Square having four right angles.]
Rectifying, [a. Right (make)]
 Chymical—O. VI. 6. A.
Rector, [Governour]
Recum- { Leaning }
 bency, { Truſt }
Recuſant.
 [adj. Refuſing (perſon)]
 [Schiſmatic]
Red. Q. II. 2.
 —breaſt. Bi. V. 5.
 —lead, [Cinnabar]
 —ſtart. Bi. V. 5. A.
Redargution, [Reproof]
Redbreaſt. Bi. V. 5.
Redeem.
 Action of God. AS. I. 7.
 [Back-buy]
 [Buy liberty]
 [Un-captivate]
 [Un- a. ſlave]
Redeliver, [Back- deliver]
Redemand, [Back-demand]
Redemption, [Redeeming] AS. I. 7.
Redolent, [Sweet]
Redouble, { a. Double }
 { Repeat }
Redoubt. RM. VI. 6.
 —ed, [Excellent]
 ſp. in Reputation]
 ſp. for Fortitude]
Redound, [a. Event]
Redreſs, { Remedy }
 { Amendment }
Redſhank. Bi. VII. 4.
Redſtart. Bi. V. 5. A.
Redwing. Bi. III. 5. A.
Reduce.
 { Cauſe }
 { Make }
 { Again-make }
 [Bring back]
Redundant.
 [adj. Exceſs]
 [Superfluous]

Reduplicate.
 [a. Double]
 [Repeat]
Reed. HL. III. 7.
 Burr——HL. III. 15. A.
 flowring—HL. V. 4.
 ſweet ſmelling—HL. III. 11.
 —mace. HL. III. 15.
Re-edifie, [Again-build]
Reek.
 [Heap]
 [Vapour]
Reel.
 [Stagger] Mo. II. 4, O.
 [a. Skein]
 a—[adj. a. { (inſtr.) }
 { Skein } { (jug.) }
Re-entry, { Again— }
 { Back -- } { entry }
Re-eſta- { Again— } { eſta-
 bliſh, { back— } { bliſh }
Refection.
 [Refreſhment]
 Feeding. Pr. I. 1. A.
Refectory, [adj. meal (place)]
Refell, [Confute]
Refer.
 [a. Relation]
 [a. Arbitrator (make)]
Reference, [a. Arbitrator (make)]
Refine.
 [a. Pure (make)]
 [Un- a. ſediment]
Reflect, [a. Mag. II. 9.]
 [Look back]
 [Again-conſider]
Reflecti- { Reflecting }
 on, { a. Reputation (corr.) }
Reflux, [Ebbing]
Reform. RO. VI. 7.
Refraſſed, Mag. II. 9. A.
Refractorineſs.
 [Perverneſs]
 [Contumacy]
Refrain, [Abſtain]
Refrane, [Proverb]
Refreſh.
 op. to wearineſs. TA. V. 8.
 [Mend]
 [Renew]
Refrigerate, [Cool]
Refuge, [To-flying] ſp. for ſafety
 Place, [adj. { Safe } (place)
 { Protection }
Refulgent, [Shining]
Refund. TA. IV. 5. A.
Refuſe.
 [Denying]
 [Rejecting]
 [Abdicating]
 [Power of firſt buying]
 The——[Worſt part]
Refute, [Confute]
Regal, [adj. King]
Regard.
 [a. Relation]
 in that—[Therefore] Conj. III. 3. A.

in—of. Pron. I. 2.
 [Eſteem]
 [Reſpect]
 [Obſerve]
 —leſs, [Careleſs]
Regene- { Again beget }
 rate, { a. Ha. V. }
Regent, [Inſtead-King]
Regiment.
 [Government]
 [Militia]
 as a—of ſouldiers. RM. IV 2. A.
Region, [Country] W. III. A.
 —of the air, [Part]
Regiſter, [Notary]
Regrate, [Buy to ſell (corr.)]
Regreſs, [Again-come]
Regret.
 [Grudging]
 [Nolleity]
 [Averſation]
Regular. RE. II, 6.
Regularity. TM. V. 4.
Regulate, [a. Rule]
Regulus Criſtatus. Bi. VI. 4.
 —non criſtatus. Bi. VI. 4. A.
Rehearſe.
 [Repeat]
 [Again-ſay]
 [a. Narration]
Reject. AS. IV. 5. O.
 [Abdicate]
Reign.
 [a. King]
 King's [time]
Reimbark, [Into a. ſhip again]
Reimburſe, [Pay]
Rein.
 Horſe——[adj. Cohibiting (arm)
 [Cord of Bridle]
 [Kidney] PG. VI. 7.
 Running of the—[Flux]
Reindeer. Be. II, 4. A.
Reinforce, [Again-ſtrengthen]
Reinveſt, [Again-inveſt]
Rejoyce, [v. Joy]
Rejoynder, [Again-anſwer]
Raiſter, [Horſeman]
Reiterate, [Repeat]
Relapſe, { Again— } { fall }
 { Back— }
 [Again-ſicken]
 [a. Apoſtaſie]
Relate.
 [a. Relation]
 [Tell]
 [Pertain to]
Relation. T. L. 8.
 —Oeconomic. RO.
 —of Conſanguinity. RO. I.
 —of Affinity. RO. II.
 —of Superiority and Inferiority. RO. III.
 —of Equality. RO. IV.
 —Civil. RC.
 —Judicial. RJ.
 —Military. RM.
 —Naval. RN.
 —Eccleſiaſtic. RE.
 [Narration]

[Re-

RE   RE   RE

[Report]
Relative, [adj. Relation]
Relaxation.
  [Loofning]
  [Eafe]
  [Refrefhing]
Releafe.
  [adj. a. Liberty]
  [Un-ty]
  [Un-imprifon]
  [Un-captive]
  [Acquit]
Releef, [Relieving]
  High- { [Protube- } { [augm.]
  Low-   rance   [dim.]
Relegation. RJ. VI. 5. A.
Relent.
  [Soften]
  { a. Pity
  { a. Repent } (inc.)
Rely, [v. Confidence]
Relick, [Refidue (thing)]
Relict.
  [Refidue]
  [Widow]
Relief, vid. Releef.
Relieve.
  [a. Adjuvant]
  [Refresh]
  [a. Alms]
  —guard, [Renew g.]
  —town. RM. I. 4. O.
Religion. RE. II.
  Natural—RE. II. 1.
  Gentil—RE. II. 2.
  Jewifh—RE. II. 3.
  Chriftian—RE. II. 4.
  Mahometan—RE. II. 5.
Religious, [adj. Religion (hab.]
a—perfon. Regular. RE. II. 6.
Relinquifh.
  { Leave
  { Let go
  { Abandon
  [a. { Defertion
     { Dereliction]
Relifh, [Taft]
Reluctancy.
  [Nolleity]
  [Averfation]
Remain.
  [a. { Permanent
     { Refidue]
  [Stay]
Remainder, [Refidue]
Remark, [Obferve]
  —able, { Obfervable
     { Excellent]
Remedy. TA. III. 9. A.
Remember.
  [a. Memory]
  [a. Exprefs]
Remiffion.
  —of fault. RJ. II. 9. O.
  —of debt, TA. IV. 9. O.
Remiffenefs.
  op. to Intenfenefs. TM. I. 8. D.
  [Slightnefs] Ha. III. 4. E.
  [Sloth] Ha. IV. 5. D.

Defect of juftice. Man. I. 1. D.
Remit, [Send] (fp. back)
  [v. { Remiffion
     { Remiffenefs]
Remnant, [Refidue]
Remonftrance, [adj. a. Publicnefs (make) writing]
Remora. Fi. VI. 8. A.
  [adj. { Impedient
     a. { Staying } (thing)
Remorfe. AS. VI. 4.
Remotenefs. Sp. II. 3. O.
Remove, { motion
  [From- { ition]
Remunerate, [Reward]
Rencounter, [Meeting] fp. fudden]
Rend, [Tear]
Render.
  [a. Efficient]
  [Yield]
  —as taken. RM. II. 6. D.
  [Give]
  [Back-give]
  [Repeat]
  —leffon, [Repeat l.]
  [Compenfate]
  —like for like, [Compenfate]
  [Tranflate]
  —account, [a. Account]
  —a reafon, [Shew reafon]
  —thanks, [a. Gratitude]
Rendezvous.
  [Convention] fp. Military]
  [Convention (place)]
Renegado.
  [Revolter]
  [Apoftate]
Renegue, [Abdicate]
Renew.
  [a. New]
  [Repair]
  [Repeat]
Rennet, [adj. a. Fermenting (thing) of Calf's ftomach]
Renovation, [Renewing]
Renown.
  { Reputation
  { Fame } (augm.)
Renounce.
  [Abdication]
  [Rejection]
Rens, [Wafh (dim.)]
Rent.
  [Tear]
  [Revenue]
  [Hire]
Renverfe, [Reverfe]
Repay, { Un-disburfe
  { Back-pay]
Repair.
  { Reftore
  { Mend] TA. II. 9.
  { Compenfate]
  [Go]
  in good—— [In g. ftate]
Reparation, [Repairing]
  to give—[Compenfate]
Repaft, { Eating
  { Refection]

Repeal, [Un-law]
Repeat. TA. II. 6. A.
  —leffon, [Say l.]
Repel, [Back-drive]
Repentance. AS. VI. 4. A.
Repeople, [Again-inhabited (make)]
Repercuf- { Back-ftrike]
  fion, { a. reflex]
Repete, vid. Repeat.
Repetition, [Repeat]
Repine, { op. to Alacrity
  { Averfation (augm.)
Replenifh, [Fill]
Repletion, [Filling]
Replevy, [Un-arreft]
Reply, [Again-anfwer]
Report.
  [Rumour]
  [Narration]
  [Reputation]
  —of a gun, [Sound of gun]
Repofe.
  [Put]
  [Lay down]
  [Reft]
  [v. Confidence]
Repofitory, [adj. Laying-up (place)]
Reprehenfion. RO. V. 7. O.
Reprefent. TA. II. 8.
Reprefs.
  [Reftrain]
  [Subdue]
Reprieve, [Procraftinate Execution]
Reprize, [Diminution of payment]
Letters of—[Commiffion for Compenfation for loffes by bootying]
Reprobate, [Rejected]
Reproch. RJ. IV. 8.
Reproving, [Reprehenfion]
Reptile, [adj. Creeping (thing)]
Republic, [adj. RC (thing)]
Repudiate.
  [Reject]
  [Abdicate]
  [Un-marry]
Repug- { Oppofite
  nant, { Contrary]
Repullulate.
Repulfe.
  [Back-driving]
  [Denial]
Reputation. Ha. II. 4.
Repute.
  [a. Opinion]
  [Efteem]
Requeft, [Petition]
  Mafter of—, [Receiving (Off.) of Petitions]
Requiem, [Reft]
Require.
  [Demand]
  [Command]
Requi- { Neceffary
  fite, { Expedient]
Requite, [Compenfate]
Rere, [Hinder-part]
Rere-boil'd, [Boil'd (dim.)]

Rere-

RE   RE   RE

Reremouse, [Bat]
Rereward, [Hinder part of army]
Rescind, [Spoil]
Rescript, [Edict]
Rescue.
  [Deliver]
  [Un-{captive / prisoner}]
Resemble.
  [Like]
  [Compare]
Resent, [a. Apprehension]
Reserch, [Inquisition]
Reserve.
  [Keep, {part / till another time}]
  [Except]
  ——*of souldiers.* RM. IV. 5. A.
  ——*edness.* Man. IV. 4. D.
Reside.
  [Inhabit]
  [v. Present]
Residue. TM. VI. 7. O.
Resign.
  [Let go]
  [Assign]
  [Yield]
  [Deliver]
  ——*to God,* [a. Self-denial]
Resin. PP. I. 6. A.
Resisting. RM. I. 3. O.
Resolve
  [Un- a. doubt (make)]
  [a. {Solution / Answer}]
  [Purpose] AS. IV. 4.
  [a. Result]
Resolute, [adj. {pret. Resolve / Constancy / Fortitude}]
Resolution.
  [Resolving]
  [Resoluteness]
Resort, [Come (freq.)]
Resound, [Sound (augm.)]
Resource, [Again-rising]
Respect.
  [Relation]
  Deference. Man. V. 4.
  in—of, [For] Prep. I. 2. A.
Respiration. Mo. III. 2.
Respite, {Time of Intermission / At times Sp. I. 8. O. / Interval sp. of ease}
  to— [Protract]
Resplendent, [Shining]
Responsal, [Answer]
Responsible, [adj. Paying (pot.)]
  I will be—for, [I stipulate for]
Rest.
  op. to Motion. M. O.
  [Stay]
  [Desist]
  [a. Period]
  ——*in Mu-{Silence (sign) / sic,* Period (dim.)}
  ——*of gun,* [Stick for supporting gun.]

to {be / see} that—[{p. / a.} Quieting]
  [Lean]
  ——*upon,* {a. Confidence / Trust}
  the—[The residue]
Restauration.
  [Restoring]
  [Mending]
Restharrow, [Cammock] HS. III. 14.
Resty.
  vid. *Restive.*
Restitution.
  [Restoring] TA. II. 7.
  [Compensating] TA. II. 7. A.
Restiveness.
  [Disingenuity]
  [Disobedience]
  [Contumacy]
Restorative, [adj. a. Restoring (apt.) Medecine]
Restore. TA. II. 7.
  ——*to* {Estate / Favor / Health / Liberty / Life} {re-adj. / p.} {Estate / Favor / Health / Liberty / Life} (make)
Restrein.
  [Diminish]
  sp. Liberty] Ha. II. 1. O.
  [a. {Cohibit / Impedience / Shortness / Narrowness}]
  {holding / exempting / limiting / excepting}
Restreint, {a. restreining / p. restreining}
  [Imprisonment (dim.)]
Restriction, [Limitation]
Restringent, [Binding] Mo. IV. O.
Result.
  [Event]
  [Summe]
  [Illation]
Resume.
  [Again—{take} / Back—]
  [Again—begin / Re—]
  [Repete]
Resurrecti- {Again— / on, Re—} life
Retail, [Sell parts (segr.)]
Retaliation, [Compensation]
Retard, {Late / a. Slow} (make)
Retching, [Stretching]
  [Pandiculation]
  [Vomiting (end)]
Retchlesness.
  [Improvidence] Man. III. 2. O.
  [Carelesness]
  [Sloth]
Retein.
  [Hold]

  [Keep] TA. V. 5.
  as his Lawyer, [Bespeak sp. with earnest]
  ——*to* {Pertinence / adj. Dependent}
Reteiner, [Dependent]
Retenti-{Holding / on, Keeping}
Retentive {Holding / faculty, Keeping} (pot.)
Retinue, {Waiters / Dependants} (agg.)
Retire.
  [Back-go]
  [Go] TA. VI. 1. O.
  ——*for safety]* RM. II. 2. D.
  ——*for* {Concealment / Privacy / Solitariness}
Retired, [adj. pret. retire]
  [Solitary]
Retirement.
  [a. Retire]
  [adj. Retire (place)]
Retort.
  *to—*D. VI. 7. A.
  a—[Crooked (vess.) adj Bottle (fig.)]
Retract
  [Back-draw]
  [Recant] D. VI. 9. O.
  sp. part]
Retreat.
  [a. Retire]
  [adj. Retire (place)]
Retrench.
  [From-cut]
  sp. part.]
  [a. {Ablatum / Diminution}]
Retribution [Compensate]
Retrive, {again-/ re-} finde
Retrograde, [back-going]
Retrospection, [Considering past (thing)]
Return.
  [re-{be / come / go}]
  [Repent]
  [again-{be / come / go}]
  [a. {Turn T. VI. 8. / Reciprocation T. VI. 8. A. / Answer / Retort / Repeat / Restore / Compensate / Refund / Pay}]
  ——*Money,* [Lend m. to be paid in another (place)]
  ——*to life,* [re-live]
  [re-{cause / doe / give}]
Reveal.
  [Revelation] AS. I. 6.
  [Shew-

[Shewing] TA. I. 8.
Reveils, { Sound (fig) for
  { Music } waking
  { (make)
Revelation. AS. I. 6.
Revel, { a. Man. II. 5. O.}
  { a. Riotousness }
  { p. Late in the night}
  —rout, [Sound (augm.) of a.
    riot]
  —s, [adj. Night recreations
    { p. of dancing}
Revenge. AS. V. 9. A.
Revenue. Po. A.
Reverberate,
  [Re-strike]
  [Reflect (make)]
Reverence. Man. V. 3.
  Sir- [Dung]
Reverend, [adj. p. Reverence
  (apt.)]
Reverse,
  to —
    { law
  Annull, [Un- { decree }
    { sentence]
  [Turn] AC. VI. 8. A.
  the — [Hinder part]
Reversion.
  { Right of fut. possession}
  { Potentialness]
  [Residue]
Revert,
  [Return]
  [Be right of fut. possession]
Revy, [More-bet]
  { See}
Review, [again { Consider }
  { Examin]
Revile. RJ. IV. 9.
  { See}
Revise, [Again { Consider }
  { Examin]
Revive, { Life }
  [re-a. { Vigor]
Reunion, [re-a. One]
Reunite, { One }
  [re-a. { Wholeness]
Revoke,
  [Recall]
  [Recant]
  [a. Nothing]
  — { law } [Un- { law}
    { sentence } a. { sentence]
Revolt,
  [a. Apostate]
  [a. Rebellion]
Revolve, { (freq.) }
  [Consider { (augm.)]
Revolution,
  [Vertiginous]
  [p. till the same situation]
  [Altering]
Revulsion { pulling }
  [From- { motion]
Reward. Ha. I.
Rhapsody [Confused mixture]
Rhetoric, [Speaking (art.) adv
  Ornate]
Rhetorician, [Teaching (artist)
  of speaking ornately]
Rheubarb, vid. Rubarb.

Rheum, [Catarrh]
Rheumatic, [adj. Catarrh]
Rheumatism. S. IV. 4. A.
Rhinocerot. Be. II. 6.
——Fly Ex. V. 1.
Rhomb,
  Line, [Line of Vergency]
  Figure, [Square having all its
    sides equal, but no right An-
    gles]
Rhomboide, [Square having its 2
  opposite Angles equal, but
  not all its sides equal]
Ri. HL. II. 1. A.
Rial.
Rib,
  —of Animal. PG. IV. 4. A.
  —of Ship, [Direct beam of
    Ship.]
Ribaldry, [Unchastity]
Riband. Pr. IV. 6.
Rives, [Red Gooseberries]
Rice,
  Plant. HL. II. 3. A.
  Jugament, [adj. a. Skein (ju-
    gament)]
  [Branch smear'd with Bird-
    lime]
Rich,
  [adj. Riches]
  [adj. Price (augm.)]
Riches. Ha. II. 2.
Rick, [Heap]
Rickets. S. IV. 8.
Rid,
  [adj. pret. riding]
  to—
    [Empty] O. II. 7. O.
    [Un- { burden }
      { tangle]
    [a. Liberty] Ha. II. 1.
    [Deliver] AS. I. 5.
    get- { Escape }
      { Obtain liberty]
    [Dispatch] TA. IV. 5.
    —way, [Dispatch his
      journey]
Riddance, { a. }
  { p. } rid]
Ridden, [adj. p. ride]
Riddle [Speech obscured with
  figure]
Ride,
  —on horse, &c. Mo. II. 7.
  —at anchor. RN. VI. 5.
Rider,
  [adj. riding (person)]
  [Lowest adj. horse (Off.)]
Money (kinde)
Ridge,
  Bank. Mag. V. 7.
  —bone, [Back bone]
  [Upper { Margin }
    { Side]
Ridiculous, [adj. p. Laugh (apt.]
Ridgeling, [Having only one te-
  sticle]
Riding, vid. Ride,
  [Shire (part)]
Rife, { Frequent }
  { Obvious]
Riffraff.

[Worst part. TM. VI. 1. O.
[Sorry (augm.) discourse]
Rifle,
  [Spoil] RM. II. 5. E.
  Dice.
Rift, [Chink through clea-
  ving]
Rig,
  [a. Rigging]
  [Wanton (fem.)]
Rigging. RN. IV.
Right,
  Subst. RC. IV.
  Adj.
  [Streight] Mag. III. 1.
  adj. { Justice }
    { Equity]
  { True }
  { Good }
  { Genuine }
  { Natural }
  { Simple }
  { Perfect }
  { Due }
  { Worthy }
  { Lawful }
  { Congruous }
  { Regular }
  { Pure }
  —angle. Mag. III. 3.
  —hand, [adj. right side h.]
  —side. Sp. II. 9.
  make—[Repair]
  Set (to—S.) [Repair]
  adv. Right.
  —in the nick, [adv. perfect
    in the nick] &c.
Righteousness,
  [Holiness] Ha. V. 3.
  [Vertue moral] Man. I.
  { Justice }
  { Equity]
Rightful, { Justice }
  [adj. { Equity]
Rigid, [adj. Rigor]
Rigor,
  Stiffness. AC. IV. 4. D.
  op. to { Justice. Man. I. 1. E.
    { Equity. Man. I. 2. O.
  op. to { Gratiousness Man. VI.
    1. O.
    { Clemency. Man. VI.
    8. O.
Rill, [Stream (dim)]
Rimm, [Margin]
  —of the belly, [Membrane of
    the b.]
Rime,
  Verse D. III. 5. A.
  [Mist that freezes in falling]
  El. III. 5. A.
Rince, [Wash (dim.)]
Rind. PP. I. 5.
Ring,
  to—
  Neuter. Q. III. 2.
  Active, [a. Ring.]
  —all in, [a. Ring the last
    (time)
  —in peal, [a. Ring adv. [Har-
    mony]
  —out, [a. Ring (augm.)]

RO

a—of bells, [Suit of bells]
a—figure. Mag. V. 2.
—*bone*, [Bone in Horses foot]
—*dove.* Bi. III. 1. A.
—*finger*, [Fourth finger]
—*leader*, [Principal]
—*tail*, [Buzzard having white streak on his train]
—*worm*, [Tetter]
all in a— [adj. Circle (fig.)]
bog—[Pin adj. p.Circle (fig.)]
ride the—[Ride adv. Circle (fig.)]
Rinse. [Wash (dim.)]
Riot.
  [a. Riotousness]
  [Sedition]
Riotousness. Man. III. 4. E.
Rip.
  [Unsow]
  [Open by cutting]
Ripeness. NP. VI. 4.
Ripier, [Carrier of fish]
Rise.
  *the—*Source. Sp. II. 4. A.
  to—[v. Rising]
    { Upward-go
    { More-adj. p. High]
  arise. AC. VI. 1.
    { Birth
    { Beginning
  [adj. p. { Being
    { Increase]
    { Grow   (lique)
  as Hill, { Upward-adj. ob-
  as Fountain, { [Spring]
    { appear (inc.) a-
  as Sun, { bove Horizon
    { above-adj. Hori-
    { zon (inc.)]
Rising, [v. Rise]
  { Protuberance] Mag. IV. 3.
  { Top] Sp. III. 7.
  —*of a hill,* [Oblique (part) of h.]
  Hill, [Mountain (dim.)]
  { Tumor] S. III.
  { Inflation] S. I. 5. A.
Barm, [adj. a. Fermenting (thing)]
Insurrection, [Rebellion (inc.)]
Resurrection, [Re-life]
Risk, { Essaying
  { Danger]
Rite, [Circumstance]
  sp. { Customary]
  { Solemn]
Ritual, [Book of Ceremonies]
Rival. RO. II. 2. A.
Rive, [Cleave]
Rivel, { Wrinkle
  { Furrow]
River. W. IV. 7.
Rivet, [Fasten pin by flatting the point of it]
Rivulet, [Stream (dim.)]
Ro.
Of Fish.
  Soft—[Milk]
  hard—[Spawn]
Beast. Be. II. 5.

RO

Roan horse.
Rob. R]. III. 7.
Robe, [Loose upper (vest) sp. Solemn]
Robin red breast. Bi. V. 5.
Robins. RN. IV. 5.
Robusti- { Strong
  ous, { Hardy]
Rock.
  Stone. W. III: 3.
  [Staff of adj. Spinning (ma-
  te—[a. Volutation] (chin)
Roch. Fi. IX. 9. A.
  —*Allum,* [Allum of the rock]
Rochet.
  Fish, [Red Gournet]
  Vest, [Bishops upper adj. Linen (vest)]
Rocket. HS. IV. 7.
  *base—*HF. I. 11. A.
  double—[Dames Violet] HS. IV. 2.
Rod.
  [Wand] PP. I. 4. A.
  Measure, [16 foot & ½]
  [adj. Whipping (instr.)] of branches (aggr.]
Rode.
  [Public way]
  —*for Ships,* [adj. Resting (place) for ships]
Rodomon- { Oversaying
  tade, { Glorying]
Rogation, [Week of walking about the bounds]
Rogue.
  [Begger]
    { Wandring
  [adj. { Vice   (person)
    { Fraud]
  [adj. Scurril (person)]
Roial; [adj. King]
  the—s of a Stag.
Roialty, [Prerogative sp. of King]
    { Riotousness
Roister, [a. { Insolence
    { Magisterialness]
Roll.
  to—
    [a. Vertigination]
    —*land.* O. III. 2. A.
    —*a Swathe about one,* [Clothe adv. Helical]
    [a. Volutation]
  as Ship—RN. VI. 7. A.
  { adj. a. Rolling (instr.)
  { adj. p. Roll (thing)
  [Cylinder]
    —*of paper,* &c. [Paper, &c. adj. p. Cylinder (fig.) by Vertigination]
  [Catalogue]
  [adj. Ring (fig.) ornament] sp. adj. p. Twist.]
Roller, [Cylinder]
  sp. adj. p. Vertigination (apt.)
  sp. for rolling] O. III. 2. A.
Rolling { Subs. } role]
  { Adj. }

RO

  —*eye* { [adj. mo- { eye
  —*tongue* { tion (apt. { tong.
  —*Press,* [adj. rolling (machin) for Printing]
Rolls.
  [Catalogue of judicial causes and proceedings]
  [adj. No- { things
  tary { (place)]
  Master of the—
Romb, vid. **Rhomb.**
Romance, [Feigned Narration]
Rome, [Wander]
Rood.
  [Stick]
  Measure, [16 foot & ½]
  [Wooden pillar]
  [Wooden Image of Christ crucified]
Roof.
  —*of house.* PO. III. 8.
  —*trees,* [Rafters that support the goof]
  —*of mouth,* [Palat] PG. III. 5.
Rook.
  to—[a. Fraud]
  a—[Crow that feeds on corn]
  Chess.
Room.
  { Space
  { Place] sp. Sufficient
  to make—[Prepare place in a house. Po. III. 2.
  of Predecessor. TG. VI. 6.
Roost, [Birds adj. sleeping (place)]
Root.
  Proper. PP. I. 1.
    to { *take—* { [v. Root]
    —*out* { out-pluck the
    —*up* { Roots]
    —*of a* { the Number which multiplied by it self produces that other number.]
    { the side] Mag. II. 3. A
  Extraction of—
  —*of the tongue,* [bottom of t.]
  Hebrew—[Primitive H. word]
Rope.
  a—[Cord (augm.]
  —*of onions,* [Onions (aggr.)]
  to— [v. Sliminess]
Ropy, [adj. Sliminess]
Rore, { Sound
  { Exclamation } (augm.]
Ros Solis, [Sun-dew]
Rosary.
Rose. Sh. I. 2.
  —*Cake,* [Caput mort. of distilled roses.]
  —*water,* [distilled w. of roses]
  Guelder—Sh. II. 12.
  holy—Sh. VI. 1.
  our Ladies—Sh. VI. 8.
  Sweet mountain—Sh. VI. 5. A.
  —*Bay,* [Oleander] Sh. VI. 1. A
  —Campion, Sh. III. 2.
  —*of Jericho,* Sh. VI. 8.
Rosemary. Sh. VI. 4.
Rose noble, Money [kind]

O o o   Rose

RO — RO — RU

Rosewood. Tr. VII. 4. A.
Rosewort. HL. VIII. 2. A.
Rosy, [adj. Rose]
Rosin. PP. L 6. A.
Rost.
— *ing.* Pr. III. 3.
rule the— { Power }
{ a. Authority }
Rot.
to— [v. Rottenness]
the— among sheep]
Rota.
Rotation, { Vertigination }
{ Wheeling }
Rote.
by— [With- { Rules }
out— { a. Reason }
Rottenness.
Putrefaction. NP. V. 2. O.
Taft or Smell. Q. IV. 7. O.
Rotundation, [From cutting the less parts]
[sp. the parts not-aliquot]
Rotundity, [Roundness]
Rove, [Wander]
Rover,
[Wanderer]
at—s [Not adj. a. Object]
[adj. Sea. adj. Robbing (person)]
Rough.
Proper.
— *to feeling,* { Having unequal Surface }
Q. VI. 2. D.
— *cast,* [Rough p. plaster]
— *draught,* { Picturing }
{ First Writing }
— *hew,* [First cutting]
— *mason.*
— *Sea,* [adj. p. wave (aug.) Sea.]
— *way.*
[Hairy]
— *footed.*
— *to taft.* Q. IV. 3.
Moral.
[Fierce]
{ Rigorous }
{ Churlish }
{ Morose }
{ Magisterial }
{ Rustic }
{ Insolent }
{ Supercilious }
{ Harsh }
{ Austere }
[Angry]
Tranf.
{ Unpleasant }
{ Violent] T. V. 5. O.
{ Not-wrought }
{ Homely }
to—up [Reprehend adv. Anger (like)]
Rouncival, [Great (augm.)]
Round Proper, [not-adj. p. angle]
More perfect.
[adj. { Sphere } (fig.)]
{ Oval }
{ Bowl }
— *ish,* [Hill { Sphere } (fig.)]
whole top { Oval }
is adj. { Bowl }

[adj. { Cylinder } (fig.)]
{ Tube }
[adj. Cone (fig.)]
[adj. { Circle } (fig.)]
{ Ring }
{ Wheel }
[adj. { Spiral } (fig.)]
{ Helix }
Less perfect.
[Crooked]
[adj. Bow (fig.)]
[adj. { Parabola } (fig.)]
{ Hyperbole }
{ Ellipsis }
adv.
— *about,* [On every side]
turn— { Vertiginate }
{ Turn adv. Vertigination }
Winde
to—
— *hair,* [adj. equal (make) by clipping]
— *a place,* [about-go]
Round improper.
[Perfect]
— *blow,* [b. (augm.)]
— *number.*
— *Sum,* [Sum (augm.)]
adv.
tell him—ly, [Tell h. plainly]
go—ly on, [Pro- { Let
ceed without { Hesitation)]
to—one in the ear, [Whisper]
a—in music, [Continued circling (like) Song]
a—of a ladder, [Step of L.]
Roundelay.
Roundhouse. RN. II. 4. A.
Roundish, [Round (dim.)]
Rounds.
Rouse.
{ Rise (make) }
{ a. Impulsive }
Rout.
[Confused multitude]
[Overthrow]
to—
{ Fly (make) }
{ Unorder Army }
[Snore]
— *as beg,* [Un-root plants]
Route, vid. *Rouse.*
Row.
of Fish.
hard— [Spawn]
soft— [Milt]
of *bodies,* [Series]
[Rank]
[File]
to— [a. Motion { Oars) (make) with { Pole }
a—Barge.
Rowel.
a— [adj. Wheel (fig.) adj. pricking (jug.)]
to—a horse.
Rowen hay, [Second mowen hay]
Rowll, vid. *Roll.*
Ru.
Herb, vid. *Rue.*
to— { a. Repentance }
{ Wish un-done }

Rub.
a—
[adj. Impediment (thing)]
[adj. Protuberance (thing)]
to—
Scrub. O. V. 8.
—*along,* [Go] sp. adv. difficulty
—*off,* [From-rub]
—*at Cards.*
Rubarb. HF. I. 1.
Monk's— [Patience]
Rubbers, [Two Games]
Rubbish
Rubble
[Confused ruine]
[Worst part]
Rubellio. Fi. V. 4. A.
Ruby. St. IV. 2.
Rubrick, [Rules for direction in red Letters]
Rudder. RN. II. 3. A.
Ruddy, [Red (dim.)]
Ruddle { Red Oker }
{ Cinnabar }
Ruddock, [Red breast] Bi. V. 5.
Rude.
[Homely]
{ Not-taught }
{ Unlearned }
{ Ignorant }
{ Unskilful }
{ Morose }
{ Rustic }
Rudiment, { Element. D. I. 1 }
{ adv. First adj. p. Learner (thing) }
Rue. HS. V. 13.
Goates— HS. III. 8.
Meadow— HF. I. 12.
Ruff.
Vest.
Bird. Bi. VII. 4. A.
Fish. Fi. IX. 6. A.
at cards.
to—
Ruffian.
{ Bawd }
{ Ribald }
{ Swagger }
Ruffle.
[a. { Roughness } (make)]
{ Confusion }
[a. Sound of Silk (vest)]
Ruful, [adj. { Grief } (make)]
{ Pity }
Rug, [Tufted bed (vest)]
Rugged, vid. *Rough.*
Ruine, [a. { Ruines }]
{ Destruction }
{ Poverty }
—*s.* Po. II. O.
Ruinous, [adj. Ruine]
Rule.
Sentence. D. IV. 5.
{ Law }
{ Edict }
—*ed case,* [Condition adj. p. rule (ought) according to exemplar.]
according to— [Regular]
{ Power }
{ Authority }
to—

RU

to— { Direct / Govern }
instrument, [adj. a. Measuring (instr.)]
to— [a. Line with adj. a. measuring (instr.)]
Ruler.
 [Magistrate]
 [adj. a. Measuring (instr.)]
Rumb, vid. *Rhomb.*
Rumble, [Confused noise]
 sp. as of rolling]
Ruminate. Mo. III. 5. A.
 [Consider]
Rummage, [Move things for seeking]
Rumor. D. V. 3. A.
Rump, [Bone at the end of the Vertebræ]
 —of bird. PP. V. 8.
 —of beef.
Rumple, { Unsmooth / a. Furrow }
Run [ition (swift)
 sp. of Animal
 Proper. Mo. II. 1. A.
 [Fly] RM. II. 3. D.
 Ition
 —the { adven- / ture / risk } { to-ition / essay / submit to } { the danger }
 [Become]
 —a ground.
 —ashore.
 —mad.
 [Continue]
 —his course.
 [Proceed]
 [Increase] *as weeds—*
  [a. Contagion]
 [Abound]
 [Exceed] *as long—*
 [Spread] O. II. 6. O.
 { Stream } *as —ing water*
 { Weep } *as —ing eye*
 { Drop }
 { Let go } *as —ing nose*
 [Spend]
 hath—his course.
v. *Swiftness.*
 —a division { Sing } *a division*
  { Swiftly } { Play } *(tion)*
 [Thrust] (imp.)
 [Dispatch]
 —about { Spread, sp. by adj.
  p. dissolving]
 —all— { after-ition
 —after { follow (augm.)
  Pursue }
 —against { run
  thrust (imp.) against]
 —at { thrust (imp. at)
  assault }
 { *large,* [Abound] (cy)
 random, [v. Exorbitantish,* [Fence with
 —away, [Fly] (spears)
 —before { Become before]
  Prevent }
 —down, [a. Falling by thrusting (imp.)

SA

—in discourse, [Posing]
—with blood, [Streaming with b.]
—forth, { Let-go / Spill }
—in, [Prick]
 —debt { Become } *being* / Increase } *debtor* }
 —upon { Thrust (imp.)
  one, { Storm }
 —off, { From-ition / Digression }
 —on { Proceed / Increase } (ly)
 —over { Through-ition (swiftness) / Let-go Sp. through fulness (exc.)
 —out,
 —as Prodigal [Spend (exc.)]
 —as Vessel, [Let-go]
 —in discourse, [Abound]
 — { his course { Finish }
  his length,
 —through, [a. hole by thrusting (imp.)]
 —to ruine, [Become ruinous]
 —up, [Increase (sp. adv. Soon)
  [Begin hastily]
 —upon, { Storm }
Runagate, [Apostate]
Runaway, [Fugitive]
Rundle, [Round thing]
 sp. { Circle / Ring }
Rundlet, [Barrel (dim.)]
Rung. RN. II. 1. A.
Runner.
 Bird.
 [Upper stone of Mill]
Runt, [Bull (dim.)]
Rupture, [Breaking]
 a— S. VI. 8.
 —wort. HF. I. 17.
Rural, [adj. Country]
Rush. HL. III. 12. A.
 *Flowering.—*HL V. 6.
 to— { Running / Thrusting } (imp.)
Russet, [Gray]
 { sp. adv. Natural }
Rust. Mes. IV. 4.
 —of bacon [Rottenness (inc.)]
Rustic, { Country / [adj. Rusticity]
Rusticity. Mn. IV. 9. D.
Rustle, [Sound of confused motion]
Rustful, { Pity / [adj. a. Grief } (apt) (tion)
Rustless, [Pitiless]
Rut of Cart, [Sign of Wheel having gone]
Rutting, [Coition] sp. of Deer]

S.

Sabbath, { Day of rest / Festivity }
 sp. Weekly]
 Jewish—[The 7th day of the week]

SA

 Christian—[The first day of the week]
Sabbatical year, [7th year]
Sable.
 [Black Martin]
 [Skin of Black Martin]
 [Black]
Sacerdotal, [adj. Priest]
Sack, [Bag (augm.)
 [Course hairy-cloth]
 —cloth.
 [Spanish Wine]
 to—[Spoile] RM. II. 5. E.
Sackbut.
Sachel, [bag (dim.)]
Sachettus. Fi. V. 10. A.
Sacrament. RE. VI. 4.
 the—[Eucharist]
 { Holy }
Sacred, { Consecrated }
Sacrifice. RE. VI. 3.
Sacriledge, { Theft } of consecrated / Robbery } (things)
Sad.
 —Disposition
 [adj. Melancholy]
 [adj. Seriousness]
 [adj. { Dulness / Lumpishness }
 [adj. Grief]
 —color { Dark / Black } (dim.)
 —bread, [Dense (exc.)]
Saddle. Po. V. 8.
 —back, [Hollow backed]
 —tree, [adj. wood (part) of S.]
 Pack—[Saddle for burdens (augm.)
Saddler, [adj. Saddle (mech.)]
Safe.
 [adj. Safety]
 —and sound, { Healthy / Whole }
 —Conduct { Compact of safe return (pot.) / Licence for safe passing }
 —guard, { Safety / [Uppermost adj. riding (vest) of woman]
 a—[Box]
Safety. T. V. 3.
Saffron, [Crocus] HL. IV. 7. A.
 *bastard—*HF. III. 5.
 *—meadow—*HL. IV. 7.
Sag, [Move (dim.)
 sp. backward]
Sagacity. Ha. III. 1.
Sagapenum, [Concrete juice of Giant Fennel]
Sage.
 Herb. HF. VI. 1.
 —of Jerusalem. HL. IX. 3.
 *Wood—*HF. VII. A.
 [adj. { Wise / Sober }
Sagittarius, [Ninth of the 12 parts of the Zodiac]
Say.
to—
 [Speak] AC. III. 1.

—*by*

SA

—*by heart*, [Say adv. memory.]
—*less than true*, [Undersay]
—*more than true*, [Oversay]
—*nay*, [a. Negation]
—*nothing*, [a. Silence]
that is to—— Conj. IV. 3.
[Essay] TA. III. 4. A.
Subst.
[Adage]
Part. TM. VI. 3.
Stuff.
Saying, { adj. Spoken (thing) / Sentence }
Sail.
—of Ship, &c. RN. II. 6.
—*yard*. RN. III. 2.
main—[Principal S. of Ship.]
mizzen—[S. of hinder (part) of Ship]
Sprit—[S. of forepart of ship]
top—[Highest S.]
hoise—[Up-lift S.]
strike—[a. fall the S.]
[Ship]
to—Mo. II. 7. A.
Sailer. RN. V. 8.
Saim, [Soft fat of hog]
Sainfoin. HS. III. 5. A.
Saint. RE. III. 5.
—*s bell*.
Sake [end] T. II. 6.
for the—*of*. Prep. I. 2. A.
Saker.
Hawk.
Ordinance.
Sal, vide Salt.
—*armoniac*. St. V. 6.
—*Gemme*. St. V. 2. A.
Salable, [adj. p. Sell (apt.)]
Salacity, [Lust (Pron.)]
Salad.
[Sawce of herbs]
[adj. head (armor]
Salamander.
Land—Be. VI. 5.
Water—Be. VI. 5. A.
Salary, [Wages]
Sale, [Sell.]
Saleable, (Fit to) adj. p. Sell (apt.)
Saligot. [Water-Nut]
Saline, { Salt / [adj. { Saltishness] }
Salivate, { Spit / Drivel } (make)
Sallet, vid. Salad.
Sally. RM. I. 6. A.
Sallow.
Tree. Tr. VI. 9. A.
Color, [yellow (dim.) adj. Sallow (like)]
Salmon. Fi. IX. 2.
Salomons Seal. HL. VII. 7.
Salpa, Fi. V. 2. A.
Salt, vid. Sal.
Subst. St. V. 1. A.
—*Armoniac*. St. V. 6.
—*Peeter*, [Nitre] St. V. 1.

SA

—*wort*, [Glassort]
Bay—[Coursest S. (kind)]
Drinous—St. V. 5.
Vessel.
—*Sellar*, [adj. Table, adj. Salt vessel]
Trencher—[adj. Trencher, adj. Salt (vessel)]
adj.
—*taste*, [adj Q. IV. 5.]
—*Marshes*, [Marshes]
Saltrive.
Salve. Pr. VI. 4.
to—[a. sound (make)]
Salvation.
[Deliverance]
[Safety]
Everlasting bliss. Ha. I. 4.
Salvediction. AC. V. 8.
Salvo, { Exempting / Exception }
Salute. AC. V. 3.
—*at meeting*. AC. V. 8.
—*at parting*. AC. V. 8. A.
Samarre, [Upper most loose adj. Woman (vest)]
Same. Pron. II. 2. 2.
—*ness*, [Identity]
of the—*time*, [Simultaneous]
Sampbier. HF. V. 2. A.
Golden flowred—HF. III. 10. A.
Sample
Sampler } Exemplar. T. II. 3.
Sanamunda. Sh. VI. 2.
Sanctifie.
[adj. Holiness (make)]
[Consecrate]
Sanction, { Law / Edict }
Sanctity, [Holiness]
Sanctuary.
[Temple]
sp. Inner (part) of it
[adj. a. Safety (place) for offenders]
Sand. St. I. 8.
—*eeles*. Fi. VI. 4. A.
the—*s*, Strand. W. III. 6.
Quick—*s*. W. III. 7.
—*blind*.
Sandal, [Lamin for the bottom of foot]
Sandarach. St. VI. 5.
Sanders.
Red—Tr. VII. 3.
Yellow—Tr. VII. 3. A.
Sandover, [Scum of glass]
Sanguin.
[adj. Blood] PG. I. 6.
[Merry]
Sanguinary, [adj. a. RJ. III.]
Sanhedrin, [Council]
Sanicle. HL. VI. 9.
bears ear—HS. VIII. 3.
Spotted—HL. VIII. 4.
Turkshire—[Butterwort] HL. VI. 7.
Sanity.
[Health]
[Soundness]
Sap.
Subst.

SA

[Juice] PP. I. 7.
—*of tree*, [adj. juice (part) of tree]
to—[Undermine]
Saphena vein, [Vein at the Ankle]
Saphire. St. IV. 5.
White—St. IV. 1. A.
Sapience, [Wisdom]
Saphic.
Saracens Confound [Comfrey] HL. IX. 4.
Sarcasm [Mock]
Sarcocolla. Tr. VIII. 2. A.
Sarda, [Chalcis] Fi. III. 12. A.
Sardius. St. III. 3.
Sardonix.
Sargus. Fi. V. 3.
Sarplier, [adj. packing cloth]
Sarsaparilla, [Root of herb like pricking Bindweed]
Sartorian Operation. O. V.
Sassafras. Tr. III. 10.
Satan, [Devil] W. I. 2. O.
Sate. AC. V. 5. A.
Sated, [adj. { augm. / p. fill { exc. }]
Satelles. W. II. 8. A.
Saturday, [Seventh day]
Satiate, [a. Sufficience]
Satiety, [a. Sufficience]
Satisfaction.
[Sufficience]
Mind-quieting. AS. III. 5.
[Conviction]
[Payment]
[Restitution]
Satisfy, [a. Satisfaction]
Satin.
[Smooth shining Silk]
Herb [Bulbonach] HS. VI. 2.
Satura. W. II. 4.
Satyr.
[adj. { Mocking / Reproving } Verse (aggr.)]
[Baboon] Be. III. 1.
Satyrion, [Orchis] HL. IV. 8.
Savage, { Fierce / Cruel }
Sauce. Pr. II. 2.
Sauce alone HS. IV. 8.
Saucer, [Shallow dish sp. for Sauce]
Saucy, { Impudent / Irreverent }
Sauridge, vid. Sausage.
Save.
General.
—*from danger*, [a. Safety] T. V. 3.
—*from* { lost / hurt } { Preserve } AS. L. 4.
—*one's oath*, [pt. himself from perjury]
incumbent, [Deliver] AS. I. 5.
imminent.
as to it, [prevent] TA. III. 9.
as to { him } { Defend } BO. VI. 5. / Protect } a. Man. VI. 4
Special,

SC

Special, as to
Estate, {Lay up] TA. V. 4.
{Keep] TA. V. 5.
from spoiling. RM. II. 5.
from spending. Ta. V. 3.
Liberty. RM. II. 6.
Event of War. RM. II. 7.
Soul.
from Sin, [Redemption] AS. I. 7.
from Hell, [Salvation] Ha. I. 4.
Comparate.
[Exempt] TA. II. 7. O.
{Except] D. IV. 5. O.
Conj. [Unless]
Prep. [Besides]
Savin. Sh. III. 10. A.
Saving, vid. *Save.*
Savingness, [Frugality]
Savior, [adj. a Save (person)
Savor.
[Taft] Q. IV.
[Smell] Q. IV. A.
Savory.
[adj. Savor (perf.
Winter——HF. VI. 7. A.
Saurus. Fi. IV. 7. A.
Sausage, [Pudding of minced Hogg's flesh]
Saw.
to—O. IV. 3. A.
—duft, [Powder made by sawing]
——
[adj. Sawing (instr.]
—wort. HF. III. 3.
Fifh. Fi. I. 2.
an old—[Adage]
I.—[I am adj. pret. See]
Sawyer, [adj. Sawing (mech.]
Saxifrage.
Burnet— HF. IV. 12.
Golden—Fl. VI. 10. A.
White—HL. VI. 10.
Scab. S. III. 1. A.
Scabbard, [Case for Sword]
Scabious. HF. II. 13.
Scaffold. Po. II. 6. A.
Scalado, [Storming with Ladders]
Scalde.
[a. Heat (excess) sp. with Liquor]
[Un-a, {skin feather hair} with hot liquor.]
—*head,* [Un-haired head sp. with scurf]
Scale.
—*of fish,* PP. IV. 1.
—*of bone,* [Scale ʃ Fragment (like) ʅ Chip } of bone]
—*of metal,* Met. IV.
to—[Un-adj. a. Scale]
Dish of the librating (jug.]
Pair of—s, [Librating (jug.]
[Ladder]
—*as of miles, &c.* [Line adj. p. part for measuring distances]

SC

to—{Climb] {Storm]
sp. with Ladder.]
Scallion, [Onion (dim.]
Scalp, [Pate] PG. III. 1. A.
—*ing iron,* [adj. Iron. adj. Scratching (instr.]
Scamble.
[Catch (end) adv. Confusion]
[a. Confusion by cutting (corr.]
Scamony. HS. VII. 6. A.
Scan.
{Consider] {Examin]
—*verse* [a. Measure v.]
Scandal, {Tempting Occasioning} to sin]
Scandalous. RE. III. 5. O.
Scant, [adj. {Scarcity Deficience Narrowness}
adv. [Scarce] adv. V. 2.
Scantling.
[Little]
[Say] TM. VI. 2.
[Measure] Mea. II.
[Proportion]
Scape, [Escape]
a—[Fart]
Scapula, [Shoulder] PG. IV. 1.
Scar, [pret. p. Wound (sign]
Scarab } Ex. V.
Scarabee
great water—Ex. V. 8.
little water—Ex. V. 8. A.
Scarce.
[Scarcity]
[adj. {Seldomness Rareness]
[adv. {Adv. V. 2. adv. Difficulty]
Scarcity, TM. I. 2. D.
Scare, [a. Fear]
—*crow,* [adj. Vanity (thing) for a. fear]
Scarf. Pr. IV. 6. A.
Scarlet, [Bright red]
—*Oke,* [Holm]
Scarifie. Mo. IV. 6. A.
Scatches, [Leg-lengthning sticks]
Scate. Fi. II. 5.
Scath, [Hurt]
Scatter. O. II. 5. O.
Come in—ing, [Came (segr.]
Scavel, [adj. hungry (exc.]
Scavinger, [adj. a. Cleanliness (Off.) of streets]
Sceleton, [Frame of dead bones]
Scene,
[a. Player (room)
[The place represented]
[The home of any action] (thing)
[Chapter of adj. p. Player (thing)
Scepter, [adj. King (sign)
[Stick]
Sceptic, {Incredulity Doubting (apt.]
Schedule, [Paper (lam.]
Scheme, [Figure]

SC

sp-{Lined] {Pictured]
Schism, [Schismatic (thing)
Schismatic. RE. III. 2. O.
Scholar.
[Learner]
[adj. Learning (person]
—*of a Colledge,* [Stipendiated Learner]
—*ship,* [Learning]
Scholastic, [Learned (like)
Scholast, [adj. a. Commentary (dim.]
School.
Greater place, [University]
—*man,* [adj. University Divine]
Lesser place, [RC. III. 6. A.]
—*boy,* [Learner at School]
—*master,* [Teacher of School]
[Sect]
Schreight, [Missle bird] Bi. III. 3.
Sciatica, [Gout in the Hip]
Science, [Ha. VI. 1. A.
Liberal—[adj. Learning Science]
Scimiter, [Crooked Sword]
Scink, [Small-headed Lizard (kind)
Scintilla volantes. El. 1. 5. A.
Sciolist, [adj. Science (dim.]
Scion, [Branch] PP. L. 3.
Schirrhus. S. III. 4. A.
Scissors, [adj. Clipping instr.]
Scocheon, vid. *Scutcheon.*
Scoff, {Reproch] {Mock]
Scold, {a. Contention (voice.] {Reprove (exc.]
Scole, [Fishes (aggr.]
Scolop. Ex. VIII. 5.
Scolopendra. Ex. II. 10.
Sconse,
[Mult]
Military place. RM. VI. 2.
[adj. Hanging. adj. supporting (instr.] for Candle]
{Pate] {adj. Head (vest]
Scoop. Pr. V. 7. A.
Scope.
{End] T. II. 6. {Object] T. VI. 2.
{Liberty Space Sufficient] Place]
Scorbutica [Scurvy]
Scorch, {Fire the outside [adj. a. {Heat (exc.]
Scordium. HF. VII. 8.
Score.
[adj. Reckoning (thing]
[Stick notched (freq.] for reckoning]
{in apoſ.} [Debtor]
—*up.*
quit—s, [Ballancing]
[Twenty]
Scoria. Met. IV. 3.

Scorn,

SC   SE   SE

Scorn, { Contemn] AS. IV. 2.
{ a. Indignation]
Scornfulness, [Superciliousness]
Scorpæna. Fi. IV. 11. A.
Scorpioides. Fi. III. 14. A.
Scorpion. Ex. II. 5. A.
— grass. HS. III. 12.
— water — Ex. I. 9.
Fish.
greater — Fi. V. 6.
lesser — Fi. V. 6. A.
Constellation [8th. (part) of the Zodiac.]
Scot.
[Shot]
[Tax]
Scotfree.
[adj. p. Immunity from payment]
[not-adj. { Hurt
p. { Punishment]
Scotomy, [Vertigo] S. IV. 5.
Scoul, [Lowring]
Scoundrel, [adj. Sorry (person)]
Scour,
a— [Shallow (part) of swift river]
to—
{ Wash } (augm.)
{ Rub }
[adj. { Purity]
a. { Brightness]
sp. by { Washing } (augm.)
{ Rubbing }
[Dung (exc.)]
Scourge, [Whip]
a— [adj. Whipping (instr.)]
Scourse, [Exchange]
Scout. RM. III. 5.
Scrag, { Tooth
{ Rough protuberance]
Scraggy, [Lean (augm.)]
Scray, [Sea Swallow] Bi. IX. 9. A.
Scrall, [Write (corr.)]
Scramble, [Climbe (corr.)]
Scrap, { Residue]
{ Fragment]
Scrape, { Rub]
{ Scratch]
{ Shave (corr.)]
— for favour, [Fawning]
— out, { Spoil } by
{ as Nothing } [scratching]
— together, { adv. Scrapingness]
[Gather } Rapaciously.]
a— [Trap]
Scrapingness. Man. III. 2. E.
Scrat, [Of both sexes]
Scratch. AC. II. 6. A.
the — es [Disease in horse's heels]
Scrawl, [Writing (corr.)]
Scream, { Acute voice (augm.)]
{ Exclamation]
Screech, [v. acute exclamation (augm.)]
— Owl, [Owl]
Screeking, [acute sound of Solids rubbing together]

Screen, [adj. a. shadow (jug.)]
Screw, vid. Scrue.
Scribble, [Write (corr.)] sp. [swift-
Scribe, { Notary]
{ adj. writing (Off.)]
Scrip, [Bag]
Scripture. RE. VI. 1.
Scrivener, [adj. Writing (mech.)]
Scrole, [Paper (lam.)]
[Catalogue]
Scrophula, [King's Evil]
Scrophularia, [Pilewort]
Scrue. O. I. 6.
— into, [Into-wriggle]
— out, [Obtain by-a. Craft]
Scrub, [Rub (augm.)]
a— [Sorry (person)]
Scruple.
Weight. Mea. III. 2.
[Doubt (dim.)]
practical. AS. III. 5. O. (Pron.)
Scrupulousness, { Doubting }
{ Scruple }
{ Incredulity }
Scrutiny, { Inquisition }
{ Examining }
Scud, [v. Ition swiftly]
Scuffle, { Mutiny }
{ Confused fighting (dim.)]
Scull.
[Bone { Head
of { Pate]
[adj. { Head } (armor)
{ Pate }
— of fish, [Fishes (aggr.)]
Sculk, [v. Concealing]
Sculler, [Boat adj. p. Oar by one man]
Scullery, [adj. Washing (room) of adj. Cookery vessel]
Scullion, [Cook's Servant]
Sculpture, [Carving]
Scum. TM. VI. 3.
a— [Sorry (person)]
Scummer, [Spoon for taking away the Scum]
to— [Dung]
Scooper. RN. II. 7. A.
Scurf. S. II. 6. A.
Scurrility, Man. IV. 9. E.
Scurvy.
Disease. S. VI. 4.
— grass. HL. VI. 13.
adj. { Sorry }
{ Evil }
Scut, [Tail] PP. VI. 6. A.
Scutcheon.
[Picture of shield]
[Area of painted degree]
— in building. (sign)
Scuttle.
[Basket]
— of Ship. RN. II. 6. A.
to — water, [Un-defile w. by motion]
Sea. W. IV. A.
— bat, [Flying fish]
— bells
— bindweed } HL. VI. 13. A.
— Calf. Be. V. 3. A.
— Card.
— Coast, [adj. Shore Countrey.]

— Cob. Bi. IX. 9.
— Cole.
Herb. HL. VI. 13. A.
Stone. St. VI. 3. A.
— Cow.
— Cormorant.
— Devil. Fi. II. 4. A.
— dragon. Fi. IV. 8.
— drake, [Cormorant]
— ear.
Animal. Ex. VII. 8.
Plant. HL. I. 13.
— fan. HL. I. 15.
— faring man. RN. V.
— frog. Fi. II. 4. A.
— grass. HL. I. 14.
— green, [Green adj. Sea (like)
— gull. Bi. IX. 9.
— hog, [Porpois]
— lettice. HL. I. 12.
— man. RN. V.
— mew. Bi. IX. 9.
— moss. HL. I. 12.
— navelwort. HL. I. 11. A.
— nettle. Ex. VI. 6. A.
— onion. HL. IV. 13.
— raven, [Cormorant]
— sick, [Sick through motion upon the sea.]
— swallow. Bi. IX. 9. A.
— toad. Fi. II. 4. A.
— weed, [S. moss]
— withywinde. HL. VI. 13. A.
arm of the —
[Bay] W. IV. 5.
[Fretum] W. IV. 5.
calm — W. IV. 1.
narrow — [Fretum] W. IV. 5.
Seal, [adj. RC. VI. 5. (instr.)]
Fish, [Sea-calf] Be. V. 3. A.
Sealing. RC. VI. 5. A.
Seam,
[adj. p. sowing (thing)]
— of the head.
— of Ship. RN. II. 8.
[Hog's fat]
Seamster, [adj. Sowing (mech.)]
Sear, [Dry (exc.)]
to — [Harden with a. fire]
— ed Conscience, [Unconscionableness.]
Searce, [Sift] O. VI. 1. A.
[adj. Sift (instr.)]
Search.
[Seek]
[a. Inquisition]
[Try] { Transf. TA. II. 5. A.
{ Judic. R] II. 4. A.
— ing, [Sagacity]
Season.
[Time]
adj. Congruity (time)
{ Time (perf.)
in— { Perfect]
out of— { adv. { Corrupt]
— of the year, [Year (part)
sp. adj. Congruity
to— { a. Salt] Q. IV. 5.
{ a. Condite] Pr. III. 9. A.
Seasonable, [adj. Season]
Seat. [adj.

SE

[adj. p. Sitting (jug.]
Stool} Po. VI. 5.
Chair} P. VI. 6.
[Situation] Sp. III.
Sebesten. Tr. II. 5. A.
Secant. Mag. II. 4.
Secession, [Separation]
Seclude, { Out-shut
Exempt
Except}
Second.
[adj. Two]
Every — [Every adv. turn adj. two]
Subst.
— of a degree.
in Magn. [3600ᵗʰ (part) of a Degree]
in Time. [60ᵗʰ part of a Minute]
[adj. Accessorines. { Fighter
Speaker
Doer of any thing}
to — {Do any thing adv.} { Accessorines
Immediate after}
Secondary, [adj. Two (kind]
Secundine. PP. VI. 7. A.
Secre- { Concealing
cy, { Taciturnity]
Secret.
{ Concealed]
{ adj. p. Taciturnity]
Secreta- { Notary]
ry, { adj. Writing (Off.]
Sect, { Faction
Schism]
Sectary, [Schismatic]
Section, [adj. p. Cut (part)
Part of Book. D. III. 2. A.
Sector.
Secular.
[Temporal] RE. O.
[Laic] RE. II. O.
[Not-regular. RO. IV. 6.]
Secundine. PP. VI. 7. A.
Secure.
{ Safe]
{ Confident]
{ Assured]
{ Fearless]
{ Heedless]
{ Careless]
to — { Security]
[a. { Imprisonment]
Security, { Safety]
{ Confidence]
{ &c.
{ Sponsion]
{ Mortgage]
Sedan. Po. V. 3.
Sedate, [adj. p. { Quiet]
{ Content]
{ Satisfaction]
Sedentary, [adj. Sitting]
Sedge, { Flagg
{ Reed}
Sediment. TM. VI. 3. A.
Sedition. RJ. III. 3. A.
Seduce. RO. VI. 1. O.
Sedulity, [Diligence]

SE

See.
{ v. Sight]
{ a. Heedfulness]
— to, [a. Heedfulness]
— you do it, [a. Heedfulness that you do it]
fair to — to, [Beautiful]
go to — [Visit]
a — [Bishops City]
Seed.
— of Plants. PP. III. 6.
— plot, [adj. p. Sowing (place)
— time, [adj. Sowing (time)
run to, [a. Seed]
— of Animal. PG. I. 4.
Seeing.
Sight. NP. III. 1.
[adj. a. Sight]
— that, [Whereas]
Seek. TA. I. 7.
{ Inquisition
— to do — { Design } to do]
{ Endeavour
— to him, [Interest him]
Seeling.
of Room. Po. III. 8. A.
of Ship, [Heeling] RN. VI. 7.
— birds eye, [Sow together the Eyelids]
Seem. TA. I. 9. A.
Seem- { Beautiful
ly, { Decent]
Seen, [adj. p. Sight]
to be — { Shew
by { Manifest]
well — in, [Skilled (perf.]
Seer, [Prophet]
Seeth, [Boyl]
— over, [Spill by Seething]
Segment, [From-adj. p. Cut (part)
Segregate. TM. III. 6.
— ing, [Separate] TA. II. 1. O.
Seigniory, [Magistrate (place)
Seise, { Take to possess]
{ Arrest]
Seizin. RC. V. 8. A.
Seldom. Sp. I. 7. O.
[Rare] Sp. II. 6. O.
Select, [Elect]
Selenite. St. II. 5.
Sell. RC. V. 3.
Self.
him — [Him him]
beside — [adj. { Dotage
{ Frenzy
{ Madness]
my — [Me me]
thy — [Thee thee]
by it — [Solitary
adj. Understand-
he is him —) ing (perf.]
[He is) In State (perf.]
{ Pride]
Selfconceit, { Esteem (exc.) of self]
Selfdenial. Ha. V. 3.
Self-nds, [Selfishness]
Selfheal. HF. VII. 16.

SE

Selfishness. Ha. V. 3. O.
Selflove, [Love of Self]
{ Disobedience]
Selfwill, { Contumacy] }
{ Pertinacy]
Selvage, [Margin of cloth]
Semblable, [Like]
{ So]
Semblably, { Also]
{ Accordingly]
Semblance, { Seeming
{ Likeness]
Sembreef.
Semicircle, [Half Circle]
Semicolon. D. I. 5. A.
Seminary.
{ Seed (place)
{ Education (place)
Semination, [Sowing]
Sena. Sh. IV. 4.
bastard — Sh. IV. 4. A.
Senary, [Six]
Senate, [Council]
Send. TA. VI. 4.
— for one, [Call by one sent]
Senembi. Be. VI. 3. A.
Seneschal, [Steward]
Sengreen, [House-leek] HL, VIII. 1.
Indented — HL. VIII. 4. A.
Senior.
[More old]
[Superior]
[p. through more age]
Sennight, [Week]
Sense.
— of a word, [Meaning]
Faculty.
— internal. NP. II.
— common — NP. II. 1.
— external. NP. III.
Sp. [Feeling]
Sensible.
[adj. a. { Common sense }
{ Understanding } (apt.]
[adj. p. { Common sense }
{ Understanding } (pot.]
— Quality. Q.
Sensitive.
— Soul. W. I. 5.
— faculty.
Internal. NP. II.
External. NP. III.
— plant. HS. III. 8. A.
— action. AC. II.
Senseless.
[adj. Stupor]
[Not adj. p. Understanding (pot.]
Sensual, [adj. Sensuality]
Sensuality. Man. II. 1. O.
Sent.
{ pret.
{ adj. p } Send]
[Smell]
Sentence.
[Opinion]
Clause. D. III. 1. A.
— in Court. RJ. II. 5. A.
Sententious, [Abounding in short sentences.]

Senti-

SE | SE | SE

Sentiment.
- { Understanding }
- { Common sense }
- { Apprehension }
- { Opinion }

Sentinel
Sentry } RM. III. 7.

Servi, [Mustard seed]
Separate. TA. II. 1. O.
- { Segregate }
- { Abstract }
- { a. Schismatic }
- { Excommunicate }

Separatists, [Schismatic]
Sepiment. RM. VI. 4.
Seps Serpt.
September, [9th month]
Septenary, [Seven]
Septuagint, [Seventy Translators]
Septuple, [Sevenfold]
Sepulchre, [adj. { thing } { place }]
  Intombing
Sepulture, [Burying]
Sequel, { Following, Event, Illation }
Sequence, [Following adv. Series]
Sequestration, [Depositing with not-party]
Seraglio, [Palace of the Mahometan King]
Seraphim, [Angel]
Serenade, [a. Music near ones adj. sleeping (place)]
Serene.
- { Clear }
- { Bright }
- { Gracious } adj. Man. VI. 1.

Serjant.
[pursevant] RJ. III. 6.
—*at arms,* [Most adj.-Superiority. RJ. III. 6.]
—*of Law,* [Most adj.-Superiority Graduate of common Lawyers]
[Chief pleader (kind)]
[Highest degree of Pleaders (kind)]
—*of feet.* RM. III. 4.

Series. TM. III. 7.
Serinus. Bi. VI. 1. A.
Seriousness.
  The Disposition. NP. IV. 3.
  The Virtue { Sobriety, Gravity }
Sermon, [adj. p. Preaching (thing)]
Sermountain. HF. IV. 7.
Serous, [adj. Serum]
Serpent. Be. VI. 6.
  Sea—Fi. VI. 2.
Serpentine, [adj. Serpent]
—*Line,* { Spiral } Mag. III. 9.
         { Helix } Mag. III. 9. A.
Serve.
[v. { Slave, Servant, Souldier }]
—*as to wages.*
  [adj. p. Hiring]

as to work, [a. { Slave, Servant, Souldier }]
  [a. { Subjection, Obedience }]
  —God, { Obedience, Worship } [a. God]
  [Wait]
  { Carry }
  { Deliver }
  —*Process.*
  —*up to Table.*
  —*wine.*
  { Furnish }
  { Sell }
  —*one with ware,* [Sell w. to one]
as to use, Transf.
  [Action]
  —*one,* { a trick in his kind }
  [v. adj. { Adjuvant, Profitable }]
  v. adj. { Congruous, Convenient }
  —*when time*—s.
  [v. adj. Stead]
  —{ for instead of }
  [v. adj. { Sufficience, Pertinence }]
  —*for such a use.*

Servant. RO. III. 7. O.
  [Suitor] RO. III. 2.
  [Beneficiary] RO. III. 8. O.
Service.
  [v. { Servant }
   a. { Souldier }
   a. Obedience]
  divine—[d. worship]
  Waiting.
  { first, second } —[meats (aggr. carried adv. { first, second }]
  [v. adj. { Adjuvant, Profitable }]
  [a. Benefactor]
  —*doing one a*
  [p. Use]
  [Berry of Service-tree]
  —*Tree.* Tr. I. 4.
  Common—Tr. I. 4. A.
Serviceable, [adj. { pot., Service { pron. }]
Servile, [adj. { Servant, Slave, Villain }]
Servingman, [Servant for waiting]
Servitor, [Servant]
Servitude, [p. Slave (thing)]
Serum. PG. I. 2.
Seseli, [Hartwort]
Sessions, [Convention] RC. III. sp. for RJ.
Set.
[Cause, sp. by motion to be { Place in a } { sp. of Situation } { Rest }]
[Cause to be so]

—*a copy,* [a. Exemplar (make)]
—*a song,* [a. Tune (make) for a l.]
—*fast,* [Fast (make)]
—*free,* [a. Liberty (make)]
—*open,* [Open (make)]
—*packing,* [From-go (make)]
—*Right,* { Put (perf.), adj. Right }
—*upright,* [Upright (make)]
{ Design, Appoint }
  sp. according to Contract.]
—*an allowance,* [appoint an all.]
—*a fine on,* [Appoint, &c.]
—*a form,* [appoint a form]
[Offer]
  sp. for p. { Hire, Sell }
[Esteem] AS. II. 8.
—*Light by,* [Contemn] AS. II. 8. A.
{ a. Place, Put }
—*himself,* { a. place h., Purpose } (augm.)
—*ones* { Put ones, &c. a. Adjuvant }
hand to { Write under }
-*Birds*
-*Travellers, &c.* } observe the place of { B., Tr. }
[a. { Situation, Figure }]
—*a bone* { Place, Situate } (perf.)
—*a bowle.*
—*a Ruff,* { Situation, Figure } (perf.)
[Motion] Mo.
  as Current, [v. Motion]
  as Boatman } Thrust
  as Horse · { (imp) with hands, feet }
[a. ition (make)]
[Rest] Mo. O.
Plant.
  the Root. O. III. 6.
  the Grain. O. III. 6. A.
[Sit (make)]
[a. { Steadiness } Q. VI. 6.
    { Fastness } Q. VI 6. E.]
—*fast,* { a. Fast (make), Imprison }
—*about* { a. Begin, a. Endeavor (inc.) }
against, { v. opposite, a. Segregate }
—*apart* { Reserve, Appropriate }
—*aside,* a. Segregate }
{ Exempt, Except }
{ Reject, Forsake }

—a1

SE | SE | SH

—*at* [a. Impulsive]
—*at liberty*, [adj. a. Liberty (make)]
—*nought*, [Contemn]
—*ods*, [Un-a. peaceable (make)]
—*peace*, [Un- {War / Fight / Contention}]
—*by* [Esteem] (make)
—*the ears*, [a. contention (make)]
—*down*- {Down-ition(make) / Write}
—*farther off*, [More-distant (make)]
—*forth*, Vid. *out*.
[v. {Go / Travel} (inc.)]
[a. Manifest]
[a. Publick (make)]
[a. Ornate (make)]
[Praise]
—*for-* [v. Travel {(inc.)}
ward [a. Proceed]
—*in* [Begin]
—*order*, [a. Order]
—*off*, vid. *forth*.
—*farther off*, [More-distant (make)]
—*on*, vid. *upon*.
{Impulsive / Incourage}
[adj. a. edge (make)]
—*edge*, [a. Stupor]
[Begin]
—*fire*, [a. fire (make)]
—*foot* {Cause (inc.)}
—*over the fire*, [Place above the fire]
—*a fine on*, [a. Mulct]
—*out*, vid. *forth*.
[Out-ition (make)]
—{Ship / Souldier} {furnish Sh. / & send So.}
—*to* {To-put / Operate (end)}
—{Hire / Sale}
—*work*, {a. Operate (make) / Operate (inc.)}
—*anes band*.
—*toge-* {Joyn}
ther, {a. One (make)}
—*by the ears*, [a Contention (make)]
—*up*, [Begun]
{Repeat / Restore}
—*again*,
—*a building*, [Build]
—*a fashion*.
—*a trade*.
—*one instead of another*, [a. Room]
—*upon his* {Lift
Legs, {a. Upright}
—*upon*, vid. *on*.
—*a person*, {Assault / Offend (end)}
&c.
—*a thing* {Resolve / Undertake / Attempt}
Subst

{Aggregate / Series / Suit}
[Game]
{Cards.
—*at* {Dice.
Sun—[Under-a. Horizon] Adj.
{Purposed / Designed / Appointed / sp. by consent]
—*allowance*.
—*Battle*.
—*Company*.
—*Fight*,
—*Form*,
—*Place*.
—*Price*.
—*Purpose*.
—*Resolution*.
—*Speech*
—*Time*.
He is——[Has lost the game]
Sun is——[S. is under the Horizon]
Well——[adj. p. figure (perf.)]
Setter.
[adj. Setting (person)]
Theefs—spy
[Dog. adj. Observing (apt.) the place of Birds]
Settle. {v.
{a.
{Cause
{Confirm
[adj. Permanence]
—*ones estate*, [Assign the fut. right of it sp. by sealed adj. Obligation (thing)]
—*to a busi-* {Prepare for permanence in a b}
ness, {Permanent (inc) in it.}
{Staying / Dwelling}
as Bird, {Rest / Stand}
[adj. {Staidness / Fastness}
as grounds {Precipitate / Sediment}
[Habit]
{Sobriety / Gravity}
Subst. [Long Chair]
—*bedstead*, [Bedstead adj. p. folding (apt.)]
Setling, vid. *Settle*.
[Sediment]
Seven. Mes. I. 7.
Sevenfold, [Seven (kind)]
Sevennight, [Week]
Seventeen. 17.
Seventh, [adj. Seven]
Seventy. 70.
Sever.
{Separate / Segregate}
[adj. Solitary (make)]
[a. {Difference / Diversity}]

Several.
[adj. {Difference / Diversity}]
[adj. p. Sever]
Severity. Man. VI. 7.
[Rigor]
Sewee.
[adj. {Order (Off.) of a. / -Suit} meats]
[Sink] Po. II. 9. A.
Sewer, {Hard / Dried} {Fat}
Sex. NP. VI. 1.
Sextant, [Sixth part of Circle]
Sextary, [Roman measure] about a pint]
Sextile, [Distance ' of a great Circle]
Sexton, [adj. Sweeping (Off.) of Temple]
Sextuple, [Sixfold]
Shackles, [Bonds]
Shad. Fi. III. 11.
Shade
Shadow {Q. I. 2.
—in painting, [Shadow (like)]
Shaft.
[Cylinder]
[Arrow]
[Cone]
[Pyramid]
[Steeple]
of Coach, &c. Po. V. 5.
Shagg, [Rough hair]
Bird, Bi. IX. 5. A.
Shake.
Proper. Mo. VI. 3. A.
—*Hands*. AC. V. 5. A.
—*down*, [Down-a.ition(make) with shaking]
—*off*, [Abandon]
—*in pieces*, [Break with shaking]
—*to* {shaking}
—*up*, [Reprehend severely]
[Tremble]
Shake- {Cloched (freq.) with
rag, {torn (vest)
{Beggar
Shall. fut.
Shale.
a—[Pod] PP. III. 3. A.
to—[Un-a. pod]
Shallop, [Ship (dim.)]
Shalot. HL. IV. 10.
Shallow.
Not deep. TM. II. 3. A.
a—{Shallow (place in the sea) / Bank} W. III. 5. A.
Not wise, [adj. Folly] (inst.)
Shalm, [adj. Tube adj. Music]
Shamble, [a. Butchering (place)]
Shame.
Affection. AS. VI. 2. A.
Cause, [Infamy]
Shamefaced, [adj. {Shame (apt.) / Modesty / Sheepishness}]
Shameful, [adj. Shame]
Shameless, [adj. Impudence]
Shamois, [Goat (kind) having small horns hooked at the end]
Shank

SH SH SH

Shank.
of Animal. PG. V. 5.
of Plant, [Stalk]
Shape, [Figure]
Share.
[Part] sp. adj. Proportioned]
to— { Divide }
{ Distribute }
{ Partner (make) }
Pubes, PG. IV. 7. A.
—bone, [Bone of the sh.]
Plow—[adj. Cutting (part) of the adj. plowing (jug.]
Sharer, [Partner]
Shark.
Fish. Fi. I. 3.
[adj. a. Fraud (person)
sp. impudently spending anothers]
Sharp.
[adj. Acute Angle]
[adj. { Point }
{ Edge }]
[adj. { Cutting }
{ Pricking (apt.) }]
of Animal, [adj. Vigor]
—sighted.
—of hearing.
—voice, [Shrill]
—in music. Q. III. 5. E.
of taste. Q. IV. 4.
[Hungry]
of mind [Sprightly]
[Sagacious]
{ Severe }
{ Austere }
{ Cruel]
Sharpen, [a. Sharp (make)]
Sharpling, [Stickleback]
Shat- { Shake into parts (dim.)
ter, { Bruise (freq.)
Shave. O. IV. 1.
—grass, [Horse tail]
Shaver, [adj. Shaving (person)
a notable—[Extraordinary (corr.)]
Sheaf, [Aggregated (thing)
sp. by together-p. bind]
Shear, [Clip]
Shears, [adj. Clipping (instr.)]
Sheard, { Fragment of earthen}
{ Piece { en vessel }
Sheat.
Rope. RN. IV. 5. A.
—Anchor, [Last anch.]
—fish. Fi. VI. 6.
[Young hog]
Sheath.
a—[Case]
—fish. Ex. VIII. 8. A.
—flies wing, [Crust of fly w.]
to—[into-a-case]
—a ship. RN. VI. 3.
Shed.
{ Lose. }
{ Let go. }
{ Spill. }
{ Lose. }
—tears, { Drop tears }
{ Weep }
—water, [Spill w.]
a—[House (dim.) (sp. not walled]

Shee, { He (fem.) }
{ Female }
Sheep. Be. II. 2.
—Cote, [House for sheep]
—Fold, [About-sepimented (place) for sheep]
—Hook, [Shepherds Hook]
Sheepishness. Man. III. 7. E.
Sheere, [Clip]
—water, [Simple water]
—wind, [adj. Cutting (like) wind]
Sheet, [Lamin]
—of Linnen, [adj. L.Bed(vest]
Shell.
of Animal.
of Oyster, &c. PP. IV. 2.
of Lobster, [Crust] PP. IV. 2. A.
Egg—[Crust of Egg]
of Vegetable.
—of Nut, [Stone] PP. II. 2. A.
—of Bean, &c. [Cod] PP. III. 5. A.
—of Grain, [Husk] PP. III. 3.
Shellaple. Bi. IV. 5. A.
Sheldrake. Bi. IX. 2.
Shelf.
Boord. Po. VI. 4. A.
Flat in the Sea, [Bank] W. III. 5.
Shelter.
[adj. a. Safety (place)]
[adj. { Protection }]
{ a. { Defence }
sp. (place)
Shelving, [Oblique]
Shent, [adj. p. Reprehend]
Shepherd, [Herdman of sheep]
—s bodkin, [Cranes bill]
—s fly. Ex. IV. 8.
—s needle, [Venus comb] HS. I. 5. A.
—s purse. HS. VI. 3. A.
—s rod. HF. VIII. 2. A.
Sheriff, [adj. Shire (Off.)]
Shew.
Gene- { a. Know (make) }
ral, { Un-a. Conceal }
TA. I. 8.
Perfect, [Manifest] TA. I. 9.
Publick, [a. Public (make)]
—what is not, [a. Appearance]
—Otherwise { a. Seeming] TA. I. 9. A.
than it is { a. Hypocrisie }
to sense.
by signes, [a. Sign]
[a. Finger (sign)]
by like, [Represent]
to the ear.
[Narration]
[Interpretation]
[Probation]
to the { Offer to be seen }
eye { a. See (make) }
—sights, [a. Sights]
—tricks, [a. Prestigiator]
to the mind, [Revelation]

Impro- { Do }
per, { Give }
—mercy, [a. Mercy]
Shy, [adj. Reservedness]
Shide of wood, [Thick piece of w.]
Shield, [Buckler]
to— { Defend }
{ Protect }
—of Brawn.
Shift.
a—
[Means] sp. (corr.)
[a. { Craft }
[a. { Fraud }
make—to[Obtain to]
Put to his—s, [Necessitated to difficult (things)]
to— { Change }
{ Alter }
—place, [Go]
—per { Escape }
—ion, { Deliver }
—thing. { Prevent { alter- }
{ Remedy { ing }
—for, [Provide for]
—off { Delay }
{ Avoid }
{ Frustrate }
sp. adv. Craft
Shifter, [Crafty person]
sp. Living by craft]
Shilling. Mea. IV. 3.
Shin, [Forepart of Leg]
Shine, [a. Brightness]
Shingle, [adj. wood (lamin) for
—s [Tetter] (roof)
Ship. RN. I. 1. A.
—wrack { Destruction } of
{ Ruine } Ship]
—wright, [adj. Ship (mech.)]
Shire. RC. III. 4.
Shirt, [Inmost Linnen (vest)]
Shittle, [Inconstant]
vid. Shuttle.
Shive, [Chip]
Shiver.
to—[Tremble]
—in { Shake } into
pieces { Break } chips]
a—[Chip]
Shock.
—of Corn, [Heap of c.]
—of battel, [Battel (imp.)]
Shod, { adj. pret. } Shoo]
{ adj. p. }
Shog, [Move (imp.)]
Shole.
[Shallow (place)]
[Fishes (aggr.)]
Shoo.
[adj. Leather adj. Foot (vest)]
—ing born, [On-drawing (instr.) for shoo.]
horse—[Under-foot(armam.) for horse]
Shook, [adj. p. pret. Shake]
Shoot.
{ Move } { swiftly }
{ Fly }
Out— { Cast }
{ Powre }

SH · SH · SI

Sh
as { Bow (b.) / Gun [a. g.] / Ordinance (q.) }
—one. RJ. V. 2. A.
as Star { Suddenly / Swiftly } [fall]
as Plant, [a. Sprout]
{ Defift }
—off, { a. Gunner }
—up, [Grow fwiftly]
a— { Sprout] PP. II. 5. / Branch] PP. I. 3. / Sucker] PP. I. 2. A. }
Hog (young)
Shop, [adj. { Mechanic / Merchant } (room)]
—*keeper*, [Merchant]
Shore.
of land. W. III. 6.
of water. W. IV. 6.
bird. Bi. V. 2.
to—*up*, [a. Prop]
Shorn, [adj. Clip]
Short.
{ op. to long, [adj. TM. II. 1. O] / Low / Little / Lefs / [adj. Epitome] / Soon / Tranfitory / —*ly*, { Soon / [adv. Future (dim.)] }
—*breathing* / —*windednefs* } S. V. 1.
be —— { a. Fewnefs / *with* { a. Harfhnefs } words }
come— }
fall— } { v. long (def.) / v. fhort (exc.) }
[adj. Defect]
[be more fhort]
fp. than it was expect-ed]
keep — [a. Cohibiting]
Shorten, [a. Short (make)]
Shot.
{ adj. p. pret. / adj. p. } Shoot }
[Bullet]
[adj. a. pay (thing)]
—*free*, [adj. p. Immunity from paying]
Shotten, [Having fpawned]
Shove, [Thruft]
—*net*, [Net for catching fifh] fp. by thrufting and lift-ing it.]
Shovel, [Up-take- { Fluid / ing (vas) { Gramulous } (things) }
—*er*. Bi. VIII. 6.
Should, [Mood { Duty / of { Neceffity }]
Shoulder.
of *trunk*. PG. IV. 1. A.
—*blade*, [Broad bone of—]
Joynt, PG. V. 1. A.
to—— [Thruft up with fhoul-der]

—*up*, { Prop / [a. Support (end.)] }
Showr. El. VI. 2. ⊕.
Shout.
[Voice (augm.)]
[Exclamation (imp.)]
fp. for joy]
Show, vid. *Shew*.
Shread, [Mince] Po. III.
● 6. A.
a—[Chip (dim.)]
Shreek, { Acute exclamation (imp.) }
Shreeve, { a. Confefs (make) / Examin for a. confefs (make) / fp. adv. Solitary to Prieft }
Shrew, { Morofenefs (fem.) / [adj. Contention] }
—*moufe*, [Long-fnouted vene-mous moufe (kind)]
Shrewd.
[Crafty]
[Hurtful]
—*turn*, { a. Hurtfulnefs }
Shrift, [a. Shreeve]
Shrill, [adv. { Sound (augm.) / acute adj. { Exclamation }]
Shrimp.
[Little]
Fifh. Ex. VI. 4.
River—Ex. II. 11. A.
Shrine, [Cafe]
fp. of Image]
Shrink.
{ Gefture. AC. VI. 3. / Pofture. AC. VI. 3. A. }
[adj. Denfity]
[adj. Diminifh]
[Back-draw]
[Retire]
Shrivel, [Wrinkle]
Shroud.
—*of a Ship*. RN. IV. 1.
[adj. Shrouding (thing)]
[Outmoft adj. Linnen (veft) of the dead]
to—[Cover]
fp. for protection]
Shrovetide.
[adj. Shreeving (time)]
[adj. Feaft (time) next before Lent]
Shrub. Sh.
to—[a. Cudgel]
Shrugging. AC. IV. 7. A.
Shuddering. [Trembling]
Shuffle, [Mingle confufedly]
fp. by motion (freq.)
Shun, [Avoid (end.)]
Shut, vid. *Clofe*.
—*ing*. O. II. 4.
—*in of the day*, [Evening]
—*up*, { Shutting (augm.) / a. Conclafion }
Shuttle.
[adj. p. Caft (apt.) adj. Wea-ving (inftr.)]
[adj. p. Motion (apt.)]
—*Cock.*
—*headed*, [Inconftant]

Sybil, [adj. Paganifm Prophet (fem.)]
Sick, [adj. Sicknefs]
Sickle, [adj. Reaping (inftr.)]
Sickly, [adj. { (apt.) / Sicknefs { (freq.) }]
Sicknefs.
in *body*. S.
the—[Plague]
in mind. TA. V. 7. O.
Side.
Part. Sp. III, 4.
—*of a Figure*. Ma. II. 3. A.
—*of ones body*, PG. IV. 5.
Page, [Surface]
[Margin]
—*blow* adj. oblique ftriking]
—*long*, [adj. Side]
—*wayes*, { Afide / [adj. Obliquity] }
—*of the Country*, [Part of the Country]
—*of the hill*, [Oblique (part) of the h.]
—*of* { River / Sea } [Shore]
kin by the Mothers—[Kin by the Mother]
on this— { Citerior / Prep. VI. 2. }
on that—{ Ulterior / Prep. VI. 2, O. }
on the { Oppofite / *other*— { Prep. VI. 3. O. }
on eve- { Environing / *ry*— } Prep. III. 4. O.
on my—[For (Prep. II. 3.)
inc.]
to—[a. { Faction / League / Acceffory }]
Sider, [Wine of Apples]
Sidefmen, [Churchwardens adj. adjuvant (Off.)]
Siege.
Leaguer. RM. I. 4.
[a. Dunging]
Sift.
Searce. O. VI. 1. A.
[Examin]
—*out*, [Find by examin-ing]
Sigh. AC. IV. 6. E.
Sight.
{ Sence. NP. III. 1. / a. Seeing }
—*of the eye*, [adj. Seeing (part) of eye]
—*of a gun*, [Through-adj. p. See (apt.) gun (part)]
Seeing—*s*. Mo. V. 7.
Sigil, [adj. Wizarding feal]
Signature, [a. Sign]
Signe.
Mark. T. VI. 5.
—*of an affection*, AC. IV. [Conftellation]
—*in the Zodiac*, 1/12 of the Zodiac]
to—RG. VI. 1.
Signet, [Seal (dim.)]
P p p 2 *Signi-*

SI   SI   SK

S*ignifie.*
  [a. Sign]
  [a. Meaning]
  [Narrate]
Silence.
  op. to Sound. Q. III. O.
  Virtue, [Taciturnity]
Silk. Pr. IV. 3.
  —*man,* [adj. Silk (merc.]
  —*worm.* Ex. III. 6. A.
  —*Grass,* [Upright Dogs-bane]
  HS. IV. 3. A.
Sill, [adj. Foundation Beam]
Sillabub, [Drink of milk { wine } coagulated with { &c.]
Silly, [adj. Folly]
Silver. Met. I. 2.
  quick—Met. III. 1.
  —*weed,* [Wild Tansey]
Silurus. Fi. VI. 6.
Similar, [All of one kind]
Simile, [adj. Translatitious (thing)
Similitude, [Likeness]
Simnel.
Simony, [Buying (corr.) of religious (thing)
Simper, [Smile]
Simple.
  [adj. Simpleness]
  —*figure.* Mag. III.
  [Simple medicinal (thing)
  sp. Herb]
  to—[Know (end.) the growing herbs]
Simpleness
Simplicity
  { Singleness }
  { Primitiveness }
  op. to mixture. T. III. 8.
  { Purity }
  { Homeliness }
  { Sorriness }
  op. to figurateness. D. III. 7. O.
  [Sincerity]
  { Folly }
  { Unskilfulness }
  { Unlearnedness }
  { Unexpertness }
Simulation, [a. Hypocrisie]
Simultaneous. Sp. I. 2.
Sin { v. } { a. }
  { Ungraciousness }
  { Unholiness }
  { Vice }
  [Evil action]
Since.
  [Before } this time]
  [After }
  —*that,* [Whereas]
Sincerity. Ha. IV. 4.
Sine. Mag. II. 6.
Sinew. PG. II. 5.
Sinful, { Ungracious }
  { Unholy }
  { Vicious }
Sing. AC. III. 5.
  as the ears—[Ring (like)
Singe [Burn { (incept.) }
  { Outside }
  { Hair }

Single.
  { One (kind) }
  { Simple }
  { Singular }
  { Solitary }
  { Onely }
  —*combate,* [Duelling]
  —*life,* [Cœlibate] RO. II 2. A.
  a—[Tail of Deer]
Singular.
  { Excellent }
  { Unlike all others }
  —*number.* TM. III. 2.
Singularity, { Affectation of being unlike others }
  { Conceitedness }
Sinister.
  [Left side]
  [Malign]
  [Censoriousness]
  [adj. Adversity]
Sink, [Down-ition under water.]
  Proper. Mo. I. 4. O.
  [Soke]
  —*into ones mind,* [Be fixed in ones m.]
  —*ing paper,* [Porous (augm.) (Drown)]
  Improper, [Fall] sp. (inc.)
  —*under the burden.*
  [adj. p. Dent]
  [Diminution]
  [Ruining (inc.)]
  a—Po. II. 9. A.
Sinnet, [Cord (augm.) of three Cords together twisted]
Sinople.
  Subst. [Cinnabar]
  adj. [Green]
Sip.
  [Drink (dim.)]
  [Suck (dim.)]
Sippet, [Bread (lam.) adj. p. Soke (apt.)
Siquis, [adj Paper (lam.) publish'd for finding lost (things)]
Sir, [Voc. adj. Dignity (person)]
Sire, [Parent (male)]
Sirname, [adj. Parent name]
Sirra, [Voc. Mean (person)]
Sise, [Six]
Siskin, [Finch green]
Sister, [Brother (fem.)]
Sisterhood, [Corporation (fem.)]
Sitting.
  { Gesture. AC. VI. 5. }
  { Posture. AC. VI. 5. A. }
  —*as Commissioners,* [Together fitting]
  —*as a hen,* [a. Fotion by upon fitting.]
  —*down,* [Sitting]
  —*out,* [Not playing]
  —*up,* { Rising }
  { adj. Permanence out of bed. }
  as Bird, { Rest }
  { Stand }
  [Permanence]

—*hard at it,* [adj. a. Diligente. adv. permanence]
Site
Situation { Sp. III.
Sith that, [Whereas]
Sithe, [adj. Reaping (instr.)]
Sive, [adj. Sifting (instr.)]
Sivet, [Sweat of the Civet Cat]
  —*cat.* Be. IV. 4. A.
Six. Mea. I. 6.
Sixfold, [Six (kind)]
Sixt, [adj. Six]
Sixteen, 16.
Sixty, 60.
Size.
  { Proportion }
  { Measure }
  Gummy liquor, [adj. a. varnish (thing)]
  sp. of boil'd Leather]
to—
  [a. Size]
  [Sear the Seams]
assize, [Convention of shire for adj. R] (things)
Sizers, [adj. Clipping (instr.)]
Skein. Mag. VI. 7. A.
Skeleton, [Frame of bones]
Skew, [Oblique]
Sky.
  [Æther] El. II. 1.
  [Heaven]
Skill.
  [Science]
  [Art]
  [Learning]
  it—*eth not,* [It is not adj. importance]
Skiller. Pr. V. 6. A.
Skim, [Unskum]
Skin.
  Hide. PG. II. 3.
  —*and bone,* [Lean (exc.)]
to—
  [Un-a. skin]
  [Cover with skin]
  [Membrane] PG. II. 3. A.
  [Husk] PP. II. 3.
Skink, [Scink]
to—[Powre for p. drinking]
Skinker, [adj. Waiting (Off.) that skinketh]
Skinner, [adj. Skin (merc.)]
Skip.
  [Leap]
  —*Jack,* [Sorry man (dim.)]
  [Omit]
Skipper, { Sailer } RN. V. 8.
  { Master } RN. V. 4.
Skirmish. RM. I. 8.
Skirret. HF. IV. 11. A.
Skirt, [Margent]
  —*of doublet,* [Lower Margent of d.]
Skittish.
  [adj. { Leap } (pron.)
  { Kick }
  { Disingenious }
  { Wanton }
Skreen.
  —*for corn,* [adj. Seperating (jug.)]
  —*between Rooms,* [adj. Separating (sep.)]

Sku,

SL

Sku, [Oblique]
Slab, { Moor
[adj. { Bog } (place)
Slabber.
  [Let-go Spittle]
  [Wet (corr.)
  [Defile]
Slack.
  { Loose }
  { Limber }
  [adj. { Remission }
         { Diminution }
  [adj. { Slight }
         { Neglect }
  [adj.a. { Slow }
           { Protract }
  [adj. a. Cunctation]
Slay, [a. Die (make)
  —*of weavers loom.*
Slake, [a. Remission]
  —*fire* { Un- { fire } (dim)
  —*thirst* { a. { thirst }
Slander, [Calumny]
Slank.
  [Thin]
  Herb, [Wrack]
Slant, [Oblique]
Slap, { Strike }
         { Cudgel }
  —*up* { Eat { greedily }
         { Lick { (corr.)
Slash.
  Cut in many places. Pr. III.
  5. A.
  { Cut deep }
  { Whip }
Slate. St. I. 5.
Slattering.
  { a. Slightness }
  { Carelesness }
  { Improvidence } Man. III.
  2. D.
Slave. RC. I. 9. O.
Slaver, vid. **Slabber.**
Slaughter, [a. Die (make)
  —*house,* [adj. Butchering
              (room)
Slaunder, [Calumny]
Sleave.
  —*silk,* [Not-spun S.]
  —*fish.* Ex. IX. 3.
  red—Ex. IX. 3. A.
Sleazy, [Loose]
Sled. Po. V. 4.
Sledge, [Hammer (augm.]
Sleek, [Smooth (augm.]
  —*stone,* [adj. stone adj. a.
              smoothing (inftr.]
Sleep. AC. II. 3. A.
  [Numness]
Sleepy, { Sleep (apt.)
            [adj. { Sluggardliness]
Sleering, [Crafty oblique a. eye
                manner]
Sleet. El. VI. 4. A.
Sleeve, [adj. arm (vest]
Sleeve- { Impertinence]
  less { Vain]
Sleight, vid. **Slight.**
  [a. { Craft }
       { Art }
Slender.

SL

[Thin] TM. II. 5. O.
{ Remiss }
{ Not sufficient]
Sleve.
  —*silk,* [Not-spun S.
  —*fish.* Ex. IX. 3.
  red—Ex. IX. 3. A.
Sly, { Crafty }
        { Reserved]
Slicing.
  Cut. Pr. III. 6.
  —*chip* { From-sliced (part
           { Chip }
           { sp. Thin]
  iron—
  to—[Dung]
Sliding, [Motion swift whose
              parts are not seen]
  Proper. Mo. II. 5.
  —*knot,* [k. un-adj. p.ty (apt.)
             by pulling]
  —*as water,* { a. Stream adv. si-
                 lence.
  —*away* { from { -ition { silence }
  —*back* { back } adv. { concea-
                                 (ling
  —*by* [beside { -ition { silence
  —*over* [over } adv. { concea-
                                 (ling
Slight, vid. **Sleight.**
  [Thin (augm.)
  { Little }
  { Deficient]
  [Loose]
  { Sorry }
  { Remiss }
  [adj. Vanity]
  [Homely]
 * Moral, [adj. Ha. III. 4. E.]
  [Careless]
  to—
    { Contemn }
    [a. Disrespect]
    —*works,* [Spoil w.]
Slim, [Long thin]
Slime, [adj. a. Sliminess (thing]
Sliminess. Q. VI. 4.
Sling, [adj. Casting (inftr.)
  pair of—*s,* [adj. Lifting (inftr.)
                 for Carriage
                 sp. of Barrels]
Slink, [Abortive Bull (young]
  —*away* { from { -ition adv.
  —*back* { back } Concealing]
Slip.
  Proper, [Slide (dim.]
         { Stumble through sliding
           (dim.]
         { Err }
         [Omit]
  —*away,* { From }
  —*back,* { Back } Rion adv.
  —*by,* { Beside } Concealing]
  —*off,* { From- }
  —*on,* { Upon- } ition, &c.]
    — { cloth }
    — { Clothes { un-cloth }
                    (swiftly)
  give one the—[From ition adv.
                   Concealing
  let— { Let go }
         { Lose }

SL

  sp. through Carelesness]
  a—[v. Slip]
  —*of plant,* [Branch]
  to— { Cut }
         [From { Pull }
  [Cord with Loop in the end]
  —*knot,* [Tied (part) for a·
              Loop (make)
Slipper, [adj. Foot (vest) not
              adj. p. ty (pot.]
Slipperiness.
  { Smoothness }
  { Unctuousness }
  [adj. Let go (pron.)
  [Lightness.] Ha. IV. 7. D.
Slit, { Cleft }
         { Chink }
  to— { Cleave }
         { a. Chink]
Slive, [Chip]
Slo, [Plum of Slow tree]
  —*tree.* Sh. I. 4.
Slop, [Loose adj. Thigh (vest]
Sloping, [Oblique]
Slot, [adj. Foot (sign) of stag]
Sloth.
  [Laziness] NP. IV. 6. O.
  Negligence. Ha. IV. 5. D.
  [Sluggardliness] Man. II. 4. O.
  Beast. Be. III. 2. A.
Sloven, [adj. Slovenliness
            (male)
  —*liness.* Man. II. 6. O.
Slouch, { Great (corr.)
           { adj. Rusticity (person]
Slough.
  { Bog }
  { Abandoned skin]
Slow.
  op. to swift. NP. V. 9. O.
  op. to soon, [Late]
  [adj. Protracting]
Slow-worm. Be. VI. 8.
                                { Negligence }
Slubber, [a. { Unskilfulness }
                 { Slovenliness }
  —*over,* Per- { Negligently }
            form { Unskilfully }
                   { Slovenly }
Sluce, [Stream stopping (jug.]
                   { Sluggishness }
Slug, [adj. { Sluggardliness }
                 { Slowness }
  —*abed,* [adj. Man. II. 4. D.
            (person]
Sluggard, [adj. Sluggardliness
                 (person]
Sluggardliness.
  Proper. Man. II. 4. ⊙.
  [Negligence]
  [Slowness]
              { Sluggardliness }
Sluggishness, { Laziness }
                    { Lumpishness }
                    (dim.]
Slumber, { (dim.]
              [Sleep, { (inc.]
Slung, { adj. a. pret. } fling]
           { adj. p. }
Slunk, { adj. a. pret. } flink]
           { adj. p. }
              Slur,

SM

Slur, { Fraud]
{ Affront]
Slurry, { Difgrace]
{ Defile]
Slut.
{ Woman (corr.]
[adj. Sluttifhnefs (fem.]
Sluttifhnefs. Man. II. 6. D.
Smack.
[Sound of feparating the lips]
[Kifs]
[Taft. Q. IV. (dim.]
a—of it, [p. adjunct (dim.]
Small.
[Little]
—nat. Tr. III. I.
[Fine]
cut— { Cut into pieces
{ Mince } (dim]
—*as—beer,* [Weak]
—*number,* [Few]
—*wares,* { Wares (dim.]
{ Little (things) of
value (dim]
Smallage. HF. IV. 9. A.
Smaragd, [Emerald]
Smart. AC. II. 8. A.
—in difcourfe, [adj. Vigor]
—of taft, { Vigor]
[adj. { Frefhnefs]
Smatch, [Taft (dim.]
Smatter, [Skill (dim.]
Smear. O. V. 6. A.
[a. Defiled (make]
Smell.
Senfe. NP. III. 3.
—*out,* [Find by fm.]
a—feaft, [Flatterer for p.
feaft]
Object. Q. IV.
[a. Unfavorinefs]
Smelt.
{ pret.
{ adj. p. } [Smell]
Fifh. Fi. IX. 2. A.
Smile. AC. XIV. 2.
Smirking, [Smiling adv. mirth]
Smite, [Strike]
Smith, [adj. a. Fabrile (perfon]
Smock, [Inmoft linnen (veft]
{ p. of man (fem.]
Smoke. El. II. 3. A.
[Fume]
{ Exhalation]
{ Vapor]
Smooth.
Proper, [adj. Q. VI. 2. E.]
of behaviour, { Courtefie]
[adj. { Complaifance]
Smother, [Stifle]
Smug, { Cleanly
{ Ornate } (augm.]
Smut { [Defile with black
Smutch { (dim.]
Smutty, [Defiled with black
(dim.]
Snacket, [Hafp of Cafement]
Snaffle, [Bridle]
Snail. Ex. I. 2. A.
—*Trefoil.* HS. III. 15.
water— Ex. VII. 1. A.
Sea— Ex. VII. 4.

SN

Snake. Be. VI. 7.
—*weed.* HL. VII. 3.
—*wood.* Tr. VII. 2. A.
Snap.
[Bite (imp.]
[Sound of bite (imp.]
—*dragon.* HS. VIII. 6.
Snaphans, [Gun with Fire-
lock]
Snap- { adj. Biting (apt.]
pifh, { Morofe]
[adj. Rafh anger]
Snare, [Loop for entangling]
[Trap]
Snarle.
[adj. Anger (voice) of Dog]
[adv. a. Con- { Knit]
fufion, { Entangle]
Snatch, [Catch (imp.]
by—es, [Sp. I. 8. O. (imp.].
Sneak, { Look } adv. Conceal-
{ Go } ing (end.]
into corners, [adj. p. Conceal
(end.]
Sneaking- { Sheepifhnefs]
nefs, { Abjectnefs]
Sneer- { Diffembling } [Smiling]
ing, { Crafty
Sneezing. Mo. IV. 1.
[White Hellebore]
—*wort.* HL. VII. 1.
HF. II. 10.
Auftrian— HF. III. 2. A.
Snib, { Secret } [reprehend]
{ Short
Sniff, [Suck-up breath (imp.)
with nofe]
Snip, [Chip]
to— { [From-cut chip]
{ a. Tuft margent by cut-
ting.]
Snipe } Bi. VII. 7. A.
Snite
Snivel, [Fluid exerement of the
nofe]
Snore } Mo. III. 2. A.
Snort
Snot, [Confiftent excrement of
the nofe]
Snow. El. III. 4. A.
—*drop,* [Bulbous violet] HL.
IV. 5. A.
Snout.
[Nofe] PG. III. 3. A.
[Trunk] PP. V. 4. A.
Snudge.
[Crumpled]
Snuff.
[Suck up the breath with
nofe]
[Huff] AC. IV. 6.
take in— { Difpleafed }
{ Be Angry }
—*of Candle,* { (with)
{ [Burning end of
the Wick of Candle]
to— [From- { adj. Afhes }
cut the { Shadowing }
(end of. &c.]
Snuffers, [adj. Bright (inftr.]
Snuffle, [a. Voice through the
nofe]

SO

So.
op. to *as,* Adv. L. 3. O.
—*that* { If]
{ Conditionally that]
op. to *how,* Adv. II. 1. O.
—*Long.*
—*Many.*
—*Much.*
—*Oft.*
And—forth. Conj. IV. 2. O.
So fo, [Indifferently]
Soake, vid. *Soke.*
Soar, [Fly high]
Sob. Mo. III. 4.
Sober, [adj. Sobriety]
Sobriety,
in temper, [Serioufnefs]
In Judgment. Ha. III. 3.
In drink. Man. II. 3.
In converfation, [Gravity]
Soccage.
Sociable.
[adj. Homiletical vertue]
[adj. { Companion
{ Society } (apt.]
Society.
[Companion (abft.]
Community. RC. III. A.
[Corporation]
Sock, [Inner adj. foot (veft]
Socket, [Hollow (part) for con-
taining]
Sod, [adj. p. Boil]
a— [Lump covered with grafs]
Sodain, vid. *Sudden.*
Sodering. O. IV. 4.
Sodomy. RJ. III. 6. A.
Soft.
Proper, [adj. Q. VI. 1. E.
[Gentle]
{ Merciful]
{ Meek]
{ Courteous]
{ Complaifant]
{ Gracious]
{ Clement]
{ Dull]
{ Lazy]
{ Nice]
{ Weak]
{ Slow]
{ Foolifh]
{ Cowardly]
{ Impatient]
{ Sheepifh]
{ Pufillanimous]
Sobo. Int. III. 1.
Soil.
{ Land]
{ Land (kind]
[adj. a. Manuring (thing]
to— [Manure]
[adj. a. Defiling (thing]
to— [adj. { Defiled }
{ a. { Spotted }
(make)
—*of Boar,* [adj. Foot (fign)
of Boar adj. pret. going]
take—as Deer, [Go into wa-
ter]
Sojourn, [a. Gueft]
Soke.

Steep.

SO   SO   SO

Steep. O. V. 7.
[Drink (augm.)
   [a. Drunkenness]
Solace.
  [Comfort]
  [Mirth]
Soland Goose. Bi. IX. 4.
Solar, [adj. Sun] W. II. 2. A.
Sold, { [adj. a. pret.] } [Sell]
    { [adj. p.] }
Soldier, RM. III.
Sole.
  alone, [Solitary]
  —of foot   } [Bottom (part)
  —of shoo }
Fish. Fi. VIII. 1.
  Spotted—Fi. VII. 1. A.
to—
  —a bowl, [a. b. (place) for volutation (inc.)
  —ones ear, [Pull (augm.)—]
  —a shoo, [to- sow bottom (part)
Solecism, [a. Grammar (corr.)]
Solemn, [adj. T. VI. 3. A.]
  —look, [adj. Gravity, face (manner)
Solemnity. T. VI. 3. A.
Solemnize. a. T. VI. 3. A.
Solicite.
  [Instead { Action
        { Business
        { augm.]
  [Intreat, 2freq.]
Solicitous, [adj. Carking]
Solicitude [Carking]
Solid.
  Body. Ma. I. 4.
  [Massie
  [Sufficient
  [Judicious
  [Grave]
Soliloquy, [Alone-speaking]
Solitary. RO. IV. 2. O.
Solitude.
  [Solitary (abstr.)
  [Not-inhabited Countrey]
Solstice, [Motion (time) of Sun in Tropic]
Solve, [a. Solution]
Soluble.
  [adj. Dunging (apt.)
  [adj. p. Solution (pot.)
Solution. D. VI. 5. O.
Solutive, [adj. a. Dunging (apt.)
Some.
  —one. Pron. II 3. O.
  —certain. Pron. II. 3.
  —body, [—(person)
  —time,
    [in some (time)
    [adv. at times] Sp. I. 8. O.
  —what
    [—(thing)
    { Little (part)
    { (dim.)
  —while
    [Through some (time)
    [adv. Permanence (dim.)
Son.
  [Child] sp. (male)
  —in Law, [adv. Affinity Son

God the.—— G. II.
Song, [adj. p. Sing (thing)
  sp. verses (aggr.)
Sonorous, [adj. Sound (augm.)]
Sontic.
  [Hurtful (augm.)
  [adj. a. Impotent]
Soon. Sp. I. 4.
  —at night, [in the evening]
Soop, [Drink by sucking (imp.)
Soot. El. IV. 3. A.
Sooth, [Truth]
Soothing, [Assentation]
Soothsayer, [adj. Wizarding (person)
  sp. by signes]
Sop, [Soked bread (lam.)
to—[Soke]
Sope, Pr. VI. 5.
  —wort. HL. VII. 3. A.
Sophism, [a. Argumentation (corr.)
Sophisticate.
  { a. Spurious}
  { Forge}
  [Make worse by mixture]
Sophistry, [adj. Se- { (Art)
  duce (apt.) a. ar-{
  gumentation { (Manner)
Sorb, [Service]
Sorce- { Witchcraft { sp. by a.
ry, { Wizarding { Lots]
Sordidness.
  [Slovenliness, [Man. II. 6. D.
  Baseness. Man. III. 4. D.
  [Pusillanimity] Man. III. 8. D.
Sore.
  [adj. Pain]
  [Fierce]
  [augm.
  —afraid, [afr. (augm.)
  to—[Fly high]
a—
  [Ulcer
  [Deer (male) of the fourth year]
Sorel, [Deer (male) of the third year]
Sorites, [Syllogism (aggr.)]
Sorrel. HF. I. a.
  —colour.
French—HF. I. 2. A.
Sorry,
  [adj. Grief
  Contemptible. TM. I. 4. D.
Sorrow, [Grief]
Sort.
  { Kind
  { Species
to— { Kinds
  [a. { Species } (tegr.)
  [Manner]
  after a— { Manner}
  [in some { Relation]
Sortition, [a. Lots]
Sot.
  [Fool (augm.)
  [Dull (augm.)
  [adj. Dotage (person)
  [Drunkard]
Souce, [Pickle]

Soverain,
  [Chief]
  [King]
  [Excellent]
Sought, { [adj. a. pret.] } [Seek]
     { [adj. p.] }
Souldier, RM. III.
  —fish. Ex. VI. 5.
Soule. W. I. 3.
  Vegetative—W. I. 4.
  Sensitive—W. I. 5.
  Rational—W. I. 6.
Sound.
  adj. Sanity, [adj. NP. V. 2.]
  [adj. Health]
  [Whole]
  { Perfect}
  { Great}
  [Solid]
  [Sincere]
a—
  Noise. Q. III.
  Articulate. Q. III. 3. A.
  Fretum. W. IV. 5.
  [Condited stomach of Codfish]
to—
  [Sound (make)   (on)
  —well   } [a { Reputati-
  —ill   { { Infamy]
  [Essay for knowing the depth]
  [Essay for knowing by conference]
Sour.
  as Vinegar, [adj. Q. IV. 4.]
  as green Fruit, [adj. Q. IV. 3.]
  [Morose]
  Look—[Lowr]
Source.
  [Original]
  [Fountain]
  [Rise]
South. Sp. III. 2. O.
  —ern wood. HF. II. 10.
Sow.
  [Hog. Be. II. 4. (fem.)
  —gelder, [Un-adj. a. Testicle (mech.)
  —'s bred. HL. VI. 6. A.
  —thistle. HF. III. 14.
  Insect. Ex. II. 9.
  —of Lead. [Cast (thing)—]
Sowe.
  as Land, &c. O. III. 4.
  as Cloth, &c. O. V. 4.
  —up, { Shut
      { Joyn } by sowing]
Souse, [Pickle]
Sowger, [adj. Mending (mech.) for adj. Foot (vest.)
Sowthistle. HF. III. 14
Space. Sp.
  Interval, [Between—space]
Spacious, [Ample]
Spade, [adj. famin adj. digging (instr.)
Spada marina. Fi. VI. 8.
Spay, [Un-a. testicle]
Spaid, [Red Deer (male) of the third year]
Spalt, { Spelter] Met. III. 4.
                 Span.

SP · SP · SP

Span.
[Measure by extending the fingers]
[Prepare adj. Gun (machin) by a. vertiginating]
Spangle, [Little round adj. metal (lamin]
Spaniel, [Dog hunting birds by smell]
Spanish picktooth. HF. V. 11.
Spar.
(Lapis Selenites) or [Muscovia glass]
[Bolt (augm.]
Spare.
{ Not-used }
{ Abundant }
—time, [adj. Leisure (time)]
[adj. Lean]
—ribs.
to ——
Not-punish, [a. Clemency]
Not-spend, [Save] TA. V. 3.
Not-use, [Abstain]
{ Leave }
{ Want }
Sparingness, [Frugality]
Spark. El. I. 1. A.
[Gallant (person)]
Sparkles El. I. 1. A.
Sparrow, Bi. IV. 3.
Mountain— Bi. IV. 3. A.
—bill, [Pin (dim.)]
—hawk, [Least long winged h.]
—mouth'd, [Wide-mouth'd]
Sparus. Fi. V. I. A.
Spathula, [adj. a. spreading (lamin.]
Spatterdashes, [adj. outward-buttoned Leg (vest]
Spavin. S. III. 9.
Spawl, Spit (augm.)
Spawn. PP. IV. 8. A.
—er, [Fish (fem.)]
Speaking. AC. III. 1.
—against, [a. Contradiction]
—for, [Intercession]
—in the nose,[a. Voice through the n.]
—with, [Conference]
Speaker,
[adj. Speaking (person)]
—in Parliament, [Speaking (Off.]
Spear. [Pike]
boar— } [Pike for { b.]
fish— } hunting { f.]
Kings— [Asphodel]
—mint.
Special.
[Principal]
[Particular]
op. to general, [adj. TM. III. 4.]
Specialty, [Bond] RC. VI. 5.
Species. T. I. A.
Specifie.
[Name the particulars]
[a. Example] D. IV. 8. A.
Specifical, [adj. a. Species]

Specious, [adj. Seeming (perf.]
Speck, { Spot (dim.)
Speckled, Q. II. 6.
Spectacle.
[Sight] No. V. 7.
[adj. Glass (instr.) for helping the sight]
Spectator.
[adj. Seeing (person)]
[adj. Mo. V. 7. (person)]
Specula- { Meditation
tion, { Inquisition
Speech.
{ Speaking }
{ Spoken (thing) }
—less, [Not-adj. Speak(pot.]
[Oration]
[Language]
Speed.
{ Swiftness }
{ Soonness }
{ Dispatch }
[Event (kind)]
good— [Prosperity]
—well. HS. VI. 11.
Female—well. HS. VIII. 9. A.
Speight, [Woodpecker]
Spell.
[Charm]
to— AC. III. 4. A.
Spelt.
Spelter. Met. III. 4.
Spence { Room } for adj. sustentation ord.
{ Box }
Spend. TA. V. 3. O. (things)
[a. Decay (make)]
[a. Diminution]
—Time— [v. Time.]
Spendthrift, [adj. Squandering (person)]
Sperage.
Sperme. PG. I. 4.
Spermaceti.
Spew, [Vomit]
Sphacelus. S. I. 8.
Sphear. Mag. III. 5.
Cœlestial, [Orb] W. VI. A.
Sphyrana. Fi. IV. 7.
Spy.
a— RM. III. 5. A.
to—
[a. Spy]
{ a. Eye. }
{ Sight }
{ Observe }
(sp. adv. Concealed)
Spice. Pr. II. 4.
to— [Powder]
sp. with Spice
a— of a dis- { Beginning——
ease, { Degree (dim.)
{ (of disease)
Spicknel. HF. V. 4.
Spider, Ex. II. 5.
—wort. HI. V91. A.
Crustaceous— Ex. VI. 9. A.
Sea— Ex. VI. 9.
Water— Ex. II. 4.
Spignel. HF. V. 4.
Spigot, [Tap]
Spike, [Lavender]
Spikenard.

Spill.
Shed. O. II. 8. O.
[Mar]
Spin. O. V. 1. A.
—out time, [Protract]
as a top, [p. Vertiginate]
Spinach. HF. I. 8.
Spinal, [adj. Backbone]
Spindle, [adj. Vertiginating adj. axis (pin) of adj. spinning (mach.]
—tree. Sh. II. 10. A.
Spink, [Chaffinch]
Spinster, [adj. Spinning (mech.]
Spiral. Mag. III. 9.
{ Cone }
Spire { Pyramid }
[Steeple]
to— as corn, [v. ear (inc.]
Spirit.
Immaterial substance. W. I.
holy— G. III.
{ Angel }
{ Devil }
[Soul]
Animal— PG. I. 1.
—s extracted. Pr. II. 7.
{ Disposition }
{ Temper }
{ Sprightliness }
{ Vigor }
Spiritual,
[adj. Spirit]
Ecclesiastical. RE.
—Persons Eccl. RE. II.
Spirituous,
[adj. Spirit. PG. I. 1.]
[adj. Freshness]
Spirt, [Syringe] O. I. 6. A.
for a— { adv. Transitoriness (imp.]
Spit.
Excretion. Mo. IV. 4.
[Roasting (instr.]
—Fish, [Lucius Marinus]
—deep, [Deep the length of ad]. digging (lam.]
{ Malignity }
Spite, { Hatred }
{ Envy }
in-[adv. { Enemy
{ Contempt]
—of { Contrary to ones will }
[adj. Coaction]
Spittle.
[adj. p. Spit (thing)]
[House of sick (persons)]
Spitter, [Smooth horned Red Deer (young)]
Splayfooted, [adj. Oblique footed]
Spleen. PG. VI. 5. A.
—wort. HL. I. 7. A.
Rough— HL. I. 6. A.
Splendid, [Bright]
Splendor, [Brightness]
Splenetic.
[Sick in the Spleen]
[Hypochondriac]
[Adj. Anger]
Spindletree. Sh. II. 10. A.

splent.

SP | SP | ST

Splent.
[Lamin]
{sp. adj. Furrow (fig.)
[Chip]
Splinter, [Chip]
Split, [Cleave]
[Chink]
Spodium, Met. V. 2.
Spoil.
[Mar]
—for use. TA. II. 9. O.
Harras. RM. II. 5. D.
Spoke.
[adj. {pret. } {speak}]
{sp.}
—of wheel. Po. V. 7. A.
Spokesman, [Instead-speaker]
Spondyl. Ex. VIII. 4. A.
(Vertebra) PG. IV. 3. A.
Fish. Ex. VIII. 4. A.
Sponk, [Touchwood]
Sponsion.
[Paction]
Suretiship. RC. VI. 6.
Spontaneity. AS. IV. 9.
Spool of weaver.
Spoon. Pr. V. 8.
—*bill.* Li. VIII. 6.
Sport.
[a. Wanton]
[Play]
[Recreation]
[Game]
[Mirth]
Sportful, [Wanton]
Spot, [adj. a. Spottedness (thing)]
Spotted, [adj. Q. I. 5. O.]
—*fever,* [Malignant f.]
Spouse, {Betrothed } (fem.)
{Married}
Spout.
{Concave (thing) for out-}
{Tube } {stream-}
{Narrow (vas } {ing.}
[Faucet]
—of *Rain.* El. VI. 3.
to—{Powre } Stream
{Syringe } (dim.)
Sprain, [a. place (corr.)]
sp. by stretching (exc.)
Sprat, [Herring (young)]
Sprawling.
[Creeping]
{Lying}
{Reverse}
spread.
Unheap. O. II. 6. O.
{Stretch} AC. VI. 2.
{Be extended} AC. VI. 2. A
[a. Publick (make) A.
[a. Contagion]
Sprig, [Eranch (dim)] PP. I. 3.
Sprightliness. NP. IV. 2.
Spring.
[adj Beginning (part)]
—of *the year.* Mea. V. 2.
—*Day*—[Day (incept.)]
[Rise] Sp. II. 4. A.
—*Fount.* W. IV. 3. A.
[Increase]
—*Tide,* {Tide} {New} of the
{at the} {Full} Moon}

Motion. O. I. 7.
—of *Lock,* [adj. Spring (inst.)]
to—
{Sprout}
{Grow}
[Leap] Mo. I. 5.
—*forth,* [Being (inc.)
—*from,* {Effect}
{be } Descendent]
—*a leak,* {v. Chink } (inc.)
{v. Crack }
—*a mine,* [Find a m.]
—*Partridges,* {Rise } (make)
{Fly } Partr.
Springal; [adj. Adolescency male]
Springe, [Trap of threads]
Sprinkle.
[Scatter drop]
{Baste}
{Powder}
Sprit.
Boul—(RN. II. 4.)
—*Sail.*
Sprout. PP. II. 5.
Spruce, [Ornate (augm.)]
Sprung, {a. pret.} Spring
{adj. p.}
Spu, [Vomit]
Spud, [Short Knife]
Spume, [Froth]
Spun, {a. pret.} Spin
{adj. p.}
Spunge. HL. I. 11.
Spungy, [Porous]
Spunk, [Match]
Spur.
—of *Bird.* PP. V. 5.
—of *a boot,* [adj. heel (arm.) of horseman]
to—[Impulsive]
Spurge. HS. V. 11.
—*Laurel.* Sh. III. 5.
—*Olive.* Sh. III. 6.
—*Tree.* Sh. IV. 6.
Spurket, RN. II. 8. A.
Spurious. adj. T. III. 4. op.
Spurn, [Strike with foot]
Spurry. HL. IX. 10. A.
Spurt, vid. Spirt.
Squab, [adj. Fat (augm.)]
to—[Break]
sp. by down casting]
Squabble, [a. Contention (corr.)]
Squadron. RM. III. 4. A.
Squall, [Exclamation]
Squalid, {Slovenly}
{Defiled}
Squander,
in spending. Man. III. 3. D.
not lay up. TA. V. 4. O.
Square.
Proper.
Plain. Mag. V. 1. A.
Solid, [Cube]
Carpenters—[c. adj. Squaring instr.]
Improper.
[Spread] AC. IV. 2. A.
—*out of*—[Exorbitant]
—*dealing,* [a. Justice]
to—[a. square (make)]

—*with,* [a. Congruous]
Squash, [Break]
{sp. by down casting}
Squar.
[Sit]
a—[Sate]
[Bruise]
{sp. by down casting.}
adj.
[Thick short]
Squatino-Raia. Fi. II. 3. A.
Squeak {v. Exclamation
Squeal { acute]
Squeamish.
[adj. Loathing (apt.)]
{sp. of meats}
[adj. Niceness]
Squeezing {Compressing}
{Straining}
Squib.
(found)
[adj. Gunpowder (instr.) for
[Jest]
Squill. HL. IV. 13.
Squilla Mantis. Ex. VI. 4. A.
Squinancy. S. IV. 9.
Squinant, [Camels-hay]
Squint, [a. Eye (manner) oblique (corr.) (man)
Squire, [Middle (kind) of Gentle-
Squirrel. Be. III. 3.
Squirt, [a. Syringing]
Squirting, [Sorry]
St. Int. III. 1. O.
Stab, RJ. V. 4.
Stability.
{Steadiness}
{Fastness}
{Constancy}
Stable.
[adj. Stability]
[adj. Horse (room)]
Stablish.
[adj. Stability (make)]
[a. Confirmation]
Stack, [Heap]
Stacbas.
Golden—HF. II. 5.
Staff, [Stick] PP. I. 4.
—of a *Song,* [Section of S.]
Stag. Be. II. 3. A.
—*Beetle.* Ex. V. 1. A.
Stage.
[Scaffold]
[adj. a. Player Room]
—*Play,* [adj. Player sight]
[Journey]
[adj. Staying (place)]
Staggering. Mo. II. 4. O.
{Doubting}
{Wavering}
Staggers.
Staggerwort, [Ragwort]
Stagnate, [v. Stagnum]
Stagnum. W. IV. 7. A.
Stay, {u.} {Continue rest}
{a.} {Discontinue motion}
Continue, [Duration]
—*Little while,* [Transitoriness]
—*Long time,* [Permanence]
—*for ever,* [Perpetuity]

Qqq   the

ST   ST   ST

the same being. T. I. 7.
the same degree. T. I. 8.
the same goodness. T. I. 9.
the same place. TA. VI. O.
[Stand his ground] RM. II. 2.
[Keep the field] RM. II. 9.
[Home] sp. II. 4.
[Dwelling] Po. I. A.
[Rest] Mo. O.
Discontinue.
{ Cohibitive }
{ Impedient }
[Obstruction]
{ Hold }
{ Keep }
——Injuriously. RJ. IV. 3 A.
[Protract]
[Desist]
——{ Adhere }
——by, { Constancy }
——for, [Wait expecting]
——{ Bear }
——up, { Prop }
——upon, [Lean]
a—[adj. a. Stay (thing)
great—{ Adjuvant
to one { Refreshing
Bring to that—[a. State]
Keep at a—TM. I. 9.
{ Serious }
Staid, { Sober }
{ Grave }
Staies.
——of a ship. RN. IV. 1. A.
Stain.
[Dying] O. V. 3. A.
[a. Spottedness]
[a. Colour (corr.)]
[Defile]
[Infamy]
Stairs. Po. IV. 1.
Stake.
[Stick] PP. I. 4.
[Wager]
——down, [a. wager in present money, &c.]
Stale.
[Old]
sp. corr.]
——Beer, [B. ripe (augm.)]
[Urine]
sp. Old u.]
[adj. Alluring (thing)]
Stalk.
a—
——of plant, [Stock] PP. I. 2.
——of leaf or flower. PF. II. 7.
to——
Walk lofty. No. II. 3.
{ Covered }
[Go { Concealed }
Stall.
{ Room }
{ Table }
sp. for selling things]
Head—[adj. head (part) of bridle]
Stallion, [Horse kept for generation]
Stamen. PP. II. 6. A.
Stammel, [Red (dim.)]
Stammer, [Stutter]

Stamp.
[Pound] Mo. VI. 5.
——with foot, [Pound with sole of foot]
[Contusion]
[Print] AC. III. 7. A.
Coin, [a. money with striking]
Stanch.
{ Cohibit }
{ Desist (make) }
sp. { Dropping }
{ Streaming }
[adj. { Taciturnity }
{ Reservedness }
Stand, Be for some time, unmoved, in posture direct. AC. VI. 1. A.
[Being]
[Duration]
——little while, [Transitoriness]
——long time, [Permanence]
——of long—ing, [ad]
[Rest]
——still.
[Stay]
——ones ground. RM: II. 2.
[Stagnate]
——ing water, [Stagnum]
[Consist] Q. V. 5.
[Place]
[Situation]
[Posture]
[Direct] Mag. II, 8. E.
[Grow]
——er, [Tree left for growth]
——ing corn, [Not reaped]
——about, [Protract]
——against, [Resist]
{ Help }
——by, { Defend } (person)
——er by, { Not-concerned }
——for, [adj. Faction]
——child, [Be Godfather]
——degree, [Be Candidate]
——preferment, [Obtain
——in (end) p.]
[p. Price]
{ Permanence }
[adj. { Constancy }
{ Obstinacy }
sp. in affirming]
——Doubt, [adj. Doubt]
——Fear, [adj. Fear]
——good-{ Adjuvant
stead { Useful }
——the way, [Impedient]
——off, { adj. aversion }
{ Demurring }
——out.
[Be constant] { Opposing }
sp. { Resisting }
{ Not-yield }
{ Hold-out }
[Be protuberant]
——to
[Be constant]
{ Assist }
{ Defend }
{ Compensate }
{ Refund }
——under, [Bear]

——up, { Stand }
{ Rise }
——upon.
{ Esteem }
{ Value }
[adj. Permanence disputing]
——with, [adj. Permanence treating]
a—[adj Standing (place)
——for drink, [adj. bearing (jug.)
——of Pikes, [RM. IV. of p.]
Bear a—TM. I. 7.
{ Stand }
{ Stay } Doubling]
Keep at a—TM. I. 9.
Make a—[Stay (imp.)]
Standard.
[adj. Standing]
[Ensign]
sp. adj. King]
——bearer, [Ensign] RM. III. 2.
sp. adj. King]
[adj. Permanence]
Measure. Mea. II. 4.
Standergrass, [Satyrion]
Standish, [adj. Ink (vess)
sp. Not-adj. p. carry (apt.)
Stannery, [adj. Tin (place)
Stanza, [Section of Poem]
Staphylinus. Ex. V. 7.
Staple.
for bolt, &c. Po. IV. 6. A.
figure. Mag. IV. 5.
[Publick sale]
Star.
Proper. W. II. 1.
fixed—W. II. 2.
wandring—[Planet]
day—[Venus]
Morning—{ Venus }
Evening—{ Venus }
Blazing—
Star. W. II. 3. A.
Meteor. El. I. 2.
falling—El. I. 2. A.
Herb.
——of Bethlehem, [Ornithogalon]
——wort. HF. III. 9.
Sea—HF. III. 10.
Fish. Fi. VIII. 6.
——in forehead, [Star (like) sign in foreh.]
Starboard, [Right side]
Starch. Pr. VI. 5. A.
Stare. Bi. III. 4.
to—AC. IV. 1.
as hair [Direct]
sp. adv. Confusion]
Stareling, [Stare] Bi. III. 4.
Stark.
[Stiff]
(aug.)
——Dead, [Whole dead]
Start, [Move (imp.) { Fear } (on)
sp. through { Admiration sign. AC. IV. 5.
[Move (imp.]
{ Run (inc.) }
——a Hare, [Raise a H.]
——aside
——back { a. Levity }

Abandon

ST   ST   ST

{ Abandon }
{ Forsake }
—*up*, [Rise (imp.)]
get the—[Ob- { Precedence }
           tain { Superiority }
Starter, [adj. a. Levity (person)]
Starting hole, [Way of escape]
Startle, [Fright (imp.)]
Startup, [Outmost Leg (vest) for warmth]
Starve. RJ. V. 5.
Starveling, [Lean (augm.)]
Starwort. HF. III. 9.
Sea—HF. III. 10.
State.
  General.
    [Quality]
    [Condition]
    [Circumstances]
    Extraordinary, [Solemnity]
    All together. T. VI. 4.
  Personal.
    [Age]
    { Disposition }
    { Temperament }
    [Dignity]
    { Degree }
    { sp. of } { Nobility }
            { Gentility }
    Take—*upon him*, [Arrogate, &c.]
    [Revenues (aggr.)]
    { Right }
    { Possession }
  Civil. RC
    the—*s*, [Chief Magistrates (aggr.)]
  Ecclesiasticals. RE.
    —*of Religion*. RE. III.
Stately.
  [Noble]
    [adj. Solemnity]
    [adj. Generosity]
  [Proud]
  { Superfluous }
Static, [adj. Measuring (art.)]
Station, { Resting } { (place) }
         { Standing }
Stationary, [adj. Standing]
Stationer, { Paper } (Merc.)
       [adj. { Book }
Statue, [Image]
Statuary, [adj. Image (mech.)]
Stature, [Height (manner)]
Statute.
  [Law]
  [Morgage]
Stave.
  —*a barrel*, [Unbottom a b.]
  —*off*, { Off-keep }
       { a. Distance }
  sp. with staff.
Stavesacre. HS. I. 4. A.
Stead.
  as Successor. T. VI. 6.
  as Substitute. T. VI. 6. A.
  in—*of*. Prep. II. 1. A.
  in no—{ Helpful }
         [Not { Useful }
Steadfast.
  { Steady }
  { Fast }

To look—*ly*, [a. Eye adv. heedfulness]
Constant]
Steady.
  Not-loose. Q. VI. 6.
  go—Mo. II. 4
  Not-light, [Constant]
Steake, [Fried flesh]
Steal.
  [a. Theft]
  { Come }
  { Goe } (adv. Concealing)
Stealth, [Theft]
  To come by—[Come adv. Concealing]
Steam, [Exhalation] El. II. 2.
Steed, [Horse (perf.)]
Steel. Met. II. 3.
  [adj. Steel (Instr.)]
Steep { Oblique (dim.) }
     { Almost-perpendicular }
  to—[Soke]
Steeple. Po. II. 3. A.
  —*figure*, { Cone }
        { Pyramid }
Steer, [Bull (young)]
  to—*a ship*, [Direct with the Rudder]
Steerage, [adj. Rudder (room)]
Stellion, [Spotted Lizard]
Stem.
  [Descen- { (aggr.) }
    dants, { (kind) }
  —*of a plant*, [Stock] PP. I. 2.
  —*of a ship*. RN. II. 2.
  [Austere]
Stench, [Unsavouriness]
Step.
  { a. Motion }
  { a. Going } Mo. I. 1.
  —*in*, { Come }
       { Enter } (sp. suddenly)
  foot—[adj. foot (sign)]
a—
  figure. Mag. V. 8. A.
  { Father adv. affinity }
  —*father* { Mother's husband }
        { Mother adv. affinity }
  —*mother* { Father's wife }
Sterility, [Barrenness]
Sterling, [adj. p. Authority by Law]
Stern.
  [Austere]
  sp. Face (manner)
  —*of a ship*. RN. II. 2. A.
Stew. Pr. III. 2. A.
a—
  [adj. Bathing (room)]
  [adj Keeping (place) for fish]
Steward, [adj. Revenue (Off.)]
Stewes, [adj. Fornication (house)]
Sty.
  [adj. Hog (house)]
  [Pustle within the eye-lid]
Stibium, [Glass (like)] O. VI. of Antimony]
Stick.
  to—
  [a. { Clamminess }
    { Gluing }

Stay.
  { Doubt }
  —*at* { Demur }
  —*in*, [Into-fasten]
  —*out*, [Protuberance]
  —*through*, { Prick }
        { Stab }
  —*to* { adhere }
     { v. Constant }
  —*with Cloves*, &c. [Lard with cl. &c.
a—PP. I. 4.
Stickadove, [Cassidony] HF. VI. 5. A.
  { Endeavour (augm.) }
Stickle, { a. Business }
     { a. Intercession }
  —*back*. Fi. IX. 13. A.
Stiff.
  op. to Limber. Q. V: 6. D.
  —*gale of wind*. El. VI. T.
  [adj. Rigor] AC. IV. 5. D.
  [Stout]
  [Zealous]
  [Rigid]
  [Pertinacious]
  —*necked*.
  { Disobedient }
  { Contumacious }
Stifle. RJ. V. 6.
Stigmatize. RJ. V. 6. A.
Stile, [Transverse septiment for over-p. ition]
Still.
  [Calm]
  { Gentle }
  [adj. { Silence }
     { Taciturnity }
  { Peaceable }
  { adj. Quieting }
  [adv. { Permanence }
     { Perpetuity }
  [Yet]
  [Distill]
Stilborn, [Abortive]
Stilletto, [Short sword (dim.)]
Stilts, [Leg-lengthning sticks]
Stimulate, [a. Impulsive]
Sting. PP. V. 5. A.
Stink, [a. Unsavouriness]
Stint.
  { Cohibit }
  { Limit }
  [Remit]
  [Cease]
  Bird. Bi. VII. 6. A.
Stipend, [Wages]
  to—RO. VI. 4. A.
Stipulation, [Sponsion]
Stir.
  [Move]
  [Endeavour]
  [Provoke]
  —*up*, [a. Impulsive]
  { Troubles }
  —*s* { Sedition }
Stirrop. Po. V. 8. A.
stitch.
  Disease, [Cramp]
  Pain, [Pricking]
  [Sowing]

through—

ST

through—{Totally / Perfectly}
—*wort*. HS. V. 9.
Stithy, [Supporting (instr.) of hammer'd (thing)]
Stoat. Be. IV. 7.
Stoccado.
Stock.
—*of plant*. PP. I. 2.
[Descendents {aggr. RO. I. / (kind. 1. O.}]
[Chief {Revenue / Possessions}]
[adj. a. Gain (thing)]
Laughing—[adj. p. Laugh (thing)]
Stockdove. Bi. III. 2.
Stockfish.
Stockgilliflower. HS. IV. 1.
Stockings, [adj. Leg (vest)]
Stocks, [Prison for the feet]
stoic.
stole.
{adj a. pret. / adj. p.} Steal]
[Long loose (vest)]
Stolidity, [Folly]
Stoln, [adj. p. Theft]
Stomach.
Ventricle. PG. VI. 4.
[Appetite]
[Anger]
[Courage]
Stomacher, [adj. Brest (vest)]
Stone. St.
Common—St. I.
middle sort of—St. II.
Precious—
—*less transparent*. St. III.
—*more transparent*. St. IV.
Weight. Mea. III. 6.
—*pitch*, [Hard p.]
Disease. S. VI. 7.
—*of a plum*. PP. II. 2. A.
Testicle. PG. VI. 8. A.
to—one, [Throw stones at one]
—*to death*. RJ. V. 2.
Stonebow, [Cross-bow (dim.)]
Stonebuck, [Goat (kind) having angular knotted horns]
Stonecrop. HL. VIII. 5.
Stonefern.
Stonesmiche. Bi. V. 8.
Stonewort.
Stool.
Seat. Po. VI. 5.
Close——[Stool (like) adj. dunging (vess.)]
going to—[a. Dunging]
Stoop. AC. VI. 4.
—*as Barrel*, [a. Oblique]
Stop.
[Stay]
[a. Impediment]
[a. {Binding / Obstruction}]
[Fill]
—*up*, [Shut]
[a. Period]
to make {Stay (make) / Hinder}
d—

ST

Stopple, {adj. Stopping (pin) / Tap}
Storax, Tr. IV. 2. A.
Store.
[Provisions]
[Multitude]
[Abundance]
to—[Lay up]
Story, [adj. p. Narration (thing)]
of building. [Degree of rooms]
Stork. Bi. VIII. 1. A.
Storm. El. VI. 4.
to——
Chafe, {Be angry (augm.) / v. Anger (voice)}
[Assault] RM. I. 6.
Stote. Be. IV. 7.
Stove.
Room. Po. II. 5.
[Box {Heating / Drying}]
Stout.
Active. NP. IV. 6.
{Strong / adj. Fortitude}
{Hardy / Obstinate}
[Perverse] NP. IV. 1. O.
[Proud]
[Contumacious]
Stow, {Lay up / Heap}
Stradle. Mo. II. 3. A.
Straggle, [Wander]
Stray, {Wander / Err.}
Straight, vid. *Streight*.
Strain, vid. *Strein*.
Strake, [Variegating line]
—*of Cart-wheel*, [Ring—]
Strand, [Shore] W. III. 6.
Strange.
{Not-adj. Custom / Extraordinary}
[Seldom]
[Not-expected]
[New]
[adj. Stranger]
Stranger. RO. IV. 4. O.
Strangle. RJ. V. 8. A.
Strangury. S. VI. 7. A.
Strap, [adj. Leather thong]
—*of Boot*, [Loop for on-drawing]
Strappado. RJ. VI. 3. A.
Stratagem. RM. I. 9.
Stratifying. Pr. III. 8.
Straw. Pt. V. 1. A.
—*worm*, [Cadew] Ex. III. 4. A.
to—{Scatter / Spread}
Strawberry. HS. IX. 1.
—*tree*. Sh. III. 4.
Streak, Line.
—*of Cart-wheel*, [Ring—]
—*in the sky*. El. V. 4.
Stream. W. IV. 7.
—*er*. RN. III. 8.
Street. Po. II. 7.
Streight.
op. to crooked,[adj.Ma.III.1.]

ST

[Narrow]
Strict, [adj. Rigor]
—*against*. Prep. VI. 3. A.
—*forward*. [adj. Proceeding adv.]
—*way*, [adv. fut. (dim.)]
a——
[Perplex difficulty]
{Necessity / Distress}
[Fretum] W. IV. 5.
Strein.
{a. Intend / Endeavour (augm.)}
[Hurt by endeavouring (augm.)]
{Depress (augm.) / Compress}
[Arrest goods]
Percolate. O. VI. 4.
a—[Degree]
—*of musick*, [Part of tune]
Strength.
[Power]
—*of body*.
{Vigor / Strength} NP. V. 7.
—*of mind*.
{Sprightliness / Fortitude}
Military.
{Forces} RM. IV.
{Places} RM. VI.
{Importance / Intenseness}
{Taste / Smell} (augm.)
[a. Drunkenness (spc.)]
Strenuous,
[adj. {Sedateness / Diligence}]
[adj. {Strength / Fortitude}]
Stress, {Endeavour (augm.) / Depression / Gravity}
Stretch.
{Extend / Pandiculation} Mo. III. 6. O.
{Long / Broad / Ample} (make)
{Coaction / Wrest}
Strew—{Scattering / Powdering}
Striated. Q. II. 6. A.
Stricken, [adj. p. strike]
—*in* {Age, [Old] adj. Mea. VI. 4. / Love, [adj. Love (augm.)] / Years, [Old (augm.)]}
—*with amazement*, [Extasied]
Strict.
{Perfect / Regular (augm.) / Rigorous / Severe}
Stricture.
{Touch (dim.) / Comment (dim.)}
Stride, [Stradle]
Strife, {Contention / a. Emulation}

loose—

ST

loose—
yellow—HS. V. 12. A.
Strike.
Proper. Mo. VI. 4.
{ Knock
{ Pound
{ Peck
{ Stab
{ Cudgel
{ Cause
{ Move } [imp.]
as Sail, { a. Downward }
{ Fall (make) }
—*a bargain*, [a. Paction]
—*blind*, [Blind (make)]
—*a colour*, [cause a c.]
—*corn*, [a. Even the surface
sp. by upon motion of
straight (thing.]
—*fire*, [Cause to sparkle]
—*heat*, [Cause h.]
—*in*, vid. *Stricken*.
{ Come
{ v. Friend } Suddenly
{ Bargain
[Stab]
—*off*.
—*account*, { Ballance }
{ Acquit }
—*ones head*, [Behead]
—*out*.
[Spoil]
[Unwrite]
—*to the heart*.
[a. Passion (augm.)]
[Stab]
—*up*.
[Begin] sp. Music.]
[a. Paction]
—*ones heels*, [Fall (make)
sp. by wrestling.]
—*with*, vid. *Stricken*.

[Bushel]
[Stick for a. Even (make)]
String.
[Cord]
[Fibre]
Strip.
[Un- { Skin
a. { Clothe]
[a. Privative]
Stripe, [Stroke]
—*ed*, [Variegated with lines]
Stripling, [adj. Adolescence
(male)
Strive.
{ Contention }
[a. { Emulation }
{ Endeavour (augm.) }
{ a. Diligence }
—*against*, [Resist]
—*for*, [Obtain (end)]
Stroy, [Destroy]
Stroke.
a—[Striking]
bear a. great [adj. power]
to—[Wipe with hand]
Stromateus, Fi. III. 15.
Strong.
. [adj. Strength]
—*hold*. RM. VI.

ST

Strow, [Scatter]
Struck, vid. *Stricken*.
Structure, [Building]
Struggle.
[Wrestle]
[Strive]
Strumpet, [adj. Fornication
(fem.)
Strung, { adj. a. pret. }
{ adj. p. } String
Strut.
[Swell with fullness]
[Stalk]
[Go proudly]
Stub.
[Bottom (part) of stock]
[Fragment of stick]
Stubble.
Stalk, [adj. p. residue after
reaping]
—*goose*, [adj. Autumn fatted
Goose]
Stubborn.
[Contumacious]
[Obstinate]
[Perverse]
Stuck, { adj. a. pret. } Stick
{ adj. p. }
Stud, [Protuberance (dim.)]
Student, [adj. a. Learning (end)
Study.
{ Endeavour }
{ a. Diligence }
{ Meditation }
{ a. Considerateness }
Closet, [adj. meditation
(room)
Studious, [adj. Study (apt.)]
Stuff.
[Matter]
—*of cloathing*.
woollen—Pr. IV. 1.
Hairy—Pr. IV. 1. A.
[Utensils]
[adj. Filling (thing)]
to—[Fill by into-thrusting]
Stum, [Wine not-adj. pret. Fermenting]
Stumble, Mo. II. 5. A.
Stump.
[adj. Residue { Cutting
(part) after { Felling]
Stupidity.
[Dulness]
[Numness] S. IV. 6. A.
Op. to common sense. NP. II.
1. O.
Stupifie, [adj. a. Stupidity(make)
Stupor, [Numness] S. IV. 6. A.
Stuprate, [adj. a. Fornication]
Sturdy.
{ Bold }
{ Valiant }
[Obstinate]
[Strong]
Sturgeon. Fi. I. 8.
Stutter. AC. III. 2.
Stygian, [adj. Hell]
[Discourse]
Style, { Writing } (manner)
{ Sentence }
to—[Name] sp. of Dignity]

SU

of a flower. PP. II. 6.
Styptic.
[Astringent]
[adj. Acerbity]
Su.
{ Intreat }
{ Petition }
for { Marriage, [a. Sutor]
{ Preferment, [a. Candidate]
{ in law, [a. Action]
Suasory, [adj. Persuade]
Subaltern, [Inferior]
Subcontrary, [Opposite together-
true (pot.)
Subdeacon, [Next RE. II. under
deacon
Subdivide, { Parts }
{ divide the { Species }
Subdue, { a. Victory }
{ Conquer }
Subduction, [a. Ablation]
Subject.
op. to præd. D. II. 5.
op. to adjunct. T. VI. 1.
Liable, [adj. p. Subject (pot.)]
op. to Governour. RC. I. 1. O.
{ [adj. a. Subjection] }
{ [adj. a. Obedience }
{ Submission] }
Subjection. Man. V. 5.
Subjoin, [After-join]
Subjunctive.
Subliming,
Sublimation, } O. VI. 7.
Sublime.
Sublimity, [Height]
Submission.
[Humility]
[Subjection]
op. to conquest. RM. II. 7. D.
to { Action. TA. IV. 1. A.
{ Suffering. Man. V. 8.
Submissive, [adj. Submission]
Submit, [a. Submission]
Subordinate, [Inferior]
sp. in Series.]
Suborn. RJ. IV. 6. A.
Subpœna, [Citation with express
threatning]
Subscribe,
[Under-write]
[Sign]
Subsidy, [Tax]
Subsidiary, { Adjuvant }
[adj. { Relieving]
Subsist.
[Being]
sp. Absolute]
sp. Permanent]
[v. Substance]
[Maintain himself]
Substance.
[Predicament. T. I. 5.
[Matter] T. II. 7.
[Possessions] Po.
Substantial.
[adj. Substance]
[adj. p. matter (perfect)]
[Of suffici- { Wisdom }
ent { Possessions]
Substi.

SU | SU | SU

Substitute, [adj. Stead. TG. VI. 6.
A. (person)]
Substract, { a. Ablatum }
          { Diminish }
Substruction, [Under-building]
Subter- { Escape }
fuge,   { Solution (corr.) }
Subterraneous, [Under-adj. earth]
Subtle.
  [Fineness]
  [a. Craftiness]
Subvert.
  [Destroy]
  [Ruine]
Suburb.
  [City (part) without the walls]
Suck.
  Proper. Mo. III. 3. A.
  —in, [Suck]
  —up.
  —the breath. AC. IV. 6. D.
  give— [Lactation]
Succedane- { Instead-of coming }
ous,   { adj. Succeed }
Succeed.
  Be after, Mag. I. 2. D.
  Be Successor, [a. T. VI. 6.]
  Come by Succession. RC. IV. 2. A.
  [Be Event]
  —ill, [adj. Adversity]
  —well, [adj. Prosperity]
Success.
  [Effect]
  [Event]
  —of war. RM. II.
  [Prospering]
Succession. RC. IV. 2. A.
Successive, [adj. Succeed, adv. Series]
Successor, [adj. a. Succeed (person)]
Succinct, { Brief (perf.) }
            { adj. Epitomy }
Succor, { Adjuvant }
          { adj. Relieve }
Succory. HF. II. 16. A.
  Gum— HF. III. 11. A.
Succuba, [adj. Coition (fem.)]
Succulent, [adj. Juice]
Succus nutritius. PG. I. 2. A.
Such.
  [of that { Quality }
          { Quantity }]
  [of the { same } { quality }
          { like } { quantity }]
  —as it is, [Such soever]
Suck, vid. Suc.
  [a. Suction]
  —up the breath. AC. IV. 6. D.
  give— [Lactation]
Sucker.
  Branch. PP. I. 2. A.
  —of a Pump, [adj. Sucking (part)]
Sucket, [Confection]
Suckle, [Lactation]
Suction. Mo. III. 3. A.
Sud, [Froth]
Sope — d.

Suddain.
  [Soon]
  [Swift]
  [adj. Dispatch]
Sudorific, [adj. a. Sweat (make)]
Suet, [Hard Fat]
Suffer.
  [Passion]
  —affliction, [adj. p. affliction].
  —persecution, [adj. p. Persecution]
  —punishment, [adj. p. punishment]
  —execution, [adj. p. Execution]
  { Licence }
  { Toleration }
  { Not-hinder }
  —to take, [Yield] TA. IV. 1.
  —to do, [Submit] TA. IV. 1. A.
  { Meekness }
  { Condescension }
  { Patience }
  { Submission }
Sufferance, { Licence }
              { Toleration }
Suffice, [adj. Sufficience]
Sufficience. TM. I. 3.
Sufficient, [adj. Sufficience]
  —man, [Of { Wisdom }
            { Riches }]
Suffocate.
  [Stifle]
  [Strangle]
Suffocation of the womb. S. VI. 9. A.
Suffragan, [Instead Bishop]
Suffrage, [Consent (sign)]
Suffumigation, [Fuming]
Suffusion, [Spreading]
Sug, [Sea-flea] Ex. II. 11. A.
Sugar. Pr. II. 3.
Suggest.
  { Think }
  { Remember } (make)
  [Dictate]
Suit.
  { Intreaty }
  { Petition }
  —in law, [Action]
  Aggregate. TM. III. 8.
  to—with, [adj. v. Congruity]
Suitable, { Conveniency }
            { adj. Congruity }
Suiter.
  [adj. { Intreating } (person)
        { Petitioning }]
  —for marriage. RO. II. 2.
  [Candidate] RC. I. 4. A.
Sullen.
  [Disingenuous]
  [Morose]
  [Contumacious]
Sully.
  [a. Colour (corr.)]
  [Defile]
Sulphur. St. V. 7.
  —wort, [Peucedanum]
Sultan, [Ring]
Sultry, [Hot (exc.)]

Sum.
  —of money, [Money (aggr.) total— TM. VI. 6. A.
Sumach. Tr. III. 2. A.
  Red— Sh. V. 5. A.
Summary, [Epitome]
  —ly, [Briefly]
Summer. Mea. V. 2. A.
  [Principal beam]
Summer- { Leap }
fault,   { Vault }
Summon, [a. Citation]
Summum jus. Man. I. 2. O.
Summer, [adj. Citation (Off.)]
Sumpter, [adj. Riding (apt. box)]
Sumptuary, [adj. Spend]
Sumptuous.
  [adj. { Spend }
        { Price } (augm.)]
  [Generous]
Sun.
  True. W. II. 2. A.
  —Shine, [Brightness]
  to— [Open to the Sun]
  appearing— [Parelius]
Sunday, [First day of the week]
Sunder, [Separate]
Sundew. HL. VI. 8. A.
Sundry, [adj. Diversity]
Sunflower. HF. II. 1.
Sung, { a. pret. } { Sing }
          { adj. p. }
Sunk, { a. pret. } { Sink }
          { adj. p. }
Sup.
  [Suction]
  [Drink adv. Suction]
  [adj. Evening meal]
Superabound, [more-abound]
Superciliousness. Man. VI. 3. O.
Supereminence, [Superiority]
Supereroga- { a good more-than duty }
tion,   { Deserve for others }
Superfetation, [Again-conception of impregnated (fem.)]
Superficial.
  [adj. Superficies]
  { slight }
  { Careless }
Superficies.
  Surface
  [Outside]
Superfine, [Fine (augm.)]
Superflui- { Excess }
ty,   { Abundance }
Superinducing, [Again-marrying of married (person)]
Superintend.
  [adj. p Office]
  [p. to observe what others do in their Offices]
Superintendent.
  [adj. Superintending (person)]
  [Bishop]
Superiority. TM. I. 5. E.
  Relation of— RO. III.
Superlative.

[Most-

SU | SU | SW

[Most—{Great / Excellent}]
[Principal]
Supernal, {Upper side / Top} [adj.]
Supernatation, [Upon-swimming]
Supernatural, {Above- adj. nature / adj. Miracle}
Supernumerary, [Beside the due number]
Superscription, [Upon-write]
Super-{Desist / Omit} *sede*,
Superstition. RE. IV. E.
Superstructure, [Upon-building]
Supervene, [Whilst-event]
Supine, [Careless]
Supper, [adj. Evening meal]
——*of the Lord*, [Eucharist]
Supplant.
  [a. Fraud]
  [Dispossess by fraud]
Supple, {Soft / Limber}
Supplement, {adj. Supplying (thing) / Vantage}
Supply.
  [a. Adjuvant]
  [adj. a. Perfect]
  [Un-deficient (make)]
  [Again-fill]
  [Relieve]
  [Compensate]
  [Repair]
  [a. Room] T. VI. 6.
Suppliant, [adj. a. Petition (person)]
Supplicate.
  [Intreat]
  [a. Petition]
Support.
  [Bear]
  [a. Adjuvant]
  [a. Patron]
  [Maintain]
Supposing.
  [Thinking]
  [v. Opinion]
  [v. Supposition]
Supposition. D. VI. 3.
Supposititious, [Forged]
Suppository, [Cylinder (dim.) Medicinal]
Suppress.
  [a. Victory]
  [Conquer]
  [Conceal]
Suppuration, [Ripening of rotten (thing)]
Supremacy, [Right of being most principal]
Supreme, [Most principal]
Surbate, {Un-skin by motion / Bruise} {(freq.)}
Surcease, [Desist]
Surcharge, [Burden (exc.)]
Surcingle, {About- adj. p. binding (arm.) / sp. for horse}
Surcoat, [adj. Upper (vest)]

Surd, [adj. Deafness]
——*number*, [Root not-expressible by numbers]
Sure,
  {Certain / Assured / Betrothed / Constant / Faithful}
  [Fast]
  [Safe]
Surely, [Truly] adv. I. 2. O.
Surety, [adj. {Sponsion (person)}]
Surface, {Superficies / Outside}
Surfeit.
  [Sickness] {Eating / Drinking / through Labor} (exc.)
  [Excess]
  [Gluttony]
Surge, [Wave (augm.)]
Surgeon. RC. II. 3. A.
Surly, {Fierce / Morose / Supercilious}
Surmise.
  [Opinion]
  [Conjecture]
  [Distrust]
  [Jealousie]
Surmount, [v. Superior]
Surname, [adj. Family name]
Surpass.
  [a. Excess]
  [Excell]
  [Superiority]
  [Better]
Surplice, [Upper linnen (vest) of Ecclesiastic (person)]
Surplus.
  [Residue]
  [Vantage]
Surprise.
  {Take / Arrest} [Unexpectedly]
  sp. by {Stratagem / Ambush}
Surque-dry, {Pride / Insolence}
Surrender.
  [Let go]
  [Yield]
  [Submit]
  [Deliver]
Surreptitious, {Theft / [adj. Forg-y]}
Surrogate, [Substitute]
Surround, {About-go / a. Circle}
Survey.
  [a. Eye]
  [Consider]
  [Measure]
Surveyer.
  [Officer for observing others]
  sp. in building
  [adj. Measuring (artist)]
Survive, [Continue after-living]
Suspect.
  [Distrust]

[Diffidence]
[Jealousie]
[a. Censoriousness]
Suspence,
  [Doubtful Expectation]
  [Demurring]
  [Wavering]
Suspend. RE. V. 4.
Suspition, vid. *Suspect*.
Sustein.
  [Bear]
  [Maintain]
  [Suffer]
  [a. Patience]
Sustenance, {adj. nourishing (thing)}
Sustentation,
Ordinary. Pr. I.
Extraordinary. Pr. II.
Sutable, [Congruous]
Suture—{Series / Sewed Line}
Swabber. RN. V. 7.
Swaddle, [About-bind adj. bottom (like)]
  [Cudgel]
Swag, {adj. p. Oblique / sp. with shaking (imp.)}
Swage, [a. Remission]
Swagger.
  [a. Insolence]
  [a. Glorying (corr.)]
Sway.
  [Power]
  [Authority]
  [Direction]
  [a. Magistrate]
  [a. Oblique (make)]
Swain.
  [adj. Country (person)]
Swallow.
  Bird. Bi. V. 1.
  ——*tail*, [adj. Mag. IV. 4. end of beam]
  ——*wort*. HS. IV. 14. A.
  Sea—BI. IX. 9. A.
  ——*fish*. Fi. III. 6. A.
  ——*ing*. Mo. III. 7. A.
  [Gulf]
Swan. Bi. IX. 1.
Swap, [Exchange]
Swarm, {Aggregate / [adj. Multitude]} (thing)
Swart, [Dark (dim.)]
Swarth, [Ridge of mowen grass, &c.]
Swashbuckler, [adj. Boasting (person) of fighting]
Swathe, [About-bind adv. bottom (like)]
Swear. RC. VI. 4.
Sweat. Mo. IV. 5.
Sweeping, [Brushing]
Sweet.
  Proper. Q. IV. 1.
  ——*bread*, [Glandule] PG. II. 7. A.
  ——*meats*, [Banquet (thing)]
  [adj. Love]
  [p. Delectation]
  ——*heart*, [Suiter]
  [adj. a. Pleasure]
  ——*music*.
  [adj.

SY · TA · TA

[adj. a. Courtefie]
Swell.
  [Tumor]
  [v. Protuberance]
Swelter, [a. heat (exc.)]
Swerve, [Err]
Swift, [adj. Swiftnefs]
  Bird. Bi. V. 14.
Swiftnefs. NP. V. 9.
Swill, [Drink (augm.)]
  —for fwine, [Drink for fwine]
Swimming. Mo. I. 4.
  Difeafe, [Vertigo]
Swine, [Hog (kind)]
  —s bread, [Sow-bread]
  —s grafs, [Knot-grafs]
  —Pipe, [Redwing] Bi. III. 5. A.
Swing. Mo. VI. 3.
Swinging, { Striking / Whipping / Cudgelling } (aug.)
  adj. [Great (augm.)]
Swingle, [adj. Striking (part) of adj. threfhing (inftr.)]
Swipe, [adj. Lifting (inftr.) on direct Pole]
Switch, [Wand] PP. I. 4. A.
  to—[Cudgel with wand]
Swivel, [Wheel]
Swoln, [adj. p. Swell]
Swoon. S, V. 5. A.
Sword.
  Proper. RM. V. 2. A.
  Put to the—[a. Dy (make) with fword]
  —of Bacon. [Skin of Bacon]
  —fifh. Fi. I. 2. A.
  green—[Graffie land]
Sworn, {p. pret.} [Swear]
Swum, [pret. Swim]
Swung, [pret. Swing]
Sycamore. Tr. VI. 6. A.
Sycophant. [adj. Fawning Accufer]
Syllable. D. I. 3.
Syllogifm. D. IV. 7.
Sylvan, [adj. Woods (perfon)]
Symbol, [Sign]
  {p. adj.} { Private / Obfcure / p. Concealing }
Symbolizing, [adj. Congruity]
Symmetry, [Proportion (perf.)]
Sympathy, { Congruity / Friendfhip / Together-fuffering } (pron.)
  { Pity / Congratulation / fp. Concealed }
Sympho-ny, { Concord / Harmony }
Symptoms [Simultaneous fign]
  fp. corr.
Synagogue, [adj. Jews] { Church / Convention Ecclefiaftic / Temple }
Synchronifm, [Narration of fimultaneous (things)]

Syndic, [Magiftrates Affeffor]
Synedrium, [adj. Jews principal Council]
Synod, [Council Ecclefiaftic]
Synonym, [Of fame meaning]
Synopfis, [Epitome]
Syntax, [Together-joyning of Integrals]
Syren.
Syringe, [Tube for fyringing]
Syringing. O. I. 6. A.
Syrt, [Quickfands] W. III. 7.
Syrup. Pr. II. 3. A.
Syftem, [Epitome]

T.

T Abaces. HS. VII. 11.
Tabernacle, [Tent]
Tabid, [adj. Confumption]
  Lamin
Table, {fp. adj. Treffel (fig.) / fp. for a meal.}
  Lamin.
  for upon-writing.
  —Book, [Book of Lamins upon-adj. p. writing (apt.)]
  [Catalogue]
  for upon-playing.
  Pair of —s, [adj. Mo. V. 2. A. (jug.)]
  —man, [adj. Mo. V. 2. A. (inftr.)]
  Play at—s. Mo. V. 2. A.
  Adj. Treffel (fig.) Po. VI. 4.
  Meat.
  Plentiful—
  to— { Hoft / [a. Gueft] }
Tabler, Gueft
Tablet, [Flat Gem]
Tabor, Tabret } [Drum (dim.)]
Taca mabaca. Tr. VIII. 7. A.
Tachygraphy, [Swift writing (art.)]
Tach, { Hook / Loop }
Tacit.
  [adj. Silence]
  [Underftood] adj. D. III. 8. O.
Taciturnity. Man. IV. 5.
Tack.
  [Pin (dim.)]
  hold-[Hold out] RM. II. 4.
  to—[Faften]
    fp. with pin (dim.)
  [Turn]
Tacks of fhip. RN. IV. 7.
Tackling, [Armament]
  —of fhip, [Rigging]
Tactic, [War (art)]
  fp. of Ordering. RM. IV.
Tactil, [adj. Feeling]
  —Quality. Q. V.
Tadpole, [Toad (young)]
Tædium. AS. V. I. O.
Tania major. Fi. VI. 3.

  —minor. Fi. VI. 3. A.
Taffety, [Silk adj. Sound (apt.) in p. motion]
Tag, [Pin of ftring]
  —&—rag, [Rabble]
Tail. PP. VI. 6. A.
  to—[Tie by the tail]
Tailor, [adj. Clothing (mech.)]
Taint.
  [a. Contagion]
  [adj. Rottennefs (make)]
  [Defile]
Take, Caufe {out of anothers to be & —in ones own poffeffion}
Proper.
  without confent. TA. I. 4.
  Judicially.
  Perfon or Goods, [a. Arreft]
  Part for Whole, [a. Seifin]
  Injurioufly, [Ufurp]
  Militarily.
  Perfon, [Captivate]
  Place. RM. II. 4. E.
  Goods, [a. Booty]
  with confent.
  { Receive / Accept }
  Improper.
  { Undertake / Think / Efteem }
  [Elect]
  [Find]
  { To— / Into- } ition
  [Obtein]
  fp. its end
  [Pleafe]
  [Have]
  [Ufe]
—account, [Reckon (make)]
—the air, [Go into the open Air]
—Breath, [a. Breath]
—Exceptions, { Except / adj. v. Difplicence }
—fire, [adj. v. fire (inc.)]
    adj. p. Power
—Head, adj. Difobedience (inc.)
—Heart, [adj. p. Encouragement]
—Heavily, [adj. a. Grief for]
—Heed, { a. Heedfulnefs / Obferve }
—his heels, [Fly]
—the height, [Meafure the h.]
—hold, [a. Hand (inc.)]
—horfe.
  as a man, [Up-ition upon his h.]
  as mate, [v. Coition]
    v. Difplicence
  —ill, { Efteem not-adj. friend }
—Leave, [a. Valediction]
—Notice, [Obferve]
—Oath, [Swear]
—pains, { a. Diligence / Operation (augm.) }
    —place,

TA | TA | TE

—*place*, [Precede]
—*a pride*, [Glorying]
—*Prisoner*, [Captivate]
—*a Purse*.
 [Steal a purse]
 [Rob money]
—*Root*, [a. Root]
—*shipping*, [into a ship]
 { Discover defect }
—*tardy*, { Find adj. pref. acti- }
—*warning*, { Warning } (on)
 [adj. p. { Heedfulness }
—*Water*.
 [Into-take water]
 [Go into water]
 [Navigate (inc.)]
—*well*, { Delectation }
 [adj. p. { Consent }
—*away*.
 [a. Privative]
 { Diminish }
 { a. Ablatum }
 { Imitate }
—*forth*, { Proceed to learn }
—*in*.
—*a town*. RM. II. 4. E.
 { Undertake }
—*band*, { Attempt }
—*Pieces*, [Separate the parts]
—*Writing*, [Write]
—*off* { From-take }
 { Diminish }
—*on*. { Grief }
 [a. { Anger } (sign)
 { To-ition }
—*to*, { Confidence }
—*Mercy*, [Be merciful to]
—*Wife*, [Marry]
—*up*.
 [Lifting take]
 [Reprehend] sp. angerly]
—*Cloth*, [Buy &c. without paying]
—*money*, [Borrow money]
—*a quarrel*, [Un-adj. a. contention (make)]
—*his rest*, [Rest]
—*time*, [Spend t.]
—*upon him*, [Claim]
Taken, [adj. p. Take]
 —*for*, [In- { Thought }
 stead— { Judged }
—*with*.
 as with diseases, [Sick]
 as with pleasure, [Pleased with (augm.)]
Talc. St. II. 5. A.
Tale.
 [Narration] sp. adj. fiction]
 [Number]
—*bearer*, [Backbiter]
Talent.
 [Natural power]
 [Acquired Habit]
Talio, [Compensation]
Talisman, [adj. Wizarding Image]
Talk, { Speech }
 { Conferring }
 { Discourse }
Talkative, [adj. Loquacity]

Tall, [High]
—*wood* [Blocks]
Tally, [Notched stick for reckoning]
Tallow, [Hard Fat]
 sp. for Candle (make)
Talon, [Claw] PP. V. 3.
Tamarind. Tr. VI. 2. A.
Tamarisk. Sh. V. 2.
Tame, [adj. Tameness]
to— { Tame (make) }
 { Conquer }
Tameness.
 Disposition, [Gentleness]
 Vice.
 op. to Fortitude, [Cowardize]
 op. to Peaceableness. Man. IV. 3. E.
Tan.
 [a. Yellowness (corr.)]
 { Make } Leather Oak
 { by juice } Brasil
 { Prepare } of &c.
Tang, [Taste (dim.)]
 sp. Unsavoriness (dim.)
Tangent. Mag. II. 4.
Tangible, [adj. p. touch (pot.)]
Tangle. O. II. 2. A.
Tankard, [Pot having cover]
Tanner, [adj. a. Leather (mech.)]
Tansy. HF. II. 12.
 Maudlin—HF. II. 4 A.
 Wild—HF. IX. 1.
Tap.
 [Striking (dim.)]
 to—[Strike (dim.)]
 Spiggot. Pr. V. 7.
—*House*, [adj. { House }
 Selling { Room } of Ale]
 to—[Stream (make)]
 sp. by into-thrusting faucet]
Tape, [Narrow Ribbon]
Taper.
 [adj. Wax candle]
 [Conical]
Tapestry, [adj. Room (vest) woven with pictures]
Tapster, [adj. Selling (Off.) of Beer, &c.]
Tar, [Black li- { Fir } trees out-
 quid Rosin { Pine } drawn by
 of { &c. } fire]
Tarantula, [Spider (aug.) adj. poison (apt.) by biteing]
Tardy.
 { Slow }
 { Late }
 [Guilty]
 take—[Find adj. pref. action]
Tare, [Worst part]
Tares. HL. III. 5.
Target, [Buckler]
Tarragon. HF. II. 10. A.
Tarras.
 [adj. Walking (place) on Building]

[Courser plaister adj. p. hard (apt.) in water]
Tarry.
 [Stay]
 —*for*, [Wait]
 { Delay }
 { Protract }
Tart.
 [adj. Austereness] Q. IV. 3.
 a—[Py of fruits]
 sp. of sowr f.]
 { Severe }
 { Austere } Man. VI. 8. O.
Tartar. St. V. 4.
Task, { Appointed } operation
 { Undertaken } business
 —*work*, [adv. Aggregate (segr.)]
Tassel, { Tuft }
 { Tufted Button }
 —*of hawk*, vid. *Teircel*]
Taste.
 the Sense. NP. III. 4.
 Sensible quality. Q. IV.
 to— { a. Taste }
 { a. Essay (sp. by tasting)]
—*er*
 [before adj. tasting (off.)]
 [Cup (dim.) for essaying by taste]
Tatter, [adj. { freq. }
 { Tear } augm.]
 a—[Fragment from adj. p. tear]
Tattle, [a. Loquacity]
 sp. Uncertain]
Tavern, [adj. Wine (merc.) house]
Taught, { adj. a. pret. }
 { adj. p. } Teach
Taunt.
 [Mock]
 [Reproach]
 [Reprove { Mock }
 adv. { Reproach }
Taurus, [Second of the 12 parts of the Zodiac]
Tautology, [Repetition of words]
 sp. Vain]
Taw, { Beat }
 { Rub }
 sp. for Lithberness (make)
Tawny, [Dark yellow]
Tax.
 [Proportion]
 Payment public. RC. V. 9. A.
 [Price]
 to—
 { a. Tax }
 { Accuse }
 { Reproach }
Teach, [a. Teacher]
 —*er*. RO. III. 3.
Teal. Bi. IX. 3. A.
Team, [Series] sp. of drawing beasts]
 —*of ducks*, [Aggregate of ducks (young)]
Tear.

Rrr

TE — TE — TH

a—[adj. p. Weeping drop]
Job's—s.
—*ing.* Mo. VI. 6. A.
Teat, [Dug] PG. IV. 2. A.
  (sp. Nipple of it)
Teazle. HF. VIII. 1.
Technical, [adj. Art]
Tedious.
  Irksom, [adj. a. AS. V. 1. O. (apt.)
  Tiring, [adj. a. Wearying (apt.)]
  { Long } (exc.)
  { Slow }
Teeming, [adj. p. pret. impregnate]
Teeth, [plur. Tooth]
Teint, vid. Taint.
Telescope, [Tube for seeing remote (things)]
Tell.
  [Say to.]
  [a. Narration]
  cannot—[Know not]
  [a. { Openness
       { Loquacity }]
  [a. { Discover
       { Shew }]
  —*tale* { Blab
         { Informer }
  [admonish]
  a. Number
Tellina. Ex. VIII. 6, A.
Temerity, [Rashness]
Temper.
  natural—NP.
  —*of mind.* NP. IV.
  —*of body.*
  resp. Individ. NP. V.
  resp. Propagation. NP. VI.
  Just—TM. I. 8.
  [Disposition]
  out of—[Sick (dim.)]
  to—
    [Mix]
    [a. Mediocrity (make)]
    [Moderate]
Temperament, [Temper]
Temperance. Man. II. 1.
Temperate.
  [adj. Temperance]
  { adj. Mediocrity
  { Moderation }
  —*Heat, &c.* Q. V. 1, &c.
Tempest. El. VI. 7. A.
Temple. Po. II. 4.
Templer. PG. III. 7, A.
Temporal.
  [Secular] adj. RE. O.
  [Transitory]
  [adj. Temples.]
Temporality, [Secular estate]
Temporary, [Transitory]
Temporize, { adj. a. Congruity
            { Alter } with times
Tempt.
  [Try
   Allure } [sp. into a. vice]
   Seduce]
Ten.

Tenacity.
  [Keeping (apt.)]
  [Perniciousness]
Tenant, [Hirer of { Farm
                   { House
                   { Land }]
Tench. Fi. IX. 7. A.
  Sea—Fi. VI. 4.
Tend.
  [v. Tendency]
  [Wait]
  [v. Leisure]
Tendency. Sp. III A.
Tender.
  { Soft }
  { Brittle }
  [adj. p. Hurt (apt.)]
  { Gentle }
  { Nice }
  { Compassionate }
  { Merciful }
  { Courteous (augm.) }
  { Clement }
  { Fond }
  [adj. Aversati- { Hurting
    on from   { Offending }]
  to—
    [a. Tender]
    [Offer]
Tendon. PG. II. 2. A.
Tendrel. PP. II. 7. A.
Tenement, [Farm]
Tenent, [adj. Affirmed (thing)]
Tennice, [Balling with adj. net (fig.) striking (instr.)]
Tennon, [Protuberance (dim.) in the end of beam]
Tenor.
  { Contained (thing) }
  { Sum }
  { Meaning }
  —*in musick,* [next (part) above the Base]
Tent.
  Tabernacle. Po. II. 1. A.
  —*work,* [White Maiden hair] HL. L 5.
  [Pin of Down (like) for stopping wound]
Tenter, [Hooked Pin]
Tenth, [adj Ten]
Tenuity, [Thinness]
Tenure, [Right (kind)]
Tepid. Q. V. 1.
Terce, vid. Tierce.
Tergiversation.
  [Deny]
  [Forsake]
  sp. { Cowardly
      { Unfaithfully }
  [Demur]
Term]
  [Limit]
  [Time]
  sp. limited]
  [adj. R] (time)
  [Word]
  [Name]
  { Conditions }
  —*s* { State }

Coming off upon equal—
  RM. II. 1.
Termi- { Desist
nate   { End }
Termination, [Ending (part)]
Ternary, [Three]
Terrene,
Terrestrial, } [adj. Earth]
Terrible, [adj. a. fear (make)
  Herb. Sh. VI. 3.
Terrier.
  [Catalogue of lands]
  [Dog for hunting beasts out of holes in the earth]
Terrifie, [adj. a. Fear (make)]
Territory, [adj. authority place]
Terse.
  [Wiped]
  [Clean]
  [Smooth]
Tertian, [Returning every second day]
Test.
  [Trial]
  [Vessel (dim.) for trial by melting]
Testaceous, [adj. Shell. PP. III. 2.
Testament.
  [adj. Bequeathing writing]
  [Scripture] RE. VI. 1.
Testator, [adj. Bequeathing (person)]:
Testy, [Morose]
Testicle. PG. VI. 8. A.
Testifie, [a. Witness]
Testimo- { Witnessing
ny   { Witnessed } (thing)
Testimonial.
  [adj. Witnessing (thing)]
  [sp. Writing]
Tester.
  [adj. Covering (jug.) of bedstead]
  [Half shilling]
Tet, vid. Tear.
Tether, [adj. tying (thing for the leg)]
Tethya. Ex. IX. 6.
Tetter. S. III. 2. A.
Tew, [Pull (augm.)]
Text.
  [adj. Subject writing]
  [adj. Scripture sentence]
Texture, [Weaving]
  sp. (manner)
Thanks, [a. Gratitude]
—*fulness,* [Gratitude]
Thanksgiving, [a. Gratitude]
—*to God.* RE. IV. 3.
That.
  [the] Art. II.
  [he] Pron. I. 3.
  that. Pron. II. 1. O.
  —*same,* [Same]
  [Which] Pron. III. 2. A.
  that. Conj. III. 1.
Thatch, [adj. Straw roof]
to—[a. Roof with straw]
Thaumaturgic, [operation (art) of things adj. p. admiration (apt.)]
Thawing

TH | TH | TH

Thawing.
 [Un-a. frost
 Dissolving]
The. Art. II.
Theater, {Sights
 {a. Player} Place]
 [adj.
Thee, [Thou]
Theef, [adj. Theft (person)
Thievery}
Theft} RJ. III. 7. A.
They}
Them} Pron. I. 3. pl.
Theme, [Subject} Speaking
 {adj. p.} Writing]
Then.
 Comparative, Adv. III. 1. O.
 [at that time]
 how— {How therefore]
 {what Next]
 if—[If {Therefore]
 {Next].
Thence.
 {thing
 From that {time ,
 {place]
Theology, [Divinity]
Theologue, [Divine]
Theorem, [Rule adj. Theory]
Theo— Meditation]
 ry, {Inquisition
 {sp. adj. a. Science (apt.]
There, [in a Thing
 that a Place]
 —*about.* Adv. V. 3.
 —*fore.* Conj. III. 3. O.
 —*in* {in }
 —*of* {of } it]
 —*upon.*
 [Upon it]
 [Upon that] Conj. IV. 1. O.
Thesis.
 [Proposition
 [Positive sentence]
Thi, [adj. Thou]
Thick,
 as to magnitude. TM. II. 5.
 as to number, [adj. multi-
 tude]
 as to time, [Frequent]
 [as to place, [Obvious]
 as to parts.
 Their greatness, [adj. Courseness]
 Their nearness to each other,
 [adj. Density]
 the cause of it.
 In Arids, [Fulling]
 In Liquids, [Coagulating]
 our sence of them, [adj. Opa-
 the sence it self. (city)
 —*of hearing,* [Dull of hearing]
Thick- {Shrubs (aggr.]
 et, {Woods (dim.]
Thigh. PG. V. 4.
Thill, [Shafts} Shafts
Thiller, [The horse between the
Thimble, [adj. {armam.} for
 Finger, {armor} sow-
Thin, (ing]
 as to magnitude. TM. II. 5. O.
 [Lean]
 as to number, [adj. Fewness]

as to time, [Seldom]
 as to place, [Rare]
 as to parts
 their nearness, [Rare]
 their bigness, [Fine]
 The cause of it.
 In Arids.
 In Liquids, [Dissolving]
 Our sense of it, [Transparent]
Thine, [adj. Thou]
Thing. T. I. 2.
 (Thing)
Think.
 [Cogitation. AS. II. 1.
 [v. Opinion]
 me—s, [I am adj. opinion]
 [adj. v. Perswasion]
 [Consider]
 [v. Meditation]
 [Esteem]
 —*good* {Approve]
 {Consent]
 —*much,* [adj. v. Nolleity]
 —*well of,* { (aug.]
 {Esteem} good]
Third, [adj. Three]
Thirsting. AC. II. 2.
Thirteen, 13.
Thirty. 30.
This. Pron. II. 1.
Thistle. HF. III. 1.
 Fullers— [Tezzle]
 Globe—HF. VIII. 2.
 Sow—HF. III. 14.
Thither, [To that place]
 —*ward,*] [Toward that place]
Thlaspi. HS. VI. 3.
Thong. Pr. IV. 8.
 Fi. II. 2. A.
Thorn.
 Prickle. PP. I. 3. A.
 Tree.
 Black—Sh. I. 4.
 Box—Sh. I. 6. A.
 Buck—Sh. I. 7.
 Christs—Sh. I. 6.
 Ever green—Sh. III. 4.
 Goats—Sh. IV. 9.
 Purging—Sh. I. 5.
 White—Sh. I. 3. A.
 —*Apple.* HS. VII. 7. A.
Thornback. Fi. II. 2. A.
Thornback Dog. Fi. I. 1.
Thorpe, [Village]
Those, {He]
 [Plur. {That]
Thou. Pron. I. 2.
Though, [Although] Conj. II. 2.
Thought, v. [Thinking]
 {Anxiety]
 —*Taking* {Heedfulness]
Thoughtfulness, [Thinking (aug.]
 {Heedfulness
 {Carking]
Thousand. 1000.
 —*pound.*
 in weight. Mea. III. 8.
 in money. Mea. IV. 7.
Thrall, [Slave]
Thrasonical, [Boasting Coward]
Thrave, [24 Sheaves]
Thred.

 Rrr 2

to—*a needle,* [Through-put
 thred]
Thred- } Worn to the
 bare, } threads].
 [Un-adj. p. Wool by
 wearing]
Threatning. RO. V. 6. O.
Three. Mea. I. 3.
 —*Fold,* [Three (kind)]
Threescore. 60.
Thresh. O. III. 5.
Threshold. Po IV. 3.
Thrice, [adv. Three]
Thrill.
 [Bore]
 [v. Inward trembling (like)
 found]
Thrift.
 [Frugality]
 Herb. HF. II. 14. A.
Thrifty, [adj. Frugality]
Thrive.
 [adj. p. Prosperity]
 {Increase
 {Become rich]
 {Grow]
 {adj. v. Vigour]
Throb, [Pulse of the heart]
 sp. Pulse (augm.]
Throne, [adj. King Chair]
Throng, [Dense multitude]
 {Thrust]
 —*to* { a. Density]
Throstle, [Thrush]
Throat PG. III. 5. A.
 Set out—[Exclamation]
 —*Boil,* [Protuberance of the
 —*wort.* HS. VII. 7. A. (th
Th-ottle, [Protuberance of the
 Rough Artery]
 —*to*— [Strangle]
 sp. by compressing throat]
Through.
 Prep. IV. 3.
 {Perfect]
 {Total]
 {Only]
 —*ly through,* [Through both
 sides]
 —*fare,* [Through-passage]
 —*out,* {Perfect]
 [adv. {Whole]
 —*Paced* {Perfect]
 {Only—} ambling]
 —*stitch,* [Perfect]
 quite—[Through both sides]
 [for] Prep. I. 2. A.
 {Impulsion]
 [By {Means } of]
 [With] Prep. I. 1. A.
 [Over] Prep. III. 3.
 [By] Prep. I. 2.
Through wax. HF. IV. 14.
 Codded—HS. IV. 6. A.]
Throw.
 [Cast] Mo. VI. 2.
 —*a dart,* [a. Dart]
 —*down,* [a. Fall]
 —*Person,* [Precipitate]
 —*Building,* [a. Ruine]
 —*forth* {Unpossess]
 —*out* {
Pang, [Pain (imp.] *Thrum*

TI   TI   TO

Thrum, [Tuft]
Thrush, Bi. III. 3. A.
  Sea— Fi. V. 9.
Thrusting. O. I. 4. O.
  —*forth* [Un-possess]
  —*out* {Un-possess}
  Himself in, [Usurp]
  —*into*, {Prick / Stab}
  —*through*, {Stab}
  [Through Wound]
Thumb, {First / biggest} Finger]
Thump.
  [Strike]
  sp. with obtuse (thing)
  [Sound of striking]
Thunder. El. I. 3. A.
  —*Bolt* {Long (dim.)} Pebble (kind)
  —*stone* {
Thursday, [5ᵗʰ day of the week]
Thus.
  [In this manner]
  —*far*, [Until / this {time / place}]
Thwack, {Strike / Cudgel}
Thwart.
  [adj. {Transverse / Cross}]
  [Contrary]
  [adj. Disingenuity]
  to—
  [Oppose]
  [Contradict]
Ty.
  Knit. O. II. 2.
  [Bind]
  [Oblige]
Tice, [Allure]
Tick, vid. *Tike*.
Ticket, [adj. Written (dim.)]
Tickling. AC. II. 8.
Tide.
  motion of the Sea. W. IV. 6. A.
  season, [Time]
  good— [Festival]
Tidings, [Narration]
  sp. of new (thing)
Tierce, {½ of a Hogshead}
Tiercel, [Hawk (male)]
Tiffany.
Tigh, [Laugh (exc.)]
Tight
  {Whole / Stiff}
Tike.
  [adj. {Countrey / Rusticity} (person)]
  Insect. Ex. II. 6.
  Sheep— Ex. II. 6. A.
  Bed—[Case of Bed]
Tile. St. I. 5. A.
  to— [a roof with Tiles]
Till.
  a— in a Chest, [Box (dim.)]
  adj. drawn (apt.)
  adv. [Until]
  to—
  [a. Prop]
  [Allure]

{a. Agriculture}
{a. Plow}
—*ed Land*, [Arable]
Tillage, [Agriculture]
Tilt.
  a—[adj. Cloth roof]
  to—[Fence with Spear]
  —*a vessel*, [adj. a. Oblique v.]
Tilth, {State} (sp. of Land)
  Land in—(L. adj. p. agriculture (perf.)
Timber [Wood for building]
  —*of fir* [aggregate—]
Timbrel, [adj. Music (instr.)]
Time.
  Space. Sp. I.
  —*to come*, &c. [Future, &c.]
  at—*s*. Sp. I. 8. O.
  at all—*s*, [adv. Perpetuity]
  often—*s*, [adv. Frequency]
  Some—*s*, [adv. Rarity]
  {Date}
  {Duration}
  {Age}
  for a—[adv. Transitory]
  Long—[adv. Permanence]
  —*in music*.
  measure of— Men. V.
  {Leisure / Opportunity}
  in—{adv. time / (perf.)}
  in good—{
  out of—[adv. time (corr.)]
  [Action in the—]
  First, [f. action]
  the—, [adj time (things)]
Time. Herb. HF. VI. 4.
Timely.
  [Opportune]
  [Early]
Timeserving, vid. *Temporizing*.
Timidi-{Fear (apt.) / Cowardise}
ty, {
Timorous, [adj. Timidity]
Tin. Met. I. 3.
  —*glass*, [Bismute] Met. III. 3.
  to—*a.* surface with Tin (fam.)
Tinca marina. Fi. VI. 4.
Tincture.
  [Dying]
  [Coloured Liquor]
  [Colour]
Tind, [v. Fire (inc.)]
Tinder, [Charred Linen]
Tine, [Toothed (pin)]
Ting, [Ring (dim.)]
  sp. adv. acute]
Tingle. AC. II. 9. A.
Tinker, [adj. Wandring. adj. metal (mech.)]
Tinkle, [Ring (dim.) sp. Acute]
Tinsel, [Cloth between-woven with Copper silver (like)]
Tintamar, [Jangling sound (augm.)]
Tip. Sp. III. 7.
  to—
  [a. Tip]
  [a. Fall by striking with adj. p. cast (thing)]
Tipper.
Tippling, {Drinking (freq.) / a. Drunkenness}

Tipstaff, [Marshal]
Tiring.
  [Wearying]
  —*for hawk*, [adj. a appetite (thing) by adj. p. pecking.]
  [a. Clothing]
  —*woman*, [Hair— {Order / Ornate} (mech.)]
Tissick. S. V. 2.
Tissue, [Cloth between-woven with Gold]
Tit.
  Bird.
  crested— Bl. VI. 8. A.
  long-tail'd— Bi. VI. 8.
  [Horse (dim.)]
  to—*over*, [Fall]
Tithe, [Tenth (part)]
Tithymal, [Spurge] HS. V. 11.
Titillation, [Tickling]
Title.
  [Name]
  sp. of Dignity]
  [Right]
Titmouse. Bi. VI. 7.
  great— Bi. VI. 6.
Tittle.
  [Point]
  [Most-little (thing)]
  —*tattle*, [adj. Loquacity (thing)]
Titular, [adj. name]
To.
  Prep.
  [For]
  —*the end*, [For the e.]
  —*that*, [That]
  [In]
  to {*day* / *morrow*} [in {this day / next day}]
  [Of] Prep. I. 1.
  according, Prep. II. 1.
  in— Prep. IV. 1.
  an— Prep. II, 1.
  —*and* {toward / to} {several places}
  fro, {
  Subst. [Finger of foot]
  —{*do* / *say*}, &c. {Doing / Saying} &c.]
Toad.
  Beast. Be. VI. 2. A.
  —*'s flax*. HS. VIII. 6. A.
  —*Stool*, [Mushrom] HL. I. 1.
  —*fish*. Fi. II. 4. A.
Tobacco. HS. VII. 11.
  —*pipe*.
  —*fish*. Fi. III. 13. A.
Tod, [28 pounds]
Together. Adv. IV. 1.
  —*with*. Prep. II. 2.
Toy.
  [Vain (thing)]
  [adj. Valour (dim.)]
  to—[a. Wantonness]
Toil.
  [Net]
  [Labour (augm.)]
Token.
  [Sign]
  [adj. Witness (sign)]
                   [Pawn

TO · TO · TR

[Pawn]
[Gift] sp. sent
Told, { adj. a. pret. } Tell
     { adj. p. }
Tole, vid. *Toll.*
  [adj. Paid (part) out of adj. p.
  grinding (thing)
  [Tribute]
  —*booth*, [Prison]
Tolerable.
  [adj. p. Patience (apt.)]
  Indifferent]
Toleration. RG. IV. 9.
Toll, vid. *Tole.*
to—
  [Ring (dim.)]
  [Allure]
Tomb, [adj. Entombing (place)]
Tome, [Book] D. III. 3. A.
Tone.
  [Voice (manner)]
  [Distance between two notes]
Tong. PG. III. 4.
  —*tied*, [Dumb through not-
  motion (pot.) of tong]
  Dogs—HM. II. 3.
  [Language]
  —*of a ballance*, [Direct pin of
  ballance]
Tongs, [adj. Taking (*jug.*) for
adj. fire (things)]
Tonfills, [Glandules] adj. PG.
III. 9. A.
  place of them. PG. III. 9. A.
Too.
  [adv. Excess]
  [Also] Conj. IV. 2.
Tool, [Instrument]
Tooth. PG. III. 4. A.
  —*and nail,* { Diligence }
  —   { adv. { Fierceness }
  —*som,* [adj. Taste (perf.)]
Eye—[Longest]
figure. Mag. IV. 2.
  —*wort.* HS. IV. 2. A.
  —*without Leaves.* HL. V. 8. A.
Top.
  Highest. Sp. III. 7.
  —*of a ship.* RN. III. 1. A.
  { Best part }
  { Principal }
  [Conc. adj, p. vertiginate
  (apt.) by ad. p. whipping]
to—
  [Cut off the top]
  [a. Superiority]
  [a. Stay]
Topaz. St. IV. 3. A.
Tophus. St. I. 5.
Topic.
  —*medicine,* [m. applicable to
  the Sick (part)]
  [adj. Invention (place { of ar-
  [Foundation (like   { gu-
                         ment)]
Topsy turvy, [With top adj. p. un-
dermost]
Torch, { Wax } Candle
         { Pitch } (augm.)
Torment { Pain (augm.) }
          { Torture   }
Tormentil. HF. IX. 2. A.

Torn, [adj. p. Tear]
Tornado. Wind.
Torpedo. Fi. II. 1. A.
Torpid, { Num'd }
          { Dull }
Torrent, [Stream (augm.) sp.
transitory]
Torrid, [Hot (augm.)]
Tortion, [Twisting]
Tortois. Be. VI. 1.
Torture, { RJ. VI. 1. }
           { Pain (augm.) }
Toss, { Cast upward }
        { a. Volutation }
  —*pot,* [adj. Drunkenness (per-
         (son)]
Toste, [Roste]
  sp. without vertigination]
Total, { Whole }
[adj.   { Sum }
Totter, { Shake }
          { Stagger }
Touch.
  [Feeling] NP. III. 3.
  [Sense]
  Extern. NP. III.
  Intern. NP. II.
  [Anger]
  [Tactil quality]
  —*active.* Q. V.
  —*paffive.* Q. VI.
  [v. Contiguity]
  [Essay]
  { a. { Experience] }
  {   { Try   }
  the—[p. Experience]
  —*stone.* St. I. 6. A.
  [v. Pertinent]
  —*ing,* [Concerning] Prep.
  I. 3. A.
  { Little }
  { Say   }
to— { Speak little of }
     { a. Object (dim.) }
  —*wood,* [Fungus of tree for
  a. fire (inc.]
Touchy, [Morose]
Toughness. Q. VI. 5. E.
Touze, [Pull (augm.)]
Tow, vid. *Towe.*
Toward.
  [That adv. way]
  —*ly,* [adj. Learn (apt.)]
  { About. Adv. } V. 3.
  { Almost Adv. } V. I.
Towe, [Hemp prepared for adj.
  p. spinning]
to—[Draw with cord]
Towel, [Linnen for wiping]
Tower. Po. II. 3.
Town. RG. III. 2. A.
  —*s men* { adj. Town (person) }
          { Citizen   }
Towre, [Fly high]
Towze, vid. *Touze.*
Toze, [Loosen by pulling (freq.)]
Trabs. El. I. 4.
Trace.
  Harness. Po. V. 9. A.
to— { Follow   }
     { Hunt } by track]]
Traburus. Fi. IV. 8. A.

Track, { Foot } (sign)
[adj.   { Wheel }
Tract.
  [Country] W. III. A.
  [Written Discourse]
  —*of time,* [Time (augm.)]
                (Gentle)
Tractable, { Courteous }
             { adj. p. Govern (apt.) }
Trade.
  [Profession. RG. II. { sp. Un-
  Art. Ha. VI. 3.   { learned }
  to—[a. Merchant]
  —*winde,* [Constant w.]
Tradition,
  [Narration] sp. Successive]
  Ecclesiastic. RE. VI. 1. A.
Traduce,
  [Reproach]
  [Calumniate]
Traffick, { Merchant }
            { a. Commerce }
Tragedy, [Play adv. a. Grief end-
  ing]
Tragical, [adj. a. Grief
  sp. in the Ending]
Tragicomedy, [adj. a. Grief play
  adv. mirth ending]
Tragopogon. HA. I. 8. A.
Tray. Pr. V. 4. A.
Trail, [Draw on the ground]
  sp. for a. Sent (make)]
Train.
  —*of garment,* [Long hinder
  part of g.]
  bird's—PP. V. 2. A.
  Series
  —*of powder.*
  Aggregate.
  [Waiters (aggr.)]
  —*of an Army.* RN. IV. 7.
  [Allurement]
to—
  { a. Teacher }
  { Educate   }
  { Entice   }
Traytor, { Perfidiousness }
  [adj.   { Treason   }
                              (person)
Tralatitious. D. III. 6. O.
Tramel, [Net adj. p. carry (apt.)
between two (persons)]
Trample.
  —*on a. foot*
  [a. Sound (augm.) with a.
  foot (augm.)]
Trance, [Extasie]
Tranquility.
  [v. Quieting (abstr.)]
  [Contentation]
Transaction, [a. Business]
Transcendent. T.
  [Excellent]
Transcribe, [a. Type writing]
Transfer.
  { Remove }
  { Deliver }
  { Alienate }
Transfigure, [Alter the form]
Transgress.
  [a. Excess]
                                    a. Dif-

TR

{ a. Disobey}
{ a. Violate}
{ a. Sin}
Transient, [Transitory]
Transition. D. V. 9.
Transitory. Sp. I. 6, O.
Translation. D. V. 5.
  vid. *Transfer*.
Transmarine, [Beyond adj. Sea]
Transmigration, [ition from one (place) to another (place)]
Transmit, { Derive } from, &c.]
         { a. ition }
Transmutation, [Altering]
Transom, [Transverse beam]
Transparent. Q. I. 4.
—*stone*, vid. *Stone*.
Transpiration. Mo. IV. 3. A.
Transplant, [Re-move { (Place) into another { (Countrey)]
Transport.
  [Carry into another Countrey]
  [a. Extasie]
Transpose, { Exchange } the
           { Alter   }
           { Place }
           { Order }
Transubstantiation, [Altering the substance]
Transverse. Ma. II. 8. D.
Trap. PO. VI. 8. A.
—*door*, [Door adj. p. open with lifting]
Trappings, [adj. a. Ornate (arm.)]
Trash.
  [Sorry]
  [Worst part]
  [Filth]
Travel.
  [Journey] TA. VI. 3.
  sp. into forreign Countreys]
  [Labour]
  [Parturition]
Travellers Joy. Sh. V. 7. A.
Traverse.
  to—[a. Transverse]
  —*Sutt*, [Denying the action].
Treachery.
  op. to fidelity. Man. IV. 2. D
  op to Loyalty. Man. V. 6. D.
Treacle, [Physical mixture of vipers, &c.]
Tread.
  [a. Foot]
  —*down*, [a. Prostrate by upon- a. foot.]
  [Goe]
  [v. Coition]
    sp. as bird (male)]
Treason. RJ. III. 2.
Treasure, { Money } { (place)
            { Riches } { (aggr.)
  —*r*, [adj. keeping (Off.) of money]
Treat.
  [a. Object]
  [Entertain]
  in order to a Bargain. RC. VI. 1. A.

TR

Treaty, [a. Treat]
Trea- { Written   }
tise, { Printed   } Discourse]
Treble.
  [Threefold]
  —*in Music*. Q. III. 1. E.
Treddle, [Navel of fut. Chick in egg.]
Tree. Tr.
  —*of life*. Tr. V. 6. A.
  —*of saddle*,[adj. wood (part) of s.]
Trefoil.
  bean—Sh. IV. 3.
  Hedgbog—HS. III. 15. A.
  Shrub—Sh. IV. 3. A.
  Snail—HS. III. 15.
  Starheaded—HP. VIII. 5. A.
Trey. Pt. V. 4. A.
  [Three]
Trembling. AC. IV. 5. E.
Trench, [Ditch]
Trencher. Pr. V. 9.
  —*friend*, [Flatterer for victuals]
  —*man*, [Eater]
Trepan.
  [adj. boring (instr.) for headbone]
  to—[allure { Hurt } into p. { Danger }]
Trepidation, [Trembling]
  sp. through fear]
Trespass.
  { a. Excess}
  { Disobey}
  { Violate}
  { a. Sin}
  { Injury}
Tress.
  [Lock of hair]
  [Tassel (like)]
Tressle. Mag. V. 5.
Trevet, [Stool with three legs (like)]
Try.
  { Consider }
  { Examine } TA. II. 5. A.
  —*at law*. RC. II. 4. A.
  Prove. TA. II. 5. A.
  { Essay }
  { a. Experience }
  —*out*, [Try the utmost]
  Refine, [Separate the course (parts)]
Triangle. Mag. V. 1.
Tribe, [Society]
  sp. from one progenitor]
Tribula- { Adversity }
tion,   { Misery   }
Tribunal, [Seat of Judge]
Tribune, [adj. Regiment (Off.)]
Tribute. RC. V. 9.
Trice, [Instant]
Trick.
  { a. Craft }
  { a. Prestigiator }
  { Action } { (dim.)
  { thing } { (corr.)
  to—[a. Ornate]
Trickle, [Drop]
  sp. adv. Series]

TR

Trident, [Halbert with three teeth]
Trifle.
  [Vain (thing)]
  [Thing of no value]
                 { Wantonness}
  —*ing*, [a   { Sloth}
                { Lightness}
                { Cunctation}]
Trigger.
  [adj. { Staying   } (instr.
        { Impediment} of vertigination)]
  [Sign of standing (place)]
Trill, [Tremble (like) with voice]
Trim, [adj. Ornate]
  —*ing a boat*, [a. Ballancing]
  —*ing a ship*—RN. VI. 4. A.
Trine, [Distance { of a great Circle]
Tringa.
  —*major*. Bi. VII. 5.
  —*minor*. Bi. VII. 5. A.
Trinity, [Three (abstr.)]
Trinkets, [Sorry { Instruments }
                   { Things }
                   { Utensils }
Trip.
  [a. Slide (make)
  [Stumble (dim.)
  —*along*, [Walk nimbly]
Tripe, [Prepared stomach of beast]
Tripartite, [Three (kind)]
Triple, [Threefold]
Trivial.
  { Ordinary }
  { Common }
  { Sorry }
  { Vain }
Triumph. RM. II. 8.
Triumvi- { Government } of to-
rat,   { Magistracy } gether-three (persons)
Trochisc, [Round lamin (dim.)]
Trochus. Ex. VII. 6.
         { adj. a. pret. }
Trod, { adj, p.   } [Tread]
Troy weight, [w. of 12 ounces in a pound]
Troll, [Ition adv. Smooth]
  [Hunt fish with adj. vertiginating (mach,)]
Troop.
  Company. RM. IV. 3.
  [Aggregate]
Trooper, [Horseman] RM. III. 1. A.
Trope, [a. Tralatitious]
Trophee. RM. II. 8. A.
Tropic.
  —*of Cancer*. W. VI. 6.
  —*of Capricorn*. W. VI. 6. A.
Trot.
  a—[adj. Decrepit (fem.)]
  to—Mo. II. 2. A.
Trotter. [Foot]
  sp. of Sheep]
Trouble.
  Molest. TA. V. 9. O.
  —*in*—[adj. p. TA. V. 9. O.]
  { Adversity}
  { Misery}   Grief

TR

{Grief}
{Remorse}
{Anxiety}
—*water*, [Un-a. quiet]
Trouble-⎰adj. a. Trouble (apt.)
som, ⎱Contentious]
Trough, [Long Trey]
Trout. Fi. IX. 3.
Trowel. [adj. spreading (instr.) of Mortar]
Trowle, vid. Troll.
True, [adj.] ⎰Truth⎱ ⎱Genuine⎰
Truant.
[Wanderer]
[Slothful (person)] HL. I. 2.
Trubs. HL. I. 2.
Truce, ⎰Transitory peace⎱ ⎱Between-space of quiet⎰
Truchman, [Interpreter]
Truck, [Exchange]
Truckle, [Wheel of pully]
to——
under-⎰Be⎱ ⎱Ly⎰
[Submit]
Trucu-⎰Fierce⎱(augm.)
lent, ⎱Cruel⎰
Truffe, Trubs. HL. I. 2.
Truly. Adv. I. 2. O.
Trull, [Common adj. fornication (fem.)]
Tramp.
[Trumpet]
[adj. Victory (kind) of Cards]
Trumpe-⎰Sorry (things)⎱
ry, ⎱Worst part⎰
sp. (aggr.)
Trumpet, [adj. Trumpeter (instr.)]
Trumpeter. RM. III. 3. A.
Fish. Fi. IV. 10.
Trunche-⎰Short thick stick⎱
on, ⎱adj. Cudgelling (inst.)⎰
Trundling, ⎰Upon wheels⎱
[motion] ⎱adv. Vertiginating⎰
Trunk.
Body.
—of *plant*, [Stock] PP. I. 2.
—of *animal*. PG. IV.
[Box]
Chest. sp. with convex adj. covering (thing)
[Tube]
snout. PP. V. 4. A.
Truss.
⎰Together—⎱ ⎰Tie⎱
⎱Up— ⎰ ⎱ ⎰
[a-aggregate by tying]
—of *hay*, [adj. p. bound (aggr.) of h.]
Trust.
[Believe]
v. Confidence] AS. III. 4.
—*with*, [Deposit]
—*for*, [Lend]
Trusty, [Faithful]
Truth. T. III. 1.
in—Adv. I. 2. O.
Tub Pr. V. 3. A.

TU

—*fish* Fi. IV. 5.
Tube
Round—Mag. V. 9. O.
Square—Mag. V. 9.
Tuberous, [adj. Protuberance (freq.)]
Tuck, ⎰Long adj. pricking (apt.) (Sword)⎱
of *a ship*. RN. II. 9.
to—[Fasten the extremity]
Tuesday, [Third day of the week]
Tuff Taffate, [Tufted Taffata]
Tuft.
Tassel. Mag. IV. 6.
—of flower. PP. II. 6.
[Aggregate]
Tugg, ⎰(augm.)⎱
[Pull] ⎱(imp.)⎰
Tuition, ⎰Guardian⎱
⎱[a. Teacher]⎰
Tulip. HL. IV. 3.
Tumbling. Mo. II. 6. A.
Tumbler, [Dog hunting lesser beasts by agility]
[Præstigiator by tumbling]
Tumbrel, [Cart]
Tumor. S. III.
Tumult.
[Sedition]
[Confused multitude]
Tumultuary.
[Seditious sudden]
Tun.
[Barrel (augm.)]
[Measure]
Weight. Mea. III. 9.
Tune. Q. III. 6.
to—Prepare (perf.)
—*able*, [adj. Music]
Tunhoof, [Ground-Ivy] HL. VI. 11.
Tunicle, [Membrane]
Tunnage, [Tribute]
Tunnel, [Concave Cone]
—of *Chimney*, [Concave (part) of ch.]
Tunny. Fi. III. 4.
Turbant, [adj. head (vest)]
Turbinated, [About—spiral adj. Cone]
Turbith. Tr. VI. 11. A.
Turbith.
Turbo. Ex. VII. 5. A.
Turbu-⎰Sedition⎱
lent, ⎱Contentious⎰
Turbut. Fi. VII. 3.
Turcois. St. III. 5.
Turdus. Fi. V. 9.
Turf, [Grassie clod]
Turgid, ⎰Tumor⎱
[adj.] ⎱Protuberance⎰
[Full (augm.)]
Turks Cap, [Martagon] HL. IV. 2. A.
Turky. Bi. II. 2. A.
[Trouble]
Turmoil,⎰Operation (augm.)⎱
⎱Business (augm.)⎰
Turn.
op. to proceed. TA. VI. 2. O.
—*head*, [Resist]

TU

Gesture. AC. VI. 8.
—*inside out*.
—*upside down*.
[Fold]
—*down*.
—*up*.
[Dig]
—*up the ground*.
⎰Bend⎱
⎱Curve⎰
[a.⎰Helical⎱ ⎱Spiral⎰]
[a. Volutation]
[a. Vertigination]
—*Spit*.
—*with a Lave*. O. IV. 7. A.
—*er*, [adj.—ing (mech.)]
[Change]
—*into*
[Become]
[v. Convert]
[v. Apostate]
[Translate]
—*away*, [From—]
—*back*, [Back—]
—*over*
—*out*, [Eject]
—*up*
a—[Turning]
[Alteration]
at every—
[Office]
a good—[a. Benefactor]
an ill—[Mischief]
Course. T. VI. 7.
by—*s*, [adv. Course]
Turnament, [Game of horsemen mutually assaulting with spears]
Turnep. HS. IV. 4.
Turnpike. RM. VI. 8.
Turpentine, ⎰Larch⎱ Tree
[Liquid ⎱Turpentine⎰ out-
resin of] Pine drawn
by incision
—*tree*. Tr. III. 3. A.
Turpitude, [Indecency (augm.)]
Turnstile, [adj. p. Vertiginate (apt) transverse cross]
Turret.
[Tower (dim.)]
fig. Mag. VI. 3. A.
Turtle.
Bird. Bi. III. 2. A.
Beast. Be. V. 1. A.
Tush. ⎰I. 3.⎱
Int. ⎱II. 3. A.⎰
Tusk, [Long Tooth]
Tut, vid. Tush.
⎰Protection⎱
Tutelary, [adj. a.⎱Defence⎰
⎰Safety⎱
Tuty.
Tutor, ⎰Guardian⎱
⎱Teacher⎰
Tutsan. HS. V. 8.
Tutty, [Flowers (aggr.) together-tied]
Twayblade. HL. VII. 5. A.
Twain, [Two]
Twang, [Ring]
Tweez, [Box of instruments (dim.)]

Twelve

VA | VA | VE

Twelve.
T —*month*, [Year]
wenty.
Twibill, [adj. pecking (inftr.]
Twice, [Two times]
Twig, [Wand] PP. I. 4. A.
Twilight, Q. I. 1;
Twins, [Two together-born]
Twine, { Twift sp. mutu- / Embrace ally.]
Twinge, { Pull / Pain } [imp.]
Twinkle, [Un-appear (freq.]
Twirl, [Vertiginate (imp.]
Twift.
 the—[Share]
 to—O. V. 1.
Twit, [Upbraid]
Twitch.
 [Pull (imp.]
 [Pain] AC. II. 9.
Twittle, [Chirp (dim.]
Two. Mea. II. 2.
 —fold, [Two (kind)]
Tygre. Be. IV. 2.
Tympany. S. VI. 3. A.
Type. T. II. 3. A.
 [Letter-printing (inftr.]
Typographical, [adj. Printing]
Tyranny. Man. VI. 4. O.
Tyrant.
 [Kingfhip, adj. Ufurping (perfon]
 [adj. Man. VI. 4. O. (perfon]

V.

V*Acant.*
 [Empty]
 [Not- { Furnifhed / Ufed]
 [adj. Leifure]
Vacation.
 { adj. Leifure / not-adj. RC. } (time)
Vacillation, [Staggering] Mo. II. 4. O.
Vacuity, [Emptinefs]
Vagabond, [adj. Wandering (perfon]
Vagary.
 [v. Wandring]
 [a. Conceitednefs]
Vail, vid. Veil.
 —s [adj. Van- { Profits / tage Revenue]
 sp. befides -wages]
Vain.
 [adj. Vanity]
 —glory, [Glorying (corr.]
 vid. Vein.
Vallens, [About- adj. hanging (veft) of the upper Margin of the Bedfted]
Vale, [Valley] W. III. 1. D.
Valediction. AC. V. 8. A.
Valerian. HF. IV. 8.
Valet, [adj. Waiting (Off.]
Valiant, [adj. Fortitude]

Validi- { Sufficience / ty, Efficience } (apt.]
Valley. W. III. 1. D.
Valour.
 Worth. Mea. IV.
 [Fortitude]
Value.
 Worth. Mea. IV.
 to—
 { Efteem / a. { Valour / Price]
Vamp, [Mend { Adding / by Renewing part]
Van.
 [Forepart]
 sp. of army]
 [Winnowing (jug.]
Vane, [Flag for fhewing the vergency of the wind]
Vanifh, [Un-appear]
Vanity.
 { Frivoloufnefs. T. IV. 5. O.
 { Not-profitablenefs
 { Fruftrating (abftr.]
 { Wantonnefs
 { Conceitednefs]
 op. to gravity. Man. IV. 6. O.
Vanquifh, { Victory / a. { Conqueft]
Vantage. TM. VI. 2. A.
Vantcurrier. RM. IV. 5.
Vantgard, [Forepart of army]
Vapor.
 [Exhalation] El. II. 2. A.
 [Glorying]
Vardingale.
Vary.
 v. Diverfity]
 [Alter]
 [a. Contention]
Varia- { adj. Alter (apt.] / ble, Inconftant]
Variance, [Contention]
Variegated, Q II. 5.
Variety, [Diverfity]
Varix. S. III. 8.
Varlet, [Sorry (perfon]
Varnifh. O. IV. 8. A.
Varvels, vid. Vervels.
Vaffal.
 [Subject]
 [Villain]
Vaft, [Ample (augm.]
Vat { Tub / Vate Barrel } (augm.]
Vault. Po. II. 8.
 to—
 [a. Vault]
 [Leap] Mo. V. 5. A.
Vaunt.
 [Glorying]
 sp. corr.]
 [a. Infolence]
 —gard, vid. Vantgard.
Vauward, [Forepart of army]
Vaumure. RM. VI. 4.
Ubiquity. Sp. II. 9.
Udder, [Dug] PG. IV. 2. A.
Veal.
 [Calf]
 [Flefh of Calf]

Veer.
 [Turn]
 { Let-go / Out-put } more { Sail / Cord]
Vegetable, [Plant] W. V. 2.
Vegetation.
 [adj. p. Vegetative foul (make]
 [a. Vigor]
Vegetative.
 [Plant] W. V. 2.
 —Soul. W. I. 4.
 its actions. AC I.
Vegetous, [Vigor]
Vehemence.s
 [Intenfenefs]
 [Fiercenefs] Ha. III. 4. D.
Vehicle, [adj. Carrying (thing]
Veil.
 a— [adj. Covering thing]
 sp. chin]
 to—
 [Cover]
 [a. Refpect (fign]
Vein.
 —of animal. PG. II. 4.
 opening a—[a. Bleeding]
 Mo. IV. 6.
 —of { Metal / Stone } Vein (like) { m / line of— } S
 in the earth]
 { Temper] NP. IV.
 { Difpofition }
 [Style]
Vellam, [Paper of Calves skin]
Velleity. AS. IV. 2.
Vellication.
 [Pulling (freq.]
 [Twitching] AC. II. 9.
Velvet, [Silk adj. p. furface with fhort tufts]
Venal { adj. p. { pot.] / Vendible Sell apt.]
Vending, [Selling]
Veneration.
 [Reverence]
 [Worfhip]
Venery.
 [Coition]
 [Hunting]
Vengeance.
 [a. Revenge]
 [Punifhment]
Venial, [adj. p. { pot.] / Forgive apt.]
Venifon, [Flefh of hunted beafts]
Venom, [Poifon]
Vent.
 { Wind / Exhalation }
 [Hole for { Wind / out- a. Exhal.]
 [Sent] Q. IV. A.
 to—
 [a. Vent]
 in— { ition / out- (make)
 sp. Air]
 [Sell]
Ventiduct, [adj. { (jug.] / a. wind tube]
Ventilation, [Winnowing]

Vento-

VE

Ventosity, [Wind (abstr.)]
Ventricle.
  [Hollow (place)]
  [Stomach] PG. VI. 4.
Venture.
  [Danger]
  [Fortune]
  [Essay]
  sp. {its danger}
       {ones fortune}
  at a—[adv. {its danger}
              {ones fortune}
   Essaying
Venturous.
  [Dangerous]
  [adj. Essaying (apt.) danger]
  [Bold]
  [Rash]
Ven.
  [Thrust (imp.)]
  [Stab (end)]
Venus. W. II. 5. A.
  —*comb*. HS. I. 5. A.
  —*flax*.
  —*Looking glass*. HS. V. 3.
  —*Shell*. Ex. VII. 7.
Veracity. Man. IV. 1.
Verb. D. II. 3.
Verbal, [adj. Word]
Verbatim, [adv. Word (segr.)]
Verbosity.
  [a. word (exc.)]
  [Loquacity]
Verderer, [adj. Forrest (Off.) assessor]
Verdict.
  [Sentence]
  [Opinion]
Verdigreece. Met. IV. 5.
Verdure.
  [Greenness]
  [Vigor]
Verge.
  [Margin]
  [Capacity]
  [Stick]
Verging. Sp. III. A.
Verger, [Before—adj. Walking (Off.)]
Very.
  [Self]
  [same]
  (augm.)
  [True]
  [Genuine]
  —*ly*. } Adv. I. 2. O.
  in—*deed* }
Verifie.
  [a. Truth (make)]
  [Perform]
  {Prove}
  {Confirm}
Verity. T. III. 1.
Verjuice. Pr. II. 5. A.
Vermilion. Met. III. 5. A.
Vermin.
  [Insects]
  sp. Hurtful]
  [Hurtful Animals]
Vernacular, {Nation}
  [adj. ones {Tribe} (place)]
Vernal.
  [adj. Spring]

VE

Vernish, [adj. a. Vernishing (thing)]
  —*ing*. O. IV. 8. A.
Verse.
  Part of Book. D. III. 2.
  op. to Prose. D. III. 4. O.
Versicle, [Verse (dim.)]
  (p. adj. preceding)
Versifie, [a. D. III. 4. O.]
Version, [Translation]
Vertebra. PG. IV. 3. A.
Vertical.
  [adj. Top]
  —*point*, [Upper pole of the Horizon]
  [adj. vertex. Ma. II. 2.
Vertiginous.
  [adj. Vertigo]
  —*motion*. O. I. 5.
Vertigo. S. IV. 5.
Vertue.
  [Habit (perf.)]
  infused. Ha. V.
  acquired.
   intellectual. Ha. VI.
   moral. Man. I.
  Respecting the body. Man. II.
  Respecting the state and dignity. Man. III.
  Homiletical.
  —*Common*. Man. IV.
  —*belonging to superior*. Man. V.
  —*belonging to Inferior*. Man. VI.
  Instruments of—Ha. II.
  Affections of—
   —*Intellectual*—Ha. III.
   —*Moral*—Ha. III.
  [Efficacy]
Verven. HS. V. 9.
Vervels, [adj. Leg bonds of Hawk]
Verule, [adj. Lamin ring]
Vesicle, [Bladder (dim.)]
Vespers, [adj. Evening worship]
Vessel.
  General, Pr. V.
  —*of animal body*, [adj. containing (apt.) hollow (parts)]
   —*Heterogeneous*. PG. VI.
   —*Homogeneous*. PG. II.
  [Ship]
Vestment, [Clothing]
Vestry, [adj. Clothing (room)]
Vesture, [Clothing]
Vetch. HS. II. 3.
  bitter—HS. II. 4.
  Crimson grass—HS. III. 7.
  hatched—HS. III. 6.
  Kidney—
  Milk—HS. III. 3. A.
  Yellow wild—HS. II. 6.
Veternus. S. IV. 2.
Vex.
  [a. {Angry} {(make)}
      {Grieved}
  [Molest]
  [a. Anxiety]
Ugly {Deformed} (augm.)
       {Indecent}

VI

Vy.
  {a. Emulation}
  {Provoke}
  [More—a. wager]
Vial.
  [adj. Glass bottle (dim.)]
  [adj. Music (instr.) to be sounded with bow]
Viands, [Victuals]
Vibrate, [Swing.] Mo. VI. 3.
Viburnum. Sh. I. 5.
Vicar.
  [Deputy]
  [Second (kind) Presbyter]
Vice.
  [Moral] Man. I. O.
  {Feign'd fool}
  {adj. Scurrility (person)}
  [adj. Holding (mach.)]
Vice—[instead]
Vicegerent, [Substitute]
Viceroy, [Instead-King]
Vitiate.
  [Vitious make]
  [Unchast (make)]
  [Mar]
Vicinity.
  [Neighborhood]
  [Neerness]
Vicount, [Nobleman of the fourth Degree]
Vicissitude.
  {a. Turn} T. VI. 8.
  {Alteration, adj. turn}
Victim, [Sacrifice]
Victor, [adj. RM. II. E. (person)]
Victory, [adj. RM. II. 1. E. (thing)]
  get the—RM. II. 1. E.
Victualler, [adj. {(Off.)} {(Merc.)} Victuals]
Victualling house, [House of adj. Victuals (merc.)]
Victuals. Pr. I.
  fall to his—[Eat]
View.
  [a. ey] PG. III. 2.
  [Observe]
  [Examine]
Vigilance.
  Abstinence. Man. II. 4.
  [Heedfulness]
Vigils.
  [a. Vigilance]
  [adj. p. Wake night before festival]
  [Day before the Festival]
Viger, NP. V. 4.
Vile.
  [adj. Valor (dim.)]
  [Sorry]
  [Vicious]
Vilifie.
  {a. Disrespect}
  {Contemn}
Village, [Houses (aggr.)]
  [Parish]
Villain.
  Lowest degree of Commonalty, RC. I. 8.
  [Sorry (person)]
  Sff   [Wicked

VI

[Wicked (person)]
Vindicate.
[a. { Defendant } { Advocate } { Shew Innocence }]
Vindictiveness, [a. Revenge (apt.)]
Vine. Sh. II. 1.
Vinegar. Pr. II. 5.
Vinew'd, { Mouldy } { Musty }
Vintage.
[Gathering grapes]
[a. Wine (make)]
Vintner, [adj. wine (merc.) sp. adv. segregate]
Vineyard, [Orchard of Vines]
Violate, TA. III. 6. O.
Violence. T. V. 5. O.
in Motion. Mo. VI.
[Coaction]
[Fierceness] Ha. III. 4 D.
Violet. HL. VI. 5.
bulbous—HL. V. 5. A.
dames—HS. IV. 2.
Violin, [Vial (dim)]
Viol,
[adj. Music (instr.) to be sounded with Bow] vid. *Vial.*
Viorna, [Travellers Joy] Sh. 1. 7.
Viper. Be. VI. 7. A.
—s *grass,* [Scorsonera]
Virago, [Man (like) woman]
Virga, Meteor. El. V. 4.
Virgin.
[Not-married] RO. II. 1.
[Chaste unmarried] RO. II. 1. A.
{ First } { New }
—*honey,* [First h. of Bees]
—*parchment,* [p. made of the skin of an abortive]
[Undefiled]
—*s bower,* [Clematis] Sh. V. 7.
Virginals, [Chest (like) adj. Music (instr.) with metalline string]
Virginity. RO. II. 1. A. (abstr.)
Virgo, [6th of the 12 parts of the Zodiac]
Virility.
age of manhood. Mea. VI. 3.
[Male (abstr.)]
Virtue, vid. Vertue.
Virulent.
[adj. Poison]
[adj. Malice]
Visage.
Face. PG. III. 1.
[Face (manner)]
[Seen (part)]
Visard, [Factitious face]
Viscous, [Clammy]
Visible, [adj. p. See (pot.)]
Vision.
[Seeing]
{ adj. apparence (thing) } { adj. p. See Revelation }
Visit. AC. V. 1.

UN

[About-ition for a Discipline]
Visor of Helmet, [Up—adj. fold (apt.) adj. forehead (part)]
Vital, [adj. life]
Vitiate, vid. Vicia^t.
Vitrifie, [a. Glass (make)]
Vitriol. St. V. 3.
Vivacity, [Long life (apt.)]
Vivifie, [a. Live]
Viviparous, [adj. parturition adj. living (thing)]
Ulcer. S. I. 7.
Ulterior. Sp. II. 2. D.
Ultimate { Remote } { Latter } [Most—]
Umber.
Fifth. Fi. IX. 4. A.
Colour
Umbilical, [adj. Navel] PG. IV. 6. A.
Umbles, [Inwards] PG. VI.
Umbra. Fi. IV. 2. A.
Umbrage.
[Doubting]
{ Distrust } { Jealousie }
Umbrella, [adj. Shadowing (jug.)]
Umpire, [Sole arbitrator]
Un—vid. In—
[Not—]
[Not-yet]
Unable, [adj. Impotence]
Unacceptable.
[Not-] { Against } acceptable
[adj. Displicence]
Unaccessible, [Not-adj. p. come]
Unaccustomed, [Not-accustomed]
Unacquainted, [Stranger]
Unadvised, [Rash] adj. Ha. IV. 1. D.
Unallowed, [Not-allowed]
Unanimous, [adv. { Opinioned } { Identity— } Minded]
Unappeasable, { Peaceableness } [Not-adj. p. { Meekness }]
Unapt, [Not-apt]
Unapproachable, [Not-adj. p. Neerness]
Unarm— { Not- } { Un- } armed
Unassured, [Not-assured]
Unassuaged, [Not-assuaged]
Unavoidable, [Not adj. p. escape (pot.)]
Unauthorize, [Un-a. Authority]
Unawares { Heeding } [Not—{ Expecting } taken at—[Surprized]
Unbar, [Un-a. bar]
Unbelief. AS. II. 4. O.
[Incredulity] Ha. III. 2. D.
[Infidelity] Ha. V. 4. O.
Unbend, [Un-bend]
Unbeam, [Un-a. Stupor]
Unbeseem, [v. Indecency]
Unbesot, [Un-a. Dotage]
Unbewitch, [Un-a Witchcraft]
Unbidden, [Not-bidden]

UN

[adj. Spontaneity]
Unbind, [Un-a. bind]
Unblameable, [Not-adj. p. blame (pot.)]
Unblind, [Un-a. blind (make)]
Unbuild, [Not-build]
Unbolt, [Un-a. bolt]
Unbound, [Not-adj. p. bind]
Unbounded, [Not-adj. p. bound]
Unbowel, [Un-a. bowel]
Unbrace, [Un-a. brace]
Unbridle, [Un-a. bridle]
—*d,* [Irregular]
Unbroken, [Not-adj. p. break]
Unbuckle, [Un-a. Buckle]
Unburden, [Un-a. burden]
Unburied, [Not-adj. p. buried]
Unbutton, [Un-a. button]
Uncalled, [Not-adj. p. call]
Uncapable, [Not-capable]
Uncase, [Un-a. case]
Uncaught, [Not-adj. p. catch]
Uncertain.
[Not-certain]
[Doubtful]
[Wavering]
Unchain, [Un-a. chain]
Unchangeable, [Not-adj. p. alter]
Uncharitableness. Ha. V. 6. D.
Uncharm, [Un-a. Wizard]
Unchastness. Man. II 7. D.
Unchewed, [Not-chewed]
Uncircumcision, [Not- p. circumcision]
Uncircumspect, [Careless]
Uncivil.
[Morose]
[Rustic]
Uncle RO. I. 3.
Unclasp, [Un-a. clasp]
Unclean.
[adj. Defilement]
[Unchast]
Unclose, [Un- a. close]
Uncloth- { Not- } { Un- } clothed
Uncomely, [Indecent]
Uncomfortable [adj. Discomfort]
Uncompounded, [Simple]
Unconceivable, [Not-adj. p. apprehension]
Uncondemned, [Not-condemned]
Unconquerable, [Not-adj. p. conquer (pot.)]
Unconscionable. NP. I. 3. O.
Unconstant. adj. Ha. IV. 7. D.
Unconstrained, [Not-adj. p. coaction]
Uncorded, [Not-adj. p. cord]
Uncorrected, [Not-adj. p. correction]
Uncorrupt.
[Not-corrupted]
[Sincere]
[Impartial]
Uncover. O. II. 3. O.
Uncouple, [Un-joyn]
Uncourteous.
[Not-courteous]
[Rustic]
Uncouth.
[Not-adj. custom]
[adj.

UN   UN   UN

[adj. Stranger]
[New (corr.)]
[Extraordinary (corr)]
Unction, Anointing
Uneasiness,
  to feeling. Q. VI. 4. D.
  to taste. Q. IV. 2.
Uncurable, [Not-adj. p. cure (pot.]
Undaunted, [Not-adj. p. fear (pot.]
Undecent. adj. T. V. 2. O.
Undecided, [Not-decided]
Undefiled.
  [Not-defiled]
  [Pure]
Undefrayed, {[Paid] [Not-Refunded]}
Under.
Proper. Prep. VI. 1. O.
—*foot*
—*hand* {Private} {adv. Concealed}
—*hand and seal,* [Under written and sealed]
[Within]
Contain —it. [c. within its capacity]
[Below]
—*age* {of adj. pupil age}
—*years*
{Less.} {Too little}
—*bid*
—*price.*
—*sell.*
—*value.*
[Lower]
—*leather.*
—*lid of eye.*
—*lip.*
—*side.* Sp. III. 5. O.
—*woods.*
{Inferior} {Subordinate}
—*Butler.*
—*Officer.*
—*Sheriff.*
[Dependent]
[Subject]
bring—{Subject Conquer} {make}
Keep—
Under—{v. Subject go, Suffer.}
Underhand, {Private} {adv. Concealed}
Underlay, [Mend by under-putting]
Underleather, [Lower Leather]
Underling. RO. III. O.
Undermine, RM. I. 5.
—*craftily,* [a. Treachery]
Undermost, [Most-adj. under part]
Underneath, Prep. VI. 1. O.
Underpart. Sp. III. 5. O.
Underpin, [Instead-a.foundation]
Underprop, [a-prop]
Undersay. Man. IV. 1. D.
Undersell, [Sell for less.]

Underset, [a. Prop]
Undersheriff, [Inferior adj. shire Off.]
Underside. Sp. III. 5. O.
Understand,
a. Intellect. NP. I. 1.
give {Narrate}
to—{Know (make)}
Omit. D. III. 8. O.
[Suppose]
Understanding,
Faculty. NP. I. 1.
action of {Speculative. AS. II. the—Practical. AS. III.}
Understood,
{adj.-a. pret. adj. p.} {Understand}
Omitted. D. III. 8. O.
Undertake. TA. III. 1. A.
—*for,* [a. Sponsion]
—*to do* [Oblige himself by promise]
Underva—{Value less than due lue, Contemn}
Underwoods, {Lower Young} {woods}
Undeserved, [Not-deserved,]
Undeserving. [Unworthy]
Undetermin—{adj. Liberty ed, Not-determined}
Undigested, [Not-digested]
Undischarged, [Not-discharged]
Undiscreet, [Foolish]
Undistinct, [Not-distinct]
Undivi—{Not-divided ded, Entire}
Undo.
[Un-do]
[Un-ty]
[Loosen]
{Spoil} {a. poverty (augm.)}
Undone,
[adj. p. Undo]
[Not-done]
Undoubted, [Not-doubted]
Undress, [Un cloth]
Undue. T. IV. 3. O.
Undulate.
Figure. Mag. IV. 9.
Motion, [a. Wave] W. IV. 1. E.
Undutiful. Man. V. 1. D.
Uneasie, [Difficult]
Unequal,
[Not-equal]
[Not-equitable]
Unestimable, Not-{Worthily adj. p. Esteem Sufficient- (pot.) ly}
Unevenness. Q. VI. 2. O.
Unevitable, [Not adj. p. escape (pot.]
Unexcusable, [Not-adj. p. excuse (pot.]
Unexecuted, [Not-executed]
Unexpected, [Not-expected]
Unexpert. Ha. VI. 4. D.
Unfaithful. Man. IV. 2. O.
Unfashion—{Not-figured ed, Figured (corr.}
Unfast—{Not- fast-ned, Un— ned}

Unfeather—{Not- feather-ed, Un-- ed}
Unfeigned.
{Not-feigned} {Sincere}
Unfetter—{Not- fetter-ed, Un-- ed}
Unfinished, [Not-finished]
Unfit, [Not-congruous]
Unfitting, [Indecent]
Unfix, [Un-fix]
Unfold, [Un-fold]
[Explain]
Unformed, [Not-formed]
Unfortified, [Not-fortified]
Unfortunate, Fortune (corr.) {adj. Adversity}
Unfriendly, [Not-adj. friend]
Unfruitfulness.
barrenness. NP. VI. 3. O.
[Unprofitableness]
Unfurnish—{Not- furnish-t, Un-- ed}
Ungainful, [Not-adj. a.gain (apt.]
Ungarnisht, [Not-adj. p. ornate]
Ungentle, [Not gentle]
Ungird—{Not-t, Un- adj. p. Bound}
Unglew, [Un-a. glue]
Ungodly,
{Graceless}
{Unholy}
Ungraciousness. Ha. V. O.
Unguent, {adj.-anointing (thing) Salve}
Unhabitable, [Not-adj.p.dwelling]
Unhallowed (pot.)
[Profaned]
[Unholy]
Unhand—{Deformed som, Indecent}
Unhappiness, [Misery]
Unharness, [Un-a. armament]
Unhealthy, [Not-healthy]
Unheard, [Not-adj. p. hearing]
Unheeded, [Not-heeded]
Unholy. Ha. V. 2. O.
Unhorse, {Down-put from horf Un-a. ride (make)}
Unhurt, [Not-hurt]
Unhusbanded, [Not-adj. p. agriculture]
Unicorn, [One-horned beast]
Uniform, [adv. (Figure Identity) Manner] adj. p. {Circumstance}
Uniformity, [Identity (manner)]
Unimaginable, [Not-adj. p. imagination (pot.]
Unimitable, [Not-adj. p. imitation (pot.]
Uninhabited, [Not- adj. p. dwelling]
Unjoyn, [Separate]
Unjoynt,
[Un-a. joynt]
[Separate the parts]
Union.
[a. One]
{Peaceableness} {League}

S ſſ a   *Uni-*

UN

Unison, [adj. p. Identity adj. a sound]
Unit, [One]
Unite, [a. one (make)]
Unity, [One (abst.)]
Universe, [Whole world]
Univer- ⎰ adj. Universality
sal, ⎱ Whole]
Universality. TM. III. 3. O.
University. RC. III. 6.
Univocal, [Of one signification]
Unjust, [adj. Injustice]
Unkennel, [Un-a. bed (room)]
Unkind.
[Uncharitable]
[Discourteous] adj. Man. IV. 7. O.
[Not-adj. friend]
Unkle. RO. I. 5.
Unknit, [Un-ty]
Unknown, [Not-known]
Unlace, ⎰ Un— ⎰ a. Lace]
       ⎱ Not- ⎱ a. String]
Unladen, [Un-adj. burdened]
Unlaw- ⎰ Not—   ⎰
ful,   ⎱ Against- ⎱ Lawful]
Unlearn, [Un-a. Learner]
Unlearned. Ha. VI. 5. D.
Unleavened, [Not-leavened]
Unless. Conj. I. 3. O.
Unlike, [adj. Unlikeness]
—ness. TM. V. 1. O.
Unlike- ⎰ Not—   ⎰ True
ly,   ⎱ Against- ⎱ (like)]
Unlimited.
     ⎰ Limited]
Not- ⎰ Cohibited]
     ⎱ Determined]
[Infinite]
Unlined, ⎰ Not- ⎰ lined]
           ⎱ Un- ⎱
Unload, [Un-a. burden)
Unlock, ⎰ Un-a. lock]
          ⎱ Open-with key
Unlook for, [Un-a. p. expected]
Unloose, [Loose]
Unlove- ⎰ Not—   ⎰ adj. p. love
ly,   ⎱ Against ⎱ (apt.)
Unlucky, ⎰ Fortune ⎰
[adj.   ⎱ Event   ⎱ (corr.
Unmake, ⎰ a. Efficient]
          ⎱ Un- a. Creation]
Unmannerly, ⎰ Rusticity
              ⎱ [adj. Disrespect]
Unman ⎰ Not—   ⎰ man
ly,   ⎱ Against- ⎱ (male)
Unmannured, [Not-manured]
Unmarried.
[Not-adj. pret. married]
[Divorced]
[adj. Celibate]
Unmask, [Uncover the face]
Unmatchable, [Not adj. p. equal (pot.)]
Unmeasurable.
[Not-adj. Measure (pot.)]
[Infinite]
Unmeet, [Indecent]
Unmerciful, [adj. Cruelty]
Unmindful, [Not- adj. remembring]

Unmingled, ⎰ Simple]
             ⎱ Pure]
Unmoveable, [Not-adj. p. move (pot.)]
Unnail'd, ⎰ Not- ⎰ nail'd]
            ⎱ Un- ⎱
Unnatural, [Against-natural]
Unnecessary, ⎰ Not-necessary]
Unneedful,   ⎱
Unnoble, [Against-noble]
Unoccupied, [Not- ⎰ Business]
adj. p. ⎱ Use]
Unorderly.
[Confused]
[Irregular]
Unpack- ⎰ Not- ⎰ (that bound toge
ed,   ⎱ Un- ⎱ aggregated)
Unpaid, [Not-paid]
Unpainted, [Not-painted]
Unpair- ⎰ Not- ⎰
ed,   ⎱ Un-   ⎱ companioned]
(p. (perf.)
Unpardonable, [Not adj. p. pardon (pot.)]
Unpeaceable. Man. IV. 3. O.
Unpeople, [Un-adj. p. Dwelling]
Unperformed, [Not-performed]
Unpinned, ⎰ Not- ⎰ fastened with
            ⎱ Un- ⎱ pin]
Unplant- ⎰ Not- ⎰
ed,   ⎱ Un- ⎱ planted]
Unpleasant- ⎰ Ha. II. 3. O.
ness,   ⎱ T. IV. 2. O.
Unpleasing, [adj. Displicence]
Unpolished, [Not-polished]
Unpolluted, [Not-defiled]
Unprepared, [Not-prepared]
Unprofitable, [Not-profitable]
Unprosperous.
[Not-prosperous]
[Adverse]
Unproved, [Not-proved]
Unprovided, [Not-provided]
Unpunish, [Not-punish]
Unquenchable, [Not-adj. p. quench (pot.)]
Unquiet,
[Against-quiet]
[adj. Molesting]
Unrank- ⎰ Not- ⎰
ed,   ⎱ Un- ⎱ ranked]
Unravel, [Un-intangle]
Unready, ⎰ Prepared
           ⎱ Clothed]
Unreasonable.
[Irrational]
Not—— ⎰
Against- ⎱ adj. Equity
in commanding, [Man. VI. 6. O.]
⎰ [Irregular]
⎱ [adj. Excess]
Unreclaimed, [Not—r.]
Unrecompensed, [Not—r.]
Unreconcileable, [Not—r.]
Unrecoverable, [Not—r.]
Unredeemed, [Not—r.]
Unregarded, [Not—r.]
Unremedied, [Not—r.]
Unrepaired, [Not—r.]
Unreproved, [Not—r.]

Unrestored, [Not—r.]
Unreturned, [Not—r.]
Unrevealed, [Not—r.]
Unrevenged, [Not—r.]
Unrewarded, [Not—r.]
Unrighteousness.
[Injustice]
[Unholiness]
Unripeness. NP. VI. 4. D.
Unrivet- ⎰ Not- ⎰ rivetted]
ed,   ⎱ Un- ⎱
Unroll, ⎰ Un-   ⎰ roule]
          ⎱ Back- ⎱
Unroot- ⎰ Not- ⎰
ed,   ⎱ Un-   ⎱ (r.]
Unruly.
[Irregular]
[Rebellious]
[Disobedient]
Unsad- ⎰ Not- ⎰
ed,   ⎱ Un- ⎱ (r.]
Unsafe, [Dangerous]
Unsaid.
[Not-said]
[Recanted]
Unsalt- ⎰ Not—(.)
ed,   ⎱ Un-
Unsalted, [Not—r.]
Unsatiated, [Not—(.]
Unsavouriness. Q. IV. 1. O.
Unseal- ⎰ Not- ⎰
ed,   ⎱ Un- ⎱ (r.]
Unsearchable, [Not-adj. p. searched (pot.)]
Unseasonable, [adj. Time (cor.)]
Unseemly, [Indecent]
Unseen, [Not—(.]
              ⎰ Not- adj ⎰ pot)
Unserviceable, ⎱ p. use   ⎱ apt)
              (Not-fast)
              (Unprofitable)
Unsetled, ⎰ Loose]
            ⎱ Light]
Unsheath, [Un-a. Case]
Unshod, ⎰ Not- ⎰ adj. p. Shoo]
          ⎱ Un- ⎱
Unshorn, [Not-clipped]
Unskilfulness. Ha. VI. 3. O.
⎰ Unlearnedness]
⎱ Inexperience]
Unsociable, [adj. Man. IV. O.]
Unsound.
⎰ Not-found]
⎱ Rotten]
Unsow- ⎰ Un—   ⎰
ed,   ⎱ Not- ⎱ Sowed]
Unspeakable, [Not-adj. p. speak (pot.)]
Unspent, [Not-spent]
Unspot- ⎰ Not-spotted]
ted,   ⎱ Clear]
Unsta- ⎰ Not-constant]
ble,   ⎱ Light]
Unstaid, [Light]
Unstained, [Not-stained]
Unstead- ⎰ Not-constant]
fast,   ⎱ Light]
Unsteady, [Not-steady]
Unstirred, [Not-stirred]
Unstitch- ⎰ Not- ⎰ sowed]
ed,   ⎱ Un- ⎱
Unstopped,

UN VO UP

Unstopped, [a. Open]
Unstrung, {Not— / Un—} Strung]
Unstuf- {Not— / Un—} Stuffed]
fed,
Unsubdued, [Not-subdued]
Unsufferable, [Not-adj. p. suffer (pot.)
Unsure, {Certain / [Not-] Safe}
Unsuita- {Not-congruous / Disagreeable]
ble,
Unswath- {Un— / Not—} swath-ed]
Unsworn, [Not-sworn]
Untamed, [Fierce]
Untangle, [Un-tangle]
Untaught, {Not-taught / Ignorant}
Unteach- {Dull / Incredulous]
able,
Unthankfulness, [Ingratitude]
Unthought of, [Not-thought of]
Unthriftiness, [Squandring]
Unti- {Not— / Un—} Tied]
ed,
Until. Adv. III. 2. O.
—*now*, [Until this time]
Untilled, [Not-tilled]
Untimely, [Not-timed (perf.]
—*birth*, Abortion]
Unto, [To / Speaking]
Untold, [Not-adj.p. Narration / Number]
Untouched, [Not-touched]
{*Untowardness* / *Untractableness*} {Incredulity / Contumacy]
{Disingenuity / Dulness / Fierceness / Incredulity / Fierceness / Pertinacy / Undutifulness / Disobedience / Contumacy]
Untrim- {Not-ornate / Homely]
med,
Untrue, {Not-true / False]
Untrus- {Not— / Un—} trussed]
fed,
Untrusty, [Treacherous]
Untruth, [Falshood]
Untuna- {Not-harmonious / adj. Discord]
ble,
{*Untwined*, Not- / *Untwisted*, Un—} twisted]
Unvaluable, {Value / Price} (pot.)
[Not-adj. p
Unvanquisht, [Not-vanquisht]
Unvaried, [Not-varied]
Unveil, [Uncover]
Unversed [adj. Inexperience]
Unusual.
{Extraordinary / Not-customary / Seldom / Not-common]
Unutterable, [Not- adj. p. express (pot.)]
Unwalled, [Not-walled]

Unwary, [Careless]
Unwashed, [Not-washed]
Unwasted, [Not-wasted]
Unwearied, [Constant]
Unweaved, [Not-weaved]
Unwel- {Not-welcom / adj. a. Displicence]
com,
Unweildy.
{Lumpish / Slow}
[Not-adj. p. motion (apt.)
Unwholsom, [adj. a. sickness (apt.)
Unwilling.
[adj. {Nolleity / Aversion}
[adj. Coaction]
Unwind, [Un-wind]
Unwise, [adj. Folly]
Unwisht for, [Not-wisht].
Unwit- {Not-knowing / Ignorant}
ting,
Unwonted, [Not-adj. p. Custom]
Unworthiness. TG. IV. 6. O.
Unwrap, [Un-fold]
Unwreath, [Un-twist]
Unwrinkle, [Un-wrinkle]
Unwritten, [Not-written]
Unwrought, {Not-wrought / Homely]
Unyoke, {Un-yoke / Separate]
Vocabulary, [adj. Catalogue Book of words]
Vocal, [adj. Voice]
Vocati- {Calling / Profession]
on,
Vocative, [adj. Calling]
Vogue, {Reputation / Rumor]
Voiage, {Sailing / Travelling]
Voice.
Proper. Q. III. 3.
Song of 3—s, [Song for 3 together-singing (persons)
Suffrage, [Consent (sign)]
Void.
adj.
[Empty]
—*of*, [Without]
[Not-possest]
[adj. {Frustrate / Vanity / Nothing]
to——
[a. Empty]
[Un-possess]
[Go]
[Banish]
[Purge]
[Dung]
[Spoil]
adj. Nothing (make)
Voider, [Dish (aug.) Shallow sp. for carrying adj. meat (things)
Voidance, [Un-possessing]
Volatil.

[Flying]
[adj. a. Exhalation (apt.)]
Volly, [Together-shootings (aggr.)
Volubility, [Agility / sp. of tongue]
Volum, [Book]
Voluntary, {Will / Spontaneity]
[adj.
Voluptuousnes, [Sensuality]
Volutation. O. I. 5. A.
Vomiting. Mo. IV. 9.
Voraci- {Rapacity / Gluttony]
ty,
Vorago, [Whirlpool]
Votary, [adj. pret. Vowing (person)
Vote.
Wish, [Velleity]
Suffrage, {Consent (sign) / sp. by speaking]
Vouch.
[a. Protestation]
[a. Sponsion]
Vouchsafe, [Condescend]
Vow. RE. IV. 1.
Vowel. D. I. 2.
Up, {Upward ver- / Upperside} gent, toward / Top]
[Direct]
—*on end*,
he is—
[adj. p. pres. motion]
Bell {b. / is in}
Hare {is— / h.} motion
Name {n.} on]
from {Beginning / Part / Imperfection / end / whole / perfection]
till
{Finally / Wholly / Perfectly]
—*and* {to and fro / divers ways]
down,
—*by the root*, [Together with the r.]
—*hill*, [Upward on the hill]
—*to*, [Until at]
Barrel— [Lay up in Barrel]
Blow—
{a. Tumor / a. Inflation / Upward cast / Overthrow]
sp. b. firing Gunpowder]
Bring— {Begin / Educate]
Burn, [b. perfectly]
Clap— {Bargain / Finish]
Give— {Yield / Submit / Let-go]
Knit— {K. together / Finish]
Lay— {Put on the heap / Store- TA. V. 4.]
Lift—[Lift]

Put—

UR | Ur | WA

Put— {a. case / a. patience}
Rift— [Rife]
Roufe— [Rife (make)]
Sit— [Sit direct]
Sow— {Sow together / Shut by fowing}
Stay— [Bear]
Stand— [Stand]
Stir— {Provoke / a. Impulfive}
Ty— {Together-ty / Shut by tying}
Upbraid. RJ. IV. 8, A.
Uphold, {Bear / Prop}
Upholfter, [adj. Bed (mech.)]
Upland, [adj. Mountain Countrey]
Upon.
  Accuf.
  Grow— [Ufurp]
  Look— [a. Sight]
  [Concerning]
  agree——
  [Toward]
  —that hand, [t. that fide]
  [To]
  Happen——
  Prep. VI. 1.
  come— [Affault]
  Run— {Affault / Storm}
  [After]
  —this, [after th.]
  worde—word.
Upper.
  Proper.
  —end, [Top]
  —fide. Sp. III. 5.
  [Superior]
  —hand, [adj. Dignity (place)]
  Get the— [a. Victory]
Upright.
  [Direct]
  ly— [ly adj. reverfe]
  [adj. {Sincerity / Integrity}]
  —Deal- {Equity / ing Juftice}
Uprifing, [Rifing]
Uproar, [Sedition]
Upfhot, [Event]
Upfide, [Upperfide]
  [Lying]
  —down, [Upfide down turned]
Upfitting.
  [Sitting direct]
Upftart, (New corr.)
Upward. Prep. V. 1.
Uranofcopus. Fi. IV. 11.
Urbanity. Man. IV. 9.
Urchin.
  [Hedgehog]
  [Little forry (perfon)]
Ure.
  [Cuftom of ufeing]
Ureter, [adj. Urining Vein]
Urge.
  [a. Impulfive (augm.)]

[a. Fiercenefs]
[Intreat (augm.)]
[Angry (make)]
Urgent.
  [Intenfe]
  [Fierce]
Urine, [Piffed (thing)]
  Salt of—St. I. 5.
Urinal, [Glas (vefs.) for Urine]
Urn, [adj. Figulatory Pot]
  [p. for burying Afhes]
Urtica. Ex. IX. 6. A.
Urus, [Bull (kind) bearded]
Us, [We]
Ufage.
  [Ufe (manner)]
  [Entertaining (manner)]
  [Cuftom]
Ufe.
  [Ufing]
  Ufus fructus]
  Intereft, [Rent of money]
  Lend upon— [Lend for hire]
  Take upon— [a. hire]
  [Manner]
  [p. adj. Cuftom]
  [Cuftom]
  in— [adj. Cuftom]
  Out of, [Un-adj. Cuftom]
  [Habit]
  [Practife]
  to— TA. V. 6.
  [Apply]
  [Entertein]
  [Accuftom]
  [Practife]
Ufher.
  [adj. Preceding (Off.)]
  —in {In-bring / Precede}
  [Acceffory Teacher]
Ufual.
  [adj. p ufe (freq.)]
  [Cuftomary]
  {Common / Ordinary}
Ufufructuary, [adj. Ufus fructus (perfon)]
Ufurp. RJ. IV. 3.
Ufury, [Hire of money]
Ufus fructus. RC. IV. 5. A.
Utenfil. Po. VI.
Uterine, [adj. Womb] PG. VI. 9.
Utility, [Profit-ablenefs]
Utmoft.
  [Moft-adj. Outfide]
  [Extream]
  [Moft]
  [Whole]
Utopia, [adj. p. Fiction Country (perf.)]
Utter.
  [adj. Outfide]
  [adj. Extream]
  [Whole]
  to—
  {Out-put / Shew}
  {Speak / Exprefs}
  [a. Narration]

{Alienate / Sell}
Utterance, [Speak-ing {pot. / manner}]
Uttermoft, vid. *Utter.*
Vulgar, [Common]
  —People, [Rabble]
Vulnerary, [adj. Wound]
Vulture. Bi. I. 1. A.
Uvula, [adj. Flefh Cylinder (dim.) for fhutting the windpipe]
Uxorious, [Fond of Wife]

W.

Wad, [adj. heap (thing) together-tied]
Waddle, [Walk {Volutation / adv. Duck (like)}]
Wade, {In— River, / Walk through &c.}
Wafer, [Thin (lamin)]
  [p. of Pudding (kind)]
Waft, [Carry over-water]
Wag, {Motion / Shaking} (dim.)
  a— [adj. Urbanity (perfon)]
Wage.
  —Law, [a. Suit]
  —Souldiers, [Bargain with S.]
  —War, [a. War]
Wager. RC. VI. 8.
Wages. RC. V. 6. A.
Waggle, [Wag (dim.)]
Wagon, [Wain]
Waife, [Abandoned (thing)]
Wagtail. Bi. V. 7.
Tellow. Bi. V. 7. A.
Way,
  [adj. ition (place)]
  [factitious way. Po. II. 7. A.
  —faring, [adj. Travelling]
  —man, [adj. Travelling (perfon)]
  —Free. Sh. II. 2.
  —Laying, [a. Ambufh]
  give—
  [*not—* {Refift / Oppofe}]
  [Submit]
  go his— [Go]
  Lead {Lead / Before-go}
  make— [Prepare w.]
  fhew the— [Direct in the w.]
  By {Acceffority / adj. Digreffion}
  In the— [Hindring]
  Set in the— [Direct]
  on the—
  Bring on the— [Accompany in the beginning of his journey]
  Go on his— [Proceed]
  Out of the—
  [Befide the fcope]
  {Erring / Wandring} [avoid-

WA

[Avoiding]
 [adj. a. Loſing]
[Diſtance]
 —great—[Remote]
 —about, [Curve (augm.
 —off, [Remote (augm.)
[Vergency]
 many—s, [adv. Diverſity
  vergent]
{ Kind }
{ Manner }
{ Means }
{ Method }
Wail, [a. Sor- { (Voice)
 row { (ſign)
Wain. P. V. I. A.
Wainſcot, [Wooden lining of a
 Room]
Wait.
 [Stay] TA. V. I. O.
     by
 Stay, { With { one. AC.
     For { V. I. A.
  Companion, [a. com-
   panion]
as { Dependent, [a. de-
   pendent]
  Servant, [a. Ser-
   vant]
Lay — [a. Ambuſh]
Waits, [Wakening Muſic.]
Waiward, { Diſingenuity }
 [adj. { Moroſeneſs]
Wake.
 awaken.
 [End ſleep]
 [Begin to wake]
 not-ſleep. AC. II. 4.
 [adj. p. Wake night before fe-
  ſtival]
 [adj. Country feſtival]
 —Robin. HL. V. 9. A.
Wakeful, adj. p. wake (apt.)
 [Vigilant]
Walk.
 Proper. Mo. II. 2.
 a— { Walking place }
  fetch a—[Go for a walk]
 as Ghoſt, [appear]
Wale, [Ridge of threeds in
 cloth]
Wall. Po. III. 6.
 [Sepiment]
 [Rampier]
 [Partition]
 —creeper, [Woodpecker] of a
  long ſlender bill, about the
  bigneſs of a Sparrow]
 —eyed, [White eyed]
 —flower. HS. IV. 1. A.
 —Louſe, [Puniſe] Po. III. 6.
 —Nut, Tr. IV. 1. A.
 —Rue, [White Maiden hair]
  HL. I. 5.
 —wort, [Danewort]
Wallet, [Riding bag]
 ſp. Open in the middle]
Walnut, Tr. IV. 1.
Wallowing, [Volutation]
Wambling, [Volutation]
 { Loathing }
 { Averſation } (dim.)

WA

Wan, { Pale }
 { Dead like }
Wand. PP. I. 4. A.
Wander. TA. VI. 3. A.
Wane, [Decreaſe]
Want.
 [Have occaſion to uſe]
 Not have. TA. I. 5. O.
 [Not have enough]
 { Scarcity }
 { Defect }
 [Poverty]
 —little of [Almoſt.]
 a—[Mole]
Wantonneſs.
 Playwardneſs, NP. IV. 3. Q.
 [Unchaſtity]
Wapentake, [Hundred]
War. RM.
 Man of—
  [Souldier]
 Ship. RN. I. 6.
Warbling, [Trembling (like)
 voice]
Ward.
 { Defend }
 { Protect }
 —off, [Defend from]
 { Guard] RM. III. 6. 1
 { Watch] RM. III. 6.
 [Together adj. ought,
  Guard City (part)
 [Impriſonment (place)
 [Pupil]
 —of key, { Cavity } in the la-
       { Notch } min of
             the key.
 —of a lock, [Curve (lamin)
  within L.
Warden, { adj. Keeping (Off.) }
     { Magiſtrate }
 —tree, [Pear (kind)
Warder.
 [adj. Keeping (Off.)
 [adj. { Guard } (perſon)
      { Watch }
Wardrobe, [adj. Keeping (Room)
 of clothing]
Ware.
 [adj. p. Sell (thing)
 [a. Imperat-heedfulneſs]]
Warfare, [War]
Warineſs.
 [Heedfulneſs]
 [Reſervedneſs]
 [Frugality]
Warlike, [adj. War]
Warm.
 [Temperate]
 { Fierce (dim.) }
 { Zealous }
Warn. RO. V. 4. A.
 —to appear, [Citation]
Warp.
 the—[Direct threed]
 to—[Bend]
Warrant.
 [Written Command]
 [Sponſion]
Warranty, [Paction for ſafe
 (make)
Warren, [Park for Rabbets]

WA

Warrener, [adj. Park (Off.) of
 Rabbets]
Warrier, [Souldier]
Wart. S. III. 5.
Was, [Am having-been]
Waſh. O. V. 4.
 —es. W. III. 6. A.
 hog—[Broth for hogs]
Waſp. Ex. IV. 2.
 —iſh, [Moroſe]
 —like fly. Ex. IV. 3. A.
Waſſail, [adj. Country Banquet]
Waſt.
 Girdleſtead, [Middle (part)
  of trunk]
 —of a ſhip. RN. II. 5.
 Not— { Uſed }
    { Inhabited }
 —land,
 [Superfluous]
 —water.
 to—
 { Decay }
 { Diminiſh }
 [Booty]
 { Mar }
 { Deſtroy }
  [a. Ruine]
  [Spend (corr.)]
  [Squander]
Waſteous, [Thin adj. Trunk (veſt]
Waſtful, [adj. Squandering]
Watch.
 to—
 [Wake]
 [a. Vigilance]
 { a. Heedfulneſs }
 { Obſerve }
 a. { Guard }
   { Watch }
 —for, [Expect waiting]
 —with, [Wait waking]
 a—[a. Watch]
 —man, [adj. { (perſon) }
       { Watching } { (Off.) }
 Perſons,
 -for cuſto- { [Guard] }
       dy of { Places, RM. III. }
           6. A.
 --word, { (adj. word (ſign) of
         Watch]
       { time (ſign) by
        word]
 { Clock without Bell }
 { adj. Pocket Clock }
Watchet, [Blue (kind)
Watchfulneſs.
 (Vigilance)
 [Heedfulneſs]
 [Diligence]
Water.
 Element. El. III.
 the—W. IV.
 Running—[Scream]
 ſtanding—[Pool]
 by— { Swimming }
    { Sailing }
 in a—[adj. Sweating (aug.)
 under—[Covered with—]
 —bank.
 —beetle. Ex. V. 8.
 —Chein, [Chain (dim.)
   —Courſe,

WA

—**Course**, {Stream / Aqueduct}
—**Furrow**, [Trench for drein]
—**Hen**, [Moorhen] Bi. VIII. 9.
—**Lilly**.
—**man**, [adj. Rowing (person)]
—**Nut**
—**Pepper**.
—**Raile**
—**Rat**
—**Scorpion**. Ex. I. 9.
—**Shoot**, {Barren branch (dim.)}
—**Snail**. Ex. VII. 1. A.
—**Spider**. Ex. II. 4.
to —
—**Cattle**, [Drink (make) c.]
—**garden**, [a. Wet (make) the surface with —]
—**meat** in [Soke] with {water}
Urin.
to make — [v. Urination]
[Out — [Distilled thing]
[adj. [Washing (thing)] sp] Medicinal]
mo uth —
Watery
Waterish [adj. Water]
—**blood**, [Serous blood]
—**tast**, [adj. water (like t.)]
Wattle, [s. Weaving sticks (dim.)]
{Gill} PG. V. 7. A.
Wave. W. IV. 1. E.
—**ing**.
{Undulation
Shaking (dim.)
Aversion
Avoiding}
Waver. AS. IV. 4. O.
Wax.
Subst. El. III. 7. A.
ear — [Excrement of the ear]
to —
[a. wax]
{Begin (inc.)}
[Increase]
[v. Event]
Waxe, [Wreath] sp. of Straw
Weakness.
[Impotence]
Feebleness, NP. V. 7. O.
{Remissness
Deficiency}
Weale, {Being (perf.) / Happiness}
Wealth.
[Riches]
Common —
[adj. RC. (thing)]
[Common prosperity]
[Government by the people]
Wean, [Teach to abstain]
—**a child**, [Un- a. suckle Child]
Weapon. RM. V. 1.
Wear.
{Lessen
Worse } by use]
Decay}

WE

—**out**, [Spoil by use]
—**as clothes**, [v. Clothing] Pr. IV.
—**in his pocket**, [Carry] Mo. VI. 1.
—**as Ring, &c**. [with p. Ornate] TM. II. 6.
a — [adj. Taking (mach.) of fish]
Weary.
to — TA. V. 8. O.
—**of** [Sick of] adj. TA. V. 7. O.
Wearish tast, [Unsavory t.]
Weasand, [Wind-pipe] PG. VI. 1. A.
Weather.
[Guelt Sheep] Be. II. 2.
Temperament of Air. El. VI.
—**Cock**, [Shewing (jug.) of the vergency of the wind]
—**glass**, [adj. Glass (instr.) for shew- } Heat } of the ing } Cold } air]
to — **one**, [a. patience]
Weave.
—**ing**. O. V. 2.
—**er**.
[adj. Weaving (mech.) Fish. Fi. IV. 8.
Web, [Woven (thing)]
Cob — [Woven (thing) of Spider]
[White spot in the eye]
Wed, [a. Marriage]
Wedding, [adj. Marriage solemnity]
Wedge.
[Prism sp. for cleaving]
—**of Silver**.
to — **in**.
[In-thrust (augm.)
[In-fasten] sp. by prisms in-thrusted about it]
Wedlock, [Marriage]
Wednesday, [4th day of the week]
We. Prep. I. 1. A.
Weed.
[Sorry garment]
[Herb]
sp. {Unprofitable / Hurtful}
—**ing**. O. III. 3. A.
Week.
—**of time**. Mea. V. 4. A.
—**of Candle**, [adj. p. flame (apt.) string (part)]
Weel, [adj. Taking (machin) for fish]
Weeld.
[Handle]
[Swing]
Ween,
[a. Opinion]
[a. Supposition]
Over — [a. Pride]
Weeping. AC. IV. 3. O.
Weesel. Be. IV. 7. A.
Weevel. Ex. V. 1. A.
Weigh.
v. mot. III.
—**with Balances**. O. I. 2.
[Be heavy] v. Q. V. 4.

WE

—**anker**, [Lift a.]
—**down**, [Depress]
[Consider]
Weight.
Gravity. Q. V. 4. E.
Measure of. Mea. III.
Measuring (instr.) Mea. III. A.
{Gold } Weight perfectly equal]
Standing }
[Importance]
Weighty, [adj. Weight]
Welk, [Periwinkle] Ex. VII. 6. A
Welkin, [Sky]
well.
{Good}
[adv. { Regular}
{Sufficient}
—**a day**. Int. II. 2. O.
—**advised**, [a. Confederate]
—**beloved**, [Loved]
—**born** {Noble } man]
{Gentle }
—**come** {Accepted (perf.)
{adj. a. Delectation}
to — **one**.
[Joy. AS. VI. 6. (sign) for his coming]
[Entertain (perf.)]
—**fare**, [Being (perf.)]
—**favoured**, [adj. Decent (fig.)]
—**in health**, [adj. Health]
—**in years**, [adj. Old (dim.)]
—**nigh**, [Almost] Adv. V. 1.
—**now** }
—**then** } Int. III. 2. O.
—**to pass**, [Rich (dim.)]
—**willing**
—**wishing** } adj. Favour
as — Adv. II. 1.
a — W. IV. 3.
Welt, [Margin]
sp. made by sowing]
Welter, [v. Volutation]
Wen. S. III. 5.
Wench.
[adj. {Childhood / Adolescence} (fem.)]
[Sorry (fem.)]
[adj. Fornication (fem.)
to — [a. Fornication]
Went, [adj. pret. go]
Wept, [adj. pret. weep]
Were.
[are having been]
it — [It might be]
as it — Adv. IV. 2. O.
West. Sp. III. 1. O.
Wet. Q. V. 2. E.
Whale. Fi. I, 1.
—**of the river**, [Sheatfish] Fi. VI. 6.
Wharf, [adj. River haven]
Wharfinger, [adj. Wharf (Off.)]
What.
{Interrog. Pron. III. 1. A.
{Relative. Pron. III. 2. A.
—**manner of**, } manner
[of what } kind]
—**soever**. Pron. III. 3. A.

WH

—*a poor shift*, [How sorry a Shift]
Wheal.
 [Pustle] S. III. 1.
 —*worm.* Ex. II. 7. A.
Wheat. HL. II. 1.
 Buck—— HF. I. 3.
 Cow——
 Indian—[Maiz] HL. II. 2.
Wheat-ear. Bi. V. 6. A.
Wheat-grass. HL. III. 3.
Wheedle.
 [adj. Fawning adv. Fraud]
Wheel.
 Figure. Mag. V. 3. A.
 to—[Vertiginate]
  —*about* { Turn
   Go in crooked
   (Line)
 —*of Cart*, &c. Po. V. 6.
 —*Barrow.* [One wheel'd Cart]
 to break on the—R J. V. 9. A.
Wheeze, [a. Asthma with sound (augm.)]
Whey.
 [Serum] PP. I. 2.
Whelk.
 [Pustle] S. III. 1.
Whelm.
 [Cover] (augm.)
Whelp, { Dog
  Lion } (yong)
  &c.
When.
 [At what time]
 [Whereas] Conj. IV. 1.
Whence.
 [From what place]
 —*soever,* [From whatsoever place]
Where.
 What.
 —*by,* [By what]
 —*in,* [in what]
 —*of,* [of what]
 —*to,* [to what]
 —*as.* Conj. IV. 1.
 —*fore.* Conj. III. 3.
 [in what place]
 —*soever,* [In whatsoever place]
 any—[In any place]
 every—Sp. II. 8.
 no—Sp. II. 8. O.
Wherl } [adj. Vertigination
Whern } (jug.)
Wherret, [Striking sp. with hand]
Wherry, [Boat adj. p. row (apt.) with 2 Oars]
Whether.
 —*of the two,* [Who of the two]
 { Affirm. Conj. I. 1.
 Negat. Conj. I. 1. O.
 —*or no.* Conj. I. 1. or Conj. I. 1. O.
 Disjunctive Indefinite. Conj. II. 3. A.

WH

—*a poor shift,* [How sorry a Whet.
 { adj. p. tooth
 as point { (make)
 { adj. a. pricking
 { (apt.)
 { adj. p. edge
 as edge, { (make)
 { adj. a. Cutting
 { (apt.)
 —*Stone.* St. I. 6.
Why, [Wherefore]
Which.
 Interrog. Pron. III. 1. A.
 Relative. Pron. III. 2. A.
Whiffler, [Disguised adj. waiting (Off.) with Candle]
Whig.
 [Drink of acid whey]
While.
 [Time]
 { sp. between]
 a good
 a great }—adv. permanent]
 a long
 — { *age* } [adv. old]
   { *since*
 a little }—[adv. transi
 a short } tory]
 — { *ago* } [adv. new]
   { *since*
 mean—[in the middle time]
 after a }—[after some
 within a } time]
 after } *a little*—[adv.
 within } soon]
 after } *a long*—[adv.
 within } late]
 { a. Cunctation)
 to—*Off.* { Delay
 { Protract]
Whilst. Adv. III. 3.
Whimper, [Acute (dim.) grief (voice)]
Whimsy.
 [a. Fancy (corr.)]
 [adj. Conceitedness [(thing)]
Whin.
 [Furz]
Whine, [acute } desire
 (dim.) } grief
 (voice)]
Whip.
 [adj. Whipping (instr.)]
 Figure. Mag. IV. 7.
 [adj. hand (part) of Rudde]
 to—
 Punish. RJ. VI. 2.
 [a. Agility]
 [about-wind threed]
 —*a top,* [Vertiginate t. with adj]. Mag. IV. 7. (instr.)
Whipsaw, [Saw (dim.)]
Whirl.
 —*bone,* [Bone covering the knee]
 —*pool.* W. IV. 1. D.
 —*wind.* El. II. 4. A.

WH

 [Vertiginate (augm.)]
 [Cast adv. Vertiginating]
Whirligig.
Whirtle. Sh. III. 3. A.
Whisk.
 [Move (imp.)]
 [Brush by striking]
Whisker, [Great]
 [Mustache]
Whisper. AC. III. 3.
 —*er,* [adj.] { Whispering
  { Backbiting
   (person)
Whist. Idt. III. 1. O.
Whistle.
 [Whistling (instr.)]
 [sp. adj. Tube (fig.)]
 —*ing.* Q. III. 4 A.
Whit, [Least]
 any—[adv. any]
 every— } all]
  { adv. } whole]
White.
 —Colour. Q. I. 1. E.
 —*bread,* [Fine bread]
 —*lead,* [Ceruse]
 —*liver'd,* [adj. Coward]
 —*meats,* [adj. milk victuals]
 —*pot,* [Fluid! Pudding]
 —*ing.*
 [White (make)
 Fish. Fi. III. 2. A.
Whither.
 [To what place]
 —*soever,* [To whatsoever place]
Whitlow.
 [Bile on the finger]
 —*grass.*
Whitsontide, [adj. Festivity (time) for pret. Descension of the Holy Ghost]
Whittler, [adj. a. white (mech. of Linen]
Whittle, [Cut (corr.)]
 —*'d,* [Drunk]
Whizz,
 [adj. Hissing (voice)]
Who.
 Interrog. pron. III. 1. A.
 Relative. Pron. III. 2. A.
 —*So*
 —*soever* } Pron. III. 3. A.
Whole.
 Total. TM. VI.
 { Entire] NP. V. 1.
 { adj. Soundness] NP. V. 2.
 Sum.
 —*Sale,* [Selling adv. aggregate]
 —*ly* } Whole]
  { adv. } All]
Wholesom, { Health]
  { adj. Soundness]
Whom, vid. *Who.*
Whoop, [v. Exclamation (augm.)]
Whore.
 [adj. fornication (fem.)]
 T t t   —*dom,*

WI

―*dom*, [Fornication]
―*monger*, [adj. fornication (male)]
Whurtle, Sh. II. 2.
Sweet―Sh. II: 6. A.
Whose, { adj. } { of } { who }
Whosoever, Pron. III. 3. A.
Wicked, { Graceless, Unholy, Vicious (augm.) }
Wicker, [Woven (thing) of wands]
  [p. adj. Ozier]
Wicket.
  [Door (dim.)]
Wide.
  [Ample]
  ―*open*, [Wholly open]
  [Remote]
  ―*from the matter*, [Impertinent (augm.)]
Widgin. Bi. IX. 3.
Widow. RO. II. 5.
  ―*Wail*. Sh. III. 6. A.
Wield.
  [Handle]
  [Govern]
Wife,
  [Married (fem.)]
  house―
  [Miftress of family]
  good― { Providence }
  [adj. { Frugality (fem.) }
  [Woman (corr.)]
Wight, [Person]
Wild.
  ―*ness*.
  { Wantonness }
  { Fierceness }
  { Conceitedness }
  { Lightness }
  { Riotousness }
  { Barbarousness }
  { Irregularness }
  [Impertinence (augm.)]
  ―*fire*, [Confection of wetted Gunpowder]
  ―*plant*, [Naturally growing]
Wilderness, [Not-adj. p. Dwelling (place)]
Wilding, [Naturally growing Apple]
Wile, [a. Craft]
Will.
  { Future tense }
  { Mood III. }
  Faculty. NP. I. 4.
  Act. AS. IV.
  { Inclination }
  { Velleity }
  { Purpose }
  { Desire }
  { Command }
  Good―[favour]
  ―*with a good*―[adv. Alacrity]
  Ill―[Malignity]
  ―*with an ill*―[adv. Grudging]

WI

[Testament]
―*with a Will*. El. I. 6.
Wilful.
  [Fierce]
  [Pertinacious]
  [adj. Disobedience (apt.)]
  [Not-adj. p. { Perfwade } { Diffuade }
  (apt.)
Willingness.
  [Will (abstr.)]
  [Spontaneity]
  [Alacrity]
Willow.
  Tree. Tr. VI. 9.
  Herb.
  Cudded―HS. IV. 3.
  Spiked―Sh. V. 1. A.
Wimble. [adv. p. Vertigination Boring (inftr.)]
Wimple.
Win.
  { Obtain }
  { Gain | }
  ―*a Victory*, [a. Victory]
  { Take }
  { Conquer }
  { Perfwade }
  { Allure }
Wince, [Strike with heels]
Winch, [adv. Ver- { Pulling } tiginated { Scruing } (machin)]
Wind.
  Proper. El. II. 4.
  ―*fall*, { Fall } [adj. p. { Event } fp. by wind]
  ―*flower*, [Anemony] HF. IX. 3.
  ―*mill*, [Mill adj. p. operation (make) by the wind]
  Side― [Oblique―]
  Whirl―El. II. 4. A.
  { Air (augm,) }
  { Vapor }
  { Fume }
  ―*gall*.
  ―*in the guts*, [Colic]
  [Breath]
  ―*pipe*, PG. VI. 1. A.
  fetch―[a. Refpiration]
  long ―
  fhort ―ed]
  [Sent]
  is in the―*of* [Difcover (inc.)] *to*―
  ―*a born*, [a. found h.]
  [fmell] fp. (inc.)
  [v. Crooked]
  { Parabolical }
  v, { Hyperbolical }
  { Elliptical }
  [Turn]
  ―*ing way*.
  [Fold]
  ―*ing fheet*, [adj Linen (veft) for adj. buried (person)]

WI

[v. { Round } { Circular }]
[Vertiginate]
[v. Undulated]
[Wriggle]
―*in and* { Turn } *out* { Wriggle }
  adv. Diverfity]
―*up and down*.
[Infinuate]
―*into one*.
―*one out of*
[v. { Spiral } { Helical }]
[Twifting]
[v. { Bottom } { Skein }]
[Glomerate]
―*up*, [End]
―*a Bottom*, [a. Bottom]
―*a Skein*, [a. Skein]
―*a Watch*.
Windle. Mag. IV. 5. A.
Windlafs, [Pulley]
Window. Po. IV. 2. A.
Wine. Pr. II. 6.
Wing. PP. V. 2.
―*of an army*, [adj. fide (part) of Army]
Wink.
[Shut eye]
[Sign by fhutting eye]
―*at*.
[Seem not to obferve]
[Not― { Correct } { Punifh }]
Winnow. O. III. 5. A.
Winter. Mea. V. 3. A.
―*cherry*.
―*Gillyflower*.
―*Green*. HL. VI. 8.
to― { Permanence } *through* { Dwelling } *the winter*]
Wipe.
Stroke. O. V. 8. A.
―*clean*, [a. Clean by wiping]
―*out*, { Annihilate } *by*―*ing*]
         { Spoil }
[a. Fraud]
[Jeer]
Wire, [adj. Metal threed]
Wife.
[Manner]
[adj. Wifdom]
Wifdom. Ha. VI. 2.
Wifh,
a. { Will }
   { Defire }
―*one to* { Advife } *one*
         { Command } &c.
―*well to* [a. Favour]
[a. Velleity]
Wifp.
[Wreath]
fp. of Straw]
[Inflammation of the eyelid]

Wift,

WI

Wist, [Pret. know]
Wistly,
{ Steddily }
Wit,
[Understanding]
&a. { Fancy
     Invention } (person)
[Sprightliness]
{ Wisdom
  Art }
—*less,* [Without— adj. wit]
in ones—s, [adj. Understanding (perf.)
out of ones—s [Mad]
little— [Wit (def.)]
Pleasant— [Facetiousness]
Searching— [Sagaciousness]
to— [Conj. IV. 3.]
Witch, [adj. R]. III. 1. (person)
—*Craft.* RJ. III. 1.
With.
{ Fight
  Run }
[Against]
[Fight—]
[by] Adv. I. 1. A.
—*much pain,* [adv. Painful]
together—Adv. II. 2.
—*all* { With it
         Also. }
a— [Twisted Wand]
Withdraw.
{ Abstain
  Cease } Giving]
[Take away]
sp. Concealing]
[Remove]
[Depart]
[Retire]
sp. adv. Concealing]
-ing Room. [Inner Room]
Wither.
[Decay]
sp. through { Nutrition
              Moisture
              (def.) }
Withers of a horse, [Convex (part) between the shoulders]
Withhold,
{ Hold
  Detention }
[a. Impedient]
Withy,
Willow. Tr. IV. 6.
Sallow. Tr. IV. 6. A.
Within.
[On this side] Prep. VI. 2.
in. Prep. IV. 1. A.
—*a little,* [Almost]
Without.
Not with. Prep. II. 2. O.
—*doubt,* [adv. Certain]
Not within. Prep. IV. 2. A.
Beyond. Prep. VI. 2. A.

WO

Withstand.
{ Oppose
  Resist }
[a. Impedient (end)]
Withwind.
Witness. RJ. I. 7. A.
Wittal, [Consenting to his Wifes Adultery]
Witty.
[adj. Wit]
Witting.
[adj. Knowledge]
Witwal.
[Wood speit] Bi. I. O.
Wizarding. RJ. III. 1. A.
Wo. { Misery
       Grief }
Woad. HS. VI. 8.
Woful { Misery
         Grief }
[adj. { Misery
        Grief }]
Wolfe.
Beast. Be. V. 1. A.
—*bane.* HS. I. 3.
Berry bearing — [Herb Christopher] HS. IX. 5.
wholesom—HS. I. 3. A.
Winter—HS. I. 4.
[Cancer] S. III. 4.
Woman, [Man. W. V. 5. [female]
—*s,* { age
       estate } Man. VI. 2.
—*s, Sex.* NF. VI. 2. O.
Womb. PG. VI. 9.
Wonder.
[Admiration]
Wont.
[Custom]
Woo.
[a. Suitor]
Wood.
Part of Tree. PP. I. A.
Place of Trees. Po. I. 7.
—*man* } [adj. Po. I. 7.
—*ward* } (Off.)
[Trees (aggr.)]
Woodbind. Sh. II. 8.
Upright—Sh. II. 8. A.
Woodcock. Bi. VII. 7. A.
Woodculver, [adj. Wood-pigeon]
Wood, { Angry (exc.)
         Mad }
Woodfretter.
Woodlark. Bi. IV. 1. A.
Woodlouse.
Woodman. adj. Po. I. 7. A.
Woodpecker. Bi. IX. 9.
Woodpile.
[Heaped wood (aggr.)]
Woodroof. HL. IX. 10.
Woodsear.
Woodsorrel.
[Three-leav'd Sorrel]
Woodspeight. Bi. IX. 9.
Woodward, [adj. Po. I. 7. (Off.)]
Woodworm, [Wood-boring insect (dim.)
Woof, [Transverse threeds of woven (thing)]

WO

Wool. PP. VI. 1. A.
—*en cloth.* Pr. IV. 1.
Word.
Proper. D. II. 4.
at
in }*a*—[Briefly]
in—*only,* [adv. Hypocrisie]
by—*of mouth,* [adv. present speaking]
by—[Proverb (corr.)]
[Watchword]
[Narration]
bring } b.
send } f. [Narration]
[Promise]
Work.
{ a. action
  v. efficient }
[Operation] O.
          { a. Efficient more operation
make—{ Do adj. must. undone (things)
[a. Mechanic
 sp. for Ornatenes]
[Embroider]
[Ferment]
a—
[adj. p. work (thing)
[Book]
Workman, [adj. Work (person)]
sp. (perf.)
—*ship,* { Work
          sp. (perf.) }
World.
The Universe of Creatures. W.
The Globe of earth and waters. W. II. 7.
The earth. W. III.
a—*of* [adj. Multitude (aug.)]
Worldly.
[adj world]
[adj. Scraping
{ Graceless
Worldling { Selfish } (person)
{ Covetous }
Worm.
Insect.
bear—Ex. III. 8. R.
belly—Ex. I. 1. A.
blam—
churr—[Evechurr] Ex. II. 2. A.
earth—Ex. I. 1.
Gally—
palmer—Ex. III. 8. A.
Silk—Ex. III. 6. A.
Skipping—Ex. III. 7.
Wheal—Ex. II. 7. A.
[Spiral Pin]
Wormseed.
Treacle.—HS IV. 13.
Wormwood. Sh. V. 3.
Worn, { adj. a. pret.
         adj. p. } Wear]
Worry, [Shake in teeth]
Worse. TM. L. 6. D.
—*and*—[adj. Worse]

WO　　　　WR　　　　YE

Worship.
　Dignity]
　[a. Reverence]
　adoration. RE. IV.
Worshipful.
　[adj. Dignity]
　[Gentleman (kind)]
Worst.
　[Most evil]
　—part. TM. VI. 1. O.
　to—
　[Overthrow]
Worsted.
　[Fine threeds of Wool]
Wort.
　[Herb]
　ale ⎫
　　　⎬ [not yet fermented]
　beer ⎭
Worth
　⎧ Worthiness ⎫
　⎨ Excellence ⎬
　⎪ Valor ⎪
　⎨ Price ⎬
　⎩ Riches ⎭
Worthiness. TM. IV. 6.
Worthless, [Sorry]
Wote, [Know]
Woven, [adj. p. Weave]
Would.
　—ing, [Velleity]
　—god, [I with]
　I—[Have it]
　[Mood conditional III]
Wound.
　hurt. S. I. 2.
　adj. a. pret. ⎫
　　　　　　　⎬ Wind]
　adj. p. 　　 ⎭
Wrack.
　Spoil ⎫
　Ruine ⎬
　sp. of Ship ⎭
　go to—[Wracked (inc.)]
　Herb. HL. I. 14.
Wrangle.
　[a. Contention]
　sp. in words]
Wrap, ⎧ Fold ⎫
　　　 ⎨ Cover by folding ⎬
　—about, [About fold]
　—up.
　⎧ Together-fold ⎫
　⎨ Cover by folding ⎬
　[Tangle]
　[a. Obscure]
Wrath.
　[Anger (augm.)]
Wreath.
　[Twist]
　a—[Cylinder about spiral]
Wreck, ⎧ Perform ⎫
　　　 ⎨ Execute ⎬
Wren. Bi. VI. 3.
Wrench.
　[Violent ⎧ extend ⎫
　　　　　⎨ open ⎬
　　　　　⎩ ⎭
　sp. by lifting]

[Hurt by violently extending]
Wrest.
　[Coaction]
　sp. by twisting]
　[Interpret (corr.)]
　—from.
　[From-take by wresting]
　[Extort]
Wrestle. Mo. V. 6.
Wretch, [adj. wretchedness (person)]
Wretchedness.
　[Misery]
　[Penuriousness (augm.)]
　[Sorriness]
Wry.
　[Oblique]
　[Crooked]
　—neck, [Woodpecker (kind) adj. holding (freq.) his head adv. oblique]
Wriggle.
　, as Reptils. Mo. I. 6.
　to denote affection. AC. IV. 4.
　—out, ⎧ Go ⎫ [out adv. wriggling]
　　　　⎨ Get ⎬
Wrinch, vid. Wrench.
Wringing.
　[a. Compression]
　sp. adv. Twisting]
　—from one.
　[From take violently,
　sp. by wringing]
　[Extort]
　—pain, [p. as if by wringing]
Wrist. FG. V. 3. A.
Writ.
　[Commission for arresting]
　holy—[Scripture]
Writing. AC. III. 7.
　a—[Written thing]
　Deed. RC. VI. 5.
Writhing, vid. Wreathing.
Wrong.
　[Irregular]
　[Evil]
　⎧ Evil (kind) ⎫
　⎨ a. Injustice ⎬
　⎩ Injury ⎭
　in the—[adj. erring]
Wroth, vid. Wrath.
Wrought ⎧ adj. a. pret. ⎫ work]
　　　　⎨ adj. p. 　　 ⎬
Wrung, ⎧ adj. a. pret. ⎫ wring]
　　　 ⎨ adj. p. 　　 ⎬

Y.

Yard.
　[Stick]
Sail—RN. III. 2.
　[3 foot]
　—land.
　[Court] Po. III. 3.
　FG. VI. 8. (male)
Yarn, [Threed adj. p. weave (apt.)]
Yarrow.
　[Millefoil]
Yawn. Mo. III. 6.
Yea.
　affirmat. Adv. I. 1.
　[Rather] Adv. III. 1.
Yee. Pron. I. 2. A.
Yeeld.
　Suffer to take. TA. IV. 1.
　⎧ Sold 　　　⎫ for]
　⎨ Demised 　⎬
　—account, [a. Account]
　—Fruit, [a. Fruit]
　⎧ a. Subjection ⎫
　⎨ Submit 　　 ⎬
　⎧ Grant ⎫ D. VI. 3. O.
　⎨ Assent ⎬ AS. II. 3.
　⎩ Confess ⎭ D. VI. 9.
　as Garrison. RM. II. 4. D.
　as Prisoner. RM. II. 6. D.
　as Conquer'd RM. II. 7. D.
　—up the Ghost, [Dy]
　⎧ Diminish ⎫
　⎨ Remit 　 ⎬
　as in moist weather, [v. moistness]
　as to the touch, [v. Yieldingness]
Yeeldingness.
　[Yield (apt.)]
　[Softness] Q. VI. 1.
Yeer. Mea. V.
　in—s [Old] adj. Mea. VI. 4.
Yeest, ⎧ adj. ferment- ⎫ Ale ⎫
　　　 ⎨ ing (thing) of ⎬ Beer ⎬
Yell, [Exclaim]
Yellow. Q. II. 2. A.
　the—s
　—hammer. Bi. IV. 2.
Yelp, [a. voice as dog (young)]
Yeoman. RC. I. 6. A.
　—of the Larder, &c. [Officer of the L. &c.]
Yerk, ⎧ Cast ⎫ (imp.)
　　　 ⎨ Strike ⎬
Yern, [adj. p. Motion]
　sp. with ⎧ Pity ⎫
　　　　　⎨ Desire ⎬
Yes. Adv. I. 1.
Yesterday, [adj. preceding day]
Yet.
　Nevertheless Conj. II. 2. O.
　⎧ Before ⎫ this time]
　⎨ Till 　 ⎬

Yew,

YE

Yew, [Sheep Be. II. 2. (fem.)]
—*tree*. Tr. V. 3.
Yex, [Hiccough]
Yoke.
{ [Neck-binding (jug.)]
{ [Together-two].
Yolk, [Yellow (part) within the Egg]
Yong, vid. *Young*.
Yonker, [Young (perſon)]
—*of ſhip*. RN. V. 8. A.
Yore, [Old] Sp. I. 3. O.
You, { Thou }
     { Yee }
Young.
—*of age*, [adj. youth]
—*ones*, [Children]
[New]
—*begin-* { Learner }
     ner, { Beginner }
Your, [adj. You]
Youth.

ZE

Under age { Infancy. Mea. VI. 1.
          { Childhood. Mea. VI. 1. A.
Of age   { Adoleſcence. Mea. VI. 2.
          { Youth. Mea. VI. 2. A.
a—[adj. Youth (perſon)]
—*full*, [adj. Youth (like)]

Z.

Z*any*, [adj. Scurril (perſon)]
Zeal. AS. VI. 1.
Zedoary.
Herb, [Root of an Indian Iris]
Tree. Tr. VI. 11.

ZO

Zelot, [adj. Zeal (perſon) ſp. ſ corr.
Zenith, [Upper Pole of the Horizon]
Zink, [Spelter] Met. III. 4.
Zodiac. W. VI. 3. A.
Zoilus, [Cenſurer (corr.)]
Zone.
[Girdle]
[Space of earth, &c.]
frigid—[Space of earth between pole and polar Circle]
temperate—[Space of earth between Polar Circle and Tropic]
torrid—[Space of earth between the two Tropics]
Zoophyte, [Plant-Animal]
Zyris.

FINIS.

www.ingramcontent.com/pod-product-compliance
Lightning Source LLC
Chambersburg PA
CBHW021221300426
44111CB00007B/382